The Essentials of Lifespan Development

To my parents, Philip & Irene Kuther

Sara Miller McCune founded SAGE Publishing in 1965 to support the dissemination of usable knowledge and educate a global community. SAGE publishes more than 1000 journals and over 600 new books each year, spanning a wide range of subject areas. Our growing selection of library products includes archives, data, case studies and video. SAGE remains majority owned by our founder and after her lifetime will become owned by a charitable trust that secures the company's continued independence.

Los Angeles | London | New Delhi | Singapore | Washington DC | Melbourne

The Essentials of Lifespan Development

Lives in Context

Tara L. Kuther

Western Connecticut State University

SAGE

Los Angeles | London | New Delhi
Singapore | Washington DC | Melbourne

SAGE

FOR INFORMATION:

SAGE Publications, Inc.
2455 Teller Road
Thousand Oaks, California 91320
E-mail: order@sagepub.com

SAGE Publications Ltd.
1 Oliver's Yard
55 City Road
London, EC1Y 1SP
United Kingdom

SAGE Publications India Pvt. Ltd.
B 1/I 1 Mohan Cooperative Industrial Area
Mathura Road, New DSelhi 110 044
India

SAGE Publications Asia-Pacific Pte. Ltd.
18 Cross Street #10-10/11/12
China Square Central
Singapore 048423

Printed in the United States of America

ISBN: 978-1-0718-7060-0

Library of Congress Control Number: 2022906659

Acquisitions Editor: Jessica Miller

Content Development Editor: Emma Newsom

Project Editor: Veronica Stapleton Hooper

Copy Editor: Diana Breti

Typesetter: diacriTech

Cover Designer: Gail Buschman

Marketing Manager: Victoria Velasquez

This book is printed on acid-free paper.

22 23 24 25 26 10 9 8 7 6 5 4 3 2 1

BRIEF CONTENTS

PART VIII LATE ADULTHOOD AND ENDINGS

DETAILED CONTENTS

PART IV MIDDLE CHILDHOOD

PART V ADOLESCENCE

PART VIII LATE ADULTHOOD AND ENDINGS

PREFACE

The Essentials of Lifespan Development: Lives in Context is the result of 25 years of classroom discussions with students about the nature of development during our lifetime. Many students find lifespan development inherently interesting as they have observed, experienced, or anticipate experiencing the topics we discuss. Sharing observations and personal experiences is fun and engaging. But sometimes our individual experiences don't completely match the theoretical and research conclusions we discuss. How do we make sense of the differences? In class, as well as in this text, I adopt a contextual perspective to help students understand variability in development and to make sense of the growing body of findings in lifespan development.

THEMES: CONTEXT AND APPLICATION

The Essentials of Lifespan Development: Lives in Context focuses on two key themes that promote understanding of how humans develop through the lifespan: the centrality of context and the applied value of developmental science. These two themes are highlighted throughout the text as well as in critical thinking features. In addition, an accessible writing style helps students to grasp these complex issues.

Contextual Perspective

The most central tenet of development is that it occurs in context. At all points in life, human development is the result of dynamic transactions among individuals; their physical, cognitive, and socioemotional capacities; and the web of interacting contexts in which they are immersed, such as family, peers, school, neighborhood, society, culture, and history. *The Essentials of Lifespan Development: Lives in Context* discusses these processes, emphasizing how individual factors combine with the people, places, circumstances, and time in which we live to influence development. A contextual approach can provide the back story to development and help us understand why individuals vary. In addition, the emerging body of research on intersectionality in development offers opportunities to shed light on these complex processes and their role in development.

This contextual theme is infused throughout the text and highlighted specifically in critical thinking questions that appear at the end of each section. *Thinking in Context: Biological Influences* items ask students to consider how biological factors, such as brain development, physical development, and health, interact with context to produce developmental outcomes. *Thinking in Context: Lifespan Development* items examine developmental theory and themes, including applying Bronfenbrenner's bioecological systems theory to understand real-world problems, as well as the role of culture in development. In recent years, discussions of culture, diversity, and individual differences have expanded to consider intersectionality and its impact on the development of children, adolescents, and adults. *Thinking in Context: Intersectionality* calls attention to the ways in which race, ethnicity, gender, sexual orientation, and socioeconomic status overlap to determine opportunities and outcomes.

Applied Emphasis

The field of lifespan developmental science is unique because so much of its content has immediate relevance to our daily lives. Students may wonder: Do the first three years shape the brain for a lifetime of experiences? Is learning more than one language beneficial to children? Do people's personalities change over their lifetimes? Do adults go through a midlife crisis? How common is dementia in older adulthood? Moreover, findings from lifespan developmental science have been applied to inform social policies that affect us all. *The Essentials of Lifespan Development: Lives in Context* engages students by exploring these and many more real-world questions. This theme is integrated throughout the text and highlighted specifically in a fourth type of end-of-section critical thinking question. *Thinking in Context: Applied Developmental Science* items ask students to apply the course content by considering cases, designing research studies, and explaining the material to different audiences and contexts.

Accessible Writing Style

Having taught at a regional public university since 1996, I write in a style intended to engage diverse undergraduate readers like my own students. I attempt to write in the same voice as I teach, carefully structuring sections to build explanations and integrating content with examples that are relevant to students. I regularly use my own texts in class, students work with me in preparing elements of each text, and my students' responses and learning guide my writing. My experience teaching 12 courses during the COVID-19 pandemic in Spring 2020 and the 2020–2021 academic year reinforced (for me) the importance of accessible, concise textbooks. Like many faculty, I was able to record only so many videos for my asynchronous classes, so I relied heavily on my text, asynchronous discussion posts, and, for the classes where available, SAGE Vantage, which enabled students to interactively read the text.

Cutting Edge Research

Our knowledge of human development is rapidly expanding. My aim is to select, highlight, and integrate cutting-edge findings with existing theory and research. Because new research has its foundation in classic work, I integrate the two to present a unified story of what is currently known in developmental science. *The Essentials of Lifespan Development: Lives in Context* contains about 2,000 references published since 2018, including more than 700 published since 2020.

PEDAGOGICAL FEATURES

My day-to-day experiences in the classroom have helped me to keep college students' interests and abilities at the forefront. Unlike many textbook authors, I teach four classes each semester (and have done so since 1996). I taught my first online course in 2002. My daily exposure to multiple classes and many students helps keep me grounded in the ever-changing concerns and interests of college students. I teach a diverse group of students. Some live on campus but most commute. Most of my students are ages 18 to 24, but my classes also include many so-called adult learners over the age of 24. Many are veterans, a rapidly increasing population at my institution with unique perspectives and needs. I have many opportunities to try new examples and activities. I believe that what works in my classroom will be helpful to readers and instructors. I use the pedagogical elements of *The Essentials of Lifespan Development: Lives in Context* in my own classes and modify them based on my experiences.

Critical Thinking Questions

In March 2020, my institution, like most in the U.S., suddenly transitioned to an entirely online campus. Like many faculty across the country and world, I taught my four-course load entirely online during the 2020–2021 academic year. Interacting with students in many asynchronous courses (sprinkled with a small handful of classes that met partially on Zoom) inspired the multifaceted critical thinking feature *Thinking in Context*, which includes four types of items that highlight critical themes in developmental science. *Thinking in Context* items encourage readers to compare concepts, apply theoretical perspectives, and consider applications of the research findings presented. They appear at the end of each main section within each chapter and highlight the following previously described themes:

- Thinking in Context: Biological Influences
- Thinking in Context: Lifespan Development

- Thinking in Context: Applied Developmental Science
- Thinking in Context: Intersectionality

Learning Objectives and Summaries

Core learning objectives at the beginning of each section provide clear goals for readers. The end-of-chapter summary returns to each learning objective, recapping the key concepts presented in the chapter.

Careers Related to Developmental Science

To say that my students are interested in careers—what they will do after college—is an understatement. Students often don't know where to begin in considering possible careers. The applied feature *Lifespan Development at Work* introduces students to more than 35 careers that are related to or benefit from an understanding of developmental science. Beginning with a discussion of transferrable skills and fields, this feature appears at the end of each Part: Beginnings, Infancy, Early Childhood, Middle Childhood, Adolescence, Early Adulthood, Middle Adulthood, Late Adulthood, and Death.

It is my hope that this volume will improve instructors' and students' experiences in and out of class—and that students will be inspired to apply the findings of developmental science to their lives.

- Thinking in Context: Applied Developmental Science
- Thinking in Context: Intersectionality

Learning Objectives and Summaries

Core learning objectives at the beginning of each section provide clear goals for readers. The end-of-chapter summary is keyed to each learning objective, recapping the key content presented in the chapter.

Careers Related to Developmental Science

To say that my students are interested in careers—what they will do after college—is an understatement. Students often don't know where to begin in considering possible careers. The applied feature, *Careers in Developmental Science*, introduces students to more than 35 careers that are related to or benefit from an understanding of developmental science. Beginning with a discussion of transferable skills and fields, this feature appears at the end of each part: Beginnings, Infancy, Early Childhood, Middle Childhood, Adolescence, Early Adulthood, Middle Adulthood, Late Adulthood, and Death.

It is my hope that this volume will improve instructors' and students' experiences in and out of class—and that students will be inspired to apply the findings of developmental science to their lives.

ACKNOWLEDGMENTS

This book has benefited from the input of many bright, enthusiastic, and generous people. I am fortunate to work with a talented team at SAGE and I am grateful for their support. I thank Lara Para for her steadfast encouragement, Katherine Hepburn for her marketing wizardry, and Reid Hester for bringing me to the SAGE family. Michele Sordi encouraged me to write the first edition of *Lifespan Development: Lives in Context* and I am forever grateful for her confidence. Emma Newsom's talent in managing the many moving pieces keeping this project (and me!) on track is beyond par. Thank you! Jessica Miller provided a patient supportive ear and invaluable guidance in making the many decisions involved in writing this book.

I am especially appreciative of those who have shared their feedback and helped me to improve this book. Lauren Schwarz provided invaluable assistance in a variety of capacities, from brainstorming and literature searches to organization, record keeping, and a range of creative (and frequently tedious) tasks. I thank Gabrielle Johnson for her meticulous review and update of the Glossary and her contributions to the careers feature, including brainstorming, gathering, and organizing the data. Thanks, Gabby, for your creativity and positive vibes.

I thank my students for their engagement in and out of class. Our discussions inform these pages. I am especially appreciative of those who have shared their feedback. Thank you to the many instructors who have reviewed and provided feedback on these chapters.

Finally, I thank my family, especially my parents, for their unwavering support. Most of all, I am thankful for the support of my husband, Fred, for his optimism, patience, encouragement, and love. There's no one I'd rather quarantine with.

SAGE thanks the following expert reviewers, who provided detailed recommendations in their areas of expertise with a focus on multicultural and cross-cultural findings and diversity in development:

Dr. Cassendra Bergstrom completed her Ph.D. in educational psychology at the University of Northern Colorado (UNC), where she is now an assistant professor. She held a post-doctoral research position working on a National Science Foundation grant through the Math and Science Teaching Institution, also at UNC. Dr. Bergstrom's research focuses on the intersection of motivation and learning environments, with a recent focus on equity. Her publications and presentations stem from research projects on the topics of transformative experience, goal orientation, and problem-based learning (PBL) environments. Dr. Bergstrom currently teaches undergraduate psychology courses, as well as graduate courses in educational psychology.

Dr. Flora Farago is an assistant professor of Human Development and Family Studies at Stephen F. Austin State University, with a background in developmental psychology and early childhood education. Her teaching and research interests center on children's prejudice and stereotype development and anti-bias curricula surrounding race and gender. Dr. Farago is particularly interested in the link between research and community activism. She collaborates with colleagues and organizations nationally and internationally, including the Indigo Cultural Center, the Jirani Project, and the Girl Child Network, to promote racial and gender equity.

Dr. Jessamy Comer is a lecturer at Rochester Institute of Technology in Rochester, New York. She has been teaching developmental psychology for more than a decade, as well as many other undergraduate and graduate courses. Her area of research interest and specialization is parent-child relationships, particularly during adolescence. She earned her B.A. in psychology from Baylor University in Waco, Texas, and she earned her M.A. and Ph.D. in developmental psychology from the University of Rochester in Rochester, New York. She is also a recipient of the Helen and Vincent Nowlis Award for Excellence in Teaching.

Kathy Erickson is a University of Arizona faculty member teaching in the Human Services and Family Studies departments. Professor Erickson's master's degree is in holistic psychology, with an emphasis on mindfulness and addiction. She has an undergraduate degree in counseling with a minor in holistic education. For two decades Kathy worked with adolescents in education and social services settings. She introduced students to biofeedback and mindfulness techniques to help them develop mechanisms to alleviate and manage stress. She is committed to the value of integrating mindfulness throughout all aspects of one's life as well as in the courses she teaches.

Dr. Merranda Romero Marín is an associate professor in the Department of Family and Consumer Science at New Mexico State University where she teaches courses ranging from lifespan development to multicultural family life education and clinical courses in marriage and family therapy. She is a licensed psychologist and a licensed marriage and family therapist specializing in the treatment of post-traumatic stress disorder (PTSD). Her areas of research include understanding the impact of poverty on children and family systems, the effects of trauma on family and community systems, multicultural counseling, and individual and family resilience.

Dr. Robert S. Weisskirch, MSW, Ph.D. is a professor of human development in the Liberal Studies Department at California State University, Monterey Bay. His research interests focus on language brokering, ethnic identity and acculturation, developmental perspectives on romantic relationships, how technology affects relationships (i.e., parent-adolescent relationships, sexting, and romantic relationships), and pedagogy of adolescent development. He received his Ph.D. in human development from the University of California, Davis, a master of social work from San Diego State University, and a Multiple Subjects teaching credential and B.A. in psychology from the University of California, Irvine.

Dr. Sarah Savoy is an associate professor of psychology at Stephen F. Austin State University, where she teaches courses in developmental, social, and health psychology. Her research concerns topics such as social and cognitive processes that contribute to the development of disordered eating as well as stigma related to eating disorders and obesity.

SAGE wishes to thank the following reviewers for their valuable contributions to the development of this first edition:

Elaine Cassel, Lord Fairfax Community College
Kim Cassie, University of Oklahoma
Christine Feeley, Farmingdale State College
Lora Garrison, Rogers State University
Krisztina Jakobsen, James Madison University
Melanie Keyes, Eastern Connecticut State University
Martha Low, Winston-Salem State University
Eirini Papafratzeskakou, Mercer County Community College
Sanjay Paul, Bethune-Cookman University
Amy Skinner, Troy University
Matthew Westra, Metropolitan Community College, Longview
Brenda Whitehead, University of Michigan, Dearborn

SAGE also expresses special appreciation to reviewers of *Lifespan Development*, whose thoughtful feedback is reflected here in these chapters:

Marita Andreassen, Inland Norway Univ. of Applied Sciences
Linda Aulgur, Westminster College
Stephen Baker, St. Francis University
Cassendra Bergstrom, University of Northern Colorado
Carla Bluhm, College of Coastal Georgia
Jamie Borchardt, Tarleton State University
Kelly Champion, Northern Illinois University
Ashley Cosentino, Chicago School of Prof. Psychology
Christine Weinkauff Duranso, California State University–San Bernardino

Naomi Ekas, Texas Christian University
Mike Figuccio, CUNY Queensborough
Robert Gall, Grace University
Janice Gallagher, Ivy Tech Community College
Theresa Garfield, Texas A&M San Antonio
Surinder Gill, California State University, Sacramento
Jessica Grady, Pacific University
Jerry Green, Tarrant County College
David Hanbury, Averett University
Janice Hargrove-Freile, Lonestar State University
Erin Harmeyer, Louisiana State
Crystal Harris, Governors State University
Jerry Haywood, Fort Valley State University
Cynthia Jacox, Alamo College
Benjamin Jeppsen, University of Nevada, Reno
Cristina Joes-Kampfner, Eastern Michigan
Lakitta Johnson, Jackson State University
Jeff Kellogg, Marian University Indianapolis
Linda Krajewski, University of Redlands
Nancy Lamphere, Caldwell Community College & Technical Institute
Robyn Long, Baker University
Geraldine Lotze, Virginia Commonwealth University
Merranda Marin, New Mexico State University
Robert Martinez, Alamo College
Robert Martinez, University of the Incarnate Word
Alan Meca, Old Dominion University
Jennifer Butler Moss, Emporia State University
Maribeth Palmer-King, SUNY Broome
Melanie Palomares, University Of South Carolina
Michelle Pilati, Rio Hondo College
Gary Popoli, Stevenson University
Kathy Phillippi-Immel, University of Wisconsin Colleges
Carolynn Pravatta, Collin College
Katie Purswell, Texas State University
Martha Ravola, Alcorn University
Mary Schindler, Sonoma State University
Brittney Schrick, University of Arkansas Cooperative Extension Service
Staci Simmelink-Johnson, Walla Walla Community College
Nina Slota, Fairmont State University
Patrick Smith, Virginia Community College
Brooke Spangler-Cropenbaker, Miami University
Catherine Steinbock, Eastern Wyoming College
Tara Stoppa, Eastern University
Elizabeth Tinsley, Marquette University
Marcia Tipton, Milwaukee Area Technical College
Debra Tower, University of Oklahoma
Katherine Volk, Lesley University
Bridget Walsh, University of Arkansas Cooperative Extension Service
Shauna Nefos Webb, Milligan College

ABOUT THE AUTHOR

Tara L. Kuther is professor of psychology at Western Connecticut State University where she has taught courses in child, adolescent, and adult development since 1996. She earned her Ph.D. in developmental psychology at Fordham University. Dr. Kuther is fellow of the Society for the Teaching of Psychology (APA, Division 2), has served in various capacities in the Society for the Teaching of Psychology and Society for Research on Adolescence, and is the former chair of the Teaching Committee for the Society for Research in Child Development. In addition to the award-winning book, *Lifespan Development: Lives in Context,* Dr. Kuther is also the author of *Child and Adolescent Development in Context; Adolescence in Context;* and *Lifespan Development in Context: A Topical Approach.* Her research interests include social cognition and risky activity in adolescence and adulthood. She is also interested in promoting undergraduate and graduate students' professional development. Her books *The Psychology Major's Handbook* and *Careers in Psychology: Opportunities in a Changing World* (with Robert Morgan) are intended to help students navigate the challenges of pursing undergraduate and graduate degrees in psychology.

1 UNDERSTANDING HUMAN DEVELOPMENT: APPROACHES AND THEORIES

Source: istock/Hispanolistic

Think back over your lifetime. How have you grown and changed over the years? Do your parents describe you as having been a happy baby? Were you fussy? What are some of your most vivid childhood memories? Were your adolescent years a stressful time? What types of changes do you expect to undergo in your adult years? Will you have a spouse? Will you have children? What career will you choose? How might these life choices and circumstances influence how you age and your perspective in older adulthood? Will your personality remain the same or change over time? In short, how will you change over the course of your lifespan?

WHAT IS LIFESPAN HUMAN DEVELOPMENT?

LEARNING OBJECTIVE

1.1 Outline five principles of the lifespan developmental perspective.

This is a book about **lifespan human development:** how people grow, change, and stay the same throughout their lives, from conception to death. When people use the term ***development***, they often mean the transformation from infant to adult. However, development does not end with adulthood. We continue to change in predictable ways throughout our lifetime, even into old age. Developmental scientists who study human development seek to understand these lifetime patterns of change.

We progress through many stages in life (see Table 1.1). The stages may have different labels and different sets of developmental tasks, but all have value and influence each other. The changes that we undergo during infancy, for instance, influence how we experience later changes, such as those during adolescence and beyond. Each stage of life is important and accompanied by its own demands and opportunities.

Change is perhaps the most obvious indicator of development. The muscle strength and coordination needed to play sports increases during childhood and adolescence, peaks in early adulthood, and begins to decline thereafter, declining more rapidly from middle to late adulthood (Gabbard, 2018). There also are ways in which we change little over our lifetimes. Some personality traits are highly stable over the lifespan, so that we remain largely the "same person" into old age (Schwaba & Bleidorn, 2018; Wortman et al., 2012).

TABLE 1.1 ■ Stages in Human Development

Life Stage	Approximate Age Range	Description
Prenatal	Conception to birth	Shortly after conception, a single-celled organism grows and multiplies. This is the period of the most rapid physical development as basic body structures and organs form, grow, and begin to function.
Infancy and toddlerhood	Birth to 2 years	The newborn is equipped with senses that help it to learn about the world. Physical growth occurs and motor, perceptual, and intellectual skills develop. Children show advances in language comprehension, problem solving, self-awareness, and emotional control. They become more independent and interested in interacting with other children and form bonds with parents and others.
Early childhood	2 to 6 years	Children grow steadily, their muscles strengthen, and they become better at coordinating their bodies. Memory, language, and imagination improve. Children become more independent and better able to regulate their emotions. Family remains children's primary social tie, but other children become more important and new ties to peers are established.
Middle childhood	6 to 11 years	Growth slows, but strength and athletic ability increase dramatically. Children show improvements in their ability to reason, remember, read, and use arithmetic. As children advance cognitively and gain social experience, they understand themselves in more complex ways compared with younger children. As friendships develop, peers and group memberships become more important.
Adolescence	11 to 18 years	Adolescents' bodies grow rapidly. They become physically and sexually mature. Although some immature thinking persists, adolescents can reason in sophisticated and adultlike ways. Adolescents are driven to learn about themselves and begin the process of discovering who they are. Peer groups increase in importance.
Early adulthood	18 to 40 years	Physical condition peaks and then shows slight declines with time. Lifestyle choices play a large role in influencing health. Most young adults join the workforce, marry or establish a longterm bond with a spouse, and become parents. The timing of these transitions varies. Adolescents in Western industrialized societies often experience an extended transition to adulthood (called **emerging adulthood**), spanning from ages 18 to 25 and as late as age 29.
Middle adulthood	40 to 65 years	In middle adulthood, people begin to notice changes in their senses, physical stamina, and sexuality. Basic mental abilities, expertise, and practical problem-solving skills peak. Career changes and family transitions require that adults continue to refine their understandings of themselves. Adults help children to become independent; then they adapt to an empty nest and assist elderly parents with their health and personal needs.
Late adulthood	65 years and beyond	Most older adults remain healthy and active. Reaction time slows, and although most older adults show a decline in some aspects of memory and intelligence, an increase in expertise and wisdom compensates for losses. Most older adult friendships are old friendships, and these tend to be very close and a source of support. Adults adjust to retirement, changes in health, and personal losses (such as the death of a loved one), as well as search for meaning in their lives.
Death		Death is a process that includes the stopping of heartbeat, circulation, breathing, and brain activity. A person's death causes changes in his or her social context—family members and friends must adjust to and accept the loss.

Lifespan human development can be described by several principles. Development is (1) multidimensional, (2) multidirectional, (3) plastic, (4) influenced by multiple contexts, and (5) developmental science is multidisciplinary (Baltes et al., 2006; Overton & Molenaar, 2015).

Development Is Multidimensional

Consider the many changes that mark each period of development and it is apparent that development is *multidimensional*. That is, development includes changes in multiple domains or areas of development. **Physical development** refers to body maturation and growth, such as body size, proportion, appearance, health, and perceptual abilities. **Cognitive development** refers to the maturation of thought processes and the tools that we use to obtain knowledge, become aware of the world around us, and solve problems. **Socioemotional development** includes changes in personality, emotions, views of oneself, social skills, and interpersonal relationships with family and friends. These areas of development overlap and interact. Brain maturation, a physical development, underlies advances in cognitive development, which enable adolescents to become better at understanding their best friend's point of view and to show more prosocial helpful behavior (Tamnes et al., 2018). In turn, adolescents become more empathetic and sensitive to their friends' needs and develop a more mature friendship, influencing socioemotional development (see Figure 1.1; Tamnes et al., 2018).

Development Is Multidirectional

Development is commonly described as a series of improvements in performance and functioning, but in fact development is *multidirectional*, meaning that it consists of both gains and losses, growth and decline, throughout the lifespan (Baltes et al., 2006; Overton & Molenaar, 2015). Throughout life, there is a shifting balance between gains, or improvements in performance (common early in life), and losses, or declines in performance (common late in life; Baltes et al., 2006; Zacher et al., 2019). At all ages individuals can compensate for losses by improving existing skills and developing new ones (Boker, 2013). The speed at which people think tends to slow in late adulthood, but their increases in knowledge and experience enable older adults to compensate for the loss of speed when completing everyday tasks (Krampe & Charness, 2018; Margrett et al., 2010).

Development Is Plastic

Development is characterized by **plasticity**: It is malleable, or changeable. Frequently the brain and body can compensate for illness and injury. In children who are injured and experience brain damage, other parts of the brain may take on new functions (Petranovich et al., 2020). Older adults who have experienced a decline in balance and muscle strength can regain and improve these capabilities through exercise (McAuley et al., 2013; Sañudo et al., 2019). Plasticity tends to decline as we age, but it does not disappear entirely. Plasticity makes it possible for individuals to adjust to change and to demonstrate **resilience**, the capacity to adapt effectively to adverse contexts and circumstances (Luthar et al., 2015; Masten, 2016).

FIGURE 1.1 ■ Domains of Development

Advances in physical, cognitive, and socioemotional development interact, permitting children to play sports, learn more efficiently, and develop close friendships.

Physical | Cognitive | Socioemotional

Source: iStock/ Essentials; iStock/ Signature; Jupiter/ Pixland/Thinkstock

Some plasticity is retained throughout life. Practicing athletic activities can help older adults rebuild muscle and improve balance.

Reuters/Mariana Bazo

Development Is Influenced by Multiple Contexts

Context refers to where and when a person develops. Context encompasses many aspects of the physical and social environment, including family, neighborhood, country, and historical period. It includes intangible factors—characteristics that are not visible to the naked eye, such as values, customs, ideals, and culture. To understand individuals' development, we must look at their context, including the subtle, less easily perceived aspects.

Were you encouraged to be assertive and actively question the adults around you, or were you expected to be quiet and avoid confrontation? How large a part did spirituality or religion play in your family's life? Did it shape your parents' childrearing practices and your own values? How did your family's economic status affect your development? These questions examine the home context, critical for our development. We are also embedded in other contexts that influence us and that we influence, such as peer group, school, neighborhood or community, and culture. Our development occurs within the contexts in which we live, a theme that we will return to throughout this book.

Sociohistorical Context

The multitude of contextual factors that interact over the life course can be organized into three categories: age-graded influences, history-graded influences, and nonnormative influences (Elder & George, 2016; Elder et al., 2016).

Age-graded influences are closely tied to chronological age and are largely predictable. Most individuals walk when about 1 year old and reach puberty in early adolescence. Similarly, most women reach menopause in their late 40s or early 50s. Age-graded influences tend to be most influential early and late in life. Although these influences are often tied to biology, social milestones can also form age-graded influences. Most people in the United States enter school at about 5 years of age, graduate from high school and enter college at about age 18, and retire during their 60s. Some age-graded influences are context-dependent. Adolescents in suburban and rural contexts commonly get driver's licenses at age 16, but this may not be true of adolescents in urban settings where driving may be less common.

The term *history-graded influence* refers to how the time in which we live and the unique historical circumstances of that period affect our development. History-graded influences include wars, epidemics, advances in science and technology, and economic shifts such as periods of depression or prosperity (Baltes, 1987). For instance, the COVID-19 pandemic shaped individuals' health behaviors, such as wearing face coverings, standing further away from others, and refraining from handshakes and hugs. School closures during the pandemic posed risks to children's and adolescents' academic and social development as well as their mental health (Golberstein et al., 2020; Lee, 2020). Even temporary changes such as these are contextual influences that shape our world and our development. The effect of historical events on development depends in part on when they occur in a person's life (Elder et al., 2015). Older adults may experience the COVID pandemic differently than younger people, given their lifelong experiences as well as their heightened risk for infection (Pfefferbaum & North, 2020). For many older adults, the pandemic is a period of great loneliness.

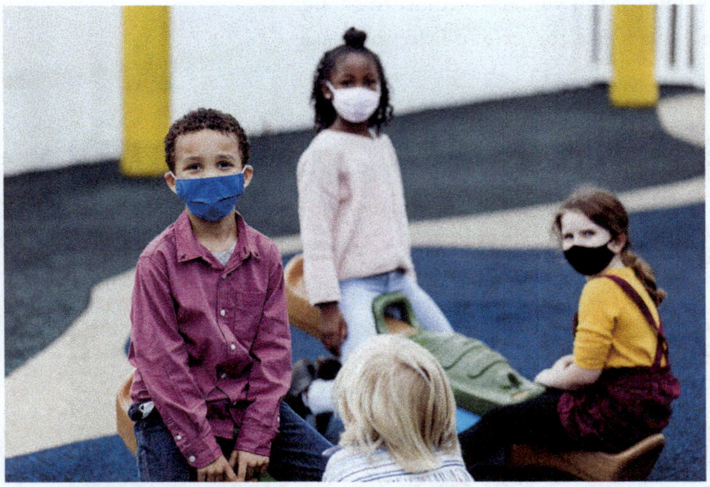

The COVID-19 pandemic is an example of a sociohistorical influence that contributes to cohort, or generational, differences in development.

istock/kali9

Contextual influences tied to specific historical eras explain why generations, such as "Baby Boomers" and "Millennials," differ from each other. A generation is also known as a **cohort** (a group of people born around the same time). Members of a cohort are similar in ways that people born at other times are not. For example, adults who came of age during the Great Depression and World War II tend to have particularly strong views on the importance of the family, civic-mindedness, and social connection (Rogler, 2002).

Take a moment to think about what role larger historical events have played in your development. Consider the Black Lives Matter Movement, begun in 2013; the legalization of same-sex marriage in the United States in 2015; the school shooting in Newtown, Connecticut in 2012; the election of the first African American president of the United States in 2008; and the terrorist attacks of September 11, 2001. How have historical events influenced you and those around you? Can you identify ways in which, because of historical events, your cohort may differ from your parents' cohort? Your grandparents' cohort?

Whereas age-graded and history-graded influences are common to all people, or all members of a cohort, individuals also have experiences that are unique to them. *Nonnormative influences* are experiences or events that happen to a person or a few people. Nonnormative influences include experiencing the death of a parent in childhood, widowhood in early adulthood, winning the lottery, or illness. Nonnormative events are not predictable and are not easily studied, as they are not experienced by most people—and the nature of nonnormative events varies widely. With age, nonnormative influences become more powerful determinants of development.

Cultural Context

Like sociohistorical context, the cultural context is a broad influence on the development of all people at all ages in life. **Culture** refers to a set of customs, knowledge, attitudes, and values that are shared by members of a group and are learned early in life through interactions with group members (Markus & Kitayama, 1991). We are immersed in culture, which influences all of our contexts and includes the processes used by people as they make meaning or think through interactions with group members (Mistry et al., 2016; Yoshikawa et al., 2016).

Development varies dramatically with cultural context (Keller, 2017). The cultural context in which individuals live influences the timing and expression of many aspects of their development, even physical developments such as walking, which was long thought to be a matter of biological maturation (Mistry, 2013). In Uganda, infants begin to walk at about 10 months of age, in France at about 15 months, and in the United States at about 12 months. These differences are influenced by parenting practices that vary by culture. African parents tend to handle infants in ways that stimulate walking, by playing games that allow infants to practice jumping and walking skills (Hopkins & Westra, 1989; Super, 1981).

Development and culture are fused and mutually interact, with culture inherent in all **domains of development** and a contributor to the context in which we are embedded, transmitting values, attitudes, and beliefs that shape our thoughts, beliefs, and behaviors (Mistry & Dutta, 2015). There are many cultures, or subcultures, within each society (Oyserman, 2016, 2017). North American culture is not homogeneous; many subcultures exist, defined by factors such as ethnicity (e.g., African American, Asian American), religion (e.g., Christian, Muslim), geography (e.g., southern, midwestern), and others, as well as combinations of these factors.

Developmental Science is Multidisciplinary

Psychologists, sociologists, anthropologists, biologists, neuroscientists, and medical researchers all conduct research that is relevant to understanding aspects of human development. Consider cognitive development. Children's performance on cognitive measures, such as problem solving, is influenced by their physical health and nutrition (Anjos et al., 2013; Biddle et al., 2019), interactions with peers (Holmes et al., 2016), and neurological development (Stiles et al., 2015), findings from the fields of medicine, psychology, and neuroscience, respectively. To understand how people develop at all periods in life, developmental scientists must combine insights from all of these disciplines.

Thinking in Context: Lifespan Development

1. Describe your own development. Provide personal examples that illustrate the multidimensional nature of your own development. In what ways has your development illustrated multidirectionality? Plasticity?

2. Consider the societal and cultural events that your parents may have experienced in their youth. What technology was available? What historical events did they experience? What were the popular fads of their youth? What influence do you think these sociohistorical factors may have had on your parents' development? Compare their sociohistorical context with the one in which you were raised. What historical and societal events may have influenced you? What events have shaped your generation?

3. Consider your own experiences with culture. With which culture or subculture do you identify? How much of a role do you think your cultural membership has had in your development?

4. Why might some people say that the U.S. has no culture? What do you think?

BASIC ISSUES IN LIFESPAN HUMAN DEVELOPMENT

LEARNING OBJECTIVE

1.2 Explain three basic issues in developmental science.

Developmental scientists agree that people change throughout life and show increases in some capacities and decreases in others from conception to death. Yet they sometimes disagree about how development proceeds and what causes developmental changes. Developmental scientists' explanations of how people grow and change over their lives are influenced by their perspectives on three basic issues, or fundamental questions, about human development:

(1) Do people change gradually, often imperceptibly, over time, or is developmental change sudden and dramatic?

(2) What role do people play in their own development? How much are they influenced by their surroundings, and how much do they influence their surroundings?

(3) To what extent is development a function of inborn genetic characteristics, and to what extent is it affected by the environment in which individuals live?

The following sections examine each of these questions.

Development Is Characterized by Continuous and Discontinuous Change

Do children slowly grow into adults, steadily gaining more knowledge and experience and becoming better at reasoning? Or do they grow in spurts, showing sudden, large gains in knowledge and reasoning capacities? Some aspects of development unfold slowly and gradually over time, demonstrating **continuous change**. For example, children slowly gain experience and learn strategies to become quicker at problem solving (Siegler, 2016). Similarly, middle-aged adults experience gradual losses of muscle and strength (Keller & Engelhardt, 2013). Others aspects of development are best described as **discontinuous change**, characterized by abrupt change, with individuals of various ages dramatically different from one another. Puberty transforms children's bodies into more adult-like adolescent bodies (Wolf & Long, 2016), infants' understanding and capacity for language is qualitatively different from that of school-aged children (Rudman & Titjen, 2018), and children make leaps in their reasoning abilities over the course of childhood, such as from believing that robotic dogs and other inanimate objects are alive to understanding that life is a biological process (Beran et al., 2011; Zaitchik et al., 2014). As shown in Figure 1.2, a discontinuous view of development emphasizes sudden transformation, whereas a continuous view emphasizes gradual and steady changes.

It was once believed that development was either continuous or discontinuous, but not both. Today, developmental scientists agree that development includes both continuity and discontinuity (Lerner et al., 2014). Whether a particular developmental change appears continuous or discontinuous depends, in part, on our point of view. Consider physical growth. We often think of increases in height as involving a slow and steady process; each month, an infant is taller than the prior month, illustrating continuous change. However, as shown in Figure 1.3, when researchers measured infants' height every day, they discovered that infants have growth days and nongrowth days—days in which they show rapid change in height interspersed with days in which there is no change in height—illustrating

FIGURE 1.2 ■ Continuous and Discontinuous Development

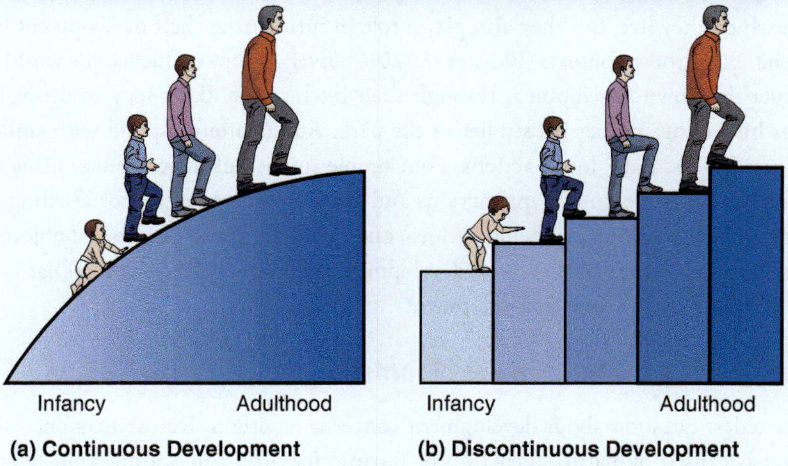

Adapted from End of the Game (2014) Child Development 101 – History and Theory, https://endofthegame.net/2014/04/15/child-development-101-history-and-theory/3/

FIGURE 1.3 ■ Infant Growth: A Continuous or Discontinuous Process

Infants' growth occurs in a random series of roughly 1-centimeter spurts in height that occur over 24 hours or less. The overall pattern of growth entails increases in height, but whether the growth appears to be continuous or discontinuous depends on our point of view.

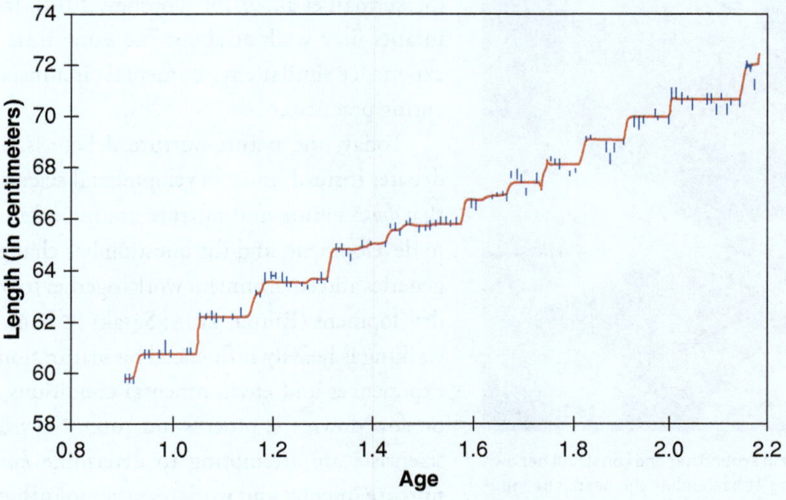

Source: Lampl et al (1992).

discontinuous change (Lampl et al., 2001). In this example, monthly measurements of infant height suggest gradual increases, but daily measurements show spurts of growth, each lasting 24 hours or less. Thus, whether a given phenomenon, such as height, is described as continuous or discontinuous depends on perspective. Most developmental scientists agree that some aspects of development are best described as continuous and others as discontinuous (Miller, 2016).

Individuals Are Active in Development

Do people have a role in influencing how they change over their lifetimes? That is, are people active in influencing their own development? Taking an active role means that they interact with and influence the world around them, create experiences that lead to developmental change, and thereby influence how they change over the lifespan. Alternatively, if individuals take a passive role in their development, they are shaped by, but do not influence, the world around them.

The prevailing view among developmental scientists is that people are active contributors to their own development (Lerner et al., 2014; Overton, 2015). People are influenced by the physical and social contexts in which they live, but they also play a role in influencing their development by interacting with, and changing, those contexts (Elder et al., 2016). Even infants influence the world around them and construct their own development through their interactions. Baby Joey smiles at each adult he passes by as his mother pushes his stroller in the park. Adults often respond with smiles, use "baby talk," and make faces. Baby Joey's actions, even simple smiles, influence adults, bringing them into close contact, making one-on-one interactions and creating opportunities for learning. By engaging the world around them, thinking, being curious, and interacting with people and objects, infants and children are "manufacturers of their own development" (Flavell, 1992, p. 998). That is, they play an active role in influencing their own development.

Nature and Nurture Influence Development

Perhaps the oldest question about development concerns its origin. Researchers once asked whether development is caused by nature (genetics) or nurture (environment), a question referred to as the **nature-nurture debate**. Explanations that relied on nature pointed to inborn genetic traits and maturational processes as causes of developmental change. For example, most infants take their first steps at roughly the same age, suggesting a maturational trend that supports the role of nature in development (Payne & Isaacs, 2016). An alternative explanation for developmental change emphasized nurture—the environment. Although most infants begin to walk at about the same time, environmental conditions can speed up or slow down the process. Infants who experience malnutrition may walk later than well-nourished infants, and those who are given practice making stepping or jumping movements may walk earlier (Siekerman et al., 2015; Worobey, 2014). In other words, infants may walk at about the same time because they experience similar environmental circumstances and parenting practices.

It's easy to see how this baby can influence the world around her and construct her own development through her interactions. By smiling at each adult she sees, she influences her world because adults are likely to smile, use "baby talk," and play with her in response.

istock/monkeybusinessimages

Today, the nature-nurture debate is, in fact, not a debate. Instead, most developmental scientists now agree that *both* nature and nurture are important contributors to development, and the question has changed to how do genetics and environment work together to influence child development (Rutter, 2014; Sasaki & Kim, 2017). Thus, walking is heavily influenced by maturation (nature), but experiences and environmental conditions can speed up or slow down the process (nurture). Now developmental scientists are attempting to determine *how* nature and nurture interact and work together to influence how people grow and change throughout life (Bjorklund, 2018b; Lickliter & Witherington, 2017).

Thinking in Context: Lifespan Development

1. Identify ways in which you have changed very gradually over the years. Have there been times when you showed abrupt change, such as in physical growth, strength and coordination, thinking abilities, or social skills? In other words, in what ways is your development characterized by continuity? Discontinuity?
2. Provide examples of how a child might play an active role in his or her development. How do children influence the world around them?

Thinking in Context: Biological Influences

1. How is nature and nurture reflected in your own development? What traits, abilities, or behaviors do you believe are influenced by inborn factors? What role did the physical and social environment play in your development?
2. Consider similarities and differences among your family members. How might they reflect the interaction of nature and nurture?

THEORETICAL PERSPECTIVES ON HUMAN DEVELOPMENT

LEARNING OBJECTIVE

1.3 Summarize five theoretical perspectives on human development.

Over the past century, scientists have learned much about how individuals progress from infants, to children, to adolescents, and to adults, as well as how they change throughout adulthood. The great body of research in the field of lifespan human development has been organized into several theoretical perspectives to account for the developmental changes that occur over the lifespan.

Psychoanalytic Theories

Psychoanalytic theories describe development and behavior as a result of the interplay of inner drives, memories, and conflicts we are unaware of and cannot control. Freud and Erikson are two key psychoanalytic theorists.

Freud's Psychosexual Theory

Sigmund Freud (1856–1939), a Viennese physician, believed that much of our behavior is driven by unconscious impulses (impulses that are outside of our awareness). He described development as the progression through a series of *psychosexual stages*, periods in which unconscious drives are focused on different parts of the body, making stimulation to those parts a source of pleasure. Freud explained that the task for parents is to strike a balance between overgratifying and undergratifying a child's desires at each stage, to help the child develop a healthy personality with the capacity for mature relationships throughout life. Notably, Freud did not study children; his **theory** grew from his work with female psychotherapy patients (Crain, 2016). Today Freud's ideas about psychosexual development and emphasis on childhood sexuality are unpopular and not widely accepted (Westen, 1998). In addition, it is not possible to conduct research examining Freud's ideas because unconscious drives and other psychosexual constructs cannot be directly observed and tested (Miller, 2016).

Sigmund Freud (1856–1939), the father of the psychoanalytic perspective, believed that much of our behavior is driven by unconscious impulses.

Library of Congress

Erik Erikson (1902–1994) posited that, throughout their lives, people progress through eight stages of psychosocial development.

Jon Erikson/Science Source

Erikson's Psychosocial Theory

Erik Erikson (1902–1994) was influenced by Freud, but he placed less emphasis on unconscious motivators of development and instead focused on the role of the social world, society, and culture (see Table 1.2). According to Erikson, throughout their lives, individuals progress through eight *psychosocial stages* that include changes in how they understand and interact with others, as well as changes in how they understand themselves and their roles as members of society (Erikson, 1950). Each stage presents a unique developmental task, which Erikson referred to as a crisis or conflict that must be resolved. How well individuals address the crisis determines their ability to deal with the demands made by the next stage of development. For example, children's success in achieving a sense of trust in others influences their progress in developing a sense of autonomy, the ability to be independent and guide their own behavior.

Regardless of their success in resolving the crisis of a given stage, individuals are driven by biological maturation and social expectations to the next psychosocial stage. No crisis is ever fully resolved, and unresolved crises are revisited throughout life. Although Erikson believed that it is never too late to resolve a crisis, resolving a crisis from a previous stage may become more challenging over time as people focus on current demands and the crises of their current psychosocial stages.

Erikson's theory includes the role of society and culture, largely ignored by Freud. Erikson based his theory on a broad range of cases, including larger and more diverse samples of people than did Freud. Erikson's theory is criticized as difficult to test because many crises are not easily observed. It has nonetheless sparked research on specific stages, such as the development of identity during adolescence (Crain, 2016). Erikson's lifespan theory of development holds implications for every period of life. We will revisit his theory throughout this book.

TABLE 1.2 ■ Psychoanalytic Theories of Development

Approximate Age	Freud's Psychosexual Theory		Erikson's Psychosocial Theory	
0 to 18 months	Oral	Basic drives focus on the mouth, tongue, and gums. Feeding and weaning influence personality development. Failure to meet oral needs influences adult habits centering on the mouth (such as fingernail biting, overeating, smoking, excessive drinking)	Trust vs. Mistrust	Infants learn to trust that others will fulfill their basic needs (nourishment, warmth, comfort) or to lack confidence that their needs will be met.
18 months to 3 years	Anal	Basic drives are oriented toward the anus, and toilet training is an important influence on personality development. If caregivers are too demanding or too lax, individuals may develop issues of control such as a need to impose extreme order and cleanliness on their environment or extreme messiness and disorder.	Autonomy vs. Shame and Doubt	Toddlers learn to be self-sufficient and independent though toilet training, feeding, walking, talking, and exploring or to lack confidence in their own abilities and doubt themselves.
3 to 6 years	Phallic	In Freud's most controversial stage, basic drives shift to the genitals. The child develops a romantic desire for the opposite-sex parent and a sense of hostility and/or fear of the same-sex parent. The conflict between the child's desires and fears arouses anxiety and discomfort. It is resolved by pushing the desires into the unconscious and spending time with the same-sex parent and adopting his or her behaviors and roles, adopting societal expectations and values. Failure to resolve this conflict may result in guilt and a lack of conscience.	Initiative vs. Guilt	Young children become inquisitive, ambitious, and eager for responsibility or experience overwhelming guilt for their curiosity and overstepping boundaries.

Approximate Age	Freud's Psychosexual Theory		Erikson's Psychosocial Theory	
6 years to puberty	Latency	This is not a stage but a time of calm between stages when the child develops talents and skills and focuses on school, sports, and friendships.	Industry vs. Inferiority	Children learn to be hard working, competent, and productive by mastering new skills in school, friendships, and home life or experience difficulty, leading to feelings of inadequacy and incompetence.
Adolescence	Genital	With the physical changes of early adolescence, the basic drives again become oriented toward the genitals. The person becomes concerned with developing mature adult sexual interests and sexual satisfaction in adult relationships throughout life.	Identity vs. Role Confusion	Adolescents search for a sense of self by experimenting with roles. They also look for answers to the question, "Who am I?" in terms of career, sexual, and political roles or remain confused about who they are and their place in the world.
Early adulthood			Intimacy vs. Isolation	Young adults seek companionship and a close relationship with another person or experience isolation and self-absorption through difficulty developing intimate relationships and sharing with others.
Middle adulthood			Generativity vs. Stagnation	Adults contribute to, establish, and guide the next generation through work, creative activities, and parenting or stagnate, remaining emotionally impoverished and concerned about themselves.
Late adulthood			Integrity vs. Despair	Older adults look back at life to make sense of it, accept mistakes, and view life as meaningful and productive or feel despair over goals never reached and fear of death.

Behaviorist and Social Learning Theories

In response to psychoanalytic theorists' emphasis on the unconscious as an invisible influence on development and behavior, some scientists pointed to the importance of studying observable behavior rather than thoughts and emotion, which cannot be seen or objectively verified. Theorists who study **behaviorism** examine only behavior that can be observed and believe that all behavior is influenced by the physical and social environment. Consider this famous quote from John Watson (1925), a founder of behaviorism:

> Give me a dozen healthy infants, well formed, and my own specified world to bring them up in and I'll guarantee to take any one at random and train him to become any type of specialist I might select—doctor, lawyer, artist, merchant, chief, and yes, even beggar-man and thief, regardless of his talents, penchants, tendencies, abilities, vocations, and race of his ancestors. (p. 82)

Watson believed that by controlling an infant's physical and social environment, he could control the child's destiny. Behaviorist theory is also known as *learning theory* because it emphasizes how people and animals learn new behaviors as a function of their environment.

Operant Conditioning

Perhaps it is human nature to notice that the consequences of our behavior influence our future behavior. A teenager who arrives home after curfew and is greeted with a severe scolding may be less likely to return home late in the future. A child who is praised for setting the dinner table may be more likely to spontaneously set the table in the future. These two examples illustrate the basic tenet of B. F. Skinner's (1905–1990) theory of operant conditioning, which holds that behavior becomes more or less probable depending on its consequences. According to Skinner, a behavior followed by a rewarding or pleasant outcome, called **reinforcement**, will be more likely to recur, but one followed by an aversive or unpleasant outcome, called **punishment** will be less likely to recur.

In a classic study conducted by Albert Bandura, children who observed an adult playing with a bobo doll toy roughly imitated those behaviors, suggesting that children learn through observation.

Mirrorpix/Contributor/Getty Images

Operant conditioning explains how we learn skills and habits, but developmental scientists tend to disagree with operant conditioning's emphasis on external events (reinforcing and punishing consequences) over internal events (thoughts and emotions) as influences on behavior (Crain, 2016). Controlling people's environments can influence their development, but change can also occur from within, through people's own thoughts and actions. Children, adolescents, and adults can devise new ideas and learn independently without experiencing reinforcement or punishment, consistent with the lifespan concept that individuals are active contributors to their development.

Social Learning Theory

Like behaviorists, Albert Bandura (1925–2021) believed that the physical and social environments are important, but he also advocated for thought and emotion as contributors to development. According to Bandura's **social learning theory**, people actively process information—they think and they feel emotion—and their thoughts and feelings influence their behavior. The physical and social environments influence our behavior through their effect on our thoughts and emotions. We can learn by thinking about the potential consequences of our actions. Teenagers who break their curfew and are met by worried parents may experience remorse, and remorse may make them less likely to come home late in the future. We do not need to experience punishment or reinforcement to change our behavior (Bandura, 2012).

One of Bandura's most enduring ideas about development is that people learn by observing the consequences of others' actions, which he referred to as **observational learning** (Bandura, 2010). Children who observe violence rewarded, such as a child grabbing (and successfully obtaining) another child's toy, may imitate what they see and use aggressive means to take other children's toys. A child observer might be less likely to imitate a child who takes another child's toy if the aggressor is scolded by a teacher and placed in time out.

Bandura also contributed to the field of lifespan human development with his concept of **reciprocal determinism**, according to which individuals and the environment interact and influence each other (Bandura, 2011, 2018). Bandura viewed individuals as active in their development because development is a result of interactions between the individual's characteristics, his or her behavior, and the physical and social environment (see Figure 1.4).

People's characteristics influence their behavior and the environments they seek. Their environments also influence their characteristics. Personal characteristics (e.g., inquisitiveness) influence behavior (e.g., asking lots of questions), which influences the environment (e.g., receiving interesting responses from other people). Those responses, in turn, influence behavior (asking questions and further engaging others) and personal characteristics (increasing or decreasing inquisitiveness).

FIGURE 1.4 ■ Bandura's Model of Reciprocal Determinism

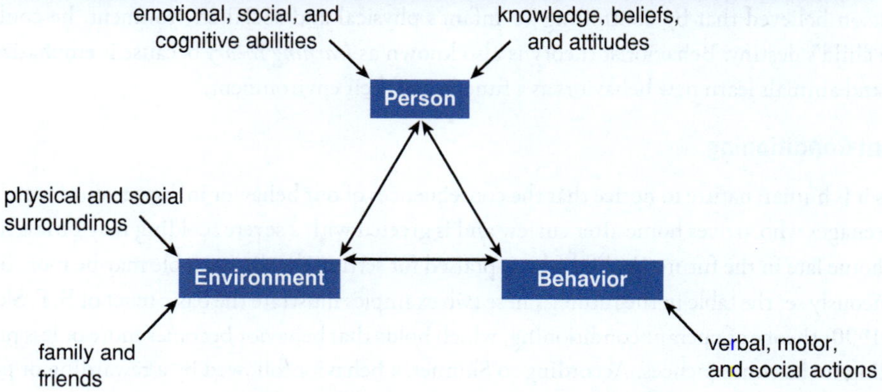

Concepts such as observational learning, reinforcement, and punishment are powerful means of explaining human behavior and hold implications for parents, teachers, and anyone who works with people of any age. Social learning theory and reciprocal determinism illustrate the role that individuals play in their own development, a more complex explanation for development and behavior. We will revisit these concepts in later chapters.

Jean Piaget (1896–1980) believed that children's drive to explore and understand the world around them propels them through four stages of cognitive development.

Bill Anderson/Science Source

Cognitive Theories

Cognitive theorists view cognition (thought) as essential to understanding people's functioning across the lifespan.

Piaget's Cognitive-Developmental Theory

Swiss scholar Jean Piaget (1896–1980) was the first scientist to systematically examine infants' and children's thinking and reasoning. Piaget believed that to understand children, we must understand how they think because thinking influences all behavior. Piaget's **cognitive-developmental theory** views children and adults as active explorers of their world, driven to learn by interacting with the world around them and organizing what they learn, thereby contributing to their own cognitive development.

Piaget proposed that children's drive to explore and understand the world propels them through four stages of cognitive development (see Table 1.3). His concept of cognitive stages and the suggestion that children's reasoning is limited by their stage has implications for education—specifically, the idea that effective instruction must match the child's developmental level.

Information Processing Theory

According to **information processing theory**, the mind works in ways similar to a computer in that information enters and then is manipulated, stored, recalled, and used to solve problems (Halford & Andrews, 2011). Unlike the theories we have discussed thus far, information processing theory is not one theory that is attributed to an individual theorist. Instead, there are many information processing theories, and each emphasizes a different aspect of thinking (Callaghan & Corbit, 2015; Müller et al., 2015; Ristic & Enns, 2015). Some theories focus on how people perceive, focus on, and take in information. Others examine how people store information, create memories, and remember information. Still others examine problem solving—how people approach and solve problems in school, the workplace, and everyday life.

TABLE 1.3 ■ Piaget's Stages of Cognitive Development

Stage	Approximate Age	Description
Sensorimotor	Birth to 2 years	Infants understand the world and think using only their senses and motor skills, by watching, listening, touching, and tasting.
Preoperations	2 to 6 years	Preschoolers explore the world using their own thoughts as guides and develop the language skills to communicate their thoughts to others. Despite these advances, their thinking is characterized by several errors in logic.
Concrete Operations	7 to 11 years	School-aged children become able to solve everyday logical problems. Their thinking is not yet fully mature because they are able to apply their thinking only to problems that are tangible and tied to specific substances.
Formal Operations	12 years to adulthood	Adolescents and adults can reason logically and abstractly about possibilities, imagined instances and events, and hypothetical concepts.

According to information processing theorists, we are born with the ability to process information. Our mental processes of noticing, taking in, manipulating, storing, and retrieving information do not show the radical changes associated with stage theories. Instead, development is continuous or gradual. We become more efficient at attending to, storing, and processing information during the childhood years and these processes tend to slow during the adult years (Luna et al., 2015). Brain maturation contributes to changes in our information processing abilities. Experience and interaction with others also contributes by helping us learn new ways of managing and manipulating information.

Contextual Theories

Contextual theories emphasize the role of the sociocultural context in development. Recall that people of all ages are immersed in a system of social contexts and are inseparable from the cultural beliefs and societal, neighborhood, and familial contexts in which they live.

Vygotsky's Sociocultural Theory

Writing at the same time as Piaget, Russian scholar Lev Vygotsky (1896–1934) offered a different perspective on development, especially cognitive development, that emphasized the importance of culture. Recall that culture refers to the beliefs, values, customs, and skills of a group; it is a product of people's interactions in everyday settings (Markus & Kitayama, 2010). Vygotsky's (1978) **sociocultural theory** examines how culture is transmitted from one generation to the next through social interaction. Children interact with adults and more experienced peers as they talk, play, and work alongside them. Through these formal and informal dialogues, children learn about their culture and adopt their culture's perspectives and practices, learning to think and behave as members of their society (Rogoff, 2016). Over time, they become able to apply these ways of thinking to guide their own actions, thus requiring less assistance from adults and peers (Rogoff et al., 2014).

Like Piaget, Vygotsky emphasized that children are actively participate in their development by engaging with the world around them. However, Vygotsky also viewed cognitive development as a social process that relies on interactions with adults, more mature peers, and other members of their culture.

Lev Vygotsky (1896–1934) emphasized the importance of culture in development. Children actively engage their social world, and the social world shapes development by transmitting culturally relevant ways of thinking and acting that guide children's thought and behavior.

Heritage Image Partnership Ltd/Alamy Stock Photo

Bronfenbrenner's Bioecological Systems Theory

Similar to Vygotsky, Urie Bronfenbrenner (1917–2005) believed that individuals are active in their own development. Bronfenbrenner's **bioecological systems theory** posits that development is a result of the ongoing interactions among biological, cognitive, and socioemotional changes within individuals and their changing contexts, including home, school, neighborhood, culture, and society (see Figure 1.5) (Bronfenbrenner & Morris, 2006). Bronfenbrenner proposed that all individuals are embedded in, or surrounded by, a series of contexts: home, school, neighborhood, culture, and society. Contexts are organized into a series of systems in which individuals are embedded and that interact with one another and the person to influence development.

At the center of the bioecological model is the individual. **Ontogenetic development** refers to the changes that take place within individuals' interacting biological, cognitive, and socioemotional traits. Physical development, such as brain maturation, may influence children's cognitive development, such as reasoning and the ability to consider other people's perspectives, which in turn may influence social development, such as the ability to have more complex and intimate friendships. Social development can then influence cognitive development, as children learn from each other. Ontogenetic development is influenced by, but also influences, the many contexts in which we are embedded (Bronfenbrenner & Morris, 2006).

FIGURE 1.5 ■ Bronfenbrenner's Biecological Systems Theory

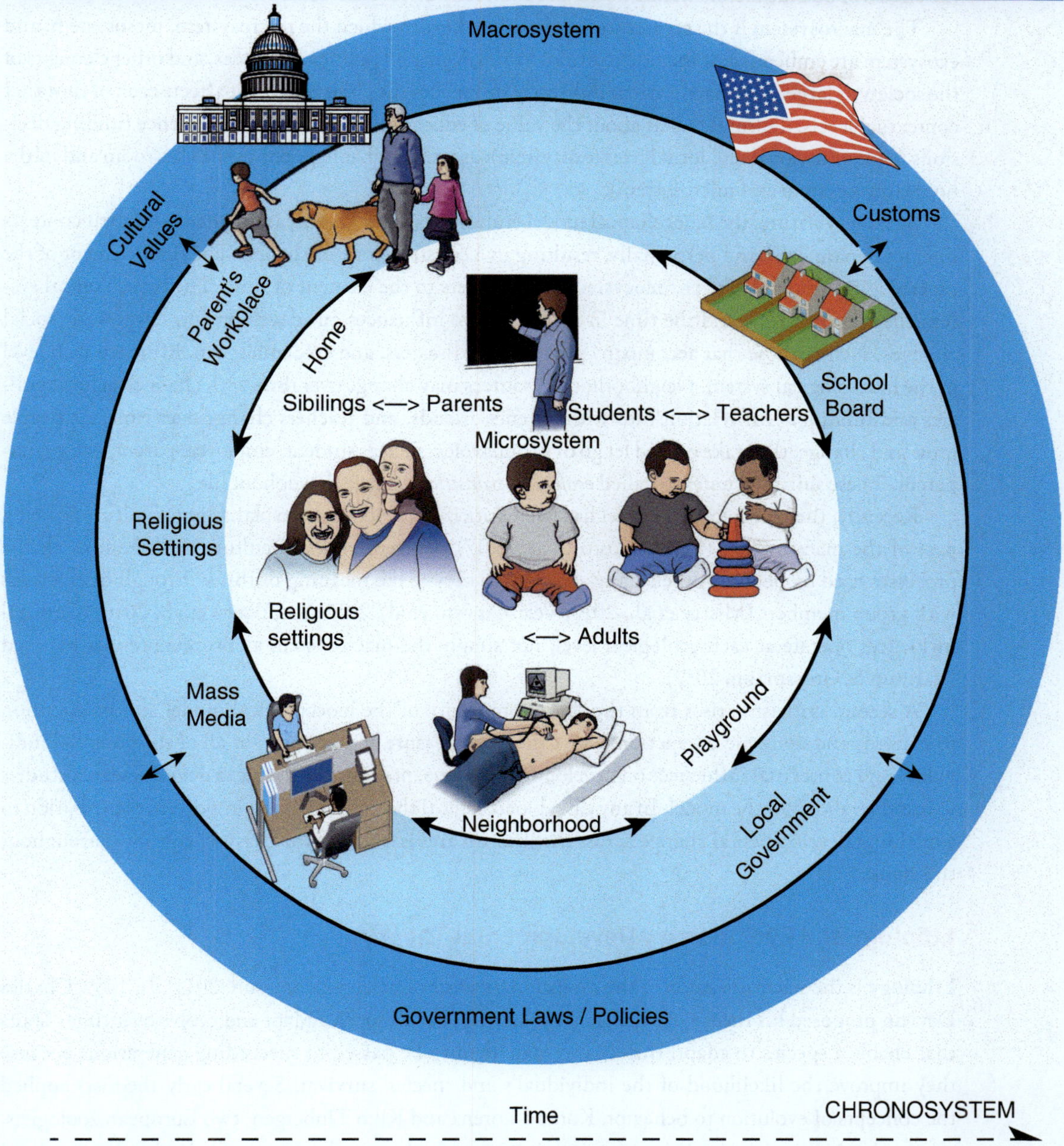

Source: Adapted from Bronfenbrenner and Morris (2006).

Perhaps the most visible context is the **microsystem**, the innermost level of the bioecological system, which includes interactions with the immediate physical and social environment surrounding the person, such as family, peers, school, and work. Because the microsystem contains the developing person, it has an immediate and direct influence on his or her development. Peer relationships can influence a person's sense of self-esteem, social skills, and emotional development.

Microsystems naturally interact. Experiences in the home (one microsystem) influence those at school (another microsystem). These interactions comprise the **mesosystem**, which refers to the relations among microsystems or connections among contexts, such as home, peer group, school, work, and neighborhood. Like the microsystem, the mesosystem has a direct influence on the individual because he or she is a participant in it.

The **exosystem** consists of settings in which the individual is not a participant but that nevertheless influence him or her. The availability of funding for schools, an exosystem factor, indirectly affects children by influencing the availability of classroom resources. The exosystem illustrates how the effects of outside factors trickle down and indirectly affect individuals.

The **macrosystem** is the greater sociocultural context in which the microsystem, mesosystem, and exosystem are embedded. It includes cultural values, legal and political practices, and other elements of the society at large. The macrosystem indirectly influences the child because it affects each of the other contextual levels. Cultural beliefs about the value of education (macrosystem) influence funding decisions made at national and local levels (exosystem), as well as what happens in the classroom and in the home (mesosystem and microsystem).

By its very nature, the bioecological model is always shifting because individuals and their contexts interact dynamically and perpetually, resulting in a constant state of change. The final element of the bioecological system is the **chronosystem**, which refers to the element of time. The bioecological system changes over time and the time in which we live influences our development. Large-scale social changes, such as those that accompany war, natural disasters, and epidemics, can influence each level of the bioecological system. Neighborhood resources may change over time with changes in local policies and funding. Our relationships with parents, friends, and teachers change over time. As people grow and change, they take on and let go of various roles, such as student, employee, parent, and grandparent. These shifts in contexts, called *ecological transitions*, occur throughout life.

Recently, the bioecological model has been criticized for its vague explanation of culture as being part of the macrosystem (Vélez-Agosto et al., 2017). Current views of culture describe it as all the processes used by people in their daily activities as they make meaning or think through interactions with group members (Mistry et al., 2016; Vélez-Agosto et al., 2017; Yoshikawa et al., 2016). Cultural influences operate at each ecological level, not simply the macrosystem as Bronfenbrenner believed (Varnum & Grossmann, 2017).

A second criticism arises from the sheer complexity of the bioecological model and its attention to patterns and dynamic interactions. We can never measure and account for all of the potential individual and contextual influences on development at once, making it difficult to devise research studies to test the validity of the model. In any case, bioecological theory remains an important contribution to explaining developmental change across the lifespan and is a theory that we will consider throughout this book.

Ethology and Evolutionary Developmental Theory

Ethology is the scientific study of the evolutionary basis of behavior (Bateson, 2015). In 1859, Charles Darwin proposed his theory of evolution, explaining that all species adapt and evolve over time. Traits that enable a species to adapt, thrive, and mate tend to be passed to succeeding generations because they improve the likelihood of the individual's and species' survival. Several early theorists applied the concepts of evolution to behavior. Konrad Lorenz and Kiko Tinbergen, two European zoologists, observed animal species in their natural environments and noticed patterns of behavior that appeared to be inborn, emerged early in life, and ensured the animals' survival. For example, shortly after birth, goslings imprint to their mother, meaning that they bond to her and follow her. Imprinting aids the goslings' survival because it ensures that they stay close to their mother, get fed, and remain protected. Mothers instinctively stay close to the nest so that their young can imprint (Lorenz, 1952).

John Bowlby (1969) believed that humans also display biologically preprogrammed behaviors that have survival value and promote development. Crying, smiling, and grasping are inborn ways that infants get attention from caregivers as caregivers naturally respond to these cues, ensuring that infants will be safe and cared for. These behaviors have adaptive significance because they meet infants' needs and promote the formation of bonds with caregivers, ensuring that the caregivers will feel a strong desire and obligation to care for them (Bowlby, 1973). In this way, innate biological drives and behaviors work together with experience to influence adaptation and, ultimately, an individual's survival.

Another theory, **evolutionary developmental theory**, applies principles of evolution and scientific knowledge about the interactive influence of genetic and environmental mechanisms to understand the changes people undergo throughout their lives (Bjorklund, 2018a; Witherington & Lickliter,

2016). From an evolutionary development perspective, genes and context interact in an ever-changing way so that it is impossible to isolate the contributions of each to development (Witherington & Lickliter, 2016). Although all of our traits and characteristics are influenced by genes, contextual factors influence the expression of genetic instructions, determining whether and how genes are shown. Contextual factors such as gravity, light, temperature, and moisture can influence how genes are expressed and therefore how individuals develop (Meaney, 2017). For instance, in some reptiles, such as crocodiles, sex is determined by the temperature at which the organism develops. Eggs incubated at one range of temperatures produce male crocodiles and at another temperature produce female crocodiles (Pezaro et al., 2017). In this way a contextual factor (temperature) determines how genes are expressed (sex).

Shortly after birth, goslings imprint to their mother, meaning that they bond to her and will follow her to ensure they will be fed and remain protected. Ethologists propose that animal and human caregiving behaviors have an evolutionary basis.

iStock/EmilyNorton

According to evolutionary developmental theory, genetic factors and biological predispositions interact with the physical and social environment to influence development, and natural selection determines which genes and traits are passed on to the next generation (Bjorklund, 2018a; Witherington & Lickliter, 2016). People are viewed as active in their development, influencing their contexts, responding to the demands for adaptation posed by their contexts, and constantly interacting with and adapting to the world around them. The relevance of both biological and contextual factors to human development is indisputable, and most developmental scientists appreciate the contributions of evolutionary developmental theory (DelGiudice, 2018; Frankenhuis & Tiokhin, 2018; Legare et al., 2018). The ways in which biology and context interact and their influence on development changes over the course of the lifetime will be discussed throughout this book. Table 1.4 summarizes the theories of human development discussed.

TABLE 1.4 ■ Comparing Theories of Human Development

	Is development influenced by nature or nurture?	Are individuals active or passive in their development?	Is development continuous or discontinuous?
Freud's psychosexual theory	*Greater emphasis on nature*: People are driven by inborn drives, but the extent to which the drives are satisfied influences developmental outcomes.	*Passive*: People are driven by inborn instincts and are not active participants in their development.	*Discontinuous*: Stages
Erikson's psychosocial theory	*Both nature and nurture*: Biological and social forces propel people through the stages and social and psychosocial influences determine the outcome of each stage.	*Active*: People are active in their development because they interact with their social world to resolve psychosocial tasks.	*Discontinuous:* Stages
Behaviorist theory	*Nurture*: Environmental influences shape behavior.	*Passive*: People are shaped and molded by their environment.	*Continuous:* Gradual process of learning new behaviors
Bandura's social learning theory	*Both nature and nurture:* Inborn characteristics and the physical and social environment influence behavior.	*Active*: Individuals are influenced by the environment but also play an active role in their development through reciprocal determinism.	*Continuous:* Gradual process of learning new behaviors

	Is development influenced by nature or nurture?	Are individuals active or passive in their development?	Is development continuous or discontinuous?
Piaget's cognitive-developmental theory	*Both nature and nurture*: An innate drive to learn coupled with brain development leads people to interact with the world. Opportunities provided by the physical and social environment influence development.	*Active*: Individuals actively interact with the world to create their own schemas.	*Discontinuous:* Stages
Information processing theory	*Both nature and nurture:* People are born with processing capacities that develop through maturation and environmental influences.	*Active*: People attend to, process, and store information.	*Continuous:* Gradual increase of skills and capacities
Vygotsky's sociocultural theory	*Both nature and nurture*: People learn through interactions with more skilled members of their culture; capacities are influenced by genes, brain development, and maturation.	*Active*: Individuals actively interact with members of their culture.	*Continuous:* Continuous interactions with others lead to developing new reasoning capacities and skills.
Bronfenbrenner's bioecological systems theory	*Both nature and nurture:* People's inborn and biological characteristics interact with an ever-changing context to influence behavior.	*Active*: People interact with their contexts, being influenced by their contexts but also determining what kinds of physical and social environments are created and how they change.	*Continuous*: People constantly change through their interactions with the contexts in which they are embedded.
Ethology and evolutionary developmental theory	*Both nature and nurture*: Genetic programs and biological predispositions interact with the physical and social environment to influence development, and Darwinian natural selection determines which genes and traits are passed on to the next generation.	*Active:* People interact with their physical and social environment.	*Both continuous and discontinuous:* People gradually grow and change throughout life, but there are sensitive periods in which specific experiences and developments must occur.

Thinking in Context: Applied Developmental Science

Just after delivering a healthy baby girl, Maria and Fernando are overwhelmed by the intense love they feel for her. Like most new parents, they also worry about their new responsibility. They hope that their baby will develop a strong, secure, and close bond to them. They want their baby to feel loved and to love them.

1. What advice would a psychoanalytic theorist give Maria and Fernando? Contrast psychoanalytic with behaviorist perspectives. How might a behaviorist theorist approach this question?
2. How might an evolutionary developmental theorist explain bonding between parents and infants? What advice might an evolutionary developmental theorist give to Maria and Fernando?
3. Considering bioecological systems theory, what microsystem and mesosystem factors influence the parent-child bond? What role might exosystem and macrosystem factors take?

RESEARCH IN HUMAN DEVELOPMENT

LEARNING OBJECTIVE

1.4 Describe the methods and research designs used to study human development and the ethical principles that guide developmental science research.

Developmental scientists conduct research to gather information and answer questions about how people grow and change over their lives. They devise theories to organize what they learn from research and to suggest new **hypotheses** to test in research studies. By conducting multiple studies over time, developmental scientists refine their theories about lifespan human development and determine new questions to ask.

Methods of Data Collection

Scientists use the term *data* to refer to the information they collect. How can we gather data about children, adolescents, and adults? Should we simply talk with our participants? Watch them as they progress through their days? Hook them up to machines that measure physiological activity such as heart rate or brain waves? Developmental scientists use a variety of different methods, or measures, to collect information.

Observational Measures

Some researchers collect information by watching and monitoring people's behavior. Developmental scientists employ two types of observational measures: naturalistic observation and structured observation.

Scientists who use **naturalistic observation** observe and record behavior in natural, real-world settings. Coplan et al. (2015) studied peer interaction patterns in children by observing 9- to 12-year-old children in the schoolyard during recess and lunch. They recorded the children's activity and interaction with peers and found that children who were consistently unengaged with peers tended to show high levels of problems, such as anxiety, depression, and loneliness, as reported by both the children and their mothers.

A challenge of using naturalistic observation is that sometimes the presence of an observer causes those being observed to behave unnaturally. This is known as *participant reactivity.* One way of reducing the effect of participant reactivity is to conduct multiple observations so that the children get used to the observer and return to their normal behavior.

Naturalistic observation permits researchers to observe patterns of behavior in everyday settings, such as whether one particular event or behavior typically precedes another. Naturalistic observation is a useful way of studying events and behaviors that are common. Some behaviors and events are uncommon or are difficult to observe, such as physical aggression among adults, requiring a researcher to observe for very long periods of time to obtain data on the behavior of interest. For this reason, many researchers make structured observations.

Structured observation entails observing and recording behaviors displayed in a controlled environment, a situation constructed by the experimenter. Children might be observed in a laboratory setting as they play with other children or complete a puzzle-solving task. The challenges of identifying and categorizing which behaviors to record are similar to those involved in naturalistic observation. The laboratory environment permits researchers to exert

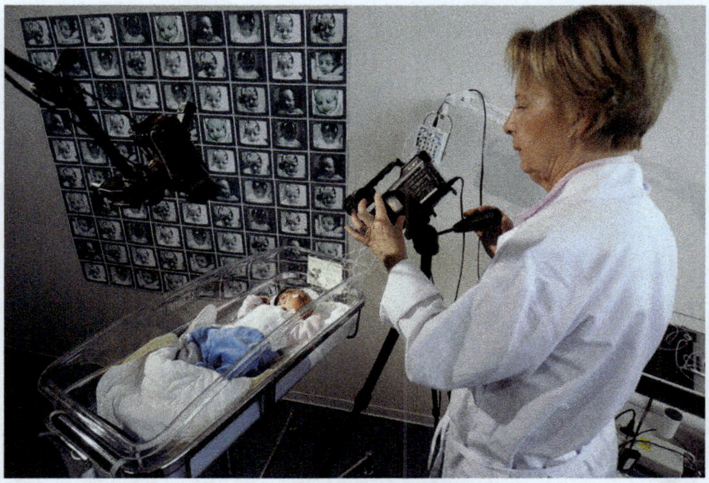

This researcher is using a video camera to observe and record the facial expressions a newborn baby makes while they sleep.

Thierry Berrod, Mona Lisa Production/Science Source

more control over the situation than is possible in natural settings. One challenge to conducting structured observations is that people do not always behave in laboratory settings as they do in real life.

Self-Report Measures

Interviews and questionnaires are known as self-report measures because the person under study answers questions about his or her experiences, attitudes, opinions, beliefs, and behavior. Interviews can take place in person, over the phone, or over the Internet.

One type of interview is the **open-ended interview**, in which a trained interviewer uses a conversational style that encourages the participant, or the person under study, to expand his or her responses. Interviewers may vary the order of questions, probe, and ask additional questions based on responses. The scientist begins with a question and then follows up with prompts to obtain a better view of the person's reasoning (Ginsburg, 1997).

Open-ended interviews permit participants to explain their thoughts thoroughly and in their own words. They also enable researchers to gather a large amount of information quickly. Open-ended interviews are very flexible but this poses a challenge: When questions are phrased differently for each person, responses may not capture real differences in how people think about a given topic and instead may reflect differences in how the questions were posed and followed up by the interviewer.

In contrast, a **structured interview** poses the same set of questions to each participant in the same way. On the one hand, structured interviews are less flexible than open-ended interviews. On the other hand, because all participants receive the same set of questions, differences in responses are more likely to reflect true differences among participants and not merely differences in the manner of interviewing.

To collect data from large samples of people, scientists may compile and use **questionnaires**, also called surveys, made up of sets of questions, typically multiple choice. Questionnaires can be administered in person, online, or by telephone, email, or postal mail. Questionnaires are popular data collection methods because they are easy to use and enable scientists to collect information from many people quickly and inexpensively. Scientists who conduct research on sensitive topics, such as sexual interest and experience, often use questionnaires because they can easily be administered anonymously, protecting participants' privacy. For example, the Monitoring the Future Study is an annual survey of 50,000 8th-, 10th-, and 12th-grade students that collects information about their behaviors, attitudes, and values concerning drug and alcohol use (Miech et al., 2017). The survey permits scientists to gather an enormous amount of data, yet its anonymity protects the adolescents from the consequences of sharing personal information that they might not otherwise reveal.

Despite their ease of use, self-report measures are not without challenges. Questionnaires rely on a person's ability to read and understand questions and provide responses. Sometimes people give socially desirable answers: They respond in ways they would like themselves to be perceived or believe researchers desire. Self-report data, then, may not always reflect people's true attitudes and behavior. Some argue that we are not always fully aware of our feelings and therefore cannot always provide useful insight into our own thoughts and behavior with the use of self-report measures (Newell & Shanks, 2014).

The interviewer may ask a child about their own experiences, opinions, and behavior. Interviews and questionnaires are known as self-report measures.

damircudic/ Getty Images

Physiological Measures

Our body responses are an important source of information that can be used to understand psychological phenomena. Physiological measures offer important information increasingly used in developmental research because cognition, emotion, and behavior have physiological indicators. Do you feel your heart beat more rapidly or your palms grow sweaty when you give a class presentation? Increases in heart rate and perspiration are physiological measures of anxiety. Other researchers might measure cortisol, a hormone triggered by the experience of stress (Simons et al., 2017).

Eye movements and pupil dilation can also indicate attention and interest. Researchers who employ physiological measures might use pupil dilation as a measure of interest in infants and physiological arousal in adults (Wetzel et al., 2016; Feurer et al., 2017). Physiological measures of brain activity are a particularly promising source of data. Several tools are used to study the brain:

Electroencephalography (EEG): Measures electrical activity patterns produced by the brain via electrodes placed on the scalp. Researchers study fluctuations in activity that occur when participants are presented with stimuli or when they sleep.

Computerized tomography scan (CT scan): Compiles multiple x-ray images to create a 3-D image of a person's brain, including brain structures, bone, brain vasculature, and tissue.

Positron emission tomography scan (PET scan): Involves injecting a small dose of radioactive material into the participant's blood stream to monitor the flow of blood. Blood flows more readily to active areas of the brain, illustrating which parts of the brain are active as participants view stimuli and solve problems.

Functional magnetic resonance imaging (fMRI): Measures brain activity using a powerful magnet combined with radio waves to measure blood oxygen level. Active areas of the brain require more oxygen-rich blood, so an increased flow of oxygenated blood shows which parts of the brain are active as individuals complete cognitive tasks.

Diffusion tensor imaging (DTI): Uses an MRI machine to track how water molecules move in and around the fibers connecting different parts of the brain, measuring the thickness and density of the brain's neural connections.

An advantage of physiological measures is they do not rely on verbal reports and generally cannot be faked. A challenge to physiological measures is that although physiological responses can be recorded, they may be difficult to interpret. For instance, excitement and anger may both cause an increase in heart rate. Data collection methods are summarized in Table 1.5.

TABLE 1.5 ■ Data Collection Methods

	Advantage	Disadvantage
Observational Measures		
Naturalistic observation	Gathers data on everyday behavior in a natural environment as behaviors occur	The observer's presence may influence the children's behavior. No control over the observational environment.
Structured observation	Observation in a controlled setting	May not reflect real-life reactions and behavior
Self-Report Measures		
Open-ended interview	Gathers a large amount of information quickly and inexpensively	Nonstandardized questions. Characteristics of the interviewer may influence participant responses.
Structured interview	Gathers a large amount of information quickly and inexpensively	Characteristics of the interviewer may influence children's responses.
Questionnaire	Gathers data from a large sample more quickly and inexpensively than by interview methods	Some participants may respond in socially desirable or inaccurate ways.
Physiological Measures	Assesses biological indicators and does not rely on participant report. Difficult to fake responses.	May be expensive, difficult for researchers to access, and difficult to interpret.

Research Designs

In addition to determining the research question and deciding what information to collect, scientists must choose a research design—a technique for conducting the research study.

Case Study

A **case study** is an in-depth examination of a single person (or small group of individuals). It is conducted by gathering information from many sources, such as through observations, interviews, and conversations with family, friends, and others who know the individual. A case study may include samples or interpretations of a person's writing, such as poetry or journal entries, artwork, and other creations. A case study provides a rich description of a person's life and influences on his or her development. It is often employed to study individuals who have unique and unusual experiences, abilities, or disorders. Conclusions drawn from a case study may shed light on an individual's development but may not be generalized or applied to others. Case studies can be a source of hypotheses to examine in large-scale research.

Correlational Research

Are children with high self-esteem more likely to excel at school? Are older adults with more friends happier than those with few? Are college students who work part-time less likely to graduate? All of these questions can be studied with **correlational research**, which permits researchers to examine relations among measured characteristics, behaviors, and events. In one study, scientists examined the relationship between physical fitness and academic performance in middle school students and found that children with higher aerobic capacity scored higher on achievement tests than did children with poorer aerobic capacity (Bass et al., 2013). Note that this correlation does not tell us *why* aerobic capacity was associated with academic achievement. Correlational research cannot answer this question because it simply describes relationships that exist among variables; it does not enable us to reach conclusions about the causes of those relationships. It is likely that other variables influence both a child's aerobic ability and achievement (e.g., health), but correlation does not enable us to determine the causes for behavior—for that we need an experiment.

Experimental Research

Scientists who seek to test hypotheses about *causal* relationships, such as whether media exposure influences behavior or whether hearing particular types of music influences mood, employ **experimental research**. An experiment is a procedure that uses control to determine causal relationships among variables. Specifically, one or more **independent variables** thought to influence a behavior of interest are changed, or manipulated, while other variables are held constant. Researchers can then examine how the changing variable influences the **dependent variable**, the behavior under study. If the behavior changes as the variable changes, this suggests that the variable caused the change in the behavior. That is, a cause and effect relationship has been demonstrated.

Researchers experimentally manipulate which children play with violent video games to determine their effect on behavior.

istock/ sakkmesterke

Gentile et al. (2017) examined the effect of playing violent videogames on children's physiological stress and aggressive thoughts. Children were assigned to play a violent videogame (*Superman*) or a nonviolent videogame (*Finding Nemo*) for 25 minutes in the researchers' lab (independent variable). The researchers measured physiological stress as indicated by heart rate and cortisol levels before and after the children played the videogame (dependent variable). The researchers found that children who played violent videogames showed higher levels of physiological stress than did the children who played nonviolent videogames. They concluded that the type of videogame changed children's stress reactions.

Developmental scientists conduct studies that use both correlational and experimental research. Studying development requires that scientists pay close attention to age and how people change over time, which requires the use of specialized research designs, as described in the following sections.

Developmental Research Designs

Does personality change over the lifespan? Do children outgrow shyness? Are infants' bonds with their parents associated with their adult relationships? These questions require that developmental scientists examine relationships among variables over time.

Cross-Sectional Research Design

A **cross-sectional research study** compares groups of people of different ages at a single point in time. Suppose a researcher wanted to know how alcohol use changes from early to late adolescence, from age 12 to 18. To study this question the researcher might visit a school system and administer a survey about alcohol use to students aged 12, 14, 16, and 18. By analyzing the survey, the scientist can describe *age differences* in alcohol use and identify how 12-year-olds differ from 18-year-olds today. However, the results do not tell us whether the observed age differences in alcohol use reflect age-related or developmental change. In other words, we do not know whether the 12-year-olds in this sample will show the same patterns of alcohol use as the current 18-year-olds when they are 18, six years from now.

Cross-sectional research permits age comparisons, but participants differ not only in age but in cohort. In developmental science, a cohort is a group of people of the same age who are exposed to similar historical events and cultural and societal influences. Cohorts refer to generations, but we can also speak of smaller cohorts based on factors such as the year of entry to school. In this example, the 12-year-olds and the 18-year-olds are different ages, but they are also in different cohorts, so the two groups may differ in reported alcohol use because of development (age-related changes) or cohort (group-related changes). Perhaps the 12-year-olds received a new early prevention program at school that was not available to the 18-year-olds when they were 12. The difference in alcohol use between 12-year-olds and 18-year-olds might then be related to the prevention program, a cohort factor, and not to age. Cross-sectional research is an important source of information about age differences, but it cannot provide information about age-related changes because participants are assessed only once.

Longitudinal Research Design

A **longitudinal research study** follows the same group of participants over many points in time. Returning to the previous example, to examine how alcohol use changes from 12 to 18 years of age, a developmental scientist using longitudinal research might administer a survey on alcohol use to 12-year-olds and then follow up two years later when they are 14, again when they are 16, and finally when they are 18. If a researcher began this study in 2022, the last round of data collection would not occur until 2028.

Longitudinal research provides information about age-related change because it follows individuals over time, enabling scientists to describe how the 12-year-olds' alcohol use changed as they progressed through adolescence. However, longitudinal research studies only one cohort, calling into question whether findings indicate developmental change or whether they are an artifact of the cohort under study. Was the group of 12-year-olds that the scientist chose to follow for six years somehow different from the cohorts or groups of students who came before or after? Because only one cohort is assessed, it is not possible to determine whether the observed changes are age-related changes or changes that are unique to the cohort examined. Research designs and developmental research designs are summarized in Table 1.6.

TABLE 1.6 ■ Comparing Research Designs

Design	Strengths	Limitations
Research Designs		
Case Study	Provides a rich description of an individual	Conclusions may not be generalized to other individuals
Correlational	Permits the analysis of relationships among variables as they exist in the real world	Cannot determine cause and effect relations
Experimental	Permits a determination of cause-and-effect relations	Data collected in artificial environments may not represent behavior in real-world environments.
Developmental Research Designs		
Cross-sectional	More efficient and less costly than the longitudinal design. Permits the determination of age differences.	Does not permit inferences regarding age change. Confounds age and cohort.
Longitudinal	Permits the determination of age-related changes in a sample of participants assessed for a period of time.	Time consuming and expensive. Participant attrition may limit conclusions. Cohort-related changes may limit the generalizability of conclusions.

Thinking in Context: Applied Developmental Science

Lua is interested in understanding academic achievement in elementary school students. Specifically, she believes that too much screen time harms students' achievement.

1. How might Lua gather information to address her hypothesis?
2. What are some of the challenges of measuring behaviors such as screen time?
3. What kind of research design should Lua use? What are the advantages and disadvantages of this design?
4. Suppose Lua wanted to know the long-term correlates of screen time. How might she study this question?

RESEARCH ETHICS

LEARNING OBJECTIVE

1.5 Discuss principles of research ethics and the ethical issues that may arise in developmental science research.

In addition to conducting research that is scientifically sound, developmental scientists must adhere to standards of ethical conduct in research.

Ethical Principles for Research

Several basic ethical principles guide developmental scientists' work: (1) to do good and avoid harm; (2) **responsibility**, (3) integrity, (4) justice, and (5) **respect for autonomy** (American Psychological

Association, 2010; Society for Research in Child Development, 2021). Developmental scientists are obligated to do good and to avoid doing harm. Researchers must protect and help the individuals, families, and communities with which they work by maximizing the benefits and minimizing the potential harms of their work. Participating in research must never pose threats to individuals beyond those they might encounter in everyday life.

Second, developmental scientists must act responsibly by adhering to professional standards of conduct, clarifying their obligations and roles to others, and avoiding conflicts of interest. Developmental psychologists who conduct research with children and parents must clarify their role as scientists and not counselors or therapists. Researchers' responsibility extends beyond their participants to society at large to ensure that their research findings are accurately portrayed in the media. The principle of responsibility means that researchers must attempt to foresee ways in which their results may be misinterpreted and correct any misinterpretations that occur (Lilienfeld, 2002; Society for Research in Child Development, 2007)

The principle of integrity requires that scientists be accurate, honest, and truthful in their work by being mindful of the promises they make to participants and making every effort to keep their promises to the people and communities with which they work. In addition, the risks and benefits of research participation must be spread equitably across individuals and groups. This is the principle of justice. Every participant should have access to the contributions and benefits of research. When a treatment or intervention under study is found to be successful, all participants must be given the opportunity to benefit from it.

Perhaps the most important principle of research ethics is respect for autonomy. Scientists have a special obligation to respect participants' autonomy—their ability to make and implement decisions. Ethical codes of conduct require that researchers protect participants' autonomy by obtaining **informed consent**—participants' informed, rational, and voluntary agreement to participate. Soliciting informed consent requires providing the individuals under study with information about the research study, answering questions, and ensuring that they understand that they are free to decide not to participate in the research study and that they will not be penalized if they refuse.

Ethical Issues in Studying Lifespan Human Development

Each period in the lifespan poses unique ethical concerns for researchers. Common and pressing ethical challenges include soliciting consent, maintaining participant confidentiality, and protecting participants from harm.

Informed Consent

Respecting people's autonomy also means protecting those who are not capable of making judgments and asserting themselves. Parents provide permission for their minor children to participate because researchers (and lawmakers) assume that minors are not able to meet the rational criteria of informed consent. Although children cannot provide informed consent, researchers respect their growing capacities for decision making in ways that are appropriate to their age by seeking **child assent**—children's agreement to participate (Tait & Geisser, 2017). For toddlers or young children, obtaining assent may involve simply asking if they want to play with the researcher (Brown et al., 2017). With increasing cognitive and social development, children are better able to understand the nature of science and engage meaningfully in decisions about research participation. Discussions about research participation should be tailored to children's development, including offering more detailed information and seeking more comprehensive assent as children grow older (Roth-Cline & Nelson, 2013).

Studying adolescents often raises unique ethical questions because they are minors, generally requiring parental consent. Adolescent research participants are often very concerned about how their information and samples will be used, and in particular, whether information would be shared with their parents (Crane & Broome, 2017). Sometimes seeking consent from parents may interfere with researchers' goals or may pose risks to minor participants. In one study, LGBT adolescents believed that participating in research on sexuality and health is important for advancing science, yet indicated that they would not participate if guardian permission were required, citing negative parental attitudes or not being "out" about their LBGT identity (Macapagal et al., 2017).

In response to these ethical challenges, researchers frequently obtain **passive consent** for conducting research on sensitive topics with adolescents. Passive consent procedures typically involve notifying parents about the research and requiring them to reply if they do *not* want their child to participate. Studies that examine sensitive topics, such as risky behaviors, may benefit from the use of passive consent procedures because they are associated with more diverse samples of adolescents that better represent the population (Liu et al., 2017).

Adults also sometimes require accommodations for providing informed consent. Traumatic brain injury, dementia, mental illness, some physical illnesses, and advanced age can impair adults' capacities to provide informed consent (Prusaczyk et al., 2017). In such cases, researchers seek assent by providing the participant with meaningful information in a format that they can understand (as well as obtaining consent from a surrogate decision maker). Cognitive capacities can often fluctuate and, in the case of traumatic brain injury patients, often improves (Triebel et al., 2014). Researchers must be prepared to tailor their explanations to the participant's fluctuating competence.

Confidentiality

Ethical issues may arise when researchers' desire to learn about development and solve problems conflicts with their need to protect research participants. Researchers generally promise participants **confidentiality**—that their responses will remain confidential and will not be disclosed to others. Suppose a researcher studying adolescents learns that a participant is in jeopardy, whether because she is engaging in health-compromising behaviors (e.g., cigarette smoking, unsafe driving, or unhealthy behavior), contemplating suicide, or engaging in illegal or harmful activities (e.g., drug addiction, stealing, or violence). Is the researcher responsible for helping the adolescent? Does the researcher have a duty to disclose the risk to an outside party who can help the adolescent, such as parents? Does the researcher's promise of confidentiality outweigh the duty to disclose? Adolescents and parents tend to have different opinions about research disclosures; parents often want to receive their children's research information, but adolescents tend to report wanting to withhold private and sensitive findings (Brawner et al., 2013).

Researchers who study risky and health-compromising behaviors *expect* to encounter participants who are engaged in potentially dangerous activities. Helping the adolescent might involve removing him or her from the study and potentially compromising the study. Adolescents generally expect that researchers will maintain confidentiality (Fisher et al., 1996); violating their confidentiality may be harmful.

Issues with confidentiality are common when studying adolescents, but they arise throughout the lifespan. Suppose a researcher is studying older adults in a nursing home and discovers illicit substance dependence in an adult who is also taking many medications? Or a sexual relationship of an adult who experiences bouts of dementia? Or suicidal thoughts in a middle-aged parent?

Ethical guidelines published by research and medical associations address researchers' obligations to help and not harm and to protect participants' confidentiality, but they generally fail to offer specific recommendations about how researchers can manage the conflicting duties to maintain confidentiality and disclose participant problems (Hiriscau et al., 2014; Sharkey et al., 2017). Instead, researchers must decide for themselves how to balance their sometimes conflicting obligations to their participants. Table 1.7 summarizes the rights of research participants.

Thinking in Context: Applied Developmental Science

1. Suppose, as part of your research, you wanted to interview children at school. What ethical principles are most relevant to examining schoolchildren? What challenges do you anticipate in conducting this work?

2. You are tasked with collecting observations and interviews of older adults to evaluate a health program at a nursing home. What ethical issues can you anticipate? What principles are most pertinent?

TABLE 1.7 ■ Rights of Research Participants

Right	Description
Protection from harm	Research participants have the right to be protected from physical and psychological harm. Investigators must use the least stressful research procedure in testing hypotheses and, when in doubt, consult with others.
Informed consent	Participants have the right to be informed about the purpose of the research, expected duration, procedures, risks and benefits of participation, and any other aspects of the research that may influence their willingness to participate. When children are participants, a parent or guardian must provide informed consent on behalf of the child, and the investigator should seek assent from the child.
Confidentiality	Participants have the right to privacy and to conceal their identity on all information and reports obtained in the course of research.
Information about the results	Participants have the right to be informed of the results of research in language that matches their level of understanding.
Treatment	If an experimental treatment under investigation is believed to be beneficial, participants in control groups have the right to obtain the beneficial treatment.

Sources: American Psychological Association, 2010; Society for Research in Child Development, 2007.

Thinking in Context: Intersectionality

Some ethical concerns are more pressing for some participants and in some studies than others. Consider a study examining sexuality. People of different ages and characteristics might vary in their concerns about confidentiality in sexuality research.

1. To what extent do you think adolescents, adults, and older adults might vary in their concerns about sharing their sexual interests, beliefs, and behaviors??
2. What other variables might be associated with different perspectives on the value of confidentiality? Might you expect cultural differences in concerns about confidentiality? Might factors like sexual orientation, religion, gender, race, or ethnicity relate to concerns about confidentiality in sexuality research? Why or why not?

APPLIED DEVELOPMENTAL SCIENCE AND INTERSECTIONALITY

LEARNING OBJECTIVE

1.6 Describe the field of applied developmental science and the role of intersectionality in development.

In its early years, the study of human development emphasized laboratory research devoted to uncovering universal aspects of development by stripping away contextual influences. This *basic research* was designed to examine how development unfolds, with the assumption that development is a universal process with all people changing in similar ways and in similar timeframes. In the early 1980s, influenced by contextual theories (such as Bronfenbrenner's bioecological approach) and the growing assumption that people are active in their development (a cornerstone of lifespan developmental theory), developmental scientists began to examine developmental processes outside of the laboratory (Lerner et al., 2015). As developmental scientists engaged in *applied research,* it quickly became apparent that there are a great many individual differences in development that vary with myriad contextual influences. We also learned that developmental research findings can be applied to improve people's lives.

Applied Developmental Science

Applied developmental science is a field of study that examines the lifelong developmental interactions among individuals and their contexts and applies these findings to prevent and intervene in problems and promote positive development (Fisher et al., 2013). Applied developmental scientists study pressing social issues, such as promoting the development of preterm infants, determining children's capacity to provide courtroom testimony, promoting safe sex in adolescents and emerging adults, and aiding older adults' and their adult children's adjustment to disability (Fisher, et al, 2013; Lerner, 2012). By its very nature, applied developmental science is multidisciplinary because real-world problems are complex and require the expertise of scientists from many fields, such as human development, psychology, medicine, biology, anthropology, and more.

Applied developmental scientists are especially interested in promoting healthy development over the lifespan. That is, they seek to enhance the life chances of diverse groups of individuals, families, and communities. Many children, adolescents, and adults are affected by social problems that can impede healthy development, such as hunger, poor nutrition, pervasive poverty, and inadequate access to education, health care, and community services (Aizer, 2017; Gauvain, 2018; Golinkoff et al., 2017; Huston, 2018). It is through applied research that scientists have come to appreciate the full range of contextual influences on development and how lifelong opportunities and outcomes vary with factors such as sex, ethnicity, socioeconomic status, and age.

Applied developmental scientists also work to understand and address the systemic disparities in opportunities that people experience over the lifespan (Fisher et al., 2012). They seek to promote equity and social justice, the basic human right of individuals to have access to opportunities, experiences, and resources that maximize their potential for growth, health, and happiness across the life course (Brown et al., 2019; Smith & Smith Lee, 2019). Individuals' access to support and opportunity varies dramatically with race, sex, and other factors. Equity and social justice involve recognizing and addressing these disparities and the complex factors that contribute to them.

Intersectionality and Development

We are all members of multiple intertwined social categories, such as gender, race, age, and sexual orientation. Our understanding and experience of each category is influenced by our membership in other categories. Adolescents' understanding and experience of gender may be filtered through the lens of their membership in another social category, such as ethnicity. Latina girls' views of themselves and their worlds may be quite different from those of Latino boys as well as girls of other ethnicities, such as Black and white girls. In this example, the intersection of ethnicity and gender influences girls' self-understanding and experience. Power and opportunity are enmeshed with social categories such as ethnicity and gender. Latina girls' views of themselves reflect not simply their sex and ethnicity, but the relative power ascribed to girls and persons of color in U.S. society.

Our unique experiences and perspectives are influenced by **intersectionality**, which describes the dynamic interrelations of social categories—gender, race and ethnicity, sexual orientation, socioeconomic status, immigration status, age, and disabilities—and the interwoven systems of power and privilege that accompany social category membership (Crenshaw, 1989). An intersectional perspective draws attention to inequities in power, opportunity, privilege, and disadvantage that accompany social category membership and are experienced as racism, sexism, classism, heterosexism, and more, to shape individuals' lived experiences (Roy, 2018; Santos & Toomey, 2018; Syed & Ajayi, 2018).

Central to intersectionality are the assumptions that (1) all individuals have multiple identities that converge; (2) within each identity is a dimension of power or oppression; and (3) identities are influenced by their sociocultural context (Abrams et al., 2020; Else-Quest & Hyde, 2016). Identities overlap and systems of oppression, such as racism and sexism, may interlock. Individuals therefore experience multiple overlapping identities and may struggle against intertwined systems of oppression and bias (Rosenthal, 2016).

The effects of social category membership are not experienced universally, but vary with context (Ghavami et al., 2016; Godfrey & Burson, 2018). Intersectionality is inherently tied to context.

These students attend the same school, but their experiences may vary greatly with intersectional factors such as race, ethnicity, and gender.

istock/ franz12

Social categories such as gender, race, and sexual orientation may be more salient and meaningful in some contexts and at some times than others, creating distinct experiences for subgroup members with implications for development (Crenshaw, 1989; Syed & Ajayi, 2018). For instance, intersecting expectations about race and gender may uniquely shape how Black boys are perceived and treated in classroom settings; their experience is unique from that of boys of other races and ethnicities and that of Black girls—with implications for their academic performance, development, and long-term outcomes (Roy, 2018). Likewise, Black boys' classroom experiences might vary with context (rural, suburban, or urban) and geographic location (North, South, Midwest, or coastal United States).

Until recently, people of color have either been largely excluded from research studies or grouped with participants of all ethnicities and races, masking differences and contributing to a sense of invisibility (Grzanka, 2020; Roberts et al., 2020; Syed et al., 2018). One analysis of articles published between 2006 and 2010 in leading developmental science journals (*Developmental Psychology, Child Development*, and *Developmental Science*) found that only 14% included samples that were predominantly people of color and a surprisingly high 28% did not mention the racial/ethnic composition at all (Nielsen et al., 2017).

The study of intersectionality sheds light on how discrimination, marginalization, oppression, and privilege combine to influence individuals' experiences in unique ways across the lifespan (Crenshaw, 1989). Intersectionality is an emerging approach in **developmental science,** with a small but rapidly growing body of research that recognizes the many ways that gender, ethnicity and race, sexual orientation, socioeconomic status, and disability interact to influence development (Godfrey & Burson, 2018; Grzanka, 2020). Throughout this book we will examine development through an intersectional lens whenever possible.

Thinking in Context: Intersectionality

1. Consider the social categories of which you are a member (perhaps gender, race, or ethnicity, socioeconomic status, or religion). Which are most important to you? How might these social categories interact to influence your experiences?
2. Consider our discussion of research methods earlier in this chapter. What are some of the challenges of studying the real-world problems addressed by applied developmental science? Do any special considerations arise when studying development through an intersectional lens?

CHAPTER SUMMARY

1.1 Outline five principles of the lifespan developmental perspective.

Development is a lifelong process. It is multidimensional, multidirectional, plastic, influenced by the multiple contexts in which we are embedded, and multidisciplinary.

1.2 Explain three basic issues in developmental science.

Developmental scientists take different perspectives on three views. First, in what ways is developmental change continuous, characterized by slow and gradual change, or discontinuous, characterized by sudden and abrupt change? Second, to what extent do people play an active role in their own development, interacting with and influencing the world around them? Finally, is development caused by nature or nurture? Most developmental scientists agree that some aspects of development appear continuous and others discontinuous, that individuals are active in influencing their development, and that development reflects the interactions of nature and nurture.

1.3 Summarize five theoretical perspectives on human development.

Psychoanalytic theories emphasize inner drives. Freud's psychosexual theory emphasizes psychosexual stages. Erikson's psychosocial theory suggests that individuals move through eight stages of psychosocial development across the lifespan, with each stage presenting a unique psychosocial task, or crisis. Behaviorist and social learning theories emphasize environmental influences on behavior, specifically operant conditioning, as well as observational learning. Piaget's cognitive-developmental theory describes cognitive development as an active process that proceeds through four stages. Information processing theorists study the steps involved in cognition: perceiving and attending, representing, encoding, retrieving, and problem solving. Contextual and systems theories look to the importance of context in shaping development. Vygotsky's sociocultural theory emphasizes interactions with members of our culture in influencing development. Bronfenbrenner's bioecological model explains development as a function of the ongoing reciprocal interaction among biological and psychological changes in the person and his or her changing context. Evolutionary developmental psychology integrates Darwinian principles of evolution and scientific knowledge about the interactive influence of genetic and environmental mechanisms.

1.4 Describe the methods and research designs used to study human development and ethical principles that guide developmental science research.

A case study is an in-depth examination of an individual. Interviews and questionnaires are called self-report measures because they ask the persons under study questions about their own experiences, attitudes, opinions, beliefs, and behavior. Observational measures are methods that scientists use to collect and organize information based on watching and monitoring people's behavior. Physiological measures gather the body's physiological responses as data. Scientists use correlational research to describe relations among measured characteristics, behaviors, and events. To test hypotheses about causal relationships among variables, scientists employ experimental research. Developmental designs include cross-sectional research and longitudinal research. Researchers must maximize the benefits to research participants, minimize the harms, be accurate and honest in their work, and respect participants' autonomy, including seeking informed consent and child assent.

1.5 Discuss principles of research ethics and the ethical issues that may arise in developmental science research.

Researchers must maximize the benefits to research participants and minimize the harms, safeguarding participants' welfare. They must be accurate and honest in their work and respect participants' autonomy, including seeking informed consent and child assent. In addition, the benefits and risks of participation in research must be spread equitably across individuals and groups. Specific ethical concerns about informed consent, the use of passive consent, and how to protect participant confidentiality arise in conducting research in lifespan development.

1.6 Describe the field of applied developmental science and the role of intersectionality in development.

Applied developmental science examines the lifelong interactions among individuals and their contexts and applies these findings to prevent and intervene in problems and promote positive development in people of all ages. Our unique experiences and perspectives are influenced by intersectionality, the dynamic interrelations of social categories—gender, race and ethnicity, sexual orientation, socioeconomic status, immigration status, and disabilities—and the interwoven systems of power and privilege that accompany social category membership. Individuals experience multiple overlapping identities and struggle against intertwined systems of oppression and bias. Intersectionality is inherently tied to context because the personal importance of social categories and the meaning ascribed to them vary with context. The study of intersectionality sheds light on how discrimination, marginalization, oppression, and privilege combine to influence individuals' experiences in unique ways across the lifespan.

KEY TERMS

applied developmental science (p. 28)
behaviorism (p. 11)
bioecological systems theory (p. 14)
case study (p. 22)
child assent (p. 25)
cognitive-developmental theory (p. 13)
cognitive development (p. 3)
cohort (p. 5)
context (p. 4)
continuous change (p. 6)
correlational research (p. 22)
cross-sectional research study (p. 23)
culture (p. 5)
dependent variable (p. 22)
development (p. 1)
developmental science (p. 29)
discontinuous change (p. 6)
domains of development (p. 5)
emerging adulthood (p. 2)
ethology (p. 16)
evolutionary developmental theory (p. 16)
experimental research (p. 22)
hypotheses (p. 19)
independent variable (p. 22)
information processing theory (p. 13)
Informed consent (p. 25)
lifespan human development (p. 1)
longitudinal research study (p. 23)
naturalistic observation (p. 19)
observational learning (p. 12)
open-ended interview (p. 20)
passive consent (p. 26)
physical development (p. 3)
plasticity (p. 3)
psychoanalytic theories (p. 9)
punishment (p. 11)
questionnaire (p. 20)
reciprocal determinism (p. 12)
reinforcement (p. 11)
resilience (p. 3)
respect for autonomy (p. 24)
responsibility (p. 24)
social learning theory (p. 12)
sociocultural theory (p. 14)
socioemotional development (p. 3)
structured interview (p. 20)
structured observation (p. 19)
theory (p. 9)

2 BIOLOGICAL AND ENVIRONMENTAL FOUNDATIONS AND PRENATAL DEVELOPMENT

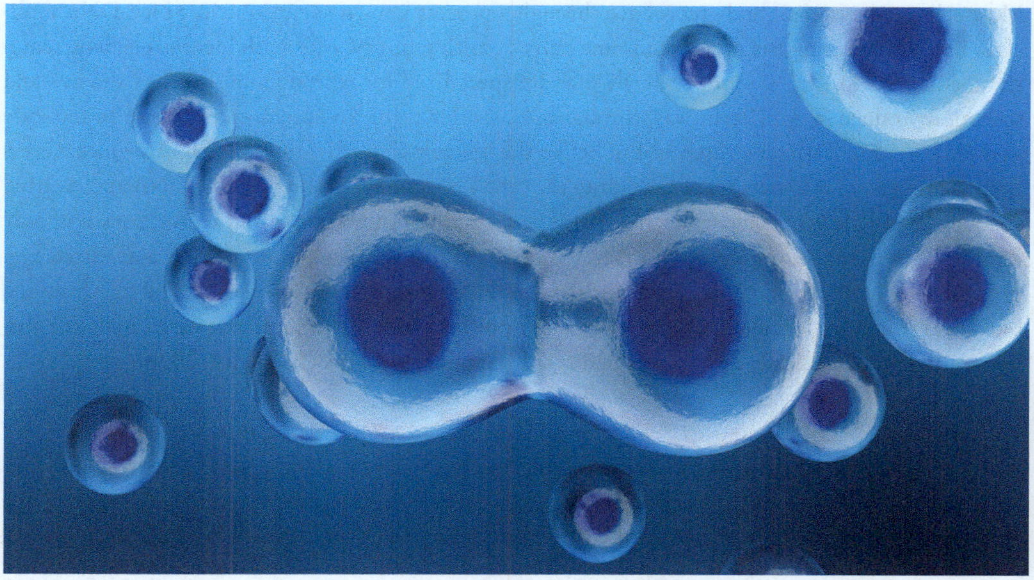

istock/luismmolina

"Rico and Remmy couldn't be more different," marveled their mother. "People are surprised to find out they are brothers." Rico is tall and athletic, with blond hair and striking blue eyes. His older brother, Remmy, has a smaller frame and wears thick glasses over his dark brown eyes. She wondered, "Where did Rico get such blue eyes and blond hair? He looks different from everyone in our family. Maybe I did something different when I was pregnant with him? Eat or do something unusual?" In this chapter, we examine processes of genetic inheritance that can help us understand how members of a family can share a great many similarities and also many differences. We also explore the process of **prenatal development**, or how a single cell develops into a newborn.

GENETIC FOUNDATIONS OF DEVELOPMENT

LEARNING OBJECTIVE

2.1 Discuss patterns of genetic inheritance and examples of genetic disorders and chromosomal abnormalities.

We are born with a hereditary "blueprint" that influences our development and determines our traits, such as appearance, physical characteristics, health, and even personality.

Genetics

The human body is composed of trillions of units called cells, each with a nucleus containing 23 matching pairs of rod-shaped structures called **chromosomes** (Finegold, 2019). Each chromosome holds the basic units of heredity, known as genes, composed of stretches of **deoxyribonucleic acid (DNA)**, a complex molecule shaped like a twisted ladder or staircase. **Genes** carry the plan for creating all of the traits that organisms carry. It is estimated that 20,000 to 25,000 genes reside within the chromosomes, comprising the human genome and influencing all genetic characteristics (Taneri et al., 2020). People around the world share 99.9% of their genes (Lewis, 2017; National Human Genome Research Institute, 2018). Although all humans share the same basic genome, every person has a slightly different code, making him or her genetically distinct from other humans.

Cell Reproduction

Most cells in the human body reproduce through a process known as **mitosis,** in which DNA replicates itself, duplicating the 46 chromosome pairs, resulting in new cells with identical genetic material (Sadler, 2018). **Gametes**, or sex cells that are specialized for reproduction (such as the ova and sperm), reproduce in a different way, through **meiosis**. First, the 46 chromosomes begin to replicate as in mitosis, duplicating themselves. But before the cell completes dividing, the DNA segments cross over, moving from one member of the pair to the other, essentially "mixing up" the DNA and creating unique combinations of genes (Finegold, 2019). The resulting gametes, ova and sperm, consist of only 23 single, unpaired sex chromosomes. At fertilization ova and sperm join to produce a fertilized egg, or **zygote**, with 46 chromosomes forming 23 pairs, half from the biological mother and half from the biological father. Each gamete has a unique genetic profile, and it is estimated that individuals can produce millions of genetically different gametes (U.S. National Library of Medicine, 2020).

Sex Determination

Twenty-two of the 23 pairs of chromosomes are matched pairs (see Figure 2.1). They contain similar genes in almost identical positions and sequence, reflecting the distinct genetic blueprint of the biological mother and father. The 23rd pair of chromosomes are not identical because they are sex

FIGURE 2.1 ■ Chromosomes

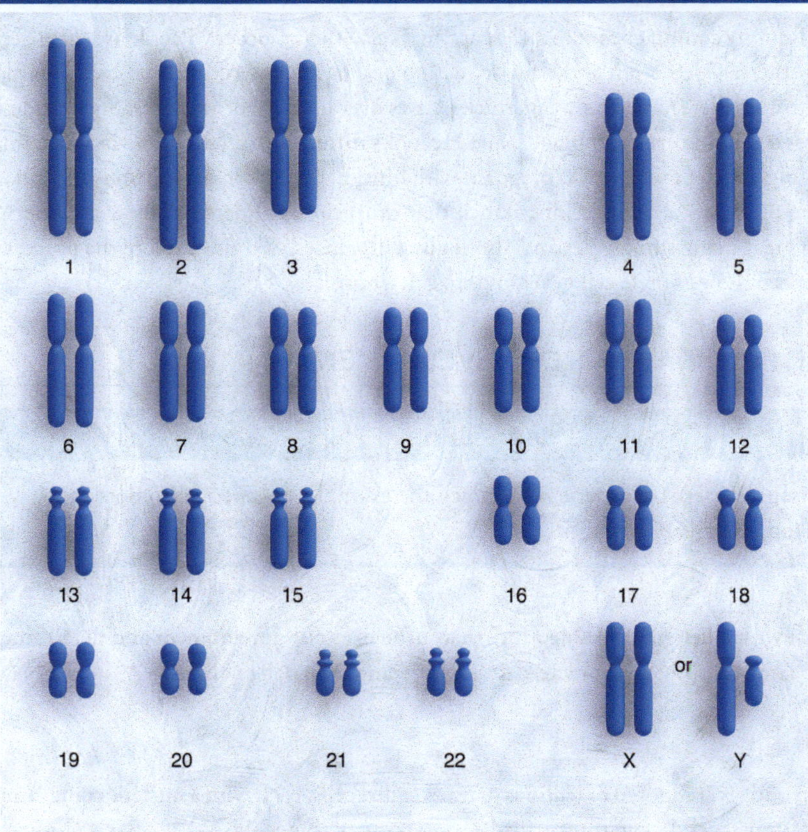

istock/somersault18:24

chromosomes that specify the genetic sex of the individual. In females, sex chromosomes consist of two large X-shaped chromosomes (XX). Males' sex chromosomes consist of one large X-shaped chromosome and one much smaller Y-shaped chromosome (XY).

Because females have two X sex chromosomes, all their ova contain one X sex chromosome. A male's sex chromosome pair includes both X and Y chromosomes; therefore, one half of the sperm males produce contain an X chromosome and one half contain a Y. The Y chromosome contains genetic instructions that will cause the fetus to develop male reproductive organs. Thus, whether the fetus develops into a boy or girl is determined by which sperm fertilizes the ovum. If the ovum is fertilized by a Y sperm, a male fetus will develop, and if the ovum is fertilized by an X sperm, a female fetus will form (see Figure 2.2).

Patterns of Genetic Inheritance

Researchers are just beginning to uncover the instructions contained in the human genome, but we have learned that traits and characteristics are inherited in predictable ways.

Dominant-Recessive Inheritance

Some genes are passed through **dominant-recessive inheritance** in which some genes are *dominant* and are always expressed regardless of the gene they are paired with. Examples of dominant genes include those for dark (brown or black) hair color and brown eyes. Other genes, such as for blond or red hair and blue eyes, are *recessive* and will be expressed only if paired with another recessive gene (see Figure 2.3 and Table 2.1).

Incomplete Dominance

Incomplete dominance is a genetic inheritance pattern in which both genes jointly influence the characteristic (Knopik et al., 2017). Consider blood type. Neither the alleles for blood type A nor B dominate each other. A person with the alleles for blood types A and B will express both A and B alleles and have blood type AB.

Polygenic Inheritance

Most characteristics result from the interaction of many genes, known as **polygenic inheritance**. Examples of polygenic traits include height, intelligence, personality, and susceptibility to certain forms of cancer (Bouchard, 2014; Flint et al., 2020; Penke & Jokela, 2016). As the number of genes that contribute to a trait increases, so does the range of possible traits. Table 2.2 summarizes the three patterns of inheritance.

FIGURE 2.2 ■ Sex Determination

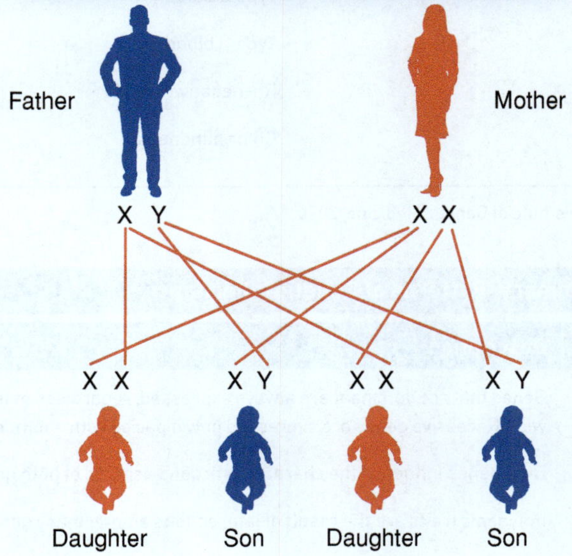

FIGURE 2.3 ■ Dominant-Recessive Inheritance

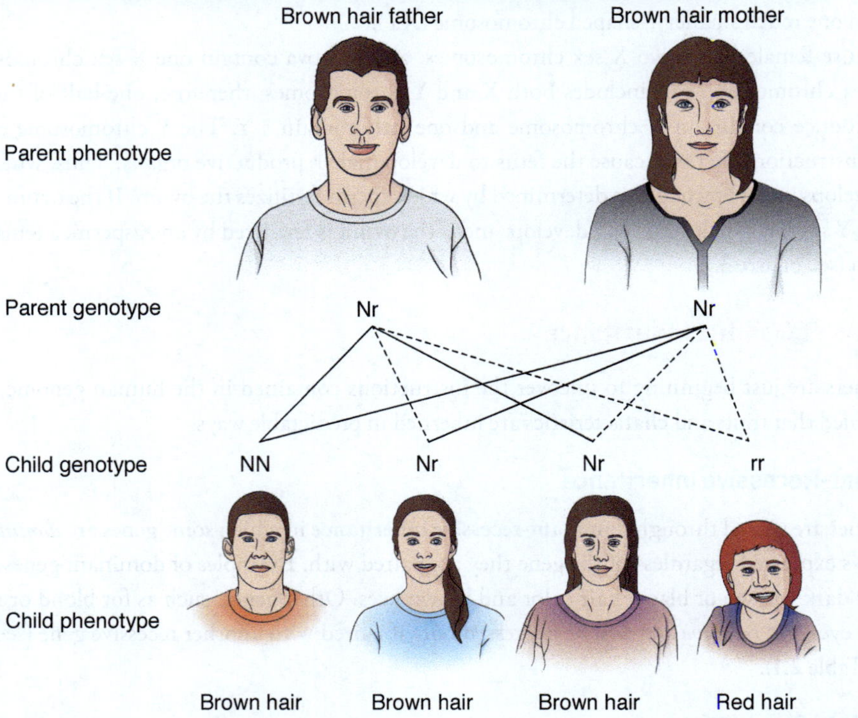

TABLE 2.1 ■ Dominant and Recessive Characteristics

Dominant Trait	Recessive Trait
Dark hair	Blond hair
Curly hair	Straight hair
Hair	Baldness
Non-red hair	Red hair
Facial dimples	No dimples
Brown eyes	Blue, green, hazel eyes
Second toe longer than big toe	Big toe longer than second toe
Type A blood	Type O blood
Type B blood	Type O blood
Rh-positive blood	Rh-negative blood
Normal color vision	Color blindness

Source: McKusick-Nathans Institute of Genetic Medicine, 2020.

TABLE 2.2 ■ Summary: Patterns of Genetic Inheritance

Inheritance Pattern	Description
Dominant-recessive inheritance	Genes that are dominant are always expressed, regardless of the gene they are paired with. Recessive genes are expressed only if paired with another recessive gene.
Incomplete dominance	Both genes influence the characteristic, and aspects of both genes appear.
Polygenic inheritance	Polygenic traits are the result of interactions among many genes.

Chromosomal and Genetic Problems

Many disorders are the result of chromosomal abnormalities passed through genetic inheritance. Many hereditary and chromosomal abnormalities can be diagnosed prenatally. Others are evident at birth or can be detected soon after an infant begins to develop. Some are discovered only over a period of many years.

Disorders and abnormalities that are inherited through the parents' genes are passed through the inheritance processes that we have discussed. Some are highly visible and some may go unnoticed throughout an individual's life.

Dominant-Recessive Genetic Disorders

Recall that in dominant-recessive inheritance, dominant genes are always expressed regardless of the gene they are paired with and recessive genes are expressed only if paired with another recessive gene. Some diseases are inherited through dominant-recessive patterns (see Table 2.3). Few severe disorders are inherited through dominant inheritance because individuals who inherit the allele often do not survive long enough to reproduce and pass it to the next generation. One exception is Huntington disease, a fatal disease in which the central nervous system deteriorates (Ghosh & Tabrizi, 2018; McKusick-Nathans Institute of Genetic Medicine, 2020). Individuals with the Huntington allele develop normally in childhood, adolescence, and young adulthood. Symptoms of Huntington disease do not appear until age 35 or later. By then, many individuals have already had children, and one half of them, on average, will inherit the dominant Huntington gene.

TABLE 2.3 ■ Diseases Inherited Through Dominant-Recessive Inheritance

Disease	Occurrence	Mode of Inheritance	Description	Treatment
Huntington disease	1 in 20,000	Dominant	Degenerative brain disorder that affects muscular coordination and cognition	No cure; death usually occurs 10 to 20 years after onset
Cystic fibrosis	1 in 2,000–2,500	Recessive	An abnormally thick, sticky mucus clogs the lungs and digestive system, leading to respiratory infections and digestive difficulty	Bronchial drainage, diet, gene replacement therapy
Phenylketonuria (PKU)	1 in 10,000–15,000	Recessive	Inability to digest phenylalanine, which, if untreated, results in neurological damage and death	Diet
Sickle cell anemia	1 in 500 African Americans	Recessive	Sickling of red blood cells leads to inefficient distribution of oxygen throughout the body that leads to organ damage and respiratory infections	No cure; blood transfusions, treat infections, bone marrow transplant; death by middle age
Tay-Sachs disease	1 in 3,600–4,000 descendants of Central and Eastern European Jews	Recessive	Degenerative brain disease	None; most die by 4 years of age

Source: McKusick-Nathans Institute of Genetic Medicine, 2020.

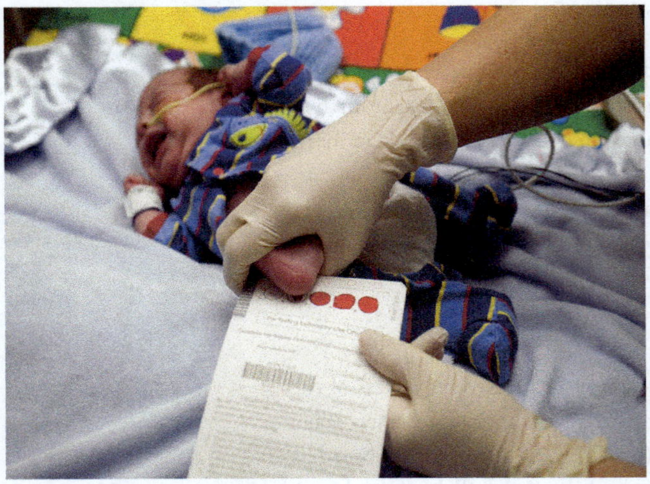

A blood sample to detect PKU is taken from this newborn. Phenylketonuria (PKU) is a genetic disorder in which the body lacks the enzyme that breaks down phenylalanine. Without treatment, the phenylalanine builds up to toxic levels and can damage the central nervous system.

Marmaduke St. John / Alamy Stock Photo

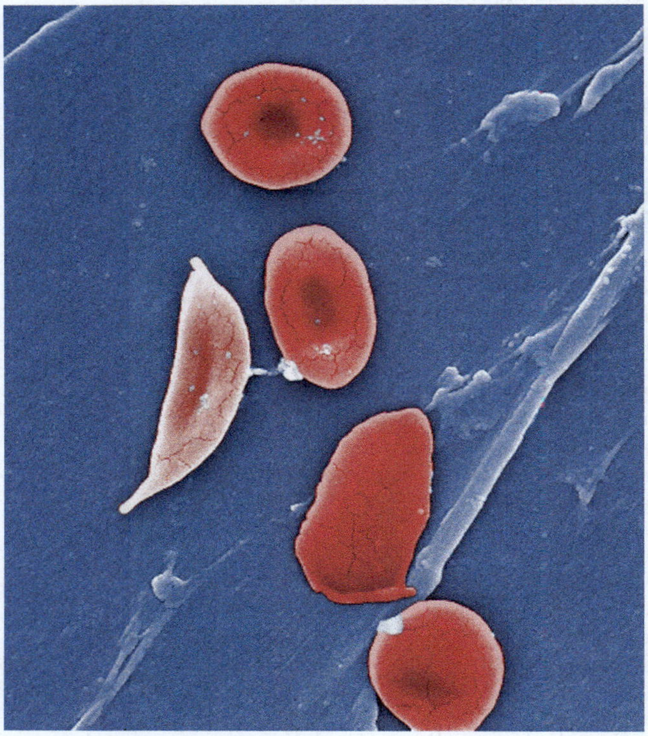

Recessive sickle cell alleles cause red blood cells to become crescent shaped and unable to distribute oxygen effectively throughout the circulatory system. Alleles for normal blood cells do not mask all of the characteristics of recessive sickle cell alleles, illustrating incomplete dominance.

BSIP SA / Alamy Stock Photo

Phenylketonuria (PKU) is a common recessive disorder that prevents the body from producing an enzyme that breaks down phenylalanine, an amino acid in proteins (McKusick-Nathans Institute of Genetic Medicine, 2020). Without treatment the phenylalanine builds up quickly to toxic levels that damage the central nervous system, contributing to intellectual developmental disability, once known as mental retardation, by 1 year of age. The United States and Canada require all newborns to be screened for PKU (Camp et al., 2014).

PKU illustrates how genes interact with the environment to produce developmental outcomes. Intellectual disability results from the interaction of the genetic predisposition and exposure to phenylalanine from the environment (Blau, 2016). Children with PKU can process only very small amounts of phenylalanine. If the disease is discovered, the infant is placed on a diet low in phenylalanine. Yet it is very difficult to remove nearly all phenylalanine from the diet. Individuals who maintain a strict diet usually attain average levels of intelligence, though they tend to score lower than those without PKU (Hofman et al., 2018; Romani et al., 2017). Some cognitive and psychological problems may appear in childhood and persist into adulthood (Christ et al., 2020; Erlich, 2019; Ford et al., 2018; Hawks et al., 2018; Jahja et al., 2017). The emotional and social challenges associated with PKU, such as the pressure of a strict diet and surveillance from parents, may worsen these symptoms, and dietary compliance tends to decline in adolescence when young people push boundaries and seek independence (Medford et al., 2017).

The **sickle cell trait**, carried by about 5% of African American newborns (and relatively few Caucasians or Asian Americans) causes another recessive disorder, sickle cell anemia (Ojodu et al., 2014). In sickle cell anemia, red blood cells become crescent, or sickle, shaped. Cells that are sickle shaped cannot distribute oxygen effectively throughout the circulatory system and can cause inflammation and damage the blood vessels (Ware et al., 2017). Unlike other recessive disorders, the genes for normal blood cells do not mask all of the characteristics of recessive sickle cell genes. This is known as incomplete dominance. People who carry a single recessive sickle cell gene do not develop full-blown sickle cell anemia but may show some symptoms, such as reduced oxygen distribution throughout the body and exhaustion after exercise (Xu & Thein, 2019; Chakravorty & Williams, 2015).

X-Linked Genetic Disorders

A special instance of the dominant-recessive pattern occurs with genes that are located on the X chromosome (Shah et al., 2017). Recall that males (XY) have both an X and a Y chromosome. Some recessive genetic disorders, like the gene for red-green colorblindness, are carried on the X-chromosome (see Table 2.4). Males are more likely to be affected by X-linked genetic disorders because they have only one X chromosome and therefore any genetic marks on their X chromosome are displayed. Females (XX) have two X chromosomes; a recessive gene located on one X chromosome will be masked by a dominant gene on the other X chromosome. Females are therefore less likely to display X-linked genetic disorders because both of their X chromosomes must carry the recessive genetic disorder for it to be displayed.

TABLE 2.4 ■ Diseases Acquired Through X-Linked Inheritance

Syndrome/Disease	Occurrence	Description	Treatment
Color blindness	1 in 12 males	Difficulty distinguishing red from green; less common is difficulty distinguishing blue from green	No cure
Duchenne muscular dystrophy	1 in 3,500 males	Weakness and wasting of limb and trunk muscles; progresses slowly but will affect all voluntary muscles	Physical therapy, exercise, body braces; survival rare beyond late 20s
Fragile X syndrome	1 in 4,000 males and 1 in 8,000 females	Symptoms include cognitive impairment; attention problems; anxiety; unstable mood; long face; large ears; flat feet; and hyperextensible joints, especially fingers	No cure
Hemophilia	1 in 3,000–7,000 males	Blood disorder in which the blood does not clot	Blood transfusions

Source: McKusick-Nathans Institute of Genetic Medicine, 2017.

Fragile X syndrome is a dominant-recessive disorder carried on the X chromosome (Hagerman et al., 2017; Salcedo-Arellano et al., 2020). Because the gene is dominant, it need appear on only one X chromosome to be displayed, so it occurs in both males and females. Fragile X syndrome (FXS) is the most common inherited form of intellectual disability (Doherty & Scerif, 2017), and children with Fragile X syndrome tend to show moderate to severe intellectual disability and problems with executive function (Schmitt, Shaffer, Hessl, & Erickson, 2019; Raspa et al., 2017). Several behavioral mannerisms are also common, including poor eye contact and repetitive behaviors such as hand flapping, hand biting, and mimicking others, behaviors also common in individuals with autistic spectrum disorders (Hagerman et al., 2017; Salcedo-Arellano et al., 2020). Fragile X syndrome is often codiagnosed with autism; it's estimated about 40%–60% of boys and 16%–20% of girls with Fragile X syndrome meet the diagnostic criteria for autism (Bagni & Zukin, 2019; Kaufmann et al., 2017).

Hemophilia, a condition in which the blood does not clot normally, is another example of a recessive disease inherited through genes on the X chromosome (McKusick-Nathans Institute of Genetic Medicine, 2020; Shah et al., 2017). Daughters who inherit the gene for hemophilia typically do not show the disorder because the dominant gene on their second X chromosome promotes normal blood clotting (d'Oiron, 2019). Sons who inherit the gene will display the disorder because the Y chromosome does not have the corresponding genetic information to counter the hemophilia gene.

Chromosomal Abnormalities

Chromosomal abnormalities are the result of errors during cell reproduction or damage caused afterward. Occurring in about 1 of every 1,500 births, the most widely known chromosome disorder is trisomy 21, more commonly called **Down syndrome** (de Graaf et al., 2017; McKusick-Nathans Institute of Genetic Medicine, 2020). Down syndrome occurs when a third chromosome appears alongside the 21st pair of chromosomes. Down syndrome is associated with marked physical, health, and cognitive attributes, including a short, stocky build; a round face; almond-shaped eyes; and a flattened nose

Down syndrome is the most common cause of intellectual disability. Interventions that encourage children to interact with their physical and social environment can promote motor, social, and emotional development.

istock/ mediaphotos

(Antonarakis et al., 2020; Bull, 2020). Children with Down syndrome tend to show delays in physical and motor development relative to other children, and health problems such as congenital heart defects, vision impairments, poor hearing, and immune system deficiencies (Diamandopoulos & Green, 2018; Morrison & McMahon, 2018; Roizen et al., 2014; Zampieri et al., 2014).

Down syndrome is the most common genetic cause of intellectual developmental disability (Vissers et al., 2016), but children's abilities vary. Infants and children who participate in early intervention and receive sensitive caregiving and encouragement to explore their environment show positive outcomes, especially in the motor, social, and emotion areas of functioning (Bull, 2020; Næss et al., 2017; Wentz, 2017).

Some chromosomal abnormalities concern the 23rd pair of chromosomes: the sex chromosomes. These abnormalities result from either an additional or missing sex chromosome. Given their different genetic makeup, sex chromosome abnormalities yield different effects in males and females (see Table 2.5).

Klinefelter syndrome, in which males are born with an extra X chromosome (XXY), occurs in 1 in 1,000 males (McKusick-Nathans Institute of Genetic Medicine, 2020; Wistuba et al., 2017). Many males are unaware they have the disorder until they are tested for infertility in adulthood (Bird & Hurren, 2016; Gravholt et al., 2018). Severe characteristics of Klinfelter syndrome include a high-pitched voice, short stature, feminine body shape, breast enlargement, and infertility (Bonomi et al., 2017). As adults, men with Klinefelter syndrome are at risk for a variety of disorders that are more common in women, such as osteoporosis (Juul et al., 2011).

Jacob's syndrome, also known as XYY syndrome, causes men to produce high levels of testosterone (McKusick-Nathans Institute of Genetic Medicine, 2017; Pappas et al., 2017). Most men with XYY syndrome are unaware that they have a chromosomal abnormality. The prevalence of XYY syndrome is uncertain given that most men go undiagnosed.

Females are susceptible to a different set of sex chromosome abnormalities. About 1 in 1,000 females are born with three X chromosomes, known as **triple X syndrome** (McKusick-Nathans Institute of Genetic Medicine, 2020; Wigby et al., 2016). Women with triple X syndrome tend to be about an inch or so taller than average with unusually long legs and slender torsos, as well as normal development of sexual characteristics and fertility. Some may score lower on intelligence tests or have learning difficulties. Because many cases of triple X syndrome often go unnoticed, little is known about the syndrome.

The sex chromosome abnormality known as **Turner syndrome** occurs when a female is born with only one X chromosome (McKusick-Nathans Institute of Genetic Medicine, 2020). Girls with Turner syndrome show abnormal growth patterns. They show delayed puberty, their ovaries do not

TABLE 2.5 ■ Sex Chromosome Abnormalities

Male Genotype	Syndrome	Description	Prevalence
XO	Turner	Abnormal growth patterns, delayed puberty, lack of prominent female secondary sex characteristics, and infertility. Short adult stature, webbing around the neck.	1 in 2,500 females
XXX	Triple X	Grow about an inch or so taller than average with unusually long legs and slender torsos, and show normal development of sexual characteristics and fertility. Because many cases of triple X syndrome often go unnoticed, little is known about the syndrome	Unknown; many cases go unnoticed.
Female Genotype	**Syndrome**		
XXY	Klinefelter	High-pitched voice, short stature, feminine body shape, and infertility. Increased risk for osteoporosis and other disorders that are more common in women.	1 in 1,000 males
XYY	Jacob's Syndrome	Accompanied by high levels of testosterone	Unknown; many cases go unnoticed.

develop normally, they do not ovulate and are infertile (Culen et al., 2017; Davis et al., 2020). As adults, they are short in stature and often have small jaws with extra folds of skin around their necks (webbing) and lack prominent female secondary sex characteristics such as breasts (Gravholt et al., 2019). Its prevalence is estimated to be 1 in 2,500 worldwide (National Library of Medicine, 2019). If Turner syndrome is diagnosed early, regular injections of human growth hormones can increase stature, and hormones administered at puberty can result in some breast development and menstruation (Culen et al., 2017; Klein et al., 2020).

Mutation

Not all inborn characteristics are inherited. Some result from **mutations**, which are sudden changes and abnormalities in the structure of genes that occur spontaneously or may be induced by exposure to environmental toxins such as radiation and agricultural chemicals in food. It is estimated that as many as one half of all conceptions include mutated chromosomes (Taneri et al., 2020). Most mutations are fatal—the developing organism dies very soon after conception, often before the woman knows she is pregnant (Sadler, 2018).

Sometimes mutations are beneficial. This is especially true if the mutation is induced by stressors in the environment and provides an adaptive advantage to the individual. For example, the sickle cell gene (discussed earlier in this chapter) is a mutation that originated in areas where malaria is widespread, such as Africa (Ware et al., 2017) and serves a protective role against malaria (Uyoga et al., 2019). Children who inherited a single sickle cell allele were more resistant to malarial infection and more likely to survive and pass it along to their offspring (Croke et al., 2017; Gong et al., 2013). The sickle cell gene is not helpful in places where malaria is not a risk.

Thinking in Context: Biological Influences

1. Consider your own physical characteristics, such as hair and eye color. Are they indicative of recessive traits, or dominant ones? Do you think that you might be a carrier of recessive traits? Why or why not?
2. Recall from Chapter 1 that most developmental scientists agree that nature and nature interact to influence development. Choose a genetic or chromosomal disorder discussed in this section and explain how it illustrates the interaction of genes and context.

Thinking in Context: Lifespan Development

Chromosomal and genetic problems can result in a variety of impairments. How might contextual factors, such as a supportive environment, aid individuals' development? Describe a specific problem or mutation. What environmental conditions might best promote healthy adjustment for individuals with this disorder?

Thinking in Context: Applied Developmental Science

Your friend, a "study buddy," is confused about the differences between disorders that are passed through genetic inheritance and chromosomal abnormalities. Explain how genetic disorders are transmitted, including examples. What are some examples of chromosomal disorders?

HEREDITY AND ENVIRONMENT

LEARNING OBJECTIVE

2.2 Describe behavior genetics and interactions among genes and environment, such as gene-environment correlations, gene-environment interactions, and the epigenetic framework.

Our **genotype**, or genetic makeup, inherited from our biological parents, is a biological contributor to all of our observable traits, from hair and eye color to personality, health, and behavior. However, genotypes alone do not determine our **phenotype**—the traits, characteristics, or personality that we display. Phenotypes result from the interaction of genotypes and our experiences.

Behavior Genetics

Behavior genetics is the field of study that examines how genes and experience combine to influence the diversity of human traits, abilities, and behaviors (Knopik et al., 2017; Plomin, 2019). Behavior geneticists assess the hereditary contributions to behavior by conducting selective breeding and family studies.

Selective breeding studies entail deliberately modifying the genetic makeup of animals to examine the influence of heredity on attributes and behavior. Mice can be bred to be very physically active by mating highly active mice only with other highly active mice or to be sedentary by breeding mice with very low levels of activity with each other (Schwartz et al., 2018). Selective breeding in rats, mice, and chickens has revealed genetic contributions to many traits and characteristics, such as aggressiveness, emotionality, sex drive, and maze learning (Bubac et al., 2020).

Behavior geneticists conduct *family studies* to compare people who live together and share varying degrees of relatedness. Two kinds of family studies are common: twin studies and adoption studies (York, 2020). *Twin studies* compare identical and fraternal twins to estimate how much of a trait or behavior is attributable to genes. Identical twins are genetically identical; they share 100% of their genes. Fraternal twins share 50% of their genes; they are genetically similar to non-twin siblings. If genes affect a given attribute, identical twins should be more similar than fraternal twins because identical twins share identical genes whereas fraternal twins share about half of their genes.

Adoption studies compare the degree of similarity between adopted children, their biological parents whose genes they share (50%), and their adoptive parents with whom they share an environment but not genes (York, 2020). If the adopted children share traits with their biological parents even though they were not raised by them (and do not share an environment), it suggests that the traits are genetic. If the children share traits with their adoptive parents, it indicates the traits are influenced by the environment.

Genes contribute to many traits, such as sociability, temperament, emotionality, and susceptibility to various illnesses including obesity, heart disease and cancer, anxiety, poor mental health, and a propensity to be physically aggressive (Bralten et al., 2019; Goodarzi, 2018; Morneau-Vaillancourt et al., 2019; Purves et al., 2019; Trucco et al., 2018). Yet even traits with a strong genetic component, such as growth, body weight, and height, are modified by environmental circumstances and opportunities that influence whether genetic potentials are realized (Dubois et al., 2012; Jelenkovic et al., 2016). Even identical twins who share 100% of their genes are not 100% alike because of the influence of environmental factors, which interact with genes in a variety of ways.

Gene-Environment Correlations

Genes and environment influence development and behavior independently, but they also are correlated. Environmental factors often support hereditary traits (Briley et al., 2019; Saltz, 2019; Scarr & McCartney, 1983). Gene-environment correlation refers to the finding that many genetically influenced traits tend to be associated with environmental factors that promote their development (Lynch, 2016). That is, genetic traits influence children's behavior, which is often supported or encouraged by the environment (Knafo & Jaffee, 2013). There are three types of gene-environment correlations: passive, reactive, and active.

Parents create homes that reflect their own genotypes. Because parents are genetically similar to their children, the homes that parents create support their own preferences but also correspond to their child's genotype—an example of a *passive gene-environment correlation* (Wilkinson et al., 2013). It is a passive **gene-environment correlation** because it occurs regardless of the child's behavior. For example, parents might provide genes that predispose a child to develop musical ability and then create a home environment that supports the development of musical ability, such as by playing music in the home and owning musical instruments (Corrigall & Schellenberg, 2015; see Figure 2.4). This type of

FIGURE 2.4 ■ Gene-Environment Correlation

The availability of instruments in the home corresponds to the child's musical abilities, and they begin to play guitar (passive gene-environment correlation). As they play guitar, they evoke positive responses in others, increasing their interest in music (evocative gene-environment correlation). Over time, they seek opportunities to play, such as performing in front of an audience (niche picking).

iStock/Signature/iStock/Essentials/iStock/Essentials

gene-environment correlation tends to occur early in life because parents create rearing environments for their infants and young children.

People naturally evoke responses from others and the environment, just as the environment and the actions of others evoke responses from the individual. In an *evocative gene-environment correlation*, a child's genetic traits (e.g., personality characteristics such as openness to experience) influence the social and physical environment, which shape development in ways that support the genetic trait (Pieters et al., 2015; Saltz, 2019). A child with a genetic trait for music talent will evoke pleasurable responses (e.g., parental approval) when she plays music; this environmental support, in turn, encourages further development of the child's musical trait.

Children also take a hands-on role in shaping their development. Recall from Chapter 1 that a major theme in understanding human development is the finding that individuals are active in their development; here we have an example of this theme. As children grow older, they have increasing freedom to choose their own activities and environments. An *active gene-environment correlation* occurs when the child actively creates experiences and environments that correspond to and influence his or her genetic predisposition. For example, the child with a genetic trait for interest and ability in music actively seeks experiences and environments that support that trait, such as friends with similar interests and after-school music classes (Corrigall & Schellenberg, 2015). This tendency to actively seek out experiences and environments compatible and supportive of our genetic tendencies is called **niche picking** (Saltz, 2019; Scarr & McCartney, 1983).

Gene-Environment (G x E) Interactions

Although behavior geneticists have learned a great deal about genetic influences on behavior, effects are often unpredictable (Flint et al., 2020). The effects of genes vary with environmental influences and not all genotypes respond to environmental influences in the same way (Fowler-Finn & Boutwell, 2019). Consider a classic study that followed a sample of boys from birth to adulthood and found that

Not all children exposed to adversity experience negative outcomes. Genes, such as MAOA, influence children's sensitivity to maltreatment.

FatCamera/ Getty Images

the effects of experiencing childhood maltreatment varied with boys' genotypes. The boys who experienced maltreatment were twice as likely to develop problems with aggression, violence, and to even be convicted of a violent crime—but only if they carried a specific form of the gene that controls monoamine oxidase A (MAOA), an enzyme that regulates chemicals in the brain. These findings have been replicated in another 30-year longitudinal study of boys (Fergusson et al., 2011) as well as a meta-analysis of 27 studies (Byrd & Manuck, 2014).

MAOA gene-environment interactions influence other mental health outcomes such as antisocial personality disorder and depression (Beach et al., 2010; Cicchetti et al., 2007; Manuck & McCaffery, 2014; Nikulina et al., 2012). **Gene-environment interactions** determine the effects of many genes. For example, the 5-HTTLPR gene, responsible for regulating specific chemicals in the brain, interacts with environmental factors to influence parenting sensitivity, depression, stress, and responses to trauma (Baião et al., 2020; Li et al., 2013). Genes and the environment work together in complex ways to determine our characteristics, behavior, development, and health (Morgan et al., 2020; Ritz et al., 2017).

Epigenetic Framework

As we have seen, development is influenced by the dynamic interaction of biological and contextual forces. Genes provide a blueprint for development, but phenotypic outcomes—individuals' characteristics—are not predetermined; they vary with environmental factors. Recently scientists have determined that environmental factors do not simply interact with genes to determine people's traits Instead, they *determine how* genes are expressed through a process known as **epigenetics** (Carlberg & Molnar, 2019; Moore, 2017). The epigenome is a molecule that stretches along the length of DNA and provides instructions to genes, determining how they are expressed, that is, whether they are turned on or off.

At birth, each cell in our body turns on only a fraction of its genes. The epigenome instructs genes to be turned on and off over the course of development and also in response to the environment (Meaney, 2017). Epigenetic mechanisms determine how genetic instructions are carried out to determine the phenotype (Lester et al., 2016; Pinel et al., 2018). Environmental factors such as toxins, injuries, crowding, diet, and responsive parenting can influence the expression of genetic traits by determining which genes are turned on and off (O'Donnell & Meaney, 2020).

Epigenetic processes also influence human development. Consider brain development (O'Donnell & Meaney, 2020). Providing infants with a healthy diet and opportunities to explore the world will support the development of brain cells, governed by epigenetic mechanisms that switch genes on and off. Conversely, epigenetic changes that accompany exposure to toxins or extreme trauma might suppress the activity of some genes, potentially negatively influencing brain development. In this way, brain development is influenced by epigenetic interactions among genes and contextual factors that determine infants' phenotypes (Lerner & Overton, 2017). These complex interactions are illustrated in Figure 2.5 (Dodge & Rutter, 2011). Interactions between heredity and environment change throughout development, as does the role we play in constructing environments that support our genotypes, influence our epigenome, and determine who we become (Lickliter & Witherington, 2017).

Perhaps the most surprising finding emerging from animal studies of epigenetics is that the epigenome can be passed by males and females from one generation to the next (Legoff et al., 2019; Szyf, 2015). This means that what you eat and do today could affect the epigenome—the development, characteristics, and health—of your children, grandchildren, and great-grandchildren (Bošković & Rando, 2018; Grover & Jenkins, 2020; Vanhees et al., 2014).

FIGURE 2.5 ■ Epigenetic Framework

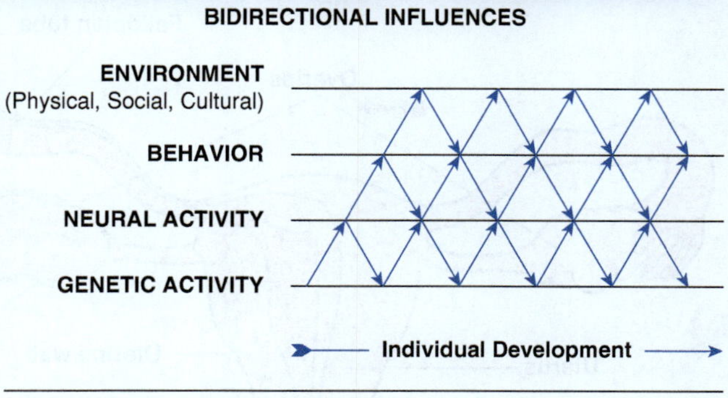

Source: Gottlieb, 2007.

Thinking in Context: Lifespan Development

1. Describe a skill or ability at which you excel. How might your ability be influenced by your genes and your context?
   - **a.** Identify passive gene-environment correlation that may contribute to your ability. How has your environment influenced your ability?
   - **b.** Provide an example of an evocative gene-environment correlation. How have you evoked responses from your context that influenced your ability?
   - **c.** Explain how your ability might reflect an active gene-environment correlation.
   - **d.** Which of these types of gene-environment correlation do you think best accounts for your ability? Why?

Thinking in Context: Biological Influences

1. Considering the research on epigenetics, what can you do to protect your epigenome? What kinds of behavioral and contextual factors might influence your epigenome?
2. If some genes may be protective in particular contexts, should scientists learn how to turn them on? Should scientists learn to turn off genes that might increase risks in particular contexts? Why or why not?

Thinking in Context: Applied Developmental Science

Imagine that you are a researcher planning to conduct a twin study and an adoption study on intelligence, personality, academic achievement, or another topic. What are the advantages and disadvantages of each method? What are some challenges in obtaining participants for these studies? Using the twin approach, how might you determine the genetic and environmental influences on your topic of interest? How does this differ in adoptive studies?

What conclusions do you draw about these types of studies? Which do you prefer and why?

PRENATAL DEVELOPMENT

LEARNING OBJECTIVE

2.3 Describe the three periods of prenatal development.

Prenatal development is a dramatic process in which a single cell transforms and grows into a **neonate**, or newborn. Conception, the union of ovum and sperm, marks the beginning of prenatal development. Over the next 38 weeks, the human progresses through several periods of development from fertilization to birth.

FIGURE 2.6 ■ Female Reproductive System

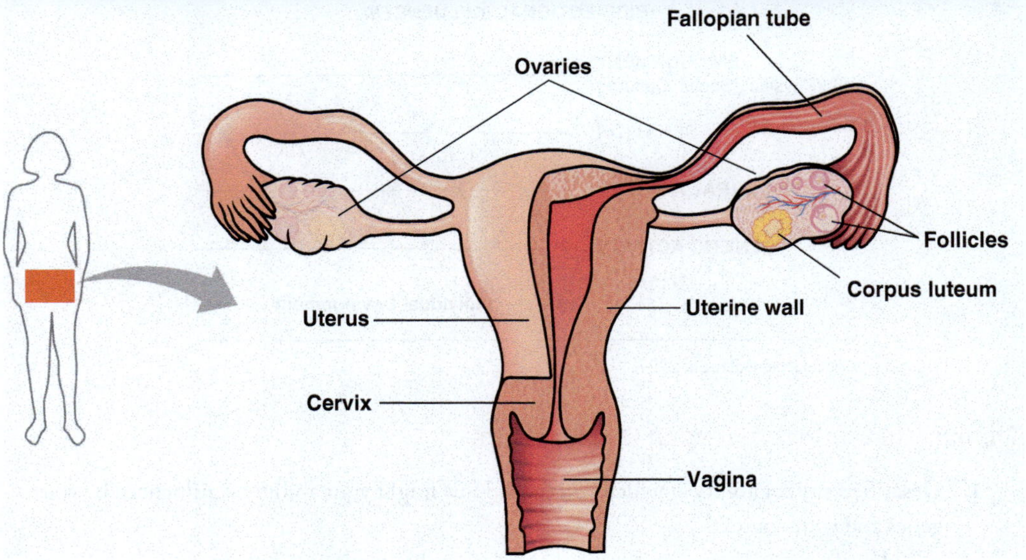

Conception

A woman can conceive only during a short window of time each month. About every 28 days, an ovum bursts from one of the ovaries into the long, thin fallopian tube that leads to the uterus; this event is known as ovulation (see Figure 2.6). Over several days, the ovum travels down the fallopian tube, which connects the ovaries to the uterus, while the woman's hormones cause the lining of the uterus to thicken in preparation for the fertilized ovum (Sadler, 2018). If fertilization does not occur, the lining of the uterus is shed through menstruation about 2 weeks after ovulation.

Conception, of course, also involves the male. Each day a man's testes produce millions of sperm, which are composed of a pointed head packed with 23 chromosomes' worth of genetic material and a long tail. During ejaculation, about 360 million, and as many as 500 million, sperm are released, bathed in a protective fluid called semen (Moore et al., 2019). On average, only about 300 sperm reach the ovum within the fallopian tubes, if an ovum is present (Webster et al., 2018). As soon as one sperm penetrates the ovum the sperm's tail falls off, and the sperm's genetic contents merge with that of the ovum. After fertilization, the zygote rapidly transforms into a multicelled organism. Prenatal development takes place over three developmental periods: (1) the germinal period, (2) the **embryonic period**, and (3) the fetal period.

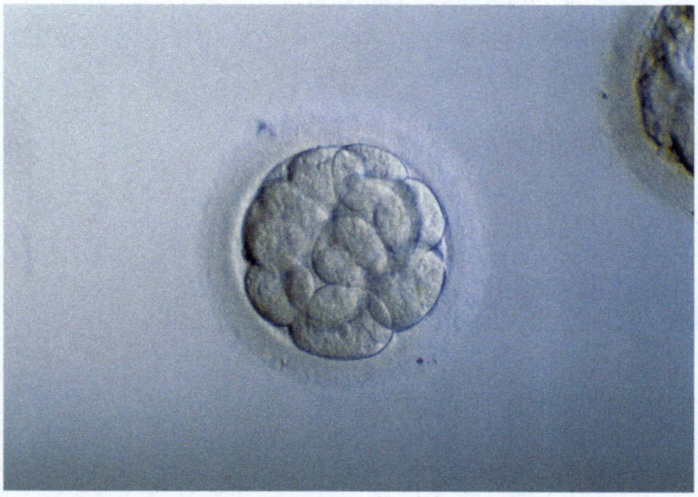

This ball of cells, known as a morula, is formed at about three days after conception. Each of these cells is identical. Differentiation has not yet begun.

Pascal Goetgheluck/Science Source

Germinal Period (0 to 2 Weeks)

During the **germinal period**, also known as the period of the zygote, the newly created zygote begins cell division as it travels down the fallopian tube, where fertilization took place, toward the uterus. About 30 hours after conception, the zygote then splits down the middle, forming two identical cells (Webster et al., 2018). This process is called cleavage, and it continues at a rapid pace. The two cells each split to form four cells, then eight, and so on (see Figure 2.7).

After four days, the organism consists of about 60 to 70 cells formed into a **blastocyst**, a fluid-filled ball of cells surrounding an inner cluster of cells from which the embryo will develop. **Implantation**, in which the blastocyst burrows into the wall of the uterus, begins at about day 6 and is complete by about day 11 (Moore et al., 2019).

FIGURE 2.7 ■ Germinal Period

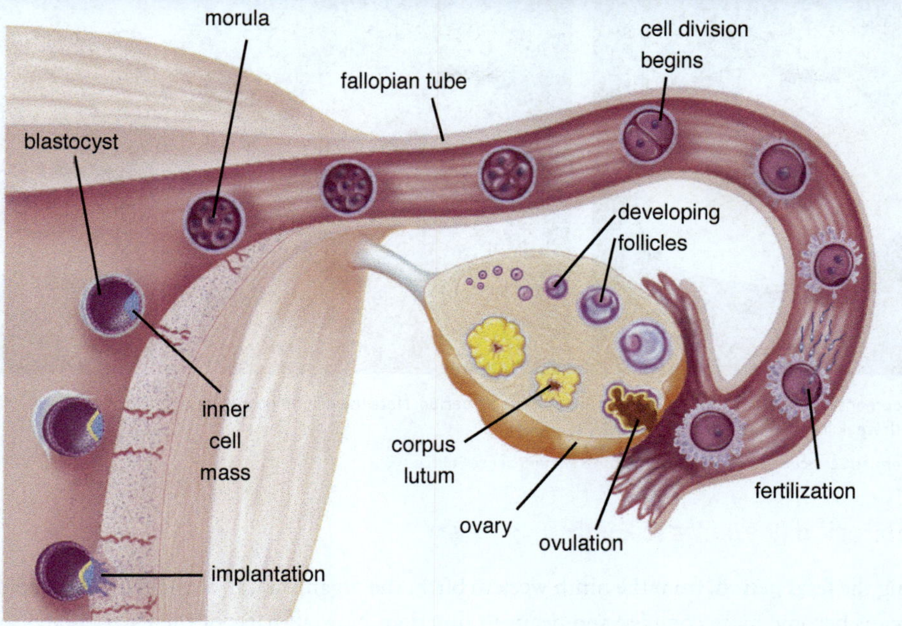

Embryonic Period (3 to 8 Weeks)

After implantation, during the third week after conception, the developing organism, now called an **embryo,** begins the most rapid period of structural development in the lifespan. The mass of cells composing the *embryonic disk* forms layers, which will develop into all the major organs of the body. The *ectoderm*, the upper layer, will become skin, nails, hair, teeth, sensory organs, and the nervous system. The *endoderm*, the lower layer, will become the digestive system, liver, lungs, pancreas, salivary glands, and respiratory system. The middle layer, the *mesoderm*, forms later and will become muscles, skeleton, circulatory system, and internal organs.

As the embryo develops, support structures form to protect it, provide nourishment, and remove wastes. The **amnion**, a membrane that holds amniotic fluid, surrounds the embryo providing temperature regulation, cushioning, and protection from shocks. The **placenta**, a principal organ of exchange between the mother and developing organism, begins to form. It will act as a filter, enabling the exchange of nutrients, oxygen, and wastes to occur through the umbilical cord, and as a protective barrier, preventing some toxins from entering the embryo's bloodstream.

About 22 days after conception marks a particularly important change: The ectoderm folds to form the **neural tube**, which will develop into the central nervous system (brain and spinal cord; Webster et al., 2018). The head can be distinguished and a blood vessel that will become the heart begins to pulse and blood begins to circulate throughout the body. During days 26 and 27, arm buds appear, followed by leg buds on days 28 through 30 (Sadler, 2018). The brain develops rapidly and the head grows faster than the other parts of the body during the fifth week of development. The eyes, ears, nose, and mouth begin to form during the sixth week. Upper arms, forearms, palms, legs, and feet appear.

During the seventh week a ridge called the **indifferent gonad** appears that can develop into the male or female genitals, depending on the fetus's sex chromosomes (XY for males and XX for females; Moore et al., 2019). The sex organs take several weeks to develop. The external genital organs are not apparent until about 12 weeks.

At the end of the embryonic period, 8 weeks after conception, the embryo weighs about one-seventh of an ounce and is 1 inch long. All of the basic organs and body parts have formed in a very rudimentary way. The embryo displays spontaneous reflexive movements, but it is still too small for the movements to be felt by the mother (Hepper, 2015). Serious defects that emerge during the embryonic period most often occur before the pregnancy is detected, are the result of chromosomal abnormalities, and often cause a miscarriage (loss of the embryo; Chou et al., 2020).

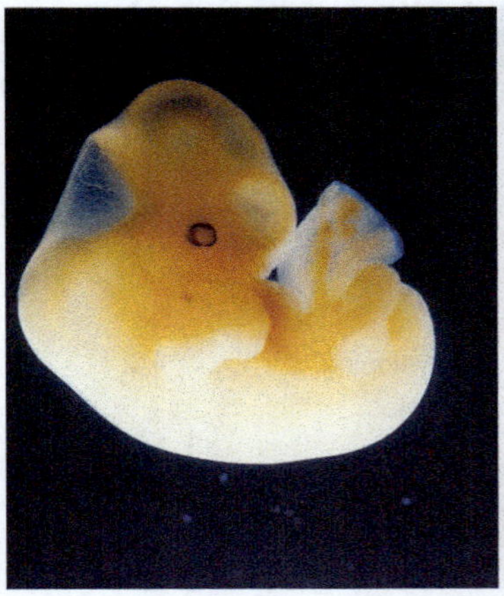
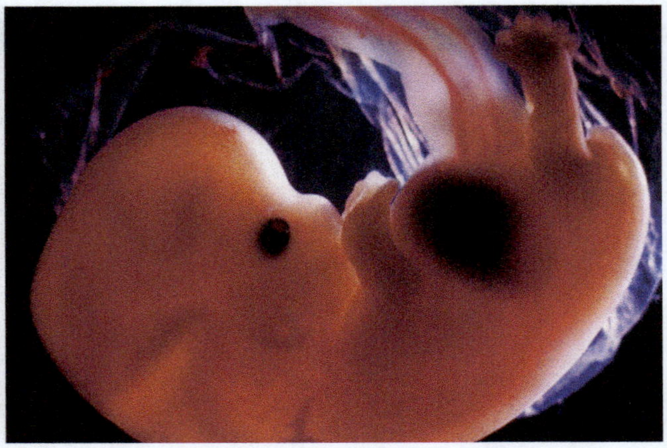

Development proceeds very quickly during the embryonic period. Note the dramatic changes from the fifth week (left) to the seventh week (right) of prenatal development.

Petit Format/Science Source; Professor Pietro M. Motta/Science Source

Fetal Period (9 Weeks to Birth)

During the **fetal period**, from the ninth week to birth, the organism, called a **fetus**, grows rapidly, and its organs become more complex and begin to function. Now all parts of the fetus's body can move spontaneously, the legs kick, and the fetus can suck its thumb (an involuntary reflex; Sadler, 2018).

By the 14th week, limb movements are coordinated, but they will be too slight to be felt by the mother until about 17 to 20 weeks. The heartbeat gets stronger. Eyelids, eyebrows, fingernails, toenails, and tooth buds form. During the last 3 months of pregnancy, the fetal body grows substantially in weight and length; specifically, it typically gains more than 5 pounds and grows 7 inches (Moore et al., 2019). At about 28 weeks after conception, the cerebral cortex develops convolutions and furrows, taking on the brain's characteristic wrinkly appearance (Andescavage et al., 2016). The fetal brain wave pattern shifts to include occasional bursts of activity, similar to the sleep-wake cycles of newborns.

Prenatal Diagnosis

Prenatal development is monitored through several methods. The most widespread and routine diagnostic procedure is **ultrasound**, in which high-frequency sound waves directed at the mother's abdomen provide clear images of the womb represented on a video monitor. Ultrasound enables physicians to observe the fetus, measure fetal growth, judge gestational age, reveal the sex of the fetus, detect multiple pregnancies (twins, triplets, etc.), and determine physical abnormalities in the fetus. Many deformities can be observed, such as cardiac abnormalities, cleft palate, and microencephaly (small head size). At least 80% of women in the United States receive at least one prenatal ultrasound scan (Sadler, 2018). Three to four screenings over the duration of pregnancy are common to evaluate fetal development. Repeated ultrasound of the fetus does not appear to affect growth and development (Abramowicz, 2019; Stephenson, 2005).

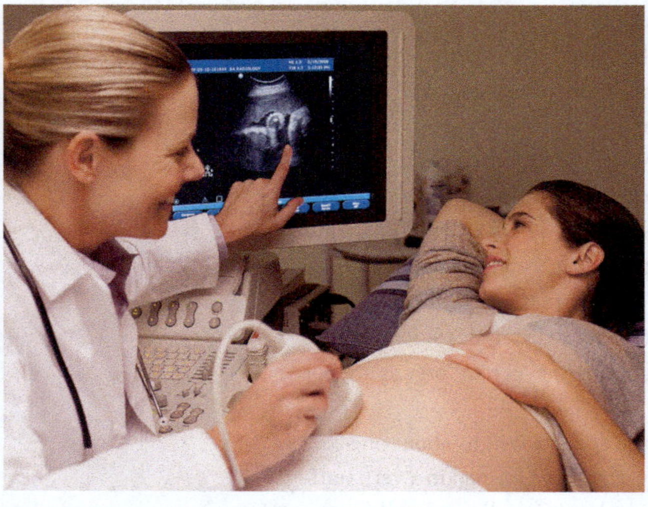

Ultrasound technology provides clear images of the womb, permitting physicians to observe the fetus, measure fetal growth, judge gestational age, reveal the sex of the fetus, detect multiple pregnancies, and determine physical abnormalities in the fetus.

iStock/Chris Ryan

Fetal MRI applies MRI technology (see Chapter 1) to image the fetus's body and diagnose malformations (Aertsen et al., 2020). It is often used as a follow-up to ultrasound imaging to provide more detailed views of suspected abnormalities (Milani et al., 2015). Unlike ultrasound, fetal MRI can detect abnormalities throughout the body, including in the central nervous system (Griffiths et al., 2017; Masselli et al., 2020). Fetal MRI is safe for mother and fetus in the second and third trimesters but is expensive and has limited availability in some areas (Patenaude et al., 2014).

Amniocentesis involves sampling the amniotic fluid surrounding the fetus by extracting it from the mother's uterus through a long, hollow needle that is guided by ultrasound as it is inserted into the mother's abdomen (Odibo, 2015). The amniotic fluid contains fetal cells, which are grown in a laboratory dish to create enough cells for genetic analysis. Genetic analysis is then performed to detect chromosomal anomalies and defects. Amniocentesis is less common than ultrasound, as it poses greater risk to the fetus, but it is safe (Homola & Zimmer, 2019). It is recommended for women aged 35 and over, especially if the woman and partner are both known carriers of genetic diseases (Vink & Quinn, 2018a). Usually amniocentesis is conducted between the 15th and 18th week of pregnancy. Conducted any earlier, an amniocentesis may increase the risk of miscarriage (Akolekar et al., 2015). Test results generally are available about two weeks after the procedure because it takes that long for the genetic material to grow and reproduce to the point where it can be analyzed.

Chorionic villus sampling (CVS) also samples genetic material and can be conducted earlier than amniocentesis, between 9 and 12 weeks of pregnancy (Vink & Quinn, 2018b). CVS requires obtaining a small amount of tissue from the chorion, part of the membrane surrounding the fetus, by using a long needle inserted either abdominally or vaginally, depending on the location of the fetus. Results are typically available about one week following the procedure. CVS is relatively painless and, like amniocentesis, has a 100% diagnostic success rate. Generally, CVS poses few risks to the fetus. (Salomon et al., 2019; Shim et al., 2014). However, CVS should not be conducted prior to 10 weeks gestation as some studies suggest an increased risk of limb defects and miscarriages (Shahbazian et al., 2012).

Noninvasive prenatal testing (NIPT) screens the mother's blood to detect chromosomal abnormalities in the fetus. Cell-free fetal DNA (chromosome fragments that result in the breakdown of fetal cells) circulates in maternal blood in small concentrations (Hartwig et al., 2017; Warsof et al., 2015). Testing can be done after 10 weeks; it's typically done between 10 and 22 weeks. Given that the test involves drawing blood from the mother, there is no risk to the fetus. The use of NIPT has increased dramatically in the U.S. and other countries (Hui et al., 2017). NIPT can provide accurate sex determination but cannot detect as many chromosomal abnormalities as amniocentesis or CVS and with less accuracy (Hartwig et al., 2017; Villela et al., 2019). Pregnant women and their partners, in consultation with their obstetrician, should carefully weigh the risks and benefits of any procedure designed to monitor prenatal development (see Table 2.6).

TABLE 2.6 ■ Methods of Prenatal Diagnosis

	Explanation	Advantages	Disadvantages
Ultrasound	High-frequency sound waves directed at the mother's abdomen provide clear images of the womb projected on to a video monitor.	Enables physicians to observe the fetus, measure fetal growth, reveal the sex of the fetus, and to determine physical abnormalities in the fetus.	Many abnormalities and deformities cannot be easily observed.
Amniocentesis	A small sample of the amniotic fluid containing fetal cells is extracted from the mother's uterus. The fetal cells are grown in a laboratory dish and analyzed.	Permits a thorough analysis of the fetus's genotype. There is 100% diagnostic success rate.	Safe, but poses a greater risk to the fetus than ultrasound, especially if conducted before the 15th week of pregnancy.
Chorionic villus sampling (CVS)	A small amount of tissue is sampled from the chorion, grown in a laboratory dish, and studied to detect chromosomal abnormalities.	Permits a thorough analysis of the fetus's genotype. There is 100% diagnostic success rate. CVS can be conducted earlier than amniocentesis, between 10 and 12 weeks.	It is safe but may pose a risk of spontaneous abortion and limb defects when conducted prior to 10 weeks' gestation.
Fetal MRI	Uses a magnetic resonance imaging scanner to record detailed images of fetal organs and structures.	Provides the most detailed and accurate images available	It is expensive, but safe.
Noninvasive prenatal testing (NIPT)	Cell-free fetal DNA is examined by drawing blood from the mother.	There is no risk to the fetus. It can diagnose several chromosomal abnormalities.	It cannot detect the full range of abnormalities and may be less accurate than other methods.

Sources: (Akolekar et al., 2015; Chan et al., 2013; Gregg et al., 2013; Odibo, 2015; Shahbazian et al., 2012; Shim et al., 2014; Theodora et al., 2016)

Thinking in Context: Lifespan Development

What might be some of the implications of the timing of prenatal development—that is, when the major body systems develop—for the behavior of pregnant women and those who are considering becoming pregnant?

Thinking in Context: Applied Developmental Science

1. Petra noticed that her abdomen has not grown much since she became pregnant three months ago. She concluded that the fetus must not undergo significant development early in pregnancy. How would you respond to Petra?
2. Suppose that you are a health care provider tasked with explaining prenatal diagnostic choices to a 38-year-old woman pregnant with her first child. How would you explain the various choices? What information would you provide about their purpose and the advantages and disadvantages of each? Which tests are most relevant to your patient? What would you advise? Why?

ENVIRONMENTAL INFLUENCES ON PRENATAL DEVELOPMENT

LEARNING OBJECTIVE

2.4 Explain how exposure to environmental factors can influence the prenatal environment and provide examples.

Prenatal development unfolds along a programmed path, a predictable pattern of change, but it can be disrupted by environmental factors called **teratogens**. A teratogen is an agent, such as a disease, drug, or other environmental factor, that can cause prenatal abnormalities, defects, and even death.

Principles of Teratology

Several principles can account for the varied effects of exposure to teratogens on prenatal development (Moore et al., 2019; Sadler, 2018).

Critical Periods

The developing organism is more susceptible to the harmful effects of teratogens during certain stages of development(Nelson & Gabard-Durnam, 2020). The embryonic period is the most sensitive stage of development (Webster et al., 2018). In addition, each organ of the body has a sensitive period during which it is most susceptible to damage from teratogens such as drugs, alcohol, and environmental contaminants (see Figure 2.8). Once a body part is fully formed, it is less likely to be harmed by exposure to teratogens, but some body parts, like the brain, remain vulnerable throughout prenatal development.

Dose

The amount of exposure (i.e., dosage) to a teratogen influences its effects. Generally, the greater the dose and the longer the period of exposure, the more damage to development, but teratogens also differ in their strength. Some, like alcohol, display a powerful dose-response relationship so that larger doses, or heavier and more frequent drinking, predictably result in greater damage (Bandoli et al., 2019).

Individual Differences

Individuals vary in their susceptibility to particular teratogens based on the genetic makeup of both the organism and mother, as well as the quality of the prenatal environment. Organisms might show a range of responses to a given teratogen, such that some show severe defects, others more mild defects, and some may display normal development (Kaminen-Ahola, 2020).

FIGURE 2.8 ■ Critical Periods in Prenatal Development

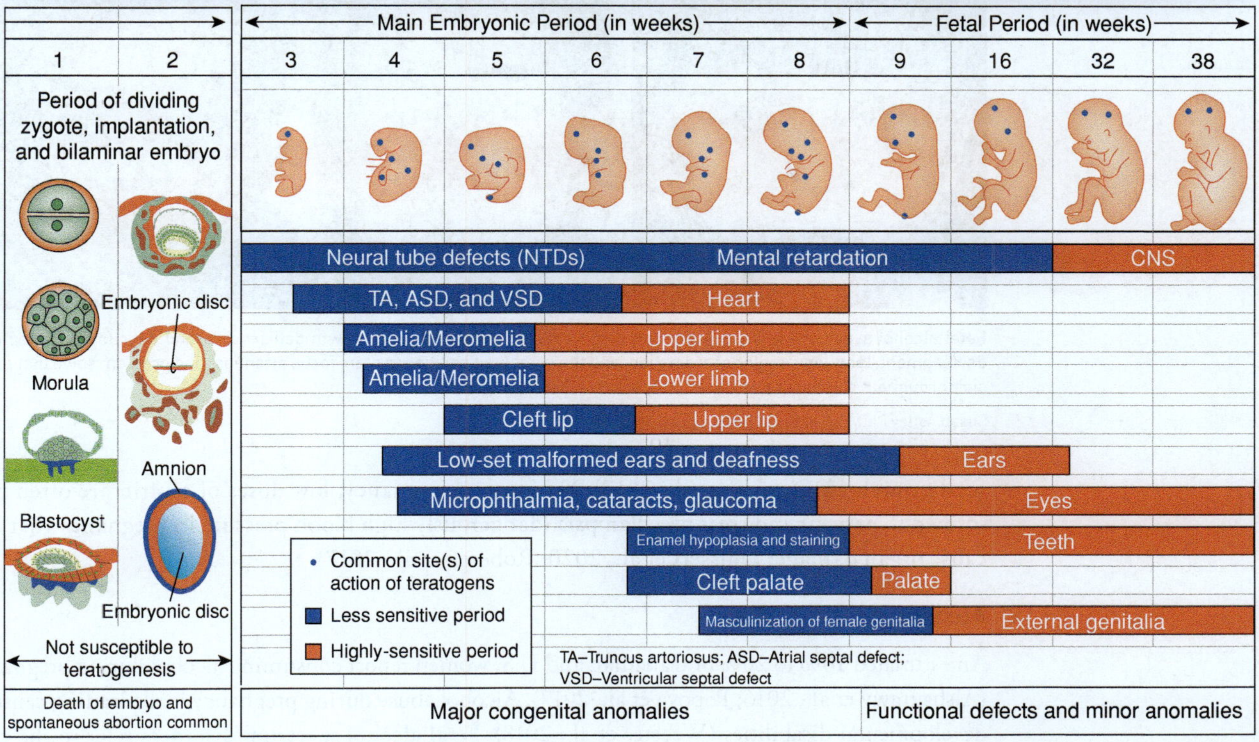

Adapted from Moore et al, 2019

Types of Teratogens

Prenatal development can be influenced by many contextual factors: maternal consumption of over-the-counter (OTC), prescription, and recreational drugs; illness; environmental factors; and more.

Prescription and Nonprescription Drugs

More than 90% of pregnant women take prescription or OTC medications (Servey & Chang, 2014; Stanley et al., 2019). Prescription drugs that can act as teratogens include antibiotics, certain hormones, antidepressants, anticonvulsants, and some acne drugs (Tsamantioti & Hashmi, 2020).

Nonprescription drugs, such as diet pills and cold medicine, can also act as teratogens, but research on OTC drugs lags far behind research on prescription drugs, and we know little about the teratogenic effect of many OTC drugs (Tsamantioti & Hashmi, 2020). Caffeine, found in coffee, tea, cola drinks, and chocolate, is the most common OTC drug consumed during pregnancy. Prenatal caffeine exposure is associated with smaller size for gestational age (Modzelewska et al., 2019) and large doses are associated with an increased risk for miscarriage and low birthweight (Chen et al., 2014; Chen et al., 2016; Qian et al., 2020).

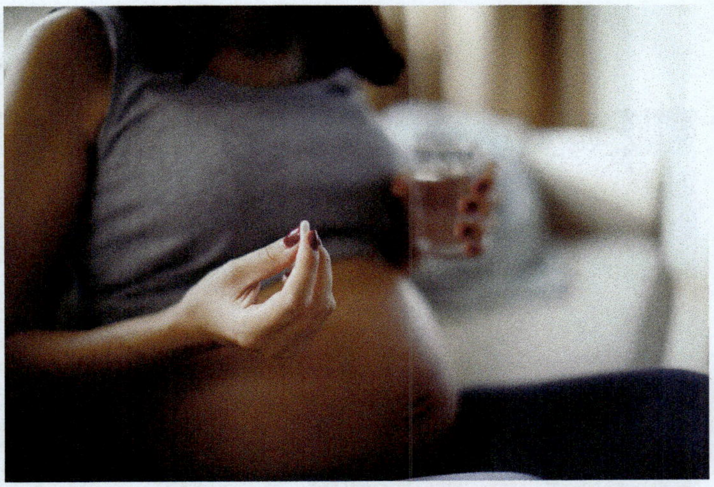

More than 90% of pregnant women take prescription or over-the-counter (OTC) medications. The findings regarding the teratogenic effects of drugs are mixed, with some studies suggesting potential harm and others suggesting no ill effects of a given drug. In addition, low doses of aspirin may have benefits in treating preeclampsia and high blood pressure during pregnancy.

iStock/ damircudic

Some drugs show complicated effects on development. High doses of aspirin early in pregnancy are associated with increased risk of miscarriage and poor

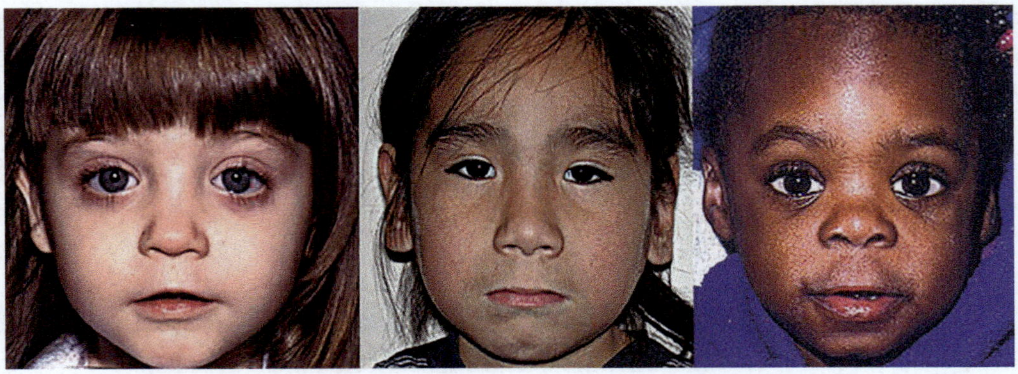

Fetal alcohol syndrome is associated with distinct facial characteristics, growth deficiencies, and deficits in intellectual development, language, motor coordination, and the combined abilities to plan, focus attention, and problem solve that persist throughout childhood and into adulthood.

Susan Astley PhD/University of Washington

fetal growth (Antonucci et al., 2012). Yet later in pregnancy, low doses of aspirin are often prescribed to prevent and treat preeclampsia (dangerously high blood pressure in pregnancy that can cause organ damage; Loussert et al., 2020; Roberge et al., 2017).

Alcohol

An estimated 10% to 20% of Canadian and U.S. women report consuming alcohol during pregnancy (Alshaarawy et al., 2016; Popova et al., 2017). Alcohol abuse during pregnancy is the leading cause of developmental disabilities (Webster et al., 2018). **Fetal alcohol spectrum disorders** refer to the continuum of effects of exposure to alcohol, which vary with the timing and amount of exposure (Hoyme et al., 2016). Fetal alcohol spectrum disorders are estimated to affect as many as 2% to 5% of younger schoolchildren in the United States and Western Europe (May et al., 2014, 2018).

Fetal alcohol syndrome (FAS) is a cluster of defects that occur with heavy prenatal exposure to alcohol. FAS is associated with physical characteristics (often small head circumference, short nose, and small midface), growth deficiencies, and deficits in motor coordination and in a range of cognitive abilities that affect attention, planning, and problem solving (Gupta et al., 2016; Loock et al., 2020; Wozniak et al., 2019). Cognitive and behavioral problems can persist from childhood and adolescence through adulthood (Dejong et al., 2019; Mamluk et al., 2017; Mattson et al., 2019). Children exposed to smaller amounts of alcohol prenatally may display *fetal alcohol effects*, which are some but not all of the problems of FAS (Hoyme et al., 2016).

There appears to be no safe level of drinking (Sarman, 2018; Shuffrey et al., 2020). Even less than one drink per day has been associated with poor fetal growth, preterm delivery, and abnormal brain activity in newborns (Mamluk et al., 2017; Shuffrey et al., 2020).

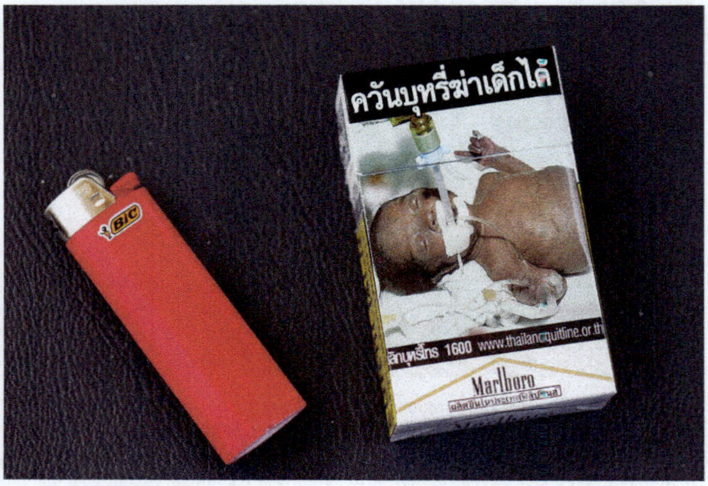

Smoking cigarettes during pregnancy can have adverse consequences.

iStock/Jan-Otto

Cigarette Smoking and E-Cigarette Use

About 7% to 10%, and in some studies as many as 17%, of women report smoking cigarettes during pregnancy (Agrawal et al., 2019; Kondracki, 2019). Fetal deaths, premature births, and low birthweight are nearly twice as frequent in mothers who are smokers than in those who do not smoke (Juárez & Merlo, 2013; Soneji & Beltrán-Sánchez, 2019). Infants exposed to smoke while in the womb are prone to congenital heart defects, respiratory problems, and sudden infant death syndrome and, as children, show more behavior problems, attention difficulties, and lower scores on intelligence and achievement tests (Froggatt et al., 2020; He et al., 2017; Sutin et al., 2017). Even babies born to light smokers (one to five cigarettes per day) show poorer fetal growth and higher rates of low birthweight than do babies born to nonsmokers (Berlin et al., 2017; Brand et al., 2019; Tong et al., 2017). Maternal smoking during pregnancy shows epigenetic effects on offspring, influencing predispositions to illness and disease in childhood, adolescence, and even middle adulthood (Joubert et al., 2016; Kaur et al., 2019; Nguyen et al., 2018).

About 10% to 15% of women report using e-cigarettes during pregnancy and the prevalence is rising (Wagner et al., 2017; Whittington et al., 2018). E-cigarettes are commonly believed to be "safer" than cigarettes, but exposure to e-cigarette vapor prenatally has similar toxic effects on prenatal development as traditional cigarettes, including increased risk for asthma and cognitive and neurological problems (Church et al., 2020; Greene & Pisano, 2019; Nguyen et al., 2018)

Marijuana

About 4% to 7% of pregnant women report using marijuana (Brown et al., 2017; Young-Wolff et al., 2019). The main active ingredient of marijuana, THC, readily crosses the placenta to affect the fetus (Alvarez et al., 2018). Marijuana use during early pregnancy negatively affects fetal growth, birthweight, and preterm birth, and is associated with a thinner cortex in late childhood (El Marroun et al., 2018). There are long-term neurological effects including impairments in attention, memory, and executive function as well as impulsivity in children, adolescents, and young adults (Grant et al., 2018; Sharapova et al., 2018; Smith et al., 2016).

Cocaine

Prenatal exposure to cocaine is associated with low birthweight, impaired motor skills and reflexes, and reduced brain volume at birth and in infancy (dos Santos et al., 2018; Grewen et al., 2014). Exposure has long-term effects on children through its effect on brain development, particularly the regions associated with attention, arousal, regulation, and executive function (Bazinet et al., 2016). It has a small but lasting effect on attention, emotional control, and behavioral problems through early adolescence and even emerging adulthood (Buckingham-Howes et al., 2013; Min et al., 2014; Richardson et al., 2015, 2019; Singer et al., 2015)

Opioids

Opioids are a class of drugs that include the illegal drugs heroin and synthetic opioids such as fentanyl, as well as prescription pain relievers, such as oxycodone and morphine. Prenatal exposure to opioids is associated with low birthweight, smaller head circumference, and altered brain development (Azuine et al., 2019; Monnelly et al., 2018; Towers et al., 2019). Newborns exposed to opioids prenatally may show signs of addiction and withdrawal symptoms, including tremors, irritability, abnormal crying, disturbed sleep, and impaired motor control (Conradt et al., 2019; Raffaeli et al., 2017). As children and adolescents they tend to show difficulty with attention, learning, managing arousal, and behavioral control; show more emotional and behavior problems than peers; and have reduced brain volume and smaller cortical surface area (Levine & Woodward, 2018; Nygaard et al., 2018; Sirnes et al., 2017; Yeoh et al., 2019).

Maternal Illness

Not all teratogens are drugs. Depending on the type and when it occurs, an illness experienced by the mother during pregnancy can have grave consequences for the developing fetus. Rubella (German measles) prior to the 11th week of pregnancy can cause a variety of defects, including blindness, deafness, heart defects, and brain damage, but after the first trimester, adverse consequences are less common (Bouthry et al., 2014; Singh, 2020). Chicken pox can produce birth defects affecting the arms, legs, eyes, and brain; mumps can increase the risk of miscarriage (Mehta, 2016; Webster et al., 2018). Some sexually transmitted infections (STIs), such as syphilis, can be transmitted to the fetus during pregnancy (Tsimis & Sheffield, 2017). HIV, the virus that causes acquired immune deficiency syndrome (AIDS), a disease affecting the immune system, can be transmitted during birth and through bodily fluids, including by breastfeeding.

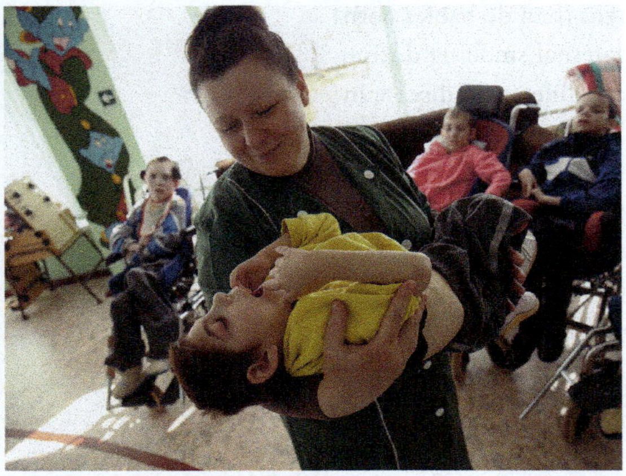

Prenatal exposure to radiation increases genetic mutation, leading to impaired development. After the nuclear power accident at Chernobyl, a significant rise in congenital conditions, or birth defects, were reported.

Sean Gallup / Staff/ Getty Images

Environmental Hazards

Prenatal exposure to chemicals, radiation, air pollution, and extremes of heat and humidity can impair development. Exposure to heavy metals, such as lead and mercury, is associated with lower scores on tests of cognitive ability and higher rates of childhood illness (Sadler, 2018; Vigeh et al., 2014; Xie et al., 2013). Prenatal exposure to radiation can cause genetic mutations and is associated with Down syndrome, reduced head circumference, intellectual disability, reduced cognitive and school performance, and heightened risk for cancer from childhood through adulthood (Black et al., 2019; Chang et al., 2014).

Contextual Factors and Teratogens

Our discussion of teratogens thus far has examined the effects of each teratogen independently, which is misleading because infants are often exposed to multiple teratogens. Most infants exposed to opioids or cocaine were also exposed to other substances, including tobacco, alcohol, and marijuana, making it difficult to isolate the effect of each drug on prenatal development. The effects of prenatal exposure to drugs are also influenced by parenting and other postnatal factors (Lee et al., 2020). Once contextual factors in the home and neighborhood, such as parenting, the caregiving environment, socioeconomic status, and exposure to violence are controlled, child and adolescent behavior problems are reduced and often eliminated (Brodie et al., 2019; Buckingham-Howes et al., 2013; Calhoun et al., 2015). Disentangling the long-term effects of prenatal exposure to substances, subsequent parenting, and contextual factors is challenging.

In addition, we must be cautious in interpreting findings about illicit drug use and the effects on prenatal development because race and ethnicity, maternal age, socioeconomic status, and region combine to influence the immediate and long-term outcomes of prenatal substance use for women and their infants. Many U.S. states treat maternal substance use as fetal abuse and construct laws that threaten women who use substances with involuntary treatment or protective custody during pregnancy (Atkins & Durrance, 2020; Seiler, 2016). About one-half of U.S. states classify controlled substance use during pregnancy as child abuse and require that substance use by pregnant mothers be reported to child protective services, which may lead to removing the newborn from parental custody or even terminating parental rights altogether (Guttmacher Institute, 2020).

Policies criminalizing maternal substance use discriminate against women of color and those in low socioeconomic brackets; low-income African American and Hispanic women are disproportionately tested and reported to child protective services for substance use (Paltrow & Flavin, 2013) (Hoerr et al., 2018; Rebbe et al., 2019). Criminal sanctions for maternal drug use can discourage women from seeking prenatal and postnatal care and undermine the physician-patient relationship (American College of Obstetricians and Gynecologists, 2011; American Medical Association, 2014). In contrast, women who live in states that adopt multiple policies, including those that reward abstention, invest in family and community supports, and promote contact with health care and social support services, hold the most promise for encouraging women to seek treatment and for promoting health outcomes (Bada et al., 2012; Hui et al., 2017; Kozhimannil et al., 2019)

Maternal and Paternal Influences on Prenatal Development

A pregnant woman's characteristics, such as her nutritional status, emotional well-being, and age, may also influence prenatal outcomes.

Nutrition

Most women need to consume 2,200 to 2,900 calories per day (and gain about 25 to 30 pounds in total) to sustain a healthy pregnancy (Kaiser et al., 2008). Yet about 14.3 million United States households (about 11%) reported food insecurity in 2018 (United States Department of Agriculture, 2019).

Fetal malnutrition is associated with poor growth before and after birth as well as effects that can last into adulthood (Han & Hong, 2019; Kim et al., 2017).

In addition to calories, specific nutrients are also needed for healthy prenatal development. Folic acid (a B vitamin) is essential in preventing neural tube defects. **Spina bifida** occurs when the lower part of the neural tube fails to close and spinal nerves begin to grow outside of the vertebrae, often resulting in paralysis and malformations in brain development and impaired cognitive development (Avagliano et al., 2019; Donnan et al., 2017). Another neural tube defect, **anencephaly**, occurs when the top part of the neural tube fails to close and all or part of the brain fails to develop, resulting in death shortly after birth (Avagliano et al., 2019). Neural tube defects can be prevented by consuming 0.4 to 0.8mg of folic acid daily. Many foods are fortified with folic acid, but a dietary supplement is safe and ensures that prenatal needs are met (Bibbins-Domingo et al., 2017).

Emotional Well-Being

Exposure to chronic and severe stress during pregnancy, such as from living in unsafe environments, experiencing traumatic life events, or exposure to racism and discrimination, poses risks for prenatal development, including low birthweight, premature birth, and a longer postpartum hospital stay (Lima et al., 2018; Schetter & Tanner, 2012). Long-term exposure to stress hormones in utero is associated with higher levels of stress hormones at birth and in infancy (Kapoor et al., 2016; McGowan & Matthews, 2018; Nazzari et al., 2019).

Infants prenatally exposed to high levels of maternal stress experience higher rates of emotional and behavior problems in infancy, childhood, and adolescence and increased risk for neurodevelopmental disorders such as autism and attention deficit disorder (Hentges et al., 2019; MacKinnon et al., 2018; Madigan et al., 2018; Manzari et al., 2019). Prenatal stress may also have epigenetic effects on development, influencing stress responses throughout the lifespan and perhaps transmitting them across generations (DeSocio, 2018).

Children who experience prenatal stress also tend to experience postnatal stress, making it difficult to separate their effects on children (Hartman et al., 2020; Lin et al., 2017). Children who are exposed to prenatal stress show greater emotional problems when they are also exposed to postnatal maternal depression and anxiety, as compared with those who are exposed to less maternal postnatal depression (Hartman et al., 2020). Contextual factors that influence pre- and postnatal maternal depression, such as exposure to poverty, racism and discrimination, and environmental stressors, are also experienced by children and influence their development and reactions to stress.

Maternal Age

Since 1990, the birth rate has increased for women ages 35 to 39 and 40 to 44 (Hamilton et al., 2017; see Figure 2.9). The risk of birth complications increases in the late 30s and especially after age 40. Women who give birth after the age of 40 are at greater risk for pregnancy and birth complications, including hypertension, gestational diabetes, and miscarriage, than are younger women (Londero et al., 2019; Magnus et al., 2019; Marozio et al., 2019).

Their newborns are at increased risk for low birthweight, preterm birth, respiratory problems, and other conditions requiring intensive neonatal care (Frederiksen et al., 2018; Grotegut et al., 2014; Kenny et al., 2013; Khalil et al., 2013). The risk of having a child with Down syndrome also increases sharply with maternal age, especially after age 40 (Diamandopoulos & Green, 2018; Hazlett et al., 2011; see Figure 2.10). Although risks for complications rise linearly with each year (Yaniv et al., 2011), it is important to know that the majority of women over age 35 give birth to healthy infants.

Paternal Characteristics

Fathers influence prenatal development indirectly, such as through secondhand smoke and their interactions with pregnant mothers (Braun et al., 2020; Glover & Capron, 2017). Biological fathers also influence prenatal development directly. Advanced paternal age (over 40) is associated with damage to sperm and DNA and an increased risk for birth defects, chromosomal abnormalities, and developmental disorders (Brandt et al., 2019; Herati et al., 2017; Rosiak-Gill et al., 2019). Alcohol use, substance use, smoking, and exposure to toxins can impair sperm production and quality, including increasing

FIGURE 2.9 ■ Birth Rates by Age of Mother, United States, 2017

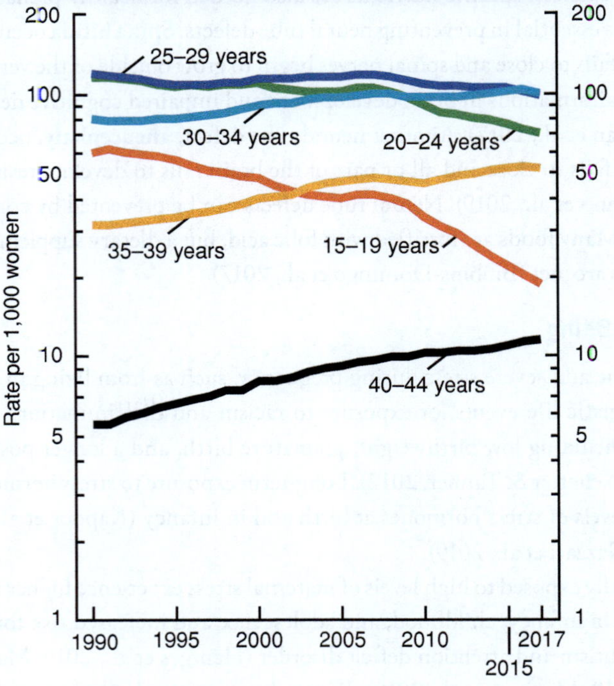

Source: Martin et al, 2018.

FIGURE 2.10 ■ Maternal Age and Down Syndrome

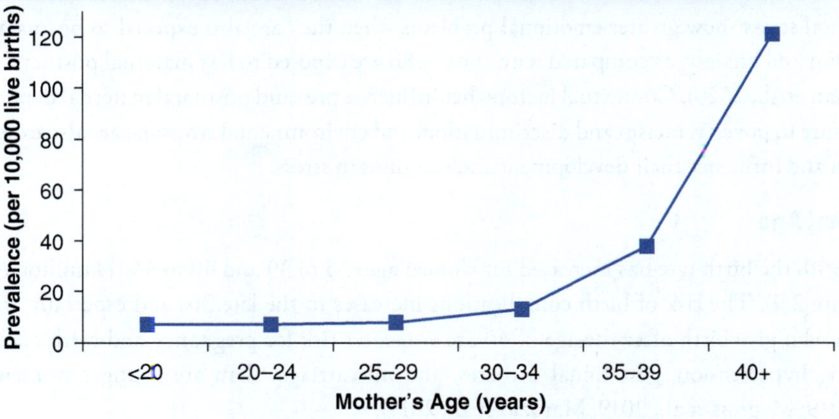

Source: Centers for Disease Control and Prevention, 2019.

the risk of DNA damage and mutations (Beal et al., 2017; Borges et al., 2018). In addition to DNA, fathers (and mothers) pass on epigenetic markers that can influence their offspring's health throughout life and may even be passed to their offspring's children (Estill & Krawetz, 2016).

Prenatal Care

Prenatal care, a set of services provided to improve pregnancy outcomes and engage the expectant mother, family members, and friends in health care decisions, is critical for the health of both mother and infant. Prenatal care visits typically include a physical exam, weight check, and diagnostic procedures, such as ultrasound, to assess the fetus's health. These visits also provide women the opportunity to ask questions and obtain health care information and advice about nutrition, prenatal care, and preparing for birth.

About one-quarter of pregnant women in the United States do not obtain prenatal care until after the first trimester; 6% obtain prenatal care at the end of pregnancy or not at all (U.S. Department of Health and Human Services, 2014). Inadequate prenatal care is a risk factor for low birthweight and preterm births as well as infant mortality during the first year (Partridge et al., 2012; Xaverius et al., 2016). The use of prenatal care predicts pediatric care, and thereby health and development, throughout childhood (Deaton et al., 2017).

Common reasons for insufficient prenatal care include lacking health insurance (Baer et al., 2018), difficulty in finding a doctor, lack of transportation, demands of caring for young children, poor prior experiences in the health care system, and family crises (see Figure 2.11; Daniels et al., 2006; Heaman et al., 2015; Mazul et al., 2017). Black and Latina women report nearly twice as many barriers to accessing care as white women (Fryer et al., 2021).

There are significant ethnic and socioeconomic disparities in prenatal care. Prenatal care is closely linked with maternal education (see Figure 2.12; Blakeney et al., 2019).

FIGURE 2.11 ■ Reasons for Delayed Prenatal Care Among Women, 2009–2010

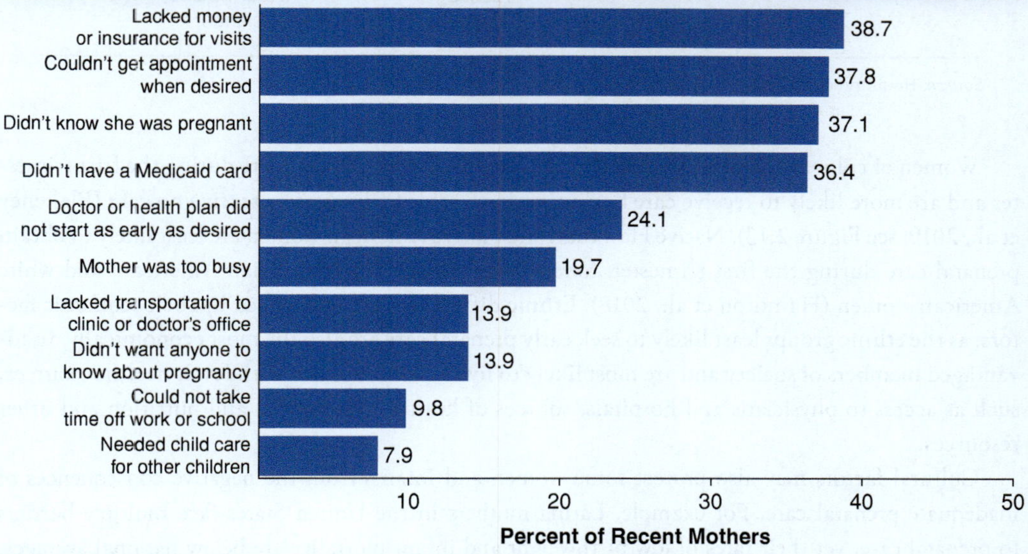

Source: U.S. Department of Health and Human Services, 2013.

FIGURE 2.12 ■ Timing of Prenatal Care Initiation, by Maternal Education, 2012

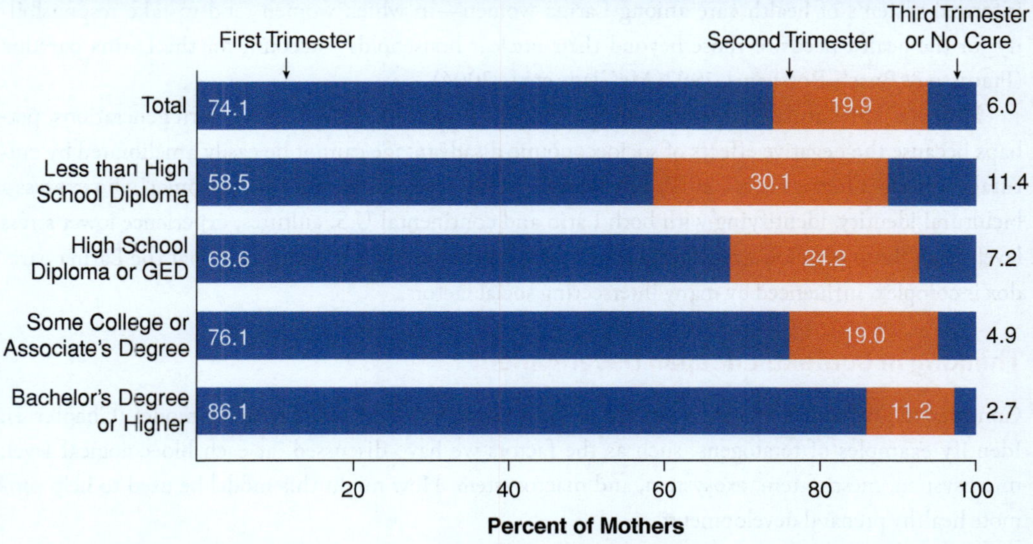

Source: U.S. Department of Health and Human Services, 2015

FIGURE 2.13 ■ First Trimester and Late Prenatal Care by Race and Ethnicity, 2018

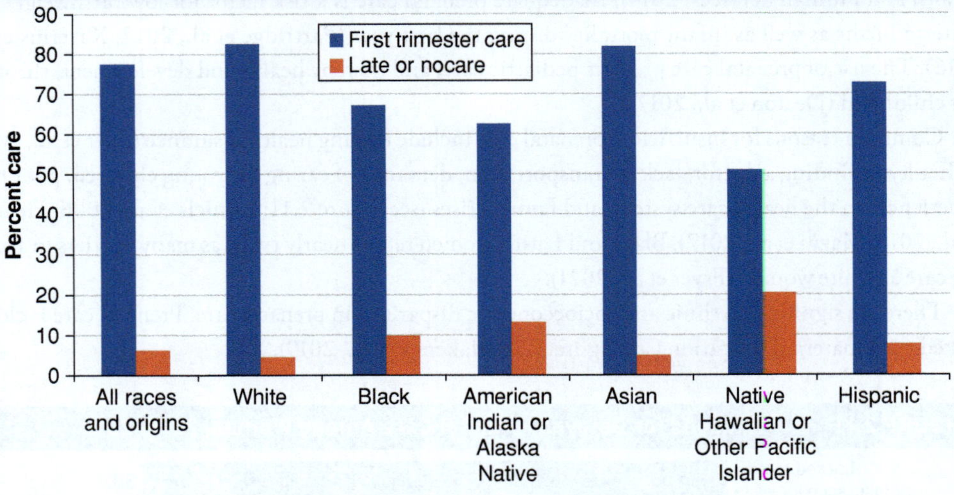

Source: Hamilton et al, 2018.

Women of color are disproportionately less likely to receive prenatal care during the first trimester and are more likely to receive care beginning in the third trimester or receive no care (Blakeney et al., 2019; see Figure 2.13). Native Hawaiian and Native American women are least likely to obtain prenatal care during the first trimester, followed by Black, Hispanic, Asian American, and white American women (Hamilton et al., 2018). Ethnic differences are influenced by socioeconomic factors, as the ethnic groups least likely to seek early prenatal care are also the most economically disadvantaged members of society and are most likely to live in communities with fewer health resources, such as access to physicians and hospitals, sources of health information, and nutrition and other resources.

Cultural factors may also protect some women and infants from the negative consequences of inadequate prenatal care. For example, Latina mothers in the United States face multiple barriers to prenatal care, yet their rates of low birthweight and infant mortality are below national averages. This is known as the *Latina paradox.* These favorable birth outcomes are striking because Latinos as a group are among the most socioeconomically disadvantaged ethnic populations in the United States (McGlade et al., 2004; Ruiz et al., 2016). Protective cultural factors, such as strong social support, support for maternity, the norm of selfless devotion to the maternal role (known as *marianismo*), and informal systems of health care among Latina women—in which women tend to take responsibility for the health needs of those beyond their nuclear households—account for the Latina paradox (Fracasso & Busch-Rossnagel, 1992; McGlade et al., 2004).

However, the Latina birth advantage may decline in subsequent American-born generations, perhaps because the negative effects of socioeconomic disadvantage cannot be easily ameliorated by cultural supports (Hoggatt et al., 2012; Sanchez-Vaznaugh et al., 2016). Yet Latina women who express a bicultural identity, identifying with both Latin and continental U.S. cultures, experience lower stress levels than those with low acculturation (Chasan-Taber et al., 2020), suggesting that the Latina paradox is complex, influenced by many intersecting social factors.

Thinking in Context: Lifespan Development

Consider the influence of teratogens from the perspective of Bronfenbrenner's model (Chapter 1). Identify examples of teratogens, such as the factors we have discussed, at each bioecological level: microsystem, mesosystem, exosystem, and macrosystem. How might this model be used to help promote healthy prenatal development?

Thinking in Context: Intersectionality

1. The issue of substance use in pregnant women is complicated. Consider the effects of teratogens on fetuses and the rights of pregnant women. How might they conflict? How do issues of justice and equity influence whether women are likely to be discovered, receive treatment, and/or be charged with maltreatment? Are all women, regardless of age, ethnicity and race, and SES, equally likely to be discovered and charged? Why or why not?
2. What are some examples of barriers to receiving prenatal care? In what ways do factors such as race, ethnicity, socioeconomic status, and culture influence whether women receive prenatal care? Would you expect all women—white, Asian American, Black, Hispanic, Pacific Islander, and Native American—to experience and perceive similar barriers? Why or why not? What environmental factors might contribute to these differences?

Thinking in Context: Applied Developmental Science

Suppose that you plan to study the presence and effects of teratogens on prenatal development. Choose a teratogen that you believe is most relevant to prenatal health.

1. How might you measure the fetus's or embryo's exposure to the teratogen? What effects would you study?
2. To what degree are other teratogens likely to be present? How might this complicate your results?
3. How will you obtain participants (pregnant women)? How might you ensure that your participants are diverse in terms of race, ethnicity, and SES? Are there other relevant variables on which women might differ?
4. In what ways might interactions among race, ethnicity, and SES influence your results? Why or why not?

CHILDBIRTH

LEARNING OBJECTIVE

2.5 Summarize the process of childbirth and the risks for, and characteristics of, low birthweight infants.

At about 40 weeks of pregnancy, or 38 weeks after conception, childbirth, also known as **labor**, begins.

Labor

Labor progresses in three stages. The first stage of labor, dilation, is the longest. It typically lasts 8 to 14 hours for a woman having her first child; for later-born children, the average is 3 to 8 hours. Labor begins when the mother experiences regular uterine contractions spaced at 10- to 15-minute intervals. Initial contractions may feel like a backache or menstrual cramps or may be extremely sharp. The amniotic sac, a membrane containing the fetus surrounded by fluid, may rupture at any time during this stage, often referred to as the "water breaking." The contractions, which gradually become stronger and closer together, cause the cervix to dilate so that the fetus's head can pass through, as shown in Figure 2.14.

The second stage of labor, delivery, begins when the cervix is fully dilated to 10 cm and the fetus's head is positioned at the opening of the cervix—known as "crowning." It ends when the baby emerges

FIGURE 2.14 ■ Stages of Labor

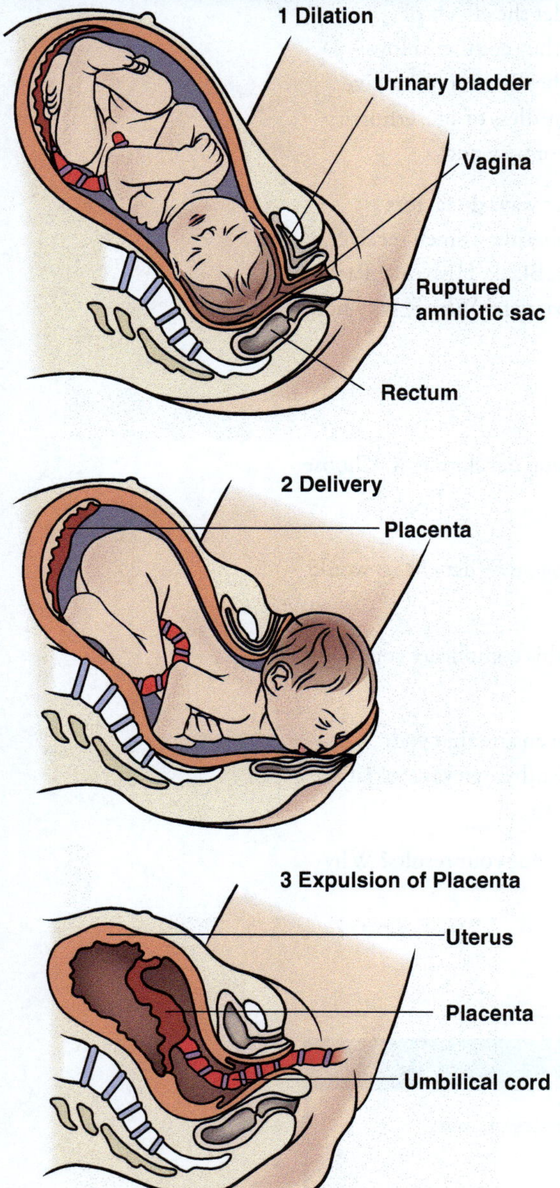

completely from the mother's body. It is during this stage that the mother typically feels an urge to push or bear down with each contraction to assist the birth process.

In the third stage of labor, shortly after birth, the placenta separates from the uterine wall and is expelled by uterine contractions.

Medication During Delivery

Medication is administered in more than 80% of births in the United States (Declercq et al., 2014). There are two main types of medications administered during labor. *Analgesics*, such as tranquilizers, reduce the perception of pain and can help the mother relax. But these drugs pass through the placenta to the fetus and are associated with decreases in heart rate and respiration (Hacker et al., 2016). Newborns exposed to some medications show signs of sedation and difficulty regulating their temperature (Gabbe et al., 2016).

Anesthetics are painkillers that block overall sensations or feelings. General anesthesia (getting "knocked out") blocks consciousness entirely; it is no longer used because it is transmitted to the fetus and can slow labor and harm the fetus. Today, the most common anesthetic is an **epidural**, in which a pain-relieving drug is administered to a small space between the vertebrae of the lower spine, numbing the woman's lower body. Epidurals are associated with a longer delivery as they weaken uterine contractions and may increase the need for a **cesarean section**, as discussed next (Gabbe et al., 2016; Herrera-Gómez et al., 2017). Epidurals do not appear to affect newborns (Wang et al., 2018). The American College of Obstetricians and Gynecologists (2017) has concluded that the proper administration of medication poses few risks to the newborn and pain medication should be available to all women.

Cesarean Delivery

Sometimes a vaginal birth is not possible because of concerns for the health or safety of the mother or fetus. A cesarean section is a surgical procedure that removes the fetus from the uterus through the abdomen. About 32% of U.S. births were by cesarean section in 2018 (Hamilton et al., 2018; Martin et al., 2018). Cesarean sections are performed when labor progresses too slowly, the fetus is in breech position (legs first) or transverse position (crosswise in the uterus), the head is too large to pass through the pelvis, or the fetus or mother is in danger (Jha et al., 2015; Visscher & Narendran, 2014). Babies delivered by cesarean are exposed to more maternal medication and secrete less of the stress hormones that occur with vaginal birth, which are needed to facilitate respiration, enhance circulation of blood to the brain, and help the infant adapt to the world outside of the womb.

Natural Childbirth

Natural childbirth is an approach to birth that emphasizes preparation by educating mothers and their partners about childbirth, helping them to reduce their fear, and teaching them pain management techniques that do not rely on medication. The most widely known natural childbirth method, the Lamaze method, entails teaching pregnant women (and partners) about their bodies, including detailed anatomical information, as well as breathing techniques, with the intent of reducing anxiety and fear. Many women seek the help of a **doula,** a caregiver who provides support to an expectant mother and her partner throughout the birth process (Kang, 2014). The doula is present during birth, whether at a hospital or other setting, and helps the woman carry out her birth plans. The presence of a doula is associated with less pain medication, fewer cesarean deliveries, and higher rates of satisfaction in new mothers (Gabbe et al., 2016; Kozhimannil et al., 2016). Many women combine medication with natural childbirth methods, such as breathing techniques.

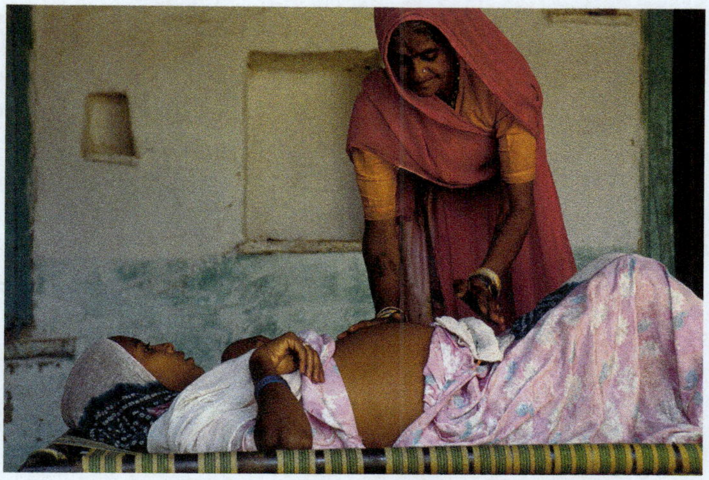
A midwife prepares a mother to give birth in her home. Birth practices vary by culture.
Viviane Moos / Getty Images

Home Birth

Although common in nonindustrialized nations, home birth is rare in the U.S., comprising 1.5% of all births in 2016 in the United States (MacDorman & Declercq, 2016). Most home births are managed by a **midwife**—a health care professional, usually a nurse, who specializes in childbirth. Midwives provide health care throughout pregnancy and supervise home births. A healthy woman who has received prenatal care and is not carrying twins is unlikely to encounter problems and may be a good candidate for a home birth (Wilbur et al., 2015). Although unpredictable events can occur and immediate access to medical facilities can improve outcomes, studies from Europe indicate that home birth is not associated with greater risk of perinatal mortality. However, home birth is far more common in many European countries than in the United States (20% in the Netherlands, 8% in the United Kingdom, and about 1% in the United States; Brocklehurst et al., 2011; de Jonge et al., 2015). The few U.S. studies that have examined planned home birth compared with hospital birth have found no difference in neonatal deaths, and women who have a planned home birth report high rates of satisfaction (Jouhki et al., 2017; Zielinski et al., 2015).

Apgar Score

Immediately after birth, newborns are evaluated to determine their **Apgar score**, which provides a quick overall assessment of the baby's health. The Apgar score is composed of five subtests: appearance (color), pulse (heart rate), grimace (reflex irritability), activity (muscle tone), and respiration (breathing). The newborn is rated 0, 1, or 2 on each subtest for a maximum total score of 10 (see Table 2.7). A score of 4 or lower means that the newborn is in serious condition and requires immediate medical attention. The rating is conducted twice, 1 minute after delivery and again 5 minutes after birth; this timing ensures that hospital staff will monitor the newborn over several minutes. A low Apgar score is associated with an increased risk of neonatal death, but an increase in score after 10 minutes lowers the risk of problems (Chen et al., 2014). More than 98% of all newborns in the United States achieve a 5-minute score of 7 to 10, indicating good health (Martin et al., 2013).

TABLE 2.7 ■ Apgar Scoring System

	Rating (Absence–Presence)		
Indicator	**0**	**1**	**2**
Appearance (color)	Blue	Pink body, blue extremities	Pink
Pulse (heart rate)	Absent	Slow (below 100)	Rapid (over 100)
Grimace (reflex irritability)	No response	Grimace	Coughing, crying
Activity (muscle tone)	Limp	Weak and inactive	Active and strong
Respiration (breathing)	Absent	Irregular and slow	Crying, good

Source: Adapted from Apgar, 1953.

Low-Birthweight Infants: Preterm and Small-for-Date Babies

About 8% of infants born in the United States each year are low birthweight (Martin et al., 2018). Infants are classified as **low birthweight** when they weigh less than 2,500 grams (5.5 pounds) at birth; **very low birthweight** refers to a weight less than 1,500 grams (3.5 pounds); and **extremely low birthweight** refers to a weight less than 750 grams (1 lb. 10 oz.). Low-birthweight (LBW) infants may be **preterm** (premature, i.e., born before their due date) or **small for date** (full term but have experienced slow growth and are smaller than expected for their gestational age). Low birthweight is the second leading cause of infant mortality (Murphy et al., 2018; Mathews & MacDorman, 2013).

Contextual Risks for LBW

Socioeconomic status is associated with LBW. In the United States, socioeconomic status is associated not simply with income, but with access to social services, such as health care, that determine birth outcomes. In one international comparison of U.S. births with those in the UK, Canada, and Australia—countries with health care and social services available to all individuals—the most disadvantaged women in all four countries were more likely to give birth to LBW infants, but SES was most strongly linked with LBW in the United States, where health care is privatized (Martinson & Reichman, 2016).

Socioeconomic disadvantage interacts with race and ethnicity in complex ways to influence LBW in the U.S. (see Figure 2.15). In 2016, non-Hispanic Black infants were more than twice as likely to be born low birthweight (11%) than non-Hispanic white and Hispanic infants (5% and 6%, respectively; Womack et al., 2018). SES plays a role in these differences, but it is not the whole story. In one study, LBW rates were higher for non-Hispanic Black mothers than non-Hispanic white mothers, but the racial difference declined (but did not disappear) when the researchers took into account

FIGURE 2.15 ■ Gestational Age and Birthweight, by Race and Ethnicity: United States, 2018

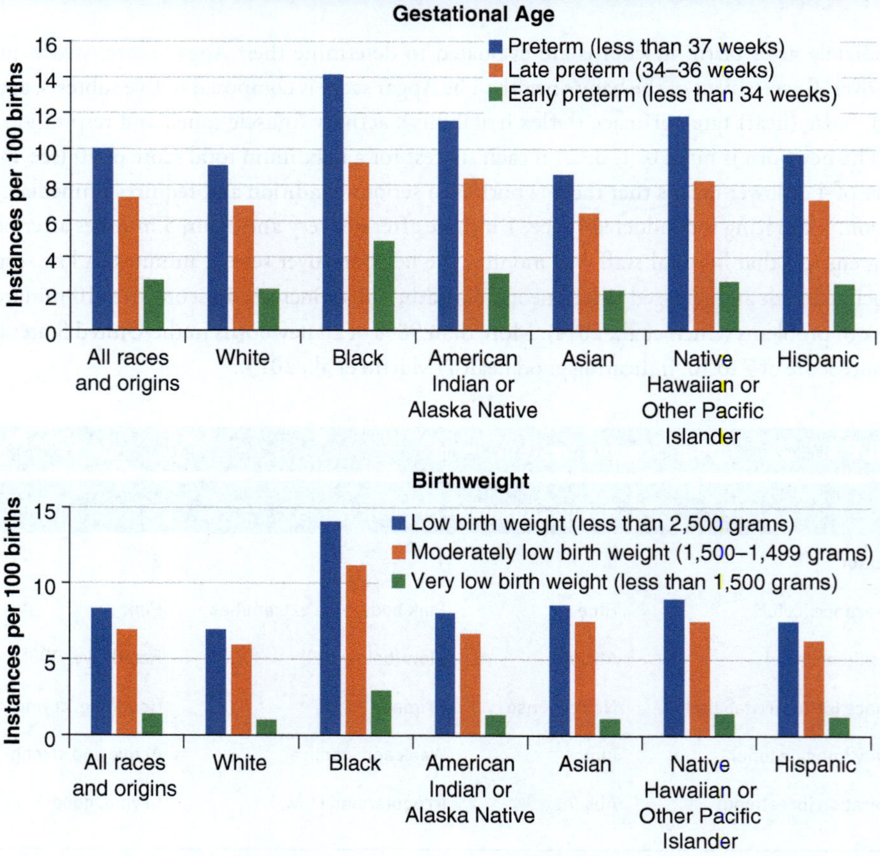

Source: Centers for Disease Control and Prevention; National Center for Health Statistics.

financial and relationship stresses, suggesting a role for SES in racial differences, but also the presence of other factors (Almeida et al., 2018). In another study of more than 10,000 Californian women, the most economically disadvantaged Black and white women showed similar LBW rates, but increase in income was more strongly associated with improvement in LBW rates among white than Black women (Braveman et al., 2015). As SES advantage increased for both white and Black women, the racial disparity in LBW outcomes grew. Racial differences in LBW are not only a function of income, but also of other factors such as racism and discrimination (Ncube et al., 2016; Ramraj et al., 2020).

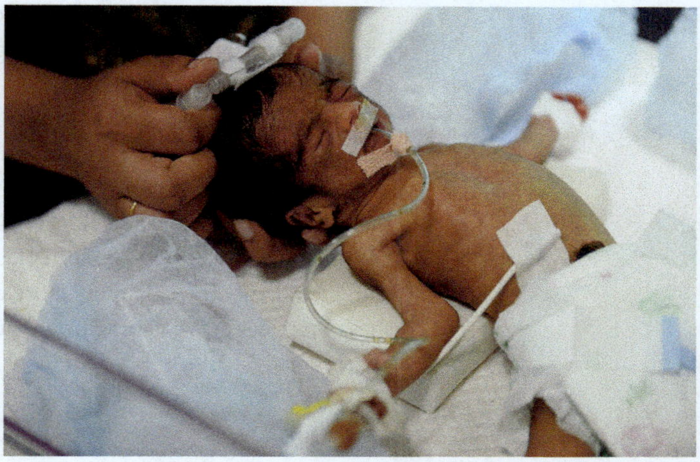

Low birthweight infants require extensive care. They are at risk for poor developmental outcomes and even death.

AFP Contributor / Contributor/ Getty

Characteristics of LBW Infants

At birth, LBW infants often experience difficulty breathing and have difficulty maintaining homeostasis, a balance in their biological functioning. (Charles et al., 2018). The deficits that LBW infants experience correspond closely to the infant's birthweight (Hutchinson et al., 2013). LBW infants are at higher risk for poor growth, cerebral palsy, seizure disorders, neurological difficulties, respiratory problems, and illness (Adams-Chapman et al., 2013; Charles et al., 2018; Durkin et al., 2016; Miller et al., 2016). They often experience difficulty in self-regulation and cognitive problems that may persist into adulthood (Eryigit Madzwamuse et al., 2015; Hutchinson et al., 2013; MacKay et al., 2010).

As children and adolescents, they are more likely to show problems with inattention, hyperactivity, and experience emotional and behavioral problems (Jaekel et al., 2018; Mathewson et al., 2017; Franz et al., 2018). They tend to show poor social competence and poor peer relationships, including peer rejection and victimization in adolescence (Georgsdottir et al., 2013; Ritchie et al., 2015; Yau et al., 2013). As adults, LBW individuals may experience social difficulties and may score high on measures of anxiety (Eryigit Madzwamuse et al., 2015; Mathewson et al., 2017).

Parenting a LBW infant is stressful because such infants tend to be easily overwhelmed by stimulation and difficult to soothe (Howe et al., 2014; Gardon et al., 2019). LBW infants are slow to initiate social interactions and do not attend to caregivers, looking away or otherwise resisting attempts to attract their attention (Eckerman et al., 1999; Provasi, 2019). Because LBW infants often do not respond to attempts to solicit interaction, they can be frustrating to interact with and are at risk for less secure attachment to their parents (Jean & Stack, 2012; Wolke et al., 2014). Research also indicates that they may experience higher rates of child abuse, partly because of their special needs but also because the risk factors for LBW, such as prenatal exposure to substances or maternal illness, also pose challenges for postnatal survival and are themselves are associated with abuse (Cicchetti & Toth, 2015; Puls et al., 2019)

Promoting Positive Outcomes for LBW Infants

The parenting context is an important influence on LBW infant health (Pierrehumbert et al., 2003; Provasi, 2019). When mothers have knowledge about child development and how to foster healthy development, are involved with their children, and create a stimulating home environment, LBW infants tend to have good long-term outcomes (Benasich & Brooks-Gunn, 1996; Jones et al., 2009; Lynch & Gibbs, 2017). A study of LBW children showed that those who experienced sensitive parenting showed faster improvements in executive function and were indistinguishable from their normal-weight peers by age 5; however, those who experienced below-average levels of sensitive parenting showed lasting deficits (Camerota et al., 2015). In contrast, longitudinal research has found that LBW children raised in unstable, economically disadvantaged families tend to remain smaller in stature, experience more emotional problems, and show more long-term deficits in intelligence and academic performance than do those raised in more advantaged homes (Taylor et al., 2001).

Interventions to promote the development of LBW children often emphasize helping parents learn coping strategies for interacting with their infants and managing parenting stress (Chang et al., 2015; Lau & Morse, 2003). One intervention common in developing countries where mothers may not have access to hospitals is **kangaroo care**, in which the infant is placed vertically against the parent's chest, under the shirt, providing skin-to-skin contact (Charpak et al., 2005). As the parent goes about daily activities, the infant remains warm and close, hears the voice and heartbeat, smells the body, and feels constant skin-to-skin contact. Kangaroo care is so effective that the majority of hospitals in the United States offer kangaroo care to preterm infants. Babies who receive early and consistent kangaroo care grow more quickly, sleep better, score higher on measures of health, and show more cognitive gains throughout the first year of life (Boundy et al., 2015; Jefferies, 2012; Sharma et al., 2019).

Thinking in Context: Lifespan Development

1. Ask adults of different generations, perhaps a parent or an aunt and a grandparent or family friend, about their birth experiences. How do these recollections compare with current birthing practices?
2. A basic tenet of development is that individuals are active in their development, influencing the world around them (see Chapter 1). Consider LBW infants: How might their characteristics and abilities influence their caregivers? Why is caring for LBW infants challenging?
3. Parental responses to having a LBW infant influence the child's long-term health outcomes. How might contextual factors influence parents' responses? What supports from the family, community, and broader society can aid parents in helping their LBW infants adapt and develop healthily?

Thinking in Context: Applied Developmental Science

Create a birth plan for a healthy woman in her 20s. What type of birth will you choose? Why? How might you address pain relief? Consider a healthy 39-year old woman; in what ways might your birth plan change (or not)? Why?

CHAPTER SUMMARY

2.1 Discuss patterns of genetic inheritance and examples of genetic disorders and chromosomal abnormalities.

Some genes are passed through dominant-recessive inheritance, in which some genes are dominant and will always be expressed and others are recessive, only expressed if paired with another recessive gene. Incomplete dominance is a genetic inheritance pattern in which both genes influence the characteristic. Polygenic traits are the result of interactions among many genes. Genetic disorders carried through dominant-recessive inheritance include PKU (recessive allele) and Huntington disease (dominant allele). Some recessive genetic disorders are carried on the X chromosome. Males are more likely to be affected by X-linked genetic disorders. Examples of X-linked disorders include hemophilia, Fragile X, and color blindness. Some disorders, such as trisomy 21, known as Down syndrome, are the result of chromosomal abnormalities. Abnormalities resulting from additional or missing sex chromosomes include Klinefelter syndrome, Jacob's syndrome, triple X syndrome, and Turner syndrome. Other disorders result from mutations—genetic abnormalites that may occur randomly or as the result of exposure to toxins.

2.2 Describe behavior genetics and interactions among genes and environment, such as gene-environment correlations, gene-environment interactions, and the epigenetic framework.

Behavior genetics is the field of study that examines how genes and experience combine to influence the diversity of human traits, abilities, and behaviors. Behavior genetic research includes three types of studies: selective breeding studies, family studies, and adoption studies. Genetics contributes to many traits. Passive, evocative, and active gene–environment correlations illustrate how traits often are supported by both our genes and environment. People's genes and environment interact in complex ways such that the effects of experience may vary with a person's genes. The epigenetic framework is a model for understanding the dynamic ongoing interactions between heredity and environment whereby the epigenome's instructions to turn genes on and off throughout development are influenced by the environment.

2.3 Describe the three periods of prenatal development.

Conception occurs in the fallopian tube. During the germinal period, the zygote begins cell division and travels down the fallopian tube toward the uterus. During the embryonic period, from weeks 2 to 8, the most rapid developments of the prenatal period take place. From 9 weeks until birth, the fetus grows rapidly, and the organs become more complex and begin to function. There are several diagnostic methods used to examine the developing organism: ultrasound, amniocentesis, chorionic villus sampling, fetal MRI, and noninvasive prenatal testing (NIPT) screens.

2.4 Explain how exposure to environmental factors can influence the prenatal environment and provide examples.

Teratogens include diseases, drugs, and other agents that influence the prenatal environment to disrupt development. Generally, the effects of exposure to teratogens on prenatal development vary depending on the stage of prenatal development and dose. There are individual differences in effects, different teratogens can cause the same birth defect, a variety of birth defects can result from the same teratogen, and some teratogens have subtle effects that result in developmental delays that are not obvious at birth or not visible until many years later. Prescription and nonprescription drugs, maternal illnesses, and smoking and alcohol use can harm the developing fetus. Prenatal development can also be harmed by factors in the environment as well as by maternal and paternal characteristics and behaviors.

2.5 Summarize the process of childbirth and the risks for, and characeritics of, low birthweight infants.

Childbirth progresses through three stages. The first stage of labor begins when the mother experiences regular uterine contractions that cause the cervix to dilate. During the second stage, the fetus passes through the birth canal. The placenta is passed during the third stage. Medication is used in most births, often in combination with breathing and relaxation techniques characteristic of natural births. About one third of U.S. births are by cesarean section. There are two types of low-birthweight infants: those who are preterm and those who are small for date. Low-birthweight infants struggle to survive and experience higher rates of sensory, motor, and language problems; learning disabilities; behavior problems; and deficits in social skills into adolescence. The long-term outcomes for low birthweight infants vary considerably and depend on the environment in which the children are raised.

KEY TERMS

amniocentesis (p. 49)
amnion (p. 47)
anencephaly (p. 55)
Apgar score (p. 61)
behavior genetics (p. 42)
blastocyst (p. 46)
cesarean section (p. 60)
chorionic villus sampling (CVS) (p. 49)
chromosomes (p. 33)
deoxyribonucleic acid (DNA) (p. 34)
dominant-recessive inheritance (p. 35)
doula (p. 60)
Down syndrome (p. 39)
embryo (p. 47)
embryonic period (p. 46)
epidural (p. 60)

epigenetics (p. 44)
extremely low birthweight (p. 62)
fetal alcohol spectrum disorders (p. 52)
fetal alcohol syndrome (FAS) (p. 52)
fetal MRI (p. 48)
fetal period (p. 48)
fetus (p. 48)
Fragile X syndrome (p. 39)
gametes (p. 34)
gene-environment correlation (p. 42)
gene-environment interactions (p. 44)
genes (p. 34)
genotype (p. 42)
germinal period (p. 46)
hemophilia (p. 39)
implantation (p. 46)
incomplete dominance (p. 35)
indifferent gonad (p. 47)
Jacob's syndrome (p. 40)
kangaroo care (p. 64)
Klinefelter syndrome (p. 40)
labor (p. 59)
low birthweight (p. 62)
meiosis (p. 34)
midwife (p. 61)
mitosis (p. 34)
mutations (p. 41)
natural childbirth (p. 60)
neonate (p. 45)
neural tube (p. 47)
niche picking (p. 43)
noninvasive prenatal testing (NPT) (p. 49)
phenotype (p. 42)
phenylketonuria (PKU) (p. 38)
placenta (p. 47)
polygenic inheritance (p. 35)
prenatal care (p. 56)
prenatal development (p. 33)
preterm (p. 62)
sickle cell trait (p. 38)
small for date (p. 62)
spina bifida (p. 55)
teratogens (p. 50)
triple X syndrome (p. 40)
Turner syndrome (p. 40)
ultrasound (p. 48)
very low birthweight (p. 62)
zygote (p. 34)

PART 1 LIFESPAN DEVELOPMENT AT WORK: FOUNDATIONS OF LIFESPAN HUMAN DEVELOPMENT

One of the tenets of lifespan development is that it is a multidisciplinary field, integrating findings from many settings. In this feature that appears at the end of each major part of this book, we explore some of the career choices for students interested in lifespan development.

Students with interests in human development select many different college majors, such as human development and family studies, psychology, social work, education, nursing, and more. What these diverse fields hold in common, beside a grounding in human development, is training in transferable skills that are valuable in a variety of employment settings.

Transferable Skills

Just as it sounds, a *transferable skill* is one that can *transfer* or be applied in multiple settings. Employers value transferable skills. Consider the top five attributes that employers seek in potential employees, shown in Table 1.

It might be quickly apparent that none of these attributes refers directly to any specific college major. Instead, these are skills that students of all disciplines who study human development have the opportunity to hone. Let's take a closer look at some of these transferable skills.

Perhaps not surprising, the skill employers view as most valuable is *problem solving.* Individuals who are successful at problem solving can gather and synthesize information from a variety of sources. They learn to weigh multiple sources of information, determine the degree of support for each position, and generate solutions based on the information at hand. Effective problem solving relies on *analytical skills.* Exposure to diverse perspectives and ideas about human development trains students to think flexibly and to accept some ambiguity because solutions to complex problems are often not clear cut.

Students in human development fields learn *teamwork skills* to work with others in coursework and placements. For example, nursing, psychology, and human development and family studies students

TABLE 1 ■ Top 5 Attributes Employers Prefer in Applicants

Desired Attribute	Percentage of Employers Endorsing
Problem-solving skills	91
Ability to work in a team	86
Strong work ethic	80
Analytical/quantitative skills	79
Communication skills (written)	78

Source: (NACE, 2020)

may work together as lab members. Education students may collaborate on group projects, such as designing curricula, and social work students may get hands-on experience working with others in field placements. These valuable experiences foster the ability to effectively work with teams, a skill coveted by employers in all fields.

Students in human development and family studies, psychology, social work, education, and nursing take coursework relevant to their discipline, but success in each of these fields requires a *strong work ethic* and good *communication skills*. Succeeding in challenging courses like anatomy and physiology, research methods, and statistics requires dedication and consistent work. Oral and written communication skills are developed in coursework, but also in field and practicum experiences when students learn to communicate with children, adolescents, adults, and supervisors.

Lifespan Development Fields

As we consider career opportunities in lifespan development, we break them into several areas: education; health care and nursing; social work, counseling, and psychology ; and research and advocacy.

Education

Perhaps the most obvious career for students interested in human development is educator, or teacher. Educators who work with young children include *early childhood educators* and *preschool teachers*. Educators who work with older children and adolescents include *elementary school teachers* and *high school teachers*. Some educators specialize in working with children with specific developmental needs (*special education teachers*). Other teachers specialize in teaching English as a Second Language (*ESL teachers*) and work with children, adolescents, and adults. Becoming a teacher requires a bachelor's degree and certification.

Career and technical education teachers provide vocational training to adolescents and adults in subjects such as auto repair, cosmetology, and culinary arts. *Adult literacy teachers* instruct adults in literacy skills such as reading and writing. *GED teachers or instructors* help students earn their GED certificate, a high school equivalency diploma.

The education field also includes careers in administration, overseeing educational programs and educators. *Preschool and childcare center directors* work with early childhood educators to design educational plans for young children, oversee staff, and prepare budgets and are responsible for all aspects of the program. *Elementary school principals, middle school principals,* and *high school principals* oversee all school operations, including the work of teachers and other personnel, curricula, and daily school activities, and they promote a safe and productive learning environment.

Perhaps the most visible career at the college level is *college professor*. Becoming a professor requires education beyond the bachelor's degree, sometimes a master's degree but more typically a doctoral degree. However, there are many opportunities to work on a college campus with a bachelor's degree. For example, every college and university sponsors student activities, such as clubs, student government, and fraternities and sororities. *Student activities directors*, or *directors of student services*, oversee the development and organization of the college or university's extracurricular programs, including approving funding for student activities and overseeing students and staff who organize and supervise student activities. *Resident directors* oversee the residence halls, ensuring that they are safe, supportive environments for students living on campus.

Health Care and Nursing

An understanding of human development is helpful to all who work in health care settings. There are many kinds of nurses, and nurses of any specialty can benefit from understanding development. Examples of nurses who specialize in human development include *geriatric nurses*, who provide care for elderly patients. *Pediatric nurses* work with infants, children, and adolescents. *Neonatal nurses* provide care to infants who are born preterm, low birthweight, or suffer health problems, from birth until they are discharged from the hospital. A *nurse midwife* provides gynecological care, especially concerning pregnancy, labor, and delivery.

All physicians must learn about human development as part of their medical education, but only some specialize in working with people of particular ages. *Obstetrician-gynecologists* are physicians who specialize in female reproductive health, pregnancy, and childbirth. *Pediatricians* treat infants, children, and adolescents and *geriatricians* treat older adults. *Psychiatrists* are medical doctors who treat patients, conduct therapy, and prescribe medication to patients. To specialize, physicians must complete additional training, often a fellowship after earning their medical degree and obtaining licensure.

Allied health is a field of health care whose functions include assisting, facilitating, or complementing the work of nurses, physicians, and other health care specialists. *Recreational therapists* assess clients and provide recreational activities to individuals with physical or emotional disabilities in a variety of medical and community settings. *Physical therapists* design and provide treatments and interventions for individuals suffering pain, loss of mobility, or other physical disabilities. *Occupational therapists* help patients with physical, developmental, or psychological impairments, helping patients develop, recover, and maintain skills needed for independent daily living and working. Physical therapists and occupational therapists must earn graduate degrees, but *assistant physical therapists* and *assistant occupational therapists* may be hired with specialized associate degrees and certification.

Other allied health care specialists include *speech-language pathologists,* who assess, diagnose, and treat speech, language, and social communication disorders in children, adolescents, and adults. A speech-language pathologist must earn a graduate degree and *assistant speech-language pathologists* may be hired with associate or bachelor's degrees with specialized coursework and certification, depending on U.S. state. *Child life specialists* typically work in hospital settings, helping children and families adjust to a child's hospitalization by educating and supporting families in the physically and emotionally demanding process of caring for hospitalized or disabled children. An entry-level position as child life specialist requires a bachelor's degree and certification.

Knowledge about health and development is also needed to become a health educator. *Health educators* design and implement educational programs (classes, promotional pamphlets, community activities) to educate individuals and communities about healthy lifestyles and wellness.

Social Work, Counseling, and Psychology

Children and adolescents have different needs and abilities to communicate than adults and older adults. Professionals who work closely with individuals must understand how they change over their lives.

Social workers help people improve their lives by identifying needed resources (such as housing or food stamps) and providing guidance. *Clinical social workers* also conduct therapy and implement counseling treatments with individuals and families. Entry-level social workers earn a bachelor's degree whereas clinical social workers must earn a graduate degree and seek licensure.

There are many different types of counselor positions, which generally require master's degrees. *Mental health counselors* help people manage and overcome mental and emotional disorders. *School counselors* help elementary, middle, and high school students develop skills to enhance personal, social, and academic growth. *Marriage and family therapists* focus on the family system and treat individuals, couples, and families to help people overcome problems with family and relationships. *Substance use counselors* help people who suffer from addictions, helping them to recover and modify behaviors through individual and group therapy sessions.

Applied behavior analysts apply scientific principles of learning to modify people's behavior to improve social, communication, academic, and adaptive skills in children, adolescents, and adults. They teach parents, teachers, and support professionals how to implement behavioral procedures, skills, and interventions. A position as an applied behavior analyst requires a graduate degree. *Assistant behavior analysts* support the work of applied behavior analysts. They assist in gathering data or information about clients, monitoring client progress and maintaining records, and administering assessments and treatment under the supervision of the applied behavior analysts.

Psychologists are doctoral-level mental health professionals. *Clinical psychologists* and *counseling psychologists* conduct therapy with children, adolescents, adults, and families. Clinical psychologists specialize in treating mental disorders and counseling psychologists emphasize helping people adjust to life changes. *School psychologists* work within school settings, assessing individuals' learning and mental health needs; collaborating with parents, teachers, and school administrators; designing interventions to improve students' well-being; and counseling students. *Applied developmental psychologists* may, depending on their training, assess and treat children, adolescents, and adults and design and evaluate intervention programs to address problems and enhance the development of people of all ages.

Research and Advocacy

Developmental scientists design and conduct research on social problems and apply their findings to advocate on behalf of individuals and families. They are employed at social service agencies, nonprofits, and think tanks conducting research to gather information about social problems and policies; assess and improve programs for children, youth, and families; and write reports and other documents to inform policymakers and the public. Some work as program directors and administrators for these programs. Others assess programs.

Some developmental scientists head nonprofit organizations as *foundation directors*. They develop goals and strategies in line with the foundation's mission statement and oversee all activities within an organization, including program delivery, program evaluation, finance, and staffing. Other developmental scientists work as *grant writers*, submitting proposals to fund programs. Organizations that award grants to others have *grant directors* who oversee the funding process by analyzing grant proposals, communicating with applicants, and determining which proposals are suitable for funding.

Developmental scientists conduct research in a variety of settings. Some work at universities and apply their research findings to help people. For example, a *researcher* might conduct experiments in a lab to identify influences of electronic cigarette use on children, adolescents, and adults and then apply the findings to develop prevention programs tailored to each age group. Developmental scientists who work for the government might evaluate government-supported social media health initiatives (such as those targeting distracted driving) or educational initiatives, such as the effects of providing free kindergarten to children.

Developmental scientists working in business and industry help companies design materials such as toys, products, and media that fit people's needs and abilities. They might determine the developmental appropriateness of toys and provide insight into children's abilities or examine children's and parents' reactions to particular toys, advertising, and promotional techniques. Others might provide developmental and educational advice to creators of children's media, such as by interpreting research on children's attention spans to inform creative guidelines for television programs such as *Sesame Street*.

Developmental scientists also assist companies in developing and marketing products that are appropriate for older adults. A consultant might suggest modifying the design of product packaging by using contrasting colors and larger print easier for older adults to read. A developmental scientist might research ways of modifying a car's dashboard to include displays and knobs that can be easily viewed and used by older adult drivers.

CAREERS IN GENETICS AND PRENATAL DEVELOPMENT

Genetic Counselor

As we have seen in Chapter 2, many chromosomal abnormalities are passed through genetic inheritance. Genetic counselors help assess the risk of an individual or couple passing a genetic disorder to their offspring.

Genetic counselors interview individuals and couples to gather information about their family history, educate them about the risks for particular genetic conditions in their offspring, and inform them about the different genetic tests available to them. Genetic counselors also help individuals and couples understand that results of DNA and other laboratory tests and the potential implications for offspring. Genetic counselors typically work in a hospital or clinic setting but may work in private practice.

Genetic counselors typically have a master's degree in genetics or genetic counseling from a program certified by the Accreditation Council for Genetic Counseling and pass a national certification exam. Some genetics counselors specialize in particular area, such as cancer, psychiatric, or genomic health. The median annual wage for genetic counselors was $85,700 in May 2020 (U.S. Bureau of Labor Statistics, 2021).

Midwife

A midwife is a health care professional who supports and cares for women throughout their pregnancy, including delivering babies during childbirth. They collaborate with other health care professionals, including obstetricians, nurses, and hospital staff.

There are two main paths to becoming a midwife, with different levels of expertise, certification, and autonomy. Some midwives are referred to as direct-entry midwives because, after earning a bachelor's degree, they are trained and certified (through the North American Registry of Midwives) but do not have a nursing degree. The legal status and requirements to become a direct-entry midwife vary by state, but many states do not permit midwives without nursing degrees. Carefully research state requirements before choosing this option.

The second path to becoming a midwife is to earn a nursing degree and complete a master's program in nurse-midwifery education. A certified nurse-midwife can practice independently in every state. Most people are familiar with the labor and delivery activities of nurse-midwives. Nurse-midwives may focus on all or part of pregnancy and birth, from preconception to postpartum. The nurse-midwife practice includes a variety of services: reproductive health visits, preventative care, and post-menopausal care. They can prescribe medication and admit or discharge patients if needed.

Nurse-midwives can work in a variety of settings, including hospitals, birth centers, health centers, and in private practice. The median annual wage for nurse-midwives was about $111,000 in 2020 (U.S. Bureau of Labor Statistics, 2021).

Doula

Doulas provide physical, emotional, and educational support to expectant mothers prior to birth, during labor, and immediately after birth through the first few weeks. Doulas provide education about labor, medication, and comfort during the birth process. Doulas also support the partner and family to aid their participation in the birth process.

The educational requirements to become a doula include a high school degree and completion of a doula education program. Some employers prefer college credits or a degree. Doulas work in hospitals, private practices, birth centers, or community organizations. Doulas' earnings vary with work setting, experience, and location. A common national hourly rate is about $45 per hour, as high as $70 in large urban cities and as low as $25 per hour in small towns.

3 PHYSICAL AND COGNITIVE DEVELOPMENT IN INFANCY AND TODDLERHOOD

AJ_Watt/ Getty

Over the first year of life infants progress from newborns unable to raise their heads to infants who can sit up on their own, then crawl, pull themselves up to stand, and eventually walk. Infants' rapid advances in growth, perceptual capacities, and motor skills enable them to interact with their world and learn in new ways. Their abilities to think, use language, and interact with objects and people will change dramatically over the next two years. In this chapter, we will explore the physical and cognitive developments that occur during infancy and toddlerhood.

PHYSICAL GROWTH AND HEALTH IN INFANCY AND TODDLERHOOD

LEARNING OBJECTIVE

3.1 Discuss patterns of and influences on physical growth and brain development during infancy and toddlerhood.

Perhaps the most obvious change that infants undergo during the first year of life is very rapid growth.

Growth Trends

By compiling information about the height and weight of large samples of children from diverse populations, researchers have determined that growth follows distinct patterns. **Growth norms** are

FIGURE 3.1 ■ Body Proportions Throughout Life

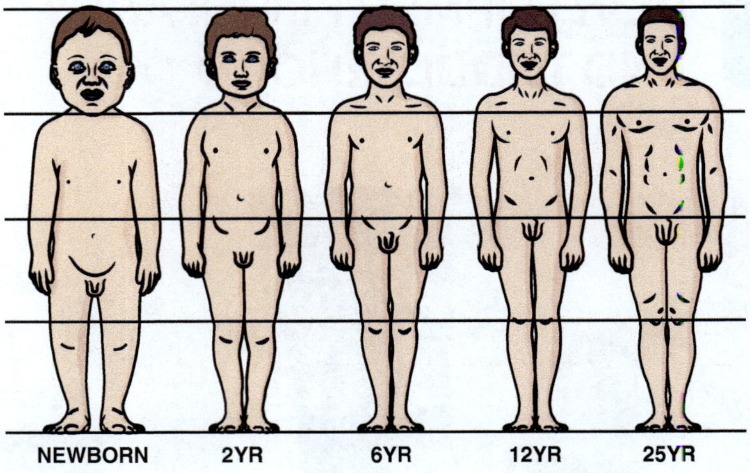

Adapted from Huelke, 1998.

expectations for typical gains and variations in the height and weight of children based on their chronological age and ethnic background.

In the first few days after birth, newborns shed excess fluid and typically lose 5% to 10% of their body weight. After this initial loss, infants gain weight quickly. Infants typically double their birth weight at about 4 months of age, triple it by 12 months, and quadruple it by 2.5 years (Kliegman & Geme, 2020). The average 3-year-old weighs about 31 pounds. The greatest growth spurt of the lifespan occurs during the first year of life with gains in height of 10 to 12 inches, making the average 1-year-old child about 30 inches tall (Ohta, 2019). Most children grow about 5 inches during their second year of life and 3 to 4 inches during their third. To parents, growth may appear slow and steady, but it instead tends to occur in spurts in which an infant or toddler can grow up to one quarter of an inch overnight (Lampl et al., 2001). At about 2 years of age, both girls and boys have reached one half of their adult height (Kliegman & Geme, 2020).

FIGURE 3.2 ■ Cephalocaudal and Proximodistal Development

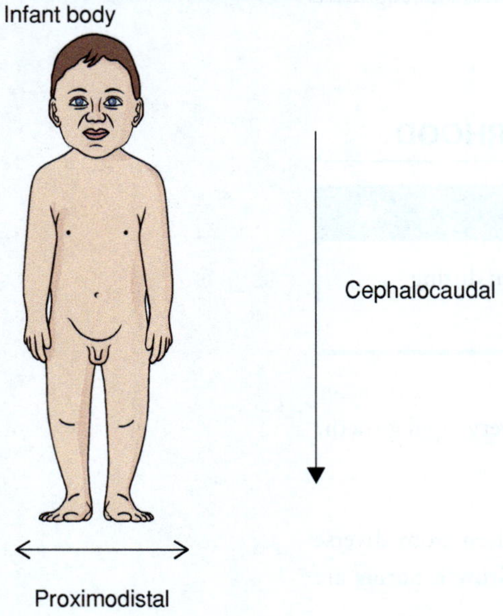

Patterns of Growth

Over the course of infancy children get larger and heavier, but growth is uneven. Different parts of the body grow at different rates. Growth during the prenatal period and infancy proceeds in two systematic patterns. **Cephalocaudal development** refers to the principle that growth proceeds from the head downward. The head and upper regions of the body develop before the lower regions. Recall that during prenatal development, the fetus's head grows before the other body parts (see Chapter 2). Even at birth, the newborn's head is about one-fourth the total body length (see Figure 3.1). As the lower parts of the body develop, the head becomes more proportionate to the body. By 3 years of age, the child is less top-heavy.

Proximodistal development refers to the principle that growth and development proceed from the center of the body outward (see Figure 3.2). During prenatal development, the internal organs develop before the arms and legs. After birth, the trunk grows ahead of the arms and legs, and the arms and legs tend to grow ahead of the hands and feet.

Growth is largely maturational, but it can be influenced by health and environmental factors, such as socioeconomic status (Von Holle et al., 2020). Today's children grow taller and faster than prior generations and the average adult is taller today than a century ago. Increases in children's growth over the past century are influenced by contextual changes such as improved sanitation, access to medical care, and nutrition (Mummert et al., 2018).

Nutrition

The first two years of life are a critical window for adequate caloric intake and good nutrition, to promote optimal health and development throughout childhood. The USDA (Dietary Guidelines Advisory Committee, 2020) and American Academy of Pediatrics (2012) recommend that infants be breastfed exclusively for the first 6 months and for breasteeding to continue, preferably, for one year.

Breastfeeding

More than 80% of women in the United States breastfeed their newborns, nearly two-thirds continue to breastfeed after 6 months, and more than one-third are still breastfeeding at 12 months (Centers for Disease Control, 2019; Centers for Disease Control and Prevention, 2017). In the U.S., breastfeeding practices vary by maternal age, education, and socioeconomic status (Dinour et al., 2020; Hauck et al., 2011), with the lowest rates of breastfeeding among low-income mothers, mothers who are young, and mothers with low levels of education (Victora et al., 2016). Black mothers are less likely to breastfeed than Hispanic and white mothers (Beauregard et al., 2019; Centers for Disease Control and Prevention, 2013; McKinney et al., 2016). They are disproportionately likely to face barriers to breastfeeding, such as health care settings that provide poor information about and support for breastfeeding as well as breastfeeding restrictions at work (Jones et al., 2015; Lind et al., 2014; Pérez-Escamilla et al., 2016).

Breastfeeding offers benefits for mothers and infants. Mothers who breastfeed have lower rates of diabetes, cardiovascular disease, depression, and some cancers (Louis-Jacques & Stuebe, 2018; Sattari et al., 2019). Breast milk contains immunizing agents that protect infants against infections, and breastfed infants tend to experience lower rates of allergies and gastrointestinal symptoms, lower risk of obesity, and fewer visits to physicians (Cabinian et al., 2016; Qiao et al., 2020; Turfkruyer & Verhasselt, 2015). Some studies suggest that infants breastfed for more than 6 months perform better on tests of cognitive and language ability from early childhood through adolescence, compared with their formula-fed counterparts, but the differences are small (Jenkins & Foster, 2014; Lenehan et al., 2020; Min Kim & Choi, 2020).

Although pediatricians recommend breastfeeding, it is not essential for a healthy infant. Many mothers do not breastfeed, whether by choice or circumstance. Infant formula is a safe and healthy alternative to breast milk. By about 5 to 6 months, infants begin to consume "solid food," usually vitamin- and iron-fortified baby cereal mixed with breast milk or formula.

Good nutrition promotes growth and development. Inadequate nutrition and medical problems pose threats to healthy development.

Breastfeeding is associated with many health benefits for infants and mothers and provides opportunities for infant-mother bonding.

iStock/SelectStock

Malnutrition

Malnutrition has devastating effects on physical growth, including **growth stunting**, a severely reduced growth rate. Malnourished children show cognitive deficits as well as impairments in motivation, curiosity, language, and the ability to effectively interact with the environment throughout childhood and adolescence and even into adulthood (Galler et al., 2012; Peter et al., 2016).

Malnourishment damages neurons, as shown in Figure 3.3, and the resulting neurological and cognitive deficits from early malnutrition last. Some of the damage caused by malnutrition can be lessened if nutrition is reinstated early. However,

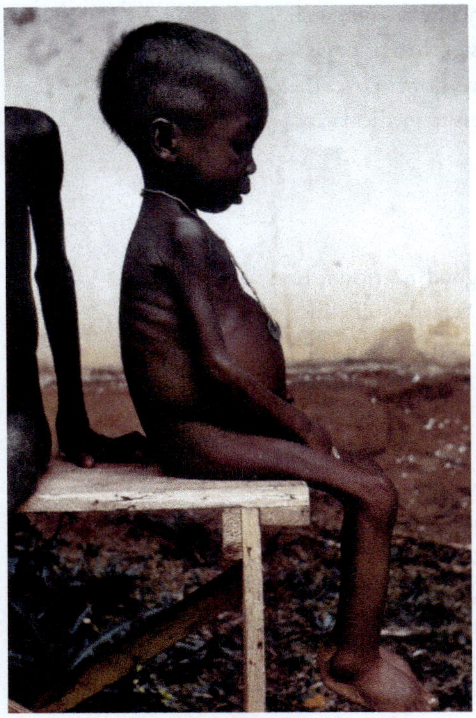

This child suffers from an extreme nutritional deficiency, kwashiorkor. Early treatment can reduce the deficits associated with kwashiorkor, but most children will not reach their full potential for height and growth.

Dr. Lyle Conrad, Centers for Disease Control and Prevention, Atlanta, Georgia, USA Public Health Image Library (PHIL); ID: 6901 http://phil.cdc.gov/

FIGURE 3.3 ■ Effects of Malnourishment on Brain Development

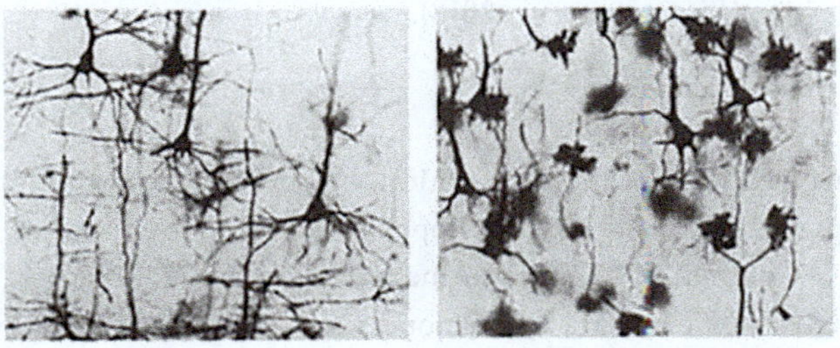

Source: de Onis and Branca (2016).

long-term difficulties in attention, learning, and intelligence often remain, even into middle adulthood (Schoenmaker et al., 2015; Waber et al., 2014).

Malnutrition is most common in developing countries, but it is also found in some of the world's wealthiest countries. Because of socioeconomic factors, many children in the United States and other developed countries are deprived of diets that support healthy growth (Ngandu et al., 2019). In 2017, about 16% of U.S. households with children were categorized as *food insecure*. That is, they lacked consistent access to food to support a healthy lifestyle for all members of the family at some point during the year (Coleman-Jensen et al., 2018). As shown in Figure 3.4, rates of food insecurity are higher in Black and Hispanic households (22% and 18%, respectively) and those headed by single parents (20% for homes headed by single men and 30% for those headed by single women). In the United States and other developed nations, food insecurity is linked with stunted growth, poor school performance, and health and behavior problems (Shankar et al., 2017; Zhu et al., 2017).

Infant Mortality

The leading causes of infant death account for more than two-thirds of deaths and include birth defects, low birthweight, sudden infant death syndrome, respiratory distress, and unintentional injuries (Singh & Yu, 2019). Over the past century in the U.S., infant mortality, or death, has declined for infants of all races and ethnicities. Despite declines, there are large racial disparities in infant mortality rates (see Figure 3.5). In 2017, infants of non-Hispanic Black women showed the highest rates of mortality—more than twice that of infants of non-Hispanic white women and Hispanic women and nearly three times that of non-Hispanic Asian women (Ely & Hoyert, 2018). Infants of Native American/Alaskan Native and Native Hawaiian/Pacific Islander women also showed high rates of mortality.

There are large educational disparities in infant mortality that have increased in recent decades. Infants whose mothers have less than a high school degree show more than double the rate of mortality as those with mothers with a college degree (Singh & Yu, 2019). Likewise, the large income differences linked with education are associated with a higher risk of infant mortality. Poverty rates are at least two times higher among Black, Hispanic, Native Hawaiian/Pacific Islander, and Native Americans/Alaskan Natives than non-Hispanic whites (Semega et al., 2020). However, infant mortality rates are highest in Black infants across all income levels (Kothari et al., 2017). Infant mortality is also higher in rural counties than urban counties in the U.S. (Ely & Hoyert, 2018).

Similar to our discussion of prenatal care (see Chapter 2), structural factors influence the racial and ethnic differences that characterize infant mortality. Poverty and its interweaving with stress and trauma, poor environmental quality and exposure to pollution, and exposure to discrimination pose

FIGURE 3.4 ■ Food Insecurity in the United States, 2017

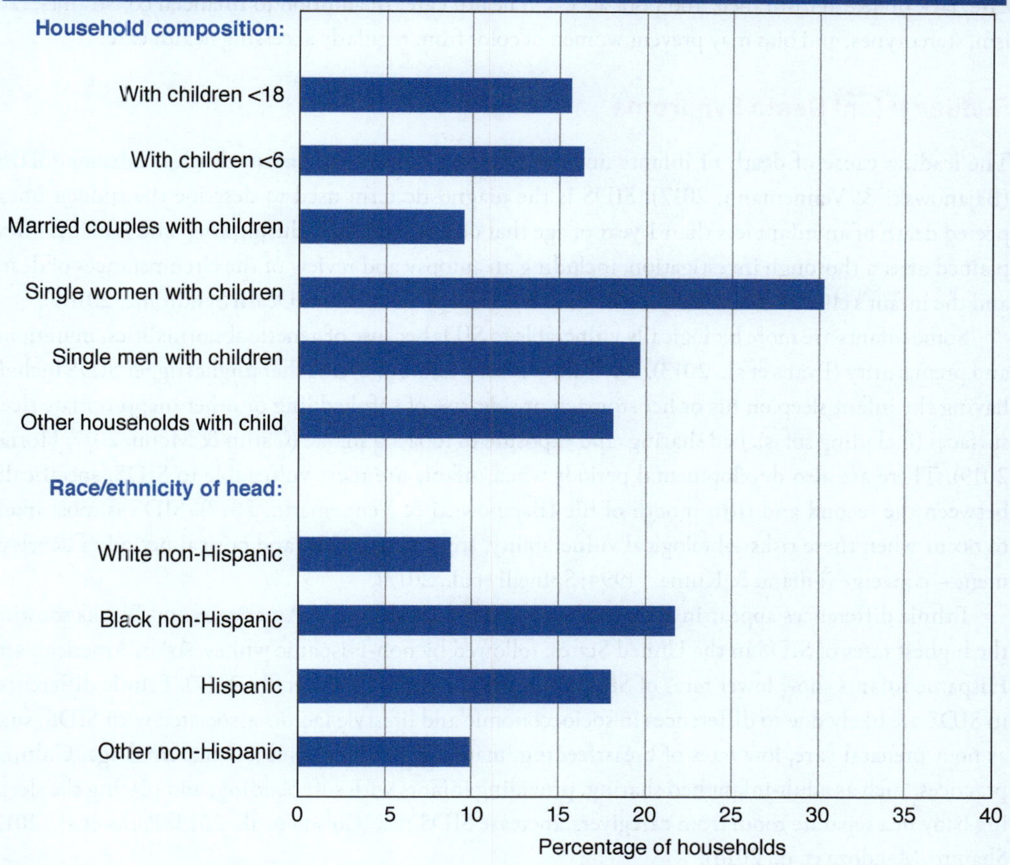

Source: Coleman-Jensen et al. (2018).

FIGURE 3.5 ■ Infant, Neonatal, and Postneonatal Mortality Rates, by Race and Hispanic Origin: United States, 2017

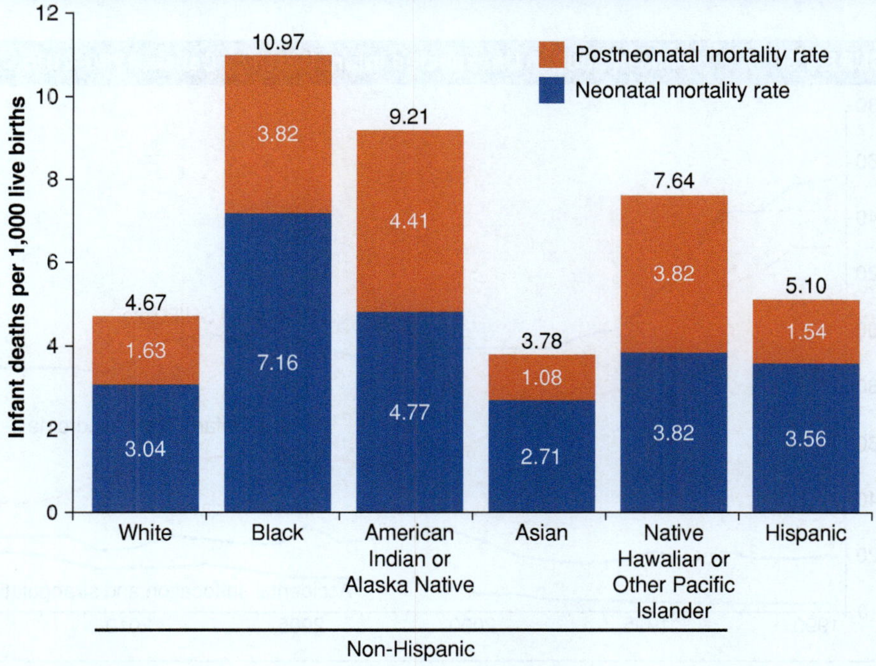

Source: Ely and Hoyert (2018).

risks to maternal and infant health. Risk factors for infant mortality also include little to no prenatal care, lack of health insurance, and poor access to health care. In addition to financial constraints, racism, stereotypes, and bias may prevent women of color from regularly accessing health care.

Sudden Infant Death Syndrome

The leading cause of death of infants under the age of 1 is **sudden infant death syndrome (SIDS)** (Bajanowski & Vennemann, 2017). SIDS is the diagnostic term used to describe the sudden unexpected death of an infant less than 1 year of age that occurs seemingly during sleep and remains unexplained after a thorough investigation, including an autopsy and review of the circumstances of death and the infant's clinical history (Moon & Task Force on Sudden Infant Death Syndrome, 2016b).

Some infants are more biologically vulnerable to SIDs because of genetic abnormalities, mutations, and prematurity (Evans et al., 2013). Environmental stressors or events that might trigger SIDS include having the infant sleep on his or her stomach or side, use of soft bedding or other inappropriate sleep surfaces (including sofas), bed sharing, and exposure to tobacco smoke (Carlin & Moon, 2017; Horne, 2019). There are also developmental periods when infants are most vulnerable to SIDS, specifically between the second and fifth month of life (Bajanowski & Vennemann, 2017). SIDS is most likely to occur when these risks—biological vulnerability, triggering events, and critical period of development—converge (Filiano & Kinney, 1994; Spinelli et al., 2017).

Ethnic differences appear in the prevalence of SIDS, with Native Americans and Blacks showing the highest rates of SIDS in the United States, followed by non-Hispanic whites. Asian American and Hispanic infants show lower rates of SIDS than white infants (Parks et al., 2017). Ethnic differences in SIDS are likely due to differences in socioeconomic and lifestyle factors associated with SIDS, such as poor prenatal care, low rates of breastfeeding, maternal smoking, and low maternal age. Cultural practices, such as adult-infant bed sharing, providing infants with soft bedding, and placing the sleeping baby in a separate room from caregivers, increase SIDS risk (Colson et al., 2013; Parks et al., 2017; Shapiro-Mendoza et al., 2014).

In the 1990s, SIDS declined dramatically after the American Academy of Pediatrics (1992) recommended that infants be placed for sleep in a nonprone position (i.e., a supine position: on their backs) as a strategy to reduce the risk of SIDS (see Figure 3.6). Initiated in 1992, the "Back to Sleep" campaign publicized the importance of nonprone sleeping. Between 1992 and 2001, the SIDS rate declined dramatically in the United States and other countries that implemented nonprone sleeping campaigns,

FIGURE 3.6 ■ Trends in Sudden Unexpected Infant Death by Cause, 1990–2015.

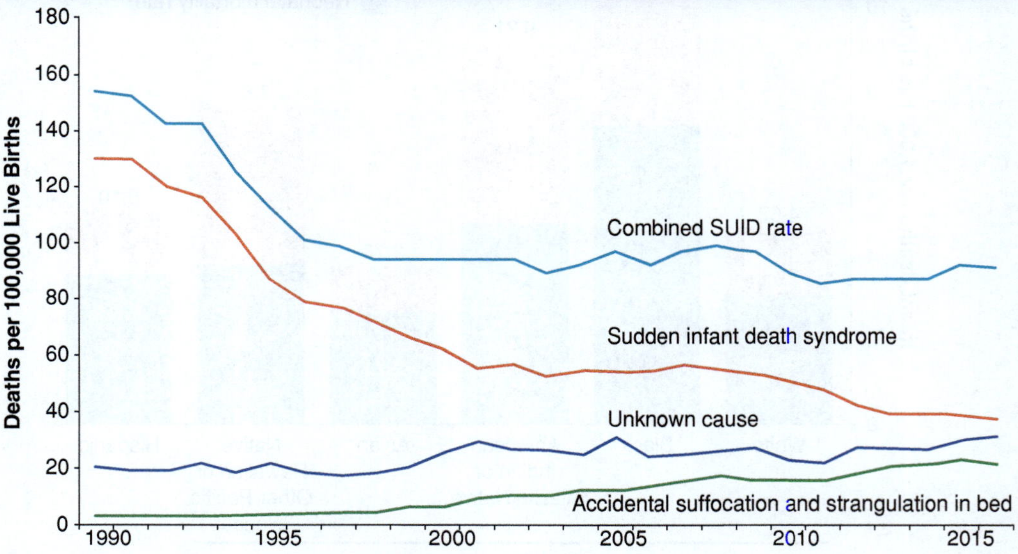

Source: Centers for Disease Control and Prevention; National Center for Health Statistics; National Vital Statistics System.

consistent with the steady increase in the prevalence of supine sleeping, illustrating the important role of contextual factors on development (Bajanowski & Vennemann, 2017; Bergman, 2015; Moon & Task Force on Sudden Infant Death Syndrome, 2016a). In addition to placing infants on their backs to sleep, other recommendations for a safe sleep environment include the use of a firm sleep surface, avoidance of soft bedding and infant overheating, and sharing a room with the infant without sharing a bed (Horne, 2019).

Brain Development

At birth, the brain is about 25% of its adult weight, and it grows rapidly throughout infancy, reaching about 70% of its adult weight by 2 years of age (Lyall et al., 2015). As the brain develops, it becomes larger and more complex.

The Neuron

The brain is made up of billions of cells called **neurons**. Neurons are specialized to communicate with one another to make it possible for people to sense the world, think, move their body, and carry out their lives. As shown in Figure 3.7, neurons have distinct structures that set them apart from other cells and enable the communicative functions characteristic of neurons. Dendrites are receptors that carry signals from other neurons to the cell body, which carries out the basic functions of the cell. Axons are tube-like structures that carry signals away from the cell body to other neurons (Stiles, 2017). When the signal reaches the end of the axon, it triggers the release of a neurotransmitter, a chemical that crosses the gap between neurons known as the synapse, to communicate with the dendrites of another neuron (Carson, 2014).

Processes of Neural Development

Neurogenesis, the formation of neurons, begins before birth. We are born with more than 100 billion neurons, more than we will ever need—and more than we will ever have at any other time in our lives. Some of our neurons die, but neurogenesis continues throughout life and new neurons are formed, although at a much slower pace than during prenatal development (Kolb, 2020).

At birth, the networks of neurons are simple, with few connections, or **synapses**, between neurons (Kolb et al., 2016). Neurons change in two ways. The dendrites grow and branch out, increasing synapses with other neurons, a process called **synaptogenesis** (see Figure 3.8). The most active areas of synaptogenesis during the first five weeks of life are in the sensorimotor cortex and subcortical parts of the brain, which are responsible for respiration and other essential survival processes (Remer et al., 2017). The visual cortex develops very rapidly between 3 and 4 months and reaches peak density by 12 months of age. The prefrontal cortex—responsible for planning and higher thinking—develops more slowly and is not complete until early adulthood (Tamnes et al., 2017b).

FIGURE 3.7 ■ The Neuron

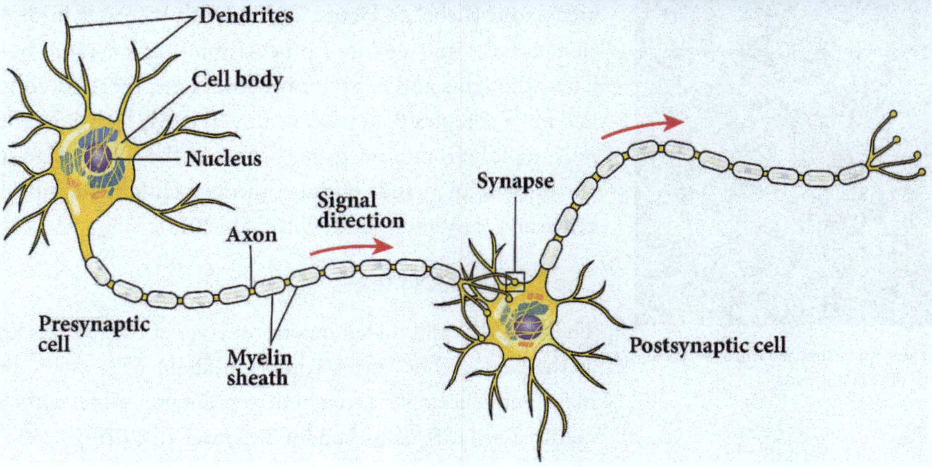

FIGURE 3.8 ■ Synaptogenesis From Birth to Age 2

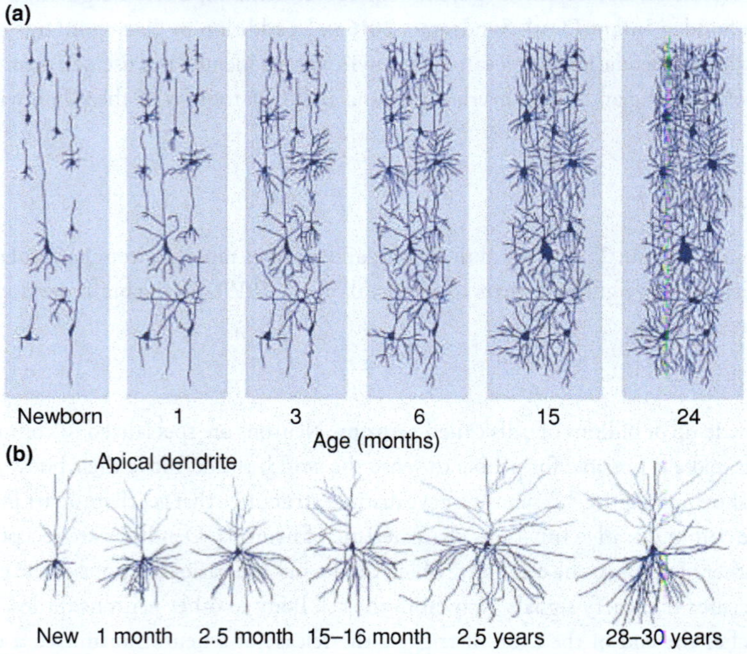

Source: Gilmore et al, 2018.

In response to stimulation from the outside world, the number of synapses initially rises meteorically in the first year of life, and the dendrites increase 500% by age 2 (Schuldiner & Yaron, 2015). This explosion in connections in the early years of life means that the brain makes more connections than it needs, in preparation to receive any and all conceivable kinds of stimulation (Kolb, 2020). Those connections that are used become stronger and more efficient, while those unused eventually shrink, atrophy, and disappear. This loss of unused neural connections is a process called **synaptic pruning**, which can improve the efficiency of neural communication by removing "clutter"—excess unused connections. Little-used synapses are pruned in response to experience, an important part of neurological development that leads to more efficient thought (Lyall et al., 2015).

A second process of brain development is **myelination**, in which axons become coated with fatty substance called **myelin** that speeds the transmission of neural signals and communication among neurons (Gibb & Kovalchuk, 2018). Myelination begins prenatally but accelerates after birth (Gilmore et al., 2018). Myelination contributes to advances in neural communication because axons coated with myelin transmit neural impulses more quickly than unmyelinated axons (Lebel & Deoni, 2018). With increases in myelination, infants and children process information more quickly. Their thoughts and behavior become faster, more coordinated, and more complex (Chevalier et al., 2015). Myelination proceeds most rapidly from birth to age 4, first in the sensory and motor cortex in infancy, and continues through childhood into adolescence and early adulthood (Qiu et al., 2015).

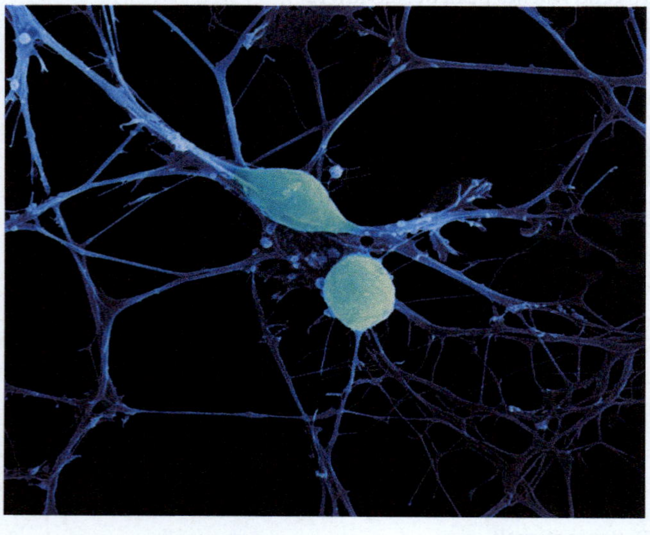

We are born with more than 100 billion neurons, more than we will ever need—and more than we will ever have at any other time in our lives.

Dennis Kunkel Microscopy/Science Source

The Cerebral Cortex

The wrinkled and folded outermost layer of the brain is known as the **cortex**. The cortex comprises about 85% of the brain's mass and develops throughout childhood; some parts don't mature until early adulthood (Gilmore et al., 2018).

The cortex is composed of different structures, called lobes, that are specialized with differing functions. The four lobes work together but develop on different timetables. The sensory and motor areas (such as the visual cortex regions of the occipital lobe) tend to develop first. The frontal lobe, specifically a part called the **prefrontal cortex**, develops throughout infancy, childhood, and adolescence, maturing in early adulthood (Hodel, 2018; Tamnes et al., 2017a). The prefrontal cortex is the part of the brain responsible for higher thought, such as planning, goal setting, controlling impulses, and using cognitive skills and memory to solve problems (see Figure 3.9).

Experience and Brain Development

Stimulation and experience are key components needed to maximize neural connections and brain development throughout life, but especially in infancy. Experience plays a powerful role in brain development in at least two ways. First, brain organization depends on experiencing certain basic events early in life, such as opportunities to hear language, see the world, touch objects, and explore the environment (Hodel, 2018; Kolb, 2020; Maurer, 2017). This is known as **experience-expectant brain development**. All infants around the world need these basic experiences during specific times in development, known as **sensitive periods**, to develop normally, and it is difficult to repair errors that are the result of severe deprivation and neglect (Hensch, 2018; McLaughlin et al., 2017; Nelson et al., 2019).

A second type of development, **experience-dependent brain development**, refers to the growth that occurs in response to learning experiences (Bick & Nelson, 2017). Experience-dependent development is the result of lifelong experiences that vary by individual based on contextual and cultural circumstances (Kolb et al., 2014). Exposure to enriching experiences, such as interactive play with toy cars and other objects that move; hands-on play with blocks, balls, and cups; and stimulating face-to-face play can all enhance children's brains, increasing activity in the prefrontal cortex, which is responsible for thought and reasoning (Bernier et al., 2016; Kolb, 2018). Poor stimulation, such as exposure to deprivation and trauma, are experiences that can have lasting negative effects on brain development (Harker, 2018).

The brain develops in response to experiences that are unique to each individual, such as playing with specific toys or participating in social interactions.

iStock/doble-d

Thinking in Context: Lifespan Development

How does the incidence of SIDS illustrate the interaction of biological and contextual risk factors? Identify examples of contextual influences on the risk for SIDS, such as the home environment, cultural practices, and policies and educational campaigns.

FIGURE 3.9 ■ The Human Brain

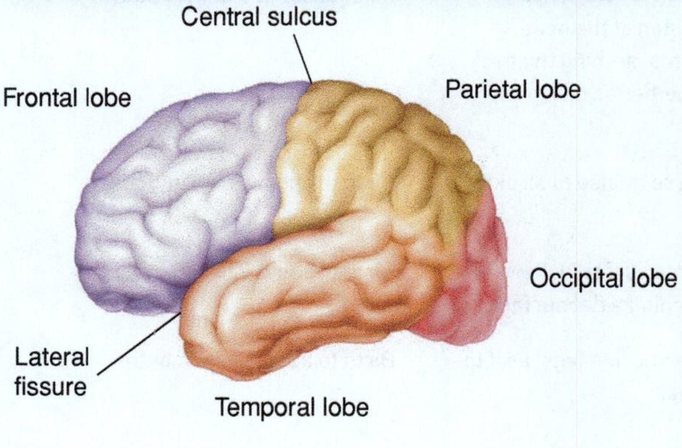

Thinking in Context: Biological Influences

Marta hopes to promote her baby's brain development. Explain the processes that influence infants' brain development and the role of experience in brain development. What advice do you give Marta?

Thinking in Context: Intersectionality

1. To what degree are demographic factors, such as socioeconomic status, geographics, and education, related to infant mortality? What are some ways in which these demographic factors intersect with race and ethnicity?
2. How do you account for the finding that Black infants are most at risk for infant mortality regardless of family income? What are some contextual factors that might influence the high rates of mortality in Black infants?

MOTOR DEVELOPMENT IN INFANCY AND TODDLERHOOD

LEARNING OBJECTIVE

3.2 Compare and contrast biological, contextual, and dynamic systems explanations for motor development in infancy and toddlerhood.

Newborns are equipped to respond to the stimulation they encounter in the world. The earliest way in which infants adapt is through the use of their **reflexes**, involuntary and automatic responses to stimuli such as touch, light, and sound. Each reflex has its own developmental course (Payne & Isaacs, 2020). Some disappear early in life and others persist throughout life (see Table 3.1). Infants show individual differences in how reflexes are displayed, specifically the intensity of the response. The reflexes of preterm newborns suggest a more immature neurological system than that of full-term newborns (Barros et al., 2011). The absence of reflexes may signal neurological deficits.

TABLE 3.1 ■ Newborn Reflexes

Name of Reflex	Response	Developmental Course
Palmar grasp	Curl fingers around objects that touch the palm	Birth to about 4 months, when it is replaced by voluntary grasp
Rooting	Turn head and tongue toward stimulus when cheek is touched	Disappears over first few weeks of life and is replaced by voluntary head movement
Sucking	Suck on objects placed into the mouth	Birth to about 6 months
Moro	Startle response in reaction to loud noise or sudden change in the position of the head, results in throwing out arms, arching the back, and bringing the arms together as if to grasp something	Birth to about 5 to 7 months
Babinski	Fans and curls the toes in response to stroking the bottom of the foot	Birth to about 8 to 12 months
Stepping	Makes stepping movements as if to walk when held upright with feet touching a flat surface	Birth to about 2 to 3 months
Swimming	Holds breath and moves arms and legs, as if to swim, when placed in water	Birth to about 4 to 6 months

Gross Motor Development

Gross motor development refers to the ability to control the large movements of the body, actions that help us move around in our environment. Like physical development, motor skills evolve in a predictable sequence. By the end of the first month of life, most infants can reach the first milestone, or achievement, in motor development: lifting their heads while lying on their stomachs. After lifting the head, infants progress through an orderly series of motor milestones: lifting the chest, reaching for objects, rolling over, and sitting up with support (see Table 3.2).

Notice that these motor achievements tend to reflect a cephalocaudal progression of motor control, proceeding from the head downward (Payne & Isaacs, 2020). Milestone charts describe group trends in motor development, but an individual infant's development often diverges from group norms (Adolph et al., 2018). For example, although crawling usually precedes walking, some infants skip crawling altogether or crawl after walking (Adolph & Robinson, 2015).

Success at initiating forward motion by crawling (6–10 months) is particularly significant for both infants and parents. Infants vary in how they crawl (Adolph & Robinson, 2015). Some use their arms to pull and legs to push, some use only their arms or only their legs, and others scoot on their bottoms. Once infants can pull themselves upright while holding on to a chair or table, they begin "cruising," or moving by holding on to furniture to maintain their balance while stepping sideways. In many Western industrialized countries, most infants walk alone by about 1 year of age. Most beginning walkers tend to walk in short spurts, a few steps at a time, often ending in the middle of the floor (Cole et al., 2016). Independent walking holds implications for cognitive, social, and emotional development, as it is associated not only with more attention and manipulation of objects but also with more sophisticated social interactions with caregivers, such as directing mothers' attention to particular objects and sharing objects.

TABLE 3.2 ■ Motor Skills Timetable

Average Age Achieved	Motor Skill
2 months	Lifts head Holds head steady when held upright
3 months	Pushes head and chest up with arms Rolls from stomach to back
4 months	Grasps cube
6 months	Sits without support
7 months	Rolls from back to stomach Attempts crawling Uses opposable thumb to grasp objects
8 months	Achieves sitting position alone Pulls to a stand
9 months	"Cruises" by holding on to furniture
10 months	Plays patty-cake
11 months	Stands alone
12 months	Walks alone
14 months	Builds tower of two cubes Scribbles
17 months	Walks up steps
18 months	Runs

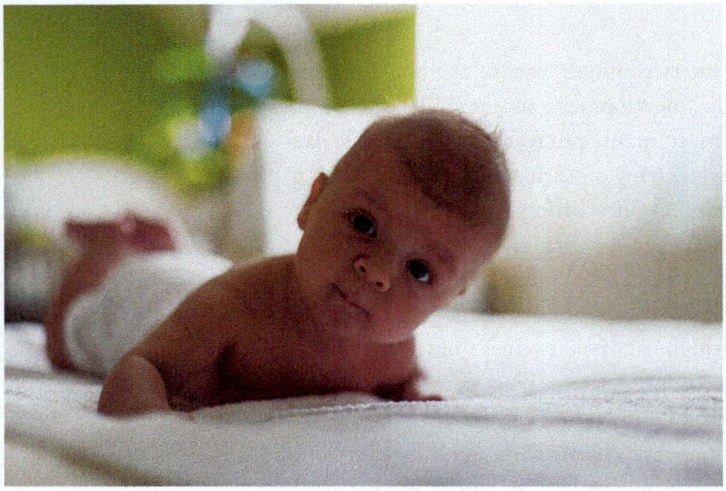

By the end of the first month of life, most infants can lift their head while lying on their stomach.

iStock/aywan88

Fine Motor Development

Fine motor development refers to the ability to control small movements of the fingers such as reaching and grasping. Voluntary reaching plays an important role in cognitive development because it provides new opportunities for interacting with the world. Like other motor skills, reaching and grasping begin as gross activities and are refined with time. Newborns begin by engaging in *prereaching*—swinging their arms and extending them toward nearby objects (Ennouri & Bloch, 1996; von Hofsten & Rönnqvist, 1993). Newborns use both arms equally and cannot control their arms and hands, so they rarely succeed in making contact with objects of interest (Lynch et al., 2008). Prereaching stops at about 7 weeks of age.

Voluntary reaching appears at about 3 months of age and slowly improves in accuracy. Infants reach for and bump objects, and eventually some are accidentally grasped (Juett & Kuipers, 2019). At 5 months, infants can successfully reach for moving objects. By 7 months, the arms can reach independently, and infants are able to reach for an object with one arm rather than both (Spencer et al., 2000). By 10 months, infants can reach for moving objects that change direction (Fagard et al., 2009).

As they gain experience with reaching and acquiring objects, infants develop cognitively because they learn by exploring and playing with objects—and object preferences change with experience. As infants gain more experience with reaching, they tend to shift their interest from large objects and spend more time looking at and touching smaller objects (Libertus et al., 2013). With experience, infants' attention moves away from the motor skill (like the ability to coordinate their movement to hit a mobile) to the object (the mobile), as well as to the events that occur before and after acquiring the object (how the mobile swings and how grabbing it stops the swinging or how batting at it makes it swing faster). In this way, infants learn about cause and how to solve simple problems. Motor development illustrates the complex interactions that take place between maturation and contextual factors.

Biological Influences on Motor Development

Motor development is influenced by genetics. Identical twins, who share the same genes, have more similarities in the timing and pace of motor development than do fraternal twins, who share half of their genes (Smith et al., 2017). But the differences are small.

Maturation plays a very strong role in motor development. Preterm infants reach motor milestones later than do full-term infants (Gabriel et al., 2009). Cross-cultural research also supports the role of maturation because around the world, infants display roughly the same sequence of motor milestones despite broad environmental differences. Among some Native Americans and other ethnic groups around the world, it is common to follow the tradition of tightly swaddling infants to cradleboards and strapping the board to the mother's back during nearly all waking hours for the first 6 to 12 months of the child's life. Although this might lead one to expect that swaddled babies will not learn to walk as early as babies whose movements are unrestricted, studies of Hopi Native American infants have shown that swaddling has little impact on when Hopi infants initiate walking (Dennis & Dennis, 1991; Harriman & Lukosius, 1982). Such research suggests that walking is very much biologically programmed. Samples of young children in the United States show no ethnic or socioeconomic status differences in gross motor skills such as running, hopping, kicking, and catching (Kit et al., 2017).

Contextual Influences on Motor Development

Much of motor development is driven by maturation, yet opportunities to use motor skills are essential. In a classic naturalistic study of institutionalized orphans in Iran who had spent their first 2 years of life lying on their backs in their cribs and were never placed in sitting positions or played with, none of the 1- to 2-year-old infants could walk, and fewer than half of them could sit up; the researchers also found that most of the 3- to 4-year-olds could not walk well alone (Dennis, 1960). Recent research suggests that infants raised in orphanages score lower on measures of gross motor milestones at 4, 6, and 8 months of age and walk later compared with home-reared infants (Chaibal et al., 2016).

Practice can enhance motor development (Lobo & Galloway, 2012). Newborns show improvement in stepping after practicing on a treadmill (Siekerman et al., 2015). When infants from 1 to 7 weeks of age practice stepping reflexes each day, they retain the movements and walk earlier than infants who receive no practice (Vereijken & Thelen, 1997; Zelazo, 1983). Practice in sitting has a similar effect (Zelazo et al., 1993). Similarly, infants who spend supervised playtime prone on their stomachs each day reach many motor milestones, including rolling over and crawling, earlier than do infants who spend little time on their stomachs (Hewitt et al., 2020; Kuo et al., 2008).

Practice contributes to cross-cultural differences in infant motor development. Different cultures provide infants with different experiences and opportunities for development. in many cultures, including several in sub-Saharan Africa and in the West Indies, infants attain motor goals like sitting up and walking much earlier than do North American infants. Among the Kipsigi of Kenya, parents seat babies in holes dug in the ground and use rolled blankets to keep babies upright in the sitting position (Keller, 2003). The Kipsigis help their babies practice walking at 2 to 3 months of age by holding their hands, putting them on the floor, and moving them slowly forward. Notably, Kipsigi mothers do not encourage their infants to crawl; crawling is seen as dangerous as it exposes the child to dirt, insects, and the dangers of fire pits and roaming animals. Crawling is therefore virtually nonexistent in Kipsigi infants (Super & Harkness, 2015). Similarly, infants of other sub-Saharan villages, such as the !Kung San, Gusii, and Wolof, are also trained to sit using holes or containers for support and are often held upright and bounced up and down, a social interaction practice that contributes to earlier walking (Lohaus et al., 2011).

Even simple aspects of the childrearing context, such as choice of clothing, can influence motor development. In the 19th century, 40% of American infants skipped crawling, possibly because the long, flowing gowns they wore impeded movement on hands and knees (Trettien, 1990). One study of 13- and 19-month-old infants compared their gait while wearing a disposable diaper, a thicker cloth diaper, and no diaper (Cole et al., 2012). When naked, infants demonstrated the most sophisticated walking with fewer missteps and falls. While wearing a diaper, infants walked as poorly as they would have done several weeks earlier had they been walking naked. In sum, motor development is largely maturational, but subtle differences in context and cultural emphasis play a role in its timing.

Although this infant spends most of his waking hours tightly swaddled and carried on his mother's back, he will walk at about a year of age, similar to babies who are not swaddled.

Norman Barrett / Alamy Stock Photo

Motor Development as a Dynamic System

Every motor behavior, such as walking, has a long history and is not a stand-alone achievement. Motor milestones, such as the ability to crawl, might look like isolated achievements, but they actually develop systematically and build on each other, with each new skill preparing an infant to tackle the next (Thelen, 1995, 2000). Infants' first steps may seem like a sudden new ability, but they are the result of continuously combining and experimenting with many existing abilities and skills (Adolph et al., 2018). According to **dynamic systems theory**, motor development reflects an interaction among developmental domains, maturation, and environment (Thelen, 1995, 2000; see Figure 3.10). Simple motor skills are combined in increasingly complex ways, permitting advances in movement, including a wider range and more precise movements that enable babies to more effectively explore and control their environments.

Separate abilities are blended to create more advanced opportunities for exploring the environment. The abilities to sit upright, hold the head upright, sense an object using binocular vision, match motor movements to vision, reach out an arm, and grasp are all combined into coordinated reaching movements to obtain a desired object (Corbetta & Snapp-Childs, 2009; Spencer et al., 2000). Motor skills become more specialized, coordinated, and precise with practice, permitting infants to reach for an object with one hand without needlessly flailing the other (D'Souza et al., 2017).

Motor development reflects goal-oriented behavior because it is initiated by infants' desires to accomplish something, such as picking up a toy or moving to the other side of the room. Infants try out behaviors and persist at those that enable them to move closer to the goal, practicing and refining the behavior. New motor skills provide new possibilities for exploring the environment and new interactions with caregivers that influence opportunities. Motor skills do not develop in isolation; rather, they are influenced by the physical and social context in which they occur. Differences in caregiver interactions and caregiving environments affect children's motor skills, the form they take, the ages of onset, and the overall developmental trend (Adolph & Franchak, 2017).

Therefore, from a dynamic systems perspective, motor development is the result of several processes: central nervous system maturation, the infant's physical capacities, environmental supports, and the infant's desire to explore the world. It is learned by revising and combining abilities and skills to fit infants' goals. Infants have goals and opportunities that are particular to their specific environments, leading to individual differences (Adolph & Franchak, 2017). Infants might respond to slippery hardwood floors by crawling on their stomachs rather than all fours or by shuffling their knees rather

FIGURE 3.10 ■ Motor Development as a Dynamic System

The infant's abilities to reach out an arm, stretch, and grasp combine into coordinated reaching movements to obtain desired objects. Motor development progresses to sitting, crawling, walking, and eventually to running, all reflections of infants' blending and coordinating abilities to achieve self-chosen goals, such as obtaining toys, and all tailored by environmental supports and challenges.

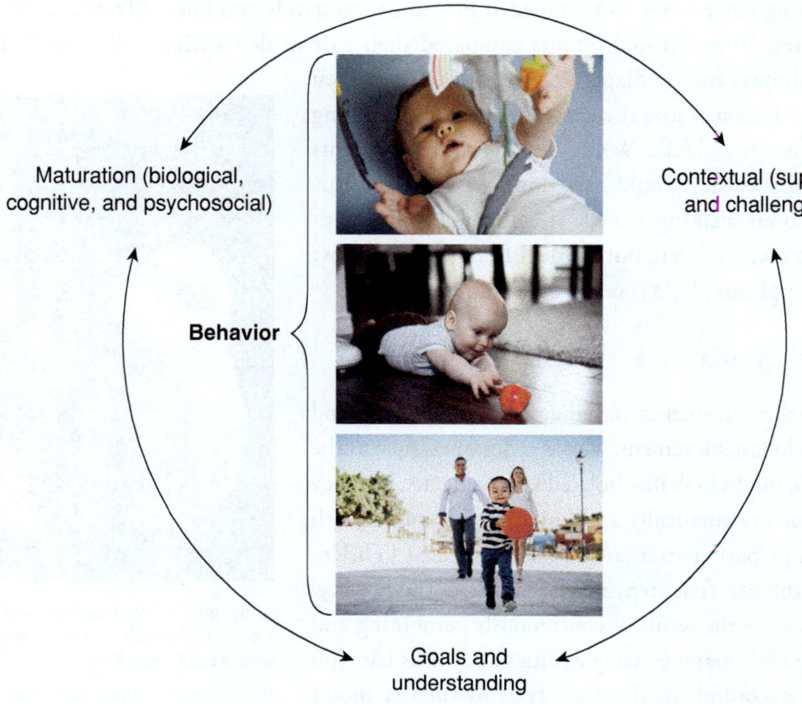

iStock/ Essentials Collection; iStock/ Essentials Collection; Can Stock Photo Inc./ harishmarnad than raising each. Infants attain the same motor tasks at about the same age, yet differ in how they approach each task (Berger et al., 2007). By viewing motor development as dynamic systems of action produced by infants' abilities, goal-directed behavior, and environmental supports and opportunities, we can account for the individual differences that we see in motor development.

Thinking in Context: Lifespan Development

1. From a bioecological systems perspective (see Chapter 1), describe contextual influences on motor development. How do factors in infants' microsystem and exosystem influence their motor skills? How might exosystem factors play a distal, or distant, influence on motor skills? Identify macrosystem cultural factors that might influence an infant's development.
2. How might a fine motor skill, such as learning to use a spoon, reflect the interaction of maturation and sociocultural context?

Thinking in Context: Applied Developmental Science

Carmen is concerned because her 14-month-old baby is not walking. All of the other babies she knows have walked by 12 months of age. What would you tell Carmen?

SENSATION AND PERCEPTION IN INFANCY AND TODDLERHOOD

LEARNING OBJECTIVE

3.3 Describe infants' developing sensory abilities.

Meeting the pediatrician for the first time in her young life, newborn Kerry stared intently at the object the doctor held about 6 inches from her face. "I think she sees it!" said her surprised mother. "She most certainly does," said the doctor. "Even as a newborn, your Kerry can sense the world better than you realize." Newborns can see, hear, smell, taste, and respond to touch, but it is unclear how they perceive sensory stimuli.

Developmental researchers draw a distinction between sensation and perception. **Sensation** occurs when our senses detect a stimulus. Our sensory organs—the eyes, ears, tongue, nostrils, and skin—convert stimuli, whether visual, auditory, taste, olfactory (smell), or tactile (touch), into electrical impulses that travel on sensory nerves to the brain where they are processed. **Perception** refers to the sense our brain makes of the stimulus and our awareness of it. The newborn is equipped with a full range of senses, ready to experience the world. They can both detect and perceive stimuli, but many of their abilities are immature relative to those of adults. Yet infants' sensory abilities develop rapidly, achieving adult levels within the first year of life (Johnson & Hannon, 2015).

Methods for Studying Infant Perception

How do researchers study infant perception? The simplest method is through *preferential looking tasks*, which are experiments designed to determine whether infants prefer to look at one stimulus or another. Consider an array of black and white stripes. As shown in Figure 3.11, an array with more stripes (and therefore, many more narrow stripes) tends to appear gray rather than black and white because the pattern becomes more difficult to see as the stripes become more narrow. Researchers determine infants' **visual acuity**, or sharpness of vision or the ability to see, by comparing infants' responses to stimuli with different frequencies of stripes because infants who are unable to detect the stripes lose interest in the stimulus and look away from it.

FIGURE 3.11 ■ Visual Acuity

Researchers and pediatricians use stimuli such as the Teller Acuity Cards illustrated here to determine what infants can see. Young infants attend to stimuli with wider lines and stop attending as the lines become smaller.

Source: Leat et al. (2009).

Another method of studying infant perception relies on infants' capacity for **habituation**, a gradual decline in the intensity, frequency, or duration of a response to a repeated, unchanging stimulus. To examine whether an infant can discriminate between two stimuli, a researcher presents one until the infant habituates, or gets used to it. Then a second stimulus is presented. If **dishabituation**, or the recovery of attention, occurs, it indicates that the infant detects that the second stimulus is different from the first. If the infant does not react to the new stimulus by showing dishabituation, it is assumed that the infant does not perceive the difference between the two stimuli. The habituation method is very useful in studying infant perception and cognition, and it underlies many of the findings discussed in this chapter.

Other ways of studying infant perception rely on technology, such as the physiological measures discussed in Chapter 1, including EEG and fMRI. Recently researchers have begun to study infants' eye movements and pupillary response to draw inferences about sensation and perception (Kaldy & Blaser, 2020; Wetzel et al., 2016). The pupil, the opening that allows light into the eye, dilates or changes shape in response to light. It also dilates in response to arousal, when the individual is interested in a stimulus, which can reveal what infants can sense and perceive.

Vision

At birth, vision is the least developed sense, but it improves rapidly. Newborn visual acuity is approximately 20/400 (Farroni & Menon, 2008). Preferential-looking studies show that infants reach adult levels of visual acuity between 6 months and 1 year of age (Mercuri et al., 2007). Improvement in vision is due to the increasing maturation of the structures of the eye and the visual cortex, the part of the brain that processes visual stimuli.

Newborns are born with preferences for particular visual stimuli. Newborns prefer to look at patterns, such as a few large squares, rather than a plain stimulus such as a black or white oval shape (Fantz, 1961). Newborns also prefer to look at faces, and the preference for faces increases with age (Frank et al., 2009; Quinn et al., 2018).

How infants explore visual stimuli changes with age (Colombo et al., 2015). Until about 1 month of age, infants tend to scan along the outer perimeter of stimuli. When presented with a face, the infant's gaze will scan along the hairline and not move to the eyes and mouth. This is known as the **externality effect** because infants scan along the outer contours of complex visual stimuli. By 6 to 7 weeks of age, infants study the eyes and mouth, which hold more information than the hairline, as shown in Figure 3.12 (Hunnius & Geuze, 2004). Similarly, the ability to follow an object's movement with the eyes, known as visual tracking, is very limited at birth but improves quickly. By 2 months of age, infants can follow a slow-moving object smoothly, and by 3 to 5 months, their eyes can dart ahead to keep pace with a fast-moving object (Agyei et al., 2016; Richards & Holley, 1999). The parts of the brain that process motion in adults are operative in infants by 7 months of age (Weaver et al., 2015).

Like other aspects of vision, color vision improves with age. Newborns see color, but they have trouble distinguishing among colors. Early visual experience with color is necessary for normal color perception to develop (Colombo et al., 2015; Sugita, 2004). Habituation studies show that by 1 month of age, infants can distinguish among red, green, and white (Teller, 1997). By 2 to 3 months of age, infants are as accurate as adults in discriminating the basic colors of red, yellow, and blue (Matlin & Foley, 1997; Teller, 1998). By 3 to 4 months of age, infants can distinguish many more colors as well as distinguish among closely related colors (Bornstein & Lamb, 1992; Haith, 1993). Seven-month-old infants detect color categories almost as well as adults; they can group slightly different shades (e.g., various shades of blue) into the same basic color categories as adults do (Clifford et al., 2009).

Depth perception is the ability to perceive the distance of objects from each other and from ourselves. Depth perception is what permits infants to successfully reach for objects and, later, to crawl without bumping into furniture. By observing that newborns prefer to look at three-dimensional objects than two-dimensional figures, researchers have found that infants can perceive depth at birth (Slater et al., 1984). Three- to 4-week-old infants blink their eyes when an object is moved toward their face, as if to hit them, suggesting that they are sensitive to depth cues (Kayed et al., 2008; Náñez & Yonas, 1994). Infants learn about depth by observing and experiencing motion.

A classic series of studies using an apparatus called the *visual cliff* demonstrated that crawling influences how infants perceive depth. The visual cliff, as shown in Figure 3.13, is a Plexiglas-covered table bisected by a plank so that one side is shallow, with a checkerboard pattern right under the glass, and the other side is deep, with the checkerboard pattern a few feet below the glass (Gibson &

FIGURE 3.12 ■ Externality Effect and Face Perception

The externality effect refers to a particular pattern of infant visual processing. When presented with a complex stimulus, such as a face, infants under 2 months of age tend to scan along the outer contours, such as the hairline. Older infants scan the internal features of complex images and faces, thereby processing the entire stimulus.

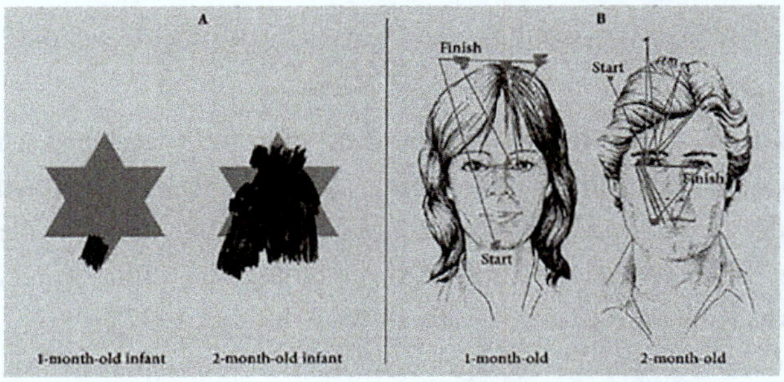

Source: Shaffer (2002, p. 190); Adapted from Salapatek (1975).

Newborns see color but they have trouble distinguishing among colors.

Phanie / Alamy Stock Photo

FIGURE 3.13 ■ Visual Cliff

Three-month-old infants show a change in heart rate when placed face down on the glass surface of the deep side of the visual cliff, suggesting that they perceive depth, but do not fear it. Crawling babies, however, move to the shallow side of the visual cliff and refuse to cross the deep side of the visual cliff.

Walk, 1960). In this classic study, crawling babies readily moved from the plank to the shallow side but not to the deep side, even if coaxed by their mothers, suggesting that they perceive the difference in depth (Walk, 1968). The more crawling experience infants have, the more likely they are to refuse to cross the deep side of the visual cliff (Bertenthal et al., 1984).

Does this mean that babies cannot distinguish the shallow and deep sides of the visual cliff until they crawl? No, because even 3-month-old infants who are too young to crawl distinguish shallow from deep drops. They becomequiet and their heart rate decreases when they are placed face down on the deep side compared to the shallow side of the cliff (Dahl et al., 2013). The young infants can distinguish the difference between shallow and deep drops but do not have the experience to understand the difference (Adolph et al., 2014). As infants gain experience crawling, their perception of depth changes. Newly walking infants avoid the cliff's deep side even more consistently than do crawling infants (Dahl et al., 2013; Witherington et al., 2005). Recent views have suggested that infants avoid the deep side of the cliff not out of fear but simply because they perceive that they are unable to successfully navigate the drop; fear might be conditioned through later experiences, but infants are not naturally fearful of heights (Adolph et al., 2014; LoBue & Adolph, 2019).

Hearing

The capacity to hear develops in the womb; in fact, hearing is the most well-developed sense at birth. Newborns are able to hear about as well as adults (Northern et al., 2014). Shortly after birth, neonates can discriminate among sounds, such as tones (Hernandez-Pavon et al., 2008). By 3 days of age, infants will turn their head and eyes in the general direction of a sound, and this ability to localize sound improves over the first 6 months (Clifton et al., 1994; Litovsky & Ashmead, 1997).

As we will discuss, the process of learning language begins at birth, through listening. Newborns are attentive to voices and can detect their mother's voice. Newborns only 1 day old prefer to hear speech sounds rather than similar-sounding nonspeech sounds (May et al., 2018). Newborns can perceive and discriminate nearly all sounds in human languages, but from birth, they prefer to hear their native language (Kisilevsky, 2016). Brain activity in the temporal and left frontal cortex in response to auditory stimuli indicates that newborns can discriminate speech patterns, such as differences in cadence among languages, suggesting an early developing neurological specialization for language (Gervain et al., 2008; Gervain & Mehler, 2010).

Touch

Compared with vision and hearing, we know much less about the sense of touch in infants. In early infancy, touch, especially with the mouth, is a critical means of learning about the world (Piaget, 1952). The mouth is the first part of the body to show sensitivity to touch prenatally and remains one of the most sensitive areas to touch after birth.

Touch, specifically a caregiver's massage, can reduce stress responses in preterm and full-term neonates and is associated with weight gain in newborns (Álvarez et al., 2017). Skin-to-skin contact with a caregiver has an analgesic effect, reducing infants' pain response to being stuck with a needle for vaccination (Pandita et al., 2018). Although it was once believed that newborns were too immature to feel pain, we now know that the capacity to feel pain develops even before birth. In one study fetuses as early as 24 weeks of age observed with sophisticated ultrasound technology showed facial expressions suggesting distress or pain in response to a needle prick (Reissland et al., 2013).

Smell and Taste

Smell and taste receptors are functional in the fetus and preferences are well developed at birth (Bloomfield et al., 2017). Just hours after birth, newborns display facial expressions signifying disgust in response to odors of ammonia, fish, and other scents that adults find offensive (Steiner, 1979). Within the first days of life, newborns detect and recognize their mother's odor (Macfarlane, 1975; Marin et al., 2015). Infants are calmed by their mother's scent. Newborns who smelled their mother's odor displayed less agitation during a heel-stick test and cried less afterward than infants presented with unfamiliar odors (Rattaz et al., 2005). Familiar scents are reinforcing and can reduce stress responses in infants (Schaal, 2017). The scent of breast milk can slow heart rate in premature neonates who are under stress (Neshat et al., 2016).

Infants show innate preferences for some tastes (Ross, 2017). Both bottle-fed and breastfed newborns prefer human milk—even milk from strangers—to formula (Marlier & Schaal, 2005). Newborns prefer sugar to other substances, and a small dose of sugar can serve as an anesthetic, distracting newborns from pain (Forestell, 2017). Experience can modify taste preferences, beginning before birth: Fetuses are exposed to flavors in amniotic fluid that influence their preferences after birth (Beauchamp & Mennella, 2011; Forestell, 2016). In one study, the type of formula fed to infants influenced their taste preferences at 4 to 5 years of age (Mennella & Beauchamp, 2002). Infants who were fed milk-based formulas and protein-based formulas were more likely to prefer sour flavors at 4 to 5 years of age compared with infants who were fed soy-based formulas, who, in turn, were more likely to prefer bitter flavors.

Intermodal Perception

All stimuli we encounter involve more than one type of sensory information. We see a dog but we also hear its bark. Not only are infants able to sense in multiple modalities, but they are able to coordinate their senses. **Intermodal perception** is the process of combining information from more than one sensory system (Johnson & Hannon, 2015). Sensitivity to intermodal relations among stimuli is critical to perceptual development and learning—and this sensitivity emerges early in life (Lewkowicz et al., 2010). Infants expect visual, auditory, and tactile information to occur together (Sai, 2005). Newborns turn their heads and eyes in the direction of a sound source, suggesting that they intuitively recognize that auditory and visual information co-occur and provide information about spatial location (Newell, 2004).

Newborns show a preference for viewing their mother's face at 72, 12, and even just 4 hours after birth (Pascalis et al., 1995). It was once believed that infants' preference for their mother's face was innate. However, in one study neonates were able to visually recognize their mother's face only if the face was paired with their mother's voice at least once after birth (Sai, 2005). Thus, intermodal perception is evident at birth because neonates coordinate auditory (voice) and visual stimuli (face) to recognize their mother. They quickly remember the association and then demonstrate a preference for her face even when it is not paired with her voice. Infants also integrate touch and vision very early in life. One-month-old infants prefer to look at smooth or nubby pacifiers that they had previously sucked, suggesting that they could match tactile and visual stimuli (Meltzoff & Borton, 1979).

Although young infants show impressive capacities to integrate visual and tactile information, these senses are not completely integrated at birth. Newborns can visually recognize an object previously held but not seen, but they cannot tactually recognize an object previously seen and not held, suggesting that intermodal relations among senses are not bidirectional at birth (Sann & Streri, 2007). Instead, development may be triggered by experience.

Infant-Context Interactions and Perceptual Development

We have seen that individuals are embedded in and interact dynamically with their context. Developmental scientists James and Eleanor Gibson applied ecological theory to perceptual development, emphasizing that perception arises through interactions with the environment (Adolph & Kretch, 2015). The Gibsons argued that individuals do not build a representation of the world by collecting small pieces of sensory information; rather, the environment itself provides all the information needed. Individuals perceive the environment directly, without constructing or manipulating sensory information.

Perception arises from action. Infants actively explore their environment with their eyes, moving their heads and, later, reaching their hands and, eventually, crawling. Perception provides the information infants need to traverse their environment. Through their exploration, infants perceive **affordances**—the nature, opportunities, and limits of objects (Gibson & Pick, 2000). The features of objects tell infants about their affordances and their possibilities for action, such as whether an object is squeezable, mouthable, catchable, or reachable.

Infants explore their environment systematically, searching to discover the properties of the things around them (Savelsbergh et al., 2013). From this perspective, perception arises from action, just as it influences action (Gibson, 1979). Exploration and discovery of affordances depends on infants' capacities for action, which is influenced by their development, genetics, and motivation. A large pot might offer a 10-year-old child the possibility of cooking because the child has learned this capacity (e.g., has observed cooking) and can perceive this affordance (or use) of the pot. In contrast, an 18-month-old infant may perceive very different affordances of the pot, such as a drum to bang or a bucket to fill, based on the child's capacities. We naturally perceive affordances, such as knowing when a surface is safe for walking, by sensing information from the environment and coordinating it with our body sensations, such as our sense of balance (Kretch et al., 2014). In this way, our perception of affordances and the opportunities for exploration influence how we move and interact within our environments and, ultimately, our opportunities for learning (Adolph & Kretch, 2015).

Thinking in Context: Lifespan Development

Intermodal perception and the perception of affordances illustrate how infants are active participants in their own development (see Chapter 1). Discuss this statement and provide examples.

Thinking in Context: Applied Developmental Science

How might parents and caregivers design caregiving environments that are tailored to infants' early sensory capacities and stimulate development? What advice would you give on how to design such an environment for a newborn? For a 6-month-old infant?

Thinking in Context: Biological Influences

Consider visual development from the perspective of evolutionary developmental psychology, as passed through generations by natural selection (see Chapter 1).

1. How might patterns of visual development, such as face perception, object exploration, color vision, and depth perception, illustrate adaptive functioning, from an evolutionary perspective?
2. Might the nature of early immature visual functioning have an adaptive purpose? How might the timing and transition to more mature visual function serve infants' adaptation?

COGNITIVE DEVELOPMENT IN INFANCY AND TODDLERHOOD

LEARNING OBJECTIVE

3.4 Describe the cognitive achievements of infancy and toddlerhood from the perspective of cognitive-developmental, core knowledge, and information processing theories.

Can newborns think? What is thinking like in infancy? Infants actively engage in their development by interacting with people and objects around them. Several theories examine infants' emerging cognitive capacities.

Piaget's Cognitive-Developmental Theory

Swiss scholar Jean Piaget (1896–1980) was the first scientist to systematically examine children's thinking. Piaget viewed infants and children as active explorers who learn by interacting with the world, building their own understanding of everyday phenomena, and applying it to adapt to the world around them.

Processes of Development

According to Piaget (1952), infants and children are active in their own development because they engage other people and the world, adapting their ways of thinking in response to their experiences. Through these interactions, individuals organize what they learn to construct and refine their own **cognitive schemas**, or concepts, ideas, and ways of interacting with the world. The first schemas are inborn motor responses, such as the reflex response that causes infants to close their fingers around an object when it touches their palm. As infants grow and develop, these early motor schemas are transformed into cognitive schemas, or thoughts and ideas. At every age, we rely on our schemas to make sense of the world, and our schemas are constantly adapting and developing in response to our experiences. We adapt our cognitive schemas to the environment in two ways: assimilation and accommodation.

Assimilation involves integrating a new experience into an existing cognitive schema. Sometimes we encounter information or a new experience that fits with and can easily be incorporated into an existing concept or way of thinking. Other times we encounter experiences or information that do not fit within an existing cognitive schema, so we must change the schema, adapting and modifying it in light of the new information. This process is called **accommodation**.

The processes of assimilation and accommodation enable people to adapt to their environment (see Figure 3.14). People—infants, children, and adults—constantly integrate new information into their schemas (assimilation) and continually encounter new information that requires them to modify their schemas (accommodation). Piaget proposed that people naturally strive for **cognitive equilibrium**, a balance between the processes of assimilation and accommodation. When assimilation

FIGURE 3.14 ■ Assimilation and Accommodation

Bobby sees a cat that fits his schema for kitty (left). He has never seen a cat like this before (middle). He must accommodate his schema for kitten to include a hairless cat (right).

istock/ GlobalP; istock/ YouraPechkin

and accommodation are balanced, individuals are neither incorporating new information into their schemas nor changing their schemas in light of new information; instead, our schemas match the outside world and represent it clearly. But a state of cognitive equilibrium is rare and fleeting. More frequently, people experience a mismatch, or **cognitive disequilibrium**, between their schemas and the world.

Disequilibrium leads to cognitive growth because the mismatch between schemas and reality leads to confusion and discomfort, which motivate children to modify their cognitive schemas so that their view of the world matches reality and cognitive equilibrium is restored. Children's drive for cognitive equilibrium is the basis for cognitive change, propelling them through the four stages of cognitive development proposed by Piaget (refer to Chapter 1). With each advancing stage, children create and use more sophisticated cognitive schemas, enabling them to think, reason, and understand their world in more complex ways.

During the sensorimotor stage, infants demonstrate object permanence, the understanding that objects exist outside of sensory awareness.

Doug Goodman/Science Source

Sensorimotor Reasoning

During the sensorimotor stage, from birth to about 2 years old, infants learn about the world through their senses and motor skills. To think about an object, they must act on it by viewing it, listening to it, touching it, smelling it, and tasting it. Piaget (1952) believed that infants are not capable of **mental representation**—thinking about an object using mental pictures. They also lack the ability to remember and think about objects and events when they are not present. Instead, to think about an object, an infant must experience it through both the visual and tactile senses. The sensorimotor period of reasoning involves a slow pattern of growth through which infant cognition progresses from simple reflexes to intentional action and mental representation.

A hallmark milestone of the sensorimotor period is **object permanence**, the understanding that objects continue to exist outside of sensory awareness (e.g., when they are no longer visible). According to Piaget, infants younger than 8 months of age do not yet have object permanence—out of sight is literally out of mind. An infant loses interest and stops reaching for or looking at a small toy after it is covered by a cloth. Not until 8 to 12 months will an infant search for hidden objects, thus displaying object permanence. This development is an important cognitive advance because it signifies a capacity for mental representation, or holding images and thoughts within the mind.

The final key development of this stage is **representational thought**, the ability to use symbols such as words and mental pictures to represent objects and actions in memory. In developing this ability, infants are freed from immediate experience: They can think about objects that they no longer see directly in front of them. Children can think through potential solutions and create new solutions without engaging in physical trial and error but simply by considering the potential solutions and their consequences.

Piaget's recognition that infants are active participants in their development and that motor action and thinking are inextricably linked is still accepted by today's developmental scientists (Libertus et al., 2016). Today developmental scientists believe that mental representation develops earlier than Piaget suggested (Carey et al., 2015). Research tasks that examine infants' looking behavior conclude that even young infants 4 months of age show an awareness of object permanence, suggesting that young infants' cognitive abilities are more remarkable than Piaget realized (Baillargeon, 2004; Bremner et al., 2015).

Core Knowledge Theory

Some developmental scientists suggest that infants are born with limited learning capacities such as a set of perceptual biases that cause them to attend to features of the environment that will help them to learn quickly (Bremner et al., 2015). Developmental scientists who support the **core knowledge theory** believe that infants are born with several innate knowledge systems, or core domains of thought, that promote early rapid learning and adaptation (Spelke, 2016).

According to core knowledge theorists, infants learn so quickly and encounter such a great amount of sensory information that some prewired evolutionary understanding, including the early ability to learn rules, must be at work (Spelke, 2017). By studying infants' looking behavior in response to series of stimuli, core knowledge researchers have found that young infants have a grasp of the physical properties of objects, including the knowledge that objects do not disappear out of existence (permanence), cannot pass through another object (solidity), and will fall without support (gravity; Baillargeon et al., 2016). Infants are also thought to have an early ability to discriminate number, distinguishing between small and large numbers of items (Cheung & Ansari, 2020; Christodoulou et al., 2017; Spelke, 2017).

Increasingly, infants are viewed as statistical learners, able to apply basic inferences to quickly identify patterns in the world around them (Köster et al., 2020; Saffran & Kirkham, 2018). When those statistical inferences do not match their perception, they may be driven to learn and retain information because they are naturally motivated to create and test new hypotheses about the world around them (Sim & Xu, 2019; Stahl & Feigenson, 2019). It is important to note that this is not a conscious process; infants do not know that they are experimenting and engaging in the scientific method. Instead, infants are driven to learn. When confronted with confusing events, they spontaneously devise explanations and compare those explanations with what they perceive (Köster et al., 2020).

Information Processing Theory

Information processing theorists describe cognition as a set of interrelated components that permit people to process information—to notice, take in, manipulate, store, and retrieve. Newborns are ready to learn and adapt to their world because they are born information processors. With development, we get better at moving information through our cognitive system in ways that enable us to adapt to our world.

Attention

Attention refers to our ability to direct our awareness. We encounter constant stimulation from the world around us. The ability to focus on specific stimuli and switch attention is critical for selecting and maintaining information in our minds so that it can be processed (Oberauer, 2019). Infants show more attentiveness to dynamic stimuli—stimuli that change over time—than to static, unchanging

The toy keys have captured this infant's attention. Infants are most attentive to dynamic stimuli—stimuli that change over time—than to static, unchanging stimuli.

iStock/kamsta

stimuli (Reynolds et al., 2013). By around 10 weeks of age, infants show gains in attention. As infants' capacities for attention increase, so do their preferences for complex stimuli and stimuli that move, such as faces and video clips (Courage et al., 2006). Attention is influenced by neurological development, including advances in myelination and development in the brain areas underlying attentional control (Dowe et al., 2020; Reynolds & Romano, 2016). Attention is vital to thought and plays a role in memory and learning (Fisher, 2019).

Memory

There are several forms of memory. When we encounter and attend to stimuli, information enters **working memory**. Information in working memory is held and "worked on" or processed. Working memory is responsible for manipulating (considering, comprehending), encoding (transforming into a memory), and retrieving (recalling) information and it includes the subjective sense of "thinking" (Baddeley et al., 2019). The capacity of working memory (how much it can hold) is limited to a small amount of information. Just as our thoughts are constantly changing, so are the contents of working memory. The capacity of working memory dramatically increases between 6 months of age, when infants can reliably recall a single item, to 12–14 months, when infants can reliably recall three objects, similar to some adults (Kibbe, 2015; Oakes & Luck, 2013; Radvansky, 2017). The durability of working memory also increases rapidly from 6 to 12 months and continues to increase through age 2 (Bjorklund & Myers, 2015; Reznick, 2009).

Long-term memory refers to the ability to recall information encountered some time in the past. One type of long-term memory, **recognition memory**, the ability to recognize a previously encountered stimulus, appears early in life. Neonates can recall visual and auditory stimuli (Muenssinger et al., 2013; Streri et al., 2013). With age, infants require fewer trials or presentations to recall a stimulus and are able to retain material for progressively longer periods of time (Cuevas & Sheya, 2019; Howe, 2015).

Long-term memory is assessed using tasks that measure **deferred imitation**, or imitating a model after a delay. The infants watch an experimenter engage in a novel behavior with an unfamiliar object. After a period of time the infants are given the object. If they display the novel behavior more often than infants who have not viewed the object, it suggests that they have formed a long-term memory of the object and action. Results from deferred imitation studies suggest that infants can form memories that last a year and sometimes longer (Bauer et al., 2000, 2002). With age, infants can remember more complicated sets of actions, with fewer exposures, and for a longer period of time (Cuevas & Sheya, 2019).

Young infants were taught to kick their foot to make an attached mobile move. When tested one week later, the infants remembered and kicked their legs vigorously to make the mobile move.

istock/ Vera Livchak

Generally, with age, infants create memories more quickly and retain them for longer periods, but at all ages infants are more likely to recall events that take place in familiar surroundings in which they are actively engaged and that are emotionally salient (Courage & Cowan, 2009; Learmonth et al., 2004; Rose et al., 2011). As we develop, we amass a great deal of information in long-term memory, organize it in increasingly sophisticated ways, and encode and retrieve it more efficiently and with less effort.

Categorization

As infants are bombarded with a multitude of stimuli, encountering countless new objects, people, and events, they form concepts by naturally grouping stimuli into classes or categories. **Categorization**—grouping different stimuli into a common class—is an adaptive mental process that allows for organized storage of information in memory, efficient retrieval of that information, and the capacity to respond with familiarity to new stimuli from a common class (Owen & Barnes, 2021; Quinn, 2016). Infants naturally categorize information, just as older children and adults do (Rosenberg & Feigenson, 2013). Without the ability to categorize, we would have to respond anew to each novel stimulus we experience.

Infants' earliest categories are based on the perceived similarity of objects (Rakison & Butterworth, 1998). Three-month-old infants categorize pictures of dogs and cats differently based on perceived differences in facial features (Quinn et al., 1993). By 4 months, infants can form categories based on perceptual properties, grouping objects that are similar in appearance, including shape, size, and color (Quinn, 2016; Rekow et al., 2020). As early as 7 months of age, infants use conceptual categories based on perceived function and behavior (Mandler, 2004). Seven- to 12-month-old infants use many categories to organize objects, such as food, furniture, birds, animals, vehicles, kitchen utensils, and more, based on both perceptual similarity and perceived function and behavior (Bornstein & Arterberry, 2010; Mandler & McDonough, 1998; Oakes, 2010).

Researchers also use sequential touching tasks to study the conceptual categories that older infants create (Perry, 2015). Research using sequential touching procedures has shown that 12- to 30-month-old toddlers organize objects first at a global level and then at more specific levels. They categorize at more inclusive levels (e.g., animals or vehicles) before less inclusive levels (e.g., types of animals or types of vehicles) and before even less inclusive levels (e.g., specific animals or vehicles; Bornstein & Arterberry, 2010). Infants' and toddlers' everyday experiences and exploration contribute to their growing capacity to recognize commonalities among objects, group them in meaningful ways, and use these concepts to think about and solve problems. Recognizing categories is a way of organizing information that allows for more efficient thinking, including storage and retrieval of information in memory (Owen & Barnes, 2021). Therefore, advances in categorization are critical to cognitive development. The cognitive abilities that underlie categorization also influence language development as words represent categories, or ways of organizing ideas and things. Table 3.3 summarizes the development of information processing skills in infancy.

Context and Cognitive Development

The social and cultural contexts in which infants are embedded provide opportunities for social interactions that affect how infants think and view their world (Veissière et al., 2019).

Culture

Children's social learning opportunities are facilitated and constrained by culture (Kärtner et al., 2020; Legare et al., 2015). Research with Western samples suggests that caregivers promote children's learning through shared attention, directing their attention to objects by using clear visual cues such as pointing and alternating their gaze between the infant and object. However, emphasis on instruction, stimulation, and engagement with infants during object play is more common in Western cultures, such as Germany and Greece, than nonwestern cultures, such as rural Cameroon and rural India (Keller et al., 2009). Visual face-to-face contact is common in Western communities, yet many nonwestern communities, such as the !Kung, Gusii, and Samoan communities, emphasize physical contact with infants instead (Konner, 2017).

In many communities, learning may occur without direct adult instruction and often through observation, without any direct instructional cues (Gaskins & Paradise, 2010; Kärtner et al., 2020). Children who grow up in cultural communities where observational learning is valued, such as in agricultural communities where children learn to participate in household tasks at an early age, tend to become skilled observational learners, even as infants, which influences how they process stimuli in

TABLE 3.3 ■ Changes in Information Processing Skills During Infancy

Ability	Description
Attention	Attention increases steadily over infancy. From birth, infants attend more to dynamic than static stimuli. During the second half of their first year, infants attend more to complex stimuli such as faces and video clips. Attention is linked with diffuse frontal lobe activity in young infants and localized frontal lobe activity by 7.5 months of age. Individual differences appear at all ages and are stable over time. Attention is associated with performance on visual recognition memory tasks.
Memory	Memory improves with age. Three-month-old infants can remember a visual stimulus for 24 hours. By the end of the first year, infants can remember a visual stimulus for several days or even weeks. Infants are most likely to remember events in familiar, engaging, and emotionally salient contexts.
Categorization	Infants first categorize objects based on perceived similarity. By 4 months, infants can form categories based on perceptual properties such as shape, size, and color. By 6 to 7 months of age, infants' brain waves correspond to their identification of novel and familiar categories. Seven- to 12-month-old infants can organize objects such as food, furniture, animals, and kitchen utensils, based on perceived function and behavior. Twelve- to 30-month-old infants categorize objects first at a global level and then at more specific levels. Infants categorize objects at more global and inclusive levels (such as motor vehicles) before more specific and less inclusive levels (such as cars, trucks, construction equipment). The use of categories improves memory efficiency.

their world. Although all infants learn from their social world, the means by which they learn appears to vary by cultural context.

Screens and Digital Media

Technology offers new contexts that influence our thoughts, actions, and development. Many infants and young children engage with screen-based media. The American Academy of Pediatrics advises that parent avoid screen time other than video chatting for children younger than 18 to 24 months (American Academy of Pediatrics Council on Communications and Media, 2016). Exposure to screen media is associated with increased risk of obesity, reduced sleep and poor sleep, language delays, and poor performance on tests of inhibition, the ability to stop responding to a stimulus (Anderson & Subrahmanyam, 2017; Cheung et al., 2017; Domingues-Montanari, 2017).

Media is so pervasive today that some developmental scientists argue that it is no longer simply an influence on infants' and children's development, but a fundamental context in which development unfolds (Barr, 2019). Infants and toddlers spend 1 to 2 hours a day engaged with screen media, including television and tablets, and are exposed to more than 5 hours daily of background television intended for adults (Courage, 2017). Even very young infants attend to video material, as its movement, color, and rapid scene changes are attractive (Courage, 2017).

Infant-directed videos and programming offer educational content embedded in an engaging video format and are often advertised as aids to babies' brain development, intelligence, and learning

(Fenstermacher et al., 2010; Vaala & LaPierre, 2014). Longitudinal studies, however, suggest that there is no evidence of long-term benefits of media use in infancy (DeLoache et al., 2010; Ferguson & Donnellan, 2014).

Infants learn more readily from people than from televisions and tablets. Infants experience a **transfer deficit,** sometimes called the video deficit, because they are less able to transfer what they see on the screen to their own behavior than what they learn through active interactions with adults (Barr, 2010). The transfer deficit applies to a variety of domains, such as imitation, language learning, and object retrieval tasks (Barr, 2013; 1). When parents and infants practice joint media engagement, such as parents watching videos with their infants and talking to them about the content, the infants spend more time looking at the screen and learn more from the media (Barr, 2019; Linebarger & Vaala, 2010). The video deficit declines over early childhood, but infants and young children benefit more from engaging with sensitive caregivers than from screens of any kind.

Infants and toddlers learn more from interaction with their parents and other caregivers than they do watching infant-directed educational content.

iStock/LucaLorenzelli

Child Care and Cognitive Development

In the United States, more than half of all mothers of infants under 1 year old, and more than two-thirds of mothers of children under 6, are employed (U.S. Bureau of Labor Statistics, 2016). The infants and young children of working mothers are cared for in a variety of settings: in center-based care, in the home of someone other than a relative, or with a relative such as a father, grandparent, or older sibling (Federal Interagency Forum on Child and Family Statistics, 2014). A common misconception is that nonfamilial center-based care is damaging to children's development. But this belief is not supported by research. A longitudinal study of more than 1,300 children conducted by the National Institute of Child Health and Development (NICHD) revealed that infants' developmental outcomes are influenced more by characteristics of the family, such as parenting, maternal education, and maternal sensitivity, than by the type of child care (Axe, 2007; DeHaan, 2006).

Quality of child care predicts children's development; it includes factors such as a low child-to-teacher ratio, positive teacher-child interactions, and specific efforts to stimulate children (Banghart et al., 2020). Infants and young children exposed to poor-quality child care score lower on measures of cognitive and social competence, regardless of demographic variables such as parental education and socioeconomic status (Banghart et al., 2020; NICHD Early Child Care Research Network, 2005). In contrast, high-quality child care is associated with gains in cognitive and language development over the first three years of life and can even compensate for lower quality and chaotic home environments (Berry et al., 2016; Gialamas, Mittinty, Sawyer, Zubrick, & Lynch, 2014; Mortensen & Barnett, 2015; Watamura, Phillips, Morrissey, McCartney, & Bub, 2011).Quality of care predicts measures of cognitive, emotional, and social competence later in childhood and academic grades and behavioral adjustment in adolescence (Vandell, Belsky, Burchinal, Steinberg, & Vandergrift, 2010; Vandell, Burchinal & Pierce, 2016).

Unfortunately, high-quality childcare is expensive. From 2012 to 2016, the annual cost of center-based care in the United States ranged from about $6,000 in Arkansas to $22,000 in Washington, D.C. (Schulte & Durana, 2016; Child Care Aware of America, 2014). The few public subsidies for child care available in the United States are tied to economic need. Despite this, children from low-SES families and neighborhoods tend to have poor access to quality care (Cloney, Cleveland, Hattie, & Tayler, 2016).

Thinking in Context: Lifespan Development

1. Recall from Chapter 1 that developmental scientists vary in whether they view development as continuous and gradual or as discontinuous and stage-like. Consider cognition in infancy. To what degree do you view it as continuous or discontinuous? Why?

Thinking in Context: Applied Developmental Science

1. What kinds of toys and activities would you recommend to caregivers who want to entertain infants while helping them develop skills in attention, memory, or categorization?
2. Marla sat her 12-month-old infant down to watch a program on a tablet computer. "I need a break, and it's educational," she reasoned. What do you think? What are the pros and cons of infant screen use? What advice would you give? Is it ever ok? Why or why not?

LANGUAGE DEVELOPMENT IN INFANCY AND TODDLERHOOD

LEARNING OBJECTIVE

3.5 Summarize patterns of language development during infancy and toddlerhood.

Language development has important implications for the child's cognitive, social, and emotional development. Gaining the ability to use words to represent objects, experiences, thoughts, and feelings permits children to think and to communicate with others in increasingly flexible and adaptive ways.

Early Preferences for Speech Sounds

Newborn infants are primed to learn language. They attend to speech and prefer to hear human speech sounds, especially their native language, as well as stories and sounds that they heard prenatally (May et al., 2018). Infants naturally notice the complex patterns of sounds around them and organize sounds into meaningful units. They recognize frequently heard words, such as their names (Kuhl, 2015).

Although infants can perceive and discriminate the sounds that comprise all human languages at birth, their developing capacities and preferences are influenced by context (Hoff, 2015). As they are exposed to their native language, they become more attuned to the sounds (and distinctions between sounds) that are meaningful in their own language and less able to distinguish speech sounds that are not used in that language (Werker et al., 2012). Infants who experience high-quality interactions with their mothers, characterized by frequent speech, show a narrowing earlier, as early as 6 months of age (Elsabbagh et al., 2013). Native-language discrimination ability between 6 and 7 months of age predicts the rate of language growth between 11 and 30 months (Kuhl, 2015).

Emerging Speech

Prelinguistic Communication

At birth, crying is the infant's only means of communication. Infants soon learn to make many more sounds, like gurgles, grunts, and squeals. Between 2 and 3 months of age, infants begin **cooing**, making deliberate vowel sounds like "ahhhh," "ohhhh," and "eeeee." Infants' first coos sound like one long vowel. These vocal sounds are a form of vocal play; they are likely to be heard when babies are awake, alert, and contented. With age, the quality of coos changes to include different vowel-like sounds and combinations of vowel-like sounds (Owens, 2019). **Babbling**—repeating strings of consonants and vowels such as "ba-ba-ba" and "ma-ma-ma"—begins to appear at about 6 months of age.

At first, babbling is universal. All babies do it, and the sounds they make are similar no matter what language their parents speak or in what part of the world they are raised. However, infants soon become sensitive to the ambient language around them, and it influences their vocalizations (Chen & Kent, 2010). By the end of the first year, infants' babbling sounds more like real speech as they begin to vary the pitch of their speech in ways that reflect the inflections of their native language (Andruski et al., 2013).

Babies learn language by hearing others speak and by modifying their babbling in response to caregiver interactions.

Eric Scouten / Alamy Stock Photo

Language acquisition is a socially interactive process: Babies learn by hearing others speak and by noticing the reactions that their vocalizations evoke in caregivers (Hoff, 2015; Kuhl, 2016). Social interaction elicits cooing, and infants modify their babbling in response to caregiver interactions (Tamis-LeMonda et al., 2014). When mothers of 9½-month-old infants speak in response to their infants' babbling, infants restructure their babbling, changing the phonological pattern of sounds in response to their mothers' speech (Goldstein & Schwade, 2008).

Language development follows a predictable pattern, from prelinguistic communication to learning words to stringing words together to communicate with others.

First Words

Throughout language development, babies' **receptive language** (what they can understand) exceeds their **productive language** (what they can produce themselves; Tamis-Lemonda & Bornstein, 2015). That is, infants understand more words than they can use. Research suggests that infants may understand some commonly spoken words as early as 6 to 9 months of age, long before they are able to speak (Bergelson & Swingley, 2012; Dehaene-Lambertz & Spelke, 2015).

At about 1 year of age, the average infant speaks his or her first word. At first, infants use one-word expressions, called **holophrases**, to express complete thoughts. A first word might be a complete word or a syllable. Usually, the word has more than one meaning, depending on the context in which it is used. "Da" might mean, "I want that," "There's Daddy!" or "What's that?" Caregivers usually hear and understand first words before other adults do. The first words that infants use are those that they hear often or are meaningful for them, such as their own name, the word no, or the word for their caregiver. Infants reared in English-speaking homes tend to use nouns first, as they are most concrete and easily understood (Waxman et al., 2013).

Learning Words: Semantic Growth

By 13 months of age, children begin to quickly learn the meaning of new words and understand that words correspond to particular things or events (Woodward et al., 1994). Infants learn new words through **fast mapping**, a process of quickly acquiring and retaining a word after hearing it applied a few times (Kan & Kohnert, 2008; Marinellie & Kneile, 2012). At 18 months, infants are more likely to learn a new word if both they and the speaker are attending to the new object when the speaker introduces the new word (Baldwin et al., 1996). Two-year-olds have been shown to be able to learn a word even after a single brief exposure under ambiguous conditions (Spiegel & Halberda, 2011) or after overhearing a speaker use the word when talking to someone else (Akhtar et al., 2001). Between 24 and 30 months, infants can learn new words even when their attention is distracted by other objects or events (Moore et al., 1999). Children's knowledge and interests influence their vocabulary development. They are more likely to learn words that are related to those they know and label objects, actions, and events that they find interesting (Mani & Ackermann, 2018).

FIGURE 3.15 ■ Number of Words Known as a Function of Time for Individual Children

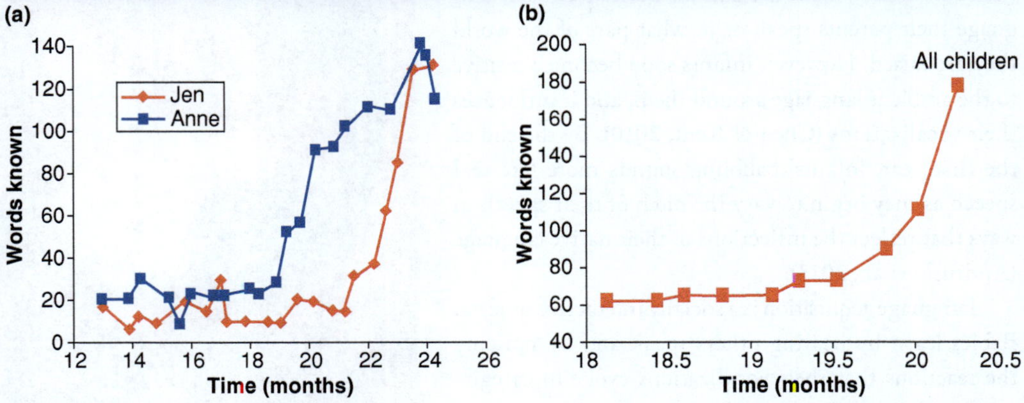

Source: Samuelson & McMurray, 2017.

Fast mapping improves with age and accounts for **vocabulary spurt**, or naming explosion—a period of rapid vocabulary learning that occurs between 16 and 24 months of age (Owens, 2019). During this period, infants apply their word-learning strategies to learn multiple words of varying difficulty seemingly at once. Within weeks, a toddler may increase her vocabulary from 50 words to more than 400 (Bates et al., 1988). As shown in Figure 3.15, infants vary in the speed of word acquisition, with some showing a rapid increase in vocabulary before others (Samuelson & McMurray, 2017). In addition, although fast mapping helps young children learn many new words, their own speech lags behind what they can understand because young children have difficulty retrieving words from memory (McMurray, 2007).

Two-Word Utterances

At about 21 months of age, or usually about 8 to 12 months after they say their first word, most children compose their first simple two-word sentences, such as "Kitty come," or "Mommy milk." **Telegraphic speech**, like a telegram, includes only a few essential words. Like other milestones in language development, telegraphic speech is universal among toddlers. Children around the world use two-word phrases to express themselves.

Language development follows a predictable path, as shown in Table 3.4. Between 20 and 30 months of age, children begin to follow the rules for forming sentences in a given language. Soon they become more comfortable with using plurals, past tense, articles (such as *a* and *the*), prepositions (such as *in* and *on*), and conjunctions (such as *and* and *but*). By 2½ years of age, children demonstrate an awareness of the communicative purpose of speech and the importance of being understood (Owens, 2019). Table 3.4 summarizes language milestones in infancy.

Language Development in Bilingual Infants

How is language learning influenced by exposure to two languages? Language development is promoted through exposure to speech during frequent, high-quality social interactions. In bilingual babies the amount of infant-directed speech heard in one-to-one interactions influences the growth of that language but is unrelated to growth of the second language (Kuhl & Ramirez, 2016). For example, hearing lots of high quality Spanish in interactions with a caregiver predicts the growth of Spanish but not English.

Typically, infants exposed to two languages from birth babble and produce their first words at the same time as a those exposed to one language. Notably, bilingual infants retain the ability to discriminate phonetic speech sounds of other languages long after monolingual peers have narrowed their perception to native language sounds (Garcia-Sierra et al., 2011; Petitto et al., 2012).

Bilingual infants' vocabulary develops in similar ways as monolingual infants' (Kuhl & Ramirez, 2016). Infants' language skills reflect the quantity of language that they hear. The rate of vocabulary

TABLE 3.4 ■ Language Milestones

Age	Language Skill
2–3 months	Cooing
6 months	Babbling
1 year	First word Holophrases
16–24 months	Vocabulary spurt Learn new words by fast mapping
21 months	Telegraphic speech
21–30 months	Syntax

and grammatical growth in bilingual children correlates with quality and quantity of speech that they hear in each language (Ramírez-Esparza et al., 2017) Although bilingual infants tend to show a smaller vocabulary than monolingual infants in a single language when both languages are considered, bilingual children do not lag behind monolingual peers (Hoff et al., 2012; Hoff & Core, 2015). Moreover, some research suggests that bilingual infants are better at learning new words than their monolingual peers (Singh et al., 2018). Their exposure to the sounds of multiple languages contributes to their ability to flexibly learn new sounds.

Influences on Language Development: Interactionist Perspective

Language development is a complex process reflecting the dynamic interplay of two factors: children's biological capacities and the social context in which they are reared. A newborn's ability to discriminate a wide variety of speech sounds and prefer human speech and the sounds of his or her native language over those of other languages suggests an inborn sensitivity to language. Yet the language that an infant learns and the pace of learning are influenced by environmental factors.

Biological Influences

The brain is wired for language at birth. Speech sounds produce more activity in the left side of both newborn and adult brains (Vannasing et al., 2016; Dehaene-Lambertz, 2017). Two areas in the left hemisphere of the brain are vital for language: Broca's and Wernicke's areas (Friederici, 2017). **Broca's area** controls the ability to use language for expression. Damage to this area inhibits the ability to speak fluently, leading to errors in the production of language. Wernicke's area is responsible for language comprehension. Damage to **Wernicke's area** impairs the ability to understand the speech of others and sometimes affects the ability to speak coherently. Although the brain plays a crucial role in language capacities, it cannot completely account for language development. Multiple genes associated with language development work together and are influenced by environmental factors and experience (Dediu & Christiansen, 2016; Fisher, 2017).

Linguist Noam Chomsky (1959, 2017) proposed that infants are born with a **language acquisition device (LAD)**, an innate facilitator of language that contains a storehouse of rules, **universal grammar**, that apply to all human languages. The LAD enables infants to quickly and efficiently analyze everyday speech and determine its rules, regardless of whether their native language is English, German, Chinese, or Urdu (Yang et al., 2017). When infants hear language spoken, they naturally notice its linguistic properties, and they acquire it. The LAD can account for children's unique utterances and the unusual grammatical mistakes they make in speaking because children are biologically primed to acquire language and do not rely on learning. However, researchers have not identified the LAD or universal grammar that Chomsky thought underlies all languages, and there are more individual differences in language learning and in languages than Chomsky proposed (Dąbrowska, 2015; Ibbotson & Tomasello, 2016). Moreover, language does not emerge in a finished form. Instead, children learn

Through infant-directed speech, adults attract infants' attention by using shorter words and sentences, higher and more varied pitch, repetition, and a slower rate. Infants prefer listening to infant-directed speech, and infant-directed speech appears cross-culturally.

istock/ damircudic

to string words together over time based on their experiences as well on as trial and error (Tomasello, 2012). Although language development has biological influences, it is also influenced by the contexts in which infants are immersed.

Contextual Influences

Language development occurs in a social context. Most adults naturally speak to young infants in a sing-song way that attracts their attention. **Infant-directed speech** uses repetition, short words and sentences, high and varied pitch, and long pauses (Thiessen et al., 2005). Infants prefer listening to infant-directed speech than to typical adult speech, and they prefer adults who use infant-directed speech (Schachner & Hannon, 2011). Infant-directed speech exaggerates sounds, helping infants hear and distinguish sounds, and enables them to map sounds to meanings (Estes & Hurley, 2013; Kitamura & Burnham, 2003; Peter et al., 2016).

Adults naturally talk to infants and infant-directed speech has been documented in many languages and countries, including Kenya, Fiji, and the United States (Broesch & Bryant, 2015; Bryant et al., 2012; Kuhl et al., 1997). The pattern of infant-directed speech is similar across cultures such that adults can discriminate it from adult-directed speech even while listening to a language they do not speak.

There are also some cultural differences in the use of infant-directed speech. In Samoa, infants are not addressed directly by caregivers until they begin to crawl. Parents tend to interpret their vocalizations as indicators of physiological state rather than as attempts to communicate. Because of the status hierarchy in Samoa, child-directed speech is uncommon in adults because it would reflect someone of higher status (i.e., an adult) adjusting his or her speech to someone of lower status (Ochs & Schieffein, 1984). Instead, older children are tasked with responding to infants' utterances, and it is largely older children who talk with infants (Lieven & Stoll, 2010). Similarly, the Kaluli of Papua New Guinea do not engage in infant-directed speech (Fitneva & Matsui, 2015). Infants are held oriented outward rather than toward the mother. When infants are addressed by others, the mother speaks for the infant in a high-pitched voice but does not use simplified language. Only when children themselves begin to talk do parents start talking to them, and then they focus on teaching them what to say (Ochs & Schieffein, 1984).

Parents from different cultures vary in how often they respond to their infants, but parental response patterns that are warm, consistent, and contingent on infant actions predict positive language development in infants across cultures.

Spencer Robertson/Newscom

Although parents from different cultures vary in how often they respond to their infants, parental response patterns that are warm, consistent, and contingent on infant actions are associated with positive language development in infants across cultures (Rodriguez & Tamis-LeMonda, 2011). Parental responsiveness to infants' vocalizations predicts the size of infants' vocabularies, the diversity of infants' communications, and the timing of language milestones (Tamis-LeMonda et al., 2014). Children whose mothers address a great deal of speech to them develop vocabulary more rapidly, are faster at processing words they know, and are faster at producing speech than children whose mothers speak to them less often (Hurtado et al., 2008; Weisleder & Fernald, 2013). The number of words and different grammatical structures used in maternal speech, as well as grammatical complexity, predict the size of children's vocabulary and understanding of grammar (Hadley et al., 2011; Huttenlocher et al., 2010).

Parents do not reliably reinforce correct grammar, but they tend to communicate in ways that tell young children when they have made errors and show how to correct them (Saxton, 1997). Adults often respond to children's utterances with expansions, which are enriched versions of the children's statements. If a child says, "bottle fall," the parent might respond, "Yes, the bottle fell off the table." Adults also tend to **recast** children's sentences into new grammatical forms. "Kitty go," might be recast into, "Where is the kitty going?" When children use grammatically correct statements, parents maintain and extend the conversation (Bohannon & Stanowicz, 1988). When adults recast and expand young children's speech, the children tend to acquire grammatical rules more quickly and score higher on tests of expressive language ability than when parents rely less on these conversational techniques (Abraham et al., 2013; Bohannon et al., 1996).

In sum, an interactionist approach to language development emphasizes the dynamic and reciprocal influence of biology and context. Infants are equipped with biological propensities and information processing capacities that permit them to perceive and analyze speech and learn to speak. Infants are motivated to communicate with others, and language is a tool for communication. Interactions with others provide important learning experiences, which help infants expand their language capacities and learn to think in ways similar to members of their culture (Fitneva & Matsui, 2015).

Thinking in Context: Lifespan Development

1. What role do other domains of development hold in influencing infants' language development? Consider motor development, perception, and cognition. How might advances in these domains influence infants' emerging language abilities? Can language development influence other areas of development?

2. Language is biologically programmed to unfold without instruction. Discuss this statement, applying what you know about biological and contextual influences on language. Do you agree or disagree with the statement? Explain.

Thinking in Context: Applied Developmental Science

1. What can parents do to promote language development in their infants? Provide advice to parents in light of the interactionist perspective, including the role of infant-directed speech and parental responsiveness.

CHAPTER SUMMARY

3.1 Discuss patterns of and influences on physical growth and brain development during infancy and toddlerhood.

Growth proceeds from the head downward (cephalocaudal) and from the center of the body outward (proximodistal). Breastfeeding is associated with many benefits for mothers and infants, but many women experience barriers to breastfeeding. At about 6 months infants begin to eat solid foods. Malnourishment is associated with growth stunting and impaired learning, concentration, and language skills throughout childhood and adolescence.

The brain develops through several processes: neurogenesis (the creation of neurons), synaptogenesis (the creation of synapses), pruning (reducing unused neural connections), and myelination (coating the axons with myelin to increase the speed of transmission). Experience shapes the brain structure through pruning. Sleep also plays a role in brain development. Although infancy is a particularly important time for the formation and strengthening of synapses, experience shapes the brain structure at all ages of life.

3.2 Compare and contrast biological, contextual, and dynamic systems explanations for motor development in infancy and toddlerhood.

Infants are born with reflexes, each with its own developmental course. Gross and fine motor skills develop systematically and build on each other, with each new skill preparing the infant to tackle the next. Much of motor development is influenced by maturation, but infants benefit from contextual factors such as opportunities to practice motor skills. Different cultures provide infants with different experiences and opportunities for practice, contributing to cross-cultural differences in motor development. Viewing motor development as dynamic systems of action produced by an infant's abilities, goal-directed behavior, and environmental supports and opportunities accounts for the individual differences that we see in motor development

3.3 Describe infants' developing sensory abilities.

Visual acuity, pattern perception, visual tracking, and color vision improve over the first few months of life. Neonates are sensitive to depth cues and young infants can distinguish depth, but crawling stimulates the perception of depth and the association of fear with sharp drops. Newborns can perceive and discriminate nearly all sounds in human languages, but from birth, they prefer to hear their native language. Intermodal perception is evident at birth as infants can combine information from more than one sensory system.

3.4 Describe the cognitive achievements of infancy and toddlerhood from the perspective of cognitive-developmental, core knowledge, and information processing theories.

According to the **cognitive-developmental perspective**, cognitive development occurs through the processes of assimilation and accommodation. During the sensorimotor stage, from birth to about 2 years old, infants learn about the world through their senses and motor skills, and infant cognition progresses from simple reflexes to intentional action and mental representation, as indicated by object permanence. According to the information processing approach, we are born with the ability to attend and remember, and these abilities improve rapidly. Infants are able to categorize objects, at first based on the perceived similarity. Later on in their first year, infants use conceptual categories based on perceived function and behavior and apply them to organize objects, such as food, furniture, birds, animals, vehicles, kitchen utensils, and more.

3.5 Summarize patterns of language development during infancy and toddlerhood.

Newborns are able to hear all of the sounds of which the human voice is capable, but their ability to perceive nonnative speech sounds declines over the first year of life. Infants progress from cooing to babbling to first words. Infants learn words through fast mapping, but their own speech lags behind what they can understand. At about 21 months of age, most children compose their first simple two-word sentences (telegraphic speech). Learning theory posits that language is learned through operant conditioning. Nativist theorists propose that the human brain has an innate capacity to learn language. An interactionist perspective integrates nature and nurture, noting that we have innate perceptual biases for discriminating and listening to language and are reared in a social context in which adults use infant-directed speech to facilitate language development.

KEY TERMS

accommodation (p. 91)
affordances (p. 90)
assimilation (p. 91)
attention (p. 93)
babbling (p. 98)
Broca's area (p. 101)
categorization (p. 95)
cephalocaudal development (p. 72)
cognitive disequilibrium (p. 92)
cognitive equilibrium (p. 92)
cognitive-developmental perspective (p. 104)
cognitive schemas (p. 91)
cooing (p. 98)
core knowledge theory (p. 93)
cortex (p. 79)
deferred imitation (p. 94)
dynamic systems theory (p. 84)
experience-dependent brain development (p. 79)
experience-expectant brain development (p. 79)
externality effect (p. 87)
fast mapping (p. 99)
fine motor development (p. 82)
gross motor development (p. 81)
growth norms (p. 71)
growth stunting (p. 73)
habituation (p. 86)

holophrases (p. 99)
infant-directed speech (p. 102)
intermodal perception (p. 89)
language acquisition device (LAD) (p. 101)
long-term memory (p. 94)
mental representation (p. 92)
myelin (p. 78)
myelination (p. 78)
neurogenesis (p. 77)
neurons (p. 77)
object permanence (p. 92)
perception (p. 85)
prefrontal cortex (p. 79)
productive language (p. 99)
proximodistal development (p. 72)
recast (p. 103)
receptive language (p. 99)
recognition memory (p. 94)
reflexes (p. 80)
representational thought (p. 93)
sensation (p. 85)
sensitive periods (p. 79)
sudden infant death syndrome (SIDS) (p. 76)
synapses (p. 77)
synaptic pruning (p. 78)
synaptogenesis (p. 77)
telegraphic speech (p. 100)
transfer deficit (p. 97)
universal grammar (p. 101)
visual acuity (p. 85)
vocabulary spurt (p. 100)
Wernicke's area (p. 101)
working memory (p. 94)

4 SOCIOEMOTIONAL DEVELOPMENT IN INFANCY AND TODDLERHOOD

Halfpoint Images/ Getty Images

As a newborn, Terrence expressed distress by spreading his arms, kicking his legs, and crying. When he did this, his mother or father would scoop him up and hold him, trying to comfort him. Terrence began to prefer interacting with attentive adults who cared for him. Soon baby Terrence began to smile and gurgle when held. In turn, Terrence's parents played with him and were delighted to see his animated, excited responses. As a toddler, his emerging language skills enabled Terrence to express his needs in words. He quickly learned that words are powerful tools that can convey emotions ("I love you, Mommy"). Terrence became able to express his ideas and feelings to everyone around him, making for new and more complex relationships with his parents and siblings.

As Terrence illustrates, in the first two years of life, babies learn new ways of expressing their emotions. They become capable of new and more complex emotions and develop a greater sense of self-understanding, social awareness, and self-management. These abilities influence their interactions with others and their emerging social relationships. These processes collectively are referred to as *socioemotional development.* In this chapter, we examine the processes of socioemotional development in infancy and toddlerhood.

PSYCHOSOCIAL DEVELOPMENT IN INFANCY AND TODDLERHOOD

LEARNING OBJECTIVE

4.1 Analyze the psychosocial tasks of infancy and toddlerhood.

According to Erik Erikson (1950), as we travel through the lifespan we proceed through a series of psychosocial crises, or developmental tasks. As discussed in Chapter 1, how well each crisis is resolved influences psychological development and how the individual approaches the next crisis or developmental task. Erikson believed that infants and toddlers progress through two psychosocial stages that influence their personality development: **trust versus mistrust** and **autonomy versus shame and doubt**.

Trust Versus Mistrust

From the day she was born, each time Carla cried, her mother or father would come to her bassinet, rock her, check her diaper, and feed her if necessary. Soon, Carla developed the basic expectation that her parents would meet her needs. According to Erikson (1950), developing a sense of trust versus mistrust is the first developmental task of life. Infants must develop a view of the world as a safe place where their basic needs will be met. Throughout the first year of life, infants depend on their caregivers for food, warmth, and affection. If parents and caregivers attend to the infant's physical and emotional needs and consistently fulfill them, the infant will develop a basic sense of trust in her caregivers and, by extension, in the world in general.

If caregivers are neglectful or inconsistent in meeting infants' needs, they will develop a sense of mistrust, feeling that they cannot count on others for love, affection, or the fulfillment of other basic human needs. The sense of trust or mistrust developed in infancy influences how people approach the subsequent stages of development. Specifically, when interaction with adults inspires trust and security, babies are more likely to feel comfortable exploring the world, which enhances their learning, social development, and emotional development (Gedge & Abell, 2020).

Autonomy Versus Shame and Doubt

Two-and-a-half-year-old Shane is an active child who vigorously explores his environment, tests new toys, and attempts to learn about the world on his own. At dinnertime, he wants to feed himself and gets angry when his parents try to feed him. Each morning, Shane takes pleasure in attempting to dress himself and expresses frustration when his mother helps. Shane is progressing through the second stage in Erikson's scheme of psychosocial development—autonomy versus shame and doubt—which is concerned with establishing a sense of autonomy, or the feeling that one can make choices and direct oneself.

Toddlers walk on their own, express their own ideas and needs, and become more independent. Their developmental task is to learn to do things for themselves and feel confident in their ability to maneuver in their environment. According to Erikson (1950), if parents encourage toddlers' initiative and allow them to explore, experiment, make mistakes, and test limits, toddlers will develop autonomy, self-reliance, self-control, and confidence. If parents are overprotective or disapprove of their toddlers' struggle for independence, the children may begin to doubt their abilities to do things by themselves, may feel ashamed of their desire for autonomy, may passively observe, and may not develop a sense of independence and self-reliance.

Children take pride in completing self-care tasks, such as tooth brushing, all by themselves, developing a sense of autonomy.

iStock/dszc

Both trust and autonomy develop out of warm and sensitive parenting and developmentally appropriate expectations for exploration and behavioral control (Lewis & Abell, 2020). Without a secure sense of trust in caregivers, toddlers will struggle to establish and maintain close relationships with others and will find it challenging to develop autonomy. Much of the research on parenting examines mothers, but fathers' interactions with infants also support autonomy development (Hughes et al., 2018). Parenting practices that promote the development of autonomy in infants and toddlers include explaining problems in developmentally appropriate ways, teaching different ways of communicating empathy, and modeling desired behaviors (Andreadakis et al., 2019). These practices also help infants and toddlers internalize rules and learn how to regulate or direct their behavior (Meuwissen & Carlson, 2019). Children who develop a sense of individuality and confidence in their own abilities to meet new challenges are better equipped to interact with and adapt to the world around them.

Thinking in Context: Applied Developmental Science

1. What kinds of behaviors on the part of parents promote a sense of trust in infants? What would you advise new parents to do to help their infants develop trust?
2. Do trust-promoting activities, such as attentiveness and cuddling, also foster a sense of autonomy in infants? Why or why not?

Thinking in Context: Lifespan Development

Families are immersed in contexts that differ in many ways: urban, suburban, or rural, with varying levels of socioeconomic status, access to health resources, safety, and exposure to racism and discrimination.

1. How might these differences and parents' experiences influence their interactions with infants and their infants' psychosocial development?
2. Would you expect infants in each of these contexts to demonstrate trust and autonomy in similar ways? Why or why not?

EMOTIONAL DEVELOPMENT IN INFANCY AND TODDLERHOOD

LEARNING OBJECTIVE

4.2 Describe emotional development and the role of contextual influences on emotional development in infants and toddlers.

What emotions do infants feel? Infants cannot describe their experiences and feelings, which makes studying their emotional development quite challenging. Most people show their emotions on their faces, such as by smiling or frowning. If we use facial expressions as a guide to what emotions infants might feel, the first and most reliable emotion that newborns show is distress. They cry, wail, and flail their arms and bodies, alerting caregivers to their need for attention. Newborns also show interest with wide-eyed gazes when something catches their attention, and they smile when they are happy.

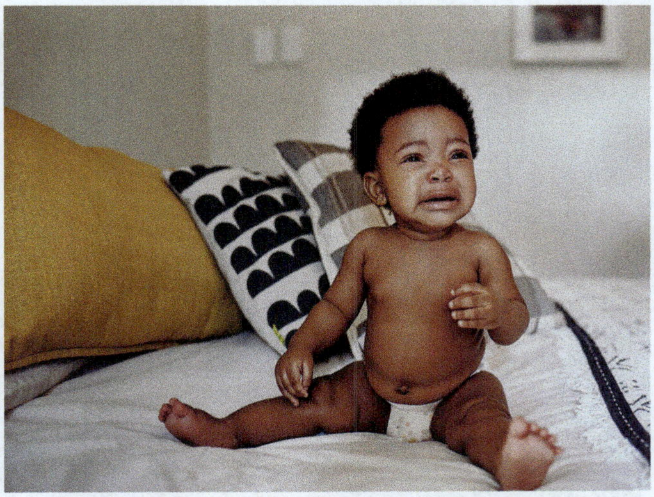

Even young infants exhibit a wide range of emotions. Observation of newborn facial expressions suggests that newborns experience interest, distress, disgust, and happiness or contentment. Between 2 and 7 months of age, they begin to display other emotions, such as anger, sadness, surprise, and fear.

mapodile/ Getty Images

Infants' Emotional Experience

Are we born with the ability to feel emotions? Newborns show facial expressions that are associated with interest, distress, disgust, and happiness or contentment (Izard et al., 2010). Infants' facial expressions are remarkably similar to those of adults (Sullivan & Lewis, 2003), but we do not know whether internal emotional states accompany their facial expressions. We cannot ask infants what they feel, so it is not clear whether newborns experience the emotions that their faces show.

Basic Emotions

Basic emotions, also known as primary emotions (happiness, sadness, interest, surprise, fear, anger, and disgust) are

TABLE 4.1 ■ Milestones in Emotional Development

Approximate Age	Milestone
Birth	Basic emotions Discriminates mother
2–3 months	Social smile Distinguishes happiness, anger, surprise, and sadness
6–8 months	Fear, stranger anxiety, and separation protest occur
7–12 months	Social referencing
18–24 months	Self-conscious emotions appear. Develops vocabulary for talking about emotions

universal, experienced by people around the world (Cordaro et al., 2018; Lench et al., 2018). Basic emotions emerge in all infants at about the same ages and are seen and interpreted similarly in all cultures that have been studied, suggesting that they are inborn (Izard et al., 2010). Between 2 and 7 months of age, infants begin to display anger, sadness, joy, surprise, and fear.

Research with adults suggests that emotions are the result of interactions among richly connected, subcortical brain structures, including the brainstem and the limbic system, as well as parts of the cerebral cortex (Celeghin et al., 2017; Kragel & LaBar, 2016). These structures develop prenatally and are present in animals, suggesting that emotions serve a biological purpose, are crucial to survival, and are likely experienced by infants (Rolls, 2017; Turner, 2014).

Emotions develop in predictable ways (see Table 4.1). Although basic emotions are thought to be inborn, the ways that they are expressed and the conditions that elicit them change during the first few months of life. In adults, smiling indicates happiness. Newborns smile, and smiling is one of the most important emotional expressions in infancy. Newborn smiles are reflexive, involuntary, and linked with shifts in arousal state (e.g., going from being asleep to drowsy wakefulness), and they occur frequently during periods of rapid eye movement (REM) sleep (Challamel et al., 2020; Kawakami et al., 2008). At about 3 weeks, infants smile while awake and alert and in response to familiarity—familiar sounds, voices, and tastes (Sroufe & Waters, 1976).

During the second month of life, as infants' vision improves, they smile more in response to visual stimuli—sights that catch their attention, such as bright objects coming into view (Sroufe, 1997). The **social smile**, which occurs in response to familiar people, emerges between 6 and 10 weeks of age and is an important milestone in infant development because it shows social engagement (Messinger & Fogel, 2007). The social smile plays a large role in initiating and maintaining social interactions between infants and adults, especially by enhancing caregiver–child bonding. Parents are enthralled when their baby shows delight in seeing them, and the parents' happy response encourages their baby to smile even more (Beebe et al., 2016).

Smiling is one of the most important emotional expressions in infancy because it plays a role in initiating and maintaining social interactions between infants and adults.

iStock/quavondo

As infants grow, laughs begin to accompany their smiles, and they laugh more often and at more things. Infants may show clear expressions of joy, or intense happiness, as early as 2 ½ months of age while playing with a parent and at 3 to 4 months of age in response to stimuli that they find highly arousing (Messinger et al., 2019). At 6 months of age, an infant might laugh at unusual sounds or sights, such as when Mommy puts a bowl on her head or makes a funny face. Laughing at unusual events illustrates the baby's increasing cognitive competence as he or she knows what to expect and is surprised when something unexpected occurs. By 1 year of age infants can smile deliberately to engage an adult.

Negative emotions change over time as well. Distress is evident at birth when newborns experience the discomfort of hunger, a heel prick, or a chilly temperature. Anger appears at about 6 months of age and develops rapidly, becoming more complex in terms of elicitors and responses (Dollar & Calkins, 2019). Initially, physical restrictions, such as being restrained in a high chair or being dressed, can elicit anger. The inability to carry out a desired act, such as unsuccessfully reaching to obtain a desired toy, can also provoke frustration and anger. Between 8 and 20 months of age, infants gradually become more reactive, and anger is more easily aroused (Braungart-Rieker et al., 2010). They become aware of the actions of others, so that anger can be elicited by others' behavior. An infant may become upset when Mommy goes to the door to leave, or when Grandma takes out the towels in preparation for bath time. During the second year of life, temper tantrums become common when the toddler's attempts at autonomy are thwarted and he or she experiences frustration or stress. The anger escalates with the child's stress level (Potegal et al., 2007). Some toddlers show extreme tantrums, lie on the floor, scream, and jerk their arms and legs. Other children's tantrums are more subtle. They may whine, mope, and stick out their lower lip. Similar to adults, infants' emotional expressions are tied to their own experiences and infants display emotional responses to stimuli that are unique to them (Camras, 2019).

Self-Conscious Emotions

Emotional development is an orderly process in which complex emotions build on the foundation of simple emotions. The development of **self-conscious emotions**, or secondary emotions—such as empathy, pride, embarrassment, shame, and guilt—depends on cognitive development, as well as an awareness of self. Self-conscious emotions do not begin to emerge until about 15 to 18 months, and they largely develop during the second and third years of life (Lewis, 2019). In order to experience self-conscious emotions, toddlers must be able to have a sense of self, observe themselves and others, be aware of standards and rules, and compare their behavior with those standards (Lewis, 2016). Feelings of pride, for example, arise from accomplishing a personally meaningful goal, whereas guilt derives from realizing that one has violated a standard of conduct. Parental evaluations are the initial basis for many secondary emotions (Goodvin et al., 2015).

Emotion Regulation

As children become aware of social standards and rules, **emotion regulation**—the ability to control their emotions—becomes important. How do infants regulate emotions? During the first two to three months of life, infants manage negative emotions by sucking vigorously on their hands or objects. At about three months of age, infants start to use voluntary motor behaviors, such as turning their bodies away from distressing stimuli (Baker, 2018).

Smiling is also thought to serve a purpose in regulating emotions, as it allows infants to control aspects of a situation without losing touch with it. When infants get excited and smile, they often look away briefly. This involuntary behavior may be a way of breaking themselves away from the stimulus and allowing them to regroup, preventing overstimulation. Smiling is associated with a decline in heart rate, suggesting that it is a relaxation response to decrease infants' level of arousal.

Whereas 6-month-old infants are more likely to use gaze aversion and fussing as primary emotion regulatory strategies, 12-month-old infants are more likely to use self-soothing (e.g., thumb sucking, rocking themselves) and distraction (chewing on objects, playing with toys). Responsive caregiving that acts on behalf of children's responses, helping them orient or move toward or away from overwhelming stimuli, can help infants and toddlers regulate their emotions (Stifter & Augustine, 2019). With advances in cognition and motor control the infant can explore the environment by walking, initiate social interactions, and remember past experiences (Baker, 2018). By 18 months of age, toddlers actively attempt to change the distressing situation, such as by moving away from upsetting stimuli, and the begin to use distraction, such as by playing with toys or talking (Crockenberg & Leerkes, 2004; Feldman et al., 2011). The caregiving environment plays a large role in infants' and toddlers' emerging abilities to engage in self-regulation. Warm and supportive interactions with parents and other caregivers can help infants understand their emotions and learn how to manage them.

Social Interaction and Emotional Development

Infants and young children often need outside assistance in regulating their emotions. Interactions with parents and caregivers helps infants understand and learn to manage their emotions.

Sensitive Caregiving

Caregivers help infants regulate their emotions by using soothing behaviors and minimizing their exposure to overwhelming stimuli. Sensitive responses coupled with soft vocalizations aid 3-month-old infants in regulating distress (Spinelli & Mesman, 2018). Sensitive caregivers respond to infants' emotional reactions and try to satisfy their needs, attempt to elicit positive responses and minimize negative ones, and seek to maintain an optimal level of arousal (stimulating but not overwhelming) in their infant (Baker, 2018). When mothers responded promptly to their 2-month-old infants' cries, these same infants, at 4 months of age, cried for shorter durations, were better able to manage their emotions, and stopped crying more quickly than other infants (Jahromi & Stifter, 2007). Caregiver sensitivity predicts self-regulation in infancy into middle childhood (Morawska et al., 2019). Responsive parenting that is attuned to infants' needs helps infants develop skills in emotion regulation, especially in managing negative emotions like anxiety, as well as their physiological correlates, such as accelerated heart rate (Feldman et al., 2011).

Parents help their infants learn to manage emotions through a variety of strategies, including direct intervention, modeling, selective reinforcement, control of the environment, verbal instruction, and touch (Stifter & Augustine, 2019; Waters et al., 2017). These strategies change as the infants grow older. Touching becomes a less common regulatory strategy with age, whereas vocalizing and distracting techniques increase (Meléndez, 2005). When mothers provide guidance in helping infants regulate their emotions, the infants tend to engage in distraction and mother-oriented strategies, such as seeking help, during frustrating events (Thomas et al., 2017). Parents who model emotion regulation strategies, such as distraction, are more likely to have toddlers who use those strategies to soothe themselves in stressful situations (Schoppmann et al., 2019).

Parent-Infant Interaction

Parent-infant interactions undergo continuous transformations over time. Infants' growing motor skills influence their interactions with parents, as well as their socioemotional development. Crawling, creeping, and walking introduce new challenges to parent-infant interaction and socioemotional growth (Adolph & Franchak, 2017). As crawling begins, parents and caregivers respond with happiness and pride, positive emotions that encourage infants' exploration. As infants gain motor competence, they wander further from parents (Thurman & Corbetta, 2017). Crawling increases a toddler's capability to attain goals—a capability that, while often satisfying to the toddler, may involve hazards.

As infants become more mobile, emotional outbursts become more common. Parents report that advances in locomotion are accompanied by increased frustration as toddlers attempt to move in ways that often exceed their abilities or are not permitted by parents (Clearfield, 2011; Pemberton Roben et al., 2012). When mothers recognize the dangers posed to toddlers by objects such as houseplants, vases, and electrical appliances, they sharply increase their expressions of anger and fear, often leading to fear and frustration in their toddlers. Parents actively monitor toddlers' whereabouts, protect them from dangerous situations, and expect them to comply—a dynamic that is often a struggle, amounting to a test of wills. At the same time, these struggles help the child to begin to develop a grasp of mental states in others that are different from his or her own.

Changes in emotional expression and regulation are dynamic because the changing child influences the changing parent. In particular, mothers and infants systematically influence and regulate each other's emotions and behaviors. Mothers regulate infant emotional states by interpreting their emotional signals, providing appropriate arousal, and reciprocating and reinforcing infant reactions. Infants regulate their mother's emotions through their receptivity to her initiations and stimulation and by responding to her emotions (Bornstein et al., 2011, 2012). By experiencing a range of emotional interactions—times when their emotions mirror those of their caregivers and times when their emotions are different from those of their caregivers—infants learn how to transform negative emotions into neutral or positive emotions and regulate their own emotional states (Guo et al., 2015).

Responsive parenting helps infants learn to manage their emotions and self-regulate.
iStock/AleksandarNakic

Social Referencing

Early in life, infants become able to discriminate facial expressions that indicate emotion. In one study, although 2-day-old infants initially did not show a preference for a happy or disgusted face, after being habituated to either a happy or disgusted face they successfully discriminated between the two, suggesting an early sensitivity to dynamic faces expressing emotions (Addabbo et al., 2018). Likewise, newborns are able to discriminate happy faces from fearful ones (Farroni et al., 2007). It is thought that infants are innately prepared to attend to facial displays of emotion because such displays are biologically significant and the ability to recognize them is important for human survival (Leppanen, 2011). Between 2 and 4 months of age, infants can distinguish emotional expressions such as happiness as opposed to anger, surprise, and sadness (Bornstein et al., 2013). At 6 ½ months, infants can identify and match happy, angry, and sad emotions portrayed on faces and also body movements indicating emotion (Hock et al., 2017).

Beyond recognizing the emotional expressions of others, infants also respond to them. Between 6 and 10 months of age, infants begin to use **social referencing**, looking to caregivers' or other adults' emotional expressions to find clues for how to interpret and respond to ambiguous events (Ruba & Repacholi, 2019;Walle et al., 2017). Social referencing influences infants' emotional reactions and, ultimately, behavior. When toddlers grab the sofa to pull themselves up, turn, and then tumble over as they take a step, they look to their caregivers to determine how to interpret their fall. If caregivers respond with fearful facial expressions, infants are likely to also be fearful, but if caregivers instead smile, infants will probably remain calm and return to their attempts at walking. The use of social referencing is one way that infants demonstrate their understanding that others experience emotions and thoughts.

Older infants tend to show a negativity bias when it comes to social referencing. That is, they attend to and follow social referencing cues more closely when the cues indicate negative attitudes toward an object, compared with neutral or happy attitudes (Vaish et al., 2008). Infants' behavior may be more influenced by the emotional message conveyed in the vocal information than the facial expressions themselves, especially within the context of fearful messages (Biro et al., 2014; Ruba & Repacholi, 2019).

How infants employ social referencing changes with development. Ten-month-old infants show selective social referencing. They monitor the caregiver's attention and do not engage in social referencing when the adult is not attending or engaged (Stenberg, 2017). At 12 months, infants use referential cues such as the caregiver's body posture, gaze, and voice direction to determine to what objects caregivers' emotional responses refer (Brooks & Meltzoff, 2008). Twelve-month-old infants are more likely to use a caregiver's cues as guides in ambivalent situations when the caregiver responds promptly to the infants' behavior (Stenberg, 2017). Social referencing reflects infants' growing understanding of the emotional states of others; it signifies that infants can observe, interpret, and use emotional information from others to form their own interpretation and response to events.

Experiencing adversity early in life may have epigenetic effects on the genes that regulate responses to stress. The caregiving environment also influences the developing stress response system and can buffer the negative effects of trauma.
REUTERS / Alamy Stock Photo

Exposure to Early Life Stress

Many infants live in stressful contexts and are exposed to adversity, including maltreatment, poverty, and violence. Very young infants likely do not recall specific experiences and events, but early exposure to trauma may affect infants' development in ways that can last a lifetime. Whereas maladaptive contexts may pose risks of physical harm to children, with negative influences on brain development, trauma poses invisible long-term risks to children's emotional development and mental health (Juruena et al., 2020; Mueller & Tronick, 2019).

Early trauma may exert a biological effect on emotional development. The experience of early social adversity may have epigenetic effects, controlling the genes that regulate the endocrine system, which controls hormone production and release at all ages in life (Agorastos et al., 2019; Conradt, 2017). Infancy may be a particularly plastic time in development, with heightened potential for epigenetic changes that may sensitize individuals' responses to stress throughout a lifetime (Laurent et al., 2016).

Not all infants respond to early life stress with heightened reactivity. Some infants exposed to trauma show lower levels of stress hormones and reduced reactivity to stress (Turecki & Meaney, 2016). The timing and intensity of adversity influences developmental outcomes. Exposure to particularly intense chronic stress early in development can lead to hyperactive stress responses that may be followed by blunted responses (Laurent et al., 2016). These dulled responses may reflect adaptations to chronically stressful situations. Unpredictable stressors, on the other hand, may lead to heightened stress reactivity as the individual adapts to volatile and unexpected situations (Blair, 2010). Both heightened and blunted stress responses may be adaptive attempts to nonoptimal caregiving environments, yet these adaptations may carry behavioral costs, such as heightened distress when confronted with stress and longer term anxiety and depressive symptoms, which negatively affect developmental trajectories (Laurent et al., 2016).

Early life stress poses risks to emotional development, but the caregiving environment also influences the developing stress response system. Mothers buffer and regulate infants' hormonal and behavioral responses to threats (Howell et al., 2017). Sensitive mothers tend to have infants who display better self-regulation during stressful events; intrusive mothers tend to have the opposite effect (Enlow et al., 2014). Sensitive caregiving can reduce the negative epigenetic effects of early life stress (Janusek et al., 2019;Provenzi et al., 2020). Warm parenting within a predictable stimulating environment with supportive adults and family can help infants develop the self-regulation skills to adapt to adverse contexts. Unfortunately, trauma often disrupts the caregiving system, making adaptation quite difficult.

Cultural Influences on Emotional Development

As we have already seen, emotional development does not occur in a vacuum. Contextual factors, including culture, influence how infants interpret and express emotions, as well as what emotions they feel.

Caregiver Responsiveness

Cultures often have particular beliefs about parenting, including how much responsiveness is appropriate when babies cry and fuss, and expectations about infants' abilities to regulate their own emotions (Halberstadt & Lozada, 2011). The !Kung hunter-gatherers of Botswana, Africa, respond to babies' cries nearly immediately (within 10 seconds), whereas Western mothers tend to wait a considerably longer period of time before responding to infants' cries (e.g., 10 minutes; Barr et al., 1991). Fijian mothers tend to be more responsive than U.S. mothers to negative facial expressions in their infants (Broesch et al., 2016). Gusii mothers believe that constant holding, feeding, and physical care are essential for keeping an infant calm, which in turn protects the infant from harm and disease; therefore, like !Kung mothers, Gusii mothers respond immediately to their babies' cries (LeVine et al., 1994). Infants from non-Western cultures are thought to cry very little because they are carried often (Bleah & Ellett, 2010). In one study, infants born to parents who were recent immigrants from Africa cried less than U.S. infants, suggesting cultural differences that may influence infant cries (Bleah & Ellett, 2010).

Caregivers' responses to infant cries influence infants' capacity for self-regulation and responses to stress. Babies who receive more responsive and immediate caregiving when distressed show lower rates of persistent crying, spend more time in happy and calm states, and cry less overall as they approach their first birthday (Axia & Weisner, 2002; Papoušek & Papoušek, 1990). Yet, the form that responsiveness takes can vary with culture and socialization goals.

Emotional Socialization

Every society has a set of **emotional display rules** that specify the circumstances under which various emotions should or should not be expressed (Safdar et al., 2009). We are socialized to learn and enact these rules very early in life through interactions with others. Interactions among parents and infants are shaped by the culture in which they live, which, in turn, influences the emotional expressions they share and display (Bornstein, Arterberry, & Lamb, 2013).

Western cultures tend to emphasize autonomy and independence. Parents in these cultures tend to encourage emotional expression in their children, often through modeling. When North American mothers play with their 7-month-old babies, for instance, they tend to model positive emotions, restricting their own emotional displays to show joy, interest, and surprise (Malatesta & Haviland, 1982). They also are more attentive to infants' expression of positive emotions, such as interest or surprise and respond less to negative emotions (Broesch et al., 2016). Italian mothers tend to welcome and encourage infants' self-expressive smiles and coos (Bornstein et al., 2012). Through early interactions with caregivers, children learn about the stimuli that elicit emotions, what emotions to show, and how to regulate emotions (Yang & Wang, 2019).

East Asian cultures tend to deemphasize emotional expression, viewing it as disruptive to group harmony. Parents in these cultures tend to express emotion less frequently. In one study, Chinese immigrant parents' emotional expressivity was related to their cultural orientation (Chen et al., 2015). Parents who were positively oriented toward American culture tended to show more emotional expression whereas those who were oriented more toward Chinese culture tended to be less emotionally expressive. Similar observations of emotional expressivity of mothers and their 4-month-old infants during face-to-face interactions showed European American mothers spent more time displaying positive affect and less time expressing neutral or negative affect than did Chinese mothers who had recently immigrated to the U.S. (Liu et al., 2013). Mothers' interactions and emotional expressivity varied with their cultural orientation. Second-generation Chinese immigrant mothers or those who had immigrated to the U.S. more than 10 years ago showed similar patterns of emotional expressivity as European American mothers (Liu et al., 2013).

Which emotions are considered acceptable, as well as how they should be expressed, differs by culture and context (Yang & Wang, 2019). Whereas North American parents tickle and stimulate their babies, encouraging squeals of pleasure, the Gusii and Aka people of Central Africa prefer to keep babies calm and quiet. They engage in little face-to-face play and look away as infants display peaks of positive emotion (Hewlett et al., 1998; LeVine et al., 1994). Cameroonian Nso parents, members of a rural farming culture, expect calmness from children (Keller & Otto, 2009). Infants' emotional expressions are not reciprocated by adults, and Cameroonian Nso

In some cultures, infants cry very little, perhaps because they are in constant contact with their mothers.

VW Pics / Contributor/ Getty Images

infants soon learn to display calm, sober faces. Although at surface glance, it might appear as if Nso adults ignore their infants' emotional expressions, that is not the case. Instead, Nso parents and infants display a different path toward emotional expression and emotional regulation than Western infants (Lavelli et al., 2019). Nso infants are often in body contact with their mothers, and their emotional expressions are monitored more by maternal body attention than visual attention (Keller, 2019). It is through these patterns of body contact that Nso infants experience interactional warmth and learn emotional regulation, as compared with the visual interactions that characterize Western infant-parent dyads.

The specific emotional display rules that infants learn, whether to express or restrain strong positive and negative emotions, varies with culture. Cultures also specify the conditions under which emotions should be shown and the stimuli that should evoke emotion.

Stranger Wariness

Many infants around the world display **stranger wariness** (also known as *stranger anxiety*), a fear of unfamiliar people. In many, but not all, cultures, stranger wariness emerges at about 6 months and increases throughout the first year of life, beginning to decrease after about 15 months of age (Bornstein et al., 2013; Sroufe, 1977). Locomotion—infant success in crawling or walking—tends to precede the emergence of stranger wariness, suggesting interconnections among motor and emotional development (Brand et al., 2020). From an evolutionary perspective, stranger wariness may have emerged to protect infants as they became able to initiate new interactions with unknown and potentially unsafe adults (Hahn-Holbrook et al., 2010).

Whether infants show stranger wariness depends on the infants' overall temperament, their past experience, and the situation in which they meet a stranger (Thompson & Limber, 1991). The pattern of stranger wariness varies among infants. Some show rapid increases and others show slow increases in stranger wariness; once wariness has been established, some infants show steady decline and others show more rapid changes. Twin studies suggest that these patterns are influenced by genetics because the patterns of change are more similar among monozygotic twins (identical twins who share 100% of their genes) than dizygotic twins (fraternal twins who share 50% of their genes; Brooker et al., 2013).

Among North American infants, stranger wariness is generally expected by parents and caregivers. Infants of the Efe people of Zaire, Africa, show little stranger wariness. This is likely related to the Efe collective caregiving system, in which Efe babies are passed from one adult to another, relatives and nonrelatives alike (Tronick et al., 1992), and the infants form relationships with the many people who care for them (Meehan & Hawks, 2013). In contrast, babies reared in Israeli kibbutzim (cooperative agricultural settlements that tend to be isolated) tend to demonstrate widespread wariness of strangers. By the end of the first year, when infants look to others for cues about how to respond emotionally, kibbutz babies display far greater anxiety than babies reared in Israeli cities (Saarni et al., 1998). In this way, stranger wariness may be adaptive, modifying infants' drive to explore in light of contextual circumstances (Easterbrooks et al., 2012).

As attachments form, infants become more wary and display "stranger anxiety" when in the presence of unfamiliar people. In many, but not all, cultures stranger wariness emerges at about 6 months and increases throughout the first year of life.

YOSHIKAZU TSUNO/AFP/Getty Images

Stranger wariness illustrates the dynamic interactions between the individual and context (LoBue & Adolph, 2019). Infants' emotionality and temperamental style, tendencies toward social interaction, and, of course, past experience with strangers are important. Parental expectations and anxiety also matter. Infants whose mothers report greater stress reactivity, who experience more anxiety and negative affect in response to stress, show higher rates of stranger wariness (Brooker et al., 2013; Waters et al., 2014). Characteristics of the stranger (e.g., his or her height), the familiarity of the setting, and how quickly the stranger approaches influence how the infant appraises the situation (LoBue et al., 2019). Infants are more open when the stranger is sensitive to the infant's signals and approaches at the infant's pace (Mangelsdorf, 1992). Not all infants show stranger wariness. Instead, whether, how, and how long infants demonstrate emergence of stranger wariness is the result of the complex interplay among individual characteristics, experiences, and context (LoBue & Adolph, 2019). Much of emotional development is the result of the interplay of infants' emerging capacities and the contexts in which they are raised.

Thinking in Context: Lifespan Development

1. Identify examples of how infants' emotional development is influenced by their interactions within their social and cultural contexts. Identify two examples of factors or experiences that promote healthy emotional development and one that might hinder emotional development. Explain your choices.

2. How might social referencing and stranger wariness reflect adaptative responses to a particular context? Why does stranger wariness vary among children and cultures?

3. In what ways might emotional display rules, such as those regarding the display of positive and negative emotions, illustrate adaptive responses to a particular context? Consider the context in which you were raised. What emotional displays do you think are most adaptive for infants?

TEMPERAMENT IN INFANCY AND TODDLERHOOD

LEARNING OBJECTIVE

4.3 Discuss the styles and stability of temperament including the role of goodness of fit in infant development.

"Joshua is such an easygoing baby!" gushed his babysitter. "He eats everything, barely cries, and falls asleep without a fuss. I wish all my babies were like him." The babysitter is referring to Joshua's temperament. **Temperament**, the characteristic way in which an individual approaches and reacts to people and situations, is thought to be one of the basic building blocks of emotion and personality (Strelau, 2020). Temperament has strong biological determinants; behavior genetics research has shown genetic bases for temperament (Saudino & Micalizzi, 2015). Yet the expression of temperament reflects reciprocal interactions among genetic predispositions, maturation, and experience (Goodvin et al., 2015; Rothbart, 2011). Every infant behaves in a characteristic, predictable style that is influenced by his or her inborn tendencies toward arousal and stimulation as well as by experiences with adults and contexts (Planalp & Goldsmith, 2020). In other words, every infant displays a particular temperament style.

Styles of Temperament

Begun in 1956, the New York Longitudinal Study is a pioneering study of temperament that followed 133 infants into adulthood. Early in life, the infants in the study demonstrated differences in nine characteristics that are thought to capture the essence of temperament (Buss & Plomin, 1984; Chess & Thomas, 1991; Goldsmith et al., 1987):

- *Activity level.* Some babies wriggle, kick their legs, wave their arms, and move around a great deal, whereas other babies tend to be more still and stay in one place.
- *Rhythmicity.* Some infants are predictable in their patterns of eating, sleeping, and defecating; other babies are not predictable.

- *Approach-withdrawal.* Some babies tend to approach new situations, people, and objects, whereas others withdraw from novelty.
- *Adaptability.* Some babies get used to new experiences and situations quickly; others do not.
- *Intensity of reaction.* Some babies have very extreme reactions, giggling exuberantly and crying with piercing wails. Other babies show more subdued reactions, such as simple smiles and soft, whimpering cries.
- *Threshold of responsiveness.* Some babies notice many types of stimuli—sights, sounds, and touch sensations—and react to them. Other infants notice few types of stimuli and seem oblivious to changes.
- *Quality of mood.* Some babies tend toward near-constant happiness while others tend toward irritability.
- *Distractibility.* Some babies can be easily distracted from objects or situations while others cannot.
- *Attention span.* Some babies play with one toy for a long time without becoming bored, whereas others get bored easily.

Some aspects of infant temperament, particularly activity level, irritability, attention, and sociability or approach-withdrawal, show stability for months and years at a time and, in some cases, even into adulthood (Lemery-Chalfant et al., 2013; Papageorgiou et al., 2014). Infants' growing ability to regulate their attention and emotions holds implications for some components of temperament, such as rhythmicity, distractibility, and intensity of reaction. The components of infant temperament cluster into three profiles (Thomas & Chess, 1977; Thomas et al., 1970):

- **Easy temperament:** Easy babies are often in a positive mood, even-tempered, open, adaptable, regular, and predictable in biological functioning. They establish regular feeding and sleeping schedules easily.
- **Difficult temperament:** Difficult babies are active, irritable, and irregular in biological rhythms. They are slow to adapt to changes in routine or new situations, show intense and frequent unpleasant moods, react vigorously to change, and have trouble adjusting to new routines.
- **Slow-to-warm-up temperament:** Just as it sounds, slow-to-warm-up babies tend to be inactive, moody, and slow to adapt to new situations and people. They react to new situations with mild irritability but adjust more quickly than do infants with difficult temperaments.

Although it may seem as if all babies could be easily classified, about one-third of the infants in the New York Longitudinal Study did not fit squarely into any of the three categories but displayed a mix of characteristics, such as eating and sleeping regularly but being slow to warm up to new situations (Thomas & Chess, 1977; Thomas et al., 1970).

Another influential model of temperament, by Mary Rothbart, includes three dimensions (Rothbart, 2011; Rothbart & Bates, 2007):

- Extraversion/surgency—the tendency toward positive emotions. Infants who are high in extraversion/surgency approach experiences with confidence, energy, and positivity, as indicated by smiles, laughter, and approach-oriented behaviors.
- Negative affectivity—the tendency toward negative emotions, such as sadness, fear, distress, and irritability.
- Effortful control—the ability to focus attention, shift attention, and inhibit responses in order to manage arousal. Infants who are high in effortful control are able to regulate their arousal and soothe themselves.

From this perspective, temperament reflects how easily we become emotionally aroused or our reactivity to stimuli, as well as how well we are able to control our emotional arousal (Rothbart, 2011). Some infants and children are better able to distract themselves, focus their attention, and inhibit impulses than others. The ability to self-regulate and manage emotions and impulses was shown to be associated with positive long-term adjustment, including academic achievement, social competence, and resistance to stress, in both Chinese and North American samples (Chen & Schmidt, 2015). Generally speaking, a difficult temperament poses risks to adjustment (MacNeill & Pérez-Edgar, 2020). Preterm infants are predisposed to experience difficult temperaments as they tend to show greater arousal, difficulty focusing their attention, and trouble regulating their arousal than full-term infants (Cassiano et al., 2020; Reyes et al., 2019).

Infant temperament tends to be stable over the first year of life but less so than childhood temperament, which can show stability over years, even into adulthood (Bornstein et al., 2019; Strelau, 2020). In infancy, temperament is especially open to environmental influences, such as interactions with others (Bornstein et al., 2015; Gartstein et al., 2016). Young infants' temperament can change with experience, neural development, and sensitive caregiving (e.g., helping babies regulate their negative emotions; Jonas et al., 2015; Thompson et al., 2013). As infants gain experience and learn how to regulate their states and emotions, those who are cranky and difficult may become less so. By the second year of life, styles of responding to situations and people are better established, and temperament becomes more stable. Temperament at age 3 remains stable, predicting temperament at age 6 and personality traits at age 26 (Dyson et al., 2015).

Context and Goodness of Fit

Like all aspects of development, temperament is influenced by reciprocal reactions among individuals and their contexts. An important influence on socioemotional development is the **goodness of fit** between the child's temperament and the environment around him or her, especially the parents' temperaments and child-rearing methods (Chess & Thomas, 1991).

The specific behaviors that comprise adaptive parenting vary with the infants' temperament (MacNeill & Pérez-Edgar, 2020). Infants are at particular risk for poor outcomes when their temperaments show poor goodness of fit to the settings in which they live (Rothbart & Bates, 1998). If an infant who is fussy, difficult, and slow to adapt to new situations is raised by a patient and sensitive caregiver who provides time for him or her to adapt to new routines, the infant may become less cranky and more flexible over time. The infant may adapt her temperament style to match her context so that later in childhood she may no longer be classified as difficult and no longer display behavioral problems (Bates et al., 1998). If, on the other hand, a child with a difficult temperament is reared by a parent who is insensitive, coercive, and difficult in temperament, the child may not learn how to regulate her emotions and may have behavioral problems and adjustment difficulties that worsen with age, even into early adolescence and beyond (Pluess et al., 2010). When children are placed in low-quality caregiving environments, those with difficult temperaments respond more negatively and show more behavior problems than do those with easy temperaments (Poehlmann et al., 2011).

Infant temperament is influenced by and influences the bond with caregivers (Le Bas et al., 2020). Goodness of fit at 4 and 8 months of age predicts a close bond with caregivers at 15 months (Seifer et al., 2014; Takács et al., 2020). An infant's temperament tends to be stable over time because certain temperamental qualities evoke certain reactions from others, promoting goodness of fit. "Easy" babies usually get the most positive reactions from others, whereas babies with a difficult temperament receive mixed reactions (Chess & Thomas, 1991). An "easy" baby tends to smile often, eliciting smiles and positive interactions from others, including parents, which in turn reinforce the baby's "easy" temperamental qualities (Planalp et al., 2017; Wittig & Rodriguez, 2019). Conversely, a "difficult" baby may evoke more frustration and negativity from caregivers as they try unsuccessfully to soothe the baby's fussing. Mothers who view their 6-month-old infants as difficult may be less emotionally available to them (Kim & Teti, 2014). Babies' emotionality and negative emotions predict their mothers' perception of parenting stress and poor parenting behaviors (Oddi et al., 2013; Paulussen-Hoogeboom et al., 2007). Mothers of difficult infants may question their own parenting competence (Takács et al., 2019).

Temperament can also be related to mothers' own temperament, as well as their expectations about their infants and their ability to parent (Grady & Karraker, 2017). In one study, mothers who, *prior to giving birth*, considered themselves less well-equipped to care for their infants were found to be more likely to have infants who showed negative aspects of temperament, such as fussiness, irritability, and difficulty being soothed (Verhage et al., 2013). This suggests that perceptions of parenting may shape views of infant temperament—and thereby shape temperament itself. In other research, three months after giving birth, new mothers' feelings of competence were positively associated with infant temperament. Mothers' beliefs about their ability to nurture are shaped by the interaction between their infants' traits and their own parenting self-efficacy, as well as their opportunities for developing successful caregiving routines (Verhage et al., 2013). This contextual dynamic has been found to hold true across cultures. Both British and Pakistani mothers in the United Kingdom reported fewer problems with their infants' temperaments at 6 months of age when the mothers had a greater sense of parenting efficacy and displayed warmer and less hostile parenting styles (Prady et al., 2014).

Socioemotional development is a dynamic process in which infants' behavior and temperament styles influence the family processes that shape their development. Sensitive and patient caregiving is not always easy with a challenging child, and adults' own temperamental styles influence their caregiving. A poor fit between the caregiver's and infant's temperament can make an infant fussier and crankier. When a difficult infant is paired with a parent with a similar temperament—one who is impatient, irritable, and forceful—behavioral problems in childhood and adolescence are likely (Rubin et al., 1998; Strelau, 2020).

Cultural Differences in Temperament

Researchers have observed consistent cultural differences in temperament that are rooted in cultural norms for how individuals are perceived. Japanese mothers, for example, view their infants as interdependent beings who must learn the importance of relationships and connections with others (Rothbaum et al., 2000). North American mothers, on the other hand, view their task as shaping babies into autonomous beings (Kojima, 1986). Whereas Japanese mothers tend to interact with their babies in soothing ways, discouraging strong emotions, North American mothers are active and stimulating (Rothbaum et al., 2000). Differences in temperament result, such that Japanese infants tend to be more passive, less irritable and vocal, and more easily soothed when upset than North American infants (Kojima, 1986; Lewis et al., 1993b; Rothbaum et al., 2000). Culture influences the behaviors that parents view as desirable and the means that parents use to socialize their infants (Chen & Schmidt, 2015; Kagan, 2013). Culture, therefore, plays a role in how emotional development—in this case, temperament—unfolds.

Asian cultures often prioritize low arousal and emotionality and socialize infants in line with these values. Chinese American, Japanese American, and Hmong children tend to display lower levels of irritability, less physical activity, but also lower levels of positive emotions, and they engage in more self-quieting and self-control than do European American children (Friedlmeier et al., 2015; Slobodskaya et al., 2013; Super & Harkness, 2010). Similarly, a recent comparison of toddlers from Chile, South Korea, Poland, and the United States showed that the South Korean toddlers scored highest on measures of control, combined with low levels of activity (Krassner et al., 2017).

If infants from Asian cultures engage in more self-soothing, are they more temperamentally resistant to stress? One study examined levels of the hormone cortisol in infants receiving an inoculation (Lewis et al., 1993a). Cortisol, which is released as part of the fight-or-flight response, is often used as a marker of stress. Four-month-old Japanese infants showed a pronounced cortisol response, suggesting that they were experiencing great stress, coupled with little crying. The U.S. infants, on the other hand, displayed intense behavioral reactions to the pain and took longer to calm down, yet they displayed a lower cortisol response. In other words, although the Japanese babies appeared quiet and calm, they were more physiologically stressed than the U.S. infants. It seems that cultural views of the nature of arousal and emotional regulation influences parenting behaviors and ultimately infants' responses to stressors (Friedlmeier et al., 2015).

What constitutes an adaptive match between infant temperament and context—goodness of fit—is sometimes surprising. Consider the Maasai, an African semi-nomadic ethnic group. In times of drought, when the environment becomes extremely hostile, herds of cattle and goats die, and infant mortality rises substantially. Under these challenging conditions, infants with difficult temperaments tend to survive at higher rates than do those with easy temperaments. Infants who cry and are demanding are attended to are fed more and are in better physical condition than easy babies, who tend to cry less and therefore are assumed to be content (Gardiner & Kosmitzki, 2018). Thus, the Maasai infants with difficult temperaments demonstrate higher rates of survival because their temperaments better fit the demands of the hostile context in which they are raised. Temperament, therefore, must be considered in context.

Culture plays a role in emotional development. Japanese mothers tend encourage their infants to develop close ties and depend on their assistance whereas North American mothers tend to emphasize autonomy.

Dukas/Universal Images Group via Getty Images

Thinking in Context: Lifespan Development

1. Under what conditions might temperament change, if at all? Is it possible for an infant with a difficult temperament to grow into a young child with an easy temperament? Why or why not? What experiences might cause temperament to mellow or become more easygoing?
2. Can an "easy" child shift to show a difficult temperament? Explain.
3. In what ways does temperament—and preferences for particular forms of temperament—vary across cultures? How might these differences reflect adaptations to specific contextual conditions?
4. To what extent do temperaments and preferences for particular temperaments occur across the many contexts within the U.S.? Are some infant temperaments a better fit for some contexts than others? Why or why not?

ATTACHMENT IN INFANCY AND TODDLERHOOD

LEARNING OBJECTIVE

4.4 Examine the development of attachment and influences on attachment stability and outcomes in infancy and toddlerhood.

Raj gurgles and cries out while lying in his crib. As his mother enters the room he squeals excitedly. Raj's mother smiles as she reaches into the crib, and Raj giggles with delight as she picks him up. Raj and his mother have formed an important emotional bond, called attachment. **Attachment** refers to a lasting emotional tie between two people who each strive to maintain closeness to the other and act to ensure that the relationship continues.

Attachment relationships serve as an important backdrop for emotional and social development. Our earliest attachments are with our primary caregivers, most often our mothers. It was once thought that feeding determined patterns of attachment. Freud, for example, emphasized the role of feeding and successful weaning on infants' personality and well-being. Behaviorist theorists explain attachment as the result of infants associating their mothers with food, a powerful reinforcer that satisfies a biological need. Certainly, feeding is important for infants' health and well-being and offers opportunities for the close contact needed to develop attachment bonds, but feeding itself does not determine attachment.

In one famous study, baby rhesus monkeys were reared with two inanimate surrogate "mothers": one made of wire mesh and a second covered with terrycloth (see Figure 4.1). The baby monkeys clung

FIGURE 4.1 ■ Harlow's Study: Contact Comfort and the Attachment Bond

This infant monkey preferred to cling to the cloth-covered mother even if fed by the wire mother. Harlow concluded that attachment is based on contact comfort rather than feeding.

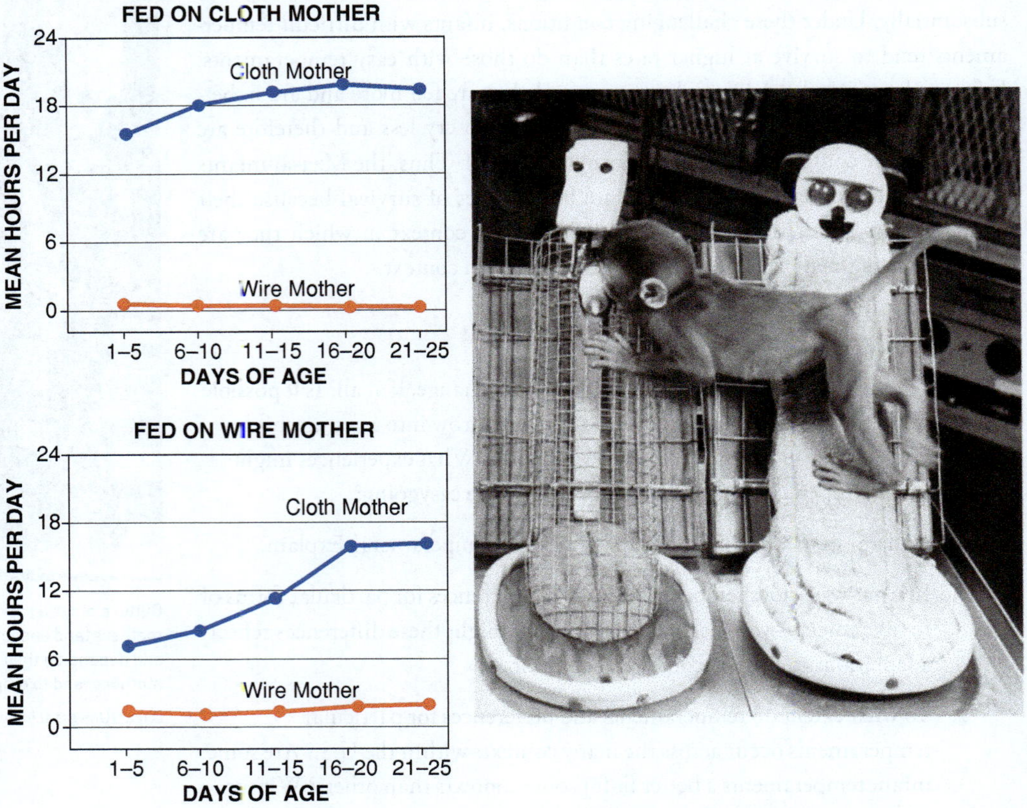

Source: Harlow, 1958; Photo Researchers, Inc./Science Source

to the terrycloth mother despite being fed only by the wire mother, suggesting that attachment bonds are not based on feeding but rather on contact comfort (Harlow & Zimmerman, 1959). So how does an attachment form, and what is its purpose?

Bowlby's Ethological Theory of Attachment

John Bowlby, a British psychiatrist, proposed that early family experiences influence emotional disturbances not through feeding practices, conditioning, or psychoanalytic drives, but via inborn tendencies to form close relationships. Specifically, Bowlby (1969; 1988) developed an ethological theory of attachment that characterizes it as an adaptive behavior that evolved because it contributed to the survival of the human species. Inspired by ethology, particularly by Lorenz's work on the imprinting of geese (see Chapter 1) and by observations of interactions between monkeys, Bowlby posited that humans are biologically driven to form attachment bonds with other humans. An attachment bond between caregivers and infants ensures that the two will remain in close proximity, thereby aiding the survival of the infant and, ultimately, the species. From this perspective, caregiving responses are inherited and are triggered by the presence of infants and young children.

Infants' Signals and Adults' Responses

From birth, babies develop a repertoire of behavior signals to which adults naturally attend and respond, such as smiling, cooing, and clinging. Crying is a particularly effective signal because it conveys negative emotion that adults can judge reliably, and it motivates adults to relieve the infants' distress. Adults are innately drawn to infants, find infants' signals irresistible, and respond in kind. One recent study found that nearly 700 mothers in 11 countries (Argentina, Belgium, Brazil, Cameroon, France, Kenya, Israel, Italy, Japan, South Korea, and the United States) tended to respond to their infants' cries and distress by picking up, holding, and talking to their infants (Bornstein et al., 2017). Infants' behaviors, immature appearance, and even smell draw adults' responses (Kringelbach et al., 2016). Infants, in turn, are attracted to caregivers who respond consistently and appropriately to their signals. During the first months of life, infants rely on caregivers to regulate their states and emotions—to soothe them when they are distressed and help them establish and maintain an alert state (Thompson, 2013). Attachment behaviors provide comfort and security to infants because they bring babies close to adults who can protect them.

Magnetic resonance imaging (MRI) scans support a biological component to attachment because first-time mothers show specific patterns of brain activity in response to infants. Mothers' brains light up with activity when they see their own infants' faces, and areas of the brain that are associated with rewards are activated in response to happy, but not sad, infant faces (Strathearn et al., 2008). In response to their infants' cries, U.S., Chinese, and Italian mothers show brain activity in regions associated with auditory processing, emotion, and the intention to move and speak, suggesting automatic responses to infant expressions of distress. (Bornstein et al., 2017).

Secure Base, Separation Anxiety, and Internal Working Models

The formation of an attachment bond is crucial for infants' development because it enables infants to begin to explore the world, using their attachment figure as a **secure base**, or foundation, to return to when frightened. When infants are securely attached to their caregivers, they feel confident to explore the world and to learn by doing so. As clear attachments form, starting at about 7 months, infants are likely to experience **separation anxiety** (sometimes called *separation protest*), a reaction to separation from an attachment figure that is characterized by distress and crying (Lamb & Lewis, 2015). Infants may follow, cling to, and climb on their caregivers in an attempt to keep them near.

Separation anxiety tends to increase between 8 and 15 months of age, and then it declines. This pattern appears across many cultures and environments as varied as those of the United States, Israeli kibbutzim, and !Kung hunter-gatherer groups in Africa (Kagan et al., 1994). It is the formation of the attachment bond that makes separation anxiety possible, because infants must feel connected to their caregivers in order to feel distress in the caregivers' absence. Separation anxiety declines as infants develop reciprocal relationships with caregivers, increasingly use them as secure bases, and can understand and predict parents' patterns of separation and return, reducing their confusion and distress.

The attachment bond developed during infancy and toddlerhood influences personality development because it comes to be represented as an **internal working model**, which includes the children's expectations about whether they are worthy of love, of whether their attachment figures will be available during times of distress, and how they will be treated. The internal working model influences the development of self-concept, or sense of self, in infancy and becomes a guide to relationships throughout life (Bretherton & Munholland, 2016).

Ainsworth's Strange Situation

Virtually all infants form an attachment to their parents, but Canadian psychologist Mary Salter Ainsworth proposed that infants differ in **security of attachment**—the extent to which they feel that parents can reliably meet their needs. Like Bowlby, Ainsworth believed that infants must develop a dependence on parents, viewing them as a metaphorical secure base, in order to feel comfortable exploring the world (Salter, 1940). To examine attachment, Mary Ainsworth developed the **Strange Situation**, a structured observational procedure that reveals the security of attachment when the infant is placed under stress. As shown in Table 4.2, the Strange Situation is a heavily structured observation task consisting of eight 3-minute-long episodes. In each segment, the infant is with the parent (typically the mother), with a stranger, with both parent and stranger, or alone. Researchers observe infants' exploration of the room, their reaction when the mother leaves the room, and, especially, their responses during reunions, when the mother returns.

TABLE 4.2 ■ The Strange Situation

Event	Attachment Behavior Observed
Experimenter introduces mother and infant to playroom and leaves.	
Infant plays with toys and parent is seated.	Mother as secure base.
Stranger enters, talks with caregiver, and approaches infant.	Reaction to unfamiliar adult.
Mother leaves room; stranger responds to baby if upset.	Reaction to separation from mother.
Mother returns and greets infant.	Reaction to reunion.
Mother leaves room.	Reaction to separation from mother.
Stranger enters room and offers comfort to infant.	Reaction to stranger and ability to be soothed by stranger.
Mother returns and greets infant. Tries to interest the infant in toys.	Reaction to reunion.

On the basis of responses to the Strange Situation, infants are classified into one of several attachment types (Ainsworth et al., 1978):

- **Secure Attachment:** The securely attached infant uses the parent as a secure base, exploring the environment and playing with toys in the presence of the parent, but regularly checking in (e.g., by looking at the parent or bringing toys). The infant shows mild distress when the parent leaves. On the parent's return, the infant greets the parent enthusiastically, seeks comfort, and then returns to individual play. About two-thirds of North American infants who complete the Strange Situation are classified as securely attached (Lamb & Lewis, 2015).
- **Insecure-Avoidant Attachment**: Infants who display an insecure-avoidant attachment show little interest in the mother and busily explore the room during the Strange Situation. The infant is not distressed when the mother leaves and may react to the stranger in similar ways as to the mother. The infant ignores or avoids the mother on return or shows subtle signs of avoidance, such as failing to greet her or turning away from her. About 15% of samples of North American infants' responses to the Strange Situation reflect this style of attachment (Lamb & Lewis, 2015).
- **Insecure-Resistant Attachment**: Infants with an insecure-resistant attachment show a mixed pattern of responses to the mother. The infant remains preoccupied with the mother throughout the procedure, seeking proximity and contact, clinging even before the separation. When the mother leaves, the infant is distressed and cannot be comforted. During reunions, the infant's behavior suggests resistance, anger, and distress. The infant might seek proximity to the mother and cling to her while simultaneously pushing her away, hitting, or kicking. About 10% of North American infants tested in the Strange Situation fall into this category (Lamb & Lewis, 2015).
- **Insecure-Disorganized Attachment**: A fourth category was added later to account for the small set of infants (10% or below) who show inconsistent, contradictory behavior in the Strange Situation. The infant with insecure-disorganized attachment shows a conflict between approaching and fleeing the caregiver, suggesting fear (Main & Solomon, 1986). Infants showing insecure-disorganized attachment experience the greatest insecurity, appearing disoriented and confused. They may cry unexpectedly and may show a flat, depressed emotion and extreme avoidance or fearfulness of the caregiver.

Attachment-Related Outcomes

Mary Salter Ainsworth (1913–1999) believed that infants differ in their security of attachment. She created the Strange Situation to measure infants' security of attachment.

JHU Sheridan Libraries/Gado/Getty Images

Secure parent-child attachments are associated with positive socioemotional development in infancy, childhood, and adolescence. Preschool and school-age children who were securely attached as infants tend to be more curious, empathetic, self-confident, and socially competent, and they will have more positive interactions and close friendships with peers (Groh et al., 2017; Veríssimo et al., 2014). The advantages of secure attachment continue into adolescence. Adolescents who were securely attached in infancy and early childhood are more socially competent; tend to be better at making and keeping friends and functioning in a social group; and demonstrate greater emotional health, self-esteem, ego resiliency, and peer competence (Boldt, Kochanska, Yoon, & & Koenig Nordling,2014; Sroufe, 2016; Stern & Cassidy, 2018).

In contrast, insecure attachment is associated with heightened physiological reactivity and maladaptive responses to interpersonal stressors, including elevated cortisol levels, a response to stress (Groh & Narayan, 2019). Insecure attachment in infancy, particularly disorganized attachment, is associated with long-term negative outcomes, including less positive and more negative affect, poor emotional regulation, poor peer relationships, poor social competence, and higher rates of antisocial behavior, depression, and anxiety from childhood into adulthood (Cooke et al., 2019; Groh et al., 2017; Wolke et al., 2014; Zajac et al., 2020). Insecure attachments tend to correlate with difficult life circumstances and contexts—such as parental problems, low SES, and environmental stress that persist throughout childhood and beyond—that influence the continuity of poor outcomes (Granqvist et al., 2017). One longitudinal study suggested that infants with an insecure-disorganized attachment at 12 and 18 months of age were, as adults, more likely to have children with insecure-disorganized attachment, suggesting the possibility of intergenerational transmission of insecure attachment (and associated negative outcomes; Raby et al., 2015).

Conversely, attachment is not set in stone. Quality parent-child interactions can at least partially make up for poor interactions early in life. Children with insecure attachments in infancy who experience subsequent sensitive parenting show more positive social and behavioral outcomes in childhood and adolescence than do those who receive continuous care of poor quality (Sroufe, 2016). In addition, infants can form attachments to multiple caregivers, with secure attachments perhaps buffering the negative effects of insecure attachments (Boldt et al., 2014).

Influences on Attachment

The most important determinant of infant attachment is the caregiver's ability to consistently and sensitively respond to the child's signals (Ainsworth et al., 1978; Behrens et al., 2011). Infants become securely attached to mothers who are sensitive and offer high-quality responses to their signals, who accept their role as caregiver, who are accessible and cooperative with infants, who are not distracted by their own thoughts and needs, and who feel a sense of efficacy (Gartstein & Iverson, 2014). Mothers of securely attached infants provide stimulation and warmth and consistently synchronize or match their interactions with their infants' needs (Beebe et al., 2010). Secure mother-infant dyads show more positive interactions and fewer negative interactions compared with insecure dyads (Guo et al., 2015). The goodness of fit between the infant and parent's temperament influences attachment, supporting the role of reciprocal interactions in attachment (Seifer et al., 2014).

Infants who are insecurely attached have mothers who tend to be more rigid, unresponsive, inconsistent, and demanding (Gartstein & Iverson, 2014). The **insecure-avoidant attachment** pattern is

The most important determinant of infant attachment is the caregiver's ability to respond to the child's signals consistently and sensitively.

iStock/aywan88

associated with parental unavailability or rejection. **Insecure-resistant attachment** is associated with inconsistent and unresponsive parenting. Parents may respond inconsistently, offering overstimulating and intrusive caregiving at times and unresponsive care that is not attentive to the infant's signals at other times. Frightening parental behavior (at the extreme, child abuse) is thought to play a role in insecure-disorganized attachment (Duschinsky, 2015). Disorganized attachment is more common among infants who have been abused or raised in particularly poor caregiving environments; however, disorganized attachment itself is not an indicator of abuse (Granqvist et al., 2017; Lamb & Lewis, 2015).

Attachment is complex and influenced by contextual factors outside the parent-infant relationship. Conflict among parents is associated with lower levels of attachment security (Tan et al., 2018). Insecure attachment responses may represent adaptive responses to poor caregiving environments (Weinfield et al., 2008). Not relying on an unsupportive parent (such as by developing an insecure-avoidant attachment) may represent a good strategy for infants. Toddlers who show an avoidant attachment tend to rely on self-regulated coping rather than turning to others, perhaps an adaptive response to an emotionally absent parent (Zimmer-Gembeck et al., 2017). Mental health problems can influence parents' emotional availability.

Maternal Depression and Attachment

Caregiver depression poses risks for attachment. Depression is not simply sadness; rather, it is characterized by a lack of emotion and a preoccupation with the self that makes it difficult for depressed mothers to recognize their infants' needs and provide care. Both mothers and fathers can become depressed, but most of the research examines mothers. The hormonal and social changes that accompany pregnancy and new motherhood place women at risk for postpartum depression—depression that occurs in the months after childbirth. However, depression can occur at any time in life.

Mothers who are depressed tend to view their infants differently than nondepressed mothers and independent observers (Newland et al., 2016). They are more likely to identify negative emotions (i.e., sadness) than positive emotions (i.e., happiness) in infant faces (Webb & Ayers, 2015). Challenging behaviors, such as fussiness and crying, and difficult temperaments tend to elicit more negative responses from depressed mothers (Newland et al., 2016). When depressed and nondepressed mothers were shown images of their own and unfamiliar infants' joy and distress faces, mothers with depression showed blunted brain activity in response to their own infants' joy and distress faces, suggesting muted responses to infants' emotional cues (Laurent & Ablow, 2013). Depressed women tend to disengage faster from positive and negative infant emotional expressions (Webb & Ayers, 2015).

In practice, mothers who are depressed tend to be less responsive to their babies, show less affection, use more negative forms of touch, and show more negative emotions and behaviors such as withdrawal, intrusiveness, hostility, coerciveness, and insensitivity (Jennings et al., 2008). Given the poor parent-child interaction styles that accompany maternal depression, it may not be surprising that infants of depressed mothers show a variety of negative outcomes, including insecure attachment, overall distress, withdrawn behavior, poor social engagement, and difficulty regulating emotions (Barnes & Theule, 2019; Granat et al., 2017; Leventon & Bauer, 2013). They tend to show greater physiological arousal in response to stressors, difficulty reading and understanding others' emotions, and are at risk for later problems in development (Liu et al., 2017; Prenoveau et al., 2017; Suurland et al., 2017).

The ongoing reciprocal interactions between mothers and infants account for the long-term negative effects of maternal depression (Granat et al., 2017). In one study, maternal depressive symptoms 9 months after giving birth predicted infants' negative reactions to maternal behavior at 18 months of age and, in turn, higher levels of depressive symptoms on the part of mothers when the children reached 27 months of age (Roben et al., 2015).

Yet low sensitivity is not always associated with poor outcomes. Infants sometimes develop secure attachments to caregivers who are less sensitive but meet their basic needs, and they maintain a calm, regulated state (Cassidy et al., 2005). A study of 4.5-month-old infants from predominantly Black, white, and Hispanic low-socioeconomic-status homes found that caregiver provision of a secure base (meeting basic needs and fostering a sense of calm) predicted attachment even in the presence of caregiver insensitivity (Woodhouse et al., 2020). Infants' brains may be predisposed to form attachments, regardless of the quality of care (Opendak & Sullivan, 2019). In addition, infants develop attachments to other members of the family system, such as fathers (Cabrera et al., 2014; Lickenbrock & Braungart-Rieker, 2015; Dagan & Sagi-Schwartz, 2018).

Depression is characterized by a lack of emotion and a preoccupation with the self that makes it challenging for depressed mothers to care for their infants and recognize their infants' needs.

iStock/monkeybusinessimages

Father-Infant Attachment

At birth, fathers interact with their newborns much like mothers do. They provide similar levels of care by cradling the newborn and performing tasks like diaper changing, bathing, and feeding the newborn (Combs-Orme & Renkert, 2009). This is true of fathers in Western contexts as well as those in non-Western contexts, such as the Kadazan of Malaysia and Aka and Bofi of Central Africa (Hewlett & MacFarlan, 2010; Hossain et al., 2007; Tamis-LeMonda et al., 2009).

Early in an infant's life, fathers and mothers develop different play and communicative styles. Fathers tend to be more stimulating and physical while mothers are more soothing (Feldman, 2003; Grossmann et al., 2002). Fathers tend to engage in more unpredictable rough-and-tumble play that is often met with positive reactions and arousal from infants; when young children have a choice of an adult play partner, they tend to choose their fathers (Feldman, 2003; Lamb & Lewis, 2016).

Differences in mothers' and fathers' interaction styles appear in many cultures, including France, Switzerland, Italy, and India, as well as among White non-Hispanic, African American, and Hispanic American families in the United States (Best, House, Barnard, & Spicker, 1994; Hossain et al., 1997; Roopnarine et al., 1992). Interaction styles differ more in some cultures than in others. German, Swedish, and Israeli kibbutzim fathers, as well as fathers in the Aka ethnic group of Africa's western Congo basin, are not more playful than mothers (Frodi et al., 1983; Hewlett, 2008; Hewlett et al., 1998; Sagi et al., 1985). Furthermore, overall and across cultures, most of the differences between mothers and fathers are not large (Lamb & Lewis, 2016).

Fathers tend to have different interaction styles than mothers. Father-infant interaction tends to be play oriented. This is true of fathers in Western contexts as well as those in non-Western contexts, such as the Kadazan of Malaysia and Aka and Bofi of Central Africa.

iStock/ kate_sept2004

Father-child interaction is associated with social competence, independence, and cognitive development in children (Cabrera et al., 2018; Sethna et al., 2016). Fathers provide opportunities for babies to practice arousal management by providing high-intensity stimulation and excitement, like tickling, chasing, and laughing (Flanders et al., 2009). Fathers who are sensitive, supportive, and appropriately challenging during play promote father-infant attachment relationships (Lickenbrock & Braungart-Rieker, 2015; Olsavsky et al., 2020). When fathers are involved in the caregiving of their infants, their children are more likely to enjoy a warm relationship with their father as they grow older, carry out responsibilities, follow parents' directions, and be well adjusted. Similar to findings with mothers, sensitive parenting on the part of fathers predicts secure attachments with their children through age 3 (Brown et al., 2012; Lucassen et al., 2011; Olsavsky et al., 2020). The positive social, emotional, and cognitive effects of father-child interaction continue from infancy into childhood and adolescence (Cabrera et al., 2018; Sarkadi et al., 2008). In addition, an infant's secure attachment relationship with a father can compensate for the negative effects of an insecure attachment to a mother (Dagan & Sagi-Schwartz, 2018; Kochanska & Kim, 2013; Boldt et al., 2014).

Stability of Attachment

Attachment patterns tend to be stable over infancy and early childhood, especially when securely attached infants receive continuous responsive care (Ding et al., 2014; Marvin et al., 2016). However, the loss of a parent, parental divorce, a parent's psychiatric disorder, and physical abuse, as well as changes in family stressors, adaptive processes, and living conditions, can transform a secure attachment into an insecure attachment pattern later in childhood or adolescence (Feeney & Monin, 2016; Lyons-Ruth & Jacobvitz, 2016).

Contextual factors such as low SES, family and community stressors, and the availability of supports influence the stability of attachment through their effect on parents' emotional and physical resources and the quality of parent–infant interactions. (Booth-LaForce et al., 2014; Thompson, 2016; Van Ryzin et al., 2011). Securely attached infants reared in contexts that pose risks to development may develop insecure attachments, and insecure attachments tend to continue in risky contexts (Pinquart et al., 2013). An insecure attachment between child and parent can be overcome by changing maladaptive interaction patterns, increasing sensitivity on the part of the parent, and fostering consistent and developmentally appropriate responses to children's behaviors.

Cultural Variations in Attachment Classifications

Attachment occurs in all cultures, but whether the Strange Situation is applicable across cultural contexts is a matter of debate. Research has shown that infants in many countries, including Germany, Holland, Japan, and the United States, approach the Strange Situation in similar ways (Sagi et al., 1991). In addition, the patterns of attachment identified by Ainsworth occur in a wide variety of cultures in North America, Europe, Asia, Africa, and the Middle East (Bornstein et al., 2013; Cassibba et al., 2013; Huang et al., 2012; Jin et al., 2012; Thompson, 2013).

Nevertheless, there are differences. Insecure-avoidant attachments are more common in Western European countries, and insecure-resistant attachments are more prevalent in Japan and Israel (Van Ijzendoorn & Kroonenberg, 1988). (see Figure 4.2) This pattern may result from the fact that Western cultures tend to emphasize individuality and independence, whereas Eastern cultures are more likely to emphasize the importance of relationships and connections with others (collectivism). Individualist and collectivist cultural perspectives interpret children's development in different ways (Keller, 2018). Western parents might interpret insecure-resistant behavior as clingy, whereas Asian parents might interpret it as successful bonding (Gardiner & Kosmitzki, 2018).

The behaviors that characterize sensitive caregiving vary with culturally specific socialization goals, values, and beliefs of the parents, family, and community (Keller, 2019; Mesman et al., 2016). Puerto Rican mothers often use more physical control in interactions with infants, such as picking up crawling infants and placing them in desired locations, over the first year of life than do European American mothers. They actively structure interactions in ways consistent with long-term socialization goals oriented toward calm, attentive, and obedient children. Typically, attachment theory conceptualizes this type of control as insensitive, yet physical control is associated with secure attachment status at 12 months in Puerto Rican infants (but not white non-Hispanic infants; Carlson & Harwood, 2003; Harwood et al., 1999). Similarly, German mothers operate according to the shared cultural belief that infants should become independent at an early age and should learn that they cannot rely on the mother's comfort at all times. German mothers may seem unresponsive to their children's crying, yet they are demonstrating sensitive childrearing within their context (Grossmann et al., 1985). In other words, the behaviors that reflect sensitive caregiving vary with culture because they are adaptations to different circumstances (Rothbaum et al., 2000).

FIGURE 4.2 ■ Cross-Cultural Variations in Attachment

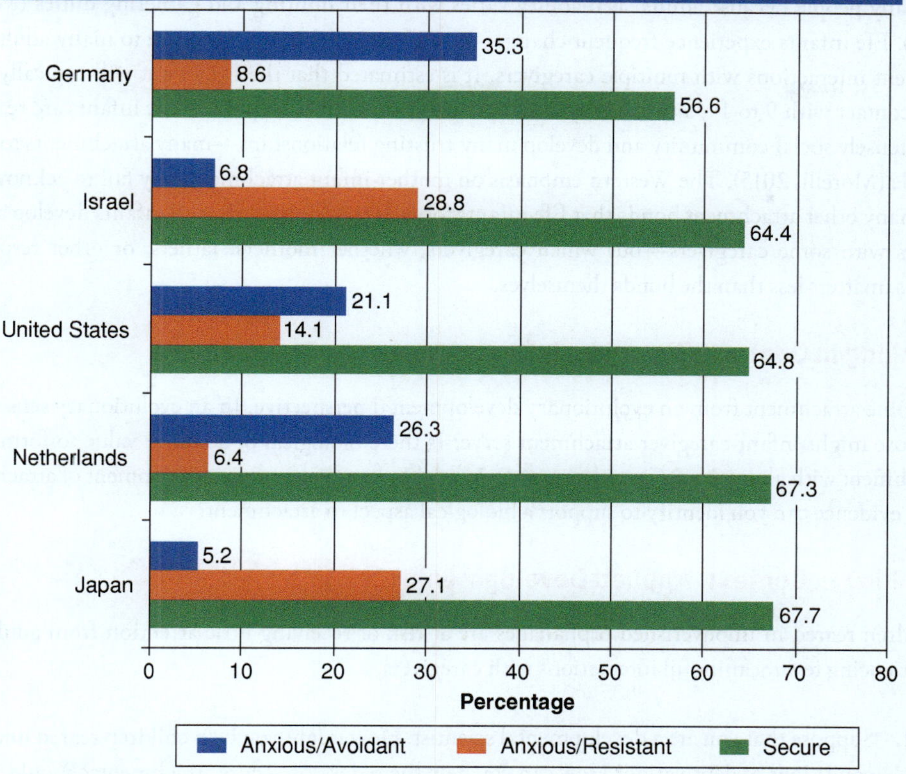

Adapted from Van Ijzendoorn & Kroonenberg, 1988.

Many Japanese and Israeli infants become highly distressed during the Strange Situation and show high rates of insecure resistance. Resistance in Japanese samples of infants can be attributed to cultural childrearing practices that foster mother-infant closeness and physical intimacy that leaves infants unprepared for the separation episodes; the Strange Situation may be so stressful for them that they resist comforting (Takahashi, 1990). In other words, the Strange Situation may not accurately measure the attachment of these infants. Similarly, infants who are raised in small, close-knit Israeli kibbutz communities do not encounter strangers in their day-to-day lives, so the introduction of a stranger in the Strange Situation procedure can be overly challenging for them. At the same time, kibbutz-reared infants spend much of their time with their peers and caregivers and see their parents infrequently, and therefore they may prefer to be comforted by people other than their parents (Sagi et al., 1985).

Dogon infants from Mali, West Africa, show rates of secure attachment that are similar to those of Western infants, but the avoidant attachment style is not observed in samples of Dogon infants (McMahan True et al., 2001). Dogon infant care practices diminish the likelihood of avoidant attachment because the infant is in constant proximity to the mother. Infant distress is promptly answered with feeding and infants feed on demand, so mothers cannot behave in ways that would foster avoidant attachment.

Dogon infants from Mali, West Africa, show rates of secure attachment that are similar to those of Western infants, but the avoidant attachment style is not observed in samples of Dogon infants because infants are in constant proximity to mothers, who respond to infant distress promptly and feed infants on demand.

Danita Delimont / Alamy Stock Photo

Although most research on attachment has focused on the mother-infant bond, we know that infants form multiple attachments (Dagan & Sagi-Schwartz, 2018).

Consider the Efe foragers of the Democratic Republic of Congo: In their culture, infants are cared for by many people because adults' availability varies with their hunting and gathering duties (Morelli, 2015). Efe infants experience frequent changes in residence and camp, exposure to many adults, and frequent interactions with multiple caregivers. It is estimated that the Efe infant will typically come into contact with 9 to 14, and as many as 20, people within a 2-hour period. Efe infants are reared in an intensely social community and develop many trusting relationships—many attachments to many people (Morelli, 2015). The Western emphasis on mother-infant attachment may fail to acknowledge the many other attachment bonds that Efe infants form. It is important that all infants develop attachments with some caregivers—but which caregivers, whether mothers, fathers, or other responsive adults, matters less than the bonds themselves.

Thinking in Context: Biological Influences

Examine attachment from an evolutionary developmental perspective. In an evolutionary sense, what purpose might infant-caregiver attachment serve? Is there biological or adaptive value to forming an attachment with a caregiver? Considering emotional development and the development of attachment, what evidence can you identify to support a biological aspect to attachment?

Thinking in Context: Applied Developmental Science

Children reared in impoverished orphanages are at risk of receiving little attention from adults and experiencing few meaningful interactions with caregivers.

1. Suppose that you are a developmental scientist. How might you help children reared under conditions of deprivation? How can you help them develop secure attachments? Would you develop an intervention? Work with infants case by case?
2. There are many children in the U.S. who experience neglect, trauma, and poor interactions with caregivers. Compare these cases with the extreme deprivation of children reared in impoverished orphanages. What similarities and differences might you expect? Would you intervene and treat these two groups of children in the same way?

Thinking in Context: Intersectionality

Many conclusions about infant-parent interactions and attachment are based on research conducted with white non-Hispanic families.

1. To what extent do you think observations of infant-parent interactions in white non-Hispanic families apply to families of color?
2. Consider interactions among race and ethnicity, socioeconomic status, religion, and cultural views of parenting. What similarities and differences in parent-infant interactions might you expect?
3. How might parents' experiences within the community, such as exposure to violence, discrimination and racism, and poverty, as well as social support and connection, influence their interactions with infants and young children?

THE SELF IN INFANCY AND TODDLERHOOD

LEARNING OBJECTIVE

4.5 Differentiate the roles of self-concept, self-recognition, and self-control in infant development.

What do babies know about themselves? When do they begin to know that they have a "self"—that they are separate from the people and things that surround them? We have discussed the challenges that researchers who study infants face. Infants cannot tell us what they perceive, think, or feel. Instead, researchers must devise ways of inferring infants' states, feelings, and thoughts. As you might imagine, this makes it very challenging to study infants' conceptions of self, as well as their awareness and understanding of themselves.

Self-Awareness

Camille, 4 months of age, delights in seeing that she can make the mobile above her crib move by kicking her feet. Her understanding that she can influence her world suggests that she has a sense of herself as different from her environment (Rochat, 1998). Before infants can take responsibility for their own actions, they must begin to see themselves as physically separate from the world around them.

Some developmental researchers believe that infants are born with a capacity to distinguish the self from the surrounding environment (Meltzoff, 1990; Rochat, 2018). Newborns show distress at hearing a recording of another infant's cries but do not show distress at hearing their own cries, suggesting that they can distinguish other infants' cries from their own and thereby have a primitive notion of self (Dondi et al., 1999). Newborns' facial imitation, that is, their ability to view another person's facial expression and produce it (see Chapter 3), may also suggest a primitive awareness of self and others (Meltzoff, 2007; Rochat, 2013, 2018). It is unclear whether these findings suggest that newborns have self-awareness because infants cannot tell us what they know.

Others argue that an awareness of oneself is not innate but emerges by 3 months of age (Neisser, 1993). Infants' sense of body awareness emerges through interactions and body contact with their mothers (Montirosso & McGlone, 2020). Some researchers believe that this emergence is indicated by infants' awareness of the consequences of their own actions on others (Langfur, 2013). As infants interact with people and objects, they learn that their behaviors have effects. With this awareness, they begin to experiment to see how their behaviors influence the world around them, begin to differentiate themselves from their environments, and develop a sense of self (Bigelow, 2017).

Self-Recognition

How do we know whether self-awareness is innate or develops in the early months of life? One way of studying self-awareness in infants is to examine infants' reactions to viewing themselves in a mirror. **Self-recognition**, the ability to recognize or identify the self, is assessed by the "rouge test." In this experiment, a dab of rouge or lipstick is applied to an infant's nose without the infant's awareness, under the pretext of wiping his or her face. The infant is then placed in front of a mirror (Bard et al., 2006). Whether the infant recognizes himself or herself in the mirror depends on cognitive development, especially the ability to engage in mental representation and hold images in one's mind. Infants must be able to retain a memory of their own image in order to display self-recognition in the mirror task. If the infant has an internal representation of her face and recognizes the infant in the mirror as herself, she will notice the dab of rouge and reach for her own nose.

Mirror recognition develops gradually and systematically (Brandl, 2018). From 3 months of age, infants pay attention and react positively to their mirror image, and by 8 to 9 months of age they show awareness of the tandem movement of the mirror image with themselves and play with the image, treating it as if it is another baby (Bullock & Lutkenhaus, 1990). Some 15- to 17-month-old infants show signs of self-recognition, but it is not until 18 to 24 months that most infants demonstrate self-recognition by touching their nose when they notice the rouge mark in the mirror (Cicchetti et al., 1997). Does experience with mirrors influence how infants respond to the rouge test? Interestingly, infants from nomadic tribes with no experience with mirrors demonstrate self-recognition at the same ages as infants reared in surroundings with mirrors (Priel & deSchonen, 1986). This suggests that extensive experience with a mirror is not needed to demonstrate self-recognition in the mirror task. In addition, research with Canadian toddlers shows that their performance on the mirror task is unrelated to their experience with mirrors in the home (Courage et al., 2004).

This toddler recognizes herself in the mirror, as shown by her touching the rouge mark on her face.

Thierry Berrod, Mona Lisa Production/Science Source

Mirror recognition is not the only indicator of a sense of self—and may not be the earliest indicator. A recent study suggests that self-recognition may develop before infants can succeed on the mirror task (Stapel et al., 2017). Eighteen-month-old infants viewed photographs of their own face, the face of an unfamiliar infant, the face of their caregiver, and the face of an unfamiliar caregiver, while their brain activity was registered via electroencephalography (EEG). The infants showed more brain activity in response to their own face, suggesting self-recognition, yet only one-half of these infants succeeded on the mirror task. By 18 to 24 months of age, children begin to recognize themselves in pictures and refer to themselves in the pictures as "me" or by their first names (Lewis & Brooks-Gunn, 1979). One study of 20- to 25-month-old toddlers showed that 63% could pick themselves out when they were presented with pictures of themselves and two similar children (Bullock & Lutkenhaus, 1990). By 30 months of age, nearly all of the children could pick out their own picture.

The mirror recognition task recruits areas in the brain associated with self-reflection in adults. Toddlers who exhibit mirror self-recognition show increased functional connectivity between frontal and temporoparietal regions of the brain, relative to those toddlers who do not yet show mirror self-recognition, suggesting that mirror self-recognition may be a good indicator of a sense of self in infancy (Bulgarelli et al., 2019).

With advances in self-awareness, toddlers begin to experience more complex emotions, including self-conscious emotions such as embarrassment, shame, guilt, jealousy, and pride (Lewis & Carmody, 2008). An understanding of self is needed before children can be aware of being the focus of attention and feel embarrassment, identify with others' concerns and feel shame, or desire what someone else has and feel jealousy toward them. In a study of 15- to 24-month-old infants, only those who recognized themselves in the mirror looked embarrassed when an adult gave them overwhelming praise. They smiled, looked away, and covered their faces with their hands. The infants who did not recognize themselves in the mirror did not show embarrassment (Lewis, 2011). A developing sense of self and the self-conscious emotions that accompany it leads toddlers to have more complex social interactions with caregivers and others; all of which contribute to the development of self-concept.

Emerging Self-Concept

In toddlerhood, between 18 and 30 months of age, children's sense of self-awareness expands beyond self-recognition to include a **categorical self**—a self-description based on broad categories such as sex, age, and physical characteristics (Stipek et al., 1990). Toddlers describe themselves as "big," "strong," "girl/boy," and "baby/big kid." Children use their categorical self as a guide to behavior. Once toddlers label themselves by gender, they spend more time playing with toys stereotyped for their own gender. Applying the categorical self as a guide to behavior illustrates toddlers' advancing capacities for self-control.

At about the same time as toddlers display the categorical self, they begin to show another indicator of their growing self-understanding. As toddlers become proficient with language and their vocabulary expands, they begin to use many personal pronouns and adjectives, such as "I", "me," and "mine," suggesting a sense of self in relation to others (Bates, 1990). Claims of possession emerge by about 21 months and illustrate children's clear representation of "I" versus other (Levine, 1983), a milestone in self-definition and the beginnings of self-concept (Rochat, 2010).

Self-Control

Self-awareness and the emerging self-concept permit self-control, as one must be aware of oneself as separate from others to comply with requests and modify behavior in accordance with caregivers' demands. In order to engage in self-control, the infant must be able to attend to a caregiver's instructions, shift his or her attention from an attractive stimulus or task, and inhibit a behaviour. Cortical development, specifically development of the frontal lobes, is responsible for this ability (Posner & Rothbart, 2018). Between 12 and 18 months, infants begin to demonstrate self-control by their awareness of, and compliance with, caregivers' simple requests (Kaler & Kopp, 1990).

Although toddlers are known for asserting their autonomy, such as by saying no and not complying with a caregiver's directive, compliance is much more common (Kochanska, 2000). Paradoxically, when parents encourage autonomous, exploratory behavior, their children are more likely to show compliance with parental instructions in toddlerhood through early childhood (Laurin & Joussemet, 2017). Secure attachment relationships and warm parenting are associated with effortful control, likely because securely attached infants feel comfortable exploring their environment, which promotes autonomy (Frick et al., 2018; Pallini et al., 2018). Toddlers' capacities for self-control improve rapidly. Delay-of-gratification tasks suggest that between 18 and 36 months, toddlers become better able to control their impulses and wait before eating a treat or playing with a toy (Białecka-Pikul et al., 2018; Cheng et al., 2018).

Infants make great strides in socioemotional development over the first two years of life, as summarized in Table 4.3. Infants' advances in emotional expression and regulation represent the interaction of biological predispositions, such as inborn capacities for basic emotions and temperament, and experience—particularly parent-child interactions, the contexts in which they are raised, and the goodness of fit between infants' needs and what their contexts provide. Infants' gains in emotional and social development and a growing sense of self form a socioemotional foundation for the physical and cognitive changes that they will experience in the early childhood years.

Thinking in Context: Lifespan Development

1. Provide examples of how infants' developing sense of self reflects interactions among temperament, emotional development, and attachment.
2. Compare families in Western cultures that emphasize individuality and Eastern cultures that value collectivism. How might parents and other adults interact with babies and promote a sense of self? How might babies in each of these cultures come to understand themselves? Might you expect differences within a culture, such as intersectional differences among infants in the US?
3. How might contextual factors, such as those that accompany being raised in an inner city, suburban neighborhood, rural environment, or nomadic society, influence infants' developing sense of self? Would you expect the same pattern of development for self-recognition, self-concept, and self-control across all contexts? Why or why not?

TABLE 4.3 ■ The Developing Self

Concept	Description	Emergence
Self-concept	Self-description and thoughts about the self	Begins as a sense of awareness in the early months of life
Self-awareness	Awareness of the self as separate from the environment	Innate or develops in the early months of life
Self-recognition	The ability to recognize or identify the self; typically tested in mirror recognition tasks	18–24 months
Categorical self	Self-description based on broad categories such as sex, age, and physical characteristics; indicates the emergence of self-concept	18–30 months

Source: Adapted from Butterworth, 1992.

CHAPTER SUMMARY

4.1 Analyze the psychosocial tasks of infancy and toddlerhood.

The psychosocial task of infancy is to develop a sense of trust. If parents and caregivers are sensitive to the infant's physical and emotional needs and consistently fulfill them, the infant will develop a basic sense of trust in his or her caregivers and the world. The task for toddlers is to learn to do things for themselves and feel confident in their ability to maneuver themselves in their environment. Psychosocial development is supported by warm and sensitive parenting and developmentally appropriate expectations for exploration and behavioral control.

4.2 Describe emotional development and the role of contextual influences on emotional development in infants and toddlers.

Newborns display some basic emotions, such as interest, distress, and disgust. Self-conscious emotions, such as empathy, embarrassment, shame, and guilt, depend on cognitive development, as well as an awareness of self, and do not emerge until about late infancy. With development, infants use different and more effective strategies for regulating their emotions. At about 6 months old, infants begin to use social referencing. Social referencing occurs in ambiguous situations, provides children with guidance in how to interpret the event, and influences their emotional responses and subsequent actions. Parents socialize infants to respond to and display their emotions in socially acceptable ways. The emotions that are considered acceptable, as well as ways of expressing them, differ by culture and context.

4.3 Discuss the styles and stability of temperament including the role of goodness of fit in infant development.

Temperament, the characteristic way in which an individual approaches and reacts to people and situations, has a biological basis. Children are classified into three temperament styles: easy, slow to warm up, and difficult. Temperament is influenced by the interaction of genetic predispositions, maturation, and experience. Temperament tends to be stable but there are developmental and individual differences. An important influence on socioemotional development is the goodness of fit between the child's temperament and the environment around him or her, especially the parent's temperament and child-rearing methods.

4.4 Examinethe development of attachment and influences on attachment stability and outcomes in infancy and toddlerhood.

From an ethological perspective, attachment is an adaptive behavior that evolved because it ensures that the infant and caregiver will remain in close proximity, aiding the survival of the infant. Using the Strange Situation, infants are classified as securely attached or insecurely attached (insecure-avoidant, insecure-resistant, or insecure-disorganized). Secure attachments in infancy are associated with social competence and socioemotional health. Attachment patterns are seen in a wide variety of cultures around the world, but the behaviors that make up sensitive caregiving vary depending on the socialization goals, values, and beliefs of the family and community, which may vary by culture. Generally, infants become securely or insecurely attached to caregivers based on the caregiver's ability to respond sensitively to the child's signals.

4.5 Differentiate the roles of self-concept, self-recognition, and self-control in infant development.

The earliest notion of self-concept—self-awareness—is evident in a primitive fashion at 3 months of age. Self-recognition, as indicated by mirror self-recognition, develops gradually and systematically in infants, but it is not until 18 to 24 months that a majority of infants demonstrate self-recognition in the mirror test. Once children have a sense of self, they can experience more complex emotions, such as self-conscious emotions. Self-awareness permits self-control as one must be aware of oneself as an agent apart from others to comply with requests and modify behavior in accord with caregivers' demands.

KEY TERMS

attachment (p. 121)
autonomy versus shame and doubt (p. 108)
basic emotions (p. 109)
categorical self (p. 132)
difficult temperament (p. 118)
easy temperament (p. 118)
emotion regulation (p. 111)
emotional display rules (p. 115)
goodness of fit (p. 119)
insecure-avoidant attachment (p. 125)
insecure-disorganized attachment (p. 124)
insecure-resistant attachment (p. 126)
internal working model (p. 123)
secure attachment (p. 124)
self-conscious emotions (p. 111)
self-recognition (p. 131)
separation anxiety (p. 123)
slow-to-warm-up temperament (p. 118)
social referencing (p. 113)
social smile (p. 110)
Strange Situation (p. 123)
stranger wariness (p. 116)
temperament (p. 117)
trust versus mistrust (p. 108)
secure base (p. 123)
security of attachment (p. 123)

PART 2 LIFESPAN DEVELOPMENT AT WORK: INFANCY AND TODDLERHOOD

There are many opportunities to work with infants and their families. Some include daily contact, such as childcare, and others entail more infrequent contact, such as in the health fields.

Childcare Director

Visitors to childcare centers are most familiar with the childcare worker or teacher who cares for infants and toddlers. Who hires and supervises the childcare workers? Who creates and administers programs? Who oversees the operations of the center? Childcare directors or administrators may not have daily contact with each infant, but their work affects infants and parents each day.

Childcare directors are responsible for operating and leading the work of a childcare center. They play a lead role in constructing the center's mission statement, the philosophy that guides the center's work. Childcare directors lead teachers in creating instructional resources to use in class and develop policies such as scheduling of outside time, naps, and other activities. They are also responsible for the running the business, including advertising, maintaining financial records, and directing human resources. Directors may market the center, take parents on tours of the facility, write budgets, and prepare annual reports. Human resource activities include hiring, overseeing, and evaluating employees and mediating disputes.

The requirements for becoming a childcare director vary by state and center. Some require a bachelor's degree (or higher) in early childhood education. Others require a high school diploma. Some states and centers may require experience as a childcare staff member before becoming a director. Most require directors of childcare centers to have certification, such as the National Administration Credential (NAC), which requires completion of a 45-hour course. The 2020 median salary for childcare directors was about $49,000 (U.S. Bureau of Labor Statistics, 2021).

Social Worker

Social workers work with individuals and families of all ages, providing counseling and identifying and helping them access needed resources. Social workers are advisers who advocate for others to during transitions, crisis situations, and challenging circumstances. They help families navigate often-confusing federal and state programs to obtain needed assistance, such as access to the WIC program, a federal program to promote the health of low-income women, infants, and children by providing nutritious food, housing assistance, medical treatment, and other aid. Social workers may engage in education and individual and group counseling sessions on topics such as parenting and coping skills. A bachelor's degree may offer preparation for entry-level positions in social work; a master's degree in social work (MSW) will provide many more opportunities, including independent practice as a clinical social worker.

Clinical social workers provide psychological treatment, including diagnosing and treating psychological, emotional, and behavioral disorders and working with doctors and other medical professionals. They are employed in a variety of settings, including hospitals, schools, community mental health centers, social service agencies, and private practice. Licensed clinical social workers (LCSW) must have a master's degree and pass a certification exam. The median salary for clinical social workers was about $57,000 in 2019 (Graves, 2020).

Pediatric Nurse

There are many different kinds of nurses. Some specialize to work with specific populations, such as infants and children. Becoming a nurse requires earning an associate degree or bachelor's degree in nursing, obtaining experience, and passing a licensing exam. The associate degree prepares nurses for entry-level positions. Some employers prefer nurses with bachelor's degrees in nursing. Bachelor's degrees provide more opportunities to advance. Becoming certified as a registered nurse (RN) opens additional opportunities (and pays a higher salary). Certification as a registered nurse requires two years of experience and passing an exam.

Pediatric nurses are RNs who specialize in caring for patients from infancy through adolescence. Pediatric nurses perform physical examinations, measure vital statistics, educate parents and caregivers, and work alongside other health care providers, such as physicians, to promote children's health and well-being. Because their patients are so young, pediatric nurses often develop close connections with them and their families. An understanding of development is critical to the work of pediatric nurses because infants, children, and adolescents have different abilities and needs—and these change with development.

Pediatric nurses are found in hospitals, clinics, private practice, schools, and more. Becoming a pediatric nurse entails completing nursing school, gaining experience, and completing a licensure exam. In addition, pediatric nurses typically complete the Certified Pediatric Nurse Examination to demonstrate their competence. In 2020 the median pay for all registered nurses was about $75,000, but salaries vary with education, experience, and geographic location (U.S. Bureau of Labor Statistics, 2021).

Pediatrician

Just as there are many types of nurses, there are many medical specialties and types of physicians (or doctors). Becoming a physician requires attending medical school for four years after obtaining a bachelor's degree. In addition to passing a licensure examination, physicians complete a 3-year (or longer) residency program to gain hands-on experience and training within a specialty. Some seek additional specialty certification by completing a board examination. Pediatricians specialize in treating infants, children, and adolescents.

Pediatricians provide treatment to infants, children, and adolescents to treat illnesses but also to improve their overall health and well-being. They perform tasks like routine checkups, provide immunizations and medications, order tests, refer patients to specialists for specific injuries or illnesses, and speak with parents about their child's treatment options. They assess children's growth, determine whether it is in the appropriate range, and if it is not, devise treatment plans. Pediatricians work in hospital settings, clinics, and independent practice. Pediatricians earned a median salary of about $185,000 in 2020 (U.S. Bureau of Labor Statistics, 2021).

5 PHYSICAL AND COGNITIVE DEVELOPMENT IN EARLY CHILDHOOD

Orbon Alija/ Getty Images

George's parents watched with pride as their 4-year-old son kicked the soccer ball to the other children. George has grown from a bowlegged, round-tummied, and top-heavy toddler into a strong, well-coordinated young child. His body slimmed, grew taller, and reshaped into proportions similar to that of an adult. As a toddler, he often stumbled and fell, but George can now run, skip, and throw a ball. He has also gained better control over his fingers; he can draw recognizable pictures of objects, animals, and people. As his vocabulary and language skills have grown, George has become more adept at communicating his ideas and needs.

How do these developments take place? In this chapter, we examine the many changes that children undergo in physical and motor development as well as how their thinking and language skills change.

PHYSICAL GROWTH AND HEALTH IN EARLY CHILDHOOD

LEARNING OBJECTIVE

5.1 Discuss patterns of physical growth and influences on growth and health, including nutrition, physical activity, sleep, and illness and injury.

George's abilities to run, skip, and manipulate his fingers to create objects with Play-Doh illustrate the many ways that children learn to control their bodies. George is also growing bigger and stronger day by day, though the speed of growth is not as dramatic as when he was younger.

In early childhood children get taller, stronger, and better able to control their bodies. Their developing motor skills permit them to engage in new activities and interact with others in new ways.

Body Growth

Although young children grow at a slower pace than infants, substantial growth occurs in early childhood. From ages 2 through 6, the average child grows 2 to 3 inches taller and gains nearly 5 pounds in weight each year. The typical 6-year-old child weighs about 45 pounds and is about 46 inches tall.

Body proportions change during early childhood as the body "catches up" with the head. The proportion of body fat to muscle changes. Young children become more lean and both boys and girls gain muscle and lose fat. By 5 years of age, girls have slightly more fat than boys and boys more muscle (Lloyd et al., 2019). The cephalocaudal trend of infancy continues as the trunk, arms, and legs grow rapidly and body proportions become similar to those of adults. As a result, over early childhood young children's bodies become less top-heavy, their bodies slim and legs become longer, and they start to take on proportions that are similar to adults.

Children's height and rate of growth is closely related to that of their parents (Kliegman et al., 2016). Ethnic differences in growth patterns appear in developed nations such as England, France, Canada, Australia, and the United States (Natale & Rajagopalan, 2014). Generally, children of African descent tend to be tallest, followed by children of European descent, then Asian, then Latino. However, there are many individual differences. Even within a given culture, some families are much taller than others (Stulp & Barrett, 2016). It is difficult to assess ethnic differences in growth patterns of children in developing nations because malnutrition and growth stunting are common (de Onis & Branca, 2016). Contextual factors, such as access to nutrition and health care, also influence body growth.

Brain Development

Early childhood is a period of rapid brain growth, but at a slower rate than infancy. The increase in synapses and connections among brain regions helps the brain to reach 90% of its adult weight by age 5 (Dubois et al., 2013). In early childhood, the greatest increases in cortical surface area is in the frontal and temporal cortex, which play a role in thinking, memory, language, and planning (Gilmore et al., 2018). Children's brains tend to grow in spurts, with very rapid periods of growth followed by little growth or even reductions in volume due to synaptic pruning (Jernigan & Stiles, 2017; Kolb, 2020). Little-used synapses are pruned in response to experience, an important part of neurological development that leads to more efficient thought.

Pruning and remolding of synapses continues in response to experience, leading to more efficient thought. The natural forming and pruning of synapses enables the human brain to demonstrate **plasticity**, the ability of the brain to change its organization and function in response to experience (Di Cristo & Chattopadhyaya, 2020; Stiles, 2017). Young children given training in music demonstrated structural brain changes over a period of 15 months that correspond with increases in music and auditory skills (Hyde et al., 2009). Plasticity enables the young child's brain to reorganize itself in response to injury in ways that the adult's brain cannot.

The immature young brain offers opportunities for plasticity but is also uniquely sensitive to injury. If a part of the brain is damaged at a critical point in development, functions linked to that region will be irreversibly impaired. Generally speaking, plasticity is greatest when neurons are forming many synapses, and it declines with pruning (Kolb et al., 2019). Overall, the degree to which individuals recover from an injury depends on the injury, its nature and severity, age, experiences after the injury, and contextual factors supporting recovery, such as interventions (Bryck & Fisher, 2012).

Myelination contributes to many of the changes that we see in children's capacities. As the neuron's axons become coated with fatty myelin, neurons are better able to communicate, and children's thinking becomes faster, more coordinated, and complex (Kolb, 2020; Chevalier et al., 2015). Patterns of myelination correspond with the onset and refinement of cognitive functions and behaviors (Dean et al., 2014). Myelination proceeds most rapidly from birth to age 4, first in the sensory and motor cortex, and then spreads to other cortical areas through childhood, continuing though adolescence and into early adulthood (Qiu et al., 2015; Reynolds et al., 2019).

Lateralization, the process of the hemispheres becoming specialized to carry out different functions, becomes more pronounced in early childhood and is associated with children's development (Kolb, 2020). Infants generally display a hand preference, left or right, which tends to strengthen with use over the lifespan. Hemispheric domination increases over childhood and the left hemisphere tends to dominate over the right in most adults (Duboc et al., 2015). Language tends to be lateralized to the left hemisphere in adults, and lateralization predicts children's language skills. Young children who show better performance on language tasks use more pathways in the left hemisphere and fewer in the right than those who are less skilled in language tasks (Walton et al., 2018).

Climbing requires strength, coordination, and balance.
Michele Oenbrink / Alamy Stock Photo

Motor Development

The refinement of motor skills that use the large muscles of the body—as well as those that require hand-eye coordination and precise hand movements—is an important developmental task of early childhood.

Gross Motor Skills

Between the ages of 3 and 6, children become physically stronger, with increases in bone and muscle strength. As the parts of the brain responsible for sensory and motor skills develop, children gain balance and coordination and can run, stop suddenly and turn, jump, hop, and climb. Young children are driven to move and to practice motor skills. Three-year-old children show the highest level of activity in the lifespan (Gabbard, 2018). As they grow and gain competence in their motor skills, young children become more coordinated and begin to show interest in balancing games and those that involve feats of coordination, such as running while kicking a ball. Coordinating complex movements, like those entailed in riding a bicycle, is challenging for young children as it requires controlling multiple limbs, balancing, and more. By age 5, most North American children can throw and catch a ball, climb a ladder, and ride a tricycle. Some 5-year-olds can even skate or ride a bicycle (Gabbard, 2018).

There is continuity in motor development throughout childhood. Motor experience and achievements in infancy are associated with motor skills in early childhood. Children who learn to crawl early tend to show more advanced motor skills in early childhood than their late-crawling peers (Payne et al., 2016). Boys and girls show similar motor abilities, with subtle differences. Boys tend to be more active than girls and can typically throw a ball and kick better as well as jump farther than girls. Girls, on the other hand, tend to be better at coordinated activities such as balancing on one foot. The games that boys and girls are typically encouraged to play contribute to sex differences in motor skills. For example, boys often have more practice in games involving balls and girls often play balancing games, such as hopscotch. Preschoolers who regularly engage in moderate to vigorous physical activity tend to show better gross motor coordination (Silva-Santos et al., 2019). Advances in gross motor skills help children move about and develop a sense of mastery of their environment, but it is fine motor skills that permit young children to take responsibility for their own care.

Fine Motor Skills

Motor development follows the proximodistal principle (see Chapter 3). Children gain motor control from the body outward toward the fingers and toes. Fine motor skills rely on controlling and coordinating the small muscles of the body. The ability to button a shirt, pour milk into a glass, assemble puzzles, and draw pictures all involve eye-hand and small muscle coordination. As children get better at these skills, they are able to become more independent and do more for themselves. Young children become better at grasping eating utensils and become more self-sufficient at feeding. Many fine motor skills are very difficult for young children because they involve both hands and both sides of the brain. Tying a shoelace is a complex act requiring attention, memory for an intricate series of hand movements, and the dexterity to perform them. Although preschoolers struggle with this task, by 5 to 6 years of age, most children can tie their shoes (Payne et al., 2016). Recent research suggests that children's fine motor ability influences cognition. Dexterity is associated with reasoning, and children's ability

TABLE 5.1 ■ Summary of Motor Skill Development Milestones in Young Children

Age	Gross Motor Skill	Fine Motor Skills
2–3 years	Walks more smoothly, runs but cannot turn or stop suddenly, jumps, throws a ball with a rigid body and catches by trapping ball against chest, rides push toys using feet	Unzips large zippers, puts on and removes some clothing, uses a spoon
3–4 years	Runs, ascends stairs alternating feet, jumps 15 to 24 inches, hops, pedals and steers a tricycle	Serves food, can work large buttons, copies vertical line and circle, uses scissors
4–5 years	Runs more smoothly with control over stopping and turning, descends stairs alternating feet, jumps 24 to 33 inches, skips, throws ball by rotating the body and transferring weight to one foot, catches ball with hands, rides tricycle and steers effectively	Uses scissors to cut along a line, uses fork effectively, copies simple shapes and some letters
5–6 years	Runs more quickly, skips more effectively, throws and catches a ball like older children, makes a running jump of 28 to 36 inches, rides bicycle with training wheels	Ties shoes, uses knife to cut soft food, copies numbers and simple words

to use their fingers to aid in counting predicts their mathematical skills (Fischer et al., 2018, 2020; Martzog et al., 2019).Young children's advances in motor skills are summarized in Table 5.1

Nutrition and Eating Habits

Young children require a healthy diet, with the same foods that adults need. Most children in developed nations eat enough calories, but their diets often contain insufficient vitamins and minerals, such as Vitamin D, calcium, and potassium, and excessive calories and sugar (Hess & Slavin, 2014). Children's food preferences are influenced by their experiences, and long-lasting attitudes about food are often formed in early childhood. Repeated exposure to sweet and salty snacks increases children's preference for sugary and salty foods (Remington et al., 2012). In one study of 96 childcare centers, 90% served high-sugar or high-salt food or did not serve whole grains in a day's meals (Benjamin Neelon et al., 2012). Nutrient-dense snacks, such as cheese, yogurt, or hummus, can increase children's intake of nutrients without contributing to dietary excess.

Young children require a healthy diet, which can be accompanied by an occasional junk food splurge.

Jose Luis Pelaez Inc/ Getty Images

From ages 2 to 6, young children's appetites vary with their growth. Children's appetite is usually very good during active growth periods, but their appetite declines as their growth slows (Marotz, 2015). This decline is normal, but often an undue concern for parents. Children eat when they are hungry and should be provided with frequent opportunities to eat. When a child doesn't finish breakfast, a small nutritious mid-morning snack can make up for lost nutrients. Generally, preschool children tend to balance their eating, making up for short periods of little food intake with greater consumption later (Ball et al., 2017).

Young children are often sensitive to the sensory quality of foods, including appearance, texture, and shape (Marotz, 2015). Children often dislike trying new foods. Encouraging children to try a new food several times over a few weeks can help them become familiar with the taste and texture, which can increase the likelihood of eating the new food. Involving children in meal preparation can improve children's interest in and acceptance of new foods.

Physical Activity

Young children's play often involves physical activity, with important benefits for development. Physical activity enhances growth and is consistently associated with advances in motor development, fitness, and bone and skeletal health (Carson et al., 2017). The recently updated Physical Activity Guidelines for Americans (U.S. Department of Health and Human Services, 2018) advises that preschool children require daily physical activity and advises a target of about 3 hours of activity (at any level ranging from light, such as walking at a comfortable place, to vigorous, such as running) per day. Over the course of a day, a child might go for a walk with a caregiver, engage in active play with peers, and practice dancing and balancing games in preschool. Canada, the United Kingdom, and the Commonwealth of Australia have published similar recommendations (U.S. Department of Health and Human Services, 2018).

Unfortunately, only about half of children meet the physical activity guidelines (Hesketh et al., 2017; Pate et al., 2015). One important predictor of physical activity is time spent outdoors. Children are more active when they are enrolled in care centers that schedule more than one hour of outside time each day (Copeland et al., 2016). Access to safe play environments is also associated with greater physical activity. Children who live in homes with yards engage in more physical activity than those who live in apartments, and yard size is positively associated with children's level of physical activity (Miller et al., 2020). Children from low-income homes tend to spend less time outdoors, engage in less physically active play, and spend more time in sedentary behaviors, such as watching television, as reported by parents (Lindsay et al., 2017). Although children of color are more likely to reside in communities that may pose challenges to outside play, ethnic and racial differences are not apparent in preschoolers' physical activity (Pate et al., 2015).

Sleep

Sleep duration naturally declines about 20% from infancy into early childhood (Honaker & Meltzer, 2014). The American Academy of Sleep Medicine advises that young children 3 to 5 years of age should sleep 10 to 13 hours (including naps) each day (Paruthi et al., 2016). Most young children meet these goals, sleeping 10 to 11 hours each night (Magee et al., 2014).

Some children experience sleep problems, such as awakening often, difficulty falling asleep, and poor sleep duration. Poor sleep may have a cascading effect on development through its influence on brain function. Sleep problems pose risks to young children's cognitive development, including problems with attention, working memory, and slower processing speed (Schumacher et al., 2017). Sleep deprivation affects the connectivity between the prefrontal cortex and parts of the brain responsible for emotion, resulting in overreactive and exaggerated emotional responses to positive and negative stimuli, poor emotional self-regulation and impulsivity, and increased risk for anxiety (Berger et al., 2012; Keefe-Cooperman & Brady-Amoon, 2014; Miller et al., 2015; Vaughn et al., 2015). These emotional problems can, in turn, interfere with sleep in a perpetual cycle, with increasing negative effects for young children (Magee et al., 2014). Providing a consistent sleep routine, limiting evening access to electronic screens, perhaps offering a security object such as a stuffed animal, and providing understanding and affection can help children develop healthy sleep habits.

Illness and Injury

Young children's immune systems are still developing and they are more susceptible to germs and tend to experience more frequent colds and illnesses than older children and adults. Most colds must run their course. Preventing dehydration and treating a child's discomfort is appropriate treatment for a cold and flu. Aspirin must never be administered to young children because it places children at risk to develop Reye's syndrome, a rare condition in which the brain and liver swell.

Immunization prevents serious, sometimes fatal, diseases that were once common, such as measles. A measles outbreak in 20 U.S. states in 2019 illustrated the value of immunization for preventing illness (Centers for Disease Control, 2019). Measles, thought to be eliminated in the U.S. in 2000, spread quickly among unvaccinated children and adults. In New York City, one child was thought to be the source of the infection that affected more than 500 other children (New York City Department of Health, 2019).

Many young children are exposed to toxins that can harm development. Exposure to indoor and outdoor air pollutants, such as cigarette smoke, carbon monoxide, particulate matter, and car exhausts, negatively affects children's respiratory health, causes breathing problems and asthma (a chronic disease involving the inflammation of the lungs (Goldizen et al., 2016; Landrigan et al., 2019). Peeling lead paint can expose children to lead chips or dust that contaminates their surroundings. Lead is associated with serious damage to the brain that can result in long-term problems in cognition, learning, and behavior, including disorders such as ADHD and behavioral problems such as delinquency, in childhood, adolescence, and even adulthood (Thapar et al., 2013; Reuben et al., 2017; Zhang et al., 2013;). Although lead is no longer included as an ingredient in household paint, older houses still contain lead paint. Children from low socioeconomic–status homes are more likely to live in older housing and be exposed to lead paint as well as other toxins that can have long-term negative effects on children's health and well-being (Landrigan et al., 2019; Suk et al., 2016).

The leading cause of death in young children is accidents. Drowning is the most common cause of accidental death, followed by car accidents, unintentional suffocation, and fire (Centers for Disease Control and Prevention, 2017). The most common nonfatal injuries that require a visit to the emergency room are falls (Centers for Disease Control and Prevention, 2018).

A variety of individual and contextual influences place children at risk for injury. Children who are impulsive, overactive, and difficult, as well as those diagnosed with attention deficit hyperactivity disorder (ADHD), experience higher rates of unintentional injuries (Acar et al., 2015; Lange et al., 2016; Morrongiello et al., 2006). Children's risk of injury increases when their parents report feeling little control over their behavior (Acar et al., 2015). Poor parental and adult supervision is closely associated with childhood injury (Ablewhite et al., 2015; Morrongiello et al., 2006). Neighborhood disadvantage, specifically low SES and lack of resources, such as safe playgrounds, is associated with higher rates of injuries, bone fractures, and injury-related death in children in the U.S., Canada, and the UK (Lyons et al., 2000; McClure et al., 2015; Rees et al., 2020; Stark et al., 2002).

Thinking in Context: Biological Influences

1. Identify similarities and differences in patterns and processes of brain development in infancy (see Chapter 4) and early childhood.
2. A parent to a 3-year-old informs you, "I'd like to take advantage of the plasticity of the early childhood brain." Explain the concept of plasticity. Should the parent "take advantage" of it? How? What do you tell the parent?

Thinking in Context: Applied Developmental Science

Provide advice to a parent of a 4-year-old. Specifically, give four tips to parents regarding young children's needs for nutrition, physical activity, and sleep. Each recommendation should include advice and an explanation of why the tip is important.

Thinking in Context: Intersectionality

All young children have the same basic health needs, but some children experience disproportionately greater risks for poor health than their peers. Discuss this statement, examining the effect of some of the disparities associated with race, ethnicity, and SES, on factors such as risk for illness and injuries and other health behaviors. How do contextual factors contribute to health risks and how might contextual factors reduce the risk for poor health outcomes?

COGNITIVE-DEVELOPMENTAL AND SOCIOCULTURAL REASONING IN EARLY CHILDHOOD

LEARNING OBJECTIVE

5.2 Compare Piaget's cognitive-developmental and Vygotsky's sociocultural perspectives on cognitive development in early childhood.

Four-year-old Timothy stands up on his toes and releases his parachute toy, letting the action figure dangling from the parachute drift a few feet from him and collapse on the floor. "I'm going to go up high and make it faster," he says, imagining standing on the sofa and making the toy sail far into the clouds. He stands on the sofa and releases the toy, which sails a bit further this time. "Next time he'll jump out of the plane even higher!" Timothy thinks, excitedly. His friend Isaiah calls out, "Let's make him land on the moon! He can meet space people!"

Timothy and Isaiah can plan, think of solutions to problems, and use language to communicate their ideas. They learn through play by interacting with people and objects around them. From the cognitive-developmental perspective, young children's thought advances beyond the sensory and motor schemes of infancy to include more sophisticated representational thought.

Piaget's Cognitive-Developmental Perspective: Preoperational Reasoning

According to Piaget, preoperational reasoning appears in young children from about ages 2 to 6. **Preoperational reasoning** is characterized by a dramatic leap in the use of symbolic thinking that permits young children to use language, interact with others, and play using their own thoughts and imaginations to guide their behavior. It is symbolic thought that enables Timothy and Isaiah to use language to communicate their thoughts and desires—and it is also what allows them to send their toy on a mission to the moon to visit with pretend space people.

Characteristics of Preoperational Reasoning

Young children in the preoperational stage show impressive advances in representational thinking, but they are unable to grasp logic and cannot understand complex relationships. Children who show preoperational reasoning tend to make several common errors, including egocentrism, animism, centration, and irreversibility.

Egocentrism "See my picture?" Ricardo asks as he holds up a blank sheet of paper. Mr. Seris answers, "You can see your picture, but I can't. Turn your page around so that I can see your picture. There it is! It's beautiful," he proclaims after Ricardo flips the piece of paper, permitting him to see his drawing. Ricardo did not realize that even though he could see his drawing, Mr. Seris could not. Ricardo displays **egocentrism,** the inability to take another person's point of view or perspective. Egocentric children view the world from their own perspectives, assuming that other people share their feelings, knowledge, and even physical view of the world.

A classic task used to illustrate preoperational children's egocentrism is the **three-mountain task.** As shown in Figure 5.1, the child faces a table facing three large mountains. A doll is placed in a chair across the table from the child. The child is asked how the mountains look to the doll. Piaget found that young children in the preoperational stage demonstrated egocentrism because they described the scene from their own perspective rather than the doll's. They did not understand that the doll would have a different view of the mountains (Piaget & Inhelder, 1967).

Animism Egocentric thinking can also take the form of **animism**, the belief that inanimate objects are alive and have feelings and intentions. "It's raining because the sun is sad and it is crying," 3-year-old Melinda explains. Children accept their own explanations for phenomena as they are unable to consider another viewpoint or alternative reason.

FIGURE 5.1 ■ The Three-Mountain Task

Children who display preoperational reasoning cannot describe the scene depicted in the three mountains task from the point of view of the teddy bear.

FIGURE 5.2 ■ Appearance vs. Reality: Is It a Cat or Dog?

Young children did not understand that Maynard the cat remained a cat despite wearing a dog mask and looking like a dog.

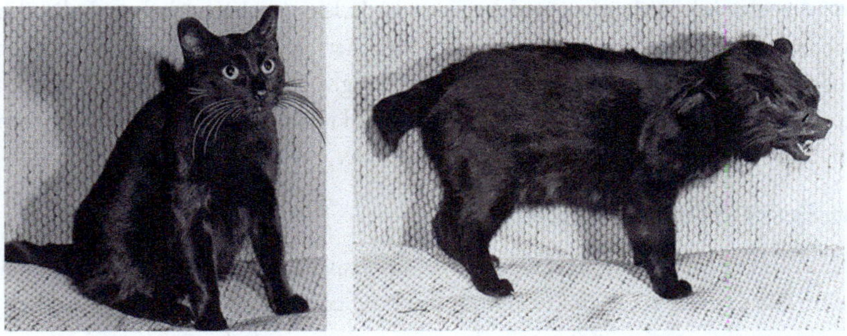

Source: (DeVries, 1969).

Centration Preoperational children exhibit **centration**, the tendency to focus on one part of a stimulus or situation and exclude all others. A boy who believes that if he wears a dress he will become a girl focuses entirely on the appearance (the dress) rather than the other characteristics that make him a boy.

Centration is illustrated by a classic task that requires the preoperational child to distinguish what something appears to be from what it really is, the appearance-reality distinction. In a classic study illustrating this effect, DeVries (1969) presented 3- to 6-year-old children with a cat named Maynard (see Figure 5.2). The children were permitted to pet Maynard. Then, while his head and shoulders were hidden behind a screen (and his back and tail were still visible), a dog mask was placed onto Maynard's head. The children were then asked, "What kind of animal is it now?" "Does it bark or meow?" Three-year-old children, despite Maynard's body and tail being visible during the transformation, replied that he was now a dog. Six-year-old children were able to distinguish Maynard's appearance from reality and explained that he only *looked* like a dog.

One reason that 3-year-old children fail appearance-reality tasks is they are not yet capable of effective dual encoding, the ability to mentally represent an object in more than one way at a time (Flavell et al., 1986). For example, young children are not able to understand that a scale model (like a doll house) can be both an object (something to play with) and a symbol (of an actual house; MacConnell & Daehler, 2004).

Irreversibility "You ruined it!" cried Johnson after his older sister, Monique, placed a triangular block atop the tower of blocks he had just built. "No, I just put a triangle there to show it was the top and finish it," she explains. "No!" insists Johnson. "OK, I'll take it off," says Monique. "See? Now it's just how you left it." "No. It's ruined," Johnson sighs. Johnson continued to be upset after his sister removed the triangular block, not realizing that by removing the block she has restored the block structure to its original state. Young children's thinking is characterized by **irreversibility**, meaning that they do not understand that reversing a process can often undo it and restore the original state.

Preoperational children's irreversible thinking is illustrated by their performance on tasks that measure **conservation**, or the understanding that the physical quantity of a substance, such as number, mass, or volume, remains the same even when its appearance changes (see Figure 5.3). In a typical conservation of liquids task, a child is shown two identical glasses. The same amount of water is poured into each glass. After the child agrees that the two glasses contain the same amount of water, the liquid from one glass is poured into a taller, narrower glass and the child is asked whether one glass contains more liquid than the other. Young children in the preoperational stage reply that the taller narrower glass contains more liquid. Why? It has a higher liquid level than the shorter, wider glass has. They center on the appearance of the liquid without realizing that the process can be reversed by pouring the liquid back into the shorter, wider glass. They focus on the height of the water, ignoring other aspects such as the change in width, not understanding that it is still the same water.

Characteristics of preoperational children's reasoning are summarized in Table 5.2.

FIGURE 5.3 ■ Additional Conservation Problems

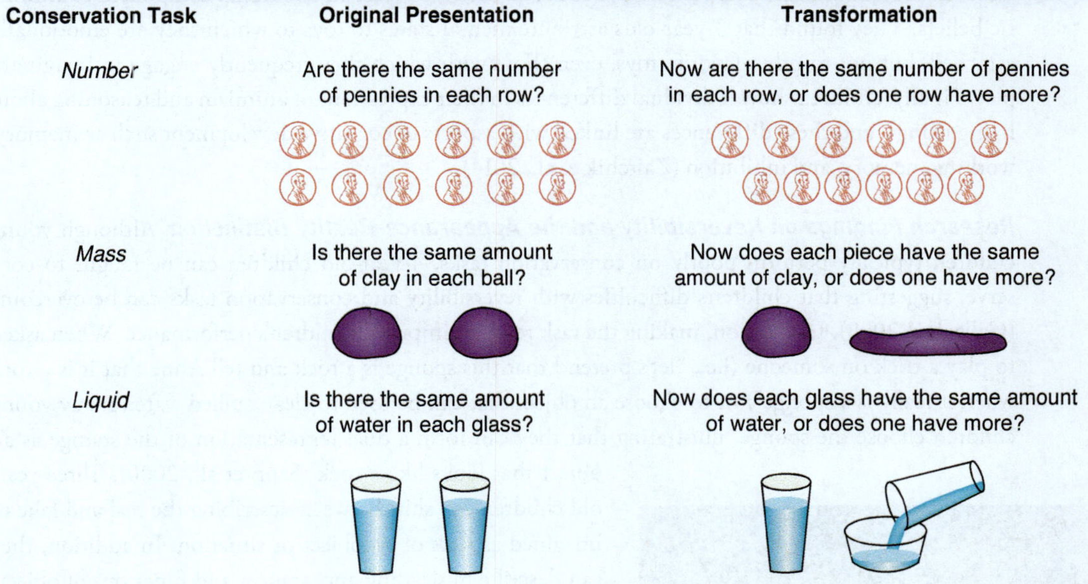

TABLE 5.2 ■ Characteristics of Preoperational Children's Reasoning

Characteristic	Description
Egocentrism	The inability to take another person's point of view or perspective
Animism	The belief that inanimate objects are alive and have feelings and intentions
Centration	Tendency to focus attention on one part of a stimulus or situation and exclude all others
Irreversibility	Failure to understand that reversing a process can often undo a process and restore the original state

Evaluating Preoperational Reasoning

Research with young children has suggested that Piaget's tests of preoperational thinking underestimated young children. Success on Piaget's tasks appears to depend more on the child's language abilities than his or her actions. As we discussed earlier, to be successful at the three-mountain task the child must not only understand how the mounds look from the other side of the table, but must be able to communicate that understanding. Appearance reality tasks require not simply an understanding of dual representation, but the ability to express it. However, if the task is nonverbal, such as requiring reaching for an object rather than talking about it, even 3-year-old children can distinguish appearance from reality (Sapp et al., 2000).

Research Findings on Egocentrism and Animism Simple tasks demonstrate that young children are less egocentric than Piaget posited. When a 3-year-old child is shown a card that depicts a dog on one side and a cat on another, and the card is held up so that the researcher can see the cat and the child can see the dog, the child correctly responds that the researcher can see the cat (Flavell et al., 1981). When the task is relevant to children's everyday lives (i.e., hiding) their performance suggests that they are not as egocentric as Piaget posited (Newcombe & Huttenlocher, 1992). Other research suggests that 3- to 5-year-old children can learn perspective-taking skills through training and retain their perspective-taking abilities 6 months later (Mori & Cigala, 2016).

Likewise, 3-year-old children do not tend to ascribe life-like qualities to inanimate objects, even when the object is a robot that can move (Jipson et al., 2016). Most 4-year-old children understand that animals grow, and even plants grow, but objects do not (Backschneider et al., 1993). Sometimes young children provide animistic responses. Gjersoe et al. (2015) suggest an emotional component to animistic beliefs. They found that 3-year-olds attribute mental states to toys to which they are emotionally attached, but not to other favorite toys, even those with which they frequently engage in imaginary play. Finally, children show individual differences in their expressions of animism and reasoning about living things, and these differences are linked with aspects of cognitive development such as memory, working memory, and inhibition (Zaitchik et al., 2014).

Research Findings on Reversibility and the Appearance-Reality Distinction Although young children typically perform poorly on conservation tasks, 4-year-old children can be taught to conserve, suggesting that children's difficulties with reversibility and conservation tasks can be overcome (Gallagher, 2008). In addition, making the task relevant improves children's performance. When asked to play a trick on someone (i.e., "let's pretend that this sponge is a rock and tell Anne that it is a rock when it really is a sponge") or to choose an object that can be used to clean spilled water, many young children choose the sponge, illustrating that they can form a dual representation of the sponge as an object that looks like a rock (Sapp et al., 2000). Three-year-old children can shift between describing the real and fake or imagined aspects of an object or situation. In addition, they can describe misleading appearances and functions of objects in response to natural conversational prompts, as compared with the more formal language in the typical prompts used in traditional appearance-reality tasks (e.g., "What is it really and truly?"; Deák, 2006). In sum, preschoolers show an understanding of the appearance-reality distinction and it develops throughout childhood (Woolley & Ghossainy, 2013).

Children learn culturally valued skills by interacting with and helping skilled partners.

Javier Mamani / Contributor/ Getty Images

Vygotsky's Sociocultural Perspective

According to Russian psychologist Lev Vygotsky, we are embedded in a cultural context that shapes how we think and who we become. Mental activity—cognition—is influenced by culture, specifically, the cultural tools that members of a cultures share (Robbins, 2005; Vygotsky, 1978).

Cultural tools include physical items such as computers, pencils, and paper but also ways of thinking about phenomena, including how to approach math and scientific problems, as well as language itself. Spoken language, the ways in which members of a culture communicate about their world, is a cultural tool that shapes thought. Children's lived experiences—their interactions with cultural tools and other members of their culture—influence their views of the world and their process of thinking (Rogoff et al., 2018). A critical assumption is that spoken language is a cultural tool that shapes how we think.

Guided Participation and Scaffolding

Children learn how to use the tools of their culture through social experience, by interacting with more experienced partners who provide guidance and assistance in completing tasks. Children learn through **guided participation** (also known as an *apprenticeship in thinking*), a form of sensitive teaching in which partners are attuned to the needs of children and help them accomplish more than the children could do alone (Rogoff, 2014). As novices, children learn from more skilled, or expert, partners by observing them and asking questions. In this way, children are apprentices, learning how others approach problems. Expert partners provide **scaffolding**, or assistance that is tailored to the child's needs and permits children to bridge the gap between their current competence level and the task at hand (Mermelshtine, 2017). Consider a child working on a jigsaw puzzle. The child is stumped, unsure of the next step. Suppose a more skilled partner, such as an adult, sibling, or another child who has more experience with puzzles, provides a little bit of assistance, a scaffold. The expert partner might point to an empty space on the puzzle and encourage the child to find a piece that fits that spot. If the child remains stumped, the partner might point out a piece or rotate it to help the child see the relationship. The partner acts to engage the child and provides support to help the child finish the puzzle, adjusting responses in light of the child's emerging competence.

Scaffolding occurs in formal educational settings, but also informally, any time more skilled persons adjust their interactional style to guide children to complete a task that they could not complete alone (Rogoff et al., 2016). Mothers vary their scaffolding behaviors in response to children's attempts at tasks. They spontaneously use different behaviors depending on the child's attention skills, using more verbal engagement, strategic questions, verbal hints, and verbal prompts when children show difficulty paying attention during a task (Robinson et al., 2009). Moreover, maternal reading, scaffolding, and verbal guidance are associated with 2- to 4-year-olds' capacities for cognitive control and planning (Moriguchi, 2014). Parents and childcare providers often provide this informal instruction, but anyone who is more skilled at a given task, including older siblings and peers, can promote children's cognitive development (Rogoff et al., 2016). Collaboration with more skilled peers improves performance on cognitive tasks such as card-sorting tasks, Piagetian tasks, planning, and academic tasks (Sills et al., 2016).

Zone of Proximal Development

As Vygotsky (1934/1962) explained, "What the child can do in cooperation today, he can do alone tomorrow" (p. 104). Effective scaffolding works within the **zone of proximal development**, which is the gap between children's competence level—what they can accomplish independently—and what they can do with the assistance of a skilled partner. With time, children internalize the scaffolding lesson and learn to accomplish the task on their own—and their zone of proximal development shifts, as shown in Figure 5.4. Adults tend to naturally provide children with instruction within the zone of proximal development (Rogoff, 2014). Adults reading a book to a child tend to point to items, label and describe characters' emotional states, explain, ask questions, listen, and respond sensitively, helping the child understand challenging material that is just beyond what the child can understand on his or her own (Silva et al., 2014).

The quality of scaffolding influences children's development. In one study of preschool teachers and children, the degree to which the adult matched the child's needs for help in playing predicted more autonomous play on the part of children over a 6-month period (Trawick-Smith & Dziurgot, 2011). Adults may act intentionally to encourage and support children's learning (Zuckerman, 2007).

FIGURE 5.4 ■ Zone of Proximal Development

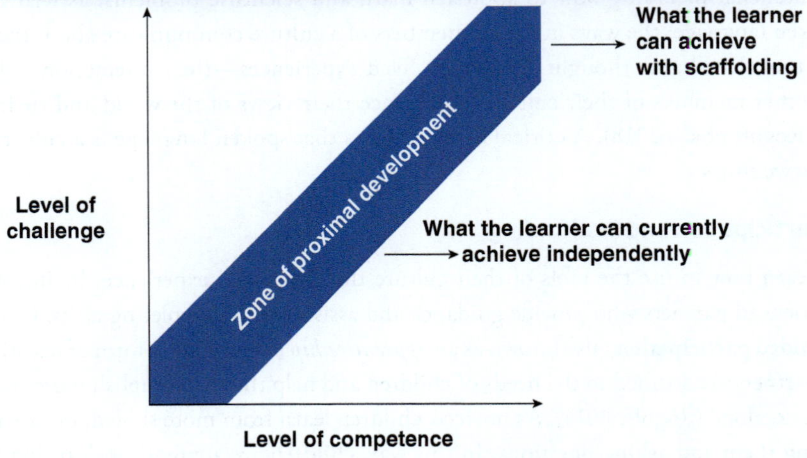

Source: Adapted from Vygotsky, 1978.

Parents' guidance acts as a scaffold within the zone of proximal development to help children accomplish challenging tasks. Soon children become able to complete the task independently.

Takamitsu GALALA Kato/ Getty Images

One study of parents and young children visiting a science museum found that when parents provided specific guidance in considering a conservation of volume problem, such as discussing the size of the containers, asking "how" and "why" questions, and talking about simple math, children were more likely to give correct responses to scientific reasoning problems, including those involving conservation (Vandermaas-Peeler et al., 2016).

Parents and preschool teachers can take advantage of the social nature of learning by assigning children tasks that they can accomplish with some assistance, providing just enough help so that children learn to complete the tasks independently. This helps to create learning environments that stimulate children to complete more challenging tasks on their own (Wass & Golding, 2014). Through guided play, teachers encourage exploration and guide children with comments encouraging them to explore, question, or extend their interests (Bodrova & Leong, 2018).

Private Speech

As Leroy played alone in the corner of the living room, he pretended to drive his toy car up a mountain and said to himself, "It's a high mountain. Got to push it all the way up. Oh no! Out of gas. Now they will have to stay here." Young children like Leroy often talk aloud to themselves, with no apparent intent to communicate with others. This self-talk, called **private speech**, accounts for 20% to 50% of the utterances of children ages 4 to 10 (Berk, 1986). Private speech serves developmental functions. It is thinking. Young children use self-talk to guide their own learning (Vygotsky, 1934/1962).

Private speech plays a role in self-regulation, the ability to control one's impulses and appropriately direct behavior; this increases during the preschool years (Berk & Garvin, 1984). Children use private speech to plan strategies, solve problems, and regulate themselves so that they can achieve goals. Children are more likely to use private speech while working on challenging tasks and attempting to solve problems, especially when they encounter obstacles or do not have adult supervision (Winsler et al., 2009). As children grow older, they use private speech more effectively to accomplish tasks. Children who use private speech during a challenging activity are more attentive and involved and show better performance than children who do not (Alarcón-Rubio et al., 2014). In one study, 4- and 5-year-old children completed a complex multistep planning task over six sessions. Children who used on-task private speech showed dramatic improvements between consecutive sessions (Benigno et al., 2011).

Although Vygotsky considered the use of private speech a universal developmental milestone, further research suggests that there are individual differences, with some children using private speech little or not at all (Berk, 1992). Preschool girls tend to use more mature forms of private speech than boys. The same is true of children from middle-income households as compared with children from low-income households (Berk, 1986). This pattern corresponds to the children's relative abilities in language use. Talkative children use more private speech than do quiet children (McGonigle-Chalmers et al., 2014). Bright children tend to use private speech earlier, and children with learning disabilities tend to continue its use later in development (Berk, 1992).

During elementary school, children's private speech becomes a whisper or a silent moving of the lips (Manfra & Winsler, 2006). Private speech is the child's thinking and eventually becomes internalized as *inner speech*, or word-based internal thought, a silent internal dialogue that individuals use every day to regulate and organize their behavior (Al-Namlah et al., 2012). Inner speech plays a role in cognitive processing, including short-term memory, planning, and executive function (Alderson-Day & Fernyhough, 2015). Children's use of inner speech varies with the task at hand. They are most likely to use inner speech when completing difficult problems and tasks (Vissers et al., 2020). As the task becomes more familiar and automatic, the accompanying inner speech declines. Inner speech is common in adults; we use words in our thoughts. . We tend to use more inner speech, and even private speech (talking out loud to ourselves), when completing challenging tasks, supporting its use in self-guidance and self-regulation (Racy et al., 2020). One of the educational implications of private speech is that parents and teachers must understand that talking to oneself or inaudible muttering is not misbehavior but, rather, indicates an effort to complete a difficult task or self-regulate behavior.

Evaluating Vygotsky's Sociocultural Perspective

Although relatively unknown until recent decades, Vygotsky's ideas about the sociocultural nature of cognitive development have influenced prominent theories of development, such as Bronfenbrenner's bioecological theory (Bronfenbrenner, 1979). They have been applied in educational settings, supporting the use of assisted discovery, guiding children's learning, and cooperative learning with peers. Effective instruction targets the zone of proximal development; most teachers intuitively seek to help students grasp new concepts that are seemingly out of reach (Taber, 2020).

Similar to Piaget's theory, Vygotsky's theory has been criticized for a lack of precision. The mechanisms or processes underlying the social transmission of thought are not described (Göncü & Gauvain, 2012). Moreover, constructs such as the zone of proximal development are not easily testable (Wertsch, 1998). In addition, underlying cognitive capacities, such as attention and memory, are not addressed. It is understandable that Vygotsky's theory is incomplete, as he died of tuberculosis at the age of 37. We can only speculate about how his ideas might have evolved over a longer lifetime. Nevertheless, Vygotsky provided a new framework for understanding development as a process of transmitting culturally valued tools that influence how we look at the world, think, and approach problems.

Thinking in Context: Lifespan Development

What role does context take in Piaget's and Vygotsky's theories? To what extent is cognitive development influenced by the sociocultural contexts in which children live, according to Piaget and Vygotsky?

Thinking in Context: Applied Developmental Science

1. Suppose that you are a preschool teacher inspired by both Piaget and Vygotsky. Which of their ideas would you choose to incorporate into your classroom? Explain.

2. If children can be taught to respond correctly to problems assessing animism, egocentrism, or conservation, should they? Why or why not?

INFORMATION PROCESSING IN EARLY CHILDHOOD

LEARNING OBJECTIVE

5.3 Describe information processing abilities during early childhood.

From an information processing perspective, cognitive development entails developing mental strategies to guide one's thinking and use one's cognitive resources more effectively. In early childhood, children become more efficient at attending, encoding and retrieving memories, and problem solving.

Attention

Early childhood is accompanied by dramatic improvements in attention, particularly **sustained attention**, the ability to remain focused on a stimulus for an extended period of time (Rueda, 2013). Young children often struggle with selective attention. **Selective attention** refers to the ability to systematically deploy one's attention, focusing on relevant information and ignoring distractors. Young children do not search thoroughly when asked to compare detailed pictures and explain what is missing from one. They have trouble focusing on one stimulus and switching their attention to compare it with other stimuli (Hanania & Smith, 2010). Young children who sort cards according to one dimension such as color may later be unable to successfully switch to different sorting criteria (Honomichl & Zhe, 2011). Young children's selective attention at age 2½ predicts working memory and response inhibition at age 3 (Veer et al., 2017). The ability to selectively focus and sustain attention predicts academic skills at the beginning and end of preschool (Shannon et al., 2020).

Working Memory and Executive Function

Young children simply get better at thinking. Recall from Chapter 3 that working memory is where all thinking or information processing takes place. Working memory consists of a short-term store (*short-term memory*), a processor, and a control mechanism known as the **central executive**, responsible for executive function, directing the flow of information and regulating cognitive activities, such as planning (Baddeley, 2016; Miyake & Friedman, 2012). Children get better at holding information in working memory, manipulating it, inhibiting irrelevant stimuli, and planning, which allows them to set and achieve goals (Carlson et al., 2013). With advances in executive function, children become more skilled at controlling and deploying their cognitive resources to serve their goals (Doebel, 2020).

Short-term memory is commonly assessed by a memory span task in which individuals are asked to recall a series of unrelated items (such as numbers) presented at a rate of about 1 per second. The greatest lifetime improvements on memory span tasks occur in early childhood. In a classic study, 2- to 3-year-old children could recall about two digits, increasing to about five items at age 7, but only increasing another two digits, to seven, by early adulthood (Bjorklund & Myers, 2015).

With improvements in selective attention and increases in short-term memory, young children are able to manipulate more information in working memory and become better at planning, considering the steps needed to complete a particular act, and carrying them out to achieve a goal (Plebanek & Sloutsky, 2019; Rueda, 2013). Preschoolers can create and abide by a plan to complete tasks that are familiar and not too complex, such as systematically searching for a lost object in a yard (Wellman et al., 1979). But they have difficulty with more complex tasks. Young children have difficulty deciding where to begin and how to proceed to complete a task in an orderly way (Ristic & Enns, 2015). When they plan, young children often skip important steps. One reason why young children get better at attention, memory, and cognitive tasks is they get better at inhibiting impulses to engage in task-irrelevant actions and can stay focused on a task.

Improvements in executive function, working memory, and response inhibition influence how young children understand, interact with, and respond to others. Preschool children who score high on measures of executive function tend to show greater social competence, including more adaptive responses to peer conflict, than other children (Caporaso et al., 2019). Young children's awareness, understanding, expression, and regulation of emotions, known as emotional competence, are also related to their executive function and contribute to social development (Li et al., 2020). Children who are skilled in self-regulation tend to be better able to control their impulses and adjust to school (Savina, 2020).

Memory

Young children's memory for events and information acquired during events, **episodic memory**, expands rapidly (Roediger & Marsh, 2003; Tulving, 2002). A researcher might study episodic memory by asking a child, "Where did you go on vacation?" or "Remember the pictures I showed you yesterday?" **Recognition memory**, the ability to recognize a stimulus one has encountered before, is nearly perfect in 4- and 5-year-old children, but they are much less proficient in **recall memory**, which is the ability to independently generate a memory of a stimulus encountered before without seeing it again (Myers & Perlmutter, 2014).

Memory Strategies

Why do young children perform so poorly in recall tasks? Young children are not very effective at using **memory strategies**, the cognitive activities that make us more likely to remember (Schwartz, 2018). Rehearsal—repeating items over and over—is a strategy that older children and adults use to recall lists of stimuli. Children do not spontaneously and reliably apply rehearsal until after the first grade (Bjorklund & Myers, 2015). Preschool-age children can be taught strategies, but they generally do not transfer their learning and apply it to new tasks (Titz & Karbach, 2014). This utilization deficiency seems to occur because of their limited working memories and difficulty inhibiting irrelevant stimuli. They cannot apply the strategy at the same time as they have to retain both the material to be learned and the strategy to be used. Instead, new information competes with the information the child is attempting to recall (Aslan & Bäuml, 2010). Overall, advances in executive function, working memory, and attention predict strategy use (Stone et al., 2016).

Young children do not always show more poor performance relative to adults. In one study, parents read a novel rhyming verse and a word list as their 4-year-old children's bedtime story on 10 consecutive days. When asked to recall the verse, the 4-year-old children outperformed their parents and a set of young adults who also listened to the verse (Király et al., 2017). The children and adults did not differ in their ability to recall the gist of the verse. Unlike adults, young children are immersed in a culture of verse and rely on oral transmission of information, likely underlying their skill relative to adults.

Autobiographical Memory

Autobiographical memory refers to memory of personally meaningful events that took place at a specific time and place in one's past (Bauer, 2015). Autobiographical memory emerges as children become proficient in language and executive function and develops steadily from 3 to 6 years of age (Nieto et al., 2018). By age 3, children can retrieve and report specific memories, especially those that have personal significance, are repeated, or are highly stressful, such as an accident and visit to the emergency room (Nuttall et al., 2014; Schwartz, 2018; Goodman et al., 1990). Eight-year-old children have been found to accurately remember events that occurred when they were as young as 3½ years of age (Goodman & Aman, 1990). Events that are unique or new, such as a trip to the circus, are better recalled; 3-year-old children will recall them for a year or longer (Fivush et al., 1983). But frequent events tend to blur together.

By age 3, children are able to retrieve and report memories of specific experiences, especially those that have personal significance, such as a fun day at a fair.

sarra22/ Getty Images

The way adults talk with the child about a shared experience can influence how well the child will remember it (Fivush, 2019; Haden & Fivush, 1996). Parents with an elaborative conversational style discuss new aspects of an experience, provide more information to guide a child through a mutually rewarding conversation, and affirm the child's responses. They may ask questions, expand on children's responses, and help the child tell their story. Three-year-olds of parents who use an elaborative style engage in longer conversations about events, remember more details, and tend to remember the events better at ages 5 and 6 (Fivush, 2011). Elaborative reminiscing is associated with children's ability to provide more detailed personal memory, both concurrently and longitudinally (Wu & Jobson, 2019).

Memory Suggestibility

Children's ability to remember events can be influenced by information and experiences that may interfere with their memories. These can include conversations with parents and adults, exposure to media, and sometimes intentional suggestions directed at changing the child's view of what transpired. Children as young as 3 years have been called upon to relate their memories of events that they have experienced or witnessed, including abuse, maltreatment, and domestic violence (Pantell & Committee on Psychosocial Aspects of Child and Family Health, 2017). How suggestible are young children? Can we trust their memories?

Repeated questioning may increase suggestibility in children (La Rooy et al., 2011). In one study, preschoolers were questioned every week about events that had either happened or not happened to them; by the 11th week, nearly two-thirds of the children falsely reported having experienced an event (Ceci et al., 1994). Preschool-age children may be more vulnerable to suggestion than school-age children or adults (Brown & Lamb, 2015). When children were asked if they could remember several events, including a fictitious instance of getting their finger caught in a mousetrap, almost none of them initially recalled these events. After repeated suggestive questioning, more than half of 3- and 4-year-olds and two-fifths of 5- and 6-year-olds said they recalled these events—often vividly (Poole & White, 1991, 1993).

In some cases, children can resist repeated suggestion. In one study, 4- and 7-year-old children either played games with an adult confederate (e.g., dressing up in costumes, playing tickle, being photographed) or merely watched the games (Ceci & Bruck, 1998). Eleven days later, each child was interviewed by an adult who included misleading questions that were often followed up with suggestions relevant to child abuse. Even the 4-year-olds resisted the false suggestions. Children also vary. Some children are better able to resist social pressure and suggestive questioning than others (Uhl et al., 2016). Children with intellectual impairments show greater suggestibility than their nonimpaired peers (Klemfuss & Olaguez, 2018).

Repeated questioning about an event that may or may not have happened may increase suggestibility in children.

G Scammell / Alamy Stock Photo

Children are more vulnerable than adults, but adults are not entirely resistant to suggestion. Indeed, in some situations, adults are *more* likely than children to make quick associations between suggestive details about unexperienced events and prior experiences, making them more vulnerable to suggestion (Otgaar et al., 2018). Like children, adults who are exposed to information that is misleading or inconsistent with their experiences are more likely to perform poorly during memory interviews—and repeated questioning has a similar effect on performance (Wysman et al., 2014).

Theory of Mind

Over the childhood years, thinking becomes more complex. In particular, children become increasingly aware of the process of thinking and of their own thoughts. **Theory of mind** refers to children's awareness of their own and other people's mental processes. This awareness of the mind can be considered under the broader concept of **metacognition**, which is knowledge of how the mind works and the ability to control the mind (Lockl & Schneider, 2007).

Young children's theory of mind grows and changes between the ages of 2 and 5 (Bower, 1993; Flavell et al., 1995; Wellman, 2017). Three-year-old children understand the difference between thinking about a cookie and having a cookie. They know that having a cookie means that one can touch, eat, or share it, while thinking about a cookie does not permit such actions (Astington, 1993). Young children also understand that a child who wants a cookie will be happy upon receiving one and sad upon not having one (Moses et al., 2000). Similarly, they understand that a child who believes he is having hot oatmeal for breakfast will be surprised upon receiving cold spaghetti (Wellman & Banerjee, 1991).

False Belief

Young children do not yet understand people can hold different beliefs and that some may be incorrect. Three-year-old children tend to perform poorly on **false-belief tasks**, which are tasks that require them to demonstrate the understanding that another person can have an incorrect belief. In a classic false-belief task, young children are presented with a Band-Aid box and are surprised to find that it contains pencils rather than Band-Aids (see Figure 5.5). Then they are asked, "What will other children think when they receive the Band-Aid box?" Children who have not yet developed a theory of mind will believe that other children will share their knowledge and expect the Band-Aid box to hold pencils (Flavell, 1993). The children do not yet understand that the other children hold different, false beliefs. In addition, young children will tend to claim they knew all along that the Band-Aid box contained pencils (Birch, 2005). They confuse their present knowledge with their memories or prior knowledge and have difficulty remembering ever having believed something that contradicts their current view (Bernstein et al., 2007).

Theory of mind as evidenced by false-belief tasks emerges at about 3 years of age and shifts reliably between 3 and 4 years of age (Grosse Wiesmann et al., 2017). By age 3, children can understand that two people can believe different things (Rakoczy et al., 2007). Four-year-old children can understand that people who are presented with different versions of the same event develop different beliefs (Eisbach, 2004). By age 4 or 5, children become aware that they and other people can hold false beliefs (Moses et al., 2000).

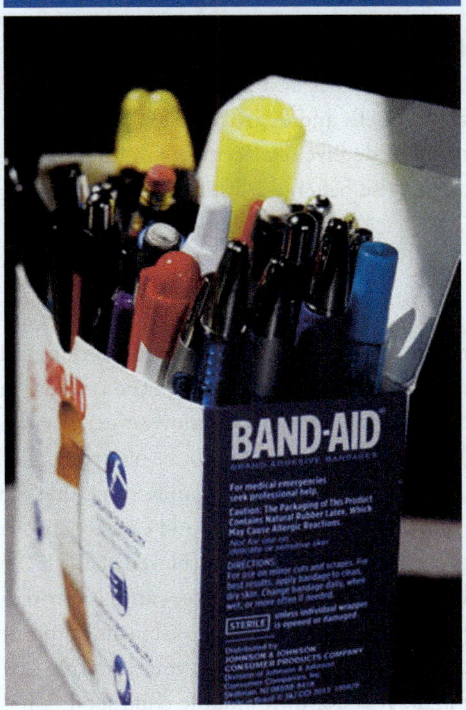

FIGURE 5.5 ■ False-Belief Task

Advanced cognition is needed for children to learn abstract concepts such as belief. Performance on false-belief tasks, such as the Band-Aid box task, is associated with measures of executive function, the abilities that enable complex cognitive functions such as planning, decision making, and goal setting (Doenyas et al., 2018; Sabbagh et al., 2006). Advances in executive functioning facilitate children's abilities to reflect on and learn from experience and promote development of theory of mind (Benson et al., 2013). Children's performance on false-belief tasks is closely related to language development and competence in sustaining conversations (Hughes & Devine, 2015). Preschoolers with more advanced scores on theory of mind measures are more likely than their less advanced peers to share resources and play cooperatively with friends (Etel & Slaughter, 2019; Vonk et al., 2020). Children's cognitive abilities influence their social relationships.

Context, Culture, and Theory of Mind

Children in many countries, including Canada, India, Thailand, Norway, China, and the United States, show the onset and development of theory of mind between the ages of 3 and 5 (Callaghan et al., 2005; Wellman et al., 2011). Children's interactions with people in their immediate contexts can also influence the development of theory of mind. Children who are securely attached to a caregiver show more advanced theory of mind skills than children with insecure attachments (Szpak & Białecka-Pikul, 2020). Everyday conversations aid children in developing a theory of mind because such conversations tend to center on and provide examples of mental states and their relationship with behavior. When parents and other adults speak with children about mental states, emotions, and behaviors, as well as discuss causes and consequences, children develop a more sophisticated understanding of other people's perspectives (Devine & Hughes, 2019, 2018; Sodian et al., 2020). In addition, siblings provide young children with opportunities for social interaction, pretend play, and practice with deception. Children with siblings perform better on false-belief tests than do only children (McAlister & Peterson, 2013). Success in false-belief attribution tasks is most frequent in children who are the most active in shared pretend play (Schwebel et al., 1999).

Children can be trained in perspective taking. Conversation about deceptive objects (e.g., a pen that looked like a flower) improves performance on false-belief tasks When children are presented with a series of deceptive objects and are shown the appearance and real states of the objects, along with explanation, 3-year-olds showed improvements on false-belief tasks(Lohmann & Tomasello, 2003). Discussion emphasizing the existence of a variety of possible perspectives in relation to an object can improve performance on false-belief tasks—dialogue can facilitate the development of theory of mind (Bernard & Deleau, 2007). Other studies have engaged North American and European children in discussions about the thoughts, beliefs, and desires of characters in stories, especially stories in which characters play tricks to surprise or deceive one another. Children who receive the training improved their performance in subsequent false-belief tasks (Liu et al., 2008; Milligan et al., 2007; Slaughter & Perez-Zapata, 2014).

Metacognition

Theory of mind is a precursor to the development of metacognition, or knowledge of how the mind works (Lecce et al., 2015). Young children know that the mind is where thinking takes place. Between 3 and 5, children come to understand that they can know something that others do not (essential for success on false-belief tasks), that their thoughts cannot be observed, and that there are individual differences in mental states (Pillow, 2008). They begin to understand that someone can think of one thing while doing something else, that a person whose eyes and ears are covered can think, and that thinking is different from talking, touching, and knowing (Flavell et al., 1995). However, young children's understanding of the mind is far from complete. Three- and 4-year-old children do not understand that we think even when we are inactive. They look for visible indicators of thinking—perhaps one reason why teachers of young children refer to "putting on your thinking cap"—and assume their absence indicates the absence of thought. It is not until middle childhood that children understand that the mind is always active (Flavell, 1999). Likewise, preschoolers tend to think of the mind as simply a

TABLE 5.3 ■ Development of Information Processing Skills During Early Childhood

Skill	Description
Attention	Young children are better able to focus and sustain their attention to complete tasks but have difficulty with complex tasks that require them to switch their attention among stimuli.
Memory	Young children's limited capacity to store and manipulate information in working memory influences their performance on memory and problem-solving tasks. Young children show advances in recognition memory and the ability to use scripts, but recall memory lags behind because they are not able to effectively use memory strategies. They often can be taught memory strategies but do not spontaneously apply them in new situations. Episodic memory emerges in early childhood, but the extent and quality of memories increase with age.
Theory of mind	Theory of mind refers to children's awareness of their own and other people's mental processes. When researchers use vocabulary that children are familiar with, observe them in everyday activities, and use concrete examples and simple problems such as those involving belief and surprise, it is clear that young children's understanding of the mind grows and changes between the ages of 2 and 5.
Metacognition	Young children demonstrate a growing ability for metacognition, or understanding the mind - their own and others' minds. Young children's abilities are limited, and they tend to fail false-belief and appearance-reality tasks, suggesting that their abilities to understand the mind and predict what other people are thinking are limited.

container for items, but older children tend to see the mind as an active constructor of knowledge that receives, processes, and transforms information (Chandler & Carpendale, 1998).

Young children show limited knowledge of memory functions, contributing to their poor performance on memory tasks. Four-year-olds recognize that increasing the number of items on a list makes recall more difficult and that longer retention intervals increase the likelihood of forgetting (Pillow, 2008). But they know little about the effectiveness of deliberate memory strategies. Whereas 6- and 7-year-olds demonstrated an understanding of the role of deliberate practice in memory—and practiced without being prompted, 5-year-olds showed an understanding of deliberate practice and some capacity to practice, but 4-year-olds showed neither of these capabilities (Brinums et al., 2018). The advances that take place in information processing during early childhood are summarized in Table 5.3.

Thinking in Context: Lifespan Development

1. In what ways does children's context influence the development of theory of mind? What are some cultural differences in theory of mind and what kinds of interactions promote the development of theory of mind?
2. Might cultural differences in interactions relevant to theory of mind occur within the U.S.? To what extent do you think U.S. children experience cultural and contextual differences in interactions that might shape the development of theory of mind?

Thinking in Context: Applied Developmental Science

1. What are the practical implications of young children's capacities for attention and memory? Consider specific types of memory, memory strategies, and suggestibility.
2. How can information processing theory be applied in the classroom? From an information processing perspective, how should preschool classrooms be organized and what can teachers do to help children learn?

YOUNG CHILDREN'S LANGUAGE DEVELOPMENT

LEARNING OBJECTIVE

5.4 Summarize young children's advances in language development, including dual language learning and contextual influences on language development.

Toddlers transitioning from infancy to early childhood tend to use telegraphic speech. They learn to use multiple elements of speech, such as plurals, adjectives, and the past tense. Children's vocabulary and grammar become dramatically more complex during early childhood, enabling them to communicate, but also think, in new ways.

Vocabulary

At 2 years of age, the average child knows about 500 words; vocabulary acquisition continues at a rapid pace. The average 3-year-old child has a vocabulary of 900 to 1,000 words. By 6 years of age, most children have a vocabulary of about 14,000 words, which means that the average child learns a new word every 1 to 2 hours, every day (Owens, 2020). How is language learned so quickly? Children continue to use fast mapping (see Chapter 3) as a strategy to enable them to learn the meaning of a new word after hearing it once or twice, based on contextual association and understanding (Kucker et al., 2015). Fast mapping improves with age.

Children learn words that they hear often, that label things and events that interest them, and that they encounter in contexts that are meaningful to them (Ackermann et al., 2020; Mani & Ackermann, 2018). Preschoolers can learn words from watching videos with both human and robot speakers, but they learn more quickly in response to human speakers (Moriguchi et al., 2011), especially when the speaker responds to them, such as through videoconferencing (e.g., Skype; Roseberry et al., 2014). Children learn best in interactive contexts with parents, teachers, siblings, and peers that entail turn taking, joint attention, and scaffolding experiences that provide hints to the meaning of new words (MacWhinney, 2015).

Another strategy that children use to increase their vocabulary is **logical extension**. When learning a word, children extend it to other objects in the same category (Owens, 2020). When learning that a dog with spots is called a Dalmatian, a child may refer to a Dalmatian bunny (a white bunny with black spots) or a Dalmatian horse. Children tend to make words their own and apply them to all situations they want to talk about. At about age 3, children demonstrate the **mutual exclusivity assumption** in learning new words: They assume that objects have only one label or name. According to mutual exclusivity, a new word is assumed to be a label for an unfamiliar object, not a synonym or second label for a familiar object (Markman et al., 2003). In one study, young children were shown one familiar object and one unfamiliar object. They were told, "Show me the X"; X was a nonsense syllable. The children reached for the unfamiliar object, suggesting that they expect new words to label new objects rather than acting as synonyms (Markman & Wachtel, 1988). Four and 5-year-old children continue to apply the mutual exclusivity principle, but they can also understand that a given object can have multiple labels (Kalashnikova et al., 2016).

At around 5 years of age, many children can infer the meanings of words given the context. They can quickly understand and apply most words they hear.

RayArt Graphics / Alamy Stock Photo

By 5 years of age, if a word is used in context or explained with examples, most children can learn it. Preschoolers learn words by making inferences given the context—and inferential learning is associated with better retention than learning by direct instruction (Zosh et al., 2013). Certain classes of words are challenging for young children. They have difficulty understanding that words that express comparisons—tall and short or high and low—are relative in nature and are used in comparing one object to another. Thus, the context defines their meaning, such that calling an object tall is often meant in relation to another object that is short. Children may erroneously interpret *tall* as referring to all tall things and therefore miss the relative nature of the term (Ryalls, 2000). Children also have difficulty with words that express relative place and time, such as *here, there, now, yesterday*, and *tomorrow.* Despite these errors, children make great advances in vocabulary, learning thousands of words each year.

Grammar

Young children quickly learn to combine words into sentences in increasingly sophisticated ways that follow the complex rules of grammar (de Villiers & de Villiers, 2014). Three-year-old children tend to use plurals (cats), possessives (cat's), and past tense (walked; Park et al., 2012). They also tend to understand the use of pronouns such as *I, you*, and *we.*

Similar to telegraphic speech, young children's sentences are short, leaving out words like *a* and *the.* Their speech is more sophisticated than telegraphic speech because they include some pronouns, adjectives, and prepositions. Four- and 5-year-olds use four- to five-word sentences and can express declarative, interrogative, and imperative sentences (Turnbull & Justice, 2016). Context influences the acquisition of syntax. Four-year-old children will use more complex sentences with multiple clauses, such as "I'm resting because I'm tired," if their parents use such sentences (Huttenlocher et al., 2002). Parental conversations and support for language learning are associated with faster and more correct language use (MacWhinney, 2015). Children often use run-on sentences, in which ideas and sentences are strung together.

"See? I goed on the slide!" called out Leona. **Overregularization errors** such as Leona's are very common in young children. They occur because young children are still learning exceptions to grammatical rules. Overregularization errors are grammatical mistakes that young children make because they are applying grammatical rules too stringently (Owens, 2020). For example, to create a plural noun, the rule is to add *s* to the word. But there are many exceptions to this rule. Overregularization is expressed when children refer to *foots, gooses, tooths*, and *mouses*, which illustrates that the child understands and is applying the rules. Adult speakers find this usage awkward, but it is actually a sign of the child's increasing grammatical sophistication. And despite all of the common errors young children make, one study of 3-year-olds showed that nearly three-quarters of their utterances were grammatically correct. The most common error was in making tenses (e.g., *eat/eated, fall/falled*; Eisenberg et al., 2012). By the end of the preschool years, most children use grammar rules appropriately and confidently.

In addition to advances in vocabulary and grammar, children demonstrate increasingly sophisticated understanding of the pragmatics of language, or how to use language to communicate effectively (Owens, 2020). Young children engage the people around them in conversation. They get better at turn taking, alternating between listening and speaking. Parents often marvel at the sophistication of their "baby's" thoughts. Young children carry on conversations about objects, their surroundings, and their feelings, although the content of their conversations is limited by their cognitive skills, especially egocentrism. Young children find it difficult to take another's perspective. As children's ability to think ahead and consider the future improves, they can increasingly talk about things that have not yet happened, such as a trip or party. Preschoolers recognize the need to adjust their speech to their conversational partner, such as speaking more simply to a toddler sibling than a peer or an adult.

Bilingual Language Learning

Children who are exposed to two languages build distinct language systems from birth (MacWhinney, 2015). The pace of learning two languages is influenced by the degree to which the two languages differ, how often the child hears each language, and how clearly the speakers enunciate speech sounds (Pace et al., 2020; Petitto et al., 2012; Werker, 2012).

Typically, bilingual children have words in both languages for the same thing, which conflicts with the mutual exclusivity assumption that characterizes most children's vocabulary learning. A bilingual child might say "all done" in English and "*pau*" in Hawaiian. In contrast, monolingual children learn synonyms for words much later (Littschwager & Markman, 1994). This difference suggests that bilingual children are aware that the words are part of two separate language systems and that a label is appropriate to a specific language. Bilingual children also learn two sets of rules for combining words (grammar) and do not appear to mix the grammatical rules for the two languages. For example, bilingual children learning French and German do not incorrectly use German words with French syntax or vice versa (Meisel, 1989). Moreover, bilingual children tend to select the appropriate language to use with other speakers, suggesting that they are aware that they know two languages (and that others may not; Genesee & Nicoladis, 2007).

The course of language development, including the pattern of vocabulary and grammatical development in each language, tends to follow the developmental path for each language (Conboy & Thal, 2006; Parra et al., 2011). The pace of simultaneous language learning is not the same as learning one language. Similar to acquiring one language, the rate of acquisition for two languages depends on the quantity and quality of the input in each language (Hoff & Core, 2015; Hoff, 2020).

Frequently bilingual children hear one language spoken more than another; in their dominant language, they may seem similar to monolingual children in terms of development. But because children who hear two languages will tend to hear less of either language than their monolingual peers, their rate of growth in each language tends to be slower than those who hear and acquire a single language. That is, a bilingual child may hear Spanish two-thirds of the time and English one-third of the time, whereas a child learning English hears English 100% of the time. Bilingual children therefore hear less of each language than monolingual children and tend to lag behind monolingual children in vocabulary and grammar in each language, when measured separately (Hindman & Wasik, 2015; Hoff et al., 2012). However, the combined vocabularies for both languages are similar in size to the vocabulary of monolingual children; some research suggests that the total vocabulary growth in bilingual children may be greater than that of monolinguals (Bosch & Ramon-Casas, 2014; Hoff et al., 2014). Gaps in vocabulary and grammatical development between monolingual and bilingual children persist but narrow through the school years, especially with continued and consistent exposure to two languages (Hoff et al., 2014; Gathercole & Thomas, 2009).

Race, Socioeconomic Status and Language Development

Like all other forms of development, language is influenced by the many contexts in which children are embedded, especially the home. Household socioeconomic status is related to children's language development. Mothers with higher incomes, higher education levels, and more prestigious careers tend to direct a greater amount of language and more diverse and complex language to their young children than mothers of low SES (Hart & Risley, 1995; Rowe, 2018). Children from low-SES backgrounds score more poorly on standardized language measures and tests as early as 3 years of age, which can contribute to lifelong differences in competence (Golinkoff et al., 2019). Although the quality of maternal language input predicts children's language development from infancy through late childhood, it is important to note that there is considerable variation in maternal speech within each SES group (Rowe, 2018; Schwab & Lew-Williams, 2016).

Socioeconomic status, race, and ethnicity are interrelated, yet many studies fail to consider the complex ways in which they overlap. SES is confounded with race in many studies. That is, if the families from low-SES contexts also happen to be families of color, it can be difficult to determine whether a set of findings are related to SES differences, racial and ethnic differences, or a combination of both. Conclusions about the quality of mother-infant interactions in low-SES contexts may lead researchers to erroneously conclude that African American mothers talk less with their young children simply because the low-SES mothers also tended to be African American. Early studies that confounded SES and race concluded that African American mothers speak less to their children, ask fewer questions, and elicit lower quality speech than other mothers (Anderson-Yockel & Haynes, 1994; Brooks-Gunn

& Markman, 2005). Yet in these early studies, it was impossible to determine whether maternal language is related to SES, race, or both.

One recent study of maternal language input disentangled maternal education and race by examining four groups of mothers: African American and non-African American mothers with a high school education or less and African American and non-African American mothers with education beyond high school (Vernon-Feagans et al., 2020). In this study, maternal education accounted for differences in maternal language input. There were no racial differences in maternal language input within each educational level, despite large income differences between African American and non—African American mothers within each education level. Maternal education, rather than race, may be the driver of early maternal language input and the source of the word gap (Hindman et al., 2014; Vernon-Feagans et al., 2020). Interventions to help mothers promote their children's language development emphasize child-directed speech during play and activities such as shared book reading (Dowdall et al., 2020; Hindman et al., 2016). Interventions to help mothers promote their children's language development emphasize child-directed speech during play and activities such as shared book reading (Dowdall et al., 2020; Hindman et al., 2016).

Thinking in Context: Lifespan Development

1. How might advances in language development influence other domains of development, such as cognitive or socioemotional development?
2. How might children's everyday experiences in the home, school, and community influence language development? Provide examples.
3. Compare the normative changes in vocabulary and grammar for young children learning one language with those learning two languages. Do you think language development unfolds in similar ways for monolingual and bilingual language learners? Why or why not?

Thinking in Context: Intersectionality

1. From an intersectional perspective, race and ethnicity, education, and poverty intersect with power, including dominant beliefs about what is normative and what kinds of family interactions are preferred. Considering intersectionality, why do some researchers question the 30 million word gap?
2. Given recent findings illustrating the interactive influence of race and SES on young children's language development, what interventions do you suggest to help young children and their parents? Why do we see these patterns, what might influence them, and what can we do to help young children?

EARLY CHILDHOOD EDUCATION

LEARNING OBJECTIVE

5.5 Identify and explain various approaches to early childhood education.

In the United States, many children attend kindergarten prior to entering elementary school, but only 15 states require children to complete kindergarten (Education Commission of the States, 2014). Early education is important for children's cognitive, social, and emotional development. Preschool programs provide educational experiences for children ages 2 to 5.

Child-Centered and Academically Centered Preschool Programs

There are two general approaches to early childhood education. **Academically centered preschool programs** emphasize providing children with structured learning environments in which teachers deliver direct instruction on letters, numbers, shapes, and academic skills. **Child-centered preschool** programs take a constructivist approach that encourages children to actively build their own understanding of the world through observing, interacting with objects and people, and engaging in a variety of activities that allow them to manipulate materials and interact with teachers and peers (Kostelnik et al., 2015). Through play, children learn by doing and learn to problem solve, get along with others, communicate, and self-regulate.

Montessori schools, first created in the early 1900s by the Italian physician and educator Maria Montessori (1870–1952), exemplify the child-centered approach, in which children are viewed as active constructors of their own development and are given freedom in choosing their activities (Lillard, 2020). Teachers act as facilitators, providing a range of activities and materials, demonstrating ways of exploring them, and providing help when the child asks. The Montessori approach is credited with fostering independence, self-regulation, and cognitive and problem-solving skills (Ackerman, 2019).

In contrast, problems have been documented with teacher-directed rigid academic programs. Children immersed in such programs sometimes show signs of stress such as rocking, may have less confidence in their skills, and may avoid challenging tasks compared with children who are immersed in more active forms of play-based learning (Stipek et al., 1995). Such programs are also negatively associated with reading skills in first grade (Lerkkanen et al., 2016).

Instead of a purely academic approach, many practitioners advocate for a **developmentally appropriate practice**, which tailors instruction to the age of the child, recognizing individual differences and the need for hands-on active teaching methods (Kostelnik et al., 2015). Teachers provide educational support in the form of learning goals, instructional support, and feedback, but they also emphasize emotional support and help children learn to manage their own behavior (Anderson & Phillips, 2017). Moreover, teachers are provided with explicit instruction in how to teach and the teaching strategies needed to support young children's literacy, language, math, social, and self-regulatory development (Markowitz et al., 2018). Responsive child-centered teaching is associated with higher reading and math scores during first grade (Lerkkanen et al., 2016).

Effective early childhood educational practice is influenced by cultural values (Gordon & Browne, 2016). In the United States, a society that emphasizes individuality, a child-centered approach in which children are given freedom of choice is associated with the most positive outcomes (Marcon, 1999). Yet in Japan, the most effective preschools tend to foster collectivist values and are society-centered with an emphasis on social and classroom routines, skills, and promoting group harmony (Holloway, 1999; Nagayama & Gilliard, 2005). Japanese preschools prepare children for their roles in society and provide formal instruction in academic areas as well as art, swordsmanship, gymnastics, tea ceremonies, and Japanese dance. Much instruction is teacher directed, and children are instructed to sit, observe, and listen. Teachers are warm but address the group as a whole rather than individuals. This structured approach is associated with positive outcomes in Japanese children (Holloway, 1999; Nagayama & Gilliard, 2005), illustrating the role of culture in influencing outcomes of early childhood education. Even within a given country such as the United States, there exist many ethnicities and corresponding cultures, such as those of Native Americans and Mexican Americans. In each case, instruction that is informed by an understanding of children's home and community culture fosters a sense of academic belongingness that ultimately influences academic achievement (Gilliard & Moore, 2007; Gordon & Browne, 2016).

In this Montessori classroom, children explore and play together.
Lori Wolfe/The Herald-Dispatch via Associated Press

Early Childhood Education Interventions

Recognizing that young children's developmental needs extend beyond education, one of the most successful early childhood education and intervention programs in the United States, **Project Head Start**, was created by the federal government to provide economically disadvantaged children with nutritional, health, and educational services during their early childhood years, prior to kindergarten (Ramey & Ramey, 1998). Parents of Head Start children also receive assistance, such as education about child development, vocational services, and programs addressing their emotional and social needs (Zigler & Styfco, 2004).

Over the past four decades, a great deal of research has been conducted on the effectiveness of Head Start. The most common finding is that Head Start improves cognitive performance, with gains in IQ and achievement scores in elementary school (Zhai et al., 2011). Compared with children who do not participate in Head Start, those who do so have greater parental involvement in school, show higher math achievement scores in middle school, are less likely to be held back a grade or have problems with chronic absenteeism in middle school, and are more likely to graduate from high school (Duncan et al., 2007; Joo, 2010; Phillips et al., 2016). Head Start is associated with other long-lasting social and physical effects, such as gains in social competence and health-related outcomes, including immunizations (Huston, 2008). Yet some research has suggested that the cognitive effects of Head Start may fade over time such that, by late childhood, Head Start participants perform similarly to control group low–socioeconomic status children who have not participated in Head Start (U.S. Department of Health and Human Services, & Administration for Children and Families, 2010). Early intervention may not compensate for the pervasive and long-lasting effects of poverty-stricken neighborhoods and inadequate public schools (Schnur & Belanger, 2000; Welshman, 2010). At the same time, long-term advantageous effects of attending Head Start include higher graduation rates and lower rates of adolescent pregnancy and criminality for low-income children who attend Head Start compared with their control group peers (Duncan & Magnuson, 2013). Despite these findings, only about one-third of poor children are enrolled in Head Start, and this proportion has shrunk over the past decade, as shown in Figure 5.6.

Additional evidence for the effectiveness of early childhood education interventions comes from the Carolina Abecedarian Project and the Perry Preschool Project, carried out in the 1960s and 1970s. Both of these programs enrolled children from families with incomes below the poverty line and emphasized the provision of stimulating preschool experiences to promote motor, language, and social skills as well

FIGURE 5.6 ■ Number of Children (in Thousands) Enrolled in Head Start and Early Head Start, and Children Enrolled as a Percentage of Children in Poverty, 2006–2014.

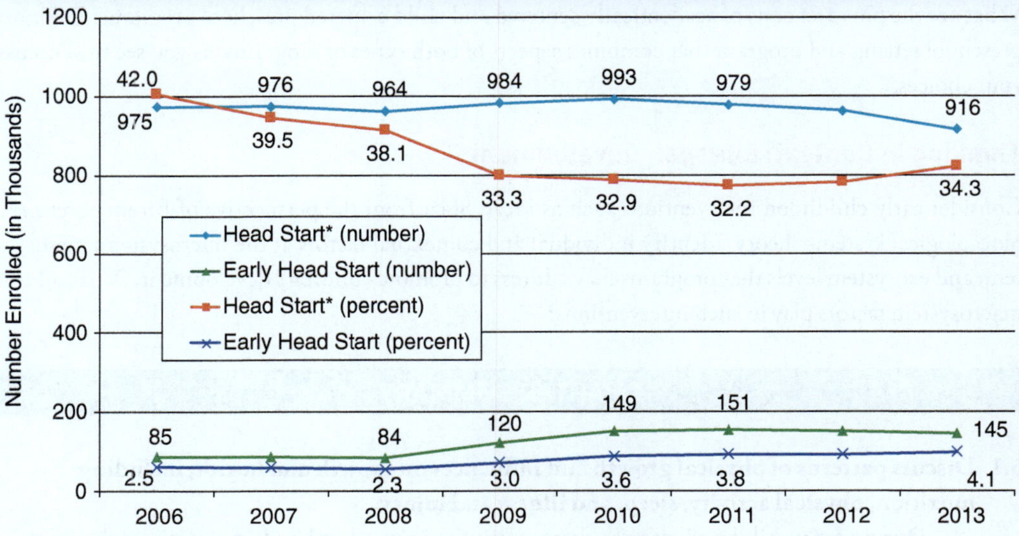

Source: United States Department of Health and Human Services

Children who attend Head Start programs have early educational experiences that improve cognitive and social skills and prepare them for kindergarten and elementary school.

Laura Dwight / Alamy Stock Photo

as cognitive skills, including literacy and math. Special emphasis was placed on rich, responsive adult-child verbal communication as well as nutrition and health services from birth to school age. Children in these programs achieved higher reading and math scores in elementary school than their nonenrolled peers (Campbell & Ramey, 1994). As adolescents, they showed higher rates of high school graduation and college enrollment, as well as lower rates of substance abuse and pregnancy (Campbell et al., 2002; Muennig et al., 2011). At ages 30 and 40, early intervention participants showed higher levels of education and income (Campbell et al., 2012; Schweinhart et al., 2005). Researchers continue to study and apply the Abecedarian approach in today in playgroups, preschools, and other settings (Page et al., 2019; Sparling & Meunier, 2019).

The success of early education intervention programs has influenced a movement in the United States toward comprehensive prekindergarten (preK). Young children who participate in high-quality preK programs enter school with greater readiness to learn and score higher on reading and math tests than their peers (Gormley et al., 2010). Although all young children appear to benefit from preK, children from low-income homes benefit the most (Slicker & Hustedt, 2019).

During 2017–2018, 44 states provided preschool programs (Friedman-Krauss et al., 2019). However, not all children in these states had access to preschool. Rates of enrollment of 3- and 4-year-olds ranged from a high of 69% of children in Vermont to 5% or less in 11 other states. A few states, including Oklahoma, Vermont, and Florida, provide universal access to preK to all children, and many more states are moving in this direction (Williams, 2015). Beginning in the fall of 2017, New York City initiated a city-funded "3-K for all" program of free full-day preschool for all 3-year-olds (Taylor, 2017). Although some research suggests that half-day and more intense full-day programs do not differ in academic and social outcomes, full-day preschool incorporates the benefit of free childcare to working parents that is likely of higher quality than they might have otherwise been able to afford (Leow & Wen, 2017). Funding public preschool programs is daunting, but the potential rewards are tremendous.

Thinking in Context: Applied Developmental Science

What are the pros and cons of academically centered and child centered preschool programs? Design a preschool setting and program that combines aspects of both types of programs, as you see fit. Discuss your choices.

Thinking in Context: Lifespan Development

Consider early childhood interventions such as Head Start from the perspective of Bronfenbrenner's bioecological systems theory. Identify individual and contextual factors at the microsystem, mesosystem, and exosystem levels that programs may address to promote children's development. What role do macrosystem factors play in such interventions?

CHAPTER SUMMARY

5.1 Discuss patterns of physical growth and influences on growth and health, including nutrition, physical activity, sleep, and illness and injury.

During early childhood, growth slows relative to infancy and body proportions change as young children gain muscle and become leaner. Advances in gross motor skills permit young children to balance and coordinate their bodies and engage in more complicated physical activities, such as throwing and catching balls. As children's fine motor skills improve, they learn to write and engage in self-care activities such as buttoning a shirt. Synaptogenesis, pruning, myelination, and lateralization continue in early childhood and contribute to enhanced plasticity. Most children in developed nations eat enough calories, but their diets are often insufficient in vitamins and minerals. Physical activity enhances growth and is consistently associated with advances in motor development, fitness, and health. Sleep problems pose risks to young children's development, such as cognitive difficulties, including problems with attention, working memory, and slower processing speed. Young children tend to experience more colds and illnesses than older children. Exposure to toxins can harm children's physical and cognitive development. Unintentional injuries (accidents), are the leading cause of death in young children.

5.2 Compare Piaget's cognitive-developmental and Vygotsky's sociocultural perspectives on cognitive development in early childhood.

Piaget explained that children in the preoperational stage of reasoning are able to think using mental symbols, but their thinking is limited because they cannot grasp logic. Simplified and nonverbal tasks demonstrate that young children are more cognitively advanced and less egocentric than Piaget posited. From Vygotsky's sociocultural perspective, children's learning occurs through guided participation, scaffolding within the zone of proximal development. With time, the child internalizes the lesson and learns to accomplish the task on his or her own. In this way cognitive development entails actively internalizing the tools of our culture.

5.3 Describe information processing abilities during early childhood.

The ability to sustain attention improves in early childhood through the preschool years. Episodic memory also improves steadily, but young children's limited working memory makes it difficult for them to use memory strategies. Autobiographical memory develops steadily and is accompanied by increases in the length, richness, and complexity of recall memory. Advances in theory of mind enable children to understand that people can believe different things, that beliefs can be inaccurate, and that sometimes people act on the basis of false beliefs. Children thereby become able to lie or use deception in play.

5.4 Summarize young children's advances in language development, including dual language learning and contextual influences on language development.

Young children apply strategies such as logical extension and the mutual exclusivity assumption to increase their vocabulary rapidly. Young children quickly move from telegraphic speech to combining words into sentences in increasingly sophisticated ways, using multiple elements of speech, such as plurals, adjectives, and the past tense, yet they often make overregularization errors. Parental conversations and support for language learning are associated with faster and more correct language use. At the end of the preschool years, most children use the main grammar rules appropriately and confidently. Children who are exposed to two languages build two distinct systems with similar patterns of development. The rate of acquisition for two languages depends on the quantity and quality of the input in each language. When considering one language, bilingual children tend to show a gap in vocabulary compared to their monolingual peers; when both languages are considered the gap closes. Contextual factors, such as parental education and SES, contribute to language development.

5.5 Identify and explain various approaches to early childhood education.

Child-centered preschool programs encourage children to manipulate materials, interact with teachers and peers, and learn by doing through play. Academically oriented preschool programs provide children with structured learning environments in which they learn letters, numbers, shapes, and academic skills via drills and formal lessons. Head Start and other early childhood education interventions can promote children's learning and development.

KEY TERMS

academically centered preschool programs (p. 160)
animism (p. 143)
appearance-reality distinction (p. 80)
autobiographical memory (p. 151)
central executive (p. 150)
centration (p. 144)
child-centered preschool (p. 160)
conservation (p. 145)
developmentally appropriate practice (p. 160)
egocentrism (p. 143)
episodic memory (p. 151)
false-belief tasks (p. 153)
guided participation (p. 147)
irreversibility (p. 145)
lateralization (p. 138)
logical extension (p. 156)
memory strategies (p. 151)
metacognition (p. 153)
Montessori schools (p. 160)
mutual exclusivity assumption (p. 156)
overregularization errors (p. 157)
plasticity (p. 138)
preoperational reasoning (p. 143)
private speech (p. 148)
Project Head Start (p. 161)
recall memory (p. 151)
recognition memory (p. 151)
scaffolding (p. 147)
selective attention (p. 150)
sustained attention (p. 150)
theory of mind (p. 152)
three-mountain task (p. 143)
zone of proximal development (p. 147)

6 SOCIOEMOTIONAL DEVELOPMENT IN EARLY CHILDHOOD

FluxFactory/ Getty Images

"Oww!" Logan cried out as he tripped. "Are you ok?" asked his mother. Logan nodded, "I'm ok but I don't like that step." "I agree," smiled Logan's mother, marveling at how Logan has matured. Just a short while ago he would react to frustration by crying. Now he used words to express his wants and needs, at least most of the time. Early childhood is a time of transition from the dependence of infancy and toddlerhood to the increasing capacities for autonomy and emotional regulation characteristic of childhood. How do young children learn to understand and control their emotions? Do they experience the same complex emotions that older children and adolescents experience? What is the role of parents in children's emotional and social development? What is the function of play in development? In this chapter, we explore children's experience and understanding of their social and emotional world and how socioemotional development changes over the early childhood years.

EMERGING SENSE OF SELF

LEARNING OBJECTIVE

6.1 Describe young children's sense of initiative, self-concept, and self-esteem.

When assigned a task, such as dusting off a bookcase shelf, 3-year-old Shawna calls out, "I'll do it!" After completing the task, she proudly proclaims, "I did it!" The autonomy that Shawna developed during the toddler years has prepared her to master the psychosocial task of the preschool years: developing a sense of initiative (Erikson, 1950).

Psychosocial Development in Early Childhood

During Erikson's third psychosocial stage, **initiative versus guilt,** young children develop a sense of purpose and take pride in their accomplishments. As they develop a sense of initiative, young children make plans, tackle new tasks, set goals (e.g., climbing a tree, writing their name, counting to 10), and work to achieve them, persisting enthusiastically in tasks, whether physical or social, even when frustrated (Lambert & Kelley, 2011).

Much of the work of this stage occurs through play. During play, young children experiment and practice new skills in a safe context and learn to work cooperatively with other children to achieve common goals (Syed & McLean, 2018). Children in all societies practice adult roles in play, such as mother, father, doctor, teacher, and police officer (Gaskins, 2014). Hopi Indian children pretend to be hunters and potters, and the Baka of West Africa pretend to be hut builders and spear makers (Roopnarine et al., 1998). The sense of pride that children feel from accomplishment fuels their play and fosters curiosity. Children become motivated to concentrate, persist, and try new experiences, such as climbing to the top of the big kid slide and sliding down by themselves. Through play, children also learn how to manage their emotions and develop self-regulation skills (Goldstein & Lerner, 2018).

During early childhood, children come to identify with their parents and internalize parental rules (Paulus, 2020). Young children feel guilt when they fail to uphold rules and when they fail to achieve a goal. If parents are controlling—not permitting children to carry out their sense of purpose—or are highly punitive, critical, or threatening, children may not develop high standards and the initiative to meet them (Mounts & Allen, 2019). Instead, children may be paralyzed by guilt and worry about their inability to measure up to parental expectations. They may develop an overly critical conscience and be less motivated to exert the effort to master new tasks.

Children who develop a sense of initiative demonstrate independence and act purposefully. Their success in taking initiative and the feeling of competence and pride that accompanies it contributes to young children's developing sense of self.

Self-Concept

Three- and 4-year-old children tend to understand and describe themselves concretely, using observable descriptors including appearance, general abilities, favorite activities, possessions, and simple psychological traits (Harter, 2012). Ryder explains, "I'm 4 years old. I have black hair. I'm happy, my doggie is white, and I have a television in my room. I can run really fast. Watch me!" Ryder's self-description, his **self-concept,** is typical of children his age. Soon children begin to include emotions and attitudes in their self-descriptions, such as "I'm sad when my friends can't play," suggesting an emerging awareness of their internal characteristics (Thompson & Virmani, 2010).

Participating in household work is one way in which children develop initiative, a sense of purpose, and pride in their accomplishments.

iStock/Rawpixel

Children naturally notice physical differences in themselves and others associated with race, such as skin color and hair color and texture. Three and 4-year-old white children tend to express racial preferences in the form of a pro-white bias (Perszyk et al., 2019; Williams & Steele, 2019). Young children of color may also demonstrate preferences for lighter skin or internalize racial biases (Jordan & Hernandez-Reif, 2009; Kaufman & Wiese, 2012). Bias declines dramatically in late childhood, about age 9 (Aboud & Steele, 2017; Williams & Steele, 2019). Why does it occur? Young children are immersed in a world that sends messages about the characteristics and acceptability of skin color. Although research is just beginning to examine how information about race and racial preferences influences young children's sense of self, it is likely that young children internalize race-related messages into their early understanding of self. Without awareness, parents often communicate racial biases to children (Pirchio et al., 2018). Adults also tend to delay conversations about race because they underestimate children's understanding and processing of race (Sullivan et al., 2010). Parents and teachers can counter discriminatory messages by adopting an anti-bias framework that includes learning about race through storybook reading and discussion (Beneke et al., 2019).

Children's conceptions of themselves are influenced by their interactions with parents and the cultural context in which they are raised. In one study, preschool through second-grade U.S. and Chinese children were asked to recount autobiographical events and describe themselves in response to open-ended questions (Wang, 2004). The U.S. children often provided detailed accounts of their experiences. They focused on their own roles, preferences, and feelings and described their personal attributes and inner traits positively. In contrast, Chinese children provided relatively skeletal accounts of past experiences and focused on social interactions and daily routines. They often described themselves in neutral or modest tones, referring to social roles and context-specific personal characteristics. These differences are consistent with cultural values of independence in the United States and collectivism in China. In another study, U.S. preschool children reported feeling more sadness and shame in response to failure and more pride in response to success than did Japanese preschool children (Lewis et al., 2010). The Japanese preschool children displayed few negative emotions in response to failure but showed self-conscious embarrassment in response to success. Culture influences how children come to define and understand themselves and even the emotions with which they self-identify (Thompson & Virmani, 2010).

Self-Esteem

Young children tend to evaluate themselves positively. That is, they generally have a high sense of **self-esteem**. For example, 3-year-old Dorian exclaims, "I'm the smartest! I know all my ABCs! Listen! A, B, C, F, G, L, M!" Like Dorian, many young children are excited but also unrealistically positive about their abilities, underestimating the difficulty of tasks and believing that they will always be successful (Harter, 2012). Preschoolers often fail to recognize deficits in their abilities and tend to view their performance favorably, even when it is not up to par (Boseovski, 2010). Even after failing at a task several times, they often continue to believe that the next try will bring success.

Young children's overly optimistic perspective on their skills can be attributed to their cognitive development, secure attachment with caregivers, and the overwhelmingly positive feedback they usually receive when they attempt a task (Goodvin et al., 2008; Verschueren, 2020). These unrealistically positive expectations serve a developmental purpose: They contribute to young children's growing sense of initiative and aid them in learning new skills. Young children maintain their positive views about themselves because they do not yet engage in **social comparison**. In other words, they do not compare their performance with that of other children. With advances in cognition and social experience, children begin to learn their relative strengths and weaknesses, and their self-evaluations become more realistic (Rochat, 2013). Between ages 4 and 7, children's self-evaluations become linked with their performance. In one study, children's self-evaluations declined when they failed tasks assigned by an adult as well as those they perceived as important (Cimpian et al., 2017). Sensitive parenting that supports children's attempts at difficult tasks emphasizes the value of effort and helps children identify and take pride in success that promotes self-esteem.

Thinking in Context: Lifespan Development

1. In what ways might young children's inaccurate views of themselves and their abilities be adaptive? Is there a benefit to having an overoptimistic view of oneself in early childhood?
2. How might young children's views of themselves influence their ability to tackle the psychosocial task of this stage, developing a sense of initiative?
3. How does a growing sense of initiative help children? How might it influence their behavior at home, school, and with peers?

EMOTIONAL DEVELOPMENT IN EARLY CHILDHOOD

LEARNING OBJECTIVE

6.2 Discuss the development of emotional understanding, regulation, and empathy in early childhood.

Young children's advances in cognitive development and growing sense of self influence the emotions they show and the contexts in which they display these emotions. Moreover, young children come to understand people and social relationships in more complex ways, leading to new opportunities for emotional development. Emotional development includes an increasing awareness and management of emotion, as well as an ability to recognize others' emotions and infer causes and consequences of others' emotions (Camras & Halberstadt, 2017).

Emotional Understanding

Donald begins to cry as his mother leaves, dropping him off at preschool. Watching Donald, Amber explains to her mother, "Donald is sad because he misses his mommy," and she brings Donald a toy. "Don't be sad," she says. By 3 to 4 years of age, children recognize and name emotions based on their expressive cues. By age 4, children begin to understand that external factors (such as losing a toy) can affect emotion and can predict a peer's emotion and behavior (such as feeling sad and crying or feeling angry and hitting things; Goodvin et al., 2015).

The emergence of theory of mind has profound implications for emotional development. As children begin to take other people's perspectives, they can apply their understanding of emotions to understand and help others, such as recognizing that a sibling is sad and offering a hug. Children's growing understanding of the mind leads them to appreciate the role of internal factors, such as desires, on emotion and behavior (Wellman, 2017). By age 5, most children understand that desire can motivate emotion, and many understand that people's emotional reactions to an event can vary based on their desires.

Theory of mind influences the development and expression of self-conscious emotions, such as pride and guilt. Self-conscious emotions emerge as children become aware of rules and standards that define socially appropriate behavior and that others have expectations for their behavior (Muris & Meesters, 2014). In response to success, children's joy may be accompanied by the self-conscious emotion of pride. Likewise, shame results from recognizing that poor outcomes are the result of their behavior.

Children's interactions with siblings offer important opportunities to practice identifying emotions, decoding the causes of emotions, anticipating the emotional responses of others, and using their emotional understanding to influence their relationships and affect the behavior of others (Kramer, 2014). Young children also often enact emotions in pretend sociodramatic play, providing experience and practice in understanding emotions and their influence on social interactions (Goodvin et al., 2015). Pretend play with siblings and peers gives children practice in acting out feelings, considering others' perspectives, and implementing self-control, regulating aggression, and improving the children's understanding of emotion (Hoffmann & Russ, 2012;). Sociodramatic play is associated with emotional control in preschoolers and predicts predicted their expressiveness, knowledge, and emotional control one year later (Goldstein & Lerner, 2018; Lindsey & Colwell, 2013).

Interactions with caregivers also plays a role in advancing children's understanding of emotions. When parents talk to their preschoolers about emotions and explain their own and their children's emotions, the children are better able to evaluate and label others' emotions and show better adjustment, as rated by teachers (Camras & Halberstadt, 2017; Thompson et al., 2020). The preschool classroom offers many opportunities for children to learn about emotions through play, modeling, and direct instruction (Valiente et al., 2020). Book-reading, accompanied by dialogue about the characters, their emotions, and their motivations can help advance preschoolers' emotional understanding (Pons et al., 2019; Schapira & Aram, 2020). Preschool teachers also engage in emotion coaching, helping young children to understand the emotions they feel and see in others (Silkenbeumer et al., 2018; Yelinek & Grady, 2019).

Emotion Regulation

Over the course of childhood, children make great strides in regulating their emotions and become better able to manage how they experience and display emotions. Advances in emotion regulation are influenced by cognition, executive function, theory of mind, and language development. By age 4, children can explain simple strategies for reducing emotional arousal, such as limiting sensory input (covering their eyes), talking to themselves ("It's not scary"), or changing their goals ("I want to play blocks," after having been excluded by children who were playing another game; Thompson & Goodvin, 2007). Emotion regulation strategies are a response to emotions, change with age, and also influence children's emotional experience (Eisenberg et al., 2015).

Skills in emotion regulation are associated with social competence and overall adjustment (Deneault & Ricard, 2013). Emotional regulation plays a key role in children's ability to adapt to their environment, including the novel demands of the school setting (Harrington et al., 2020). Children who are able to direct their attention and distract themselves when distressed or frustrated become well-behaved students and are well liked by peers (McClelland & Cameron, 2011).

Parents are important resources for emotional management in early childhood. Mothers' emotional awareness and management skills influence children's emotional regulation skills (Crespo et al., 2017). Parents who are responsive when children are distressed, who frame experiences for children (e.g., by acting cheery during a trip to the doctor), and who explain expectations and strategies for emotional management both model and foster emotion regulation (Sala et al., 2014). In contrast, dismissive or hostile reactions to children's emotions prevent them from learning how to manage and not be overwhelmed by their emotions (Zeman et al., 2013).

Empathy

In early childhood, young children develop the cognitive and language skills that permit them to reflect on emotions, talk about emotions, and convey feelings of **empathy**, the ability to understand someone's feelings (Main & Kho, 2020; Stern & Cassidy, 2018). Empathy is linked with the perspective-taking ability that emerges with theory of mind. The child must imagine another's perspective in order to understand how that person feels (Eisenberg et al., 2015). A secure attachment to a caregiver helps children develop the emotional understanding and regulation skills on which empathy depends (Ştefan & Avram, 2018). Parents who provide supportive and compassionate responses to children's emotions foster the development of empathy in children (Hu et al., 2020).

Empathy influences how young children make judgments in their social world. Children who score higher on measures of empathy tend to rate moral transgressions involving physical and psychological harm as more serious and are more likely to rate unfairness as more deserving of punishment than other children (Ball et al., 2017). Empathy develops during early childhood. For example, 3-year-old children protest when an agent responds to a hurt child by laughing, but not when the agent ignores the hurt child; but 5-year-old children rate *both* the antisocial agent and the agent that ignored the needy child negatively (Paulus et al., 2020). Children who feel empathy for another person often are primed to engage in **prosocial behavior**, voluntary behavior intended to benefit another, as discussed later in this chapter. (Eisenberg et al., 2015).

Thinking in Context: Lifespan Development

Cognitive development influences how young children understand and regulate their emotions, as well as their capacity for empathy. Examine these interrelations, especially the role of theory of mind in young children's emotional experience.

Thinking in Context: Applied Developmental Science

How can we help children learn strategies for self-control? Provide suggestions for how parents, childcare providers, and preschool teachers can help children understand and learn to regulate their emotions.

MORAL DEVELOPMENT AND BEHAVIOR IN EARLY CHILDHOOD

LEARNING OBJECTIVE

6.3 Summarize perspectives on moral development and behavior, including prosocial and aggressive behavior.

How do young children learn to distinguish right from wrong? How do they acquire a sense of morality? **Moral reasoning**, or judgments of right and wrong, is influenced by children's cognitive abilities and develops in a predictable pattern (Skitka et al., 2016). Two-year-old children categorize behavior as good or bad. They respond with distress when viewing or experiencing aggressive or potentially harmful actions (Kochanska et al., 1995). By age 3, children judge a child who knocks another child off a swing intentionally as worse than one who does so accidentally (Yuill & Perner, 1988). They begin to show an understanding of and respect for basic normative standards, such as treating play partners fairly, enforcing social norms such as sharing, and feeling guilty when they violate them (Tomasello, 2018). Four-year-old children can understand the difference between truth and lies (Bussey, 1992). By age 5, children are aware of many moral rules, such as those regarding lying and stealing. They also demonstrate conceptions of justice or fairness (e.g., "It's my turn," "Hers is bigger," "It's not fair!"). How do these capacities develop?

Moral Reasoning

The cognitive-developmental perspective views moral development through a cognitive lens and examines reasoning about moral issues: Is it ever right to steal even if it would help another person? Is lying ever acceptable? Similar to cognitive development, children are active in constructing their own moral understanding through social experiences with adults and peers (Dahl, 2018; Killen et al., 2015). Young children's reasoning about moral problems changes with development as they construct concepts about justice and fairness from their social interactions (Dahl, 2019; Gibbs, 2003).

Cognitive-developmental theorist Jean Piaget (1932) studied children's moral development—specifically, how children understand rules. He observed children playing marbles, a common schoolyard game in Piaget's time, and asked them questions about the rules. Piaget found that preschool-age children's play was not guided by rules. The youngest children engaged in solitary play without regard for rules, tossing and rolling the marbles about as they pleased. Piaget posited that moral thinking develops in stages similar to those in his theory of cognition.

By 6 years of age, children show **heteronomous morality** (also known as the morality of constraint). As children first become aware of rules, they view them as sacred and unalterable. At this stage, moral behavior is behavior that is consistent with the rules set by authority figures. Young children see rules, even those created in play, as absolute and behavior as either right or wrong; they view the violation of rules as meriting punishment regardless of intent (DeVries & Zan, 2003; Nobes & Pawson, 2003). Young children may proclaim, without question, that there is only one way to play softball: As their coach advocates, the youngest children must be first to bat. Preschoolers will hold to this rule, explaining that it is simply the "right way" to play.

Moral theorist Lawrence Kohlberg (1969, 1976) investigated moral development by posing hypothetical dilemmas about justice, fairness, and rights that place obedience to authority and law in conflict with helping someone. Is stealing ever permissible—even in order to help someone? Young children demonstrate the first level of Kohlberg's stages of moral reasoning: **preconventional reasoning**. Similar to Piaget, Kohlberg argued that young children's behavior is governed by self-interest; they want to avoid punishment and gain rewards. "Good" or moral behavior is a response to external pressure. Young children have not internalized societal norms, and their behavior is motivated by desires rather than internalized principles. The ability to take other people's perspectives contributes to advances in moral development. We will examine Kohlberg's perspective in greater detail when we discuss middle and late childhood.

How adults discuss moral issues, such as truth telling, harm, and property rights, influences how children come to understand these issues. When adults, especially parents, discuss moral issues in ways that are sensitive to the child's developmental needs, children develop more sophisticated conceptions of morality and advance in their moral reasoning (Janssens & Dekovic, 1997; Padilla-Walker & Memmott-Elison, 2020).

Social Learning and Moral Behavior

All behavior, including moral behavior, can be influenced by modeling and reinforcement, which are social learning processes (Bandura, 1977; Grusec, 1992). Bandura and McDonald (1963) demonstrated that the moral judgments of young children could be modified through a training procedure involving social reinforcement and modeling. Parents and others naturally dole out reinforcement and punishment that shapes the child's behavior. Modeling also plays a role in children's moral development. Adults and other children serve as models for the child, demonstrating appropriate (and sometimes not!) actions and verbalizations. When children observe a model touching a forbidden toy, they are more likely to touch the toy. Some research suggests that children who observe a model resisting temptation are less likely to do so themselves (Rosenkoetter, 1973). However, models are more effective at encouraging rather than inhibiting behavior that violates a rule or expectation. Children are more likely to follow a model's transgressions rather than his or her appropriate behavior.

Children are more likely to imitate models they view as competent and powerful (Bandura, 1977). They are also more likely to imitate models that are perceived as warm and responsive rather than cold and distant (Yarrow et al., 1973). Over the course of early childhood, children develop internalized standards of conduct based on reinforcements, punishments, and observations of models (Bandura, 1986; Mussen & Eisenberg-Berg, 1977). Those adopted standards and moral values are then internalized and used by children as guides for behavior (Grusec & Goodnow, 1994). In this way, children's behavior is shaped to conform with the rules of society.

Prosocial Behavior

Prosocial behavior is behavior intended to help others. At 18 months of age, prosocial behavior is simple, such as the tendency to help adults, even unfamiliar experimenters, by picking up markers that have fallen (Thompson & Newton, 2013). Between 18 and 24 months of age, toddlers show increasingly prosocial responses to others' emotional and physical distress, but their responses are limited to their own perspective (Eisenberg et al., 2015). That is, they tend to offer the aid that they themselves would prefer, such as bringing their own mother to help a distressed peer (Hepach et al., 2012).

At 3½ years of age, children show more complex forms of **instrumental assistance**, or tangible help. Compared to 18-month-old children, 3½-year-olds are more likely to help an adult by bringing a needed object, to do so autonomously without the adult's specific request, and to select an object appropriate to the adult's need (Svetlova et al., 2010). Young children may engage in prosocial behavior for egocentric motives, such as the desire for praise and to avoid punishment and disapproval. With development, children become less egocentric and more aware of others' perspectives (Imuta et al., 2016). Young children's prosocial behavior becomes motivated by empathy and concern for others as well as internalized societal values for good behavior (Eisenberg et al., 2013).

In addition to helping, children display prosocial behavior by sharing. Three-year-old children conceptualize fair sharing as strict equality; each child should get the same amount of candy, no matter what (Damon, 1977; Enright et al., 1984). Despite endorsing norms of sharing, 3-year-old children tend to favor themselves (Smith et al., 2013). Four- and 5-year-olds believe in an obligation to share, but they often allocate rewards based on observable characteristics, such as age, size, or other obvious physical characteristics (e.g., "The oldest should get more candy"). When told that they must make an unequal distribution, 5-year-olds tend to share more with others whom they expect will reciprocate and more with friends than with peers they dislike (Paulus & Moore, 2014). They are also more likely to share with friends and persons known to them than strangers.

Like adults, young children's judgments about whether to help are influenced by considerations such as people's welfare and needs as well as the situation (Dahl & Paulus, 2019). Young children

One example of prosocial behavior is sharing. Sharing becomes more equitable and complex with development.

iStock/FatCamera

share more with children and adults who show prosocial behaviors such as sharing and helping others, and they view helping as less acceptable if the recipient is trying to steal (Dahl & Brownell, 2019; Kuhlmeier et al., 2014). Notably, young children's perspectives on sharing shifts from an emphasis on equality to equity, and they begin to consider others' wealth and distribute more resources to poor others than rich others (Paulus et al., 2018). Children who have more contact with children of lesser wealth are more likely to allocate resources based on wealth, allocating more to a low-wealth peer than high-wealth peer (Elenbaas, 2019).

Early childhood prosocial behavior is associated with positive peer relationships, mental health, and social competence in preschool and beyond (Malti & Dys, 2018). Prosocial children tend to show low levels of aggressive and problem behaviors. They tend to be successful in school and score high on measures of vocabulary, reading, and language—perhaps because prosocial children are friendly and engage in interaction with teacher and peers (Eisenberg et al., 2015; Miller & Hastings, 2020).

Influences on Prosocial Behavior

Prosocial behavior is influenced by many interacting factors. Emotional influences on prosocial behavior include empathy and concern for others, which emerge in toddlerhood. Self-conscious emotions, such as guilt and pride, influence prosocial behavior. In response to guilt, 2- and 3-year-olds are motivated to repair damage that they have caused and repair relationships with others, such as by apologizing (Vaish & Hepach, 2020; Vaish, 2018). At about 3–5 years of age, children begin to anticipate guilt in response to wrongdoing, which predicts prosocial behavior such as sharing (Malti & Dys, 2018). When 3- and 4-year-old children feel pride in response to an achievement, they are more likely to offer spontaneous help to a person in need (Ross, 2017).

Prosocial behaviors, such as sharing, comforting, and helping, emerge through everyday interactions with caregivers (Dahl & Brownell, 2019). Rich interactions with parents engage the emotions, cognitions, and behaviors critical to prosocial responding (Brownell, 2016). The secure attachment that accompanies warm, sensitive parenting aids in the development of emotional regulation, a predictor of empathy and prosocial responding (Beier et al., 2019; Spinrad & Gal, 2018). Parents of prosocial children draw attention to models of prosocial behavior in peers and in media, such as in storybooks, movies, and television programs. As suggested earlier, parents may also describe feelings and model sympathetic concern and the use of language to discuss feelings. Young children whose parents do these things are more likely to use words to describe their thoughts and emotions and attempt to understand others' emotional states (Taylor et al., 2013).

Parents also actively encourage prosocial behavior by including young children in their household and caregiving activities (Dahl, 2015). Parents' encouragement of children's participation in household cleanup routines predicts children's willingness to help another adult in a new context (Hammond & Carpendale, 2015). Children's prosocial behavior emerges out of prosocial activity shared with adults, and parental encouragement promotes its development (Brownell, 2016).

Siblings offer opportunities to learn and practice helping and other prosocial behavior (Hughes et al., 2018). Older siblings who display positive emotional responsiveness promote preschoolers' emotional and social competence. Researchers have observed that children with siblings tend to develop a theory of mind earlier than those without siblings (Kramer, 2014). As we have seen, the perspective-taking and cognitive skills that comprise theory of mind promote emotional understanding and prosocial behavior.

The broader social world also influences the development of prosocial behavior. Collectivist cultures, in which people live with extended families, work is shared, and the maintenance of positive relationships with others is emphasized, tend to promote prosocial values and behavior more so than do cultures that emphasize the individual, as is common in most Western cultures (Eisenberg et al., 2015). One study of mother-child dyads in Japan and the United States found that the Japanese mothers of 4-year-old children tended to emphasize mutuality in their interactions, stressing the relationship (e.g., "This puzzle is difficult for us. Let's see if we can solve it."). In contrast, the U.S. mothers tended to emphasize individuality (e.g., "This puzzle is hard for you, isn't it? Let's see you try again."; Dennis et al., 2002). These different styles influence how children display empathy, whether as sharing another's emotion or simply understanding another's emotion.

These cultural differences extend to children's reasons for sharing. When Filipino and American fifth graders were presented with hypothetical scenarios that required them to determine how resources should be shared, both the Filipino and American children preferred equal division of the resources regardless of merit or need (Carson & Banuazizi, 2008). However, the children offered different explanations for their choices. U.S. children emphasized that the characters in the scenario preformed equally and therefore deserved equal amounts of the resources, reflecting U.S. culture's emphasis on individuality and merit. Filipino children, on the other hand, tended to be more concerned with the interpersonal and emotional consequences of an unequal distribution, in line with their culture's emphasis on the collective and the importance of interpersonal relationships (Carson & Banuazizi, 2008).

Aggressive Behavior

Although their capacities for empathy and prosocial responses increase, young children commonly show **aggressive behavior**—behavior that harms or violates the rights of others. Most infants and children engage in some physically aggressive behaviors—hitting, biting, or kicking—some of the time (Tremblay et al., 2004). Some aggression is normal and not an indicator of poor adjustment.

The most common form of aggression seen in infancy and early childhood is **instrumental aggression**—aggression used to achieve a goal, such as obtaining a toy. Instrumental aggression is often displayed as physical aggression (Hay et al., 2011). A child who grabs a crayon out of another child's hand is often motivated to obtain the crayon, not to hurt the other child. In addition to fighting over toys, preschool children often battle over space ("I was sitting there!"). Instrumental aggression increases from toddlerhood into early childhood, around age 4, as children begin to play with other children and act in their own interests. Indeed, instrumental aggression usually occurs during play. It is often displayed by sociable and confident preschoolers, suggesting that it is a normal aspect of development.

By ages 4 to 5, most children develop the self-control to resist aggressive impulses and the language skills to express their needs. Now physical aggression declines and verbal aggression becomes more frequent (Eisner & Malti, 2015). **Verbal aggression** is a form of **relational aggression**, intended to harm others' social relationships (Ostrov & Godleski, 2010). In preschool and elementary school, relational aggression often takes the form of name calling and excluding peers from play (Pellegrini & Roseth, 2006).

Most children learn to inhibit aggressive impulses; however, a small minority of children show high levels of aggression (e.g., repeated hitting, kicking, biting) that increase during childhood (Tremblay, 2014). Young children who show high levels of aggression are more likely to have experienced coercive parenting, family dysfunction, and low income; they are also

In the preschool years, children may engage in instrumental aggression when they want to obtain an object, such as the toy in this picture.

iStock/Zabavna

more likely to have mothers with a history of antisocial behavior and early childbearing (Wang et al., 2013). Children who do not develop the impulse control and self-management skills to inhibit their aggressive responses may continue and escalate aggressive behavior over the childhood years and show poor social and academic outcomes during the school years and beyond (Gower et al., 2014).

Thinking in Context: Lifespan Development

Compare the social learning and cognitive-developmental perspectives on moral development.

1. What are the strengths and weaknesses of each?
2. In your view, is moral development better explained by modeling and reinforcement or by changes in thinking? Explain.
3. Aggession is inborn and prosocial behavior is learned. Agree or disagree? Explain.

FAMILIES IN EARLY CHILDHOOD

LEARNING OBJECTIVE

6.4 Compare styles of parenting and discipline and their associations with child outcomes.

The home context and family relationships, especially the parent-child relationship, play a large role in shaping children's social and emotional development.

Parenting Styles

Parenting style is the emotional climate of the parent-child relationship—the degree of warmth, support, and boundaries that parents provide. Parenting style influences parents' efficacy, their relationship with their children, and their children's development. Parenting styles are displayed as enduring sets of parenting behaviors that occur across situations to form childrearing climates. These behaviors combine warmth and acceptance with limits and rule setting in various degrees. In a classic series of studies, Diana Baumrind (1971, 2013) examined 103 preschoolers and their families using interviews, home observations, and other measures. She identified several parenting styles and their effects on children (see Table 6.1).

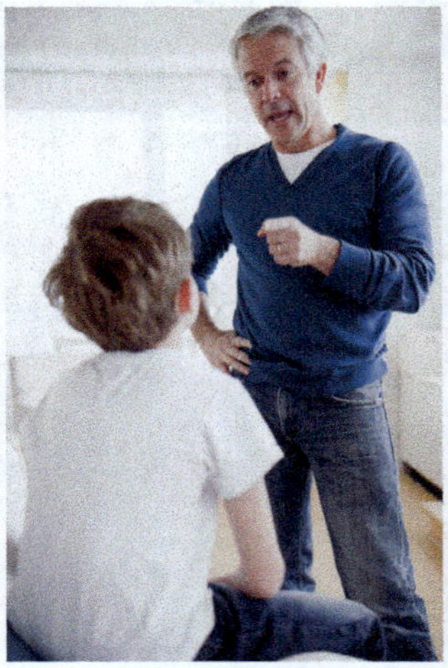

Parenting style is an important influence on development. Authoritarian parenting emphasizes rigid strictness over warmth. Uninvolved parenting can make children feel invisible. Extreme forms of uninvolved parenting constitute neglect.

Jamie Grill/ Getty Images; istock/ LightFieldStudios

TABLE 6.1 ■ Parenting Styles

Parenting Style	Warmth	Control
Authoritative	High	Firm, consistent, coupled with discussion
Authoritarian	Low	High, emphasizing control and punishment without discussion or explanation
Permissive	High	Low
Indifferent	Low	Low

Authoritarian Parenting Style

In Baumrind's classification, parents who use an **authoritarian parenting style** emphasize behavioral control and obedience over warmth. Children are to conform to parental rules without or question, simply "because I say so." Violations are often accompanied by forceful punishment, such as yelling, threatening, or spanking. Parents with an authoritarian style are less supportive and warm and more detached, perhaps even appearing cold.

Children raised by authoritarian parents tend to be withdrawn, mistrustful, anxious, and angry (Rose et al., 2018). They tend to interact with peers in disruptive ways and react with hostility in response to frustrating peer interactions (Gagnon et al., 2013). Children reared with harsh, controlling parenting show more behavioral problems and display less prosocial behavior than other children, from early childhood into adolescence (Baumrind et al., 2010; Pinquart, 2017; Wong et al., 2020). Moreover, parents and children influence each other. As parenting becomes more harsh, children tend to display more behavior problems, which tends to increase negative interactions with parents.

Permissive Parenting Style

Parents who adopt a **permissive parenting style** are warm and accepting, even indulgent. They emphasize self-expression and have few rules and behavioral expectations for their children. When rules are set, they often are not enforced or are enforced inconsistently. Parents with a permissive parenting style often allow children to monitor their own behavior. Autonomy is not granted gradually and in developmentally appropriate ways. Instead, children are permitted to make their own decisions, such as deciding their bedtime or monitoring their screen time, at any early age, often before they are able. Many children lack the self-regulation capacities to appropriately limit their activity. Compared with their peers, preschoolers raised with a permissive parenting style tend to be more socioemotionally immature than their peers, more rebellious, impulsive, and bossy, and show less self-control, self-regulatory capacity, and persistence (Hoeve et al., 2011; Piotrowski et al., 2013). A permissive parenting style also places children at risk for poor school achievement and more behavior problems, posing long-term risks for development (Jewell et al., 2008).

Uninvolved Parenting Style

Parents with an **uninvolved parenting style** focus on their own needs rather than those of their children. Parents who are under stress, emotionally detached, or depressed often lack time or energy to devote to their children, putting them at risk for an uninvolved parenting style (Baumrind, 2012). Uninvolved parents provide little support or warmth, exert little control, and fail to recognize their children's need for affection and direction. As a result, young children reared in neglectful homes show less knowledge about emotions than do children raised with other parenting styles (Sullivan et al., 2010). At the extreme, uninvolved parenting is neglectful and a form of child maltreatment. Uninvolved parenting can have negative consequences for all forms of children's development—cognitive, emotional, social, and even physical.

Authoritative Parenting Style

The most positive developmental outcomes are associated with what Baumrind termed the **authoritative parenting style**. Authoritative parents are warm and sensitive to children's needs but also are firm in their expectations that children conform to appropriate standards of behavior. While exerting firm, reasonable control, they engage their children in discussions about standards and grant them developmentally appropriate levels of autonomy, permitting decision making that is appropriate to the children's abilities (Baumrind, 2013). When a rule is violated, authoritative parents explain what the children did wrong and impose limited, developmentally appropriate punishments that are closely connected to the misdeed. Authoritative parents value and foster children's individuality. They encourage their children to have their own interests, opinions, and decisions, but ultimately, they control the children's behavior.

Children of authoritative parents display confidence, self-esteem, and curiosity, and score higher on measures of social skills, prosocial behavior, executive function, and academic achievement; these positive effects persist throughout childhood into adolescence (Helm et al., 2020; Pinquart & Gerke, 2019; Sosic-Vasic et al., 2017; Wong et al., 2020). Parents in a given household often share a common parenting style, but when they do not, the presence of authoritative parenting in at least one parent buffers the negative outcomes associated with the other style and predicts positive adjustment (Hoeve et al., 2011; McKinney & Renk, 2011).

Discipline

Discipline refers to the methods a parent uses to teach and socialize children toward acceptable behavior. Learning theory can account for the effect of parents' discipline strategies on children's behavior. Specifically, the consequences of a child's behavior, whether it is reinforced or punished, influence the child's future behavior. Effective reinforcement must be viewed as rewarding to the child and can be tangible, such as money or candy, or intangible, such as attention or a smile. To change a child's behavior, reinforcement must be administered consistently when the desired behavior occurs. Eventually the reinforcement becomes internalized by the child and the behavior itself becomes reinforcing, associated with pleasurable feelings and, eventually, a positive feeling of accomplishment.

Time out removes the child from overstimulating situations and stops inappropriate behaviors without humiliating him or her. Time out is effective when it is accompanied by explanation and a warm parent-child relationship.

istock/ sdgamez

Physical Punishment

Physical punishment, also known as corporal punishment or spanking, is against the law in more than 50 countries (Grogan-Kaylor et al., 2018), yet hotly contested in other countries. Parents in many countries within Asia, Africa, the Middle East, and North and South America report that spanking is acceptable, appropriate, and sometimes necessary (Hicks-Pass, 2009; Oveisi et al., 2010). In the United States, the majority of adults report that they were spanked as children without harm, and 80% of a sample of U.S. parents report spanking their young children (Gershoff et al., 2018). Why the controversy on spanking if it occurs in most cultures?

Research suggests that physical punishment tends to increase compliance only temporarily. Longitudinal research suggests that physical punishment is associated with behavior problems in infancy, toddlerhood, and early childhood through age 5 and internalizing problems (such as anxiety and depression), externalizing problems (such as aggression), low self-esteem, and antisocial behavior in childhood, adolescence, and even adulthood (Choe et al., 2013; Lee et al., 2013; Mendez et al., 2016). Parents often punish children for aggressive behavior, yet physical punishment models the use of aggression as an effective way of resolving conflict and other problems, teaching children that might makes right (D'Souza et al., 2016; Sege & Siegel, 2018). Parents who reported using physical discipline were nearly three times as likely to report aggressive behaviors like hitting and kicking in their young children than parents who did not use physical discipline (Thompson et al., 2017).

Physical punishment is damaging to the parent-child relationship (Balan et al., 2017; Coley et al., 2014; Gershoff & Grogan-Kaylor, 2016; Sege & Siegel, 2018; Laible et al., 2020). When a parent loses self-control and yells, screams, or hits a child, the child may feel helpless, become fearful of the parent, avoid him or her, and become passive. One recent analysis concluded that the effects of physical punishment are similar to those of child maltreatment and that parents should avoid physical punishment and health professionals and policymakers should advocate against it and devise means of educating parents about its negative effects (Gershoff et al., 2018).

What can parents do about their children's undesirable behavior? While physical punishment is not advised, noncorporal punishment can be effective, in small doses and within specific contexts. To be effective, punishment should occur immediately after the dangerous behavior, be applied calmly and consistently, be clearly connected to the behavior, and be explained to the child. The purpose of such punishment is to keep the child from engaging in the dangerous behavior, to make him or her comply but not to feel guilt.

Despite estimates that the vast majority of parents spank their children, recent evidence with a sample of more than 16,000 parents suggests that the use of spanking has declined dramatically over the past 25 years (Mehus & Patrick, 2020; see Figure 6.1). These findings are encouraging, but pediatricians and developmental scientists agree that parents can benefit from education about alternative discipline strategies.

Inductive Discipline

Inductive discipline refers to methods that use reasoning; they are effective alternatives to spanking in changing a child's behavior (AAP Committee on Psychosocial Aspects of Child and Family Health, 1998; Lawrence et al., 2020). Examples of inductive methods include helping children find and use words to express their feelings. Another inductive method is to provide children with choices (e.g., peas or carrots), permitting them to feel some control over the situation and be empowered. Parents who use inductive techniques model effective conflict resolution and help children to become aware of the consequences of their actions. Inductive methods are very effective in helping children to internalize rules and standards and adopt positive social skills (Choe et al., 2013; Tompkins & Villaruel, 2021). The use of inductive discipline is part of the authoritative parent's repertoire (Lawrence et al., 2020).

The American Association of Pediatrics recommends that parents positively reinforce good behavior and, when necessary, discourage inappropriate behavior with the use of time out, removal of privileges, and verbal reprimands aimed at the behavior rather than the child (AAP Committee on Psychosocial Aspects of Child and Family Health, 1998; Sege & Siegel, 2018). Time out from

FIGURE 6.1 ■ **Trends in the Prevalence of Spanking**

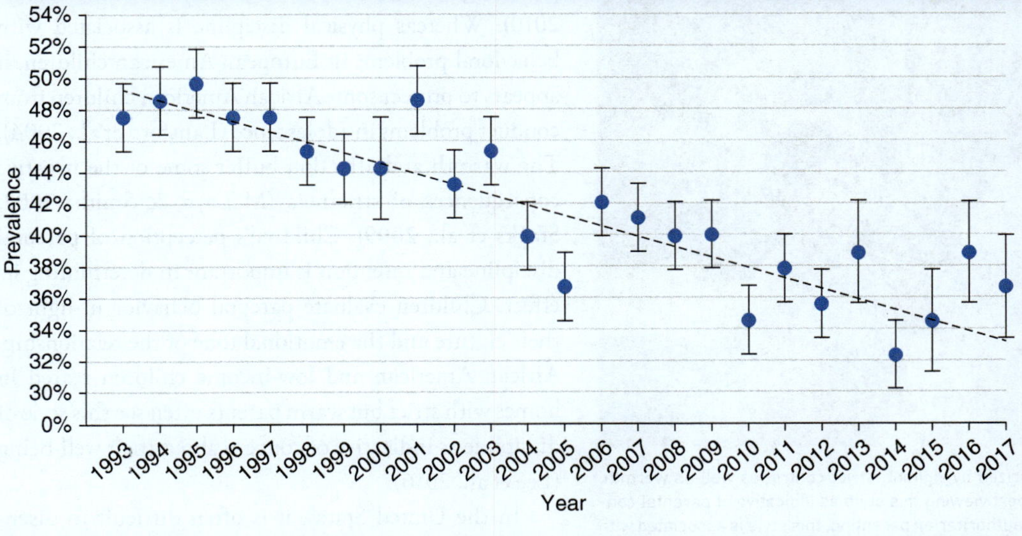

Source: Adapted from Mehus & Patrick, 2020.

reinforcement, commonly referred to as time out, entails removing a child from the situation and its rewarding stimuli, including social contact, for a short period of time (Dadds & Tully, 2019). Implemented correctly, time out is effective in reducing inappropriate behavior (Lawrence et al., 2020; Morawska & Sanders, 2011).

Effective punishment is administered calmly, privately, and it is accompanied by an explanation so that the child understands the reason for the punishment (Baumrind, 2013). Overall, developmental professionals agree that discipline that relies on a warm parent-child relationship, clear expectations, communication, and limit setting is most effective in modifying children's behavior.

Culture, Context, and Parenting

The strategies parents use to control children's behavior vary with the parent's and child's personalities, the age of the child, the parent-child relationship, the parent's knowledge about child development, and cultural customs and expectations (Vally & El Hichami, 2020). One concern that researchers have regarding discussions of discipline is that there is not just one effective way to parent. Instead, there are many cultural variations in parenting, and the effectiveness of disciplinary techniques may differ by cultural context (Cauce, 2008).

Chinese parents tend to describe their parenting as relatively controlling and not emphasizing individuality and choice (Chao, 2001). They are directive and view exerting control as a way to teach children self-control and encourage high achievement (Huntsinger et al., 1998). Yet most Chinese parents couple the emphasis on control with warmth (Xu et al., 2005). Authoritative parenting is associated with emotion regulation, cognitive and social competence, and fewer behavioral problems in young children from collectivist cultures, such as Indonesia and China, and individualist cultures, such as Australia and the United States (Haslam et al., 2020). In contrast, authoritarian parenting and power assertive discipline are associated with difficulties in emotion regulation, poor social competence, anxiety, poor behavior, and poor academic achievement in children of diverse cultures and countries, including China, the U.S., Australia, the European Union, and 25 countries in Africa (Cheah et al., 2009; Dede Yildirim et al., 2020; Gu & Kwok, 2020; Haslam et al., 2020).

Is strict control always harmful to North American children? Researchers have identified a disciplinary style common in African American families that combines strict parental control with affection (Tamis-LeMonda et al., 2009). Sometimes referred to as "no-nonsense parenting," this style stresses obedience and views strict control as important in helping children develop self-control and attentiveness. African American parents who use controlling strategies tend to raise children who are more cognitively mature and socially competent than their peers who are raised in other ways. This difference is particularly apparent in children reared in low-income homes and communities, where vigilant, strict parenting enhances children's safety (Weis & Toolis, 2010). Whereas physical discipline is associated with behavioral problems in European American children, it appears to protect some African American children from conduct problems in adolescence (Lansford et al., 2004). The warmth and affection buffer some of the negative consequences of strictness (McLoyd & Smith, 2002; Stacks et al., 2009). Children's perception of parental discipline and intention is important in determining its effect. Children evaluate parental behavior in light of their culture and the emotional tone of the relationship. African American and low-income children reared in homes with strict but warm parents often see this style of discipline as indicative of concern about their well-being (Lee et al., 2016).

No-nonsense parenting is characterized by vigilant, strict control as well as warmth. African American children often report viewing this style as indicative of parental concern about their welfare and, unlike authoritarian parenting, this style is associated with positive outcomes—especially within challenging community contexts.

istock/ kali9

In the United States, it is often difficult to disentangle the effects of culture and neighborhood context on parenting behaviors in African American families because African American families are disproportionately represented in disadvantaged neighborhoods. Does strict discipline embody cultural beliefs about parenting? Or is it a response to raising children in a disadvantaged environment (Murry et al., 2008)? Parental perceptions of danger and their own distress influence how they parent (Cuellar et al., 2013). Parenting behaviors, including discipline, must be considered within a cultural and environmental context, as parenting is not "one size fits all" (Sorkhabi, 2005).

Child Maltreatment

Child maltreatment, also known as *child abuse*, is any intentional harm to a minor (an individual under 18 years of age), including actions that harm the child physically, emotionally, sexually, and through neglect (U.S. Department of Health and Human Services, 2016). Many children experience more than one form of abuse.

- Physical abuse refers to any intentional physical injury to the child, and can include striking, kicking, burning, or biting the child, or any other action that results in a physical impairment of the child.
- Sexual abuse refers to engaging in any sexual activity, coerced or persuaded, with a child. It also includes inappropriate touching or comments.
- Neglect occurs when a child is deprived of adequate food, clothing, shelter, or medical care.

Each year, there are about 700,000 confirmed cases of abuse or neglect in the United States (U.S. Department of Health and Human Services, 2020). This number is alarming, but it likely underestimates the incidence of abuse because many children experience maltreatment that is not reported. Parents are the most common perpetrators of maltreatment (in more than 90% of cases, on average), with relatives other than parents and unmarried partners of parents constituting an additional 8% of perpetrators (U.S. Department of Health and Human Services, 2016). Moreover, abuse often is not a one-time event; some children experience maltreatment that persists for years.

Effects of Child Maltreatment

The physical effects of abuse often are immediate, ranging from bruises to broken bones to internal bleeding and more. Some physical effects are long lasting. Injuries and prolonged stress can impair brain development and functioning and increase the risk for attention deficit/hyperactivity disorder (ADHD), emotional regulation problems, conduct disorder, and learning and memory difficulties (Cicchetti & Toth, 2015; Hein & Monk, 2017). Chronic maltreatment is related to impairment of brain structures that play a role in regulating emotion, cognition including working memory, processing speed, and language, as well as visual-spatial and motor skills (Cabrera et al., 2020).

Abuse is also associated with academic problems, such as poor school readiness, poor learning and problem-solving skills, and, later, academic failure (Widom, 2014). School-age children who are maltreated tend to score lower on standardized math and reading tests, are more likely to be identified as needing special education, and are more likely to be held back at least one grade (Ryan et al., 2018).

Maltreatment has negative effects on children. The socioemotional effects are especially daunting and long lasting.

istock/ fizkes

The socioemotional effects of child maltreatment are especially daunting and long lasting. Young children who are abused tend to have poor coping skills, low self-esteem, and difficulty regulating their emotions and impulses, and they show more negative affect, such as anger and frustration, and less positive affect than other children (Barth et al., 2007). They tend to have difficulty understanding their own and other people's emotions and often have difficulty making and maintaining friendships (Cicchetti & Banny, 2014). Children and adolescents who are abused also are at risk for a range of psychological disorders, such as anxiety, eating, and depressive disorders as well as behavioral problems in adolescence (Carlson et al., 2015; Cecil et al., 2017; Jones et al., 2013).

Risk Factors for Child Maltreatment

Risk factors for child abuse exist at multiple levels of context: the child, parent, community, and society, as shown in Figure 6.2 (Cicchetti, 2016). Rather than any one factor causing maltreatment, it is the accumulation of risk factors that increases the likelihood of child abuse (Vial et al., 2020; Yang & Maguire-Jack, 2018).

Certain characteristics of children place them at increased risk for abuse. Children with special needs, such as those with physical and mental disabilities, preterm birth status, or serious illness, require a great deal of care that can overwhelm or frustrate caregivers, placing such children at risk of maltreatment. Similarly, children who are temperamentally difficult, inattentive, overactive, or have other developmental problems are also at risk because they are especially taxing for parents (Font & Berger, 2014).

Abuse takes place within the context of adult, most often parent, and child interactions. Parental characteristics may increase the likelihood for abuse. Parents who abuse their children tend to perceive them as stubborn and noncompliant and may evaluate children's misdeeds severely, leading them to use strict and physical methods of discipline (Casanueva et al., 2010). They often lack knowledge about

FIGURE 6.2 ■ Bioecological Perspective of Risk Factors for Child Maltreatment

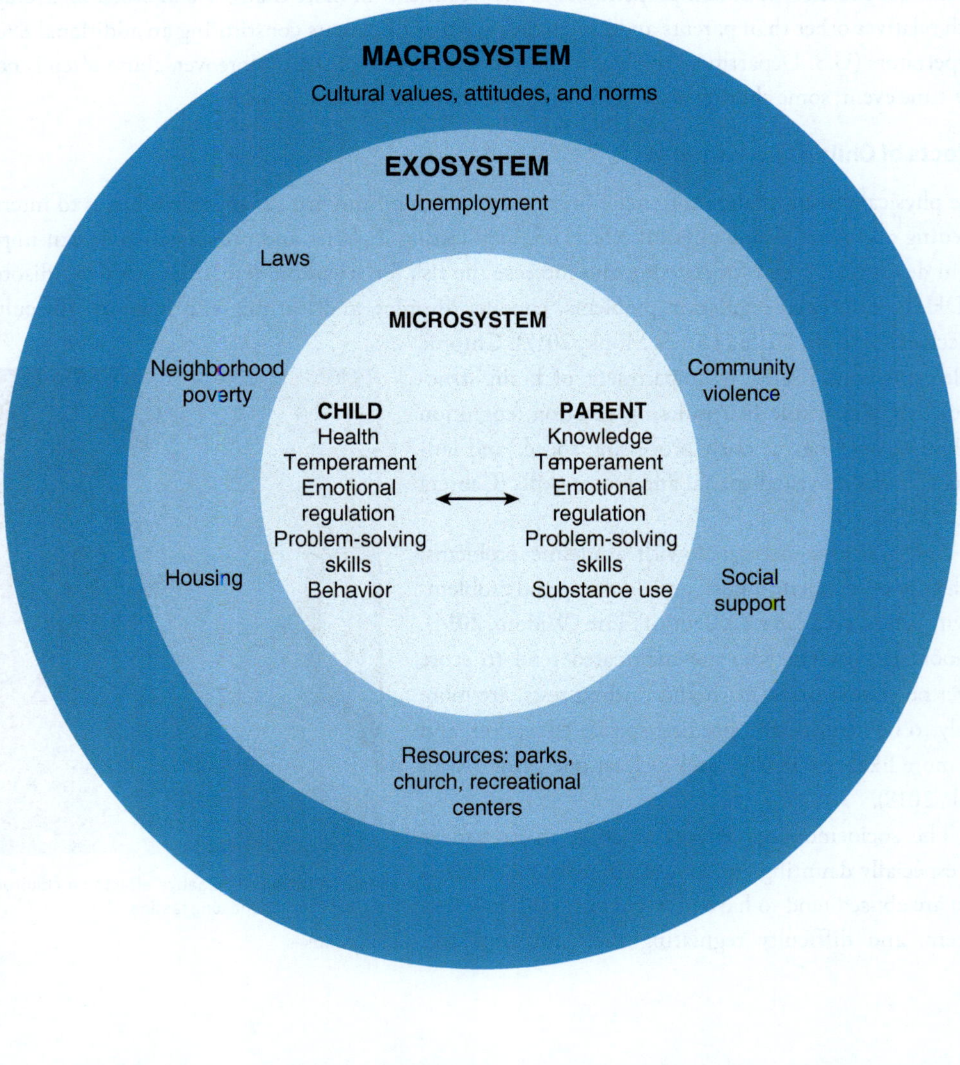

child development and have unrealistic expectations for their children. They may be less skilled in recognizing emotions displayed on their children's faces; find it difficult to recognize, manage, and express their own feelings appropriately; and have poor impulse control, coping, and problem-solving skills (Wagner et al., 2015). The goodness of fit between children's and parents' characteristics influences their relationship and the likelihood of abuse. Parental temperaments and characteristics that clash with those of the child can be a catalyst for abuse when parents have poor emotional regulation and impulse control.

Risk factors for abuse within the home context include marital instability, poverty, and household members who engage in drug and alcohol abuse (Cicchetti & Toth, 2015). Children who are raised in homes in which adults come and go—multiple marriages, separations, and revolving romantic partners—are at higher risk of abuse, especially sexual. However, abuse also occurs in intact middle-class families, yet it is often undetected and unreported (Hinkelman & Bruno, 2008). Income loss, involuntary job loss, parental stress, and parental burnout also predict maltreatment (Griffith, 2020; Schenck-Fontaine & Gassman-Pines, 2020).

Community factors, such as inadequate housing, violence, and poverty, pose threats to family well-being and place children at risk for abuse (Cuartas, 2018; Widom, 2014). Neighborhoods with few community-level support resources, such as parks, childcare centers, preschool programs, recreation centers, and churches, increase the likelihood of child maltreatment (Molnar et al., 2016). In contrast, neighborhoods with a low turnover of residents, a sense of community, and connections among neighbors support parents and protect against child maltreatment (van Dijken et al., 2016).

At the societal level, several factors contribute to the problem of child abuse. Legal definitions of violence and abuse and political or religious views that value independence, privacy, and noninterference in families may influence the prevalence of child abuse within a given society (Tzeng et al., 1991). Social acceptance of violence—for example, as expressed in video games, music lyrics, and television and films—can send the message that violence is an acceptable method of managing conflict.

Overall, there are many complex and interacting influences on child maltreatment at all contextual levels (Vial et al., 2020; Yang & Maguire-Jack, 2018). As risk factors accumulate, the potential for abuse increases. Table 6.2 provides a nonexhaustive list of signs of abuse. Not all children who display one or more of the signs on this list have experienced maltreatment, but each sign is significant enough to merit attention.

All U.S. states and the District of Columbia identify **mandated reporters**, individuals who are legally obligated to report suspected child maltreatment to the appropriate agency, such as child protective services, a law enforcement agency, or a state's child abuse reporting hotline (Child Welfare Information Gateway, 2013). Individuals designated as mandatory reporters typically have frequent contact with children: teachers, principals, and other school personnel; childcare providers; physicians, nurses, and other health care workers; counselors, therapists, and other mental health professionals; and law enforcement officers. Of course, anyone can, and is encouraged to, report suspected maltreatment of a child.

Thinking in Context: Applied Developmental Science

1. Under what circumstances do you think it is appropriate to punish a young child? Identify examples of nonphysical punishment that you believe are appropriate under each circumstance.
2. Parents have a range of tools in their "parenting tool box," but deciding which tool to use is often challenging. Provide examples of an instance in which inductive discipline would be effective. Reinforcement? Time out? Another form of nonphysical punishment?

Thinking in Context: Lifespan Development

Child abuse is a problem with a complex set of influences at multiple bioecological levels. The most effective prevention and intervention programs target risk and protective factors in the child, parent,

TABLE 6.2 ■ Signs of Child Abuse and Neglect

The Child	• Exhibits extremes in behavior, such as overly compliant or demanding behavior, extreme passivity, withdrawal, or aggression • Has not received help for physical or medical problems (e.g., dental care, eyeglasses, immunizations) brought to the parents' attention • Has difficulty concentrating or learning problems that appear to be without cause • Is very watchful, as if waiting for something bad to happen • Frequently lacks adult supervision • Has unexplained burns, bruises, broken bones, or black eyes • Is absent from school often, especially with fading bruises upon return • Is reluctant to be around a particular person or shrinks at the approach of a parent or adult • Reports injury by a parent or another adult caregiver • Lacks sufficient clothing for the weather • Is delayed in physical or emotional development • States that there is no one at home to provide care
The Parent	• Shows indifference and little concern for the child • Denies problems at home • Blames problems on the child • Refers to the child as bad or worthless or berates the child • Has demands that are too high for the child to achieve • Offers conflicting, unconvincing, or no explanation for the child's injury • Uses harsh physical discipline with the child or suggests that caregivers use harsh physical discipline if the child misbehaves • Is abusing alcohol or other drugs

Adapted from Child Welfare Information Gateway, 2019.

and community. Referring to the bioecological model, discuss factors at each bioecological level that might be incorporated into prevention and intervention programs to prevent child abuse and promote positive outcomes (microsystem, mesosystem, exosystem, and macrosystem).

Thinking in Context: Intersectionality

Your friend explains, "Authoritative parenting is a luxury for the privileged."

1. What is authoritative parenting?
2. What contextual factors might influence whether a parent adopts an authoritative style of parenting? Consider individual and contextual factors, such as immediate and extended family, socioeconomic status, work, neighborhood, culture, and society, as well as prior experience and personality.
3. How might experiences with racism and social injustice influence adults' views of their roles as parents, beliefs about what behaviors are important to foster in their children, and how to protect children from injustice and foster resilience?
4. Why might some argue that authoritative parenting is a luxury? What do you think?

GENDER STEREOTYPES, GENDER DIFFERENCES, AND GENDER TYPING

LEARNING OBJECTIVE

6.5 Examine influences on gender typing and discuss ways of reducing gender stereotyping.

Many people use the terms *sex* and *gender* interchangeably, but to developmental scientists, sex and gender have distinct meanings. **Sex** is biological and determined by genes—specifically, by the presence or absence of a Y chromosome in the 23rd pair of chromosomes—and is indicated by the genitals. **Gender**, on the other hand, is determined by socialization and the roles that the individual adopts. Our examination of the role of gender in development begins with a basic question: How do boys and girls differ?

Sex Differences

Despite common views, boys and girls are more alike than different (Leaper, 2013). The largest sex difference is in socioemotional functioning. From an early age, girls are better able to manage and express their emotions than boys (Else-Quest et al., 2012; Thompson & Voyer, 2014). Sex differences in aggression have been observed in toddlerhood (Hyde, 2014). Preschool-aged boys tend to show more physical and verbal aggression, whereas girls tend to demonstrate more relational aggression—excluding a peer from social activities, withdrawing friendship, spreading rumors, or humiliating the person (Ostrov & Godleski, 2010).

Intelligence tests show no differences between boys and girls, but small differences appear on specific tasks. Girls tend to perform better at verbal and mathematical computation tasks as well as those requiring fine motor skills (Miller & Halpern, 2014). Boys tend to perform better on a specific type of spatial reasoning task—mental rotation, or the ability to recognize a stimulus that is rotated in space (Hines, 2015; Lauer et al., 2019).

In all, there are few differences between boys and girls. There is also a great deal of variability within each sex—more so than between the sexes. In other words, there are a greater number and variety of differences among boys than between boys and girls.

Gender Stereotypes and Gender Typing

Although they share many similarities, boys and girls—and men and women—are often treated differently. Beliefs about gender roles sometimes reflect **gender stereotypes**, the rigid expectations and judgments of the activities, attitudes, skills, and characteristics appropriate for men and women in a given culture. Gender stereotypes appear in many cultures (Guimond et al., 2013; Lockenhoff et al., 2014).

Children show awareness of gender stereotypes as early as age 2, and stereotype knowledge increases during the preschool years as children acquire gender role norms, a process called **gender typing** (Liben et al., 2013). By 5 or 6 years of age, children have extensive knowledge of the activities and interests stereotyped for men and women (Blakemore et al., 2009). They express this knowledge as rigid rules about the behavior appropriate for boys and girls (Baker et al., 2016).

Biological Influences on Gender Typing

From an evolutionary perspective, males adapted to become aggressive and competitive because these traits were advantageous in securing a mate and thereby passing along their genetic inheritance (Côté, 2009). Females became more nurturing because caring for young ensured that their genes survived to be passed along to the next generation.

Males secrete higher levels of testosterone than females, which can account for boys' tendency to be more aggressive than girls. When females are exposed to male sex hormones prenatally (e.g., in the case of congenital adrenal hyperplasia, a genetic disorder that causes excess androgen production), they show more active play and fewer caregiving activities in early childhood compared with their female peers (Hines et al., 2016). Hormonally influenced differences in behavioral styles influence play styles; children choose to play with children who have similar styles, resulting in a preference for same-sex playmates (Berenbaum, 2018). In this way, biological factors influence the behaviors that are associated with gender roles. Other explanations for gender role development rely on understanding children's thinking, as described in the next section.

Cognitive Influences on Gender Typing

From the cognitive-developmental perspective, children's understanding of gender is constructed in the same manner as their understanding of the world: by interacting with people and things and thinking about their experiences. Most children develop the ability to label gender groups and to use gender labels in their speech between 18 and 24 months of age (Martin & Ruble, 2010).

Gender Identity and Gender Constancy

Gender identity—awareness of whether one is a boy or a girl—occurs at about age 2 (Bussey, 2013). Once children label themselves as male or female, they classify the world around them, as well as their own behavior, according to those labels (e.g., like me, not like me; Kohlberg, 1966). In this way, children construct their own understandings of what it means to be a boy or a girl and thereby begin to acquire gender roles. By 2 to 2½ years of age, once children have established gender identity, they show more interest in gender-stereotyped toys (e.g., dolls for girls, cars for boys) and a preference for playing with children of their own sex (Silva & Alves, 2020b; Zosuls et al., 2009). Between ages 3 and 5, children show an increase in stereotype knowledge, which is associated with evaluating their own gender more positively and ultimately showing more gender stereotyped preferences and behavior (Halim et al., 2013; Halim et al., 2017).

Young children's beliefs about gender tend to focus on appearance. They often believe that wearing a dress, for example, can change a child from boy to girl. With advances in cognition, children demonstrate **gender constancy**, the understanding that gender does not change—that they will always be the same regardless of appearance, activities, or attitudes (Kohlberg, 1966). Initially, gender constancy may further gender typing, as children become more aware of and pay more attention to gender norms (Arthur et al., 2009). When children understand that gender remains stable over time, and when they view their own gender positively, they are more likely to show gender rigidity, such girls insisting on wearing dresses and boys refusing to wear anything with a hint of femininity (Halim et al., 2014, 2018).

As children develop positive other-gender attitudes, they tend to show less gender rigidity and less gender-stereotyped behavior (Halim et al., 2017). A full understanding of gender constancy includes the awareness that a person's sex is a biological characteristic, which typically occurs by about 7 years of age (Halim, 2016; Silva & Alves, 2020a). Children with a more mature grasp of gender constancy may be less afraid to engage in cross-gender-typed activities because they understand that their gender will still remain the same despite their interests or behavior (Halim et al., 2017).

Gender Schema

Once children develop the ability to label their sex, they begin to form a **gender schema**, a mental structure that organizes gender-related information, representing children's understanding of what it means to be a boy or girl (Canevello, 2016; Weisgram, 2016). As children apply their gender schema they notice more differences between boys and girls, such as preferred clothes, toys, and activities. Children also notice that their culture classifies men and women as different and encompassing gendered roles. Children use their gender schemas as guides for their behavior and attitudes, and gender typing occurs. When given gender-neutral toys, children first try to figure out whether they are boys' or girls' toys before deciding whether to play with them (Miller et al., 2006). When told that an attractive toy is for the opposite sex, children will avoid playing with it and expect same-sex peers to avoid it as well. Young children play with peers who engage in similar amounts of gender-typed activities (e.g., playing dress-up, playing with tools) and, over time, engage in increasingly similar levels of gender-typed activities, contributing to sex segregation in children's play groups (Martin et al., 2013).

Gender schemas are such an important organizing principle that they can influence children's memory. Preschool children tend to notice and recall information that is consistent with their gender schemas (Liben et al., 2013). Children who see others behaving in gender-inconsistent ways, such as a boy baking cookies or a girl playing with toy trucks, often will misrecall the event, distorting it in ways that are gender consistent. They may not even recall gender-inconsistent information (Signorella & Liben, 1984). Not until around age 8 do children notice and recall information that contradicts their gender schemas. Yet even elementary school children have been shown to misrecall gender-inconsistent story information (Frawley, 2008). Clearly, children's knowledge and beliefs about gender and gender roles influence their own gender role and behavior. However, the world around the child also holds implications for gender role development.

Contextual Influences on Gender Typing

A contextual approach to understanding gender development emphasizes social learning and the influence of the sociocultural context in which children are raised. Social learning theory emphasizes the importance of models in acquiring gender-typical behavior (Bandura & Bussey, 2004). Children observe models—typically the same-sex parent, but also peers, other adults, and even characters in stories and television programs. They use models as guides to their own behavior, resulting in gender-typed behavior. Feedback from others serves as reinforcement. Sometimes parents or other adults directly teach a child about gender-appropriate behavior or provide positive reinforcement for behaving in sex-consistent ways: Boys get approval for building bridges and running fast, whereas girls get approval for preparing a make-believe meal or keeping a pretty dress neat. Each of these contextual factors also influences the cognitive components of gender, such as gender schema.

Parents

Boys and girls have different social experiences from birth (Martin & Ruble, 2010). Parents perceive sons and daughters differently and have different expectations for them. Boys' rooms tend to be filled with toys that emphasize action and competition, such as cars, trains, and sports equipment, and girls tend to receive toys that focus on cooperation, nurturance, and physical attractiveness, such as baby dolls, toy kitchens, and play makeup (Hanish et al., 2013; MacPhee & Prendergast, 2019). In one study, 3- and 5-year-old children identified "girl toys" and "boy toys" and predicted that their parents would approve of their playing with gender-appropriate toys and disapprove of choices to play with cross-gender toys (Freeman, 2007).

Gender-consistent behavior is socially regulated through approval. Parents tend to encourage boys' independent play, demands for attention, and even attempts to take toys from other children. In contrast, parents tend to direct girls' play, provide assistance, refer to emotions, and encourage girls to participate in household tasks (Hines, 2015). Boys tend to be more strongly gender socialized than girls. Although both boys and girls tend to play with sex-typed toys for their gender, over childhood boys, but not girls, tend to increase the time spent playing with sex-typical toys (i.e., "boy toys"; Todd et al., 2018). Parents, especially fathers, tend to show more discomfort with sex-atypical behavior in boys (e.g., playing with dolls) than girls (e.g., playing with trucks; Basow, 2008).

Parents often have different expectations for boys and girls and encourage their children to play with gender-appropriate toys.

iStock/gregoryelang

Dutch fathers with strong stereotypical gender role attitudes tended to use more physical control strategies with their 3-year-old boys than with girls, whereas fathers with counter-stereotypical attitudes used more physical control with girls; this differential treatment predicted gender differences in aggression one year later (Endendijk et al., 2017).

Societal forces, such as children's television and movies, tend to depict the world as gender stereotyped.
Diane Bondareff/ Associated Press

Activist Jazz Jennings, although assigned male at birth, identifies as a transgender woman. Noam Galai / Contributor/ Getty

Peers

As early as age 3, children reinforce gender-typed behavior with praise, imitation, or participation (Hanish et al., 2013). Young children tend to show more disapproval of boys who engage in cross-gender behavior than girls (Hanish et al., 2013). Preschoolers often act as gender enforcers, excluding boys and girls who engage in cross-gender activities. Children who spend more time with gender-enforcing peers tend to play more with same-sex peers and show more gender stereotyped attitudes than other children (Xiao et al., 2019).

Girls and boys show different play styles that contribute to gendered preferences in playmates. Boys use more commands, threats, and force; girls use more gentle tactics, such as persuasion, acceptance, and verbal requests, which are effective with other girls but ignored by boys (Leaper, 2013). Girls, therefore, may find interacting with boys unpleasant, as boys pay little attention to their attempts at interaction and are generally nonresponsive. Differences in play styles influence boys' and girls' choices of play partners and contribute to sex segregation (Martin et al., 2011). Peer and parental attitudes tend to be similar and reinforce each other, as both are part of a larger sociocultural system of socialization agents (Bandura & Bussey, 2004).

Media

Children's television, books, and G-rated movies tend to depict the world as gender stereotyped, and these media depictions can promote gender-typed behavior in children (Ward & Grower, 2020) (Golden & Jacoby, 2018). Typical children's media displays more male than female characters, with male characters in action roles such as officers or soldiers in the military and female characters as more likely to have domestic roles, be in romantic relationships, be described as meek, or be in need of help (which is usually provided by male characters; England et al., 2011; Evans, 1998; Filipović, 2018; Tsao, 2020). Coloring books display similar patterns, with more male than female characters, and male characters are depicted as older, stronger, more powerful, and more active than female characters (e.g., as superheroes vs. princesses; Fitzpatrick & McPherson, 2010). One study of 4- and 5-year-old children found that viewing and playing with Disney princess media and toys was associated with more female gender–stereotypical behavior in girls one year later, even after controlling for initial levels of gender-stereotypical behavior (Coyne et al., 2016).

Transgender Identity

Recently, increased attention has been drawn to **transgender** children—those who do not identify with their chromosomal sex but instead identify with the other gender. The prevalence of transgender identity is not well documented, but it appears to be rare (about 0.5% to 1% of adults; Conron et al., 2012; Gates, 2011). It is not clear how many children adopt a transgender identity, but it is accurate to conclude that the majority of children adopt a **cisgender** identity, one that is congruent with their chromosomal sex.

Transgender children's gender development is quite similar to that of cisgender children (Olson & Gülgöz, 2018). Like gender-typical children, transgender children show preferences for peers, toys, and clothing typically associated with their expressed gender, choose stereotypically gendered outfits, and report that they are more similar to children of their expressed gender than to children of the other gender (Fast & Olson, 2018; Olson et al., 2015).

Although parents, peers, and teachers tend to discourage gender nonconformity in children, transgender children resist such pressure, viewing gender as inborn and insisting on their gender identity (Gülgöz et al., 2019; Spivey et al., 2018). While in the past parents may have ignored children's wishes or outright prohibited them from adopting a transgender identity, some parents today adopt a different approach, permitting their children to "socially transition" to the gender identity that feels right to them. This type of social transitioning is reversible and nonmedical. It may entail changing the pronoun used to describe a child, the child's name, and the child's appearance, including hair and clothing. In this way, children are raised according to their gender identity rather than their chromosomalsex.

Whether or not parents should support children's desire to live presenting as their gender identity is hotly debated (Steensma & Cohen-Kettenis, 2011; Zucker et al., 2012). The few studies that have examined transgender children have found that older children who have *not* socially transitioned reported increased rates of anxiety and depression, with more than 50% of older children in some samples falling in the clinical range of internalizing symptoms (Ryan et al., 2010; Simons et al., 2013). In contrast, studies of transitioned transgender children suggest levels of depression and anxiety similar to gender-consistent children and overall norms (Olson et al., 2016). Parental affirmation and support is associated with positive mental health in transgender children (Durwood et al., 2017; Fuss et al., 2015). A sense of acceptance and the ability to live as one's perceived gender may buffer the stresses that tend to accompany gender nonconformity.

Reducing Gender Stereotyping

Young children are immersed in a gendered world and they quickly learn and internalize messages about gender as they interact with people and things around them. Parents who wish to reduce gender stereotyping in their children must begin by examining their own views and gender-related behavior. Parents can model gender neutral attitudes and beliefs by engaging in nontraditional activities, such as men baking cookies and women taking out the garbage. Parents can encourage mixed-gender play dates that include a broad range of activities.

Teachers can organize classrooms to be less gender salient, such as by encouraging all children to take turns playing in the kitchen, block area, and sandbox. Some preschools are committed to creating "gender-neutral" classroom environments in which teachers typically refrain from using gendered language and actively work to counteract gender stereotypes. Children in these settings typically show more gender-neutral behaviors and attitudes (Shutts et al., 2017).

In addition to encouraging children to befriend boys and girls and play with a wide range of toys, including nontraditional toys, parents and teachers can help children recognize gender stereotyping and sexism in the world around them (Bigler & Pahlke, 2019). Parents and teachers can point out and correct stereotypes. Opportunities arise daily. When 4-year-old Aaron insisted, "Only boys can be doctors!" his father replied, "Is that true? Remember Dr. Lopes? She's a woman—and a doctor. And remember the nurse who gave you a shot, Aaron?" "He's a man." "Yes, and he's a nurse. Men can be nurses and women can be doctors." Young children encounter messages about gender daily. Each of these instances is an opportunity to reduce stereotyping and encourage children to be more flexible and tolerant. Table 6.3 summarizes theoretical explanations of gender role development.

Thinking in Context: Biological Influences

1. Discuss the evidence for sex differences in young children. What biological influences contribute to gender in early childhood? Do parents, teachers, peers, and other contexts play a role? Why or why not?
2. In your view, is gender a function of nature, nurture, or an interaction? Explain.

TABLE 6.3 ■ Influences and Explanations for Gender Role Typing

Biological	Describes gender role development in evolutionary and biological terms. Males adapted to become more aggressive and competitive and females more nurturing as it ensured that their genes were passed to the next generation. Gender differences may also be explained by subtle differences in brain structure as well as differences in hormones.
Cognitive	The emergence of gender identity leads children to classify the world around them according to gender labels, and they begin to show more interest in gender-appropriate toys. Children show an increase in stereotype knowledge, evaluate their own gender more positively, and demonstrate rigidity of gender-related beliefs. Gender constancy furthers gender typing as children attend more to norms of their sex. According to gender schema theory, once children can label their sex, their gender schema forms and becomes an organizing principle. Children notice differences between males and females in preferred clothes, toys, and activities, as well as how their culture classifies males and females as different and encompassing different roles. Children then use their gender schemas as guides for their behavior and attitudes, and gender typing occurs.
Contextual	Contextual explanations rely on social learning and the influence of the sociocultural context in which children are raised. Males and females have different social experiences from birth. Gender typing occurs through socialization, through a child's interpretation of the world around him or her, and modeling and reinforcement from parents, peers, and teachers.

Thinking in Context: Applied Developmental Science

1. What advice do you give to a parent who is concerned about gender-atypical behavior, such as a boy who is interested in playing with dolls or a girl who wishes to play with trucks and dress like a superhero?
2. Provide advice to parents and teachers on how to reduce gender stereotyping in young children. Your advice should include the home, peer, and childcare or school contexts.

PLAY AND PEER RELATIONSHIPS IN EARLY CHILDHOOD

LEARNING OBJECTIVE

6.6 Discuss the forms play takes in early childhood and its influence on cognitive and socioemotional development and relationships.

In early childhood, the social world expands to include peers. Play offers important learning opportunities for young children.

Play and Development

Play contributes to physical, cognitive, and socioemotional development. Running, jumping, and balancing games help young children develop their motor skills and strengthen their muscles and bones. Children learn how to use their muscles, control their bodies, coordinate their senses, and practice new motor skills.

Young children's emerging cognitive and social abilities make certain types of play possible. In make believe or **representational play,** children often pretend that one object is something else. Understanding that an object, such as a block, can also symbolize something else, such as a make-believe telephone, is a cognitive feat that prepares children for learning symbols such as letters and numbers (Berk & Winsler, 1995; Vygotsky, 1986). Following the "rules" of pretend play, that a block is a telephone, gives children practice in controlling their impulses and regulating their own behavior.

Young children's cognitive and emotional capacities, such as their growing theory of mind and ability to control their emotions, enables them to join peer groups easily, manage conflict, and select and keep playmates (Schlesinger et al., 2020). Preschool children can join groups and play cooperatively to observe the rules in simple games, such as Simon Says, matching games, and games with spinners and dice (Rubin et al., 2015). Successfully playing with peers requires that young children match their behavior to that of their peers and the setting (Coplan & Arbeau, 2009). During play children learn to take other children's perspectives; manage challenging situations; control impulses; regulate emotions; learn to express their thoughts, desires, and emotions; and problem solve (Coplan & Arbeau, 2009).

Types of Play

Advances in social development in early childhood enables children to include others in their play. Social play develops over a series of steps that take place from the ages of 2 through 5 (Parten, 1932). Toddlers' play is characterized by *nonsocial activity*, including inactivity, onlooker behavior, and solitary play. *Parallel play* then emerges, in which children play alongside each other but do not interact. Play shifts to include social interaction in *associative play*, in which children play alongside each other but exchange toys and talk about each other's activities. Finally, *cooperative play* represents the most advanced form of play because children play together and work toward a common goal, such as building a bridge or engaging in make-believe play (Fehr et al., 2020). These forms of play emerge in order but are not a strict developmental sequence because later behaviors do not replace earlier ones (Yaoying & Xu, 2010). Solitary play declines with age but may take up to a third of kindergarteners' playtime (Dyer & Moneta, 2006).

With advances in reasoning and opportunities to interact with other children, the most advanced type of play, **sociodramatic play**, emerges. In sociodramatic play, children interact with other children, taking on roles and acting out stories (Lillard, 2015;Vasc & Lillard, 2020). They imitate people and experiences they have had or observed. Representational play is part of sociodramatic play as children make believe that they are adults, animals, or super heroes and incorporate pretend objects into their play. Sociodramatic play is social, involving two or more children, and it is interactive, requiring children to talk with each other as they act out their stories. It emerges in early childhood and becomes more frequent and more complex from ages 3 to 6, often with intricate storylines (Rubin et al., 2015).

By pretending to be mothers, astronauts, cartoon characters, and other persons, children learn how to explain their ideas and emotions and develop a sense of self-concept as they differentiate themselves from the roles they play (Coplan & Arbeau, 2009). Practicing being sad, angry, or afraid in pretend scenarios helps children develop emotional control (Goldstein & Lerner, 2018). Both boys and girls engage in sociodramatic play, with girls engaging in more such play than boys. Sociodramatic play offers important opportunities for development as children learn through social interactions. Children model higher level thinking and interaction skills, scaffold less-skilled peers, and help them to reach their potential (Vygotsky, 1978). Sociodramatic play helps children explore social rules and conventions, promotes language skills, and is associated with social competence (Gioia & Tobin, 2010; Newton & Jenvey, 2011).

Some sociodramatic play is accompanied by **rough-and-tumble play**, characterized by vigorous physical activity—running, climbing, chasing, jumping, and play fighting (St. George & Fletcher, 2020). Children's rough-and-tumble play is seen around the world and can be distinguished from aggression by the presence of a play face, smiling, and laughing (Pellegrini, 2013). Rough-and-tumble play serves developmental purposes. It is carefully orchestrated and requires self-control, emotional regulation, and social skills. Children learn how to assert themselves, interact with other children, and engage in physical play without hurting other children (Ginsburg, 2007). Rough-and-tumble play exercises children's gross motor skills and helps them to develop muscle strength and control. Research with animals has shown that rough-and-tumble play elicits positive affect that buffers the effects of stress, suggesting that it promotes resilience (Burgdorf et al., 2017).

Rough-and-tumble play, which includes running, climbing, chasing, jumping, and play fighting, is seen around the world.

iStock/yellowsarah

This child is pretending to be an astronaut. She is involved in sociodramatic play and is learning to act out a role.

iStock/Choreograph

Both boys and girls engage in rough-and-tumble play, but boys do so at much higher rates. In one observation of preschool children, about 80% of the instances of rough-and-tumble play occurred in boys (Tannock, 2011). It is estimated that preschool children engage in rough-and-tumble play 5% of play time in the preschool period, rising to about 10% in late childhood and falling to about 4% in adolescence (Pellegrini, 2013).

Rough-and-tumble play often accompanies sociodramatic play (Fehr et al., 2020). Many children engage in superhero play, pretending to be media characters with extraordinary abilities, including strength, the ability to fly, or to transform themselves into other beings. Children act out scenarios, running, jumping, and chasing. They take turns pretending to be "bad guys" and "good guys" (Frost et al., 2012). Similar to other forms of sociodramatic play, superhero play promotes children's emotional and social development. Children pretend to be powerful characters and pretend to experience different emotions, advancing their understanding of and ability to regulate their emotions (Vasc & Lillard, 2020). Superhero play promotes friendships between children as they share their common interests and cooperate with each other.

Early Friendships

Over the preschool years social play becomes more common, and children have more playmates, longer play episodes, and more varied contacts (Pellegrini, 2013). Most young children can name a friend (Quinn & Hennessy, 2010). Young children generally understand friends as companions who live nearby and share toys and expectations for play. Friends are a source of amusement and excitement. Friends share with each other, imitate each other, and initiate social interactions with each other (van Hoogdalem et al., 2013). As children enter preschool, they spend more time interacting with peers, especially same-sex peers. Although researchers emphasize the proximity and play dimensions of young children's friendships, some research suggests that preschool friendships can be characterized by emotional qualities such as support and closeness, and high-quality friendships are more likely to endure over the school year (Sebanc et al., 2007; Wang et al., 2019). Through peer interactions, young children gain social competence, communication, and emotional regulation skills that permit them to have more complicated—and rewarding—relationships in later childhood and adolescence (Schlesinger et al., 2020).

Imaginary companions or friends are common in early childhood, as early as ages 2 to 3, and occur in about 40% of young children (McAnally et al., 2020; Taylor et al., 2009). Children appear to come up with them on their own. Imaginary companions often represent extensions of real people known to the child, especially those who the child admires or characters from stories, television, or movies. Imaginary companions are usually human, although they may take the form of animals, aliens, and monsters (Gleason et al., 2000). The sense of what an invisible friend looks like is stable and can be retained for years.

Relationships with imaginary friends appear to resemble those with real friends and provide similar benefits, especially companionship (Gleason & Kalpidou, 2014). Children create realistic relationships with their imaginary companions that include pretend conflicts, feeling angry with them, and finding them unavailable to play (Taylor, 1999). Their similarity with real friends has sometimes caused concern in parents and professionals who fear that children create imaginary companions because they are lonely and have no playmates. However, research suggests that children with pretend friends are particularly sociable by nature and do not differ from other children in terms of the number of playmates or peer acceptance (Gleason & Kalpidou, 2014). By interacting with imaginary companions, children may practice social interactions, social roles, and emotions (Gleason, 2017). In fact, children with imaginary companions are better at communicating with peers and show more advanced theory of mind and understanding of emotion than their peers (Davis et al., 2014; Giménez-Dasí et al., 2016)

Imaginary friends are common in early childhood and are indicative of a child's creativity and imagination.
Bob Daemmrich / Alamy Stock Photo

Although children around the world play, peer activities take different forms in different cultures. Children in collectivist societies tend to play games that emphasize cooperation. Children in India often engage in sociodramatic play that involves acting in unison coupled with close physical contact. In a game called *bhajtto*, for instance, the children imaginatively enact a script about going to the market, pretending to cut and share a vegetable, and touching each other's elbows and hands (Roopnarine et al., 1994). In contrast, children from Western cultures that tend to emphasize the rights of the individual are inclined to play competitive games such as follow the leader, hide and seek, and duck, duck, goose! Play, like other aspects of development, is shaped by the context in which it occurs.

Thinking in Context: Applied Developmental Science

1. Educate a group of parents about the value of play in early childhood. Discuss some of the developmental functions of play. Do different types of play provide different benefits? Provide suggestions on how parents can support their children's play.
2. "Five-year-old children can't have friends," argued Janelle, "they're too young." Respond to Janelle. What do we know about young children's relationships and capacities for friendship?

CHAPTER SUMMARY

6.1 Describe young children's sense of initiative, self-concept, and self-esteem.

Young children's psychosocial task is to develop a sense of initiative rather than guilt, a sense of purpose, and pride in their accomplishments. Young children tend to understand and describe themselves concretely and have unrealistically positive views about their abilities. As children gain life experience and develop cognitively, their self-evaluations become more realistic and correlated with skills, accomplishments, evaluations by others, and other external indicators of competence.

6.2 Discuss the development of emotional understanding, regulation, and empathy in early childhood.

Young children become better able to understand their own and others' emotions. Skills in emotion regulation influence adaptation and are associated with social competence and overall adjustment. Parents are important resources for emotional management. Empathy, the ability to understand someone's feelings, is linked with the perspective-taking ability and influences how young children make judgments in their social world. Empathy can motivate prosocial behavior.

6.3 Summarize perspectives on moral development and behavior, including prosocial and aggressive behavior.

Moral behavior can be influenced and shaped through observation, reinforcement, and punishment. The cognitive-developmental perspective examines reasoning about moral issues, specifically concerns of justice. Kohlberg explained that young children display preconventional moral reasoning, motivated by self-interest. Young children in diverse cultures can differentiate moral concerns from social conventions or social customs. Social experiences with parents, caregivers, siblings, and peers help young children develop conceptions about justice and fairness. Prosocial behavior is often first motivated by egocentric motives, to gain praise and avoid punishment. With development, prosocial behavior becomes motivated by empathy and internalized societal perspectives of good behavior. Parents of prosocial children model prosocial behavior and empathetic concern. Aggression, especially instrumental aggression, is common in early childhood. By age 4, most children have developed the self-control to express their desires and to wait for what they want, moving from using physical aggression to expressing desires with words.

6.4 Compare styles of parenting and discipline and their associations with child outcomes.

Parenting styles are enduring sets of parenting behaviors. Authoritarian parents emphasize control and obedience over warmth and raise children who tend to be withdrawn and anxious and often react to frustration with hostility. Parents who are permissive are warm and accepting but have few rules and expectations for children, resulting in children with little self-control who are immature, impulsive, and rebellious. Uninvolved parents provide little support or warmth and little control, with negative consequences for all forms of development. Authoritative parents are warm and sensitive to children's needs but also are firm in their expectations that children conform to appropriate standards of behavior. Children of authoritative parents show the most positive outcomes. Parenting behaviors must be considered within their cultural context as parenting is not one-size-fits-all.

6.5 Examine influences on gender typing and discuss ways of reducing gender stereotyping.

There are few sex differences between boys and girls—and men and women—yet stereotyped gender roles appear in all societies. Biological explanations of gender development cite evolutionary perspectives and examine hormones as contributors to sex differences in psychological and behavioral functioning. Cognitive-developmental perspectives on gender development posit that children's understanding of gender is constructed in the same manner as their understanding of the world, by interacting with the world and thinking about their experiences. Cognitive explanations of gender development focus on the gender schema as a guide for their behavior and attitudes. Contextual explanations of gender development emphasize the influence of various contextual settings and socialization. Parents and teachers who wish to reduce gender stereotyping in their children must examine their own views and gender-related behavior, create environments where gender is less salient, encourage children to play with both boys and girls and a wide range of toys, and directly address gender stereotypes as they arise.

6.6 Discuss the forms play takes in early childhood and its influence on cognitive and socioemotional development and relationships.

Play contributes to physical, cognitive, and socioemotional development. Young children's emerging cognitive and social abilities make certain types of play, such as representational play, possible. During play children learn to take other children's perspectives; manage challenging situations; control impulses; regulate emotions; learn to express their thoughts, desires, and emotions; and problem solve. The most advanced type of play is sociodramatic play, in which children interact with other children, take on roles, and act out stories. Sociodramatic play helps children explore social rules and conventions, promotes language skills, and is associated with social competence. Sociodramatic play is sometimes accompanied by rough-and-tumble play—running, climbing, chasing, jumping, and play fighting. Young children generally understand friends as companions who live nearby and share toys and expectations for play. Preschool friendships can be characterized by emotional qualities such as support and closeness and can endure over the school year.

KEY TERMS

PART 3 LIFESPAN DEVELOPMENT AT WORK: EARLY CHILDHOOD

Many people with interests in early childhood enter early childhood education to work directly with young children. Below are other opportunities for helping young children and creating materials to educate and entertain them.

Early Childhood Educator

Early childhood educators work as preschool teachers as well as in educational programs and interventions designed to promote school readiness, such as Head Start.

Preschool teachers prepare young children for kindergarten by introducing them to the classroom environment and helping them acclimate to it. Preschool teachers create educational and social programs to promote young children's cognitive and socioemotional development. They employ different educational techniques, such as storytelling, educational play, and media, to teach children, help them develop their creativity, and help them improve their social competencies and self-esteem. They provide children opportunities to interact with each other and help them resolve conflicts. They record children's progress, identify needs, and communicate with parents.

Early childhood educators also work in educational programs and interventions outside of preschools, such as Head Start. Head Start is a free, federally funded program that is designed to help 3- to 5-year-old children from impoverished homes prepare (or get a "head start") for entry to school. Like preschool teachers, Head Start teachers develop and administer curriculum, such as teaching letters and numbers; record children's progress; report developmental concerns; and meet with parents. They also support the mission of Head Start, promoting the health and well-being of underserved children and their families. Head Start helps children and their parents access health and family services, such as medical and dental care, healthy meals and snacks, and support for parents.

About three-quarters of Head Start teachers hold bachelor's degrees, but the qualifications to become a preschool teacher vary by state and school (U.S. Bureau of Labor Statistics, 2021). While some private schools might require an associate degree, public schools generally require a bachelor's degree in early childhood education or a related field and completion of a licensure exam. The median wage for preschool teachers was about $32,000 in 2020, but salaries vary by state and school (U.S. Bureau of Labor Statistics, 2021).

Speech-Language Pathologist

Speech-language pathologists work with children and adults who have problems with speech and communication. Their patients may be unable to speak at all or may have problems such as stuttering, unusually high-pitched voice, difficulty making specific sounds, or difficulty swallowing. Speech-language pathologists assess and diagnose speech difficulties, create and carry out treatment plans, and monitor patient progress, modifying the treatment plan as needed. They also counsel individuals and families on how to cope with communication and swallowing disorders.

Many speech-language pathologists work in schools, evaluating children for speech and language disorders and working with teachers, school personnel, and parents to carry out individual and group programs and provide counseling and support. Speech-language pathologists also work in hospitals, private practice, or nursing and residential care.

Becoming a speech-language pathologist requires a master's degree from a speech-language pathology program accredited by the Council on Academic Accreditation in Audiology and Speech-Language Pathology. To practice graduates must also be licensed through their state licensing board, which typically requires supervised experience and an exam. In some states, speech-language pathologists who work in schools may need a teaching certification. The median annual wage for speech-language pathologists was $80,480 in 2020 (U.S. Bureau of Labor Statistics, 2021).

Developmental Psychologist

When most people think of psychologists, they think of therapists. However, there are many different kinds of psychologists, and many are not therapists, but they help people by conducting research and a variety of applied activities. Psychologists study human behavior, including physical, cognitive, and socioemotional functioning, and apply their findings to improve people's lives. Developmental psychologists study people of all ages to learn about how their behavior changes over the lifetime. The topics and findings discussed throughout this book are the result of research in developmental psychology.

How do you become a psychologist? The specific method varies by psychology subfield, but all psychologists attend graduate school and earn doctoral degrees. Earning a doctoral degree typically takes four to five years of study that includes two to three years of coursework and one or two comprehensive exams that test students' knowledge of the field and ability to think critically about it. Upon completing coursework and exams, students begin the final requirement: a dissertation, which is an independent research project that makes new discoveries and a unique contribution to the field.

Developmental psychologists study people from conception to death. Many specialize in a particular age, such as young children, and/or a specific topic, such as emotional development. Developmental psychologists often conduct research in university settings on a variety of topics such as memory, executive function, behavioral problems such as aggression, emotional regulation, and attachment. Some of this research is described as basic, intended to further knowledge and theory. Others conduct applied research, designed to be applied to children in the real world.

A developmental psychologist might study patterns of aggression in the preschool environment. Which children show the highest rates of aggression? What characteristics do they share? What events typically occur prior to aggressive acts? How do teachers' and children's responses influence aggressive behavior? Developmental psychologists might collect observational data; interview children, teachers, and parents; and may administer cognitive or social assessments of children labeled as aggressive. This research might be shared in scientific journals and be described in books such as this. Developmental psychologists may also make suggestions for children and teachers in a specific classroom. They might design interventions to help children, teachers, and parents manage young children's aggression. These interventions might be applied to a particular classroom or as an intervention carried out at many preschools.

Developmental psychologists who conduct research are found in various settings including universities, hospitals, social service settings, government, and more. Some developmental psychologists engage in toy and media-related research, as discussed next.

Toy and Media Research

Some toys captivate young children yet fail to interest older children. How do companies create toys that meet the specific interests of children of a given age? It requires knowledge of development to make toys fun and educational. Some companies employ people to conduct toy development research. These researchers might speak with children about their interests and assess children's reactions to prototypes of toys or current toys in the market. They might conduct focus groups with parents and children to determine their views about specific products and to get feedback on toy designs. The resulting knowledge is used to improve the product. They may also determine how to market particular toys based on their observations of children.

These same techniques may be applied in creating children's media. An understanding of development helps media creators design television and other media to fit children's attention spans and interests. Focus groups and observations can help media creators design effective media. People in toy and media research might hold the job title of *market research analyst*, which earned a median salary of about $66,000 in 2020 (U.S. Bureau of Labor Statistics, 2021). These positions may have other titles, so reviewing the organizational structure of specific companies is a useful way of learning about opportunities in these areas.

7 PHYSICAL AND COGNITIVE DEVELOPMENT IN MIDDLE CHILDHOOD

istock/ Imgorthand

"I scored a goal today!" 8-year-old Kimani exclaimed. Now that she can run faster and kick a ball farther than ever before, Kimani enjoys playing on her elementary school soccer team and is becoming more skilled in the sport. Kimani hopes to attend soccer camp this summer. Not only does she like playing soccer but she also likes learning about her favorite soccer players and memorizing game-related statistics. Advances in cognition have led Kimani to enjoy other hobbies that require concentration and planning, such as making complex collages and playing video games with intricate plots. An increasingly sophisticated vocabulary, emerging social reasoning skills, and an ability to understand other people's perspectives aid Kimani in expressing herself and communicating her needs. Is Kimani a typical school-age child? In this chapter, we examine the physical and cognitive changes that children undergo in middle childhood, from about ages 6 to 11.

PHYSICAL DEVELOPMENT AND HEALTH

LEARNING OBJECTIVE

7.1 Identify changes in physical and motor development and health during middle childhood.

In middle childhood, physical development is more subtle and continuous than earlier in life. School-age children's bodies gradually get bigger, and they show advances in gross and fine motor development and coordination.

Body Growth

Growth slows considerably in middle childhood. As in infancy and early childhood, growth follows a cephalocaudal pattern, proceeding from the head downward (Kliegman et al., 2016). In middle childhood, children grow 2 to 3 inches and gain 5 to 8 pounds per year, so that the average 10-year-old child weighs about 70 pounds and is about 4.5 feet tall. In late childhood, at about age 9, girls begin a period of rapid growth that will continue into adolescence. During this time, girls gain about 10 pounds a year, becoming taller and heavier than same-age boys. As we will discuss in Chapter 11, not until early adolescence, at about age 12, do boys enter a similar period of rapid growth. As children grow taller, their body proportions become more like those of adults, slimmer and with longer limbs.

Brain Development

The human brain reaches about 95% of its adult size by about age 6. Brain volume increases throughout middle childhood into early adolescence, especially in the **prefrontal cortex** (Stiles, 2017). Located in the frontal lobe, behind the forehead, the prefrontal cortex is responsible for executive function, the highest level of thinking. Executive function plays a role in attention, working memory, reasoning, planning, and inhibition (Perlman et al., 2016).

With experience and learning, new neural connections form. Synaptogenesis and the accompanying rise in synaptic density is responsible for increases in **gray matter**, unmyelinated neurons, and cortical thickness in middle childhood (Di Cristo & Chattopadhyaya, 2020). As in earlier periods of life, unused synapses are pruned, or eliminated (Mills et al., 2016). Pruning and the accompanying streamlining of connectivity leads older children to show more focused brain activity on cognitive tasks, as compared with young children who tend to show diffuse patterns of activity throughout multiple parts of the brain (Gibb & Kovalchuk, 2018). As children use fewer regions of the brain they free up processing capacity, leading to improvements in working memory (Ullman et al., 2014).

Myelination continues throughout middle childhood. Myelinated brain tissue is known as **white matter** because myelin, the fatty substance that coats neurons, is white. Insulating neurons with myelin increases the speed of neural transmission and contributes to more efficient processing of information. As a result, children's performance on cognitive tasks improves (Gibb & Kovalchuk, 2018). Myelination increases throughout the brain but, like synaptogenesis, it is especially prominent in the prefrontal cortex (Cafiero et al., 2019). Myelination continues throughout adolescence and into early adulthood.

Brain development, therefore, has clear implications for how children think and learn.

Motor Development

Like growth, motor development advances gradually throughout childhood with increases in body size and strength. During the school-age years, the gross motor skills developed in early childhood refine and combine into more complex abilities, such as running and turning to dodge a ball, walking heel to toe down the length of a balance beam and turning around, or creating elaborate jump rope routines that include twisting, turning, and hopping (Gabbard, 2018). Advances in flexibility, balance, and agility enable children to bend their bodies to do a somersault or carry out a dance routine; balance to jump rope; demonstrate agility to run and change speed and direction rapidly; and have the strength to jump higher and throw a ball farther than ever before (see Figure 7.1).

School-age children build model cars, braid friendship bracelets, and learn to play musical instruments—all tasks that rely on advances in fine motor control. Fine motor development is particularly important for penmanship. By third grade, most children can write in cursive (writing using

FIGURE 7.1 ■ Gross Motor Skills

In middle childhood, gross motor skills combine and become more complex, permitting faster running, higher jumping, and greater coordination, such as the ability to balance on a balance beam.

Source: Hill Street Studios/ Getty Images; iStock/ Ridofranz; Westend61/ Getty Images flowing strokes and connected letters, sometimes referred to as *script*). As computers are increasingly used in classrooms, handwriting has become less commonly used in class and several states have eliminated instruction in cursive writing in favor of keyboard instruction. However, research suggests that cursive writing stimulates neural connections that promote learning (Chemin, 2014; Ose Askvik et al., 2020). Success in cursive writing is associated with academic achievement, especially in reading and writing (Dinehart, 2015; Semeraro et al., 2019).

Brain development plays a role in advancing motor skills. The pruning of unused synapses contributes to increases in motor speed and reaction time so that 11-year-old children tend to respond twice as quickly as 5-year-old children (Payne & Isaacs, 2020). Growth of the **cerebellum** (responsible for balance, coordination, and some aspects of emotion and reasoning) and myelination of its connections to the cortex contribute to advances in gross and fine motor skills and speed (Hull, 2020; Tiemeier et al., 2010). The cerebellum plays a role in learning sequences of behaviors and refining movement (Li et al., 2019). Brain development improves children's ability to inhibit actions, which enables children to carry out more sophisticated motor activities that require the use of one hand while controlling the other, such as throwing a ball, or that require the hands to do different things, such as playing an instrument.

In addition to maturational advances in physical growth and brain development, motor development is also influenced by contextual factors, such as nutrition, opportunities to practice motor skills, socioeconomic status, and health (Ferreira et al., 2018). Children in different contexts have different opportunities to practice motor skills through vigorous physical play and other activities (Laukkanen et al., 2014). In addition, there are long-term implications of motor development for other domains of development. In one study, children's motor development and activity at age 8 predicted measures of cognitive development and academic achievement 8 years later, at age 16 (Kantomaa et al., 2013).

Physical Activity in Middle Childhood

Regular physical activity promotes physical and motor development and health throughout childhood and the lifespan. The Physical Activity Guidelines for Americans recommends that children get 60 minutes or more of moderate to vigorous physical activity daily (U.S. Department of Health and Human Services, 2018). During the school years physical activity is often interwoven into outdoor play carried out with peers on playgrounds, school yards, and recreation centers. Running and chasing games, dancing, biking, jumping rope, and other games such as playing basketball increase children's heart rate and improve cardiovascular health, bone and muscle strength, blood pressure, and immune system health (Bangsbo et al., 2016; Caldas & Reilly, 2018; Eather et al., 2020).

Physical activity, especially cardiovascular (aerobic) exercise, is associated with cognitive and psychological health (Drollette & Hillman, 2020; Poitras et al., 2016). Children who engage in regular physical activity score higher on measures of attention, memory, and executive function, especially planning and cognitive control (Carson et al., 2013; Janssen et al., 2010; van der Niet et al., 2015). Short bouts of moderate cardiovascular activity, such as running and chasing, are associated with improved attention and executive function and improved classroom performance (Bangsbo et al., 2016; Hillman et al., 2019) (Mavilidi et al., 2020). In addition, physical activity has been linked to higher levels of self-esteem and lower levels of anxiety, which in turn are associated with higher academic performance in the classroom (Biddle & Vergeer, 2020; Caldas & Reilly, 2018).

Unfortunately, the majority of children and adolescents in the U.S. do not meet the recommended guidelines of at least 60 minutes of moderate to vigorous physical activity every day. Only about one-quarter of children and adolescents age 6 to 15 are at least moderately active for 60 minutes per day on at least 5 days per week, with activity dropping with age, such that only 8% of 12- to 15-year-old adolescents meet the guideline (Kann et al., 2014). Declines in physical activity begin in middle childhood, about age 7, and are frequently displaced by screen time (Farooq et al., 2018).

Children have opportunities to engage in physical activity at school, most often during physical education (PE) classes. PE is structured and designed to educate students about movement, fitness, and health. On days when elementary schoolchildren have PE, they are more active and take more steps: more than one-third as many steps and two-thirds as many moderately vigorous steps as on non-PE days (Calvert et al., 2018; Castillo et al., 2015). Support for physical education varies, with many schools increasingly devoting less time to PE in favor of academic activities. Moreover, when PE is offered, schoolchildren tend to spend only about one-third of PE classes engaged in moderately vigorous physical activity (Hollis et al., 2016).

Childhood Injuries and Mortality

Middle childhood is a healthy time in development, with 89% of U.S. school-age children in very good or excellent health (Parasuraman et al., 2020). In addition, childhood mortality declines after infancy, and mortality overall has declined over the last four decades (Child Trends, 2019b). As shown in Figure 7.2, the mortality, or death, rate for children ages 5 to 14 is about one-half of the rate for infants and young children age 1 to 4 and about one-quarter that of adolescents age 15 to 19. Unintentional injuries from accidents are the most common cause of death in children and adolescents in the United States, causing about one in five deaths (Dellinger & Gilchrist, 2018; Xu et al., 2016).

Rates for nonfatal injuries vary dramatically with age and are highest in infancy and adolescence (specifically, ages 15 to 19) and decreases into emerging adulthood (ages 20 to 24; Centers for Disease Control and Prevention, 2019). At all ages, boys experience more injuries than girls, likely due to their higher levels of activity and risk taking. Motor vehicle accidents are the most common source of injury at all ages. Other common types of injuries also vary with age, as shown in Figure 7.3. Falls are the most common source of injuries in children ages 5 to 9; from age 10 to 14, children are equally likely to be injured by a fall or be struck by an object or person.

A web of individual and contextual influences place children at risk of injury (Schwebel, 2019). Unintentional injuries are more common in children who are impulsive, overactive, and difficult, as well as those diagnosed with ADHD (Lange et al., 2016). Poor parental and adult supervision is closely associated with childhood injury. Many injuries occur at school, accounting for more than 20% of school-age children's visits to the emergency room (Zagel et al., 2019). Overall, children from low socioeconomic status homes have higher rates of injury and mortality than do other children because of poor access to health care, poor nutrition, and stressful home and neighborhood environments (Braudt et al., 2019; Mahboob, Richmond, Harkins, & Macpherson, 2021; Yuma-Guerrero et al., 2018).

Disadvantaged neighborhoods may also contribute to children's injuries due to factors that increase overall injury risk, such as poor maintenance of streets and sidewalks and poor design or maintenance of housing and playgrounds. In addition to having fewer opportunities to be active, children in disadvantaged neighborhoods often have inadequate access to sources of healthy nutrition; this combination of circumstances can interfere with the development of healthy, strong bodies.

FIGURE 7.2 ■ **Childhood Mortality in the United States, 1980–2017**

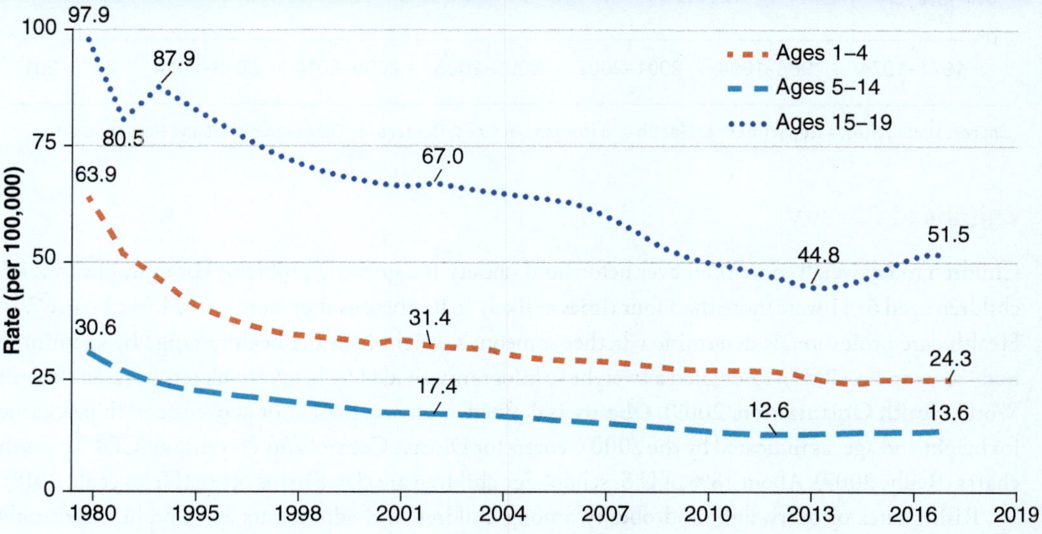

Source: Centers for Disease Control and Prevention, 2019.

FIGURE 7.3 ■ Leading Causes of Nonfatal Injury, in the United States, Ages 1–14, 2018

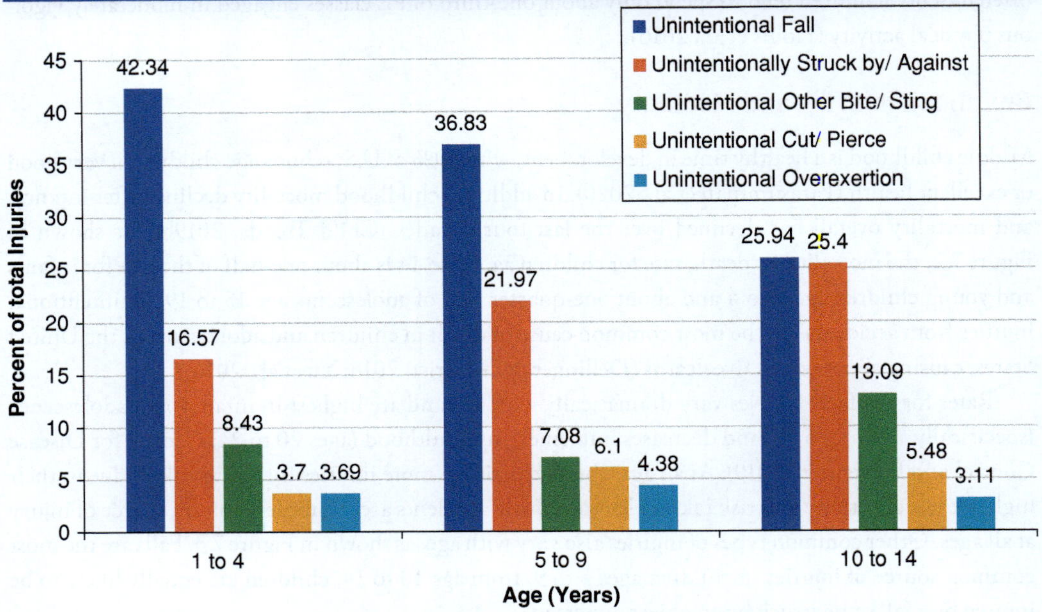

Source: Centers for Disease Control and Prevention, 2020.

FIGURE 7.4 ■ Percentage of Children Ages 2 to 19 Who Are Obese, 1971–2016

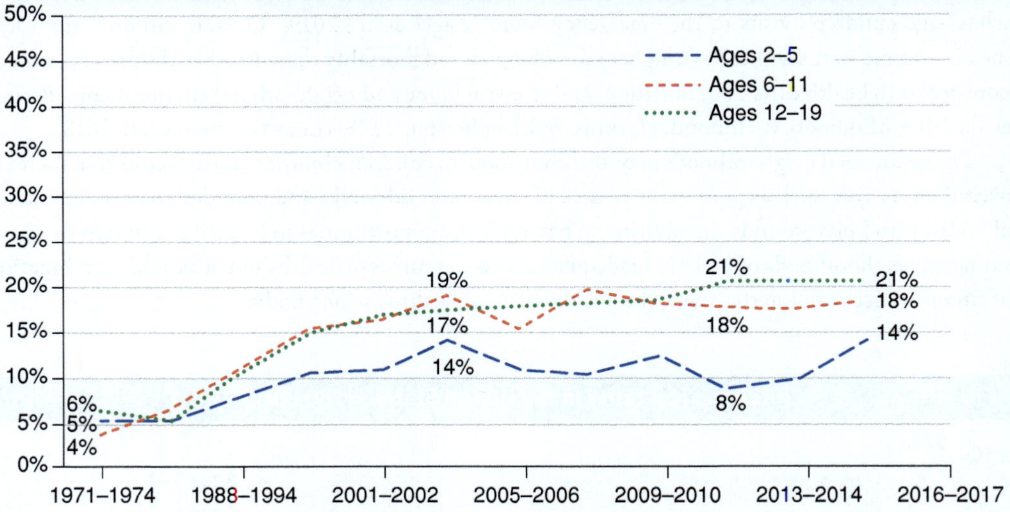

Source: United States Department of Health and Human Services; Centers for Disease Control and Prevention.

Childhood Obesity

Children today weigh more than ever before and obesity is a growing problem. For example, in 2015 children aged 6–11 were more than four times as likely to be obese as they were in 1971 (see Figure 7.4). Health care professionals determine whether someone's weight is in the healthy range by examining **body mass index (BMI),** calculated as weight in kilograms divided by height in meters squared (kg/m^2; World Health Organization, 2009). **Obesity** is defined as having BMI at or above the 95th percentile for height and age, as indicated by the 2000 Centers for Disease Control and Prevention (CDC) growth charts (Reilly, 2007). About 18% of U.S. school-age children are classified as obese (Hales et al., 2018).

Rising rates of overweight and obesity among children and adolescents are a problem not only in the United States but internationally, including countries in Europe, Australia, South America, and parts of Asia and Africa (Di Cesare et al., 2019; Garrido-Miguel et al., 2019; Spinelli et al., 2019; Xu et al., 2018). Obesity is also becoming more common in developing nations, such as India, Pakistan, and China, as they adopt Western-style diets higher in meats, fats, and refined foods and as they show the increased snacking and decreased physical activity linked with watching television and screen use (Afshin et al., 2017).

Child and adolescent obesity is associated with short- and long-term health problems, including heart disease, high blood pressure, orthopedic problems, and diabetes (Pulgarón, 2013). Obese children and adolescents are at risk for peer rejection, depression, low self-esteem, and body dissatisfaction (Harrist et al., 2016; Pulgarón, 2013; Quek et al., 2017). The majority of obese youngsters do not outgrow obesity but instead become obese adults (Simmonds et al., 2016).

Heredity plays a strong role in obesity, but contextual factors also place individuals at risk for obesity and interact with biology to determine whether genetic predispositions to weight gain are fulfilled (Albuquerque et al., 2017; Goodarzi, 2018). The effects of SES may interact with individuals' genetic predispositions. In one study, children who were carriers of a particular allele of the *OXTR* gene had greater BMI when reared in low-SES environments but had the lowest BMI when reared in high-SES homes (Bush et al., 2017). Community-level influences on obesity include the lack of safe playgrounds with equipment that encourages activity and even the proximity of fast-food restaurants to schools (Alviola et al., 2014; Black et al., 2015; Fan & Jin, 2014).

Physical activity also contributes to body weight, and it tends to decline beginning in middle childhood, about age 7 (Farooq et al., 2018). Screen time increases with age, and the sedentary nature of screen time and snacking that tends to accompany it place children at risk for overweight and obesity (Rideout, 2015; Robinson et al., 2017).

Programs that effectively reduce obesity in children and adolescents target their screen time and increase their physical activity and time spent outdoors. In addition, successful programs teach children about nutrition and help them to reduce their consumption of high-calorie foods and increase their consumption of fruits and vegetables (Kumar & Kelly, 2017; Lobstein et al., 2015). To prevent obesity, parents should monitor their children's activities and engage in physical activities with them such as walking, biking, and swimming.

Thinking in Context: Biological Influences

1. The contributions of biology (nature) and context (environment) are perhaps most easily recognizable as influences on physical development. Discuss and provide examples of biological and contextual influences on aspects of physical development.
2. Zoe believes that there is a "fat gene" that alone determines the risk of obesity in middle childhood. Compare Zoe's belief with we know about influences on obesity.

Thinking in Context: Lifespan Development

1. What physical activities did you engage in as an elementary school student? How did your interests and abilities change over middle and late childhood? How do you account for these changes?
2. What role might contextual factors in the home, school, peer, or neighborhood context have had in influencing your physical activity? What opportunities did your contexts provide for your physical activity? Did any pose risks, perhaps preventing activity?
3. Development takes place through dynamic interactions between the individual and the world around him or her. Consider childhood obesity in light of these interactions. What are some of physical and socioemotional correlates of childhood obesity? How might these outcomes influence children's subsequent interactions with the people, objects, and places around them?

Thinking in Context: Intersectionality

What are some reasons why children from disenfranchised groups experience a higher risk for injury and injury-related mortality? How are household socioeconomic status and neighborhood socioeconomic status related to the risk for injury and injury-related death?

DEVELOPMENTAL DISABILITIES

LEARNING OBJECTIVE

7.2 Compare common developmental disabilities and discuss the relevance of contextual influences for disability.

Developmental disabilities are a variety of conditions that are due to impairments in physical functioning, learning, language, and behavior (Zablotsky & Black, 2020). They begin early in life and are usually lifelong. Over the past half century, the nature of childhood disability has dramatically shifted. Advances in medicine and improvements in public health, including prenatal diagnostic tests, information about teratogens and prenatal development, and access to medical care, have spurred a decline in rates of physical disabilities in children, such as cerebral palsy, limb and other birth defects, and sensory impairments (Houtrow et al., 2014). Although physical disabilities have declined, disabilities related to neurodevelopmental conditions have risen, resulting in an overall increase in childhood disability in recent decades, including the past decade (Graham et al., 2017; Houtrow et al., 2014; Zablotsky et al., 2019). As shown in Figure 7.5, the most common developmental disabilities are neurodevelopmental conditions (ADHD and learning disorders).

Attention Deficit/Hyperactivity Disorder

Attention-deficit/hyperactivity disorder (ADHD) is the most commonly diagnosed neurodevelopmental disorder in children, diagnosed in about 10% of schoolchildren in the United States (Visser et al., 2014; Zablotsky et al., 2019). ADHD is characterized by persistent difficulties with attention and/or hyperactivity/impulsivity that interferes with performance and behavior in school and daily life (Hinshaw, 2018). Difficulty with attention and distractibility may manifest in different ways among children, but it may include failing to attend to details, making careless mistakes, not appearing to listen when spoken to directly, not following instructions, or difficulty organizing tasks or activities.

FIGURE 7.5 ■ Common Developmental Disabilities

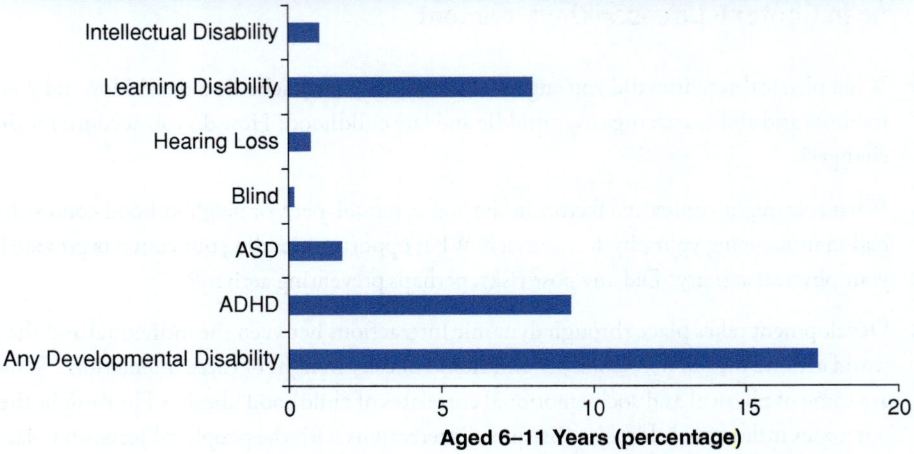

Source: Adapted from Zablotsky et al., 2019.

Impulsivity may include frequent fidgeting, squirming in seat, and leaving seat in class; often running or climbing in situations where it is not appropriate; talking excessively, often blurting out an answer before a question is completed; and having trouble waiting a turn (Antshel, 2020; Luo et al., 2019). Although most children show one or two symptoms of inattention or hyperactivity at some point in their development, a diagnosis of ADHD requires consistent display of a minimum number of specific symptoms over a 6-month period, and the symptoms must interfere with behavior in daily life (American Psychiatric Association, 2013; Hinshaw, 2018).

ADHD is associated with differences in brain development, specifically structural abnormalities in parts of the brain responsible for attentional and motor control (Jacobson et al., 2018). ADHD has biological causes and is nearly 80% heritable, or genetic (Aguiar et al., 2010; Schachar, 2014). Research studying identical twins in which only one twin was diagnosed with ADHD has suggested a role for epigenetics in determining the degree to which genetic propensities are expressed (Aranda, 2008; Mirkovic et al., 2020; Tistarelli et al., 2020). Environmental influences on ADHD may include premature birth, maternal smoking, drug and alcohol use, lead exposure, and brain injuries (Cabral et al., 2020; Huang et al., 2018; Tarver et al., 2014).

Stimulant medication is the most common treatment for ADHD. Stimulant medication increases activity in the parts of the brain that are responsible for attention, self-control, and behavior inhibition (Hawk et al., 2018). Behavioral interventions can help children learn strategies to manage impulses and hyperactivity, direct their attention, and monitor their behavior (Antshel, 2020; Evans et al., 2018).

Autism Spectrum Disorders

Autism spectrum disorders (ASD) are a family of neurodevelopmental disorders that range in severity and are characterized by deficits in social communication and a tendency to engage in repetitive behaviors (Lord et al., 2020). About 1 in 68 U.S. children are diagnosed with ASD, with males about four times as likely to be diagnosed as females (Masi et al., 2017). The social and communication impairments vary widely, from minor difficulties in social comprehension and perspective taking to the inability to use verbal or spoken language. A common characteristic of ASD is repetitive behavior, such as rocking, hand-flapping, twirling, and repeating sounds, words, or phrases. (Hall, 2018; Hodges et al., 2020). Some children with ASD experience sensory dysfunction, feeling visual, auditory, and tactile stimulation as intense and even painful.

ASD is likely influenced by multiple interacting genetic and environmental factors (Cheroni et al., 2020; Grove et al., 2019). Prenatal exposure to teratogens, maternal infection, and advanced maternal and paternal age have been associated with increased risk for ASD (Bölte et al., 2019; Wang et al., 2017a). Infants born prematurely and of low birth weight carry a higher risk for ASD in addition to other neurodevelopmental disorders (Agrawal et al., 2018). It is critical to note that, contrary to a popular misconception, ASD is not caused by vaccination (Hodges et al., 2020; Hviid et al., 2019)

ASD is associated with atypical brain development characterized by altered neural connectivity and sensitivity (Bourgeron, 2015; Hahamy et al., 2015; Zhang & Roeyers, 2019). Sensorimotor areas of the brain tend to show heightened connectivity, perhaps accounting for the sensory difficulties and motor features associated with ASD (Hull et al., 2017; Khan et al., 2015). The areas of the brain responsible for inhibitory control and self-regulation tend to show less connectivity, suggesting that children with ASD may experience difficulty controlling impulses (Voorhies et al., 2018). There are also fewer neural connections within and reduced

Children with ASD may benefit from instruction that emphasizes modeling, hands-on activities, and concrete examples.

istock/ KatarzynaBialasiewicz

interconnectivity among areas involved in detecting facial expressions, social behavior, emotion, social communication, and perspective taking (Cheng et al., 2015; Dajani & Uddin, 2016; Sato & Uono, 2019). Collectively these neurological differences mean that children with ASD may experience a poor theory of mind (Hodges et al., 2020; Kana et al., 2015). That is, they may find it difficult to consider mental states, which is essential to communication.

Children with ASD often show difficulties with working memory, requiring additional time to process information (Wang et al., 2017b). They may benefit from instruction that emphasizes modeling, hands-on activities, and concrete examples and teaches skills for generalizing learning from one setting or problem to another (Kent et al., 2020; Lord et al., 2020).

Specific Learning Disorder

A **specific learning disorder (SLD)** is diagnosed when children demonstrate a measurable discrepancy between aptitude and achievement in a particular academic area given their age, intelligence, and amount of schooling (American Psychiatric Association, 2013). Children with SLDs have difficulty with academic achievement despite having normal intelligence and sensory function. An estimated 1 in 5 children in the United States has a specific learning disorder (Horowitz et al., 2017). SLDs can be manifested in several ways, reflecting different patterns of brain function, and influence reading, writing skills, mathematics, and other cognitive skills (Grigorenko et al., 2020).

Developmental dyslexia is the most commonly diagnosed SLD. Children with dyslexia have difficulty reading, with reading achievement below that predicted by age or IQ. Children with dyslexia demonstrate age-inappropriate difficulty in matching letters to sounds and difficulty with word recognition and spelling despite adequate instruction and intelligence and intact sensory abilities (Peterson & Pennington, 2012; Ramus, 2014). During speech tasks, they use different regions of the brain than other children, and they are often have difficulty recognizing that words consist of small units of sound, strung together and represented visually by letters (Richlan, 2019; Schurz et al., 2015) Dyslexia is estimated to affect 5% to nearly 18% of the school population, boys and girls equally. Successful interventions include not only training in phonics but also supporting emerging skills by linking letters, sounds, and words through writing and reading from developmentally appropriate texts (Snowling, 2013).

A similar common SLD is **developmental dyscalculia**, a disorder that affects mathematics ability. Dyscalculia is thought to affect about 5% of students and is less well understood than developmental dyslexia (Kaufmann et al., 2013; Rapin, 2016). Children with developmental dyscalculia find it challenging to learn mathematical concepts such as counting, addition, and subtraction and often have a poor understanding of these concepts (Gilmore et al., 2010; Kucian & von Aster, 2015). In early elementary school, they may use relatively ineffective strategies for solving math problems, such as using their fingers to add large sums. Research suggests that it is influenced by brain connectivity and suboptimal recruitment of regions needed for mathematical cognition, working memory, and executive function, especially visuospatial short-term memory and inhibitory function (Castaldi et al., 2020; McCaskey et al., 2020; Menon, 2016). Children with dyscalculia are usually given intensive practice to help them understand numbers, including the use of an abacus (a counting tool consisting of a frame with beads) to help visualize numbers, but there is much to learn about this disorder (Bryant et al., 2016; Fuchs et al., 2017; Lu et al., 2020).

Developmental dysgraphia is a disorder that affects writing abilities. It is closely related to dyslexia and may manifest as difficulties with spelling, poor handwriting, and trouble conveying thoughts on paper, leading children to show writing performance below that expected based on their grade (Döhla et al., 2018; Döhla & Heim, 2016). Developmental writing disorders occur in about 7% to 15% of school-aged children and is more common in boys (Horowitz et al., 2017). Similar to dyslexia, dysgraphia indicates difficulties with working memory and executive function, especially response inhibition; however, fMRI scans suggest different patterns of brain connectivity (Richards et al., 2015).

Writing relies on motor and sensory skills; teachers and parents can help children with dysgraphia by focusing on these skills (Berninger & Wolf, 2009). Providing a choice of pens and pencils, paper with raised lines as a sensory guide to help children learn to write within the lines, and training in keyboard skills can aid children with dysgraphia.

Context and Disability: Race and Socioeconomic Status

Contextual influences such as access to health resources plays a role in the prevalence and treatment of childhood disability. Children in low socioeconomic–status homes are more likely to be diagnosed with neurodevelopmental disabilities than children of high SES (Durkin et al., 2017; Zablotsky et al., 2019, 2020). Rates of disability are higher among children in rural communities, which tend to offer fewer health and social services, than urban communities (Zablotsky et al., 2019; Zablotsky & Black, 2020).

Non-Hispanic white children are most likely to be diagnosed with ADHD and ASD, followed by non-Hispanic Black children; Hispanic children are least likely to be diagnosed. Learning disabilities show a different patten whereby non-Hispanic Black children are more likely to be diagnosed with learning disabilities than non-Hispanic white children, who in turn are more likely to be diagnosed than Hispanic children (Bax et al., 2019; Zablotsky et al., 2019).

Despite these findings, researchers are hesitant to draw conclusions about racial and SES differences in disability. Black children may experience similar rates of developmental disabilities, but may be less likely to be diagnosed than white children (Bax et al., 2019; Morgan et al., 2017). SES and race are intertwined, and families in low-SES homes and communities may lack access to professionals to evaluate and diagnose their children. Schools in disadvantaged neighborhoods are more likely to be overcrowded, with fewer resources to identify children with special needs. In addition, race and ethnicity may influence teachers' and school staffs' interpretation of children's performance in the classroom. Racial biases about intelligence or academic ability may play a role in under-identifying Black children for developmental disability screening (Slobodin & Masalha, 2020). Teachers and staff may be unaware of racial biases that may influence their judgment. They may be more likely to attribute disruptive behavior to attentional difficulties in white children and to learning difficulties or oppositional behavior in Black children (Bax et al., 2019; Fadus et al., 2020; Fish, 2019). In this way, white children may be channeled toward assessment for attention problems, and be diagnosed with ADHD, and Black children to be evaluated for learning disabilities and behavioral problems—both with potentially lifelong consequences.

Thinking in Context: Biological Influences

Discuss the alterations in brain development that comprise developmental disabilities. What is the role of epigenetics in developmental disabilities?

Thinking in Context: Applied Developmental Science

Consider the characteristics of ASD and ADHD. How might classroom behavior and performance differ among children with ASD and ADHD? Do these children interact with other children in similar ways? How might their peer relations and friendships differ?

Thinking in Context: Intersectionality

Marked racial and ethnic differences occur in diagnoses of developmental disorders, with white children more likely to be diagnosed with some disorders and children of color, especially Black children, more likely to be diagnosed with others. How might these findings be related to issues of social justice? Consider issues such as access to assessment and intervention, biases about intellect, and expectations for behavior problems. Which children are most likely to receive which diagnoses? What might underlie these differences?What might be some long-term consequences of these differences?

COGNITIVE DEVELOPMENT IN MIDDLE CHILDHOOD

LEARNING OBJECTIVE

7.3 Discuss school-age children's capacities for reasoning and processing information.

Children's ability to take in, process, and retain information expands dramatically in middle childhood. They grasp the world around them in new, more adultlike ways and become capable of thinking logically, although their reasoning remains different from that of adults. Children become faster, more efficient thinkers, and they develop more sophisticated perspectives on the nature of knowledge and how the mind works.

Piaget's Cognitive-Developmental Theory: Concrete Operational Reasoning

When children enter Piaget's **concrete operational stage of reasoning**, at about age 6 or 7, they become able to use logic to solve problems but are still unable to apply logic to abstract and hypothetical situations. Older children's newly developed ability for logical thinking enables them to reason about physical quantities and is evident in their skills in classification and conservation.

Classification is the ability to understand hierarchies, to simultaneously consider relations between a general category and more specific subcategories. Now children can compare multiple items across several dimensions at once. Several types of classification skills emerge during the concrete operational stage: transitive inference, seriation, and class inclusion.

The ability to infer the relationship between two objects by understanding each object's relationship to a third is called **transitive inference**. Present children with three sticks: A, B, and C. Demonstrate that Stick A is longer than Stick B and Stick B is longer than Stick C. Children who reason at the concrete operational stage do not need to physically compare Sticks A and C to know that Stick A is longer than Stick C. They use the information given about the two sticks to infer their relative lengths (Wright & Smailes, 2015). Transitive inference emerges earlier than other concrete operational skills. By about 5 years of age, children are able to infer that A is longer than C (Goodwin & Johnson-Laird, 2008). Skills in transitive inference contribute to children's growing understanding of mathematics and ability to understand relations among quantities and make inferences based on those relations (Schwartz et al., 2020).

Seriation is the ability to order objects in a series according to a physical dimension such as height, weight, or color. Ask a child to arrange a handful of sticks in order by length, from shortest to longest. Four- to 5-year-old children can pick out the smallest and largest stick but will arrange the others haphazardly. Six- to 7-year-old children, on the other hand, arrange the sticks by picking out the smallest, and next smallest, and so on (Inhelder & Piaget, 1964).

In the concrete operational stage children become capable of classification, and can organize these rocks across several dimensions, such as size, color, type or location.

istock/ Ja_Het

Class inclusion involves understanding hierarchical relationships among items. Suppose that a child is shown a bunch of flowers, seven daisies and two roses. She is told that there are nine flowers; seven are called daisies and two are called roses. The child is then asked, "Are there more daisies or flowers?" Preoperational children will answer that there are more daisies, as they do not understand that daisies are a subclass of flowers. By age 5, children have some knowledge of classification hierarchies and may grasp that daisies are flowers but still not fully understand and apply classification hierarchies to correctly solve the problem (Deneault & Ricard, 2006). By about age 8, children not only can classify objects, in this case flowers, but also can make quantitative judgments and respond that there are more flowers than daisies (Borst et al., 2013).

Perhaps the most well-known skill that emerges during the concrete operational stage is conservation, the understanding that the physical properties of objects, such as mass or volume, do not change despite superficial changes in appearance. In a classic conservation problem, a child is shown two identical balls of clay and watches while the experimenter rolls one ball into a long hotdog shape. When asked which piece contains more clay, a child who reasons at the preoperational stage will say that the hotdog shape contains more clay because it is longer. Eight-year-old Julio, in contrast, notices that the ball shape is shorter than the hotdog shape, but it is also thicker. He knows that the two shapes contain the same amount of clay. At the concrete operational stage of reasoning, Julio understands that certain characteristics of an object do not change despite superficial changes to the object's appearance. An understanding of reversibility—that an object can be returned to its original state—means Julio realizes that the hotdog-shaped clay can be reformed into its original ball shape.

Most children solve this conservation problem of substance by age 7 or 8. At about age 9 or 10, children also correctly solve conservation of weight tasks (after presenting two equal-sized balls of clay and rolling one into a hotdog shape, "Which is heavier, the hotdog or the ball?"). Conservation of volume tasks (after placing the hotdog- and ball-shaped clay in glasses of liquid: "Which displaces more liquid?") are solved last, at about age 12. The ability to conserve develops slowly, and children show inconsistencies in their ability to solve different types of conservation problems.

Culture and Concrete Operational Reasoning

Piaget believed that all children around the world progressed through the same cognitive developmental stages at the same pace. Today's researchers find that the cultural context in which children are immersed plays a critical role in development (Goodnow et al., 2015). Children around the world demonstrate concrete operational reasoning, but experience and specific cultural practices play a role in how it is displayed (Manoach et al., 1997). Schooling influences the rate at which principles are understood. Children who have been in school longer tend to do better on transitive inference tasks than same-age children with less schooling (Artman & Cahan, 1993). Formal education is associated with similar patterns of emerging cognitive operations in children from developed and developing countries, including Britain, Greece, Australia, Pakistan, and Zimbabwe (Mpofu & van de Vijver, 2000; Shayer et al., 1988).

Studies of children in non-Western cultures, especially those without formal schooling, suggest that they achieve conservation and other concrete operational tasks later than children from Western cultures. In Papua New Guinea, conservation of number (typically first to emerge) appears approximately three years later than in Western samples, while mastery of more complex tasks (e.g., conservation of area, volume) appears up to six years later (Shea, 1985). Cultural differences in children's performance on tasks that measure concrete operational reasoning may be influenced by methodology (e.g., how questions are asked and the cultural identity of the experimenter) rather than reflect children's abilities (Gauvain et al., 2015). Generally, children perform better when they are assessed using their native language (Gardiner & Kosmitzki, 2018). For instance, when 10- and 11-year-old Canadian Micmac Indian children were tested in English on conservation problems (substance, weight, and volume), they performed worse than 10- to 11-year-old white English-speaking children. But when tested in their native language, by researchers from their own culture, the children performed as well as the English-speaking children (Collette & Van der Linden, 2002).

Children are more likely to display logical reasoning when considering substances and materials with which they are familiar (Rogoff, 2003). Mexican children who make pottery understand at an early age that clay remains the same when its shape is changed. They demonstrate conservation of substance earlier than other forms of conservation (Fry & Hale, 1996) and earlier than children who do not make pottery (Hitch et al., 2001; Leather & Henry, 1994). These different developmental trends reflect cultural differences in the skills that are adaptive and valued within particular societies (Dasen, 1994; Molitor & Hsu, 2019).

These school-age children can process and retain information more accurately and quickly than younger children.

iStock/JohnnyGreig

Information Processing

In contrast to cognitive-developmental theory, which views cognitive development as a stage-like process, information processing theorists see development as entailing quantitative changes in the efficiency of cognition. School-age children can take in more information, process it more accurately and quickly, and retain it more effectively than younger children. They are better able to determine what information is important, attend to it, and use their understanding of how memory works to choose among strategies to retain information more effectively.

Working Memory and Executive Function

Children's working memory expands rapidly but is more limited than that of adults. By 8 years of age, children on average recall about half as many items as adults (Kharitonova et al., 2015). Steady increases in working memory and executive function continue throughout childhood and are responsible for the cognitive changes seen during childhood. Advanced executive function capacities enable older children to control their attention and deploy it selectively, focusing on the relevant information and ignoring other information, compared with younger children, who are easily distracted and fidget (Ristic & Enns, 2015). Children not only get better at attending to and manipulating information, but they get better at storing it in long-term memory, organizing it in more sophisticated ways and encoding and retrieving it more efficiently and with less effort. They are also able to prioritize information in working memory, devoting more resources to attend to and manipulate information deemed valuable (Atkinson et al., 2019).

Improvements in memory, attention, and processing speed are possible because of brain development, particularly myelination and pruning in the prefrontal cortex and corpus callosum (Crone & Steinbeis, 2017; Perone et al., 2018). Between ages 3 and 7, children show increasing prefrontal cortex engagement while completing tasks that measure working memory (Perlman et al., 2016). Neural systems for visuospatial working memory, auditory working memory, and response inhibition differentiate into separate parts to enable faster and more efficient processing of these critical cognitive functions (Crone & Steinbeis, 2017; Tsujimoto et al., 2007). Older children are quicker at matching pictures and recalling spatial information than younger children, and they show more activity in the frontal regions of the brain compared with younger children (Farber & Beteleva, 2011). Development of the prefrontal cortex leads to advances in response inhibition, the ability to withhold a behavioral response inappropriate in the current context. These advances improve children's capacity for self-regulation, controlling their thoughts and behavior.

Advances in working memory and executive function are associated with language, reading, writing, and mathematics skills (Allen et al., 2019; Berninger et al., 2017; Peng et al., 2018). The demands of formal schooling, such as learning in a classroom with peers, directing attention to a teacher's lesson, following directions and completing independent work, rely on working memory and executive function skills. Academic success is influenced by working memory and executive function, yet the school context also promotes these cognitive abilities. Working memory shows greater advancements during the school year than summer months (Finch, 2019).

Metacognition and Metamemory

Whereas young children tend to see the mind as a static container for information, older children view the mind in more sophisticated terms, as an active manipulator of information. Development of the prefrontal cortex influences children's growing capacities for metacognition. Children become mindful of their thinking and better able to consider the requirements of a task; determine how to tackle it; and monitor, evaluate, and adjust their activity to complete the task (Ardila, 2013). At about 5 to 7 years of age, children become able to spontaneously monitor the cognitive demands of tasks and allocate their effort accordingly (Niebaum & Munakata, 2020).

Metamemory, an aspect of metacognition, includes the understanding of one's memory and the ability to use strategies to enhance it. Metamemory improves steadily throughout the elementary school years and contributes to advances in memory (Cottini et al., 2018; Schneider & Ornstein, 2015). Kindergarten and first-grade children understand that forgetting occurs with time and studying improves memory, but not until they are age 8 or 9 can children accurately evaluate their knowledge and apply it to learn more effectively. Older children perform better on cognitive tasks because they can evaluate the task; determine how to approach it given their cognitive resources, attention span, motivation, and knowledge; and choose and monitor the use of memory strategies that will permit them to successfully store and retrieve needed information (Schneider & Pressley, 2013). These abilities improve with neural maturation and experience.

Memory Strategies

Advances in executive function, working memory, and attention enable children to use memory strategies—cognitive activities ("tricks") that make them more likely to remember (Coughlin et al., 2018). Common memory strategies include rehearsal, organization, and elaboration. **Rehearsal** refers to systematically repeating information in order to retain it in working memory. A child may say a phone number over and over so that he does not forget it before writing it down. Children do not spontaneously and reliably apply rehearsal until after the first grade (Miller et al., 2015; Morey et al., 2018). Shortly after rehearsal appears, children start to use organization, categorizing or chunking items to remember by grouping them by theme or type, such as animals, flowers, and furniture. When memorizing a list of words, a child might organize them into meaningful groups, or chunks—foods, animals, objects, and so forth. Growth in working memory is partially attributed to an increase in the number of chunks children can retain with age (Cowan et al., 2010). A third strategy, **elaboration**, entails creating an imagined scene or story to link the material to be remembered. To remember to buy bread, milk, and butter, a child might imagine a slice of buttered bread balancing on a glass of milk. It is not until the later school years that children use elaboration without prompting and apply it to a variety of tasks (Schneider & Ornstein, 2015). As metacognition and metamemory skills, and the executive function that underlies these abilities, improve, children get better at choosing, using, and combining memory strategies, and their recall improves dramatically (Stone et al., 2016).

Context and Cognition

As children go about their daily lives they acquire increasing amounts of information, which they naturally organize in meaningful ways. As children learn more about a topic, their knowledge structures become more elaborate and organized, while the information becomes more familiar and meaningful. It is easier to recall new information about topics with which we are already familiar, and existing knowledge about a topic makes it easier to learn more about that topic (Ericsson & Moxley, 2013). During middle childhood, children develop vast knowledge bases and organize information into elaborate hierarchical networks that enable them to apply strategies in more complex ways and remember more material than ever before—and more easily than ever before. Fourth-grade students who are experts at soccer show better recall of a list of soccer-related items than do students who are soccer novices, though the groups of children do not differ on the non-soccer-related items (Schneider & Bjorklund, 1992). The soccer experts tend to organize the lists of soccer items into categories; their knowledge helps them to organize the soccer-related information with little effort, using fewer resources on organization and permitting the use of more working memory for problem solving and reasoning. Novices, in contrast, lack a knowledge base to aid their attempts at organization. Children's experiences, then, influence their memory, thinking, and reasoning.

The strategies that children use to tackle cognitive tasks vary with culture. In fact, daily tasks themselves vary with our cultural context. Children in Western cultures receive lots of experience with tasks that require them to recall bits of information, leading them to develop considerable expertise in the use of memory strategies such as rehearsal, organization, and elaboration. In contrast, research shows that people in nonwestern cultures with no formal schooling do not use or benefit from instruction in memory strategies such as rehearsal (Rogoff & Chavajay, 1995). Instead, they refine memory skills that are adaptive to their way of life. They may rely on spatial cues for memory, such as when recalling items within a three-dimensional miniature scene. Australian aboriginal and Guatemalan Mayan children perform better at these tasks than do children from Western cultures (Rogoff & Waddell, 1982). Culture and contextual demands influence the cognitive strategies that we learn and prefer, as well as how we use our information processing system to gather, manipulate, and store knowledge. Children of all cultures amass a great deal of information, and as they get older, they organize it in more sophisticated ways and encode and retrieve it more efficiently and with less effort.

Thinking in Context: Lifespan Development

1. In what ways might children's increasing ability to apply logic influence their social relationships and their interactions with others?
2. How do children's surroundings influence their thinking? Consider your own experience: How have aspects of your surroundings—culture, neighborhood, media, home, school, and peers—influenced specific aspects of your thinking, such as what strategies you use and your capacities for metacognition? Give at least three specific examples of how your context has influenced your cognitive development.

Thinking in Context: Applied Developmental Science

Imagine that you are an elementary school teacher. How would cognitive-developmental and information processing theories influence your teaching? What parts of each theory do you think are most useful for helping children learn in a classroom setting?

INTELLIGENCE IN MIDDLE CHILDHOOD

LEARNING OBJECTIVE

7.4 Summarize views of intelligence including the uses, correlates, and criticisms of intelligence tests.

At its simplest, **intelligence** refers to an the ability to adapt to the world in which we live (Sternberg, 2014). Some experts include physical, social, and problem-solving abilities in their definitions of intelligence. Intelligence is most commonly assessed through the use of **intelligence tests (IQ tests)**, which measure intellectual aptitude, an individual's capacity to learn.

Intelligence Tests

Individually administered intelligence tests are conducted in a one-on-one setting by professionally trained examiners. The most widely used individually administered measures of intelligence today are a set of tests constructed by David Wechsler, who viewed intelligence as "the global capacity of a person to act purposefully, to think rationally, and to deal effectively with his environment" (Wechsler, 1944, p. 3). The children's test, the Wechsler Intelligence Scale for Children (WISC-V), is appropriate for children aged 6 through 16. In addition to the WISC, there are Wechsler tests for preschoolers (the Wechsler Preschool and Primary Scale of Intelligence, or WPPSI) and adults (the Wechsler Adult Intelligence Scale, or WAIS; Beaujean & Woodhouse, 2020).

The WISC-V is composed of 10 subtests that comprise an overall measure of IQ as well as five indexes: verbal comprehension, visual spatial, fluid reasoning, working memory, and processing speed (Wechsler, 2014a). The WISC tests verbal abilities that tap vocabulary and knowledge and factual information that is influenced by culture. It also tests nonverbal abilities that are thought to be less influenced by culture, for example arranging materials such as blocks and pictures. The nonverbal subtests require little language proficiency, which enables children with speech disorders and those who do not speak English to be fairly assessed. Supplemental subtests are included to aid examiners in further assessing a child's capacities in a given area. Table 7.1 presents the subtests and sample items that comprise the WISC-V. By carefully examining a child's pattern of subtest scores, a professional can determine whether a child has specific learning needs, whether gifted or challenged (Flanagan & Alfonso, 2017).

Intelligence tests are often administered individually, one-on-one.

BSIP / Contributor/ Getty Images

The WISC is standardized on samples of children who are geographically and ethnically representative of the total population of the United States, creating norms that permit comparisons among children who are similar in age and ethnic background (Beaujean & Woodhouse, 2020; Sattler, 2014). In Canada, an adapted WISC, standardized with children representative of the Canadian population, is available in English and French (Wechsler, 2014b). The WISC has been adapted and used in many other countries, including the United Kingdom, Greece, Japan, Taiwan, Sweden, Lithuania, Slovenia, Germany, Austria, Switzerland, France, and the Netherlands, with few differences (Van de Vijver et al., 2019; Georgas et al., 2003). During the COVID-19 pandemic, procedures for remote administration of the WISC online were developed and tested with U.S. children, with comparable overall estimates of IQ (Wright, 2020).

IQ scores are correlated with academic achievement. Children with high IQs tend to earn higher-than-average grades at school and are more likely to stay in school (Kriegbaum et al., 2018; Mackintosh, 2011). School, in turn, provides children with exposure to information and ways of thinking that are valued by the majority culture and reflected in IQ tests. Same-age children with more years of schooling tend to have higher IQs than their less-educated peers and correlations between IQ and school achievement tests tend to increase with age, suggesting that schooling is also an influence on IQ (Cliffordson & Gustafsson, 2008;Sternberg et al., 2001; Sternberg, 2020). IQ rises with each year spent in school, improves during the school year, and drops over the summer vacation (Flynn & Sternberg, 2019; Huttenlocher et al., 1998). The seasonal drop in IQ scores each summer is larger for children from low-SES homes (Nisbett et al., 2013).

TABLE 7.1 ■ Sample Items Measuring the Five Wechsler Intelligence Scale for Children Indices

WISC-V Index	Sample Item
Verbal Comprehension Index (VCI)	Vocabulary: What does amphibian mean?
Visual Spatial Index (VSI)	Block design: In this timed task, children are shown a design composed of red-and-white bocks, are given a set of blocks, and are asked to put together the blocks in order to copy the design.
Fluid Reasoning Index (FRI)	Matrix reasoning: Children are shown an array of pictures with one missing. They must select the picture that completes the array.
Working Memory Index (WMI)	Digit span: Children are read lists of numbers and asked to repeat them as heard or in reverse order.
Processing Speed Index (PSI)	Coding: In this timed task, children are shown a code that converts numbers into symbols and are asked to transcribe lists of numbers into code.

Individual and Group Differences in IQ

A consistent and controversial finding in the intelligence literature is that African American children as a group tend to score 10 to 15 points below non-Hispanic white Americans on standardized IQ tests (Rindermann & Thompson, 2013). The IQ scores of Hispanic children as a group tend to fall between those of children of African American and non-Hispanic white descent, and the scores of Asian American children tend to fall at the same level or slightly higher than those of non-Hispanic white children (Neisser et al., 1996; Nisbett et al., 2013).

It is important to remember that emphasizing differences between groups overlooks important facts. For one thing, individuals of all races and ethnicities show a wide range of functioning, from severely disabled to exceptionally gifted. In addition, the IQ scores of children of all races and ethnicities overlap. At least 20% of African American children score higher on IQ than all other children, whether African American or non-Hispanic white (Rindermann & Thompson, 2013). Because there are more differences among African American children and among non-Hispanic white children than between the two groups, many researchers conclude that group comparisons are meaningless (Daley & Onwuegbuzie, 2011). Contextual differences associated with race and ethnicity, including socioeconomic status, are more important influences on intelligence scores than race itself (Henry et al., 2020).

Contextual Influences on IQ

Like all facets of development, intelligence is influenced by dynamic interactions among genetic or biological factors and context (Dubois et al., 2012; Plomin et al., 2016). The heritability of IQ tends to vary with context (Sauce & Matzel, 2018). Genes appear to play a large role in determining IQ scores of children from high-SES homes but play less of a role in determining IQ scores for children in low-SES homes (Nisbett et al., 2013). Because high-SES homes tend to provide more educational resources and a high quality intellectual environment, including greater child-directed speech and cognitive stimulation, children are more likely to achieve their genetic potential for IQ. Therefore, differences in IQ among children reared in high-SES homes are more likely due to genetics. Children from impoverished homes often lack consistent access to the basic support needed for intellectual development, such as nutrition, health care, and stimulating environments and activities. In these cases, IQ scores are often more heavily influenced by the context and opportunities that children have experienced than their genetic endowment (Nisbett et al., 2013; Sauce & Matzel, 2018). African American children are disproportionately likely to live in poverty, and impoverished children's IQ scores tend to be more influenced by the disadvantaged contexts in which they are immersed than by the genes with which they are born (Flynn & Sternberg, 2019). Socioeconomic status contributes to IQ through differences in culture, nutrition, living conditions, school resources, intellectual stimulation, and life circumstances such as the experience of discrimination (Kriegbaum et al., 2018; Plomin & Deary, 2015).

Children are immersed in contexts that send subtle and overt messages about the nature of intelligence, the characteristics of individuals deemed intelligent, and stereotypes about group differences in intelligence. Children's awareness of negative stereotypes may influence their performance on intelligence tests. Specifically, children may underperform because of fear or worry that they might confirm negative stereotypes about their group (Spencer et al., 2016; Steele & Aronson, 1995). This is known as **stereotype threat**. When children are administered a verbal task, African American and Hispanic American children who are aware of negative ethnic and racial stereotypes perform more poorly than European American peers when they are told the task is a "test" examining academic ability than when they are told that it is "not a test." (McKown & Strambler, 2009; McKown & Weinstein, 2003; Wasserberg, 2014). On the other hand, children who reject negative stereotypes and believe that the stereotypes do not apply to them demonstrate higher engagement and achievement (Nasir et al., 2017).

Although theorized as an influence on academic performance in children of color, stereotype threat may also apply to other intersectional categories, such as socioeconomic status and gender (Jaxon et al., 2019). Children from low-SES homes who are aware of negative stereotypes about socioeconomic status and ability tend to perform more poorly on standardized tests, such as IQ, and academics (Durante & Fiske, 2017). Girls who believe negative stereotypes about girls' ability to do math tend to show poorer mathematics achievement than girls who reject gender stereotypes (Herts et al., 2020).

TABLE 7.2 ■ Multiple Intelligences

Intelligence	Description
Verbal-Linguistic Intelligence	Ability to understand and use the meanings and subtleties of words ("word smarts")
Logical-Mathematical Intelligence	Ability to manipulate logic and numbers to solve problems ("number smarts")
Spatial Intelligence	Ability to perceive the visual-spatial world accurately, to navigate an environment, and judge spatial relationships ("spatial smarts")
Bodily-Kinesthetic Intelligence	Ability to move the body skillfully ("body smarts")
Musical Intelligence	Ability to perceive and create patterns of pitch and melody ("music smarts")
Interpersonal Intelligence	Ability to understand and communicate with others ("people smarts")
Intrapersonal Intelligence	Ability to understand the self and regulate emotions ("self-smarts")
Naturalist Intelligence	Ability to distinguish and classify elements of nature: animals, minerals and plants ("nature smarts")

Source: Gardner, 2017.

Alternative Views of Intelligence

Arguments about the cultural bias of IQ tests have led some researchers to reconsider what it means to be intelligent. Howard Gardner and Robert Sternberg propose that intelligence entails more than academics. Their theories link intelligence to everyday problem solving.

Multiple Intelligences

A skilled dancer, a champion athlete, an award-winning musician, and an excellent communicator all have talents that are not measured by traditional IQ tests. According to Howard Gardner (Gardner, 2017; Gardner et al., 2018), intelligence is the ability to solve problems or create culturally valued products. Specifically, Gardner's **multiple intelligence theory** proposes at least eight independent kinds of intelligence, shown in Table 7.2. Multiple intelligence theory expands the use of the term *intelligence* to refer to skills not usually considered intelligence by experts and has led to a great deal of debate among intelligence theorists and researchers (Kaufman et al., 2013).

According to multiple intelligence theory, each person has a unique pattern of intellectual strengths and weaknesses. A person may be gifted in dance (bodily-kinesthetic intelligence), communication (verbal-linguistic intelligence), or music (musical intelligence), yet score low on traditional measures of IQ. Each form of intelligence is thought to be biologically based, and each develops on a different timetable (Gardner, 2017). Assessing multiple intelligences requires observing the products of each form of intelligence (e.g., how well a child can learn a tune, navigate an unfamiliar area, or learn dance steps), which at best is a lengthy proposition and at worst is nearly impossible (Barnett et al., 2006). Through extended observations, an examiner can identify patterns of strengths and weaknesses in individuals and help them understand and achieve their potential (Gardner et al., 2018).

According to multiple intelligence theory, intelligence spans beyond book smarts to include artistic abilities, such as the ability to mold a pot from clay.

istock/ lyosha_nazarenko

FIGURE 7.6 ■ Triarchic Theory of Intelligence

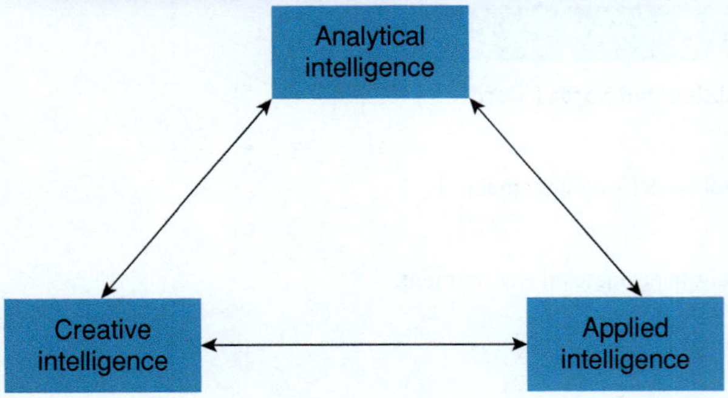

The theory of multiple intelligences is an optimistic perspective that allows everyone to be intelligent in his or her own way, viewing intelligence as broader than book-learning and academic skills. Educators who adopt this view may create enriching educational experiences that target the many forms that intelligence may take and help students to develop a range of physical, creative, and academic talents (Cavas & Cavas, 2020). The theory of multiple intelligences has been criticized as not being grounded in research (Waterhouse, 2006). Neuroscientists, however, have noted that each type of intelligence corresponds to specific neurological processes, suggesting a biological basis for multiple intelligences (Shearer, 2020; Shearer & Karanian, 2017). Ultimately, a critical contribution of multiple intelligence theory is the recognition that IQ tests measure a specific set of mental abilities and ignore others.

Triarchic Theory of Intelligence

People who are intelligent are able to adapt to the demands of their environment. Theorist Robert Sternberg (1985) describes intelligence as a set of mental abilities that permits individuals to adapt to any context and to select and modify the sociocultural contexts in which they live and behave. Sternberg's **triarchic theory of intelligence** poses three interacting forms of intelligence: analytical, creative, and applied (Sternberg, 2011; Sternberg, 2020; Figure 7.6). Individuals may have strengths in any or all of them.

Analytical intelligence refers to information processing capacities, such as how efficiently people acquire knowledge, process information, engage in metacognition, and generate and apply strategies to solve problems. *Creative intelligence* taps insight and the ability to deal with novelty. People who are high in creative intelligence respond to new tasks quickly and efficiently. They learn easily, compare information with what is already known, come up with new ways of organizing information, and display original thinking. *Applied intelligence* influences how people deal with their surroundings: how well they evaluate their environment, selecting, modifying, and adapting it to fit their own needs and external demands; revising plans on the fly; and using whatever resources are available. Intelligent people apply their analytical, creative, and applied abilities to suit the setting and problems at hand (Sternberg, 2018). Some situations require careful analysis, others the ability to think creatively, and yet others the ability to solve problems quickly in everyday settings. Many situations tap more than one form of intelligence.

Traditional IQ tests measure analytical ability, which is thought to be associated with school success. However, IQ tests do not measure creative and practical intelligence, which predict success outside of school. Some people are successful in everyday settings but less so in school settings and therefore may obtain low scores on traditional IQ tests despite being successful in their careers and personal lives. In this way, traditional IQ tests can underestimate the intellectual strengths of some children (Sternberg, 2020).

Thinking in Context: Lifespan Development

1. To what extent do you think the WISC subscales match the content taught in elementary school classes? What kinds of experiences might help children improve their verbal comprehension skills? How about spatial reasoning, fluid reasoning, working memory, and processing speed? Are some abilities more easily modified than others? In your view, do schools offer opportunities for children to modify the abilities assessed by the WISC?

2. To what degree do you think children's responses to questions on IQ tests like the WISC are influenced by factors other than their intelligence? What are some factors that might influence responding? Might hunger or tiredness matter? What about the test environment? Factors within the home? School? Neighborhood?

3. Compare and contrast the multiple intelligence and triarchic perspectives on intelligence. What is the role of context in each theory? In your view, which theory most effectively integrates biological and contextual influences on intelligence?

LANGUAGE DEVELOPMENT IN MIDDLE CHILDHOOD

LEARNING OBJECTIVE

7.5 Discuss language development during middle childhood, including learning a second language.

School-age children expand their vocabulary and develop a more complex understanding of grammar, the rules that enable combining words to express ideas and feelings. Children's understanding of pragmatics—how language is used in everyday contexts—grows and becomes more sophisticated during middle childhood.

Vocabulary

School-age children's increases in vocabulary are not as noticeable to parents as the changes that occurred in infancy and early childhood. Nevertheless, 6-year-old children's vocabularies expand by four times by the end of the elementary school years and six times by the end of formal schooling (Clark, 2017).

Children learn that many words can describe a given action, but the words often differ slightly in meaning (e.g., walk, stride, hike, march, tread, strut, and meander; Hoff, 2015). They become more selective in their use of words, choosing the right word to meet their needs. As their vocabularies grow, children learn that some words can have more than one meaning, such as *run* ("The jogger runs down the street," "The clock runs fast," etc.). They begin to appreciate that some words have psychological meanings as well as physical ones (e.g., a person can be smooth, and a surface can be smooth). This understanding that words can be used in more than one way leads 8- to 10-year-old children to understand similes and metaphors (e.g., a person can be as "cold as ice" or "sharp as a tack"; Katz, 2017).

Everyday experiences shape our vocabulary, how we think, and how we speak. Words are often acquired incidentally from speaking with others and reading rather than through explicit vocabulary instruction (Owens, 2020). Reading is a primary source of vocabulary expansion in school-age children (Sparapani et al., 2018; Wasik et al., 2016). Some complex words, such as scientific terms, require the acquisition of conceptual knowledge over repeated exposure in different contexts. One study examined 4- to 10-year-old children's knowledge of two scientific terms, eclipse and comet, before and after the natural occurrence of a solar eclipse. Two weeks after the solar eclipse and without additional instruction, the children showed improvement in their knowledge of eclipses but not comets; older and younger children did not differ in their knowledge (Best et al., 2006). Similar to infants and young children, older children learn words through exposure.

Children's vocabulary expands and becomes more complex during the school years.
iStock/FangXiaNuo

Grammar

Older children become increasingly aware of and knowledgeable about the nature and qualities of language, known as metalinguistic awareness (Simard & Gutiérrez, 2018). Language arts classes in elementary school teach children about the parts of language and the syntax of sentences, aiding children as they further develop their ability to think about their use of language. By 8 years of age, children can analyze the grammatical acceptability of their utterances and spontaneously self-correct many of their errors (Hanley et al., 2016).

In middle childhood, school children become better able to understand complex grammatical structures. They begin to use the passive voice ("The dog is being fed"), complex constructions such as the use of the auxiliary *have* ("I have already fed the dog"), and conditional sentences ("If I had been home earlier, I would have fed the dog"; Clark, 2017). Despite these advances, school-age children often have difficulty understanding spoken sentences whose meaning depends on subtle shifts in intonation (Turnbull & Justice, 2016). An example can be found in the sentence, "John gave a lollipop to David, and he gave one to Bob." With the emphasis placed on "and," the sentence can be taken to mean that John gave a lollipop to both David and Bob; whereas if the emphasis is on "he," the sentence can be assumed to mean that John gave a lollipop to David, and David gave a lollipop to Bob.

Experience with language and exposure to complex constructions influence grammatical development. Most English-speaking children find passive-voice sentences (such as "The boy was struck by the car") difficult to understand and therefore master passive-voice sentences later than other structures (Armon-Lotem et al., 2016). In contrast, the Inuit children of Arctic Canada hear and speak the Inuktitut language, which emphasizes full passives; they produce passive voice sentences in their language sooner than do children from other cultures (Allen & Crago, 1996). The culture and language systems in which children are immersed influence their use of language and, ultimately, the ways in which they communicate. Throughout middle childhood, sentence structure and use of grammar becomes more sophisticated, children become better at communicating their ideas, and their understanding of pragmatics improves.

Pragmatics

Pragmatics refers to the practical application of language to communicate (Owens, 2015). With age and advances in perspective-taking skills that come with cognitive development, children are more likely to change their speech in response to the needs of listeners. When faced with an adult who will not give them a desired object, 9-year-old children are more polite in restating their request than are 5-year-old children (Ninio, 2014). Children speak to adults differently than to other children, and they speak differently on the playground than in class or at home. In addition, older children begin to understand that there is often a distinction between what people say and what they mean.

One example of pragmatics that develops in middle childhood is the use of *irony*, choosing a word or expression that conveys the opposite of its literal meaning. Many contextual, linguistic, and developmental factors influence the processing and comprehension of irony, such as the ability to interpret intonation and facial expressions as well as the capacity to evaluate how well a statement matches the situation (Pexman, 2014). Children at the ages of 5 to 6 become capable of recognizing irony when they are able to understand that a speaker might believe something different from what has been said. Yet most children at this age tend to interpret irony as sincere, relying on the person's statement and disregarding other cues in the story, such as intonation and gestures. Cognitive development permits children to detect the discrepancy between what the speaker says and what he or she believes. Children's ability to understand ironic remarks continues to develop through middle childhood, and by age 8, children can recognize and use irony (Glenwright & Pexman, 2010). However, even in adolescence, the understanding of irony is still developing; children as old as 13 do not reliably distinguish irony, which is intended to joke or mock, from deception, which is intended to conceal information (Filippova & Astington, 2008).

Bilingual Language Learning

About one in three U.S. children under the age of 17 speaks a language other than English at home (Child Trends, 2019a). Of these, about one in five struggle with speaking English at school (Federal Interagency Forum on Child and Family Statistics, 2017). How should children be taught a second language? In the United States, English as a Second Language (ESL) is most often taught to children by English immersion, which places foreign-language-speaking children in English-speaking classes, requiring them to learn English and course content at the same time. Some studies suggest that immersion is associated with a loss in children's native language use (Baus et al., 2013). Reductions in native language use associated with immersion may predict slower development of executive function (Kubota et al., 2020).

Another approach is **dual-language learning** (also called two-way immersion), in which English-speaking and non-English-speaking students learn together in both languages and both languages are valued equally. Advocates of dual-language learning argue that bringing a child's native language into the classroom sends children the message that their cultural heritage is respected and strengthens their cultural identity and self-esteem (Ramírez, 2020). Children exposed to dual-language immersion tend to retain their native language while learning the new language, and native language skill may contribute to developing skills in the new language (Castro et al., 2011; Mancilla-Martinez et al., 2020). Dual-language immersion approaches, which encourage students to retain their native language while learning English, are more effective than immersion approaches at promoting successful learning of English as well as overall academic achievement (Relji et al., 2015). Children's skills in their native language transfer to influence literacy and skills in the new language (Macswan et al., 2017).

In dual language learning, two languages are used for instruction. English-speaking and non-English-speaking students are taught in their native language and a second language.

AP Photo/Paul T. Erickson

Learning a second language during childhood may affect proficiency in the first or native language. This is true even when children are encouraged to retain their native language. In some cases that first language declines or is lost. In others the second language may become dominant, used more often (Hoff, 2015). Alternatively, children's competence in both languages may steadily improve, with the second increasingly more rapidly (Oppenheim et al., 2020). One study followed children in Southern California who first learned Spanish at home and then began to learn English at school at 5 years of age (Kohnert & Bates, 2002). The children improved their proficiency in both Spanish and English but made faster progress in English, so that by middle childhood, they were more proficient in English.

The ability to speak more than one language is thought to have cognitive advantages. Individuals who master two or more languages tend to score higher on measures of memory, **selective attention**, analytical reasoning, mathematics, and cognitive flexibility (Bialystok, 2020; Hartanto et al., 2018). Bilingual children tend to score higher on measures of executive function, particularly the ability to control attention and ignore misleading information (Barac et al., 2014; Bialystok, 2015). Although a recent study found that 9- and 10-year-old children did not show a bilingual advantage for executive function (Dick et al., 2019), the ability to communicate with others is undoubtedly beneficial for development. When children can speak, read, and write in two or more languages, they are able to participate in the contexts and cultures in which they are immersed.

Thinking in Context: Lifespan Development

1. In what ways does language development illustrate the interaction of developmental and contextual factors? Give some examples related to school-age children's language development.
2. Children's advances in language enable them to have more complicated relationships with parents and peers. Discuss the social implications of gains in vocabulary, grammar, and pragmatics.
3. In your view, why is learning a second language beneficial for children's development? Why is it associated with cognitive gains? Can you identify other benefits?

LEARNING AND SCHOOLING IN MIDDLE CHILDHOOD

LEARNING OBJECTIVE

7.6 Examine approaches to education, including reading and math as well as educating children with special needs.

The school context exposes children to new ideas and opportunities to learn from teachers and peers. Teachers help older children grasp complex ideas by building on what children already know, identifying connections between new material and prior knowledge, and keeping pace with their growing abilities. Older children become proficient at reading, writing, and mathematics. Children's early experiences in school, especially the transition to first grade, influences their academic achievement throughout elementary school and beyond.

Approaches to Education

Similar to early childhood education programs, elementary school instruction varies. Some classrooms emphasize teacher-centered instruction and others student-centered instruction. Classrooms that are teacher-centered emphasize direct instruction from a teacher who selects the instructional strategies and conveys information to students (Powell, 2019). Learning activities typically include drills, quizzes, presentations, and recitations of definitions, facts, and lists. Children's learning is assessed through quizzes and exams that often involve selecting responses, such as multiple choice or fill-in-the-blank items. Critics of teacher-centered instruction argue it encourages passive learning by overemphasizing teacher talk and learning and comprehending facts rather than higher-level thinking (Burden & Byrd, 2019). Today facts are easily available via the internet. Children need to develop skills in evaluating and applying information (Borich, 2017).

A second approach, often referred to as a student-centered approach, is the constructivist classroom, influenced by Piaget and Vygotsky's perspectives on cognitive development. Constructivist instruction involves students in their own learning (Powell, 2019). Children are viewed as active constructors of their own understanding through interactions with their worlds. Constructivist student-centered instruction engages children in problem-solving activities in which they investigate a problem, examine data or information relevant to the problem, and devise conclusions. Teachers ask questions to encourage student exploration and nurture reflection and thought about the process rather than emphasize a single correct answer. Constructivist approaches also encourage peer interaction. Cooperative learning, role playing, simulations, and debates permit students to interact, share their ideas, and learn from one another (Burden & Byrd, 2019).

Reading and Mathematics Instruction

Changes in reading and mathematics instruction over the past several decades illustrate the distinction between direct teacher-centered instruction and constructivist student-centered instruction. The effectiveness of each method of instruction may vary with the subject material.

In past generations, most children were taught to read via **phonics instruction**, lessons and drills that emphasized learning the patterns of sound combinations in words. Children learned the sounds of each letter, memorized language rules, and sounded out words (Brady, 2011; Ehri, 2020). In the late 1980s, the whole-language approach to reading instruction was introduced. In this approach, literacy is viewed as an extension of language, and children learn to read and write through trial-and-error discovery that is similar to how they learn to speak—without drills or learning phonics. The emphasis on children as active constructors of knowledge is appealing and in line with cognitive-developmental theory. Today, the whole-language approach is still in widespread use, and many teachers are not trained in phonics instruction. However, the research comparing the two approaches has offered little support for whole-language claims and overwhelming support for the efficacy of phonics training in improving children's reading skills (Cunningham, 2013). An approach that integrates phonics instruction with unstructured opportunities to engage with reading materials holds promise and may end the so-called reading war debate on reading instruction (Alexander, 2020; Solity, 2020).

A substantial number of U.S. children are poor readers and thereby at risk for poor academic achievement. In 2019, more than one-third of fourth-grade students were unable to meet basic standards for reading at their grade level (National Center for Education Statistics, 2020b). Early reading deficits influence all areas of academic competence (math, writing, science, etc.), and children who experience early difficulties in reading often remain behind (Child et al., 2019; Rabiner et al., 2016; Vanbinst et al., 2020). Children's attitudes, interests, and motivation in reading and writing tend to decline over the school years; the drop occurs more rapidly in worse readers (Wigfield et al., 2016; Wigfield & Eccles, 2020). Deficits in reading skill are associated with social adjustment problems, and this association increases over time (Haft et al., 2016; Westrupp et al., 2020). Poor reading achievement is associated with behavioral problems, including engaging in bullying, two to three years later (Guo et al., 2015; Turunen et al., 2019). Children with poor reading skills tend to have poor vocabularies, which may make it more difficult for them to successfully interact with peers (Benner et al., 2002; Sparapani et al., 2018).

Advances in cognitive development underlie older children's achievements in math, reading, and other academic skills.

iStock/Choreograph

In past generations, math was also taught through rote learning activities such as drills, memorization of number facts (e.g., multiplication tables), and completion of workbooks. Many children found these methods boring or restrictive; they learned to dislike math and did not perform well. In 1989, the National Council of Teachers of Mathematics modified the national mathematics curriculum to emphasize mathematical concepts and problem solving, estimating, and probability; teachers were to encourage student interaction and social involvement in solving math problems. The emphasis changed from product—getting correct answers quickly—to process—learning how to understand and execute the steps in getting an answer. Teachers often use strategies that involve manipulatives—opportunities for students to interact physically with objects to learn target information—rather than relying solely on abstraction. Such strategies have been shown to be effective in enhancing problem solving and retention (Carbonneau et al., 2013).

In contrast with research findings about the whole-language approach to reading, changes in the mathematics curriculum are supported by student achievement, as fourth-grade students' mathematical skills have improved over the last two decades. Between 1990 and 2015, the proportion of fourth-grade students performing at or above the proficient level increased from 13% to 41%, and the proportion that could not do math at their grade level fell from 50% in 1990 to 19% in 2015 (National Center for Education Statistics, 2020a). Although these represent important gains, nearly one in five U.S. schoolchildren is still deficient in math skills, suggesting that there is more work to be done. The past decade has seen new educational initiatives that emphasize math and reading instruction coupled with frequent assessments of student achievement, to ensure that progress is made and children do not fall through the cracks.

Access to Digital Technology and Learning

All school-age children in the U.S. have access to computers or tablets at school and broadband internet is available to all schools (National Science Foundation, 2018). But not all schools provide access to current technology and the quality of internet access varies across school systems. Schools in rural areas and low-SES communities are less likely to have access to current technology or may have fewer opportunities to access computers and tablets, given fewer resources.

Computers and tablets offer children new learning opportunities. Effective educational applications engage children and foster active learning through discovery. For example, children may learn social studies, math, and science by playing and reflecting on computer simulations, games, and interactive cartoons (Chauhan, 2017; Hwang et al., 2015; Outhwaite et al., 2017). Perhaps not surprising, children report preferring tablet learning to traditional classroom instruction (Dunn et al., 2018). Digital learning environments are especially effective in fostering learning outside of the classroom, at home (Chauhan, 2017; Daoud, Starkey, Eppel, Vo, & Sylvester, 2021). Computer and tablet-based games and interventions improve attention, working memory, and other cognitive skills (Ramos & Melo, 2019; Roberts et al., 2016).

Unfortunately, children's home access to technology varies with geography and socioeconomic status (Katz et al., 2018). About one-quarter of rural families report access to highspeed internet is a major problem and an additional third report it is a minor problem (Anderson, 2018). Although more than 90% of families with school-age children living in low-SES homes report having internet access, more than half of these families report that their connectivity is constrained by interrupted or slow service, outdated devices, or having to share devices (Rideout & Katz, 2016). Inequity in home access to technology is often referred to as the "homework gap" because of the challenges that students face when trying to do their homework. Inequities increase as teachers incorporate more technology-based learning into assignments, and the effects magnify with each grade (Moore et al., 2018). Children with poor access to technology at home typically report using their smart phone and cellular data plan, a poor substitute for computers and high-speed internet. School and community initiatives that provide children with tablets or inexpensive computers for home use hold promise for improving children's access to technology and closing the homework gap (Wenger, 2018).

The large socioeconomic differences in children's access to technology and internet became apparent during the COVID-19 pandemic, which closed schools in many states and forced schoolchildren to quickly transition to remote learning from home (Masonbrink & Hurley, 2020). As of this writing, there is little research available on the effects of remote learning during the pandemic, but it is likely that negative effects will be exacerbated in children who lack reliable access to digital technology, such as tablets and computers, and high-speed internet.

Educating Children With Special Needs

School systems must meet the needs of a diverse population of children, many with **special education** needs. Children with intellectual and learning disabilities require assistance to help them overcome obstacles to learning. The U.S. Individuals with Disabilities Education Improvement Act mandates that children with disabilities must receive services to determine their educational needs, devise an individualized education plan (IEP), and provide educational opportunities similar to those experienced by children without disabilities (Forbringer, 2020).

Special education classrooms that practice inclusion integrate all children into a regular classroom with additional teachers and educational support that is tailored to learning disabled students' special needs. Students with learning disabilities learn more and demonstrate more social advancement in inclusion settings.

iStock/ monkeybusinessimages

An IEP is a plan that is tailored to each student's specific abilities and educational needs. It is a written plan created by a team of individuals, including a school psychologist or school counselor, the child's teacher, parents, and sometimes other professionals, such as vision or hearing specialists, depending on the child's disability. The IEP is specialized, goal-directed, and guided by student performance (Heward, 2018). At least once each year the team of school staff, professionals, and parents convene to assess the child's progress and revise the IEP accordingly.

In the United States and Canada, legislation mandates that children with disabilities are to be placed in the "least restrictive" environment, or classrooms that are as similar as possible to classrooms for children without learning disabilities. Whenever possible, children are to be educated in the general classroom, with their peers, for all or part of the day and provided with a teacher or paraprofessional specially trained to meet their needs

(Mastropieri & Scruggs, 2017). This is known as inclusion. Children's responses to inclusion vary with the severity of their disabilities as well as the quality and quantity of support provided in the classroom (Lewis et al., 2017). Most experts agree that inclusion works best when children receive instruction in a resource room that meets their specialized needs for part of the school day and the regular classroom for the rest of the school day (Heward, 2018). When children are placed in regular classrooms with peers of all abilities, they have multiple opportunities to learn from peers and may be better prepared to learn and work alongside people of all abilities (Salend, 2015). Interaction with peers and cooperative learning assignments that require children to work together to achieve academic goals help students with learning disabilities learn social skills and form friendships with peers.

Thinking in Context: Lifespan Development

1. What are some reasons why U.S. children score poorly on reading comprehension and mathematics? In your experience, what techniques are most effective in helping children learn?
2. Identify challenges in providing children with special needs education in the least restrictive environment. As an educator, how might you balance the special needs of the child with those of the other children in class?

CHAPTER SUMMARY

7.1 Identify changes in physical and motor development and health during middle childhood.

Growth and motor development advances gradually throughout middle childhood. Brain volume continues to increase, especially in the prefrontal cortex. Synaptogenesis, pruning, and myelination contribute to cognitive efficiency. Children's body movements become more fluid and coordinated. Increases in fine motor skills influence children's interests and enable them to write fluidly. Motor development is influenced by contextual factors, such as nutrition, opportunities to practice motor skills, and health. Most children do not meet recommended guidelines for physical activity. Childhood obesity is associated with short- and long-term physical and psychological health problems. Most children do not grow out of obesity. Programs that are effective at reducing childhood obesity decrease children's television and video game use, increase their physical activity, and teach children about nutrition.

7.2 Compare common developmental disabilities and discuss the relevance of contextual influences for disability.

The most common developmental disability is attention-deficit/hyperactivity disorder (ADHD), characterized by persistent difficulties with attention and/or hyperactivity and impulsivity that interferes with performance and behavior in school and daily life. Autism spectrum disorders (ASD) are a family of disorders that range in severity and are characterized by deficits in social communication and a tendency to engage in repetitive behaviors. Specific learning disorders are diagnosed in children who demonstrate a measurable discrepancy between aptitude and achievement in a particular academic area. There are several SLDs that influence reading (developmental dyslexia), writing skills (developmental dysgraphia), mathematics (developmental discalcula), and other cognitive skills. Developmental disabilities are influenced by genetic factors, but racial and SES differences in diagnoses illustrate the role of context.

7.3 Discuss school-age children's capacities for reasoning and processing information.

At about age 7, children enter the concrete operational state of reasoning, permitting them to use mental operations to solve problems, think logically, demonstrate several different kinds of classification skills, and make advances in solving conservation tasks. Concrete operational reasoning is found in children around the world, but experience, specific cultural practices, and education play a role in development. Brain maturation leads to improvements in executive functioning and attention, memory, response inhibition, and processing speed. As children's understanding of their own thinking and memory increase, they get better at selecting and using mnemonic strategies and become more planful. Experience influences how children organize information and the strategies they use.

7.4 Summarize views of intelligence including the uses, correlates, and criticisms of intelligence tests.

IQ tests measure intellectual aptitude and are often used to identify children with special educational needs. IQ predicts school achievement, how long a child will stay in school, and career attainment in adulthood. Persistent group differences are found in IQ scores, but contextual factors, such as socioeconomic status, living conditions, school resources, culture, and life circumstances, are thought to account for group differences. Multiple intelligence theory and the triarchic theory of intelligence conceptualize intelligence as entailing a broader range of skills than those measured by IQ tests.

7.5 Discuss language development during middle childhood, including learning a second language.

Vocabulary expands fourfold during the elementary school years. School-age children learn words through contextual cues and by comparing complex words with simpler words. Understanding of complex grammatical structures, syntax, and pragmatics improves in middle childhood with experience with language and exposure to complex constructions, and children become better communicators. Many children speak more than one language and bilingualism is associated with cognitive benefits. Dual-language approaches to language learning are more effective than immersion approaches at teaching language and promoting academic achievement in children.

7.6 Examine approaches to education, including reading and math as well as educating children with special needs.

Teacher-centered classrooms emphasize direct instruction whereas constructivist classrooms involve students in their own learning. Although phonics methods are highly effective in teaching reading, most schools employ the whole-language approach. A substantial number of U.S. children are poor readers and about one in five is deficient in math skills. All schools offer access to technology, but quality varies and children's home access to technology varies with geography and socioeconomic status. In the United States and Canada, legislation mandates that, whenever possible, children with developmental learning disabilities are to be educated in the general classroom, with their peers, for all or part of the day. The nature of inclusion varies with the severity of the disability as well as the quality and quantity of support provided in the classroom.

KEY TERMS

attention-deficit/hyperactivity disorder (ADHD) (p. 204)
class inclusion (p. 208)
classification (p. 208)
developmental dysgraphia (p. 206)
developmental dyslexia (p. 206)
elaboration (p. 211)
intelligence (p. 212)
pragmatics (p. 218)
rehearsal (p. 211)
seriation (p. 208)
special education (p. 222)
cerebellum (p. 200)
concrete operational stage of reasoning (p. 208)
developmental dyscalculia (p. 206)
dual-language learning (p. 219)
Flynn effect (p. 208)
gray matter (p. 198)
intelligence tests (IQ tests) (p. 212)
metamemory (p. 211)
multiple intelligence theory (p. 215)
obesity (p. 202)
phonics instruction (p. 220)
prefrontal cortex (p. 198)
selective attention (p. 219)
specific learning disorder (SLD) (p. 206)
stereotype threat (p. 214)
transitive inference (p. 208)
triarchic theory of intelligence (p. 216)
white matter (p. 198)

8 SOCIOEMOTIONAL DEVELOPMENT IN MIDDLE CHILDHOOD

iStock/ FatCamera

Middle childhood, ages 6 to 11, represents an important transition in children's conceptions of themselves and their abilities. School-age children construct more advanced views of themselves, moral orientations, and understanding of relationships than young children. Their friendships become based on emotional qualities, such as affection, trust, and loyalty. Relationships with parents remain important in middle childhood, influencing adjustment across a range of family structures and settings. In this chapter, we examine ways in which family and peer contexts shape school-age children's socioemotional development.

PSYCHOSOCIAL DEVELOPMENT IN MIDDLE CHILDHOOD

LEARNING OBJECTIVE

8.1 Describe school-age children's self-conceptions, self-evaluations, and motivation.

According to Erik Erikson (1950), school-age children face the psychosocial crisis of industry verses inferiority. Children must learn and master skills that are valued in their society, such as reading, mathematics, writing, and using computers. Success at culturally valued tasks influences children's feelings of competence and curiosity as well as their motivation to persist and succeed in all of the contexts in which they are embedded. When children are unable to succeed or when they receive consistently negative feedback from parents or teachers, they may lose confidence in their ability to succeed and be productive at valued tasks (inferiority). Children's sense of industry influences their self-concept, self-esteem, and readiness to face the physical, cognitive, and social challenges of middle childhood.

Self-Concept

In middle childhood, self-concept shifts from concrete descriptions of behavior to trait-like psychological constructs (e.g., popular, smart, good looking). Consider this school-age child's self-description: "I'm pretty popular... That's because I'm nice to people and helpful and can keep secrets. Mostly I am nice to my friends, although if I get in a bad mood I sometimes say something that can be a little mean" (Harter, 2012b, p. 59). Like most older children, this child's self-concept describes abilities and personality traits rather than specific behaviors.

Older children include both positive and negative traits, unlike younger children who tend to describe themselves in all-or-none terms. Through interactions with parents, teachers, and peers, children learn more about themselves (Pesu et al., 2016). Older children come to understand that their traits can vary with the context—that a person can be nice or mean, depending on the situation. The all-or-none trait descriptions in early childhood transform into complex integrations of psychological traits in middle to late childhood. By about 9 years of age, children describe and evaluate themselves across a range of domains, including a physical self-concept (referring to physical attributes and attractiveness), academic self-concept (school performance), athletic self-concept (physical skills), social self-concept (social relationships with peers and others), and beliefs about behavioral conduct (whether they can behave appropriately; Harter, 2012a, 2012b). Children's self-concept is associated with their behavior.

Self-Esteem

Generally speaking, self-esteem tends to increase into late childhood, from age 4 to 11 years (Orth et al., 2018). Whereas preschoolers tend to have unrealistically positive self-evaluations, school-age children's sense of self-esteem becomes more realistic (Boseovski, 2010). Older children's growing ability to take other people's perspectives enables them to consider their abilities more objectively. Children evaluate their characteristics, abilities, and performance in comparison with peers, which influences their overall sense of competence (Harter, 2012b). Children also receive feedback about their abilities from parents, teachers, and peers, and this affects their self-esteem (Hart, Atkins, & Tursi, 2006; Thomaes et al., 2010). Self-esteem is influenced by children's ability to balance feedback from themselves and others. Children whose self-evaluations depend heavily on approval from others are likely to have low self-esteem (Moore & Smith, 2018).

Beliefs about the self become more closely related to behavior (Davis-Kean et al., 2009). Self-esteem is influenced by children's self-evaluations as well as by the importance they assign to the particular ability being evaluated. This is illustrated by a child's comment, "Even though I'm not doing well in those subjects, I still like myself as a person, because Math and Science just aren't that important to me. How I look and how popular I am are more important" (Harter, 2012b, p. 95). Children tend to report feeling most interested in activities in which they perform well and areas that they view as their strengths (Denissen et al., 2007).

Positive parent-child interactions and a secure attachment to parents predict a positive sense of self-esteem throughout childhood (Harris et al., 2017; Krauss et al., 2020; Magro et al., 2019). Warm parents express positive emotions and acceptance and foster in their children the feeling that they matter. Children internalize the view of themselves as worthy individuals, and this internalized view is at the core of self-esteem (Brummelman, 2017). The home environment influences self-esteem throughout the lifespan. In one longitudinal study, the quality of the early home environment through the first 6 years of life predicted self-esteem at age 8 through early adulthood, age 28 (Orth, 2017).

Children's ratings of self-esteem vary with ethnic, contextual, and cultural factors. Many African American children experience adverse contextual conditions such as poverty, unsafe neighborhoods, ongoing stressors, and the experience of racism and discrimination. These conditions may influence African American children's tendency to score lower on measures of self-esteem than white and Hispanic children (Kenny & McEachern, 2009). Cultural factors also influence self-esteem. Although Chinese and Japanese children tend to show greater academic achievement than North American children, Chinese and Japanese children tend to score lower in self-esteem. One reason may be that competition is high and Asian children experience great pressure to achieve (Stevenson et al., 2000). In addition, Asian cultures emphasize collectivism, social harmony, and modesty, and they do not encourage children to use social comparison to enhance their self-esteem (Toyama, 2001). Instead, children are encouraged to praise others, including their peers, while minimizing attention to themselves in order to foster and maintain relationships (Falbo, Poston, Triscari, & Zhang, 1997).

The cultural emphasis on individuality characteristic of North America contributes to children's high self-esteem. However, when parents overvalue their children's attributes, overpraise their performance, and overencourage them to stand out from others, children may develop a sense of narcissism, viewing themselves as superior to others (Brummelman, 2017). Children's self-esteem is best fostered within the context of warm and accepting parent-child interactions, parental encouragement for realistic and meaningful goals, and praise that is connected to children's performance (Brummelman & Sedikides, 2020).

Achievement Motivation

Children's sense of industry and emerging sense of self influence their **achievement motivation**, the willingness to persist at challenging tasks and meet high standards of accomplishment (Wigfield et al., 2015). How children attribute or account for their successes and failures is important for sustaining motivation and ultimately influencing their achievement. Children who adopt **internal attributions**, emphasizing their own role in the outcome, and a **growth mindset,** a belief that they can change, tend to have a strong **mastery orientation**, a belief that success stems from trying hard and that failures are influenced by factors that can be controlled, like effort (Haimovitz & Dweck, 2017). When faced with challenges, children who are mastery oriented focus on changing or adapting their behavior (Muenks et al., 2018). They can bounce back from failure and take steps, such as learning study strategies to improve their exam scores, to improve their performance.

In contrast, a **learned helplessness orientation** is characterized by **external attributions,** such as believing luck is responsible for success, and a **fixed mindset**, the belief that one's ability cannot be changed. (Dweck, 2017; Dweck & Yeager, 2019). Children who show learned helplessness are overwhelmed by challenges, are overly self-critical, feel incompetent, and avoid challenging tasks (Yeager & Dweck, 2012). Poor performance, in turn, can confirm children's negative views of their ability and their sense of helplessness. Our views about our abilities and our explanations for our successes and failures are influenced by our interactions with the people around us.

Some children respond to success and failure in maladaptive ways. Children who attribute success to factors such as luck and failure to factors such as ability are at risk to develop a learned helplessness orientation.

iStock/FatCamera

Parents influence children's achievement through their own beliefs and attitudes about ability, success, and failure (Haimovitz & Dweck, 2016). Children raised by parents with a fixed view of abilities are more likely to view their abilities as fixed and unchangeable and are more likely to show a learned helplessness orientation than children raised by parents with a growth mindset (Pomerantz & Dong, 2006). When parents believe that ability cannot be changed, they tend to provide few opportunities for children to improve and may ignore positive changes that children show. Failing to provide opportunities to problem solve or intervening when a child tries a challenging task may inhibit children's desire to succeed and may foster helplessness (Orkin et al., 2017).

Warm and supportive parenting that fosters autonomy can help children to recognize their worth, appreciate their own competence, and develop a mastery orientation.

istock/ JohnnyGreig

The type of feedback parents provide plays a large role in influencing children's beliefs about ability. Frequently parents and other adults praise children for success by emphasizing traits ("You're so smart! You did it!"). This is known as *person praise* because it focuses on the qualities of the individual. Although well-meaning adults use person praise simply to make children feel good, it instead can lead children to intensify beliefs in a fixed mindset ("I'm good at this task because I'm smart." Or "I failed because I'm not smart"; Haimovitz & Dweck, 2017). In the face of failure or criticism, person praise can result in an increased sense of learned helplessness because it implies that ability is fixed (Dweck & Yeager, 2019). *Process praise*, in contrast, emphasizes the role of effort, a nonfixed ability, in success ("Great job! You studied hard and your performance shows it!). Process praise fosters a growth mindset (Brummelman & Sedikides, 2020).

Socioeconomic status (SES) influences children's motivation through the availability of opportunities and resources and through parents' behavior. Research has shown that children who grow up in high-SES families are more likely than their middle- or low-SES peers to show a greater mastery orientation and higher levels of achievement motivation, as well as better academic performance and greater involvement in organized activities after school (Wigfield et al., 2015). Children require not only opportunities to try new things but also parents who are aware of and able to take advantage of opportunities (Archer et al., 2012; Simpkins et al., 2013). Parents in low-SES families often work jobs that involve long hours, rotating and nonstandard shifts, and high physical demands. As a result, many low-SES parents lack the energy and time to devote to children, and they may be unaware of opportunities or unable to take advantage of them (Parra-Cardona et al., 2008).

Teachers who form close, warm relationships with students promote academic motivation and engagement (Heatly & Votruba-Drzal, 2019). When students view their teachers as unsupportive, they are more likely to attribute their performance to external factors, such as luck or the teacher, and to withdraw from class participation. As students' achievement declines, they further doubt their abilities, creating a vicious cycle between helpless attributions and poor achievement. Teachers support a mastery orientation in students when they are warm and helpful and when they attribute children's failure to lack of effort (Wentzel, 2002). Teachers who relate failure to their students' effort, are supportive of their students, and stress learning goals over performance goals are more likely to have mastery-oriented students (Meece et al., 2006).

Thinking in Context: Lifespan Development

How does cognitive development influence self-concept, self-esteem, and achievement motivation? Identify aspects of socioemotional development that might influence development in these areas.

Thinking in Context: Intersectionality

1. How might a learned helplessness orientation form? Identify examples of how early and later experiences in and out of the home might place a child at risk for a learned helplessness orientation.
2. How might children's experiences vary across environments and SES?
3. What role might race and ethnicity play in the development of achievement motivation? For example, consider stereotype threat (see Chapter 7). What risks might children of color face in developing a mastery orientation?
4. What kinds of experiences might help children develop positive views of their own abilities?

MORAL DEVELOPMENT IN MIDDLE CHILDHOOD

LEARNING OBJECTIVE

8.2 Examine the process of moral development in childhood, including children's reasoning about fairness and justice.

Advances in cognitive development enable children to reason logically about people, things, and events they encounter. Children also become able to reason about social problems. Is it wrong to lie? Can a lie ever be helpful? Just as children take an active role in their cognitive development, they actively construct their own moral understanding from their social interactions with adults and peers (Dahl, 2018, 2019; Killen & Smetana, 2015). Many developmental scientists approach moral development from a cognitive-developmental perspective, examining how children reason about moral issues concerning justice and fairness.

Reasoning about Rules: Piaget's Theory

As discussed in Chapter 6, cognitive-developmental theorist Jean Piaget (1932) believed that moral thinking develops in stages similar to those in his theory of cognition. He studied children's understanding of fairness, especially how they think about rules. Piaget observed children's schoolyard play and found that very young children's play was not guided by rules. But by 6 years of age, children enter the first stage of Piaget's theory of morality, **heteronomous morality** (also known as the morality of constraint). In this stage, children view rules as sacred and unalterable. Rules are created by authority figures and are viewed as having always existed. Moral behavior abides by the rules, without exception.

As elementary school children spend more time with peers and become better at taking their friends' perspectives, their understanding of rules becomes more flexible. In middle childhood, at about age 7, children enter the second stage of Piaget's scheme, **autonomous morality** (also known as the morality of cooperation). Now children begin to see rules as products of group agreement and tools to improve cooperation. Older children are likely to recognize that a rule that the youngest children must be the first to bat at the piñata at a children's party is a way to help the youngest children, who are less likely to be successful. Some children might agree that the rule promotes fairness, while others might argue to abandon the rule as it gives younger children an unfair advantage. At this stage, children view a need for agreement on rules and consequences for violations. Piaget's theory of moral reasoning inspired Lawrence Kohlberg, who created perhaps the best-known theory of moral reasoning.

Conceptions of Justice: Kohlberg's Theory of Moral Reasoning

Influenced by Piaget, Lawrence Kohlberg (1969, 1976) adopted a cognitive developmental perspective of moral development. He proposed that children construct their understanding of moral development through their interactions with others. Children's cognitive development determines how they reason, or make decisions, about issues of fairness.

Recall from Chapter 6,Kohlberg investigated moral development by posing hypothetical dilemmas about justice, fairness, and rights that place obedience to authority and law in conflict with helping someone. Is stealing ever permissible—even in order to help someone? Individuals' responses change with development; moral reasoning progresses through a universal order of six stages, grouped into three levels that represent qualitative changes in conceptions of justice.

Beginning in early childhood and persisting until about age 9, children demonstrate Level 1 of Kohlberg's scheme: **preconventional reasoning**. Young children are motivated d by self-interest. In Stage 1, children's moral judgments are first drivenby the desire to avoid punishment ("Don't steal because you don't want to go to jail"). Next, children become motivated by rewards, or concern about what others can do for them if they comply (Stage 2). Children who demonstrate preconventional reasoning account for "good" or moral behavior as a response to external pressure. At this point children have not internalized societal norms, and their behavior is motivated by desires rather than internalized principles.

At about age 9 or 10, children transition to Level 2 of Kohlberg's scheme, **conventional moral reasoning**. Children are now able to take others' perspectives and are motivated by reciprocity, seeking to be accepted and avoid disapproval. Rules maintain relationships. At Stage 3, children uphold rules in order to please others, gain affection, and be a good person—honest, caring, and nice. The Golden Rule motivates their behavior: "Do unto others as you would have them do unto you." At Stage 4, which emerges in adolescence, perspective-taking expands beyond individuals to include society's rules. Older children accept rules as tools to maintain social order and believe that everyone has a duty to uphold the rules. Reasoning is no longer influenced by relationships and a desire to be a good person. Instead, rules are universal and must be enforced for everyone. Many people demonstrate conventional reasoning throughout their lives. Not everyone develops the third and final level of reasoning, postconventional reasoning, discussed in Chapter 10. Piaget's and Kohlberg's theories of moral development are compared in Table 8.1.

Distributive Justice: Reasoning About Sharing

A pervasive moral problem that children frequently encounter concerns distributive justice—how to divide goods fairly (Damon, 1977, 1988). How should a candy bar be divided among three siblings? Does age matter? Height? Hunger? How much the child likes chocolate? Children's reasoning about distributive justice undergoes predictable age-related changes. When asked how to decide rewards, 4- and 6-year-old children prefer unfair distributions that maximize their profit and award others less. By 8 years of age, children tend to prefer the fair allocation, forgoing the opportunity to allocate more to themselves (Qiu et al., 2017).

As with moral reasoning, children progress from self-serving reasons for sharing expressed in early childhood (e.g., "I get more candy because I want it" or "I share candy so that Mikey will play with me") to more sophisticated and mature conceptions of distributive justice in middle childhood (Damon, 1977). At about 7 years of age, children take merit into account and believe that extra candy should go to the child who has excelled or worked especially hard. At around 8 years of age, children can act on the basis of benevolence, believing that others at a disadvantage should get special consideration. For example, extra candy should go to the child who does not get picked to play on a sports team or a child who is excluded from an activity. Between ages 8 and 10, children begin to reflect on the need to balance competing claims, such as those of merit and need (Smith & Warneken, 2016). With age, children of all cultures increasingly prefer equitable distributions, but cultural values influence how they account for or explain their choices (Huppert et al., 2019).

Conceptions of Moral, Social, and Personal Issues

Many, but not all, of children's social concerns and conflict center on justice and fairness. Young children can differentiate between moral issues, imperatives which concern people's rights and welfare, and social conventions or customs (Smetana et al., 2018; Smetana & Braeges, 1990). By age 5, children can differentiate personal issues, matters of personal choice that do not violate rights, across home and school settings (Turiel & Nucci, 2017). Children believe that they have control over matters of personal choice, unlike moral issues whose violations are inherently wrong.

School-age children also distinguish between moral and conventional rules, judging moral rules as more absolute than conventional rules (Turiel & Nucci, 2017). Moral rules are seen as less violable, less contingent on authority, and less alterable than social conventions (Smetana et al., 2014). Children anticipate feeling positive emotions after following moral rules and are likely to label violations of moral rules as disgusting (Danovitch & Bloom, 2009). With advances in cognitive development, children can consider multiple perspectives and become better able to consider the situation and weigh a variety of variables in making decisions. They discriminate social conventions that have a purpose from those with no obvious purpose. Social conventions that serve a purpose, such as preventing injuries (e.g., not running indoors), are evaluated as more important and more similar to moral issues than social conventions with no obvious purpose (e.g., avoiding a section of the school yard despite no apparent danger; Smetana et al., 2014).

School-age children also distinguish among moral issues, such as unfair distributions, physical harm, and psychological harm (Smetana & Ball, 2019). Elementary school children judged bullying

TABLE 8.1 ■ Moral Development in Middle Childhood: Comparison of Piaget's and Kohlberg's Theories

	Piaget's Stages		Kohlberg's Levels*	
	Stage 1: Morality of Constraint	**Stage 2: Morality of Cooperation**	**Level 1: Preconventional Moral Reasoning**	**Level 2: Conventional Moral Reasoning**
Cognitive-developmental stage	Preoperational	Concrete operational	Preoperational	Concrete operational
Perspective	Individualistic. Children cannot take the perspective of others; they assume that everyone sees the world as they do.	Multiple. Children can take the perspective of others; they see that more than one point of view is possible and that others do not necessarily view issues as they do.	Individualistic. Children cannot take the perspective of others; they focus on their own needs.	Community. Children take the perspective of the community at large; there is an emphasis on societal rules and welfare.
View of justice	Absolute. Children see acts as either right or wrong, with no shades of gray. The wrongness of an act is defined by punishment.	Relative. Children see that there is often more than one point of view. Acts are seen as right or wrong regardless of punishment.	Absolute. Acts are either right or wrong, defined by punishment and rewards.	Absolute. Right or wrong acts are defined by social approval.
Understanding of rules	Rules are unalterable and sacred.	Rules are created by people and can be changed if it suits people's needs.	Rules are unalterable and imposed by authority figures.	Rules are unalterable and act to uphold the community.
Reason for compliance with rules	Rules are obeyed out of a sense of obligation to conform to authority and to avoid punishment.	Rules that are just are obeyed for their own sake rather than under threat of punishment.	Rules are followed in order to gain rewards and avoid punishment.	Rules are followed out of a sense of duty, in order to please others and gain social approval, which is more important than other rewards.

Note: *In Kohlberg's theory, each level consists of two stages. Level 3, Postconventional Moral Reasoning, is discussed in Chapter 10.

Sources: Adapted from Hoffman (1970), Kohlberg (1981), and Piaget (1932).

as wrong independent of rules and more wrong than lapses in truth telling (Thornberg et al., 2016). School-age children become increasingly able to demonstrate nuanced judgments in response to complex moral dilemmas. For example, 5- to 11-year-old children become increasingly tolerant of necessary harm; that is, violating moral rules in order to prevent injury to others (Jambon & Smetana, 2014).

Children develop and hone their understanding of justice and fairness through social interaction at home, at school, and with peers. Children regularly encounter moral and conventional issues, such as lying to a friend, not completing homework, or violating a household rule. These everyday experiences advance moral reasoning. Issue-focused discussions characterized by mutual perspective taking and opportunities to take multiple points of view help children understand their own and other children's perspectives (Dahl, 2018; Killen & Smetana, 2015). During these discussions, children are likely to encounter reasoning that is slightly more advanced than their own, which may prompt them to reconsider their own thinking and perhaps internalize the new reasoning (Padilla-Walker and Memmott-Elison, 2020).

Thinking in Context: Lifespan Development

1. In what ways might children's moral reasoning, such as preconventional or conventional moral reasoning, influence their decisions about distributive justice? Would you expect children who show more mature moral reasoning to view moral and conventional issues differently? Why or why not?
2. Many theories of moral reasoning emphasize cognition. In what ways might children's decisions about right and wrong reflect other factors, such as physical maturation or socioemotional development?

Thinking in Context: Intersectionality

1. The contexts in which children are embedded determine their opportunities for interacting with peers and adults. How might these interactions influence children's conceptions of morality and fairness?
2. Examine how children's observations and experiences with injustice, such as conditions of poverty, racism, unemployment, violence, and distrust by authority figures, might influence their views of fairness, justice, and equitable distribution of resources.
3. What challenges do parents face in promoting children's moral reasoning within contexts of injustice? Given what you know about cognition and moral development, how can parents discuss social justice with their children?

GENDER DIFFERENCES AND GENDER TYPING

LEARNING OBJECTIVE

8.3 Discuss gender differences, gender stereotypes and beliefs, and gender identity in middle childhood.

The processes of gender typing begun in infancy and early childhood continue in middle childhood. Children's understanding and beliefs about the characteristics of boys and girls and their views of their own gender change with advances in cognitive and socioemotional development, as well as experience.

Boys and Girls: Similarities and Differences

Casual observers often remark that boys and girls are different. Are they? Recall from Chapter 6, in early childhood boys and girls are more similar than different. This pattern continues in middle childhood. Although some adults may insist that boys and girls differ in abilities and behavior, research instead suggests that in childhood, and all periods of life, average sex differences in cognitive abilities and social behaviors are small or negligible (Hyde, 2014; Liben et al., 2013). There are a greater number and variety of differences among boys and among girls than there are between boys and girls (Hyde,

2016; Miller & Halpern, 2014). Therefore, generalizations about boys and girls refer to overall average differences, which may not apply to any specific boy or girl.

Although boys and girls do not differ in measures of intelligence, they may show small differences in several aspects of cognition (Halpern & LaMay, 2000). First, in all industrialized countries, girls show a slight advantage on reading comprehension and verbal fluency tasks through adolescence (Miller & Halpern, 2014; Petersen, 2018). Yet these subtle gender differences disappear as children grow up. Most tests of vocabulary and other verbal abilities show negligible or no sex difference in adults (Hines, 2015; Hyde, 2016).

Second, boys tend to outperform girls on one specific type of spatial reasoning: *mental rotation*, the ability to recognize a stimulus that is rotated in space (Roberts & Bell, 2002; van Tetering et al., 2019). Boys and girls show similar performance on other spatial tasks (Hyde, 2016; Miller & Halpern, 2014).

Third, in prior decades girls tended to perform better on tests of computational mathematics skills in childhood and boys performed better on tasks measuring mathematical reasoning in adolescence (Hyde, 2014; Leahey & Guo, 2001; Wei et al., 2012). These sex differences have disappeared, as suggested by a recent comprehensive study of children age 6 to 13 in which boys and girls demonstrated similar numerical skills (Hutchison et al., 2019). Girls' improvement in mathematical reasoning skills in recent decades accompanies the increasing emphasis by educational institutions, government, and industry on encouraging women to enter careers in the sciences, suggesting that socialization influences how children approach math (Ceci et al., 2014; Dasgupta & Stout, 2014).

Finally, the socioemotional differences in boys and girls discussed in Chapter 6 persist. Girls tend to be better at managing and expressing their emotions than boys. Throughout childhood into adulthood, girls tend to express a greater range of emotions more intensely than do boys (Birditt & Fingerman, 2003; Chaplin, 2015; Zimmermann & Iwanski, 2014). In contrast, boys tend to be more physically active and engage in more physical aggression than girls (Leaper, 2013; Scott & Panksepp, 2003).

Gender Stereotypes and Gender Beliefs

By about 5 years of age, children have extensive knowledge of the activities and interests stereotyped for men and women that are expressed as rigid rules about the behavior appropriate for boys and girls, influencing their preferences for toys, activities, and playmates (Baker et al., 2016; Blakemore et al., 2009). Children's preference for same-sex peers increases in middle childhood. Four-and-one-half-year-old children spend about three times as much time with same-sex peers as with opposite-sex peers, and this difference increases to 10 times by 6.5 years of age (Hines, 2015; Maccoby & Jacklin, 1987).

In middle childhood, knowledge of stereotypes expands to include beliefs about personality and achievement (Bussey, 2013; Serbin et al., 1993). Elementary school children describe reading, spelling, art, and music as appropriate subjects for girls and mathematics and athletics as being for boys (Kurtz-Costes et al., 2014; Passolunghi et al., 2014). Gender stereotypes influence children's preferences and views of their own abilities, such as girls' attitudes about math. Girls tend to report negative feelings about math and perceive math as a "male subject" (Cvencek et al., 2011). Despite recent initiatives to increase women's representation in quantitative fields such as science, technology, engineering, and mathematics (STEM), girls show less interest in these areas and are less likely to pursue a career in these areas than boys (Eccles & Wang, 2016).

Stereotyped attitudes, beliefs, and interests about math are influenced by early experiences with parents and teachers. Boys' exposure to toys that emphasize acting on the world, such as blocks, vehicles, and building sets, stimulate quantitative interests and abilities. Parents' and teachers' beliefs about gender influence children's attitudes, and research suggests that adults commonly hold stereotypes that girls are less likely to succeed in math than boys (Cimpian et al., 2016; Ellemers, 2018). As early as first grade, teachers consistently underrate girls' math performance relative to boys' despite a general lack of evidence for sex differences in math achievement (Cimpian et al., 2016). Adults' gender-stereotyped expectations influence their interactions with children, encouraging stereotyped behavior (Ellemers, 2018). Fortunately, from middle childhood into adolescence, as rigid beliefs about gender decline, children become more likely to report that both boys and girls can and should be good at STEM (McGuire et al., 2020).

Children who identify as transgender show similar patterns of stereotyped beliefs as children with a cisgender identity (Olson & Gülgöz, 2018). One study compared 5- to 12-year-old transgender children, their cisgender siblings, and a group of unrelated cisgender children on self-report and implicit, less controllable, measures of ability and preferences (Olson et al., 2015). When transgender children's responses were considered in light of their birth gender, their responses differed radically from the cisgender children and the stereotyped behavior typical of children their age. When transgender children's responses were evaluated in terms of their expressed gender, there was a close match to peers. The transgender children preferred peers and objects endorsed by peers who shared their expressed gender, suggesting a similar developmental trend in gender identity and preferences for transgender and cisgender children. Children who identify as transgender (and their siblings) demonstrate more flexible views of gender stereotypes than cisgender children, are less likely to endorse gender stereotypes, and view gender nonconformity as more acceptable in peers than cisgender (and unrelated) children (Olson & Enright, 2018).

Gender Constancy and Gender Typing

By around 7 years of age, children demonstrate full understanding of **gender constancy**, which is the awareness that a person's sex is a biological characteristic (Halim, 2016). Gender rigidity tends to decline as children's understanding of gender constancy develops (Ruble et al., 2007; Trautner et al., 2005). Children with a more mature grasp of gender constancy may be less afraid to engage in other-gender-typed activities than they had been previously because they understand that they will remain a girl or boy despite engaging in cross-gender-typed activities (Halim, Ruble, Tamis-LeMonda, Shrout, & Amodio, 2017). Girls tend to show more flexible gender-stereotyped beliefs than boys and over time tend to identify less strongly with feminine gender roles than do boys with masculine gender roles (Sravanti & Kommu, 2020). This trend toward flexibility in views of what males and females can do increases with age in both boys and girls (Blakemore et al., 2009).

However, becoming more open-minded about boys' and girls' gendered behavior does not mean that school-age children approve of violating gender stereotypes. School-age children tend to remain intolerant to certain violations, especially boys playing with dolls or wearing dresses and girls playing noisily and roughly, which they rate as severely as moral violations (Blakemore, 2003; Levy, Taylor, & Gelman, 1995). Yet older children tend to understand that gender-stereotyped traits and behaviors are associated with gender but are not defined by gender (Banse, Gawronski, Rebetez, Gutt, & Bruce Morton, 2010; Martin et al., 2002). At about 9 to 10 years of age, children grasp the social basis of gender roles: that they are social conventions rather than biological inevitabilities (Leaper, 2013). Now children increasingly agree that boys and girls should follow their own preferences regardless of social conventions.

Gender Identity

In middle childhood gender identity expands as children begin to compare themselves with others. Several dimensions of gender identity rise in importance: perceived same-gender typicality and perceived other-gender typicality, gender contentedness, and perceived pressure to conform to gender roles.

Children who are high in **perceived same-gender typicality** feel that they are typical of their gender and similar to same-gender peers. These children tend to show high self-esteem, high social competence, secure relationships, and little depression, and they are viewed positively by their peers as likable, prosocial, and rarely victimized (Corby et al., 2007; Perry et al., 2019; Zosuls et al., 2016). Less is known about the consequences of **perceived other-gender typicality**, or perceiving oneself as similar to the other gender. Children's perceived same-gender typicality and perceived other-gender typicality are not highly correlated; many children believe they hold characteristics typical of both genders (Martin et al., 2017; Pauletti et al., 2017). It appears that the consequences of perceived other-gender typicality depend on children's level of perceived same-gender typicality. Other-gender typicality is associated with positive adjustment when it is accompanied by perceived same-gender typicality (Martin et al.,

2017; Pauletti et al., 2017). If children do not feel typical of their gender, however, feeling other-gender typical may expose them to risks such as emotional distress, low self-esteem, peer victimization, and poor adjustment (Pauletti et al., 2017; Perry et al., 2019; Zosuls et al., 2016).

Gender contentedness refers to children's satisfaction with their gender assignment at birth (girl or boy; Egan & Perry, 2001). Generally, children who show high levels of gender contentedness show positive outcomes, such as high self-esteem, social competence, few internalizing problems (e.g., depression, social withdrawal, sadness, anxiety), secure attachments to others, and better relationships with peers (Carver et al., 2003; Cooper et al., 2013; Menon, 2011; Pauletti et al., 2017). Children who are gender nonconforming and those who identify as transgender tend to display poor gender contentedness.

Children vary in their **perceived pressure to conform to gender roles**, meaning the degree to which they feel pressure to avoid other-gender behavior, including anticipating the negative consequences (e.g., ridicule, criticism, and shaming) that may accompany engaging in behavior characteristic of the other gender. Children who perceive heavy pressure to conform to gender roles may experience adjustment problems (Pauletti et al., 2014; Perry et al., 2019). In girls, perceived pressure to conform to gender roles is associated with problems with self-esteem, depression, poor attachments to parents and friends, and poor peer relationships. Boys who perceive pressure to conform to gender roles may show higher levels of aggression, low prosocial behavior, and biases against girls. Children and their peers tend to show similar beliefs about the pressure to conform to gender roles, and their beliefs become more similar over time (Kornienko et al., 2016). Children's beliefs about pressure to conform to gender roles is socialized through their daily interactions with peers, including discussion and modeling (Schroeder & Liben, 2020).

Thinking in Context: Lifespan Development

1. How are children's sex-stereotyped attitudes and behavior as well as gender identity influenced by cognitive development? Provide examples.

2. How might contextual factors in the home, school, and neighborhood influence children's gender-related attitudes and behavior and their gender identity?

Thinking in Context: Applied Developmental Science

1. Why do many adults perceive sex differences in children despite research findings suggesting that there are few differences?

2. Explain what we know about sex differences in childhood to a parent of a 9-year-old child.

3. Willyour explanation differ depending on whether the parent is raising a son or daughter? Why or why not?

PEER RELATIONSHIPS IN MIDDLE CHILDHOOD

LEARNING OBJECTIVE

8.4 Analyze the role of friendship, peer acceptance, and peer victimization in school-age children's adjustment.

As older children's self-concepts expand and they become better able to understand and appreciate others' perspectives, they develop richer and closer relationships with peers. Older children spend more time with friends and place more importance on those relationships than do younger children (Schneider, 2016). Most school-age children have multiple friendships and are part of a peer group in school and, increasingly, out of school. Friendship and peer acceptance become important influences on adjustment.

Friendship

Friendships are a source of companionship, stimulation, and affection. In middle childhood, friendship transforms into a reciprocal relationship in which children are responsive to each other's needs and trust each other (Maunder & Monks, 2019). Friends provide each other with tangible and emotional support. Shared values and rules become important components to friendship by 9 to 10 years of age (Bagwell & Bukowski, 2018; Rubin et al., 2015a). Friends are expected to be loyal and stick up for each other. Violations of trust, such as divulging secrets, breaking promises, and not helping a friend in need, can break up a friendship. School-age children differentiate among best friends, good friends, and casual friends, depending on how much time they spend together and how much they share with one another (Rubin et al., 2015a). Older children, especially girls, tend to have fewer, but closer, friends, and by age 10, most children report having a best friend (Erdley & Day, 2017).

Close supportive friendships are associated with positive adjustment and well-being, including self-esteem and self-worth, prosocial behavior, and less peer victimization (Bagwell, 2020; Bagwell & Bukowski, 2018; Maunder & Monks, 2019). Poor friendship quality, on the other hand, is associated with poor adjustment and internalizing problems such as depression and anxiety (Schwartz-Mette et al., 2020; Troop-Gordon et al., 2019).

At all times in life friendships are rooted in similarity. Children choose friends who share interests, play preferences, and personality characteristics (Laursen, 2017). Friends show similarities in cognitive ability and intelligence, likely because these characteristics influence the capacity to take other people's perspectives and reciprocate (Boutwell et al., 2017; Ilmarinen et al., 2017). Friends also tend to share demographics, such as gender, race, and ethnicity (Rubin et al., 2015b). Friends are also a source of social comparison, permitting children to judge their competence relative to peers (Erdley & Day, 2017).

Contextual characteristics, such as the ethnic diversity of a neighborhood or school, influence children's choices of friends within and outside of their own ethnic group. In schools and neighborhoods that are ethnically, racially, and socioeconomically diverse, children are more likely to report having at least one close friend of another race (Iqbal et al., 2017; Lessard et al., 2019). School-age girls may be more likely to have ethnically diverse social networks and cross-race friendships than boys (Lee, Howes, & Chamberlain, 2007). Once established, cross-race friendships are similar to same-race friendships with regard to intimacy, companionship, and security (McDonald et al., 2013). Compared to children who do not have friends of other races, children in cross-race friendships tend to show a lower tolerance for excluding others (Killen et al., 2010) and are less prone to peer victimization (Kawabata & Crick, 2011). They also tend to feel socially and emotionally safer and less vulnerable at school (Graham et al., 2014; Munniksma & Juvonen, 2012).

Friendships often remain stable from middle childhood into adolescence, especially among children whose friendships are high in relationship quality, characterized by sharing, mutual perspective taking, and compromise (Asher & Weeks, 2018; Poulin & Chan, 2010). Nevertheless, because friendship is based largely on similar characteristics, proximity, and opportunities for interaction, many friendships may come and go as children develop new interests, competencies, and values (Laursen, 2017). They may also end as children progress into new contexts, as when they change schools, move to a different neighborhood, or even begin a new school year (Troutman & Fletcher, 2010). Friendships that take place in multiple contexts, such as school, neighborhood, and extracurricular contexts, are more likely to endure than those that occur in only one context (Meter & Card, 2016). Older children become more upset at losing a friend and find making friends more challenging than do young children (Hartup, 2006).

Friendship instability and loss, or dissolution, is associated with problems with depression, loneliness, guilt, anger, anxiety, and acting-out behaviors, yet children with psychosocial problems are at risk to experience friendship loss and, in turn, show poor adjustment (Lessard & Juvonen, 2018; Rubin et al., 2015a). Many children replace "lost" friendships with "new" friendships. In one study of fifth graders, losing a friend was associated with adjustment difficulties only when the lost friendship was not replaced by a new friendship. For these children, the lost and new friendships were largely interchangeable (Wojslawowicz Bowker et al., 2006). For many children, the importance of stable best friendships during middle childhood may have less to do with the relationship's length and more to do with simply having a "buddy" by one's side who can provide companionship, recreation, validation, caring, help, and guidance.

Friends are an important source of companionship, support, and fun in middle childhood.
Jeffrey Greenberg/UIG via Getty Images

Peer Acceptance, Popularity, and Rejection

In middle childhood, peer evaluations become vital sources of self-validation, self-esteem, and confidence (LaFontana & Cillessen, 2010). **Peer acceptance**, the degree to which a child is viewed as a worthy social partner by his or her peers, becomes important in middle childhood. Some children stand out from their peers as exceptionally well liked or exceptionally disliked.

Popularity

Children who are valued by their peers are said to be popular. **Popular children** tend to have a variety of positive characteristics—including helpfulness, trustworthiness, assertiveness, and friendliness—and are perceived as fun and prosocial (Kornbluh & Neal, 2016; Laursen et al., 2020; Lease et al., 2020). They are skilled in self-control, emotional regulation, and social information processing (van den Berg et al., 2017). That is, popular children are good at reading social situations, problem solving, self-disclosure, and conflict resolution (Blandon et al., 2010). Positive social competencies and prosocial behaviors are cyclical; children who excel at social interaction continue to do so, their peers tend to reciprocate, and positive effects on peer relationships increase (Laible et al., 2014; Wang et al., 2019).

Some popular children do not show the prosocial and empathetic characteristics typical of popularity. Some popular children are disliked (McDonald & Asher, 2018; Romera et al., 2019). Often labeled by peers and teachers as "tough," these children are socially skilled yet show antisocial and aggressive behavior (Shi & Xie, 2012). Aggressive popular children show social competencies similar to prosocial popular children, yet they also share many characteristics of children who are rejected by their peers (Kornbluh & Neal, 2016; Marks, 2017).

Peer Rejection

Children who experience **peer rejection** tend to be disliked and shunned by their peers. Children who have poor communication, emotional control, and social information processing skills are at risk for peer rejection (Bierman et al., 2014; Menting et al., 2011; van der Wilt et al., 2019). Boys and girls with behavior problems experience heightened risk for peer rejection—and peer rejection, in turn, is associated with increases in behavior problems throughout elementary school and rule breaking in adolescence (Ettekal & Ladd, 2015; Prabaharan & Spadafora, 2020). Rejected children's behavior tends to be characterized by either withdrawal or aggression.

Not all children have a best friend. Lacking close friendships is not indicative of maladjustment especially if children experience other close relationships.
Alistair Berg/ Getty Images

Common views of peer rejection characterize rejected children as socially withdrawn, passive, timid, anxious, and socially awkward. **Withdrawn-rejected children** tend to isolate themselves from peers, rarely initiate contact with peers, and speak less frequently than their peers (Rubin et al., 2009; Duffy et al., 2020). They tend to spend most of their time playing alone and on the periphery of the social scene, often because of shyness or social anxiety. When socially withdrawn children experience peer rejection, they tend to become more withdrawn and even more disliked by their peers (Coplan et al., 2013). Despite this, socially withdrawn children are just as likely to have a best friend as other children (Rubin et al., 2006).

Not all rejected children are withdrawn. **Aggressive-rejected children** are confrontational, hostile toward other children, impulsive, and hyperactive (Duffy et al., 2020). They enter peer groups in destructive ways that disrupt the group's interaction or activity and direct attention to themselves. Aggressive-rejected children tend to have difficulty taking the perspective of others, and they tend to react aggressively to slights by peers, quickly assuming hostile intentions (Fite et al., 2013; Laible et al., 2014). Children whose parents show little warmth and use coercive discipline are likely to have poor social skills, show aggressive behavior, threaten other children, and are more likely to be rejected by other children (Lansford, 2014).

Both aggressive-rejected and withdrawn-rejected children tend to misinterpret other children's behaviors and motives, have trouble understanding and regulating their emotions, are poor listeners, and are less socially competent than other children (Ladd & Kochenderfer-Ladd, 2016). Peer rejection further hinders social development by depriving children of opportunities to learn and practice social

TABLE 8.2 ■ Characteristics of Popular and Rejected Children

	Characteristic	Outcomes
Popular children	Helpful, trustworthy, assertive Cognitively skilled and achievement oriented Socially skilled, able to self-disclose and provide emotional support Good social problem-solving skills and conflict resolution skills Prosocial orientation Assume others have good intentions A minority are also antisocial and aggressive. They interact with others in a hostile way, using physical or relational aggression, and are likely to bully other children.	Positive characteristics are strengthened though experience and peer approval. Positive peer evaluations are sources of self-validation, self-esteem, confidence, and attention from peers, and they influence adjustment. Without intervention, the minority of popular children who are aggressive are likely to continue patterns of physical or relational aggression in response to peer approval and acceptance.
Withdrawn-rejected children	Passive, timid, and socially awkward Socially withdrawn, isolate themselves from others Anxious Poor social skills Fear being disliked by peers Misinterpret other children's behaviors and motives	Similar outcomes for both types of rejected children Negative characteristics are strengthened. Few opportunities to learn and practice social skills, conflict resolution, and emotional regulation Anxiety, depression, and low self-esteem Behavior problems Poor academic achievement Increased physical and relational aggression over time Withdrawal and loneliness
Aggressive-rejected children	Confrontational, hostile toward other children Impulsive and hyperactive Difficulty with emotional regulation Difficulty taking others' perspectives Assume that their peers are out to get them Poor social skills Misinterpret other children's behaviors and motives	

skills such as interacting with other children, resolving conflict, and regulating emotions (Prabaharan & Spadafora, 2020). Peer rejection is associated with short- and long-term problems, such as loneliness, anxiety, depression, low self-esteem, low academic achievement, and, in adolescence, delinquency and school dropout (Cooley & Fite, 2016; Menting, Koot, & van Lier, 2014; Schwartz, Lansford, Dodge, Pettit, & Bates, 2015). Peer rejection also places children at risk for bullying (Menesini & Salmivalli, 2017). Table 8.2 summarizes characteristics associated with popular children and those who are rejected.

Bullying

Bullying, also known as *peer victimization*, refers to an ongoing interaction in which a child repeatedly attempts to inflict physical, verbal, or social harm on another child by hitting, kicking, name-calling, teasing, shunning, or humiliating the other child (Olweus, 2013). Bullying is a problem for school-age children in many countries. Estimated rates of bullying and victimization range from 15% to 25% of children in Australia, Austria, England, Finland, Germany, Norway, and the United States (Zych et al., 2017). Physical bullying is most common in childhood, and verbal/relational forms of bullying rise in childhood and remain common in adolescence (Finkelhor et al., 2009). Cyberbullying is a type of relational bullying carried out by text or electronic communication and social media (Vaillancourt et al., 2017). Cyberbullying tends to accompany other types of bullying rather than occur independently and is more common in adolescence than childhood (Waasdorp & Bradshaw, 2015).

Children Who Bully

Boys and girls who engage in bullying tend to be impulsive and aggressive. Boys tend to show physical aggression and target both boys and girls. Girls who bully tend to target other girls, using verbal or psychological methods that threaten relationships (Murray-Close, Nelson, Ostrov, Casas, & Crick, 2016). These methods, known as **relational aggression**, include ridiculing, embarrassing, and spreading rumors.

Bullying, specifically relational aggression, can be motivated by the pursuit of high status and the desire to maintain a powerful dominant position in the peer group (Thomas et al., 2017; van der Ploeg et al., 2020). Children who are skilled at relational aggression are frequently perceived by peers as cool, powerful, and popular (Juvonen & Graham, 2014). Bullying can be helpful in maintaining prestige and high social status among peers. In support of this, many bullies report making friends easily and receive similar levels of support from their classmates as other children (Menesini & Salmivalli, 2017).

Children who bully tend to experience maladaptive and rejecting parenting, including inconsistent and poor parental involvement and support and poor supervision (Nocentini et al., 2019). Parents of bullies are more likely to prefer coercive control and physical discipline, and they tend to be permissive toward aggressive behavior, even encouraging children to retaliate for perceived provocation (Gómez-Ortiz et al., 2016; Rajendran et al., 2016).

Victims of Bullying

Victims of bullying are often perceived by their bullies and other children as different, as more quiet, inhibited, and cautious than other children (Juvonen & Graham, 2014). They often report experiencing intrusive parenting, overprotectiveness, and criticism from parents, which may increase their vulnerability to bullying (Menesini & Salmivalli, 2017). Common social characteristics of victims, such as nonassertive styles of interacting with peers, passivity, and withdrawal, and emotional characteristics, including anxiety, depression, and poor emotional control, are present in children prior to peer victimization and are then amplified by victimization (Cooley et al., 2020; Husky et al., 2020; Perren

Children who show physical forms of bullying are often reared in homes with poor supervision, coercive control, and physical discipline.

istock/ fstop123

et al., 2013). Bullying has negative emotional and academic consequences that appear as early as in kindergarten and persist throughout the childhood and adolescent years, often well after the bullying ends (Moore et al., 2017).

Many children respond to bullying by avoiding contact, such as by not going to school and refusing to go certain places (Waasdorp & Bradshaw, 2011). Older children who experience frequent victimization may respond with more intense feelings of anger and greater desires to retaliate, making them more likely to show reactive aggression, an aggressive response to an insult, confrontation, or frustration (Arseneault, 2018).

Not all victims of bullying are passive and withdrawn. Some children, **bully-victims**, share characteristics of both bullies and victims (Hymel & Swearer, 2015). There is often overlap between bullies and victims (Walters, 2020). Bully-victims often display the high levels of anxiety and depression and low rates of social acceptance and self-esteem common to other victims, but they also show more aggression, impulsivity, and poor self-control than do other victims (Swearer & Hymel, 2015; van Dijk et al., 2017). Children who are bully-victims have difficulty managing emotions, which may increase their risk for reactive aggression and acting out behaviors that invite aggressive exchanges with others. They tend to have problems in peer relationships and often are disliked by their classmates (Arseneault, 2018). Children who are bully-victims are more likely than other victimized children to experience anxiety and depression in late adolescence and in early adulthood—and even into middle adulthood (Evans-Lacko et al., 2017; McDougall & Vaillancourt, 2015).

Contextual Approaches to Bullying Intervention

Bullying occurs in a social context—usually the school—which influences its outcomes. Successful interventions to combat bullying address multiple perspectives, including victims, bullies, and other members of the school (Hutson et al., 2018; Nese et al., 2014; see Table 8.3). Interventions can help victims change their negative self-perceptions and acquire the skills needed to maintain relationships with peers and teach them to respond to bullying in ways that do not reinforce their attackers (Olweus & Limber, 2010). Successful interventions stress that victimized children are not to blame for the abuse. Parents and teachers should help children who bully learn to identify, understand, and manage their and other people's emotions, as well as direct anger in safe and appropriate ways (Hutson et al., 2018). Teachers need to be aware of bullying and willing to intervene (Espelage et al., 2014).

It is especially important to address bystanders—children who witness episodes of bullying. Bystanders who do not act reinforce bullies' behaviors and increase bullying (Kärnä et al., 2010; Salmivalli, 2014). School and class norms can influence whether bystanders intervene, especially if parents reinforce norms (Grassetti et al., 2018; Pozzoli et al., 2012). Parents tend to advise children to intervene and tell an adult in response to physical bullying and to help the victim in response (Grassetti et al., 2020) to emotional attacks. Classmates can be encouraged to support one another when bullying events occur: Rather than being bystanders or egging the bully on, they can tell a teacher, refuse to watch, and even, if safe, encourage bullies to stop.

Stopping bullying requires awareness and change within the school. Schools must review and modify practices with an eye toward identifying how class environment and procedures may maintain or increase bullying (Fink et al., 2018; Nese et al., 2014). In recognition of the pervasiveness and severity of bullying, specific bully-related policies are included in public school laws in most states. Addressing the problem of bullying requires that children, teachers, and parents voice concerns about bullying; schools develop policies against bullying; teachers supervise and monitor children during lunch and recess times; and parents learn how to identify and change victims' and bullies' behaviors.

Risks and interventions for bullying are presented in Table 8.3.

Thinking in Context: Lifespan Development

Considering Bronfenbrenner's bioecological theory from Chapter 1, what microsystem factors (such as personal characteristics), mesosystem factors (such as family and school), and exosystem factors (such as neighborhood) might lead a child to be popular or unpopular with peers? Which factors are most important, in your view?

TABLE 8.3 ■ Bullying Risks and Interventions

Bullying Risk Factor			Bullying Intervention
Child	Victim	Physically weak Younger than peers Anxious, insecure, low self-esteem, dependent Quiet, cautious, withdrawn Little prosocial behavior Poor emotional control Loneliness Unhappiness at school Fewer good friends than peers	Teach assertiveness skills. Teach children alternative responses to bullying. Teach anxiety and emotional management as well as social and coping skills.
	Bully	Above average in size More physically and verbally assertive Impulsive Domineering, hostile toward peers Little anxiety or insecurity in peer contexts Makes friends easily Hyperactive behavior Academic difficulties Poor emotional control	Teach alternatives to violence. Help children develop empathy. Teach emotional management and coping skills to reduce impulsive behavior.
Parent	Victim	Intrusive, overprotective, and/or critical parenting	Teach authoritative parenting skills. Encourage parents to aid children in being independent and developing coping skills.
	Bully	Hostile and rejecting parenting Use of physical punishment Models aggressive behavior Permissive, inconsistent response to aggressive bullying behavior	Teach authoritative parenting skills. Parent with sensitivity and consistency. Model nonaggressive behavior, interpersonal interactions, and conflict management strategies. Provide positive feedback to children for appropriate social behaviors. Use alternatives to physical punishment.
School		Groups students by physical characteristics such as height Policies that discourage reporting bullying incidents Teachers and administrators who ignore bullying Environment of negative feedback and negative attention	Stress that victims are not to blame. Teach social skills and conflict management. Promote a positive school climate that encourages students to feel good about themselves. Encourage fair discipline that is not punitive. Train teachers to identify and respond to potentially damaging victimization. Teachers use positive feedback and modeling to address appropriate social interactions. School personnel never ignore bullying behaviors. Encourage classmates to support one another and, rather than simply watch bullying events occur, tell a teacher, and refuse to watch or encourage the bully. Review and modify school practices with an eye toward identifying how school procedures may contribute to bullying.

Thinking in Context: Applied Developmental Science

1. As a parent, what might you do to lessen the likelihood that your child becomes a bully or a victim of bullying?
2. How can teachers foster a bully-free environment in their classrooms? How can teachers respond effectively to bullying? What can school principals do?

FAMILIES IN MIDDLE CHILDHOOD

LEARNING OBJECTIVE

8.5 Discuss family relationships in middle childhood and the relations among family structure and children's adjustment.

Children are embedded in families that play an important role in their development. Children's relationships with parents and siblings are dynamic and reciprocal. Children influence and are influenced by every member of their family. Families may take many forms, as described in the following sections.

Parent-Child Relationships

As school-age children become more independent, they spend less time with but remain close to their parents. Parents and school-age children tend to spend their time together engaging in task-oriented activities, such as doing homework, preparing meals, cleaning, and shopping. Interactions with parents help children rehearse and refine skills that are important for peer relationships. The parent-child relationship transforms as parents adapt their parenting styles to match their children's increased ability to reason and desire for independence. Parents tend to use less direct management and instead begin to share power—for example, by guiding and monitoring children's behavior from a distance, communicating expectations, and allowing children to be in charge of moment-to-moment decision making (Lamb & Lewis, 2015). Parents increasingly use reasoning and inductive discipline techniques, such as pointing out the consequences of a child's behavior, explaining how a child affects others, and appealing to the child's self-esteem and sense of values (Hawes & Tully, 2020).

Continuity is typical in parenting and parent-child relationships during middle childhood (Bradley et al., 2017). Patterns of harsh verbal discipline (yelling, threatening, punishment, shaming) and insensitive parenting established in early childhood tend to persist in middle childhood (Bradley & Corwyn, 2008; Lansford et al., 2013). In turn, harsh parenting styles and poor quality parent-child relationships in middle childhood tend to worsen and are associated with poor adjustment, antisocial activity, and delinquency into adolescence (Hakvoort, Bos, van Balen, & Hermanns, 2010; Keijsers, Loeber, Branje, & Meeus, 2011; Koehn & Kerns, 2018).

Similar to infancy and early childhood, middle childhood attachment to parents is associated with positive adjustment. Parents of securely attached children tend to use more behavioral and less harsh discipline strategies and support children's autonomy (Koehn & Kerns, 2018). Secure attachment is negatively associated with anxiety, depression, and behavior problems (Brumariu et al., 2018; Cortés-García et al., 2019). Children who are securely attached to parents tend to develop positive emotion regulation skills that aid them in home, peer, and school contexts (Brumariu, 2015).

Same-Sex-Parented Families

Over one-third of LGBT adults raise a child (Gates, 2015). Most children raised by LGBT parents are the biological children of the parents, as shown in Figure 8.1. However, LGBT parents are more likely to adopt children than are heterosexual parents. As a result of Obergefell v. Hodges, the landmark 2015 U.S. Supreme Court ruling that legalized same-sex marriage nationwide, every state permits joint adoption by married couples, regardless of sexual orientation.

FIGURE 8.1 ■ Percentage of Same-Sex Couple Households with Stepchildren, Adopted, or Biological Children, United States, 2019

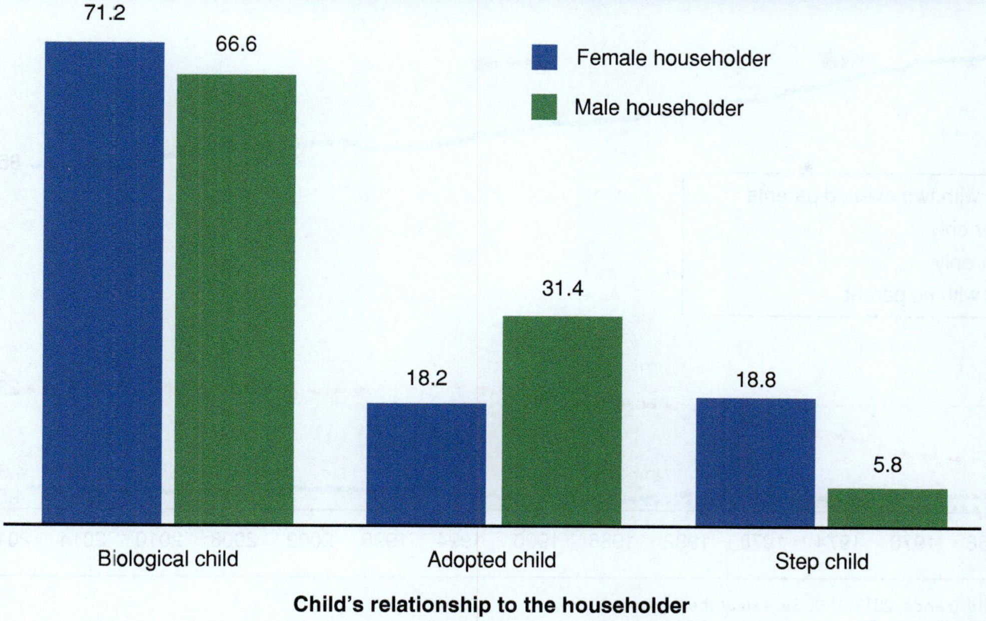

Source: Taylor, 2020.

More than three decades of research conducted in the United States, the United Kingdom, Belgium, and the Netherlands has failed to reveal important differences in the adjustment or development of children and adolescents reared by same-sex couples compared with those reared by other couples (Fedewa et al., 2014; Patterson, 2017; Perrin & Siegel, 2013). Specifically, children and adolescents raised by lesbian mothers or gay fathers do not differ from other children on measures of emotional development, such as empathy and emotional regulation (Bos et al., 2016; Farr, 2017; Imrie & Golombok, 2020). Instead, some studies have suggested that children raised by gay and lesbian parents may score higher in some aspects of social and academic competence, as well as show fewer social and behavioral problems and lower levels of aggression, than other children (Bos & Gartrell, 2020; Farr et al., 2019; Golombok et al., 2018; Mazrekaj et al., 2020; Miller et al., 2017). Moreover, children raised by lesbian mothers and gay fathers show similar patterns of gender identity and gender role development as children raised by heterosexual parents—they are not more likely to identify as gay or lesbian in adulthood (Fedewa et al., 2014; Schumm & Crawford, 2019). Researchers have concluded that a family's social and economic resources, the strength of the relationships among members of the family, and the presence of stigma are far more important variables than parental gender or sexual orientation in affecting children's development and well-being (Farr, 2017; Imrie & Golombok, 2020).

Same-sex parents show similar levels of parenting competence but often experience greater well-being as compared with heterosexual parents, often because same-sex parents tend to share household and child-rearing duties.

SHIH WEBER/SIPA/Newscom

Single-Parent Families

Over one-quarter of U.S. children under age 18 live with a single parent, most commonly with their mother (U.S. Bureau of the Census, 2018). Figure 8.2 shows the various living arrangements for households with children.

Black children are disproportionally likely to live in a single-parent home (Figure 8.3). More than one-half

FIGURE 8.2 ■ Living Arrangements of Children Under 18, 1970–2017

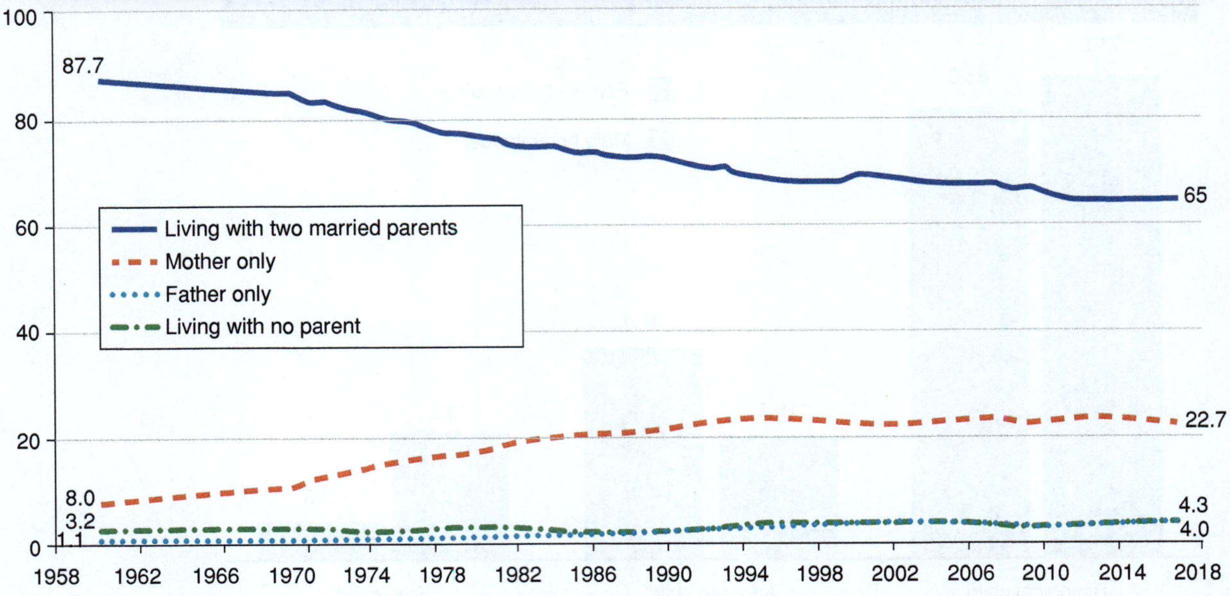

Source: Adapted from Child Trends, 2013; U.S. Bureau of the Census, 2018

of Black children live with one parent, compared with about one-third of Hispanic, one-fifth of non-Hispanic white, and 10% of Asian American children.

Single-parent families may be created through divorce or death, or the single parent may never have married. Some research suggests that children in single-parent homes tend to show more physical and mental health problems, poorer academic achievement, and more behavior problems than do children in intact two-parent families (Taylor & Conger, 2017; Waldfogel et al., 2010). Other research has found no differences in children's emotional and behavioral adjustment or the quality of mother-child relationships (Zadeh, 2020). These diverse findings are likely related to variations in levels of parenting stress that may accompany single parenthood, particularly in low-socioeconomic contexts (Peverill et al., 2021; Reiss et al., 2019).

Children in single-mother homes, regardless of ethnicity, are disproportionately likely to live in poverty (Cancian & Meyer, 2018; Damaske et al., 2017). Low socioeconomic status poses risks for academic, social, and behavioral problems. Economic disadvantage affects children in myriad ways, from having less money for books, clothes, and extracurricular activities to living in poorer school districts and neighborhoods. In addition, families headed by single mothers often experience many transitions, as single mothers tend to change jobs and homes more frequently than other mothers. Each transition poses challenges to children's adjustment (Evans et al., 2013). In addition, single mothers report more depression and psychological problems than married mothers and, when depressed, undoubtedly function less well as parents (Reising et al., 2013; Waldfogel et al., 2010). Children in single-parent homes formed by divorce also undergo transitions related to the divorce, with implications for adjustment (Golombok, & Tasker, 2015).

It is important to recognize that differences in adjustment between children raised by one or two parents are small; the vast majority of children raised in one-parent homes are well adjusted (Lamb, 2012; Zadeh, 2020). In addition, there are more differences among children in single-parent homes than between children in single-parent homes and two-parent homes. Many of the differences associated with family structure are reduced or disappear when researchers take socioeconomic status into account, suggesting that differences in child well-being across family types are strongly influenced by family income, access to resources, and the stresses that accompany economic difficulties (Ryan et al., 2015; Taylor & Conger, 2017). Increasingly women become single parents by choice. Children reared by single-by-choice parents tend to live in higher socioeconomic homes than other children reared by single parents, and they tend to experience positive adjustment and few problems (Golombok, 2017; Imrie & Golombok, 2020).

FIGURE 8.3 ■ Living Arrangements of Children, by Race and Hispanic Origin, 2017

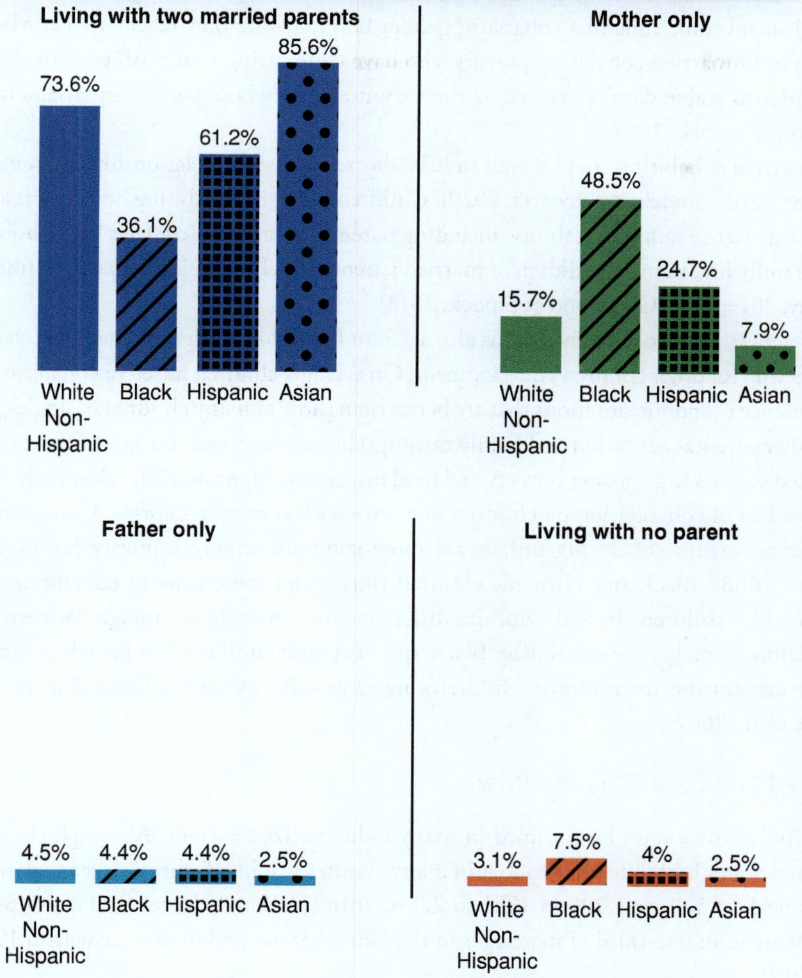

Source: Adapted from Child Trends, 2013; U.S. Bureau of the Census, 2018

Social support influences parents' ability to provide emotional support for their children and implement effective parenting strategies. In African American communities, single mothers are often integrated within their community, providing their children with opportunities to interact with many caring adult family members and friends of the family; thus, children are raised as members of a larger African American community (Jayakody & Kalil, 2002). Often, an adult male, such as an uncle or grandfather, takes on a fathering role, helping a child build competence and develop a relationship with a caring adult (Hill et al., 2003). In such families, grandmothers often are highly involved, warm, and helpful, taking on important support roles (Harper & Ruicheva, 2010). When children are close to highly involved extended family members, they develop family bonds and a sense of family honor that guides them and encourages them to succeed; this tends to hold true of all children, regardless of family structure (Jaeger, 2012).

Around 25% of children under age 18 live with a single parent, most commonly with their mother. Children raised in one-parent households are generally well-adjusted.

ANDREW HOLBROOKE/Corbis via Getty Images

Cohabiting Families

There are many kinds of families, and not all are formed through marriage. An estimated 40% children will spend some time in a cohabiting-parent family before they reach age 12 (Manning, 2015). Children of unmarried cohabiting parents who have close caring relationships with the children and whose union is stable develop as well as their counterparts whose parents' marriage is stable (Rose-Greenland & Smock, 2013).

Unmarried cohabiting couples tend to have shorter, less stable relationships than married couples (Manning, 2015; Smock & Schwartz, 2020). Children living in cohabiting households are much more likely to experience family instability, including parental separation, conflict in the home, and transitions in family life, than are children of married parents, all of which influence adjustment (Cavanagh & Fomby, 2019; Rose-Greenland & Smock, 2013).

Differences in socioeconomic status also account for children's development in cohabiting homes, just as they do for other children's development. On average, children raised in cohabiting-parent families experience economic situations that are better than those of many children in single-parent families (e.g., higher parental education and family earnings) but more economically stressful than those reared by married parents (e.g., greater poverty and food insecurity; Manning, 2015; Kennedy & Fitch, 2012).

The effect of cohabitation on children may vary with contextual norms. Consensual unions and childbearing within cohabiting unions are more common among minority families (Kennedy & Bumpass, 2008). Black and Hispanic children thus spend more time in cohabiting-parent unions than do white children. In addition, the difference in economic advantage between marriage and cohabitation is smaller for cohabiting Black and Hispanic families than for white families, perhaps partially accounting for minority children's more positive outcomes (Manning & Brown, 2006; Osborne et al., 2007).

Divorced and Divorcing Families

Since 1960, divorce rates have tripled in many industrialized nations. Although the divorce rate in the United States is high relative to that in many countries, it has declined over the past three decades from its peak of 5.3 per 1,000 in 1981 to 2.9 in 2018 (National Center for Health Statistics, 2015, 2020). More than one-third of marriages in the United States end in divorce within 15 years (Copen et al., 2012).

For many decades, it was assumed that divorce caused significant and irreparable harm to children. Most researchers today take a neutral stance, viewing divorce as a common transition that many children experience and that poses some challenges to adjustment. Research has suggested that divorce has some negative effects on children's adjustment, such as internalizing and externalizing problems, but the effects are small, vary by particular outcome, are often transient, and do not apply to all children uniformly (Amato & Anthony, 2014; Weaver & Schofield, 2015). Variations in child, parent, and family characteristics and contexts influence children's adjustment to parental divorce, but most children show improved adjustment within two years after the divorce, suggesting that the majority of children of divorce are resilient (Lamb, 2012). What initially appear to be effects of divorce are likely to be a complex combination of parent, child, and contextual factors that precede and follow the divorce, in conjunction with the divorce itself (Amato & Anthony, 2014; Zemp & Bodenmann, 2018).

Divorce triggers a reconfiguration of family roles, and parenting responsibilities shift disproportionately onto the custodial parent. After divorce, children are typically raised by their mothers and experience a drop in income that influences their access to resources and opportunities, such as after-school programs and activities (Bratberg & Tjøtta, 2008). Single-parent-headed households often move to more affordable housing, causing additional changes in children's school, community, and circle of friends, which may reduce children's access to social support and opportunities to play with friends. Custodial parents might also increase the hours they work, leading to less contact with their children. These changes contribute to inconsistencies in family routines, activities, and parental monitoring prior to, during, and after the divorce. High-quality family relationships, including positive interactions with the noncustodial parent and low levels of parent-parent conflict, can buffer children against these stressors (Bastaits & Mortelmans, 2016; Weaver & Schofield, 2015).

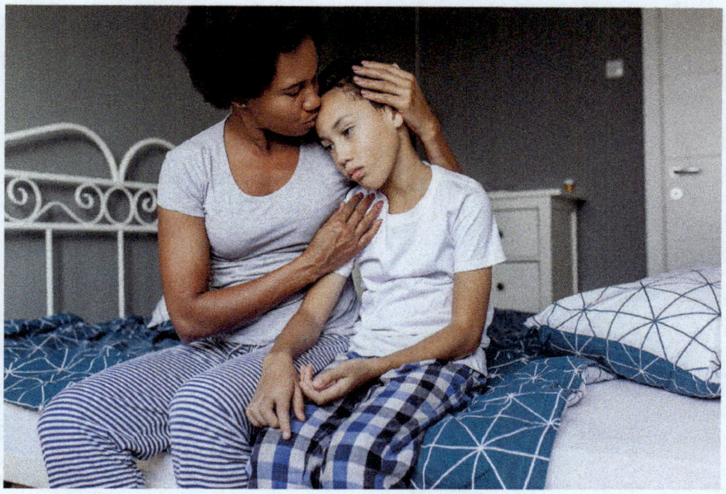

Divorce tends to be preceded by a period of parental conflict and uncertainty, and the tension may continue for several years after the divorce. These processes understandably take a toll on children's emotional and psychological health.

istock/ Riska

Divorce tends to be preceded by a period of uncertainty and tension, often characterized by increases in conflict between parents that may continue for several years after the divorce (Amato, 2010). In fact, harmful family processes, such as parental conflict, poor parent-child interactions, and ineffective parenting strategies, may precede parental divorce by as much as 8 to 12 years (Drapeau et al., 2009; Potter, 2010). These processes understandably take a toll on children's emotional and psychological health. Chronic exposure to parental conflict is associated with increased physiological arousal, an elevated stress response, and poorer adjustment (Davidson et al., 2014; Davies & Martin, 2014; Van Eldik et al., 2020). In turn, the consequences of children's difficulties adapting, such as behavior problems, can increase parental conflict (Drapeau et al., 2009). Longitudinal research following children of married parents has found that children whose parents later divorce show many of the problems typical of children of divorce, such as anxiety, depression, delinquency, and poor academics, long before the divorce takes place (Strohschein, 2005). But not all parents display high levels of conflict. When researchers take into account the quality of parenting and children's exposure to conflict, the link between parental divorce and children's adjustment lessens, suggesting that parenting strategies and relationships are more important influences on children's adjustment than divorce (Bing et al., 2009; Sanders & Kirby, 2014).

Blended Families

About 15% of U.S. children live in a blended family: a family composed of a biological parent and a nonrelated adult, most commonly a mother and stepfather (Pew Research Center, 2015). Blended families, also sometimes referred to as stepfamilies or reconstituted families, present children with new challenges and adjustments, as the multiple transitions entailed by divorce and remarriage are stressful. It is often difficult for blended families to integrate and balance the many relationships among custodial, noncustodial, and stepparents, in addition to grandparents and extended family members (Nixon et al., 2016). As stepfamilies become more complex, that is, as the number of biologically and nonbiologically related individuals in the family increases, so do challenges to children's adjustment (Brown et al., 2015).

Age influences adaptation to a blended family. School-age children and adolescents tend to display more difficulties in adjusting to remarriage than do younger children (Ganong, Coleman & Russell, 2015). Although adjusting to being part of a blended family may pose challenges, most children reared in stepfamilies do not differ from those raised in single-parent families in terms of cognitive, academic, and social outcomes (Ganong & Coleman, 2017). Many are similar to children in first-marriage families. Indeed, entering a stepfamily is associated with improved adjustment, especially when it results in an increase in family income (Ryan et al., 2015). Overall, blended families adapt more easily and children show better adjustment when stepparents build a warm friendship with the child and adopt their new roles slowly rather than rushing or forcing relationships (Doodson & Morley, 2006; Zemp & Bodenmann, 2018).

Thinking in Context: Lifespan Development

1. How do parent-child interactions change during middle childhood? Parents and children influence each other dynamically. Provide examples of how children influence their parents and are also influenced by their parents.

2. Compare children's experiences in single parent, cohabiting parent, divorcing family, and blended family homes. What opportunities and challenges does each family constellation offer for children's development?
3. Family constellations often differ in factors such as race and SES and correlates of SES, such as home and neighborhood environment and contact with adults. How might differences in contextual factors influence children's adjustment? What conclusions do you draw about the challenges of disentangling these interrelations to predict child development?

RISK AND RESILIENCE IN MIDDLE CHILDHOOD

LEARNING OBJECTIVE

8.6 Describe risks to children's development and the role of resilience in promoting adjustment to adversity.

Children are immersed in a collection of shifting contexts that influence and are influenced by them. Individual characteristics and the contexts in which children are embedded pose both opportunities and risks for development. **Risk factors** are individual and contextual variables associated with a higher likelihood of negative outcomes. In contrast, contexts also include **protective factors**, which may reduce or protect children from the poor outcomes associated with adverse circumstances. All children are exposed to both risk and protective factors, but the specific factors and their ratio varies.

Parental Incarceration

By age 14, about 1 in 14 U.S. children experiences a resident parent leaving for jail or prison (Poehlmann-Tynan & Turney, 2020). Children with parents who are incarcerated tend to show more psychological and behavioral problems, such as anxiety, symptoms of trauma, health vulnerabilities, antisocial behavior, and delinquency (Arditti & Johnson, 2020; Kjellstrand et al., 2020; Poehlmann-Tynan & Turney, 2020; Turney & Goodsell, 2018; Wildeman et al., 2018).

Children of color and low-income children are disproportionately likely to experience parental incarceration, and their adjustment to parental incarceration is associated with the contextual factors that are intertwined with race and SES (Bruns & Lee, 2019). Children with incarcerated parents often experience multiple co-occurring adversities before and after incarceration, including family instability, parental substance use, parenting stress, poverty, residential instability, and homelessness (Arditti & Johnson, 2020; Wildeman et al., 2018). The circumstances surrounding the incarceration—such as witnessing criminal activity, arrest, or judicial proceedings—may be traumatic, posing further risks to children's well-being. Children with incarcerated parents may experience stigma, and shame may impede their social interactions, relationships, and learning at school, with peers, and in the community (Turney & Goodsell, 2018).

Within the home context, incarceration increases economic hardship and strains family processes, with implications for parenting. Parental incarceration is stressful for caregivers, posing mental health risks which may negatively impact parenting. Children with incarcerated parents are more likely to experience harsh punishment and less supervision than their peers (Arditti & Johnson, 2020). They are also more likely to enter the child welfare system (Berger et al., 2016; de Haan et al., 2019). Close, nurturing relationships between youth and their caregivers can help children and families adapt to the emotional and social challenges of parental incarceration and promote children's well-being (Smith, 2019).

Parental Deployment

More than one-third of the 1.6 million active duty military members in the United States had children in 2019 (Department of Defense, 2020). A parent's deployment (transition to active duty) places great demands on the family as it includes parental separation and the risk of injury or death of the service member (Wright et al., 2013). The at-home spouse experiences additional responsibilities and stress as they adjust to single parenting. Children with deployed parents experience unique stressors, such as indirect exposure to and awareness of conflict and violence and exposure to a family member who may return from combat with psychological or physical injuries (Park, 2011).

Children with a deployed parent tend to experience more emotional and behavioral difficulties than civilian peers, and that tends to increase with deployment length (Cramm et al., 2019; Foran et al., 2017; Mustillo et al., 2016). Because deployment is associated with imminent danger of parental injury or even death, these symptoms likely are due to greater worries (Cunitz et al., 2019). Although anxiety symptoms are common, behavioral problems are more varied and not consistently found (Williamson et al., 2018). Military families tend to experience economic stability and the support of a community of other military families, which aids them in coping with adversity.

Children and families are often surprised to find that the parent's return from active duty and reintegration into the family and community is stressful for children, spouses, and marriages. Children's adjustment is influenced by the length of parental deployment and parental distress—of both the at-home spouse and returned parent (Maholmes, 2012; Williamson et al., 2018). The returning parent's adjustment influences their spouse and children. In studies of combat veterans returning from war, anger, aggression, and PTSD are frequently reported problems (Mathewson-Chapman & Chapman, 2020; Russell & Russell, 2019). PTSD symptoms affect parenting behaviors, child discipline and supervision, and involvement and interest in the child's activities, resulting in impaired parent-child interactions (Banneyer et al., 2017; Giff et al., 2019). PTSD symptoms in parents are associated with anxiety, depression, and behavioral problems in children (Cramm et al., 2019; Foran et al., 2017). Successful interventions address the family's stress and aid parent and child adjustment with education about stress, emotion regulation skills, problem-solving skills, parenting, and family communication (Creech et al., 2014).

Exposure to Community Violence

Many children are exposed to violence within their communities. Traumatic experiences may be particularly challenging for school-age children, as they are able to understand the gravity of the situation but have not yet developed the emotion regulation, abstract reasoning, and psychosocial maturity to process such events (Saraiya et al., 2013). Children exposed to acts of violence may show anxiety and symptoms of PTSD, fear of being alone, safety concerns, difficulty eating and sleeping, academic problems, and behavior problems such as aggression (Huesmann et al., 2016; Slone & Mann, 2016). Children who are exposed to community violence tend to be less socially aware, less skilled, and display more aggressive and disruptive behavior than other children (McMahon et al., 2013).

Parents influence how children process their experiences. Parents' ability to regulate their own experience of trauma and manage their stress and emotions influences children's adjustment (Halevi et al., 2016). The parental distress, frustration, and sense of helplessness that accompany community violence can compromise parenting and is associated with harsh, controlling parenting (Guo et al., 2018; Sim et al., 2018). When dealing with their own grief, fear, and anxiety, parents may be less available for physical and emotional caregiving, which in turn predicts poor child adjustment (Farver et al., 2005). They also experience heightened risk for depression, posing risks to parenting (Dempsey et al., 2016; Jacoby et al., 2017). Parents face many challenges, but those who are able to instill a sense of warmth and security are best able to support their children's needs and promote well-being (Saraiya et al., 2013). Effective interventions to combat the effects of community violence support parents and provide children with safe spaces, such as after-school community centers, that allow children to interact with each other and caring adults in a safe context that permits them to develop skills in coping, conflict resolution, and emotional regulation.

Child Sexual Abuse

Child maltreatment, discussed in Chapter 6, remains common in middle childhood. One form of maltreatment, sexual abuse, is particularly prevalent at this age. Sexual abuse refers to inappropriate touching, comments, or sexual activity, whether coerced or persuaded, with a child.

Sexual abuse may occur at any time during infancy, childhood, or adolescence, but it is most often reported in middle childhood, with about half of cases occurring between ages 4 and 12 (U.S. Department of Health and Human Services, 2018). Once considered rare, child sexual abuse is now understood as a widespread problem around the world (Hillis et al., 2016). It is estimated that about one-quarter to one-third of U.S. children under the age of 17 have experienced sexual abuse (Finkelhor et al., 2014).

Many cases are unreported (Leclerc & Wortley, 2015). Older children are more likely to disclose sexual abuse, whereas sexual abuse of young children is most likely discovered accidentally, through eyewitness detection or in response to questions (Alaggia et al., 2018). Girls are more often victims of sexual abuse, but boys are much less likely to report abuse (Gagnier & Collin-Vézina, 2016). It is often difficult for children who are sexually abused to cope and heal because sexual abuse often is not a one-time event; some children experience sexual abuse that persists for years.

Reported cases of child sexual abuse are more common in homes characterized by poverty, food and housing insecurity, marital instability, and drug and alcohol abuse (Assink et al., 2019; U.S. Department of Health and Human Services, 2018). Children who are raised in homes in which adults come and go—repeated marriages, separations, and revolving romantic partners—are at higher risk of sexual abuse. However, sexual abuse also occurs in intact families and at all socioeconomic levels. Some researchers argue that maltreatment is more likely to be discovered in children of disadvantaged families than in children at higher socioeconomic levels because disadvantaged children are likelier to come into contact with social services, such as when parents seek welfare and other forms of financial assistance or when parental substance use is discovered (Kim et al., 2018).

Perpetrators of sexual abuse are most often males whom the child knows, trusts, and has frequent contact with, such as parents, stepparents, and live-in boyfriends; stepfathers are likelier than fathers to be perpetrators (U.S. Department of Health and Human Services, 2018). Most sexual assaults occur in the home of the victim or the perpetrator, not in dark alleys or during abduction by a stranger (Kenny, 2018).

Boys and girls show similar emotional responses to sexual abuse, including symptoms of anxiety and depression and behavioral responses such as social withdrawal, aggression, sleep disturbances, poor academic achievement, and risky behaviors (Maikovich-Fong & Jaffee, 2010; Pérez-Fuentes et al., 2013; Waid-Lindberg & Mohr, 2019). Childhood sexual abuse is associated with problems in adolescence and adulthood, including depression, anxiety, PTSD, antisocial behavior, substance dependence, difficulty managing stress, risky sexual activity, and suicide attempts (Jones et al., 2013; Kenny et al., 2020; Pérez-González et al., 2017).

Child sexual abuse is most common in middle childhood. Sexual abuse often is not a one-time event; some children experience sexual abuse that persists for years.

iStock/ ljubaphoto

Prevention and early identification of sexual abuse are essential because children display more positive adjustment when it is identified and stopped early (Fryda & Hulme, 2015). Effective prevention and early identification of sexual abuse rely on training parents and teachers to recognize the signs of abuse and report suspicions to law enforcement and child protection agencies. Children tend to experience fewer long-term consequences of abuse if the child's account is believed, the abuse is stopped, and the home environment is structured, stable, and nurturing (Kenny, 2018). In addition to targeting parents, caregivers, and other adults, effective prevention programs educate children about their bodies and their right to not be touched. When children are exposed to school-based education programs that help them learn how to recognize inappropriate touches, they are more apt to report them to teachers and other

TABLE 8.4 ■ Characteristics of Effective Child Sexual Abuse Prevention Programs

Characteristic	Description
Early identification	Train parents and teachers to recognize the risk factors and early signs of sexual abuse and report suspicions to law enforcement and child protection agencies.
Educate children	Educate children in a developmentally appropriate way about their bodies and their rights to not be touched. Provide children with the vocabulary to describe their bodies. Help children learn how to recognize inappropriate touches and learn what to do if touched.
Engage parents	Educate parents and assist them in discussing sexual abuse prevention with their children. Encourage them to support school efforts by discussing school activities.
Repeat exposure	Repeatedly expose children to the material in school and at home via homework and discussions with parents.
Strengthen parenting and families	Provide parents with support, parenting education, and other resources to help them improve the bond with their child, reducing children's attention-seeking behaviors.

adults (Brassard & Fiorvanti, 2015). Table 8.4 summarizes characteristics of effective sexual abuse prevention programs.

Resilience in Middle Childhood

We have discussed a variety of risk factors that pose threats to healthy development and functioning, such as exposure to violence, child maltreatment, and poverty (Luthar et al., 2015; Masten et al., 2016). Risk factors are cumulative and their effects interact—adjustment becomes more challenging as children and families are faced with more threats (Ungar, 2015). Children show a range of outcomes in response to adversity. Poor responses include psychological, behavioral, and health problems, such as anxiety, depression, frequent illnesses and hospitalizations, poor academic achievement, and delinquent activity (Cutuli et al., 2017). Each of these, in turn, pose cascading risks to future development and adjustment.

Some children exposed to intense stressors, such as maltreatment, display little trauma and are able to manage their anxiety to succeed at home and school; they maintain high self-esteem, low levels of depression, and few behavioral problems (Cicchetti, 2016; Pérez-González et al., 2017). These children display **resilience**, the ability to respond or perform positively in the face of adversity, to achieve despite the presence of disadvantages, or to significantly exceed expectations given poor home, school, and community circumstances (Cutuli et al., 2021).

Adaptation to adversity is a dynamic process involving interactions among a child's developmental capacities and his or her changing context, which includes both risk factors and protective factors. Protective factors may help shield children from risk factors, buffering the poor outcomes that accompany adverse circumstances and contexts. Protective factors may arise from within the child, from the family or extended family, and from the community (Traub & Boynton-Jarrett, 2017; Twum-Antwi et al., 2020). Warm relationships with caregivers and other adults, active engagement at school and in the community, participation in routines, and church attendance are protective factors that promote adjustment and can reduce the negative outcomes associated with adversity (Masten & Monn, 2015; Ungar, 2015).

Resilient individuals tend to have personal characteristics that protect them from adversity and help them learn from experience, such as an easy temperament, a sense of competence, self-control, good information processing and problem-solving skills, friendliness, and empathy (Afifi & MacMillan, 2011; Domhardt et al., 2015; Masten et al., 2016; Twum-Antwi et al., 2020). A fundamental

TABLE 8.5 ■ Characteristics of Resilient Children

Individual Competencies	Family Competencies and Characteristics	School and Community Characteristics
Coping skills	Close relationships with parents and caregivers	Access to local churches
Easy temperament	Organized home	After-school programs
Emotional regulation abilities	Parental involvement in children's education	Availability of emergency services
Good cognitive abilities	Positive family climate	Mentoring programs and opportunities to form relationships with adults
Intelligence	Postsecondary education of parents	Health care availability
Positive outlook	Provision of support	Instruction in conflict management
Positive self-concept	Religiosity and engagement with the church	Opportunity to develop and practice leadership skills
Religiosity	Socioeconomic advantage	Peer programs, such as big brother/big sister programs
Self-efficacy (feeling of control over one's destiny)	Warm but assertive parenting	Programs to assist in developing self-management skills
Talents valued by others		Public safety
		Support networks outside of the family, such as supportive adults and peers
		Ties to prosocial organizations
		Well-funded schools with highly qualified teachers
		Youth programs

Source: Adapted from Child Trends, 2013.

characteristic of resilience is the ability to regulate one's emotions and behavior. Resilient individuals also have a proactive orientation, take initiative, believe in their own effectiveness, and have a positive sense of self (Brodie et al., 2019; Luthar et al., 2015; Pérez-González et al., 2017).

Children's adjustment is influenced by the balance of risk and protective factors they experience. The more risks children face, such as residing in poor and dangerous communities, the more likely they are to experience difficulties with adjustment and development.

Chris Hondros/Newsmakers

Avenues for fostering resilience include promoting children's strengths and bolstering children's executive function skills, self-appraisals, and sense of efficacy (Ellis et al., 2017; Traub & Boynton-Jarrett, 2017; Twum-Antwi et al., 2020). Resilience is accompanied by strong and supportive relationships with caregivers or adults who provide warm guidance and firm support (Arditti & Johnson, 2020; Labella & Masten, 2018). Effective supports for children at risk target parents' mental health and self-care skills, aid parents in establishing routines, promote parenting skills, and help parents understand the impact of trauma on children (Masten & Monn, 2015; Ungar, 2015).

Table 8.5 illustrates characteristics that promote resilience in children. Resilient children illustrate an important finding: Exposure to adversity in childhood does not necessarily lead to maladjustment; many children thrive despite challenging experiences.

Thinking in Context: Lifespan Development

1. Do you think the same risk and protective factors influence adjustment to different challenges, such as coping with parental incarceration, parental deployment, the experience of child maltreatment, or exposure to violence? Or do the factors that promote adaptation vary by the type of adversity? Why?
2. What are some barriers to the prevention and early reporting of child sexual maltreatment? What factors might influence children's and adults' awareness of sexual abuse? What might determine whether abuse is reported?
3. Consider the problem of community violence from a bioecological systems perspective:
   a. Identify at least one microsystem, mesosystem, and exosystem factor that might be influenced by exposure to community violence.
   b. In turn, how might microsystem, mesosystem, and exosystem factors influence children's risk of experiencing community violence?
   c. Can you identify factors at each ecological level that might help children and families cope with community violence?

CHAPTER SUMMARY

8.1 Describe school-age children's self-conceptions, self-evaluations, and motivation.

School-age children's conceptions of themselves become more sophisticated, organized, and accurate. They incorporate feedback about their abilities from parents, teachers, and peers as well as engage in social comparison to derive a sense of self-esteem. A mastery orientation, characterized by internal attribution and growth mindset, is associated with academic success. A learned helplessness orientation is associated with poor performance. Parents and teachers who are warm and supporting promote a mastery orientation.

8.2 Examine the process of moral development in childhood, including children's reasoning about fairness and justice.

By 6 years of age, children enter the first stage of Piaget's theory of morality, heteronomous morality, in which they view rules as absolute and unalterable. In middle childhood, at about age 7, children enter the second stage of Piaget's scheme, autonomous morality, when they begin to see rules as products of group agreement and tools to improve cooperation. Also adopting a cognitive-developmental perspective, Lawrence Kohlberg believed that children's reasoning about justice progresses from preconventional reasoning governed by self-interest to, in late childhood, conventional moral reasoning guided by perspective-taking and motivated by reciprocity. Children's reasoning about distributive justice also progresses from self-serving reasons to those motivated by equity. School-age children also distinguish between moral and conventional issues and those that concern personal choice.

8.3 Discuss gender differences, gender stereotypes and beliefs, and gender identity in middle childhood.

Differences in cognitive and social abilities are small or negligible in children. School-age children tend to prefer same-sex peers and express gender stereotypes that influence preferences and views of their own abilities. Children who identify as transgender show similar patterns of stereotyped beliefs as children with a cisgender identity, but transgender children demonstrate more flexible views of gender stereotypes. By around 7 years of age, children demonstrate gender constancy, the awareness that a person's sex is a biological characteristic, and gender rigidity tends to decline. At about 9 to 10 years of age, children grasp the social basis of gender roles and increasingly agree that boys and girls follow their own preferences regardless of social conventions.

8.4 Analyze the role of friendship, peer acceptance, and peer victimization in school-age children's adjustment.

In middle childhood, friendship becomes a reciprocal relationship characterized by intimacy, loyalty, and commitment. Friendships offer opportunities for children to learn relationship skills and influence children's adjustment. Peer acceptance is a source of self-validation and self-esteem. Popular children tend to be helpful, trustworthy, and bright; they are skilled in self-regulation and conflict resolution. Aggressive-rejected and withdrawn-rejected children show poor emotion regulation skills and are at risk for short- and long-term problems. Children who bully tend to be physically and verbally assertive and impulsive, whereas bullied children are more likely to be inhibited, be anxious, and have low self-esteem and poor social and emotional regulation skills. School procedures can play a role in both increasing and decreasing the prevalence of bullying.

8.5 Discuss family relationships in middle childhood and the relations among family structure and children's adjustment.

Parents tend to adapt to children's growing independence by guiding and monitoring behavior from a distance, communicating expectations, using reasoning, and permitting children to be in charge of moment-to-moment decision making. Decades of research has failed to reveal important differences in the adjustment or development of children and adolescents reared by same-sex parents. Children's adjustment is influenced by socioeconomic status and family conflict, characteristics that vary with family structure. Divorce has some negative effects on children's adjustment, but the effects are small, vary by particular outcome, and do not apply to all children. Many of children's emotional, psychological, and behavioral problems stem from exposure to parental conflict before and after the divorce.

8.6 Describe risks to children's development and the role of resilience in promoting adjustment to adversity.

All children are exposed to risk factors, which are individual and contextual variables associated with a higher likelihood of negative outcomes, and protective factors that may reduce or protect children from the poor outcomes associated with adverse circumstances, but the specific factors and their ratio varies. Parental incarceration, parental deployment, and exposure to community violence are challenging situations that pose risks to children's adjustment.

Child sexual abuse poses serious risks to children's physical, psychological, and emotional health. Some children show resilience despite experiencing adversity.

KEY TERMS

achievement motivation (p. 227)
aggressive-rejected children (p. 238)
autonomous morality (p. 229)
bully-victims (p. 240)
bullying (p. 239)
conventional moral reasoning (p. 230)
external attributions (p. 227)
fixed mindset (p. 227)
gender constancy (p. 234)
gender contentedness (p. 235)
growth mindset (p. 227)
heteronomous morality (p. 229)
internal attributions (p. 227)
learned helplessness orientation (p. 227)
mastery orientation (p. 227)
peer acceptance (p. 237)
peer rejection (p. 237)
perceived other-gender typicality (p. 234)
perceived pressure to conform to gender roles (p. 235)
perceived same-gender typicality (p. 234)
popular children (p. 237)
preconventional reasoning (p. 229)
protective factor (p. 248)
relational aggression (p. 239)
resilience (p. 251)
risk factors (p. 248)
withdrawn-rejected children (p. 237)

PART 4 LIFESPAN DEVELOPMENT AT WORK: MIDDLE CHILDHOOD

Much of older children's days are spent at school. Opportunities to work with older children are often in school settings as well as in medical and mental health settings.

Elementary Education

Elementary school teachers provide class instruction to children in grades K through 5 or 6, depending on school. Some elementary schools include children up through grade 8. Although not visible to children and parents, much of elementary school teachers' work is conducted outside of class. They develop educational goals and construct plans for each day of class, including selecting reading and other materials, developing activities, creating lectures, choosing discussion topics and preparing questions, grading student work, recording and assessing student progress, communicating with parents, and submitting reports to administrators. Most people are familiar with elementary school teachers' classroom activity, such as instructing, working to maintain student attention, managing behavior problems, and creating intellectual and emotional connections with students.

Becoming a teacher requires earning a bachelor's degree in education, which includes an internship experience in an elementary school classroom. Some colleges offer intensive 1-year programs for aspiring teachers who hold bachelor's degrees in other fields. Teachers must pass a state licensing or certification exam. Elementary school teachers earned a median salary of about $61,000 in 2020 (U.S. Bureau of Labor Statistics, 2021). Recall that the median is the middle score; half of elementary school teachers earn less than $61,000 and half earn more than $61,000.

Special Education

Special education teachers conduct the same activities as elementary school teachers, but they specialize in working with students who have special education needs, including developmental and learning disabilities. They may assist general education teachers in identifying and assessing children who may have special needs.

Special education teachers work with a team, including the parents, general teacher, counselor or school psychologist, and administrator, to create an individualized education program (IEP) for each student with special needs. The IEP is a detailed plan and set of supports that is the cornerstone of a special needs child's education. Special education teachers adjust class lessons to fit the child's needs, as outlined in the IEP. They monitor students' progress, record their observations and evaluations, update parents on students' progress, and meet with the IEP team to evaluate and adjust learning goals as needed.

Becoming a special education teacher requires a bachelor's degree in special education, including supervised teaching, and passing a certification exam. Some states require a master's degree. In 2020 special education teachers earned a median salary of about $61,000 (U.S. Bureau of Labor Statistics, 2021).

Child Life Specialist

A child's hospitalization poses many challenges for parents and families. Children are often afraid and may not understand why they are away from home and why they are ill. Parents worry about their children and balancing their responsibilities to the hospitalized child, other children, and work. Enter the child life specialist.

Child life specialists work in medical settings to help children and families navigate the process of illness, injury, disability, and hospitalization. They help children and families better understand a process, procedure, or other element of a medical experience. They provide support in the physically and emotionally demanding process of caring for hospitalized or disabled children. Child life specialists help children reduce their anxiety and promote positive development. They apply age-appropriate strategies to minimize children's trauma and improve their understanding of medical diagnoses and treatment plans. They may implement group programs, therapies, and activities with children, such as play activities to encourage free expression, and promote social and emotional development and feelings of competence.

Child life specialists collaborate with healthcare teams to coordinate and manage care. These teams may include social workers, chaplains, nurses, and doctors. They primarily work in hospitals but can also work in medical clinics, hospice, dental offices, schools, camps, and even patients' homes.

Becoming a child life specialist requires a bachelor's degree in child life studies or a related field like social work or psychology. In addition to a bachelor's degree, certification requires a 600-hour internship and a passing score on the Child Life Professional Certification Examination. In 2020 the median salary of child life specialists was about $49,000 (Association of Child Life Professionals, 2021).

Applied Behavior Analyst

Many children engage in challenging behavior that parents and teachers must curb, such as aggressive behavior, disruptive classroom behavior, and impulsivity. Applied behavior analysts identify problematic behaviors and devise treatment plans to modify those behaviors. Applied behavior analyses apply psychological principles to modify people's behavior. They work with people of all ages. Applied behavior analysts who work with children are sometimes called *child behavior specialists*.

Applied behavior analysts work to improve individuals' social, communication, academic, and adaptive skills. They assess children's behavior, work with children and parents to set goals, devise and implement treatments, and monitor change. Applied behavior analysts teach parents, teachers, and support professionals how to implement behavioral interventions, such as operant conditioning and reinforcement, at home, school, and in other settings. They observe children, monitor their progress, and write reports. They communicate with teachers, families, and staff about the children's progress and needs.

Behavior analysts often work in special education settings to help children with special needs learn to regulate their behavior. They are often members of healthcare provider teams and consult with doctors, therapists, and psychologists. They work in hospitals, private clinics, schools, in patients' homes, and in private practice.

Training to become an applied behavior analyst consists of completing a master's degree that includes coursework in behavioral analysis, completing 800–1,500 of supervised experience (depending on placement), and passing the Board Certified Behavior Analyst Exam. In some states applied behavior analysts are licensed as professional counselors. The median salary for a board certified applied behavior analyst was about $61,000 in 2021 (Salary.com, 2021).

Bachelor's degree holders may become assistant behavior analysts and support the work of applied behavior analysts, under their supervision. Assistant applied behavior analysts are required by most states to seek certification and become licensed as board certified assistant behavior analysts. A bachelor's degree with coursework in principles of learning and behavior analysis and ethics, 500–1,000 hours of supervised experience, and a passing score on the Board Certified Assistant Behavior Analyst Certification Examination are basic requirements for becoming a board certified assistant behavior analyst. The median salary for a board certified assistant behavior analyst was about $50,000 in 2021 (Salary.com, 2021).

School Psychologist

There are many different kinds of psychologists. School psychologists work with schoolchildren to improve their educational experience, mental health, and behavior.

School psychologists engage in a range of activities, such as consultation, assessment, intervention and prevention, educational or training services, research, and program development. Educational services may take the form of teaching educators classroom management techniques, learning strategies, and ways to identify at-risk children. School psychologists help teachers and schools by teaching educators how to identify children at risk for learning disorders or mental health problems, providing skills training for parents and teachers to cope with disruptive behavior, and developing school initiatives to promote student social development and create a safe environment, such as anti-bullying and substance use prevention.

School psychologists spend much of their time assessing children. They use instruments and diagnostic tools to evaluate the nature of a student's academic or behavior problem and identify the most appropriate intervention. School psychologists evaluate students' academic skills and learning aptitudes, personality and emotional development, social skills, learning environment and school climate, eligibility for special education, and effectiveness of intervention strategies. They then teach and train children, teachers, parents, and others who interact with the child.

School psychologists also provide counseling for children, parents, and families, such as family therapy, substance abuse counseling, and grief counseling. They counsel individual children and groups of children in skills training, such as social skills, coping strategies, and problem solving.

Becoming a school psychologist requires education beyond the master's degree. School psychologists obtain either a specialist-level degree or a doctoral degree. The specialist-level degree consists of 60 credits, whereas the doctoral degree entails 90 credits. Both specialist and doctoral level complete year-long 1,200-hour supervised internships. School psychologists must seek state licensure, typically by passing an exam. In 2019 school psychologists earned a median salary of about $78,000 (U.S. News & World Report, 2020).

School psychologists spend much of their time assessing children. They use instruments and diagnostic tools to evaluate the nature of a student's academic or behavior problem and identify the most appropriate intervention. School psychologists evaluate students' academic skills and learning aptitudes, personality and emotional development, social skills, learning environment and school climate, eligibility for special education, and the effectiveness of intervention strategies. They then consult with children, teachers, parents, and others who interact with the child.

School psychologists also provide counseling for children, parents, and families, such as family therapy, substance abuse counseling, and grief counseling. They counsel individual children and groups of children in skills training, such as social skills, coping strategies, and problem solving.

Becoming a school psychologist requires education beyond the master's degree. School psychologists obtain either a specialist-level degree or a doctoral degree. The specialist-level degree consists of 60 credits, whereas the doctoral degree entails 90 credits. Both specialist- and doctoral-level completers undergo a 1,200-hour supervised internship. School psychologists must seek state licensure, typically by passing an exam. In 2019 school psychologists earned a median salary of about $76,000 (U.S. News & World Report, 2020).

9 PHYSICAL AND COGNITIVE DEVELOPMENT IN ADOLESCENCE

iStock/ monkeybusinessimages

Imagine a rapid period of change during which you grow taller and heavier and develop new body proportions. These changes describe development in infancy, but also development in the second decade of life, adolescence—the transition from childhood to adulthood. In earlier historical periods (as well as in most developing societies today), childhood was followed nearly immediately by the assumption of adult roles, such as worker, spouse, and parent (Schlegel, 2008; Steinberg & Lerner, 2004). In industrialized societies, education and vocational training are required for employment, an important marker of adulthood; therefore, the passage to adulthood is more gradual. Because of this, adolescence in industrialized societies spans a great many years and can be divided into three phases: early adolescence (11 to 14 years), middle adolescence (14 to 16 years), and late adolescence (16 to 18 years). In addition, many adolescents experience an extended transition to adulthood known as emerging adulthood (age 18 to about age 25), discussed in Chapters 11 and 12 (Arnett, 2016).

PUBERTY

LEARNING OBJECTIVE

9.1 Summarize the physical changes that occur with puberty, correlates of pubertal timing, and influences on pubertal timing.

In contrast to the gradual steady pattern of growth in middle childhood, adolescence is marked by dramatic changes in physical appearance and function. **Puberty** is the biological transition to adulthood, in which adolescents mature physically and become capable of reproduction. It begins in late childhood at about age 8 or 9 in girls and roughly two years later in boys, when the brain signals the endocrine system to increase the release of sex hormones (Berenbaum et al., 2015). Levels of testosterone, responsible for male sex characteristics, and estrogen, responsible for female sex characteristics, increase in boys and girls but in different ratios, leading to different patterns of physical development. Although many people view puberty as an event, it is a process that includes many physical changes that occur over about four years but can vary dramatically from one to seven years (Mendle, 2014). Puberty entails the development of reproductive capacity, but that is not the whole story, for puberty influences a great variety of physical changes beyond those typically associated with sexual maturity, such as changes in body size, shape, and function.

CHANGES IN BODY SHAPE AND SIZE

The first outward sign of puberty is the **adolescent growth spurt**, a rapid gain in height and weight that generally begins in girls at about age 10 (as early as age 7 and as late as 14) and in boys at about age 12 (as early as age 9 and as late as 16; Tinggaard et al., 2012). During this period adolescents grow nearly as fast as infants (Das et al., 2017). The pattern and pace of growth, (see Figure 9.1) is similar for most children (Sanders et al., 2017). Because girls begin their growth spurt about two years before boys, 10- to 13-year-old girls tend to be taller, heavier, and stronger than boys their age. By starting their

FIGURE 9.1 ■ Sequence of Physical Changes During Puberty

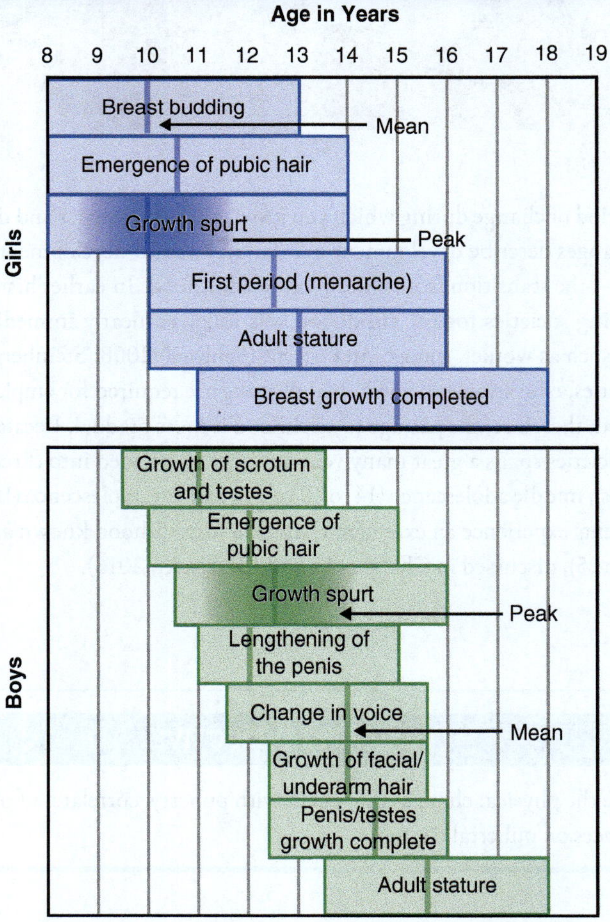

Source: Carolina Hrejsa/ Body Scientific Intl.

growth spurts two years later than girls, boys begin with an extra two years of prepubertal growth on which the adolescent growth spurt builds, leading boys to end up taller than girls (Yousefi et al., 2013). On average, the growth spurt lasts about two years, but growth in height continues at a more gradual pace, ending by about 16 in girls and 18 in boys. Adolescents gain a total of about 10 inches in height.

Young adolescents' physical maturation varies dramatically by individual.

Bob Daemmrich / Alamy Stock Photo

Different parts of the body grow at different rates. The extremities (fingers and toes) grow first; then hands and feet; then arms and legs; and finally, the torso (). Adolescents' bodies therefore tend to appear lanky and awkward, contributing to a temporary increase in clumsiness as adolescents attempt to control their quickly changing bodies. Adolescents' bodies become taller and heavier before their muscles grow stronger and their internal organs mature (DeRose & Brooks-Gunn, 2006).

Sex differences in body shape emerge during the growth spurt. Boys and girls gain fat and muscle, but in different ratios. Girls gain more fat overall, particularly on their legs and hips, so that fat comes to comprise one-fourth of their body weight—nearly twice as much as boys. Boys gain more muscle than do girls, especially in their upper bodies, doubling their arm strength between ages 13 and 18 (Payne & Isaacs, 2020). Bone density increases in both boys and girls, and the respiratory and cardiovascular systems mature. Boys become much better at taking in and using oxygen as their hearts and lungs grow larger and function more effectively and the number of red blood cells increases (Sadler, 2017). Consequently, once puberty has begun, boys consistently outperform girls in athletics (Tønnessen et al., 2015).

Emergence of Secondary Sex Characteristics

Most people associate puberty with the development of **secondary sex characteristics**, body changes that indicate physical maturation but are not directly related to fertility. Examples of changes in secondary sex characteristics include breast development, deepening of the voice, growth of facial and body hair, and, for many, the emergence of acne (Hodges-Simeon et al., 2013).

In girls, rapid increases in estrogen cause the budding of breasts, which tends to accompany the growth spurt as the first signs of puberty (Emmanuel & Bokor, 2017). Testosterone causes boys' voices to deepen. As their voices change, boys may occasionally lose control over their voices and emit unpredictable changes in pitch often experienced as high squeaks, which some refer to as the voice "breaking" (Busch et al., 2019). Girls' voices also deepen, but the change is gradual and not as noticeable as in boys (Berger et al., 2019). Oil and sweat glands become more active, resulting in body odor and acne. Hair on the head, arms, and legs becomes darker, and pubic hair begins to grow, first as straight and downy, later becoming coarse.

Maturation of Primary Sex Characteristics

Maturation of the **primary sex characteristics**, the reproductive organs, is less noticeable than secondary sex characteristics, but is the function of puberty—reproductive maturation. In girls, primary sex characteristics include the ovaries, fallopian tubes, uterus, and vagina. In boys, they include the penis, testes, scrotum, seminal vesicles, and prostate gland.

Menarche

For girls, the onset of sexual maturity occurs with **menarche**, the first menstruation. **Menstruation** refers to the monthly shedding of the uterine lining, which has thickened in preparation for the implantation of a fertilized egg. Menarche occurs toward the end of puberty, yet most adolescents and adults view it as a critical marker of puberty because it occurs suddenly and is memorable (Brooks-Gunn & Ruble, 2013).

In North America, the average age of menarche is 12.25. Most white girls experience menarche shortly before turning 13 (roughly 12.7 years of age) and the average African American girl at about 12 (Emmanuel & Bokor, 2017). Generally, Black girls tend to be heavier and enter puberty about a year earlier, reaching pubertal milestones such as the growth spurt and menarche earlier than other girls (Emmanuel & Bokor, 2017). Hispanic American girls enter puberty at about the same time as Black girls, with some studies suggesting slightly earlier menarche and others later (Biro et al., 2018; Deardorff et al., 2014). Ethnic and racial differences in the onset of puberty, the accompanying body changes, and menarche lead to variations in girls' day-to-day experiences and adjustment, but research on the intersection of ethnicity/race and pubertal timing is scant (Deardorff et al., 2019). Frequently, during the first few months after menarche, menstruation takes place without ovulation, which is the ovaries' release of an ovum (Lacroix & Whitten, 2017). However, this period of temporary sterility is variable and unpredictable.

Girls' perception and experience of menarche is influenced by their knowledge about menstruation as well their expectations (Brooks-Gunn & Ruble, 2013). Generations ago, girls tended to receive little to no information about menarche and were often surprised by it, tended to view it negatively, and were often afraid of it (Costos et al., 2002). Today, menarche still takes most girls by surprise, but most girls in Western countries have some knowledge about it and are not afraid because they have been informed about puberty by health education classes and parents (Stidham-Hall et al., 2012; Wigmore-Sykes et al., 2020).

The extent to which adolescents learn about menarche and sexuality varies by context and culture. In some cultures menstruation is a taboo subject, girls are poorly informed about menarche, and girls can be excluded from interaction with others, including attending school, when they are menstruating (Marván et al., 2017; Behera et al., 2015; Chandra-Mouli & Patel, 2017). Across cultures, girls who view menstruation negatively are more likely to experience it negatively, with more menstrual symptoms and distress (Rembeck et al., 2006).

Spermarche

In boys, the first primary sex characteristic to emerge is the growth of the **testes**, the glands that produce sperm (Tinggaard et al., 2012). About a year later, the penis and scrotum enlarge and pubic hair, a secondary sex characteristic, appears. As the penis grows, the prostate gland and seminal vesicles begin to produce **semen**, the fluid that contains sperm. At about age 13, boys demonstrate a principal sign of sexual maturation: the first ejaculation, known as **spermarche** (Gaddis & Brooks-Gunn, 1985; Tomova et al., 2011). Although some scientists argue that spermarche is similar to menarche because it marks reproductive maturation, spermarche is relatively unstudied given its association with sexual enjoyment (Chad, 2020).

We know less about boys' experience of puberty because the changes that boys experience with puberty are less easily observed than those of girls as they lack easily determined objective markers, such as menarche (Deardorff et al., 2019). Similar to girls, boys who know about ejaculation beforehand are more likely to show positive reactions, such as feeling pleasure, happiness, and pride. Unfortunately, many boys report that health education classes and parents generally do not discuss ejaculation (Omar et al., 2003; Stein & Reiser, 1994). Parents sometimes report discomfort talking with their sons about reproductive development, particularly ejaculation, because of the close link with sexual desire, sexuality, and masturbation (Frankel, 2002).

Pubertal Timing and Adolescent Development

Casual observations of adolescents reveal that, although most tend to progress through puberty at about the same time, some begin much earlier or later than others. Children who show signs of physical maturation before age 8 (in girls) or 9 (in boys) are considered early maturing, whereas girls who begin puberty after age 13 and boys who begin after age 14 are considered late-maturing adolescents (Pyra & Schwarz, 2019). Early maturation, in particular, poses challenges for both girls' and boys' adaptation.

Early Maturation

Adolescents who mature early tend to look older than their years and are more likely to be treated in ways similar to older adolescents, which they may perceive as stressful (Rudolph et al., 2014). Around the world, early maturing boys and girls show higher rates of risky activity, including smoking, alcohol and substance use, and aggressive behavior, as well as internalizing problems such as depression, than do same-age peers (Hamlat et al., 2019; Ullsperger & Nikolas, 2017). Notably, differences between early maturing adolescents and their peers dissipate over adolescence and are indistinguishable after adolescence (Dimler & Natsuaki, 2021).

Early maturation poses specific risks to girls' development. Girls who mature early relative to peers tend to feel less positively about their bodies, physical appearance, and menstruation itself, and they show higher rates of depression, anxiety, low self-esteem, and problem behavior than do girls who mature on time or late (Bucci & Staff, 2020; Copeland et al., 2019; Skoog et al., 2016). Early maturation may pose social risks for girls, such as peer exclusion as well as heightened risk of victimization by, and perpetration of, bullying (Carter, Halawah, et al., 2018; Su et al., 2018). In addition, early maturing girls tend to date earlier than their peers, are at higher risk of dating violence, and experience more sexual harassment than their peers (Chen et al., 2017; Skoog & Bayram Özdemir, 2016).

Early maturing boys tend to be athletic, popular with peers, school leaders, and confident (Stojković, 2013). There is less research on boys than on girls, but it appears that early maturing boys also experience some internalizing and externalizing symptoms, including depression and antisocial and aggressive behavior (Bucci & Staff, 2020;). Like girls, early maturing boys tend to show higher rates of problematic drinking, including consuming alcohol more frequently and in greater quantities, and becoming intoxicated more often, than their on-time and late-maturing peers (Biehl et al., 2007; Schelleman-Offermans et al., 2013).

Early maturation may be particularly challenging for adolescents of color, especially girls, who tend to enter puberty prior to other adolescents. Because they look older than their age, adolescents of color may have different experiences and perceptions of ethnic and racial stereotypes and discrimination than their on-time and late-maturing peers (Deardorff et al., 2019). Ethnicity, race, and sex likely influence how adolescents experience puberty and the effects of pubertal timing. This is an emerging area of study.

Late Maturation

In contrast to early maturation, the effects of late maturation tend to differ markedly for boys and girls. Late maturation appears to have a protective effect on girls with regard to depression (Negriff & Susman, 2011). Because late maturing girls tend to be thin, they tend to experience less teasing about their appearance and have lower rates of appearance-related anxiety as compared with other girls (Zimmer-Gembeck et al., 2018).

Findings regarding the effects of late maturation on boys are mixed and less consistent (Mendle & Ferrero, 2012). Late-maturing boys may experience more social and emotional difficulties, such as anxiety (Carter, 2015). During early adolescence, late-maturing boys may be less well liked by their peers and may be more likely than their peers to experience a poor body image, overall body dissatisfaction, and depression during early adolescence, but these effects tend to decline with physical maturation (Negriff & Susman, 2011).

Context and the Effects of Pubertal Timing

Contextual factors are thought to amplify the effects of pubertal timing on behavior (Natsuaki et al., 2015; Seaton & Carter, 2018). Some of the problems that early maturing boys and girls experience arise because they tend to seek relationships with older peers who are more similar to them in physical maturity than their classmates (Kretsch, Mendle, Cance, et al., 2016). Spending time with older peers makes early maturing adolescents, especially girls, more likely to engage in age-inappropriate behaviors, such as early sexual activity and risky sexual activity (Baams et al., 2015; Moore et al., 2014). The composition of the peer group may also matter. In one study, early pubertal development was associated with a higher risk for experiencing adolescent dating abuse when the early maturing girls' friendship groups included a higher percentage of boys, but not when the friendship groups contained few boys (Chen et al., 2017).

The school context influences the effects of pubertal timing. When elementary school teachers were shown drawings of girls at varying stages of pubertal development, many expected early developing girls to have more academic and social problems relative to other girls (Carter, Mustafaa, et al., 2018). In addition, they expected Black early developers to experience more problems than white early developers, possibly suggesting that race and ethnicity may influence adults' expectations and thereby girls' experience of early puberty. In fact, African American and Caribbean Black girls who perceive themselves as early maturing report more experiences with discrimination relative to their peers (Seaton & Carter, 2019).

Racial identity can influence the effects of pubertal timing. Among early maturing Black adolescent girls, those who reported race as an important aspect of their identity were more likely to experience depressive symptoms when they attended mixed-race schools and believed that others held Blacks in poor regard (Seaton & Carter, 2018). The stress that accompanies perceived discrimination may pose serious risks to adaptation, but the effects are complicated and depend on contextual factors. Pubertal development influences girls' sense of self and may interact with their other self-relevant beliefs—as well as the social and racial contexts in which they are immersed—to influence their responses (Seaton & Carter, 2018, 2020).

Biological and Contextual Influences on Pubertal Timing

Puberty is a complex trait influenced by many genes that interact with contextual factors (Horvath et al., 2020; Zhu et al., 2018). In support of the role of genetics, pubertal timing for both boys and girls tends to be similar to that of their parents (Wohlfahrt-Veje et al., 2016). Identical twins (who share 100% of their genes) experience menarche more closely in time than fraternal twins (who share only 50% of their genes; Kretsch et al., 2016). Heredity sets the boundaries of pubertal timing, the earliest and latest age when we might begin puberty. But the onset of puberty and whether it is early or late relative to our inherited range is influenced by more than genes. Contextual influences and life experiences play a role in determining when a child begins puberty.

Puberty is triggered by achieving a critical level of body weight, specifically body fat (Das et al., 2017). Girls with a greater body mass index (BMI), especially those who are obese, mature earlier than their peers, and girls who have a low percentage of body fat, whether from athletic training or severe dieting, often experience menarche late relative to other girls (Currie et al., 2012; Tomova, 2016).

In contrast, extreme malnutrition can prevent the accumulation of adequate fat stores needed to support pubertal development so that menarche is delayed. In many parts of Africa, menarche does not occur until ages 14 to 17, several years later than in Western nations (Tunau et al., 2012). Similarly, some research suggests that weight affects the onset and tempo of puberty in boys, with higher BMI and obesity associated with earlier puberty, but less so as compared with girls and the mechanism is not well understood (Busch et al., 2020; Lee et al., 2016; Tinggaard et al., 2012).

Adolescents' social contexts, especially exposure to stress, influence pubertal timing (Joos et al., 2018; Tremblay & Larivière, 2020). Early life stress and the experience of severe stress, such as sexual abuse and maltreatment, can speed the onset of menarche (Negriff et al., 2015; Noll et al., 2017). Similarly, poor family relationships, harsh parenting, family stress and conflict, parents' marital conflict, and anxiety are associated with early menarche in North American and European girls (Graber et al., 2010; Rickard et al., 2014). In industrialized countries such as the United States, Canada, and New Zealand, girls who are raised by single mothers experience puberty earlier than those raised in two-parent homes (Mendle et al., 2006). In addition, the absence of a biological father and the presence in the home of a biologically unrelated male, such as a stepfather or a mother's live-in boyfriend, is associated with earlier onset of menarche (Deardorff et al., 2011; Webster et al., 2014). Household stress, economic adversity, and father absence may hold similar implications for boys' pubertal development, speeding it (); there is much less research on boys' development (Joos et al., 2018).

Contextual factors outside the home also influence pubertal timing. Adolescents who live in similar contextual conditions, especially those of socioeconomic advantage, reach menarche at about the same age, despite having different genetic backgrounds (Tremblay & Larivière, 2020). Low socioeconomic status is associated with early pubertal onset in the United States, Canada, and the UK and may account for some of the ethnic differences in pubertal timing (Kelly et al., 2017; Sun et al., 2017b). For example, African American and Latina girls tend to reach menarche before white girls, but they are also disproportionately likely to live in low-SES homes and neighborhoods. Ethnic differences in the timing of menarche are reduced or even disappear when researchers control for the influence of socioeconomic status (Deardorff et al., 2014; Obeidallah et al., 2000). That is, girls growing up in low-SES contexts may experience more stress at home and in the community and may have less access to healthy foods and opportunities for safe physical activity. In developing countries such as Pakistan, Iran, India, and Indonesia, however, low socioeconomic status is associated with delayed puberty as it is also associated with undernutrition and malnutrition (Karim et al., 2021; Nasiri et al., 2020; Öztürk & Güneri, 2020; Singh & Singh, 2020).

The influence of contextual conditions and physical health in triggering puberty is thought to underlie the **secular trend**, or the lowering of the average age of puberty with each generation from prehistoric to the present times (see Figure 9.2; Ohlsson et al., 2019; Papadimitriou, 2016b). Through the 18th century in Europe, puberty occurred as late as age 17; between 1860 and 1970, the age of menarche declined by about three to four months per decade (Tanner, 1990). Since 1977 the age of menarche has declined by about six months per decade in China, and in Western countries girls' breast development began on average almost 3 months earlier per decade (Eckert-Lind et al., 2020; Meng et al., 2017).

FIGURE 9.2 ■ Secular Trend in Girls' Pubertal Development, 1830–2012

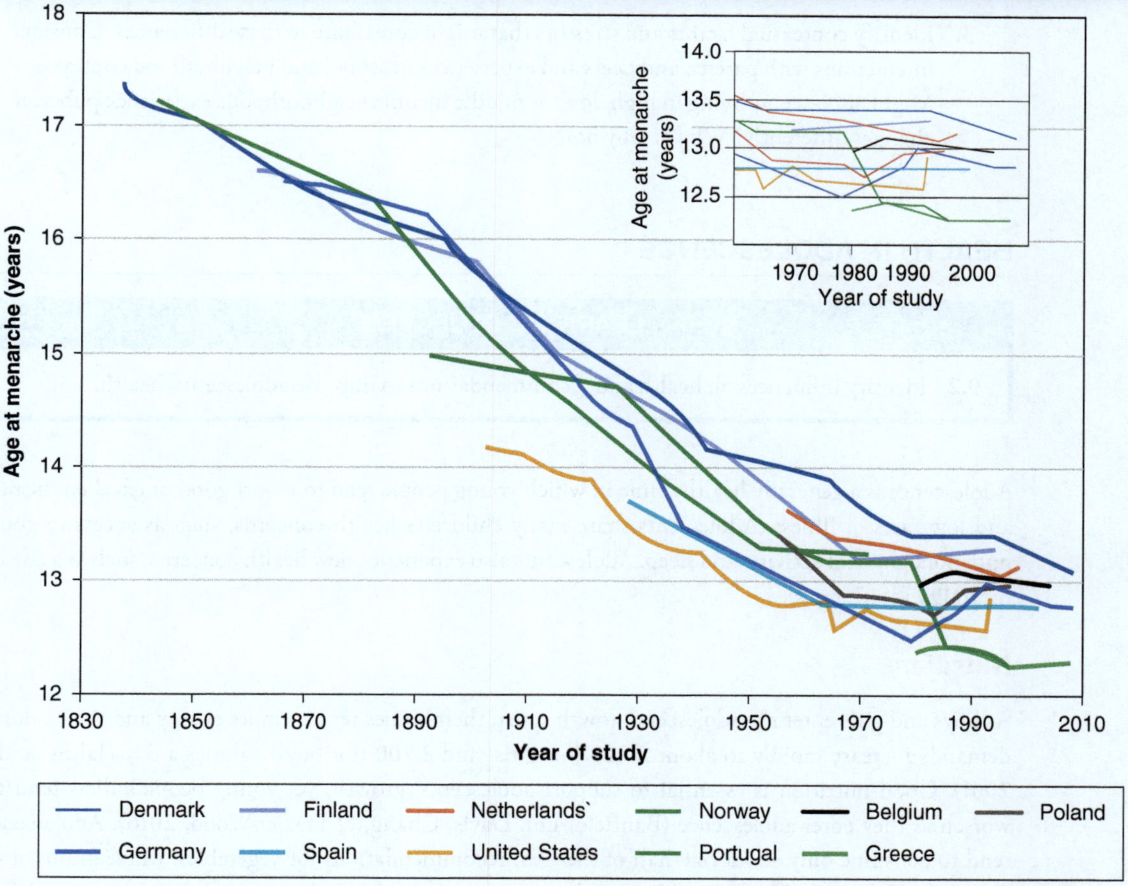

Source: Sørensen et al. (2012).

Boys in the United States and Canada begin puberty at least 1 to 1½ years earlier today than in the 1960s (Herman-Giddens, 2006; Herman-Giddens et al., 2012). The secular trend parallels increases in the standard of living and average BMI among children in developed countries and is especially influenced by the growing problem of childhood obesity (Biro et al., 2012; Bygdell et al., 2014; Ohlsson et al., 2019). The secular trend poses challenges for young people and parents because the biological entry to adolescence is lowering at the same time as the passage to adulthood is lengthening, making the period of adolescence longer than ever before. However, there are some indications that the secular trend has slowed or perhaps even stopped in many industrialized nations (Kleanthous et al., 2017; Papadimitriou, 2016a; Piras et al., 2020).

Thinking in Context: Biological Influences

Compare menarche and semenarche. How are they similar and different? Compare boys' and girls' experiences and perceptions.

Thinking in Context: Lifespan Development

In what ways might pubertal changes influence adolescents' behavior? What are some of the social implications of sex differences in body growth, such as how adolescents interact with and are treated by others? How might girls' earlier maturation contribute to sex differences in behavior?

Thinking in Context: Intersectionality

1. Examine racial and ethnic differences in pubertal development and timing.
2. In what ways do the experience and correlates of puberty vary with race and ethnicity?
3. Identify contextual factors and stressors that might contribute to these differences. Consider interactions with parents and peers and experiences in school and neighborhood contexts. Might adolescents living in high, low, or middle income neighborhoods experience pubertal changes differently? Why or why not?

HEALTH IN ADOLESCENCE

LEARNING OBJECTIVE

9.2 Identify influences on health and recommendations to improve adolescents' health.

Adolescence is a generally healthy time in which young people tend to report good or excellent health and low rates of illness. Adolescents share many children's health concerns, such as access to good nutrition, physical activity, and sleep. Adolescents also experience new health concerns, such as a rise in mortality (death rates).

Nutrition

As boys and girls enter the adolescent growth spurt, their bodies require more energy and their caloric demands increase rapidly to about 2,200 (for girls) and 2,700 (for boys) calories a day (Jahns et al., 2001). Good nutrition is essential to support adolescents' growth, yet young people's diets tend to worsen as they enter adolescence (Banfield, Liu, Davis, Chang, & Frazier-Wood, 2016). Adolescents tend to consume only about one-half of the U.S. recommendations for vegetables, whole grains, and fruits (Banfield et al., 2016). In addition, adolescents tend to skip meals, especially breakfast, and drink less milk—and this pattern increases over the high school years, especially in girls (Demissie et al., 2018; Stang & Stotmeister, 2017).

Fast food consumption tends to increase during adolescence and is associated with less consumption of fruits and vegetables, more sugary drink and snack food intake, and more sedentary activity (Gopinath et al., 2016; Scully et al., 2020). When a fast food restaurant is near a school, students in the U.S., U.K., Australia, and Finland show more irregular eating habits, greater consumption of fast food, and higher rates of overweight and obesity (Janssen et al., 2018; Virtanen et al., 2015).

Good nutrition is essential to support adolescents' growth, yet young people's diets tend to worsen as they enter adolescence.

iStock/p_ponomareva

Family meals are an important way of establishing healthy eating habits. Adolescents who eat an evening meal with parents tend to have healthier eating habits, including more fruits and vegetables, a lower BMI, and greater self-control over eating than their peers who do not share family meals (de Wit et al., 2015; Watts et al., 2017). Family dinners benefit both adolescents' and parents' well-being, including fewer depressive symptoms, lower levels of stress, and better family functioning (Utter et al., 2017, 2018). Adolescents who have more frequent meals with parents report better parent-child communication, emotional support, and connection with parents and more time spent with parents (Brown et al., 2019). Family meals offer the opportunity to turn off the television and other devices with screens, get adolescents involved with meal preparation, provide foods with higher nutritional quality, and make time for the family to talk and connect and for parents to model healthy eating (Dallacker et al., 2019). However, the frequency of family dinners drops sharply between ages 9 and 14, and family dinners have become less common in recent decades (Walton & Spencer, 2009).

Physical Activity and Exercise

Physical activity promotes cardiovascular health, muscle strength, motor control, cognitive performance, mental health, and well-being in adolescents (Esteban-Cornejo et al., 2015; McMahon et al., 2017). As in childhood, adolescents who regularly engage in physical activity show better cognitive function, including selective attention, processing speed, and general self-efficacy (Reigal et al., 2020). Physical activity is associated with brain development, including myelination and the activation of regions responsible for cognitive processes and self-regulation, which have a protective effect on mental health and are associated with reduced risk for depression (Belcher et al., 2020; Biddle et al., 2019; Valkenborghs et al., 2019).

Physical activity tends to decline beginning in middle childhood, about age 7 (Farooq et al., 2018). Maturational timing, specifically the onset of puberty, is associated with declines in physical activity and increases in sedentary behavior in boys and girls (Moore et al., 2020). Most adolescents in the U.S. do not meet the federal recommendation of at least 60 minutes of moderate to vigorous physical activity every day. It is estimated that only about 8% of 12- to 15-year-old adolescents are active for 60 minutes per day on at least 5 days per week (Kann et al., 2014). Although some teens engage in competitive sports, average levels of physical activity decrease throughout adolescence, and many adolescents engage in no regular exercise or activity (Dumith et al., 2011; Farooq et al., 2018). Schools play a role in promoting physical fitness through physical education classes. But participation in physical education is highest among students in 9th grade, decreases among 10th- and 11th-grade students, and is lowest among 12th-grade students (Kann et al., 2014).

Longitudinal research with U.S. adolescents has shown that the declines in physical activity during adolescence are consistent across contextual settings, whether rural or urban, and across SES (Metcalf et al., 2015). Adolescents of low SES are more likely to be sedentary and obese than their more affluent peers; this holds true for adolescents from a variety of developed nations, such as Canada, England,

Finland, France, and the United States (Frederick et al., 2014; Mielke et al., 2017; Wang & Lim, 2012). Socioeconomic disparities are linked with opportunities for physical activity, such as the availability of safe parks and outdoor spaces and opportunities for extracurricular activities in the school and community (Gavand et al., 2019; Watts et al., 2016). After-school and community sports teams may be more prominent and available in middle income and affluent communities.

Sleep

Adolescents are often depicted as night owls, late risers, and grumpy in the morning. Unlike many stereotypes about adolescents, common depictions of adolescent sleep patterns are often accurate. During puberty a shift occurs in adolescents' sleep patterns and preferred sleep schedule, known as a **delayed phase preference** (Carskadon & Tarokh, 2014). Delayed phase preference is triggered by a change in the nightly release of a hormone that influences sleep called **melatonin**. Adolescents who have experienced puberty tend to show a nightly rise in melatonin (and sleep) about two hours later than those who have not begun puberty. Although adolescents need about nine hours of sleep each night, most high school students in Western countries obtain seven or fewer hours of sleep on school nights (Galván, 2019). As a result, adolescents tend to report daytime sleepiness, which interferes with their cognitive and emotional functioning.

Sleep plays an essential role in the neurological processes that influence complex cognitive abilities such as working memory, cognitive flexibility, executive function, and processing speed (Fontanellaz-Castiglione et al., 2020; Galván, 2020). Insufficient sleep impairs adolescents' learning and academic achievement (Fuligni et al., 2018; Sharman & Illingworth, 2020). It also poses risks to mental health such as anxiety, irritability, and depression (Jamieson et al., 2020; Shimizu et al., 2020; Vermeulen et al., 2021). Sleep problems are also associated with risky behaviors, including cigarette smoking and alcohol and substance use, and predict the onset of heavy drinking and marijuana use up to five years later (Miller et al., 2017; Nguyen-Louie et al., 2018; Pieters et al., 2015). Moreover, "catching up" on missed sleep by sleeping longer on the weekends may be ineffective in reducing the sleep deficit and may instead increase internalizing and externalizing symptoms (Fuligni et al., 2018).

The tendency for adolescents to go to bed later has increased over the last three decades, along with the increased availability of television and electronic media that compete with sleep for adolescents' time (Bartel et al., 2015; Carskadon & Tarokh, 2014). Greater screen use at bedtime, especially heavy social media use, is associated with less sleep, including late sleep onset and wake times on school days and trouble falling back asleep after nighttime awakening (Scott et al., 2019; Vermeulen et al., 2021).

The home context also influences adolescents' sleep. Parental support and cohesive parent-child relationships are linked to longer sleep duration, less sleep variability, and less time spent awake during the night (Tsai et al., 2018). Family chaos, on the other hand, is associated with poor sleep, and, in turn, symptoms of anxiety and depression (Peltz et al., 2019).

Greater screen use at bedtime, especially heavy social media use, is associated with poor sleep, posing risks for health.

iStock/ ljubaphoto

Delaying school start times improves student school attendance, grades, and disposition. Later start times are associated with increased sleep and reduced student daytime sleepiness, depression, caffeine use, tardiness to class, and trouble staying awake (Minges & Redeker, 2016; Owens et al., 2017). In 2017, the American Academy of Sleep Medicine issued a policy statement calling on communities, school boards, and educational institutions to implement start times of 8:30 a.m. or later for middle schools and high schools to ensure that every student arrives at school healthy, awake, alert, and ready to learn (Watson et al., 2017). Scientists agree that national and international standards of secondary school start times of 8:30 a.m. or later are needed (Blake et al., 2019).

Mortality

Mortality rises substantially in adolescence, largely influenced by risky behavior (see Figure 9.3; Kochanek et al., 2017; U.S. Department of Health and Human Services, 2017). More than two-thirds of adolescent deaths are due to fatal injuries caused by accidents (such as motor vehicle, pedestrian, and unintentional poisoning, including drug overdoses), suicide, and homicide. Each of these types of fatal injuries declined in prevalence from 1999 through 2013 and has since increased (Curtin et al., 2018). Boys account for more than two-thirds of deaths.

Ethnic differences in mortality emerge in late adolescence, in both death rates and causes of fatal injuries. Black adolescents show dramatically higher rates of death by homicide than their peers (see Figure 9.3). American Indian and Alaskan Native adolescents show the highest rates of unintentional injury and suicide, as compared with other adolescents (Ballesteros et al., 2018). White non-Hispanic adolescents show higher rates of suicide than Black, Hispanic, and Asian American and Pacific Islander adolescents.

Contextual factors contribute to ethnic differences in mortality rates during adolescence. Specifically, socioeconomic status and community factors place Black and American Indian/Alaskan Native youth, who are disproportionately at risk to live in low-SES homes and communities, at risk for higher rates of mortality. Economic disadvantage is one of the most robust predictors of violence, especially in urban settings (Stansfield et al., 2017). Violence by Black adolescents may be fueled by insufficient home and neighborhood resources and exposure to violence and discrimination in the community (Rojas-Gaona et al., 2016). American Indians/Alaskan Natives also experience high levels of poverty. The perception of discrimination, difficulty acculturating or integrating native customs and beliefs with popular culture, and feeling marginalized contribute to higher rates of suicide in American Indian/Alaskan Native adolescence (Jaramillo et al., 2016; Wyatt et al., 2015).

Thinking in Context: Lifespan Development

1. Why do family meals matter for adolescent development? What role does the meal itself versus the process of a family meal play in influencing adolescent outcomes? What might family meals mean to parents?
2. Were you active in sports or other physical activities in childhood? Did your interests and behaviors change in adolescence? Why do you think many teens become less physically active? Do your own experiences and observations match these findings? How might the home, school, peer, and neighborhood context influence the extent to which adolescents engage in physical activity?

FIGURE 9.3 ■ Fatal Injuries Among Youth Aged 10–19 Years, by Intent and Race, National Vital Statistics System, United States, 2013–2015

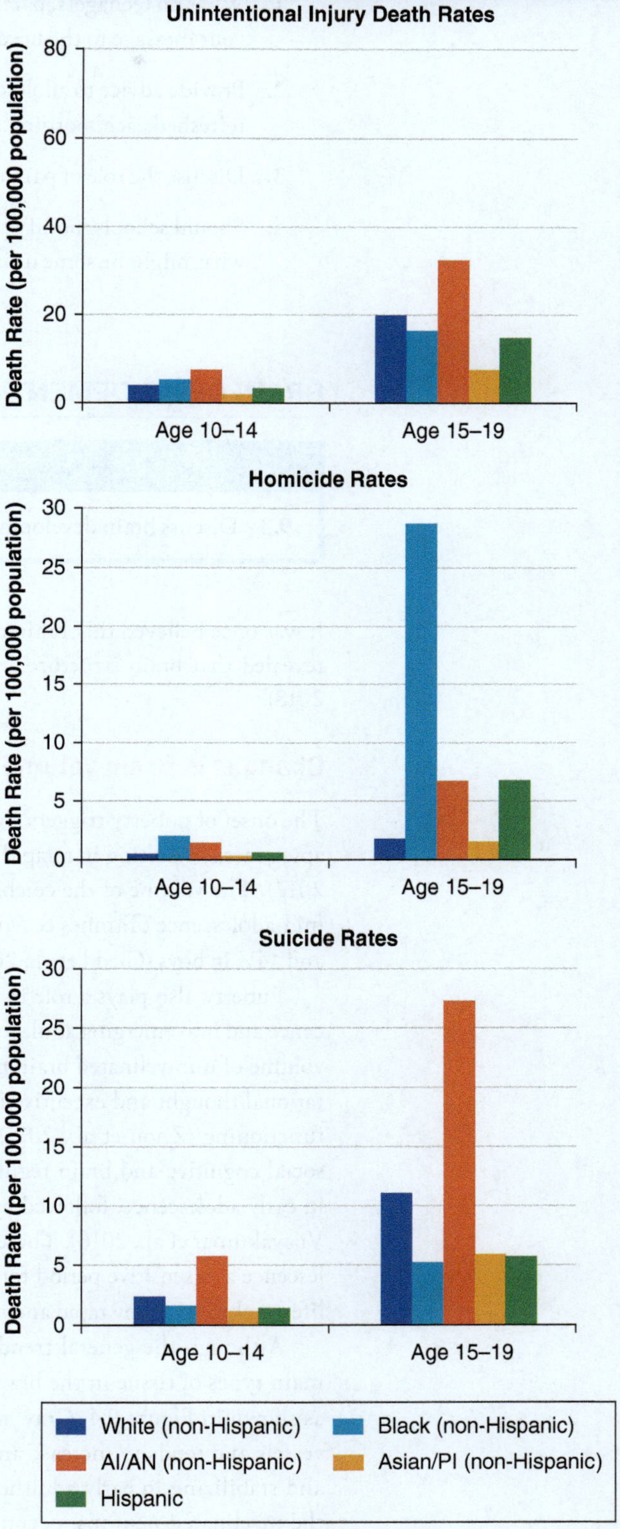

Source: Ballesteros et al., 2018.

Thinking in Context: Applied Developmental Science

You've been tasked with informing and providing advice to adolescents, parents, and schools about the importance of sleep.

1. What do teenagers, parents, and school staff need to know about sleep? How might you tailor your message to the needs, interests, and comprehension of each group?
2. Provide advice to adolescents on what they can do to improve their sleep habits and wake refreshed each morning.
3. Discuss the role of parents in influencing sleep habits. What would you advise parents?
4. Should schools modify policies to help students get healthy sleep? What might they do, and what might be some unintended consequences?

BRAIN DEVELOPMENT IN ADOLESCENCE

LEARNING OBJECTIVE

9.3 Discuss brain development during adolescence and its effect on behavior.

It was once believed that brain development ended in childhood, but advances in neuroimaging have revealed that brain structure and function changes dramatically during adolescence (Morris et al., 2018).

Changes in Brain Volume and Structure

The onset of puberty triggers a variety of neurological developments, including a second burst of synaptogenesis, resulting in a rapid increase of connections among neurons (Goddings et al., 2019; Sisk, 2017). The volume of the cerebral cortex increases about 1% each year from late childhood through mid-adolescence (Tamnes & Mills, 2020). The rate of growth peaks at about 10½ years of age in girls and 14½ in boys (Giedd et al., 2009).

Puberty also plays a role in synaptic pruning, which occurs at an accelerated rate during adolescence and into emerging adulthood (Giedd, 2018; Goddings et al., 2019). Synaptic pruning reduces the volume of unmyelinated brain matter, thins and molds the prefrontal cortex, which is responsible for rational thought and executive function, and results in markedly more efficient cognition and neural functioning (Zhou et al., 2015). The prefrontal cortex and other areas responsible for higher order social cognitive and brain regulatory functions show a burst of increase in volume and surface area in early adolescence, followed by decreases from late adolescence through the 20s (Mills et al., 2016; Vijayakumar et al., 2016). These rapid changes and the corresponding shaping of the cortex mark adolescence as a sensitive period for brain development (Fuhrmann et al., 2015); only in the first years of life are there as many rapid and significant changes.

Although the general trend is for an overall decline in cortical volume with pruning, the two main types of tissue in the brain, grey and white matter, show different developmental trajectories, as shown in Figure 9.4. **Gray matter** includes unmyelinated axons, dendrites, glial cells, and blood vessels and tends to increase and reach its greatest volume in childhood, decreasing in adolescence and stabilizing in early adulthood (Mills & Tamnes, 2018;Tamnes & Mills, 2020). **White matter**, the myelinated neurons, occupies about half of the brain; it increases linearly from late childhood through adolescence and continues to develop into early adulthood (Geeraert et al., 2019; Lebel & Deoni, 2018). Myelination is especially prominent in the prefrontal cortex and the corpus callosum, which increases up to 20% in size, speeding communication between the right and left hemispheres (Lebel & Deoni, 2018).

FIGURE 9.4 ■ Developmental Changes in Gray and White Matter Across Adolescence

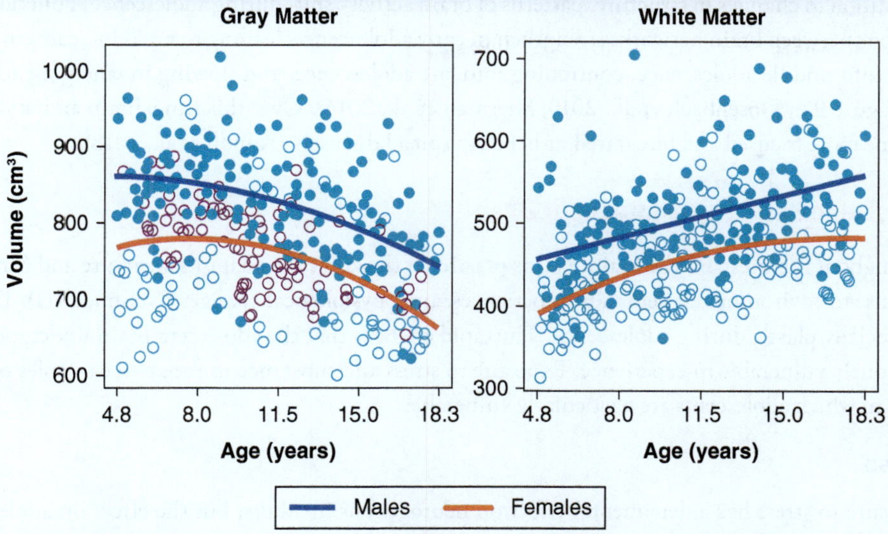

Source: Brain Development Cooperative Group (2012).

Just as in childhood, different parts of the brain develop at different times, leaving adolescents with somewhat lopsided functioning for a time (Tamnes & Mills, 2020). The prefrontal cortex requires the most time to develop, continuing maturation into emerging adulthood. Research using fMRI scans has shown substantial growth and change in cortical and subcortical structures. The **limbic system**, a set of subcortical structures responsible for emotion, undergoes a burst of development in response to pubertal hormones (see Figure 9.5; Goddings et al., 2019; Sisk, 2017). The **amygdala,** a limbic structure that plays a role in fear learning, reward, aggression, and sexual behavior, increases in volume in childhood and peaks in growth at around 12 to 14 years of age, with greater changes in boys (Campbell et al., 2021). The hippocampus, also a part of the limbic system, shows linear growth in adolescence, influencing learning, memory, and aspects of emotional function and stress reactivity. In contrast to the limbic system, which shows a burst of growth in early adolescence followed by more gradual changes during adolescence (Tamnes & Mills, 2020), the prefrontal cortex continues to develop in emerging adulthood, into the mid-20s (Blakemore & Mills, 2014). The prefrontal cortex is the seat of reasoning, cognitive control, decision making, and planning, suggesting that these sophisticated abilities continue to develop well into emerging adulthood. The different timing between the limbic system and prefrontal cortex influences adolescents' behavior, as we will discuss.

FIGURE 9.5 ■ The Human Brain

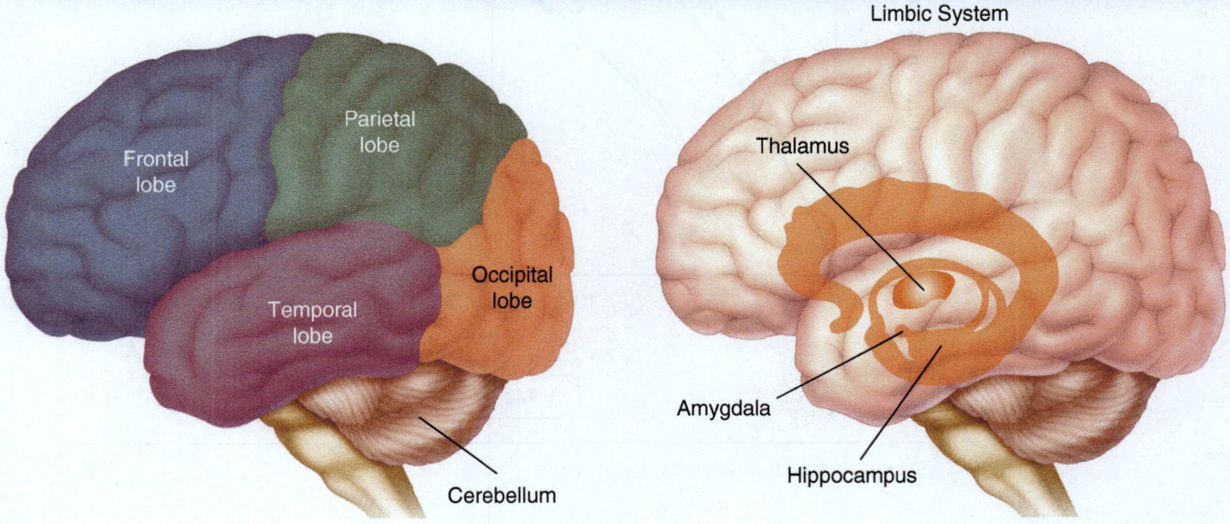

CHANGES IN BRAIN STRUCTURE AND FUNCTION

In addition to changes in structure, patterns of brain activity shift during adolescence. Functional connections between brain networks strengthen in early adolescence, leading to rapid increases in connectivity into middle adolescence, continuing into late adolescence, and slowing in emerging adulthood (see Figure 9.6; Dosenbach et al., 2010; Sherman et al., 2014). Over this time, brain activity tends to become more focused and integrated rather than spread diffusely (Kundu et al., 2018).

Experience and the Adolescent Brain

Throughout the lifespan, the brain retains **plasticity**, the ability to adapt its structure and function in response to environmental demands, experiences, and physiological changes (Nelson, 2011). The brain is especially plastic during adolescence. The rapid changes that the adolescent brain undergoes makes it uniquely vulnerable to experience. Exposure to stress and substance use are two examples of experiences to which adolescents are particularly vulnerable.

Stress

Exposure to stress has a detrimental effect on neurogenesis in adults, but the effect on adolescents is less well studied. Research with rodents suggests that exposure to stress during adolescence may reduce neurogenesis in the hippocampus, with potentially long-lasting effects for cognitive function (Hueston et al., 2017). Moreover, adolescents may be uniquely vulnerable to stress because the adolescent brain,

FIGURE 9.6 ■ Connectivity Maturation in Adolescence and Emerging Adulthood

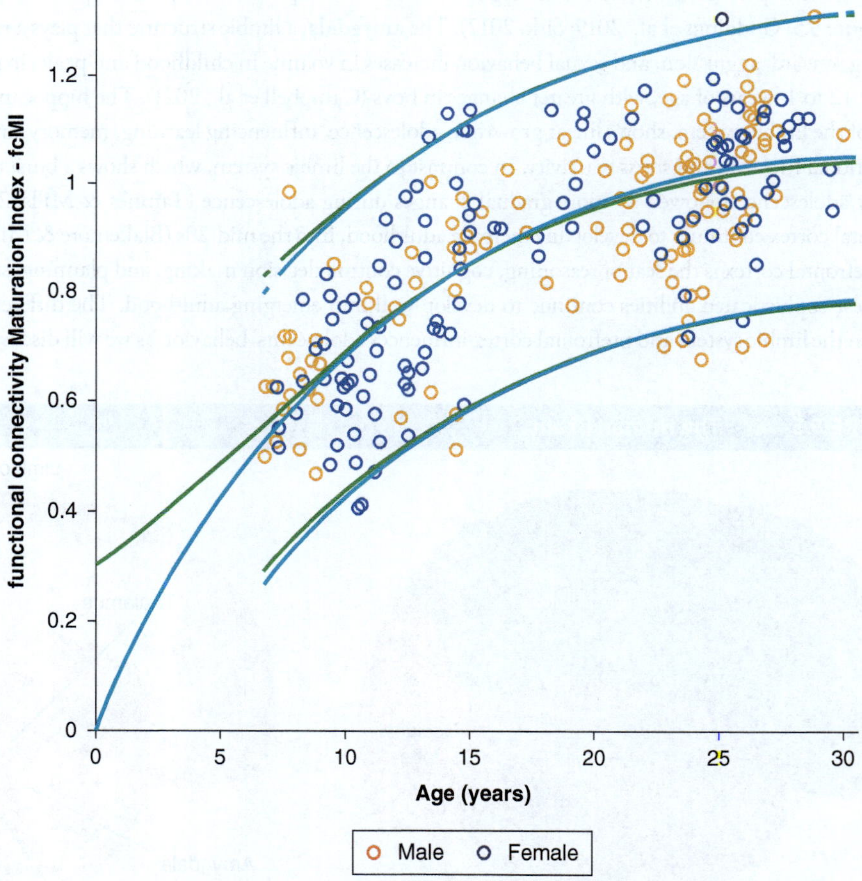

Source: Adapted from Dosenbach et al., 2010.

especially the hippocampus, amygdala, and prefrontal cortex, is particularly sensitive to stress hormones (Romeo, 2017). Exposure to stress hormones is associated with reduced volume, reduced dendritic growth, and atrophy of dendrites and thereby synapses (Romeo, 2017; Tottenham & Galván, 2016).

Socioeconomic status is a contextual factor, often a source of stress, associated with brain development from childhood through adolescence. In cross-sectional research with individuals aged 3–20 years, the number of years of parental education was positively associated with cortical surface area in many brain regions involved in language, reading, social cognition, executive functions, and spatial skills (Noble et al., 2015). The neighborhood context, specifically neighborhood disadvantage, also influences brain development, independent of parental education and household income (Vargas et al., 2020). Exposure to neighborhood disadvantage is associated with poorer performance on neurocognitive tasks that rely on the prefrontal cortex as well as increased gray matter volume in the prefrontal cortex, suggesting less synaptic pruning and therefore protracted development of the prefrontal cortex (Taylor et al., 2020; Tomlinson et al., 2020). Positive parenting can reduce the effects of family and neighborhood disadvantage, supporting the role of contextual factors as influences—risk and protective factors—on neural development (Whittle et al., 2017).

Substance Use

The adolescent brain is uniquely sensitive to the effects of alcohol and substance use. Cross-sectional and longitudinal studies have shown abnormal grey and white matter trajectories in adolescent alcohol and substance users (Guerri & Pascual, 2019; Spear, 2018; Squeglia & Gray, 2016). In one prospective 8-year study of youth ages 12 to 24, those who transitioned to heavy drinking showed accelerated decreases in gray matter volume compared with light and nondrinkers (particularly in frontal and temporal regions) and attenuated increases in white matter volume over the follow-up, even after controlling for marijuana and other substance use (Squeglia et al., 2015). This is consistent with other findings that heavy-drinking adolescents and emerging adults have systematically thinner and lower volume in prefrontal cortex, attenuated white matter development, and altered neural activity suggesting consuming alcohol in large quantities has a toxic effect on brain development (Cservenka & Brumback, 2017; Lees et al., 2020).

Similarly, marijuana use during adolescence is also associated with abnormalities in brain structure and patterns of activity and function (Takagi et al., 2016). Research has consistently shown that recreational marijuana use before the age of 18 has been linked to grey matter atrophy (Battistella et al., 2014). The prefrontal cortex and brain activation associated with inhibitory control, reward, and memory are especially affected (Chye et al., 2020). Heavy users tend to show progressively worse performance, compared to abstaining youth, on tests of complex attention, memory, processing speed, and visuospatial functioning (Cyrus et al., 2021). Adolescents who report daily marijuana use show greater impairments in executive function than adults who report similar use (Gorey et al., 2019). Earlier onset of marijuana use is associated with poorer processing speed and executive functioning by age 19, suggesting initiation of marijuana use during early adolescence (before age 16) may be more harmful to the developing brain than later initiation (Jacobus et al., 2015). We examine adolescent substance use in Chapter 10.

Brain Development and Behavior

We have seen that the limbic system, responsible for emotion, undergoes a burst of development well before the prefrontal cortex, responsible for judgment and executive control (Sisk, 2017). Full development entails the prefrontal cortex catching up to the early developing limbic system. According to the **dual systems model**, the different developmental timetables for these structures can account for many "typical" adolescent behaviors (Mills et al., 2014; Shulman et al., 2016). Volume differences between the prefrontal cortex and parts of the limbic system are associated with engagement in risky behavior (McIlvain et al., 2020). Let's take a closer look at how these changes influence adolescents' thoughts and behavior.

Socioemotional Perception

Adolescents' brains do not always enable them to accurately assess situations, leading them to respond in ways that may be puzzling to adults. Adolescents have difficulty identifying some emotions depicted in facial expressions. In studies when both adults and adolescents are shown photographs of people's faces depicting fear, adults tend to correctly identify the emotion shown in the photograph, but many of the adolescents incorrectly identify the emotion as anger (Yurgelun-Todd, 2007). Why? Functional magnetic imaging scans indicate that when adults view facial expressions, both their limbic system and prefrontal cortex are active. In contrast, scans of adolescents' brains reveal a highly active limbic system but relatively inactive prefrontal cortex relative to adults, suggesting that adolescents experience emotional activation with relatively little executive processing in response to facial stimuli indicating fear (Yurgelun-Todd, 2007).

When faced with emotionally arousing contexts and stimuli, adolescents tend to show exaggerated activity and connectivity in the amygdala relative to adults and fewer functional connections between the prefrontal cortex and amygdala, suggesting that adolescents experience more emotional arousal yet less cortical processing and control than adults (Blakemore & Mills, 2014; Marusak et al., 2017). The ability to control responses to emotionally triggering stimuli develops independently and after the ability to reason about neutral stimuli (Aïte et al., 2018). It seems that adolescents are wired to experience strong emotional reactions and to misidentify emotions in others' facial expressions, which can make communication and social interactions difficult.

Generally speaking, performance on tasks measuring sensitivity to facial expressions improves steadily during the first decade of life but dips in early adolescence, increasing in late adolescence into emerging adulthood (Cohen Kadosh et al., 2013; Motta-Mena & Scherf, 2017). Adolescents have difficulty distinguishing subtle differences in facial expressions (Lee et al., 2019). They are more likely to rate neutral adult faces negatively, similar to ratings of angry faces (Marusak et al., 2017). However, recent research suggests that adolescents are better able to process peer faces than adult faces, especially faces with a pubertal status similar to their own (Picci & Scherf, 2016). As the young adolescents' body prepares for sexual maturity, the brain's face processing system may become calibrated toward peers, potential reproductive partners, rather than caregivers.

Adolescents are neurologically primed to engage in risky behaviors.

iStock/Meinzahn

Reward Perception

Risk taking and adolescence go hand in hand, and the brain plays a large part in such behavior. In early adolescence, the balance of neurotransmitters shifts. At 9 to 10 years of age, the prefrontal cortex and limbic system experience a marked shift in levels of serotonin and dopamine, neurotransmitters that are associated with impulsivity, novelty seeking, and reward salience (Goddings et al., 2019; Luna et al., 2015). Sensitivity to rewards peaks at the same time as adolescents experience difficulty with response inhibition, the ability to control a response. A heightened response to motivational cues coupled with immature behavioral control results in a bias toward immediate goals rather than long-term consequences (Hansen et al., 2019; van Duijvenvoorde et al., 2016). The shift is larger for boys than girls and is thought to make potentially rewarding stimuli even more rewarding for teens (Steinberg, 2008). As a result, risky situations that entail an element of danger become enticing and are experienced as thrills (Spielberg et al., 2014). Adolescents may find themselves drawn to extreme sports, enjoying the high and element of the unknown when they direct their skateboard into the air for a daring turn. These same mechanisms, adolescents' attraction to novelty and enhanced sensitivity to immediate rewards, serve to increase their vulnerability to drugs and alcohol (Bava & Tapert, 2010; Geier, 2013).

Developmental shifts in risky behavior are common among adolescents around the world (Duell et al., 2018). One study examined adolescents in 11 countries in Africa, Asia, Europe, and the Americas and found that sensation seeking increased in preadolescence, peaked at around age 19, and declined thereafter (Steinberg et al., 2018). Risky activity is thought to decline in late adolescence in part because of increases in adolescents' self-regulatory capacities and the capacities for long-term planning that accompany maturation of the prefrontal cortex (Dumontheil, 2016). The shifting balance between prefrontal and limbic activity and fine-tuning of behavioral control continues into emerging adulthood (Giedd, 2018).

Thinking in Context: Biological Influences

1. Most adults blame puberty for much of adolescent behavior. Researchers point to brain development as an important influence on adolescent behavior. Discuss.
2. How might contextual factors, such as interactions with parents and peers and settings such as school and neighborhood, influence how brain development is manifested in adolescent behavior? Through what means might socioeconomic status influence brain development?

Thinking in Context: Applied Developmental Science

Uncle Bob wisecracks, "If adolescents are so smart, why do they do such dumb things?" How would you respond to Bob, considering what we know about the dual systems model and brain development and behavior?

COGNITIVE DEVELOPMENT IN ADOLESCENCE

LEARNING OBJECTIVE

9.4 Identify ways in which thinking changes in adolescence and how these changes are reflected in adolescent decision making and behavior.

Fifteen-year-old Zuri spends much of her time learning about astronomy. She wonders about the existence of dark matter—cosmological matter that cannot be observed but is inferred by its gravitational pull on objects like planets and even galaxies. Zuri's newfound ability and interest in considering complex, abstract phenomena illustrates the ways in which adolescents' thinking departs from children's. As with earlier periods, the cognitive-developmental perspective on cognition describes adolescence as entailing a transformation in thought. The information processing perspective, on the other hand, explains cognitive development in adolescence as a continuation, growth, and refinement of capacities and skills developed in childhood.

Piaget's Cognitive Developmental Theory: Formal Operational Reasoning

According to Piaget's cognitive-developmental theory, from birth we are active constructors of our cognitive schemes. Through their interactions with the world adolescents devise new, more mature schemes and undergo a transformation in thought. The result is **formal operational reasoning**, the final stage of Piaget's cognitive-developmental theory, emerging in early adolescence, at about 11 years of age (Inhelder & Piaget, 1958).

Formal Operational Reasoning

Formal operational reasoning entails the ability to think abstractly, logically, and systematically (Inhelder & Piaget, 1958). Children in the concrete operational stage reason about specific *things*—that is, concepts that exist in reality, such as how to equitably divide a bowl of pudding into five servings.

Adolescents in the formal operational stage reason about *ideas,* possibilities that do not exist in reality and that may have no tangible substance, such as whether it is possible to love equitably—to distribute love equally among several targets. (Kazi & Galanaki, 2020). Adolescents become capable of reasoning about their own thinking and even positing their own existence ("What is thinking? How do I know I exist?"). The ability to think about abstract possibilities permits adolescents to plan for the future, make inferences from available information, and consider ways of solving potential but not yet real problems.

Formal operational thought enables adolescents to engage in **hypothetical-deductive reasoning**, or the ability to consider problems, generate and systematically test hypotheses, and draw conclusions. These abilities underlie the scientific method (see Chapter 1). The tasks that Piaget constructed to study formal operational reasoning test adolescents' abilities to use scientific reasoning to approach a problem by developing hypotheses and systematically testing them. Consider his famous pendulum task (see Figure 9.7; Inhelder & Piaget, 1958). Adolescents are presented with a pendulum and are asked what determines the speed at which the pendulum swings. They are given materials and told that there are four variables to consider: (1) length of string (short, medium, long); (2) weight (light, medium, heavy); (3) height at which the weight is dropped; and (4) force with which the weight is dropped. Adolescents who display formal operational reasoning develop hypotheses that they systematically test. They change one variable while holding the others constant (e.g., trying each of the lengths of string while keeping the weight, height, and force the same). Concrete operational children, on the other hand, do not proceed systematically and fail to test each variable independently. Concrete operational children might test a short string with a heavy weight, then try a long string and light weight. Solving the pendulum problem requires the scientific reasoning capacities that come with formal operational reasoning.

FIGURE 9.7 ■ Measuring Formal Operations: The Pendulum Task

Children and adolescents are presented with a pendulum and are asked what determines the speed at which the pendulum swings. They are given materials and told that there are four variables to consider: (1) length of string (short, medium, long); (2) weight (light, medium, heavy); (3) height at which the weight is dropped; and (4) force with which the weight is dropped.

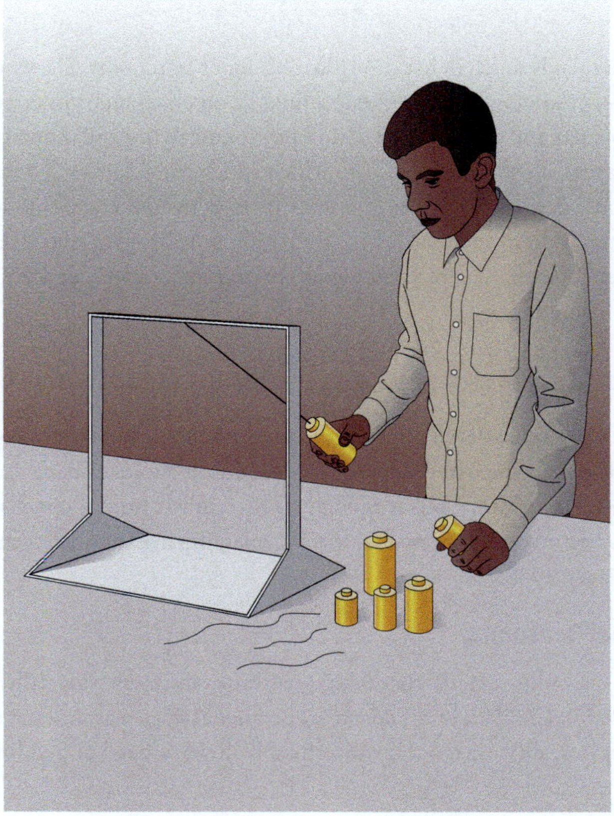

Evaluating Formal Operational Reasoning

Adolescent thinking is qualitatively different and more rational than children's thinking (Moshman, 2021). Although Piaget believed that cognitive development is a universal process, individuals show varying abilities (Kazi & Galanaki, 2020). Most adolescents and many adults do not display formal operational thinking in Piagetian hypothetical-deductive tasks (Kuhn, 2013). Does this mean that they cannot think abstractly? Likely not. Piaget (1972) explained that opportunities to use formal operational reasoning influence its development. Individuals are more likely to show formal operational reasoning when considering material with which they have a great deal of experience. For example, completing college courses is associated with gains in propositional and statistical thought, skills that are often honed in college as well as measured in Piagetian tasks (Kuhn, 2012; Lehman & Nisbett, 1990).

Adolescents' application of logic and scientific reasoning improves but is often limited compared with adults'. Although adolescents show advances in scientific reasoning, their reasoning tends to emphasize single solutions to problems rather than the multiple causal influences that tend to characterize complex real-life problems (Kuhn, 2012). For many young people, the more complex reasoning required to consider multiple influences at once, as well as a more sophisticated understanding of the nature of knowledge and scientific phenomena, arises in emerging adulthood and early adulthood, as discussed in Chapter 11.

Ultimately, the appearance of formal operational reasoning varies among individuals as well as within individuals, as it is not consistent across intellectual areas (Kazi & Galanaki, 2020). Instead, the appearance of formal operations varies with situation, task, context, and the individual's motivation (Birney & Sternberg, 2011; Labouvie-Vief, 2015; Marti & Rodríguez, 2012). Moreover, formal operational reasoning does not suddenly appear in early adolescence. Instead, cognitive change occurs gradually from childhood on, with gains in knowledge, experience, and information processing capacity (Keating, 2012; Moshman, 2021). Finally, most developmental scientists believe that the pinnacle of cognitive development is not in adolescence. Most agree that cognitive development continues throughout adulthood.

Information Processing

From the perspective of information processing theory, improvements in information processing capacities—such as attention, memory, knowledge base, and speed—enable adolescents to think faster, more efficiently, and more complexly than ever before. Specifically, brain development influences adolescents' growing capacities for executive function, permitting greater cognitive control and regulation of attention, thinking, and problem solving (Carlson et al., 2013; Crone et al., 2018), as described in the following sections.

Attention

As compared with children, adolescents show improvements in **selective attention**, the ability to focus on one stimulus while tuning out others and remaining focused even as task demands change, as well as **divided attention**, or attending to two stimuli at once (Hanania & Smith, 2010; Memmert, 2014). With increases in attention, adolescents are better able to hold material in working memory while taking in and processing new material (Barrouillet et al., 2009). Improvements in the ability to monitor information and select the most important parts of it have important implications for classroom performance. Now students can concentrate on more complex tasks, tune out giggling friends to pay attention to what the teacher is saying, determine what is important, and explain the material in their own words. Advances in information processing support adolescents' abilities to solve geometry problems, employ the scientific method, and solve other complex problems.

Advances in cognitive abilities such as executive function contribute to adolescents' increasing ability to attend in class and grasp sophisticated material.

iStock/diego_cervo

Working Memory and Executive Function

Working memory improves in early adolescence, reaching adult-like levels by about age 19, and it continues to improve into the 20s (Embury et al., 2019; Malagoli & Usai, 2018; Simmonds & Luna, 2015). Advances in working memory are largely driven by changes in the central executive and permit individuals to effectively deploy their attention and memory to solve problems.

Adolescents become better able to combine new information with information already in working memory and select and apply strategies for manipulating the information in order to understand it, make decisions, and solve problems (Andersson, 2008; Baddeley, 2016). Adolescents are more likely than children to use memory strategies such as organizing new material into patterns and connecting new material with what is already known (Camos et al., 2018). Experience contributes to cognitive advances. Adolescents know more than children, permitting them more opportunities to associate new material with old, enhancing encoding and long-term memory (Keating, 2012). These advances in knowledge and strategy use result in more sophisticated, more efficient, and quicker thinking and learning. Now adolescents can retain more information at once, better integrate prior experiences and knowledge with new information, and combine information in more complex ways (Cowan et al., 2010; Gaillard et al., 2011). Specifically, brain development influences adolescents' growing capacities for executive function, permitting greater cognitive control and regulation of attention, thinking, and problem solving (Carlson et al., 2013; Crone et al., 2018).

An important aspect of executive function is **response inhibition**, which is the ability to control and stop responding to a stimulus (Carlson et al., 2013). Response inhibition increases throughout childhood, and it shows gradual but substantial gains in adolescence through emerging adulthood (Crone et al., 2018; Malagoli & Usai, 2018). Advances in response inhibition enable adolescents to adapt their responses to the situation. They can inhibit well-learned responses when they are inappropriate to the situation, thereby speeding cognitive processing (Gyurkovics et al., 2020). Immature inhibitory processes can contribute to emotional outbursts when it seems as if adolescents speak before considering their own feelings or the potential consequences of their actions. The neurological changes that underlie response inhibition continue to develop into the 20s, and still-immature capacities for response inhibition are thought to underlie the risk-taking behavior common in adolescence (Müller & Kerns, 2015; Peeters et al., 2015).

Working memory and executive function improve with maturation and experience, but they are also influenced by contextual factors. Some research suggests that the experience of early life stress is associated with impaired inhibition in adolescence (Mueller et al., 2010). Socioeconomic status is also associated with executive function and performance on tasks that require attention switching, working memory, and response inhibition (Last et al., 2018; Theodoraki et al., 2020). Adolescents of all ethnicities who live in low-SES homes and neighborhoods may experience greater challenges in developing the cognitive control capacities needed for good decision making (Last et al., 2018; Lawson et al., 2018). Other research suggests that adolescents from high-income families show greater activation of the prefrontal cortex during working memory tasks than those from low-income families, and prefrontal activity predicted math achievement in high-income adolescents (Finn et al., 2017). Contextual factors can also buffer the negative effects of low SES. For example, low-SES adolescents who perceive greater academic support at school show better performance on executive function tasks, specifically inhibition, than their peers who perceive less support (Piccolo et al., 2018).

Processing Speed

One important way in which adolescents' thinking improves is that it gets quicker (Kail, 2008). Older adolescents process information to solve problems more quickly than younger adolescents, who are quicker than children. Processing speed reaches adult levels in middle to late adolescence, as early as 15 (Coyle et al., 2011). Changes in the brain underlie many improvements in information processing capacities. As the structure of the prefrontal cortex changes, with decreases in gray matter and increases in white matter, cognition becomes markedly more efficient (Asato et al., 2010). Myelination underlies improvements in processing speed during childhood and adolescence, permitting quicker physical and cognitive responses (Silveri et al., 2008). Compared to children, not only do adolescents show faster reaction speed in gym class, but they are quicker at connecting ideas, making arguments, and drawing conclusions. Processing speed increases and reaches adult levels at about age 15 and is associated with advances in working memory and cognition, especially reasoning (Coyle et al., 2011).

Advances in processing speed are also due to expertise. With practice, cognitive processes become automatic and require fewer cognitive resources, such as attention and working memory, and become quicker (Servant et al., 2018). Automaticity is a function of experience. Adolescents become more efficient problem solvers as they get better at understanding how their mind works (metacognition).

Advanced capacities for attention make adolescents better able to concentrate and study.

Tony Gutierrez/ Associated Press

Metacognition

Not only are adolescents better at thinking than children, they are more aware of their own thought process. Adolescents become capable of thinking about ideas and the nature of thinking itself, or metacognition (Ardila, 2013). Recall from Chapter 5 that metacognition refers to knowledge of how the mind works and the ability to control the mind. Metacognitive ability develops dramatically between ages 11 and 17 (Weil et al., 2013). As metacognition develops, adolescents become better able to think about how their mind works and are better able to be planful about their cognitive system—how they take in, manipulate, and store information (Ardila, 2013; van der Stel & Veenman, 2014). They are better able to understand how they learn, evaluate their learning, and choose and deploy strategies that enhance their memory and learning in light of the situation and problem. Adolescents' abilities to apply metacognition in real-world settings continues to develop into late adolescence and early adulthood.

The ability to think about one's thinking enables adolescents to reason about problems in new ways. By considering their own cognitive strategies and experimenting and reflecting on their experiences, adolescents begin to appreciate logical reasoning and hypothetical-deductive thinking, which they increasingly apply to everyday situations (Ardila, 2013; Kuhn, 2013; van der Stel & Veenman, 2014). The development of metacognition proficiency is associated with gains in academic performance (van der Stel & Veenman, 2013).

Social Cognition

By adolescence, young people have lots of social experience and their reasoning skills make them much better able to take other people's perspectives, or understand different viewpoints, which has implications for social relationships (Carpendale & Lewis, 2015). Perspective-taking ability is linked with working memory and cognitive control (Nilsen & Bacso, 2017). Although attending to social cues is largely automatic, attending to another person's perspective when it differs from one's own requires inhibiting our own perspective, which is an effortful process that requires the cognitive control resources in working memory (Kilford et al., 2016).

Advances in **social perspective taking** permit adolescents to better understand others, but also to grasp how they are perceived by others. Perspective-taking ability predicts peer relations, friendship, and popularity (Nilsen & Bacso, 2017). Yet, not all adolescents effectively apply their perspective-taking skills (Flannery & Smith, 2017). Similar to abstract thought, perspective-taking abilities and the ability to apply their understanding emerges gradually. Teenagers are prone to errors in reasoning and lapses in judgment, as evidenced by the emergence of adolescent egocentrism.

Adolescent Egocentrism

Although social perspective taking improves, it often develops slowly and even in a piecemeal fashion. When it comes to considering themselves, adolescents often have difficulty separating their own and others' perspectives. That is, adolescents find it difficult to distinguish their view of what others think of them from reality, what others actually think about them. They show **adolescent egocentrism**, a perspective-taking error that is manifested in two phenomena: the **imaginary audience** and the **personal fable** (Elkind & Bowen, 1979).

The imaginary audience is experienced as self-consciousness—feeling as if all eyes are on them. Adolescents misdirect their preoccupation with themselves toward others and assume that they are the focus of others' attention (Elkind & Bowen, 1979). In this way, the imaginary audience is an error in perspective taking. The imaginary audience fuels adolescents' concerns with their appearance and can make the slightest criticism sting painfully, as teens are convinced that all eyes are on them. The imaginary audience contributes to the heightened self-consciousness characteristic of adolescence (Alberts et al., 2007).

Adolescents' preoccupation with themselves also leads them to believe that they are special, unique, and invulnerable—a belief known as the personal fable (Elkind & Bowen, 1979). They believe that their emotions—the highs of happiness and depths of despair that they feel—are different from and more intense than other people's emotions and that others simply do not understand. The invulnerability aspect of the personal fable may predispose adolescents to seek risks, leading them to believe that they are immune to the negative consequences of such risky activities as drug use, delinquency, and unsafe sex (Alberts et al., 2007).

Both the imaginary audience and the personal fable are thought to increase in early adolescence, peak in middle adolescence, and decline in late adolescence (Elkind & Bowen, 1979). Yet some research suggests that adolescent egocentrism may persist into late adolescence and beyond (Schwartz et al., 2008). Indeed, in one recent study adolescents 13 to 16 showed similar levels of egocentrism as adults; they were just as likely as adults to believe that others could tell when they were lying and when they were nervous (Rai et al., 2016). Moreover, for many adolescents (and adults), the audience is not imaginary. When posting to social media, many adolescents painstakingly consider their audience and play to them by sharing content to appear interesting, well-liked, and attractive (Yau & Reich, 2018).

Decision Making

We have seen that adolescents engage in more complex thinking and approach decision making in more sophisticated ways than children. Under laboratory conditions, adolescents are capable of demonstrating rational decision making that is in line with their goals and is comparable to that of adults (Reyna & Rivers, 2008). Comparisons of adolescents and adults' decisions on hypothetical dilemmas—such as whether to engage in substance use, have surgery, have sex, or drink and drive—show that adolescents and adults generate similar consequences for each decision option, spontaneously mention similar risks and benefits of each option, and rate the harmfulness of risks in similar ways (Reyna & Farley, 2006). However, laboratory studies of decision making usually present adolescents with hypothetical dilemmas that are very different from the everyday decisions they face.

One explanation for heightened self-consciousness in adolescence is the imaginary audience, a component of adolescent egocentrism.

iStock/ skynesher

Everyday decisions have personal relevance, require quick thinking, are emotional, and often are made in the presence and under the influence of others. Recall the developmental mismatch described by the dual systems model, above.

Adolescents often feel strong emotions and impulses that they may be unable to regulate due to the still-immature condition of their prefrontal cortex (Cohen & Casey, 2017). Adolescents are susceptible to risk taking in situations of heightened emotional arousal (Figner et al., 2009; Mills et al., 2014). When faced with unfamiliar, emotionally charged situations; spur-of-the-moment decisions; pressures to conform; poor self-control; and risk and benefit estimates that favor good short-term and bad long-term outcomes, adolescents tend to reason more poorly than adults (Albert et al., 2013; Breiner et al., 2018).

We have seen that adolescents are neurologically more sensitive to rewards than adults. Adolescents tend to place more importance on the potential benefits of decisions (e.g., social status, pleasure) than on the potential costs or risks (e.g., physical harm, short- and long-term health issues; Javadi et al., 2014; Shulman & Cauffman, 2013). In the presence of rewards, adolescents show heightened activity in the brain systems that support reward processing and reduced activity in the areas responsible for inhibitory control, compared with adults (Paulsen et al., 2014; Smith et al., 2015). In fact, activity in the reward centers of the brain predicts alcohol use in 16- to 18-year-old adolescents (Swartz et al., 2020). Risky activity is thought to decline in late adolescence in part because of increases in adolescents' self-regulatory capacities and their capacities for long-term planning that accompany maturation of the frontal cortex (Albert, Chein, & Steinberg, 2013; Casey, 2015). Experience in making decisions and learning from successes and failures, coupled with developments in cognition, self-control, and emotional regulation, can lead to adolescent decision making that is more reflective, confident, and successful (see Figure 9.8).

FIGURE 9.8 ■ Influences on Adolescent Decisions

Brain Development

- Increases in cortical volume and white matter
- Decreases in gray matter
- Rapid limbic system development in early adolescence
- Prefrontal cortex matures slowly throughout adolescence into young adulthood
- Shifts in levels of neurotransmitters in early adolescence

↓

Cognitive Development

- Advances in attention, memory, processing speed, and strategy repertoire and use
- Abstract thinking
- Metacognition and metamemory
- Executive functioning

↓

Adolescent Decision-Making and Behavior

- Difficulty reading other people and identifying their emotions
- Emotionally charged responses before reasoning
- Advances in planning abilities
- Increasingly able to identify and weigh options and consider multiple sources of information
- Impulsivity and novelty seeking, but over time, improvements in response inhibition

Thinking in Context: Lifespan Development

1. Recall from Chapter 1 that themes of development interact. How might cognitive development in adolescence influence how adolescents understand the physical changes that they undergo? How do advances in cognition influence socioemotional functioning? Consider the reverse: How might aspects of cognition be influenced by socioemotional development? Physical development?
2. Consider a parent's perspective. Provide examples of how advances in information processing abilities might influence parent-adolescent interactions. What challenges and rewards might these pose for parents?
3. Despite their rapid advances in information processing and reasoning skills, in everyday life adolescents often make poor decisions. How do you account for this discrepancy? To what degree should adolescents be protected from the consequences of poor decisions? Does it depend on the situation and poor choice itself, such as a nasty fall, car accident, or serious crime? Do you draw distinctions? If so, how and why?

SCHOOL CONTEXT IN ADOLESCENCE

LEARNING OBJECTIVE

9.5 Describe the challenges that school transitions pose for adolescents and contextual influences on academic achievement and completing high school.

The structure of schools in the United States has changed dramatically since the mid-20th century. In past generations, students made only one school transition, or change of schools, from elementary school (kindergarten–Grade 8) to high school (Grades 9–12). Today, students make more school transitions than ever before. Junior high schools, comprising seventh, eighth, and ninth-grade students, were created in the 1960s and were modeled after high schools, serving as mini-high schools. In the late 1970s and 1980s, educators began to recognize that young adolescents have different educational needs than middle and older adolescents, and junior high schools began to be converted and organized into middle schools of Grades 5 or 6 through 8 or 9 (Byrnes & Ruby, 2007). Middle schools are designed to provide more flexibility and autonomy than elementary schools while encouraging strong ties to adults, such as teachers and parents, as well as offering active learning that takes advantage of and stimulates young adolescents' emerging capacities for abstract reasoning (National Middle School Association, 2003).

Shifting Contexts

The transition from elementary to middle school, and middle school to high school, entails a complete shift in contexts, including environments, teachers, standards, support, and, often, peers. School transitions tend to coincide with many developmental and contextual changes. Many young people experience puberty during the transition to middle school. Changing thought capacities, self-perceptions, and relationships as well as new responsibilities and opportunities for independence influence how adolescents adapt to school transitions. As friendships become more important, they may be disrupted when friends transition into different schools. Most adolescents experience the many changes that accompany school transitions as stressful, and academic achievement tends to decline during the transitions to middle school and high school (Booth & Gerard, 2014; Felmlee et al., 2018). In addition, student engagement and motivation tends to decline and feelings of loneliness, anxiety, depression, and stress tend to rise (Akos et al., 2014; Benner, 2011; Goldstein et al., 2015).

Grades tend to decline with each school transition; students who experience more school transitions tend to perform more poorly than peers who have changed schools less often (Rudolph et al., 2001; Seidman et al., 2003). Young adolescents enrolled in K–8 schools tend to score higher in academic achievement, specifically math and reading, than do same-grade peers who have changed schools from elementary to middle school (Byrnes & Ruby, 2007). Larger cumulative declines in academic achievement are seen when students make two school transitions before high school (elementary to middle school and middle to high school) as compared with one (K–8 elementary school to high school; Crockett et al., 1989). During transitions, students may experience an increase in anxiety or depression that may manifest as poor school attendance, lower grades, and behavior problems in school (Coelho et al., 2017; Duchesne et al., 2019). For most students, these adjustment difficulties are temporary and their achievement recovers within one to two years as they adapt to their new schools (Crosnoe et al., 2015). However, students who perceive the school transition as more stressful than their peers tend to show greater drops in motivation and academic achievement and less connectedness to school that persists well beyond the school transition (Goldstein et al., 2015). Students with lower academic ability, lower self-esteem, and who are unprepared for middle or high school are particularly vulnerable to poorer school and peer transitions, which have been associated with depressive symptoms (Coelho et al., 2017).

Stage-Environment Fit

Why are school transitions vulnerable periods for adolescents? Negative effects of school transitions occur when there is poor **stage-environment fit**. That is, adolescents experience difficulties when there is a poor match between their developmental needs and what the school environment affords in its organization and characteristics (Eccles & Roeser, 2011). The school environment, teachers, and standards change with each transition. Middle schools were intended to be tailored to the needs of early adolescents, yet many students view their middle school experiences less positively than their elementary school experiences (Byrnes & Ruby, 2007; Roeser et al., 2000).

As adolescents enter middle school and then high school, they are confronted with more stringent academic standards, and evaluation becomes more frequent and formal than in elementary school. At the same time, many students feel that they receive less support from teachers (Mueller & Anderman, 2010). Students commonly report feeling less connected to middle school teachers than elementary school teachers and view their middle school teachers as less friendly, supportive, and fair (Way et al., 2007). High school students often report that they receive less personal attention from teachers, more class lectures, fewer hands-on demonstration activities, and fewer opportunities to participate in class discussions and group decision making than they did in middle school (Gentle-Genitty, 2009; Seidman et al., 2004). Across middle and early high school, adolescents feel less connected to and less valued within their classroom and school environment (Shubert et al., 2020). Declines in teacher support across the high school transition are associated with increases in depression (Barber & Olsen, 2004).

School transitions can be a vulnerable period for adolescents, with both positive and negative effects depending on stage-environment fit.

iStock/ fstop123

Although it is tempting to blame adolescents' views about school on poor perspective taking or an immature prefrontal cortex, research suggests that many teachers' views corroborate them. Middle and junior high school teachers hold different beliefs about students than do elementary school teachers, even when they teach students of the same chronological age (Midgley et al., 1995). They are less likely to report trusting their students and are more likely to emphasize discipline than their peers who teach elementary school. Teachers' belief in their abilities as teachers declines with each grade into secondary school, which is problematic because teachers who feel competent set high expectations for students, which in turn predicts student success (Eccles & Roeser, 2015). This decline is greater for teachers in low-SES schools and communities, likely influenced by poor access to resources and increased stress adding to the challenges that at-risk students face (Cooper et al., 2010). As a result, middle school classrooms tend to be characterized by a greater emphasis on teacher control; they offer fewer opportunities for student decision making and autonomy and involve more frequent and formal evaluations than in elementary school (Eccles & Roeser, 2015). The mismatch of adolescents' changing developmental needs and school resources contributes to declines in academic performance, motivation, and overall functioning, including increases in anxiety and depressive symptoms (Benner et al., 2017; Booth & Gerard, 2014; Coelho et al., 2017).

School transitions may also entail changes in the ethnic and racial composition of schools. African American, Latinx, Asian, and white adolescents fare best in diverse schools with ethnic groups of relatively equal size (Juvonen et al., 2018). Students in diverse schools report feeling safer, less victimized, and less lonely; perceive teachers as more fair; and report more favorable attitudes toward students of other ethnicities. Changes in school demographics, particularly a mismatch between the ethnic composition of elementary and middle school or middle school and high school, can pose challenges to adolescents' adjustment (Douglass et al., 2014). High school students who experienced more ethnic incongruence when moving from middle to high school, or a change in demographics, reported feeling less connected to school over time and increasingly worried about their academic success (Benner & Graham, 2009). African American and Latinx students who moved to high schools with fewer students who were ethnically similar to themselves were most likely to experience a disconnect. This is of particular concern because African American adolescents tend to experience more risk factors to academic achievement, more difficulties in school transitions, and are more likely to fall behind during school transitions than other adolescents (Burchinal et al., 2006).

Similarly, Latinx students tend to be more sensitive to changes in the school climate and experience school transitions as more challenging than do non-Hispanic white students (Espinoza & Juvonen, 2011). One recent study found that students' academic risk during the transition to high school varied with their academic standing in middle school and their ethnicity (Sutton et al., 2018). Specifically, Black boys and Latina girls who were high achieving in middle school tended to show the greatest losses in achievement over the transition to high school, and white girls tend to show the greatest stability in academic status between middle school and high school. Risks to academic achievement tend to accumulate over time, with disadvantaged students facing disproportionate risks to achievement as they are often less prepared to meet the heightened demands of high school.

Contextual Influences on Academic Achievement

The best student outcomes occur when schools closely match adolescents' developmental needs. Small, tight-knit middle schools may reduce the alienation that some students experience during the school transition (Crosnoe et al., 2015). Small schools may also foster strong teacher-student relationships by offering more opportunities for teachers to interact with a smaller student base and help students feel that they belong in school. A sense of school belonging is associated with positive school engagement and conduct and psychological well-being (Demanet & van Houtte, 2012; Neel & Fuligni, 2013). Teachers, parents, and peers play a role in influencing adolescents' school transitions and their academic achievement.

Teachers

Teachers help adolescents during school transitions by creating a classroom environment that supports students' psychological needs (Eccles & Roeser, 2011; Madjar & Cohen-Malayev, 2016). Teachers who provide a high-quality classroom environment, including emotional support, autonomy, positive relationships with their students, and greater teaching self-efficacy, have students who show better student achievement (Alley, 2019; Yu et al., 2016). Close teacher-student relationships may help teachers feel comfortable providing opportunities for adolescents to have autonomy in classroom interactions and assignments while providing strong support.

Adolescents who report high levels of teacher support and feel connected to their schools tend to show better academic achievement and better emotional health, including lower rates of depressive and anxiety symptoms (Kidger et al., 2012; Madjar & Cohen-Malayev, 2016). They are also more likely to graduate high school (Burns, 2020). The student-teacher relationship is reciprocal: students who feel that they have a close relationship with their teacher tend to have teachers who report a similarly close relationship (Prewett et al., 2019).

Parents

Close parent-adolescent relationships serve as an important support for academic motivation and performance from childhood through adolescence for young people at all socioeconomic levels (Dotterer et al., 2014). As in other areas of development, both the overly harsh parenting of the authoritarian parenting style and the lax, permissive parenting style are associated with poor academic performance. Likewise, adolescents reared by uninvolved parents tend to show the poorest school grades (Gonzalez & Wolters, 2006; Heaven & Ciarrochi, 2008). Authoritative parenting, in contrast, is associated with academic achievement in U.S. adolescents of all ethnicities as well as in many other countries, including Argentina, Australia, Canada, China, Hong Kong, Iran, Pakistan, and Scotland (Assadi et al., 2007; Gonzalez & Wolters, 2006; Pinquart, 2017; Spera, 2005).

Parents can promote academic achievement in middle and high school students by setting high but realistic expectations and being active and involved by knowing their teens' teachers, monitoring progress, ensuring that their teens are taking challenging and appropriate classes, and expressing high expectations (Benner, 2011; Boonk et al., 2018; Karbach et al., 2013). Parent-school involvement predicts academic achievement for adolescents, regardless of socioeconomic status and ethnicity, but may be particularly beneficial for more disadvantaged youth such as those from low-SES families or with poorer prior achievement (Benner et al., 2016; Castro et al., 2015). By being involved in the school, parents communicate the importance of education; they also model academic engagement and problem solving, which can help protect against dropout.

Peers

Peer relationships and interactions also influence adolescents' school experiences and academic achievement. Adolescents tend to choose friends who share interests and similarities, such as academic achievement (Gremmen et al., 2019; Véronneau et al., 2010). Friends mutually influence each other, becoming more similar through socialization (Gremmen et al., 2017). Peer support can be a protective factor for adolescents at risk. Research with African American students has shown peer support to be related to emotional engagement in school and, indirectly, to academic outcomes (Golden et al., 2018). Adolescents who viewed their peers as having high academic values reported engaging in greater school effort. Students' grades become more similar over time in response to their connectedness (Gremmen et al., 2017). Friends can exert a positive influence on one another to increase achievement (Rambaran et al., 2017).

Authoritative parenting is associated with academic achievement in adolescents around the world.

iStock/monkeybusinessimages

School Dropout

School dropout rates in the United States have reached historic lows, with dramatic decreases for African American and Hispanic adolescents (see Figure 9.9). Nevertheless, each year about 6% of high school students drop out of school (National Center for Educational Statistics, 2017). Students of low socioeconomic status are at high risk of school dropout, and adolescents of color and immigrant students are particularly vulnerable.

Students with behavior and substance use problems are most at risk for school dropout, but many who drop out simply have academic problems, skip classes with increasing frequency, and disengage emotionally and behaviorally (Bowers & Sprott, 2012; Henry et al., 2012; Wang & Fredricks, 2014). Lack of parental involvement places students at risk for school dropout—and when parents respond to poor grades with anger and punishment, this can further reduce adolescents' academic motivation and feelings of connectedness to school (Alivernini & Lucidi, 2011).

Students who are engaged and attached to school and who participate in many school-related activities are less likely to drop out than their less-engaged peers (Janosz et al., 2008; Mahoney, 2014). Conversely, feelings of anonymity at school increase the risk of dropping out. Many of the unfavorable characteristics that students report of their high schools predict dropout: large schools, unsupportive teachers, and few opportunities to form personal relationships or to speak out in class (Battin-Pearson & Newcomb, 2000; Christenson & Thurlow, 2004; Croninger & Lee, 2001; Freeman & Simonsen, 2015); poor connections with teachers and poor support for meeting academic expectations (Jia et al., 2016); bullying and poor relationships with peers (Cornell et al., 2013; Frostad et al., 2014). Students who experience academic difficulties may be more vulnerable than their peers to the structural changes that are common during school transitions.

Although dropout is often the result of extended difficulties, there are multiple paths to drop out. Many students show few problems until a particularly disruptive event or situation, such as severe peer victimization, health problems, family instability, or long work hours, impairs their coping skills (Dupere et al., 2015). For example, a study comparing Canadian students who were recent dropouts, at-risk students who remained in school, and average students found that dropouts were more than three times more likely to have experienced recent acute stressors, suggesting that it may be these acute stressors that place students at increased risk for dropout, over and above existing contextual risks (Dupéré et al., 2018).

FIGURE 9.9 ■ Percentage of Grade 10 to 12 Dropouts Among Persons 15 Through 24 Years Old, by Race/Ethnicity: October 1976 Through 2016

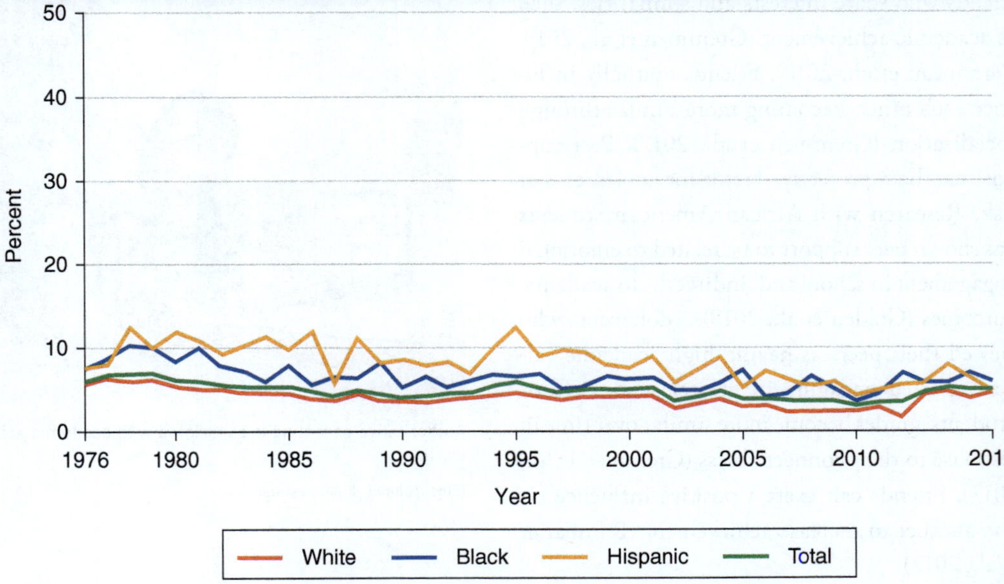

Source: National Center for Educational Statistics, 2017.

As adults, high school dropouts experience higher rates of unemployment and, when hired, earn less than high school graduates throughout adulthood. Young people who have dropped out of school have the option of taking a high school equivalency test, the General Educational Development exam (GED). The GED was developed in the late 1940s to certify that returning World War II veterans who had left high school to serve in the military were ready for college or the labor market. Although passing the GED exam can signify that a young person has accumulated the knowledge required to earn a high school diploma, GED holders do not fare as well as regular high school graduates in the labor market, and they tend to get much less postsecondary education (Tyler & Lofstrom, 2009).

Students drop out of school for a variety of reasons. Some show an extended history of problems. Others experience a disruptive event or situation that impairs their coping skills and leads to drop out.

The Fresno Bee/MCT via Getty Images

Thinking in Context: Lifespan Development

1. From your experience and observations, what challenges do adolescents face in middle and high school? How well does the environment match adolescents' developmental needs? What contextual factors might determine goodness of fit? How can we enhance the fit between adolescents' needs and school opportunities and resources?
2. Did you hold a job in high school? Describe your experience, contrasting it with what we know about adolescent employment. How might you account for any differences?
3. What can be done to help students stay in school and graduate from high school? Consider home, peer, neighborhood, and, of course, school influences. How can each of these contexts influence students' likelihood of graduating from high school?

Thinking in Context: Intersectionality

1. Discuss some of the reasons why adolescents of color and from disenfranchised groups may experience greater challenges during school transitions and poor goodness of fit. Consider intersections among race, SES, school climate, parent and teacher perceptions and expectations, as well as peers.
2. How might the factors identified above contribute to the risk for school dropout?
3. What factors do you think are most important to address to help disenfranchised adolescents and those of color?

CHAPTER SUMMARY

9.1 Summarize the physical changes that occur with puberty, correlates of pubertal timing, and influences on pubertal timing.

The most noticeable signs of pubertal maturation are the growth spurt and the development of secondary sex characteristics, such as breast development, deepening of the voice, growth of body hair, and changes in the skin. During puberty, the primary sex characteristics, the reproductive organs, grow larger and mature, and adolescents become capable of reproduction.

Pubertal timing is influenced by genetic and contextual factors. Early maturation poses challenges for both boys and girls, with more dramatic effects for girls. The consequences of early and late maturation differ dramatically for girls and boys.

9.2 Identify influences on health and recommendations to improve adolescents' health.

Adolescence is a generally healthy time in which young people tend to report good or excellent health and low rates of illness. Good nutrition and physical activity are essential to support adolescents' growth, yet young people's diets tend to worsen and sedentary behavior increases in adolescence. During puberty a shift occurs in adolescents' sleep patterns and preferred sleep schedule, known as a delayed phase preference, and adolescents tend to get less sleep than they need to support the neurological processes that influence complex cognitive abilities. Mortality rises substantially in adolescence, largely influenced by the risky behavior that commonly accompanies neurological development.

9.3 Discuss brain development during adolescence and its effect on behavior.

Changes in the volume of the cortex, interconnections among neurons, and myelination influence the speed and efficiency of thought and the capacity for executive function. According to the dual-process model, the limbic system undergoes a burst of development well ahead of the prefrontal cortex, and this difference in development can account for many "typical" adolescent behaviors. Changes in the balance of neurotransmitters that are associated with impulsivity and reward salience influence adolescent engagement in risky behavior.

9.4 Identify ways in which thinking changes in adolescence and how these changes are reflected in adolescent decision making and behavior.

Adolescents become capable of formal operational reasoning permitting hypothetical-deductive reasoning and the use of propositional logic. Research suggests that formal operational reasoning does not suddenly appear in early adolescence; instead, cognitive change occurs gradually from childhood on. Adolescents' advances in cognition are the result of improvements in information processing capacities, such as attention, memory, knowledge base, response inhibition, strategy use, speed, and metacognition. Adolescents' ability to take other people's perspectives advances, yet they also show features of adolescent egocentrism. Adolescents' decision-making competence is more advanced in laboratory settings than everyday settings, which often are charged with emotion.

9.5 Describe the challenges that school transitions pose for adolescents and contextual influences on academic achievement and completing high school.

Many students experience school transitions as stressful and academic motivation and achievement often decline. Poor stage-environment fit—the mismatch of adolescents' changing developmental needs with school resources—contributes to the challenges of school transitions. Supportive relationships with teachers and peers, authoritative parenting, and parent involvement in the school are associated with academic achievement in adolescents at all socioeconomic levels. School dropout poses challenges to young people's short- and long-term development.

KEY TERMS

adolescent egocentrism (p. 280)
adolescent growth spurt (p. 260)
amygdala (p. 271)
delayed phase preference (p. 268)
divided attention (p. 277)
dual systems model (p. 273)
formal operational reasoning (p. 275)
gray matter (p. 270)
hypothetical-deductive reasoning (p. 276)
imaginary audience (p. 280)
limbic system (p. 271)
melatonin (p. 268)
menarche (p. 261)
menstruation (p. 261)
personal fable (p. 280)
plasticity (p. 272)
primary sex characteristics (p. 261)
puberty (p. 260)

response inhibition (p. 278)
secondary sex characteristics (p. 261)
secular trend (p. 265)
selective attention (p. 277)
semen (p. 262)
social perspective taking (p. 279)
spermarche (p. 262)
stage-environment fit (p. 283)
testes (p. 262)
white matter (p. 270)

10 SOCIOEMOTIONAL DEVELOPMENT IN ADOLESCENCE

Stígur Már Karlsson /Heimsmyndir/ Getty Images

Adolescence, the period between childhood and adulthood, is a period of rapid development. Physical changes, such as puberty, are very noticeable. Other hallmarks of adolescence are less visible. The socioemotional task of adolescence is most concisely described as "figuring yourself out." Specifically, adolescents construct a sense of self and identity, an understanding of who they are and who they hope to be. Adolescents' attempts at self-definition and discovery are influenced by their relationships with parents and peers—relationships that become more complex during the adolescent years.

PSYCHOSOCIAL DEVELOPMENT: THE CHANGING SELF

LEARNING OBJECTIVE

10.1 Summarize changes in self-concept, self-esteem, identity, and morality during adolescence.

Adolescents spend a great deal of time reflecting on themselves and engaging in introspective activities, such as writing in journals, composing poetry, and posting messages, photos, and videos about their lives on social media. These activities might seem self-indulgent, but they are a means of constructing a sophisticated sense of self, which influences adolescents' emotional and social experiences.

Self-Concept

A more complex, differentiated, and organized self-concept emerges in adolescence (Esnaola et al., 2020; Harter, 2012a). Adolescents use multiple abstract and complex labels to describe themselves (e.g., witty, intelligent). As young people recognize that their feelings, attitudes, and behaviors may change with the situation, they begin to use qualifiers in their self-descriptions (e.g., "I'm sort of shy"; Balakrishnan, 2020). Adolescents' awareness of the situational variability in their psychological and behavioral qualities is evident in statements such as, "I'm assertive in class, speaking out and debating my classmates, but I'm quieter with my friends. I don't want to stir up trouble." Many young adolescents find these inconsistencies confusing and wonder who they really are, contributing to their challenge of forming a balanced and consistent sense of self.

As adolescents become able to consider the future, imagine their future lives, and wonder how they might change over time, they identify an *ideal self*, or who they aspire to be. A mismatch or discrepancy between the ideal aspirational self and real self, their perceived personal characteristics, is associated with symptoms of depression, low self-esteem, and poor school grades (Ferguson et al., 2010; Stevens et al., 2014). Supportive relationships with parents and teachers promote a positive self-concept (Dudovitz et al., 2017; Van Dijk et al., 2014).

Self-Esteem

As self-conceptions become more differentiated, so do self-evaluations. Adolescents describe and evaluate themselves overall, as well as in specific areas, such as academics, athletic ability, and social competence (Esnaola et al., 2020; Harter, 2012b). Adolescents develop a positive self-esteem when they evaluate themselves favorably in the areas that they view as important. For example, sports accomplishments are more closely associated with physical self-esteem in adolescent athletes, who tend to highly value physical athleticism, but athleticism is less closely related to self-esteem in nonathletes (Wagnsson et al., 2014). Similarly, adolescents with high academic self-esteem tend to spend more time and effort on schoolwork, view academics as more important, and continue to demonstrate high academic achievement (Preckel et al., 2013).

Self-esteem tends to decline in early adolescence, at about 11 years of age, reaching its lowest point at about 13 years of age, then rises (Orth, 2017). This pattern is true for both boys and girls of all ethnicities, with girls tending to show lower self-esteem, but for most adolescents these shifts in self-esteem are small (Bleidorn et al., 2016; Onetti et al., 2019; von Soest et al., 2016). Declines in global self-esteem are likely due to the multiple transitions that young adolescents undergo, such as body changes and the emotions that accompany those changes, as well as adolescents' self-comparisons to their peers (Schaffhuser et al., 2017). However, ethnic differences suggest more complex changes.

After a drop in early adolescence, self-esteem tends to rise from middle to late adolescence.

iStock/Rawpixel

Generally speaking, Black adolescents tend to have higher self-esteem than their other-ethnic peers (see Figure 10.1; Bachman et al., 2011; Erol & Orth, 2011). From early to late adolescence the relative position of white and Hispanic adolescents shifts, with Hispanic adolescents showing dramatic increases in self-esteem relative to white adolescents. Asian American adolescent tend to score particularly low on measures of self-esteem compared to their peers (Bachman et al., 2011). How do we account for ethnic differences in self-esteem? Despite often experiencing racism and discrimination, Black adolescents' self-esteem may be protected by their immersion in closely knit Black communities that offer young people support, guidance, and connections to adults who provide positive feedback. These connections are a source

FIGURE 10.1 ■ Self-Esteem in Black, White, and Hispanic Adolescents From Age 14–30

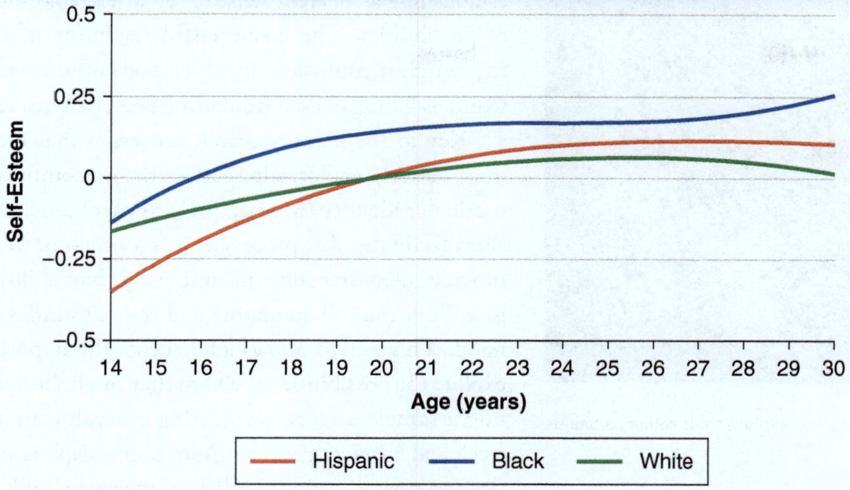

Source: Erol and Orth (2011).

of support that influences Black adolescents' self-conceptions and their feelings of worth. Hispanic adolescents are often immersed in similar communities that emphasize family ties that buffer the effect of negative experiences on adolescents' self-evaluations. Culture also plays a role in influencing Asian American adolescents' typically low self-evaluations. Asian cultures tend to emphasize interdependence and collectivism, valuing the community over the individual (Markus & Kitayama, 2010). Promoting self-esteem runs contrary to these values (Heine & Hamamura, 2007).

Adolescents' sense of self-worth influences their behavior and well-being. Adolescents with high self-esteem tend to be more confident, more willing to reject advice they deem poor, more likely to speak up, and are more sure of themselves (Baumeister & Vohs, 2018; Cvencek & Greenwald, 2020). Adolescents with high self-esteem have more self-compassion; they are kind to themselves and are more likely to perceive experiences and failures as opportunities for self-awareness rather than self-judgment (Barry et al., 2015). Low self-esteem, on the other hand, is associated with risky behavior, including alcohol and substance use (Jackman & MacPhee, 2017; Lee et al., 2018; Oshri et al., 2017). Persistently low self-esteem is associated with adjustment difficulties, such as depression, that can persist throughout adolescence (Fiorilli et al., 2019; Orth, 2017).

Family and peers are important contexts for the development of self-esteem. High-quality parent-adolescent relationships, characterized by an authoritative style and parents' emotional availability, are associated with higher estimates of self-worth and better adjustment in adolescents from the Netherlands, China, Australia, Germany, Italy, and the United States (Babore et al., 2017; Harris et al., 2015; Keizer et al., 2019; Miconi et al., 2017; Wang & Sheikh-Khalil, 2014; Wouters et al., 2013). In contrast, parent-adolescent conflict and parental feedback that is critical, inconsistent, and not contingent on behavior predict the development of poor self-esteem (Wang et al., 2016). Peer acceptance can buffer the negative effects of a distant relationship with parents (Birkeland et al., 2014). Adolescents who feel supported and well-liked by peers tend to show high self-esteem in adolescence, emerging adulthood, and young adulthood through age 35 (Gruenenfelder-Steiger et al., 2016; Sánchez-Queija et al., 2017; Vanhalst et al., 2013).

Identity

As adolescents come to understand their diverse characteristics, they undertake the psychosocial task of adolescence: they begin to organize their self-understandings to construct an **identity**, a sense of self that is coherent and consistent over time (Erikson, 1950). In establishing a sense of identity, individuals must consider their past and future and come to a sense of their values, beliefs, and goals for vocation,

Some adolescents learn about different religions and explore their religious beliefs as part of their identity search.

iStock/FatCamera

politics, religion, sexuality, and more. **Identity achievement** represents the successful resolution of this process, establishing a coherent sense of self after exploring a range of possibilities. The unsuccessful resolution of the identity search is confusion, in which one withdraws from the world, isolating oneself from loved ones, parents, and peers.

Key to the identity search process is that individuals must actively explore alternatives before committing to a particular identity (Meeus, 2011). A **psychosocial moratorium** facilitates this process as it is a time-out period that provides more freedom and autonomy than childhood but is without the full autonomy and responsibilities of adulthood. This period allows adolescents the opportunity to explore the possibilities of whom they might become. They might sample careers, considering becoming an actor one week and a lawyer the next. Adolescents explore personalities and desires, trying out different personas and styles. As adolescents explore possible identities, they identify choices and become increasingly confident about those choices over time. Identity development is a dynamic process in which individuals shift between certainty to uncertainty—as often as daily—as they explore identity alternatives and examine their feelings of commitment to a particular identity structure (Becht et al., 2017; Galliher et al., 2017).

Identity Statuses

Researchers study identity with large samples of people using interview and survey measures. The most common approach is to classify individuals' progress in identity exploration (the degree to which they have explored possible selves) and commitment (whether they have committed to specific beliefs and goals) into four categories known as **identity status** (see Table 10.1; Marcia, 1966).

The least mature status is identity diffusion (not having explored or committed to a sense of self), characterized by pervasive uncertainty with little motive for resolution (Berzonsky & Kuk, 2000). Individuals who are in the identity foreclosure status have prematurely chosen an identity without having engaged in exploration; they tend to be inflexible and view the world in black and white, right and wrong, terms. The identity moratorium status involves an active exploration of ideas and a sense of openness to possibilities, coupled with some uncertainty. The uncertainty is uncomfortable and young people are highly motivated to seek resolution and reduce the discomfort. The fourth category, identity achievement status, requires that individuals construct a sense of self through reflection, critical examination, and exploring or trying out new ideas and belief systems; it also requires that they have formed a commitment to a particular set of ideas, values, and beliefs. Identity diffusion and foreclosure become less common in late adolescence, when moratorium and identity achievement are more prevalent.

Young people typically shift among identity statuses over the adolescent years, but the specific pattern of identity development varies among adolescents (Meeus, 2011). Some adolescents remain in one identity status, such as identity moratorium, for the bulk of adolescence, while others experience multiple transitions in identity status. The most common shifts in identity status are from the least mature statuses, identity diffusion and identity foreclosure, to the most mature statuses, moratorium and achievement, in middle and late adolescence (Al-Owidha et al., 2009; de Moor et al., 2021; Yip, 2014). The overall proportion of young people in the moratorium status tends to increase during adolescence, peaking at about age 19 and declining over emerging adulthood as young people gradually commit to identities (Kroger et al., 2010).

People form a sense of identity in many different realms within both the ideological (i.e., occupation, religion, and politics) and interpersonal (i.e., friendships and dating) domains (Grotevant et al., 1982). Although Erikson emphasized identity development as a task for adolescence, researchers today believe that emerging adulthood is an important time for identity development, especially for young people who attend college (Arnett, 2016). Although the task of forming an identity is first encountered during adolescence, it is often not resolved in adolescence and the resulting identity is still not final thereafter (Kroger, 2015; Marcia, 2002). Identity is revisited and reconstructed again and again (Crocetti, 2017a). Changing life circumstances, contexts, and developmental needs spur identity development during adulthood (Carlsson et al., 2015).

Influences on Identity Development

Just as authoritative parenting fosters the development of positive self-concept and self-esteem, it also is associated with identity achievement. Adolescents who feel connected to their parents, supported, and accepted by them but who also feel that they are free and encouraged to develop and voice their own views are more likely to engage in the exploration necessary to advance to the moratorium and achieved statuses (Schwartz et al., 2015; Trost et al., 2020). In turn, as adolescents commit to identities, their relationships with parents and siblings tend to improve (Crocetti et al., 2017). The degree of freedom and support that adolescents are afforded for exploration varies with contextual factors related to family and community, such as socioeconomic status (Vosylis et al., 2020). Adolescents from high–socioeconomic status homes may have fewer responsibilities outside the home, may reside in communities with more extracurricular opportunities, and may be more likely to attend postsecondary education than their peers from low–socioeconomic homes—all factors that support the exploration needed for identity achievement (Kroger, 2015; Spencer et al., 2015).

Peers also influence identity development as they serve as a mirror in which adolescents view their emerging identities and an audience to which they relay their self-narratives (McAdams & Zapata-Gietl, 2015). When adolescents feel supported and respected by peers, they feel more comfortable exploring identity alternatives (Ragelienė, 2016). As with parents, conflict with peers harms identity development because adolescents may feel less free to explore identity alternatives and may lack a supportive peer group to offer input on identity alternatives, which can lead to undesirable identity outcomes, such as identity foreclosure or identity diffusion (Hall & Brassard, 2008).

Outcomes Associated With Identity Development

Identity achievement is associated with high self-esteem, a mature sense of self, feelings of control, high moral reasoning, and positive views of work and school (Jespersen et al., 2013; Spencer et al., 2015). In contrast, young people in the moratorium status often feel puzzled by the many choices before them (Lillevoll et al., 2013). The process of sorting through and choosing among possibilities is stressful and associated with negative mood and, at its extreme, can be paralyzing and curtail identity exploration (Crocetti et al., 2009; Klimstra et al., 2016). Young people who show identity foreclosure tend to take a rigid and inflexible stance. Unopen to new experiences, they avoid reflecting on their identity choice and reject information that may contradict their position.

Finally, while it is developmentally appropriate for early adolescents to have neither explored nor committed to a sense of identity, by late adolescence identity diffusion is uncommon and has been considered indicative of maladjustment (Kroger et al., 2010). Identity-diffused adolescents keep life on hold. They do not seek—and may even avoid—the meaning-making experiences needed to form a sense of identity (Carlsson et al., 2016). Academic difficulties, general apathy, organization and time management problems, and alcohol and substance use are associated with identity diffusion and often precede it (Crocetti, 2017b; Mercer et al., 2017).

Ethnic-Racial Identity

Race and ethnicity are important components of the sense of self for many adolescents.

Ethnic-racial identity refers to a sense of membership in an ethnic or racial group including the attitudes, values, and culture associated with that group (e.g., Latinx, Asian American, African American, European) within a specific sociohistorical context (Phinney & Ong, 2007; Rivas-Drake et al., 2014; Umaña-Taylor, 2016).

The exploration and commitment process that is key to identity achievement also underlies establishment of a sense of ethnic-racial identity (Yip, 2014). Like other components of a sense of self, ethnic-racial identity develops and changes over time as individuals explore, gain experience, and make choices in various contexts. Adolescents who learn about their culture, such as its values, attitudes,

TABLE 10.1 ■ Identity Status

		Commitment	
		Present	**Absent**
Exploration	**Present**	**Identity Achievement** Commitment to an identity after exploring multiple possibilities. Associated with an active problem-solving style, high self-esteem, feelings of control, high moral reasoning, and positive views of work and school	**Moratorium** Active exploration of identity alternatives without having committed to an identity. Associated with openness to experience, an active problem-solving style, anxiety and discomfort, and experimentation with alcohol or substance use
	Absent	**Identity Foreclosure** Commitment to an identity without having explored multiple possibilities. Associated with avoiding reflection or exploration of identity alternatives, rigidity, and a lack of openness to new information and ideas, especially if they contradict their position	**Identity Diffusion** Has neither committed to an identity nor explored alternatives. Associated with avoidance, tending to not solve personal problems in favor of letting issues decide themselves, academic difficulties, apathy, alcohol and substance use

Source: Marcia (1966); Meeus (2011).

language, and traditions, and regularly interact with parents and peers as members of a cultural community are more likely to construct a favorable ethnic-racial identity (Romero et al., 2014; White et al., 2018). In addition to exploration, the process of ethnic-racial identity development involves internalizing values from one's ethnic and racial group (Hughes et al., 2017). As adolescents develop a sense of belonging to their cultural community, they may become committed to an ethnic-racial identity.

Like other aspects of identity, ethnic-racial identity is influenced by family, peer, school, neighborhood, and societal contexts. Parents promote ethnic and cultural socialization and pride by teaching children about the history, culture, and heritage associated with their ethnicity (Huguley et al., 2019; Umaña-Taylor, 2016). Research suggests that there are group differences in ethnic socialization practices. Parents of color tend to engage in more ethnic and cultural socialization than white parents (Else-Quest & Morse, 2015; Harding et al., 2017). Black and Latinx youth and their parents report a greater emphasis on preparing adolescents to manage bias than parents of youth from other ethnic groups (Else-Quest & Morse, 2015; Hughes et al., 2009; Rivas-Drake et al., 2009).

Peers support ethnic-racial identity development by communicating experiences and beliefs about ethnicity and race, providing a sense of community that can bolster young people's sense of commitment to an ethnic-racial identity and offer a buffer against the stress of prejudice and discrimination (Jugert et al., 2020; Rivas-Drake et al., 2017).

The context outside of the home and friendship group also influences ethnic-racial identity formation. With advances in cognitive development and perspective-taking abilities, adolescents of color become increasingly aware of and sensitive to negative stereotypes about their race or ethnicity, discrimination, and inequality, all of which pose challenges to developing a positive sense of ethnic-racial identity (McLean et al., 2015). Adolescents from a variety of racial and ethnic groups, both U.S. born and immigrant, report encountering discrimination on average one or two times a week (Hughes et al., 2016; Umaña-Taylor, 2016). Adolescents of color often receive confusing messages to embrace their heritage while confronting discrimination, making the path to exploring and achieving ethnic-racial identity challenging and painful (McLean et al., 2015).

Adolescents' ethnic-racial identity and feelings about their ethnic-racial group membership influences their perceptions and experiences of discrimination (Seaton et al., 2009). Identifying with an ethnic-racial group may sensitize adolescents to discrimination (Gonzales-Backen et al., 2018). Young people who rate ethnicity/race as important to their overall sense of self, as well as those who are still in the process of exploring their identity, are more likely to report experiences with discrimination (Brittian et al., 2015; Burrow & Ong, 2010). Alternatively, the experience of discrimination may also prompt adolescents to seek information about, and increase identification with, their ethnic and racial group, rejecting negative stereotypes (Mims & Williams, 2020; Yip, 2018).

Adolescents can develop a strong sense of ethnic-racial identity by learning about their cultural heritage, including the language, customs, and shared history.

David McNew/Getty Images

A strong sense of ethnic-racial identity can reduce the negative impact of racial discrimination on adjustment, including self-concept, academic achievement, and problem behaviors, as well as act as a buffer to stress, including discrimination stress, among African American, Latinx, and multiracial adolescents (Douglass & Umaña-Taylor, 2016; Sanchez et al., 2017; Yip et al., 2019). Positive ethnic-racial identity contributes to well-being and is associated with school achievement in adolescents from diverse ethnicities, such as those of Mexican, Chinese, Latinx, African American, and European backgrounds (Kyere & Huguley, 2020; Miller-Cotto & Byrnes, 2016). Adolescents who have achieved a strong sense of ethnic-racial identity tend to show better adjustment and coping skills, including self-esteem and optimism, as well as fewer emotional and behavior problems than do those who do not or only weakly identify with ethnicity (Douglass & Umaña-Taylor, 2017; Miller-Cotto & Byrnes, 2016; Nelson et al., 2018; Zapolski et al., 2017). Ethnic-racial identity continues to influence adjustment in adulthood (Syed et al., 2013).

Gender Intensification and Transgender Identity

The identity explorations of adolescence extend to gender. With puberty adolescents' bodies change rapidly; they appear more mature and are often treated differently by others. Many young adolescents perceive greater social pressure to adhere to gender-stereotyped roles and behaviors, a phenomenon referred to as **gender intensification** (Galambos et al., 2009; Kågesten et al., 2016; Priess & Lindberg, 2018). Gender typing and gender stereotypic behavior tends to increase in early adolescence (Galambos et al., 2009; Klaczynski et al., 2020). Boys who are perceived as less masculine and girls as less feminine than peers may feel less accepted, be less popular, and experience higher rates of victimization (Smith & Leaper, 2006; Toomey et al., 2018). However, not all adolescents experience gender intensification, leading researchers to debate its existence (Korlat et al., 2021;Priess & Lindberg, 2018).

The heightened attention to gender that accompanies the onset of puberty can be distressing for adolescents with a transgender identity, posing risks for adjustment as their bodies change in ways that do not align with their gender identity (Vance et al., 2014). About 0.5% to 1% of the population of adolescents and adults identify as transgender (Crissman et al., 2017; Gates, 2011; Zucker, 2017), but the true figure may be higher.

As compared with their cisgender peers, adolescents with a transgender identity experience elevated stress and higher rates of mental health problems, including self-harm, depression, anxiety, and suicidal ideation (thinking about suicide; Becerra-Culqui et al., 2018; Price-Feeney et al., 2020; Russell & Fish, 2016; Thoma et al., 2019). Transgender adolescents commonly experience harassment, discrimination, and higher levels of peer victimization than their cisgender peers (Birkett et al., 2015; Hatchel et al., 2019; Mustanski et al., 2016).

Close supportive relationships with family and peers are associated with positive adjustment (Johns et al., 2018; Pariseau et al., 2019). Students who attend schools with clear policies against bullying, LGBT-inclusive curricula, and the presence of a gay-straight alliance (GSA) or other gender-inclusive student group, tend to report feeling more connected to adults at school and school itself, as well as report feeling safer at school and more engaged (Hazel et al., 2019;Ioverno et al., 2016; Marx & Kettrey, 2016). But only about half of U.S. secondary students report the availability of a GSA in their school (Kosciw et al., 2015).

Adolescents with a transgender identity may seek to transition to their self-identified sex.

DEREK R. HENKLE/AFP/Getty Images

Adolescents with a transgender identity may seek to transition to their self-identified sex. A **social gender transition** entails matching adolescents' everyday experience with their gender identity, such as by changing the pronoun used to describe the person, perhaps their name, and their appearance, including hair and clothing. Social transitioning and parental support of social transitions are associated with better mental health outcomes in transgender adolescents, including lower rates of anxiety and depression (Durwood et al., 2017; Russell et al., 2018; Simons et al., 2013).

A **biological gender transition** is a medical process that typically involves body changes that are induced by hormone therapy and permanent changes to the external genitals, accomplished by means of gender reassignment surgery. Older children who identify as transgender, in consultation with their parents and pediatrician, may take puberty suppressors (medication that inhibits sex hormones and prevents the onset of pubertal changes). Puberty suppression is reversible and affords transgender adolescents and their parents and medical team the time needed to explore and understand transgender adolescents' gender identity and develop coping skills (Panagiotakopoulos, 2018). Some research has suggested that puberty suppression is safe and associated with positive mental health outcomes in transgender adolescents (Bonifacio et al., 2019; Schagen et al., 2016), but there are no large long-term studies to inform professional practice (Mahfouda et al., 2017). Gender-affirming medical care is often limited outside of large cities and is expensive, posing large barriers for adolescents and their parents who seek support and treatment (Puckett et al., 2018; Safer & Chan, 2019).

Moral Development

Adolescents are confronted with moral dilemmas and opportunities for prosocial behavior daily. Recall from Chapter 8, Lawrence Kohlberg's theory of moral development examines age-related changes in reasoning about fairness and justice. Young children display preconventional reasoning, governed by self-interest. Conventional reasoning that emphasizes societal perspectives and reciprocity emerges in middle to late childhood (see Chapter 1). In adolescence, according to Kohlberg, individuals become capable of demonstrating the most advanced moral thinking, **postconventional moral reasoning**—autonomous decision making from moral principles that value respect for individual rights above all else. Postconventional moral thinkers recognize that their self-chosen principles of fairness and justice may sometimes conflict with the law and, therefore, may justify breaking the law when human life or dignity is at stake.

Lawrence Kohlberg constructed his theory of moral development using longitudinal observations and interviews of a group of boys, ages 10, 13, and 16, over three decades (Kohlberg, 1969). Kohlberg measured moral reasoning by presenting individuals with hypothetical dilemmas that examine how people make decisions when fairness and people's rights are pitted against obedience to authority and law. The Heinz dilemma is the most popular example of the hypothetical conflicts that Kohlberg used to study moral development:

> Near death, a woman with cancer learns of a drug that may save her. The woman's husband, Heinz, approaches the druggist who created the drug, but the druggist refuses to sell the drug for anything less than $2,000. After borrowing from everyone he knows, Heinz has only scraped together $1,000. Heinz asks the druggist to let him have the drug for $1,000 and he will pay him the rest later. The druggist says that it is his right to make money from the drug he developed and refuses to sell it to Heinz. Desperate for the drug, Heinz breaks into the druggist's store and steals the drug. Should Heinz have done that? Why or why not? (Kohlberg, 1969)

Kohlberg discovered that the boys' reasoning progressed through a predictable series of stages, grouped into three levels (with two stages per level). At the preconventional level, decisions are influenced by self-interest, rewards, and punishments. Children might respond that Heinz should not steal the drug because he will go to prison, or that he should steal the drug to avoid his wife's anger or to receive her affection. Conventional moral reasoning is socially driven. School-age children might argue that Heinz should steal the drug because good people help their wives or because it is his duty as a husband. Alternatively, they might say that Heinz should not steal the drug because good people do not steal or because following rules maintains social order; what would happen if everyone stole? At the postconventional level of reasoning, adolescents might explain that, although stealing is against the law, laws are intended to help people and, in this case, stealing the drug is intended to help Heinz's wife. Moreover, the value of a life is exponentially greater than that of the drug, suggesting that Heinz should steal the drug.

As they enter the postconventional level of moral reasoning, individuals view laws and rules as flexible and part of the social contract or agreement meant to further human interests (Stage 5). Laws and rules are to be followed because they bring good to people, but laws can be changed if they are inconsistent with the needs and rights of the majority. Sometimes, if laws are unjust—if they harm more people than they protect—they can be broken. The final, most advanced, and most rare stage of reasoning, Stage 6, is based on abstract ethical principles that are universal—valid for all people regardless of law—such as equality and respect for human dignity. Although advances in cognitive development make postconventional reasoning possible, the highest forms of postconventional reasoning are rare.

A great deal of research has confirmed that individuals proceed through the first four stages of moral reasoning in a slow, gradual, and predictable fashion (Boom et al., 2007; Dawson, 2002). The preconventional level tends to decline by early adolescence. Conventional reasoning, specifically Stage 3, increases through middle adolescence, and Stage 4 reasoning increases in middle to late adolescence and becomes typical of most individuals by early adulthood. Research suggests that few people advance beyond conventional (Stage 4) moral reasoning. Postconventional reasoning is rare in adults and appears as Stage 5 reasoning (Kohlberg et al., 1983). Research generally has not supported the existence of Stage 6, the hypothesized most advanced type of moral reasoning, because it was not demonstrated by participants in Kohlberg's studies, but Stage 6 represents an end-goal state to which human development strives (Kohlberg & Ryncarz, 1990).

Influences on Moral Reasoning

Moral reasoning is influenced by interactions with others in all of the contexts in which adolescents live. High-quality parent-child relationships predict advanced moral reasoning (Malti & Latzko, 2010). Reasoning advances when adolescents have opportunities to engage in discussions that are characterized by mutual perspective taking. Engaging adolescents in discussion about personal experiences, local issues, and media events—while presenting alternative points of view and asking questions—advances reasoning. Issue-focused discussions that present adolescents with reasoning that is slightly more advanced than their own prompts them to compare their reasoning with the new reasoning and often internalize the new reasoning, advancing their moral reasoning to a new level (Carlo et al., 2011). Interactions with peers in and out of school promote moral reasoning when adolescents share different perspectives and engage each other with in-depth discussions (Power et al., 1989).

Gender, Culture, and Moral Reasoning

A popular criticism of Kohlberg's theory of moral reasoning arises because his initial research was conducted with samples of boys. Early research that studied both men and women suggested gender differences in moral reasoning, with men typically showing justice-oriented Stage 4 reasoning, characterized by concerns about law and order, and women showing care-oriented Stage 3 reasoning, characterized by concerns about maintaining relationships and avoiding harming others (Gilligan, 1982; Poppen, 1974). Later research demonstrated that men and women display similar reasoning that combines concerns of justice (e.g., being fair) with those of care (e.g., being supportive and helpful), and when there are sex differences, they are very small (Jaffee & Hyde, 2000; Knox et al., 2004; Kohlberg et al., 1983; Weisz & Black, 2002). The most mature forms of moral reasoning incorporate both justice and care concerns.

Most people at least sometimes behave in ways they know they shouldn't.

iStock/FatCamera

Although the highest forms of moral reasoning appear in all cultures, people in non-Western cultures rarely score above the conventional level, specifically, Stage 3, on Kohlberg's measures (Gibbs et al., 2007). Like cognitive capacities, morality and appropriate responses to ethical dilemmas are defined by each society and its cultural perspectives. Western cultures tend to emphasize the rights of the individual (justice-based Stage 4 reasoning) and non-Western cultures tend to value collectivism, focusing on human interdependence (care-based stage 3 reasoning). Collectivist cultures tend to view moral dilemmas as a responsibility of the entire community rather than simply of the individual (Miller, 2018). Because moral values are relative to the cultural context, Stage 3 reasoning is an advanced form of reasoning in collectivist cultures because it embodies what is most valued in these cultures, concepts such as interdependence and relationships. People of different cultures are able to reason using both care and justice orientations even though cultures tend to vary in the weight they assign moral orientations, emphasizing one over another.

Moral Reasoning and Behavior

With advances in moral reasoning, adolescents are more likely to act in ways that are in line with their beliefs (Smetana et al., 2014). Adolescents who demonstrate higher levels of moral reasoning are more likely to share with and help others and are less likely to engage in antisocial behavior such as cheating, aggression, or delinquency (Brugman, 2010; Comunian & Gielen, 2000). Although adolescents who show low levels of moral reasoning are thought to be at greater risk for delinquency, findings are mixed (Leenders & Brugman, 2005; Tarry & Emler, 2007). The degree to which moral reasoning is associated with behavior varies with adolescents' beliefs about whether the behavior is a moral concern or simply a social convention or a personal choice (Berkowitz & Begun, 1994; Brugman, 2010). Adolescents' moral reasoning predicts behavior they deem to be a moral choice but not the many issues they view as personal choices.

Thinking in Context: Lifespan Development

Why is identity often referred to as the central developmental task of adolescence? What are some indicators that adolescents are undergoing this process? In your view, when do most young people complete this process? What might be indicators that it is complete?

Thinking in Context: Intersectionality

1. Why is it that a sense of ethnic-racial identity can sensitize adolescents to discrimination, a critical stressor, yet also benefit adolescents? In what ways might ethnic-racial identity act a protective factor for youths of color, promoting resilience despite hardships?
2. Consider your own sense of ethnic-racial identity. Is ethnicity or race an important part of your sense of self? Why or why not? Have you experienced shifts in your experience of race or ethnicity from childhood to adulthood?
3. Why is ethnicity and race more salient to some young people than others? Why might critics argue that not exploring racial-ethnic identity is a luxury for the privileged? Do you agree or disagree?

ADOLESCENTS AND THEIR PARENTS

LEARNING OBJECTIVE

10.2 Discuss parent-child interactions and the parent-child relationship in adolescence.

Parents must adapt their parenting strategies to match children's ability to reason and their desire for independence, both of which increase from middle childhood into adolescence. Adolescence marks a change in parent-child relationships. As they advance cognitively and develop a more complicated sense of self, adolescents strive for **autonomy**, the ability to make and carry out their own decisions, and they begin to rely less on parents. They also can demonstrate better self-understanding and more rational decision making and problem solving, creating a foundation for parents to treat adolescents less like children and grant them more decision-making responsibility. The parenting challenge during adolescence is to offer increasing opportunities for adolescents to develop and practice autonomy while providing protection from danger and the consequences of poor decisions (Kobak et al., 2017). Parents may doubt their own importance to their adolescent children, but a large body of research shows that parents play a critical role in adolescent development alongside that of peers.

Parent-Adolescent Conflict

Conflict between parents and adolescents tends to rise in early adolescence, becoming more frequent, as boys and girls seek autonomy and begin to recognize that their parents are fallible and are capable of good and bad decisions (Meeus, 2016). Adolescents report having three or four conflicts or disagreements with parents over the course of a typical day (Adams & Laursen, 2007). Parent-adolescent conflict generally centers on mundane matters: small arguments over the details of life, such as household responsibilities, privileges, relationships, curfews, cleaning of the adolescent's bedroom, choices of media, or music volume (Van Doorn et al., 2011). Conflicts over religious, political, or social issues occur less frequently, as do conflicts concerning other potentially sensitive topics (e.g., substance use, dating, sexual relationships; Renk et al., 2005). Conflict tends to peak in middle adolescence and decline from middle to late adolescence and emerging adulthood as young people become more independent and begin to better understand their parents as people (Branje, 2018).

Most adolescents and parents continue to have warm, close, communicative relationships characterized by love and respect (Hart et al., 2019). A minority of adolescents experience intense conflict with parents. In one longitudinal study, about 14% of participants reported turbulent relationships with parents characterized by low support and high conflict in early adolescence (age 12), rising to 29% at about age 16 and declining to 10% by around age 20 (Hadiwijaya et al., 2017). Although about one-third of the adolescents reported turbulent relationships in middle adolescence, the parent-child relationship showed overall continuity, and most adolescents reported that their relationships with their parents remained the same. There tends to be continuity in parenting and parent-child relationships (Huey et al., 2017). Patterns of harsh verbal discipline (yelling, threatening, punishment, shaming) and insensitive parenting established in early childhood tend to persist and worsen in middle childhood and adolescence (Lansford et al., 2013). Parent-adolescent interactions are reciprocal, with parents and adolescents influencing each other over time. Daily diaries by adolescents reveal that anger both predicts conflict with parents and is also a consequence of conflict (LoBraico et al., 2020). As parents engage in more negative interactions, adolescents focus more on angry interpersonal interactions and less on happy interactions (Lucas-Thompson et al., 2020).

Age-related shifts in conflict are supported by research with diverse samples, with some small differences (Smetana & Rote, 2019). Some research suggests that conflicts develop earlier and are more frequent among European Americans as compared with adolescents of other ethnicities and races (Smetana, 2011). Contextual factors may contribute to these differences, such as cultural values, including individualism, collectivism, family solidarity, and respect for elders, as well as neighborhood

Parent-child conflict tends to peak in middle adolescence but it is usually over mundane issues, such as housework. Most adolescents report having warm and supportive relationships with their parents.

istock/ Motortion

and community influences, including resources, socioeconomic status, and privilege. A common source of conflict for adolescents from immigrant families concerns acculturation, specifically mismatches between adolescents and parents (Chung et al., 2009; Fuligni & Tsai, 2015). Research with Latinx and Asian-heritage families suggests that parent-adolescent gaps in acculturation, when it reflects clashes in values, may lead to conflicts over everyday issues. In one study of Arab American adolescents, the larger the acculturation gap between parents and adolescents (as perceived by adolescents), the greater the conflict (Goforth et al., 2015).

Frequent arguments charged with negative emotion are harmful to adolescents (Huey et al., 2017). In adolescents of all races and ethnicities—African American, Latinx, Asian, and white—parent-adolescent conflict is associated with internalizing problems such as depression, externalizing problems such as aggression and delinquency, and social problems such as social withdrawal and poor conflict resolution with peers, poor school achievement, and, among girls, early sexual activity (Hofer et al., 2013; Moreno et al., 2017; Skinner & McHale, 2016; Weymouth et al., 2016). Severe parent-adolescent conflict is associated with an increased risk for depression in adulthood (Alaie et al., 2020).

Although severe conflict is harmful, some conflict is conducive to adolescent development, helping adolescents learn to regulate emotions and resolve conflicts (Branje, 2018). Though distressing to adolescents, moderate levels of adolescent-parent conflict are associated with better adjustment than either no conflict or very frequent conflict (Smetana & Rote, 2019). Developmentally supportive conflict is coupled with acceptance, respect, and autonomy support. Within the context of warm parental relationships, daily conflict with parents is not associated with poor adolescent well-being (Silva et al., 2020). Disagreements have a purpose: to transform adolescent-parent relationships from hierarchical in early adolescence to more symmetrical in late adolescence (Meeus, 2016).

Parenting and Adjustment

Parents' task in raising adolescents is to balance autonomy granting with guidance. Authoritative parenting best accomplishes this feat as it is characterized by warmth, support, and limits. Across ethnic and socioeconomic groups, and in countries around the world, authoritative parenting fosters autonomy, self-reliance, self-esteem, a positive view of the value of work, and academic competence in adolescents (Bornstein & Putnick, 2018; McKinney & Renk, 2011; Uji et al., 2013). Authoritative parents' use of open discussion, joint decision making, and firm but fair limit setting helps adolescents feel valued, respected, and encouraged to think for themselves (Hart et al., 2019). Parents in a household often share a common parenting style, but when they do not, the presence of authoritative parenting in at least one parent buffers the negative outcomes associated with the other style and predicts positive adjustment (Hoeve et al., 2011). Generally, emotional support by parents tends to increase and psychological control continues to decline during emerging adulthood (Desjardins & Leadbeater, 2017; Smetana & Rote, 2019).

One way in which parents' balance autonomy granting with protection is through **parental monitoring**, being aware of their teens' whereabouts and companions. Effective parental monitoring is accompanied by warmth and is balanced with respect for adolescents' autonomy and privacy. Parental monitoring coupled with autonomy support is associated with positive adjustment and overall well-being, including academic achievement, delayed sexual initiation, and low levels of substance use and delinquent activity in youth across ethnicity and socioeconomic status (Lopez-Tamayo et al., 2016; Merrin et al., 2019; Rodríguez-Meirinhos et al., 2020).

Adolescents who live in poor, high-risk communities may benefit from more active and restrictive forms of parental monitoring, such as daily discussions about activities and behavioral limit setting, which may protect them from dangers in their communities (Bendezú et al., 2018; Burton & Jarrett, 2000). Parents who exert psychological control characteristic of authoritarian parenting inhibit the development of autonomy. Authoriarian parenting is associated with low self-esteem, depression, low academic competence, and antisocial behavior in adolescence through early adulthood in young people from Africa, Asia, Europe, the Middle East, and the Americas (Bornstein & Putnick, 2018; Griffith & Grolnick, 2013; Lansford et al., 2014; Uji et al., 2013; Pinquart & Gerke, 2019).

Adolescents communicate more openly and parenting strategies are most effective when the family emotional climate is positive (Kapetanovic & Skoog, 2021). When parents monitor too closely and restrict autonomy, such as monitoring in ways that adolescents perceive as intrusive or controlling, adolescents are likely to conceal their activities from their parents, lie, and continue to do so over time (Baudat et al., 2020; Rote & Smetana, 2016). Negative parent-adolescent interactions are associated with greater concealment and secret keeping among adolescents, which in turn predicts poorer parent-child relationships over time (Dykstra et al., 2020; Rote et al., 2020). Generally speaking, adolescents with positive relationships with parents conceal less and those with negative relationships conceal more (Rote et al., 2020). In middle-SES adolescents, parental monitoring perceived as intrusive is positively associated with delinquency as well as increases in delinquency over time (Kerr et al., 2010; Willoughby & Hamza, 2011).

What is considered effective parental monitoring changes as adolescents grow older. Throughout adolescence parents and adolescents often differ in their perception of parental monitoring (De Los Reyes et al., 2019; Lippold et al., 2011). Adolescents' and parents' perceptions of parental monitoring remain mismatched, with parents, but not adolescents, reporting declines in parental solicitation of information from adolescents (Lionetti et al., 2019). From middle to late adolescence, parental knowledge and control naturally declines as adolescents establish a private sphere, spend more time out of the home, and disclose less (Masche, 2010; Wang et al., 2011). Some mild concealment may serve a developmental purpose. White lies, partial truths, and keeping secrets may be a means for adolescents to establish autonomy (Lionetti et al., 2019). Although adolescents are entitled to their own thoughts and increasing privacy, keeping many secrets from parents can be harmful. Adolescent secrecy is associated with behavior problems including substance use and delinquency (Dykstra et al., 2020; Kapetanovic et al., 2019; Marceau et al., 2020). One cross-cultural study of nearly 1,100 young adolescents from 12 cultural groups in 9 countries—China, Colombia, Italy, Jordan, Kenya, Philippines, Sweden, Thailand, and the United States—found that adolescent secrecy is associated with externalizing problems in all cultures (Kapetanovic et al., 2020).

Thinking in Context: Lifespan Development

1. Compare and contrast popular views of parent-child relationships during adolescence with the research on parenting style and parental monitoring.
2. How might the specific actions that comprise effective parenting vary with context? Consider the different circumstances in which adolescents and their parents live, such as rural, urban, and suburban communities, coupled with SES. What concerns might arise for a parent rearing an adolescent in rural poverty? Are those concerns different in urban poverty? Suburban poverty? Do the behaviors that comprise effective parenting, such as monitoring, vary with the setting? Why or why not?

ADOLESCENTS AND THEIR PEERS

LEARNING OBJECTIVE

10.3 Examine the developmental progression of peer relations in adolescence.

The most easily recognizable influence on adolescents, and that which gets the most attention from adults and the media, is the peer group. Each week, adolescents spend up to one-third of their waking, nonschool hours with friends (Hartup & Stevens, 1997).

Friendships

The typical adolescent has four to six close friends (French & Cheung, 2018). Adolescent friendships are characterized by intimacy, self-disclosure, trust, and loyalty (Bowker & Ramsay, 2018). Adolescents expect their friends to be there for them, stand up for them, and not share their secrets or harm them. Adolescent friendships tend to include cooperation, sharing, intimacy, and affirmation, which reflect their emerging capacities for perspective taking, social sensitivity, empathy, and social skills (Bukowski et al., 2020).

Boys tend to get together for activities, usually sports and competitive games, and tend to be more social and vocal in groups as compared with one-on-one situations (Rose & Asher, 2017). Girls tend to engage in more one-on-one interactions and spend their time with friends talking. Girls' friendships tend to be shorter in duration, but characterized by more closeness, than those of boys (Erdley & Day, 2017a). High-quality friendships characterized by sharing, intimacy, and open communication tend to endure over time (Hiatt et al., 2015). About one-third to one-half of friendships in early adolescence are unstable, with young people regularly losing friends and making new friendships (Poulin & Chan, 2010). After early adolescence friendships become more stable, with young people retaining the majority of their friendships over the course of a school year.

As in childhood, similarity characterizes adolescent friendships. Friends tend to be similar in demographics, such as age, ethnicity, and socioeconomic status (Bowker & Ramsay, 2018; Laursen, 2017). Close friends and best friends tend to be similar in orientation toward risky activity, such as willingness to try drugs and engage in delinquency and dangerous behaviors such as unprotected sex (de Water et al., 2017; Hiatt et al., 2017; Richmond et al., 2019; Trinh et al., 2019). Adolescent friends tend to share interests, such as tastes in music; they are also similar in academic achievement, educational aspirations, and political beliefs; and they show similar trends in psychosocial development, such as identity status (Markiewicz & Doyle, 2016; Shin & Ryan, 2014). Through interaction, friends tend to become even more similar to each other (Bukowski et al., 2020).

Most adolescents report having several close friendships that are characterized by trust, intimacy, loyalty, and companionship.

mauritius images GmbH / Alamy Stock Photo

Sometimes middle and older adolescents choose friends who are different from them, which encourages them to consider new perspectives. Cross-ethnic friendships are less common than same-ethnic friendships but are associated with unique benefits. Ethnic minority adolescents with cross-ethnic friends perceive less discrimination, vulnerability, and relational victimization and show higher rates of self-esteem and well-being over time than those without cross-ethnic friends (Bagci et al., 2014; Graham et al., 2014; Kawabata & Crick, 2011). In addition, members of cross-ethnic friendships show lower levels of and greater declines in racial prejudice over time than their peers without cross-ethnic friendships (Titzmann et al., 2015).

Close and stable friendships aid adolescents in their social adjustment (French & Cheung, 2018). By communicating with others and forming mutually self-disclosing supportive relationships, adolescents develop perspective taking, empathy, self-concept, and a sense of identity. Friends who are supportive and empathetic encourage prosocial behavior, promote psychological health, reduce the risk of delinquency, and help adolescents manage stress, such as the challenges of school transitions (Hiatt et al., 2015; Wentzel, 2014). Friendship continues to have positive benefits and the nature of friendship continues to change from adolescence into emerging adulthood and early adulthood (Miething et al., 2017).

Cliques and Crowds

This group of girls comprises a clique. In early adolescence same-sex cliques are most common. Cliques of boys and girls tend to merge in middle adolescence, creating larger integrated groups.

mauritius images GmbH / Alamy Stock Photo

During adolescence, one-on-one friendships tend to expand into tightly knit peer groups of anywhere from three to as many as nine, but most commonly around five, members who are close friends. These close-knit groups of friends are known as **cliques**. Like most close friends, members of cliques tend to share similarities such as demographics and attitudes (Lansford et al., 2009). Belonging to a peer group provides adolescents with a sense of inclusion, worth, support, and companionship (Ellis & Zarbatany, 2017).

In contrast with cliques, which are an expansion of intimate friendships, **crowds** are larger and looser groups based on shared characteristics, interests, and reputation (such as athletes/jocks, academics/brains, populars/elites, or partiers). Rather than voluntarily "joining," adolescents are sorted into crowds by their peers. The emergence of crowds is tied to cognitive development as young adolescents notice patterns of traits and behaviors in their peers, and then group their peers accordingly. Members of a crowd may or may not interact with one another, but because of similarities in appearance, activities, and perceived attitudes, their peers consider them members of the same group. Adolescent crowds have been found in nearly all U.S. secondary schools large enough to have multiple social groups (Cross, 2018). Crowds differentiate young people on the basis of behaviors such as sexual activity, academic achievement, psychiatric symptoms, and health risks such as alcohol and substance use (Jordan et al., 2019; Stalgaitis et al., 2020; Van Hoorn et al., 2017b).

Peer Conformity

As peers rise in importance in early adolescence, so does the pressure to conform, sometimes called peer pressure, peaking at about age 14 and declining through age 18 and after (see Figure 10.2; Steinberg & Monahan, 2007). Adolescents experience the greatest pressure to conform to day-to-day activities and personal choices such as appearance (clothing, hairstyle, makeup) and music. Peer influence occurs within the context of friendship (Erdley & Day, 2017b). Adolescents are more likely to conform to best friends' behavior when they share a high-quality and satisfying relationship (Hiatt et al., 2017). Adolescents tend to select peers who engage in similar behaviors and friends' behaviors become more similar over time (Gremmen et al., 2017). Adolescents' reports of risky behavior such as smoking, unsafe sexual activity, and antisocial behavior correlates with their friends' behaviors (Choukas-Bradley et al., 2014; Daspe et al., 2019; McCoy et al., 2019; van de Bongardt et al., 2014). These behaviors tend to occur in the presence of peers, raising the question of whether adolescents' risky behavior is the result of conforming to peer influence or whether it is simply a shared activity.

It is not simply peer behavior that influences adolescent behavior; it is adolescents' perceptions of peer behavior, and beliefs about peers' activities, that predict engaging in risky activities such as smoking, substance use, and even sexting—sending sexually explicit text messages (Duan et al., 2009; Maheux et al., 2020). In addition, adolescents naturally engage in more risk in the presence of peers, even without encouragement (Van Hoorn et al., 2017a). Young people vary in how they perceive and respond to peer pressure based on factors such as age, personal characteristics, and context, such as the presence of norms (Pei et al., 2020). Adolescents are especially vulnerable to the negative effects of peer pressure during transitions such as entering a new school and undergoing puberty and when they are uncertain of their status in the peer group (Brechwald & Prinstein, 2011; Ellis & Zarbatany, 2017). Young adolescents are more susceptible to peer influence than older adolescents, especially for antisocial behaviors such as delinquent activity, peaking at about age 14 (Sumter et al., 2018).

FIGURE 10.2 ■ Age Differences in Resistance to Peer Influence

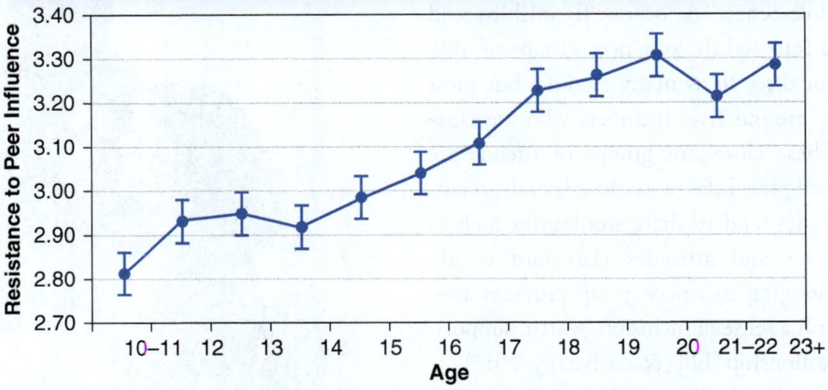

Source: Steinberg and Monahan (2007).

Peer pressure is not always negative. Adolescents also report pressure from their friends to engage in prosocial and positive behaviors such as getting good grades, performing well athletically, getting along with parents, and avoiding smoking (Brown et al., 2008; Farrell et al., 2017; Hofmann & Müller, 2018; Wentzel, 2014). They are also more likely to share and volunteer to help others in their community if they believe their friends and other students in their school volunteer (Choukas-Bradley et al., 2015; van Hoorn et al., 2016). Peer relationships are a positive force on adolescent development. Ultimately, susceptibility to peer influence tends to decline with advances in psychosocial maturity that support independent decision making.

Dating

Establishing romantic relationships is a considered a normative part of the adolescent experience. However, dating has become less common over the past three decades. As shown in Figure 10.3, the proportion of 12th-grade students who report that they do not date more than tripled between 1992 and 2017, from 15% to 49% (Child Trends, 2019a). The proportion of 10th graders who do not date has doubled during that time, and not dating has increased among 8th graders by 24%.

The declines in dating coincide with the rise of social media and video technology that permits face-to-face contact from a distance. It may be that in-person dating has transitioned to electronic forms or that adolescents do not use the term *dating* to describe romantic relationships (Twenge & Park, 2019). A shift from in-person to online relationships is concerning because online communication cannot replace in-person contact. Frequent use of technology-based communication with romantic partners is associated with lower social competence, especially among boys (Nesi et al., 2017).

Most adolescents perceive pressure to conform to peer norms for both positive and, in this example, negative behavior.

iStock/sturti

Developmental Shifts in Dating

In middle adolescence, from about age 14 to 16, romantic relationships tend to occur within a group context and through casual dating. Dating typically begins with the intermingling of mixed-sex peer groups (e.g., at parties and dances) and progresses to group dating and casual relationships, and finally one-on-one dating and romantic relationships (Connolly et al., 2013). Adolescents with larger social networks and greater access to opposite-sex peers tend to date more than those who are less social.

FIGURE 10.3 ■ Percentage of 8th, 10th, and 12th Graders Who Report They Never Date: Selected Years, 1976–2017

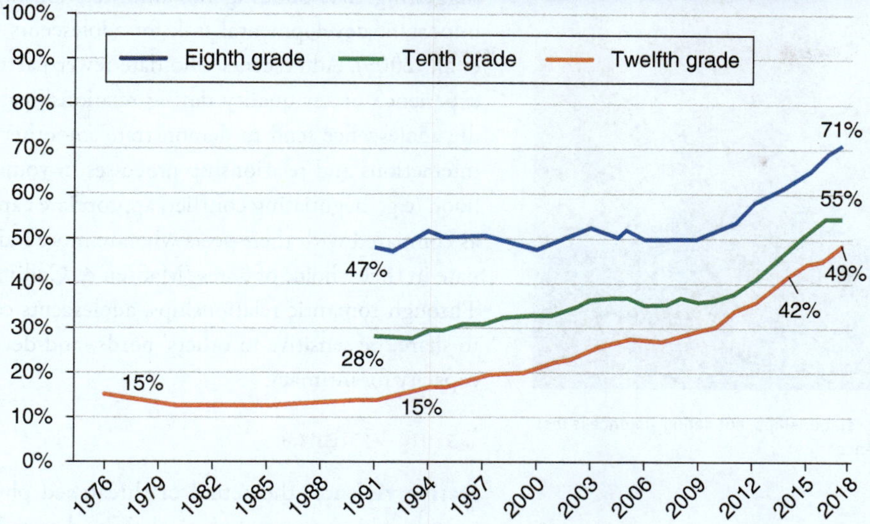

Source: Adapted from Child Trends Databank (2017).

In late adolescence, at about age 17 or 18, relationships tend to occur outside of peer groups (Furman & Rose, 2015). Relationships may become more serious over time in the sense that they become characterized by emotional bonds, become a source of intimacy, and commitment is valued (Kindelberger et al., 2020). Romantic relationships become more common with age (Furman et al., 2019).

Discussions of romantic relationships in adolescence tend to focus on heterosexual relationships. We know little about romantic relationship development in LGBT youth. Today, adolescents who are attracted to the same sex are more likely to have same-sex romantic relationships than in prior generations. However, romantic relationships among sexual minority youth may be less public because of concerns about stigmatization or being unprepared to come out to family. Adolescents with same-sex interests frequently date other-sex adolescents for a variety of reasons, such as exploration, attraction, social pressure, a desire to conceal, or because they are unready to come out (Savin-Williams, 2019; Ybarra et al., 2019). Similar to gender differences in friendship, girls' same-sex relationships tend to be closer and more intimate than boys' (Furman et al., 2019).

Dating and Psychosocial Adjustment

In middle and late adolescence, romantic relationships are associated with positive adjustment, including psychosocial maturity, positive self-concept, peer competence, fewer feelings of alienation, and good physical and mental health (Beckmeyer & Weybright, 2020; Connolly & McIsaac, 2011; Gonzalez Avilés et al., 2021). However, early dating relative to peers, prior to age 15, is associated with higher rates of poor adjustment, including alcohol and substance use, delinquency, and low academic competence, as well as depression, especially in girls (Beckmeyer & Weybright, 2020; Connolly et al., 2013). Dating off-time may interfere with developmental tasks, such as identity development, and adolescents who date early may not be able to meet the emotional demands of these relationships.

Romantic relationships are common in adolescence.

iStock/Martin Dimitrov

Many adolescents find themselves in abusive relationships, but dating violence is less likely to be reported than adult domestic violence.

istock/ Mixmike

Romantic experiences in adolescence are often continuous with romantic experiences in adulthood, suggesting that building romantic relationships is an important developmental task for adolescents (Collins et al., 2009). Adolescents who date fewer partners and experience better quality dating relationships in middle adolescence tend to demonstrate smoother partner interactions and relationship processes in young adulthood (e.g., negotiating conflict, appropriate caregiving) as compared with their peers who are more indiscriminate in their choice of dates (Madsen & Collins, 2011). Through romantic relationships, adolescents can learn to share, be sensitive to others' needs, and develop the capacity for intimacy.

Dating Violence

Dating violence, the actual or threatened physical or sexual violence or psychological abuse directed toward a current or former boyfriend, girlfriend, or dating partner, is surprisingly prevalent during adolescence. On average, about 20% of high school students have experienced physical violence, and 9% sexual violence, within a dating relationship (Wincentak et al., 2017). Both boys and girls perpetrate dating violence at roughly equal rates and within the context of relationships of mutual partner aggression in which both partners perpetrate and sustain the aggression (Sears et al., 2007; Williams et al., 2008). Girls are more likely to inflict psychological abuse and minor physical abuse (slapping, throwing objects, pinching), and boys are more likely to inflict more severe types of physical abuse, such as punching, as well as sexual abuse, making girls more likely to suffer physical wounds than boys. Physical violence tends to occur alongside psychological violence (Giordano et al., 2010).

Risk factors for engaging in dating violence include difficulty with anger management, poor interpersonal skills, exposure to family violence, and community violence (Foshee et al., 2014, 2015; Malhi et al., 2020; Vagi et al., 2013). Many of the risk factors for dating victimization are also outcomes of dating violence, such as poor self-regulation and conflict management, depression, anxiety, negative interactions with family and friends, low self-esteem, and substance use, making it difficult to determine causality (Collibee et al., 2019; Exner-Cortens et al., 2013; Malhi et al., 2020; Niolon et al., 2015). Successful interventions for dating violence help adolescents build skills in regulating their emotions, communicating effectively, and resolving conflicts (Rizzo et al., 2018; Smith-Darden et al., 2017).

Thinking in Context: Applied Developmental Science

Aunt Anne proclaims "I never want my teen to be in a clique. They're mean kids who exclude others." How do you respond? Explain the nature of friendship and the role of cliques in adolescence.

Thinking in Context: Lifespan Development

1. Identify three common misconceptions about peer relationships in adolescence. Consider issues such as cliques, crowds, peer influence, social media, and dating. Why do many people hold mistaken beliefs about these issues?
2. What might account for the decline in adolescent dating in recent decades? What contextual factors influence dating in adolescence? How might these have shifted? Some considerations might include the nature of parent-adolescent relationships, peer relationships, technology, views about romance in adolescence, identity development, and more. What do you think?

ADOLESCENT SEXUALITY

LEARNING OBJECTIVE

10.4 Analyze patterns of adolescent sexual activity including sexual orientation.

Adolescents are often depicted in media as driven by hormones and obsessed with sex. Yet sexuality is an important dimension of socioemotional development during adolescence. Sexuality encompasses feelings about oneself, appraisals of the self, attitudes, and behaviors (McClelland & Tolman, 2014). With the hormonal changes of puberty, both boys and girls experience an increase in sex drive and sexual interest (Fortenberry, 2013). Social context influences how biological urges are channeled into behavior and adolescents' conceptions of sexuality.

Sexual Activity

Sexual behaviors tend to progress in a predictable pattern from hand-holding to kissing, to touching through clothes and under clothes, to oral sex and then to genital intercourse (de Graaf et al., 2009). Contrary to the stereotypes of promiscuous sex-obsessed adolescents, most young people have sexual intercourse for the first time at about age 17 (see Figure 10.4; Guttmacher Institute, 2017).

An important trend over the past three decades is that fewer adolescents initiate sexual activity in the early years of high school. The percentage of high school students who have ever had sexual intercourse is at an all-time low (Kann et al., 2018; Witwer et al., 2018). By the time they graduate, 57% of high school students report having had sexual intercourse (Witwer et al., 2018). Only about a third of high school students report being sexually active, defined as sex within the previous three months (Child Trends Databank, 2017).

As shown in Figure 10.5, the proportion of adolescents who have ever engaged in sexual intercourse declined from 2005 to 2015. This trend is especially visible among Black adolescents and, to a lesser extent, among Hispanic adolescents, but not among white adolescents (Ethier, Kann & McManus, 2018). Racial and ethnic differences in adolescent sexual activity are intertwined with the socioeconomic and contextual factors that are correlated with race and ethnicity. Early sexual activity and greater sexual experience are more common in adolescents reared in stressful contexts, such as low-SES homes and neighborhoods where community ties are weak (Carlson, McNulty, Bellair, & Watts, 2014; Warner, 2018). For example, in one study of middle school students, experiencing a direct threat of violence in the school or community predicted early sexual initiation (Coyle, Guinosso, Glassman, Anderson, & Wilson, 2017). In addition, racial differences in rates of pubertal maturation influence sexual activity, with African American girls experiencing puberty earlier than other girls; early maturation is a risk factor for early sexual activity, as we will discuss later in this chapter (Carlson et al., 2014; Moore, Harden & Mendle, 2014). It is unclear why adolescents of color have experienced greater declines in sexual initiation and activity than white adolescents; however, racial and ethnic differences remain.

Understanding and becoming comfortable with one's sexuality is a developmental task for adolescents. In late adolescence, sexual activity is associated with positive self-esteem and well-being (Goodson et al., 2006; Vrangalova & Savin-Williams, 2011) and is not associated with psychological problems such as anxiety or depression or problem behavior (Harries et al., 2018). Although initiating sexual activity in the later high school years is not associated with poor adjustment, early sexual initiation, prior to age 16, poses risks to development. Early sexual activity is associated with attitudes that are more accepting of risk taking and engaging in more risky behaviors, such as sexual risks, alcohol and substance use, poor academic achievement, and delinquency, as well as having a larger number of sex partners relative to peers (Finer & Philbin, 2013; Harries et al., 2018; Lara & Abdo, 2016; Warner, 2018).

FIGURE 10.4 ■ Percentage of Students in Grades 9 Through 12 Who Report Ever Having Had Sexual Intercourse, 1991–2015

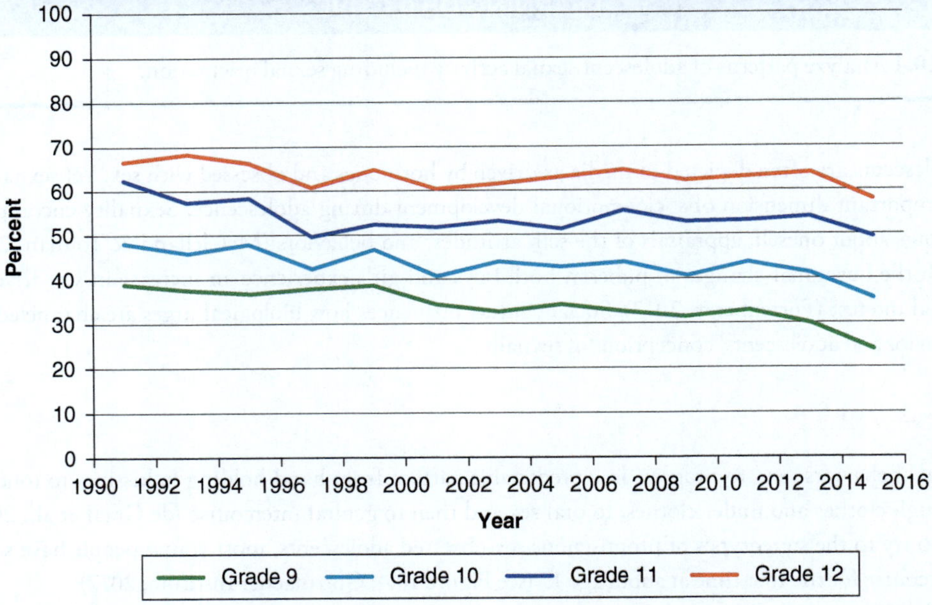

Source: Adapted from Child Trends Databank (2017).

FIGURE 10.5 ■ Ethnic Differences in Sexual Initiation, 2005–2015

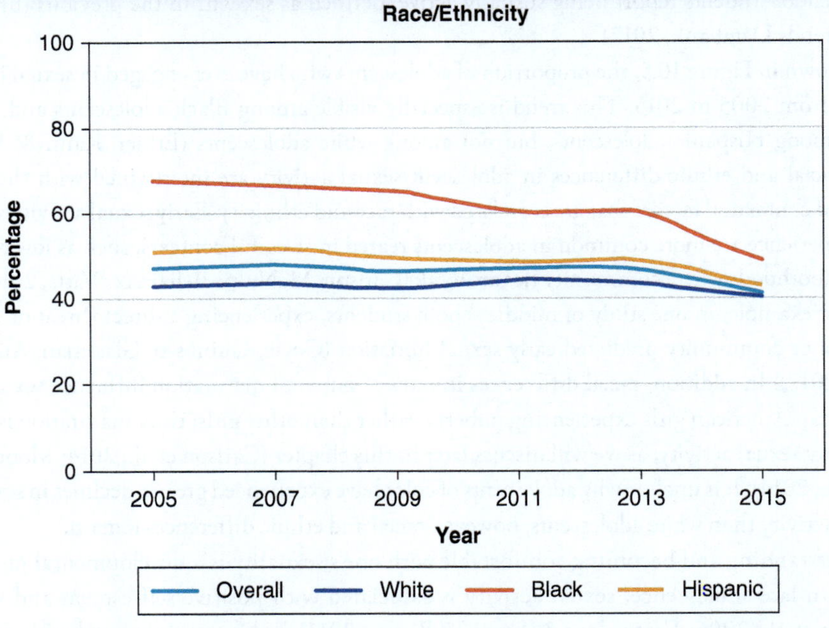

Source: Ethier et al. (2018).

Risk factors for early sexual activity in U.S. teens are early pubertal maturation, poor parental monitoring, and poor parent-adolescent communication (McClelland & Tolman, 2014; Negriff et al., 2011; Nogueira Avelar e Silva et al., 2016). Authoritative parenting, regularly shared family activities (e.g., outings, game nights, or shared dinners), parental monitoring, and parental knowledge are associated with lower rates of sexual activity (Dittus et al., 2015; Huang et al., 2011). Having sexually active peers and perceiving positive attitudes about sex among schoolmates predict initiation and greater levels of sexual activity and a greater number of sexual partners (Coley et al., 2013; Moore et al., 2014; White & Warner, 2015).

Lesbian, Gay, and Bisexual Adolescents

Adolescents' emerging sexual orientation often becomes an important contributor to their sense of self (McClelland & Tolman, 2014). **Sexual orientation** is an enduring pattern of emotional, romantic, and sexual attraction to opposite-sex partners (heterosexual), same-sex partners (gay or lesbian), or partners of both sexes (bisexual; Greenberg, 2017). Many youth enter a period of questioning in which they explore their sexuality, just as they explore other aspects of identity development (Saewyc, 2011). After a period of questioning and exploration of alternatives, adolescents may commit to a sexual orientation and integrate their sexuality into their overall sense of identity. The final stage of sexual identity development, acceptance and disclosure, may occur in adolescence, but it often occurs in emerging adulthood and afterward (Savin-Williams & Ream, 2007). However, adoption of a sexual orientation is not a clear-cut linear process. Moreover, many researchers today view sexual orientation as a dynamic spectrum, ranging from exclusive opposite-sex attraction and relations to exclusive same-sex attraction and relations, with multiple sexual orientations in between (Bailey et al., 2016; Savin-Williams, 2016). Many people are attracted to both sexes, attractions vary over time, and sexual orientation tends to be least stable in adolescence (Kaestle, 2019; Saewyc, 2011).

The onset of sexual activity can precede, co-occur with, or follow self-identification as gay or lesbian, but most often first-time sex occurs after, not before, the recognition that they are gay or lesbian (Calzo et al., 2011). Most gay and lesbian adolescents do not participate exclusively in same-sex behavior (Diamond & Savin-Williams, 2009). Reasons for heterosexual dating and activities include the desire to experiment or have fun, pressure from peers or parents, alcohol intoxication or substance use, and genuine sexual desire. The earlier adolescents identify as lesbian or gay the less likely they are to have heterosexual sex (Drasin et al., 2008).

On average, young people disclose their sexual orientation, or "come out," just prior to high school graduation (Savin-Williams & Cohen, 2015). Research suggests that some sexual minority youth may disclose their sexuality starting at around age 14 or 15, yet many wait until late adolescence or emerging adulthood (Calzo et al., 2017; Savin-Williams & Ream, 2003). Both boys and girls tend to first disclose to a female best friend, followed by another LGB person, close sibling, or male friend. Despite stereotypes, adolescents who come out to a parent are rarely met with ongoing condemnation, severe negative response, or expulsion (Savin-Williams et al., 1998). Most receive responses that range from neutral to positive (Samarova et al., 2014).

Constructing an identity as a young person who is lesbian, gay, bisexual, or transgender can be complicated by the prejudice and discrimination that many LGBT youth experience in their schools and communities (Robinson & Espelage, 2013). Perceived discrimination and victimization by peers contribute to LGBT adolescents' increased risk for psychological and behavioral problems, such as depression, self-harm, suicide, running away, poor academic performance, substance use, and risky sexual practices (Barnett et al., 2019; Collier et al., 2013; Haas et al., 2011; Plöderl et al., 2013).

Support from parents and peers can buffer the negative effects of stigmatization and victimization for LGBT individuals and is associated with high self-esteem and positive adjustment (Birkett et al., 2015; McConnell et al., 2016; Watson et al., 2019). Thus, being out may increase the risk of victimization but also offer support that promotes resilience. Disclosing one's sexual orientation can facilitate the development of identity, self-esteem, and psychological health and can often reduce distress, anxiety, and depression (Juster et al., 2013; Ueno, 2005; Vincke & van Heeringen, 2002). It can also be a means for obtaining social support and interpersonal closeness (Kosciw et al., 2015; Legate et al., 2012; Savin-Williams & Cohen, 2015).

Sexuality is central to a sense of identity. Adolescents explore their sexual feelings to understand their sexual orientation.

istock/ Marc Bruxelle

Contraceptive Use

Most sexually active high school students report using contraceptives, most commonly condoms, (Guttmacher Institute, 2014). In 2017, 84% of sexually active girls and 90% of boys reported using contraceptives (Witwer et al., 2018). Many adolescents use contraceptives only sporadically and not consistently (Pazol et al., 2015). Only about one-half of high school students report using a condom at last intercourse (Witwer et al., 2018). Common reasons given for not using contraceptives include not planning to have sex, the belief that pregnancy is unlikely, and difficulty communicating and negotiating the use of condoms (Johnson et al., 2015). Adolescents' knowledge and access to contraceptives are the best predictors of consistent use of contraceptives (Jaramillo et al., 2017). In one recent survey of nearly 800 high school superintendents, they reported that only 7% of schools offered condoms to high school students (Demissie et al., 2019).

Sexually Transmitted Infections

With sexual activity comes the risk of transmitting or acquiring sexually transmitted infections (STIs), infections passed from one individual to another through sexual contact. STIs may be caused by viruses, bacteria, or parasites. The prevalence of STIs—specifically cases of chlamydia, gonorrhea, and syphilis—are at an all-time high in the United States (Centers for Disease Control, 2018b). Although they represent only 25% of the sexually active population, 15- to 24-year-olds account for more than half of all STI diagnoses each year. Untreated STIs can result in sterility and serious, even life-threatening, illnesses such as cancer. Despite the high risk for acquiring STIs among youth, only one-third of adolescent girls and less than half (45%) of young women ages 19 to 25 report that they have discussed STIs with their health care providers (Kaiser Family Foundation, 2014).

Human papillomavirus (HPV) is the most common STI diagnosed in people of all ages and is associated with cervical cancer in women (McQuillan et al., 2017). The U.S. Centers for Disease Control and Prevention recommends HPV vaccinations for boys and girls starting at age 11. Only about half of adolescents age 13 to 17 complete the recommended regimen of three doses, perhaps because of cost and the erroneous belief that giving the vaccine might condone sexual activity (Holman et al., 2014; Walker et al., 2019).

The most serious sexually transmitted infection is **human immunodeficiency virus (HIV)**, which causes acquired immune deficiency syndrome (AIDS). Adolescents and emerging adults aged 13 to 24 represented more than one in five of new HIV diagnoses in 2017 (Centers for Disease Control, 2018a). About 85% of high school students receive education and demonstrate basic knowledge about HIV/AIDS, but most underestimate their own risks, know little about other STIs, and are not knowledgeable about how to protect themselves from STIs (Kann et al., 2014). The three ways to avoid STIs are to abstain from sex; to be in a long-term, mutually monogamous relationship with a partner who has been tested and does not have any STIs; or to use condoms consistently and correctly.

Adolescent Pregnancy

The birth rate among 15- to 19-year-old girls in the United States has dropped dramatically, from 117 per 1,000 in 1990 to 17 per 1,000 girls in 2018 (Martin et al., 2018). The decline in adolescent birth rates can be attributed to an increase in contraceptive use (Lindberg et al., 2016). Despite overall declines in the past two decades, the United States continues to have one of the highest teen birth rates in the developed world (Sedgh et al., 2015). In addition, ethnic and socioeconomic disparities place vulnerable teens at heightened risk for adolescent pregnancy and birth. Hispanic, African American, and American Indian/Alaska Native adolescents, as well as those from low-SES homes and communities—both rural and urban—have the highest adolescent birth rates in the United States (Burrus, 2018). As shown in Figure 10.6., although birthrates for all girls have declined dramatically since the 1980s, the birthrate for Hispanic and Black girls is more than twice that for non-Hispanic white girls (Child Trends, 2019b).

The risks for adolescent pregnancy are much the same as for early sexual activity (see Figure 10.7). Girls who experience menarche early, relative to peers, tend to engage in sexual behavior earlier than their same-age peers and experience higher risks of pregnancy (De Genna et al., 2011). Similarly, poor academic achievement, delinquency, substance use, depression, and affiliation with deviant peers are risk factors for early sexual activity and adolescent pregnancy (Carlson et al., 2014; Fortenberry, 2013). Low-SES homes and neighborhoods are associated with a higher risk of adolescent pregnancy, likely influenced by lack of access to health services and after-school activities and weak community ties. Recall that adolescents reared in stressful contexts tend to engage in sexual activity at earlier ages than their peers, and early sexual activity increases the risk of adverse outcomes, such as pregnancy. In addition, low levels of parental warmth and monitoring influence early sexual activity and the risk for adolescent childbirth. Girls are much more likely to become pregnant when they have an older sister who experienced adolescent pregnancy (Wall-Wieler et al., 2016). However, the home context can also serve a protective role. Involved and firm parenting during early adolescence can buffer the effects of multiple home and community risk factors on the likelihood of early sexual activity and adolescent pregnancy (East et al., 2006).

Adolescent mothers are less likely than their peers to achieve many of the typical markers of adulthood on time, such as completing high school, entering a stable marriage, and becoming financially and residentially independent (Taylor, 2009). Lack of resources such as childcare, housing, and financial support are associated with poor educational outcomes; adolescent mothers with childcare and financial resources tend to show higher educational attainment (Casares et al., 2010). Although adolescent pregnancy is associated with negative outcomes, the risk factors for adolescent pregnancy are also those that place youth at risk for negative adult outcomes in general, such as extreme poverty, family instability, and few educational and community supports (Oxford et al., 2005). It is therefore difficult to determine the degree to which outcomes are caused by adolescent pregnancy itself or the contextual conditions that are associated with it. Adolescent fathers are similar to adolescent mothers in that they are more likely than their peers to have poor academic performance, higher school dropout rates, finite financial resources, and lowered income potential (Kiselica & Kiselica, 2014).

Infants born to adolescent mothers are at risk for preterm birth and low birthweight (Jeha et al., 2015). Children of adolescent mothers tend to be at risk for a variety of negative developmental outcomes such as conduct and emotional problems, cognitive and developmental delays, and poor academic achievement (Baudry et al., 2017; Rafferty et al., 2011; Tang et al., 2016). These outcomes are

FIGURE 10.6 ■ Birth Rates for Adolescents Aged 15 to 19, 1960–2017

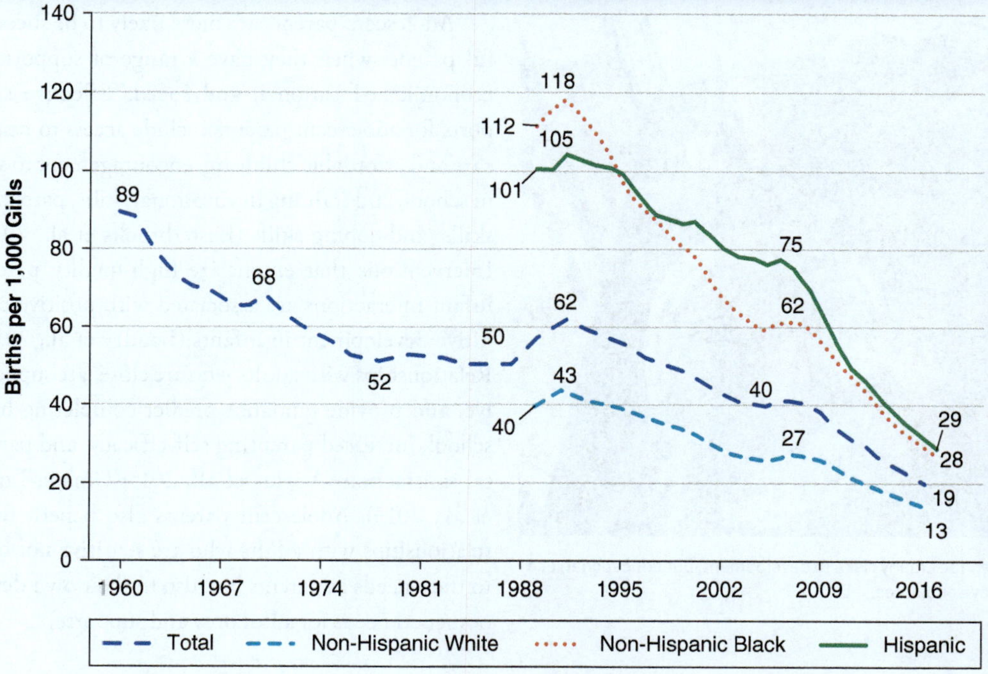

Source: Adapted from Child Trends Databank (2019b).

FIGURE 10.7 ■ Influences on Adolescent Pregnancy

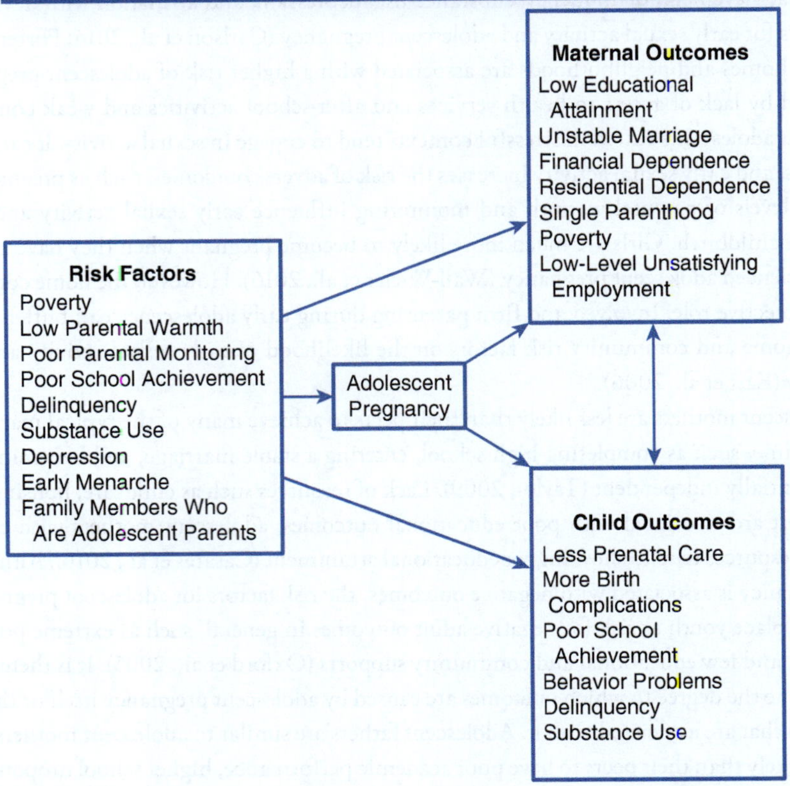

influenced by the characteristics of adolescents who are likely to become mothers, as well as the consequences of having a child at a young age (e.g., low level of maternal education, low socioeconomic status, frequent caregiver and residence changes, poor parenting; De Genna et al., 2011; Rafferty et al., 2011). But there is variability in outcomes. Many children of adolescent mothers demonstrate resilience and adjustment despite these risks (Levine et al., 2007). Positive adjustment is predicted by secure attachment, low maternal depressive symptoms, and positive parenting on the part of the mother, characterized by warmth, discussion, and stimulation.

Adolescent mothers and their children face many risks to development, but educational, economic, and social supports can improve outcomes.

ZUMA Press, Inc. / Alamy Stock Photo

Adolescent parents are more likely to be successful parents when they have a range of supports—economic, educational, and social. Effective supports for adolescent parents include access to health care and affordable childcare, encouragement to stay in school, and training in vocational skills, parenting skills, and coping skills (Easterbrooks et al., 2011). Interventions that emphasize high-quality parent-infant interactions are associated with positive cognitive development in infants (Baudry et al., 2017). Relationships with adults who are close, are supportive, and provide guidance predict completing high school, increased parenting self-efficacy, and parental satisfaction (Angley et al., 2015; Umaña-Taylor et al., 2013). Adolescent parents also benefit from relationships with adults who are sensitive not only to their needs as parents but also to their own developmental needs for autonomy and support.

Sexuality Education

Public opinion polls in the United States suggest strong support for comprehensive approaches to sex education: information about abstinence; education about sexuality, condoms, and contraception; and provision of condoms and contraception for sexually active adolescents (Kantor & Levitz, 2017; Santelli et al., 2017). Comprehensive sexuality education programs provide medically accurate information about safe sex while emphasizing age-appropriate physical, mental, emotional, and social dimensions of human sexuality (Future of Sex Education Initiative, 2012). Topics include sexual and reproductive health, consent and sexual rights, positive views of sexuality, the prevention of violence, support of diversity, and the promotion of healthy relationships (Panchaud & Anderson, 2014;American College of Obstetricians and Gynecologists, 2016; American Public Health Association, 2014; Breuner et al., 2016). Systematic reviews consistently find that comprehensive sexuality education programs tend to show efficacy in delaying initiation of intercourse in addition to promoting other protective behaviors, such as condom use (Breuner et al., 2016).

Thinking in Context: Lifespan Development

1. What might contribute to the finding that adolescents who disclose an LGBT orientation experience heightened risk of discrimination and victimization, yet often experience resilience? What role might individual and contextual factors, such as sense of self and social support, play?
2. Identify influences on adolescent sexual activity (e.g., intercourse, oral sex, contraceptive use) at each of Bronfenbrenner's bioecological levels. How might interventions apply this information to reduce sexual activity and increase safe sex practices among adolescents?

Thinking in Context: Applied Developmental Science

In health education class, your adolescent has been assigned a "baby" egg to keep "alive" for a week. Although the assignment is designed to simulate parenthood and prevent adolescent pregnancy, you have doubts.

1. Discuss risks for adolescent pregnancy.
2. Given what you know about adolescent reasoning and decision making in real-life contexts (see Chapter 11), as well as influences on adolescent pregnancy, explain why this is an effective or ineffective assignment.

PROBLEMS IN ADOLESCENCE

LEARNING OBJECTIVE

10.5 Identify common psychological and behavioral problems in adolescence.

Most young people traverse the adolescent years without adversity, but about one in five teenagers experiences serious problems that pose risks to their health and development (Lerner & Israeloff, 2007). Common problems during adolescence include eating disorders, substance abuse, depression, and delinquency.

Depression and Suicide

Although about one-third of adolescents report sometimes feeling hopeless (Department of Health and Human Services, 2019;Kann et al., 2014), a smaller number, about 13% of 12- to 17-year-old adolescents in the U.S., meet the criteria to be diagnosed with depression (American Psychiatric Association, 2013; National Institute of Mental Health, 2019). Depression is characterized by feelings of sadness, hopelessness, and frustration; changes in sleep and eating habits; problems with concentration; loss of interest in activities; and loss of energy and motivation. Depressive symptoms and rates of depression rise in early to middle adolescence and sex differences emerge, with girls reporting depression twice as often as boys (Petersen et al., 2018; Thapar et al., 2012).

Genetic factors influence susceptibility to depression in a variety of ways, such as by influencing the brain regions responsible for emotional regulation and stress responses as well as the production of neurotransmitters that play a role in depression (Lussier et al., 2021; Maughan et al., 2013). Contextual factors, such as early life stress, neighborhood disadvantage, a poor sense of efficacy in the community, low socioeconomic status, and the extended experience of stress, also influence depression (Choi et al., 2021; Li et al., 2020;Uddin et al., 2017). Relationships with parents influence adolescents' responses to stressful life events. The long-term effects of stressful life events on depression are buffered by parent-child closeness and worsened by parental depression (Ge et al., 2009; Natsuaki et al., 2014). Family support is a particularly robust protective factor against depression (Rueger et al., 2014).

Intense and long-lasting depression can lead to thoughts of **suicide**—death caused by self-directed injuries with the intent to die. Each year, suicide is among the top three causes of death in people aged 10 to 24 in the U.S. (Curtin & Heron, 2019). It is also one of the top three causes of death in many other Western countries, including Canada, the United Kingdom, and Australia (Australian Institute of Health and Welfare, 2016; Centers for Disease Control and Prevention, 2017; Office for National Statistics, 2015; Statistics Canada, 2015). Moreover, the U.S. suicide rate for adolescents and emerging adults increased by more than one-third between 2007 and 2017, from 6.8 per 100,000 people to 10.6 per 100,000 people (Curtin & Heron, 2019).

About 17% of high school students report suicidal ideation, which means they have thought about committing suicide in the past year (Child Trends Databank, 2019). Girls are more likely to report suicidal ideation (22%) than boys (17%), and about 7% of adolescents (9% girls and 5% boys) report attempting suicide. About one-third of these attempts are serious enough to require medical attention. Boys are four times more likely than girls to succeed in committing suicide (Glenn et al., 2020; Xu et al., 2014). Girls tend to choose suicide methods that are slow and passive and that they are likely to be revived from, such as overdoses of pills. Boys tend to choose methods that are quick and irreversible, such as firearms.

Adolescents who feel isolated from peers or experience bullying are at greater risk for depression and suicide.

iStock/Highwaystarz-Photography

LGBT youth, especially male and bisexual youth, experience an exceptionally high risk for suicide, with three to four times as many attempts as other youth (Miranda-Mendizábal et al., 2017; Raifman et al., 2020). In one national study, one-third to one-half of adolescents who identified as transgender reported a suicide attempt (Toomey et al., 2018). LGBT adolescents who attempt suicide often list family conflict, peer rejection, and inner conflict about their sexuality as influences on their attempts (Grossman et al., 2016; Liu & Mustanski, 2012; Mustanski & Liu, 2013; Russell & Fish, 2016). Preventing suicide relies on recognizing and treating depression and symptoms of suicide, such as those listed in Table 10.2.

TABLE 10.2 ■ Suicide Warning Signs

Any of the following behaviors can serve as a warning sign of increased suicide risk.

- Change in eating and sleeping habits
- Withdrawal from friends, family, and regular activities
- Violent actions, rebellious behavior, or running away
- Drug and alcohol use, especially changes in use
- Unusual neglect of personal appearance
- Marked personality change
- Persistent boredom, difficulty concentrating, or a decline in the quality of schoolwork
- Frequent complaints about physical symptoms, such as stomachaches, headaches, and fatigue
- Loss of interest in pleasurable activities
- Complaints of being a bad person or feeling rotten inside
- Verbal hints with statements such as the following: "I won't be a problem for you much longer." "Nothing matters." It's no use." "I won't see you again."
- Affairs are in order—giving away favorite possessions, cleaning his or her room, and throwing away important belongings
- Suddenly cheerful after a period of depression
- Signs of psychosis (hallucinations or bizarre thoughts)

Most important: Stating "I want to kill myself," or "I'm going to commit suicide."

Source: Adapted from American Academy of Child and Adolescent Psychiatry (2008).

Eating Disorders

Adolescents' rapidly changing physique, coupled with media portrayals of the "ideal" female body shape, leads many to become dissatisfied with their bodies, and the dissatisfaction often persists into emerging adulthood (Benowitz-Fredericks et al., 2012). Adolescents with a negative body image are at risk of developing **eating disorders**, mental disorders that are characterized by extreme over- or under-control of eating and behaviors intended to control weight such as compulsive exercise, dieting, or purging (American Psychiatric Association, 2013). Eating disorders, such as **anorexia nervosa**, **bulimia nervosa**, and **binge eating disorder** pose serious challenges to health.

Anorexia Nervosa and Bulimia Nervosa

Anorexia nervosa and bulimia nervosa are both characterized by excessive concern about body weight and attempts to lose weight. They differ in how this concern is manifested. Girls who suffer from anorexia nervosa have a distorted body image that causes them to starve themselves and sometimes engage in extreme exercise to achieve thinness and maintain a weight that is substantially lower than expected for height and age (American Psychiatric Association, 2013; Hagman et al., 2015). Anorexia affects about 2% of girls 19 and under; many more girls show similar behaviors and are undiagnosed (Smink et al., 2013, 2014).

Bulimia nervosa is characterized by recurrent episodes of *binge eating*—consuming an abnormally large amount of food (thousands of calories) in a single sitting coupled with a feeling of being out of control—followed by *purging*, inappropriate behavior designed to compensate for the binge, such as vomiting, excessive exercise, or use of laxatives (American Psychiatric Association, 2013). Individuals with bulimia nervosa experience dissatisfaction with body image and attempt to lose weight, but they tend to have a body weight that is normal or high-normal (Golden et al., 2015). Bulimia is more common than anorexia, affecting between 1% and 5% of girls and women across Western Europe and the United States (Kessler et al., 2013; Smink et al., 2014). Many more young people show symptoms of bulimia but remain undiagnosed (Keel, 2014).

Adolescents with eating disorders often have a distorted and negative view of their bodies coupled with an obsession with weight control and extreme weight-control behaviors.

istock/ PeopleImages

Both anorexia and bulimia are dangerous to young people's health (Bruni & Dei, 2018). The starvation and malnutrition characteristic of anorexia nervosa causes bone loss, kidney failure, heart and brain damage, and even death in about 16% of cases (Golden et al., 2015;Reel, 2012). Side effects of bulimia nervosa include nutritional deficiencies, sores, ulcers, and even holes and cancers in the mouth and esophagus caused by repeated exposure to stomach acids (Katzman, 2005).

Anorexia nervosa and bulimia nervosa occur in all ethnic and socioeconomic groups in Western countries and are increasingly common in Asian and Arab cultures (Isomaa et al., 2009; Keski-Rahkonen & Mustelin, 2016; Pike et al., 2014; Thomas et al., 2015). In the United States, white and Latina girls, especially those of higher socioeconomic status, are at higher risk for poor body image and eating disorders than are Black girls, who may be protected by cultural and media portrayals of African American women that value voluptuous figures (Smink et al., 2013). Some researchers suggest that eating disorders remain undetected and undiagnosed in Black girls because of barriers to diagnosis and treatment (Wilson et al., 2007). In addition, LGBT youth report higher rates of dangerous eating behaviors, such as fasting, diet pill use, and purging to control weight, than their heterosexual peers (Watson et al., 2017).

In some studies as many as three-quarters of adolescents diagnosed with an eating disorder continued to show symptoms five years later (Ackard et al., 2011; Herpertz-Dahlmann et al., 2015). Anorexia nervosa is difficult to treat because girls with anorexia tend to deny that there is a problem because they are unable to objectively perceive their bodies and value thinness and restraint (Berkman et al., 2007). Only about half of girls with anorexia make a full recovery, and anorexia nervosa has the highest mortality rate of all mental disorders (Smink et al., 2013).

In contrast, girls with bulimia tend to feel guilty about binging and purging and are more likely than those with anorexia to seek help (Lock, 2011; Smink et al., 2013).

Binge Eating Disorder

It is not uncommon for people to use the word *binge* in reference to their eating (e.g., "I totally binged on pizza!"). Binge eating disorder is not simply overeating. Binge eating refers to eating an extremely large amount of food in a discrete period (such as 2 hours). It is associated with a sense of feeling out of control. Binge eating typically occurs in private and tends to be accompanied by a sense of guilt, shame, self-disgust, and depression afterward. Notably, the binge eating is not accompanied by compensatory behavior, such as exercising or purging, as with bulimia nervosa (Campbell & Peebles, 2014). Binge eating disorder is diagnosed when binges occur at least once a week for three months.

Binge eating disorder is the most prevalent eating disorder and may affect up to 5% of adolescents (Marzilli et al., 2018). Although most research has examined adolescent girls, binge eating disorder may occur in 1%–2% of boys. Similar rates of binge eating are seen in adolescents of all ethnicities (Rodgers et al., 2017). Binge eating disorder emerges more frequently in early adolescence and again in emerging adulthood (Marzilli et al., 2018) and often persists from adolescence into emerging adulthood and even into middle adulthood (Goldschmidt et al., 2016).

Like other eating disorders, binge eating disorder is associated with internalizing thin body ideals, body dissatisfaction, dieting, and negative affect (Stice et al., 2017). Experiencing negative emotions may increase the risk for binge eating as high-calorie "comfort" foods may become more rewarding and enticing and binge eating may be rewarding and improve mood (Lavender et al., 2016). Binge eating is associated with chronic abdominal pain, obesity, diabetes, and other health problems associated with obesity, as well as anxiety, depression, and suicidality (Ágh et al., 2016; Forrest et al., 2017; Micali et al., 2015). Treatment for binge eating disorder addresses eating behaviors, patients' weight and shape concerns, and psychological conditions such as anxiety and depression through therapy, behavioral training, and perhaps medication (Berkman et al., 2015).

Alcohol and Substance Use

Nearly half of U.S. teens have tried an illicit drug and about two-thirds have tried alcohol by the time they leave high school, as shown in Figure 10.8. Experimentation with alcohol, tobacco, and marijuana, that is, "trying out" these substances, is so common that it may be considered normative for North American adolescents. Rates of experimentation rise during the adolescent years into emerging adulthood (Miech et al., 2017). Perhaps surprising to some adults is that a limited amount of experimentation with drugs and alcohol is common in well-adjusted middle and older adolescents and associated with psychosocial health and well-being (Mason & Spoth, 2011). Why? Alcohol and substance use may serve a developmental function in middle and late adolescence, such as a way of asserting independence and autonomy from parents, sustaining peer relationships, and learning about oneself (Englund et al., 2013; Rulison et al., 2015). Notice that many more adolescents have tried a given substance ("experimented" with it) than use it regularly. As we will see in Chapter 11, alcohol and marijuana use tend to peak in emerging adulthood and then decline (Miech et al., 2017).

Alcohol and substance use, though common, pose risks to adolescents' development. Adolescents are vulnerable to alcohol abuse because they show reduced sensitivity to the effects of alcohol that serve as cues in adults to limit their intake, such as motor impairment, sedation, social impairment, and quietness or distress (Spear, 2018). They develop a tolerance and are at risk for developing dependence on alcohol more quickly than adults (Simons et al., 2014). Alcohol and substance use are associated with negative consequences that can interfere with adolescents' development, such as academic problems; unwanted

FIGURE 10.8 ■ Lifetime Versus 30-Day Prevalence of Use of Various Drugs for 8th, 10th, and 12th Graders

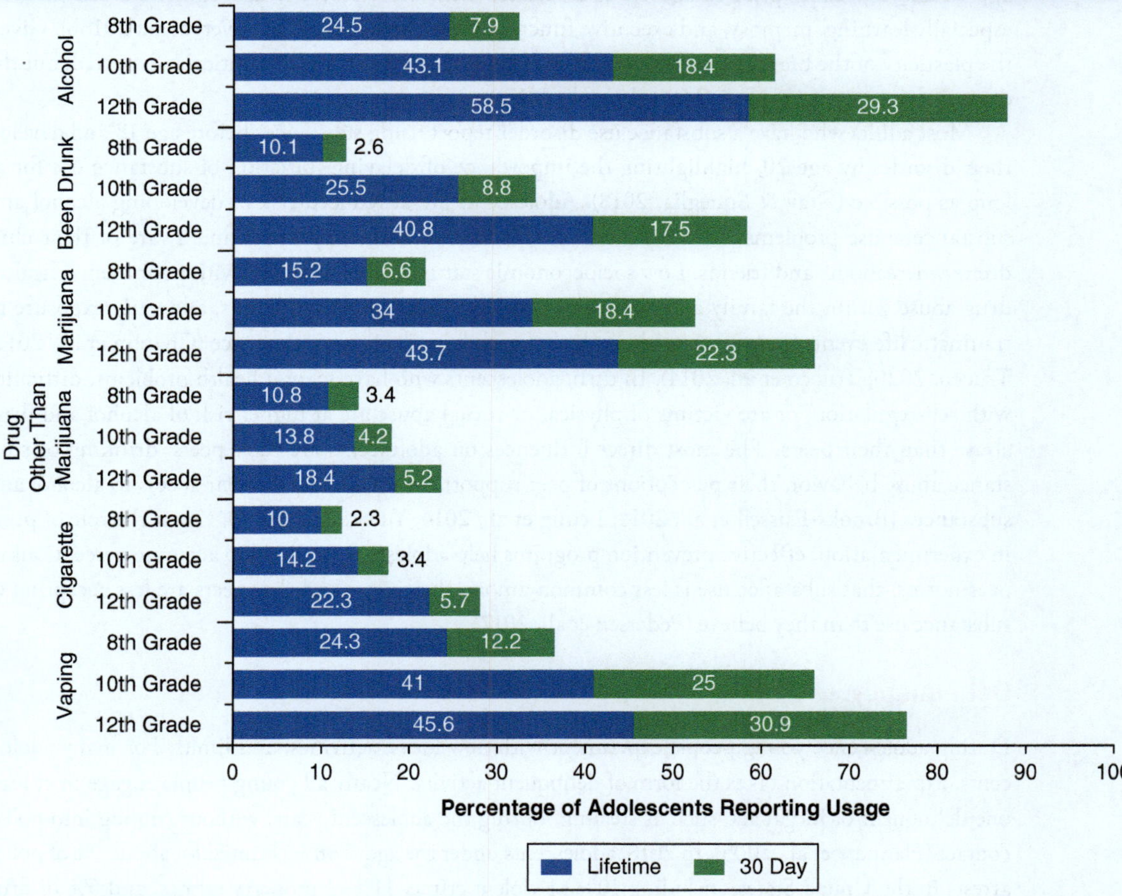

Source: Johnston et al. (2019).

Most adolescents experiment with alcohol and some try other substances.

iStock/KatarzynaBialasiewicz

sexual encounters; risky sexual activity; externalizing problems, such as aggression and delinquency; and internalizing problems, such as anxiety, depression, and suicide (Coffey & Patton, 2016; Marshall, 2014; Spear, 2018).

Alcohol use in adolescence, even moderate use, is associated with damage to the brain, including smaller brain volume and gray matter density in areas responsible for executive control, especially the frontal cortex (Cservenka & Brumback, 2017; Hamidullah et al., 2020; Müller-Oehring et al., 2018; Silveri et al., 2016a). Yet there is room for optimism because some research has shown that when alcohol use is discontinued, the adolescent brain can increase in volume and show improved executive function (Lisdahl et al., 2013). The extent and limits of this rebound effect are unclear.

Whereas regular alcohol use is associated predominantly with deficits in attention and executive function, regular marijuana use is associated with a broad set of neurocognitive deficits in attention, learning and memory, processing speed, visuospatial functioning, and executive control (Lisdahl et al., 2013; Lorenzetti et al., 2020; Meruelo et al., 2017). Alcohol and marijuana use tend to co-occur, making it difficult to disentangle the independent effects of each (Karoly et al., 2020), but, like alcohol use, regular marijuana use is associated with brain alterations, including reduced brain and gray matter volumes in the frontal lobe, followed by the parietal and temporal lobes (Lopez-Larson et al., 2012; Takagi et al., 2016). Early onset of marijuana use, before age 18 and especially prior to age 16, is associated with more severe neurocognitive consequences, especially learning, memory, and executive function (Lubman et al., 2015; Silveri et al., 2016b). Given the plasticity of the brain, some recovery of neurological function after abstention is expected, but the degree of recovery is not clear (Meruelo et al., 2017).

Most adults who have a substance use disorder report using substances before age 18 and develop their disorder by age 20, highlighting the importance of delaying initiation of substance use for as long as possible (Gray & Squeglia, 2018). Adolescents are at reduced risk of developing alcohol and substance abuse problems if their parents are involved, warm, supportive, and aware of their children's whereabouts and friends. Low socioeconomic status, family members with poor mental health, drug abuse within the family and community, disadvantaged neighborhoods, and early exposure to traumatic life events increase the risk of alcohol and drug abuse in adolescence (Chaplin et al., 2012; Trucco, 2020; Trucco et al., 2014). In turn, adolescents who have mental health problems, difficulty with self-regulation, or are victims of physical or sexual abuse are at higher risk of alcohol and drug abuse than their peers. The most direct influences on adolescents are their peers' drinking or substance abuse behavior, their perceptions of peer support for such use, and their access to alcohol and substances (Brooks-Russell et al., 2014; Leung et al., 2014; Yuen et al., 2020). Given the role of peers in experimentation, effective prevention programs help adolescents to develop accurate perceptions of peer norms: that substance use is less common among their peers and that peers are less accepting of substance use than they believe (Pedersen et al., 2017).

Delinquency

During adolescence young people experiment with new ideas, activities, and limits. For many adolescents, experimentation takes the form of delinquent activity. Nearly all young people engage in at least one delinquent or illegal act, such as stealing, during the adolescent years, without coming into police contact (Flannery et al., 2005). In 2018, adolescents under the age of 18 accounted for about 7% of police arrests in the United States, including 10% of violent crime, 11% of property crimes, and 5% of drug violations (Federal Bureau of Invesigation, 2019). Boys are about four times as likely to be arrested as girls.

As shown in Figure 10.9, juvenile arrests have declined dramatically over the past four decades, but there are large ethnic and racial differences in arrest rates (Office of Juvenile Justice and Delinquency Prevention, 2019). African American youth are disproportionately likely to be arrested as compared with white youth, and Asian American youth are least likely to be arrested (Federal Bureau of Invesigation, 2019; Office of Juvenile Justice and Delinquency Prevention, 2019). By one estimate, Latinx and Hispanic youth show similar arrest rates as white youth (Andersen, 2015). In a recent national analysis of post-arrest handling decisions by police (such as whether to release the adolescent or process the arrest and refer the adolescent to the court system), Hispanic and Latinx adolescents were more likely to be referred to the court for less severe charges, such as trespassing or loitering, than white adolescents (Claus et al., 2017). However, there were no ethnic differences in referrals for more serious charges, such as violence, weapons, and drug offenses. Differences in arrest rates may be influenced by the greater surveillance of the low-SES communities in which youth of color are likely to live and adolescents' access to fewer community resources.

Most delinquent acts are limited to the adolescent years and do not continue into adulthood (Piquero & Moffitt, 2013). Adolescents often show an increase in delinquent activity in early adolescence that is sustained by affiliation with similar peers, continues into middle adolescence, and then declines in late adolescence. With advances in cognition, moral reasoning, emotional regulation, social skills, and empathy, antisocial activity declines (Monahan et al., 2013). Some delinquent activity is common, though not all adolescents engage in delinquent or antisocial acts. Delinquent activity is more common among adolescents with a greater drive for sensation seeking, who experience poor parental monitoring, who spend more unstructured time with peers, especially antisocial peers, and who are more susceptible to peer influence (Bendezú et al., 2018; Choukas-Bradley et al., 2014; Hoeben et al., 2016; Lopez-Tamayo et al., 2016; Mann et al., 2016). Parenting that is inconsistent, controlling, and accompanied by harsh punishment can magnify impulsive, defiant, and aggressive tendencies in adolescents (Chen et al., 2013; Harris-McKoy & Cui, 2012).

Although mild delinquency is common and not necessarily cause for concern, about one-quarter of violent offenses in the United States, including murder, rape, robbery, and aggravated assault, are committed by adolescents (Office of Juvenile Justice and Delinquency Prevention, 2014). Adolescents who engage in serious crime are at risk to become repeat offenders who continue criminal activity into adulthood. Yet most young people whose delinquent activity persists and evolves into a life of crime show multiple problem behaviors that begin in childhood (Farrington & Loeber, 2000), and they typically have their first contacts with the criminal justice system by age 12 or earlier (Baglivio et al., 2014).

FIGURE 10.9 ■ Arrest Rates per 100,000 Persons Age 10 to 17, 1980–2018

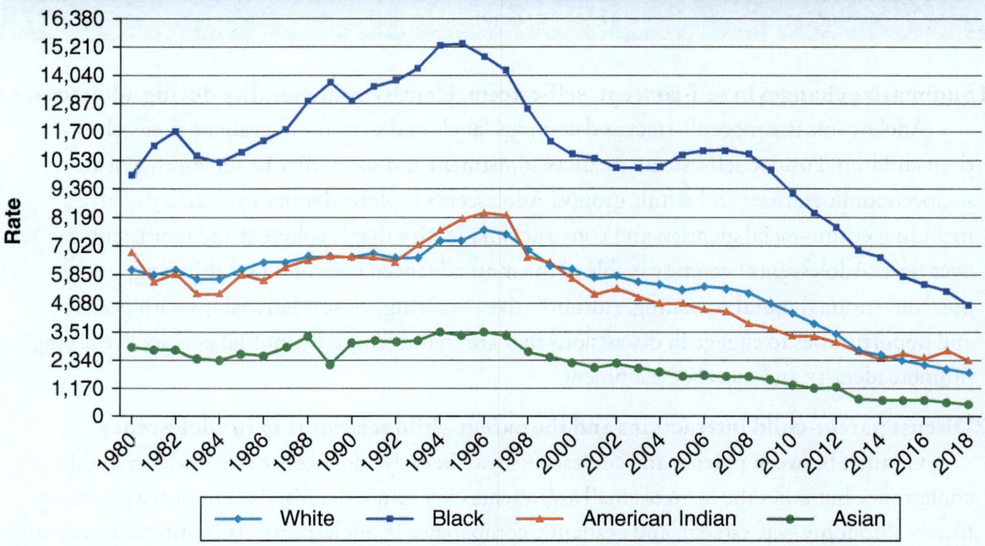

Source: Office of Juvenile Justice and Delinquency Prevention (2019).

Most adolescents engage in at least one delinquent act, such as vandalism. Delinquency tends to rise in early adolescence, peak in middle adolescence, and decline in late adolescence.

iStock/Syldavia

Addressing adolescent delinquency requires looking beyond the individual to consider the contextual factors in the community that contribute to delinquency. Communities of pervasive poverty are characterized by limited educational, recreational, and employment activities, over-policing, access to drugs and firearms, opportunities to witness and be victimized by violence, and exposure to and offers of protection and companionship by gangs that engage in criminal acts—all of which contribute to the onset of antisocial behavior (Chen et al., 2013; McCrea et al., 2019; Winters, 2020). Adolescent delinquency is a problem whose causes extend well beyond the individual adolescent.

Thinking in Context: Biological Influences

Grandpa Joe gave his 14-year-old grandson the "drugs talk." As they stood in the kitchen, he heated up a frying pan and then cracked an egg into the pan. As the egg whites and yolk sizzled in the pan, he explained, "This is your brain on drugs." Considering what we know about neurological development, is he correct? How do alcohol and drugs affect the adolescent brain?

Thinking in Context: Lifespan Development

1. How do adolescents' physical, cognitive, and social characteristics influence their likelihood of developing an eating disorder such as anorexia nervosa or bulimia nervosa? Are girls of some ethnicities or races "immune" to eating disorders? Why or why not?

2. How might we distinguish normative from atypical delinquent activity? To what degree can we predict when delinquent activity will persist beyond adolescence?

3. Are there dangers in taking the perspective that some alcohol and substance use is common and simply a part of growing up? How should parents, teachers, and professionals respond to adolescent alcohol and substance use?

CHAPTER SUMMARY

10.1 Summarize changes in self-concept, self-esteem, identity, and morality during adolescence.

Adolescents use more abstract and complex labels to describe and evaluate themselves than children. Positive self-esteem predicts adjustment and sociability in adolescents of all socioeconomic statuses and ethnic groups. Adolescents explore identity in a variety of areas, including ethnic-racial identity, and construct an identity that is coherent and consistent over time. Adolescents become capable of the most advanced level of moral thinking, postconventional moral reasoning. Authoritative parenting, close relationships with peers, and opportunities to engage in discussions that are characterized by mutual perspective taking promote identity and moral development.

10.2 Discuss parent-child interactions and the parent-child relationship in adolescence.

Conflict between parents and adolescents rises in early adolescence and peaks in middle adolescence but takes the form of small arguments over minor details. Authoritative parenting fosters autonomy, self-esteem, and academic competence in adolescents. Authoritarian parenting inhibits the development of autonomy and is linked with poor adjustment. Parental monitoring promotes well-being and is a protective factor against risky behavior.

10.3 Examine the developmental progression of peer relations in adolescence.

In adolescence, friendships are characterized by intimacy, loyalty, self-disclosure, and trust and promote positive adjustment. In early adolescence, cliques emerge and by mid-adolescence begin to include both boys and girls, creating opportunities for dating. Dating typically begins through the intermingling of mixed-sex peer groups, progresses to group dating, and then goes to one-on-one dating and romantic relationships. Both cliques and crowds, larger reputation-based groups, tend to decline in late adolescence. Susceptibility to peer conformity for both positive and negative behaviors tend to rise in early adolescence, peaks in middle adolescence, and declines thereafter.

10.4 Analyze patterns of adolescent sexual activity including sexual orientation.

Sexual activity among U.S. adolescents has declined over the past few decades. Risk factors for early sexual activity include early pubertal maturation, poor parental communication and monitoring, sexually active peers, risky behaviors, and stressful homes and neighborhoods. Despite a decline since 1990, the United States has one of the highest teen pregnancy rates in the developed world. Adolescent mothers are less likely to achieve many of the typical markers of adulthood. Children born to adolescent mothers are at greater risk for academic and behavioral problems.

10.5 Identify common psychological and behavioral problems in adolescence.

Several problems tend to rise during adolescence: depression, eating disorders, substance use, and delinquency. Girls tend to show higher rates of depression and eating disorders. Alcohol and substance use rises for both boys and girls during the adolescent years through emerging adulthood. They may serve developmental functions, but are associated with short- and long-term effects, such as accidents, academic problems, risks for dependence and abuse, and impaired neurological development. Nearly all adolescents engage in at least one delinquent activity and overall rates of delinquency rise in early adolescence and decline in late adolescence.

KEY TERMS

anorexia nervosa (p. 317)
autonomy (p. 301)
binge eating disorder (p. 317)
biological gender transition (p. 298)
bulimia nervosa (p. 317)
cliques (p. 305)
crowds (p. 305)
dating violence (p. 308)
eating disorders (p. 317)
ethnic-racial identity (p. 295)
gender intensification (p. 297)
human papillomavirus (HPV) (p. 312)
human immunodeficiency virus (HIV) (p. 312)
identity (p. 293)
identity achievement (p. 294)
identity diffusion (p. 294)
identity foreclosure (p. 294)
identity status (p. 294)
parental monitoring (p. 302)
postconventional moral reasoning (p. 298)
psychosocial moratorium (p. 294)
sexual orientation (p. 311)
social gender transition (p. 298)
suicide (p. 316)

PART 5 LIFESPAN DEVELOPMENT AT WORK: ADOLESCENCE

We have seen that adolescence is a transitional time in which young people interact in a variety of contexts, including home, school, and community. Each of these settings offers opportunities to work with adolescents.

Secondary Education: Middle School Teacher and High School Teacher

Middle school teachers typically work with students in Grades 6 through 8, but sometimes as early as 4th grade and as late as 9th grade. Secondary school teachers typically work with students in Grades 9 through 12. Many activities of elementary school, middle school, and high school teachers are similar. All develop educational goals and construct plans for each day of class, teach, record and assess student progress, communicate with parents, and submit reports to administrators. High school, and often middle school, teachers typically specialize in one, sometimes two, subjects such as English or math. They usually teach several classes of students over course of the day, whereas elementary school teachers usually teach the same group of students all day each day.

Middle schools are often smaller than high schools. Middle school teachers often have smaller classes than high school teachers (but larger than elementary school classrooms). In middle school, often entire classes of students move from teacher to teacher, so that a group of students remains together in all classes. Frequently middle school teachers work together to create a cohesive experience for students. High school students move from class to class individually. Teachers may not share the same students and may work more independently.

Middle and high school teachers are often tasked with maintaining order during breaks, such as when students change classes, during lunch periods, and in study halls. They also are frequently involved in after-school activities, such as clubs.

Becoming a middle school teacher or high school teacher requires earning a bachelor's degree in education, and often specializing in a specific subject (such as history, biology, or math), and completing an internship experience in the classroom. Teachers must pass a state licensing or certification exam. The median annual salary for middle school teachers was about $61,000 and $63,000 for high school teachers in 2020 (U.S. Bureau of Labor Statistics, 2021).

School Counselor

School counselors, sometimes called guidance counselors, help students understand and cope with social, behavioral, and personal problems. School counselors use counseling skills to identify and prevent problems and aid students in learning skills to enhance their personal, social, and academic growth. They work with parents, teachers, principals, medical professionals, and social workers to address the issues that may be inhibiting a student's learning and school performance. School counselors may provide special services such as substance abuse prevention programs, conflict management, and parenting education training, as well as supervising peer counseling programs. They work with individuals, small groups, or entire classes.

Whereas school psychologists work with students with special needs, school counselors are available to all students, often leaving their door open for students to visit as they choose. They may identify students who are in distress and may need further assistance from the school psychologist. School counselors may also play a role in helping students apply to college or make plans for after graduation.

Becoming a school counselor requires a master's degree, supervised experience, and obtaining a school counseling certification. Some states require public school counselors to have both counseling and teaching certificates. The median salary for school counselors was about $58,000 in 2020 (U.S. Bureau of Labor Statistics, 2021).

Recreation Worker

Recreation workers organize activities to help people to stay active, improve fitness, and have fun. They develop, plan, organize, and direct recreational activities for people of all ages (such as aerobics, arts and crafts, performing arts, camping, or recreational sports). Some recreation workers are camp counselors are workers who lead and supervise children and adolescents in outdoor activities such as swimming and boating, horseback riding, camping, hiking, sports, music, drama, and art. Other recreation workers might work in youth programs or church activities. In residential camps, recreation workers may assume a therapeutic role helping adolescents build social and problem-solving skills.

Recreation workers are employed in educational settings, park and recreational centers, community activity centers, health clubs and fitness centers, country clubs and medical and rehabilitation centers, including nursing homes. A position as an entry-level recreation worker generally does not require a bachelor's degree, but a college diploma creates opportunities for advancement to supervisory positions. The mean annual wage for recreation workers was about $29,000 in 2020 (U.S. Bureau of Labor Statistics, 2021).

Intervention Research

There are many prevention and intervention programs designed to promote positive development in adolescence. These programs are conducted in a variety of settings, such as schools, after-school programs, community centers, and nonprofit centers. Individuals work in these programs in a variety of ways, as workers, counselors, and social workers who implement them or as planners and researchers who create, assess, evaluate, and revise them.

Researchers may fulfill several roles in intervention research. Some researchers study social problems to provide information to other professionals who create interventions. They might study ways of preventing adolescent pregnancy or how to increase the prevalence of girls and underrepresented minorities in science, technology, engineering, and mathematics at all levels of education. Other researchers assess the effectiveness of programs. A researcher at a social service agency might examine the effectiveness of new drug-control interventions like mandatory minimum sanctions, residential and group home treatments for youthful offenders identified as drug users, and school-based prevention programs. The results of this research is used to improve programs.

Individuals interested in intervention research are employed at nonprofit agencies, universities, think tanks (research centers), and government. They conduct research to gather information about social problems and policies; assess and improve programs for children, youth, and families; and write reports and other documents to inform policymakers and the public. Researchers at educational nonprofit organizations such as the Educational Testing Service might study ways of accommodating standardized test–takers with disabilities.

Assistant research positions are often available to bachelor's degree holders. Additional education and credentialling required depends on the position. Direct service work implementing interventions might require licensure or certification as a counselor. Research skills honed in a master's program in quantitative research, psychology, human development, or another related field can enable individuals to work on research teams. Doctoral degrees offer the most opportunities to lead research teams and create programs. Applied developmental psychologists are often involved in intervention research.

Applied Developmental Psychologist

As we have discussed, developmental psychology is the study of lifespan development. Some developmental psychologists focus on applying developmental science in everyday settings. These applied developmental psychologists design and empirically evaluate programs provided by hospitals, social service agencies, mental health clinics, and schools. For example, an applied developmental psychologist might evaluate the impact of a behaviorally oriented program administered in a hospital or clinic setting, such as the effect of prenatal care and education for adolescent mothers and the effects on infant health outcomes. Others serve as consultants who provide teachers with information about behavioral management and instructional techniques appropriate for troubled adolescents.

Applied developmental psychologists also work in direct service, providing assessment, consultation, and treatment to individuals and families. They conduct developmental assessments of children and adolescents who have suffered injuries or who are suspected of having a developmental delay. Frequently, applied developmental psychologists in hospital and service settings work with a multidisciplinary team of physicians, social workers, physical therapists, and other professionals to determine the best course of treatment or intervention for patients.

Applied developmental psychologists are also found in social services agencies and court settings, where they evaluate families who wish to provide foster parenting, determine parental fitness for regaining child custody after loss of parental rights, or participate as part of a multidisciplinary team to assist children who have suffered abuse during the subsequent investigation and court process. Applied developmental psychologists conduct evaluations of children and families during divorce and child custody cases, determine the developmental status of adolescents in criminal cases in which they might be tried as adults, and serve as expert witnesses in child abuse cases, custody cases, and trials in which the defendants are children and adolescents.

A master's degree can offer preparation for many research positions and positions in program design and evaluation, as well as for engaging in developmental assessment activities under the supervision of a licensed psychologist. Doctoral degrees enable graduates to engage in more advanced research and program development activities. Applied developmental psychologists who plan careers as scientist-practitioners, such as assessing and treating individuals, must seek state licensure. Typically, licensure eligibility requires at least 4,000 hours of supervised field experience, with at least 2,000 hours post-doctoral, passing a written national examination and a written examination covering ethical and legal issues within a particular state, as well as an oral examination in some states.

11 PHYSICAL AND COGNITIVE DEVELOPMENT IN EMERGING AND EARLY ADULTHOOD

Morsa Images/ Getty Images

The transition time from adolescence to adulthood has lengthened in recent decades as education and extended career training has become more common. Emerging adulthood is a period in which young people are not adolescents but have not fully entered adulthood. Emerging adulthood spans from the end of secondary school, about age 18, to the assumption of adult roles at about age 25. The distinction between emerging adulthood and early adulthood (about age 25 to 40) is new and not agreed upon by all researchers (Arnett, 2014; Côté, 2014; Syed, 2016). Over the two decades spanning emerging adulthood and early adulthood, individuals experience many, often subtle, physical changes, as well as changes in the way they think and view the world around them. In this chapter, the term *emerging adult* will refer to individuals age 25 and under (unless otherwise specified) and *young adult* will refer to all individuals under age 40, including emerging adults (unless otherwise specified).

PHYSICAL DEVELOPMENT IN EMERGING AND EARLY ADULTHOOD

LEARNING OBJECTIVE

11.1 Summarize the physical developments of emerging and early adulthood.

All of the organs and body systems, including digestive, respiratory, circulatory, and reproductive systems, peak in functioning from emerging adulthood into early adulthood. We may not think of young adults as aging, but the biological fact is that once individuals are physically mature with growth and physical development at adult levels, **senescence**—a pattern of gradual age-related declines in physical functioning—begins (Spini et al., 2016). Measurable age-related changes in functioning occur by about age 30, but most people do not notice these until middle adulthood. Aging entails gradual changes in appearance, strength, body proportions, and fertility.

Similar to development throughout infancy, childhood, and adolescence, development in early adulthood is multidimensional and multidirectional. Different parts of the body age at different rates, and development consists of both gains and losses in strength, endurance, and motor skill. In addition, organs vary in their rate of decline (McDonald, 2014); in one individual the digestive system may show signs of aging earlier than the cardiovascular system, while it may be the other way around for another individual.

Age and physical development are closely related in childhood, but the link is much weaker in adulthood (Dodig et al., 2019). Young adults display a wide range of individual differences in physical functioning and aging (Ferrucci et al., 2020). In one study, 38-year-old young adults' biological age (a combination of physical markers such as cardiovascular fitness, BMI, and white blood cell count) ranged from 26 to 71 (Belsky et al., 2015). That is, some 38-year-old adults' bodies and physical development were similar to adults in their 20s and others were similar to adults over age 70. Differences in socioeconomic status and traumatic experiences, such as childhood poverty and chronic victimization, contributed to the rate of biological aging (Belsky et al., 2020). Other influences on the rate of aging include genetics, sociohistorical context, experience including education, health resources, and behaviors such as smoking, exercise, and diet (Bonnie et al., 2015; Gerstorf et al., 2020).

Theories of Aging: What Causes Aging?

Why do we age? It was once believed that the body "wore out" from use (Bengtson et al., 2016). On the contrary, research suggests that we must "use it or lose it." That is, regular exercise is associated with longevity in all people regardless of ethnicity or SES (Lin et al., 2020; Sanchez-Sanchez et al., 2020). Activity is a critical component of a long and healthy life.

Aging is complex and influenced by many factors. Some of aging is thought to be influenced by genetics, a biological program that unfolds over time. Parents' lifespans predict those of their children, and identical twins share more similar lifespans than do fraternal twins, suggesting a role for heredity in aging (Fedarko, 2018; Montesanto et al., 2011). Yet kin relations for markers of biological age, such as strength, respiratory capacity, blood pressure, and bone density, are relatively small as health is influenced not just by genetics but by context and lifestyle. It may be that it is not lifespan that we inherit but a set of genetic factors that interact with environmental factors to predict lifespan (Mitteldorf, 2016; Moskalev et al., 2014). Whether genetic predispositions for longevity are realized depends on environmental factors such as the availability of health care or exposure to environmental toxins, and lifestyle factors, such as diet and exercise, alcohol use, or smoking (Govindaraju et al., 2015; Li et al., 2020).

Some environmental factors cause "errors" in our functioning that influence how we age (Parker & Heflin, 2020). One account of aging relies on cellular mutation, or damage to DNA and chromosomes. Research with animals shows that cell mutations increase exponentially with age (Baines et al., 2014; Milholland et al., 2017). Cellular mutations are associated with age-related diseases and cancers (Lodato & Walsh, 2019). Some of this damage may be due to **free radicals**, highly reactive and corrosive molecules that form when oxygen corrodes a cell and strips off an electron. Free radicals destroy cellular materials in an attempt to replace the missing electrons. Free radicals may increase the likelihood of many age-related diseases such as cancer, cardiovascular disorders, and arthritis and may predict mortality (Lagouge & Larsson, 2013; Schöttker et al., 2015; Valko et al., 2016). Environmental factors may work to defend the body from free radicals by producing material that neutralizes free radicals and reduces the harm caused by them (Miura & Endo, 2010). A diet rich in antioxidants, including vitamins C and E and beta carotene, may protect against damage from free radicals (Neha et al., 2019). Aging is complex and free radicals likely account for only a proportion of change (Ziegler et al., 2015). Recent research suggests that some species tolerate moderately high levels of free radicals, perhaps because the added stress encourages cells to repair themselves, and other species show longevity despite reduced physical capacities (Van Houten et al., 2018).

Aging occurs at the cellular level. Human cells have a limited capacity to reproduce, a fact that is the basis for another explanation for aging. Human cells have the capacity to divide about 50 times in their lifespan (Hayflick, 1996). Each time the cell divides, telomeres—tiny caps of DNA located at both ends of the chromosomes—become shorter. Shorter telomeres may protect the cell from common mutations that occur with repeated divisions, but they also reduce the cell's capacity to reproduce itself (Xi et al., 2013). Telomeres that shorten past a critical length cause the cell to stop dividing all together, leading to increases in disease, cell death, and body aging (Campisi, 2013; Opresko & Shay, 2017). Telomere length is associated with dozens of cancers (Barthel et al., 2017). In this sense, telomere length may serve as a biomarker of aging (Mather et al., 2011; Xu et al., 2013). Telomeres shorten predictably over time, but telomere length is not completely programmed. Telomere length is thought to be influenced by epigenetic mechanisms—contextual factors that influence how genetic propensities are displayed (Adwan-Shekhidem & Atzmon, 2018). Stress contributes to the shortening of telomeres, as well as oxidative stress, which results from free radicals (Cannon et al., 2017). For people of all ages, regular physical activity contributes to longer telomeres, suggesting that behavioral factors can attenuate telomere shortening and thereby aspects of aging (Arsenis et al., 2017; Blackburn et al., 2015).

Another way in which aging is expressed is through changes in the immune system (Parker & Heflin, 2020). The immune system determines how the body adjusts to external stressors and pathogens encountered throughout life. With age the immune system becomes less able to differentiate healthy cells from pathology, may direct the body's defenses against healthy cells, and may ignore harmful cells (Müller et al., 2019). Chronic low-grade inflammation—immune activity that is not associated with infection or disease—is a hallmark of aging and associated with various age-related diseases including cardiovascular diseases, cancers, and diabetes. Recent research suggests that from early adulthood through late adulthood, Black adults and those of low socioeconomic status tend to show more biological indicators of aging, especially low-grade inflammation and inflammatory biomarkers, than white adults—and the disparities widen with age, suggesting the role of contextual factors and experience in immune system aging (Lam et al., 2021)

Experiments with animals suggests that diet, specifically caloric restriction, may play a role in longevity (Olmedillas del Moral et al., 2020; Speakman & Mitchell, 2011). Animal studies suggest that a nutritious diet that is extremely low in calories, with about 40% fewer calories than recommended, is associated with a longer lifespan and with less oxidative stress (resulting in fewer free radicals; Redman et al., 2018). However, the near-starvation diet is uncomfortable and may be difficult for a human adult to sustain (Golbidi et al., 2017; Pifferi & Aujard, 2019).

Physical Changes

Age-related changes in the skin are gradual, predictable, unavoidable, and begin in emerging adulthood, at about age 20. The connective tissue gradually thins, resulting in less elastic skin and some visible wrinkles around the eyes by age 30 (Tobin, 2017). The skin becomes drier as oil glands become less active. Most adults in their 30s notice lines developing on their foreheads, and by the 40s these lines are accompanied by crow's feet around the eyes and lines around the mouth—markers of four decades of smiles, frowns, laughter, and other emotions. The rate of skin aging is influenced by exposure to the elements, such as sun, heat, cold, and pollution. Exposure to the sun is thought to be the most dramatic contributor to skin aging, responsible for about 80% of skin changes and the leading cause of skin cancer (Flament et al., 2013). The use of sunscreen has been shown to retard skin aging (Pedić et al., 2020). Though more apparent in middle age, by age 30, some individuals begin to notice gray hairs, as the hair follicle cells that produce pigment, or color, become less abundant. Men who are prone to hereditary baldness typically begin balding in their 30s.

Physiological function, including muscle development and strength, tends to improve throughout the 20s, peaking at about age 30 (Kenney et al., 2020). Adults' performance on activities that require body coordination and bursts of strength, such as sprinting and playing basketball, tend to peak in the early 20s whereas those that require endurance, such as distance running, peak in the early 30s and show declines after age 40. Muscle strength, as measured by the maximum force with which one can throw a ball, shows a gradual decline beginning at about age 30 but is generally not noticeable to most people until middle age (Payne & Isaacs, 2020). Although physical abilities show a predictable pattern of change, adults vary in the rate of change in their performance. Physical activity plays a large role in maintaining weight, muscle mass, and endurance throughout adulthood.

Fertility and Reproductive Capacity

Martina holds her newborn close to her while chatting with her family who has come to visit her in the maternity ward. At 32 years of age, Martina is older than the average first-time mother; most women are in their 20s when they give birth to their first child. Births to women in their 30s and 40s have increased substantially since the early 1990s (see Figure 11.1; Martin et al., 2019). The average age at first birth has increased for U.S. women across race and ethnicity (see Figure 11.2; Matthews & Hamilton, 2016). The increase in average maternal age at birth is thought to be a result of the dramatic decline in adolescent pregnancy (see Chapter 11). Many young adults wait to have children until they have completed their education and established their careers. The maturity and financial stability that accompany the 30s can make for better parents. However, reproductive capacity peaks in the 20s and declines with age, increasing the risk for women in their mid-to-late 30s to experience difficulty conceiving (Jasienska et al., 2017).

As women's reproductive systems age, changes occur in the quality of ova and in the rate of ovulation. Although women are born with about 400,000 ova, they decay with age and chromosomal anomalies accumulate, increasing the risk of pregnancy loss, or miscarriage (Bentov et al., 2011). A common cause of female infertility is the failure to ovulate—to release an ovum into the fallopian tube. With advancing age, ovulation becomes less regular. There are also a variety of factors that can prevent ovulation; some are treatable or preventable, such as drug and alcohol abuse, environmental toxins, obesity, and being underweight. Illnesses that affect the reproductive system, such as ovarian cancer and ovarian cysts, can also make it difficult or impossible to conceive. In addition, dwindling reserves of ova can prevent conception because it is thought that the body requires a minimum level

FIGURE 11.1 ■ Births to Women Ages 18 to 39 in the United States, 1990–2018

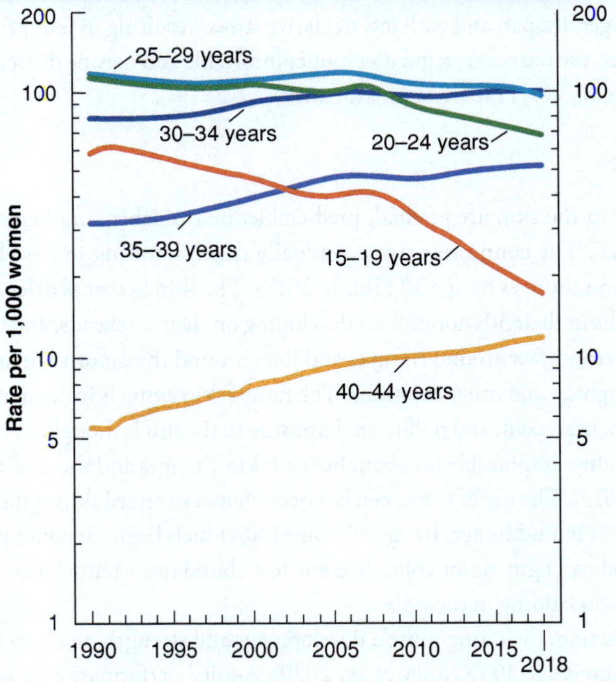

Note: Rates are plotted on a logarithmic scale.

Source: Martin et al., 2017.

FIGURE 11.2 ■ Mean Age at First Birth, by Race and Hispanic Origin of Mother: United States, 2000 and 2014

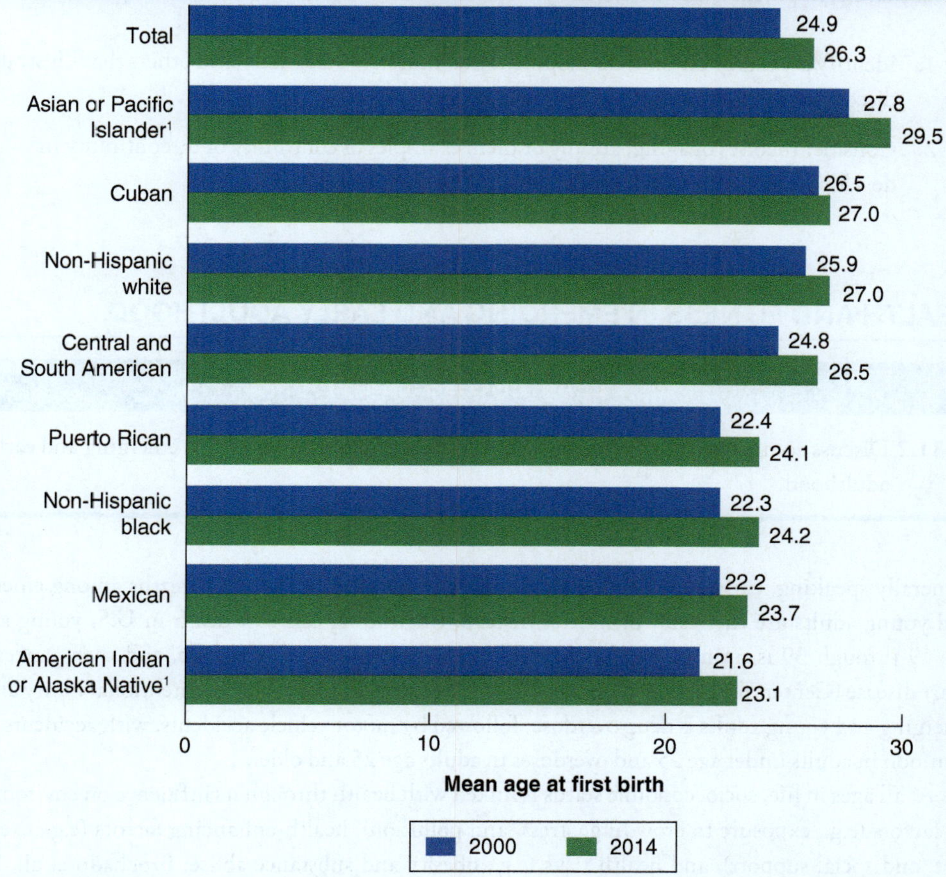

Source: Matthews and Hamilton, 2016.

of ova reserves in order to ovulate (Martins & Jokubkiene, 2017). The exact minimum is unknown and, like other aspects of physical development, may vary with genetic and contextual factors (Schuh-Huerta et al., 2012).

Men's rate of change in reproductive capacity is significantly different from that of women; most men remain able to conceive into older adulthood. In young men, sperm can be affected by anything that interferes with the functioning of the body, such as fever, stress, drug abuse, alcoholism, radiation, and environmental toxins (Ilacqua et al., 2018; Marcho et al., 2020). Exposure to these factors can reduce the number of sperm or affect their physical structure, activity, and motility. In this way, lifestyle and contextual factors contribute to young men's fertility. In addition, the number and quality of sperm produced declines in middle adulthood, beginning at about age 40 (Brahem et al., 2011; Johnson et al., 2015).

Thinking in Context: Biological Influences

1. Aging reflects the interaction of biology and context. Analyze how theories of aging support or refute this statement.
2. How does reproductive capacity—the ability to reproduce—change in men and women over early adulthood? What are some of the personal and emotional implications of the timing of physical and reproductive change for young adults?

Thinking in Context: Lifespan Development

Recall that development is characterized by continuities and discontinuities (see Chapter 1).

1. Identify aspects of physical development that illustrate continuity and others that illustrate discontinuity in emerging and early adulthood.
2. Consider theories of aging; are any of them examples of continuity or discontinuity in development?

HEALTH AND FITNESS IN EMERGING AND EARLY ADULTHOOD

LEARNING OBJECTIVE

11.2 Discuss common health concerns and the effects of physical activity in emerging and early adulthood.

Generally speaking, early adulthood is a time of good physical health. Few deaths among emerging and young adults are the result of illness. Instead, the leading cause of death in U.S. young adults age 19 through 39 is unintentional injury, followed by suicide and homicide, and then cancer and heart disease (Centers for Disease Control, 2021). The most common fatal unintentional injury among emerging and young adults is drug overdose, followed by motor vehicle accidents, with accidents most common in adults under age 25 and overdoses in adults age 25 and older.

At all ages in life, socioeconomic status is linked with health through its influence on environmental factors (e.g., exposure to crowding, stress, and pollution), health-enhancing factors (e.g., exercise, diet, and social support), and health risks (e.g., obesity and substance abuse; Brochado et al., 2017; Cornman et al., 2015). Material hardship and the perceived stress that accompanies it is associated with depression, sleep problems, and suicidal thoughts (Huang et al., 2021).

Overweight and Obesity

During his first year of college, Byron welcomed the ability to make choices about food and plan his own meals. Without his health-conscious mother's input, he was able to munch on fried chicken wings whenever he wanted. The absence of parental controls, access to an abundance of food, busy schedule, and stresses associated with life transitions (such as to college and career) makes it difficult for emerging adults to eat healthily. **Obesity**, defined as a body mass index (BMI) of 30 or above, and overweight (BMI greater than 25) have increased substantially in recent decades More than three-quarters of American adults over the age of 20 are overweight (31%), obese (43%), or severely obese (9%; Fryar et al., 2021). Young adult men and women age 20 to 39 show similar rates of obesity (about 40% each; Hales et al., 2020; see Figure 11.3). Obesity becomes more common from early to middle adulthood.

Adult obesity is influenced by the dynamic interplay of genetic and environmental factors (Herrera et al., 2011; Silventoinen & Konttinen, 2020). Worldwide, the prevalence of overweight and obesity has doubled over the past four decades, supporting the increasingly important role of the environment in obesity (Chooi et al., 2019). With advances in technology, desk jobs have replaced many jobs requiring physical labor and many people have become less active. Food has become more abundant in Western countries, especially sugary, fatty, and processed foods. Increasingly people in low- and middle-income countries consume Western diets (Ford et al., 2017). With age, it becomes more difficult to avoid overeating because caloric needs drop between the ages of 25 and 50, and the metabolic rate—the amount of energy the body uses at rest—gradually falls as muscle cells decline in number and size (Roberts & Rosenberg, 2006). A sedentary lifestyle, little physical activity, and too much screen time are closely associated with obesity (Heinonen et al., 2013; Vella et al., 2020).

FIGURE 11.3 ■ Prevalence of Obesity Among Adults Aged 20 and Over, by Sex and Age: United States, 2017–2018.

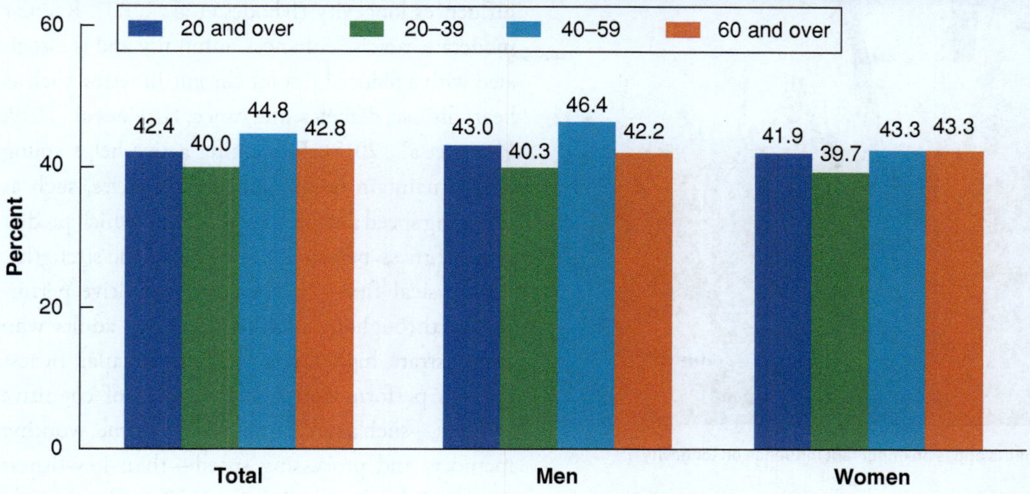

Source: Hales et al. (2020).

Contextual factors, such as neighborhood socioeconomic status, may encourage or deter health-related activities, such as engaging in outside physical activities (Gordon, 2017; Lakerveld & Mackenbach, 2017). Neighborhood disadvantage is associated with obesity through a variety of means, such as poor access to green spaces, greater access to fast food restaurants, and greater perceived stress (Kwarteng et al., 2017; Mylona et al., 2020; Walker et al., 2020). Low-income communities often have more convenience stores and fast-food restaurants than supermarkets, with fewer healthy options such as fresh fruits and vegetables (Larson et al., 2009). In addition, individuals' and families' socioeconomic status influences the risk for obesity because fruits, vegetables, and lean protein are costly relative to less healthy sweet snacks, processed foods, and refined grains (Fulgoni & Drewnowski, 2019; Rao et al., 2013).

Obesity is a serious health risk, associated with a range of health problems and illnesses such as high blood pressure; stroke; circulatory problems; diabetes; digestive disorders; arthritis; cancer; and, ultimately, early death (Cheng et al., 2016; Roh & Choi, 2020; Tchernof & Després, 2013). Obesity may also affect adults' ability to fight illnesses, such as COVID-19. Among adults diagnosed with COVID-19, obesity was associated with an increased likelihood of hospitalization and poor outcomes, including death (de Siqueira et al., 2020; Yang et al., 2021). Moreover, weight gain throughout early adulthood predicts illnesses such as cardiovascular disease and cancer as well as death in middle adulthood (Zheng et al., 2017). Obese adults often experience weight-related bias and discrimination from individuals and groups who have negative attitudes about obesity, such as the misconception that obesity is related to self-control (Cohen & Shikora, 2020; Nutter et al., 2018). Obese adults may experience more difficulty finding mates, rental apartments, and jobs than do non-obese adults (Campos-Vazquez & Gonzalez, 2020; Côté & Bégin, 2020; Puhl et al., 2011). Adults' perceptions and experience of bias predicts mental health problems, such as depression (Puhl et al., 2020; Robinson et al., 2017).

Health outcomes improve with even moderate weight loss (Orzano & Scott, 2004). Successful long-term weight loss is challenging, as indicated by the vast array of "quick" weight loss programs advertised in the media. Successful weight loss is most often a result of lifestyle changes, such as regular moderate exercise coupled with a nutritionally balanced diet low in calories and fat (Nicklas et al., 2012; Nurkkala et al., 2015). Effective weight loss interventions emphasize behaviors and encourage individuals to keep accurate records of what they eat and analyze eating patterns in their food choices (MacLean et al., 2015). Since many people overeat as a reaction to stress, training in problem-solving skills helps participants learn non-food-related ways of managing day-to-day conflicts and difficulties, as well as increasing social support to help individuals cope with challenging environments.

Exercise offers powerful health benefits and is an important influence on longevity.

iStock/verve231

Physical Activity

Physical activity offers powerful health benefits and influences longevity (Rhodes et al., 2017). Regular moderate exercise enhances immunity and is associated with a reduced risk for chronic illnesses, such as heart disease, diabetes, and cancer (Lavie et al., 2019; Piercy et al., 2018). Remaining active helps young adults maintain motor skill competencies, such as throwing speed and jumping distance, which predict overall fitness, percentage of body fat, and strength.

Physical fitness is linked to cognitive performance throughout adulthood. Young adults who demonstrate high levels of cardiovascular fitness tend to perform better on measures of cognitive abilities—such as attention, reaction time, working memory, and processing speed—than low-fitness young adults (Loprinzi et al., 2020; Stillman et al., 2020). Mental health benefits of regular physical activity include improved mood, energy, and ability to cope and lower levels of stress, anxiety, and depression (Herbert et al., 2020; Teychenne et al., 2020).

How much exercise is enough to reap health benefits, such as reduced cholesterol levels, decreased body fat, and reduced risk of developing diabetes or heart disease? U.S. national guidelines recommend 150 to 300 minutes of moderate intensity activity each week (e.g., brisk walking, raking the lawn, or pushing a lawn mower), or 75 to 150 minutes of vigorous intensity activity, plus muscle strengthening exercises on at least two days each week (U.S. Department of Health and Human Services, 2018). The activity does not have to be performed in a single block of time; it may be accumulated in 10-minute increments throughout the day. Physical activity tends to decline from adolescence into young adulthood, increasing the risk for poor health outcomes throughout adulthood (Corder et al., 2019).

The quarantines that accompanied the COVID-19 pandemic in 2020 and 2021 prevented may young adults from obtaining minimum recommended levels of physical activity. Analyses of more than 19 million daily step-count measurements from more than 455,000 users from 187 countries showed that step counts declined by more than one-quarter, and in some countries by nearly half, during the pandemic (Tison et al., 2020). Declines in physical activity and increases in sedentary activity, such as sitting for 10 hours or more daily, were associated with depressive symptoms (Maugeri et al., 2020; Schuch et al., 2020). Sedentary behavior is problematic for health because it is associated with increased risk for cardiovascular disease, diabetes, and cancer (DiPietro et al., 2019). Adults with a high BMI tended to show greater increases in sedentary activity and overeating during pandemic quarantines than adults with a lower BMI (Robinson et al., 2021). Physical activity has also shown mental health benefits for adults in quarantine. Adults who reported at least 30 minutes of moderate physical activity each day were less likely to show anxiety and depressive symptoms than their less active peers (Pieh et al., 2020; Schuch et al., 2020).

Substance Abuse

Substance use tends to rise during emerging adulthood as young people live away from their parents for the first time in their lives. Emerging adults experience the drive to explore the world at the same time as they feel pressure to complete their education, begin a career, and find a mate. These circumstances, coupled with easy access to drugs and alcohol, increase the risk of alcohol and substance abuse in emerging adulthood. In North America, use of substances such as drugs, alcohol, and tobacco tends to begin during adolescence, peak in the early 20s, and decline in the 30s (Schulenberg et al., 2020). Generally speaking, similar patterns of use during emerging adulthood occur in Australia, New Zealand, and Northern European countries (Andrews & Westling, 2016). Substance use tends to decline as young adults become parents and transition into new family roles; however, substance use remains prevalent in adulthood, with about 12% of adults aged 35 and 40reporting illicit drug use (other than marijuana) within the past year (about 30% including marijuana; Schulenberg et al., 2020). The following sections examine the most commonly used substances: alcohol, marijuana, and tobacco.

Alcohol

Alcohol is legal for young adults at age 21 in all U.S. states and is the drug of choice for most people throughout adulthood. Of particular concern to professionals are rates of **binge drinking**, defined as consuming five or more drinks in one sitting for men and four drinks in one sitting for women (U.S. Department of Agriculture & U.S. Department of Health and Human Services, 2020). Heavy drinking is defined as two or more instances of binge drinking within the past 30 days. Generally, binge drinking and heavy drinking are highest in emerging and young adulthood, with about one-third of adults aged 18 to 24 and 25 to 34, as well as one in five adults aged 35 to 44, reporting binge drinking within the past 30 days (see Figure 11.4; Substance Abuse and Mental Health Services Administration, 2014). Binge drinking is associated with negative short- and long-term consequences for physical and psychological well-being including fatal and nonfatal injuries, physical fights, driving after drinking, arrests and detentions, sexual assault, and threats to cardiovascular function, such as increased arterial stiffness (Kuntsche et al., 2017; Hwang et al., 2020).

As shown in Figure 11.5, in 2013, about 20% of 21- to 25-year-olds and 26- to 29-year-olds and about 18% of 30- to 34-year-olds reported driving under the influence of alcohol within the past year (United States Department of Health and Human Services, 2014). Each year alcohol is implicated in one-third of traffic fatalities and in 40% of all crimes (National Council on Alcoholism and Drug Dependence, 2015; National Highway Traffic Safety Administration, 2016).

Research with college students has suggested that binge and heavy drinking may be part of a "stage of life phenomenon" for which the transition out of high school increases the risk (Reckdenwald et al., 2016). As they enter college, young people experience greater exposure to drinking and encounter more peer drinking and positive peer attitudes toward alcohol, and consequently alcohol use tends to increase (Simons-Morton et al., 2016). Most emerging adults report experiencing more positive consequences of drinking (such as feeling social) than negative consequences (such as cognitive impairment), which contributes to high rates of binge and heavy drinking in this age group (Lau-Barraco et al., 2017; Lee et al., 2011). Although emerging adults who attend college tend to drink more than their non-college-attending peers (Reckdenwald et al., 2016; Simons-Morton et al., 2016), heavy drinking and alcohol-related problems are more common among emerging adults regardless of college enrollment (Merrill & Carey, 2016).

FIGURE 11.4 ■ Current, Binge, and Heavy Alcohol Use Among Persons Ages 12 and Older, by Age, 2014.

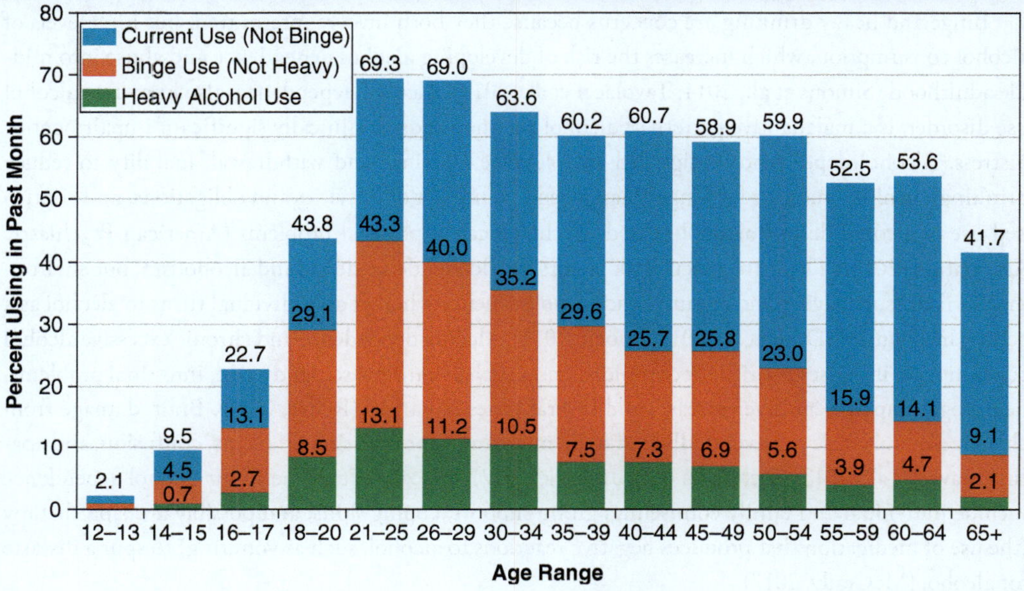

Source: Substance Abuse and Mental Health Services Administration, 2014.

FIGURE 11.5 ■ Driving Under the Influence of Alcohol in the Past Year Among People Aged 16 or Older, by Age, 2014.

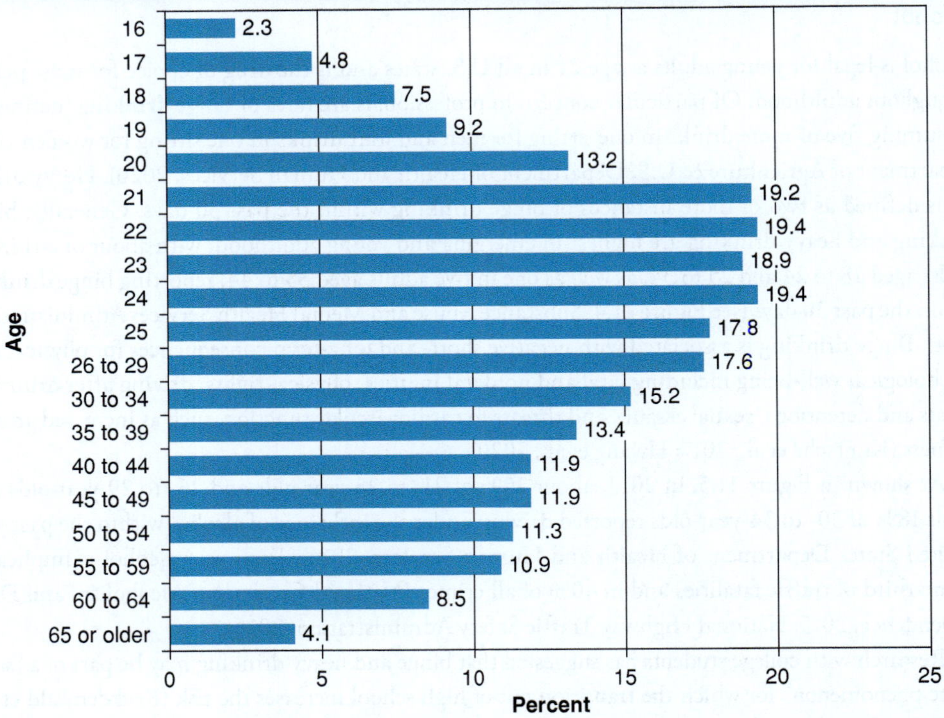

Source: Lipari et al., 2016.

Often referred to as "maturing out," alcohol use tends to decline as young people enter early adulthood. Generally, young adults in their 20s continue to drink frequently but consume less alcohol on each occasion (Arria et al., 2016). The transition to adult responsibilities such as career, marriage, and parenthood typically predicts declines in heavy drinking and alcohol-related problems (Leech et al., 2020). Yet heavy drinking and binge drinking remain prevalent in adulthood, with 14% of middle aged adults reporting binge drinking within the last month (Kanny et al., 2013). Recent research suggests that young adults who drink much more than their peers do not show the declines in drinking characteristic of maturing out (Windle, 2020).

Binge and heavy drinking are concerns because they both involve intermittent but high levels of alcohol consumption, which increases the risk of developing **alcohol dependence** and abuse into middle adulthood (Simons et al., 2014; Tavolacci et al., 2019). Alcohol dependence, also known as alcohol use disorder, is a maladaptive pattern of alcohol use that leads to clinically significant impairment or distress. Alcohol dependence is signaled by tolerance, cravings and withdrawal, inability to reduce drinking, drinking more or for longer than intended, neglect of activities and obligations, and continued use of alcohol despite alcohol-related psychological or physical problems (American Psychiatric Association, 2013). There are genetic risk factors for alcohol dependence and alcoholism, but environmental factors, behavior, and circumstances also influence whether an individual turns to alcohol as a coping mechanism (Deak et al., 2019; Enoch, 2013). Alcohol dependence and chronic excessive alcohol consumption increases the risk for chronic diseases such as cardiovascular disease, intestinal problems, neurologic impairment, liver disease, and several types of cancer (Rehm, 2011). Brain damage from chronic alcohol abuse can eventually lead to memory and concentration problems, confusion, and apathy (Stavro et al., 2013; Cservenka & Brumback, 2017). Successful treatments for alcohol dependence include individual and family counseling, group support, coping skills, and possibly aversion therapy (the use of medication that produces negative reactions to alcohol, such as vomiting) to spur a distaste for alcohol (McCrady, 2017).

Marijuana

By far the most commonly used substance, after alcohol, is marijuana, with 20% of 18- to 25-year-old emerging adults and 13% of 26- to 34-year-old young adults reporting use in the last month (Azofeifa et al., 2016; Miech et al., 2017). Young people consume marijuana for different reasons; those who cite experimentation as their primary reason tend to report fewer marijuana-related problems than do those who list coping, relaxation, and enjoyment (Patrick et al., 2016).

Marijuana use has increased rapidly among emerging and young adults over the past 15 years, correlating with changes in its legal status in U.S. states (Bae & Kerr, 2020; Kerr, Bae, et al., 2018; Kerr, Lui, et al., 2018; Leung et al., 2018). Emerging adults are more likely to report recreational use rather than medical reasons for marijuana use; medical use becomes more common with age, especially in middle adulthood (Compton et al., 2017). Similar to alcohol, marijuana use tends to decline in one's 20s, but young adults today report greater use at age 30 than prior cohorts (Terry-McElrath et al., 2018). For most young people, marijuana use is infrequent and limited in duration, but about one-quarter report continued frequent use from emerging adulthood through age 30 (Terry-McElrath et al., 2019).

Sustained marijuana use can interfere with completing the developmental tasks of young adulthood, such as reaching education and career goals, forming intimate relationships and marriage, and taking on adult roles. Heavy marijuana use is associated with lower levels of academic attainment, lower income, greater levels of unemployment, conflict with partners, and poor life satisfaction (Hall, 2014; Silins et al., 2014; Zhang et al., 2016). Cognitive effects of heavy marijuana use includes impairments in learning, memory, and thinking (Kroon et al., 2021; Lovell et al., 2020). Heavy marijuana use is also thought to interfere with executive functioning—problem solving, abstract reasoning, and judgment—and the earlier the age of onset, the greater the negative effects (Colizzi et al., 2020; Lovell et al., 2020). Finally, marijuana smokers experience many of the same respiratory problems common among tobacco smokers, such as cough, more frequent chest illnesses, and cancers (Tan & Sin, 2018). Marijuana e-cigarettes—vaping—are thought to have similar effects on pulmonary health (Traboulsi et al., 2020). Marijuana smoke contains irritants and at least 33 different carcinogens (Schwartz, 2017).

Tobacco

Smoking is the leading cause of preventable death in the United States, responsible for 1 in 5 deaths each year (Office of the Surgeon General, 2016). Nearly 90% of smokers have their first cigarette before age 18, but regular or daily smoking often does not begin until about age 20 or later, and the overall risk of initiating smoking plateaus at about age 22 and is rare after 24 (Edwards et al., 2013; U.S. Department of Health and Human Services, 2014). About 8% of emerging adults age 18 to 24 are current smokers, compared with 17% of adults age 25 to 44 years of age (Centers for Disease Control, 2020). Many smokers do not consider themselves smokers because they only engage in occasional social smoking, "bumming" cigarettes rather than buying them, and smoking in social groups rather than as a daily habit (Villanti et al., 2017). Social smokers tend to report no immediate desire to quit (Brown et al., 2011).

Why is cigarette smoking so problematic? With each cigarette, a smoker consumes one to two milligrams of nicotine, which stimulates reward pathways in the brain. Withdrawal symptoms of nicotine begin within a few hours after the last cigarette, including irritability, craving, anxiety, and attention deficits, which often send the smoker in search of another cigarette. Other withdrawal symptoms include depression, sleep problems, and increased appetite. When a smoker quits, withdrawal symptoms often peak within the first few days of smoking cessation and usually subside within a few weeks, but some people continue to experience symptoms for months. About two-thirds of cigarette smokers report interest in quitting each year and about half attempt to quit, but fewer than 1 in 10 smokers quit each year (Babb et al., 2017). The negative health effects emerge early. Smoking is associated with declines in cardiovascular function in young adulthood (Batista et al., 2020; Sumartiningsih et al., 2019).

Recently e-cigarettes have emerged as a popular alternative to tobacco cigarettes. E-cigarettes are the most commonly used tobacco product among emerging adults, with about 20% of 19- to

Smoking is highly addictive, leading many smokers to ignore health warnings.

iStock/DanBrandenburg

22-year-olds reporting use within the past 30 days, dropping to 11% at age 25–26, and 9% at ages 27–30 (Schulenberg et al., 2020). E-cigarettes aerosolize nicotine and produce a vapor that emulates that of conventional cigarette (Yamin et al., 2010). Many people view e-cigarettes as a safer alternative to conventional cigarettes (Farsalinos & Polosa, 2014; Goniewicz et al., 2013; Huerta et al., 2017). Nicotine and the aerosol created by e-cigarettes include chemicals, heavy metals, and ultrafine particles that reach the lungs and are linked to heightened cardiovascular risk and lung disease (Gawlik et al., 2018; Ghosh et al., 2018; Murthy, 2017). Moreover, e-cigarette users show increased risk for transitioning to tobacco smoking (Andrews et al., 2016; Soneji et al., 2017).

Thinking in Context: Lifespan Development

1. How do contextual and circumstantial factors relate to changes in substance use in emerging adulthood and early adulthood? How do you account for the phenomenon of "maturing out" of use in light of typical substance use patterns over early adulthood?
2. Apply the bioecological framework to explain the myriad factors that influence eating and exercise habits over early adulthood.
   - Identify factors in the microsystem, mesosystem, exosystem, and macrosystem that can act as risk and protective factors to health.
   - How do these shift from adolescence into emerging adulthood and from emerging adulthood into early adulthood?

Thinking in Context: Applied Developmental Science

1. Why does the risk for obesity and poor health behaviors, such as engaging in little physical activity or smoking, rise in early adulthood?
2. Given these factors, provide health and lifestyle advice to emerging adults. Consider the settings or contexts in which they engage and typical activities, concerns, and stressors.
3. What advice would you give to young adults in their late 20s and 30s? Compare their contexts, activities, concerns, and stressors with those of emerging adults. To what degree does your advice change?

COGNITIVE DEVELOPMENT IN EMERGING AND EARLY ADULTHOOD

LEARNING OBJECTIVE

11.3 Compare postformal reasoning, pragmatic thought, and cognitive-affective complexity.

For Alexander, a college junior majoring in biology, weighing hypotheses on evolutionary theory is easy. As he sees it, there is one account that is clearly more rational and supported by data than the others. Like most emerging adults, Alexander finds personal decisions much more difficult because many are vague and have multiple options with both costs and benefits.

As individuals progress toward adulthood, their thinking becomes increasingly flexible and practical. Adults come to expect uncertainty and ambiguity, and they recognize that everyday problems are influenced by emotion and experience rather than pure reasoning. Researchers who study adult cognition often focus on **epistemic cognition**—the ways in which individuals understand the nature of knowledge and how they arrive at ideas, beliefs, and conclusions.

Postformal Reasoning

From Piaget's cognitive developmental perspective, adolescents demonstrate formal operational reasoning, including the ability to think abstractly and to solve hypothetical problems. Although formal operational reasoning is the end point of Piaget's scheme, representing what he believed to be the most advanced form of reasoning, many researchers believe that there is much more to adult thinking than logical abstract reasoning. Researchers who adopt a cognitive-developmental perspective tend to agree that formal operations, Piaget's final stage of cognitive development, does not adequately describe adult cognition. Instead, adults develop a more advanced form of thinking known as **postformal reasoning**, which integrates abstract reasoning with practical considerations (Sinnott, 1998). Young adults who demonstrate postformal reasoning recognize that most problems have multiple causes and solutions, that some solutions are better choices than others, and that all problems involve uncertainty. People's understanding of the nature of knowledge advances along a predictable path in emerging and early adulthood, especially among college students.

When they enter college, individuals tend to view knowledge as a set of facts that hold true across people and contexts (King & Kitchener, 2016; Perry, 1970). Beginning college students tend to display **dualistic thinking,** in which knowledge and accounts of phenomena are viewed as either right or wrong with no in-between. Learning is viewed as a matter of acquiring and assessing facts. At the dualistic stage of reasoning, individuals tend to have difficulty grasping that several contradictory arguments can each have supporting evidence. The entering college student may sit through class lectures wondering, "Which theory is right?" and become frustrated when the professor explains that multiple theories each have various strengths and weaknesses.

With experience and exposure to multiple viewpoints, multiple arguments, and their inherent contradictions, individuals become more aware of the diversity of viewpoints that exist in every area of study. Their thinking becomes more flexible, and they relinquish the belief in absolute knowledge that characterizes dualistic, black and white thinking. Next, young adults move toward **relativistic thinking,** in which most knowledge is viewed as relative, dependent on the situation and thinker (King & Kitchener, 2016; Perry, 1970). Relativistic thinkers recognize that beliefs are subjective, that there are multiple perspectives on a given issue, and that all perspectives are defensible, at least to a certain extent. At first, relativistic thinkers may become overwhelmed by relativism—the great many opinions and options—and conclude that most topics are simply a matter of opinion and all views are correct. For example, they may conclude that all solutions to a problem are correct as it all depends on a person's perspective. The more mature thinker who displays **reflective judgment** acknowledges the multiple options and carefully evaluates them to choose the most adequate solution. He or she recognizes that options and opinions can be evaluated—and generates criteria to do so (Sinnott, 2003). As shown in Table 11.1, reflective judgment is the most mature type of reasoning as it synthesizes contradictions among perspectives. Although reasoning tends to advance throughout the college years, ultimately few adults demonstrate reflective judgment (Hamer & van Rossum, 2017).

Lively debate and discussion fosters the development of postformal reasoning.
iStock/ PeopleImages

TABLE 11.1 ■ Postformal Reasoning

	Understanding of Knowledge	Examples From Interviews With Young Adults
Dualistic Thinking	Knowledge is a collection of facts, and a given idea is either right or wrong.	"....theory might be convenient..., but .... The facts are what's there...and... should be the main thing."
Relativistic Thinking	Knowledge is relative, dependent on the situation and thinker, and a matter of opinion and perspective.	"I really can't [choose a point of view] on this issue. It depends on your beliefs since there is no way of proving either one... I believe they're both the same as far as accuracy." "People think differently and so they attack the problem differently. Other theories could be as true as my own but based on different evidence."
Reflective Judgment	Knowledge is a synthesis of contradictory information and perspectives whose evidence can be evaluated according to certain criteria.	"[when approaching a problem] there are probably several ways to do it. What are they? Which one's most efficient? Which one will give us the most accurate results?" "One can judge an argument by how well thought-out the positions are, what kinds of reasoning and evidence are used to support it, and how consistent the way one argues on this topic is as compared with how one argues on other topics." "It is very difficult in this life to be sure. There are degrees of sureness. You come to a point at which you are sure enough for a personal stance on the issue."

Postformal cognitive development depends on experience and metacognition, the ability to reflect on one's thought process. When individuals are exposed to situations and reasoning that challenges their knowledge and belief systems, they may be motivated to consider the adequacy of their own reasoning processes and modify them as needed (Sandoval et al., 2016). Social interaction is critical to postformal development. Discussing and considering multiple perspectives and solutions to a problem can spur individuals to evaluate their own reasoning. With maturation, young people become more likely to compare their reasoning process and justifications with others. When their justifications fall short, adults seek a more adequate explanation and adjust their thinking accordingly. Therefore postformal reasoners demonstrate the capacity for mindfulness (Sinnott et al., 2020). Advancement to postformal reasoning is associated with contextual factors: specifically, exposure to realistic but ambiguous problems with diverging information, as well as supportive guidance, such as that which is often a part of college education within Western cultures (Stahl et al., 2016; Zeidler et al., 2009).

Given that postformal reasoning is influenced by experience, not all emerging and young adults display it. For example, Chinese college students generally do not display the typical advancement from dualism to relativism to reflective judgment (Zhang, 2004). When compared with their U.S. counterparts, Chinese students tend to lack opportunities for making their own choices and decisions in many areas such as curricula, career choices, academic majors, and residential arrangements (Zhang, 1999). Experience in decision making matters. Some theorists argue that even in Western cultures, the most advanced level of postformal reasoning (commitment within relativism) may come only with graduate study and wrestling with challenging philosophical and practical problems (Hamer & van Rossum, 2017; King & Kitchener, 2016). People's reasoning advances throughout adulthood; however, reasoning and decision making are not simply cognitive endeavors, but are influenced by emotion.

Pragmatic Thought and Cognitive-Affective Complexity

Cognitive advances permit adults to reason about hypothetical and academic problems in more sophisticated ways, but they also influence young adults' everyday functioning. Adults apply their postformal reasoning abilities, specifically reflective judgment, to solve everyday problems. This ability to accept inconsistencies and use reasoning to determine the best alternatives, to apply reflective judgment in real-world contexts, is known as **pragmatic thought** (Labouvie-Vief, 2015). Managing various roles and tackling the problems of everyday life require thinking that is adaptive and accepting of contradiction. Adults must come to terms with their relative power in various contexts: At home they have autonomy and are able to carve out their own niche, whereas at work they must follow the directions of their employer. Coordinating dynamic roles as spouse, parent, friend, employee, and manager requires flexibility.

Reasoning in everyday situations is not simply a matter of logic; it is fused with emotion. Our evaluations of potential solutions to problems are influenced by our emotions—positive and negative feelings about each option. Sometimes our cognitive and emotional evaluations conflict. Over the course of adulthood, individuals become better at understanding and regulating their emotions and become less swayed by emotions, which influences their reasoning in everyday situations (Mather, 2012; Watson & Blanchard-Fields, 1998). Successfully coordinating emotion and cognition improves people's capacity to adapt to the complexities of adult life and the inherent balancing of many roles and obligations (Labouvie-Vief, 2006). This capacity to be aware of emotions, integrate positive and negative feelings about an issue, and regulate intense emotions to make logical decisions about complicated issues is known as **cognitive-affective complexity** (Labouvie-Vief, 2015; Mikels et al., 2010).

Cognitive-affective complexity increases from early adulthood through late middle adulthood. With gains in cognitive-affective complexity, adults better understand others, including their perspectives, feelings, and motivations, influencing their social relationships.

Evaluating Cognitive-Developmental Approaches to Adult Development

Similar to research on the development of formal operations, advances in postformal reasoning and cognitive-affective complexity vary among individuals. Adults are more likely than adolescents to demonstrate postformal reasoning, but not all adults reach the most advanced levels of reasoning (Hamer & van Rossum, 2017). In fact, most do not. People seem to show more mature reasoning when considering material and problems with which they have the greatest experience.

The way in which researchers ask questions influences individuals' responses and, ultimately, what is concluded about cognition (Ojalehto & Medin, 2015a). Researchers have learned that more complex responses are yielded when they ask participants to consider systems of causation using prompts such as "How are *x* and *y* related to each other and to the larger system?" as compared with prompts that encourage reasoning about individual causal links, such as "Does *x* cause *y*?" This work has shown that there is cultural variation in reasoning about causal events (Ojalehto & Medin, 2015b). Westerners tend to explain events using a single or few direct causes. In contrast, people from East Asian cultures tend to explain events as caused by multiple factors that interact, creating a ripple effect whereby one event holds many complex consequences that may not be easily anticipated (Maddux & Yuki, 2006). This reasoning is conceptually similar to the interacting systems posited by Bronfenbrenner (see Chapter 1). Other research has shown that the multi-factor interactive view of causality is present among people of many nonwestern cultural communities. For example, indigenous Itza Maya and Native American Menominee people tend to emphasize complex interactions across many entities (e.g., animal and spiritual entities), contexts (e.g., habitats), and time frames (Atran & Medin, 2008; Unsworth et al., 2012).

Likewise, cognitive-affective complexity relies on advances in emotional awareness and regulation. The ability to coordinate sophisticated emotions and cognitions vary with situations, tasks, contexts, and motivations (Labouvie-Vief, 2015). Furthermore, advanced forms of pragmatic reasoning likely do not suddenly appear but rather emerge with gains in knowledge, experience, and information processing capacity (Kuhn, 2013; Moshman & Moshman, 2011).

Thinking in Context: Lifespan Development

1. What kinds of experiences foster the development of postformal reasoning? In your view, is higher education necessary to develop the capacity for postformal reasoning? Why or why not?
2. How does cognitive-affective complexity reflect advances in both cognitive and emotional maturity? How do the various contexts in which people interact influence cognitive-affective maturity? Consider the home, peer, and school or work contexts.

Thinking in Context: Applied Developmental Science

You are a researcher who wishes to study postformal reasoning, pragmatic thought, and cognitive-affective complexity. How might you study these concepts? Who would you study? What data collection techniques would you use (see Chapter 1)? What challenges do you envision in conducting this research?

EDUCATION IN EMERGING AND EARLY ADULTHOOD

LEARNING OBJECTIVE

11.4 Explain how attending college influences young adults' development, and identify challenges faced by first-generation and nontraditional students, students with disabilities, and young adults who do not attend college.

Unlike childhood and adolescence, when education is mandated and virtually all students progress with their peers on the same schedule, educational progress is not closely associated with age in early adulthood.

Developmental Impact of Attending College

Attending college, at least for a time, has become a normative experience for emerging adults. In 2018, 69% of high school graduates in the United States enrolled in 2- or 4-year colleges (National Center for Education Statistics, 2017, 2021a). In 2018, about 13% of all college students enrolled in the United States identified as Black, 19% as Hispanic, 7% as Asian and Pacific Islander, and less than 1% as Native American or Alaska Native (55% identified as white; National Center for Education Statistics, 2021c). Students enroll in college to learn about a specific field of study (a major) and to prepare for careers, but there are other benefits of attending college. Adults of all ages often view their college years as highly influential in shaping their thoughts, values, and worldview (Patton et al., 2016). In addition to academic learning, college presents young people with new perspectives and encourages experimentation with alternative behavior, beliefs, and values. College courses often require students to construct arguments and solve complex problems, fostering the development of postformal reasoning (King & Kitchener, 2016). Attending college is associated

There are intellectual, psychological, and social benefits of attending college.
iStock/Rawpixel

with advances in moral reasoning, identity development, and social development (Lapsley & Hardy, 2017; Patton et al., 2016).

The positive impact of attending college is not simply a matter of the type of college one attends; research indicates that all institutions, public and private, selective and open enrollment, advance cognitive and psychological development (Mayhew et al., 2016). In addition, students at 2-year community colleges show cognitive and academic gains similar to those of their peers at 4-year institutions (Monaghan & Attewell, 2015). Rather than the type of institution attended, developmental outcomes are most influenced by student involvement in campus life and peer interaction in academic and social contexts. Students who are active in campus life and feel a sense of belonging tend to show greater educational attainment and often develop leadership skills (Mayhew et al., 2016; Soria & Johnson, 2017). Students who develop close friendships with other students are more likely to persist in college, succeed, and graduate (Bronkema & Bowman, 2019). Students who live in residence halls have more opportunities to interact with peers and become involved in the academic and social aspects of campus life—and show the greatest cognitive gains in the college years (Bronkema & Bowman, 2017).

Some students require more than 4 years to complete a bachelor's degree. Many students choose to take fewer courses at a time because of time constraints, special learning needs, or the need to work part or full time. Delayed time to graduation does not harm employment chances, but lengthy delays are associated with lower post-college earnings relative to on-time peers (Witteveen & Attewell, 2021). Many students do not complete college. Only about two-thirds of students who enroll in 4-year institutions graduate within 6 years and one-third of students enrolled at 2-year institutions graduate within 3 years (National Center for Education Statistics, 2020). Generally, student attrition is highest in colleges with open enrollment and those with relatively low admission requirements.

First-Generation College Students

As of 2016, 56% of college students are first-generation students, as they have parents without 4-year degrees, including 24% whose parents have never attended college (RTI International, 2019a). Students of color and those of low socioeconomic status are disproportionately likely to be first-generation college students (RTI International, 2019a). First-generation college students experience higher risk of drop out than students with parents who have earned 4-year degrees. First generation students tend to be less active in campus and extracurricular activities and less academically prepared than their peers, two factors that often aid students in adjusting to college and protect against college dropout (Feldman, 2017).

Some research suggests that first-generation college students experience more stress than their peers (Wilbur, 2021). First-generation college students often face economic circumstances that interfere with their academic success and their ability to participate on campus. First-generation students are more likely than their peers to be enrolled part time, to hold a job, and to have mixed feelings about college (Ward et al., 2012). In 2016, more than two-thirds of first-generation students were employed in a paid job (RTI International, 2019b). Financial concerns and the need to work during college predict drop out among first-generation students (Pratt et al., 2019).

Attending college is often accompanied by social challenges for first-generation students. With few family and peer models of how to succeed in college, first-generation students and students of color may feel isolated and find it difficult to understand and adjust to the college student role and expectations. First-generation students report having fewer opportunities to talk about their negative experiences and are more likely to feel guilty about their educational achievement (Jury et al., 2017).

Many students experience a cultural mismatch between their college environment, their changing sense of self, and the communities with which they identify (Phillips et al., 2016). Many first-generation college students live in families and communities characterized by norms of interdependence, where community members "look out" for one another, which often contrasts with the norms of independence that are prevalent in college environments (Stephens et al., 2012). In one study, Latinx first-generation students revealed that many experienced conflicts between their home and school values and responsibilities that interfered with their academic achievement and sense of well-being. Conflicts included providing assistance to family versus doing academic work and allocating funds to the family or for travel to see family versus allocating money for educational expenses (Vasquez-Salgado et al., 2015). Likewise, some Latinx students reported feeling guilt for attending college and not offering their families daily assistance (Covarrubias & Fryberg, 2015). At the same time, research with first-generation college students from Mexican American families suggests that perceived family support is protective and associated with positive adjustment to college, including better academic achievement and fewer depressive symptoms (Jimenez et al., 2021).

The college environment also plays a role in influencing students' transition to and success in college. Institutions that are responsive to the academic, social, and cultural needs of students help them adjust to college and, ultimately, succeed (Mayhew et al., 2016). Reaching out to at-risk students during the first weeks of college can help them to feel connected to the institution. Colleges and universities can provide opportunities for faculty and students to interact and form connections, help students to develop study skills, and assist students in getting involved on campus. Students who live on campus, see faculty as concerned with their development, establish relationships with faculty and other students, and become involved in campus life are more likely to succeed and graduate from college (Mayhew et al., 2016). When students feel that they are part of a campus community, they are more likely to persist and graduate.

Nontraditional College Students

Virtually all research on the effects of college tends to focus on what most people think of as the typical college student, age 18 through 22. But there are many paths to a college degree. About 34% of all college students are age 25 and older, including 28% of students enrolled in public 4-year colleges and 33% of students enrolled in public 2-year colleges (National Center for Education Statistices, 2021). More than one-third of nontraditional students are people of color and the majority are women (U.S. News & World Report, 2016).

Why do students return to college, or attend for the first time, in their mid-20s or beyond? Nontraditional college students tend to have some or all of the following characteristics: are older than the typical student, are independent for financial aid purposes, have one or more dependents, attend college part time, attend college online, and work full time (Rabourn et al., 2018; Radford et al., 2015). Each of these factors poses significant challenges to nontraditional students' success in college (MacDonald, 2018). They are more likely than other college students to juggle multiple life roles, such as worker, spouse, parent, and caregiver. Sometimes the demands of school, family, and work conflict. Work-related travel is often disruptive to childcare as well as academic demands, resulting in class absences and missed assignments. Also known as adult learners, nontraditional college students often seek a college degree to be eligible for higher paying and more satisfying careers (Ross-Gordon, 2011). Employers sometimes encourage employees to enroll in college to learn new skills. Some enroll in college to change career paths.

Adults return to college for many reasons, including to change career paths, obtain higher paying and more satisfying careers, learn new skills, and fulfill personal goals.

istock/ monkeybusinessimages

A growing body of nontraditional students in the U.S. are veterans, with unique challenges. Like other nontraditional learners, student veterans must prioritize and manage multiple roles, juggle stressors related to work, finances, housing, marriage, and childcare (Alschuler & Yarab, 2018; Sansone & Tucker Segura, 2020). Many student veterans experience emotional or physical health problems, such as post-traumatic stress disorder, depression, anxiety, traumatic brain injuries, or physical disabilities (Ulrich & Freer, 2020). Despite these stressors, student veterans tend to earn higher grades than their peers and show similar graduation rates as other students (54%; Institute for Veterans and Military Families, 2019).

Nontraditional students tend to be more engaged academically than their younger peers and show a readiness to learn and a problem-centered orientation toward learning that emphasizes acquiring the knowledge and skills needed for career advancement (Rabourn et al., 2018; Ross-Gordon, 2011). Older students tend to have a more complex knowledge base from which to draw and emphasize seeking meaning and applying what they learn to their lives. Their experience and multiple roles can help nontraditional learners make meaning of theoretical concepts that may be purely abstract to younger learners (Osam et al., 2017).

Many nontraditional students may find the practical details of college, such as scheduling, difficult to navigate (Osam et al., 2017). Classes that meet two or three days each week often conflict with work schedules. Evening classes often meet once per week, providing convenience at the expense of continuity and frequent contact with professors. Some students may find that required courses are offered only during the day, or they may have difficulty accessing advisors and student support services. Many colleges and universities increasingly support the needs of nontraditional students by extending student services beyond business hours, providing adequate and close parking for those students who rush from work to school, and offering affordable on-campus childcare for full- and part-time students, including evening students (Hope, 2017). Some also offer orientation programs for adult learners to provide information about support resources as well as help nontraditional students connect with one another and begin to build a social support network of peers.

Students With Developmental Disabilities

Emerging adults with developmental disabilities, such as autism spectrum disorder, ADHD, and specific learning disorders, are less likely than their peers to immediately enroll in 4-year postsecondary institutions after high school (Carroll et al., 2018). In 2015–2016, about 18% of undergraduate students under the age of 23 reported a disability (and 22% of students aged 24 and older; National Center for Education Statistics, 2019). Longitudinal research with more than 11,000 students suggests that students with disabilities are less likely than other students to graduate in 4 or 5 years; however, 6-year graduation rates are similar for students regardless of the presence of a disability (Wessel et al., 2009). Students with developmental disabilities tend to persist to graduation, but on a longer timetable than their peers, often taking fewer courses each semester and therefore requiring an extra semester or two to graduate (Knight et al., 2018).

The social and emotional challenges of entering college are often amplified for students with developmental disabilities (White et al., 2016). They frequently experience academic underachievement and high rates of remedial coursework despite being well-prepared intellectually and academically (Elias & White, 2018). This is true despite their reports of similar levels of academic engagement, such as asking questions, preparing for class, attending class, and contacting faculty. Although students with disabilities are similarly engaged with their academic work as other students, their similar levels of engagement do not translate into similar levels of achievement (McLeod et al., 2019).

Difficulties with executive functioning, common to most developmental disorders, contribute to poor outcomes (Dijkhuis et al., 2020; Lee et al., 2021). Specific features of some disabilities, such as difficulty attending for a period of time, characteristic of ADHD, or difficulty with changes in long-standing routines or environment, characteristic of autism spectrum disorder, can hamper success in college (Elias & White, 2018). Written assignments and group work may pose challenges because of difficulties with attention, executive function, and communication (McLeod et al., 2019).

Students with developmental disabilities may also struggle to manage social tasks and skills of daily living. Social interactions, making friends, and maintaining social supports may be challenging. College students with developmental disabilities tend to report lower-quality social relationships and are less likely to report having a confidant than nondisabled peers (McLeod et al., 2019). The number of social activities, such as clubs, residence life activities, and community service, is positively associated with students' sense of self-determination, autonomy, and positive adjustment, suggesting that helping students with disabilities engage with the community can aid their adjustment to and, ultimately, success in college.

Not Attending College

It can be said that attending college is part of the American dream and has become expected of many young people. Yet, in 2018 one-third of high school graduates in the U.S. did not immediately enroll in college (National Center for Education Statistics, 2021a). In 2019, only about 39% of adults held bachelor's degrees by age 29 (National Center for Education Statistics, 2021b).

Some academically well-prepared students report forgoing college because of a desire to work or a lack of interest in academics, but many cite economic barriers, such as the high cost of college or the need to support their family, as reasons for nonattendance (Bozick & DeLuca, 2011). The population of non-college-bound youth has been referred to in the literature as "forgotten" by educators, scholars, and policy makers because relatively few resources are directed toward learning about them or assisting them, as compared with college-bound young adults.

Young adults who enter the workforce immediately after high school have fewer work opportunities than those of prior generations. The rate of unemployment for high school graduates is about twice that of bachelor's degree holders (U.S. Bureau of Labor Statistics, 2015; Vilorio, 2016). In addition, many young people with high school degrees spend their first working years in jobs that are similar to those they held in high school: unskilled, with low pay and little security (Rosenbaum & Person, 2003). As illustrated in Figure 11.6, at all ages high school graduates earn less, and are more likely to be unemployed, than peers with college degrees.

The curricula of most secondary schools tend to be oriented toward college-bound students, and counseling tends to focus on helping students gain admission to college (Krei & Rosenbaum, 2000). Some argue that over the past three decades, secondary education has shifted toward emphasizing academics and reducing vocational training, leaving young adults who do not attend college ill prepared for the job market (Symonds et al., 2011). A solution proposed in the Pathways to Prosperity report from Harvard Graduate School of Education is for the U.S. educational system to support multiple pathways in the transition to adulthood (Ferguson & Lamback, 2014; Symonds et al., 2011). Opportunities for vocational training and to obtain relevant work experience will help young people try out careers and get relevant training for specific jobs. In addition, training programs should relay specific expectations for youth with regard to their responsibility in career training and decision making as well as the educational and vocational support they can expect in return (Symonds et al., 2011).

FIGURE 11.6 ■ Unemployment Rates and Earning by Educational Attainment in 2019

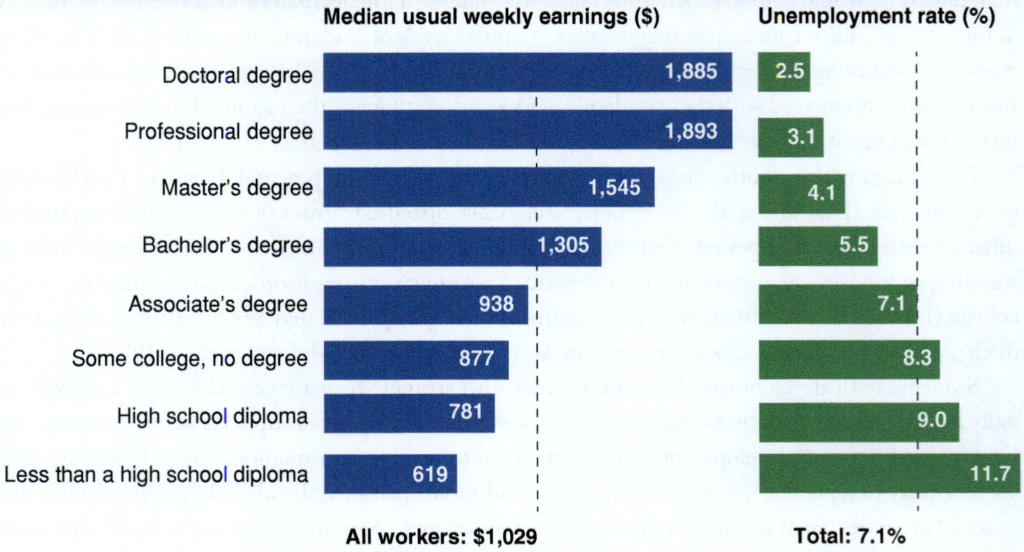

Source: U.S. Bureau of Labor Statistics (2019)

Thinking in Context: Lifespan Development

1. Consider your own experience as a college student. How has college contributed to your development? If you are a first-generation or nontraditional student, what challenges do you face? How do you overcome them?
2. Students with developmental disabilities have unique circumstances that influence their college experience and their ability to succeed in college.
    - What challenges do they face?
    - Identify personal and contextual strengths and resources that may help them to be resilient and support their success in college.
    - To what extent are some developmental disabilities associated with more difficulties in college than others?

Thinking in Context: Intersectionality

What are some reasons why first-generation and nontraditional students may experience a mismatch between their experiences within their homes and communities and the college environment?

- How do the various roles that individuals hold in their families and communities contribute to the mismatch?
- In what ways do race, ethnicity, and socioeconomic status play into first-generation and nontraditional students' college experience?

CAREER DEVELOPMENT IN EMERGING AND EARLY ADULTHOOD

LEARNING OBJECTIVE

11.5 Discuss vocational development, young adults' experiences in the workplace, and the value of work-life balance.

Selecting an occupation is one of the most important decisions that young people make. Children often fantasize about careers as astronauts, actors, and rock stars—careers that bear little resemblance to the choices they ultimately make when they grow up. How do people select occupations in real life?

Occupational Stages

Developmental theorist Donald Super proposed that the development of occupational goals progresses through five stages (Super, 1990). According to Super's model, vocational maturity reflects the degree to which an individual's occupational behaviors and status match the age-appropriate occupational stage. The first stage of occupational development, known as crystallization, begins in adolescence. Adolescents from ages 14 through 18 begin to think about careers in increasingly complex ways, considering their own interests, personality, abilities, and values as well as the requirements of each career. Similar to the exploration entailed in identity development, career exploration is at first tentative. Adolescents seek information about careers by talking with family, friends, and teachers, as well as through internet searches. They compare what they learn with their own interests.

The next stage is the specification stage (at about ages 18 to 21), in which individuals identify specific occupational goals and pursue the education needed to achieve them. As a first-year college student, Imani knew that she wanted to do something related to business but had not yet selected among several possible majors. Imani considered several business-related majors including accounting, management, and entrepreneurship and completed an internship at an investment firm before deciding to major in finance.

The third stage, implementation, typically from ages 21 to 24, is when emerging adults complete training, enter the job market, and make the transition to become employees. The developmental task of the implementation stage is to reconcile expectations about employment and career goals with available jobs. Young people may take temporary jobs or change jobs as they learn about work roles and attempt to match their goals with available positions. For example, Yolanda majored in education but found no teaching positions available at schools near her home. She accepted a temporary position running an after-school program while she applied for jobs in other cities and states. Even young adults who attain their "dream jobs" often find that they must tailor and adapt their expectations and goals in light of their career setting.

In the stabilization stage, young adults from ages 25 to 35 become established in a career; they settle into specific jobs, gain experience, and adapt to changes in their workplace and in their field of work. Toward the end of early adulthood, from age 35 and up, individuals progress through the final stage, consolidation. They accumulate experience and advance up the career ladder, moving into supervisory positions and becoming responsible for the next generation of workers.

Although a stage-oriented approach to understanding career development remains useful, it is important to recognize that career development does not follow a universal pattern. Not everyone progresses through the stages in the prescribed order and at the same pace. For many adults, career development does not progress in a linear fashion; in fact, most adults do not hold the same occupation throughout adulthood. Adults in their 50s today have had an average of 12 occupations between the ages of 18 and 52 (U.S. Bureau of Labor Statistics, 2019). Young adults can expect to change career paths one or more times throughout their lives. Nevertheless, in considering an adult's perspective on careers, it is useful to conceptualize career development as entailing the five stages outlined by Super: crystallization, specification, implementation, stabilization, and consolidation.

Influences on Vocational Choice

Many factors influence how emerging adults perceive and evaluate occupational choices, but perhaps the most important factor in selecting a career is the match between their personality traits and abilities and their occupational interests. We are most satisfied when we select occupations that match our personalities and other individual traits, such as intelligence and skills. John Holland (1997) proposed that occupational choices can be categorized by six personality types, as shown in Table 11.2. Holland explained that each personality type is best suited to a particular type of vocation. It is useful to consider careers in terms of Holland's six personality types, but most people have traits that correspond to more than one personality type and are able to successfully pursue several career paths (Hansen, 2020;

TABLE 11.2 ■ Personality and Vocational Choice

Personality Type	Vocational Choices
Investigative	Enjoys working with ideas; likely to select a scientific career (e.g., biologist, physicist)
Social	Enjoys interacting with people; likely to select a human services career (e.g., teaching, nursing, counseling)
Realistic	Enjoys working with objects and real-world problems; likely to select a mechanical career (carpenter, mechanic, plumber)
Artistic	Enjoys individual expression; likely to select a career in the arts, including writing and performing arts
Conventional	Prefers well-structured tasks; values social status; likely to select a career in business (e.g., accounting, banking)
Enterprising	Enjoys leading and persuading others; values adventure; likely to select a career in sales or politics

Spokane & Cruza-Guet, 2005). Furthermore, many careers entail a variety of skills and talents that cross the boundaries of the six-factor typology.

Career choice is the result of interactions between individual factors, such as personality, and contextual influences, such as socialization and access to economic and educational opportunities. Genetics may play a role in academic achievement and vocational interests, which in turn influence career opportunities and choices (Christensen et al., 2020; Rimfeld et al., 2016). Parents tend to share personality characteristics and abilities with their children, but they also influence children's career development through socialization (Lawson, 2018). Parents act as role models; their own occupational fields tend to influence their children's career choices (Lawson, 2018; Schoon & Polek, 2011). Parents also influence children's career development through the provision of resources and socioeconomic status (Johnson et al., 2020; Lawson, 2018).

Children in high-SES homes tend to have more educational resources, less pressure to work to aid the family, and more support and opportunities for exploring vocational options, which influences vocational choice (Jiang et al., 2019). Young people's career decisions and success are also influenced by parental support and their psychosocial development. (Garcia et al., 2015; Maier, 2005). Among low-SES first-generation college students, a sense of ethnic identity and maternal support predicted career expectations, and in turn, school engagement—the behavior needed to achieve vocational goals (Kantamneni et al., 2018).

Career development does not end with selecting a vocation. Young adults must obtain a job, learn about their role and tasks, develop proficiency, work well with others, respond to direction, and develop a good working relationship with supervisors. Work life influences young people's sense of competence, independence, and financial security and often is a source of new friendships (Brooks & Everett, 2008).

Transition to Work

Most young adults find that workplace responsibilities, expectations, and rewards are very different from the demands of high school and college. Many young adults find themselves employed in careers that are not their first choice, often explaining they simply "fell into it" or took the job that was available, without much planning or choice. First jobs frequently do not match young adults' interests and education. These mismatches are common during the early years of employment as young adults are learning about and developing their competencies and preferences and comparing them with the reality they encounter in the workplace. Even years after entering the workforce, many young adults report that are not working in a field that represented their greatest interest (Athanasou, 2002). The day-to-day tasks entailed by a given occupation often differ from young people's expectations, as entry-level

TABLE 11.3 ■ Employer vs. Student Perception of Proficiency in Career Readiness Skills, by Percentage of Respondents

	Percentage of Employers Who Rated Graduates Proficient	Percentage of Students Who Considered Themselves Proficient
Professionalism/work ethic	43	89
oral/written communications	42	79
critical thinking/problem solving	56	80
teamwork/collaboration	77	85
leadership	33	71
digital technology	66	60
career management	17	41
intercultural fluency	21	35

Source: National Association of College and Employers, 2017; National Association of Colleges and Employers, 2018.

jobs often include more clerical and other paperwork, fewer opportunities for autonomy, and lower pay than desired. The reality—that vocational expectations are not always achieved—can be a shock and can influence self-concept and occupational development as young adults revise their expectations.

The gap between young adults' career expectations and reality is related to inaccurate self-evaluations of competence and job preparedness (Tuononen et al., 2019). There is often a mismatch between employers' evaluations of their recent graduates' skills and the graduates' self-rated skills (see Table 11.3). Employers tend to rate new hires' interpersonal skills (e.g., responding to customer needs, understanding teams, and working well with others) and information use skills (e.g., locating, organizing, and using information) more poorly as compared with new hires' self-evaluations (McGarry, 2018). Early career dissatisfaction may be influenced by the potentially large divide between employers' and employees' views of employees' professionalism, oral and written communication, and critical thinking skills.

Managing expectations in light of reality often leads young adults to resign and seek alternative jobs and careers. It is not uncommon for a young adult to undergo as many as eight job changes by age 32 (U.S. Bureau of Labor Statistics, 2020c). Adults in their 40s today held, on average, five jobs between the ages of 18 and 22, three between 23 and 27, and two between 28 and 32. The median length of job tenure (time spent in a particular position) across all ages is about 4 years, on average, but it varies with age from about 3 years for young adults (aged 25 to 34) to 10 years for workers aged 55 to 64 (US Bureau of Labor Statistics, 2016, 2020a).

Today's young adults, the Millennial generation, and increasingly Generation Z, appear to hold different expectations for work than prior generations. These cohort differences include a greater preference for meaningful work, fulfilment, autonomy, opportunities for challenge and advancement, and work-life balance (Calk & Patrick, 2017; Kultalahti & Viitala, 2015). These expectations are more likely to be filled by positions requiring greater expertise and experience than entry-level positions provide and that many young adults entering the work force have (Mahmoud et al., 2020).

At this writing, the oldest members of Generation Z are entering their mid-twenties, and it is likely that their transition to the workforce will be unlike any other cohort's experience to date. The immediate effects of the COVID-19 pandemic and quarantines have included widespread furloughs, firings, remote work at home, and a dramatic rise in unemployment, especially for women, people of color, and adults with less education (Cowan, 2020). Young people may, at least temporarily, be less selective in choosing a job, which may lead to dissatisfaction. Those who work remotely may face challenges in training, interacting with coworkers, and developing relationships with supervisors. It is unknown whether the COVID-19 pandemic will result in permanent changes to the workplace, but it is a macrosystem factor likely to have a long-term influence on young peoples' work experiences.

Intersectionality and the Workplace

Women make up about half of the United States labor force, yet women earn 81 cents for every dollar men earn (PayScale, 2020b; US Bureau of Labor Statistics, 2021). When controlling for job and qualifications, white women, Hispanic women, and Black men each earn about 98 cents, and Black women earn only 97 cents for every dollar white men earn (PayScale, 2020a). Although a three-cent gap may seem paltry, it represents $1,500 of a $50,000 salary. Consider average wage increases over a lifetime and a three-cent gap can mean a difference of hundreds of thousands of dollars (PayScale, 2020a).

Women and people of color face many obstacles to career success, often collectively known as the **glass ceiling**, the invisible barrier that prevents disenfranchised people from advancing to the highest levels of the career ladder. Women and people of color are more likely than white men to fill entry-level positions and jobs that require little experience. Their numbers decline with each higher rung on the career ladder. Women in the U.S. hold about three-quarters of office and administrative support positions but only 40% of management positions (US Bureau of Labor Statistics, 2021). The effect is more striking for people of color. As shown by Figure 11.7, 55% of Asian Americans and 41% of white Americans hold managerial and professional positions, as compared with 32% of African Americans and 23% of Hispanic or Latinx Americans (U.S. Bureau of Labor Statistics, 2020b).

FIGURE 11.7 ■ Employed People by Occupation, Race, and Hispanic or Latino Ethnicity, United States, 2019

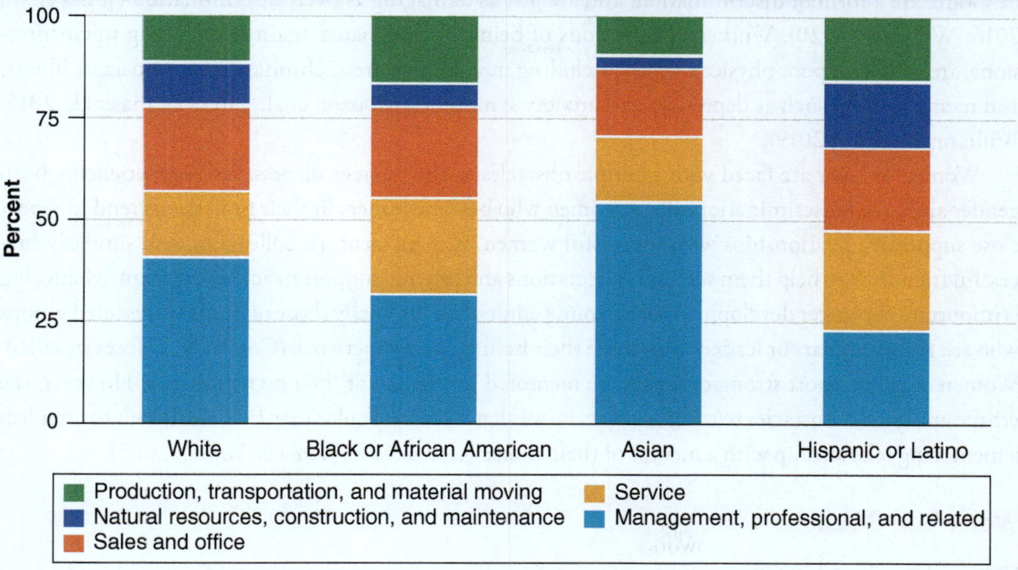

Source: U.S. Bureau of Labor Statistics (2020b)

Although laws guarantee equal opportunity, racial bias infiltrates every point of the hiring process—even how résumés are viewed. In one study, white male participants were asked to examine résumés that varied in quality (some indicated high qualifications and others low) and by the writer's race (African American, Hispanic American, Asian American, and white). The participants rated résumés from hypothetical Asian American job seekers as highly qualified for high-status jobs, regardless of the actual résumé's quality. When they were shown résumés indicating high qualifications, they rated them higher for white and Hispanic American job seekers than for African Americans. In fact, they gave African American job seekers negative evaluations regardless of résumé quality. This result indicates how racial discrimination may make it difficult for even highly qualified African American candidates to obtain jobs (King et al., 2006). In another study, college students judged recommendation letters for hypothetical job candidates of various ethnicities; the results were similarly biased against African American candidates (Morgan et al., 2013). Similarly, a recent variation found that recruiters were more likely to hire hypothetical native-born candidates for high-skill positions and hypothetical immigrant candidates for low-skill positions (Ndobo et al., 2018).

Women and people of color often face the glass ceiling, an invisible barrier preventing them from advancing to the highest levels of the career ladder.

iStock/track5

In the workplace, discrimination is often subtle, taking the form of microaggressions—brief commonplace daily slights that communicate hostile, derogatory, or negative attitudes or insults toward vulnerable groups, including people of color, women, individuals who identify as LGBTQ, and older workers (Sue et al., 2007). Perpetrators are sometimes unaware that they engage in microaggressions, conveyed through dismissive looks, gestures, and tones as well as through comments that the aggressor believes to be compliments or jokes. Examples include complimenting a Black colleague's eloquence; giving a nickname to a colleague whose name is difficult to pronounce; asking a Latinx, young, or female colleague to get coffee, take notes, or complete menial tasks that are not part of their job; or expressing surprise that an older colleague is familiar with Tik Tok (or any other new form of media). In the workplace, microaggressions may take the form of being overlooked, underrespected, and devalued because of race, gender, sexual orientation, and other identities. Microaggression messages are often so pervasive and automatic that they are dismissed as innocuous. These messages are a result of bias, of which aggressors may not be aware; are a form of discrimination; and are just as damaging as overt discrimination (Jones et al., 2016; Williams, 2020). Workers' perceptions of being discriminated against, including microagressions, are related to poor physical health, including measures of stress, chronic illness, and acute illness, and mental health, such as depressive and anxiety symptoms (Mouzon et al., 2017; Triana et al., 2015; Williams & Lewis, 2019).

Women of color are faced with multiple obstacles to their career success, often experiencing both gender and racial discrimination. Black women who become leaders in their professions tend to report close supportive relationships with successful women, such as mentors, colleagues, and similarly successful friends, who help them set high expectations and provide support in achieving them. Mentoring is important for career development of all young adults, but especially those of underrepresented groups who see few exemplars or leaders who share their heritage and experience (Combs & Milosevic, 2016). Women of color report strong desires to be mentored by women of their own ethnicity. However, the ethnic and gender obstacles to career success mean that women of color may find it difficult to establish a mentoring relationship with a mentor of their choice (Gonzáles-Figueroa & Young, 2005).

Work-Life Balance

Young adults participate in many roles: worker, friend, spouse, parent, and more. Frequently, roles conflict, such as having to work late and the desire to see friends or care for a child. **Work-life balance** refers to the effective management or balancing of multiple roles in one's work and nonwork life (Sirgy & Lee, 2018). Many discussions of work-life balance emphasize coordinating work and childrearing roles, but any adult with a life outside of work needs work-life balance.

Most parents find it challenging to meet the competing demands of family and career. Although it was once common for women to focus solely on raising children, caring for the home, and engaging with the school and community, today the majority of U.S. mothers of children under the age of 18, both married and unmarried, work (68% vs. 76% for married mothers and unmarried mothers, respectively; see Figure 11.8). Mothers with very young children are only slightly less likely to work than those with older children: more than two-thirds of mothers with children under 6 years of age and

FIGURE 11.8 ■ Working Mothers' Labor Participation 1975–2017

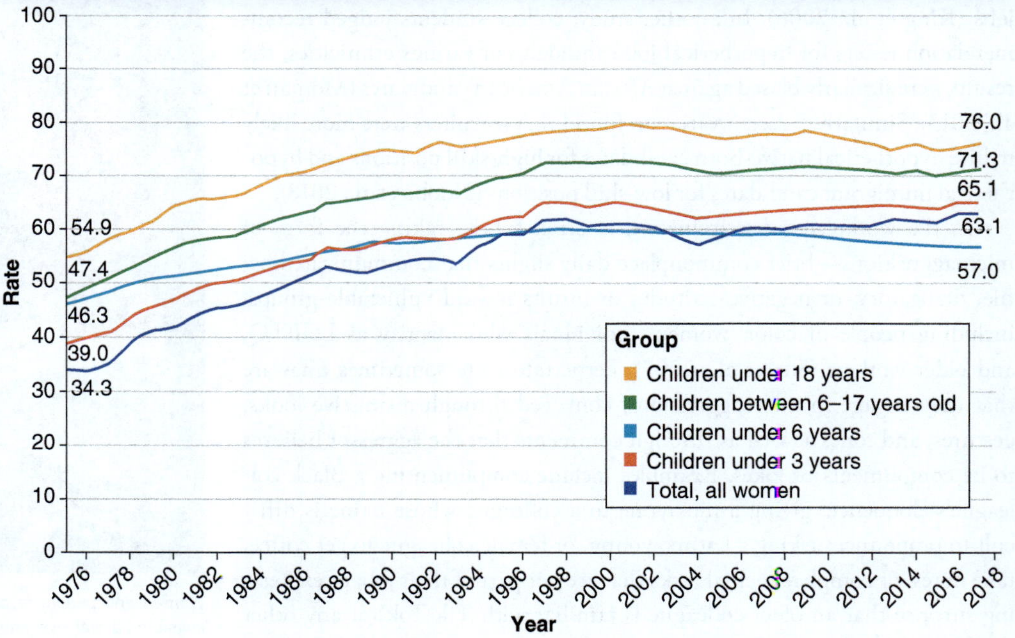

Source: U.S. Department of Labor (2020)

Flexible policies that permit employees to balance home and work responsibilities are positively associated with attendance, commitment to the organization, and work performance.

istock/ FatCamera

nearly two-thirds of mothers with an infant under a year old are in the labor force (U.S. Bureau of Labor Statistics, 2017). In addition, nearly all married fathers work and most share childcare and household responsibilities with their spouses.

Women and men report feeling conflict between work and family obligations (Shockley et al., 2017; Winslow, 2005). Adults who feel a sense of control over their work workload and schedule tend to show greater satisfaction with work-life balance and lower levels of work-life conflict (Carlson et al., 2011). A perceived loss of control accompanies a sense of role overload. More common among women, role overload refers to high levels of stress that result from attempting to balance the demands of multiple roles: employee, mother, and spouse (Higgins et al., 2010). Role overload is associated with poor health, depressive symptoms, ineffective parenting, and marital conflict (Carnes, 2017; Duxbury et al., 2018). Successfully managing multiple roles entails setting priorities, such as deemphasizing household chores and errands in favor of spending more time with children, with family and friends, and also alone (Hewitt et al., 2006). Women who best manage role overload are those who seek physical and emotional support from others (Higgins et al., 2010).

Work-life balance is a concern to adults in most Western countries. Research comparing employees across several European countries found that poor work-life balance was associated with perceived health, health complaints, and poor well-being in both men and women (Lunau et al., 2014). The reported experience of work-life balance varied by country alongside differences in national regulations regarding work hours, suggesting that workplace policies (often regulated by government) influence employees' sense of work-life balance and overall well-being. Workplace policies influence employee morale and productivity. Flexible policies that permit employees to balance home and work responsibilities (e.g., flexible starting and stopping times, opportunities to work from home, and time off to care for sick children) are positively associated with attendance, commitment to the organization, and work performance and negatively associated with distress symptoms (Allen et al., 2013; Halpern, 2005). Work flexibility, such as in scheduling, is linked with occupational status. Flexibility tends to be particularly advantageous to workers in lower-level jobs, but it is also more rare in these jobs (Kossek & Lautsch, 2018). Workplaces with onsite childcare show lower rates of employee absenteeism and higher productivity as compared with those without childcare (Brandon & Temple, 2007). When adults are able to balance work and family, they are more productive and happy workers, more satisfied spouses, better parents, and experience greater well-being at home and work (Herrenkohl et al., 2013; Lunau et al., 2014; Russo et al., 2016).

Although the ability to work flexibly from home often predicts a positive sense of work-life balance, working from home may also pose challenges. During the 2020 COVID-19 pandemic, most workplaces and schools in the U.S. transitioned to remote work and remote learning. Working from home became a necessity for many parents at the same time as children learned to attend school and complete assignments remotely, from home. These simultaneous transitions posed serious challenges for work-life balance as parents struggled to fulfill multiple roles as workers, parents, and educators. In October 2020, about 6 months into the pandemic, nearly two-thirds of working women with children under age 12 reported that handling childcare was difficult (Igielnik, 2021). Half of parents with children younger than 18 who work at home all or most of the time report finding it difficult to get their work done without interruptions since the COVID-19 outbreak started. (Parker et al., 2020). Workers with a bachelor's degree or higher were more likely to work from home during the pandemic than those without a 4-year college degree (two-thirds as compared with less than one-quarter). Parents who worked outside the home met with greater challenges in work-life balance. As childcare centers and schools closed, many were left with few choices other than family care and, sometimes, no childcare, compounding multiple stresses (Khazan & Harris, 2020).

Thinking in Context: Lifespan Development

1. How might macrosystem factors (such as economic changes, government policies, wars, or catastrophic events such as pandemics) influence young adults' employment experiences?

Thinking in Context: Intersectionality

1. Racial and gender bias and microaggressions are not limited to the workplace. What forms might discrimination take in other contexts, such as on the college campus? Have you observed or experienced microaggressions or other forms of discrimination?
2. What suggestions do you have for addressing microaggressions at college and in the workplace? To what extent might education help? What form should it take? How else might you address this problem?
3. In addition to race and gender, other forms of identity, such as age, parental status, physical or intellectual disability, and sexual orientation, are associated with greater risk for experiencing microaggressions and differential treatment in the workplace. Many identities intersect (consider a Black lesbian single parent), increasing the complexity of this problem. How can employers protect all workers and make them feel included, respected, and treated fairly? How can employers address diversity issues in the workplace and increase morale and productivity?

CHAPTER SUMMARY

11.1 Summarize the physical developments of emerging and early adulthood.

Physical development continues into the 20s when all of the organs and body systems reach optimum functioning. Age-related physical changes are so gradual that most go unnoticed by young adults. Physical strength peaks at about age 30, then gradually declines, but young adults vary in the rate of change in their performance. Men are capable of reproducing throughout life, but sperm production is impaired by factors that harm the body's functioning. In women, ovulation becomes less regular with age and is impaired by a variety of behavioral and environmental factors.

11.2 Discuss common health concerns and the effects of physical activity in emerging and early adulthood.

Obesity is influenced by hereditary and contextual factors and is a serious health risk, associated with a range of illnesses and problems. Regular exercise increases longevity, enhances immunity, and promotes stress reduction. Alcohol and substance use tend to peak in emerging adulthood and decline, but do not disappear, in early adulthood.

11.3 Compare postformal reasoning, pragmatic thought, and cognitive-affective complexity.

People's understanding of the nature of knowledge advances along a predictable path in young adulthood from dualistic thinking, to relativistic thinking, to reflective judgment. Development beyond formal operations is dependent on metacognition and experience. Pragmatic thought refers to the ability to apply reflective judgment to real-world contexts. Cognitive-affective complexity is an advanced form of thought that includes the ability to be aware of emotions, integrate positive and negative feelings about an issue, and regulate intense emotions to make logical decisions about complicated issues.

11.4 Explain how attending college influences young adults' development, and identify challenges faced by first-generation and nontraditional students, students with disabilities, and young adults who do not attend college.

Attending college is associated with advances in moral reasoning, identity development, and social development. First-generation and nontraditional college students experience a high risk of drop out. Students of color and those of low socioeconomic status are disproportionately likely to be first-generation and nontraditional college students and may perceive a cultural mismatch between their home and neighborhood context and the college environment. Emerging adults with developmental disabilities are less likely than their peers to immediately enroll in 4-year postsecondary institutions after high school, and the social and emotional challenges of entering college are often amplified for them. Young adults who enter the workforce immediately after high school have fewer work opportunities than those of prior generations.

11.5 Discuss vocational development, young adults' experiences in the workplace, and the value of work-life balance.

In addition to the development of occupational goals and personality, contextual factors such as family, socioeconomic status, and educational opportunities influence our choice of career.

The transition to work is often challenging as workplace responsibilities, expectations, and rewards are very different from the demands of high school and college and often deviate from young adults' expectations. Discrimination in the workplace is often displayed as microaggressions. Workers' perceptions of discrimination are related to poor physical and mental health. Work-life balance is a challenge for many young adults, especially those with young children. Adults who feel a sense of control over their work workload and schedule tend to show greater satisfaction with work-life balance and lower levels of work-life conflict.

KEY TERMS

alcohol dependence (p. 336)
binge drinking (p. 335)
cognitive-affective complexity (p. 341)
dualistic thinking (p. 339)
epistemic cognition (p. 339)
free radicals (p. 328)
glass ceiling (p. 350)
obesity (p. 332)
postformal reasoning (p. 339)
pragmatic thought (p. 341)
reflective judgment (p. 339)
relativistic thinking (p. 339)
senescence (p. 328)
work-life balance (p. 352)

12 SOCIOEMOTIONAL DEVELOPMENT IN EMERGING AND EARLY ADULTHOOD

Geber86/Getty Images

Early adulthood spans a great many years, from roughly age 18 to 40, and includes many significant developmental tasks. Young adults continue to learn about themselves, make decisions about relationships, family, career, and lifestyle—and transition and commit to these roles. Some young people transition to adult responsibilities very quickly, while others take a more lengthy, winding path to adopting the roles that comprise early adulthood. Young adults nurture children, spousal relationships, and friendships, which influence and are influenced by their psychosocial development. In this chapter, we take a closer look at the relationships and roles that mark early adulthood. Similar to Chapter 11, we will use the term *emerging adult* to refer to individuals age 25 and under (unless otherwise specified), and *young adult* will refer to all individuals under age 40, including emerging adults (unless otherwise specified).

EMERGING ADULTHOOD

LEARNING OBJECTIVE

12.1 Examine the features of emerging adulthood and its contextual nature.

Today, most young people reach traditional markers of adulthood, such as completing education, entering a career, becoming financially independent, and marrying and forming a family, at later ages relative to prior generations. According to researcher Jeffrey Arnett, recent social changes prolonging

Emerging adulthood is an exciting time of exploration, independence, and firsts.
iStock/swissmediavision

the transition to adulthood have created a new period of life called emerging adulthood (Arnett, 2016c). When adolescents enter emerging adulthood upon completing high school, at about 18, they are generally dependent on their parents and beginning to explore identity, romantic relationships, and careers. Fast forward to the mid-20s, the end of emerging adulthood, and most young people live independently and have identified romantic and career paths. In the interim, emerging adults occupy an "in-between" status in which they are no longer adolescents but have not yet assumed the roles that comprise adulthood. How young people traverse this stage, and how long it takes, is a result of the interaction of emerging adults' capacities and the context in which they live—family, social, economic, and community resources (Arnett, 2019; Wood et al., 2018).

Characteristics of Emerging Adulthood

Several features mark emerging adulthood as a distinct period in life. It is distinct demographically, subjectively, and psychologically (Arnett, 2019; Tanner, 2018).

Demographic Instability

Emerging adulthood is marked by instability (Arnett et al., 2014). People aged 18 to 25 have the highest rates of residential change of any age group, shifting among residences and living situations. Some emerging adults live with their parents, others live in college dormitories or in apartments with roommates or with spouses or alone. Many shift from one residential status to another repeatedly, from living with parents, to college dorms, perhaps to living with parents again or with different groups of roommates. Changes in romantic relationships are also frequent and most emerging adults experience several job changes. The instability is often challenging, experienced as stressful and potentially posing risks to mental health, such as anxiety (Tanner, 2016, 2018). Nearly one-quarter of emerging adults are diagnosed with anxiety and many more experience symptoms of anxiety (LeBlanc et al., 2020).

Subjective Sense of Feeling In Between

Surveys with people in their late teens and early 20s reveal that most do not feel fully adult. When asked if they feel like adult, most reported "in some respect yes, in some respects no," suggesting a sense of being "in between" adolescence and adulthood (Arnett, 2019; Tanner, 2018). What does it take to become an adult? Emerging adults tend to view becoming an adult as independent of traditional markers of adulthood, such as marriage, and instead based on personal characteristics such as accepting responsibility for themselves and becoming financially independent (Sharon, 2016). As young people make progress toward resolving their identity, they are more likely to perceive themselves as adults (Schwartz et al., 2013). In addition, with increasing age, emerging adults are more likely to view themselves as full-fledged adults. For example, only about one-third of 18- to 21-year-olds report that they consider themselves to be adults, as compared with more than half of 22- to 25-year-olds and more than two-thirds of 26- to 29-year-olds (Arnett & Schwab, 2012).

Identity Exploration, Self-Focus, and Optimism

Emerging adulthood is the primary time for identity exploration (Lapsley & Hardy, 2017). Although we may begin the identity search process in adolescence, it is not until emerging adulthood that most individuals have the opportunity to sample opportunities and life options. No longer under parental restrictions and without the full range of adult responsibilities, emerging adults are able to fully engage in the exploration that comprises identity development (Wood et al., 2018). As they explore alternatives, emerging adults often make changes in educational paths, romantic partners, and jobs. With identity exploration comes risk taking, such as increased substance use (Andrews & Westling, 2016; Tanner, 2018). The identity search is exciting but also often confusing, especially for emerging adults who find themselves unable to make choices about which paths to explore, or who feel that the choices they would like to make in love relationships and work are unattainable (Arnett et al., 2014).

Emerging adulthood is a time of self-focus, when young people become more autonomous and make independent decisions about events in the present and future. Emerging adults work on developing skills of daily living, gain self-understanding, and develop autonomy. Self-focus supports identity exploration (Arnett, 2019).

Although emerging adults experience many transitions, instability, and mixed emotions, most have a sense of optimism. In one study of more than 1,000 18-to-29 year-olds in the United States, 89% agreed with the statement, "I am confident that eventually I will get what I want out of life," and more than 75% agreed with the statement, "I believe that, overall, my life will be better than my parents' lives have been" (Arnett & Schwab, 2012). Optimism is an important psychological resource during a turbulent time.

Contextual Nature of Emerging Adulthood

Emerging adulthood is thought to be a response to larger societal changes in Western societies, such as increased education and later onset of marriage and parenthood, but it is not universal (Syed, 2016). Transitions do not occur at the same pace or in the same order for everyone. Young people vary with regard to when they enter careers, when they marry, and when they become parents (Eisenberg et al., 2015).

Most research on emerging adulthood has sampled college students, potentially yielding a narrow view of this period in life (Hendry & Kloep, 2010; Mitchell & Syed, 2015). College enrollment often delays residential and financial independence, as most college students tend to depend on parents for financial and often residential support. Indeed, Jeffrey Arnett (2016a) describes college as an essential playground for emerging adults, a temporary safe haven where they can explore possibilities in love, work, and worldviews without many of the responsibilities of adult life.

In contrast to college students, young people who are employed are more likely to be financially self-supporting and to live in a residence independent of parents, both markers of adulthood. Young people who drop out of high school, experience early parenthood, begin working at a job immediately after high school, or live in low-SES homes and communities may experience only a limited period of emerging adulthood or may not experience emerging adulthood at all (du Bois-Reymond, 2016; Maggs et al., 2012). Emerging adulthood may be interwoven with socioeconomic status (du Bois-Reymond, 2016). In one recent examination, emerging adults with low SES tended to show less optimism/possibilities, less self-focus, were less likely to feel that they were in between, and showed more negativity/instability and more other-focus than their high-SES peers. (Landberg et al., 2019). Other research with college students suggests that financial well-being is associated with self-focus and financial difficulties with negative perceptions and instability (Vosylis & Klimstra, 2021). Interviews with 18- to 24-year-olds who experienced homelessness, child welfare involvement, and low SES revealed that most participants sought financial stability and independence, rather than identity and career exploration (Bowen et al., 2021). The features of emerging adulthood and the objectives young people seek may vary with intersectional factors. There is a need to examine the nature of emerging adulthood in diverse populations.

Emerging adulthood may be extended into the late 20s for young people who obtain advanced training, such as attending medical school or law school, which delays entry into career, other adult roles, and financial independence. Some theorists therefore argue that emerging adulthood is not a life stage—it does not exist everywhere and for everyone—but is simply an indicator of medium to high socioeconomic status and the educational and career opportunities that accompany such status (Côté, 2014; Syed, 2016). Given that ethnicity is often interwoven with socioeconomic status, people of color may be less likely to experience emerging adulthood (du Bois-Reymond, 2016; Syed & Mitchell, 2016).

Emerging Adulthood and Culture

Although emerging adulthood is not universal, it has been observed among young people in many cultures, including many countries in North and South America, Northern and Eastern Europe, as well as Israel, China, Japan, and Malaysia (Arnett et al., 2014; Arnett & Padilla-Walker, 2015; Nelson, 2009; Sirsch et al., 2009; Swanson, 2016; Wider et al., 2021). However, definitions of adulthood and the specific features and characteristics with which young people define adulthood vary by culture, and likely within cultures, accompanying ethnic and socioeconomic differences (du Bois-Reymond, 2016; Syed & Mitchell, 2016).

Young people in developed countries tend to rate accepting responsibility for the consequences of one's actions as the most important criterion for adulthood, but other important criteria vary by culture (Nelson & Luster, 2016). North American emerging adults also rate making independent decisions and becoming financially independent as criteria for adulthood. In Argentina, young people rated the capacity to care for young children as the second–most important criteria for women (Facio & Micocci, 2003). Israeli young adults listed being able to withstand pressure as a required attribute for adulthood (Mayseless & Scharf, 2003), whereas Romanian young people reported norm compliance as an indicator of adulthood (Nelson, 2009). Chinese emerging adults rated learning to have good control of your emotions as being necessary for adulthood (Nelson et al., 2004). Yet none of these criteria were rated as necessary for adulthood by North American emerging adults (Arnett, 2003).

Emerging adulthood has been recognized in young people of many countries, but the theory of emerging adulthood is largely based on samples of youth from Western countries, especially the U.S. One recent analysis found that three-quarters of research on emerging adulthood published between 2013 and 2015 examined U.S. samples (Ravert et al., 2018). Findings obtained with Western samples can not necessarily be generalized to people in other parts of the world. Young adults from Ghana and Nigeria rate independence, the capacity to and care for a family, and norm compliance as essential to adulthood, suggesting that other cultures hold similar views of the characteristics of adulthood (Obidoa et al., 2019).

The problem of relying on and overgeneralizing findings of Western samples is not unique to research on emerging adulthood. In fact, the majority of research published tends to sample people from the English-speaking world or from Western Europe, with little representation from Latin America, Asia, Africa, or the Middle East. Henrich et al. (2010) refer to the majority of research samples published in international journals as "Western, Educated, Industrialized, Rich, and Democratic." Worldwide, few people are categorized as WEIRD, yet findings from WEIRD samples are treated as applicable to the rest of the world. The majority of studies of emerging adulthood are conducted in Western nations without attention to whether the features that mark emerging adulthood generalize to nonwestern contexts.

Frequently in nonwestern cultures, entry to adulthood is marked by rituals and is the same for everyone. Isolated hunter-gatherer communities tend to have scripted roles, responsibilities, and trajectories. Young people in these communities likely do not take time to decide what to do with their lives, engage in social experimentation, and find themselves (Schwartz, 2016). Instead, they adopt the roles ascribed to them and participate in their communities as adults. Emerging adulthood likely does not exist in these communities.

Though there are similarities, characteristics of emerging adulthood vary across cultures.
d3sign/Getty Images

Over the last two decades, the theory of emerging adulthood has remained a popular description of the period between adolescence and adulthood. Many people find it intuitively appealing to consider this time an in-between period of instability, self-focus, identity exploration, and optimism for the future. But are these features tied only to the ages of

FIGURE 12.1 ■ Mean Ratings of Features of Emerging Adulthood from Ages 18–60

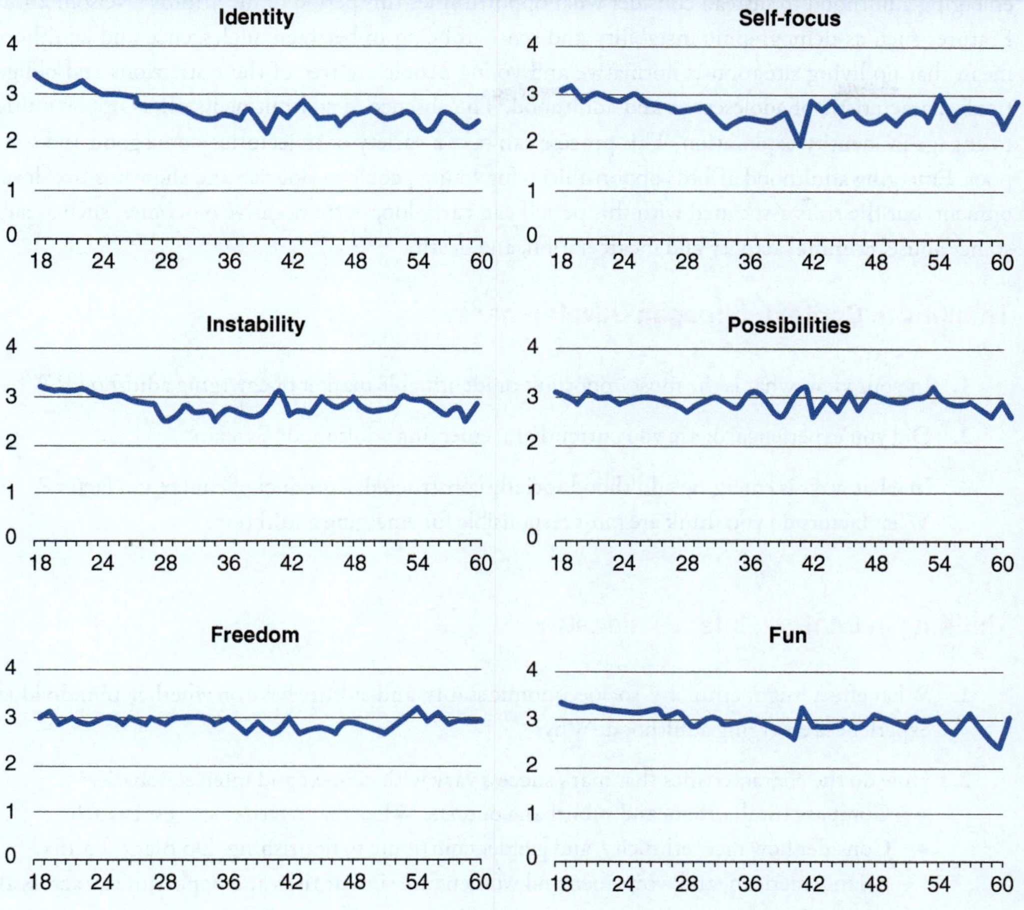

Note: The *x*-axis represents participants' age and *y*-axis represents the degree to which each feature of emerging adulthood applied to them on a scale of 1 (strongly disagree) to 4 (strongly agree).

Source: Arnett & Mitra, 2020.

FIGURE 12.2 ■ Do You Feel You Have Reached Adulthood?

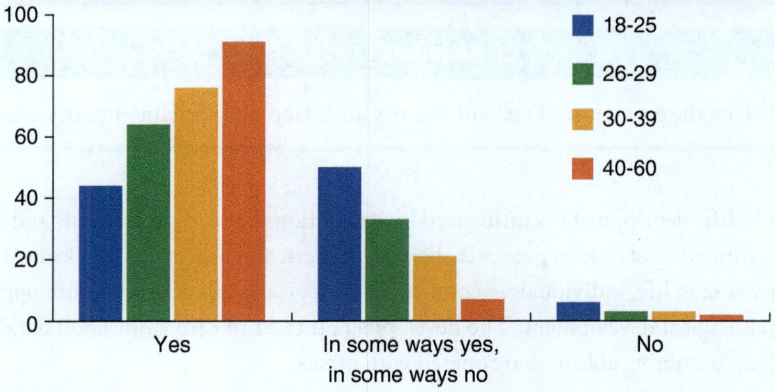

Source: Arnett & Mitra, 2018.

emerging adulthood (roughly 18 to 25)? One recent study examined individuals aged 18 to 60 and found that, although 18- to 25-year-olds endorsed nearly all criteria of emerging adulthood as relevant to them, most adults aged 26 to 60 did as well (see Figure 12.1; Arnett & Mitra, 2020). With age, individuals were more likely to rate themselves as adults (see Figure 12.2).

Developmental scientists have recently suggested moving beyond debates over the existence of emerging adulthood to instead consider what opportunities this period of life affords (Nelson, 2021). Features such as demographic instability and sense of being in-between adolescence and adulthood mean that no living situation is normative and young people are free of the restrictions and obligations characteristic of adolescence and adulthood. The absence of commitments offers opportunities to engage in identity exploration. This process can take a variety of trajectories, some good and some poor. Emerging adulthood affords opportunities for young people to flourish and show positive development, but the risks associated with this period can carry long-term negative outcomes, such as substance abuse, criminal activity and incarceration, and death.

Thinking in Context: Lifespan Development

1. In your view, what is the most important or identifiable marker of emerging adulthood? Why?
2. Did you experience, or are you currently in, emerging adulthood? Explain.
3. In what ways is emerging adulthood socially constructed, a product of contextual factors? What factors do you think are most responsible for emerging adulthood?

Thinking in Context: Intersectionality

1. What effect might ethnicity, socioeconomic status, and culture have on whether an individual experiences emerging adulthood. Why?
2. How do the characteristics that mark success vary with context and intersectionality?
   - Compare rural, urban, and suburban contexts: What characterizes success in each?
   - Consider how race, ethnicity, and gender contribute to flourishing. Do Black, Latinx, Asian American, and white men and women face similar risks and opportunities across all contexts?
3. What risks might experiences with racism, sexism, and discrimination pose for flourishing in emerging adulthood? How might we address these risks?

PSYCHOSOCIAL DEVELOPMENT

LEARNING OBJECTIVE

12.2 Discuss the psychosocial tasks of identity, intimacy, and sexuality in early adulthood.

At all points in life, development is influenced by interactions between individuals and their changing social world, consisting of family, peers, teachers, employers, and others. Erik Erikson (1950) proposed that at every phase in life, individuals encounter psychological crises that offer both opportunities and risks for psychological development. The developmental tasks of early adulthood entail developing a sense of self and becoming able to share oneself with others.

Identity Versus Role Confusion

Identity development is a defining feature of emerging adulthood. Originally conceived by Erikson (1950) as the psychosocial task of adolescence, today young people begin the identity search process in adolescence, but most do not establish a firm sense of self until emerging adulthood (Arnett, 2016a). The identity search process is extended today, relative to the mid-20th century when Erikson developed his theory. At that time, most North Americans entered the workforce after high school, marrying and starting families soon after. As we have discussed, over the past half-century, college enrollment has increased and marriage and childbirth is delayed, leading to the creation of emerging adulthood (Arnett, 2019). We adopt a sense of identity in many domains, including moral identity, religious orientation, political preference, gender and sexuality, and ethnic-racial identity (Schwartz et al., 2016).

Constructing a sense of ethnic-racial identity involves exploring one's ethnic group, including the attitudes, values, and culture associated with that group; determining what elements to internalize; developing a sense of belonging to a group; and committing to a sense of identity (Umaña-Taylor, 2016; Umaña-Taylor et al., 2014). Ethnic-racial identity may become a less central element of self over adulthood as compared with adolescence and emerging adulthood (Feliciano & Rumbaut, 2018, 2019). By their late 30s, adults vary in their sense of ethnic-racial identity, ranging from strong attachment to indifference. Individuals incorporate and interpret their experiences in light of their sense of identity, but there is little research on ethnic-racial identity from early through middle and late adulthood (Williams et al., 2020).

Identity development continues in early adulthood, with identity achievement becoming more common with age (Eriksson et al., 2020). Yet identity development remains a lifelong task, continuing to be revised and refined from early through late adulthood (Lodi-Smith et al., 2017).

Intimacy Versus Isolation

According to Erik Erikson, the major psychosocial task of early adulthood, from ages 18 to 40, is **intimacy versus isolation**: developing the capacity for intimacy and making a permanent commitment to a romantic partner. The formation of intimate relationships is associated with well-being in young adults (Busch & Hofer, 2012). The flip side—not attaining a sense of intimacy and not making personal commitments to others—is the negative psychosocial outcome of isolation, entailing a sense of loneliness and self-absorption.

Establishing an intimate relationship is a challenge for young adults, especially emerging adults who often continue to struggle with identity issues and who are just gaining social and financial independence. Because developing a sense of intimacy relies on identity development, many emerging adults who are just forming their identities are ill prepared for this task. Young people immersed in Erikson's psychosocial moratorium of identity development are exploring opportunities and are less likely to form successful intimate relationships than those whose identities have been achieved (Markstrom & Kalmanir, 2001; Weisskirch, 2018). Moreover, emerging adults generally report feeling that they are not ready for a committed, enduring relationship (Collins & van Dulmen, 2006).

Identity achievement, including a sense of self, values, and goals, predicts readiness for intimate and committed romantic relationships and the capacity to actively seek and establish them (Barry et al., 2009; Beyers & Seiffge-Krenke, 2010). Although Erikson did not draw distinctions between emerging adulthood and early adulthood, today it is clear that many young people do not enter into truly intimate relationships until they have traversed the transition from emerging adulthood to early adulthood. Furthermore, as adults form intimate relationships, they must reshape their identities to include their role as partner and the goals, plans, and interests shared with their partner. Thus, they must resolve identity and intimacy demands that may conflict. As they engage in continued identity development, they must do the work of establishing an intimate relationship—making sacrifices and compromises which may involve a temporary loss of self—before expanding the sense of self to include a partner.

A primary task of early adulthood is to establish intimate relationships with significant others.
Yasin Ozturk/Anadolu Agency/Getty Images

Some young adults postpone constructing a strong sense of identity in the relationship area and forming intimate relationships. The tendency to delay entering intimate relationships is influenced by young adults' preferences and priorities, as well as the context in which they live, including the family and friends closest to them, the opportunities available to them, and their view of broader societal expectations. As we have discussed, the transition to adulthood is longer today than ever before. Many young people may feel less pressure to commit to relationships and more comfortable waiting until their personal and financial circumstances support their decision to explore all options and commit (Laughland-Booÿ et al., 2018).

Sexuality

We have seen that today's adolescents initiate sex at older ages than recent generations. Similarly, over the past half century, consensual premarital sex among adults has become more accepted. In recent decades adults have reported more sexual partners in their lifetime, from 7 in 1988 to 11 in 2012 (Twenge et al., 2015).

Sexual Activity

Generally speaking, sexual activity is highest among people in young adulthood, from their mid-20s to mid-30s, and declines gradually for people in their 40s and again in their 50s, but the amount of decline is modest (King, 2019). It is estimated that young adults may engage in sexual activity only about one to two times a month more than do their middle-aged counterparts (Herbenick et al., 2010). Emerging adults are more likely than other young adults to report not engaging in sexual activity in the past year (see Figure 12.3; Ueda et al., 2020). By one estimate, about half of young adults who identify as gay and lesbian reported weekly sexual activity within the past year, and the majority report one sexual partner within the past year (Ueda et al., 2020). In early adulthood, the frequency of sexual activity is closely related to marital status. Married adults are more sexually active than single adults (Ueda et al., 2020). The average American married couple engages in intercourse two to three times per week when they are in their 20s, with the frequency gradually declining to about weekly in their 30s (Hyde & DeLamater, 2017). Not surprisingly, young adults report greater positive affect after sex, extending to the next day, especially with a romantic partner rather than nondating partner (Debrot et al., 2017; Vasilenko & Lefkowitz, 2018). Overall, the frequency of sexual intercourse is associated with emotional, sexual, and relationship satisfaction, as well as overall happiness, in adults (McNulty et al., 2016).

The social script of emerging adulthood as a "time to experiment" is conducive to casual sex—sexual activity outside of romantic relationships (Kuperberg & Padgett, 2016). Although often depicted as an activity unique to the current generation of young adults, casual sex has always existed, but young people now commonly refer to it as "hooking up" (Claxton & Van Dulmen, 2016). Hooking up is not consistently defined by emerging adults, but it generally refers to a brief sexual encounter that can range from kissing to intercourse, without the expectation of forming a long-term relationship or attachment (Olmstead et al., 2018). About two-thirds of college students report having experienced at least one hook up (Garcia et al., 2012; Olmstead, 2020; Kuperberg & Padgett, 2016). College students often cite benefits to hook ups, but one study of 4,000 students at 30 colleges found that men and women who reported casual sex within the previous month scored lower than their peers on measures of psychological well-being (self-esteem, life satisfaction, psychological well-being, and happiness) and higher on measures of distress (anxiety, depression; Bersamin et al., 2014). Negative emotional reactions are more common after casual encounters with nondating partners and may be more pronounced in women (Napper et al., 2016; Vasilenko & Lefkowitz, 2018). The majority of research on casual sex examines heterosexual partners; there is little work examining LGBT adults (Watson et al., 2017).

Sexual Assault

About one-third of all women will experience nonconsensual sexual activity—sexual assault or rape—in their lifetime (Smith et al., 2017). Nonconsensual sex includes instances in which the victim is coerced by fear tactics, such as threats or use of physical harm, or is incapable of giving consent due to the influence of drugs or alcohol or because of age. Nearly 80% of sexual assaults occur prior to age 25 (Breiding, Smith, et al., 2014). Underreporting of rape is high, perhaps as high as 80% (Sinozich & Langton, 2014).

Most rapes are committed by someone the victim knows (Sinozich & Langton, 2014). Alcohol, especially heavy drinking, is often involved in sexual assault by acquaintances (Wilhite & Fromme, 2021). One meta-analysis of 28 studies (with almost 6,000 participants) found that two-thirds of women rape survivors, especially those who experienced acquaintance rape, did not acknowledge that they had been raped (Wilson & Miller, 2016). Instead they used more benign labels such as "bad sex" or "miscommunication." Sexual assault is not unique to women.

Survivors of sexual assault have a higher than average risk of developing post-traumatic stress disorder (PTSD), anxiety, and depression, and of abusing alcohol and other substances (Carey et al., 2018; Kirkner et al., 2018). Women who blame themselves for the assault tend to experience more adjustment difficulties, including PTSD, depression, and self-blame (Kline et al., 2021; Mgoqi-Mbalo et al., 2017). Social support can improve adjustment and is associated with reduced PTSD symptoms over time (Dworkin et al., 2018; Orchowski et al., 2013).

Male rape is increasingly recognized and most states have revised their rape laws to be gender neutral (Hock, 2015). Men may feel a greater sense of shame and stigma than women and are even less likely than women to recognize their experience as sexual assault and less likely report being sexually assaulted (Reed et al., 2020).

Contextual influences, such as the prevalence of rape myths, can affect the frequency of sexual assault (Ryan, 2019). Rape myths are common among college students and associated with perpetrating sexual coercion and assault (O'Connor et al., 2018; Trottier et al., 2021). Young adults who buy into rape myths are less likely to provide supportive responses to victims (Grandgenett et al., 2021). Gender stereotypes of men's and women's roles, encouraging dominance, aggression, and competition in males and passivity in females, may support attitudes that are accepting of sexual violence. College students who are highly gender stereotyped and believe in strict gender roles are more likely than their peers to blame sexual assault survivors and express attitudes condoning nonconsensual sex (Seabrook et al., 2018; Vechiu, 2019). Effective sexual assault prevention educates men and women about gender socialization, the nature and impact of sexual violence, debunks rape myths, and offers suggestions on how to avoid danger and intervene as a bystander (Ryan, 2019; Stewart, 2014).

FIGURE 12.3 ■ Frequency of Sexual Activity Over the Past Year, Ages 18–44

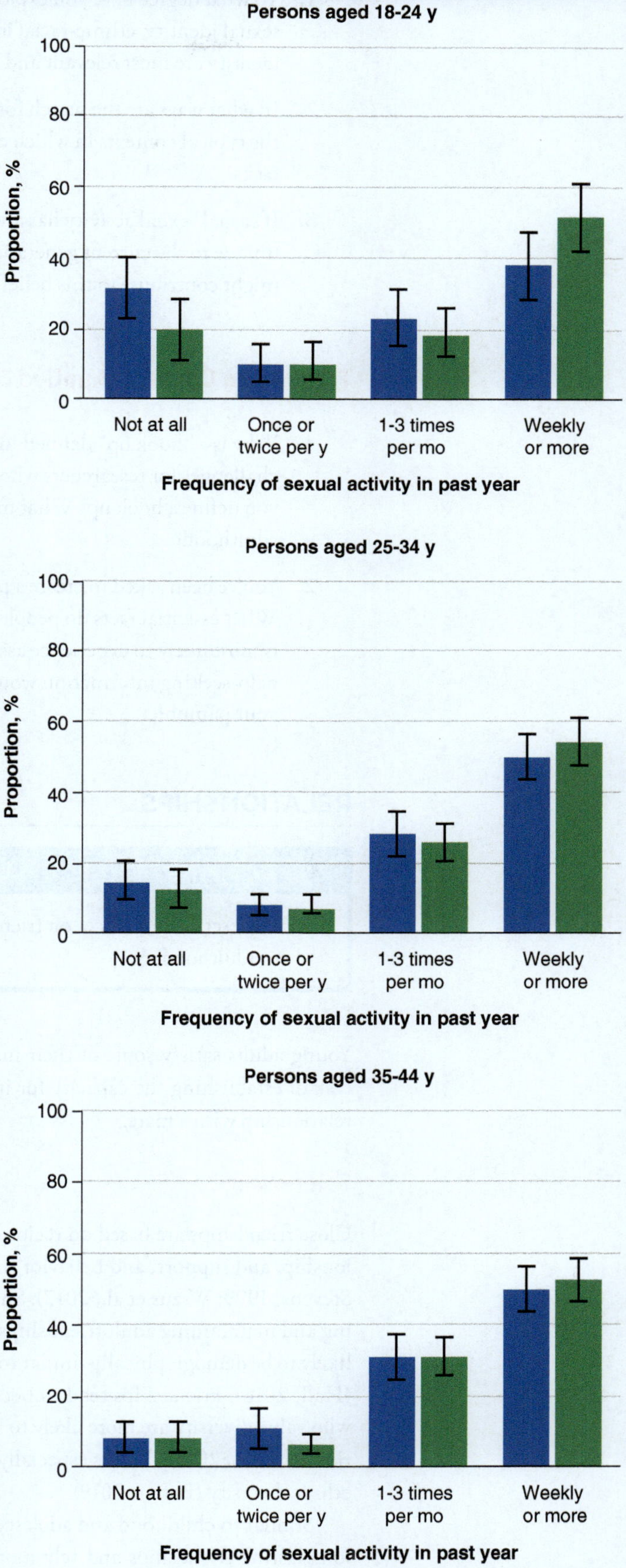

Source: Ueda et al., 2020.

Thinking in Context: Lifespan Development

1. To what degree have you explored your identity? Consider moral identity, gender identity, sexual identity, ethnic-racial identity, religious identity, and political identity. What aspects of identity are most relevant and important to you?
2. In what ways are the search for identity and a sense of intimacy complementary? How might the typical contexts in which emerging and early adults live contribute to these developmental tasks?
3. If casual sexual activity has always occurred, why do many people believe that it is new or unique to the current generation of young adults? What are some contextual factors that might contribute to this belief?

Thinking in Context: Applied Developmental Science

1. Why is a "hook up" defined in many different ways? How might the varying definitions pose challenges for researchers who wish to study sexuality? If you were a researcher, how would you define a hook up? What method would you use to gather data about hook ups in young adulthood?
2. You've been asked to create a pamphlet to address the problem of sexual coercion and assault. What essential facts do people need to know about this problem? Consider its prevalence, who is most likely to experience assault, and contextual factors that influence sexual assault. What help-seeking information would you provide? Locate an online or local resource to include in your pamphlet.

RELATIONSHIPS

LEARNING OBJECTIVE

12.3 Describe influences on friendship, mate selection, and romantic relationships in early adulthood.

Young adults satisfy some of their intimacy needs through close friendships. Yet the developmental task of establishing the capacity for intimate relationships is best fulfilled by establishing a romantic relationship with a mate.

Friendship

Close friendships are based on reciprocity, an emotional give and take that entails intimacy, companionship, and support, and behavior such as sharing, exchanging favors, and giving advice (Hartup & Stevens, 1999; Wrzus et al., 2017). Shared interests, attitudes, and values are most important to forming and maintaining adult friendships (Wrzus et al., 2017). As in other periods in life, adult friends are likely to be demographically similar to one another in factors such as age, sex, and socioeconomic status (Hall, 2016). Friendships tend to become more diverse over early adulthood (Thomas, 2019). Adults who value diversity are more likely to have friends of different ethnicities, religions, and sexual orientations (Bahns, 2019). This is especially true for college students attending campuses high in racial and ethnic diversity (Bahns, 2019).

Similar to childhood and adolescence, in early adulthood women tend to have more intimate and long-lasting friendships and rely more on friends to meet social and emotional needs than do men

In early adulthood, as in all times of life, close friendships are based on reciprocity, intimacy, companionship, and support.

iStock/DGLimages

(Hall, 2016). Men's friendships tend to center on sharing information and activities, such as playing sports, rather than intimate disclosure (David-Barrett et al., 2015). As male friendships endure to become long-lasting ties, self-disclosure increases, and the friends become closer. Men and women often become friends. Different-sex friendships can be important sources of social support but tend not to last as long as same-sex friendships. Men's friendships with women tend to decline after marriage, but women, especially highly educated women, tend to have more friendships with men throughout adulthood, especially in the workplace (Weger, 2016). Different-sex friendships are a source of companionship and support and offer opportunities to learn about gender differences in the expression of intimacy (Reeder, 2017). Across all types of friendship, relationship quality is associated with psychological adjustment and well-being, including social competence, life satisfaction, and lower levels of depression and loneliness (Gillespie et al., 2015; Holt et al., 2018).

Friendship changes over the course of early adulthood. As adults progress through their 20s and take on adult roles, they tend to see their friends less (Nicolaisen & Thorsen, 2017). Young adults who are single tend to rely more heavily on friendships to fulfill needs for social support and acceptance than do married young adults (Wrzus et al., 2017). Intimacy among close friends in early adulthood is associated with relationship satisfaction in midlife (Steinhoff & Keller, 2020). As adults establish careers and families, they often have less time to spend with friends, yet friendship remains an important source of social support and is associated with well-being, positive affect, and self-esteem throughout life (Gillespie et al., 2015; Huxhold et al., 2014).

Romantic Relationships

A psychosocial task of early adulthood is to form long-term intimate relationships that will endure throughout adulthood (Seiffge-Krenke, 2003). Generally speaking, there is continuity in relationship quality such that the quality of romantic relationships in adolescence predicts relationship quality in emerging adulthood and beyond (Shulman & Connolly, 2013). The nature of romantic relationships often changes over time. Adults may fluctuate between long-term relationships and short sexual and romantic encounters (Cohen et al., 2003; Shulman et al., 2018). Today, young adults often experience years of singlehood and dating before partnering.

Mate Selection

Upon first meeting a potential mate, men and women tend to judge attractiveness as important influences on romantic interest and desire to pursue further contact (Fletcher et al., 2014). Men and women from many cultures show similar patterns in mate preferences. Men tend to prefer a younger mate and assign greater value to physical attractiveness and domestic skills; from an evolutionary perspective, these are thought to be attributes that signal fertility and the capacity to care for offspring (Li et al., 2013). Women tend to be more cautious and choosy than men (Fletcher et al., 2014). Generally, women assign greater importance to earning potential, intelligence, height, and moral character and seek mates who are the same age or slightly older—characteristics that may increase the likelihood that a woman's offspring will survive and thrive. Over the course of early adulthood, young adults tend to become less selective about potential mates, increasing the potential of establishing romantic relationships (Sprecher et al., 2019).

Although opposites might attract, it is similarity that breeds relationship satisfaction. Most intimate partners share similarities in demographics, attitudes, and values. Perceived similarity (the degree to which individuals believe they are similar to their partner) predicts attraction to potential and current mates (Taylor et al., 2011) and is more important in mate selection than actual, measurable similarities (Tidwell et al., 2013). Common similarities among couples include personality style, intelligence, educational aspirations, and attractiveness (Markey & Markey, 2007). Romantic partners often also share similar health behaviors (such as smoking), patterns of alcohol use (including binge drinking), and tendencies toward risk taking (Bartel et al., 2017; Smithson & Baker, 2008; Wiersma et al., 2010). Not only do adults tend to choose partners who share similarities with them, but they also often become more similar to each other as their relationships develop. The more similar partners are in values such as political beliefs, the more likely they are to report being satisfied with their relationship and to remain in the relationship (Leikas et al., 2018; Lutz-Zois et al., 2006).

It is important to note that similarities in values and attitudes are critical to the success of a relationship, but demographic similarities are much less so. Research suggests that dating relationships among emerging adult partners who differ in ethnicity or race are similar in quality, conflict level, and satisfaction as those of adults who date within their ethnic or racial group (de Guzman & Nishina, 2017). Most research in this area examines college students. We know less about emerging and young adults who are not enrolled in college. In addition, although the multiracial population of the United States is rapidly increasing, we know even less about relationships among multiracial adults (Buggs, 2017).

Components of Love

There are many kinds of love, based on different combinations of three components: passion, intimacy, and commitment (Sternberg, 2004). New romantic relationships tend to be characterized by passion—the excitement that accompanies physical attraction and physiological arousal (Anderson, 2016). Passion is not always accompanied by intimacy—emotional engagement, warm communication, closeness, and caring for the other person's well-being.

Commitment, the decision that partners make to stay with one another, grows as people spend more time together, create shared goals, and solve problems together. According to theorist Robert Sternberg (2004), different combinations of these three components comprise seven different types of love, as shown in Table 12.1 and Figure 12.4.

Western ideals of love, such as those depicted in movies and television programs, include all three components. The relative proportions of these components vary over the course of a relationship and with age. Young adults tend to experience higher levels of passion in their relationships than older adults, and midlife and older adults tend to experience greater levels of commitment (Sumter et al., 2013). Novelty plays a role in the euphoria of passion. Intimacy grows with familiarity as partners get to know one another. Commitment emerges over time. Intimacy and commitment, not passion, determine the relationship's fate and the likelihood that a family will form (Hendrick & Hendrick, 2004). A study of the Hadza people of Tanzania, a hunter-gatherer community, revealed that although all of the men and women experienced all three types of love, only commitment predicted the number of children for both men and women, suggesting a reproductive purpose for commitment (Sorokowski et al., 2017).

The ratio of passion, intimacy, and commitment changes over the course of a relationship. Love persists, but its nature may shift.

Jessica Hill/For The Washington Post via Getty Images

TABLE 12.1 ■ Forms of Love

	Intimacy	Passion	Commitment	Description
Liking/friendship	X			Close friendship characterized by feelings of warmth but without a long-term commitment.
Infatuated love		X		Love characterized by passion. Many romantic relationships begin as infatuated love and later become intimate and committed. Relationships characterized by infatuated love may dissolve suddenly.
Empty love			X	Relationship characterized by commitment without love or intimacy. A more complex kind of love may dissolve into empty love. In cultures in which there are arranged marriages (partners are selected by their families on the basis of cultural values) relationships of empty love sometimes grow to include intimacy and/or passion.
Romantic love	X	X		Characterized by physical passion and emotional closeness. Many romantic relationships represent romantic love and later develop commitment.
Companionate love	X		X	Similar to friendship, this love is intimate and not passionate; it has the element of long-term commitment. It is shared by close friends who have a platonic but strong friendship. It is also characteristic of some marriages in which the passion wanes but strong feelings of emotional connection and commitment remain.

	Intimacy	Passion	Commitment	Description
Fatuous love		X	X	Relationship in which commitment is motivated by passion. It might occur in a whirlwind, quick marriage in which the couple does not have the time to form intimacy.
Consummate love	X	X	X	Ideal relationship—passion, intimacy, commitment. The couple displaying consummate love feel close and connected passion and a long-term commitment to each other. Consummate love may be difficult to maintain over time. As passion wanes, it may transform into companionate love.

Source: Adapted from Sternberg, 2004.

FIGURE 12.4 ■ Sternberg's Triangular Theory of Love

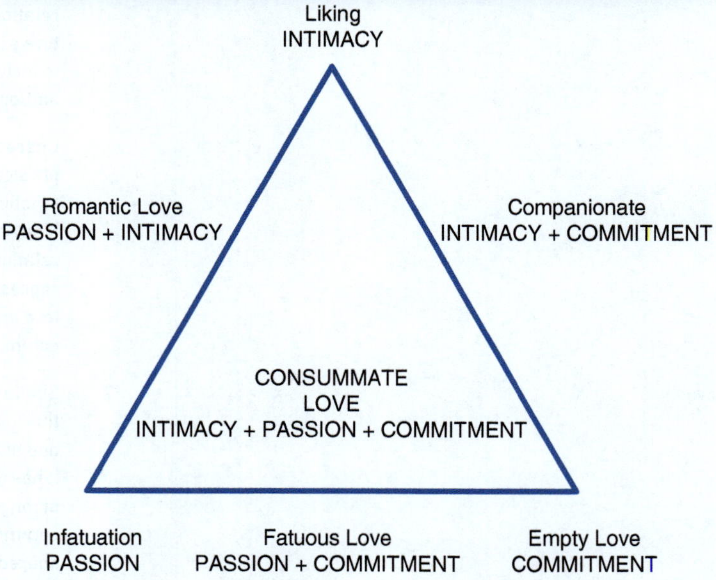

It has generally been thought that as intimacy and commitment increase, passion subsides for all couples, heterosexual and same-sex, married and unmarried (Anderson, 2016; Kurdek, 2006). Cross-sectional research with adults in 25 countries suggests subtle declines in passion over the duration of romantic relationships up to 21 years in length (Sorokowski et al., 2021; see Figure 12.5). However, love is dynamic. Other studies suggest that intimacy and passion are closely related and can fluctuate from day to day (Graham, 2011; Rubin & Campbell, 2012). Increases in intimacy predict increase in passion

FIGURE 12.5 ■ Components of Love Depending on the Relationship's Length in Adults From 25 Countries

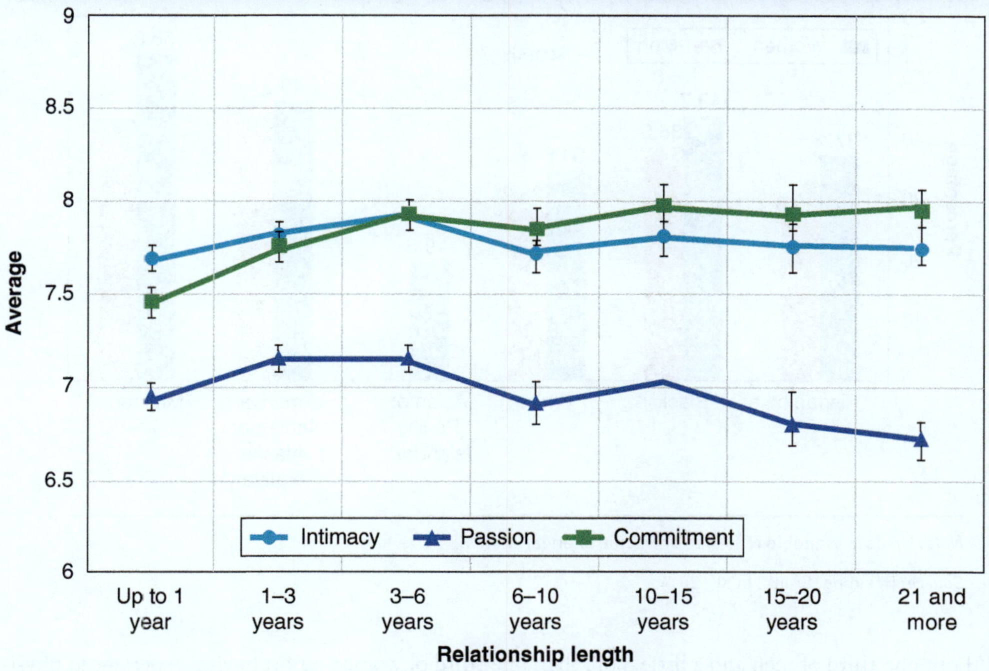

Source: Sorokowski et al., 2021.

and vice versa (Aykutoğlu & Uysal, 2017; Ratelle et al., 2013). Many couples show a long-term romantic love characterized by passion and intimacy, which in turn increases marital happiness and enhances their feelings of commitment (Acevedo & Aron, 2009). Successful couples acknowledge and appreciate the "ups" in intimacy and passion despite overall declines.

Eastern cultures such as those of China and Japan offer a different perspective on romantic love. Traditional collectivist views common in Eastern cultures value interdependence. The young person is defined through relationships and roles—such as the roles of daughter, son, sibling, husband, and wife—rather than as an individual. Because all relationships are important components of the young person's sense of self, affection is dispersed throughout all relationships, and romantic relationships are less intense than those experienced by Western young people. Chinese and Japanese young adults consider mate selection within the context of their other relationships and responsibilities to others. They are more likely than North American and European young adults to rate companionship, similarity in backgrounds, and career potential as important in choosing a partner and are less likely to rate physical attraction and passion as important factors (Dion & Dion, 1993). Similarly, dating couples in China report feeling less passion than do those in the United States but report similar levels of intimacy and commitment, which in turn predict relationship satisfaction (Gao, 2001). Finally, in a sample of Chinese adults from Hong Kong who were involved in heterosexual romantic relationships, relationship satisfaction was associated with intimacy and commitment but not passion, suggesting that conceptualizations of romantic love and relationship satisfaction may vary with culture (Ng & Cheng, 2010).

Intimate Partner Violence

Violence among intimate partners is a widespread health issue that is not limited by culture, ethnicity, socioeconomic status, sexual orientation, marital status, or gender (Ahmadabadi, Najman, Williams, Clavarino, & D'Abbs, 2021; Smith et al., 2017). **Intimate partner violence** includes physical, sexual, and emotional abuse directed at a romantic partner. Victims frequently experience several forms of violence (Krebs et al., 2011).

FIGURE 12.6 ■ Lifetime Rates of Intimate Partner Violence by Sex and Ethnicity

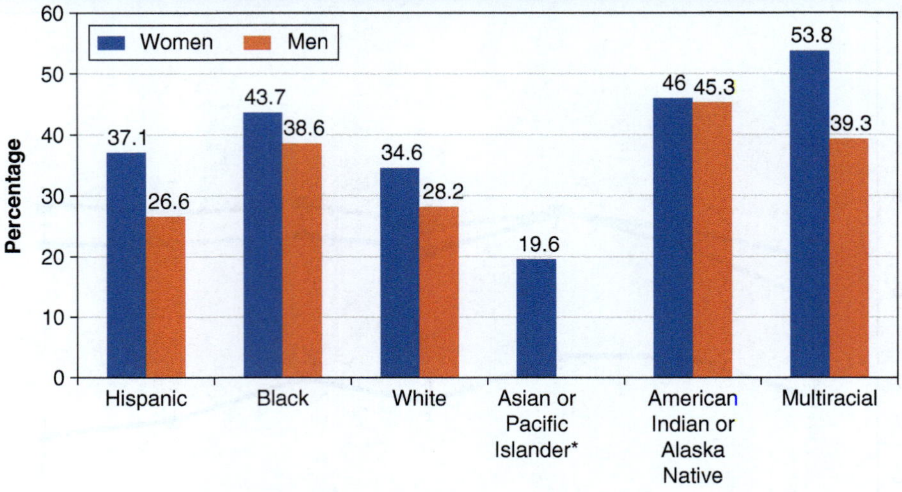

Note: No data available for Asian or Pacific Islander males.

Source: Breiding, Smith, et al., 2014.

About one-third of men and a little more than one-third of women report having experienced physical intimate partner violence, such as rape, physical violence, or stalking, at some point in their lifetime, and about 5% within the past year (Centers for Disease Control and Prevention, 2018; Smith et al., 2017). Many acts of violence are unreported. Intimate partner violence occurs in couples of all sexual orientations but is most often reported when a man harms a woman (Barrett, 2015; Smith et al., 2017). Rates of reported intimate partner violence vary by race and ethnicity, as shown in Figure 12.6. Although men and women are about equally likely to instigate episodes of intimate partner violence, women are more likely to miss work, report depression, and be injured or killed by their partners as a result of the violence (Ahmadabadi et al., 2021; Centers for Disease Control and Prevention, 2018; Jasinski et al., 2014). There is overlap between perpetrator and victim roles; many victims also engage in abusive behavior (Richards et al., 2017; Tillyer & Wright, 2013).

Intimate partner violence includes physical, sexual, and emotional abuse directed at a romantic partner. Most victims experience several forms of violence.

AP Photo/K.M. Chaudary

Research is mixed regarding the prevalence of intimate partner violence in the LGBT community, with some proposing rates similar to those in heterosexual populations and others suggesting higher rates and underreporting of violence (Barrett, 2015; Langenderfer-Magruder et al., 2016; Rollè et al., 2018). Bisexual adults experience higher risks for intimate partner violence than other sexual orientations (Turell et al., 2018). Adults who identify as transgender are at especially high risk for intimate partner violence; they are more than twice as likely to experience physical violence and two-and-a-half times more likely to experience sexual violence than cisgender adults (Peitzmeier et al., 2020). Sexual minority stress and the experience of discrimination are unique contextual contributors to violence in LGBT couples (Lewis et al., 2017; Rollè et al., 2018).

Risks for engaging in intimate partner violence include childhood exposure to domestic violence, receiving physical punishment and coercive discipline, and poor-quality relationships with parents (Shortt et al., 2016; Kaufman-Parks et al., 2018). Contextual factors that contribute to intimate partner violence include economic stressors, such as unemployment and poverty, and lack of community resources, such as poor access to services (Beyer et al., 2015; Copp et al., 2016). Intimate partner violence increased by as much as three times in many countries during the COVID-19 pandemic of 2020–2021 (Agüero, 2021; Emezue, 2020; Moreira & Pinto da Costa, 2020). Lockdowns, closing of nonessential businesses, layoffs and disruptions in employment, and imposed self-isolations and quarantines caused many couples to spend much more time together than in normal circumstances, with limited contact with other people. Victims' access to services like hotlines, crisis centers, and legal aid were scaled down by a lack of personnel or funding, and fears of catching the virus or infecting others kept many from seeking support and shelter. Evidence suggests that victims of intimate partner violence delayed reaching out to health care services until a much later stage of violence (Gosangi et al., 2021).

Cultural norms and values also influence rates of partner violence. Worldwide, about one-third of women experience intimate partner violence in their lifetimes, but rates vary widely: 16% in East Asia (including China, Japan, North Korea, and South Korea); 19% in Western Europe; 41% and 42% in South Asia (including Bangladesh, India, and Pakistan) and parts of Latin America, respectively; and 66% in Central and sub-Saharan Africa (including Chad, Congo, and Rwanda; Breiding, Chen, et al., 2014; Devries et al., 2013). Cultural norms valuing male dominance and female submissiveness, as well as differences in women's social mobility through education and career, underlie differences in prevalence rates throughout the world (Bendall, 2010; Boyle et al., 2009; Eng et al., 2010; World Health Organization, 2005). In Cambodia, the more contact and discussions couples have, the more likely are husbands to assert control and engage in intimate partner violence because women's more frequent discussion may be viewed as a violation of the cultural belief that wives are to be quiet and submissive (Eng et al., 2010).

Many communities provide services to aid victims of intimate partner violence, including crisis telephone lines, shelters, and clinics that provide counseling, support, and treatment. Yet victims of intimate partner violence often return to the relationship several times before terminating it. For perpetrators, treatment that is holistic—emphasizing individual needs and addressing motivation, communication, anger management, substance use, and problem solving—hold promise, but patterns of violence and the interactions that support them are difficult to break (Butters et al., 2021; Karakurt et al., 2019; Tarzia et al., 2020).

Thinking in Context: Lifespan Development

1. Consider friendship from adolescence through early adulthood. What similarities can you identify? How does the nature of friendship change from adolescence to emerging adulthood and to the late 20s and 30s?
2. How might developmental and contextual factors such as neighborhood, age, and life experience influence the formation and course of friendships?
3. In what ways is seeking a mate similar to and different from seeking a friend?

Thinking in Context: Intersectionality

1. Summarize the ways in which reports of intimate partner violence vary with intersectional factors such as race and ethnicity, gender, and sexual orientation.
2. How might race and ethnicity (such as in Hispanic, Asian American, or multiracial adults) combine with gender to influence the likelihood of experiencing intimate partner violence? What factors might underlie these relationships? Consider culture, socioeconomic status, and other contextual factors such as racism, discrimination, and inequity.
3. What might account for associations among gender identity, sexual orientation, and intimate partner violence? Can you identify reasons why bisexual and transgender adults are more likely to report intimate partner violence? Consider the contextual factors discussed thus far, such as culture, discrimination, and inequity.
4. Given what you know about development, context, and intersectionality, would you expect Black bisexual and transgender women to experience similar risks for intimate partner violence as Latinx or white bisexual or transgender women? Men?

ROMANTIC PARTNERSHIPS AND LIFESTYLES

LEARNING OBJECTIVE

12.4 Describe the diverse romantic situations that may characterize early adulthood, including singlehood, cohabitation, marriage, and divorce.

Most young people marry in early adulthood; others experience alternative living styles, whether by choice or circumstance—they may remain single or cohabit with a partner. Trends such as late marriage, divorce, and an increasing number of adults who choose not to marry mean that most adults in the United States will spend a large part of their adult lives single; indeed, about 8% will remain single throughout life. Couples who marry are very likely to live together before marriage. Others live together in long-term relationships that do not lead to marriage.

Singlehood

Singlehood, not living with a romantic partner, is common among U.S. young adults. In 2019, about 26% of people aged 35–39 were never married (U.S. Census Bureau, 2019). About half of single adults say they would like to get married in the future (Wang & Parker, 2014). Younger adults, under the age of 30, are more likely to say they would like to get married (66% compared with 33% of adults 30 and older). Many adults are satisfied with singlehood and do not seek a partner (DePaulo, 2014).

Compared with men, women are more likely to remain single for many years or for their entire lives. Women tend to select mates who are the same age or older, are equally or better educated, and who are professionally successful. Because of these tendencies, highly educated professional women who are financially independent may find it difficult to find potential mates whom they consider suitable (Sharp & Ganong, 2007). Some adults attribute singlehood to focusing more on career goals than marriage, disappointing romantic relationships, or to never having met the right person (Baumbusch, 2004). Some report simply preferring solitude and alone time (Timonen & Doyle, 2014). Adults who are involuntarily single, who wish to be married, may feel a sense of romantic loneliness and loss and may be concerned with singlehood's impact on childbearing (Adamczyk, 2017; Jackson, 2018).

In contrast, adults who describe themselves as single by choice tend to be self-supporting, feel a sense of control over their romantic lives, and describe singlehood as a result of not having encountered anyone they wish to marry (Sharp & Ganong, 2007). In one study, Black single women described maintaining singlehood for the purposes of growth, exploration, or safety (Moorman, 2020). Adults who are single by choice tend to report enjoying singlehood and the freedom to take risks and experiment with lifestyle changes. They also tend to associate singlehood with independence, self-fulfillment, and autonomy throughout their life course, including in old age (Timonen & Doyle, 2014).

Single adults tend to maintain more social connections with both women and men. Compared to their married peers, single adults are more likely to stay in frequent touch with parents, friends, and neighbors and to give and receive help from them, suggesting some important social benefits of singlehood (Pepping et al., 2018; Sarkisian & Gerstel, 2016). Single adults with more satisfying sex lives and friendships tend to hold more positive views of singlehood and less interest in marriage (Park et al., 2021). Satisfaction with one's single status is associated with well-being (Lehmann et al., 2015).

Cohabitation

The trend for increased education and delayed career entry that is characteristic of emerging adulthood has led to a rise in **cohabitation**, the practice of unmarried couples sharing a home. Today, more than half of adults in their 20s have lived with a romantic partner and about 70% of U.S. couples live together before marriage (Manning, 2015). Cohabitation tends to decline across early adulthood. In one recent national poll, similar percentages of emerging adults aged 18–24 cohabited (7%) as married

(9%), but marriage was the more common status among young adults aged 25–34 (41% married vs 14% cohabiting; Stepler, 2017). In contrast, cohabitation remains common throughout adulthood in some European countries: more than 75% of couples in Northern and Central Europe and the UK cohabit, and about 90% of couples in Sweden and Denmark (Hsueh et al., 2009; Manning, 2013; Popenoe, 2009).

The nature of cohabitation and its relationship with marriage is shifting. Although it was once viewed as a path to marriage, less than half of cohabiting couples report expecting to marry (Guzzo, 2014; Vespa, 2014). Marital expectations are similar for young adults at all levels of education (Kuo & Raley, 2016). Indeed, fewer cohabitating couples transition to marriage today (Guzzo, 2014; Lamidi et al., 2019). Compared with the Baby Boom cohort, in which marriage was the most common outcome of cohabitation, young adults today are more likely to end cohabiting unions through breakups than marriage (Lamidi et al., 2019).

Some young adults move in with their partners because of changes in employment or housing situations, for the sake of convenience, or in response to pregnancy (Sassler & Miller, 2011). For emerging adults, cohabitation may be an adaptive strategy for those whose lives are in transition; it permits flexibility and avoids long-term commitments, which is suitable for young people who are still transitioning to career, financial independence, and adulthood (Manning, 2020). Adults commonly cite assessing romantic compatibility, convenience, and potential improvement in finances as reasons for cohabiting (Copen et al., 2013). Black and Latinx young adults and those of low socioeconomic status are more likely to engage in long-term cohabitation as an alternative to marriage than European American young adults and those of high socioeconomic status, who are more likely to marry after a period of cohabitation (Lesthaeghe et al., 2016). Sociocultural expectations for marriage vary with contextual conditions.

Cultures differ in the acceptability of cohabitation and have different laws and policies pertaining to it. In many European countries, cohabitation is viewed not as a precursor but rather as an alternative to marriage. Cohabiting couples in those countries often hold legal rights similar to those of married couples and show similar levels of stability as married couples (Hiekel et al., 2014; Perelli-Harris & Gassen, 2012). France, Norway, and the Netherlands offer similar financial protections to married and cohabiting couples, such as insurance, social security, and, in the case of a partner's death, the right to his or her pension (Sánchez Gassen & Perelli-Harris, 2015). In contrast, cohabitation is nearly unheard-of in some countries, such as Ireland, Italy, Japan, and the Philippines, where fewer than 10% of adults have ever lived with an unmarried partner (Batalova & Cohen, 2002; Williams et al., 2007).

In the past, cohabiting couples in the United States who married tended to have unhappier marriages with a greater likelihood of divorce than noncohabiting couples (Copen et al., 2013; Jose et al., 2010; Kulik & Havusha-Morgenstern, 2011). However, these findings were largely the result of observations of Baby Boomers, whose sociocultural context viewed premarital cohabitation as taboo (Sassler & Lichter, 2020). Boomer cohabitors were likely more unconventional, risky, and rebellious than their married peers. These differences likely contributed to the greater instability of cohabiting than married unions. Research with current cohorts of young adults, specifically Millennials, has shown that cohabitation is no longer related to lower levels of marriage stability (Kuperberg, 2014; Manning et al., 2021). Couples who end cohabitation with marriage, including those with children, are no more likely to end their marriages that those who married without cohabitating prior to marriage (Musick & Michelmore, 2018).

Most young adults in North America and Europe cohabitate, or live together, in committed relationships.

MoMo Productions/ Getty Images

It is important to note that, although cohabitation is common, it usually does not last long, does not end in marriage, and is consistently shorter than marriages (Sassler & Lichter, 2020). About one-half of young adults' first cohabiting relationships last just over two years (Eickmeyer, 2019). Young adults tend to experience multiple cohabiting relationships. About three-quarters of young adults in cohabiting breakups enter new cohabiting relationships (Eickmeyer & Manning, 2018). Young adults today are more likely to have experienced a series of relationships by the time they reach age 30, compared to Boomers (Manning, 2020). Multiple cohabitation experiences mean that today's young adults have multiple opportunities to learn about relationships, learn about what works and does not work, and practice skills in navigating romantic partnerships, which can lead to more successful future relationships (Giordano et al., 2012).

Marriage

Over the past half-century, marriage rates have declined to record lows—yet nearly all adults in the United States will marry. By age 45, more than 80% of adults have married at least once, 90% have married by age 60, and more than 95% by age 80 (US Bureau of the Census, 2015). In 2020, the median age of first marriage in the United States was 28.1 for women and 30.5 for men, with dramatic increases over the past 50 years, as shown in Figure 12.7 (U.S. Census Bureau, 2020). Similar increases have occurred in other Western countries. In Canada and Sweden, the average age of marriage is 31; it is 34 in Germany and the Netherlands and 35 in Italy (United Nations, 2019).

Generally speaking, marriage offers economic, physical, and psychological benefits. Married people around the world tend to live longer, and are happier, physically healthier, wealthier, and in better mental health than nonmarried people (Grover & Helliwell, 2014; Koball et al., 2010; Vanassche et al., 2012). Nevertheless, the transition to marriage is often challenging, as newlyweds experience multiple changes during their first years of marriage, such as coordinating and making decisions about living arrangements, housework, eating habits, and sexual activity. Many newlyweds struggle with rising debt, which is associated with higher levels of conflict (Neff & Karney, 2017). Most couples report a decline in relationship satisfaction over the first year of marriage (Lavner & Bradbury, 2014). Couples who are successful at managing the transition to married life express warmth, empathy, and respect in their relationship (Gadassi et al., 2016). They are able to address differences and resolve conflicts constructively by expressing feelings calmly, listening, accepting responsibility, and compromising (Hanzal & Segrin, 2009). Partners in successful marriages are able to maintain positive emotions for their spouse even in the midst of conflict (Gottman & Gottman, 2017). In contrast, during arguments, unhappy couples easily sink into negative emotions that are overwhelming and, like quicksand, difficult to escape.

FIGURE 12.7 ■ U.S. Median Age at First Marriage, 1890 to Present

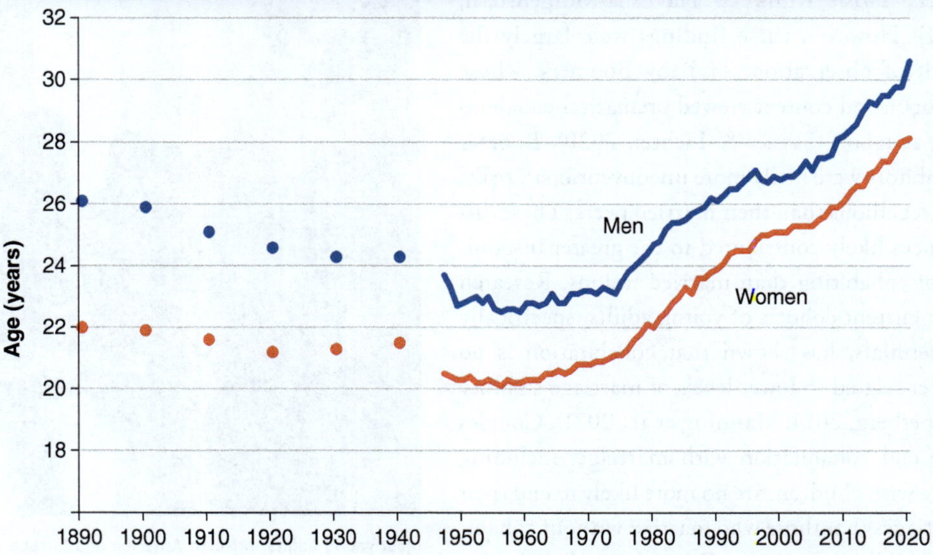

Source: U.S. Census Bureau, 2020.

The transition to marriage poses many challenges as newlyweds must negotiate household tasks, financial obligations, and new roles.

Daniel Ernst / Alamy Stock Photo

One of the best predictors of marital satisfaction and a long-lasting marriage is the partners' chronological maturity, or age. Generally speaking, the younger the bride and groom, the less likely they are to have a lifelong marriage (Smock & Schwartz, 2020). Forging an intimate relationship depends on a secure sense of identity, which many emerging adults are still developing. Marital success is also predicted by the degree of similarity between the members of the couple. Similarity in socioeconomic status, education, religion, and age all contribute to predicting a happy marriage (Gonzaga et al., 2007; van Scheppingen et al., 2019). In addition, spouses reciprocally influence each other and tend, over a lifetime of marriage, to become more similar to each other in terms of personality (Caspi et al., 1992; Lewis & Yoneda, 2021). They also become more similar in their general well-being, as measured by rates of depression, physical activity, substance use, and health, including chronic diseases such as high blood pressure and markers of aging (Bookwala & Jacobs, 2004; Ko et al., 2007; Lewis & Yoneda, 2021; Pettee et al., 2006; Umberson et al., 2018). This is true of different-sex and same-sex couples.

The quality of the marital relationship predicts mental health and well-being in both men and women (Robles, 2014). Men generally report being happier with their marriages than women, though the difference is small (Jackson et al., 2014). Satisfaction, particularly in women, tends to be highest in egalitarian relationships in which home and family duties are shared and couples view themselves as equal contributors (Helms et al., 2010; Ogolsky et al., 2014). This is particularly true in Western nations, where egalitarian marriage roles are increasingly expected (Greenstein, 2009). In dual-earner marriages today, most men take on many more childcare tasks than in prior generations, although they still spend less time than women on housework. Dual-earner couples who view themselves as equal contributors to household duties tend to divide work most equitably and report highest levels of satisfaction (Helms et al., 2010; Thielemans et al., 2021). Very unequal divisions of labor predict marital instability and dissolution (Thielemans et al., 2021). Although many couples strive for it, true equality in marriage is rare. In determining marital satisfaction, it seems that what matters more than actual equity (how household responsibilities are distributed between partners) is the perception of equity (whether partners feel that responsibilities are distributed fairly); this holds true for both members of the couple but especially for women (Amato & Irving, 2006; Greenstein, 2009; Pollitt et al., 2018).

Most of the research examining equity and marital satisfaction has studied cisgender different-sex couples. One review found that lesbian couples tended to share a more equal distribution of household labor than different-sex couples, and lesbian women tended to divide chores based on task and ability rather than typical gendered divisions (Brewster, 2017). Regardless of sexual orientation, it appears that if the division of household responsibilities feels equal, the couple is likely to report marital satisfaction.

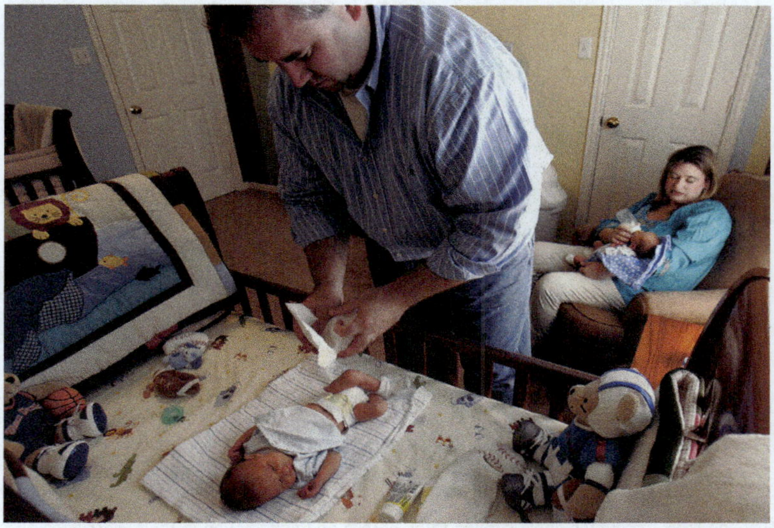

Perceived equity, the sense that work and household responsibilities are distributed fairly, predicts relationship satisfaction in married couples.

Donna McWilliam/ Associated Press

Same-Sex Marriage

Like all people, gay and lesbian adults seek love, partnership, and close intimate relationships. Intimate relationships and marriage have similar meanings for same-sex and different-sex couples, and, as noted, all couples share similar influences on marital satisfaction (Carpenter, Eppink, Gonzales, & McKay, 2021; Chen & van Ours, 2018; Cherlin, 2013). Until recently, it was very difficult to study same-sex unions because same-sex marriage was not legal in all U.S. states. Since the 2015 Supreme Court decision in *Obergefell v. Hodges*, gay and lesbian couples have begun forming legal unions through marriage (Riggle et al., 2017). The literature comparing these couples with heterosexual couples has been growing, although it is still sparse.

Studies that have compared gay, lesbian, and different-sex couples have found no significant differences in love, satisfaction, or the partners' evaluations of the strengths and weaknesses of their relationships (Frost et al., 2015; Lavner et al., 2014). Serious problems such as intimate partner violence exist in both types of relationships (Edwards et al., 2015; Kimmes et al., 2019). Moreover, the breakup rate for same-sex couples is comparable to that for different-sex couples (Rosenfeld, 2014). The available research suggests that gay and lesbian adults experience the same psychological benefits from legal marriage, civil unions, and registered domestic partnerships as different-sex couples (Riggle et al., 2010; Rostosky & Riggle, 2017). As with different-sex couples, marital satisfaction in same-sex unions is influenced by perceived equality and associated with physical and mental health, life satisfaction, and well-being (Cherlin, 2013; Pollitt et al., 2018).

The U.S. legalization of gay marriage itself plays a role in the health and psychological well-being benefits of marriage for same-sex couples (Cao et al., 2017; Frost et al., 2015; Hatzenbuehler, 2014). The stressors that individual gay men and lesbian women face, such as stigma and prejudice, are also evident at the macrosystem level, as sanctioned discrimination, most salient as the inability to marry (Wight et al., 2013). The national legalization of marriage offsets some of these stressors. This is perhaps best illustrated by research conducted prior to the national legalization of marriage. At that time, same-sex couples living in states with legally sanctioned marriage reported higher levels of self-assessed health, greater self-acceptance, and less isolation than those living in states that barred same-sex marriage (Kail et al., 2015; Riggle et al., 2017). Likewise, legally married same-sex older adult couples reported better quality of life and more economic and social resources than unmarried partnered couples (Goldsen et al., 2017). These observations of adults prior to national legalization of same-sex marriage in the United States illustrate how laws represent an important contextual influence on well-being.

Gay and lesbian couples show similar rates of love and satisfaction in their marriages and experience similar benefits of marriage as compared with heterosexual couples.

iStock/ franckreporter

Divorce

In the first few decades following the 1960s, divorce rates tripled in many Western industrialized countries, but since then they have stabilized and even declined (United Nations Statistics Division, 2014; see Figure 12.8). In the United States the divorce rate increased during the 1970s, peaking at 5.3 divorces per 1,000 people in 1981, and then declined to 2.9 divorces per 1,000 people in 2018 (Ortiz-Ospina & Roser, 2020). Despite declines in divorce rates around the world, large international differences remain. The highest divorce rate is in the Russian Federation (4.5 per 1,000 persons) and the lowest in Ireland (0.6), suggesting that social contextual factors unique to each culture play an influential role (United Nations Statistics Division, 2017). Most U.S. marriages that end in divorce do so within the first 10 years (Copen et al., 2012). By

FIGURE 12.8 ■ Divorce Rates, 1950–2018

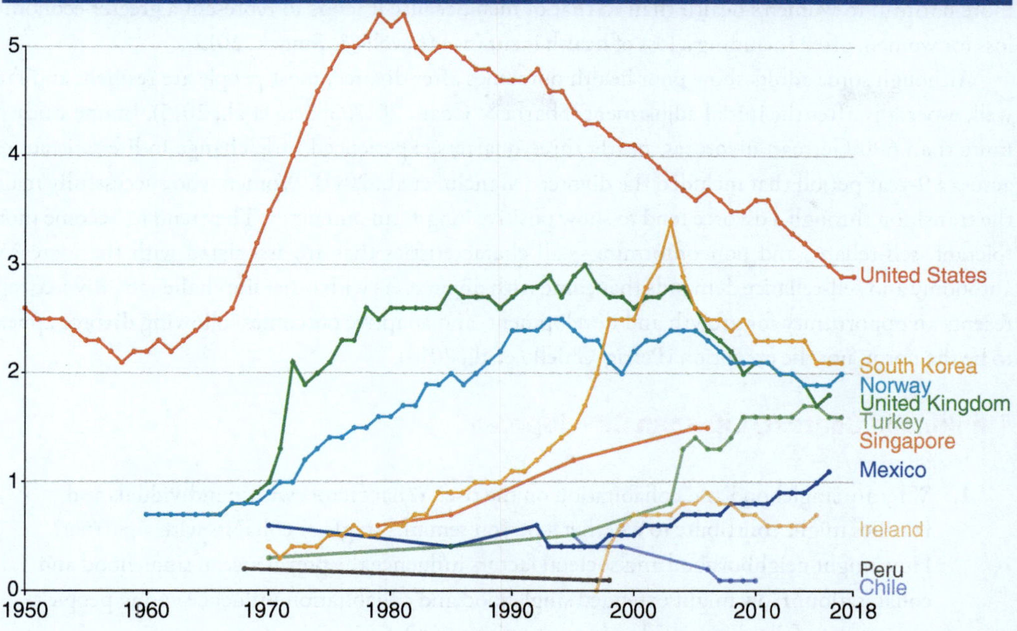

Source: Ortiz-Ospina & Roser, 2020.

45 years of age, more than one-third of men and women have been divorced (Kreider, Ellis, & U. S. Bureau of the Census, 2011).

We have seen that couples who are older and who share similarities in demographics, interests, personality, attitudes, and values are more likely to have successful marriages. Poor education, economic disadvantage, not attending religious services, and experiencing multiple life stressors and role overload are associated with increased risk of divorce (Härkönen, 2015). Adults who have experienced their parents' divorce may themselves be more prone to divorce. When adult children of divorced families marry, they may have poor coping and conflict resolution skills, experience more stress and conflict in their relationships, and be less able or willing to resolve differences (Amato, 2010; Roper et al., 2020). In addition, remarriages experience higher rates of divorce (DeLongis & Zwicker, 2017).

A critical predictor of divorce is the couple's communication and problem-solving style. Negative interaction patterns and difficulty regulating discussions predict later divorce even in newlyweds reporting high marital satisfaction, and these patterns are often evident even before marriage (Gottman & Gottman, 2017; Lavner & Bradbury, 2012). During conflict, troubled couples often experience negative emotions that are overwhelming and interfere with their connection to their partner. Unable to effectively resolve differences, when one member of the couple raises a concern, the other may retreat, reacting with anger, resentment, and defensiveness, creating a negative cycle (Ramos Salazar, 2015). Disagreements over finances are particularly strong predictors of divorce (Dew et al., 2012).

The process of divorce entails a series of stressful experiences, including conflict, physical separation, moving, distributing property, and, for some, child-custody negotiations. Regardless of who initiates a divorce, all family members feel stress and a confusing array of emotions, such as anger, despair, embarrassment, shame, failure—and, sometimes, relief (Härkönen, 2015). Recently divorced adults are prone to depression; loneliness; anxiety; an increase in risky behaviors such as drug and alcohol use; promiscuous sexual activity; and poor eating, sleeping, and working habits (Härkönen, 2015; Sbarra et al., 2015). Divorce is associated with decreased life satisfaction, heightened risk for a range of illnesses, and even a 20% to 30% increase in early mortality (Björkenstam et al., 2013; Sbarra et al., 2011; Sbarra & Coan, 2017). However, spouses in very low-quality relationships may experience divorce as a relief and show increased life satisfaction afterward (Bourassa et al., 2015). The outcomes of divorce are characterized by individual differences. The bulk of these negative effects are thought to affect only a minority of divorcing adults (Sbarra et al., 2015). Although life satisfaction tends to plummet during the divorce itself, it gradually rises after (van Scheppingen & Leopold, 2020). Divorce is thought to be more harmful to women's health than to that of men because it tends to represent a greater economic loss for women, often including a loss of health insurance (Lavelle & Smock, 2012).

Although some adults show poor health outcomes after divorce, most people are resilient and fare well, especially after the initial adjustment (Sbarra & Coan, 2017; Sbarra et al., 2015). In one study of more than 600 German divorcees, nearly three-quarters experienced little change in life satisfaction across a 9-year period that included the divorce (Mancini et al., 2011). Women who successfully make the transition through a divorce tend to show positive long-term outcomes. They tend to become more tolerant, self-reliant, and nonconforming—all characteristics that are associated with the increased autonomy and self-reliance demands that come with divorce. As with other life challenges, divorce represents an opportunity for growth and development, and adaptive outcomes following divorce appear to be the norm, not the exception (Perrig-Chiello et al., 2014).

Thinking in Context: Lifespan Development

1. Why are singlehood and cohabitation on the rise? What factors within individuals and families might contribute to whether a person remains single or cohabits with a partner? How might neighborhood and societal factors influence the prevalence of singlehood and cohabitation? How might extended singlehood and cohabitation influence young people's attainment of developmental tasks such as intimacy?
2. Provide advice to newlyweds. Given what is known about love, marriage, and divorce, what can they do to ensure a happy marriage and reduce the likelihood of divorce? Alternatively, what can someone who is facing divorce do to aid his or her transition?

PARENTHOOD

LEARNING OBJECTIVE

12.5 Compare the experiences of young adults as stepparents, never-married parents, and same-sex parents.

Having children was once considered an inevitable part of adult life, but since the 1960s, effective methods of birth control and changing cultural views on parenthood and childlessness have made having children a choice (Mills et al., 2011). Consequently, childbearing rates have declined in most industrialized nations. In the 1950s, the average number of children born to a woman in the United States was 3.8; today it is 1.8 (Central Intelligence Agency, 2021). The average number of children is even lower for many other industrialized nations, including Canada (1.6), Germany (1.5), and Japan (1.4). In contrast, rates are significantly higher in developing nations such as Niger (6.9), Chad (5.6), and Afghanistan (4.7).

Although families in many countries are growing smaller, most married adults still become parents, but later in life than ever before. The average age at which U.S. women give birth has increased over the past three decades, from 21.4 in 1970 to 26.9 in 2018 (see Figure 12.9; Martin et al., 2019; Matthews & Hamilton, 2002). However, women who postpone childbearing to their early 30s are at increased risk for experiencing fertility problems (Schmidt et al., 2012).

Becoming a Parent

The decision to have a child is influenced by personal factors, such as values, health, and financial status, as well as circumstance. About 45% of all pregnancies in the United States are unintended (Finer & Zolna, 2016). North American adults, regardless of sexual orientation, cite a variety of reasons to

FIGURE 12.9 ■ Maternal Age at First Birth in the United States, 1970–2018

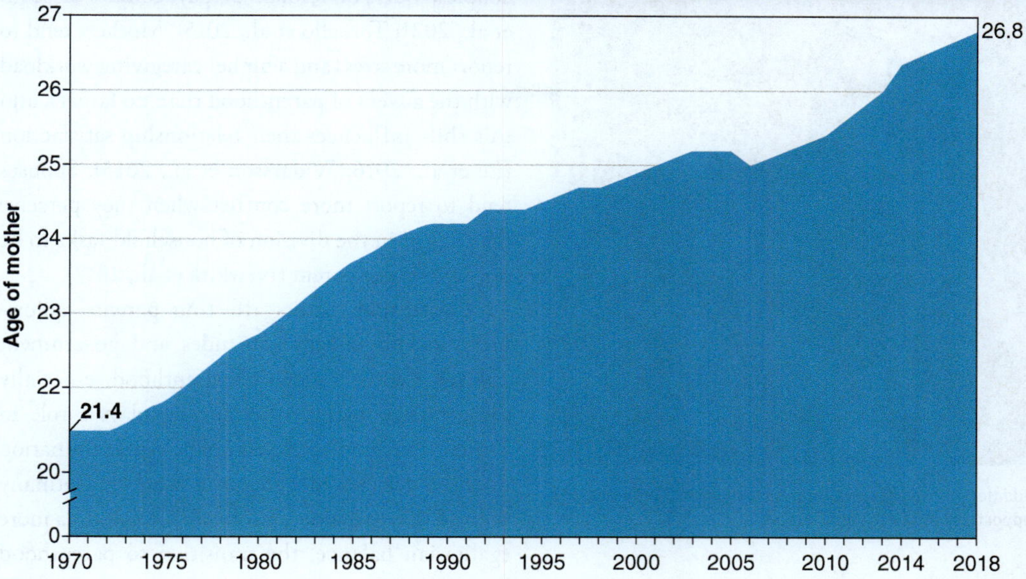

Source: Martin et al., 2019; U.S. Department of Health and Human Services, 2019.

have children, including experiencing the parent-child bond; growth, learning, and fun experiences that come with raising a child; and the desire to help someone grow into a productive adult (Gato et al., 2017; Goldberg et al., 2012; O'Laughlin & Anderson, 2001; Simon et al., 2018). Common disadvantages of parenthood include the loss of freedom and the high cost of raising a child. It is estimated that an average middle-income parent will spend about $234,000 over the course of raising a child from birth to age 18 (U.S. Department of Agriculture, 2017). Parents with incomes in the lowest third spend about $175,000 and those in the highest third spend about $372,000.

The transition to parenthood is challenging for adults of all ages. Many new parents report not feeling prepared for their infants' constant needs for attention, affection, and care or for the roller coaster of emotions ranging from joy to frustration and exhaustion that accompany parenthood (Galatzer-Levy et al., 2011; Stanca, 2012). New caregiving responsibilities are accompanied by added housework, financial demands, loss of sleep, decreased physical activity, and diminished leisure time. Such pressures are associated with a reduced sense of well-being, self-esteem, and self-control and even depression (Bleidorn et al., 2016; Nelson et al., 2014; van Scheppingen et al., 2018). Generally, women are more likely to experience declines in well-being while men tend to show more positive well-being outcomes over time (Nelson-Coffey et al., 2019). The parenthood-happiness link may be related to the workload that parenthood entails. One study of Swiss parents found that it was not the first child but a second child that was associated with declines in mothers' life satisfaction (Mikucka & Rizzi, 2020). The challenges of new parenthood are accompanied by rewards, such as experiencing a greater sense of meaning in life (Brandel et al., 2018).

The parenthood transition places stress on even the best of relationships and marriages. Parenthood is associated with sudden declines in marital satisfaction for both partners in same-sex and opposite-sex relationships (Doss & Rhoades, 2017). Conflict tends to rise in response to increased financial, household, and parental demands and decreased leisure time (Don & Mickelson, 2014; Trillingsgaard et al., 2014). Declines in satisfaction are higher in couples who experienced problems prior to the birth, have temperamentally difficult infants, and have an insecure attachment to their spouse or child (Doss & Rhoades, 2017; Simpson & Rholes, 2019).

During the transition to parenthood, most North American and European different-sex couples, even those in relatively egalitarian marriages, shift toward traditional marital roles and division of labor (Dribe & Stanfors, 2009; Katz-Wise et al., 2010; Koivunen et al., 2009). Mothers tend to do more infant care than they expect and men less; engaging in more infant care than expected is associated

Parenting includes challenges in addition to rewards, with outcomes varying in part due to contextual factors such as social support and socioeconomic status.

iStock/lewkmiller

with relationship dissatisfaction in different-sex couples, but not lesbian or gay couples (Ascigil et al., 2021; Tornello et al., 2015). Mothers tend to report more stress and a higher caregiving workload with the advent of parenthood than do fathers, and this shift influences their relationship satisfaction (Le et al., 2016; Widarsson et al., 2013). Spouses tend to report more conflict when they perceive the change in the division of household tasks to be unfair to either parent (Newkirk et al., 2017).

Contextual factors affecting parents' adjustment include cultural attitudes and government policies. Cultural views of parenthood, especially the gendered nature of childcare, plays a role in adults' transition to parenthood. An examination of three decades of parents in western Germany showed that as gender norms shifted toward a more egalitarian balance, the transition to parenthood became easier for parents to manage, and the common declines in parental happiness vanished (Preisner et al., 2020). Tangible forms of support also assist parents. Research with adults in 27 European countries suggests that parents report greater life satisfaction, less financial strain, and fewer work-life conflicts when they live in countries that offer financial benefits to families, childcare, and working time flexibility, compared with parents who live in countries that provide low levels of support (Pollmann-Schult, 2018).

Nonmarital Childbearing

About 40% of infants in the United States are born to unmarried mothers each year (up from 28% in 1990; Wildsmith et al., 2018). Since 1990, rates of nonmarital childbearing have increased for all women, but especially for white and Hispanic women. In recent years, more single professional women in their 30s have become single parents by choice. However, nonmarital childbearing is most common among women who have not attended college (see Figure 12.10; Wildsmith et al., 2018). Children in single-mother homes are disproportionately likely to live in poverty, posing significant risks to their development (Damaske et al., 2017).

Drawing conclusions about the effects of nonmarital childbearing is difficult because there are many circumstances associated with nonmarital childbearing. Unmarried noncohabitating mothers in the United States tend to have less education and are more likely to live at or near the poverty level; this is true in the European Union as well (Bernardi & Mortelmans, 2018; Chzhen & Bradshaw, 2012). Most nonmarital births occur to couples who live together in a cohabiting union but are not married (Lichter et al., 2014). Recent estimates suggest that 62% of births to never-married women are to women in a cohabiting union (Lamidi, 2016). We have seen that cohabitation affords many of the benefits of marriage, but it is often less stable than marriage and this instability is inversely associated with child health (Manning, 2015).

Although some research suggests that never-married mothers tend to be similar to married mothers in mental health (Afifi et al., 2006; Taylor & Conger, 2014), other work suggests that never-married single mothers are less happy (Baranowska-Rataj et al., 2013) and are more likely to have poor health in middle and older adulthood (Berkman et al., 2015). The experiences of never-married single mothers vary with contextual influences such as social support from family and from nonresidential fathers (Taylor & Conger, 2014, 2017). Some research suggests that Black and white nonresidential fathers tend to spend similar amounts of time with their children (Ellerbe et al., 2018). Declines in father involvement are linked with more maternal depression and lower maternal life satisfaction (Mallette et al., 2020).

FIGURE 12.10 ■ Nonmarital Childbearing Among Women, Ages 20–29, by Ethnicity and Education

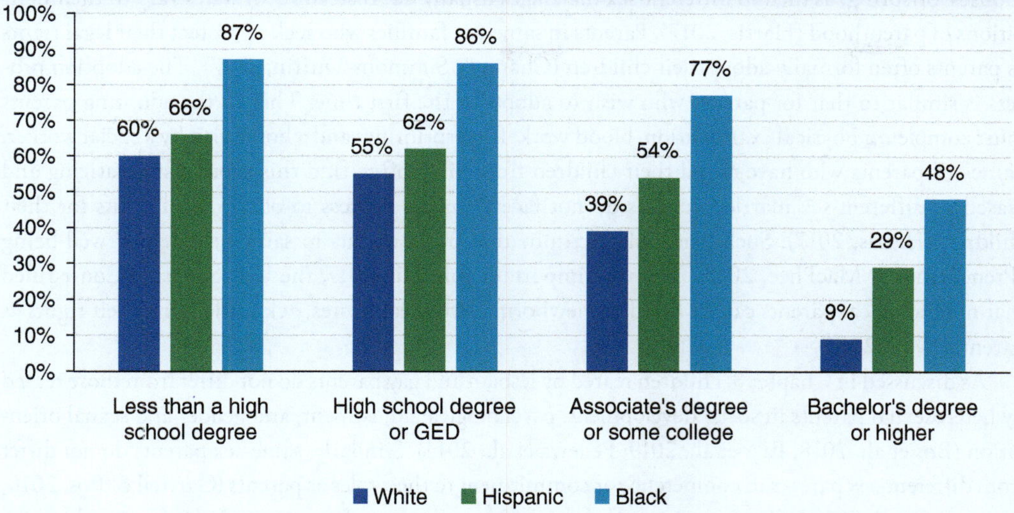

Source: Adapted from Wildsmith et al., 2018; National Center for Health Statistics, 2018.

Same-Sex Parents

About 16% of same-sex couples are raising children today (24% of lesbian and 8% of gay couples), compared with 39% of different-sex couples (Goldberg & Conron, 2018; see Figure 12.11). Gay men and lesbian women become parents through assisted reproductive technologies (see Chapter 2) and adoption; many also parent a spouse or partner's child.

Just as same-sex couples have only recently won the right to marry, it was only in 2017 that joint adoption by same-sex couples became legal in all U.S. states (Movement Advancement Project, 2018). Before this ruling most U.S. states permitted adoption by LGBT single adults, but few permitted same-sex couples to jointly adopt (Raley et al., 2013).

FIGURE 12.11 ■ Percentage of Couples Raising Children, by Sex of Couple

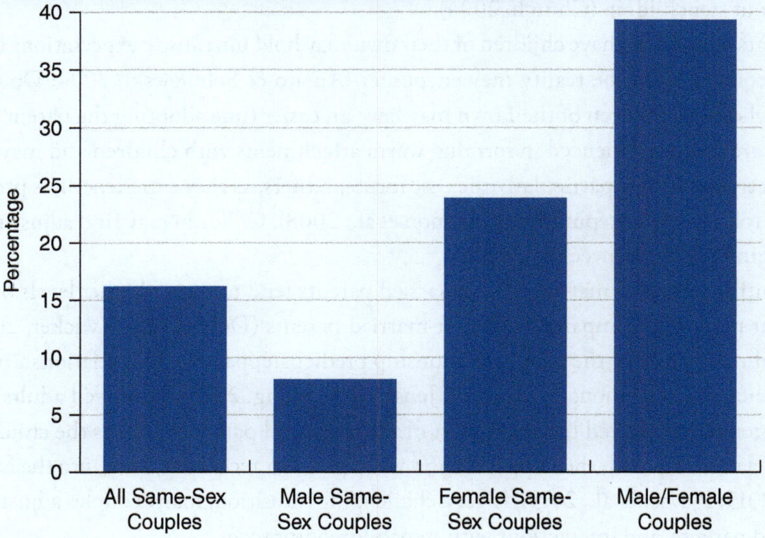

Source: Adapted from Goldberg & Conron, 2018.

Gay and lesbian couples who create families through reproductive technology face unique challenges. In many states social (nongenetic) parents do not have automatic legal connection to their spouses' offspring, as men in different-sex marriages usually do. Instead, U.S. states vary in their definitions of parenthood (Harris, 2017). Parents in same-sex families who seek to protect their legal rights as parents often formally adopt their children (Chang & Simmons-Duffin, 2017). The adoption process is similar to that for parents who wish to adopt for the first time. That is, the adopting parents must complete a physical examination, blood work, fingerprinting, and a home visit by a social worker. Same-sex parents who have raised their children from birth often find this process stigmatizing and biased as different-sex married couples do not face a similar process to obtain legal rights for their children (Harris, 2017). Such bias and discrimination poses threats to same-sex parents' well-being (Prendergast & MacPhee, 2018). In a very important ruling in 2017, the U.S. Supreme Court ruled that nonbiological parents can be listed on newborns' birth certificates, acknowledging their rights as parents (Wolf, 2017).

As discussed in Chapter 8, children reared by lesbian and gay parents do not differ from those reared by heterosexual parents in social development, psychological adjustment, and gender and sexual orientation (Bos et al., 2018; Farr et al., 2019; Fedewa et al., 2014). Similarly, same-sex parents do not differ from different-sex parents in competence or commitment to their roles as parents (Gartrell & Bos, 2010; Perrin & Siegel, 2013). The parenting role that same-sex partners take varies with the way in which the family formed. Generally speaking, the biological parent tends to assume most of the parenting responsibility when the child is the result of a previous heterosexual relationship. As parents, gay and lesbian couples tend to coparent more equally than different-sex partners; their relationship dynamics often shift based on paid work outside the home (Reczek, 2020). Same-sex couples with children may move from shared employment, decision making, and household work to differentiation between partners in childcare based on employment status and income (Van Rijn - Van Gelderen et al., 2020).

Stepparents

Stepfamilies, composed of at least one child, biological parent, and stepparent, are increasingly common. Stepparents are often challenged with the task of providing discipline outside of the warm attachment bond that characterizes most parent-child relationships. Compared with stepfathers, stepmothers tend to face particularly high levels of conflict; to be more disliked by their stepchildren; and to experience more stress, anxiety, and depression (Doodson, 2014; Shapiro & Stewart, 2011). Stepmothers may expect to take on maternal roles and develop relationships quickly. But stepparent-stepchild bonds take a great deal of time to develop, and stepmothers may feel guilty for not feeling maternal and for preferring life without stepchildren (Church, 2004).

Stepparents who do not have children of their own may hold unrealistic expectations for family life that sharply contrast with the reality they encounter (Amato & Sobolewski, 2004; Doodson, 2014). Stepparents who have children of their own may have an easier time adopting the parent role, perhaps because they are more experienced in forming warm attachments with children and may engage children in fun activities; this is particularly the case for stepfathers, as they experience less pressure to take on parenting roles than do stepmothers (Hennon et al., 2008). Children may find adjusting to stepsiblings challenging (Raley & Sweeney, 2020).

Stepparenting tests new marriages as remarried parents tend to report higher levels of tension and conflict about parenting compared with first-married parents (DeLongis & Zwicker, 2017). Marital dynamics and the quality of the couple relationship predict stepparent-child relationships and overall stepfamily functioning (Ganong et al., 2019; Jensen & Ganong, 2020). How well adults adjust to the role of stepparent is influenced by the support of the biological parent as well as the children's perception of their relationship with the stepparent and willingness to accept the adult into the family (Jensen & Howard, 2015; Pylyser et al., 2019). After a challenging transition, many couples adjust to their roles as spouses and parents, and interactions with stepchildren improve.

Childlessness

Although most adults have children, some remain childless. In 2016, 14% of all U.S. women aged 40 to 44 had not given birth to any children (Livingston, 2018). It is difficult for researchers to determine the rate of childlessness in men. Frequently childlessness is involuntary, the result of infertility or of postponing parenthood. About 13% of women aged 30 to 44 experience *impaired fecundity*, the inability to become pregnant or carry a fetus to term (National Center for Health Statistics, 2019). Some adults are childless by choice—or *childfree*, the term preferred by some. Common reasons for voluntary childlessness include the desire for flexibility and freedom from childcare responsibilities, pursuit of career aspirations, economic security, environmental reasons (e.g., not wanting to contribute to global overpopulation), and desires to preserve marital satisfaction (Stegen et al., 2021). It is unclear how many women are childless by choice.

Consistent predictors of childlessness include education and career status. High levels of education and income predict childlessness in women from Australia, the Netherlands, Finland, Germany, the UK, and the United States (Frejka, 2017; Waren & Pals, 2013). Women and men who are voluntarily childless tend to be less religious and more assertive, independent, and self-reliant than their peers, attributes which likely influence their adjustment throughout life (Avison & Furnham, 2015). Overall, adults who are childless by choice tend to be just as content with their lives as those who are parents. Positive attitudes toward childlessness are more common among adults who are college educated, childless, and female, while negative attitudes toward childlessness are more common among adults who are male, less educated, and have conservative religious beliefs (Koropeckyj-Cox et al., 2007; Koropeckyj-Cox & Pendell, 2007).

Childlessness appears to interfere with psychosocial development and personal adjustment only when it is involuntary and a result of circumstances beyond an individual's control (Roy et al., 2014). In both men and women, involuntary childlessness is associated with life dissatisfaction varying from ambivalence to regret and deep disappointment, especially when it is accompanied by self-blame, rumination, and catastrophizing (Hadley & Hanley, 2011; Koert & Daniluk, 2017; Peterson et al., 2007). The social context also matters, as the extent to which childlessness is associated with decreased psychological well-being appears to be associated with the degree to which a country and culture's norms are tolerant toward childlessness (Huijts et al., 2011; Kreyenfeld & Konietzka, 2017).

Thinking in Context: Lifespan Development

1. What personality, developmental, and life experience factors influence whether an adult will become a parent? How might contextual factors play a role in determining whether one becomes a parent and the timing of parenthood?
2. To what extent do you think national differences in family leave reflect cultural views of parenting? Why do you think family leave policies often spark debate in the United States?
3. How might the experience and effects of nonmarital childbearing vary with cohabitation? In what ways might mothers in cohabitating relationships experience parenthood differently than their noncoupled peers? How might children experience single and cohabitating parent homes differently (see Chapter8)?

Thinking in Context: Applied Developmental Science

Given what you know about children and families (such as child development and the effects of parent-child interactions, parental employment, and childcare) as well as young adults' career development, what family policies, such as the length of leave, would you suggest? How might employers help parents and foster work-life balance?

Thinking in Context: Biological Influences

1. Describe the physical and reproductive changes that women experience in early adulthood that may influence whether they become a parent. What challenges might they face and what reproductive options are available?
2. How might variations in physical development and common health issues influence young adults' likelihood of becoming parents and their adjustment to parenthood?

CHAPTER SUMMARY

12.1 Examine the features of emerging adulthood and its contextual nature.

Emerging adulthood, roughly age 18 to 25, is characterized by diversity in lifestyles, identity development, and the subjective sense of being "in between." Although emerging adulthood is observed in industrialized cultures around the world, it is not universal as it is influenced by socioeconomic status and contextual changes that have prolonged the transition into adulthood.

12.2 Discuss the psychosocial tasks of identity, intimacy, and sexuality in early adulthood.

Young adults tend to continue the identity search commonly begun in adolescence. The identity search extends to include many domains, including ethnic-racial identity. Erikson proposed that the psychosocial task of early adulthood is establishing an intimate relationship that is mutual and satisfying. Sexual activity is highest among people in young adulthood and declines modestly for people in their 40s and again in their 50s, but the amount of decline is modest. About one-third of all women will experience nonconsensual sexual activity—sexual assault or rape—in their lifetime. Contextual influences, such as the prevalence of rape myths and gender stereotypes of men's and women's roles, may influence sexual assault.

12.3 Describe influences on friendship, mate selection, and romantic relationships in early adulthood.

Like friendships in childhood and adolescence, adult friendships are based on similarity and show gender differences. Men and women from many cultures seek different characteristics in mates. Despite this, most intimate partners share similarities in demographics, attitudes, and values. Violence between intimate partners is not limited by culture, ethnicity, socioeconomic status, sexual orientation, or marital status. A variety of factors contribute to intimate partner violence including contextual factors such as poverty, unemployment, drug and alcohol abuse, and cultural norms.

12.4 Describe the diverse romantic situations that may characterize early adulthood, including singlehood, cohabitation, marriage, and divorce.

Most North Americans spend a large part of their adult lives single, and some remain single throughout life. Cohabitation has become increasingly common in the United States and is very common in most European nations. Cohabiting unions in the United States are less stable than married unions, but premarital cohabitation is not related to marital instability. Most North Americans marry. Marital success is predicted by maturity and similarity in demographic factors. Successful marriages are based on realistic expectations, flexibility, communication, and joint conflict resolution. Same-sex and different-sex couples express similar levels of satisfaction and love and experience similar health benefits to marriage. Risk factors for divorce include being at an economic disadvantage, experiencing multiple life stressors and role overload, and having poor communication and conflict resolution skills. Recently divorced adults are prone to depression, anxiety, and a variety of risky behaviors.

12.5 Compare the experiences of young adults as stepparents, never-married parents, and same-sex parents.

New parents are greeted with a host of new responsibilities and changes. The transition to parenthood is associated with declines in marital satisfaction. In dual-earner couples, the greater the degree of shared parenting responsibilities, the greater the couple's happiness. Nonmarital parenting is often accompanied by cohabitation, and the effects vary depending on maternal and contextual factors. Stepparents are often placed in the position of providing discipline without the warm attachment bond that characterizes most parent-child relationships. Same-sex parents do not differ from different-sex parents in competence or commitment to their roles as parents, and their children do not differ in adjustment, gender identity, or sexual orientation. Adults who are childless by choice tend to be as content as other adults. Involuntary childlessness is associated with poor adjustment.

KEY TERMS

cohabitation (p. 374)
intimacy versus isolation (p. 363)
intimate partner violence (p. 371)
singlehood (p. 374)

PART 6 LIFESPAN DEVELOPMENT AT WORK: EARLY ADULTHOOD

Early adulthood spans more than two decades and many different concerns, including education, career, and family. There are many opportunities to influence the lives of young adults, such as the following.

ESL Teacher

An English as a Second Language (ESL) teacher educates students whose first language is not English. They work with nonnative speakers of all ages. ESL teachers instruct students on reading, writing, and conversing in English with the goal of improving students' communication skills so that they can succeed at school, work, and in the community. They prepare lesson plans; adapt their lessons to accommodate student differences in age, ability, and progress; and prepare progress reports. ESL teachers' instructional style must be flexible to adjust to students of different ages and backgrounds. They must be knowledgeable about different cultures as they encounter students from many backgrounds. ESL teachers often act as formal and informal mentors, advisors, and liaisons to students and families who are new to a community or require assistance with communication.

ESL teachers are employed by schools, but many work with adult learners in community centers, high schools, and colleges. Becoming an ESL teacher requires a bachelor's degree, teaching internship, completion of a state licensure exam, and completion of an add-on certification to teach ESL, which requires an additional exam. The median salary for ESL teachers was $55,350 in May 2020 (U.S. Bureau of Labor Statistics, 2021).

Substance Abuse Counselor

Substance abuse counselors provide support to individuals experiencing drug and alcohol problems. They teach adults how to modify their behavior to progress toward recovery. They evaluate clients, develop treatment and recovery plans, facilitate individual and group therapy sessions, teach coping skills, monitor clients'' progress, and revise treatment plans as needed. Substance abuse counselors collaborate with psychiatrists, doctors, nurses, social workers, and departments of corrections. They are found in hospitals, individual and family services, mental health and substance abuse facilities, and state and local governments.

Substance abuse counseling requires a master's degree in substance abuse counseling, followed by 3,000 hours of supervised experience, and completion of a licensure exam. However, states vary in their requirements to practice. In many states substance abuse counselors may be employed at the bachelor's level, with certification. Frequently bachelor's level certification involves completing four courses in drug and alcohol abuse counseling, 300 to 600 hours of supervised training, and a certification exam (usually from the Association for Addiction Professionals, but some states maintain their own accreditation requirements). The median salary for substance abuse counselors was about $48,000 in 2020 (U.S. Bureau of Labor Statistics, 2021).

Professor

College and university professors engage in teaching, research, and service to the institution, but the exact combination of activities that comprise a professor's job varies by institution. Two-year community colleges tend to focus heavily on teaching with few research commitments. Professors at research universities spend most of their time conducting research and teach very little. In between these extremes are liberal arts colleges and 4-year universities that weight teaching and research responsibilities about equally, or close to it.

Like other teachers, professors do a great deal of work outside of class, including preparing lessons, lectures, class activities, and out of class assignments; loading materials onto the learning management syste;, grading; and so on. They also provide service to the department, campus, and community, such as advising students, assessing programs, and working on committees that administer and run the university.

A graduate degree is needed to become a professor. With a master's degree, it is possible to become a community college professor or to teach part time. However, faculty positions at community colleges have become more competitive in recent years; many are held by psychologists with doctoral degrees. Similarly, although master's degree holders may be hired to teach at 4-year colleges on a part-time basis, they are unlikely to be hired for full-time positions. A doctoral degree in your field of interest is the best choice. The median annual wage for professors at all settings and levels of experience was $80,790 in May 2020 (U.S. Bureau of Labor Statistics, 2021).

Student Activities Director and Resident Director

Every college and university sponsors student activities, such as clubs, student government, and fraternities and sororities. The student activities director, also known as director of student services, oversees the development and organization of the college's or university's extracurricular programs. The director identifies and implements strategies for increasing student use of services and involvement in programs. Activities include approving funding for student activities and overseeing students and staff who organize and supervise student activities. Bachelor's degree holders with less experience may be hired as *assistant director of student services.* This position reports to the student activities director and engages in similar activities but with less responsibility. The average salary for a director of student services in 2021 was about $65,000 and about $54,000 for an assistant director of student services (Salary.com, 2021a).

Residential colleges employ resident directors, full-time staff members who supervise a residence hall or dorm. They are responsible for forming a connection between academics and life by providing a safe, comfortable environment that is functional for students living on campus. They organize activities for students and staff; assist residents with problems; and train, oversee, and evaluate resident assistants, the college students who monitor the residence hall and lead their peers. Resident directors also establish student conduct policies, respond to student concerns about housing and environment, and plan and supervise student activities within and near residence halls.

Becoming a resident director requires a bachelor's degree and experience with student affairs such as organizing campus activities or having worked as a resident assistant (RA). The mean salary for resident directors was $38,000 in 2021 (Salary.com, 2021b).

Clinical Psychologist and Counseling Psychologist

There are many careers that enable professionals to provide counseling and mental health assistance. Psychologist is perhaps the best-known career. Psychologists who provide counseling are most often trained in clinical or counseling psychology. Both clinical psychologists and counseling psychologists provide individual assessment and therapy, and they create and evaluate therapeutic programs for individuals and groups. Despite these similarities, clinical and counseling psychology are two distinct fields with different emphases. Traditionally, clinical psychology focused on the assessment and treatment of mental disorders to alleviate distress and behavior problems. Counseling psychology also treats distress but works to improve well-being over the lifespan, focusing on normative functioning rather than disorder. In practice, however, clinical and counseling psychologists engage in similar counseling and therapeutic activities.

Clinical and counseling psychologists work in a variety of settings including private practices, hospitals and medical centers, community mental health centers, schools, university or college counseling centers, criminal justice settings, and specialty clinics. Some psychologists specialize in a particular age or topic, such as health psychology, geropsychology, eating disorders, or parenting problems. In addition to direct service delivery, clinical and counseling psychologists also engage in intervention and program development and evaluation. Some become administrators who manage other mental health workers or manage an entire agency or organization.

Use of the title *psychologist* requires state licensure. Clinical and counseling psychologists earn doctoral degrees, which includes supervised experience and the completion of a dissertation, which typically requires conducting original research. After obtaining a doctoral degree, clinical and counseling psychologists complete an additional year of supervised experience, then a national licensure exam. Many states require an additional state licensure exam. The median salary for clinical and counseling psychologists was about $80,000 in 2020 (U.S. Bureau of Labor Statistics, 2021).

13 PHYSICAL AND COGNITIVE DEVELOPMENT IN MIDDLE ADULTHOOD

Luis Alvarez/ Getty Images

As the basketball swooshed through the hoop, Alfonzo called out to his son, Alito, "Yeah! Your dad's still got it!" Alito raced toward his father, beating him for the rebound, "But I'm still faster." "You may be faster, but I'm experienced—and experience makes all the difference," Alfonzo challenged his son. Who is right, father or son? In many ways, both are. In this chapter, we examine the physical and cognitive changes of middle adulthood. Our discussion will largely mirror this conversation: Middle-aged adults experience mild physical and cognitive declines, but experience and wisdom often permit them to compensate for any decline in capacity.

PHYSICAL DEVELOPMENT IN MIDDLE ADULTHOOD

LEARNING OBJECTIVE

13.1 Summarize the physical changes that occur during middle adulthood.

Unlike the changes that occur in early adolescence, the physical changes that occur in middle adulthood (age 40–65) are more gradual. Like Alfonzo, adults often compensate for changes by modifying their behavior. Nevertheless, even active and vibrant middle-aged adults notice some changes in their body shape, strength, speed, and appearance. Most middle-aged adults begin to sense their own mortality, often in response to acute or chronic health conditions and especially after experiencing life-threatening health concerns. As they progress through midlife, many adults begin to think of

A common sign of presbyopia is needing to hold reading materials at a distance.

10'000 Hours/ Getty Images

their lives in terms of years left of life rather than years lived (Neugarten, 1968). Aging itself cannot be controlled, and physical declines are inevitable. But there is variability in the rate of change so that middle-aged adults often vary in appearance and function. Many middle-aged adults compensate for declines and maximize their physical capacities in order to maintain an active lifestyle.

Sensory Aging

Suddenly aware that he holds the newspaper at arm's length and still squints to read, 45-year-old Dominic wondered to himself, "When did this happen? I can't see like I used to." Like much of physical development, the changes that take place in our senses represent continuous change. Over the adult years, vision and hearing capacities gradually decline. Like Dominic, most adults notice changes in vision during their 40s and changes in hearing at around age 50. The use of corrective lenses aids vision problems, and hearing aids amplify sounds, permitting better hearing.

Vision

Dominic's need to hold the newspaper at a distance in order to read is not unusual and is related to changes in the eye that occur throughout the adult years. The cornea flattens; the lens loses flexibility; and the muscle that permits the lens to change shape, or accommodate, weakens. The result is that most adults in their 40s develop **presbyopia,** also known as farsightedness—the inability to focus the lens on close objects, such as in reading small print (Gil-Cazorla et al., 2016). By age 50, virtually all adults display presbyopia and require reading glasses or other corrective options (Kollbaum & Bradley, 2020). Most also require corrective lenses for distance. Bifocals that combine lenses for nearsightedness and farsightedness are helpful (Wolffsohn & Davies, 2019).

In addition to changes in the accommodative ability of the lens, the ability to see in dim light declines because, with age, the lens yellows, the size of the pupil shrinks, and over middle age, most adults have lost about one half of the rods (light receptor cells) in the retina, which reduces the ability to see in dim light and makes adults' night vision decline twice as fast as their day vision (Sörensen et al., 2016). As rods are lost, so too are cones (color receptive cells) because rods secrete substances that permit cones to survive (Barbur & Rodriguez-Carmona, 2015). Thus, color discrimination becomes limited with gradual declines beginning in the 30s (Paramei & Oakley, 2014). Night vision is further reduced because the vitreous (transparent gel that fills the eyeball) becomes more opaque with age, scattering light that enters the eye (creating glare) and permitting less light to reach the retina (Garcia et al., 2018). In middle adulthood, about one-third more light is needed to compensate for these changes that reduce vision (Owsley et al., 2007). All of these changes in vision make driving at night more challenging as headlights from other cars become blinding (Gruber et al., 2013).

Hearing

In addition to changes in vision, Dominic also noticed that he has difficulty hearing, at least in some situations. When he plays with his 4-year-old nephew, Dominic finds that he has to lean in close to hear the boy's speech. Sometimes he finds himself watching his teenage daughter's lips while she speaks, especially when they are having dinner in a crowded restaurant. Age-related hearing loss, **presbycusis** ("old hearing"), becomes apparent in the 50s and is caused by natural cell death that results in the deterioration of the ear structures that convert sound into neural impulses (Quaranta et al., 2015). The loss is first limited to high-pitched sounds, which enable us to distinguish between consonants such as f versus s and p versus t; as a result, the person often can hear most of a message but may misinterpret parts of it, such as names. Middle-aged adults tend to experience more difficulty hearing under conditions of background noise and perform more poorly under that condition than do young adults (Leigh-Paffenroth & Elangovan, 2011). Presbycusis hearing deficits tend to be more apparent in settings with background noise, such as a dinner party (Helfer et al., 2017). By late adulthood, hearing loss extends to all sound frequencies. Reduced sensitivity to speech sounds influences processing as older adults show less activation of the auditory cortex in response to speech as compared with younger adults (Wettstein & Wahl, 2016).

Presbycusis is age-related and influenced by genetics, but contextual factors also play a large role in hearing loss (Wang & Puel, 2020). Generally, men's hearing declines more rapidly than women's, perhaps up to twice as quickly (Zhang et al., 2020). Men's rapid hearing decline can be traced to exposure to intense noise (e.g., headphones and concerts) and loud work environments (e.g., construction, military, and transportation work). Hearing loss can be lessened and prevented by wearing protective equipment, such as earplugs, and by lowering the volume on smartphones. Urban street environments are a source of high level "city noise," such as sirens, horns, and loud trucks, trains, and other vehicles, that contribute to presbycusis and poor auditory health (Mayes, 2021). Screening to identify risk for hearing loss and early signs of hearing loss can help in delaying loss.

Skin

Changes in the skin are perhaps the most visible sign of aging in middle adulthood. Age-related changes in the skin are gradual and predictable. Most adults in their 30s notice lines developing on their foreheads, and by their 40s, these lines are accompanied by crow's feet around the eyes and lines around the mouth—markers of four decades of smiles, frowns, laughter, and other emotions. During middle adulthood the process continues: Skin becomes less taut as the **epidermis,** the outer protective layer of the skin that produces new skin cells, loosens its attachment to the thinning **dermis,** the middle layer of skin consisting of connective tissue that gives skin its flexibility (see Figure 13.1; Swift et al., 2021; Wiegand et al., 2017). Declines in elasticity are accompanied by the loss of fat in the **hypodermis,** the innermost layer of skin composed of fat, which leads to wrinkling and loosening of the skin (Robert & Labat-Robert, 2016). At the molecular level, skin aging is influenced by many of the aging factors discussed in Chapter 11, including oxidative stress, DNA damage, inflammation, and telomere shortening (Zhang & Duan, 2018).

FIGURE 13.1 ■ Layers of the Skin

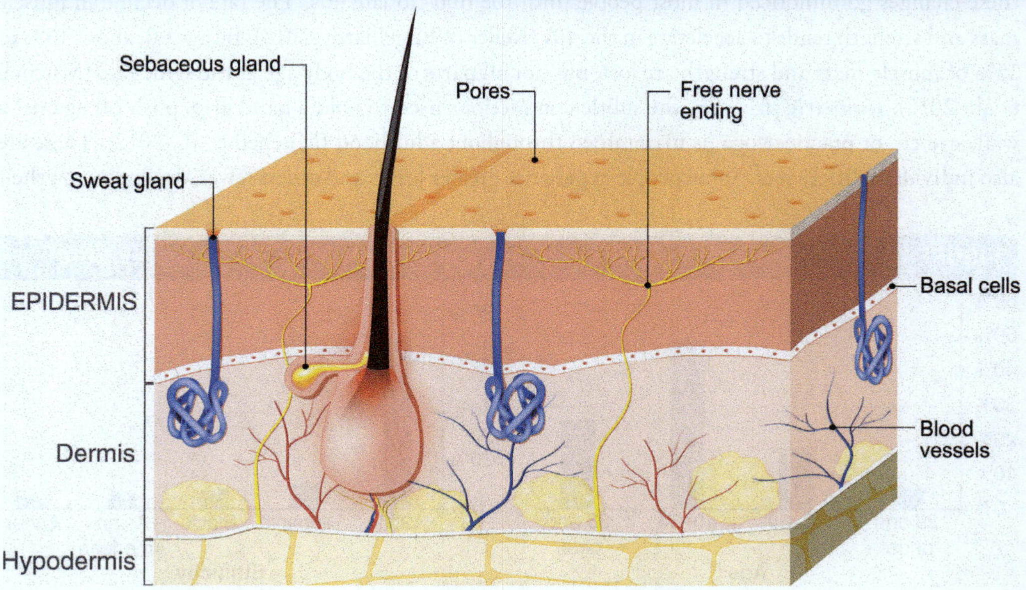

Source: iStock/ ttsz

Women tend to experience age-related changes sooner and more quickly than men. Their dermis is thinner, and as they age they experience hormonal changes that exacerbate aging, particularly a reduction in the female hormone estrogen (Castelo-Branco & Davila, 2015; Firooz et al., 2017). Although age-related changes in the skin are unavoidable, the rate of change varies dramatically with exposure to lifestyle and environmental factors, such as pollution, diet, smoking, and especially the sun's rays (McDaniel et al., 2018; Parrado et al., 2019). Exposure to the sun's rays is responsible for most of the changes in the skin that we associate with age (Zhang & Duan, 2018).

Many adults seek to improve their appearance through nonsurgical cosmetic procedures. In 2019, 18.4 million "minimally invasive" procedures—procedures that do not involve surgery—were conducted, most commonly the use of Botox injections (which paralyze facial muscles, making them unable to contract and "wrinkle"), so-called fillers (substances injected into wrinkles, temporarily filling them), and chemical peels (which remove the outermost layers of skin, to reveal smooth new skin; American Society of Plastic Surgeons, 2020). About 90% of cosmetic procedures are conducted on women and, as shown in Figure 13.2, middle-aged women are most likely to obtain cosmetic procedures (American Society of Plastic Surgeons, 2017). Nearly three-quarters of women who obtain cosmetic procedures are white.

The ethnic differences in the number of cosmetic procedures suggest that individual and contextual factors influence whether women obtain cosmetic procedures. Western cultural norms equate women's aging with a decline in physical attractiveness. There is little research on ethnic differences in cosmetic procedures, but examinations of body image suggest that at all ages, Black women tend to be more satisfied with their bodies than white women (Grabe & Hyde, 2006). As young adults, Black women report feeling less pressure to conform to Western beauty ideas as portrayed by the media and are less likely to internalize thin ideals for body shape (Warren et al., 2013). Black women may hold a multifaceted definition of attractiveness that extends beyond body size to include factors such as dress, race, and personality (Davis et al., 2010). Likewise, Black adolescent girls report defining beauty as including attitude, style, personality, and presence (Rubin et al., 2003). Cultural depictions of beauty may protect Black women from negative depictions of aging in mainstream culture. Cultural views about the wisdom that comes with age may influence adults' beliefs about their own aging and the value of cosmetic procedures. Elders, especially grandmothers, are valued in Black culture as matriarchs and sources of wisdom (Kelch-Oliver, 2011). Aging therefore may afford cultural status.

Body Composition

Muscle strength tends to peak in the 20s, followed by a small gradual decline through the 30s, but these changes go unnoticed in most people until the mid- to late 40s. The rate of decline in muscle mass and strength tends to accelerate in the 40s (Keller & Engelhardt, 2013). By age 60, about 10% to 15% of muscle mass and strength are lost, but not all parts of the body age at the same rate (Mitchell et al., 2012). **Isometric strength**, the subtle contractions used to hold a hand grip, push off against a wall, stretch, or practice yoga, is maintained throughout adulthood (Mitchell et al., 2012). There are also individual differences. Some people experience greater losses and others fewer, depending on their

FIGURE 13.2 ■ Cosmetic Procedures by Age and Ethnicity in the United States, 2016

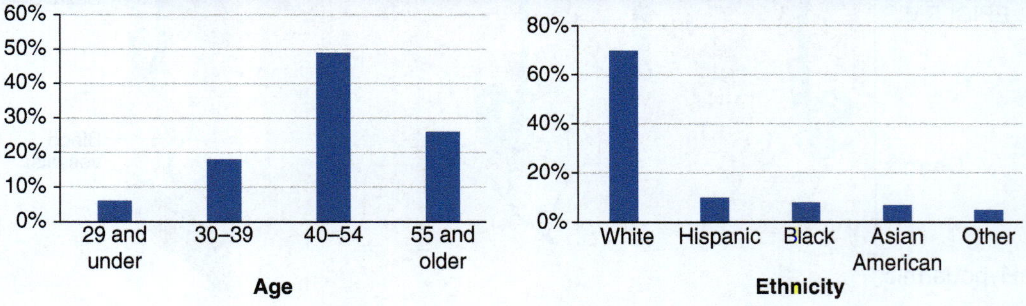

Source: American Society of Plastic Surgeons, 2017.

level of physical activity. Loss of endurance tends to occur after age 40, but the decline is generally proportionately less than that of strength (Hayslip et al., 2007).

Body composition shifts over the course of adulthood as the metabolic rate slows. Declines in muscle and bone accompany an increase in body fat. Both men and women tend to experience weight gain in middle adulthood. In men, fat accumulates on the back and upper abdomen, while women tend to experience an increase in fat in the upper arms and around the waist (Wong et al., 2020). Yet an active lifestyle with weight bearing physical activity can not only reduce muscle losses but produce gains in muscular density (Endo et al., 2020). When adults gradually reduce their caloric intake to match their reduced need for calories, such as by consuming a low-fat diet with lots of vegetables, fruits, and grains, age-related weight gain is minimized for adults, regardless of SES and ethnicity (Howard et al., 2006).

Physical activity can offset midlife losses in muscle.

Jose Luis Pelaez Inc/ Getty Images

Normal aging brings some loss of bone tissue that begins around age 40. Bone loss increases in the 50s, especially in women, whose bones have less calcium to begin with and who lose the protective influence of estrogen on bones after menopause (Gold, 2016). The bone loss that occurs with reproductive aging increases the risk of **osteoporosis**, a disorder entailing severe bone loss that leads to brittle and easily fractured bones (see Chapter 15; Sinaki, 2021). Bones become thinner, more porous, and more brittle as calcium is absorbed. As the bones that make up the vertebrae in the spinal column become thin and more brittle, the disks collapse and adults lose height, about an inch or more by age 60 and more thereafter (Hannan et al., 2012). Loss of bone density causes bones to break more easily and heal more slowly, making a broken bone more serious as we age. Losses in bone density can be slowed by behavior, such as avoiding smoking and excess drinking and engaging in weight-bearing exercise (Sinaki, 2021). Table 13.1 summarizes some of the physical changes that take place during middle adulthood.

Reproductive Aging

In middle adulthood, the level of sex hormones in the body declines in both men and women. Women experience the end of fertility. Men retain their reproductive capacity, but at a diminished level.

Reproductive Changes in Women

At about 51 years of age on average, but starting as early as age 42 and as late as 58, women experience **menopause**, the cessation of ovulation and menstruation (Santoro et al., 2021). The timing of menopause is influenced by heredity but also by lifestyle choices and contextual influences, such as exposure to pollution (Chamani & Keefe, 2019). Menopause occurs earlier in women who smoke, have not given birth, are malnourished, are exposed to pollutants, or are of lower SES (Gold et al., 2013; Grindler et al., 2015; Langton et al., 2020). A woman is said to have reached menopause one year after her last menstrual period. **Perimenopause** refers to the transition to menopause, extending approximately three years before and after menopause. It is during perimenopause that the production of reproductive hormones declines and symptoms associated with menopause first appear (McNamara et al., 2015; Santoro et al., 2021).

The first indicator of perimenopause is a shorter menstrual cycle, followed by erratic menstrual periods (Ketch et al., 2017). Ovulation becomes less predictable, occurring early or late in the cycle; sometimes several ova are released and sometimes none. This unpredictability in ovulation can sometimes lead to a "surprise" late-life pregnancy (Miller et al., 2018). Other women who waited to have children may find themselves frustrated by the unpredictability of their cycles, the accompanying difficulty getting pregnant, and the closing window of opportunity. The most common and long-lasting

TABLE 13.1 ■ Physical Development During Middle Adulthood

Physical Development	Age-Related Change
Vision	Presbyopia affects nearly all adults by age 50. Structural changes of the eye, including the cornea, lens, and retina, cause a decline in night vision.
Hearing	Presbycusis is common by the 50s with the loss first limited to high-pitched sounds and settings in which there is background noise. By late adulthood, it extends to all sound frequencies. Contextual factors, such as exposure to noise, play a role in age-related hearing loss.
Skin	Fine lines are apparent by the 30s, first on the forehead, and by the 40s as crow's feet around the eyes and lines around the mouth. Skin becomes less taut as the epidermis loosens its attachment to the dermis. The resulting loss in elasticity is accompanied by the loss of fat in the hypodermis, which leads to wrinkling and loosening of the skin. Exposure to sun rays is associated with advanced skin aging for people of all skin types and ethnicities.
Muscle	Peak muscle strength is typically reached during the 20s, followed by a gradual decline. Changes usually are not noticeable until about age 45. Loss of endurance tends to occur after age 40. Good nutrition and an active lifestyle can reduce losses and even increase muscular density.
Skeleton	Bone density peaks in the mid- to late 30s, after which adults tend to experience gradual bone loss, advancing in the 50s, especially in postmenopausal women. Losses in bone density can be slowed by behaviors such as avoiding smoking and excess drinking and by engaging in weight-bearing exercise.

symptom of perimenopause is hot flashes, in which the expansion and contraction of blood vessels cause sudden sensations of heat throughout the body accompanied by sweating (McNamara et al., 2015; Sussman et al., 2015). One-third to as many as three-quarters of U.S. women experience hot flashes, which may persist for seven or more years (Avis et al., 2015; Santoro, 2016).

Hormone Replacement Therapy **Hormone replacement therapy** is sometimes prescribed to women early in menopause to address perimenopause symptoms. Younger menopausal women aged 50–59 (or within 10 years of menopause) show benefits of HRT such as the reduction of hot flashes and other symptoms and reduced risk for cardiovascular disease without an increased risk of breast cancer or stroke (Benkhadra et al., 2015; Kotsopoulos et al., 2016; Lobo, 2017). HRT can help some postmenopausal women with health conditions such as osteoporosis, type 2 diabetes, atherosclerosis, and some cancers (Arnson et al., 2017; Gambacciani & Levancini, 2014; Panay et al., 2013). Although little research has examined ethnic differences in the effectiveness of HRT, some studies have suggested similar effects for white and Black women (Chlebowski et al., 2017; DeBono et al., 2018). Findings such as these suggest that HRT may be a reasonable option to help manage menopausal symptoms over the short term (Hickey et al., 2012). With increasing age, starting at about age 60, HRT is associated with increased risk for cardiovascular disease for some women and there is little evidence of benefits for most women (Stevenson, 2017). The U.S. Food and Drug Administration recommends that physicians prescribe the smallest dose of hormones needed to reduce menopausal symptoms and for the shortest time (Hannon, 2010). Ultimately the decision as to who should use any form of hormone replacement therapy needs to be based on the individual woman's needs, quality of life, and potential risks versus benefits.

Cultural Views of Menopause Similar to girls' reactions to menarche, how women experience menopause, whether they report severe mood changes and irritability or few psychological and physical consequences, varies with their attitudes and expectations for menopause, which are influenced by personal characteristics, circumstances, and societal views about women and aging (Delanoë et al., 2012; Nosek et al., 2012). Women who have children may view menopause as providing sexual freedom and enjoyment without the worry of contraception or pregnancy. In contrast, women who desire a family, but who have not given birth, may view menopause as the end of fertility and the possibility of child-rearing, making menopause a difficult transition (Howell & Beth, 2002). High levels of education and high SES are both associated with more positive views of menopause and fewer reports of menopausal symptoms (Goodman, 2020). Ethnicity is also related to views about menopause. African American and Mexican American women tend to hold more favorable views toward menopause than white non-Hispanic American women, often describing it as a normal part of life, one that many women look forward to (Avis et al., 2001; Sampselle et al., 2002).

Cultural depictions of menopause influence women's experience of menopause.

Ashley Cooper pics / Alamy Stock Photo

Societal and cultural views influence how menopause is perceived. In societies that value youth, women may fear the bodily changes of menopause and their perceived loss of sex appeal (Howell & Beth, 2002). On the other hand, in cultures where older women are respected and achieve social or religious power with age (e.g., powerful mother-in-law and grandmother roles), women report few complaints about menopausal symptoms (Delanoë et al., 2012). In Asian cultures, such as Japan, China, and India, where women tend to gain power and responsibility with age, women rarely report hot flashes or other menopausal symptoms (Gupta et al., 2006; Huang et al., 2010; Liu & Eden, 2007).

Similarly, Mayan women of the Yucatán achieve increased status with menopause along with freedom from child-rearing (Beyene & Martin, 2001). Many Mayan describe menopause in positive terms such as providing freedom, being happy, and feeling like a young girl again. Few report menopausal symptoms such as hot flashes (Beyene & Martin, 2001). Indeed, there is no word in the Mayan language to describe hot flashes (Beyene, 1986). Women in rural India also report menopause as a welcomed time that is accompanied by enhanced mobility, freedom from unwanted pregnancy, and increased authority (Gupta et al., 2006).

Women in Western industrialized societies tend to have mixed feelings about menopause. A sample of UK women viewed menopause in a variety of ways, as a normal biological process, a distressful transition involving identity loss, and as a liberating transformation involving biological and social change and the end of contraceptive worries (de Salis et al., 2018). Other women describe the negatives, including a loss of fertility and the physical changes that accompany it, feeling less feminine, and having a clear sign of aging (Chrisler, 2008).

When menopause is viewed as a medical event whose symptoms require treatment, women tend to view it more negatively and report more physical and emotional symptoms (Hvas & Dorte Effersøe, 2008). Recent generations of women have objected to the notion of menopause as a disease and instead view it as a naturally occurring process—a life transition (Dillaway, 2008; Hvas & Dorte Effersøe, 2008). Women's views of menopause are also colored by their experience. In the United States, postmenopausal women tend to view menopause more positively than do younger women (Avis et al., 2005). They tend to report menopause as causing few difficulties and instead view it as a beginning with positive attributes, such as being free from birth control (Rossi, 2004). This pattern may also be true cross-culturally. A study of about 1,400 women aged 40–55 from West Bengal, India revealed that postmenopausal women had more positive attitudes about menopause and aging than did perimenopausal women (Dasgupta & Ray, 2017).

Reproductive Changes in Men

Do men experience a sudden drop in reproductive ability similar to women? No. Unlike women, men's reproductive ability changes gradually and steadily over the adult years, with declines in testosterone beginning as early as age 30 in some men and continuing at a pace of about a 0.3% to 1% decrease per year to a total decline in testosterone of about 30% by age 70 (Basaria, 2013). Men's bodies produce less testosterone and they become less fertile, but about 75% of men retain testosterone levels in the normal range, with most adult males continuing to produce sperm throughout adulthood; many are able to father children into their 80s and beyond (Ehlert & Fischbacher, 2013). However, the number and quality of sperm produced declines in middle adulthood, beginning at about age 40, and offspring of older men may be at greater risk of congenital abnormalities (Almeida et al., 2017; James et al., 2021; Khan, 2017).

Although men experience gradual declines in testosterone over their lifetimes, levels can shift dramatically in response to stress and illness, creating the appearance of a "male menopause" (Shores, 2014). Stress from problems such as unemployment, illness, marital problems, children leaving home, or sexual inactivity can cause reductions in testosterone, which decreases sexual desire and responses. Low levels of testosterone may interfere with a man's ability to achieve or maintain an erection, which can influence anxiety about his sexual capacity, which can lead to further declines in testosterone (Seidman & Weiser, 2013). Sudden declines in testosterone tend to occur with stress and health problems and do not represent an inevitable biological transition (Donatelle, 2004). There is no male menopause. Regardless, media and popular views in the United States and Europe have contributed to common beliefs in a male menopause and a corresponding medicalization of masculinity in middle and older adulthood with the use of hormone and other treatments (Marshall, 2007; Vainionpää & Topo, 2006). For example, products designed to treat so-called "low T" are commonly advertised on television despite research suggesting that only about 6% to 10% of men experience symptoms of testosterone deficiency (Araujo et al., 2004; Haring et al., 2010). Similar to the medicalization of menopause, viewing normative hormonal changes experienced by men as a disease contributes to negative views of normal aging.

Thinking in Context: Lifespan Development

1. Give examples of how context may influence adults' views of the changes they experience in appearance and fertility. Consider the role of race and ethnicity, SES, culture, perceived beauty norms, views of aging, and other factors.
2. The physical changes that accompany middle adulthood can influence how adults view themselves as well as how others view and treat them. What are some of the possible implications of physical aging for adults' sense of self?

Thinking in Context: Applied developmental Science

Suppose you were invited to give a talk about the physical changes of middle adulthood to adults who are entering midlife. What information about vision, hearing, and body changes are most important for adults to know? What advice would you give for preventing or lessening the effect of these changes?

Thinking in Context: Biological Influences

Compare menopause with menarche. How is the process of menopause similar to and different from menarche? What is the role of context in shaping women's experience and perspective on each?

HEALTH

LEARNING OBJECTIVE

13.2 Identify common health conditions and illnesses during middle adulthood and the role of stress and hardiness on health.

Most middle-aged adults view themselves as healthy, but some health risks become more common (Centers for Disease Control and Prevention, 2016; Federal Interagency Forum on Aging-Related Statistics, 2016). Health status varies with contextual factors, most notably socioeconomic status. In the United States and Europe, high socioeconomic status is associated with good health (Chen & Miller, 2013; Hu et al., 2016; Mielck et al., 2014). Socioeconomic status is also related to health in low- and middle-income countries, but less so compared with high-income countries, because poor access to health resources often affects all individuals in low- and middle-income countries, across socioeconomic levels (Niessen et al., 2018; Williams et al., 2018)

Mortality

Middle-aged adults are most likely to die by cancer and heart disease, followed by unintentional injuries, of which unintentional poisoning—drug overdose—is most common (Centers for Disease Control, 2021). Life expectancy increased radically from 1900 to the early 2010s, but it has declined since 2014. The decline in life expectancy can be attributed to the increasing mortality rate among white middle-aged adults (Woolf et al., 2018). In recent decades, midlife mortality has declined dramatically for Black adults and more subtly for Hispanic adults, influenced by increased educational and socioeconomic opportunities (see Figure 13.3). Among white middle-aged adults the mortality rate increased by 9% between 2010 and 2017 (Curtin & Arias, 2018).

The rapid increase in midlife mortality is attributed to a rise in fatal drug overdoses, suicides, and alcohol-related liver diseases (Glei & Preston, 2020). Death by opioid overdose is most common (Cano, 2021). Some scientists have referred to these as "deaths of despair" because they have been concentrated among whites of low socioeconomic status and in economically depressed rural areas (Case & Deaton, 2017; Gaydosh et al., 2019). But this problem is not limited by race, socioeconomic status, and geography. Drug mortality increased most dramatically in low-SES rural counties, but rapid increases have occurred throughout the United States across race and ethnicity, socioeconomic status, and geography (Gutin & Hummer, 2020; Shiels et al., 2019).

Experts advise a combination of community- and individual-based approaches to addressing the opioid epidemic, including reducing opioid prescriptions, increasing access to substance abuse treatment, and increasing education for the public and health care professionals about the benefits of substance abuse treatment (Larney & Hall, 2019). Public information campaigns can reduce the stigma

FIGURE 13.3 ■ Mortality Trends by Race and Ethnicity Among Adults Aged 45–64: United States, 2000–2017

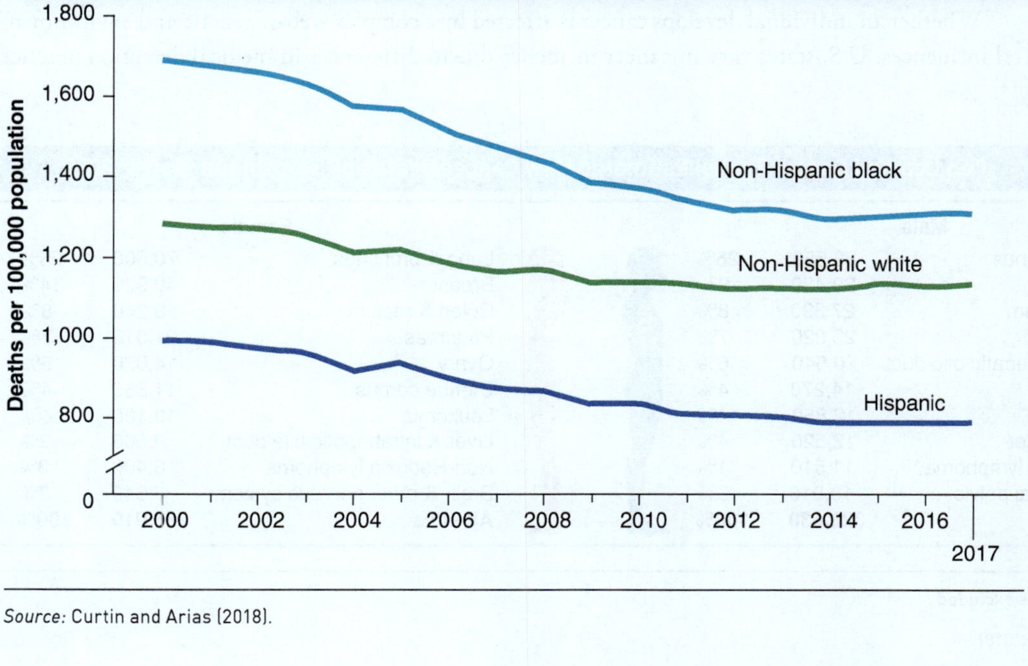

Source: Curtin and Arias (2018).

associated with seeking substance abuse treatment. In addition, although opioid overdose deaths have received the bulk of attention for increases in midlife mortality, these are just one type of "death of despair" that has contributed to the decline in life expectancy. Reducing these preventable deaths requires policies to increase access to health care and health-promoting resources, reduce unemployment and the negative effects of poverty, and increase opportunities for education and social mobility.

Common Illnesses

Cancer, cardiovascular disease, and diabetes are the leading health concerns of middle-aged adults. Note that, until recently, nearly all studies of health in adulthood were conducted on men, particularly whitemen. Women and people of color are underrepresented in research on prevention and treatment of illness. Researchers have only recently begun to address this deficit in our understanding of illness. The following sections describe what we know about common illnesses in adulthood, discussing sex and ethnic differences when possible.

Cancer

Cancer-related mortality overall has declined 26% since 1991, yet cancer remains among the top two leading cause of death in middle adulthood (Centers for Disease Control, 2021; Siegel et al., 2018). It is estimated that nearly 15% of adults will develop cancer between the ages of 50 and 69. What is cancer? Cancerous cells are abnormal cells. Everyone has some of these abnormal cells. Cancer occurs when the genetic program that controls cell growth is disrupted. When this happens, abnormal cells reproduce rapidly, undergo uncontrolled growth, and spread to normal tissues and organs (Madi & Cui, 2020; Nenclares & Harrington, 2020).

Skin cancer is the most common form of cancer. Following skin cancer, across all ages women are most likely to be diagnosed with breast, lung, and colorectal cancer and men with prostate, lung, and colorectal cancer (see Figure 13.4; National Cancer Institute, 2020). Overall, men tend to be diagnosed with cancer at a higher rate than women. Sex differences in cancer that emerge in midlife are influenced by genetics and contextual factors such as workplace exposure to toxins, health-related behaviors such as smoking, and making fewer visits to the doctor.

People of low SES tend to experience cancer at higher rates than do other adults, a difference attributable to a range of causes including inadequate access to medical care, poor diet, high levels of stress, and occupations that may place them in contact with toxins (Gupta et al., 2019; Houston et al., 2018; Kish et al., 2014). There are large ethnic differences in cancer rates: the incidence rate in Black men is 85% higher than that of Asian American men and 10% higher than non-Hispanic White men (Siegel et al., 2018).

Whether an individual develops cancer is affected by a complex web of genetic and environmental influences. U.S. states vary in cancer incidence due to differences in medical detection practice

FIGURE 13.4 ■ Ten Leading Cancer Types: Estimated New Cancer Deaths by Sex, United States, 2018

Estimated Deaths

Male			Female		
Lung & bronchus	83,550	26%	Lung & bronchus	70,500	25%
Prostate	29,430	9%	Breast	40,920	14%
Colon & rectum	27,390	8%	Colon & rectum	23,240	8%
Pancreas	23,020	7%	Pancreas	21,310	7%
Liver & intrahepatic bile duct	20,540	6%	Ovary	14,070	5%
Leukemia	14,270	4%	Uterine corpus	11,350	4%
Esophagus	12,850	4%	Leukemia	10,100	4%
Urinary bladder	12,520	4%	Liver & intrahepatic bile duct	9,660	3%
Non-Hodgkin lymphoma	11,510	4%	Non-Hodgkin lymphoma	8,400	3%
Kidney & renal pelvis	10,010	3%	Brain & other nervous system	7,340	3%
All sites	**323,630**	**100%**	**All sites**	**286,010**	**100%**

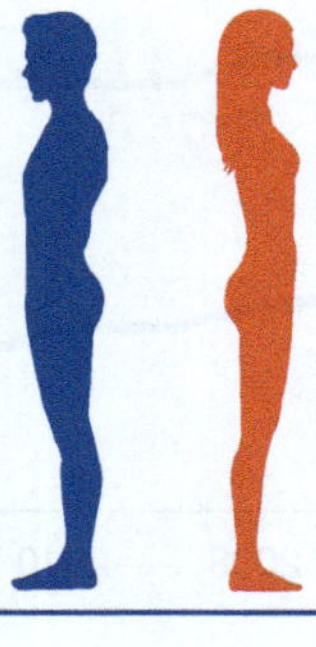

Note: Skin cancer was excluded.

Source: (Siegel et al., 2018).

and the prevalence of risk factors, such as smoking, obesity, and other health behaviors, as well as the national distribution of poverty and access to medical resources (Nguyen et al., 2016). The large geographic variation in lung cancer occurrence reflects the historical and continuing differences in smoking prevalence between states (Jemal et al., 2008). Lung cancer incidence rates in Kentucky, where tobacco is grown and is part of the local economy and smoking prevalence continues to be highest, are about 3.5 times higher than those in Utah, where smoking prevalence is lowest (Siegel et al., 2018).

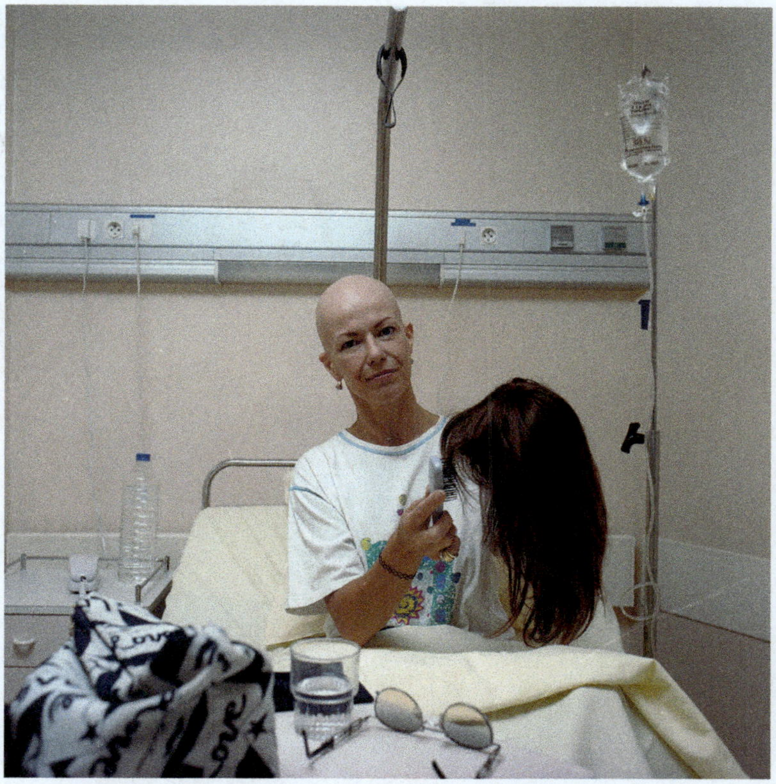

Cancer rates have declined over the last two decades and survival rates have risen to nearly three-quarters of diagnoses, but it remains a leading cause of mortality in middle age. Manuel Litran / Contributor/ Getty

Scientific breakthroughs have increased our knowledge of genetic risk factors for cancer. Women can be tested for mutations in the genes responsible for suppressing the proliferation of breast cancer cells. Genetics, however, is not destiny. Only about 35% to 50% of women who test positive for the genetic mutation actually develop breast cancer (Stephens et al., 2012). Whether a genetic risk factor for breast cancer leads to developing breast cancer can be influenced by a variety of other risk factors, such as heavy alcohol use, being overweight, the use of oral contraceptives, exposure to toxins, and low socioeconomic status (Khan et al., 2010; Nickels et al., 2013). Women who show more genetic mutations are more likely to develop breast cancer especially early in life, often before age 30 (Stephens et al., 2012). Early-onset breast cancers (prior to age 45) account for about 10% of diagnoses (Chelmow et al., 2020). They are largely inherited, are often invasive, and spread quickly.

In contrast, late-onset breast cancers, diagnosed in older adulthood, tend to grow more slowly, are less biologically aggressive, and are influenced by extended exposures to environmental risk factors and the disruptions in cell division that occur with aging (Anderson et al., 2014; Benz, 2008). Although it is commonly believed that a diagnosis of cancer is a death sentence, survival rates vary by cancer type and today's medical advances permit more people to survive cancer, defined as surviving at least 5 years after remission, than ever before.

Cardiovascular Disease

About 40% of men and women age 40–59 have heart disease (Benjamin et al., 2018). **Cardiovascular disease**, commonly referred to as heart disease, is responsible for more than one-quarter of all deaths of middle-aged Americans each year (see Figure 13.5; National Center for Health Statistics, 2015). Markers of cardiovascular disease include hypertension (high blood pressure), high blood cholesterol, plaque buildup in the arteries (atherosclerosis), irregular heartbeat, and, particularly serious, heart attack (blockage of blood flow to the heart caused by a blood clot occurring within a plaque-clogged coronary artery; Elias & Dore, 2016; Koh et al., 2010). Cardiovascular disease can also cause a stroke, a blockage of blood flow to brain cells, which can result in neurological damage, paralysis, and death. A stroke occurs when a blood clot, often originating in the coronary arteries, travels to the brain or when a clot forms in the brain itself.

Awareness of the symptoms of heart attack is critical to surviving it. The most commonly experienced symptom of heart attack is chest pain—uncomfortable pressure, squeezing, fullness, or pain in the chest that may come and go or persist (Ferry et al., 2019). Other symptoms include discomfort or pain in other areas of the upper body, especially the left arm but also the back, neck, jaw, or stomach. Shortness of breath, nausea, or light-headedness can also occur. Cardiovascular disease has been

FIGURE 13.5 ■ Cardiovascular Disease

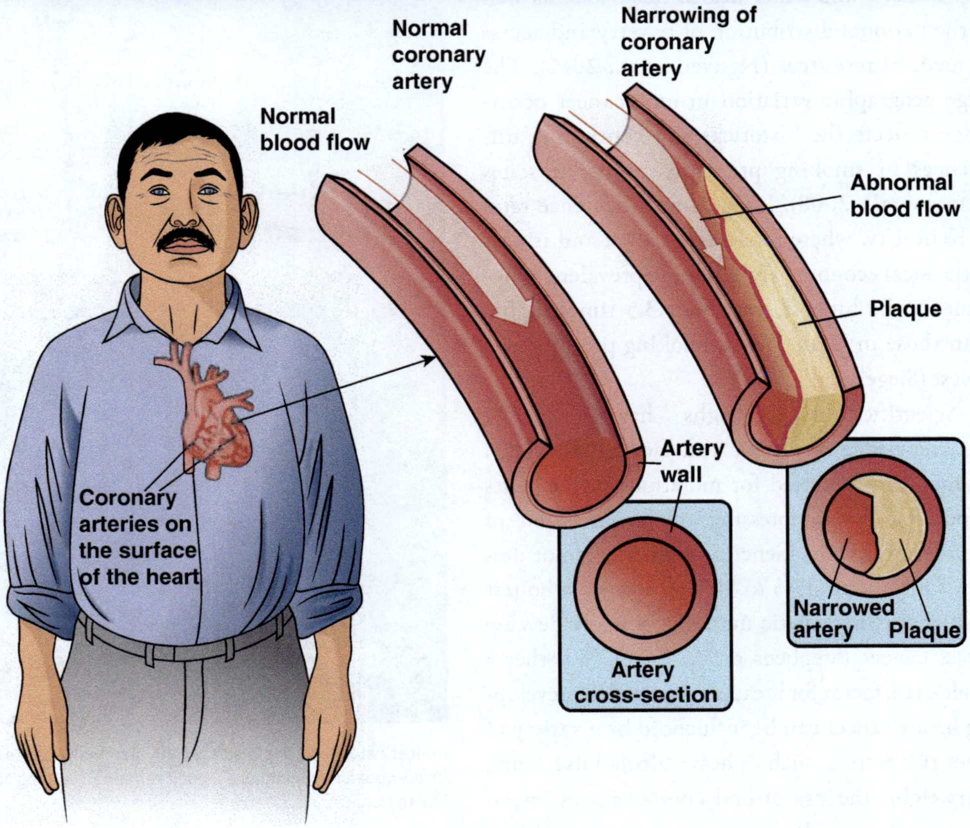

stereotypically viewed as an illness affecting men, as men are more likely to be diagnosed with cardiovascular disease, but women also experience high rates.

Many people are unaware that women tend to show different symptoms of heart attack (Smith et al., 2018). Women are less likely to report chest pain than men. When they do, women are more likely to describe it as pressure or tightness than pain (Mehta & Yeo, 2017). Women are more likely than men to report mild discomfort the left shoulder or arm, or throat or jaw, and feeling tired, nauseous, dizzy, or suddenly weak (Keteepe-Arachi & Sharma, 2017). Because of these differences, many women do not recognize their symptoms as severe and life threatening (Madsen & Birkelund, 2016). For these reasons, women are more likely than men to die from cardiovascular disease, especially heart attack (Murphy et al., 2017).

Risk factors for cardiovascular disease include heredity, age, a diet heavy in saturated and trans fatty acids, and smoking (Badimon et al., 2017; Hanson, 2019). Hypertension (high blood pressure), a risk for heart attack, occurs in more than half of U.S. adults aged 40 to 59 and three-quarters of adults over age 60 (Ostchega et al., 2017). Anxiety, psychological stress, and a poor diet have negative effects on the heart and contribute to hypertension and cardiovascular disease (Backé et al., 2012; Holt et al., 2013). As shown in Table 13.2, various behaviors can help to prevent heart disease; genetic factors also contribute to cardiovascular disease risk (Kalayinia et al., 2018).

Treatment for cardiovascular disease varies depending on the severity. Medication and behavioral changes, such as increasing physical activity, changing diet, and consuming more fish oil, may reduce hypertension and cholesterol levels (Elias & Dore, 2016). In more severe cases, surgery may be recommended. Angioplasty involves threading a tube into the arteries and inflating a tiny balloon to flatten plaque deposits against the arterial walls and enable blood to flow unobstructed. A stent is often placed to prevent the artery from narrowing again after the balloon is removed. In serious cases, a health-care provider may recommend coronary bypass surgery, in which damaged coronary blood vessels are replaced with those from the leg.

TABLE 13.2 ■ Preventing Heart Disease

Guideline	Description
Don't smoke or use tobacco.	Smokers have more than twice the risk of heart disease. Chemicals in tobacco and cigarette smoke, including nicotine and carbon monoxide, make your heart work harder by narrowing your blood vessels and increasing blood pressure, leading to atherosclerosis and potentially a heart attack.
Reduce blood cholesterol levels.	Heart disease risk increases along with blood cholesterol levels. Cholesterol contributes to the formation of plaque inside the heart's arteries, leading to atherosclerosis.
Control high blood pressure.	Blood pressure is the force of blood pushing against the walls of the arteries as the heart pumps blood. High blood pressure increases the risk of heart attack and damage to the arteries and heart.
Exercise regularly.	Exercise lowers your risk of heart disease. Regular exercise will also help lower "bad" cholesterol and raise "good" cholesterol. Research has shown that getting at least 30 minutes of moderate physical activity on five or more days of the week can help lower blood pressure, lower cholesterol, and keep your weight at a healthy level.
Follow a heart-healthy diet.	Eat a diet low in fat, cholesterol, and salt and rich in fruits, vegetables, whole grains, and low-fat dairy products. Limit red meat, a source of unhealthy fat, and increase consumption of low-fat sources of protein such as beans and fish. Fish is a source of omega-3 fatty acids, a type of healthy fat, which may decrease your risk of heart attack, protect against irregular heartbeats, and lower blood pressure.
Achieve and maintain a healthy weight.	Excess weight strains your heart and is associated with heart disease factors such as diabetes, high blood pressure, and high cholesterol.
Manage stress and anger.	Stress can increase the risk factors for heart disease. People under stress may overeat, start smoking, or smoke more than they otherwise would.

Cardiovascular or heart disease is the second most common cause of death for middle-aged adults (and third for young adults). Behavioral choices play a large role in the development of heart disease. Follow these guidelines to reduce your risk of heart disease.

Diabetes

After each meal we eat, the body digests and breaks down food, releasing glucose into the blood. Insulin, a hormone released by the pancreas, maintains a steady concentration of glucose in the blood, and excess glucose is absorbed by muscle and fat. **Diabetes** is a disease marked by high levels of blood glucose. Diabetes occurs when the body is unable to regulate the amount of glucose in the bloodstream because there either is not enough insulin produced (type 1) or the body shows insulin resistance and becomes less sensitive to it, failing to respond to it (type 2; American Diabetes Association, 2014). Symptoms of diabetes include fatigue, great thirst, blurred vision, frequent infections, and slow healing. When glucose levels become too low, hypoglycemia occurs with symptoms of confusion, nervousness, and fainting. Hyperglycemia is characterized by overly high glucose levels, also resulting in serious illness. Managing diabetes entails careful monitoring of the diet and often self-injection of insulin, which permits the body to process glucose, critical to body functioning.

About 18% of adults aged 45–64 have diabetes, rising to about 27% of adults over the age of 65 (Centers for Disease Control, 2020). Diabetes is the fifth leading cause of death among people aged 55 to 64 and sixth leading cause of death among people aged 45 to 54 and 65 and older (Centers for Disease Control, 2021). Figure 13.6 presents sex and ethnic differences in diabetes diagnoses. African American, Mexican American, and Canadian Aboriginal people are diagnosed with diabetes at higher rates than European Americans because of epigenetic factors (interactions among genetic predispositions) and contextual factors, such as differences in diet, activity levels, exposure to toxins, and health that accompany socioeconomic inequities and poverty (Cheng et al., 2019; Hill-Briggs et al., 2021). Epigenetics play a large role in influencing diabetes risk (Franks & Pare, 2016). Diabetes risk

FIGURE 13.6 ■ Diabetes Prevalence by Age, Sex, and Ethnicity

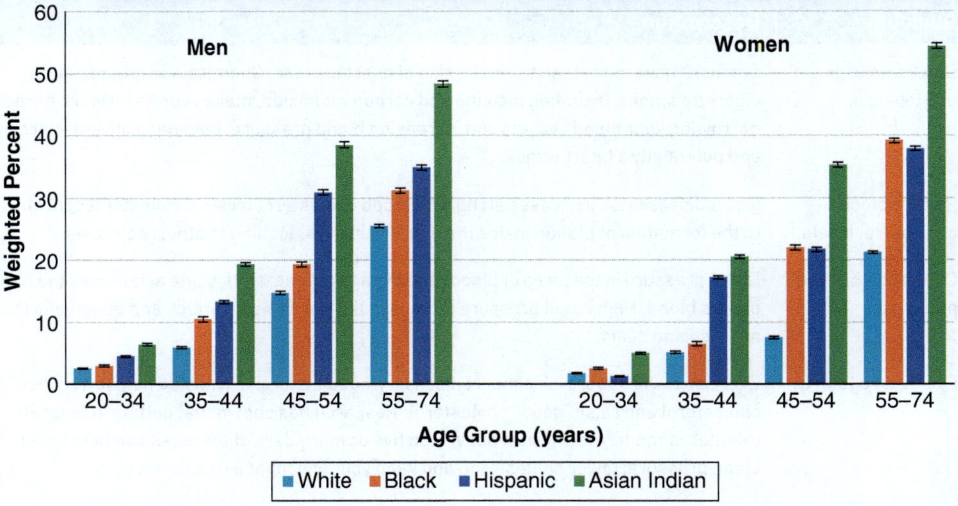

Source: Gujral et al. (2016).

is influenced by genetic propensities that interact with behaviors such as diet and exercise (Jannasch et al., 2017; Leong et al., 2016).

People with diabetes are at risk for a variety of health problems, such as heart attack, stroke, circulation problems in the legs, blindness, and reduced kidney functions (DeFronzo & Abdul-Ghani, 2011). Although women are about as likely as men to be diagnosed with diabetes, for largely unknown reasons, women with diabetes experience a much larger risk for heart attack and stroke than men (Peters et al., 2014). Diabetes has serious cognitive effects including impairments in executive function, processing speed, memory, and motor function (Biessels & Whitmer, 2020; Palta et al., 2014). Over time, diabetes is associated with accelerated brain aging, including losses of gray matter, abnormalities in white matter, and a heightened risk of dementia and Alzheimer's disease in older adults (Espeland et al., 2013; Kuehn, 2020; Roberts et al., 2014). Depression is two to three times more common among people with diabetes compared to their peers, and they are more likely to experience chronic depression (Roy & Lloyd, 2012). Adults with depression are less likely to follow dietary restrictions, comply with medication, and monitor blood glucose—behaviors associated with worse outcomes, including increased risk of mortality (Naicker et al., 2017; van Dooren et al., 2013).

Diabetes poses cognitive and health risks. Managing diabetes entails careful monitoring of the diet and often self-injection of insulin to regulate levels of glucose in the body.

iStock/ FatCamera

Maintaining a healthy weight through diet and exercise is a powerful way of preventing diabetes. Individuals can successfully manage the disease by adopting a diet that carefully controls the amount of sugar entering the bloodstream as well as engaging in regular exercise (American Diabetes Association, 2014; Jannasch et al., 2017). Frequent blood testing permits the individual to monitor his or her glucose levels and take insulin when needed to lower levels of glucose in the blood. Coping with diabetes requires a great deal of self-monitoring and self-care, but appropriate self-treatment enables adults to manage this chronic illness and live an active life.

Stress and Health

Stress is a part of every person's life. Daily hassles such as traffic, childcare difficulties, work deadlines, and conflict with family and friends are small stresses that can quickly accumulate to influence our mood, ability to cope, and views of our health (Graf et al., 2017). Often referred to as the "sandwich generation," many middle-aged adults are pressed to meet not only the multiple demands of career and family but often the demands of caring for two generations, their children and their own parents. The resulting stress can influence their mood, ability to cope, and even their health.

Stress

Stress is physiologically arousing. When people experience stress, they respond with a "fight-or-flight" stress response in which cortisol is released and the body readies for action, raising blood pressure and heart rate. The fight or flight response can motivate behavior, but if experienced daily in response to an excess of daily hassles, the cortisol response can impair health (McEwen, 2018). Middle-aged adults experience elevated cortisol responses on days that they care for their aging parents and more favorable levels of cortisol on days they care for their children, suggesting that providing daily support to parents may be particularly stressful (Fuentecilla et al., 2020). Adults' perception of daily hassles is linked with their physical health symptoms and well-being (Graf et al., 2017; Piazza et al., 2019). On days when adults experience greater stressors, they are more likely to engage in poor health behaviors such as smoking (Stubbs et al., 2017).

Chronic stress is associated with acute illnesses, such as cold and flu, as well as chronic illnesses, such as hypertension, arteriosclerosis, cardiovascular disease, cancer, and autoimmune diseases (e.g., lupus and chronic fatigue syndrome; Esler, 2017; Marsland et al., 2017; O'Connor et al., 2021). Chronic stress is associated with higher rates of anxiety and depression and can be a trigger for experiencing mental illnesses, such as bipolar disorder and schizophrenia (Gershon et al., 2013; Juster et al., 2011; Segerstrom & O'Connor, 2012). Exposure to daily stressors is linked with long-term health outcomes, higher mortality, and greater reactivity to stress, thereby worsening the stress response (Jeong et al., 2016; Mroczek et al., 2015).

Stress Reactivity

Adults vary in their sensitivity to stress. Some adults are more reactive (show greater responses) to stress than other people. The stress response and negative consequences of stress tend to be higher in adults who have experienced childhood trauma as well as those who live in low-SES communities (Agorastos et al., 2019; Schieman & Koltai, 2017). Physiological responses to stress, especially the reactive release of cortisol, can be programmed early in life (Lê-Scherban et al., 2018). Responses that may be adaptive in response to significant stressors are often maladaptive in response to mild daily stressors (O'Connor et al., 2021). Adults who show greater reactivity and slower recovery to a laboratory stressor are more likely to show poor cardiovascular health over time (Turner et al., 2020) Similarly, heightened reactivity to daily stressors is associated with biomarkers for inflammation (Sin et al., 2015).

People often respond to stress with a "fight-or-flight" response that can motivate behavior in times of danger, but if experienced in response to daily hassles it can impair physical and psychological health.

iStock/DGLimages

People who score high on measures of hostility and anger, who tend to view others as having hostile intentions and are easily angered, are more sensitive to stress and are at risk for negative health outcomes, such as heart disease and atherosclerosis (Brydon et al., 2010; Friedman & Kern, 2014). Anger is physiologically arousing—stress hormones course through the body, increasing heart rate and blood pressure. Frequent angry displays and ruminating about events that invoke anger and other negative emotions can lead to high blood pressure that persists and, ultimately, heart disease (Brydon et al., 2010; Ohira et al., 2008).

Hardiness and Stress

Some adults are better able than others to adapt to the physical changes of midlife and the stress wrought by the changes in lifestyle that accompany midlife transitions, such as juggling career with caring for children and parents. These adults display the personal characteristic that researchers refer to as **hardiness** (Maddi, 2016, 2020a). Individuals who display hardiness tend to have high self-efficacy, a sense of control over their lives and experiences. They also view challenges as opportunities for personal growth and feel a sense of commitment to their life choices.

Hardy individuals tend to appraise stressful situations more positively, viewing them as manageable; approach problems with an active, problem-focused coping style; and show fewer negative reactions to stressful situations (Maddi, 2020b; Vogt et al., 2008). The positive appraisals and sense of control that come with hardiness serve a protective function as they are associated with lower emotional reactivity, lower average blood pressure, slower progression of cardiovascular disease, and positive self-ratings of physical and mental health (Maddi, 2013; Sandvik et al., 2013). People who score low in hardiness tend to feel less control; experience more negative reactions to stressful situations; and are more likely to use an emotion-focused style of coping, such as avoidance or denial, which is maladaptive to health and functioning and is associated with higher stress in response to stimuli (Ayala Calvo & García, 2018).

Hardiness can be learned. Training in hardy skills and attitudes, such as coping, social support, relaxation and stress reduction, nutrition, and physical activity, can increase feelings of control, challenge, and commitment that are central to hardiness (Bartone et al., 2016). Hardiness has a protective effect on job burnout and can enhance adults' experiences in the workplace (Ayala Calvo & García, 2018).

Social support can buffer the negative emotional and health consequences that accompany psychological stress. It is associated with lower cortisol levels, suggesting a reduced fight-or-flight response (Ditzen et al., 2008). In addition, when people learn to control their reactions to stress by using relaxation techniques, meditation, and biofeedback, they can reduce the incidence and severity of illness (Sharma & Rush, 2014). Exercise can also reduce stress and promote health and wellness (Gerber & Pühse, 2009). Physically fit individuals show less psychological reactivity (e.g., spikes in blood pressure) and better recovery from psychological stressors than do unfit individuals (Forcier et al., 2006).

Overall, daily stress tends to decline and feelings of well-being increase in the second half of middle adulthood, from age 50 on (Stone et al., 2017). Fortunately, most people tend to show more adaptive responses to stress as they progress through middle adulthood. They learn to anticipate stressful events, take steps to avoid them, and approach stressful situations with more realistic attitudes about their ability to change them (Aldwin & Levenson, 2001). Overcoming stressful conditions and personal challenges contributes to a growing sense of self-efficacy during middle adulthood.

Individuals' sense of hardiness can be enhanced by learning stress management and coping techniques, such as meditation.

iStock/FatCamera

Thinking in Context: Intersectionality

Discuss how health in midlife is influenced by the interaction of race and ethnicity, sex, and SES. How are these factors associated with the incidence of cancer, cardiovascular disease, diabetes, and overall mortality? What are some reasons for these relationships? Consider differences in opportunities, environmental risks, supports, and exposure to injustice.

Thinking in Context: Biological Influences

Genetic tests can reveal whether an individual has a gene for an illness such as cancer. What does a positive test, suggesting the presence of the gene for an illness, mean? Considering the influence of lifestyle and epigenetics (from Chapter 2), what advice would you give to a person who has the gene for an illness such as cancer?

COGNITIVE DEVELOPMENT

LEARNING OBJECTIVE

13.3 Summarize changes in intelligence and cognitive capacities during middle adulthood, including attention, memory, processing speed, and expertise.

We have seen that there are many, mostly gradual, physical changes that occur in middle adulthood. Are the physical changes of middle adulthood accompanied by cognitive changes? Recall from Chapter 8that the Weschler Intelligence Scales measure a variety of cognitive skills and abilities that comprise intelligent adaptive functioning, such as knowledge, nonverbal abilities, and processing speed. These abilities can be grouped into two forms of intelligence: fluid and crystallized.

Fluid and Crystallized Intelligence

Intelligent people have a broad knowledge base acquired through experience and education. This accumulation of facts and information comprises **crystallized intelligence** (Horn & Cattell, 1966; Horn & Noll, 1997). Examples of crystallized intelligence include memory of spelling, vocabulary, formulas, and dates in history. People who score high on measures of crystallized intelligence not only know more but they learn more easily and remember more information than do people with lower levels of crystallized intelligence (Brown, 2016).

While crystallized intelligence refers to accumulated knowledge, **fluid intelligence** refers to a person's underlying capacity to make connections among ideas and draw inferences. Fluid intelligence permits flexible, creative, and quick thought, which enables people to solve problems quickly and adapt to complex and rapidly changing situations. Information processing abilities, such as attention, speed of analyzing information, and especially working memory capacity, influence fluid intelligence (Burgoyne et al., 2019; Ellingsen & Ackerman, 2016). Fluid and crystallized intelligence are independent components of intelligence, but they interact in the sense that the basic information processing capacities that embody fluid intelligence make it easier for a person to acquire knowledge and develop crystallized intelligence (Nisbett et al., 2013).

Fluid and Crystalized Intelligence in the Adult Years

How do intellectual abilities change during adulthood? The groundbreaking Seattle Longitudinal Study was the first to comprehensively examine intellectual change over the course of adulthood. In 1956, researcher K. Warner Schiae collected data from multiple cohorts of adults aged 22 to 70. These individuals were followed at regular intervals and new samples of adults were added every few years. Over six decades the Seattle Longitudinal Study has examined more than 5,000 men and women, yielding both cross-sectional comparisons (comparing people of different ages at once) and longitudinal data (following individuals over a 60-year period). This design enabled Schaie to study the effects of age (change over time) and cohort (change over generations; Schaie, 2013, 2016).

As shown in Figure 13.7, cognitive abilities show different patterns of change. Components of crystallized intelligence, such as verbal ability and verbal memory, increase into middle adulthood,

FIGURE 13.7 ■ Longitudinal Changes in Crystallized and Fluid Intelligence During the Adult Years

Longitudinal research shows stability over the adult years in most intellectual competencies, especially crystallized abilities, with declines occurring in late adulthood. In contrast, fluid abilities, such as perceptual speed, show steady decline throughout the adult years.

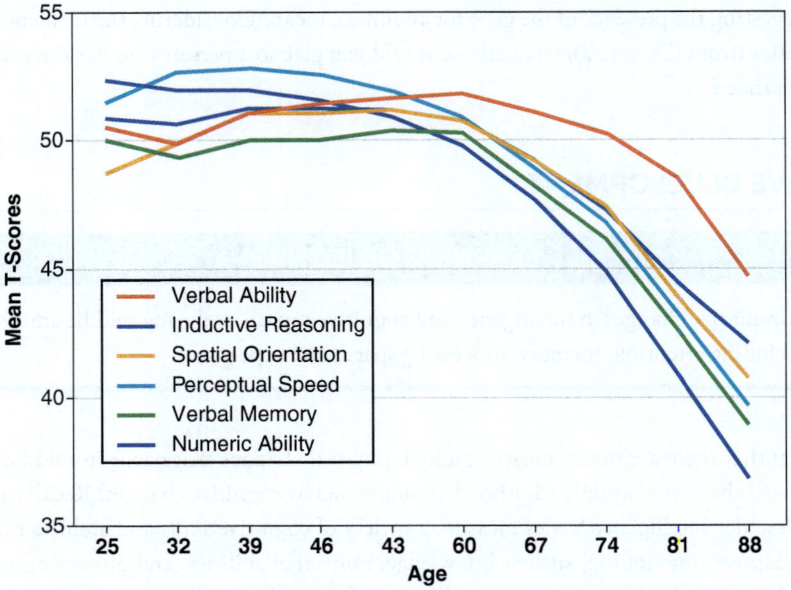

Source: Schaie (2013).

suggesting that individuals expand and retain their wealth of knowledge over their lifetimes (Schaie, 2013, 2016). Fluid intelligence, such as perceptual speed, spatial orientation, and numeric ability, decreases in early adulthood, suggesting that cognitive processing slows with age. In contrast, inductive reasoning, generally thought a fluid intellectual ability, is maintained through middle adulthood to age 60, influencing adults' abilities to adapt to their changing environments. These patterns of growth in crystallized intelligence through middle adulthood, coupled with gradual declines in fluid intelligence, have been shown in several samples (Anderson & Craik, 2017; Hartshorne & Germine, 2015). In late adulthood all intellectual abilities decline (Schaie, 2013).

Why does fluid intelligence decline during the adult years? Declines in performance on tasks measuring fluid intelligence may be due to the biological slowing of the central nervous system, including reductions in frontal lobe functioning, neural interconnectivity, and efficiency, and changes in working memory (Geerligs et al., 2014; Ramchandran et al., 2019; Unsworth et al., 2014). Although fluid intelligence shows marked declines with age, it often goes unnoticed in everyday functioning because gains in crystalized intelligence help adults compensate and adapt (Kievit et al., 2018; Zaval et al., 2015).

Overall, intellectual ability is largely maintained during the adult years, especially when individuals are engaged in complex occupational and leisure activities—which are more common among recent cohorts (Schaie, 2013; Schmiedek, 2017). One study examined adult workers over a 17-year period and found that periodically experiencing intellectual challenge in the form of novel work tasks was associated with better processing speed, working memory, and gray mater volume in areas associated with learning and that show age-related decline (Oltmanns et al., 2017).

Cohort Effects in Intelligence

The Seattle Longitudinal Study demonstrated that there are large cohort effects in intelligence, suggesting that people are getting "smarter" with each generation. Known as the *Flynn Effect*, scores on IQ measures increased by about 3 IQ points each decade from 1909–2013, as measured in 31 countries (Flynn, 1984, 2012; Pietschnig & Voracek, 2015). Meta-analyses have shown that patterns of IQ gains are closely associated with historical events. Gains were strong between World Wars I and II but showed a marked decrease during the World War II years and a rise following the 1940s, perhaps reflecting the influences of poor nutrition and marked environmental stress experienced by the general population in regions that were most affected by the World Wars (Pietschnig & Voracek, 2015; see Figure 13.8).

The Flynn effect occurs in developed countries, but the gains are especially pronounced in developing countries, such as Kenya, Sudan, China, Brazil, Argentina, and many Caribbean nations (Colom et al., 2007; Flynn, 2012; Flynn & Rossi-Casé, 2012). The generational increase in IQ is thought to be a function of contextual factors, such as changes in nutrition, health care, education, and environmental stimulation (Lynn, 2009; te Nijenhuis, 2013; Trahan et al., 2014). With each generation, young people complete more years of education and have more exposure to testing. In addition, advanced levels of education tend to emphasize logic and self-expression, which are among the skills measured by intelligence tests (Baker et al., 2015; Williams, 2013). If IQ scores are influenced by contextual improvements, such as education and health care, as living conditions optimize in industrialized countries, IQ scores should plateau (Nisbett et al., 2013). Yet a large meta-analysis of 285 studies, involving more than 14,000 participants since 1951, suggests that the Flynn effect is still at work, yielding an increase of about 2.3 IQ points each decade (Trahan et al., 2014). Likewise, studies of older adults in 10 European countries showed continued high scores relative to earlier cohorts (Hessel et al., 2018; Munukka et al., 2020).

Cognitive Development in Middle Adulthood

We have seen that middle-aged adults experience gradual shifts in intellectual abilities. What do these changes mean for cognition? Similar to findings on fluid and crystalized intelligence, age-related group differences in cognition begin to appear in midlife, but longitudinal studies do not document within-person declines in cognitive performance before the seventh decade of life (Karlamangla et al., 2014). Research on cognitive development in adulthood tends to compare the tail ends of adulthood, young adults and older adults. Most theorists assume that midlife performance falls somewhere in between that of the young and older adults. Although some evidence suggests small gradual changes in

FIGURE 13.8 ■ Gains in IQ, 1909–2013

Domain-specific IQs gain trajectories for 1909-2013. Changes are based on weighted average annual IQ changes in all available data.

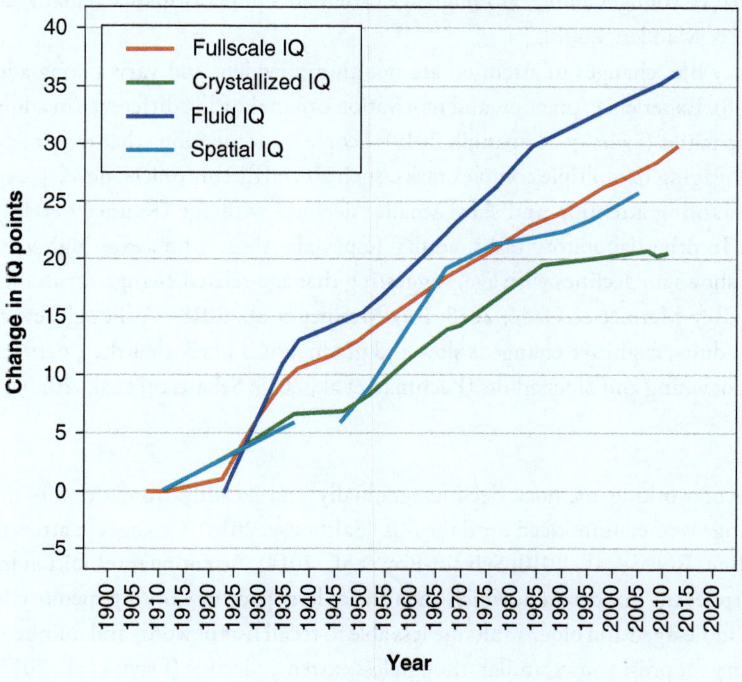

Source: Pietschnig & Voracek, 2015.

As she paints, this woman must attend carefully to the subject of her painting and her technique. She must ignore distracters and irrelevant stimuli.

David Burch/ Getty Images

cognitive abilities over midlife, few studies examine this period in life (Cornelis et al., 2019; Infurna et al., 2020; Sebastiani et al., 2020).

Attention

Researchers who study attention examine how much information a person can attend to at once, the ability to divide attention and focus from one task to another in response to situational demands, and the ability to selectively attend and ignore distracters and irrelevant stimuli. From middle adulthood into older adulthood each of these tasks becomes more difficult (Hartley & Maquestiaux, 2016; Künstler et al., 2018). Consider tasks measuring the cocktail party effect—the ability to follow one conversation and switch to another, such as at a party. When adults are presented with two streams of words to the left and right ear, they are less able to report information from either stream with age, suggesting declines in the ability to monitor two sets of stimuli, selectively attend, and switch attention (Passow et al., 2012). The deficit increases as the number of target speakers adults must listen to increases (Meister et al., 2020).

With age, adults show more difficulty inhibiting or resisting interference from irrelevant information (Campbell et al., 2020; Zanto & Gazzaley, 2017). For example, in a laboratory task, participants are presented with a series of letter combinations and told to press the space bar only when they see a particular combination (such as T-L); they are to ignore all other combinations. In such tasks, adults' performance declines steadily from the 30s on (Sylvain-Roy et al., 2014). But the stimuli and task matter in attention tasks. Adults show better performance on tasks that use social stimuli, such as photos of faces, rather than objects (Federico et al., 2021). Practice improves performance and reduces age-related decline. Training in how to divide attention between two tasks by using selective attention, switching back and forth between mental operations, improves the performance of older adults as much as that of younger adults, although age differences in performance remain (Ballesteros et al., 2017; Kramer & Madden, 2008).

In everyday life, changes in attention are not always evident and vary among adults (Kramer & Madden, 2008). Experience, practice, and motivation can make a big difference in adults' information-processing capacities (Swirsky & Spaniol, 2019). People in occupations that require detecting critical stimuli and engaging in multiple complex tasks, such air traffic controllers, develop expertise in focusing and maintaining attention and show smaller declines with age (Kennedy et al., 2010; Morrow et al., 2003). In other laboratory tasks, adults' (especially those who assess high-value information) performance shows no declines with age, suggesting that age-related changes in attentional inhibition are complex (Rey-Mermet & Gade, 2018; Rey-Mermet et al., 2018). Although few studies examine middle-aged adults, cognitive change is slow and gradual; it is likely that their performance score lies between that of young and older adults (Lachman et al., 2015; Sebastiani et al., 2020).

Memory

The capacity of working memory declines gradually and steadily from the 20s through the 80s, although change is often unnoticed until the 60s. (Salthouse, 2016). Changes in attention are related to memory decline (Rowe et al., 2010; Sylvain-Roy et al., 2014). Attentional inhibition makes it difficult to tune out irrelevant information, which then leaves less space in working memory for completing a given task. Middle-aged and older adults are less able to recall lists of words and numbers than are young adults; memory for prose shows similar, though less extreme, decline (Davis et al., 2017; Old & Naveh-Benjamin, 2008). Age differences in performance on working memory tasks can be partially explained by a decline in the use of memory strategies, specifically organization and elaboration (Chevalère et al., 2020; Craik & Rose, 2012). Both of these strategies require the person to link new information with existing knowledge. From middle adulthood into old age, adults begin to have more difficulty retrieving information from long-term memory, which makes them less likely to spontaneously use organization and elaboration as memory strategies.

Laboratory tests of memory in middle-aged adults are influenced by factors such as motivation, task, and experience. Laboratory studies may not accurately measure the everyday memory capacity of middle-aged and older adults.

BSIP/Newscom

Many laboratory tests of memory entail tasks that are similar to those encountered in school settings. Middle-aged and older adults may be less motivated by such tasks than younger adults who likely have more recent experience in school contexts. Laboratory findings, therefore, may not accurately illustrate the everyday memory capacity of middle-aged and older adults (Salthouse, 2012). When the pace of a memory task is slowed, permitting more encoding time, or when participants are reminded to use organization or elaboration strategies, middle-aged and older adults show better performance (Bartsch et al., 2019; Braver & West, 2008). In addition, the type of task influences performance. In one study, adults aged 19 to 68 completed memory tests under two conditions: a pressured classroom-like condition and a self-paced condition. When participants were shown a video and tested immediately (classroom-like condition), younger adults showed better recall than did the middle-aged adults. However, when participants were given a packet of information and a video to study on their own (self-paced condition), young and midlife adults did not differ on recall three days later (Ackerman & Beier, 2006). The midlife adults performed better when they could apply their own strategies and memorize the material at their own pace.

Age-related declines in memory evident in laboratory research are less apparent in everyday settings (Salthouse, 2012, 2016). Knowledge of facts (e.g., scientific facts), procedures (e.g., how to drive a car), and information related to one's vocation either remain the same or increase over the adult years (Schaie, 2013). Adults' experience and knowledge of their cognitive system (metacognition) enable them to use their memory more effectively. They increasingly use external supports and strategies to maximize their memory, such as by organizing their notes or placing their car keys in a designated spot where they can reliably be found (Schwartz & Frazier, 2005). As with attention, memory declines vary with the individual and task. Most adults compensate for declines and show little to no differences in everyday settings, but chronic stress and negative affect impair working memory (Lee & Goto, 2015; Rowell et al., 2016). Midlife adults who feel overwhelmed in daily life, such as those faced with many conflicting responsibilities and stressors that demand a great deal of multitasking, are more likely to rate their memory competence as poor (Vestergren & Nilsson, 2011). Mothers of children with disabilities reported more stress and showed more declines in episodic memory than other mothers (Song et al., 2016). The ability to manage distraction, a skill that can be taught, is associated with better performance on working memory tasks (Lorenc et al., 2021).

Processing Speed

The greatest age-related change in information processing capacity is a reduction in the speed of processing. Simple reaction time tasks, such as pushing a button in response to a light, reveal a steep decline (slowing of responses) from the 20s into the 90s (see Figure 13.9; Elgamal et al., 2011; Salthouse, 2016; Sebastiani et al., 2020). The more complex the task, the greater the age-related slowing of reaction time. Yet when reaction time tasks require a vocal response rather than a motor response, age-related declines are less dramatic, suggesting that reaction times may be influenced by motor speed (Low et al., 2017). In addition, adults' performance on standard tasks measuring processing speed is influenced by their capacities for attention. Adults who are highly distractible show slowed responding on standard tasks measuring processing speed, but their performance improves when tasks are designed to reduce distractions (such as by listing fewer items on a page; Lustig et al., 2006; Zanto & Gazzaley, 2017).

FIGURE 13.9 ■ Processing Speed Across the Lifespan

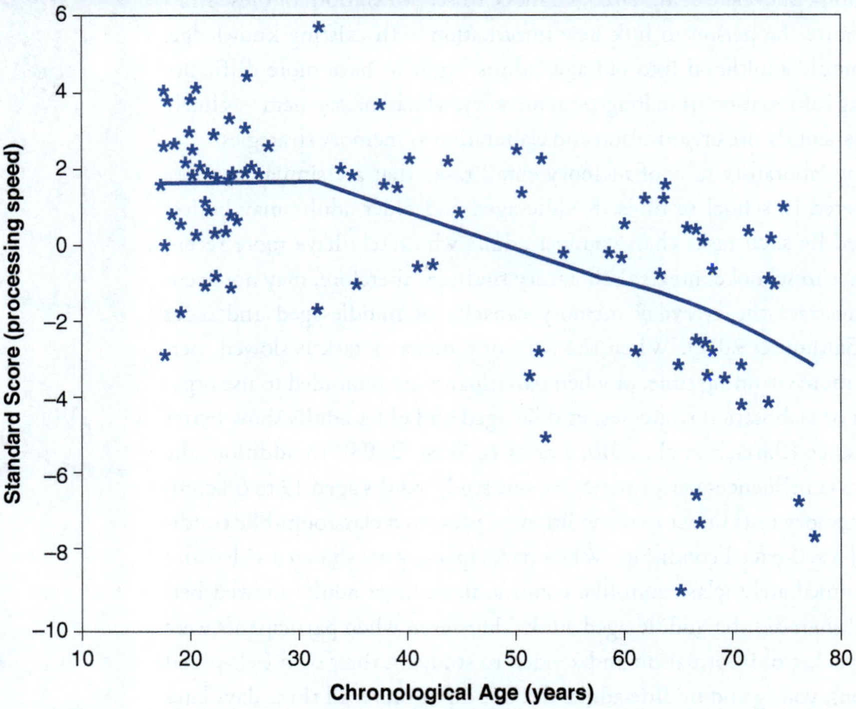

Source: Adapted from Elgamal et al, 2011.

Task-relevant factors, such as adults' interest and level of engagement, also influence adults' performance (Daniëls et al., 2020).

Changes in the brain underlie reductions in processing speed. The loss of white matter—myelinated connections—reduces processing speed (Chopra et al., 2018; Nilsson et al., 2014). In addition, the loss of neurons forces the remaining neurons to reorganize and form new, often less efficient, connections (Salthouse, 2017). Changes in processing speed influence many of the cognitive declines associated with aging. Declines in processing speed with age predict age-related declines in memory, reasoning, and problem-solving tasks (Park & Festini, 2017; Salthouse & Madden, 2013). Moreover, the relationship between processing speed and performance on cognitive tasks becomes stronger with age (Chen & Li, 2007; Salthouse & Pink, 2008).

Yet, like attention and memory, the decline in the speed of processing is not as apparent in everyday situations as it is in laboratory tests. Middle-aged and older adults proficiently engage in complex tasks every day, showing performance similar to, or better, than that of younger adults. A classic study tested 19- to 72-year-olds on two tasks: a reaction time task and a typing task. Both tasks measured their speed and accuracy. Although the middle-aged and older adults displayed slower reaction time as compared with young adults, their typing speed and accuracy were no different (Salthouse, 1984). With age, adults compensated for their slower reaction time by looking farther ahead in the material to be typed, thereby anticipating keystrokes (Salthouse, 1984). Adults naturally compensate for declines in processing speed by modifying their activities to emphasize skills that rely on accumulated knowledge and thereby honing their crystallized intelligence (Salthouse, 2016). Most people experience cognitive change as a gradual process across adulthood (Sebastiani et al., 2020).

Expertise

Over the course of midlife into old age, many adults gain extensive experience and training in a given area. They develop **expertise**, an elaborate and integrated knowledge base that underlies extraordinary proficiency in a given task (Ericsson, 2017). Experts are not distinguished by extraordinary intellect but by a combination of inherent ability and extensive knowledge and experience (Fadde & Sullivan, 2020;

Hambrick et al., 2018). Expert knowledge is transformative in that it permits an intuitive approach to problems (Ericsson, 2014). Experts' responses are automatic—well rehearsed, seemingly without thought. This automaticity enables them to process information more quickly and efficiently, and it makes complex tasks routine (Herzmann & Curran, 2011). As expertise grows, experts find that their responses become so automatic that it is hard for them to consciously explain what they do. Adults are better than children at tying shoelaces, yet children are far better than adults at explaining how to tie shoelaces (McLeod et al., 2005).

In 2009 Captain Sully Sullenberger successfully executed an emergency water landing of U.S. Airways Flight 1549 in the Hudson River off Manhattan, New York City. He explained to CBS News anchor Katie Couric: "One way of looking at this might be that for 42 years, I've been making small, regular deposits in this bank of experience, education, and training. And on January 15 the balance was sufficient so that I could make a very large withdrawal."

Todd Sumlin/MCT/Newscom

In addition to operating more intuitively and automatically, expert behavior is strategic. Experts have a broader range of strategies—and have better strategies—than novices and can better apply them in response to unanticipated problems (Ericsson & Moxley, 2013). Despite showing slower working memory, experts maintain their performance in their areas of expertise, often by relying on external supports, such as notes (Morrow & Schriver, 2007). In one study, airplane pilots engaged in a flight simulation in which they were given directions from air traffic controllers and allowed to take notes. The experienced pilots were more likely to take notes than the nonexpert pilots, and their notes tended to be more accurate and complete (Morrow et al., 2003). In actual flights comparing pilots aged 22 to 76, older pilots took more notes than younger pilots but did not differ in their ability to repeat complex instructions regarding flight plans and conditions. Similarly, expert golfers show fewer declines in performance with age as they compensate for their changing capacities (Ericsson & Pool, 2016; Logan & Baker, 2007). Longitudinal research with expert chess players showed few age effects in chess skill. Players with greater expertise and who have participated in more tournaments showed fewer age-related declines in chess performance, but they performed similarly to nonexpert chess players in other areas (Moxley & Charness, 2013; Roring & Charness, 2007). Intuitive and automatic application of a broad range of strategies permits experts to be more flexible than nonexperts. Experts are more open to deviating from formal procedures when they encounter problems. Experts often approach cases in an individualized way, varying their approach with contextual factors, and are sensitive to exceptions (Ericsson, 2017; Ormerod, 2005).

Expertise permits **selective optimization with compensation**, the ability to adapt to changes over time, optimize current functioning, and compensate for losses in order to preserve performance despite declines in fluid abilities (Baltes & Carstensen, 2003). It is expertise that enables middle-aged and older adults to compensate for declines in processing speed and memory (Ericsson & Moxley, 2013). The typists described earlier compensated for declines in reaction time by looking farther ahead in the material to be typed (Salthouse, 1984). One study examined 20- to 60-year-old food service workers in several areas: strength and dexterity, technical knowledge (e.g., of the menu), organizational skills (e.g., setting priorities), and social skills (e.g., providing professional service). Although middle-aged workers showed declines in physical abilities, they performed more efficiently and competently than did young adults, suggesting that expertise compensated for losses in physical strength and dexterity (Perlmutter et al., 1990).

As people age, they intuitively select and optimize aspects of functioning in which they excel, improving their abilities (Bugg et al., 2006; Salthouse, 1984). In addition to emphasizing their strengths, people naturally devise ways of compensating for declines in physical functioning and fluid ability. Selective optimization with compensation occurs naturally, often without the individual's awareness as their expertise permits them to adapt to developmental changes. Successful aging entails selective optimization with compensation (Freund & Baltes, 2007). The cognitive changes of middle adulthood are summarized in Table 13.3.

TABLE 13.3 ■ Cognitive Change During Middle Adulthood

Cognitive Capacity	Age-Related Change
Crystallized intelligence	Crystallized intelligence increases steadily over the adult years and declines modestly in late adulthood.
Fluid intelligence	Fluid intelligence begins to decline in the 20s and continues to decline throughout adulthood.
Attention	With age, adults show more difficulties with divided attention and inhibition. Declines tend to vary with the individual and task. Most healthy adults compensate for declines and, until old age, show few differences in everyday settings.
Working memory	The capacity of working memory declines from the 20s through the 60s. Changes in working memory are influenced by declines in attention and in the use of memory strategies, such as organization and elaboration, that occur with age. Declines tend to vary with the individual and task. Most healthy adults compensate for declines and, until old age, show few differences in everyday settings.
Processing speed	Processing speed declines steadily from the 20s into the 90s. The more complex the task, the greater the age-related decline in reaction time. Declines in processing speed with age predict age-related declines in memory, reasoning, and problem-solving tasks, and the relationship between processing speed and performance on cognitive tasks becomes stronger with age.
Expertise	With age, most adults develop and expand their expertise. It is expertise that permits middle-aged and older adults to compensate for declines in processing speed.

Thinking in Context: Lifespan Development

1. Why do we typically find large cohort differences in intellectual abilities? Consider the contextual changes that accompany recent generations. Consider your own experiences with those of your parents, grandparents, and even great-grandparents. How were your worlds different, and how might this contribute to differences on intelligence measures?
2. Uncle Mike says, "Social media is making us dumber." Considering intelligence, do you think he's correct? To what degree might technology influence generational differences in fluid and crystalized intelligence, if at all? Explain.
3. Give examples of how cognitive declines apparent in laboratory settings are less apparent in everyday life. Why do adults tend to show higher functioning in real-world settings than in the laboratory?

Thinking in Context: Applied Developmental Science

Suppose you wanted to study intelligence in middle adulthood.

1. Discuss your concerns in selecting a research design (see Chapter 1). What are some issues that you might expect using a cross-sectional design? Longitudinal?
2. Describe the sequential research design. How might you apply it in your research? What are some of the challenges you might face or concerns you might have in using this design?

Thinking in Context: Intersectionality

1. Given what we know about the relationship between stress and cognitive performance in adulthood, how might challenging and traumatizing contexts, such as those involving exposure to poverty, violence, racism, and discrimination, influence adults' functioning? What might you expect?

2. As a developmental scientist, how might you study the relation of trauma and cognitive performance? How would you define trauma? What aspects of cognition would you examine? Who would you study? Where might you obtain participants?

CAREERS IN MIDDLE ADULTHOOD

LEARNING OBJECTIVE

13.4 Discuss career-related concerns of middle-aged adults, including influences on job satisfaction, experiences with age discrimination, and planning for retirement.

Throughout adulthood, work is often the mainstay that structures people's days, contributes to a sense of identity and self-esteem, and provides a number of benefits aside from income. Through work, people have opportunities to interact with others; to display generativity by creating products, items, and ideas and by advising and mentoring others; and to contribute to the support of their families and communities. How do people's work experience and views of work change over adulthood?

Job Satisfaction

A job is a source of income, but job satisfaction is influenced by more than salary. The gender pay gap, whereby women tend to earn less than men, tends to grow with age. In 2015, among full-time workers aged 20–24, women were paid 90% of what men were paid on a weekly basis (AAUW, 2017). By the time workers reach 55–64 years of age, women are paid only 74% of what their male peers are paid. Paradoxically, women tend to show higher job satisfaction than men or, in some cases, similar levels of satisfaction to men (Donohue & Heywood, 2014; Zou, 2015). One explanation for the gender difference lies in work orientations and preferences for extrinsic versus intrinsic rewards. Men tend to emphasize the extrinsic rewards of work, such as high salaries, benefits, and achievement, and may remain in a job that they find less intrinsically satisfying because of those rewards (Linz & Semykina, 2013). Women tend to value intrinsic rewards, such as the pleasures of surmounting challenges, engaging in creative pursuits, and being productive; in midlife they report feeling more pride in their work (Magee, 2015). Job satisfaction is predicted by extrinsic rewards for men and both intrinsic and extrinsic rewards for women (Linz & Semykina, 2013). Extrinsic rewards, such as salary, are not always within adults' control, perhaps accounting for lower job satisfaction in men.

Samples of adults from the United States, Europe, China, Turkey, and Japan show that age is generally associated with increases in job satisfaction (Barnes-Farrell & Matthews, 2007). Age-related increases in satisfaction are related to shifts in reward preferences. Young adults tend to gravitate toward jobs that emphasize extrinsic rewards such as high salaries and employee benefits whereas middle-aged employees tend to place greater importance on the intrinsic rewards of work, such as friendships with coworkers, job satisfaction, self-esteem, and feeling that one is making a difference (Heidemeier & Staudinger, 2015; Kehr et al., 2018).

Age-related increases in job satisfaction are greater for professionals than blue-collar workers (Ng & Feldman, 2010). Blue-collar workers tend to have more highly structured jobs with fewer opportunities to control their activities than do white-collar workers, which may contribute to their relatively lower level of job satisfaction (Avolio & Sosik, 1999; Hu et al., 2010). Men in physically demanding occupations, such as laborers and construction workers, may find that the physical changes that occur over the course of middle adulthood make them less able to perform the tasks their jobs require (Gilbert & Constantine, 2005). In addition, older workers face increased risk of experiencing age discrimination, discussed later in this chapter.

Adults' views of themselves and their employability changes with age. They tend to perceive themselves as less employable than young adults (Peters et al., 2019). Many may hold beliefs, real or imagined, that others view them negatively as slow, out of touch, inflexible, or grumpy (Finkelstein et al., 2013). Fears about age discrimination and the difficulty of being hired in a job market competing with young, fresh, and eager young adults may increase older workers' vulnerability to job insecurity (Yeves et al., 2019). Job insecurity refers to instability and unpredictability in employment, the perceived or real potential to lose one's job as employers downsize, outsource labor, and demand that employees be more productive with less support (Shoss, 2017). Perceived job insecurity is inversely related to intrinsic and extrinsic job satisfaction and well-being (Charkhabi, 2019; Yeves et al., 2019). The negative impact of job insecurity onjob satisfaction may be higher for older workers, especially when job insecurity is related to retirement concerns (Gaines et al., 2018). Job insecurity is also associated with increased risk for burnout (Blom et al., 2018).

Job burnout refers to a sense of mental exhaustion that accompanies long-term job stress, excessive workloads, and reduced feelings of control. (Lubbadeh, 2020). Burnout is relatively frequent in professions that are interpersonally demanding and whose demands may exceed workers' coping skills, such as in the helping professions of health care, human services, and teaching (Malinen & Savolainen, 2016; Shanafelt et al., 2015). Employee burnout is a serious problem in the workplace, not simply through its association with poor job satisfaction. Burnout is linked with impairments in attention and concentration abilities, depression, illnesses, poor job performance, workplace injuries, and high levels of employee absenteeism and turnover (Deligkaris et al., 2014; von Känel et al., 2020). When workers receive social support, assistance in managing workloads and reducing stress, and opportunities to participate in creating an attractive workplace environment, they are less likely to experience job burnout (Lubbadeh, 2020).

Age Discrimination

With their increased lifespan, better health, and later childbearing relative to prior generations, middle-aged and older adults are spending more years in the workforce than their parents and grandparents. Workers over 50 are often valued for their experience, knowledge, and ability to keep cool in crisis (Dennis & Thomas, 2007). Yet older workers are also at risk to experience age discrimination in the workplace. Examples of age discrimination include older workers being turned down for a job or promotion in favor of younger workers who are paid less or being disproportionately targeted in company layoffs. Other less obvious "soft" forms of age discrimination include being excluded from important meetings and key assignments, receiving impolite remarks or jokes about age, encountering stereotypes, or being referred to as "too old" for something (Stypinska & Turek, 2017). Age discrimination in online job applications may include dropdown menus for years that go back only to a particular decade, such as the 1980s, effectively screening out anyone who graduated or had work experience before those dates (Terrell, 2017).

The Age Discrimination in Employment Act (ADEA), signed in 1967 by President Lyndon B. Johnson, specifies that employment must be based on ability and not influenced by age, thereby prohibiting age discrimination in the workplace. Although illegal, age discrimination is common. One recent study examined the prevalence of age discrimination by sending three résumés that differed only in respondent age (about ages 30, 40, and 65) to 13,000 jobs posted online in 12 U.S. cities (Neumark et al., 2017). Even though the résumés listed identical skills and experience, older candidates, especially women, were less likely to receive callbacks from employers.

Women are more likely to report experiencing age discrimination than men (Perron, 2018). Women who report age discrimination tend to report greater financial strain and lower levels of life satisfaction

(Shippee et al., 2019). Black adults are more likely to report age discrimination than Hispanic and white adults (Perron, 2018). Research with UK adults supports the finding that people of color are more likely to experience age discrimination (Drydakis et al., 2018). Age discrimination is not unique to the U.S. or UK. It has been documented in 29 countries (Bratt et al., 2018).

Age discrimination may first emerge at about age 50. One study of 15,000 adults over the age of 50 found that those in midlife, specifically ages 50–59, reported more instances of unfair treatment than the older age groups but were less likely to attribute their experiences to age discrimination (Giasson et al., 2017). Other research following adults aged 51 and older for 4 years found gradual increases in perceived age discrimination at work that were related to increases in older employees' depressive symptoms and declines in their job satisfaction and overall self-rated health (Marchiondo et al., 2019). These results suggest that there is a "wear and tear" effect in which perceptions of age discrimination tend to worsen as workers age and accumulate examples of discrimination. Employees of all ages who report age discrimination tend to experience lower job satisfaction and less perceived control at work (Taylor et al., 2017). Age discrimination experiences are associated with poor psychological well-being, health, and affect (Stokes & Moorman, 2020). Perhaps most notably, the majority of adults who experience age discrimination do not report it (Perron, 2018).

Planning for Retirement

Retirement planning is a process that often begins once the adult becomes aware that retirement is looming on the horizon, but it should begin much earlier. Retirement planning is important because retirement represents a major life transition, and adults who plan ahead for the financial and lifestyle changes that accompany retirement tend to show better adjustment and greater life satisfaction (Adams & Rau, 2011). We will examine the retirement transition and accompanying lifestyle changes in Chapter 16. Here we examine the financial planning required to fund retirement.

Although most U.S. adults will spend many years in retirement, most are not financially prepared for it. It is estimated that workers should plan for retirement income of at least 70% to 80% of their current pre-retirement income, yet about one-third of middle-class households have no savings, including nearly 20% of adults aged 55 to 61 (Wells, 2014). People with a college degree are more likely to have some retirement savings (80%) than those with some college (56%), a high school degree (47%), or no high school degree (24%; Morrissey, 2019). White non-Hispanic adults are more likely to have some retirement savings (80%) than Black (64%) or Hispanic (61%) adults, but only about half of U.S. adults report feeling that they are on track to meet their retirement goals (Federal Reserve, 2020).

Median retirement savings account balances are low for all U.S. adults. In 2015, the median retirement account savings balance among all households headed by adults aged 44–49 was $13,000; $11,000 for adults age 50–55; and about $21,000 for adults 56–61 (Morrissey, 2019). There are also large racial disparities in the amount of retirement savings, with white non-Hispanic adults having saved more than three times as much as those who are Black or Hispanic (a median of $80,000, $29,000, and $23,000, respectively; Morrissey, 2019). Income disparities associated with low levels of education and social inequities experienced by members of marginalized groups contribute to ethnic and racial differences in retirement savings.

Retirement planning is also influenced by psychological factors. Adults with more positive beliefs about their ability to control aspects of aging are more likely to financially plan for retirement than are those with an intermittent, rather than constant, awareness of the aging process (Heraty & McCarthy, 2015). The COVID-19 pandemic of 2020–2021 is likely to have long-term negative implications for retirement planning (Hanspal et al., 2020). Unexpected job losses and furloughs coupled with stock market volatility derailed some adults' financial planning, with especially detrimental outcomes for those approaching retirement age. Some adults withdrew retirement savings to make ends meet while unemployed or underemployed. Given depleted retirement accounts and gaps in savings due to the pandemic, many may defer retirement.

Thinking in Context: Lifespan Development

1. What are some of the contextual factors that might influence job satisfaction?
   - Consider the type of job, location, individual characteristics and skills, and demographic characteristics such as sex, ethnicity, and socioeconomic status.
   - What conditions are likely to predict high satisfaction? What factors might be associated with poor job satisfaction or job burnout?
   - What can be done to help adults be happier at work? What can employers do? What advice can you give workers?

2. Suppose you were to create an intervention or workshop to encourage middle-aged adults to plan for their retirement.

   - What information would you include?
   - Identify considerations in advising middle-aged adults, such as their family status (children's age and needs), physical development, health, and career status.
   - How might your workshop and advice vary based on adults' individual differences and circumstances?

CHAPTER SUMMARY

13.1 Summarize the physical changes that occur during middle adulthood.

Presbyopia and presbycusis are common in middle adulthood. Declines in strength and endurance become noticeable, but the rate and extent of change is influenced by physical activity. Men and women tend to gain body fat and lose muscle, but these changes can be offset by reducing caloric intake and remaining physically active. Bone density peaks in the mid- to late 30s, after which adults tend to experience gradual bone loss, advancing in the 50s, especially in postmenopausal women. Menopause is reached at about age 51 and is most commonly accompanied by hot flashes. The timing of menopause is influenced by heredity but also by lifestyle choices. Women's experience of menopause is influenced by many factors, including culture and the use of hormone replacement therapy. Men's reproductive ability declines gradually and steadily over the adult years, but most men continue to produce sperm throughout adulthood.

13.2 Identify common health conditions and illnesses during middle adulthood and the role of stress and hardiness on health.

Cancer and chronic health conditions, such as cardiovascular disease and diabetes, are the result of a complex web of genetic and environmental influences. Risk factors for cardiovascular disease include heredity, high blood pressure, poor diet, smoking, and psychological stress. Diabetes, marked by high levels of glucose, increases the risk for heart attack and stroke. Advances in medicine have changed the nature of disease. More people survive cancer than ever before. Medication and behavioral changes may reduce hypertension and cholesterol and glucose levels. Chronic stress is associated with acute and chronic illnesses. Training in coping, social support, relaxation and stress reduction, nutrition, and physical activity can increase feelings of control, challenge, and commitment that are central to hardiness.

13.3 Summarize changes in intelligence and cognitive capacities during middle adulthood, including attention, memory, processing speed, and expertise.

The Seattle Longitudinal Study has shown a cross-sectional drop in fluid intelligence after the mid-30s but also a longitudinal gain in crystallized intelligence in midlife that is sustained into the 60s. There are large cohort effects in intelligence, related to changes in contextual factors such as access to nutrition, health care, education, and environmental stimulation.

With age, it becomes more difficult to divide attention to engage in two complex tasks at once and focus on relevant information as well as to inhibit irrelevant information. The capacity of working memory declines with age because of a decline in the use of memory strategies and changes in attention. Processing speed declines from early adulthood through the middle to late adult years. Cognitive changes are less apparent in everyday life than in lab contexts. An expanding knowledge base, experience, and growing expertise permits most adults to show few changes in cognitive capacity in everyday contexts and demonstrate selective optimization with compensation for declines.

13.4 Discuss career-related concerns of middle-aged adults, including influences on job satisfaction, experiences with age discrimination, and planning for retirement.

Although the gender pay gap grows with age, women tend to report higher job satisfaction than men. Job satisfaction is predicted by extrinsic rewards, often uncontrollable rewards, for men and both intrinsic and extrinsic rewards for women. Age-related increases in job satisfaction are related to shifts in preferences toward intrinsic rewards. With age, job insecurity increases when older workers perceive themselves as less employable than young adults. Age discrimination may first emerge at about age 50. Women and people of color are most likely to report experiencing age discrimination. Employees of all ages who report age discrimination tend to experience lower job satisfaction and poor psychological well-being, health, and affect. Most adults who experience age discrimination do not report it. Retirement is a major life transition, and adults who plan ahead for the financial and lifestyle changes that accompany retirement tend to show better adjustment and greater life satisfaction. Most adults are not financially prepared for retirement. There are large education, income, and racial disparities in retirement savings.

KEY TERMS

cardiovascular disease (p. 401)
crystallized intelligence (p. 407)
dermis (p. 393)
diabetes (p. 403)
epidermis (p. 393)
expertise (p. 412)
fluid intelligence (p. 407)
hardiness (p. 406)
hormone replacement therapy (p. 396)
hypodermis (p. 393)
isometric strength (p. 394)
job burnout (p. 416)
menopause (p. 395)
osteoporosis (p. 395)
perimenopause (p. 395)
presbycusis (p. 392)
presbyopia (p. 392)
selective optimization with compensation (p. 413)

With age, it becomes more difficult to divide attention to engage in two complex tasks at once and focus on relevant information, as well as to inhibit irrelevant information. The capacity of working memory declines with age because of a decline in the use of memory strategies and changes in attention. Processing speed declines from early adulthood through the middle to late adult years. Cognitive changes are less apparent in everyday life than in lab contexts. An expanding knowledge base, experience, and growing expertise permits most adults to show few changes in cognitive capacity in everyday contexts and demonstrate selective optimization with compensation for declines.

13.4 **Discuss career-related concerns of middle-aged adults, including influences on job satisfaction, experiences with age discrimination, and planning for retirement.**

Although the gender pay gap grows with age, women tend to report higher job satisfaction than men. Job satisfaction is predicted by extrinsic rewards, often more tangible rewards for men and both intrinsic and extrinsic rewards for women. Age-related increases in job satisfaction are related to shifting preferences toward intrinsic rewards. With age, job insecurity increases when older workers perceive themselves as less employable than younger adults. Age discrimination may first emerge at about age 50. Women and people of color are most likely to report experiencing age discrimination. Employees of all ages who report age discrimination tend to experience lower job satisfaction and poor psychological well-being, health, and affect. Most adults who experience age discrimination do not report it. Retirement is a major life transition, and adults who plan ahead for the financial and lifestyle changes that accompany retirement tend to show better adjustment and greater life satisfaction. Many adults are not financially prepared for retirement. There are large education, income, and racial disparities in retirement savings.

cardiovascular disease (p. 401)
crystallized intelligence (p. 407)
dermis (p. 378)
diabetes (p. 403)
epidermis (p. 375)
expertise (p. 412)
fluid intelligence (p. 407)
hardiness (p. 406)
hormone replacement therapy (p. 396)
hypodermis (p. 378)
isometric strength (p. 379)
job burnout (p. 416)
menopause (p. 395)
osteoporosis (p. 377)
perimenopause (p. 395)
presbycusis (p. 382)
presbyopia (p. 382)
selective optimization with compensation (p. 413)

14

SOCIOEMOTIONAL DEVELOPMENT IN MIDDLE ADULTHOOD

Terry Vine/Getty Images

Ramon attends a parent-teacher conference at his daughter's elementary school. Lena helps her son move into his college dorm. Danielle kisses her baby on the cheek as she drops her off at childcare. Hal is ecstatic to meet his newborn grandchild. Each of these individuals is 45 years old. These middle-aged adults have very different life experiences and occupy a variety of roles: parent to an infant, parent to an older child, parent to a college student, and grandparent—yet all are middle-aged adults.

Middle adulthood spans a broad period of life, from roughly age 40 to 65. Over these two and one-half decades, we undergo many life changes. Similar to other periods in life, concerns, priorities, and developmental tasks shift over middle adulthood (Hutteman et al., 2014). The timing of these tasks varies dramatically with life circumstances. A 40-year-old parent to an infant faces different concerns than a 40-year-old parent to an emerging adult. Likewise, the experience of parenting an emerging adult may vary for a 40-year-old parent compared with a 55-year-old parent. Just as parenting tasks change over time, career concerns shift from achieving and maintaining professional status early in midlife to preparing for retirement in the late 50s and 60s. In this chapter, we explore socioemotional development in middle adulthood; changes in developmental tasks; and changes in middle adults' sense of self, personality, relationships, and career.

PSYCHOSOCIAL DEVELOPMENT IN MIDDLE ADULTHOOD

LEARNING OBJECTIVE

14.1 Examine psychosocial development in midlife, including changes in generativity, the sense of meaning in life, and sexuality.

Compared to childhood and old age, middle adulthood has come under study very recently and is perhaps the least-understood period of life (Infurna et al., 2020; Lachman et al., 2015). Middle adulthood consists of several decades during which adults hold multiple changing roles as spouse, parent, grandparent, caregiver, and worker. Developmental concerns change over the decades, yet we know relatively little about these shifts and adults' adjustment during this period. Popular views associate middle age with psychological awakening and growth, as well as crises. These conflicting views suggest that there are multiple paths through middle adulthood, many factors influence outcomes for better or worse, and well-being and life satisfaction vary among middle-aged adults.

Is Midlife Characterized by Crisis?

The 45-year-old who purchases a red convertible sports car; the middle-aged person who unexpectedly leaves a spouse and moves out of the home, beginning a new life in a new city; the midlifer who is suddenly gripped with anxiety over the future, the fear that half of life is over, and despair that life has not turned out as planned and little time remains to make changes—each of these people embodies aspects of the most popular stereotype about middle age. Depicted in television dramas and self-help magazine articles, the **midlife crisis** is proposed as a stressful time in the early to middle 40s when adults are thought to evaluate their lives. The term arose in the public consciousness in the 1970s after publication of several popular books, including *Seasons of Life*, in which Daniel Levinson (1978) articulated his theory of adult development, discussed later in this chapter.

Although the existence of a midlife crisis is widely accepted among laypersons (Wethington, 2000), research is at odds with this popular view. Surveys of adults over age 40 have revealed that only about 10% to 20% report having experienced a midlife crisis (Wethington et al., 2004). A period of crisis or psychological disturbance is not a universal midlife experience. Adults show individual differences and crises occur at various periods of life (Brim et al., 2004; McCrae & Costa, 2006; Rosenberg et al., 1999). Adults who believe that they have experienced a midlife crisis have usually experienced upheavals at other times in their lives (Freund & Ritter, 2009). Personal characteristics may determine whether middle adulthood, or any other point in life, is experienced as a crisis. Men who scored higher on measures of psychological problems earlier in adulthood were more likely to report experiencing a midlife crisis 10 years later than were men who scored lower on psychological problems (McCrae & Costa, 2006). Outside events that can occur at any time in adulthood, such as job loss, financial problems, or illness, may trigger responses that adults and their families may interpret as midlife crises (Beutel et al., 2010).

Middle adulthood is unquestionably a transition and is perhaps the most stressful time in life, given changes in adults' bodies, families, careers, and contexts. Most developmental scientists adopt the perspective that midlife represents a transition similar to the transition to adulthood; it entails creating, clarifying, and evaluating values, goals, and priorities (Lachman et al., 2015). A close examination of this kind can lead to insights about oneself, revisions in identity, and decisions to revise life plans (Rathunde & Isabella, 2017). Most adults respond to these changes by making minor adjustments, creating turning points in their lives rather than dramatic changes. If they cannot revise their life paths, they try to develop a positive outlook (Vandewater & Stewart, 2006; Wethington et al., 2004). Moreover, goals are not set in stone. Adults assess and adjust goals throughout life, often without awareness (Freund, 2017).

The concept of a midlife crisis remains popular in our culture, perhaps because it describes exciting possibilities for making major life changes, or perhaps because it is a simple explanation for the many changes that occur. Despite this, the research suggests that most adults tend to view middle adulthood as a positive time in life, as shown in Figure 14.1 (Freund & Ritter, 2009). Middle adulthood is a time of increasing life satisfaction, self-esteem, and well-being (Arnett, 2018; Lachman et al., 2015; Orth et al., 2010). Moreover, longitudinal studies show that much of personality remains stable from young adulthood through middle adulthood to older adulthood, suggesting that a period of upheaval and turmoil is not normative in midlife (Bleidorn & Hoppwood, 2019; McCrae & Costa, 2006).

FIGURE 14.1 ■ Views of Midlife, by Age

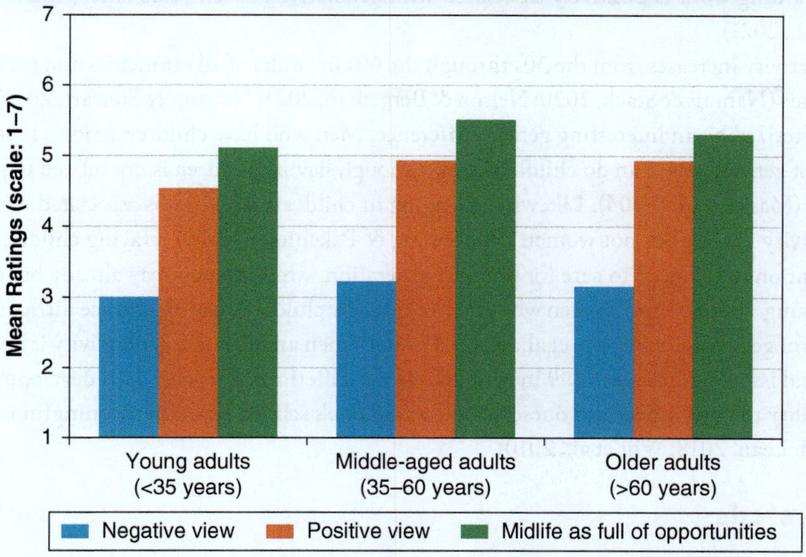

Source: Freund and Ritter (2009).

Generativity Versus Stagnation

Naomi spent several mornings each week coaching her daughter's softball team. Eduardo hired several high school students to work as interns at his firm and learn about his career path. Francesca volunteered her time at a child advocacy center, helping to write grant proposals to earn the funds needed for the center to remain open. Each of these adults is "giving back" to others. For Erik Erikson (1959), middle-aged adults face the psychosocial stage of **generativity versus stagnation**. The developmental task of this stage entails cultivating a sense of generativity, a concern and sense of responsibility for future generations and society as a whole. In early midlife, generativity is often expressed through childrearing (Syed & McLean, 2018).

Over the middle adult years, generativity expands to include a concern and commitment to the social world beyond oneself and one's immediate family to future generations and even the species itself (McAdams, 2014). Generativity fulfills adults' needs to feel needed and to make contributions that will last beyond their lifetimes, achieving a sense of immortality (Nantais & Stack, 2020). Generativity also serves a societal need for adults to guide the next generation, sharing their wisdom with youth through their roles as parents, teachers, and mentors. Adults fulfill generative needs through teaching and mentoring others in the workplace and community, volunteering, civic engagement, and engaging in creative work (Chen et al., 2019). For the active and generative, middle adulthood is the prime of life even as they experience multiple conflicting demands.

A minority of adults experience disappointment in middle adulthood. After not achieving career and family goals or finding them dissatisfying, some middle-aged adults remain self-absorbed. They focus on their own comfort and security rather than seeking challenges, being productive, and making contributions to help others and make the world a better place (Nantais & Stack, 2020). Adults who fail to develop a sense of generativity experience stagnation—self-absorption that interferes with personal growth and prevents them from contributing to the welfare of others.

Generativity is good for others, but it is also good for the middle-aged adult as it promotes personal growth (Villar, 2012). Generativity is associated with creativity. The most generative adults are proactive problem solvers who approach problems by investigating multiple solutions and exploring several options before committing to any one (Adams-Price et al., 2018; Beaumont & Pratt, 2011). Generativity is associated with life satisfaction, self-acceptance, low rates of anxiety and depression, cognitive health, and overall well-being (An & Cooney, 2006; Cox et al., 2010; Steinberg et al., 2018). Workplace experiences are reciprocally associated with the development of generativity. Generativity predicts job satisfaction and positive career outcomes (Doerwald et al., 2021), but engaging in intrinsically rewarding work is positively associated with generativity seven years later (Chen et al., 2019; Krahn et al., 2021).

Generativity increases from the 30s through the 60s in adults of all ethnicities and socioeconomic backgrounds (Nantais & Stack, 2020; Nelson & Bergeman, 2021; Newton & Stewart, 2010). However, it is characterized by an interesting gender difference. Men who have children tend to score higher in measures of generativity than do childless men, although having children is not related to generativity in women (Marks et al., 2004). Likewise, engaging in childcare activities is associated with increases in generativity in men but not women (McKeering & Pakenham, 2000). Having children may draw men's attention to the need to care for the next generation, while women may already be socialized to nurture young. But men and women who are involuntarily childless may experience difficulty developing a sense of generativity (Moore et al., 2017). For both men and women, generativity is influenced by psychosocial issues addressed earlier in life and reflects a lifetime of psychosocial development including the ability to trust others and oneself, understand one's self, and sustain meaningful relationships (Syed & McLean, 2018; Wilt et al., 2010).

Seasons of Life

Similar to Erikson, Daniel Levinson (1978, 1996) viewed development as consisting of qualitative shifts in challenges that result from the interplay of intrapersonal and social forces. Based on interviews with 40 men aged 35 to 45 and, later, 45 women aged 35 to 45, all of whom worked in a wide variety of occupations, Levinson concluded that adults progress through a common set of phases that he called **seasons of life**.

The key element of Levinson's psychosocial theory is the **life structure**, which refers to the overall organization of a person's life: relationships with significant others as well as institutions such as marriage, family, and vocation. In Levinson's model, individuals progress through several seasons over the lifespan in which their life structures are constructed, then tested and modified in response to intrapersonal and social demands.

During the transition to early adulthood (ages 17 to 22), according to Levinson, we construct our life structure by creating a dream, an image of what we are to be in the adult world, which then guides our life choices. Young adults then work to realize their dreams and construct the resulting life structure (ages 22 to 28). Levinson explained that men tend to emphasize the occupational role and construct images of themselves as independent and successful in career settings, whereas women often create dual images that emphasize both marriage and career.

The age 30 transition (28 to 33) entails a reconsideration of the life structure in which adults may shift priorities from career to family, or vice versa. Adults who do not have satisfying experiences at home or work may struggle to revise their life structure and may experience the age 30 transition as a crisis. Men tend to experience the mid- to late 30s (34 to 40) as a period of settling down, focusing on some goals and relationships and giving up others based on their values. Women were thought to remain unsettled through middle adulthood because they generally take on new career or family commitments and balance multiple roles and aspirations.

Levinson observed that as adults transition to middle adulthood (40 to 45), they become aware of the passage of time, that half of life is spent. Middle-aged adults reexamine their dreams established in early adulthood and evaluate their progress, coming to terms with the fact that they will not realize many of them. In areas where they have achieved hoped-for success, they must reconcile reality with their dream and perhaps wonder whether the experience was "worth it," or whether they are missing out on some other aspects of life. Some middle-aged adults make substantial changes to their life structure by changing careers, divorcing, or beginning a new project such as writing a book.

Many people find the seasons of life conceptualization intuitively pleasing, but it is vital to note that Levinson based his ideas on a very small sample of adults who were highly educated, white, and of high socioeconomic status (Dare, 2011). The seasons of life are likely influenced by context because the process of evaluating and revising the life structure is influenced by the social opportunities and situations around us. Contexts of disadvantage—poverty, discrimination, or limited opportunities—deplete individuals of the energy and social resources needed to examine and revise the life structure. The seasons of life model likely does not apply to all men and women across ethnicity, socioeconomic status, and social context. That said, adults who construct dreams, revise them in light of opportunity and experience, and are successful in achieving them are likely to be well positioned to focus on the developmental tasks of middle adulthood, such as becoming generative and developing a more comprehensive sense of self.

Search for Meaning

A meaningful life has purpose and makes sense to the person living it (Heintzelman & King, 2014). Adults are naturally driven to find meaning in life. A sense of meaning is motivational; is the basis for value systems that underlie goals, aspirations, and behavior; and provides people with a sense of control over their lives (Baumeister & Landau, 2018). Adults who perceive that their lives have meaning tend to show greater well-being, quality of life, life satisfaction, self-esteem, optimism, and happiness and health (Czekierda et al., 2017; Hooker et al., 2018; King & Hicks, 2021). In contrast, those who feel that their lives lack meaning are more likely to experience depression, anxiety, social isolation, and loneliness than their peers.

Belief that life has meaning is adaptive, but many people find the search for meaning challenging. Similar to the identity search, the active search for a sense of meaning is linked with openness to experience and curiosity, but also with questioning and ambiguity (Işık & Ü Zbe, 2015). Uncertainty is often experienced as stressful. Adults actively searching for meaning report greater levels of anxiety, rumination, and unhappiness and lower levels of well-being and life satisfaction than those who are not searching (Bundick et al., 2021; Steger et al., 2009, 2011). Turning points in life, the significant transitions that can be interpreted as crises, often spark meaning-making attempts (Park, 2010). Research with more than 43,000 people from 100 countries suggested that adults tend to report searching for a sense of meaning before milestone birthdays (e.g., years that end with zero, signifying exiting and entering a new decade of life; Alter & Hershfield, 2014). People not only view exiting and entering a new decade in life as triggers for meaning making, but they expect to question the meaning of life as they approach milestone birthdays in the future, and they report a greater search for meaning as they exit and enter new decades.

The search for meaning may be more challenging for midlife adults because of their many roles, responsibilities, and constraints that can interfere with exploration (Morgan & Robinson, 2013). Yet the search for meaning is a developmental task of middle adulthood. Midlife adults tend to report greater immersion in the search for meaning than do young or older adults (Battersby & Phillips, 2016; Ko et al., 2016). Self-reported sense of meaning in life tends to increase from midlife into old age. With age, adults are more likely to report the sense that they have purposeful goals and aims, feel excitement and enthusiasm for living, feel a sense of accomplishment in personally valued areas, and perceive their lives as having inherent value or worth (King & Hicks, 2021; Morgan & Robinson, 2013). It is no wonder that a sense of meaning in life is associated with positive adaptation across adulthood (Bundick et al., 2021; Heintzelman & King, 2014).

Sexuality

Sexuality is a core aspect of the sense of self throughout adulthood. Generally speaking, sexual activity occurs most frequently among young adults, from their mid-20s to mid-30s, and declines gradually for people in their 40s and again in their 50s, but the amount of decline is modest (King, 2019). Many middle-aged adults report engaging in sexual activity only one or two times less frequently each month than their younger counterparts (Herbenick et al., 2010). For midlife adults, the major predictors of sexual activity are health and having a partner (King, 2019; Smith et al., 2017). In one study of about 1,300 midlife women, those who were married or cohabiting were 8 times more likely than their single peers to be sexually active (Thomas et al., 2015). Research with adults in 20 countries suggests that the frequency of sexual intercourse is associated with emotional, sexual, and relationship satisfaction (Costa & Brody, 2012; McNulty et al., 2016). Sexual frequency is associated with greater reports of happiness, peaking for adults who engage in sexual activity once per week (Muise et al., 2016).

Generally speaking, the research literature examining sexual activity in middle adulthood is sparse as compared with emerging adulthood, and it tends to be focused nearly exclusively on heterosexual cisgender adults.

Midlife adults experience many physical and psychosocial changes that can influence sexual function (Thomas & Thurston, 2016). Declines in the sex hormones, estrogen and testosterone, can influence sexual interest and activity in men and women (Rastrelli et al., 2018; Thomas, Neal-Perry, et al., 2018). In women, declining levels of estrogen slows sexual arousal and reduces vaginal lubrication, sometimes making intercourse uncomfortable (Simon, 2011; Thomas et al., 2018a, 2018b) Women vary in sexual responses after menopause. Many report no change in sexual interest, some report increased interest, and others show declines (Avis et al., 2017; DeLamater, 2012). In one study, about half of middle-aged women experienced some symptoms of sexual dysfunction, such as changes in desire, arousal, discomfort, and satisfaction, although many women were not distressed by these changes (von Hippel et al., 2019). Adults often adapt by changing sexual behavior, such as lengthening foreplay, trying different types of activities, and using lubricants (Herbenick et al., 2011; Thomas et al., 2018a) Many adults express overall sexual satisfaction despite changes in frequency (Thomas et al., 2018a).

With age, men are more likely to experience difficulties establishing or maintaining erections (Walther et al., 2017). The prevalence of erectile dysfunction (ED) ranges from 2% to 9% in men between the ages of 40 and 49 years and 20% to 40% in men aged 60–69 years. (Shamloul & Ghanem, 2013). Men who experience ED express less happiness with their sex lives than their peers (Quinn-Nilas et al., 2018). ED is closely connected with health, especially cardiovascular disease (Fang et al., 2015; Moore et al., 2014). ED is associated with an increased risk of heart disease and stroke (Moore et al., 2014). ED is treated first with lifestyle changes to improve health, such as physical activity, diet, and behavioral change, such as quitting smoking (Krzastek et al., 2019). It is also treated with oral medication taken prior to intercourse.

Psychosocial changes, such as shifts in roles, family and work obligations, stress, and changes in body image, can influence sexual function. Midlife adults report feeling busier and more stressed than when they were younger. Many find their numerous roles make it difficult to relax and interfere with sexual activity. These potential barriers to sex are buffered by the positive psychosocial development that characterizes middle adulthood. Midlife adults often report feeling more confident and comfortable with themselves, better able to communicate their needs to partners, and better able to understand their needs than when they were younger (Thomas et al., 2018a). Maintaining a satisfying sex life in middle adulthood is important because it is associated with sexuality, sexual satisfaction, and overall well-being in older adulthood (Buczak-Stec et al., 2019; Kolodziejczak et al., 2020).

Thinking in Context: Lifespan Development

1. According to Erikson's lifespan psychosocial theory, each psychosocial stage builds on the last. How does resolution of the tasks of infancy, childhood, adolescence, and young adulthood contribute to adults' capacities to address the task of middle adulthood, developing a sense of generativity?

2. Identify instances in which a midlife crisis is depicted in popular media. Given what you know about psychosocial development, including generativity, meaning, and sexuality, identify ways in which these depictions are accurate and inaccurate. What do you conclude about the existence of the midlife crisis?

Thinking in Context: Intersectionality

Theories and research findings concerning many aspects of psychosocial development, such as generativity, the search for meaning, sexuality, and the notion of seasons of life, are based on small samples of white, often highly educated and of higher SES, adults.

1. To what degree might theories be influenced by the specific samples on which they are based? Do the demographics of the sample matter? Why or why not?
2. People live in many different contexts. What role, if any, might these differences in environments play in psychosocial development? Consider social resources and economic circumstances. What conditions might aid development? Hinder development? How might contexts of disadvantage and limited opportunities influence adults' ability to address developmental tasks?
3. How might adults' multiple identities and roles influence psychosocial development? Consider gender identities, religious identity, and racial-ethnic identity. How might participation in various roles contribute to psychosocial development? Consider adults' roles as parents, spouses, workers, friends, and adult children. In what ways might adults' psychosocial development be linked with their many identities and roles?

THE SELF

LEARNING OBJECTIVE

14.3 Describe middle adults' changing self, including self-perceptions, sense of control, and well-being.

The process of development continues throughout adulthood as self-concept becomes more complex and integrated (Lodi-Smith & Roberts, 2010). In addition to describing themselves in more complex ways, adults are increasingly likely to integrate autobiographical information and experiences into their self-descriptions as they grow older (Pasupathi & Mansour, 2006).

Self-Concept and Self-Esteem

Our beliefs about what is possible, our **possible selves**, shift over adulthood (Smith & Freund, 2002; Voss et al., 2017). Many adolescents and young adults in their 20s describe idealistic and grand aspirations—visions of fame, wealth, exceptional health, and athletic prowess. By middle adulthood, most people realize that their time and life opportunities are limited and they become motivated to balance images of their possible selves with their experiences in order to find meaning and happiness in their lives. Over their lifetimes, adults revise their possible selves to be more practical and realistic (Lapp & Spaniol, 2016), typically aspiring to competently perform the roles of worker, spouse, and parent, and to be wealthy enough to live comfortably and meet the needs of children and aging parents (Bybee & Wells, 2003).

Self-concept becomes more complicated in middle adulthood and includes subjective age, or how old we feel.

iStock/RossHelen

The sense of self is an important influence on people's overall functioning and their sense of well-being (Sneed et al., 2012). Middle-aged adults are more likely than young adults to acknowledge and accept both their good and bad qualities and feel positively about themselves (Ryff, 1991, 1995). Revised, more modest, possible selves influence adults' sense of self-esteem and well-being (Orth et al., 2010). Self-esteem increases throughout middle adulthood, with a recent meta-analysis of

FIGURE 14.2 ■ Changes in Self-Esteem

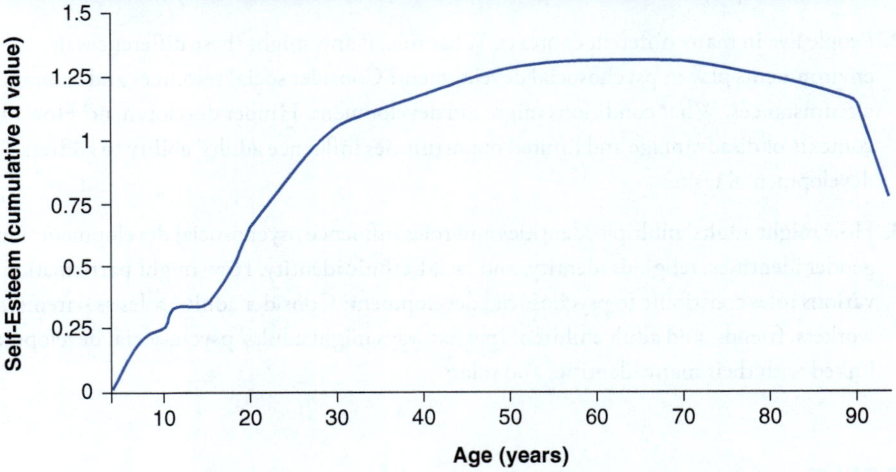

Source: Orth et al., 2018.

longitudinal studies suggesting that self-esteem increases through midlife, peaking at about 60 and remaining stable until about age 70, then declining slowly to about age 90, followed by a steep decline (Orth et al., 2018; see Figure 14.2). Notably, this pattern of lifespan change held across gender, ethnicity, country, and even birth cohort, suggesting that multiple generations of adults show similar shifts in self-esteem across their lives. Self-esteem is associated with positive emotional, social, and career outcomes throughout life, from adolescence through older adulthood (and these outcomes, in turn, tend to influence self-esteem; Harris & Orth, 2020; Orth, 2017).

Subjective Age

Subjective age—how old one feels—is an important aspect of self (Barrett & Montepare, 2015). Children, adolescents, and emerging adults tend to perceive themselves as older than their chronological age, but by age 30 adults tend to view themselves as *younger* than their chronological years. The discrepancy between subjective and chronological age increases into middle adulthood such that by late adulthood, adults from North America, Western Europe, Australia, and Africa feel, on average, 13% to 18% younger than their chronological age (Bergland et al., 2014; Shinan-Altman & Werner, 2019; Pinquart & Wahl, 2021).

Why do adults consistently identify with their younger selves? A younger subjective age may be a compensatory strategy to counteract the negative cultural messages associated with aging. Like self-concept, subjective age is multidimensional, including aspects such as physical abilities, cognition, and health. Adults are more likely to report feeling younger in areas that tend to be associated with negative age-related stereotypes, such as cognitive aging and health (Kornadt et al., 2018).

The saying, "You're only as old as you feel," appears to hold some truth in the sense that subjective age is associated with a variety of measures of health and wellness. Adults who view themselves as younger than their chronological age tend to score high on measures of well-being, mental health, and life satisfaction and even experience lower rates of mortality (Degges-White & Kepic, 2020; Keyes & Westerhof, 2012; Ryff, 2014). One national longitudinal study found that feeling 11 years older than one's age was associated with a 29% higher risk of mortality (Stephan et al., 2018). Longitudinal studies have shown that adults who reported feeling younger relative to their peers tended to show better performance and slower declines in episodic memory, executive function, and health over a 10-year period than same-age peers (Hughes & Lachman, 2018; Stephan et al., 2014). A younger subjective age is associated with feeling more control and motivation at work (Shane et al., 2019).

Why does subjective age matter? Although people cannot change their chronological age, perceiving oneself as younger or older than one actually is can alter one's perceived control over one's life and activities (Heckhausen & Brim, 1997). Perceived control, the sense that one has the power to influence one's circumstances and the course of one's life, is a powerful coping resource (Robinson & Lachman, 2017). Feeling younger than one's age can enhance one's sense of vitality and resourcefulness, enhancing motivation and confidence to pursue goals. Feeling older can activate negative stereotypes about aging, reducing one's sense of perceived control, which can lead to disengagement (Shane et al., 2019). In support of the role of subjective age as a potential protective factor in psychologically distancing oneself, one recent longitudinal study of adults surveyed prior to the COVID-19 outbreak in January, 2020 and during the outbreak in March and April, 2020 found that perceived age declined from January to March for adults who agreed that "coronavirus is only a threat to older adults." For these adults, adopting a younger subjective age may be a coping mechanism to psychologically distance themselves from old age and perceived vulnerability to a deadly illness (Terracciano et al., 2021).

Perceived Control

Perceived control, often referred to as self-efficacy, refers to individuals' expectations about the extent to which they can bring about desired outcomes (Robinson & Lachman, 2017). Control beliefs tend to rise in early adulthood, as young adults gain competence and make progress toward career and personal goals. Control beliefs tend to peak and remain stable in midlife and decline in late adulthood (Drewelies et al., 2017). Age-related declines in perceived control are related to changes in biological and social resources, like health, income, social status, bereavement, and increasing vulnerability to health problems (Lachman et al., 2015). Accurate control beliefs—the ability to realistically appraise one's situation and the controllability of one's circumstances—coupled with the ability to modify coping strategies accordingly (such as by reducing effort on unattainable goals and redirecting effort toward realistic goals) mark successful aging (Heckhausen et al., 2010; Shane & Heckhausen, 2019).

Perceived control tends to vary with gender, socioeconomic status, and race. Generally, women tend to report lower perceived control than men, likely influenced by differences in education and income (Drewelies et al., 2017). Adults with higher education and higher income tend to perceive greater control over their decisions and lives than do those with low levels of education and income (Vargas Lascano et al., 2015). Low socioeconomic status, especially poverty, poses environmental constraints, including access to basic resources, such as food, health care, and safety, that increases individuals' vulnerability to poor outcomes and reduces their sense of control. Race is associated with perceived control through SES differences, as Black adults are disproportionately likely to live in low-SES communities, and especially through experiences with racial discrimination. For many Black adults, racial discrimination is an ever-present stressor, often viewed as inescapable, with the power to decimate the sense of control (Brondolo et al., 2018; Peterson et al., 2020). Despite these trends, individuals of all races, ethnicities, genders, and SES levels show varied control beliefs, and these variations predict health outcomes.

Individuals who perceive greater control and fewer constraints on their choices and actions tend to show better physical health, greater life satisfaction, fewer depressive symptoms, and lower mortality (Infurna et al., 2011; Robinson & Lachman, 2017). This is true for all adults, regardless of race, gender, and SES. When adults with a low SES perceive a greater sense of control over their lives, their health and longevity is similar to those with a high SES (Turiano et al., 2014). Feeling in control can help people regulate their emotions and adapt to life changes, stress, and health threats, such as disease. When people view their health as controllable, they are more likely to adopt health-promoting behaviors, such as exercising regularly or going to preventative doctor's appointments (White et al., 2012). A sense of control influences health, but health also influences individuals' sense of control. In one study, self-rated health, social participation and support, and life satisfaction predicted perceived control over 11 years (Infurna et al., 2011). Likewise, adults with fewer health problems and functional limitations showed higher perceived control and less pronounced declines in perceived control over 16 years (Infurna & Okun, 2015). For most adults, perceived control remains stable throughout midlife, in one study showing only small forms of decline over a 15-year period (Drewelies et al., 2017).

In middle age, adults become less tied to gender stereotypes for their own behavior. Men tend to adopt more expressive characteristics, such as being warm and sensitive, and women adopt more instrumental characteristics, such as becoming more assertive.

istock/Mr_Jamsey

Gender Identity

Adults' views of gender and the roles they adopt tend to shift over the lifespan. Some theorists argue that adult gender roles are shaped by the parental imperative—the need for mothers and fathers to adopt different roles in order to successfully raise children (Gutmann, 1985). We have seen that most couples adopt traditional roles and division of labor after the birth of a child (Schober, 2013; Yavorsky et al., 2015). Gender differences in couples' division of labor continue throughout childhood. The American Time Use Survey found that in most couples, the mother typically spends about twice as much time as the father on both housework and childcare, whereas fathers spend more time working outside the home (37 hours as compared with 21 hours for mothers; Parker & Wang, 2013). It should be noted that fathers today spend twice as much time doing household chores as in 1965 (from an average of about 4 hours per week in 1965 to about 10 hours per week today), suggesting a shift in perceived responsibility (Parker & Wang, 2013).

As children grow up and leave the nest, adults' activities shift away from parenting. When adults are freed of the parental imperative they may become less tied to traditional gender roles (Gutmann, 1985). Over the middle adult years, individuals' identification with the masculine or feminine gender role tends to become more fluid and they may begin to integrate instrumental and expressive aspects of themselves, becoming more similar and more androgynous (James & Lewkowicz, 1995). That is, men begin to adopt more traditionally expressive characteristics, such as being sensitive, considerate, and dependent, and women adopt more traditionally instrumental characteristics, such as confidence, self-reliance, and assertiveness (Lemaster et al., 2017). In one study that followed a representative sample of third-grade Finnish children for 30 years, boys and girls adopted traditional gender characteristics in adolescence, but by age 40 the men had become less aggressive and more conforming in contrast to the women, who showed a reverse pattern of becoming more assertive (Pulkkinen et al., 2005). Longitudinal research following adults from their 30s to 80s mirrors this finding: Although there are individual differences, the average man, initially low in expressive traits, becomes more expressive across the lifespan; the average woman, initially high in expressive traits, becomes less expressive across the lifespan (Jones et al., 2011, 2017). This pattern of gender convergence increases in middle adulthood in Western nations as well as in nonwestern cultures, such as the Mayan people of Guatemala and the Druze of the Middle East (Fry, 1985).

Androgyny, integrating instrumental and expressive characteristics, provides adults with a greater repertoire of skills for meeting the demands of middle and late adulthood. Middle-aged women who may be newly independent after experiencing divorce, death of a partner, or the end of childrearing may enter the workplace, seek advancement in current careers, or enroll in college. Successfully meeting these new challenges requires self-reliance, assertiveness, and confidence. Men, on the other hand, may become more sensitive and self-reflective as they complete generative tasks of mentoring and caring for the next generation. A great deal of research has shown that androgyny predicts positive adjustment and is associated with high self-esteem, advanced moral reasoning, psychosocial maturity, and life satisfaction in later years (Bem, 1985; Lefkowitz & Zeldow, 2006; Pilar Matud et al., 2014). Men and women with androgynous gender roles have a diverse set of instrumental and expressive skills, which permits them to adapt to a variety of situations with greater ease than do those who adopt either a masculine or feminine gender role.

Life Satisfaction and Well-Being

Self-esteem increases in middle adulthood, but paradoxically, well-being shows a U-shaped curve, gradually dropping in early adulthood, reaching its lowest point in midlife, roughly the mid 40s, and rising smoothly through about age 70 (Cheng et al., 2017; López Ulloa et al., 2013; Ryff, 2014). This U-shaped age pattern has been found in 145 countries, including 109 developing countries (Blanchflower, 2021). Perhaps the overall decline in well-being in middle adulthood is related to the great many roles most middle-aged adults occupy. In Chapter 12, we discussed the challenge that role overload poses to well-being. When accompanied by a sense of control, multiple role involvement predicts positive well-being, more trusting and positive relations with others, a positive sense of life purpose, and greater overall well-being (Chrouser Ahrens & Ryff, 2006). Perceived control is associated with life satisfaction, and the multiple demands that middle-aged adults face often test their sense of control (de Quadros-Wander et al., 2013). Positive processing, a tendency to interpret events in a favorable light, is associated with high levels of well-being in middle adulthood (Lilgendahl & McAdams, 2011). Multiple roles must be accompanied by a sense of control or mastery in that area to influence well-being.

Life satisfaction tends to go hand-in-hand with well-being and it increases in midlife (Cowan, 2019). As shown in Figure 14.3, one national sample of 25- to 75-year-old adults studied over a 9e-year span found stability in life satisfaction; on average, all ages reported feeling moderate to high levels of life satisfaction in the present as well as 10 years ago and rated their satisfaction as increasing from past to present (Röcke & Lachman, 2008). A recent study of middle-aged adults found that most believed that this time in their life is stressful, but also fun and exciting, a time of freedom and when anything is possible, suggesting that positive views coexist with stress (Arnett, 2018).

Thinking in Context: Biological Influences

1. According to evolutionary developmental psychology, patterns and norms in lifespan development serve an adaptive purpose for our species. How might this be true in middle adulthood? Consider subjective age. How does people's perceived age tend to change over adulthood? How might these normative changes in subjective age (how old one feels) be adaptive?

FIGURE 14.3 ■ Adults' Mean Ratings of Their Past (10 Years Ago) and Present Life Satisfaction

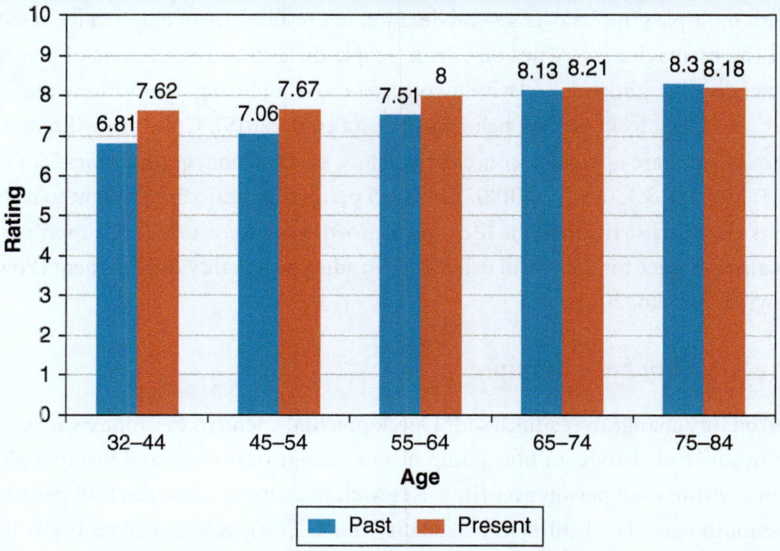

Note: The life satisfaction scale can range from 1 (low satisfaction) to 10 (high satisfaction).

Source: Röcke & Lachman, 2008.

2. Gender convergence is common across cultures. From an evolutionary developmental perspective, does gender convergence serve an adaptive purpose? Why or why not?

Thinking in Context: Intersectionality

Recall from Chapter 1 that individuals and their contexts interact reciprocally, influencing each other. How might perceived control illustrate this?

1. How might individuals' contexts and circumstances influence their sense of control? Consider family and community socioeconomic status—wealthy, middle income, low income—sense of diversity, access to resources, safety, and other relevant factors. Do these factors matter in determining perceived sense of control?
2. In what ways might the effects of contextual factors vary with intersectional characteristics, such as gender, race and ethnicity, sexual orientation, and disability status? Might Black women's experience differ from Black men's? Latina women? White women? Might education matter? Neighborhood SES and opportunities? What possible relationships can you identify? What intersectional factors might you expect to be particularly relevant in influencing adults' sense of control?
3. How do people influence their contexts? How does adults' sense of control influence their interactions with others? How might adults' interactions differ when they feel little control as compared with a strong sense of control?

PERSONALITY

LEARNING OBJECTIVE

14.2 Analyze patterns of stability and change in personality in middle adulthood.

We have seen that self-concept becomes more defined, but the content remains much the same over adulthood. Does personality show similar stability? One view of personality, evolved through research conducted with multiple samples over several decades, has resulted in an empirically based theory that has collapsed the many characteristics on which people differ into five clusters of personality traits. Traits are generally thought to be relatively consistent and enduring dispositions that are apparent in individuals' thoughts, feelings, and behaviors (Costa et al., 2019). Collectively known as the **Big 5 personality traits**, they are openness, conscientiousness, extroversion, agreeableness, and neuroticism (see Table 14.1; McCrae & Costa Jr., 2008). The Big 5 personality traits are thought to reflect inherited predispositions that persist throughout life, and a growing body of evidence supports their genetic basis; there is also evidence for the role of experience in adult personality development (Power & Pluess, 2015; Vukasović & Bratko, 2015).

Personality Stability and Change

How does personality change over adulthood? Developmental scientists examine two aspects of personality change: mean-level change, or how group means change over time, and intraindividual change, which is change within each person over time. Research examining mean levels of personality change have shown smooth age-related shifts in personality traits. The greatest changes occur in early adulthood, prior to age 30, and late adulthood (Milojev & Sibley, 2017). Personality maturation in early adulthood includes increases in conscientiousness, agreeableness, and emotional stability. Personality maturation occurs predictably during early adulthood as individuals assume adult roles and adopt

TABLE 14.1 ■ Big 5 Personality Traits

Trait	Description
Openness	The degree to which one is open to experience, ranging from curious, explorative, and creative to disinterested, uncreative, and not open to new experiences.
Conscientiousness	The tendency to be responsible, disciplined, task oriented, and planful. This trait relates to effortful self-regulation. Individuals low in this trait tend to be irresponsible, impulsive, and inattentive.
Extroversion	Includes social outgoingness, high activity, enthusiastic interest, and assertive tendencies. This trait is related to positive emotionality. On the opposite pole, descriptors include social withdrawal and constrictedness.
Agreeableness	This trait includes descriptors such as trusting, cooperative, helpful, caring behaviors and attitudes toward others. Individuals low in agreeableness are seen as difficult, unhelpful, oppositional, and stingy.
Neuroticism	This trait relates to negative emotionality. Descriptors include moodiness, fear, worry, insecurity, and irritability. The opposite pole includes traits such as self-confidence.

the mature psychological and behavioral functioning needed to succeed in those roles (Lodi-Smith & Roberts, 2007). Fulfilling responsibilities as spouses, parents, and productive workers is facilitated by emotional stability, agreeableness, and conscientiousness—and most young adults cultivate these traits. Success at work usually requires people to be on time, dress and behave professionally, and regularly produce goods or services; fulfilling these responsibilities entails conscientiousness and can also cultivate it. Investing in new roles can, over time, lead to changes in personality traits (Denissen et al., 2019). Because all societies have similar requirements for adult behavior, similar patterns of personality maturation occur in in all cultures (Bleidorn et al., 2013).

These patterns of maturation, increases in conscientiousness, agreeableness, and emotional abilities, continue much more subtly and smoothly in middle adulthood, from the 40s to early 60s, making this time a period of stability. Personality traits shift subtly during adulthood (see Figure 14.4; Soto et al., 2011). Cross-sectional studies of adults in 26 countries, including Canada, Germany, Italy, Japan, Russia, South Korea, and the United States, have found that agreeableness and conscientiousness increase and neuroticism, extroversion, and openness decline into middle adulthood, suggesting that adults mellow with age (Löckenhoff et al., 2009; McCrae & Costa, 2006; McCrae, Terracciano, & The Personality Profiles of Cultures Project, 2005; Soto et al., 2011). These patterns continue into older adulthood. Extroversion and openness to experience decline with age from 30 to 90, with the most pronounced drops after the mid-50s (Lucas & Donnellan, 2011; Mroczek et al., 2006; Srivastava et al., 2003). Conscientiousness increases from emerging adulthood to mid-adulthood, peaks between 50 and 70, and then declines; agreeableness tends to increase with age (Leszko et al., 2016; McCrae, 2002; McCrae & Costa, 2006). Thus, cross-cultural similarities in patterns of change support arguments that personality itself and age-related changes have biological origins, but cultures often share some contextual similarities.

Individual Differences in Stability and Change

Mean-level changes illustrate population-level shifts in personality trait scores, or how the group averages change across adulthood. There are also individual differences in personality traits, and these differences tend to be highly stable over periods of time ranging from 3 to 30 years (McAdams & Olson, 2010; Wängqvist et al., 2015). People tend to show rank-order stability in personality traits; their position, relative to peers, remains stable over time (Deary et al., 2013; Roberts & Mroczek, 2008). Individuals who score high relative to peers on a given trait, such as extroversion, tend to remain higher than their peers even as the group displays normative trait shifts, such as mean-level declines in extroversion across adulthood. Someone who is highly extroverted compared to peers in young adulthood, perhaps with a very active social life, will tend to be highly extroverted compared to peers in

FIGURE 14.4 ■ Age Differences in Big 5 Personality Traits

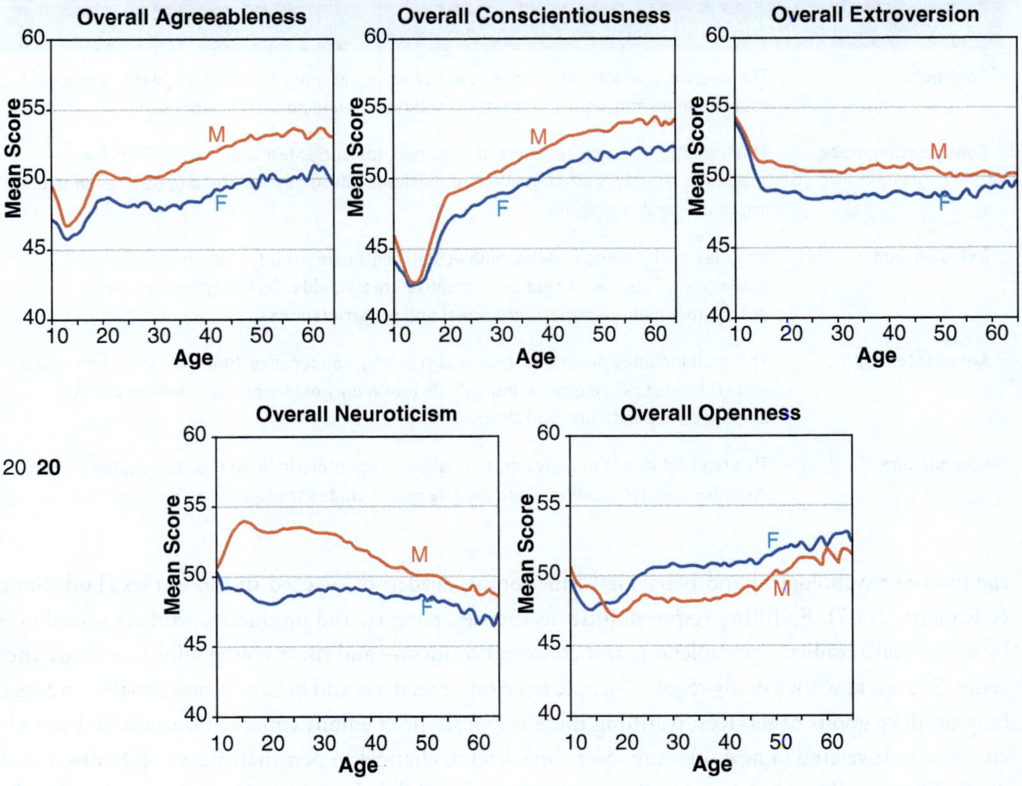

Source: Soto et al., 2011.

middle adulthood, perhaps manifested as being active in a parent-teacher organization, leading a scout troop, or participating in a book group. Although middle-aged adults as a group may show decline, individuals' rank order relative to the group tends to persist.

Individual differences characterize not only patterns of personality traits, but there are subtle individual differences in the pattern and magnitude of change (Graham & Lachman, 2012). Not all individuals follow the normative increase in conscientiousness scores over adulthood. Some people change more than others, and some change in ways that are contrary to general population trends (McAdams & Olson, 2010). One recent study found that individual differences in openness, conscientiousness, extroversion, and agreeableness were greatest in emerging adulthood, lesser in magnitude in young and middle adulthood, and smallest in magnitude in old age (Schwaba & Bleidorn, 2018). Interestingly, individual differences in emotional stability were small and remained relatively constant across adulthood.

Influences on Personality

Why do individual differences in personality tend to endure? Genetics plays a role. Research with monozygotic and dizygotic twins suggests a strong genetic component to the stability of personality (Kandler et al., 2010). Personality traits are thought to reflect inherited predispositions that first emerge as temperament in infancy (Costa et al., 2019). Most people's traits undergo subtle shifts, but personality often remains largely the same over a lifetime. Is there no role for environment in adult personality development? We have noted the potential influence of role transitions and social investments in personality maturation. Research, however, is mixed. Entering the workforce is associated with shifts in personality traits in the direction of maturation, but there are conflicting findings regarding entering a romantic relationship (Bleidorn et al., 2018; Denissen et al., 2019). At present there is no evidence for the impact of other transitions such as ending a relationship, marriage, divorce, parenthood, widowhood, job loss, or retirement on personality (Bleidorn et al., 2018).

It is commonly believed that adult personality is influenced by events and experiences over a lifetime. The logic goes that after a humiliating experience at a party, a person becomes introverted and anxious about social gatherings. Yet research suggests that experience rarely causes dramatic changes in personality and that instead, our personalities influence our choices and experiences (Bleidorn et al., 2018; McCrae & Costa, 2006). People choose behaviors, lifestyles, mates, and contexts based, in part, on their personalities, and then the outcomes of these choices and life experiences contribute to and may stabilize personality traits (Soto, 2015; Wrzus et al., 2016). Returning to the example, introverted and socially anxious people may be prone to find parties and social gatherings challenging—and in their distress they may behave in ways that increase the likelihood of humiliating experiences (e.g., grasping a cup too tightly and inadvertently spilling its contents). In this sense, stability of personality is influenced by individuals' behaviors and choice of environments as well as by environmental factors themselves (Kandler et al., 2010). Dramatic life changes, such as divorce, serious illness, or widowhood, may bring about new behaviors and patterns of traits, but more commonly such events evoke and strengthen existing patterns of traits (Mroczek et al., 2006; Roberts & Caspi, 2003).

Personality and Adjustment

Big 5 personality traits predict career, family, and personal choices in adulthood. People who are high in conscientiousness are more likely to complete college, those high in extroversion are more likely to marry, and those high in neuroticism are more likely to divorce (Hill et al., 2012; Shiota & Levenson, 2007). Personality traits are associated with coping, emotion regulation strategies, and resilience (Oshio et al., 2018). Adaptive emotion regulation strategies, such as reappraisal, problem solving, and mindfulness, are associated with higher levels of extroversion, openness to experience, agreeableness, and conscientiousness and low levels of neuroticism, whereas poor emotion regulation strategies, such as avoidance, are associated with the reverse (Barańczuk, 2019). In addition, people who are high in extroversion, agreeableness, and conscientiousness and low in neuroticism report higher levels of well-being (Cox et al., 2010).

Big 5 traits, especially low conscientiousness, even predict health and mortality (Graham et al., 2017; Strickhouser et al., 2017). Conscientiousness has an especially close association with health as it influences the behaviors persons engage in—exercise, eating habits, and risky behaviors such as smoking and substance use—and these behaviors affect the likelihood of good or poor health outcomes (Friedman & Kern, 2014; Kroencke et al., 2021; Turiano et al., 2015). In fact, conscientiousness measured in childhood predicts health in middle adulthood (Hampson et al., 2016).

Thinking in Context: Lifespan Development

1. Which personality changes are thought to comprise *personality maturation*? Why do we see similar patterns of maturation in most adults and cross-culturally?
2. How does the adoption of social roles support personality maturation?
3. What patterns of personality change do most adults show over midlife?
4. What are some influences on individual differences in personality development in adulthood?

FRIENDSHIP AND ROMANTIC RELATIONSHIPS

LEARNING OBJECTIVE

14.2 Examine friendship and spousal relationships in middle adulthood.

Middle-aged adults' changing sense of self, changing family formations, and changing roles and responsibilities in the workforce and at home influence their social relationships with friends, spouses, children, and parents.

Middle-aged adults often have less time for their friends, but friendships continue to be important sources of social support and are associated with well-being, positive affect, and self-esteem.

10'000 Hours/Getty Images

Friendships

Over the course of middle adulthood, most people spend more time with family than friends, but friendships continue to be important sources of social support and are associated with well-being, positive affect, and self-esteem (Blieszner, 2014; Huxhold et al., 2014). Like young adults, middle-aged adults tend to share demographic similarities, such as gender, with their friends (Mehta et al., 2021). Women's friendships continue to be more intimate and they report having more close friends and experience more pleasure and satisfaction in their friendships than men, whose friendships tend to center on activities (Fiori & Denckla, 2015). Work and family demands tend to reduce the available time and resources adults have for friends, leading adults to prune their social networks (Wrzus et al., 2017). The number of friends and the amount of contact with them tends to decrease. Middle-aged adults therefore report having fewer friends and spending less time with friends than young adults, but the friendships that have endured tend to be described as close, and few to none are ambivalent or troubled (Fingerman et al., 2004).

Friendship is positively associated with physical and mental health (Holt-Lunstad, 2017; King et al., 2017). Friendships offer powerful protection against stress for both men and women (Blieszner, 2014). Satisfaction with the number of friends, frequent visits with friends, and a sense of group belonging are associated with life satisfaction (Degges-White & Kepic, 2020). Adults turn to close friends for support with daily hassles as well as major stressors (Birditt et al., 2012). Increasingly, friends offer companionship and support from afar, via participation in social media, permitting interactions despite limited time (Dare & Green, 2011; Meng et al., 2017). One study found that middle-aged adults' social media use increased as their children moved out of the home, an often stressful transition, and remained high for up to 2 years later, suggesting a supportive role for online interactions (Tanis et al., 2017).

Marriage

In 1960, about 93% of adults married by age 45 (Wang & Parker, 2014). Although marriage rates have declined to record lows over the past half-century, nearly all U.S. adults will marry. Today, about 80% marry by age 45, 90% by age 60, and more than 95% by age 80 (U.S. Bureau of the Census, 2015). Similar to early adulthood, marriage is positively associated with physical and mental health for both different-sex and same-sex partners (Carpenter et al., 2021; Goldsen et al., 2017; Grover & Helliwell, 2014; Kiecolt-Glaser, 2018).

Men generally report being happier with their marriages than women, though the difference is small (Jackson et al., 2014). For both different-sex and same-sex marriages, satisfaction tends to be highest in egalitarian relationships in which home and family duties are shared and couples view themselves as equal contributors (Ogolsky et al., 2014; Pearson et al., 2014; Pollitt et al., 2018). The most satisfying marriages reflect congruence in which partners' attributes complement one another (Rammstedt et al., 2013). Successful marriage partners balance similarity and differences. Partners must share enough interests, goals, and communication styles to get along but differ in ways that generate and sustain interest.

Marital satisfaction in different- and same-sex couples tends to wax and wane over the decades (Bosley-Smith & Reczek, 2018). In middle adulthood, marital satisfaction tends to increase as child rearing tasks and stress decline, family incomes rise, and spouses get better at understanding each other and have more time to spend together (Fincham et al., 2007). The advances in emotion regulation that typically come with age may also improve the quality of marital interactions and predict satisfaction (Bloch et al., 2014; Mazzuca et al., 2019).

A mismatch in a couple's expectations and support for adult children and aging parents predicts poor marital satisfaction and conflict, which is associated with psychological distress in both different-sex and same-sex marriages (Polenick et al., 2017, 2018). Women are more influenced by their partner's distress than men—this is true in different- and same-sex relationships (Behler et al., 2019). Women tend to show greater emotional reactivity in response to conflicts, report more detailed and vivid memories of marital disagreement, and report ruminating more about arguments than men (Kross et al., 2012; Lorenz et al., 2006; Sbarra et al., 2012). Women, especially those married to men, experience more distress and depression in response to poor marital quality than men (Garcia & Umberson, 2019). Depression is closely tied to inflammation, an indicator of health, and relationship-related distress is more closely tied to inflammation among women than men (Kiecolt-Glaser, 2018).

In middle adulthood, marital satisfaction tends to increase as child rearing tasks and stress decline.

iStock/mapodile

Divorce

Divorces most often occur within the first 10 years marriage, but about 10% of marriages break up after 20 years or longer (U.S. Bureau of the Census, 2015). Different-sex and same-sex marriages show similar rates of dissolution (Balsam et al., 2017). Overall, middle-aged adults list similar reasons for divorce as do young adults: communication problems, relationship inequality, adultery, physical and verbal abuse, and desires for autonomy (Crowley, 2019; Rokach et al., 2004; Sakraida, 2005). Women are more likely than men to initiate divorce, and women who are the initiators tend to fare better than those who do not initiate the divorce (Steiner et al., 2011).

Divorce is thought to pose greater risks for women's adjustment, compared with men. Divorce tends to represent a greater economic loss for women, including a decline in household income and sharp increase in the risk of poverty (Lavelle & Smock, 2012; Leopold, 2018). Results from the 2004–2014 Health and Retirement study revealed that, after divorce, women experienced a 45% decline in their standard of living (measured by an income-to-needs ratio), whereas men's standard of living dropped by 21%. These declines persisted over time for men and only reversed for women following repartnering (Lin & Brown, 2021). Education is a protective factor for women; a high level of education is associated with positive health and adjustment, likely because of its link with SES (Symoens et al., 2014).

The process of divorce entails a series of stressful experiences for partners and family members, including conflict, physical separation, moving, distributing property, and, for some, child custody negotiations. Regardless of who initiates a divorce, all family members feel stress and a confusing array of emotions, such as anger, despair, embarrassment, shame, failure—and, sometimes, relief (Clarke-Stewart & Brentano, 2006; Härkönen, 2015). Divorce is associated with decreased well-being and life satisfaction, heightened risk for a range of illnesses, and even a 20% to 30% increase in early mortality (Grundström et al., 2021; Kiecolt-Glaser, 2018; Sbarra et al., 2011). The link between divorce and poor health is complex. Health declines after divorce, but recall that poor health is also associated with declines in marital quality prior to divorce, suggesting a reciprocal rather than causal relationship (Karraker & Latham, 2015; Tracy & Utz, 2020). In addition, poor health could impede adults' ability to work, compounding financial problems (Brown et al., 2019).

Although some adults show poor health outcomes of divorce, most people are resilient and fare well after divorce, especially after the initial adjustment (Sbarra & Coan, 2017; Sbarra et al., 2015). Adults who wanted to get divorced, are financially secure, and are in good health may experience few or no downsides to divorce, and their quality of life might even improve following divorce (Brown et al., 2019). In one study of more than 600 German divorcees, nearly three-quarters experienced little change in life satisfaction across a 9-year period that included the divorce (Mancini et al., 2011). Women who successfully make the transition through a divorce tend to show positive long-term outcomes, such as becoming more tolerant, self-reliant, and nonconforming—all characteristics that are associated with the increased autonomy and self-reliance demands that come with divorce.

Divorce is challenging, but middle-aged persons generally show less of a decline in psychological well-being and show overall better adaptation than do young adults (Wang & Amato, 2000). It may be that increases in experience, flexibility, and problem-solving and coping skills in middle adulthood aid adaptation. As with other life challenges, divorce represents an opportunity for growth and development (Baum et al., 2005; Schneller & Arditti, 2004), and adaptive outcomes following divorce appear to be the norm, not the exception (Perrig-Chiello et al., 2014).

Thinking in Context: Lifespan Development

1. Examine stability and change in friendship from adolescence through middle adulthood. Consider friendship in midlife: how is it similar and different from emerging adulthood and early adulthood (see Chapter 12)? From adolescence (see Chapter 10)? What can you conclude about friendship over these years? What aspects are continuous, or remain the same? What changes?
2. How might socioemotional development influence middle-aged adults' experience of marriage? Consider developmental tasks, such as generativity and the search for meaning; the self, such as identity and perceived control; and/or personality. How might individuals' development influence their interactions with their spouse and their marriage? Consider the reverse: How does marital experience influence socioemotional development in middle adulthood?

Thinking in Context: Applied Developmental Science

Give advice to midlife adults on what they can expect as they begin divorce proceedings. What changes might occur? To what degree will they adjust? How might your explanation vary, if at all, for men and women?

INTERGENERATIONAL RELATIONSHIPS

LEARNING OBJECTIVE

14.5 Contrast adults' relationships and roles as parents to young children, adolescents, and adults; grandparents; and adult children.

Most middle-aged adults participate in many social roles. In addition to friend and partner or spouse, midlife adults may hold roles as parents, grandparents, and adult children to aging parents. These intergenerational relationships mark middle adulthood, but they also vary considerably among adults.

Parent-Child Relationships

Parent-child relationships change dynamically over a lifetime. Just as parents become proficient at meeting children's developmental demands at a given age, children advance, posing new challenges and requiring a transformation of skills. The parenting task of middle adulthood involves launching adult children into the world and supporting children through emerging and early adulthood. A growing minority of adults postpone parenthood into middle adulthood.

Parents to Infants and Young Children

It is not uncommon today for adults in their 40s and early 50s to raise infants and young children. We have discussed the biological changes in reproductive capacity that occur throughout early and middle adulthood. Fertility declines with age, particularly in women. Midlife adults may become parents naturally, especially in the early 40s, but the probability of unassisted conception is much lower than in early adulthood and declines rapidly. Midlife pregnancy often occurs through assisted reproduction, especially in vitro fertilization with a donated egg, and adoption.

The transition to parenthood entails many changes for parents. Adults of all ages may experience an increased risk of health problems, such as obesity, stress-related reductions in immunity, and depression, but middle-aged adults are especially vulnerable to the health effects of stress (Saxbe et al., 2018; Simon & Caputo, 2019). Middle-aged parents may find the social side of their new role most challenging as their daily experiences may not match those of their peers. Midlife parents of infants may have different concerns and needs than their friends. A new mother may find that her social clock does not match those of her same-age peers who may be sending their children to college or planning for weddings and grandchildren. At the same time, a middle-aged mother may find herself much older than many of the other parents of infants she meets at childcare, play groups, and parks. For these reasons, older parents may find the social side of parenting a challenge. In addition, raising infants and young children can be stressful and emotionally and physically exhausting because they have nonnegotiable everyday needs that must be satisfied.

When asked, middle-aged parents cite benefits to being an older parent. Many have established careers with financial security, enabling flexibility in how they spend their time. Middle-aged parents also feel that they are better prepared for parenthood than they would have been at a younger age. They feel mature, competent, and generative, and they tend to be less stressed than younger parents (Mac Dougall et al., 2012). Middle-aged parents also tend to experience greater increases in life satisfaction with the birth of their children and are less prone to depressive symptoms (Luhmann et al., 2012). They tend to take a more youthful perspective, seeing middle age as extending longer and old age as starting later than do those who have children early in life (Toothman & Barrett, 2011). The most common complaints of older parents include having less energy for parenting and feeling stigmatized as older parents (Mac Dougall et al., 2012).

Children also benefit from being raised by older parents. Older parents are often in a better socioeconomic position, have more life experience, and display more hardiness than younger parents (Sanders & Turner, 2018; Zondervan-Zwijnenburg et al., 2020). Children raised by older mothers tend to be healthier, having fewer visits to the hospital, a greater likelihood of receiving all of their immunizations by 9 months of age, and higher scores on measures of cognitive, language, and social development through age 5 (Sutcliffe et al., 2012; Tearne, 2015).

The cognitive and emotional changes that take place from early to middle adulthood contribute to midlife adults' readiness to parent. In some studies, mothers who were older when their first child was born tended to demonstrate more sensitivity and positive parenting behaviors such as hugs, kisses, and praise and fewer negative ones such as threats or slaps (Barnes et al., 2013; Camberis et al., 2016). Older parents may appraise behavior problems differently, feel less distressed by them, and may be more patient and capable of setting limits for their children (Trillingsgaard & Sommer, 2018). As they enter adolescence, children of older parents display fewer externalizing problems (Zondervan-Zwijnenburg et al., 2020).

Parents to Adolescents

The parenting task shifts as children grow older. Advances in cognition and socioemotional development coupled with the tasks of seeking a sense of identity and autonomy empower adolescents to reason and engage in more sophisticated conversations, negotiations, and arguments than ever before. Recall from Chapter 10 that parent-child conflict tends to increase in early adolescence. It may not be surprising, then, that parents tend to report that adolescence is the most stressful stage of parenting (Nomaguchi & Milkie, 2020). Parental satisfaction tends to reach its lowest point in early adolescence as conflict increases most rapidly (Luthar & Ciciolla, 2016; Meier et al., 2018).

As the stresses and rewards of parenting change over childhood and into adolescence, the effects of parenthood on adults' mental and physical health also shift (Simon & Caputo, 2019). Although caring for infants and young children is physically demanding and associated with a greater sense of parenting role overload, parents of adolescents report poor life satisfaction, self-esteem, self-efficacy, and more depressive symptoms than parents of infants and young children (Nomaguchi & Milkie, 2020; Pollmann-Schult, 2014).

For many parents, part of the challenge of raising adolescents is the sharp contrast between the developmental trajectories and tasks of adolescence and those of middle adulthood. Many midlife parents begin to notice gradual declines in health and fitness, strength and mobility, and appearance and sexual appeal at the same time as their children advance toward physical maturity and show sharp increases in these characteristics. Children's puberty and physical maturation can make parents aware of the passing of time, their age, and their limited lifespan. As adolescents begin their identity search, parents may reevaluate their sense of self, priorities, and goals, revising their own sense of identity (Soenens et al., 2019; Steinberg, 2001).

Parents to Adult Children

Emerging adulthood involves a series of transitions that are simultaneously exciting and stressful for both young people and their parents. Parents of emerging adults may share more similarities in physical and mental health to parents of adolescents than to parents of adults over age 30. Parents of emerging adults tend to report more symptoms of depression and anxiety, less frequent positive emotions, lower levels of life satisfaction, and more poor health than parents of young adults age 30 and over (Simon & Caputo, 2019). During their children's early adulthood parents' relationship with children transforms, becoming more friendship-like and based on mutual support, which most parents find gratifying (Nomaguchi & Milkie, 2003). Most parents report having positive interactions with their grown children on a regular basis (Fingerman et al., 2016). Negative interactions with adult children are consistently associated with parent reports of negative affect and predict daily patterns of the stress hormone cortisol (Birditt et al., 2017).

A son's or daughter's moving out of the family home is an important experience for parents and children as it marks the child's entry to adulthood and independent living. The so-called **empty nest** is a transitional time of parenting that occurs when the youngest child leaves home (Wray, 2007). This time was once considered a difficult transition for parents, but it is also a time for improved relationships and new opportunities. Mothers tend to report the move as more stressful than fathers, but most parents adjust well to their children's transition to independent living and the resulting empty nest (Mitchell & Lovegreen, 2009; Seiffge-Krenke, 2010). Frequently the adult child's transition to independent living is gradual and nonlinear, involving intermittent moves back home (Mitchell, 2016). Parents who have adjusted well to the empty nest may find this transition distressing as it may represent a loss of autonomy or privacy. A temporary dip in parental well-being and increase in depressive symptoms is common, especially if the adult child's return is due to unemployment and economic troubles (Caputo, 2019; Tosi, 2020).

A son's or daughter's moving out of the family home is an important experience for parents and children as it marks the child's entry to adulthood and independent living. Most parents adjust well to the empty nest.

iStock/kali9

Contextual macrosystem factors such as economic recessions, wars, and pandemics influence emerging adults' behavior and living situation as well as parents' adjustment. After the economic recession that affected much of the world in 2007–2008, it became increasingly common for adult children to return home at some point in their 20s. In 2016, more than one-third of U.S. young adults aged 18 to 31 lived with their parents (Fry, 2016).

FIGURE 14.5 ■ Adults Living With Parents, 1900–2020

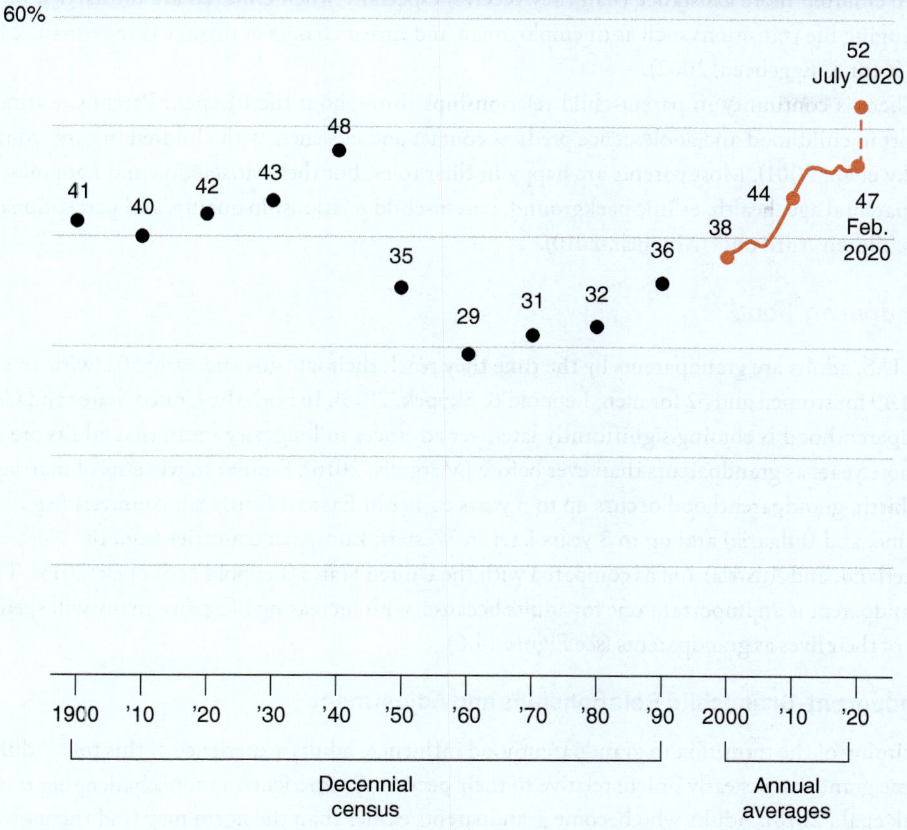

Note: "Living with a parent" refers to those who are residing with at least one parent in the household.

Source: Fry et al. (2020)

That number surged during the COVID-19 pandemic to include 52% of adults age 18–29 in July, 2020, higher than the previous peak during the Great Depression (see Figure 14.5; Fry et al., 2020). When co-residence was uncommon, living with adult "boomerang" children was associated with poor parental well-being (Pudrovska, 2009). Middle-aged parents surveyed in 2008 reported poor marital quality if an adult child was living in the home, but not when they were surveyed in 2013 as co-residence became more normative (Davis et al., 2018). Parents' well-being suffers with co-residence when they believe their grown children need too much support and should be more autonomous (Fingerman, Cheng, Wesselmann, et al., 2012; Pillemer et al., 2017).

Children's success in life influences their midlife parents' adjustment. Both mothers and fathers show negative emotional responses to their adult children's unmet career and relationship goals (Cichy et al., 2013). Adult children's problems are associated with low parental well-being, including more negative than positive affect, low levels of self-esteem, poor marital quality, and poor parent-child relationships (Bouchard, 2018; Fingerman, Cheng, Birditt, et al., 2012).

Around the world, families who live apart continue to provide various forms of emotional and physical support to one another, including advice, babysitting, loans, car repair, and more. How much support family members provide each other depends on many factors, such as attachment, relationship quality, cultural norms, and resources. *Familism*, a value characteristic of Latinx cultures, mandates that the family comes before all else and that family members have a duty to care for one another, regardless of the problem or situation, whether personal, financial, or legal (Carlo et al., 2007). Financial resources influence the level and types of support that family members provide. Families with fewer resources and those living in poverty may provide a great deal of financial and physical assistance to each other, including living together. In most nations, low-income families, including single parents, immigrants, and members of marginalized groups, are more likely to live together in three-generation households (parents, children, and grandchildren; Burr & Mutchler, 1999). Middle-aged parents tend to give children more assistance than they receive, especially when children are unmarried or facing challenging life transitions such as unemployment and career change or divorce (Fingerman & Suitor, 2017; Zarit & Eggebeen, 2002).

There is continuity in parent-child relationships throughout the lifespan. Parental warmth and support in childhood and adolescence predicts contact and closeness with children in early adulthood (Belsky et al., 2001). Most parents are happy in their roles, but their satisfaction and happiness varies with parental age, health, ethnic background, parent-child relationship quality, and perception of how their children "turn out" (Mitchell, 2010).

Grandparenthood

Most U.S. adults are grandparents by the time they reach their late 40s and early 50s (with an average age of 49 for women and 52 for men; Leopold & Skopek, 2015). In both the United States and Canada, grandparenthood is coming significantly later, yet advances in longevity mean that adults are spending more years as grandparents than ever before (Margolis, 2016). Similar to patterns of marriage and childbirth, grandparenthood occurs up to 3 years earlier in Eastern European countries (e.g., Poland, Ukraine, and Bulgaria) and up to 8 years later in Western European countries (e.g., the Netherlands, Switzerland, and Austria) and as compared with the United States (Leopold & Skopek, 2015). The role of grandparent is an important one for adults because, with increasing lifespans, many will spend one-third of their lives as grandparents (see Figure 14.6).

Grandparent-Grandchild Relationships and Adjustment

The timing of the transition to grandparenthood influences adults' experience of this role. Adults who become grandparents early or late relative to their peers may experience a more challenging transition (Hank et al., 2018). Adults who become grandparents earlier than the norm may find themselves parenting young children and adolescents while fulfilling the care and support functions of the grandparent role (Fuller-Thomson & Minkler, 2001). Grandparents offer an important source of emotional support for their grandchildren (Huo et al., 2018). The grandparent role is rewarding, and time caring for a new grandchild is associated with positive mental health (Condon et al., 2018). But many adults experience role strain as they may juggle expectations of employers, spouses, children, adult children, and grandchildren.

Grandparent involvement is associated with child well-being and adolescent adjustment (Griggs et al., 2010; Sheppard & Monden, 2019). Children and adolescents reared in divorced and single-parent homes show more positive adjustment and fewer problem behaviors when they have close nurturing relationships with grandparents (Attar-Schwartz et al., 2009; Henderson et al., 2009).

FIGURE 14.6 ■ Distribution of Grandparents by Age and Gender in the United States, 2001 and 2015

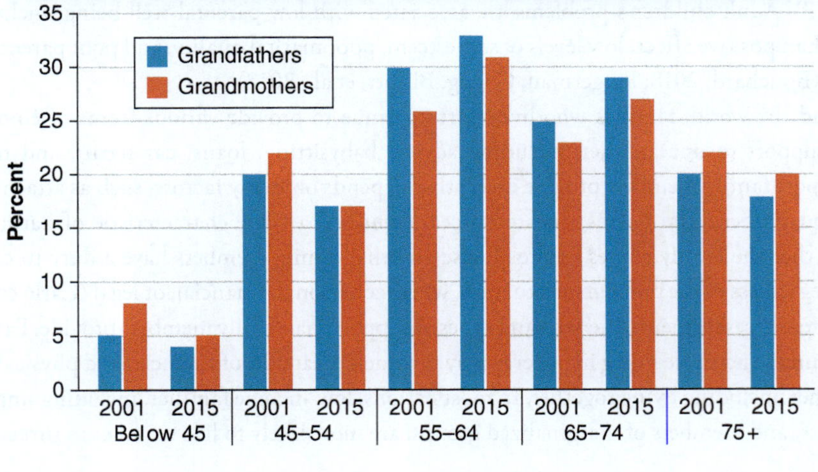

Grandparents may adopt important financial and caregiving roles in low-income and rural families (Yancura et al., 2020). In families of color, including African American, Latinx, Asian American, Native American, and Canadian Indigenous families, grandparent involvement tends to be high, especially for grandmothers, who often take on caregiver, mentor, and disciplinarian roles (Kamo, 1998; Werner, 1991; Williams & Torrez, 1998). Grandparent involvement and co-residence can ease adult children's stress, reduce feelings of work-family conflict, and aid adjustment (Mustillo et al., 2021). Some theorists argue that *grandparental investment*, the tendency for grandparents to be involved in their grandchildren's lives and transfer resources to them, stems from its provision of evolutionary benefits such as a correlation between the presence of the maternal grandmother and child survival (Coall & Hertwig, 2011).

Being a grandparent provides opportunities to enjoy spending time and playing with children without the responsibility of parenthood.

iStock/SolStock

Grandparent involvement is supported by regular contact, close relationships with grandchildren, and parental encouragement to visit with grandchildren. Grandparents who are engaged and spend time with their grandchildren tend to report high levels of life satisfaction (Moore & Rosenthal, 2015). Research with 14 European countries suggests that this is especially true for those who live in cultures with high grandparent obligations, such as Italy and Greece (Neuberger & Haberkern, 2013).

Relationships between grandparents and grandchildren are influenced by several factors, including grandparent and grandchild gender, geographic proximity, socioeconomic status, and culture. In most cultures, grandparents and grandchildren of the same sex tend to be closer than those of different sex, especially grandmothers and granddaughters. Generally, grandmothers tend to have more contact with their grandchildren than do grandfathers and they tend to report higher satisfaction with the grandparent role (Silverstein & Marenco, 2001; Soliz, 2015). Grandparents who live closer to their children tend to have closer relationships with their grandchildren than do those who have contact only on special occasions like holidays and birthdays. Yet in Western nations, most grandparents remain involved in their grandchildren's lives despite distance (American Association of Retired Persons, 2002). Because parents tend to regulate grandparent-grandchildren contact, grandparents' relationships with their adult children influence their contact and relationships with their grandchildren.

Grandparents Raising Grandchildren

About 2% of children are raised by grandparents (US Census Bureau, 2017). African American and Hispanic grandparents are more likely to be the primary caregiver for a grandchild than white non-Hispanic grandparents (Ellis & Simmons, 2014). The majority of custody arrangements are informal with no involvement from child welfare agencies. Grandparents often obtain custody of their grandchildren in response to parental absence or incapacitation from physical and mental illness, substance abuse, incarceration, or death (Hayslip et al., 2017).

The transition to parenting grandchildren is not easy, partly because parental absence is often linked with experiences that are traumatic to both grandparent and grandchild. Children in grandparent-headed homes are more likely to have experienced threats to development, such as witnessing or being victimized by violence, having a parent incarcerated or in jail, or living with someone with a mental illness or who is suicidal (Rapoport et al., 2020). Grandchildren often enter grandparent custodial arrangements with internalizing and externalizing problems, including anxiety, depression, anger, and behavior problems (Smith & Hancock, 2010; Williams, 2011). In addition, contextual factors make custodial grandparenting more difficult. Grandparent caregiver arrangements are more common in low-income communities, as kin offer a safety net for families in crisis. About one-quarter of grandparent-headed households live in poverty (US Census Bureau, 2017). Despite these challenges,

Raising a grandchild is challenging, yet custodial grandparents frequently mention a sense of satisfaction in parenting and in seeing grandchildren's accomplishments.

Nikki Kahn/Washington Post/Getty Images

custodial grandparents show similar interactions with children, emotional support, and coping skills as custodial parents (Rapoport et al., 2020).

Grandparent caregiving is not part of typical midlife development, making it particularly difficult and stressful for adults (Hayslip Jr & Blumenthal, 2016). Perhaps because of the stress, financial difficulties, grief and anger toward the parent, and feelings of social isolation, grandparent caregivers tend to suffer more mental and physical health problems than those who do not care for their grandchildren (Edwards & Benson, 2010). Grandparents who care for grandchildren with emotional and behavioral problems tend to experience higher rates of anxiety, stress, and depression, and they tend to report less life satisfaction (Doley et al., 2015). African American and Latinx grandparents tend to experience the greater risk of health problems because they are more likely to live in poverty and in disadvantaged neighborhoods, but social support can buffer some negative outcomes (Chen et al., 2015; Hayslip et al., 2015; Whitley & Fuller-Thomson, 2017).

Despite these challenges, many grandparent caregivers adjust and report positive aspects of caregiving (Hayslip et al., 2017). Many report enjoying the love and companionship of their grandchildren and the opportunity to influence their development. Some grandparents report that raising their grandchildren is easier than parenting their own children because of greater wisdom and experience, feeling more relaxed, and having more time and attention to give to grandchildren (Dolbin-MacNab, 2006). Grandparents who feel that they have a social support network to turn to for emotional and physical assistance tend to show better adjustment, fewer problems, and a greater sense of well-being and life satisfaction (Hayslip et al., 2017; Mendoza et al., 2020).

Similar to parent-child relationships, grandparent-grandchild relationships show continuity over time. Close grandparent-grandchild relationships in childhood predict close relations in adulthood (Geurts et al., 2012). Grandparents and adult grandchildren tend to agree that their relationships are close and enduring (Hayslip Jr & Blumenthal, 2016; Villar et al., 2012). Over time, contact with grandchildren tends to decline as young and middle-aged grandchildren take on time-consuming family and work roles, but affection between grandchildren and grandparents remains strong (Silverstein & Marenco, 2001; Thiele & Whelan, 2008). The grandparent role provides adults opportunities to satisfy generative needs by nurturing a new generation, enjoying spending time and playing with children without the responsibility of parenthood, and gaining a sense of immortality by passing along family and personal history as well as a second generation of progeny (Moore & Rosenthal, 2015; Soliz, 2015).

Relationships With Aging Parents

Close relationships with parents are continuous throughout life. Generally speaking, parents and adult children who have a lifetime of close and positive relations tend to remain close (Whitbeck & Hoyt, 1994). In middle age, many people look back and gain more appreciation for their parents' assistance and sacrifices over the years. Relationships between mothers and daughters, usually closer than other parent-child relationships, tend to become more intimate and complex as daughters enter middle age (Fingerman, 2000, 2001; Lefkowitz & Fingerman, 2003).

The "sandwich generation" is a popular depiction of adults' relationships with their aging parents. Middle-aged adults are viewed as scrambling to meet the needs of both dependent children and frail

FIGURE 14.7 ■ Middle-Aged Adults Provide More Emotional Support to Two Generations Than Financial Support

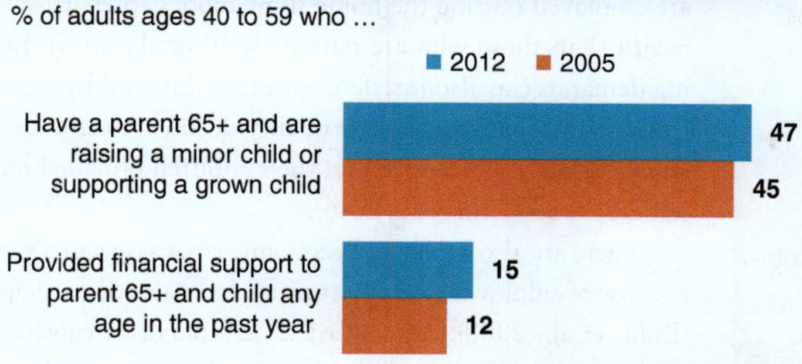

Source: Parker and Patten (2013)

elderly parents and thus are sandwiched between the two, but this picture it is not entirely accurate (Grundy & Henretta, 2006; Riley & Bowen, 2005). As they progress through midlife, adults are more likely to be parents to adult children than minor children. We have seen that adult children often require *some* assistance. About 30% of middle-aged adults provide support to both adult children and parents over the age of 65 (Friedman et al., 2017). They are more than twice as likely to provide financial support for their children than their parents, but they provide similar levels of emotional support to both generations (Birditt et al., 2017; Parker & Patten, 2013). Although the popular "sandwich" metaphor may exaggerate the number of middle-aged adults who provide *financial* support to two generations, most adults do provide *emotional* support and assistance to multiple generations (see Figure 14.7).

The care that adult children provide aging parents is influenced by the parent-child relationship as well as family circumstances, gender, and ethnicity. Adults tend to offer more care to parents who live nearby and who are widowed or have few siblings (Stuifbergen et al., 2008). Women are more likely to provide care to parents than men, especially if they live nearby (Ivery & Muniz, 2017; Pillemer & Suitor, 2014). African American and Latinx adults at all income levels are more likely than white non-Hispanic adults to provide aging parents with financial and caregiving assistance (Cohen et al., 2019; Rote & Moon, 2016). These trends likely may reflect cultural values, such as familism, which emphasizes filial reciprocity and obligation. Chinese, Japanese, and Korean women tend to provide care for their husband's aging parents, who tend to live with them (Montgomery et al., 2007; Zhan, 2004). In Thai families, intergenerational relations between older-age parents and their children remain close throughout life, with more than 70% of older persons living with or next to a child (Knodel & Chayovan, 2009).

The challenges that caregivers experience vary with cultural factors, such as filial reciprocity norms. Immigrant Chinese adults with a strong sense of filial obligation tend to experience few emotional, social, and physical caregiving burdens; this is especially true for adults who were less acculturated to the United States and the accompanying individualistic values (Guo et al., 2019). Several studies suggest racial differences in emotional adaptation to caregiving. White adults tend to report a caregiving as a greater emotional burden than Black adults, who tend to report little distress and more positive emotional aspects of caregiving, suggesting emotional resilience (Cook et al., 2018). Positive views of caregiving and emotional resilience are protective and associated with less distress, anxiety, depression, and hostility (Bekhet, 2015). However, Black and Latinx caregivers may experience more physical health problems than white caregivers (Gelman et al., 2013; Rote & Moon, 2016). Physical health disparities may be less due to caregiving than the contextual correlates of membership in a marginalized group, such as racial discrimination, poor access to health care, and fewer economic resources (Cook et al., 2018).

As adults' caregiving responsibilities increase, such as when an elderly parent develops cancer or Alzheimer's disease, they are more likely to experience conflicts among their many roles. Caregivers can feel overwhelmed by their obligations to parents, children, spouses, employers, and friends, and

Middle-aged adults often provide emotional support to their parents.

Alistair Heap/Alamy Stock Photo

this role strain is associated with anxiety and depressive symptoms, a reduced sense of personal mastery and self-efficacy, and less engagement in outside activities (Mausbach et al., 2012; Wang et al., 2011). Caregivers who are employed outside the home show more depressive symptoms and worse health than those who are retired (Kohl et al., 2019). Increases in caregiving demands can also interfere with the adult child-parent relationship. One study found that relationship quality declined over a 5-year period as older adults' disability increased and their children provided more assistance with self-care tasks (Kim et al., 2016).

There are also career and economic costs associated with caregiving, such as a loss of employment opportunities and reduced participation in paid work (Bolin et al., 2008). Among a U.S. sample of caregivers who reduced their work hours or left the workforce to care for a parent, about half reported losing income (Aumann et al., 2010). Women are more likely than men to be expected to provide care; caregiving can interfere with women's employment, causing losses in hours, earnings, and advancement. According to one estimate, women who become caregivers to their parents may lose more than $300,000, on average, in income and benefits over their lifetime (MetLife Mature Market Institute et al., 2011). Caregiving responsibilities for parents may place female caregivers at risk of living in poverty and requiring public assistance later in life (Lee et al., 2015).

For many adults, the stresses of caring for aging parents is accompanied by a positive sense of generativity and satisfaction from giving back to parents in gratitude (Grossman & Gruenewald, 2017). Positive adjustment is more likely when adults value filial obligations, view caregiving as a manageable challenge, and seek meaning in caregiving (Jones et al., 2011).

Thinking in Context: Lifespan Development

1. Midlife adults are parents to children ranging in age from infancy through young adulthood. Compare the nature of parenting at each age. What challenges do parents face at each age? Are there similarities across age? How might the challenges and benefits of parenting shift with the age of the child?
2. From a bioecological perspective, how do contextual factors influence grandparent-grandchild relationships?
   - How might factors within the adult, such as physical development, health, and socioemotional development, influence their interactions with grandchildren?
   - How might children's characteristics influence their interactions? To what extent is the goodness of fit between the child's and grandparents' characteristics relevant (see Chapter 4)? Explain.
   - Consider mesosystem factors, such as the interrelationships among child, parent, grandparent, and siblings, as well as adults' relationships with their child's spouse. How might these mesosystem relationships influence grandparents and grandchildren?
   - Identify exosystem factors in the neighborhood or community, and other settings that might affect grandparent-grandchild interactions.
   - Consider macrosystem influences: What role might cultural and societal factors play?

Thinking in Context: Applied Developmental Science

As a developmental scientist, you are charged with developing an intervention to help grandparents who are raising grandchildren.

1. What risks does raising grandchildren pose for children and grandparents?
2. What circumstances may cause children to require grandparent care? Why is raising grandchildren challenging?
3. What are some protective factors, or influences that promote positive adjustment?
4. What can be done to promote these influences and help grandparents? How would you intervene to assist grandparents? What types of support might you provide, such as education, resources, and other forms of support?

CHAPTER SUMMARY

14.1 Examine psychosocial development in midlife, including changes in generativity, the sense of meaning in life, and sexuality.

For Erik Erikson, the psychosocial task of middle adulthood is cultivating a sense of generativity, fulfilled through volunteering, teaching, and mentoring others in the workplace and community. Daniel Levinson proposed that midlife adults reexamine their life dream established in early adulthood, reevaluate their goals, and modify their life structures accordingly. Adults are naturally driven to search for meaning in life. Sexual activity tends to decline modestly over middle adulthood, but many adults report satisfaction. The most popular stereotype about middle age is the midlife crisis, a stressful time in the early to middle 40s when adults are thought to evaluate their lives. The midlife crisis is not universal and depends on individual factors and circumstances rather than age.

14.2 Describe middle adults' changing self, including self-perceptions, sense of control, and well-being.

Self-concept becomes more complex and integrated and self-esteem increases into middle adulthood, peaking at about 60. Self-esteem is associated with positive emotional, social, and career outcomes throughout life. By age 30 adults tend to view themselves as younger than their chronological years. The discrepancy between subjective and chronological age increases into middle adulthood and is associated with cognitive and physical health as well as perceived control. Control beliefs tend to peak and remain stable in midlife, and decline in late life. Perceived control tends to vary with gender, socioeconomic status, and race and is associated with physical and mental health. Gender convergence increases over middle adulthood as many adults begin to integrate masculine and feminine aspects of themselves. Androgyny predicts positive adjustment. Well-being shows a U-shaped curve, gradually dropping in early adulthood, reaching its lowest point in midlife, likely related to the many roles adults occupy. Despite changes in well-being, life satisfaction increases and is high in midlife.

14.3 Analyze patterns of stability and change in personality in middle adulthood.

Big 5 personality factors are thought to reflect genetic predispositions, but experience also plays a role in adult personality development. The greatest shifts occur in early and late adulthood. Personality maturation includes increases in conscientiousness, agreeableness, and emotional stability. These patterns continue much more subtly in middle adulthood, making this time a period of stability. Over adulthood, agreeableness and conscientiousness tend to increase and neuroticism, extroversion, and openness decline into middle adulthood, suggesting that adults mellow with age. There are also individual differences in personality traits and their magnitude of change, and these differences tend to be highly stable. People tend to show rank-order stability in personality traits. Most people's traits undergo subtle shifts, but personality often remains largely the same over a lifetime.

14.4 Examine friendship and spousal relationships in middle adulthood.

Friendships improve with age. Similar to earlier periods in life, middle-aged friends share demographic similarities, experiences, and values that make them useful sources of advice for dealing with problems. In middle adulthood, marital satisfaction in different- and same-sex couples tends to increase as child rearing tasks and stress decline, emotional regulation advances, family incomes rise, and spouses get better at understanding each other and have more time to spend together. Different-sex and same-sex marriages show similar rates of dissolution. Divorce is thought to pose greater risks for women's adjustment as it tends to represent a greater economic loss for women. Middle-aged persons show less of a decline in psychological well-being and show overall better adaptation than do young adults. Adaptive outcomes following divorce appear to be the norm, not the exception.

14.5 Contrast adults' relationships and roles as parents to young children, adolescents, and adults; grandparents; and adult children.

Midlife adults typically launch adult children into the world. Some adults postpone parenthood into middle adulthood. Their greater maturity and stability contribute to greater life satisfaction and less depression over the transition to parenthood. Parental satisfaction reaches its lowest point in early adolescence as conflict increases most rapidly. Parents of adolescents are more likely to report poor life satisfaction, self-esteem, self-efficacy, and depressive symptoms. Most parents adjust well to their adult children's transition to independent living and the resulting empty nest. Over early adulthood, relationships with children become more friendship-like, based on mutual support, and most parents are happy in their roles. Satisfaction varies with parental age, health, ethnic background, parent-child relationship quality, and perception of their children's success. Grandparents offer emotional support for their grandchildren, promoting well-being and adjustment. The grandparent role is rewarding and time caring for a new grandchild is associated with positive mental health. Relationships between grandparents and grandchildren are influenced by grandparent and grandchild gender, geographic proximity, socioeconomic status, and culture. Some grandparents raise their grandchildren, a challenging and stressful circumstance. Similar to parent-child relationships, grandparent-grandchild relationships show continuity over time. Most midlife adults provide emotional support to their parents and as their parents grow older, caregiving. The care that adult children provide aging parents is influenced by the parent-child relationship as well as family circumstances, gender, and ethnicity. For many adults the stresses of caring for aging parents is accompanied by a positive sense of generativity and satisfaction.

KEY TERMS

androgyny (p. 430)
Big 5 personality traits (p. 432)
empty nest (p. 440)
generativity versus stagnation (p. 423)
life structure (p. 424)
midlife crisis (p. 422)
possible selves (p. 427)
seasons of life (p. 424)

PART 7 LIFESPAN DEVELOPMENT AT WORK: MIDDLE ADULTHOOD

Family and career remain important in middle adulthood. In addition, many adults may first notice the physical changes associated with aging. The following opportunities address some of these issues.

Marriage and Family Therapists

Marriage and family therapists are counselors who adopt a family system perspective, the recognition that all members of a family interact and influence each other as a dynamic system, similar to the bioecological perspective that we have discussed throughout this book. When conducting therapy, marriage and family therapists consider the set of relationships in which a person is embedded. They treat many problems, such as depression, marital problems, anxiety, parent-child relationship difficulties, and substance abuse. Marriage and family therapists emphasize short-term therapy designed to change specific behaviors and patterns of communications and promote peoples' strengths.

Marriage and family therapists are found in mental health centers, hospitals, community centers, and private practice. Becoming a marriage and family therapist requires earning a master's degree in marital and family therapy, which includes an internship. They must also complete two years (3000 hours) of supervised clinical experience and pass a licensure exam to practice independently. In 2020, marriage and family therapists earned a median salary of about $52,000 (U.S. Bureau of Labor Statistics, 2021).

Physical Therapist

Physical therapists provide treatment and intervention for individuals suffering pain, loss of mobility, or other physical disabilities. They are movement experts who treat people with injuries, disabilities, and health conditions that need treatment, as well as people who want to become healthier or avoid future problems. Physical therapists examine patients, diagnose their movement difficulties, and devise treatment plans to improve their ability to move, reduce/manage pain, restore function, and prevent disability. Physical therapists conduct hands-on therapy, prescribe and demonstrate strengthening and stretching exercises, use electrical stimulation and other treatments, and engage in patient education. Physical therapists work in many settings including hospitals, outpatient clinics, homes, sports facilities, nursing homes, rehabilitation facilities, and private practices.

Physical therapy is a doctoral-level health field. To become a physical therapist, earn a Doctor of Physical Therapy degree (DPT), typically a 3-year degree, pass the National Physical Therapy Examination, and then a state licensure exam. The median annual wage for physical therapists was $91,010 in May 2020 (U.S. Bureau of Labor Statistics, 2021).

Another option for those with interest in physical therapy is to become a *physical therapy assistant.* Physical therapy assistants support the work of physical therapists in providing treatments and interventions for people suffering pain, loss of mobility, or other physical disabilities. Physical therapy assistants may provide some of the hands-on work, such as assisting patients with exercises and providing treatments. Becoming a physical therapy assistant requires completing 2 years of coursework in a physical therapy assistant program and passing an exam to become certified. The median annual wage for physical therapist assistants was $59,770 in May 2020 (U.S. Bureau of Labor Statistics, 2021).

Occupational Therapist

Occupational therapists provide rehabilitative services to patients with physical, developmental, or psychological impairments and help people having problems with movement and coordination. Whereas a physical therapist treats the muscles and physical impairment itself, occupational therapists help people adapt in everyday settings. They help people improve the motor skills, coordination, and balance involved in carrying out everyday tasks, like writing and getting dressed, which include fine and gross motor skills and motor planning.

Occupational therapists help people recovering from injuries regain skills, such as abilities lost after an accident. An occupational therapist may evaluate a patient's needs in their home and work settings to ensure that they learn the skills needed to adapt and live independently. Like other health professionals, they assess patients' problems, determine goals, create interventions to improve patients' ability to perform daily activities and reach goals, and evaluate outcomes, modifying treatments as needed.

Becoming an occupational therapist requires a master's degree in occupational therapy, passing the National Board for Certification of Occupational Therapy exam, and obtaining state licensure. The median annual wage for occupational therapists was $86,280 in May 2020 (U.S. Bureau of Labor Statistics, 2021).

An option for individuals interested in occupational therapy is to become an *occupational therapy assistant.* Occupational therapy assistants aid occupational therapist by performing support activities, such as guiding patients in stretching and exercising. Becoming an occupational therapy assistant requires the completion of a 2-year occupational therapy assistant program, followed by a certification examination (depending on state). The median annual wage for occupational therapy aides was $63,000 in 2020 (U.S. Bureau of Labor Statistics, 2021).

Human Resources

Human resources departments, also known as personnel departments, are responsible for managing an organization's employees: recruitment, administering salaries and benefits, training, and conducting research on employee needs and satisfaction. Human resources personnel work to attract the most qualified employees, match them to the jobs for which they are best suited, help them to succeed in their jobs, and ensure that the organization complies with labor laws. An understanding of human development is helpful in completing these duties. There are a variety of positions at all levels of education within human resource departments located in businesses, government, and private and nonprofit agencies.

Human resource generalists engage in all aspects of managing personnel, including recruitment, placement, training, and development. They often administer salary and benefits and develop and communicate personnel policies. *Employee relations specialists* are tasked with communicating with employees. They administer human resources policies and procedures, report employee relations issues to management, and brainstorm possible solutions. The job description of a *recruiter* includes soliciting potential employees, collecting applications and résumés for jobs, assembling applicant files, performing background checks, and sometimes participating in interviews. Recruiters may administer or oversee the administration of pre-employment assessments and tests, convey the results to management, and may contact applicants with job offers. *Training specialists,* also known as trainers and training and development analysts, deliver an organization's training programs and workshops to employees. They conduct training sessions, provide on-the-job training, maintain records of employee participation, and monitor the effectiveness of training and development programs. Median annual salaries for these human resources position are about $57,000 per year (Salary.com, 2021).

Health Psychologist

Health psychologists share similarities with clinical, counseling, school, and applied developmental psychologists. Each of these psychologists works to help people through counseling, assessment, and the design of interventions. Health psychologists work in clinical and medical settings to improve people's health.

Health psychologists' counseling work often focuses on the connection between physical and mental health. They might help patients manage pain or work through the emotional issues that accompany extreme weight loss interventions. Health psychologists help people manage the stress of experiencing a terminal illness or a family member's terminal illness or death.

Health psychologists also conduct assessments in conjunction with other medical professionals to understand a person's health behaviors and health-related problems and devise ways of improving their health. Assessments conducted by health psychologists may include cognitive and/or behavioral assessments, physical assessments, personality assessments, demographic surveys, and clinical interviews. Health psychologists may collaborate with other health professionals to devise plans to improve patients' health and address health problems.

Health psychologists develop programs to prevent or reduce health-related problems and concerns, such as smoking cessation programs, healthy eating and exercising programs, and stress management programs. They also conduct research to assess the effectiveness of prevention and intervention programs.

Becoming a health psychologist requires earning a doctoral degree in psychology, most often in clinical or counseling psychology. They then specialize in health psychology during a postgraduate internship or fellowship. Health psychologists who wish to practice must seek state licensure. Psychologists who engage in clinical activities earned a median salary of about $80,000 in 2020 (U.S. Bureau of Labor Statistics, 2021).

15 PHYSICAL AND COGNITIVE DEVELOPMENT IN LATE ADULTHOOD

iStock/ monkeybusinessimages

At 75 years of age, Sylvia lives alone in an apartment in an older adult community. Her daughter and grandchildren stop by frequently to help around the house and assist in cooking family dinners. Sylvia still drives her car to the store, church, and the senior center, but she does not drive at night and avoids driving to unfamiliar places. Sylvia has noticed that she sometimes forgets new information, like people's names, so she works hard to remember names by repeating them. Overall, she feels that she is still good at making decisions and carrying out her life on her own terms. Her grandchildren—even the oldest, who recently graduated from college—turn to her for advice and tell her she is wise. In many ways, Sylvia is the picture of successful aging.

As is the case with people at other ages in life, older adults vary in their health and functioning. Many, like Sylvia, remain free of serious physical and cognitive disabilities. All older adults experience declines in physical and cognitive areas, and many experience chronic illnesses that demand adaptation. In this chapter, we examine the physical and cognitive side of aging, including the challenges to physical and mental health that older adults face.

PHYSICAL DEVELOPMENT

LEARNING OBJECTIVE

15.1 Discuss age-related changes in the brain and body systems in late adulthood and how older adults may compensate for changes.

Senescence—physical aging—begins in early adulthood and continues gradually, often undetected, through midlife. By late adulthood most people notice changes in their appearance and functioning. A full head of silver hair, feeling out of breath after carrying groceries up a flight of stairs, and age-related ailments such as cataracts or hearing loss are not easily ignored. The processes of biological aging in midlife described in Chapter 13 continue and accelerate into late adulthood.

Appearance

The skin loses collagen and elasticity throughout adulthood and becomes more dry as oil glands become less active (Russell-Goldman & Murphy, 2020). Pigmented marks called age spots often appear on the hands and face. The skin also thins and loses the layer of fat underneath it, making blood vessels more visible and older adults more sensitive to cold (Tobin, 2017). Exposure to sunlight exacerbates these changes (Parrado et al., 2019). The nose and ears grow larger and broader in older adulthood (Farage et al., 2015). Hair whitens, and both men and women experience hair loss as hair follicles die, while thin downy hair begins to grow from the scalp follicles of men with hereditary baldness.

Body shape changes in older adulthood as fat is redistributed and accumulates in the abdomen. Sarcopenia, the age-related loss of muscle mass and strength, continues with average losses of 10% to 20% by 60 to 70 years of age and 30% to 50% from age 70 to 80 (Buford et al., 2010). As discussed later in this chapter, physical activity, especially resistance exercise, can strengthen muscles and offset losses into the 90s (Peterson & Serra, 2021).

The Senses

Our sensory abilities decline in late adulthood. Changes in vision, hearing, and taste and smell can affect older adults' everyday activities, abilities to engage in self-care tasks, and social interactions.

Vision

Similar to middle-aged adults (Chapter 13), virtually all older adults experience presbyopia and have difficulty seeing objects up close. In late adulthood, the lens yellows, the vitreous clouds, less light reaches the retina, and it becomes more difficult to see in dim light and to adapt to dramatic changes in light, such as those that accompany night driving (Owsley et al., 2018). Many adults develop **cataracts**, a clouding of the lens resulting in blurred, foggy vision that makes driving hazardous and can lead to blindness (Lin et al., 2016). Cataracts are the result of a combination of hereditary and environmental factors associated with oxidative damage, including illnesses such as diabetes and behaviors such as smoking (Ang & Afshari, 2021). By age 80, more than half of adults have cataracts (American Academy of Ophthalmology, 2011), which can be corrected through a surgical procedure in which the lens is replaced with an artificial lens.

Presbyopia tends to worsen in older adulthood, making everyday tasks such as reading fine print on a label challenging.

iStock/DaveMcDPhoto

In addition to the lens, other parts of the eye show structural changes (see Figure 15.1). Cells in the retina and optical nerve are lost with aging (Owsley et al., 2018). Some older adults experience **macular degeneration**, a substantial loss of cells in the center area of the retina, the macula, causing blurring and eventual loss of central vision (Blasiak, 2020). Hereditary and environmental factors, such as smoking and atherosclerosis, influence the onset of macular degeneration (Heesterbeek et al., 2020). Good nutrition, including a diet high in vitamins A, C, and E (found in leafy greens) and carotenoids (found in vegetables such as carrots) may protect the retina (Mares et al., 2017; Woodside et al., 2015). Laser surgery, medication, and corrective eyewear can sometimes restore some vision and treat the

FIGURE 15.1 ■ Age-Related Changes in the Eye

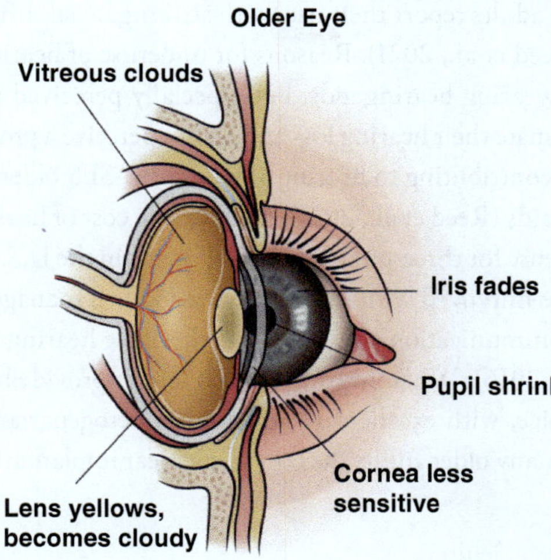

early stages of macular degeneration. However, macular degeneration is the leading cause of blindness (Mitchell et al., 2018).

Most of these changes in vision are so gradual that they may go unnoticed in people who do not visit an ophthalmologist regularly for eye examinations (Owsley et al., 2018). Substantial vision loss can have a serious effect on older adults' daily lives as it interferes not only with driving but also with reading, watching television, and doing a variety of daily activities from cooking to banking. Not surprisingly, older adults with vision loss participate less than their peers in recreational and sports activities, activities with friends and families outside the household, volunteer work, and other social activities (Jin et al., 2019). They also show higher rates of depression than their peers without visual impairments, especially when vision loss interferes with their day-to-day functioning and independence (Frank et al., 2019; van Nispen et al., 2016). Research with adults from 10 European countries linked vision loss with concentration difficulty; losing interest and enjoyment in activities; feeling fatigued, irritable, and tearful; having less hope for the future; and even wishing for death (Mojon-Azzi et al., 2008).

Hearing

Age-related hearing loss—presbycusis—typically begins in middle adulthood. By age 70 it affects about two-thirds of adults as cell losses accumulate in the inner ear and cortex (Cheslock & De Jesus, 2021). Older adults experience difficulty distinguishing high-frequency sounds, soft sounds of all frequencies, and complex tone patterns and show less activation of the auditory cortex in response to speech as compared with younger adults (Wettstein & Wahl, 2016). As in middle adulthood, men tend to suffer hearing loss earlier and to a greater extent than women (Quaranta et al., 2015). Hearing loss can greatly diminish quality of life and poses health risks. It is associated with higher risk for chronic diseases, cognitive decline, depression and mental health problems, and dementia (Bigelow et al., 2020; Brewster et al., 2020; Park et al., 2021). The inability to hear car horns and other street sounds or to hear the telephone or doorbell is a risk to safety but also to self-esteem. Turning up the volume to hear a television or radio program and then being asked by others to turn down the volume can be frustrating to older adults and their loved ones. Difficulty hearing others' speech can socially isolate older adults, reducing their social network, increasing feelings of loneliness and depression, and reducing life satisfaction.

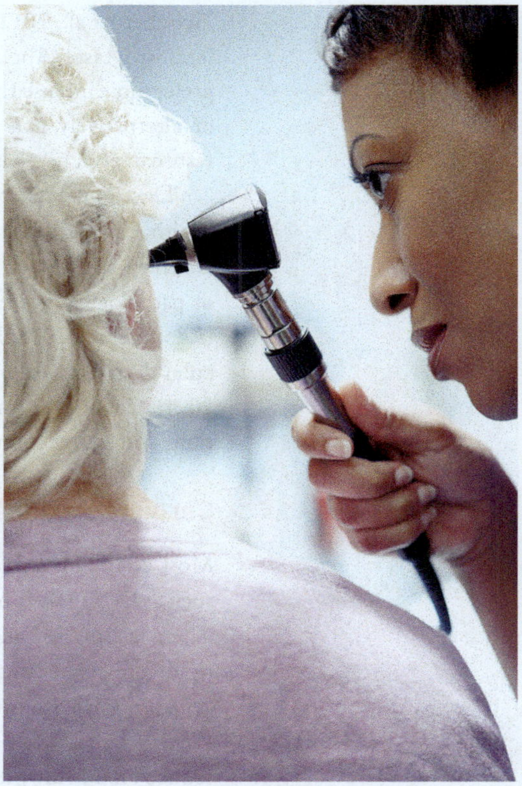

Presbycusis and other forms of hearing loss become more common in older adulthood. Hearing loss management, including examinations and communication with physicians, can improve quality of life in older adults who experience losses.

iStock/FangXiaNuo

Many older adults compensate for their hearing loss by reducing background noise, when possible, and paying attention to nonverbal cues such as lip movements, facial expressions, and body language to optimize their ability to hear and participate in conversations. Hearing aids are widely available, but only about 19% of older adults report their use, with striking racial differences (21% of white and 6% of Black older adults; Reed et al., 2021). Reasons for underuse of hearing aids include the stigma associated with being seen wearing hearing aids, but especially perceived need (Mckee et al., 2019). Many older adults underestimate their hearing loss and do not perceive a problem (Angara et al., 2021). Cost is also a driving factor contributing to hearing aid use. Low-SES older adults tend to report poor access to and use of hearing aids (Reed et al., 2021). The average cost of hearing aids is about $2,500, a potentially catastrophic expense for three-quarters of older adults in the U.S. (Jilla et al., 2021). Quality of life for older adults can be improved with successful hearing loss management, which may include education about effective communication and access to affordable hearing aids and assistive listening devices (Wettstein & Wahl, 2016). When hearing aids no longer provide benefit, cochlear implantation is the treatment of choice, with excellent results even in octogenarians (Quaranta et al., 2015). Similar to hearing aids, for many older adults the cost of cochlear implantation is prohibitive.

Smell and Taste

Sensitivity to smell declines throughout adulthood, but declines in performance are notable by about age 60 in men and 70 in women (Kondo et al., 2020; Wang et al., 2016). About one-third of adults experience substantial disruptions in their ability to smell by age 80 (Attems et al., 2015). As with much of development, individuals vary. Some show marked declines and others more gradual change. The odor itself might matter in determining adults' performance on olfactory tasks. Older adults may be as able as younger adults to identify and remember unpleasant odors, but they show decline in their abilities to identify and remember pleasant odors (Larsson et al., 2009).

Smell and taste are linked such that declines in olfactory abilities hold implications for the ability to taste. Older adults are generally less sensitive to taste as compared with young and middle-aged adults (Schubert et al., 2012). They also produce less saliva with age, resulting in a dry mouth that also interferes with taste (Abrams, 2014). Most older adults report that food seems more bland, and they tend to prefer more intense flavors, especially sweetness (de Graaf et al., 1994). They may lose interest in eating or, alternatively, may overuse salt and spicy seasonings with poor health consequences. A poor sense of taste can even be a health hazard by making it more difficult for an older adult to detect spoiled food.

Developmental changes in both smell and taste are influenced by many factors, such as general health, chronic disease, medications, and smoking (Imoscopi et al., 2012; Schiffman, 2009). Olfaction is linked with overall health and physical aging. Olfactory impairment may be an early biomarker of pathological brain aging and is associated with increased risk of cognitive decline and dementia (Adams et al., 2018; Brai et al., 2020). Loss of smell is associated with deteriorating health, cardiovascular disease, and a higher risk of mortality (Choi et al., 2021; Lafreniere & Parham, 2019; Roh et al., 2021). Changes in smell and taste, like other physical capacities, are influenced by our lifelong interactions within our contexts.

Cardiovascular, Respiratory, and Immune Systems

Most adults in their 60s become aware of changes in their cardiovascular and respiratory systems, such as feeling their heart pound and taking longer to catch their breath after running to catch a train. There is a physiological reason for this: With age, the heart experiences cell loss and becomes more rigid. The heart contains pacemaker cells that signal when to initiate a contraction; over time, these cells diminish and weaken by nearly one half, and the heart becomes less responsive to their signals (Peters et al., 2020). The arteries stiffen, and the walls accumulate cholesterol and fat plaques, which reduce blood flow; this condition is known as atherosclerosis and is a cause of heart disease (Paneni et al., 2017). As discussed in Chapter 13, cardiovascular disease may manifest as heart valve problems, arrhythmia, heart attack, and stroke. Heart disease becomes more common with age, as shown in Figure 15.2 (Benjamin et al., 2018). The nature and pace of cardiovascular system aging is influenced by epigenetics, complex interactions among genes, lifestyle, and contextual factors (Zhang et al., 2018).

FIGURE 15.2 ■ Prevalence of Cardiovascular Disease in Adults, by Age and Sex

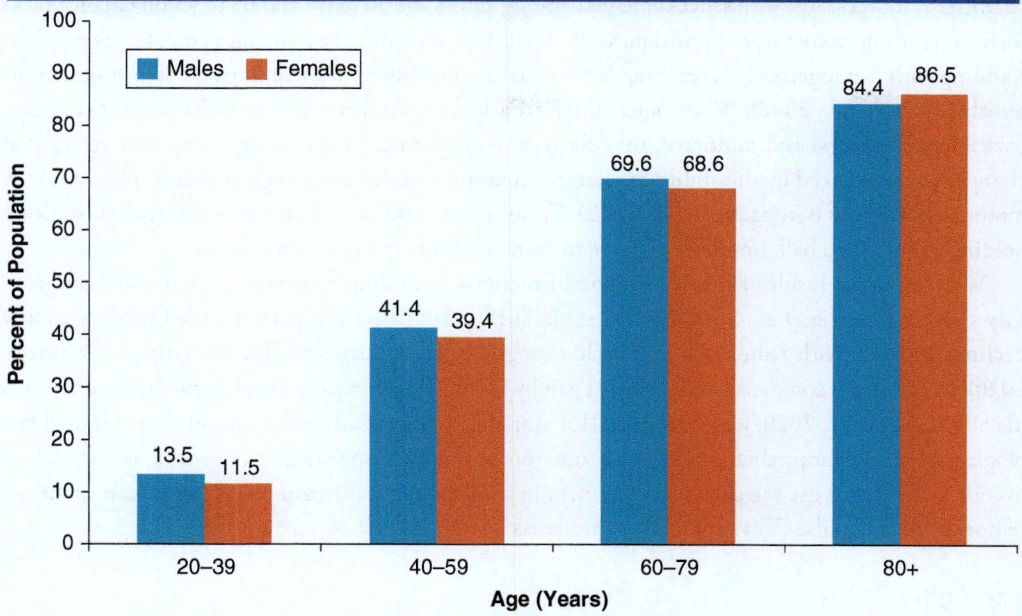

Source: Adapted from Benjamin et al. (2018).

Just as the heart undergoes changes with age, changes in the respiratory system also reduce the flow of oxygen to the body. The lungs gradually lose cells and elasticity over the adult years, substantially reducing the amount of oxygen that enters the system and is absorbed by the blood (Cho & Stout-Delgado, 2020). Older adults have more trouble breathing, feel more out of breath during physical exertion, and have a harder time catching their breath than younger adults. Experience and lifestyle influence cardiovascular and respiratory system changes. Smoking and exposure to environmental toxins increases damage to the cardiovascular and respiratory systems while physical activity and good nutrition can compensate for decreases in cardiovascular and respiratory function (Paneni et al., 2017).

With age, the immune system becomes less adaptive and efficient (Fenn et al., 2013). Declines in immune function place older adults at higher risk of diseases such as flu and pneumonia, cancers, and autoimmune diseases such as rheumatoid arthritis (Müller et al., 2019). Exposure to stress reduces immune function, and the effects increase with age: Older adults often show greater immune impairment in response to stress than younger adults (Vitlic et al., 2014). The body's T cells become less effective at protecting the body by attacking foreign substances and the immune system becomes more likely to malfunction and display an autoimmune response by turning against body tissues (Cho & Stout-Delgado, 2020). There are large individual differences in immune function. Some people retain strong immune functioning into older adulthood, but most experience at least some declines (Fenn et al., 2013).

Motor Aging

Motor skills change in predictable ways over the lifespan, with performance improving from infancy through emerging adulthood and gradually declining into late adulthood (Leversen et al., 2012). The degree of change varies among individuals. A lifetime of regular physical activity predicts greater mobility in late adulthood (Boyer et al., 2012). Physical activity can reduce age-related declines and can increase muscle and strength.

Changes in balance, the ability to control the body's position in space, play a role in age-related changes in mobility (Payne & Isaacs, 2020). Balance involves integrating sensory information with awareness of the position of one's body in space and in the surrounding environment. Changes in sensory abilities can make balance more difficult to achieve and sustain. Just as muscle strength can be improved, so can balance. Interventions that encourage exercise and promote strength and balance, such as dance and yoga, can increase balance and strength and offset loss (Čekanauskaitė et al., 2020;

Khanuja et al., 2018; Mattle et al., 2020). With age, balance requires more attention and taps more cognitive resources. Age differences emerged among adults age 50 to 64 and 65 to 75 on balance tasks such as standing from a seated position, walking 10 feet, returning and sitting as quickly as possible; standing with feet together and reaching forward as far as possible; and stepping on a step as quickly as possible (Aslan et al., 2008). When older adults are asked to perform cognitive tasks (such as counting backwards by threes) and multitask, they show even greater decrements, suggesting that age-related changes are influenced by the ability to allocate attention and that neurological change plays a role in motor performance (Granacher et al., 2012). Training on tasks with dual demands, such as walking holding a tray with a ball, improves performance and mobility (Brustio et al., 2018).

Walking is the result of many integrated functions, including neurological, muscular, and sensory systems (Holtzer et al., 2014; Sorond et al., 2015). Gait (the way a person walks) speed naturally declines with age with reductions in muscle strength, bone density, and flexibility (Payne & Isaacs, 2020). Many adults compensate for a slowed gait by taking longer steps or simplifying their movements (da Silva Costa et al., 2020; Jerome et al., 2015). Rapid declines in gait speed may indicate overall physiological declines that predict mortality because motor function, specifically gait speed, is a marker of overall health and is used in geriatric assessment in addition to measures of blood pressure, respiration, temperature, and pulse (Kuys et al., 2014; Studenski, 2011).

The Aging Brain

The brain changes in predictable ways over late adulthood. Brain volume declines as dendrites contract and are lost, accompanied by losses in synapses and glial cells (Raz & Daugherty, 2018). Glial cells provide less support to neurons and many neural fibers lose their coating of myelin, slowing communication among neurons. Declines are especially marked in the prefrontal cortex, responsible for executive functioning and judgment (Taubert et al., 2020). Myelin losses contribute to cognitive declines with aging; some myelination continues throughout adulthood, but at a slower rate, permitting some plasticity (Peters & Kemper, 2012; Wang & Young, 2014).

For most people, these neural changes are gradual. The reduction in brain volume is, on average, less than half of 1% each year throughout adulthood (Salthouse, 2011). Also, estimates of age-related changes in brain volume vary with measurement and across research studies. Some cross-sectional samples that compare adults of different ages at one time show greater age differences in brain volume than do longitudinal samples, which tend to show more continuous and gradual changes in brain volume that are less tied to age (Salthouse, 2011). Recent analyses suggest that normative volume changes are not associated with changes in verbal and nonverbal intelligence over 4 years (Jäncke et al., 2020).

Neural Compensation

Age-related changes in brain volume are not always apparent in adults' functioning. The brain retains plasticity and compensates for structural changes throughout late adulthood (Stern et al., 2019). Older adults' brains compensate for cognitive declines by showing more brain activity and using different brain areas in solving problems than younger adults (Turner & Spreng, 2012). Older adults often show brain activity (indicated in red in Figure 15.3) that is spread out over a larger area, including both hemispheres, compensating for neural losses (Daselaar & Cabeza, 2005; Reuter-Lorenz & Cappell, 2008). Sometimes neural compensation can help older adults perform as well as young adults. In one study, older adults compensated for lower levels of activity in the parietal and occipital lobes with greater activity in the frontal lobes and performed better on a working memory task than did younger adults (Osorio et al., 2010).

Adults retain **cognitive reserve**, which helps the older adult brain compensate for loss. Cognitive reserve is the ability to make flexible and efficient use of available brain resources to promote cognitive efficiency, flexibility, and adaptability (Barulli & Stern, 2013; Nair et al., 2014; Stern et al., 2019). It is a type of plasticity cultivated throughout life from experience and environmental factors. Educational and occupational attainment and engagement in leisure activities are sources of cognitive reserve that allow some adults to cope with age-related changes better than others and show more successful aging (Chapko et al., 2018; Rodriguez et al., 2019).

FIGURE 15.3 ■ Age Differences in Neural Activity During a Memory Task

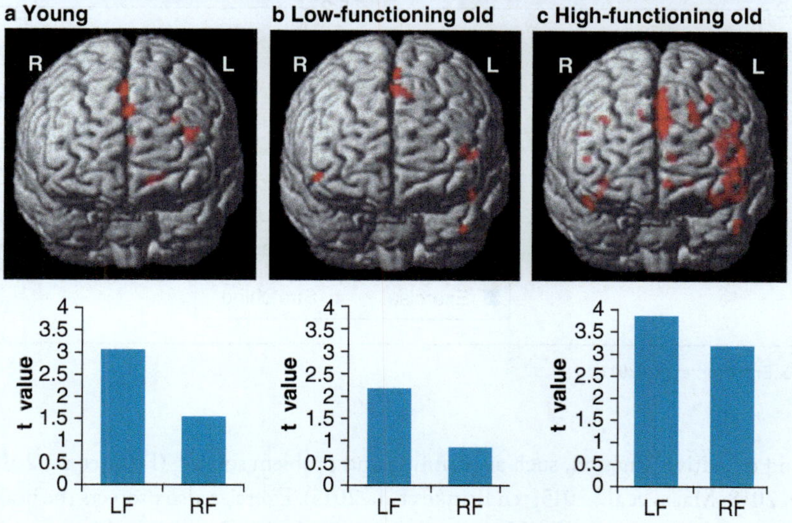

Source: Hedden and Gabrieli (2004).

Bilingualism is associated with cognitive benefits throughout life and is thought to be a marker of cognitive reserve (Bialystok, 2021). Adults who have daily experiences in using two languages, such as determining when to use one and inhibit another, show enhanced cognitive control abilities, more mental flexibility, as well as being better able to handle tasks involving switching, inhibition, and conflict monitoring (Berkes et al., 2021). In addition, bilingual older adults show preserved white matter integrity, especially in the frontal lobe, as compared with their monolingual peers (Olsen et al., 2015; Pliatsikas et al., 2015).

A particularly exciting finding is that neurogenesis, the creation of new neurons, continues throughout life (Babcock et al., 2021). New neurons are created in the hippocampus and striatum (a subcortical part of the brain responsible for coordinating motivation with body movement) and the olfactory bulb throughout life, although at a much slower rate than prenatally (Gonçalves et al., 2016; Sailor et al., 2017). Most of these neurons die off, but some survive, especially if exposed to experiences that require learning (Shors, 2014). Research with mice suggests that intense physical activity, such as running, may promote the survival of new neurons (Trinchero et al., 2017). Adult-born neurons play a distinct role in brain functions related to the hippocampus, such as memory encoding and mood regulation (Toda et al., 2019). As with neurogenesis early in life, surviving neurons migrate to the parts of the brain where they will function and create synapses with other neurons, permitting lifelong plasticity (Braun & Jessberger, 2014). It is estimated that about 2% of neurons are renewed each year (Spalding et al., 2013). The corresponding synaptogenesis is associated with learning and plays a role in cognition and in stress and emotional responses, contributing to plasticity and the maintenance of cognitive abilities and advances in psychosocial maturing in the adult years.

Promoting Brain Health

Physical health predicts neurological health and plasticity all throughout the lifespan (Braun et al., 2015). Risks to physical health, such as obesity, high blood pressure, smoking, and a sedentary lifestyle, are associated with accelerated brain aging (Bittner et al., 2021; Corlier et al., 2018). Behaviors that promote good health, such as a nutritious diet, adequate vitamin intake, and physical exercise, also promote brain health (Poulose et al., 2017).

More physically fit and active older adults tend to show greater brain volume and more efficient activity in areas key to memory and abstract thought (Erickson et al., 2010; Prakash et al., 2015). Cardiovascular exercise and activities that improve coordination are associated with increases in volume and connectivity in the frontal cortex, temporal lobe, and the hippocampus, areas responsible for

FIGURE 15.4 ■ Changes in Hippocampal Volume With Aerobic Exercise

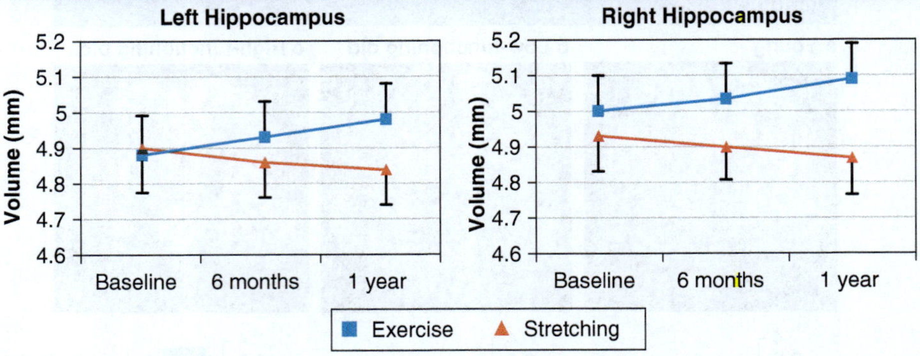

Source: Erickson et al. (2011).

memory and executive function, such as planning and problem solving (Firth et al., 2018; Kramer & Colcombe, 2018; Maass et al., 2015; ten Brinke et al., 2015). Exercise also protects the brain through its positive effect on cardiovascular health, reducing the likelihood of stroke, and increases blood flow to the brain, which protects brain function (Hsu et al., 2018).

Older adults who begin a program of moderate aerobic exercise show improvements in brain function and cognition (Loprinzi et al., 2018; Stillman et al., 2020). In one study, greater amounts of physical activity were associated with greater gray matter volume in several areas of the brain, including the prefrontal cortex and hippocampus, over a 9-year period and a reduced risk for cognitive impairment (see Figure 15.4; Erickson et al., 2010). Even light aerobic activity, such as taking walks, is associated with increased volume (Spartano et al., 2019). Moreover, it is never too late to begin an exercise program; sedentary older adults introduced to a long-term program of moderate physical activity showed increases in hippocampal volume over a 2-year period (Rosano et al., 2017). Changes in fitness levels and hippocampal volumes are associated with improvements in recognition and spatial memory (Maass et al., 2015). These exercise experiments demonstrate that the brain remains modifiable throughout adulthood and that aerobic exercise offers important opportunities for neural plasticity.

Thinking in Context: Lifespan Development

1. To what extent does the phrase "use it or lose it" apply to physical functioning in late adulthood? Provide examples considering areas such as the brain and cardiovascular, respiratory, and immune systems.
2. Contextual factors, such as socioeconomic status, influence all aspects of physical aging, including the rate and form that aging takes. Describe and provide examples of contextual factors that might influence physical development in older adulthood. To what extent do these forces operate earlier in life?

Thinking in Context: Applied Developmental Science

How might the age-related changes that adults experience in vision and hearing influence their day-to-day functioning and interactions with others? Consider adults' roles in the workplace and at home, as employees, parents, spouses, and friends. Outline some of the practical implications of these developmental changes. What can older adults (and those they interact with) do to improve their day-to-day interactions and experiences?

ATYPICAL BRAIN AGING: DEMENTIA

LEARNING OBJECTIVE

15.2 Describe common dementias and the role of contextual and intersectional factors in dementia.

Some older adults experience high rates of cell death and severe brain deterioration that characterize dementia. **Dementia** is a term referring to the progressive loss of mental abilities due to changes in the brain that influence higher cortical functions such as thinking, memory, comprehension, and emotional control, and are reflected in impaired thought and behavior, interfering with the older adult's capacity to engage in everyday activities (Alzheimer's Association, 2018; World Health Organization, 2012). In recent years scientists have recognized that there are many causes of dementia and dementia can take many forms, depending on its cause. The *Diagnostic and Statistical Manual of Mental Disorders* (DSM-5) has replaced the generic term *dementia* with *neurocognitive disorder* as a label for a set of diseases that cause brain deterioration (American Psychiatric Association, 2013). Throughout our discussion we will use the term *dementia* to refer to the cognitive symptoms that are characteristic of neurocognitive disorders.

There are about 50 million people worldwide living with dementia today, and there may be more than 150 million by 2050 (World Health Organization, n.d.). Much of the increase will be in low-income developing countries (see Figure 15.5). Worldwide, currently 60% of people with dementia live in developing countries; by 2050 this will rise to more than 70%. The fastest growth in the elderly population is taking place in China, India, and their south Asian and western Pacific neighbors (Alzheimer's Disease International, 2015). Poor access to education, health care, and nutrition contribute to geographic differences in dementia rates.

Neurocognitive disorders that cause dementia symptoms often co-occur and adults may show different forms of dementia at once (Fierini, 2020; Kang et al., 2019). The most common cause of dementia is Alzheimer's disease, followed by vascular dementia and Lewy body dementia. Neurocognitive disorders, even in their very early stages, are associated with higher rates of mortality (Andersen et al., 2010). The most common neurocognitive disorders are discussed next.

FIGURE 15.5 ■ Projected Growth in Dementia Prevalence: Low-Income vs. High-Income Countries, 2013–2050

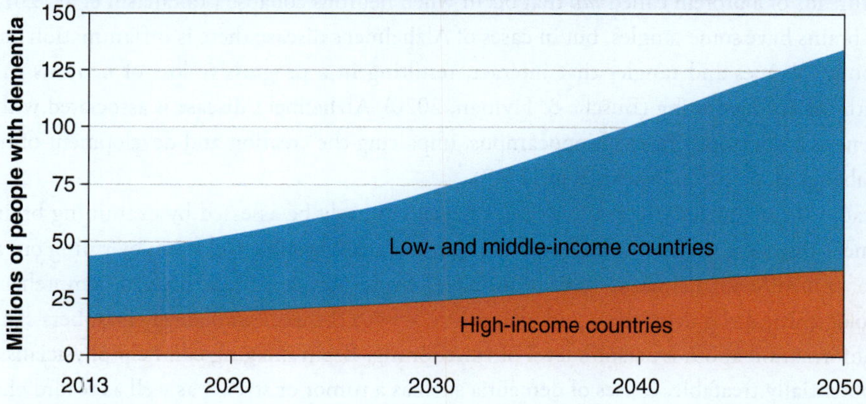

Source: Adapted from Alzheimer's Disease International (2015).

FIGURE 15.6 ■ Projected Prevalence of Alzheimer's Disease in the U.S. Population, 2010–2050

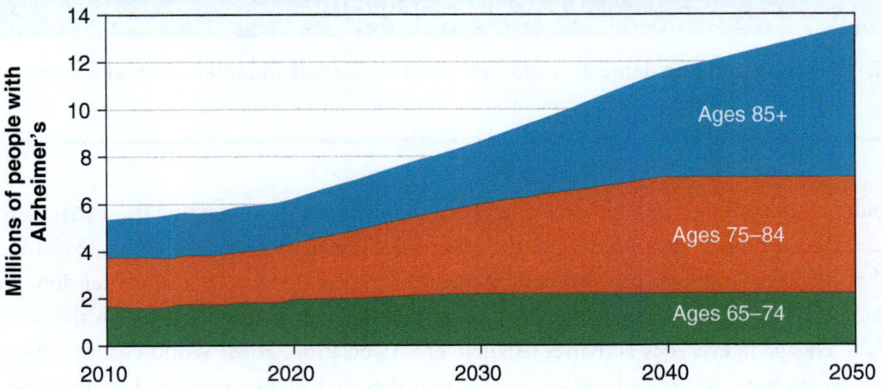

Source: Adapted from Alzheimer's Disease International (2015).

Alzheimer's Disease

Alzheimer's disease is a neurodegenerative disorder that progresses from mild to moderate cognitive declines to include personality and behavior changes, motor problems, severe dementia, and death (Abeysinghe et al., 2020). The risk of Alzheimer's disease grows exponentially with age, doubling approximately every 5 to 6 years in most Western countries. Currently 6.2 million Americans, including more than 1 in 9 people over the age of 65, have Alzheimer's disease (see Figure 15.6; Alzheimer's Association, 2021). Prevalence rates increase with age: Alzheimer's disease is diagnosed in about 5% of people age 65 to 74, 14% of those 75 to 84, and 35% of those 85 or older. People younger than 65 can also develop Alzheimer's dementia, but it is uncommon.

Diagnosis

Alzheimer's disease is characterized by widespread brain deterioration associated with inflammation and accumulations of *beta-amyloid*, a protein present in the tissue that surrounds neurons in the healthy brain (Long & Holtzman, 2019). Alzheimer's patients experience inflammation that causes the beta-amyloid to accumulate and join with clumps of dead neurons and glial cells, forming large masses called **amyloid plaques** (see Figure 15.7). It is thought that amyloid plaques disrupt the structure and function of cell membranes and contribute to the formation of **neurofibrillary tangles**, twisted bundles of threads of a protein called *tau* that occur when neurons collapse (Takahashi et al., 2017). Even healthy brains have some tangles, but in cases of Alzheimer's disease there is inflammation and a proliferation of plaques and tangles that interact, resulting in a progressive loss of neurons that interferes with brain functioning (Busche & Hyman, 2020). Alzheimer's disease is associated with altered neurogenesis and atrophy in the hippocampus, impairing the creation and development of new neurons (Babcock et al., 2021; Josephs et al., 2017).

Because the characteristic beta-amyloid plaques can only be assessed by examining brain tissue, Alzheimer's disease is generally diagnosed in living patients through exclusion: by ruling out all other causes of dementia (Alzheimer's Association, 2021). Symptoms, a medical history, comprehensive sets of neurological and cognitive tests, and conversations with the adult and family members can provide useful information about a person's level of functioning. Brain imaging can help physicians rule out other, potentially treatable, causes of dementia such as a tumor or stroke, as well as record changes in brain volume and activity (Hort et al., 2010). For example, larger than usual spaces surrounding some of the blood vessels in the brain are associated with Alzheimer's disease (Banerjee et al., 2017). MRI scans can capture images of amyloid plaques and tangles associated with diagnoses of Alzheimer's disease (Raman et al., 2016). Biomarkers—genetic or biological traces—of the disease, such as high concentrations of beta-amyloid in cerebrospinal fluid, hold promise for diagnosis but are not yet routinely used in the U.S. (Blennow et al., 2015; Frisoni et al., 2017).

FIGURE 15.7 ■ Alzheimer's Disease and the Brain

Alzheimer's disease entails a wasting of the brain, as illustrated by the decreased size in the diseased brain (top) as compared with the healthy brain (middle). Alzheimer's disease is characterized by the presence of plaques (bottom) that damage neurons and disrupt functioning.

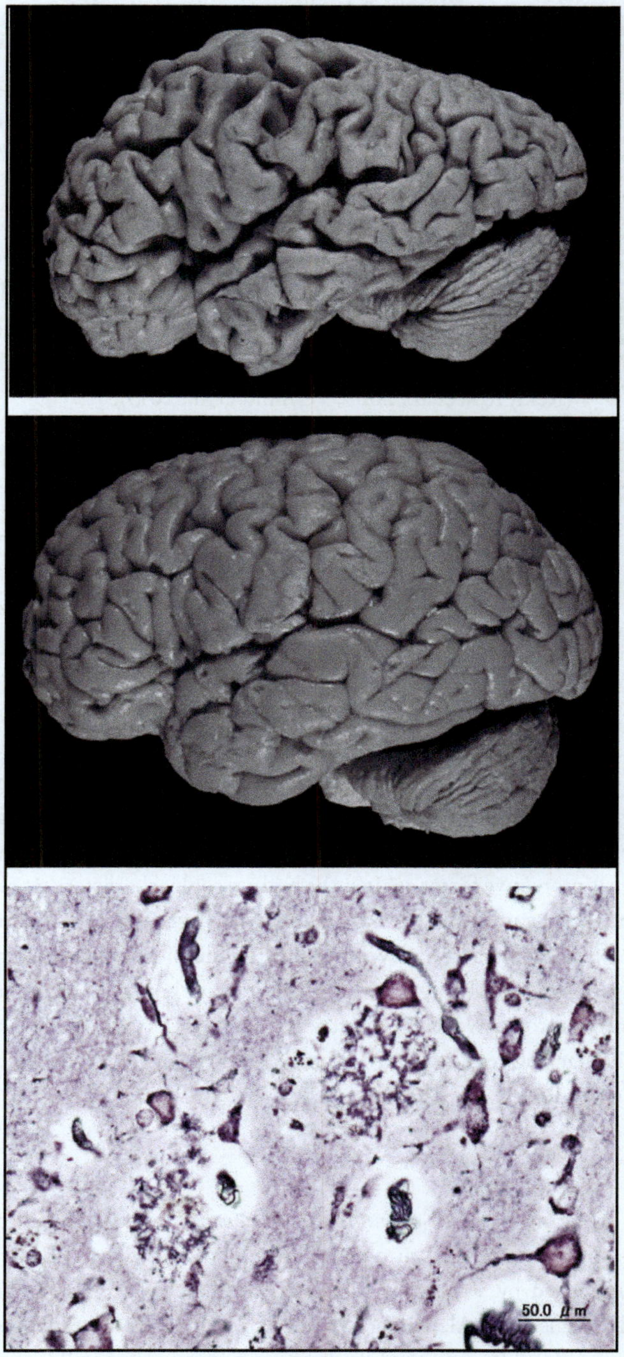

Source: Wikimedia Commons

Progression

Alzheimer's disease progresses through several predictable steps with specific patterns of cognitive and memory loss. The earliest symptoms of Alzheimer's disease are memory problems, likely because the neurological disruptions that comprise Alzheimer's disease usually begin in the hippocampus, which is influential in memory (Guzmán-Vélez et al., 2016). Memory deficits are accompanied by

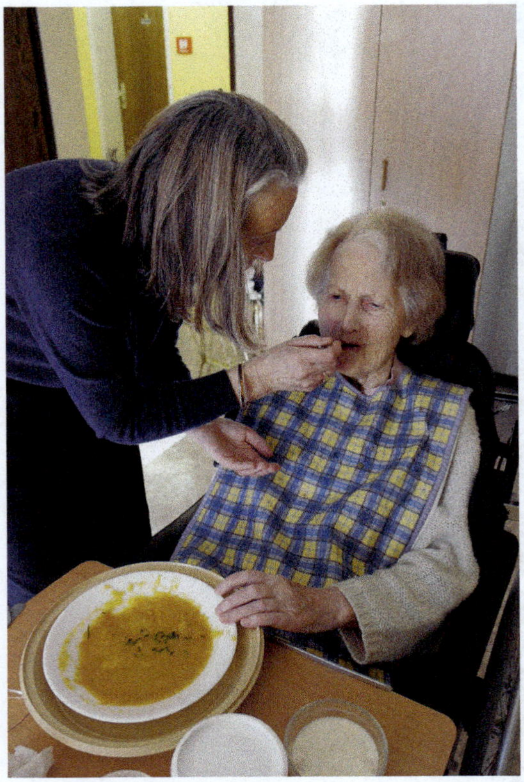

In the final stages of Alzheimer's disease, brain deterioration interferes with the individual's ability to comprehend and produce speech, to control bodily functions, and to respond to stimuli.

Tony Craddock/Science Source

impaired attentional control, which, to an outside observer, may appear as further absentmindedness and inattention, or being "lost" in one's own world (Huntley et al., 2017). Early Alzheimer's disease can be hard to distinguish from normal aging—or at least popular views and stereotypes of aging. Over time, impairments worsen and Alzheimer's patients tend to become frequently confused (Carson et al., 2015). Some adults may show unpredictable angry outbursts, paranoia, and personality changes (Tautvydaitė et al., 2017). As the disease progresses patients become unable to care for themselves. Eventually they will no longer recognize objects, faces, and familiar people (Lavallée et al., 2016). In the final stages of the disease, Alzheimer's patients lose the ability to comprehend and produce speech, to control bodily functions, and to respond to stimuli (Carson et al., 2015). They show heightened vulnerability to infections and illnesses that often lead to death. Eventually brain functions deteriorate to the point where organs fail and life cannot be sustained. The average patient progresses to the final stage of Alzheimer's disease over the course of about 10 years, with a typical range of 5 to 12 years (Rektorova et al., 2009; Vermunt et al., 2019).

Risk and Protective Factors

Alzheimer's disease has genetic influences and often runs in families (Bettens et al., 2013; Naj & Schellenberg, 2017). Several chromosomes are implicated, including the 21st chromosome. Individuals with Down Syndrome (trisomy 21) are at high risk to develop Alzheimer's disease as many show plaques and tangles in their brains as early as age 40 (Lemere, 2013; Wiseman et al., 2015). Contextual and behavioral factors also matter. Research suggests that the same factors that contribute to cardiovascular risk, such as high blood pressure and obesity, also heighten the risk for Alzheimer's disease (Li et al., 2016; Tosto et al., 2016). Good nutrition is linked with cardiovascular health and might serve a protective role against Alzheimer's disease, but research is mixed (Douaud et al., 2013; Schelke et al., 2016).

Cognitive reserve is protective factor against the brain atrophy characteristic of Alzheimer's disease (Xu et al., 2015). One recent study showed that patients with higher levels of education showed similar cognitive functioning to those with lower levels of education despite demonstrating more severe neurofibrillary tangles, suggesting that their greater cognitive reserve buffered against losses (Hoenig et al., 2017). Other influences on cognitive reserve contributing to a lower risk of Alzheimer's disease include social engagement, interacting regularly with others, as well as engaging in regular physical activity (De la Rosa et al., 2020; Khoury et al., 2019).

Vascular Dementia

Vascular dementia, sometimes known as *multi-infarct dementia*, is the second most common form of dementia and loss of mental ability in older adulthood, worldwide (O'Brien & Thomas, 2015). Vascular dementia is caused by strokes, or blockages of blood vessels in the brain (Vinters et al., 2018). Whereas individuals with Alzheimer's disease show slow and steady decrements in mental abilities, those with vascular dementia tend to show sudden, but often mild, losses with each stroke (Kalaria, 2018). As time passes, individuals tend to show improvement because the brain's plasticity leads other neurons to take on functions of those that were lost. Additional strokes usually follow, and with each stroke brain matter is lost and it becomes harder for the remaining neurons to compensate for losses (Korczyn et al., 2012).

As vascular dementia worsens, the symptoms are similar to those of Alzheimer's disease (O'Brien & Thomas, 2015). But vascular dementia is neurologically different from Alzheimer's disease. The damage caused by small strokes is visible on MRI scans and localized to specific areas of the brain (Vinters et al., 2018). Postmortem analyses of the brains of people with vascular dementia show substantial deterioration of areas of the brain and disruptions in white matter but not the widespread abundance of plaques and tangles that accompany Alzheimer's disease (Hase et al., 2018; Iadecola, 2013),

Vascular dementia is influenced by both genetic and environmental factors (Markus & Schmidt, 2019; Srinivasan et al., 2016). Obesity, diabetes, hypertension, and cardiovascular disease increase the risk of vascular dementia (Lyu et al., 2020; Turana et al., 2019). As we have discussed, genetics may influence factors that are known to be linked with vascular dementia, such as obesity, diabetes, and cardiovascular disease. Factors that prevent cardiovascular disease, such as physical activity, can also prevent or slow the progression of vascular dementia (Gallaway et al., 2017). Thus, prevention and management of vascular risks may be the best weapon in a fight against age-related cognitive decline (Corriveau et al., 2016). In addition, when symptoms of stroke arise, such as sudden vision loss, weakening or numbness in part of the body, or problems producing or understanding speech, anti-clotting drugs can prevent the blood from clotting and forming additional strokes.

Parkinson's Disease

Parkinson's disease is a brain disorder that occurs when neurons in a part of the brain called the substantia nigra die or become impaired. Neurons in this part of the brain produce the neurotransmitter dopamine, which enables coordinated function of the body's muscles and smooth movement. Parkinson's disease is characterized by a specific progression of motor symptoms including tremors, slowness of movement, difficulty initiating movement, rigidity, difficulty with balance, and a shuffling walk (Postuma et al., 2015). Parkinson's symptoms appear when at least 50% of the nerve cells in the substantia nigra are damaged (National Parkinson Foundation, 2008).

Motor symptoms typically occur in one part of the body and slowly spread to the extremities on the same side of the body before appearing on the opposite side of the body (Truong & Wolters, 2009). Because the stiffness and rigidity are first located in one part of the body, individuals may assume that it is ordinary stiffness, perhaps the result of too much activity or simply because of aging. As the disease progresses, individuals have difficulties with balance and controlling their body movements (Mirelman et al., 2019). As neurons continue to degenerate, cognitive symptoms emerge. Brain functioning declines and cognitive and speech abilities deteriorate. Research on the incidence of dementia in Parkinson's patients is mixed, but recent studies estimate that 25% to 30% of adults with Parkinson's disease will develop dementia within 10 years of diagnosis (Bove et al., 2020; Hanagasi et al., 2017).

The prevalence of Parkinson's disease and its associated dementia increases with age and Parkinson's disease is found throughout the world, with similar rates occurring in Asia, Africa, South America, Europe, North America, and Australia (Hirsch et al., 2016; Pringsheim et al., 2014; Savica et al., 2018). People diagnosed with Parkinson's disease at advanced ages tend to develop dementia earlier into their disease than do younger people, likely because of age-related differences in cognitive capacities and neural reserves (Grossman et al., 2006).

There is a genetic component to Parkinson's disease (Blauwendraat et al., 2020). Environmental influences might include exposure to heavy metals, pesticides, smoking, and substance abuse, but there are few consistent findings regarding environmental and lifestyle influences (Ball et al., 2019; Marras et al., 2019). Parkinson's is likely influenced by the complex gene-environment interactions characteristic of epigenetics (Dunn et al., 2019; van Heesbeen & Smidt, 2019). Physical activity may act as a protective factor in developing Parkinson's disease, slowing its progression, and improving motor control (Bellou et al., 2016; Paillard et al., 2015).

Boxer Muhammad Ali (1942–2016) and actor Michael J. Fox, both diagnosed with Parkinson's disease, pretend to spar before giving their testimony before the 2002 U.S. Senate Appropriations Subcommittee on Health and Human Services advocating that more funding be directed to finding a cure for the disease.

Mark Wilson / Staff/ Getty

Diagnosing Parkinson's disease is difficult because it is diagnosed by exclusion. Incorrect diagnoses are common, potentially delaying treatment for Parkinson's patients (Rizzo et al., 2015). Recent research shows that brain scans can detect changes in the substantia nigra associated with Parkinson's disease, suggesting that, in the future, such scans might be used for diagnosis (Atkinson-Clement et al., 2017). Researchers are searching for biomarkers that may be used to diagnose Parkinson's disease, but the work is still in its early stages (Miller & O'Callaghan, 2015; Parnetti et al., 2019).

Parkinson's symptoms can be treated. Deep brain stimulation, stimulating specific parts of the brain with electricity, as well as resistance training can improve some of the motor symptoms, such as poor gait and posture (Hartmann et al., 2019; Lamotte et al., 2015). Most medications either replace or mimic dopamine, which temporarily improves the motor symptoms of the disease; anti-inflammatory medications may also help reduce neurodegeneration and medication can help alleviate the symptoms of dementia (Aarsland et al., 2017; Emre et al., 2014). Medication can temporarily reduce symptoms and perhaps slow its progression, but Parkinson's disease is not curable.

Lewy Body Dementia

Lewy body dementia is thought to be about as common as vascular dementia (Walker et al., 2017). Central features of Lewy body dementia include progressive dementia that interferes with social or occupational functions and deficits on cognitive tasks, such as attention, visuospatial ability, and executive function (Bonanni et al., 2018). Unique to Lewy body dementia are fluctuations in cognition, alternating worsening and improving (Matar et al., 2020). Lewy body dementia can also be distinguished from Alzheimer's disease by the presence of visual hallucinations, cognitive symptoms that fluctuate (improving and worsening), some Parkinson's-like motor symptoms, and, especially, sleep disorders in which individuals sleepwalk and act out their dreams (Hamilton et al., 2012).

The hallmark of Lewy body dementia is the presence of Lewy bodies—spherical protein deposits —accompanied by neural loss (Walker et al., 2015). Lewy bodies are also common to Parkinson's dementia. The genetics of dementia with Lewy bodies and Parkinson's disease overlap, suggesting that the disorders are linked (Meeus et al., 2012). Unfortunately, damage caused by Lewy bodies is usually not apparent on MRI scans until very late in the disease or after death. Like other neurocognitive disorders, Lewy body dementia is diagnosed by exclusion, ruling out other causes of dementia (Bonanni et al., 2018). The search is on for biomarkers of Lewy body dementia, but research is in its early stage and there are no definitive biomarkers (Matar et al., 2020; Siderowf et al., 2018). Like other dementias, Lewy body dementia is managed but not cured. Medication can treat many of the symptoms of Lewy body dementia, such as sleep problems, hallucinations, and cognitive problems, but Lewy body dementia is a progressive neurodegenerative disease that eventually causes death.

Race, Ethnicity, and Dementia

Neurocognitive disorders know no bounds, but the risk for developing dementia symptoms varies with race, ethnicity, and sex (Quiñones et al., 2020). Women, regardless of race, ethnicity, and age, experience greater risk for developing Alzheimer's disease than men (Matthews et al., 2019; Pike, 2017). Hormonal differences may play a role in Alzheimer's risk but there is not enough research to draw conclusions (Nebel et al., 2018). Vascular dementia is more common in men, but the risk factors for vascular dementia vary among men and women. Stroke and heart disease are greater contributors in men and diabetes, hypertension, and midlife obesity in women (Gannon et al., 2019).

There are dramatic ethnic differences in the prevalence of dementia in older adults (see Figure 15.8). Overall, African Americans are twice as likely, and Hispanic populations one-and-one-half times as likely, to be diagnosed with dementia than non-Hispanic whites (Matthews et al., 2019; Mayeda et al., 2016; Mehta & Yeo, 2017).

There is a genetic component to dementias such as Alzheimer's, but genetics is not thought to influence racial and ethnic differences in rates of diagnoses (Raj et al., 2017). Instead, social and contextual factors, such as health, access to resources, socioeconomic status, and life experience play a large role in racial and ethnic differences in Alzheimer's and other dementias. High blood pressure, diabetes, and

FIGURE 15.8 ■ Estimated Prevalence of Alzheimer's Disease and Related Dementias in the U.S. Population, Aged ≥65 Years, by Sex, Race, and Ethnicity, 2014

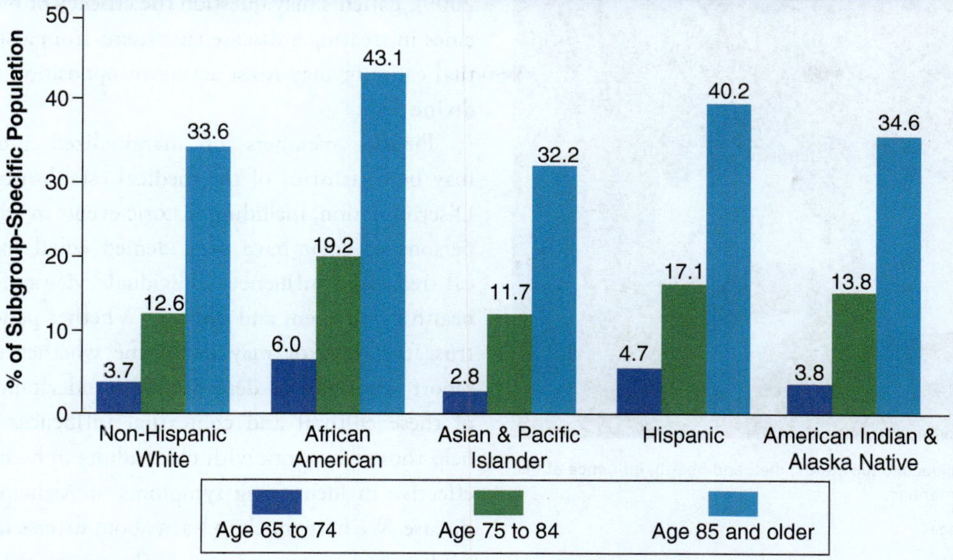

Source: Matthews et al. (2019).

cardiovascular disease, risk factors for many dementias, are more common among Black and Latinx adults (Cheng et al., 2019; Farrell et al., 2020; Hill-Briggs et al., 2021).

Differences in educational attainment, an influence on cognitive reserve, may also contribute to ethnic and racial differences in risk for dementia. One early study found that Latinx and African Americans showed higher rates of dementia than white adults, but the ethnic and racial differences disappeared once education was taken into account (Gurland et al., 1999). More recent research suggests much more complicated relationships among education, cognitive reserve, and dementia risk. A recent study of diverse older adults found that educational attainment buffered the impact of neurological deficits on memory and language only for white older adults but not for Black and Hispanic older adults (Avila et al., 2021). In addition, the neurological deficits, such as reductions in white matter and synaptic complexity, were more strongly associated with memory and language declines for Blacks than others. These results suggest that educational attainment may not be a good indicator of cognitive reserve for Black older adults and therefore may not reduce their risk of Alzheimer's disease.

Why might educational attainment be a less relevant contributor to cognitive reserve for Black older adults, compared with white older adults? Research demonstrating links between education and cognitive reserve was, like much research today, based on samples of white adults and did not consider racial and ethnic differences in education or school quality. Many Black older adults in the U.S. were born and raised in the South where Jim Crow laws enforced segregation and limited opportunities for education, health care, housing, income, and work. Poor quality education may not contribute to cognitive reserve in the same way as high-quality education, accounting for some of the racial differences in dementia. Other threats to the development of cognitive reserve include poverty and lack of resources, community stress, and exposure to early and repeated trauma in childhood, adolescence, and adulthood (Quiñones et al., 2020). These cohort or generational experiences of structural racism pose risks that educational attainment cannot override.

Other contextual factors that contribute to the higher risk for Alzheimer's disease in people of color include cultural beliefs about aging, spirituality, and views of the medical profession. Black adults are more likely than white adults to express beliefs that Alzheimer's symptoms, such as substantial memory loss, are just a normal part of aging (Connell et al., 2009; Jackson et al., 2017; Roberts et al., 2003). Differences in expectations for normative aging and Alzheimer's may contribute to delayed dementia care in Black older adults (Chin et al., 2011; Quiñones et al., 2020). Religious and spiritual beliefs may also influence views of Alzheimer's. One study found that a larger proportion of African Americans

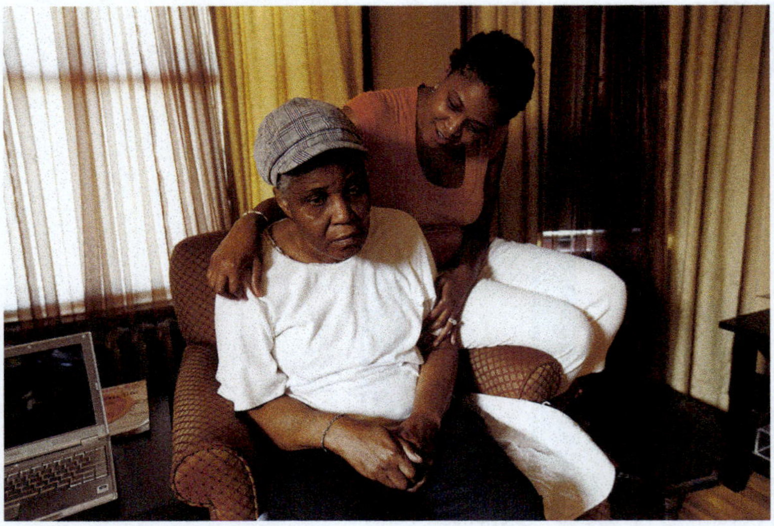

Social and cultural factors, such as socioeconomic status, diet, and health, influence ethnic differences in Alzheimer's and other dementias.

Yoon S. Byun/The Boston Globe via Getty Images

indicated that they believed "God's will" determined who developed Alzheimer's (Connell et al., 2009). Patients may question the efficacy of medicines in treating a disease that stems from a spiritual cause or may resist acting in opposition to a divine plan.

Finally, members of marginalized groups may be distrustful of the medical establishment. Discrimination, including historic events in which persons of color have been denied equal medical treatment, influences individuals' views of the health care system and doctors. Whether patients trust their doctor may determine whether they report symptoms of dementia. An understanding of these cultural and contextual influences can help those who work with older adults to be more effective in identifying symptoms of Alzheimer's disease. We have much to learn about diverse older adults' experiences and their influence on risk for dementia. It is clear that access to opportunities differ radically with race, ethnicity, and SES and influence health and susceptibility to disease and dementia.

Thinking in Context: Intersectionality

1. Describe some racial and ethnic differences in dementia rates. What are some contributors to these differences?
2. What risks to cognitive reserve might older adults of color experience? How might adults boost their cognitive reserve?
3. Considering sociohistorical context, to what extend might you expect young adults today to experience similar threats to cognitive reserve and similar risks for dementia as their grandparents? Why?

HEALTH

LEARNING OBJECTIVE

15.3 Summarize influences on health and common health issues in late adulthood.

Adults today live longer than ever before. The increase in life expectancy over the past century can be attributed to the influence of contextual factors such as advances in health care, nutrition, sanitation, and especially the reduction in infant mortality (Dong et al., 2016). Death during childbirth, a common hazard to women in the early 1900s, is rare in industrialized nations. Breakthroughs in medicine and increases in the availability of health care mean that fewer people die of common ailments such as flu, pneumonia, and heart disease. A greater understanding of the role of behavioral factors such as smoking, exercise habits, and diet also contributes to advances in longevity (White et al., 2018). Although cancer remains a leading cause of death, the cancer survival rate, defined as living 5 years after diagnosis, is higher than ever. In 2013, 69% of adults diagnosed with cancer in the United States were survivors, as compared with about one-half in 1975 (American Cancer Society, 2019).

Ages of Adulthood

Adults 90 years of age and older are the fastest growing population in Western countries. Centenarians, once an oddity, are increasingly common.

iStock/ praetorianphoto

Advances in life expectancy have led gerontologists to categorize older adults into the **young-old**, **old-old**, and **oldest-old**. The young-old, ages 65 to 74, tend to be active, healthy, and financially and physically independent. Old-old adults (75 to 84) typically live independently but often experience some physical and mental impairment. The oldest-old, adults 85 years and older, are at highest risk for physical and mental health problems and often are unable to live independently, requiring physical and social support to carry out the tasks of daily life. Although these age categories are thought to predict physical health and dependency, some adults in their mid-60s show advanced signs of aging characteristic of the oldest-old, while others in their late 80s function similarly to old-old adults. Because of this, many developmental researchers categorize older adults not by chronological age but by functioning, using terms such as **successful aging** and *impaired aging* (Kok et al., 2015).

Centenarians, individuals who live past 100 years, are becoming more common. There were 90,000 centenarians recorded in the United Stated in 2020, 25% more than the roughly 70,000 recorded in 2014 (which was about 44% more than in 2000!; PBS Newshour, 2020; Xu, 2016). The longest recorded human lifespan is 122 years (Punt, 2020). The number of centenarians is expected to rise rapidly in the coming decades. Adults 90 years of age and older are the fastest growing population in Western countries, such as Denmark, Italy, Japan, the United Kingdom, and the United States (Administration on Aging, 2014; Alejandro et al., 2015).

Centenarians tend to be healthier than their same-age peers all throughout life, often delaying the onset of mortality-related diseases and disability until well into their 90s (Ailshire et al., 2015; Brandão et al., 2017). Like all older adults, most centenarians experience chronic age-related diseases, but up to one-quarter reach age 100 with no chronic disease (Ash et al., 2015; Richmond et al., 2012). Moreover, centenarians seem to manage chronic illnesses more effectively than other older adults, with many not experiencing disability until well into their 90s (Sebastiani & Perls, 2012). In addition, about one-half to two-thirds appear to reach 100 without cognitive impairment (Ailshire et al., 2015; Corrada et al., 2010).

Longevity is influenced by both genes and lifestyle factors through epigenetics (Armstrong et al., 2017). A particular gene known as the APOE gene is associated with longevity, and centenarians show different patterns of APOE activation that may be linked with their lower likelihood of disease and longer lifespan (Arai et al., 2017; Ryu et al., 2016; Shadyab & LaCroix, 2015). Behavioral and environmental factors, such as nutrition, stress, education, and smoking, may show epigenetic effects on longevity by turning particular genes on and off (Govindaraju et al., 2015; Ishioka et al., 2016; Rea & Mills, 2018). Centenarians tend to attribute their longevity to their lifestyles, social relationships and support, and to their own attitudes about life, including optimism and adaptability (Freeman et al., 2013). Life satisfaction predicts future happiness and longevity and influences how centenarians frame their subjective evaluations of their own health status (Bishop et al., 2010; Jopp et al., 2016; Yorgason et al., 2018).

Nutrition

As adults age, their metabolism slows and their nutritional needs change. Older adults require fewer calories than younger adults, and their diets must be more nutrient dense to meet their nutritional needs with fewer calories (Bernstein, 2017). It is estimated that two-thirds of older adults in many developed countries, including Germany, Italy, Japan, the Netherlands, and the United States, are at risk for malnutrition (Kaiser et al., 2010; van Bokhorst-de van der Schueren et al., 2013). Malnutrition is associated with illness, functional disability, and mortality (Charlton et al., 2013).

Age-related declines in taste and smell may influence older adults' eating habits (Ogawa et al., 2017). As adults lose their sense of taste they may eat less food or choose stronger flavors. Nutrition surveys suggest that older adults consume more sweet and salty foods (Sergi et al., 2017). Older adults who live alone may be reluctant to shop, cook, and eat by themselves. Bereavement, social isolation, depression, and illnesses, such as cancer, are associated with malnutrition (Boulos et al., 2017; van den Broeke et al., 2018). Medication can alter older adults' nutritional needs (Reilly & Ilich, 2017). For example, medications that treat hypertension tend to deplete stores of potassium, an electrolyte critical for nervous system and organ functioning.

Vitamin and mineral supplements can fill in gaps in older adults' diet. Most (80%) older adults report taking at least one dietary supplement (Gahche et al., 2017). Vitamin D and calcium can help reduce the risk of fractures (Saad et al., 2018). The effects of vitamin supplements on cardiovascular disease and cancer are mixed, with some studies suggesting a protective effect and others none (Blumberg et al., 2018; Rautiainen et al., 2017; Woodside et al., 2015). Catechin, a polyphenol found in green tea, has an antioxidative effect and may protect against age-related declines in cognitive functions such as learning and memory, as well as progressive neurodegenerative disorders such as Parkinson's and Alzheimer's diseases (Calapai et al., 2017; Farzaei et al., 2019)

Omega-3, an oil found in fish that is high in polyunsaturated fatty acids, promotes vascular health and is associated with reductions in inflammation and reduced risk of cardiovascular disease and degenerative diseases such as arthritis and potentially Alzheimer's disease (Bernasconi et al., 2021; Lorente-Cebrián et al., 2013, 2015). In one double-blind study, healthy older adults aged 50 to 75 showed increases in executive function and improvements in white matter integrity and gray matter volume, suggesting that omega-3 may have implications for neurological health and functioning (Witte et al., 2014). Moreover, consumption of omega-3 appears to have an epigenetic effect on longevity through its action on telomeres, the caps covering the tips of DNA. Recall from Chapter 11 that telomeres shorten with every cell division until they reach a critical length, stopping cell division and preceding cell death. The consumption of omega-3 is associated with slowed and even reduced telomere shortening over 5- to 8-year periods (Farzaneh-Far et al., 2010; Paul, 2011), suggesting that cell aging can be slowed and even extended. Improved nutrition holds the promise of protection against age-related cognitive changes, but more research is needed.

Exercise

As in early and middle adulthood, exercise offers powerful health benefits in late adulthood. It is never too late to become more physically active. Older adults who begin a program of cardiovascular activity, such as walking, cycling, or aerobic dancing, show gains similar to those of much younger adults (Grootswagers et al., 2020). Weight-bearing exercise begun as late as 90 years of age can improve blood flow to the muscles and increase muscle size (Bechshøft et al., 2017; Grootswagers et al., 2020).

The physical benefits of regular exercise include increases in strength, balance, posture, and endurance and permit older adults to carry out everyday activities such as grocery shopping, lifting grandchildren, reaching for objects, and opening jars and bottles (Peterson et al., 2010). Throughout the adult years, moderate physical activity is associated with improved physiological function, a decreased incidence of disease, and reduced incidence of disability (Barengo et al., 2017; Fielding et al., 2017).

Physical activity is also good for the mind. Just as earlier in life, exercise offers older adults stress relief, protects against depression, and is associated with higher quality of life (Windle et al., 2010). Older adults who are physically active show less neural and glial cell losses throughout their cortex and less cognitive decline than do those who are sedentary (Muscari et al., 2010; Sampaio-Baptista & Johansen-Berg, 2017). Perhaps more significant is that in older adults, exercise is associated with increased hippocampal volume (Dumas, 2017; Ryan & Nolan, 2016). Older adults who participate in exercise training programs show improved cognitive function (Falck et al., 2019). Adults who engage in regular cardiovascular exercise demonstrate improved performance on tasks examining attention, executive function, processing speed, memory, and other cognitive processes (Erickson et al., 2011; Hindin & Zelinski, 2012). Moreover, dementia patients who engage in a program of physical exercise, specifically cardiovascular exercise, show improvements in cognitive function, regardless of the intervention frequency or the specific dementia diagnosis (Groot et al., 2016), suggesting that exercise has powerful benefits for cognitive health.

Exercise is associated with neural plasticity, including increases in volume and connectivity.
iStock/Mikolette

National guidelines recommend that adults of all ages do at least 150 minutes to 300 minutes of moderate-intensity or 75 minutes to 150 minutes of vigorous-intensity physical activity weekly, coupled with muscle strengthening exercise at least twice a week (U.S. Department of Health and Human Services, 2018). Older adults should modify their speed and intensity as needed. As little as 10 minutes of activity at a time counts. Exercises that maintain or improve balance are also important in promoting mobility and protecting against falls.

Chronic Illness

Chronic illnesses become more common with age. About 80% of older adults suffer from one chronic illness or another, and many have multiple diagnoses (National Council on Aging, 2021). Yet, like younger people, older adults tend to view their health as good or better (see Figure 15.9).

Arthritis

Although there are many different types of arthritis, a degenerative joint disease, the most common is **osteoarthritis**, which affects joints that we use most often: the hips, knees, lower back, and hands. The cartilage that protects the ends of bones where they meet at joints wears away and joints become less flexible and swell. Those who suffer from osteoarthritis experience a loss of movement and a great deal of pain. Aging is the most prominent risk factor for osteoarthritis; it often first appears in middle adulthood, occurring in about one-third of adults ages 45 to 64, but it becomes more common and

FIGURE 15.9 ■ Current Health Status Among Adults Aged 18 and Over in the United States, 2015

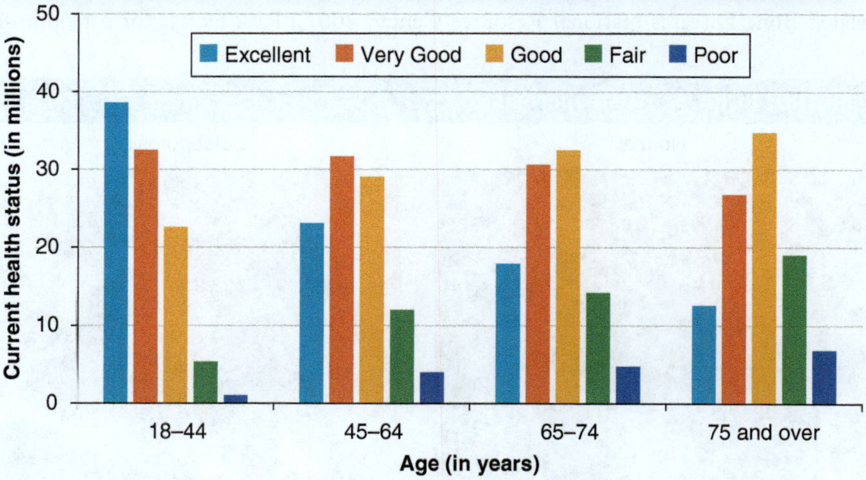

Source: Adapted from National Center for Health Statistics (2018)

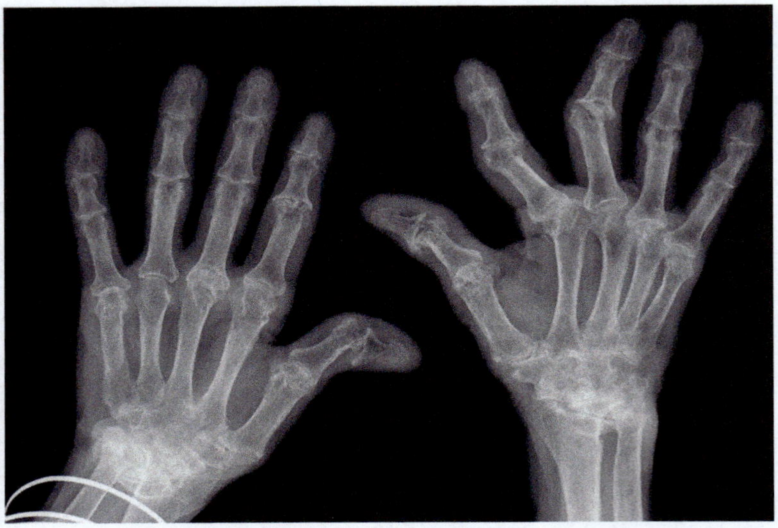

Osteoarthritis, a degenerative joint disease, often occurs in the hands, knees, and hips.

istock/ WILLSIE

worsens in severity during late adulthood (Aigner et al., 2007; Cooper et al., 2014). About half of adults aged 65 or older report a diagnosis of arthritis, and it is likely that many more cases remain undiagnosed (National Center for Health Statistics, 2018). Nearly all older adults show at least some signs of osteoarthritis, but there are great individual differences. People whose job or leisure activities rely on repetitive movements are most likely to experience osteoarthritis. Office workers who type every day might experience osteoarthritis in their hands. Runners might experience it in their knees. Obesity can place great pressure on joints.

Arthritis is a chronic disease because it is managed, not cured. Physical exercise—cardiovascular, strength, and stretching and yoga—are effective means of managing arthritis (Cheung et al., 2017; Fransen et al., 2015). When inflammation flares, more rest is needed, as well as pain relief. Rather than sedentary rest, mild physical activity helps the muscles maintain flexibility. Injection of synthetic material into a joint provides cushioning and improves movement. In severe cases the affected joint, such as the hip or knee, may be surgically replaced.

Osteoporosis

The hormonal changes that accompany menopause in midlife are associated with bone loss, increasing women's risk for **osteoporosis**, a disorder characterized by severe bone loss resulting in brittle and easily fractured bones (Sinaki, 2021; Siris et al., 2014). We tend to think of our bones as static and unchanging, but the skeleton is a dynamic organ made of living cells that continually dissolve and regenerate. In the first 10 years after menopause, women typically lose about 25% of their bone mass, largely due to menopausal declines in estrogen; this loss increases to about 50% by late adulthood (Avis et al., 2005; Vondracek, 2010). Men experience a more gradual and less extreme loss of bone because age-related decreases in testosterone, which their bodies convert to estrogen, occur slowly, and therefore the loss of bone mass that occurs with declines in estrogen occurs gradually over the adult years (Avis & Crawford, 2006; Walker, 2008).

About 30% of women and 16% of men have osteoporosis (see Figure 15.10; Wright et al., 2017), which can be identified through a routine, noninvasive bone scan. Most people—men and women—are diagnosed with osteoporosis only after experiencing bone fractures. One out of every two women and one in four men over 50 will have an osteoporosis-related fracture in their lifetime (NIH Osteoporosis and Related Bone Diseases National Resource Center, 2007). Risk factors for osteoporosis in men

FIGURE 15.10 ■ Osteoporosis

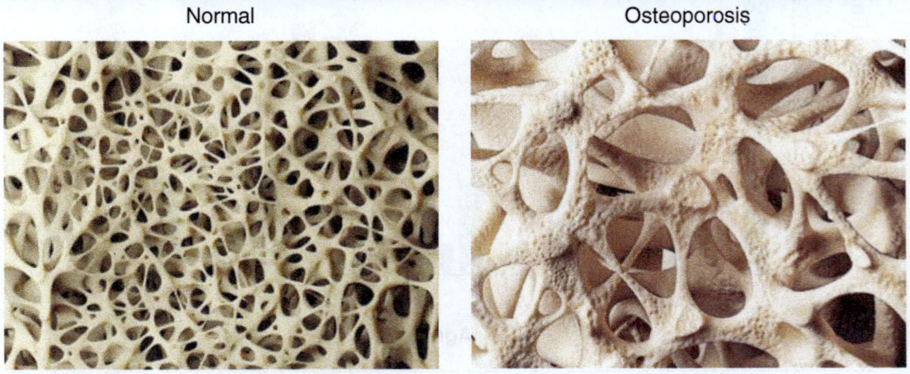

Source: istock/ eranicle

include low body mass, sedentary lifestyle, and advanced age (Cawthon et al., 2016). Because women are more widely known to be at risk, men often go undiagnosed and untreated (Liu et al., 2008).

Heredity and lifestyle contribute to the risk of osteoporosis. At least 15 genes contribute to osteoporosis susceptibility (Dong et al., 2020; Li et al., 2010). Identical twins are more likely to share a diagnosis of osteoporosis than are fraternal twins (Hsu et al., 2020). Thin, small-framed women tend to attain a lower peak bone mass than do other women and are at higher risk of osteoporosis. Other risk factors include a sedentary lifestyle, calcium deficiency, cigarette smoking, and heavy alcohol consumption (Bleicher et al., 2011; Nachtigall et al., 2013).

Lifestyle factors can reduce the risk of osteoporosis. A diet rich in calcium and vitamin D and, especially, weight bearing exercise, such as walking, jogging, dancing, and hiking, can offset postmenopausal bone loss (Sinaki, 2021). High-intensity exercise and strength training can improve bone density, muscle mass, and reduce the risk of osteoporosis (Senderovich et al., 2017). Medication can increase the absorption of calcium and slow the bone loss associated with osteoporosis in late adulthood (Tu et al., 2018).

Injuries

Deaths from unintentional injuries rise dramatically in later adulthood. They account for 45.01 deaths per 100,000 in 65- to 69-year-old adults, and a striking 365.7 per 100,000 adults age 85 and older (see Figure 15.11; Centers for Disease Control, 2018). Such injuries arise from a variety of causes, including motor vehicle accidents and falls.

Motor Vehicle Accidents

Driving a car represents autonomy. Many older adults continue to drive as long as they are able to because driving provides a sense of control and freedom. Older adults today, largely members of the Baby Boom generation, are more likely to keep their driver's licenses, make up a larger proportion of the driving population, and drive more miles than prior generations. The number of licensed drivers aged 70 and older increased by 70% between 1997 and 2019 (Insurance Institute for Highway Safety, 2021). Accidents involving older drivers, both nonfatal and fatal, have declined over the last two decades, but there remain predictable age-related increases in accidents in older adulthood. Per mile traveled, crash rates and fatal crash rates increase as drivers enter late adulthood (see Figure 15.12).

Compared with younger drivers, senior drivers are more likely to be involved in collisions in intersections, when merging into traffic, and when switching lanes (Cicchino & McCartt, 2015). Although they drive more slowly and carefully than young adults, older adults are more likely to miss traffic signs, make inappropriate turns, fail to yield the right of way, and show slower reaction time—all risks

FIGURE 15.11 ■ Fatal Unintentional Injury Rate by Age

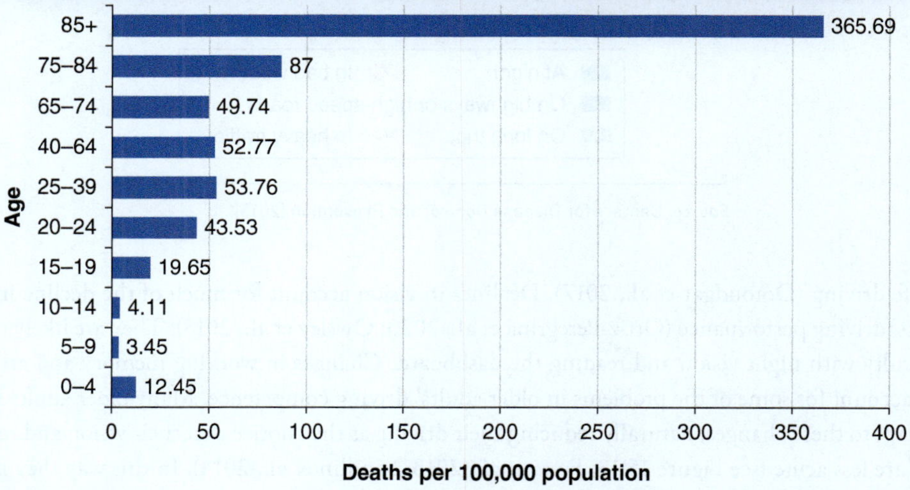

Source: Centers for Disease Control (2018).

FIGURE 15.12 ■ Rate of Vehicle Accidents per Million Miles Traveled in the United States, by Driver Age, 2017

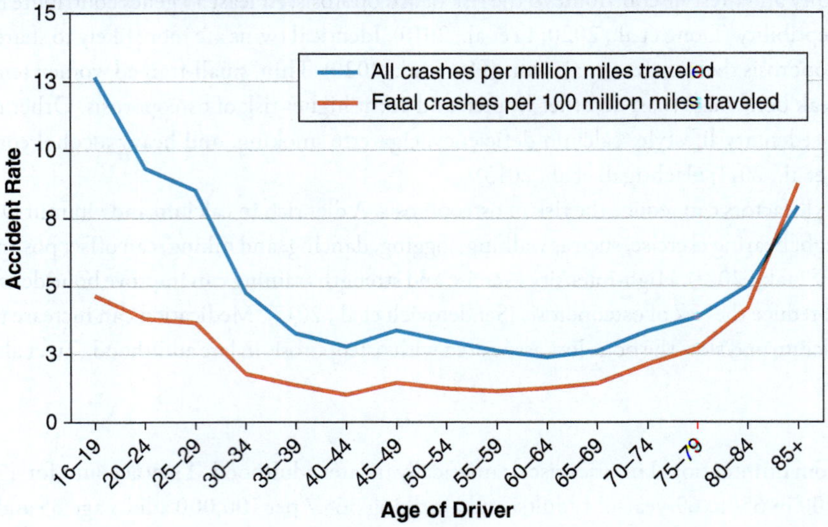

Source: Insurance Institute for Highway Safety (2021);

FIGURE 15.13 ■ Older Adult Drivers Who Tend to Avoid Driving Under Specific Conditions by Gender, 2015

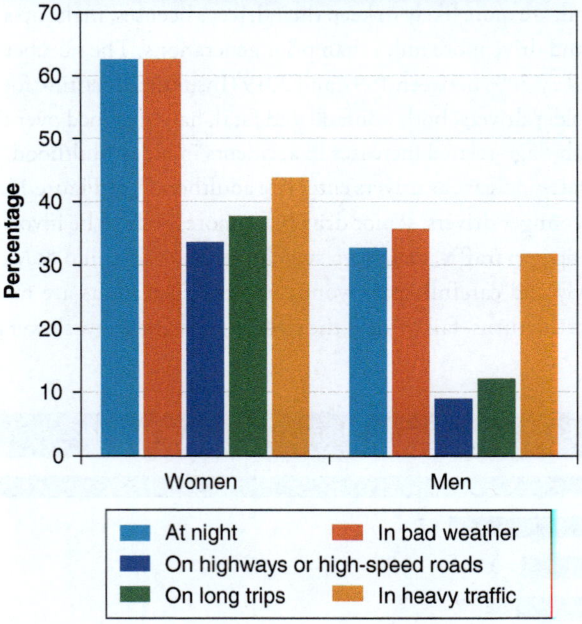

Source: Centers for Disease Control and Prevention (2015).

to safe driving (Doroudgar et al., 2017). Declines in vision account for much of the decline in older adults' driving performance (Ortiz-Peregrina et al., 2020; Owsley et al., 2018). They are likely to have difficulty with night vision and reading the dashboard. Changes in working memory and attention also account for some of the problems in older adults' driving competence. Many older adults appear to adapt to these changes, naturally reducing their driving as they notice that their vision and reaction time are less acute (see Figure 15.13; Festa et al., 2013; Sandlin et al., 2014). In this way they may, at least partially, compensate for their higher risk for motor vehicle accidents (Feng et al., 2018).

Falls

Over one-quarter of U.S. adults over the age of 65 fall each year, and falls are the leading cause of injury in older adults (Crews et al., 2016; Jin, 2018). Many aspects of aging increase the risk of falls, including changes in vision, hearing, motor skills and neuromuscular control, and cognition. Older adults are less able than their younger counterparts to balance and regulate body sway, have reduced muscular density (i.e., strength), and are less adept at navigating and avoiding obstacles (Frank-Wilson et al., 2016; Johansson et al., 2017). Declines in cognition, particularly in executive functioning and processing speed, also increase the risk of falls (Mirelman et al., 2012; Welmer et al., 2016).

Over one-quarter of U.S. older adults fall each year. Exercise programs such as Tai Chi and strength and agility training can improve older adults' strength, balance, and confidence. Environmental modifications such as addressing slippery floors, installing handrails on steps, and equipping shower/bath facilities with grip bars, can also help to prevent falls.

iStock/ fotoVoyager

Falls are a serious hazard for older adults because the natural loss of bone and high prevalence of osteoporosis increase the risk of bone fractures, especially a fractured hip. Hip fractures are particularly dangerous as they immobilize an older adult, are painful, and take a great deal of time to heal. Following hip fracture, many elderly adults lose the capacity for independent living, and up to one-quarter may die as a result of complications, such as infection, within a year after the fall (Panula et al., 2011).

After experiencing a fall, many older adults report fear of falling (Visschedijk et al., 2010). Adults who fear falling tend to become more cautious, avoiding activities that pose a risk of falling, but also limiting opportunities for physical activities that support physical health, retention of mobility, psychological well-being, and social connections (Visschedijk et al., 2010). There are a variety of ways to prevent falls and help older adults become more confident about their mobility. Exercise programs such as Tai Chi, yoga, and strength and agility training can improve older adults' strength, balance, and confidence (Kaniewski et al., 2015; Tricco et al., 2017). Environmental modifications such as addressing slippery floors, installing handrails on steps, and equipping shower/bath facilities with grip bars, can also help to prevent falls.

Thinking in Context: Lifespan Development

Recall from Chapter 1 that domains or types of development interact. Changes in one area of development hold implications for other areas of functioning. How might chronic illnesses in adulthood, such diabetes or arthritis, influence other aspects of development, like cognition or socioemotional development? How might these changes influence individuals' interactions within all of the contexts in which they are embedded?

Thinking in Context: Applied Developmental Science

Share what you know about promoting health and safety in late adulthood.

1. Explain the role of nutrition and lifestyle factors on health. What recommendations would you make to an older adult on how to promote health?
2. What risks to safety are older adults likely to experience? What safety precautions are most important?
3. What barriers might older adults face in fostering health and safety needs? Why?

COGNITIVE DEVELOPMENT

LEARNING OBJECTIVE

15.4 Analyze patterns of cognitive change in late adulthood and influences on cognitive change.

Cognition continues to change over late adulthood alongside physical development. Sensory capacities, such as vision and hearing, decline with age and are associated with age-related declines in cognition (Pichora-Fuller, 2020; Swenor et al., 2019). Sensory impairments may prevent some information from getting into the cognitive system in the first place, so that older adults may never be aware that they have missed it. Cognition changes in several predictable ways over older adulthood.

Attention

Older adults experience more difficulty dividing attention to engage in two complex tasks at once, focusing only on relevant information, than young adults (Weeks & Hasher, 2017; Wong et al., 2021). As with other capacities, age-related declines in attention are not uniform across adults and these differences predict variations in cognitive performance.

Selective attention, the ability to focus on stimuli, tuning out others, also becomes more challenging with age. Response inhibition becomes more difficult and adults find it harder to resist interference from irrelevant information to stay focused on the task at hand (Sylvain-Roy et al., 2014). Researchers have assessed attention with laboratory tasks in which participants are presented with a series of letter combinations and told to press the space bar only when they see a particular combination (such as T-L); they are to ignore all other combinations. In such tasks, adults' performance declines steadily from the 30s on. Older adults make more errors of commission (pressing the space bar after incorrect letter combinations) and omission (not pressing the space bar in response to the correct sequence) when the task is accompanied by distractors such as noise (Zanto & Gazzaley, 2019). Older adults are also slower at responding and inhibiting a response than young adults (Bloemendaal et al., 2016; Haring et al., 2013). In everyday life, these changes in attention might make older adults appear more easily distracted, less able to attend, and less able to take in information.

Working Memory

As we have discussed in prior chapters, working memory begins to decline in early adulthood, continuing through middle adulthood into late adulthood. These changes influence performance on a range of cognitive tasks including problem solving, decision making, and learning. Changes in attention influence declines in working memory because the presence of distracting information leaves less space in working memory for completing a given task (Oberauer, 2019). Individual differences in attention translate to differences in working memory and its age-related shifts (Unsworth et al., 2020).

Once material is encoded in working memory, healthy adults of all ages retain the ability to exert control over working memory—they are able to orient their attention within working memory (and stay on task; Mok et al., 2016). Problems with working memory vary with the number of tasks and task demands: The greater the number of tasks and demands, the worse the performance (Kessels et al., 2010). With age, most adults find it is more difficult to simultaneously perform a motor and cognitive task than it is to perform either task alone (Greene et al., 2020). But practice in the motor task makes it more automatic, reducing the demands on working memory. In this way, practice can reduce (but not eliminate) age-related deficits in cognitive performance (Neely & Nyberg, 2021; Voelcker-Rehage & Alberts, 2007).

Age-related decline is less apparent in cognitive tasks that are more passive and less attentionally demanding, such as digit recall and visual pattern recall tasks (Bisiacchi et al., 2008). When working memory maintenance systems are taxed, as in the case of interference, older adults perform more poorly than young and middle-aged adults. **Proactive interference** occurs when information that has previously been remembered interferes with memory for new information (Archambeau et al., 2020;

Bowles & Salthouse, 2003). Older adults are more susceptible to interference effects than are younger adults, even when they have learned the material equally well (Jacoby et al., 2010).

Context, Task Demands, and Memory Performance

Research on cognitive aging is often conducted in laboratory environments that are similar to school settings. Most older adults have little recent experience in school settings, compared with younger adults. Familiarity with laboratory and school environments may influence adults' performance on cognitive tasks. Laboratory findings, therefore, may not accurately illustrate the everyday memory capacity of middle-aged and older adults (Salthouse, 2012).

Older adults' performance varies with task complexity. Some laboratory tasks require participants to coordinate multiple cognitive tasks, such as switching attention between two sets of stimuli (such as pressing the *x* key when the number *1* appears on a screen and the *y* key when the number *2* appears). Managing multiple cognitive tasks is associated with greater disruptions in working memory in older adults as compared with younger adults (Clapp et al., 2011). Yet when older adults have the opportunity to slow down to a pace with which they feel comfortable, or when they are reminded to use cognitive strategies, they can show performance on working memory tasks similar to that of younger adults (Verhaeghen et al., 2003; Coats et al., 2021).

Laboratory findings of memory declines are less apparent in everyday settings (Salthouse, 2012). Adults retain their knowledge of facts and procedures, and they continue to learn new information and advance their expertise. Adults' experience and knowledge of their cognitive system (metacognition) enable them to use their memory more effectively (Schaie, 2013). They use external supports and strategies to maximize their memory, such as by leaving sticky notes as reminders or placing their car keys in a designated spot where they can reliably be found (Schwartz & Frazier, 2005). As with attention, memory declines vary with the individual and task.

Emotion and Working Memory

In contrast with age-related deficits in the ability to manipulate visual information, older adults show unimpaired working memory for emotional stimuli (Mikels et al., 2005). Positive mood enhances working memory capacity and older adults are better able to retain information despite exposure to task-irrelevant information when in a positive mood, yet a negative mood appears unrelated to working memory capacity (Storbeck & Maswood, 2016). Known as the **positivity effect**, there is an age-related shift in attentional preferences from emphasizing negative information in early adulthood to positive information in late adulthood (Carstensen & DeLiema, 2018).

Older adults are naturally biased toward recalling positive over negative information, while younger adults show the reverse, with more attention on the negative (Reed et al., 2014). One reason underlying the positivity effect in older adults' memories may be older adults' greater focus on managing their emotions. That is, older adults may use cognitive control mechanisms that enhance positive and diminish negative information in order to feel good (Joubert et al., 2018; Mather & Carstensen, 2005). This finding has appeared in research with Chinese and Korean adults suggesting that the positivity bias with age may appear cross-culturally (Gutchess & Boduroglu, 2015). Although they are often studied separately, emotion and cognition are intertwined (Reed & Carstensen, 2012). Emotion characterizes most real-life decisions, suggesting that older adults are likely able to focus their attention and cognitive capacities on the task at hand, if it has real-world emotional relevance, such as decisions about health care, finance, and living situations (Samanez-Larkin et al., 2009).

Long-Term Memory

Age-related changes in working memory also contribute to changes in long-term memory. As cognitive processing slows, most adults show difficulties with recall, but the various types of long-term memory show different patterns of change. Semantic memory—memory for factual material—shows little age-related decline, while episodic memory—memory for experiences—tends to deteriorate with age (Baddeley, 2020; St-Laurent et al., 2011).

Autobiographical memory shows predictable patterns of change. Generally, autobiographical memories include fewer event-specific details with age (Frankenberg et al., 2021). Older adults are more likely to recall experiences early in life, between ages 10 and 30, known as the *reminiscence bump* (Munawar et al., 2018). When older asked to discuss a personal memory or experience that comes to mind in response to cue words, such as the words *surprise* or *song*, older adults commonly recall experiences they had during adolescence and early adulthood. Similarly, when asked to create a timeline of memorable events in their lives, older adults tend to remember events from adolescence through early adulthood; they also remember recent events better than midlife events (Rubin, 2000; Schroots et al., 2004). In addition, they are more likely to remember happy events that occurred between ages 10 and 30 than those that occurred any other time in life (Berntsen & Rubin, 2002).

Why does long-term memory show a reminiscence bump? Perhaps we process events differently during our adolescent and early adult years, a time when we are constructing our identities. And perhaps we are less adept at recalling events from middle adulthood because of interference, as new memories interfere with our recall of older memories. Similarities among events may make it difficult to distinguish them. Throughout life, memory is malleable and we often revise our memories in light of new experiences. Yet it also appears that older adults recall fewer details from recent events (within the past 5 years), and different types of details, than do younger adults. This suggests that older and younger adults differ in what stimuli they attend to and select for processing (Gaesser et al., 2011; Piolino et al., 2006; Piolino et al., 2010).

Contextual factors play a role in the rate of cognitive change. Similar to findings of cohort differences in intelligence scores, there are generational differences in overall cognitive performance that are maintained throughout life (see Figure 15.14). Specifically, younger cohorts show better performance on a range of cognitive measures and less steep age-related declines (Gerstorf et al., 2011). Possible factors underlying cohort differences include secular trends in educational systems, disease prevalence, years of education, and quality of education.

Language

Language comprehension, the ability to understand spoken or written language and retrieve the meaning of words, shows little to no change with age. In fact, older adults maintain or improve their knowledge of words and word meanings, an example of the increases in crystallized intelligence that occur into older adulthood (Shafto & Tyler, 2014).

The most common language-related deficit older adults report is difficulty accurately and quickly recalling specific words while in conversation (Ossher et al., 2013; Owens, 2015). Older adults tend to produce more ambiguous references and more filled pauses (e.g., saying *um* or *er*) and reformulate their words more than young adults do (Horton et al., 2010). They use more unclear references and speak more slowly, taking time to retrieve words. They are also more prone to the *"tip-of-the-tongue" phenomenon* than young adults, in which one temporarily cannot recall a specific word but can recall words with similar meaning(Mortensen et al., 2006; Shafto et al., 2010). Older adults are more likely than younger adults to use indefinite words, such as *thing*, in place of specific names. This is likely due to deficits in working memory and slower processing speed (Salthouse & Madden, 2013).

Difficulties in retrieving words and producing language may diminish older adults' success in communicating and weaken their and others' views of their own language competence. Negative self-appraisals can promote withdrawal from social interaction. Yet similar to managing other cognitive declines, older adults often compensate for losses. They may take more time in speaking and simplify their sentences and grammar in order to devote their cognitive resources to retrieving words and producing speech that others can comprehend.

Problem Solving and Wisdom

Cognitive changes in older adulthood are also reflected in problem-solving skills. Laboratory studies of problem solving that rely on traditional hypothetical problems show declines with age (Sinnott, 2003). Yet when decisions tap into relevant experience or knowledge, older adults tend to be as effective

FIGURE 15.14 ■ Age and Cohort Differences in Cognitive Aging

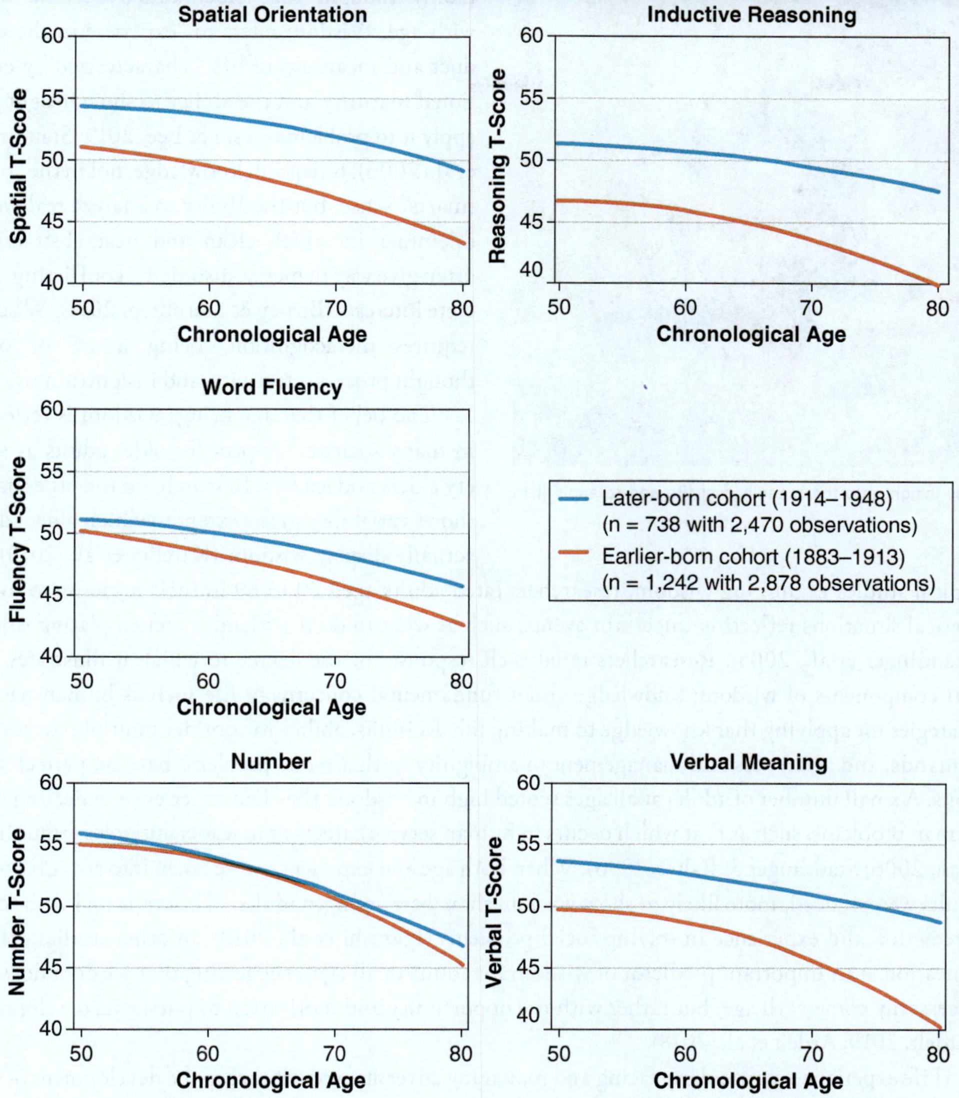

Source: Gerstorf et al. (2011).

at making decisions as younger adults (Denney et al., 1982). Examinations of problem-solving skills in everyday settings show that people remain efficient decision makers throughout adulthood. Older adults tend to show adaptive problem solving in response to health-related decisions; they are actually better than younger adults at making decisions about whether they require medical attention and seeking medical care (Artistico et al., 2010; Löckenhoff & Carstensen, 2007).

Generally speaking, adults perform better on everyday problems that are relevant to the contexts they experience in their daily lives (Artistico et al., 2010). In addition, older adults outperform young and middle-aged adults on problems set in contexts relevant to older adults, such as medical care, suggesting that age-related declines observed in laboratory settings may not be observed in everyday life. Older adults may be better at matching their strategies to their goals than are young adults, perhaps because experience and crystallized knowledge provide an extensive base for making real-life decisions and aligning goals with decisions (Hoppmann & Blanchard-Fields, 2010). In older adults, crystallized intelligence is a better predictor of performance on everyday problem-solving tasks than fluid intelligence, suggesting the importance of experience (Chen et al., 2017). Finally, older adults are more likely than younger people to report that they turn to spouses, children, and friends for input in making decisions (Strough et al., 2003).

Older adults are more likely to display insight into the meanings of life and to apply it to problems—to be wise.

iStock/ fstop123

Related to everyday problem solving, it is commonly thought that older adults become wiser with age. **Wisdom** refers to "expertise in the conduct and meanings of life," characterized by emotional maturity and the ability to show insight and apply it to problems (Jeste & Lee, 2019; Staudinger et al., 2006). It requires knowledge, not in the "book smarts" sense, but the ability to analyze real-world dilemmas in which clean and neat abstractions often give way to messy, disorderly, conflicting concrete interests (Birney & Sternberg, 2011). Wisdom requires metacognition, being aware of one's thought process, creativity, and insightfulness.

The belief that age brings wisdom is reflected in many societies' respect for older adults as society elders and leaders. Research, on the other hand, shows variability in the extent to which older adults actually display wisdom (Karelitz et al., 2010). In typical studies examining wisdom, researchers rated adults aged 20 to 89 in their response to hypothetical situations reflecting uncertain events, such as what to do if a friend is contemplating suicide (Staudinger et al., 2005). Researchers rated each response for the degree to which it illustrates several components of wisdom: knowledge about fundamental concerns of life such as human nature, strategies for applying that knowledge to making life decisions, ability to consider multiple contextual demands, and awareness and management of ambiguity in that many problems have no perfect solutions. A small number of adults at all ages scored high in wisdom; they had experience in dealing with human problems, such as that which occurs in human service careers or in leadership roles (Staudinger et al., 2006; Staudinger & Baltes, 1996). When both age and experience were taken into account, older adults were, indeed, more likely to show wisdom than were younger adults. Wisdom is tied with social interaction and experience in solving social problems (Igarashi et al., 2018). In other studies college education is an important predictor of wisdom for adults of all ages, suggesting that wisdom does not necessarily come with age, but rather with the opportunity and motivation to pursue its development (Ardelt, 2010; Ardelt et al., 2018).

Life experience, particularly facing and managing adversity, contributes to the development of wisdom. One study of people who came of age during the Great Depression of the 1930s found that, 40 years later, older adults who had experienced and overcome economic adversity demonstrated higher levels of wisdom than their peers (Ardelt, 1998). Experience, particularly expertise in solving the problems of everyday life, is associated with wisdom (Baltes & Staudinger, 2000). It is not simply experience that matters. Those who are wise are reflective; they attempt to find meaning in their experiences (Weststrate & Glück, 2017). They also have advanced cognition and emotional regulation skills, qualities that contribute to the development of wisdom but are also associated with better physical health, higher levels of education, openness to experience, positive social relationships, and overall psychological well-being (Zacher & Staudinger, 2018). What can we conclude about wisdom? Perhaps that it is a rare quality, one that can be found at all ages but that typically improves with age and is associated with well-being. And, older adults are more likely to be among the very wise.

Influences on Cognitive Change in Adulthood

Cognitive abilities tend to remain stable, relative to peers, over the lifespan. High intelligence early in life (e.g., at age 11) is predictive of intelligence in old age (through age 87; Gow et al., 2012). With advancing age comes greater diversity in cognitive ability. Centenarians, people age 100 or older, show greater variations in cognitive performance than do older adults aged 85 to 90 (Miller et al., 2010; Paúl et al., 2010). Differences in experience and lifestyle can account for many differences in cognitive change over adulthood.

Cross-sectional research shows that education, measured by years of formal schooling or by literacy levels on reading tests, is a strong and consistent predictor of cognitive performance and problem-solving tasks in old age (Kavé et al., 2008). In fact, findings from the Georgia Centenarian Study suggest that education accounted for the largest proportion of cognitive differences among the centenarians studied (Davey et al., 2010). Recall from Chapter 1 that cross-sectional and longitudinal studies often yield different results. Similar to research on cognitive change in older adulthood, the influence of education on cognitive change varies depending on whether the study is cross-sectional or longitudinal. Longitudinal research studies with older adults from Germany, Australia, and the United States, spanning 7 to 13 years in length with testing occurring at 3 to 6 time points, do not find a relationship between education and cognitive decline at older age (Anstey et al., 2003; Van Dijk et al., 2008). The effects of education are mixed and may vary with cohort, but it is generally recognized that throughout life, cognitive engagement—through mentally stimulating activities—predicts the maintenance of mental abilities (Bielak, 2010; Schaie, 2013).

Another predictor of cognitive performance and impairment across the lifespan is physical health (Blondell et al., 2014; Wang et al., 2014). Health conditions such as cardiovascular disease, osteoporosis, and arthritis are associated with cognitive declines (Baltes & Carstensen, 2003; Okonkwo et al., 2010). Longitudinal studies also suggest that poor mental health, such as depression and anxiety, is associated with declines in processing speed, long-term memory, and problem solving (Lönnqvist, 2010; Margrett et al., 2010). It is difficult to disentangle the directional effects of health and cognitive decline because people who score higher on cognitive measures are more likely to engage in health-promoting behaviors.

Interventions that train older adults and encourage them to use cognitive skills can preserve and even reverse some age-related cognitive declines. One study of participants in the Seattle Longitudinal Study examined the effects of 51 hours of cognitive training on cognitive functioning in late adulthood (Schaie, 2013). Two-thirds of adults showed gains in performance, and 40% of those who showed cognitive decline prior to the study returned to their level of functioning 14 years earlier. Training improved strategy use and performance on verbal memory, working memory, and short-term memory tasks. Most promising is that 7 years later, older adults who had received training scored higher on mental ability tests than their peers. In other research, training improved measures of processing speed and fluid intelligence and these improvements were retained over an 8-month period (Borella et al., 2010).

Older adults' improvement with intervention is often similar in magnitude to that of younger adults, including gains in working memory, sustained attention, and fewer complaints about memory (Brehmer et al., 2012). Other research suggests that gains from working memory interventions generalize to other measures of fluid intelligence (Karbach & Verhaeghen, 2014; Stepankova et al., 2014). However, one meta-analysis of 87 studies suggested that we must be cautious in drawing conclusions about cognitive interventions because post-training improvements tended to be short term, specific, and did not transfer to real-world cognitive skills (Melby-Lervåg et al., 2016).

Although older adults experience cognitive declines, there is a great deal of variability in everyday functioning and it is possible to retain and improve cognitive skills in late adulthood. Older adults who maintain a high cognitive functioning tend to engage in selective optimization with compensation: They compensate for declines in cognitive reserve or energy by narrowing their goals and selecting activities that will permit them to maximize their strengths and existing capacities. In all, healthy older adults retain the capacity to engage in efficient controlled processing of information.

Thinking in Context: Lifespan Development

1. Consider the cognitive changes that occur over the lifespan. In your view, are cognitive development, reasoning, and decision-making best described as developing continuously or discontinuously? (Recall these concepts from Chapter 1.) Why?
2. What factors might make older adults better decision makers than young adults? Worse? To what extent do contextual factors play a role in decision making?
3. An important theme of lifespan development is that development is characterized by gains and losses. How might the cognitive changes that adults experience illustrate this?

Thinking in Context: Applied Developmental Science

1. Suppose you wanted to study influences on cognitive change in late adulthood.
   - What aspects of cognition would you study?
   - What potential influences do you think are important to examine?
   - What type of design would you use? Would you follow people over time or study them once?
   - What are some challenges in conducting this research?
2. Aunt Jo proclaims, "Just like dogs, old people can't learn new tricks." Given what we know about cognition in late adulthood, do you agree or disagree? Discuss at least three aspects of cognition in your response.

CHAPTER SUMMARY

15.1 Discuss age-related changes in the brain and body systems in late adulthood and how older adults may compensate for changes.

Appearance, body shape, and the sensory organs change over late adulthood. Structural changes in the eye make it difficult to see in dim light and to adapt to dramatic changes in light. Vision may be impaired by the presence of cataracts and macular degeneration. Hearing loss from presbycusis increases from middle into older adulthood. Older adults compensate for sensory losses by modifying their behaviors and environment as well as through surgery and medication. With age, cardiovascular, respiratory, and immune systems become less efficient. Changes in balance and strength hold implications for mobility. The loss of neurons contributes to reduced brain volume, especially in the prefrontal cortex. Reductions in myelination contribute to slower communication among neurons. Cognitive reserve contributes to neural compensation. Physical health promotes brain health.

15.2 Describe common dementias and the role of contextual and intersectional factors in dementia.

Alzheimer's disease is characterized by widespread brain deterioration and the presence of beta-amyloid plaques and neurofibrillary tangles in the cerebral cortex. Vascular dementia is caused by a series of strokes. Lewy body dementia is caused by a proliferation of lewy bodies. Parkinson's disease occurs when neurons in the substantia nigra die or become impaired and are unable to produce dopamine. Dementia emerges in the late stages of Parkinson's disease. Each disease has a predictable course. Genetic and environmental factors contribute to dementia. Generally, the symptoms of dementia are treated as most cannot be cured. People of color show higher rates of dementia, influenced by factors such as segregation, unequal access to resources, racism and discrimination, which impair cognitive reserve.

15.3 Summarize influences on health and common health issues in late adulthood.

Nutrition is an important influence on immunity and overall health. Moderate physical activity is associated with improved physiological function, less disease and disability, better mental health, and higher quality of life. Nearly all older adults show signs of osteoarthritis. Injury-related fatalities rise dramatically in older adulthood. In older adulthood, brittle bones mean that falls result in fractures, especially hip fractures, which immobilize an older adult, are painful, and take a great deal of time to heal.

15.4 Analyze patterns of cognitive change in late adulthood and influences on cognitive change.

Declines in working memory are influenced by reduced sensory capacity and reduced processing speed. The various types of long-term memory show different patterns of change. People remain adaptive problem solvers throughout adulthood. Adults perform best on everyday problems that are relevant to the contexts they experience in their daily lives. Wisdom does not necessarily come with age but rather with the opportunity and motivation to pursue its development. Older adults with higher levels of education, engaging careers, and leisure activities tend to retain their mental abilities. Many physical and mental conditions are associated with cognitive decline. Older adults who maintain a high cognitive functioning tend to compensate for declines in cognitive reserve or energy by modifying their goals and activities.

KEY TERMS

Alzheimer's disease (p. 460)
amyloid plaques (p. 460)
cataracts (p. 452)
cognitive reserve (p. 456)
dementia (p. 459)
Lewy body dementia (p. 464)
macular degeneration (p. 452)
neurofibrillary tangles (p. 460)
old-old (p. 467)
oldest-old (p. 467)
osteoarthritis (p. 469)
osteoporosis (p. 470)
Parkinson's disease (p. 463)
positivity effect (p. 475)
proactive interference (p. 474)
successful aging (p. 467)
vascular dementia (p. 462)
wisdom (p. 478)
young-old (p. 467)

16 SOCIOEMOTIONAL DEVELOPMENT IN LATE ADULTHOOD AND DEATH

iStock/ monkeybusinessimages

"Hold the end, and swing it gently in time with your sister," 72-year-old Jennifer instructed her grandson as he grasped the end of the jump rope. She watched as he and his sister swung the rope and a third grandchild hopped in between them, beginning a game of jump rope. "When I was little I could jump double Dutch. Do you know what that is?" Jennifer asks her grandchildren. Jennifer thinks back in time, closes her eyes, and smiles before she begins her explanation.

In this chapter, we examine the socioemotional transitions of older adulthood, including changes in how adults view themselves, changes in the contexts in which they live, their evolving relationships, and changes in work habits. Again, it will be apparent that the reality of life in late adulthood does not conform to many of the stereotypes or commonly held views about older adults.

PSYCHOSOCIAL DEVELOPMENT

LEARNING OBJECTIVE

16.1 Summarize patterns of psychosocial development in late adulthood.

The "terrible twos" of toddlerhood, adolescent angst, and the midlife crisis are periods of development that are accompanied by stereotypes—beliefs about commonalities shared by members of a given age group. Older adulthood is no different. Ageist attitudes abound in popular culture. Stereotypes of older adults include the belief that they are lonely; lack close friends and family; have a higher rate of mood disorders; and are rigid, unable to cope with age-related declines, one-dimensional, dependent, and

FIGURE 16.1 ■ Challenges of Aging as Expected and Experienced by Older Adults

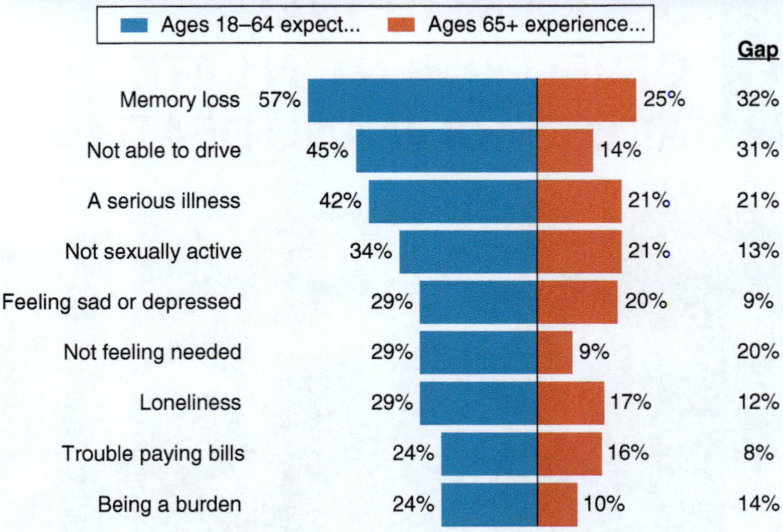

Source: Pew Research Center (2009)

cognitively impaired. These stereotypes are misguided. Older adults experience fewer challenges of aging than young and middle-aged adults expect (see Figure 16.1). However, stereotypes can influence how adults see themselves and other aspects of their psychosocial development.

Self-Concept and Self-Esteem

Self-conceptions are more multifaceted, complex, and stable in old age than at other periods of life. Although global self-esteem tends to decline in late life, most adults maintain a positive view of themselves, expressing more positive than negative self-evaluations well into old age (Orth & Robins, 2019). Old (70 to 84) and very old (85 to 103) adults rate themselves more positively than negatively in a variety of areas including hobbies, interests, family, health, and personality, and these positive self-evaluations predicted psychological well-being (Freund & Smith, 1999). Older adults tend to compartmentalize their self-concept more so than younger and middle-aged adults by categorizing the positive and negative aspects of self as separate roles, whereas younger and middle-aged adults tend to integrate them into one (Ready et al., 2012). Life experience and advances in cognitive affective complexity (see Chapter 15) underlie older adults' multifaceted self-conceptions and evaluations. The developmental task for older adults is to accept their weaknesses and compensate by focusing on their strengths. Over time, adults reframe their sense of self by revising their possible selves in light of experience and emphasizing goals related to the sense of self, relationships, and health (Smith & Freund, 2002). Adults' reports of life satisfaction and well-being typically increase into old age, along with corresponding decreases in negative affect (Darbonne et al., 2012; Jeste & Oswald, 2014).

Subjective Age

Throughout life, perceived age is an important part of our self-concept. Most older adults feel that they are younger than their years and this tendency increases with age (see Figure 16.2; Bergland et al., 2014; Shinan-Altman & Werner, 2019). On average, adults over age 60 feel up to 18%, or about 20 years, younger than their age (Pinquart & Wahl, 2021). Research with U.S., German, and Chinese adults suggests that this pattern occurs cross-culturally (O'Brien et al., 2017).

Why do older adults feel younger than their years? One reason may have to do with avoiding the self-categorization of being old (Kornadt & Rothermund, 2012). Categorizing oneself as a member of one's age group influences how individuals think about themselves, their competencies, and their future (Weiss & Lang, 2012). Given the negative stereotypes associated with aging, adults may employ strategies to avoid the negative consequences of identification with their age group, such as denying

FIGURE 16.2 ■ Subjective Age Across the Lifespan

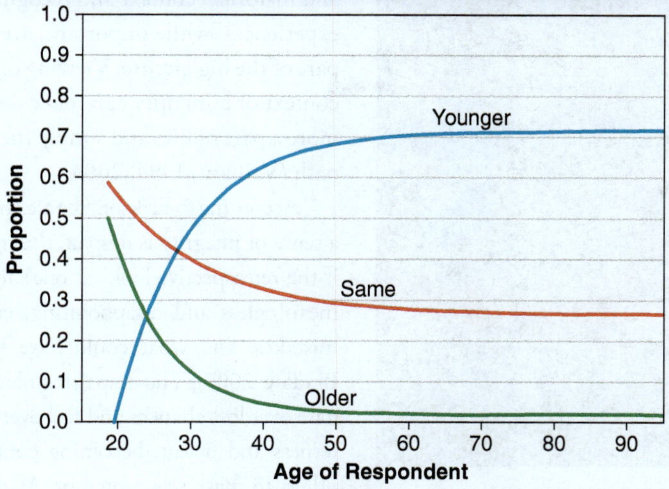

Source: Rubin & Berntsen, 2006.

or hiding their age by excluding themselves from the "old age" category (Heckhausen & Brim, 1997). Adults with more negative self-views are more likely to feel older than their years over time (Kornadt et al., 2018). In addition, individuals experiencing challenging contexts and situations, such as those experiencing financial distress, tend to report older subjective ages (Agrigoroaei et al., 2017).

Subjective age is associated with health and well-being, including the risk for cardiovascular disease, engagement in health behaviors, life satisfaction, and mortality (Stephan et al., 2018; Stephan, Sutin, Wurm, et al., 2021). Individuals who feel younger than their years are less likely to internalize negative stereotypes about aging and they remain active, which promotes good heath (Kotter-Grühn et al., 2016). Younger subjective ages are associated with physical functioning, such as grip strength (Stephan et al., 2013). Cognitive performance is also related to subjective age. Older adults who reported feeling younger relative to their peers tended to show better performance and slower declines in recall tasks over a 10-year period (Stephan et al., 2014). In contrast, an older subjective age is associated with accelerated aging; adults who feel older are biologically older than their peers (Stephan, Sutin, Luchetti, et al., 2021). Even more striking, older adults who perceived themselves as younger than their real ages showed larger gray matter volume and younger predicted brain age, as assessed by MRI scans (Kwak et al., 2018).

Subjective age is malleable in response to contextual conditions (Hughes & Touron, 2021). In one study, older adults reported feeling older after taking a working memory test but not after a vocabulary test (Hughes et al., 2013). Recall from Chapter 13 and 15 that age-related declines are seen in tasks tapping fluid intelligence, such as working memory, but not tasks tapping crystallized intelligence, such as vocabulary. More important, simply expecting to take a memory test was associated with feeling subjectively older, suggesting that perception of abilities in various domains can influence perceived age (Hughes et al., 2013). Similarly, reminders of one's aging body, such as body pain, can temporarily increase subjective age (Barrett & Gumber, 2020). Collectively, these findings suggest that the old adage, "You're only as old as you feel," is partially true as one's perception of one's own age is dynamically associated with health, well-being, and cognitive performance.

Ego Integrity

Older adults naturally engage in **life review**, reflecting on past experiences and contemplating the meaning of those experiences and their role in shaping one's life (Butler, 1963). They are tasked with processing and accepting the triumphs and disappointments of their lives and tend to become more tolerant and accepting of others, and they experience a rise in life satisfaction and well-being. Life review is integral to developing a sense of **ego integrity vs. despair**, the last stage in Erikson's (1959) psychosocial theory, in which older adults find a sense of coherence in life experiences and ultimately conclude that that their lives are meaningful and valuable (Whiting & Bradley, 2007). Adults who achieve ego

Social support from family and friends protects against the negative effects of stress, promotes longevity and life satisfaction, and enhances well-being.

iStock/Tarzan9280

integrity can see their lives within a larger global and historical context and recognize that their own experiences, while important, are only a very small part of the big picture. Viewing one's life within the context of humanity can make death less fearsome, more a part of life, and simply the next step in one's path (Vaillant, 1994, 2004).

According to Erikson, the alternative to developing a sense of integrity is despair, the tragedy experienced if the retrospective looks at one's life are evaluated as meaningless and disappointing, emphasizing faults, mistakes, and what could have been (Whiting & Bradley, 2007). The despairing older adult may ruminate over lost chances and feel overwhelmed with bitterness and defeat, becoming contemptuous toward others to mask self-contempt. As might be expected, adults who do not develop a sense of ego integrity are more likely to experience a poor sense of well-being and depression (Dezutter et al., 2014).

How does one attain ego integrity? A sense of ego integrity relies on cognitive development, such as complexity and maturity in moral judgment and thinking style, tolerance for ambiguity, and dialectical reasoning (Hearn et al., 2011). The ability to realize that there are multiple solutions to problems and recognize that one's life path may have taken many different courses is integral to developing a sense of ego integrity. Ego integrity is also predicted by social factors, including social support, generativity, and good family relationships (James & Zarrett, 2006; Sheldon & Kasser, 2001). Similar to the development of identity and generativity, ego integrity is influenced by interactions with others. When older adults relay their experiences, tell family stories from their lives, and provide advice, they have opportunities to engage in the self-evaluation that can lead to ego integrity.

Personality

As in other life periods, personality traits remain stable into late adulthood. Adults who scored high in extroversion relative to their peers at age 30 tend to continue to score high relative to their peers in old age (Graham & Lachman, 2012). Research examining the Big 5 personality traits (see Chapter 14) suggests that the stereotype of older adults becoming rigid and set in their ways is untrue. Personality traits shift subtly over the life course in response to individuals' interactions with their contexts (Mroczek, 2020). Most people experience a mellowing of personality characteristics with age. A longitudinal study that examined adults aged 60 through their 80s found that more than one-third of the sample scored highest on agreeableness in their 80s (Weiss et al., 2005). Extroversion and openness to experience decline with age from 30 to 90, with the most pronounced drops after the mid-50s (Lucas & Donnellan, 2011; Wortman et al., 2012). Conscientiousness increases from emerging to midadulthood, peaks between 50 and 70, and then declines. These findings are also supported by cross-cultural research with adults from 50 countries (McCrae et al., 2005).

Individuals' patterns of Big 5 personality traits predict physical and cognitive functioning (Mroczek et al., 2020). Conscientiousness is associated with health and longevity, as well as better performance on cognitive tasks (Bogg & Roberts, 2013; Graham et al., 2021; Mõttus et al., 2013). Neuroticism, on the other hand, is associated with worse average cognitive functioning, poor executive function, and a steeper rate of decline (Bell et al., 2020; Luchetti et al., 2015). Neuroticism also predicts increasing frailty (Stephan et al., 2017).

Big 5 personality traits show complex associations with well-being. Specifically, well-being correlates with higher levels of extroversion, agreeableness, and conscientiousness, and with lower levels of neuroticism (Cox et al., 2010). Moreover, this relationship is bidirectional. A study of 16,000 Australian adults revealed that their personality traits predicted changes in well-being, yet changes in well-being, in turn, influenced their traits (Soto, 2015). Individuals who were initially extroverted, agreeable, conscientious, and emotionally stable subsequently increased in well-being and in turn became even more agreeable, conscientious, emotionally stable, and extroverted. We have seen that well-being tends to increase over the adult years. Research from the Big 5 trait approach to personality supports this, as people in their later years tend to become happier (more agreeable and less neurotic), more self-contented and self-centered (less extroverted and open), more laid back and satisfied with what they have, and less preoccupied with productivity (less conscientious; Kandler et al., 2015; Marsh et al., 2012). This mellowing of personality aids older adults in adjusting to change, contributing to well-being (Reitz & Staudinger, 2017).

The nature of sexual expression often changes in older adulthood, but most older adults remain interested in, and satisfied by, sexual activity.

iStock/ poco_bw

Sexuality

Despite common beliefs and stereotypes, five decades of research has consistently shown that older people tend to maintain sexual interest and remain sexually capable and active well into their 80s and often 90s (DeLamater & Koepsel, 2015; Lee et al., 2016). Research conducted in Europe, the United States, Australia, and Asia confirms that many older people continue to view sexual interest and activity as important (Bauer et al., 2016; Hyde et al., 2010; Palacios-Ceña et al., 2012).

The frequency of sexual activity declines with age, but sexual satisfaction often remains unchanged (Lee et al., 2016; Thompson et al., 2011). Studies of older adults age 70 to 85 have suggested that at least one-third to one-half report having intercourse within the past year (Doskoch, 2011; Hyde et al., 2010). However, the nature of sexual expression shifts with age, encompassing an array of behaviors (e.g., self-stimulation, noncoital activity with partners) as well as sexual activity in both long-term and new relationships (McAuliffe et al., 2007; Skałacka & Gerymski, 2019). Similar to other periods of life, research on gay, lesbian, and bisexual older adults is scant. A small sample of older adults suggests similar levels of activity and satisfaction in LGB and heterosexual older adults (Brennan-Ing et al., 2021). Common reasons for lack of sexual activity include physical problems, lack of interest, partner's lack of interest, partner's physical problems, and the loss of a partner (Palacios-Ceña et al., 2012). Although challenges and sexual impairments increase with age, few older adults report distress (Srinivasan et al., 2019). Just as in middle age, good sex in the past predicts good sex in the future (Bell et al., 2017).

Many factors may diminish sexual response and satisfaction: cigarette smoking, heavy drinking, obesity, poor health, some medications, and negative attitudes toward sexuality and aging, among others (DeLamater, 2012). Many illnesses encountered in advancing age (e.g., arthritis, heart disease, diabetes, Parkinson's disease, stroke, and cancer) can have a negative impact on an individual's interest or participation in sexual activity (Syme et al., 2013; Taylor & Gosney, 2011). Sexual activity is a correlate of health, as those who report good health are more likely to be sexually active (DeLamater & Koepsel, 2015; Holden et al., 2014). However, just as during other phases of life, there is a bidirectional relationship: Sexual activity is likely to enhance health by reducing stress and improving positive affect and well-being (Debrot et al., 2017; Freak-Poli et al., 2017).

Religiosity

Older adults tend to be more active participants in religion than younger people and view prayer and personal religious activity as more important (Kaplan & Berkman, 2021). With age, U.S. adults experience an increase in religious intensity and strength of beliefs (Atchley, 2016; Bengtson et al., 2015; see Figure 16.3). Religious attendance declines in late adulthood, likely due to changes in health, mobility, and transportation (Hayward & Krause, 2013).

FIGURE 16.3 ■ Importance of Religion by Age Groups

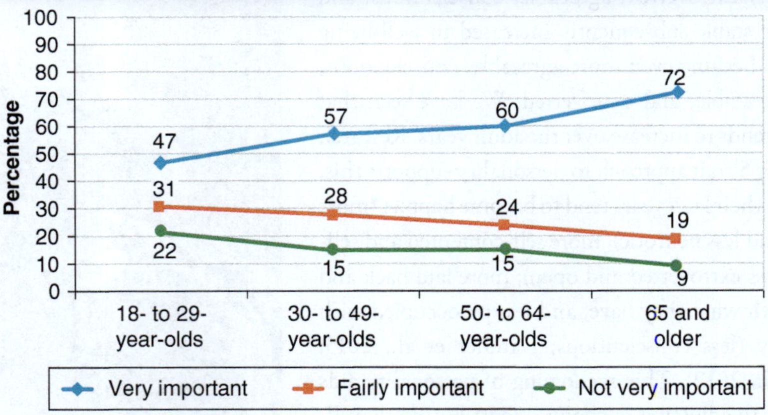

Source: Newport (2006).

In North America, marginalized groups tend to show the highest rates of religious participation. Black older adults tend to report higher levels of private religious practice and daily spiritual experiences than white older adults, as well as the belief that God controls much of the world, than do white older adults (Krause, 2005). Black older adults tended to report turning to God as both a primary source of social support and their personal consultant for health-related matters, whereas white older adults tended to report seeking assistance from family, friends, professional and community sources of support (Lee & Sharpe, 2007). Religion and religious involvement are embedded in the culture, community, and identity for Black, Latinx, and other people of color (Nguyen, 2020). In these communities, the church often provides tangible support in the form of social connections, informal health interventions, and activities that improve welfare (Cosby, 2020).

In late adulthood, religiosity is positively associated with physical activity and health, including increased telomere length (a marker of biological age) and longevity (Homan & Boyatzis, 2010; Kim et al., 2015; Wang et al., 2020). Religiosity and spirituality are also associated with well-being in older adulthood (Abu-Raiya et al., 2015; Galek et al., 2015). A strong sense of religiosity can buffer stress in the face of disadvantage and stressful life events, promote resilience, and help older adults to find meaning in life (Manning & Miles, 2018; Zimmer et al., 2016). Religiosity is also associated with optimism, a sense of self-worth, life satisfaction, and low rates of depression (Reed & Neville, 2014; Ronneberg et al., 2016; Ysseldyk et al., 2013).

Most older adults report religious or spiritual beliefs. Religiosity in older adulthood is positively associated with physical health, well-being, life satisfaction, and longevity.

iStock/ Canberk Sezer

Religiosity has a powerful protective effect on mental health for Black and Latinx older adults (Nguyen, 2020). Religious attendance may facilitate mental health through social means by increasing an older adult's connections with other people in the community, both in giving and in receiving support (Zimmer et al., 2016). Church attendance is positively associated with social network size, frequency of social contact, and perceived support, which in turn are associated with life satisfaction (Fernández Lorca & Valenzuela, 2020;Keyes & Reitzes, 2007; Lee & Sharpe, 2007). One study of nearly 1,200 older adults who attended church regularly found that most—and especially African Americans—perceived increases in the amount of emotional support they gave and received over a 7-year period and were more satisfied with the support they received (Hayward

& Krause, 2013). Social engagement and feeling part of a community are important benefits of religious service attendance.

Thinking in Context: Lifespan Development

1. Compare changes in subjective age and personality in late adulthood. To what extent do they change and stay the same? How is each associated with health and well-being? In what ways do contextual factors influence subjective age and personality?
2. What are some common or popular views about sexuality in late life? Evaluate these views in light of current evidence. To what degree do popular views reflect stereotypes versus reality? How might popular views influence older adults' experience of sexuality? Explain.

Thinking in Context: Intersectionality

With advancing age religion tends to become more important to most adults, but there are racial and ethnic differences. Discuss these differences. What role might religious participation play for older adults from marginalized groups? Why?

Thinking in Context: Applied Developmental Science

As a recreation coordinator at a local senior center, you are asked to design activities to help older adults foster a sense of ego integrity.

1. What is ego integrity and how is it achieved?
2. What kinds of activities or tasks might help older adults reflect on their lives?
3. How will you know if the activities are successful?

RELATIONSHIPS

LEARNING OBJECTIVE

16.2 Discuss features of older adults' relationships with others, including friends, spouses, children, and grandchildren.

Social and emotional connections with family and friends are essential for well-being and are important influences on adaptation and happiness. Aging places new constraints on social relationships, but most older adults find that social relationships continue to be a source of support, social interaction, and fun.

Friendships

In late adulthood, friendships become more important and more fulfilling, partly due to declines in family and work responsibilities (Adams, 2017). With more time to devote to leisure activities, friendships become more centered on activities, such as playing card games and walking, and older adults report having more fun with their friends than do younger adults (Blieszner & Ogletree, 2017). Although friends become fewer in number, older adults form new friendships throughout their lives (Robles et al., 2015). Older adults tend to report more meaningful relationships than younger adults (Fingerman & Charles, 2010; Sander et al., 2017).

Similar to younger people, older adults describe close friendships as entailing mutual interests, a sense of belonging, and opportunities to share feelings (Adams et al., 2000). Adults tend to choose

Older adults have more time to spend with friends than middle-aged adults and their friendships become more fulfilling.

iStock/ monkeybusinessimages

friends who share similarities in age, race, ethnicity, and values. With increasing age older adults are more likely to report having friends of different ages (Elliott O'dare et al., 2019; Gillespie et al., 2015). We know little about intergenerational friendships, but they likely have similar benefits as same-age friendships.

Friendships, giving and receiving support from friends, are as important to psychological health and well-being in older adulthood as family relationships (Blieszner et al., 2019; Dunbar, 2018;Santini et al., 2015). Friendship also plays a role in physical health (Adams, 2017; Kent de Grey & Uchino, 2020). Specifically, social isolation is associated with frailty and increased risk of mortality after suffering a fractured bone (Mortimore et al., 2008; Uno et al., 2021). Friendships help adults manage age-related losses in health, are associated with improved well-being and happiness, and can help older adults cope with major life events, such as bereavement at the death of a loved one (Adams & Taylor, 2015).

Marriage, Divorce, and Cohabitation

Most older adults are very satisfied in their marriages. A lifetime of shared experiences, such as raising families, navigating crises, and building memories together, brings couples closer.

iStock/PeopleImages

As parenting and employment roles are retired, older adults have more time to spend with their spouse. Marital satisfaction tends to increase from middle adulthood through late adulthood (Ko et al., 2007). Marriages in older adulthood are characterized by greater satisfaction, less negativity, and more positive interactions than in other developmental periods (Story et al., 2007). Older couples show fewer disagreements and tend to discuss disagreements with more respect and humor, resolve arguments more quickly and constructively with less resulting anger and resentment, and show more positive affect in their marital interactions than younger couples (Hatch & Bulcroft, 2004; Waldinger & Schulz, 2010).

Compared with middle-aged adults, older adults perceive more positive characteristics and fewer negative characteristics in their partners (Henry et al., 2007). They also show greater positive sentiment override; that is, they appraise their spouse's behavior as more positive than do outside observers (Story et al., 2007). Viewing one's spouse positively predicts marital satisfaction (McCoy et al., 2017). To date, research on marital satisfaction in older adulthood nearly exclusively focuses on heterosexual couples. The limited research discussed in prior chapters suggests that romantic partners share similar relationship and family processes regardless of sexual orientation; therefore, it is reasonable to assume that these patterns of increasing marital satisfaction likely apply to same-sex couples as well. For example, one recent study of gay and lesbian older adult couples found that legally married adults reported better quality of life and more economic and social resources than unmarried couples (Goldsen et al., 2017). Marital satisfaction is associated with health and lower mortality risk (Manvelian & Sbarra, 2020).

Just as marital satisfaction generally tends to increase with age, couples over the age of 65 are less likely to divorce than are younger couples. Yet the "gray divorce" rate has doubled since 1990 (Brown & Wright, 2017). Similar to younger people, older adults report divorcing because of poor communication, emotional detachment, and few shared interests (Wu & Schimmele, 2007). Contrary to popular belief, the empty nest, retirement, and chronic illnesses are not related to divorce (Lin et al., 2018). Adults in long-term marriages may find it more difficult to adjust to divorce than younger adults. Divorce poses financial challenges for couples because accumulated assets must be divided and financial security in retirement is at risk. Women face greater financial and emotional difficulties than men as they are more likely to remain single throughout the remainder of their lives (McDonald & Robb, 2004).

Rates of remarriage decline in older adulthood. Still, a substantial number of adults, particularly older men, remarry after divorce (Huyck & Gutmann, 2006). Single women, whether by divorce or widowhood, are less likely to marry than men. When older adults remarry, their unions tend to be more stable than those of younger people. The gains in maturity and perspective may contribute to a more realistic concept of marriage and support the longevity of late-life marriages (Kemp & Kemp, 2002).

Cohabitation is increasingly common among all adults. Older adults view cohabitation positively and adults over the age of 50 represent about a quarter of all cohabiting adults (Brown & Wright, 2016). Although the prevalence of cohabitation among adults over age 65 is unknown, cohabitation has nearly quadrupled among adults over age 50, from 1.2 million in 2000 to 4 million adults in 2016 (Brown et al., 2012; Stepler, 2017). Many older adults enter cohabiting relationships as an alternative to marriage (Brown & Wright, 2017)

Cohabitation is more consistently associated with positive outcomes in late adulthood as compared with early adulthood. Older adult cohabitors tend to report higher-quality relationships, perceive more fairness, more time spent alone with their partner, fewer disagreements, and a lower likelihood of heated arguments than their younger peers (Brown & Kawamura, 2010; King & Scott, 2005). Compared with younger couples, older adults who cohabit tend to be in relationships of longer duration; are more likely to have experienced the dissolution of a marriage; and tend to report fewer marriage plans, viewing the relationship as an alternative to marriage (Brown et al., 2012). Older adults may be less interested in marriage because they are past the age of childbearing. They also may be more interested in protecting the wealth they have accrued over their lifetime than they are in pooling economic resources. In late adulthood, cohabitating unions are similar to marriages in terms of adults' reports of emotional satisfaction, pleasure, openness, time spent together, perceived criticism and demands, and overall health and well-being (Brown & Kawamura, 2010; Wright & Brown, 2017).

Relationships With Adult Children and Grandchildren

Most North American older adults are parents, usually of middle-aged adults. The nature of the relationship and exchange of help changes over time, from predominantly parent-to-child assistance in childhood through early adulthood, to increasing assistance provided by adult children to their elderly parents. Adult child-to-parent assistance most often takes the form of emotional support and companionship, which helps adults cope with and compensate for losses such as disabilities and widowhood. Most older adults and their adult children keep in touch even when they are separated by great distance. Overall, adult daughters tend to be closer and more involved with parents than sons, speaking with and visiting more often than sons. In contrast with emotional support, fewer older adults receive instrumental assistance from adult children. Instead, many older adults, especially those of high socioeconomic status, continue to assist their adult children, primarily with financial assistance (Grundy & Henretta, 2006).

Family relations may take many forms. Some parents and adult children live nearby, engage in frequent contact, and endorse family obligation norms. Support is provided either primarily from parent to adult child or adult to parent. Some older adults are part of multigenerational families that include their children and grandchildren (Gilligan et al., 2018). Other families provide support at a distance when they do not live nearby, haveregular contact, endorse fewer family obligation norms, and provide mainly financial support—often from parents to children. Other family relationships are autonomous: not living nearby, engaging in little contact, little endorsement of family obligation norms, and few support exchanges. Each of these types of family relations is found in most European nations and North America (Dykstra & Fokkema, 2010).

Most older adults have grandchildren and most will see them grow into adults (AARP, 2002). Grandchildren and great-grandchildren increase older adults' opportunities for emotional support.

The quality of the grandparent relationship is influenced by the degree of involvement in the grandchild's life. A history of close and frequent contact, positive experiences, and affectionate ties predicts good adult child–grandparent relationships (Geurts et al., 2012; Sheehan & Petrovic, 2008) Adults who share close emotional ties with their grandchildren spend more time listening and providing emotional support and companionship to them as adults (Huo et al., 2018). Over time, contact with grandchildren tends to decline as young and middle-aged grandchildren take on time-consuming family and work roles, but affection between grandchildren and grandparents tends to remain strong (Thiele & Whelan, 2008).

Thinking in Context: Lifespan Development

1. To what extent are relationships continuous over adulthood (from early through late adulthood)? Consider friendship and relationships with spouses, children, and grandchildren.
   - What are some ways in which these relationships show continuity or stability?
   - Are there ways in which these relationships change? Explain.
   - How might these patterns of continuity and change influence older adults' health and well-being?
2. Why is cohabitation increasingly common among older adults? Compare older adults' experiences of cohabitation with that of younger adults. What are some similarities and differences?

SOCIAL CONTEXTS

LEARNING OBJECTIVE

16.3 Describe the social contexts in which older adults live and their influence on development.

We have seen that relationships are important sources of support and well-being in late adulthood. As in all periods in life, our interactions with others take place within a range of social contexts that influence our physical functioning, thoughts and relationships. Social contexts are important influences on development, such as changes in physical, cognitive, and social functioning, as well as adaptive functioning. The immediate contexts that influence older adults are neighborhoods and their living environments, including their homes, residential communities, or nursing homes.

Changing Social World

Social support is important for well-being. Yet social interaction tends to decline in older adulthood as social networks become smaller, focused more on family and less on peripheral relationships (Sander et al., 2017). Scientists have examined several explanations for these changes.

An early view, **disengagement theory**, is commonly held but incorrect. According to this theory, older adults are thought to disengage from society, relinquishing valued social roles and reducing interaction, as they anticipate death. At the same time, society disengages from them and this is beneficial to all (DeLiema & Bengtson, 2017). Research has shown that the central tenet of disengagement theory is not true. Rather than disengage, most older individuals prefer to remain active and engaged with others and they benefit from social engagement (Bengtson & DeLiema, 2016; Johnson & Mutchler, 2014). Disengagement does not reflect healthy development but rather a lack of opportunities for social engagement (Lang et al., 1997).

In contrast, **activity theory** says that declines in social interaction are not a result of adults' desires, but are instead a function of social barriers to engagement (DeLiema & Bengtson, 2017). When older adults lose social roles due to retirement or disability, they attempt to replace them to stay active and busy. Volunteer work and civic activity may replace career roles and protect against decline in health,

Successful aging entails remaining active and maintaining a sense of continuity in self, in habits, personalities, and lifestyles.

kali9/E+/Getty Images

psychological well-being, and mortality (Glass et al., 2006; Hao, 2008). Yet it is not simply the quantity of activity and social relationships that influences health and well-being, but the quality, and individuals differ in their needs and desires (Bengtson & DeLiema, 2016; Pushkar et al., 2010). The more active adults are in roles they value—such as spouse, parent, friend, and volunteer—the more likely they are to report high levels of well-being and life satisfaction and to live longer, healthier lives (Adams et al., 2011; Cherry et al., 2013).

Relatedly, successful aging entails not simply remaining active but maintaining a sense of consistency in self across one's past into the future, a tenet of **continuity theory** (DeLiema & Bengtson, 2017). Despite changing roles, people are motivated to maintain their habits, personalities, and lifestyles, adapting as needed to maintain a sense of continuity, that they are the same person they have always been (Breheny & Griffiths, 2017). The task is to acknowledge and minimize losses, integrate them with their sense of self, and optimize their strengths to maintain their sense of remaining the same person over time despite physical, cognitive, emotional, and social changes (Bengtson & DeLiema, 2016). Older adults therefore tend to seek routine: familiar people, familiar activities, and familiar settings. Most of older adults' friends are old friends. Engaging in familiar activities with familiar people preserves a sense of self and offers comfort, social support, self-esteem, mastery, and identity (Pushkar et al., 2010).

Another explanation for older adults' narrowing social circles rests on the uniquely human ability to monitor time. With advancing age, people become increasingly aware of their shrinking time horizon: that they have little time left to live (Zacher & Kirby, 2015). This awareness causes them to shift their goals and priorities and accounts for continuity and change in social relationships. According to **socioemotional selectivity theory**, the functions of social interactions change with age (English & Carstensen, 2016). Young adults accumulate many friends because they emphasize the information-sharing function of friendship as they are developing a sense of identity and entering social roles (Wrzus et al., 2013). With age the information-sharing aspects of social interaction become less important because older adults often have accumulated decades of knowledge. Instead it is the emotion-regulating function of social relationships—feeling good—that becomes more important during older adulthood (Carstensen & Mikels, 2005).

As perceived time left diminishes, people tend to discard peripheral relationships and focus on important ones, such as those with close family members and friends (English & Carstensen, 2014). Older adults become increasingly motivated to derive emotional meaning from life and thereby cultivate emotionally close supportive relationships and disengage from more peripheral social ties (Carstensen et al., 2011; English & Carstensen, 2016). Despite an overall decline in the number of relationships in late adulthood, this process of strengthening and pruning relationships is associated with positive well-being. It allows older adults to focus their limited time and energy on relationships that are most beneficial while avoiding those that are inconsequential or detrimental, thereby maximizing their emotional well-being. In this sense, social selectivity is an emotional regulation strategy (Sims et al., 2015).

Neighborhoods

The neighborhoods and communities in which older adults reside influence their adaptation through the provision of physical and social resources. City, suburban, and rural communities offer different opportunities and challenges. Older adults who live in the suburbs tend to be healthier and wealthier and show higher rates of life satisfaction than those who live in cities (Dandy & Bollman, 2008; DeNavas-Walt & Proctor, 2014). Yet because their neighborhoods are less compact, suburban older adults tend to walk less and show greater declines in walking with age, both of which influence health and ability to live independently (King et al., 2017). Generally, urban older adults have better access to transportation and health and social services than do those in suburban and rural settings, enhancing their opportunities for social participation (Andonian & MacRae, 2011).

One-fourth of U.S. and one-third of Canadian older adults live in rural areas where they tend to be more disadvantaged in terms of health, wealth, and availability of services, and they are less likely to live near their children than other adults (DeNavas-Walt & Proctor, 2014). But older adults who live in rural areas tend to interact with their neighbors more than their urban and suburban counterparts (Shaw, 2005). Close relationships with community members, friends, and neighbors, including frequent interaction and high levels of social support, are important emotional and material resources for rural older adults.

In urban and suburban communities, neighborhood SES is associated with older adults' physical and mental health. Canadian older adults who live in poor neighborhoods are more likely than those in affluent neighborhoods to experience arthritis, diabetes, hypertension, heart disease, depression, and stroke (Menec et al., 2010). Disordered neighborhoods are associated with poor health, including frailty, poor mental health, and increased depressive symptoms (Caldwell et al., 2018;Joshi et al., 2017; Wu et al., 2015). Neighborhood characteristics are thought to have a biological effect on health. Specifically, neighborhood SES deprivation is associated with shortened telomere length, a marker of health and longevity (Powell-Wiley et al., 2020).

Perception of neighborhood safety influences activity and health. Australian older adults who reported a sense of trust in their neighborhood and social cohesion were more likely to report recreational walking in nearby parks than were those who perceived the neighborhood as less safe (Van Cauwenberg et al., 2017). One study found that Mexican American older adults who viewed their neighborhoods positively and as safe were less likely to report poor self-rated health, controlling for both socioeconomic status and health status (Stroope et al., 2017). Older adults in more accessible and safe neighborhood contexts, including walking-friendly sidewalks, access to parks, the availability of public transportation, and low crime, are more likely to retain a higher degree mobility, health, and social activity and lower levels of depressive symptoms than those in less accessible contexts (Choi & Matz-Costa, 2017; Joshi et al., 2017; Mathis et al., 2017).

Neighborhood factors, such as walkability and access to transportation, health services, and social opportunities, influence health and ability to live independently.

istock/ U.Ozel.Images

It is worth noting that Black older adults may perceive the same neighborhoods differently than white older adults, with ramifications for health. For example, Black older adults are more likely than white older adults to describe a given neighborhood as lacking features such as accessible parks (Esposito et al., 2020). At all ages, adults' experience of a neighborhood is filtered through lenses of race, ethnicity, and gender. Racial differences in views of a given neighborhood are influenced by a lifetime of exposure to inequality, discrimination, and racism, such as segregated housing within a community. Adults who live in neighborhoods with a higher density of Black residents and more residential instability and disorder show higher rates of frailty (Caldwell et al., 2018). Moreover, the effects of neighborhood poverty and disadvantage accumulate over a lifetime, with significant implications for functional decline and mortality (Clarke et al., 2014).

Aging in Place

Most older adults prefer to age in their homes, referred to as "aging in place" (see Figure 16.4; Fields & Dabelko-Schoeny, 2016). Most older adults live in or near the home they have lived in most of their lives. As health declines, living alone poses physical and psychological risks, including social isolation and loneliness. Declines in health and widowhood often prompt older adults to relocate, but most North Americans remain in their old neighborhoods (Chappell et al., 2003). Despite the challenges, remaining in a lifelong home strengthens adults' feelings of continuity with the past, aids their sense of identity, as well as maintains connections with the community, an important source of support.

When older adults are healthy and not physically impaired, living in their own home permits them the greatest degree of control over their lives, such as choosing what and when to eat. Because of divorce, widowing, or never marrying, about one-third of North American older adults live alone, and more than one-third of women over 65 live alone (see Figure 16.5; Stepler, 2016). Older adults who live alone are more likely to worry about finances and to live in poverty. Elderly women are about 50% more likely to be poor than elderly men, and the risk of poverty increases as women age.

African American older adults are especially likely to remain in their lifelong neighborhoods and to live in poverty, but they also tend to rely on informal support systems for care, a helper network that includes spouses, children, siblings, friends, neighbors, and church members (Rasheed & Rasheed, 2003). This helper network is the basis for informal caregiving for those older persons who find

FIGURE 16.4 ■ Living Preferences Among Older Adults

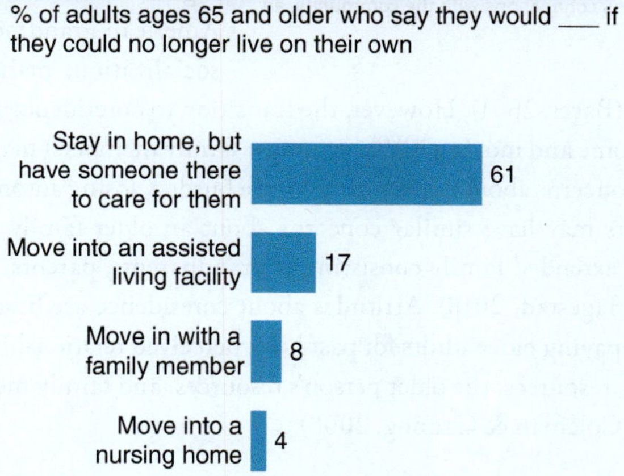

Most older adults want to age in place

Source: Stepler (2016)

FIGURE 16.5 ■ Living Arrangements of Older Adults, by Sex

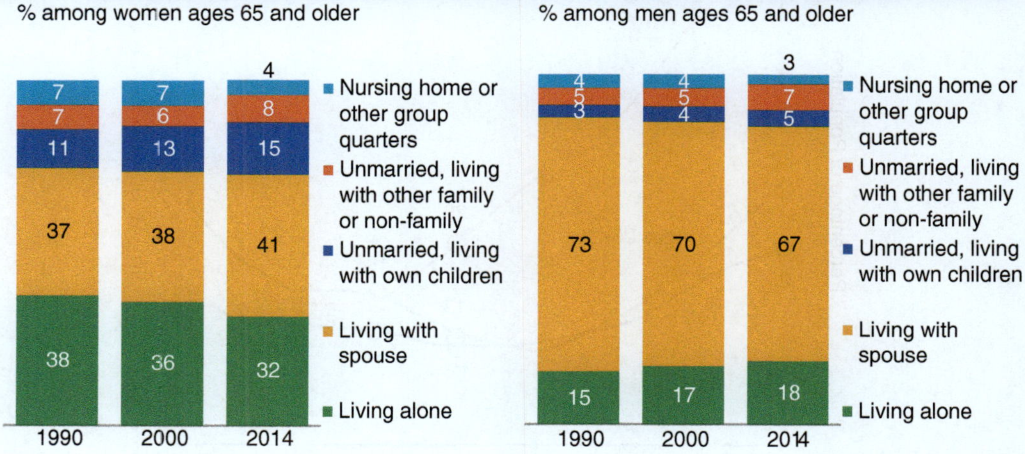

Source: Stepler (2016)

Most adults prefer to age in place and retain their independence. As health declines, living alone poses physical and psychological risks, such as social isolation and loneliness. Despite the challenges, remaining in a lifelong home strengthens elders' feelings of continuity with the past, aids their sense of identity, as well as maintains connections with the community, an important source of support.

iStock/Willowpix

themselves unable to maintain complete self-care due to illness or physical infirmities. It provides older adults with instrumental assistance, such as help in grocery shopping, transportation, and meal preparation, and expressive assistance, including emotional support, giving advice, encouragement, companionship, and prayer.

Many older adults live with kin, in intergenerational families. As discussed in Chapter 15, adult children often feel a strong responsibility to care for aging parents and grandparents, especially when the older adults have serious economic and housing needs (Postigo & Honrubia, 2010). As members of an intergenerational household, older members of a family may provide childcare and share their experience with grandchildren, adult children, and other family members (see Figure 16.6). Grandparents, particularly African American grandmothers, are important agents of socialization, maintaining the role of matriarch and kinkeeper (Barer, 2001). However, the transition to coresidence (an older family member giving up their own home and moving in with younger family members) may be challenging. The older person may have concerns about not wanting to be a burden, losing autonomy, or losing privacy; younger family members may have similar concerns about an older family member disrupting the household. The new extended family consisting of grandparents, parents, and grandchildren must find a new balance (Hagestad, 2018). Attitudes about coresidence are based on family obligation norms, beliefs about repaying older adults for past help, perceived relationship quality, other demands on the younger adults' resources, the older person's resources, and family members' sense of moral responsibility to assist (Coleman & Ganong, 2008).

FIGURE 16.6 ■ Adults Residing in Multigenerational Households in the United States, by Age, 1940–2014

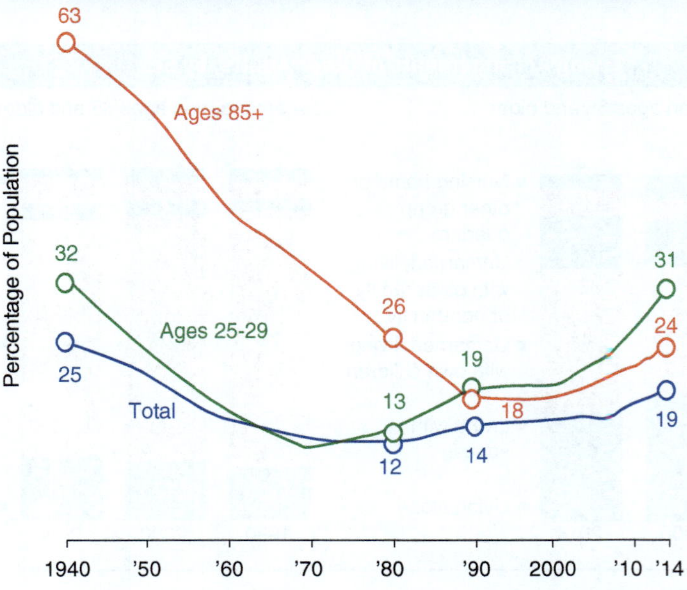

Source: Cohn and Passel (2018)

Other Housing

There are many types of residential communities and many offer several options for care. Living in a community of older adults provides opportunities for social activities, forming friendships, and offering help to peers.

iStock/CasarsaGuru

Some older adults live in residential communities for older adults, ranging from single houses, to small collections of condominiums, to large apartment complexes (Freedman & Spillman, 2014). Homes in residential communities are designed to meet older adults' physical and social needs and may include such features as grab bars in bathrooms, single-level homes, and intercoms for emergency assistance. Some homes are designed for low-income elderly and are subsidized by the government. Most communities are private businesses. Older adults rent or purchase a home and entry to a community complete with recreational facilities for socializing with other adults and obtaining assistance. Others live in congregate housing, which permits them to live independently but provides more comprehensive support, including common areas such as a dining room, recreational facilities, meals, and additional supervision and assistance with disabilities. Some older adults opt for "continuing care" communities that are designed to meet their changing needs, wherein they begin with independent housing, and when needed, transfer to congregate housing, and finally nursing home care.

Living in a community of older adults supports social activities, the formation of friendships, and provision of assistance to others, which increases a sense of competence and leadership (Ball et al., 2000; Lawrence & Schigelone, 2002). Older adults show better adaptation to living in residential communities when they share similar backgrounds and values, have frequent contact and communication with others, and feel socially integrated into the community. Supportive environments can match their changing physical abilities and offset declines in mobility and aid older adults' attempts to remain active (Fonda et al., 2002; Jenkins et al., 2002). Overall, older adults who reside in residential communities tend to show higher levels of perceived autonomy, sense of security, and quality of life as compared with those living independently in the neighborhood (van Bilsen et al., 2008). Although adults in residential settings did not differ from those in regular homes with regard to their sense of well-being or feelings of loneliness, those in residential communities participate more frequently in social activities. The main drawback to residential communities is their cost, which may entail purchasing an apartment or renting for $2,000 or more per month in the United States.

A small and declining number of older adults live in nursing homes (Toth et al., 2021). A nursing home is a facility that provides care to older adults who require assistance with daily care and health issues (Sanford et al., 2015). Nursing homes offer the greatest amount of care, 24 hours a day and 7 days a week, but also are most restrictive of adults' autonomy. Nursing homes tend to be hospital-like settings in which adults often have limited opportunities to control their schedule or interact with others, and their contact with peers generally is determined by staff. Constraints on autonomy can lead to loneliness, feelings of helplessness, and depression (Anderberg & Berglund, 2010). Most older people prefer to avoid living in nursing homes, if possible. Family members often experience guilt when they see no other choice but nursing home placement for their loved one (Seiger Cronfalk et al., 2017).

Several factors are thought to be most influential in determining the quality of life of older adults: freedom of choice and involvement in decision making, recognition of individuality, right to privacy, continuation of normal social roles, a stimulating environment, and a sense of connectedness between home, neighborhood, and community. Well-being is enhanced in nursing homes that are designed to foster a sense of control over day-to-day experiences and social life. Encouraging social interaction in communal spaces, allowing residents to furnish and deinstitutionalize their spaces with some belongings, and modifying their environments to meet their changing needs while retaining as much autonomy as possible can help residents adapt to nursing home living.

Thinking in Context: Lifespan Development

1. Individuals' social circles tend to narrow over adulthood. Why? What are some of the implications of socioemotional selectivity theory for older adults' daily interactions, relationships, and well-being?
2. Considering the full span of adulthood, from early through late adulthood, compare socioemotional selectivity theory with the positivity effect, the tendency to switch focus from negative to positive information from early adulthood through late adulthood (see Chapter 15). How are these concepts similar and different? How might they interrelate?
3. Compare aging in place with living in residential communities and nursing homes.
   - **a.** What are the advantages and disadvantages of each environment?
   - **b.** What factors, such as activities, safety, autonomy, and others, do you deem important in choosing a housing situation?
   - **c.** To what degree does an adult's age, mobility, or health influence housing decisions? How might housing decisions change over late adulthood?

Thinking in Context: Intersectionality

Contrast rural, urban, and suburban contexts.

1. What opportunities and challenges do rural, urban, and suburban contexts offer older adults?
2. What is the role of neighborhood SES in health and well-being?
3. In what ways might adults' experiences vary with race, ethnicity, and membership in a marginalized group? Why?

RETIREMENT

LEARNING OBJECTIVE

16.4 Examine influences on the timing of retirement and adaptation to retirement.

Today's adults, members of the Baby Boom generation (born 1946–1964), tend to remain working full time longer than ever before. About 28% of adults age 65 to 74 and 9% adults age 75 and older are in the workforce (U.S. Bureau of Labor Statistics, 2020). In contrast, only about 20% of adults in the generations born between 1901 and 1945 worked between ages 65 and 72 (Fry, 2019). Improved health and longevity enable adults to work many more years. However, working in late life, or retiring for that matter, are decisions that are often out of older adults' control because of finances, health, or circumstances.

Deciding to Retire

Ideally retirement is a process that begins long before the last day of employment. Under the best of circumstances, the retirement process begins with imagining the possibility of retirement and what it might be like. Adults then assess their abilities and their resources, determine when is the best time to let go of the work role, and put plans into action (Feldman & Beehr, 2011). The reality of retirement planning is that plans may change quickly and unexpectedly.

Health is a critical influence on the timing of retirement. Adults with poor health and visual and hearing impairments tend to retire earlier than their peers (Gopinath et al., 2017). The large racial and ethnic differences that we see in health over the lifespan influence retirement rates. Among U.S.

retirees, 40% of Black and 50% of Hispanic retirees indicate that poor health was at least somewhat important to their decision, as compared with 26% of white retirees (U.S. Federal Reserve, 2018).

Retirement ages tend to vary with job conditions. Workers tend to retire early from jobs that are stressful or hazardous. Many of these job have mandatory retirement ages (such as air traffic controllers, pilots, firefighters, and police officers). Older adults tend to delay retirement from jobs that are highly stimulating, take place in pleasant environments, and are a source of identity and self-esteem (American Association of Retired Persons, 2008). Some adults cite the desire to maintain a routine and enjoyment as reasons to work (Sewdas et al., 2017). Workers in professional occupations and those who are self-employed tend to stay in their jobs longer as compared with those in blue-collar or clerical positions.

A sense of control and perceived working conditions, such as feeling respected by coworkers and leaders, is associated with delaying retirement in German and Finnish older adults (Böckerman et al., 2017;Wöhrmann et al., 2017). In contrast, workers who feel devalued may feel forced from the workplace. For Black workers, experiences with discrimination over their lifetime and at work are associated with retiring early relative to peers (Gonzales et al., 2018).

Financial resources have a large influence on whether and when an older adult retires.There are large racial disparities in the amount of retirement savings, with Black and Hispanic adults having saved about one-third as much as white non-Hispanic adults (a median of $29,000, $23,000, and $80,000, respectively; Morrissey, 2019). Black older adults are disproportionately at risk to live in poverty during retirement.

Changing economics also influence older adults' abilities to retire, as personal retirement investments such as IRAs and 401(k) plans may lose value unexpectedly. The availability of Social Security influences retirement timing for women (Morrill & Westall, 2019). Social Security, enacted as part of the Social Security Act signed by President Franklin D. Roosevelt in 1935, is funded by taxes paid by workers. Social Security provides older Americans with a dependable monthly income, with automatic increases tied to increases in the cost of living. Social Security has reduced poverty rates for older Americans by more than two-thirds, from 35% in 1959 to about 9% in 2016 (Bureau of the Census, 2017; Shelton, 2013). More than 90% of U.S. retirees receive monthly Social Security benefit payments (Social Security Administration, 2018). Yet Social Security was never intended as a sole form of income, but as a supplement to income from a retirement plan, pension, and savings. Unfortunately, many older adults rely on Social Security as their primary source of income. In 2017, one-half of married older adult couples and nearly three-quarters of single adults were getting at least half of their income from Social Security; and for about one-quarter and nearly one-half, respectively, Social Security was virtually their only income (Social Security Administration, 2018). Moreover, Social Security provides critical income to older women and people of color, who are more likely than married and white older adults to rely on Social Security for 90% or more of their income (Social Security Administration, 2016).

Transition to Retirement and Adjustment

Theorists propose that the transition to retirement is a process that follows a predictable set of steps. Adults generally seek to preserve continuity in their sense of self, and this tendency influences their transition to retirement (Atchley, 1989). Adults who are more satisfied at work may see work as central to their sense of self, may experience retirement as a disruption to their sense of self, and may thereby delay retirement. As workers approach retirement they may adjust their attitudes toward work, revising their views on its importance. Work is central to many people's sense of identity, posing transitory adjustment issues for new retirees (Bordia et al., 2020).

After the retirement event, retirees may experience a short honeymoon phase marked by new interests and rest without the obligations of work. As retirees become accustomed to the reality of everyday life in retirement, these positive feelings may change to disenchantment. Over time, the adult develops a realistic view of the social and economic opportunities and constraints of retirement, and a period of reorientation occurs in which the person attempts to replace the lost work role with new activities or becomes stressed if they cannot (Richardson & Kilty, 1991). Finally, stability occurs once the retiree accommodates and adjusts to retirement.

Gains in one domain, such as increased family time, might compensate for losses in another, such as job-related status. Attitudes toward retirement may be based on adults' evaluation of the expected balance between the gains and losses associated with leaving working and being retired and the expected disruption to their lifestyle (Davies et al., 2017). The net balance of perceived gains and losses will vary between individuals, with some older adults expecting greater gains or losses than others (Pinquart & Schindler, 2007b). Given the scale and scope of potential changes across multiple life domains, attitude toward retirement is likely to be characterized by ambivalence in which individuals will hold both favorable and unfavorable attitudes (Muratore & Earl, 2015; Newman et al., 2012).

Research on retirement adjustment suggests that the majority of adults show high levels of well-being and life satisfaction and adjust well to their post-retirement life, but some adults show poor adjustment (Henning et al., 2017; Howe et al., 2010; Pinquart & Schindler, 2007a). One study of Australian retirees found several patterns of adjustment. Some retirees maintained high life satisfaction across the retirement transition (40%), others experienced declining levels of life satisfaction from a high level prior to retirement (28%), some experienced low levels of life satisfaction that declined further (18%), and some reported increasing life satisfaction from a low level prior to retirement (14%). Overall, retirees who experienced significant declines in life satisfaction tended to have worse health and less access to a range of social and economic resources prior to retirement, suggesting that preretirement experiences influence adjustment (Heybroek et al., 2015).

For individuals who find their job stressful or burdensome, retiring could be a very positive experience, a relief from ongoing strains and conflicts, energizing and fulfilling (Fehr, 2012). Also, for individuals who would like to participate more heavily in the roles of family member and community member, retirement is an opportunity for them to enjoy the rewards and responsibilities tied to those roles. Continuity in other social roles and the ability to adapt to role changes leads to few changes in life satisfaction after retirement (Reitzes & Mutran, 2004). In addition, retirement satisfaction tends to increase for most older adults over the first half dozen years after retirement (Gall, Evans, & Howard, 1997; Wang, 2007).

Many older adults report being more socially and intellectually active after retirement (Henning et al., 2021). Retirement has health benefits such as lower cardiovascular risk for both men and women, which is associated with improved cognitive functioning (Oi, 2021). Many adults show improvements in mental health, especially when they retire from jobs with poor working conditions, such as high demands, low authority, and low support (Fleischmann et al., 2020).

Influences on Retirement Adjustment

Adjustment to retirement is influenced by a complex web of factors, including characteristics of the individual, his or her social relationships, and the job (Wang et al., 2011). Some positive predictors of successful adjustment include physical health, finances, leisure, voluntary retirement, social integration, psychological health, and personality-related attributes (Barbosa et al., 2016). Positive adjustment to retirement is also associated with engagement in satisfying relationships and leisure activities—and planning ahead for the financial and social changes that come with retirement (Grotz et al., 2017; Siguaw et al., 2018;Yeung & Zhou, 2017). Workers in high-stress, demanding jobs, or those that provide little satisfaction, tend to show positive adaptation to retirement (Adams et al., 2002; Fehr, 2012). For them, retirement often comes as a relief. Those who are in highly satisfying, low-stress, pleasant jobs tend to experience more challenges in adaptation. Generally speaking, the greater the intrinsic value of the older worker's job, the lower the levels of retirement satisfaction (van Solinge & Henkens, 2008).

The characteristics of the retirement transition also matter. Many adults are taking the route of a gradual retirement, slowly decreasing their involvement and working part time, rather than an abrupt retirement (Calvo et al., 2009). Frequently this is out of financial necessity. One study of Australian retirees found that those who had retired abruptly were more likely to rate their health as having deteriorated, whereas those who had retired gradually tended to report better adjustment to retirement life (De Vaus et al., 2007). The length of the transition, whether abrupt or gradual, matters less in determining happiness after retirement than the worker's sense of control over the transition—whether the retirement is chosen or forced (Calvo et al., 2009; De Vaus et al., 2007; Quine et al., 2007). Having a sense of control over the decision to retire, as well as the timing and manner of leaving work, has an important positive impact on psychological and social well-being that lasts throughout the retirement transition (Siguaw et al., 2018).

Social support also influences adjustment. Among married retirees, relationship satisfaction aids the transition to retirement and, in turn, the increased time together that retirement brings can serve to enhance marital satisfaction. In contrast, adults who are lonely or recently divorced are more likely to experience difficulty (Damman et al., 2015; Segel-Karpas et al., 2018). Maintaining multiple roles after retirement promotes well-being (Butler & Eckart, 2007). For example, volunteer work offers older adults opportunities to share their experience, mentor others, and develop and sustain social relationships, all of which may enhance their well-being (Tang, 2008; Windsor et al., 2008).

Thinking in Context: Lifespan Development

1. Discuss individual and contextual factors that influence whether and when an older adult retires.
2. In what ways might the characteristics of jobs; individuals' education and experience; and other microsystem, macrosystem, and exosystem factors influence adjustment to retirement?

Thinking in Context: Biological Influences

How might the typical physical changes that older adults experience influence retirement decisions?

1. Consider physical changes in older adulthood, such as strength, sensory and motor abilities, and brain development (see Chapter 15). How might these changes influence adults' performance at work?
2. What kinds of jobs are most likely to be influenced by the sensory, motor, and body changes of older adulthood? By the neurological changes?
3. How might contextual factors influence the connection between physical aging and retirement decisions?

DEATH AND END-OF-LIFE ISSUES

LEARNING OBJECTIVE

16.5 Consider definitions of death and end-of-life considerations.

At its simplest, death is the absence of life. It is unavoidable, comes hand-in-hand with life, and is the final state of the lifespan. In this section, we examine death and death-related issues across the lifespan, including evolving definitions of death, how people of varying ages understand and experience death, and the bereavement processes. The circumstances that surround death and its timing in the lifespan have changed radically over the last century, alongside advances in life expectancy.

Defining Death

The actual moment of death is not easy to determine. In prior centuries, death was defined as the cessation of cardiopulmonary function. A person was dead once the heart stopped beating, now referred to as **clinical death**. Today's medical practices, including the widespread dissemination of cardiopulmonary resuscitation (CPR) techniques, have permitted many people to regain a heartbeat and be "revived" from clinical death. A heartbeat is no longer a clear marker of life, or in its absence, death. Today ventilators permit patients' hearts to continue to beat even though they cannot eat, think, or breathe on their own.

More precise definitions of death are needed. A 1968 physician-led committee at Harvard Medical School concluded that patients who meet criteria for specific severe neurological injuries, **whole brain death**, may be pronounced dead before the heart stops beating (Harvard Medical School ad Hoc Committee, 1968). Whole brain death refers to the irreversible loss of functioning in the entire brain, higher and lower brain regions, the cortex and brainstem, without possibility of resuscitation (McMahan True et al., 2001). Indicators include no spontaneous movement or respiration, no motor reflexes, no pupilar response, and a flat EEG. This definition was reaffirmed by the 2008 report of the President's Council on Bioethics. Under the Uniform Determination of Death Act, all 50 U.S. states and the District of Columbia apply the whole brain standard in defining death, thereby permitting a person to be declared legally dead and removed from life support.

The most controversial definition of death looks beyond the whole brain standard to include instances in which inadequate blood supply to the brain irreparably damages the cortex while leaving the brainstem intact and functional, such as after heart attack, drowning, or traumatic brain injury. The neurons of the brainstem often survive stressors that kill cortex neurons (Brisson et al., 2014), resulting in cortical death, or a **persistent vegetative state (PVS)**, in which the person appears awake and maintains heart rate and respiration but is not aware, due to the permanent loss of all activity in the cortex (Laureys et al., 2010). PVS patients are neither clinically dead nor meet the criteria for whole brain death, but remain biologically alive despite lacking the capacity to regain awareness and cognitive capacities (Bender et al., 2015). Because PVS does not meet the criteria for whole brain death, it is not recognized as death by U.S. legal statute (McMahan, 2001). Canada and several other countries acknowledge cortical death (Teitelbaum & Shemie, 2016). Supporters of the cortical definition of death argue that the cortex is responsible for what makes us human—thought, emotion, and personality. From this view, when higher cortical functions have ceased, these capacities are lost. Yet U.S. courts require authoritative medical opinion that recovery is not possible before terminating life-prolonging activities (Cranford, 2004). Several lengthy and dramatic court cases have caused many people to consider and communicate their own wishes regarding how they want to die.

The Dying Trajectory

There is great variability in the **dying trajectory**, or the rate of decline that people show prior to death (Cohen-Mansfield et al., 2017; Lunney et al., 2003). Dying trajectories vary by duration and descent and can be categorized into four patterns. The first trajectory is the *abrupt-surprise death*, which is sudden, unexpected, and instantaneous, such as an accident, a shooting, or a heart attack. As shown in Figure 16.7, the person shows normal functioning until a steep, catastrophic decline occurs, bringing a sudden death without warning. The dying person and his or her family have no time to prepare or adjust beforehand. A second trajectory, the *short-term expected death* is a steady predictable decline due to a terminal illness such as cancer (Teno et al., 2001). A third dying trajectory is referred to as an *expected lingering death* because it is anticipated but prolonged, such as in the case of frailty and old age. The fourth trajectory is referred to as *entry-reentry deaths* because slow declines are punctuated by a series of crises and partial recoveries; the dying person may have repeated hospital stays, returning home between stays. The dying trajectory

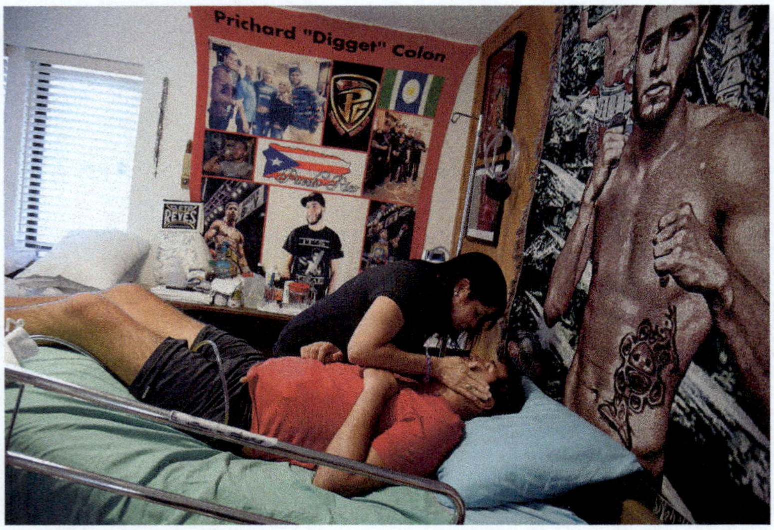

Nieves Melendez tends to her son, former professional boxer Prichard Colon, while he lies in a vegetative state after suffering a traumatic brain injury during his bout against Terrel Williams.

The Washington Post / Contributor/ Getty Images

FIGURE 16.7 ■ Theoretical Trajectories of Dying

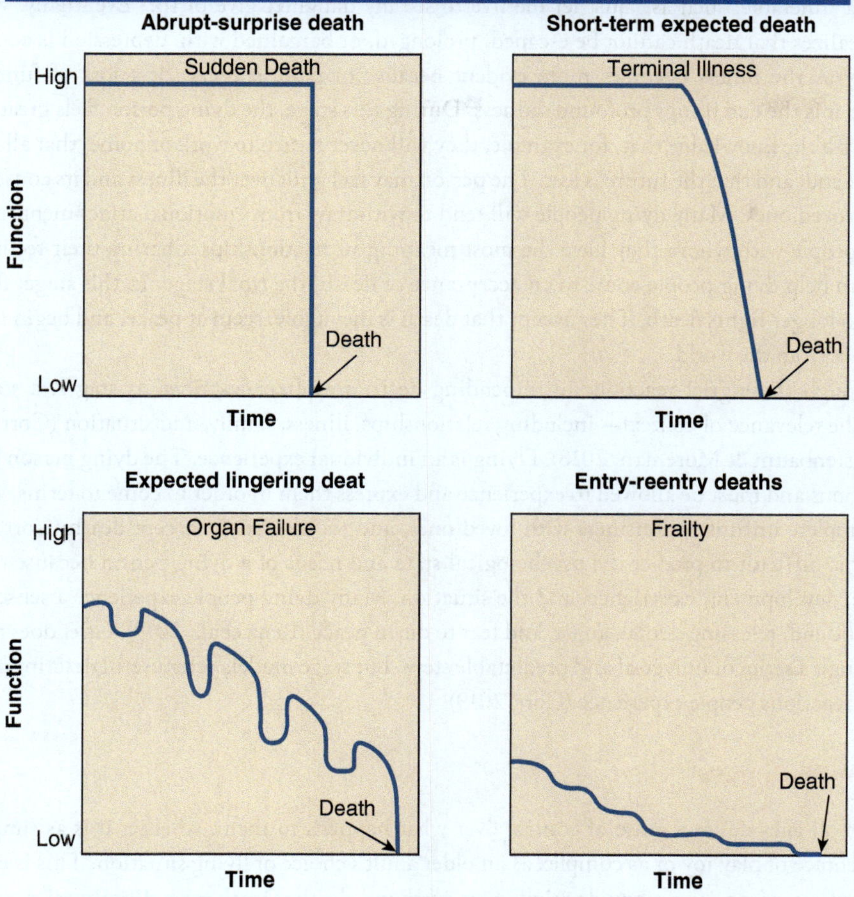

Source: Lunney et al., 2003.

influences adaptation on the part of the dying person and his or her family. Typically, the short-term expected death is most predictable and most likely to be experienced in hospice care as the lifespan is clearly identified as limited. Lingering and entry-reentry deaths are prolonged. They can tax caregivers' coping skills as such deaths are often not afforded hospice care until death is imminent.

Emotional Reactions to Dying

People tend to show a range of emotional reactions to the knowledge that they are dying. After conducting more than 200 interviews with terminally ill people, psychiatrist Elisabeth Kübler-Ross categorized people's reactions into five types or ways in which people deal with death: denial, anger, bargaining, depression, and acceptance (Kübler-Ross, 1969). Although Kübler-Ross described these grief reactions as a series of stages, not everyone experiences all of them or proceeds through them at the same pace or in the same order (Corr et al., 2019; Kübler-Ross, 1974).

Upon learning that one has a terminal illness, the first reaction is likely shock. For most people, denial ("It's not possible!") is the first stage of processing death, reflecting the initial reaction to the news. The person may not believe the diagnosis, deny that it is true, and might seek a second or third opinion. Once the dying person realizes that they are terminally ill, anger may set in. Dying people might ask themselves, "Why me?" Feeling cheated and robbed of life, the person may harbor resentment and envy toward family, friends, and caregivers, as it may seem unfair that others live while they must die. Anger is a very difficult stage, but with time and effort most dying people manage and resolve these challenging feelings.

The bargaining stage, like the other stages of dying, is common but not universal. The dying person bargains to find a way out. Perhaps a deal can be struck with God or fate. The dying person might promise to be a better person and help others if only they can survive. A parent might attempt to bargain a timetable, such as, "just let me live to see my daughter give birth." Eventually, when the person realizes that death cannot be escaped, prolonged, or bargained with, depression is common—especially as the illness becomes more evident because of pain, surgery, or a loss of functioning. Knowing it is the end brings profound sadness. During this stage, the dying person feels great loss and sorrow with the knowledge that, for example, they will never return to work or home, that all relationships will end, and that the future is lost. The person may feel guilt over the illness and its consequences for their loved ones. Many dying people will tend to withdraw from emotional attachments to all but the few people with whom they have the most meaningful relationships. Sharing their feelings with others can help dying people come to an acceptance of death, the final stage. In this stage, the dying person no longer fights death. They accept that death is inevitable, seem at peace, and begin to detach themselves from the world.

Although these grief reactions to impending death are often described as stages, a stage view ignores the relevance of context—including relationships, illness, family, and situation (Corr & Corr, 2013;Kastenbaum & Moreman, 2018). Dying is an individual experience. The dying person has myriad emotions and must be allowed to experience and express them in order to come to terms with their grief, complete unfinished business with loved ones, and to, ultimately, accept death (Corr & Corr, 2013). It is difficult to predict the psychological state and needs of a dying person because they vary with age, development, experience, and the situation. Many dying people experience a sense of calm toward the end, releasing denial, anger, and fear to die in peace (Renz et al., 2018). Grief does not progress through a series of universal and predictable steps, but stage models offer useful descriptions of the range of reactions people experience (Corr, 2019).

Death With Dignity

People of all ages desire a sense of control over what happens to them, whether it is as simple as an infant's choice of play toy or as complex as an older adult's choice of living situation. This is especially true when it comes to the many decisions that surround death. **Death with dignity** refers to ending life in a way that is true to one's preferences, controlling one's end-of-life care (Guo & Jacelon, 2014; Kastenbaum & Moreman, 2018). Given that death is not easily defined, end-of-life issues are particularly important to consider.

Advance Directives

Planning and communication are key to helping people die with dignity. Without prior communication, dying patients are often unable to express their wishes and often cannot participate in decisions about their own end-of-life care, such as pain management, life-prolonging treatment, and memorial services. The Patient Self-Determination Act (PSA) of 1990 guaranteed the right of all competent adults to have a say in decisions about their health care by putting their wishes regarding end-of-life and life-sustaining treatment in writing. Advance directives, including a living will and a durable power of attorney, are important ways of ensuring that people's preferences regarding end-of-life care are known and respected.

A **living will** is a legal document that permits people to make known their wishes regarding what medical intervention should and should not be used to prolong their lives if they are incapacitated by an illness or accident and are unable to speak for themselves. A **durable power of attorney** for health care is a document in which individuals legally authorize a trusted relative or friend (called a *health care proxy*) to make health care decisions on their behalf if they are unable to do so.

Advance directives permit patients to take control over their health care, their deaths, and what happens to their bodies and possessions after death. Caregivers benefit from advance directives because an understanding of the patients' wishes can help in decision making and reduce stress, emotional strain, and, potentially, guilt (Radwany et al., 2009). Overall, about one in three U.S. adults, including 40% to 50% of older adults, have written some form of advance directive (Gamertsfelder et al., 2016; Rao et al., 2014; Yadav et al., 2017). Yet advance directives are not just for the old or the ill. Many argue that it is the healthy—especially the young and healthy—who benefit most from living wills and health care proxies because they and their families are often unprepared for the decisions that may accompany the sudden loss of decision-making capacities and consciousness, such as from an accident (Khan, 2014).

Euthanasia

Through a living will individuals indicate when life-prolonging care may be withdrawn and under what conditions euthanasia is acceptable. **Euthanasia** ("easy death") refers to the practice of assisting terminally ill people in dying more quickly (Jecker, 2006; van der Maas, 1991). **Passive euthanasia** occurs when life-sustaining treatment, such as a ventilator, is withheld or withdrawn, allowing a person to die naturally. In **active euthanasia**, death is deliberately induced, such as by administering a fatal dose of pain medication. More than two-thirds of U.S. adults and 95% of physicians support passive euthanasia (Curlin et al., 2008; Pew Research Center, 2013). Most adults say there are at least some situations in which they, personally, would want to halt medical treatment and be allowed to die, but about a third of adults say they would tell their doctors to do everything possible to keep them alive—even in dire circumstances, such as having a disease with no hope of improvement and experiencing a great deal of pain (Pew Research Center, 2013).

Physician-Assisted Suicide

Physician-assisted suicide is a type of voluntary active euthanasia in which terminally ill patients make the conscious decision that they want their life to end before dying becomes a protracted process. Patients receive from physicians the medical tools needed to end their lives. The patient self-administers the medication. Physician-assisted suicide is legal in the Netherlands, Luxembourg, and Switzerland (Grosse & Grosse, 2015) and is often tacitly accepted in other countries.

As of 2021, the practice of physician-assisted suicide is legal in the U.S. states of California, Colorado, Hawaii, Maine, New Jersey, New Mexico, Oregon, Vermont, and Washington and the District of Columbia (Houghton, 2021). Oregon was the first U.S. state to legalize assisted suicide. Under Oregon's Death with Dignity Act, enacted in 1997, terminally ill Oregonians may end their lives through the voluntary self-administration of lethal medications, expressly prescribed by a physician for that purpose. There are strict requirements: Oregon residents must be diagnosed with a terminal illness that will kill them within 6 months. Their written request for a lethal dose of medication for ending their life must be confirmed by two witnesses unrelated to the patient or their care. After a second physician confirms the patient's diagnosis, they must wait an additional two weeks to make a second oral request before the prescription can be written.

Since the Oregon law was enacted in 1997, a total of 2,895 people have had prescriptions written and 1,905 patients have died from ingesting medication prescribed under the act (Oregon Public Health Division, 2021). Three-quarters of patients who died were over the age of 65 and the median age at time of death for all people was 72. More than three-quarters had been diagnosed with cancer. The top three concerns reported by patients as influences on their decisions were being less able to engage in activities to enjoy life, loss of autonomy, and loss of dignity (Oregon Public Health Division, 2021).

Hospice

The desire to die with dignity, minimal pain, and on one's own terms has advanced the hospice movement. **Hospice** is an approach to end-of-life care that emphasizes dying patients' needs for pain management; psychological, spiritual, and social support; and death with dignity (Connor, 2018). The philosophy of the hospice approach does not emphasize prolonging life, but rather prolonging quality of life. Although death occurs most often in hospitals, most dying people express the desire to die at home with family and friends (Weitzen et al., 2003). Dying persons have needs that set them apart from other hospital patients and hospital settings are often not equipped to meet those needs. Rather than medical treatment, dying patients require **palliative care**, focusing on controlling pain and related symptoms. Hospice services are enlisted after the physician and patient believe that the illness is terminal and no treatment or cure is possible.

Hospice services may be provided on an inpatient basis, at a formal hospice site that provides all care to patients, but they are frequently provided on an outpatient basis in a patient's home (Connor,

2018). Outpatient hospice service is becoming more common because it is cost effective and enables the patient to remain in the familiar surroundings of his or her home. Home hospice care is associated with increased satisfaction by patients and families (Candy et al., 2011). Whether hospice care is given on an inpatient or outpatient basis, the patient care team typically includes physicians, nurses, social workers, and counselors who act as spiritual and bereavement counselors to support the patient in facing his or her impending death and help the patient's loved ones cope with the loss.

Thinking in Context: Lifespan Development

1. In what ways might the developmental tasks of identity and autonomy, developing a sense of self, and the ability to make and carry out choices be embodied in end-of-life choices, such as advance directives, euthanasia, physician-assisted suicide, and hospice?
2. How might context, including culture and historical time, influence choices individuals make about end-of-life care?

Thinking in Context: Applied Developmental Science

Our knowledge of adults' experiences of death is limited.

1. What are some of the challenges in studying death, generally? Consider the research questions that can be asked, the ways of obtaining participants, and what kinds of information might be gathered.
2. In what ways is studying people's experiences with death similar to and different from other topics, like cognition or personality?

BEREAVEMENT AND GRIEF

LEARNING OBJECTIVE

16.6 Analyze typical grief reactions to the loss of loved ones and influences on the grief process.

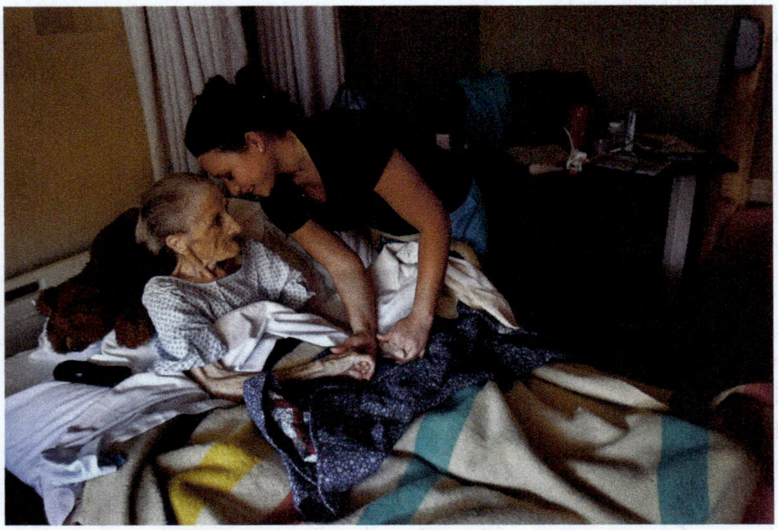

Hospice services permit dying patients to remain in their home, comfortable, and feel a sense of control in the death process. Counseling services help families assist the dying person, cope with their own needs, and strengthen connections with the dying person. Hospice services permit death with dignity that honors a loved one's wishes.

John Moore / Getty Images

One's impending death or the death of the loved one triggers an emotional response known as **grief**, which includes an array of emotions such as hurt, anger, guilt, and confusion. Most discussions of the losses that accompany death focus on the family and friends of the deceased, those left behind. Knowledge of one's impending death also brings about a grief response centered on the losses that they and their loved ones will experience.

Cultural Rituals Surrounding Death

The death of a loved one brings on **bereavement**, a state of loss. It triggers an emotional response known as grief, which includes an array of emotions such as hurt, anger, guilt, and confusion. **Mourning** refers to culturally patterned ritualistic ways of displaying and expressing bereavement, including special clothing, food, prayers, and gatherings. One of the first steps in mourning is to organize a funeral or other ritual to mark the occasion of the loved one's death; such customs are different in various cultures around the world. Mourning rituals such as the Jewish custom of sitting *shiva*—ceasing usual activity and instead mourning and receiving visitors at home for a week—provides a sense of structure to help the bereaved manage the first days and weeks of bereavement. The process of coping with the loss of a loved one is personal, complicated, and lengthy.

There is great variability in cultural views of the meaning of death and the rituals or other behaviors that express grief (Rosenblatt, 2008). Many cultures in the South Pacific do not differentiate death as a separate category of functioning. Melanesians use the term *mate* to refer to the very old, the very sick, and the dead; all other living people are referred to as *toa* (Counts & Counts, 1985). Other South Pacific cultures explain that the life force leaves the body during sleep and illness; therefore, people experience forms of death over the course of their lifetime before experiencing a final death (Counts & Counts, 1985). The Kwanga of Papua New Guinea believe that most deaths are the result of magic and witchcraft (Brison, 1995).

Perhaps the best-known death rituals were practiced by the ancient Egyptians. They believed that the body must be preserved through mummification to permanently house the spirit of the deceased in his or her new eternal life. The mummies were surrounded by valued objects and possessions and buried in elaborate tombs. Family members would regularly visit, bringing food and necessities to sustain them in the afterlife. Egyptian mummies are the most familiar, but mummies have also been found in other parts of the world such as the Andes mountains of Peru (Whitbourne, 2007).

The Bornu of Nigeria enlistfamily members to wash the deceased, wrap the body in a white cloth, and carry it to the burial ground (Cohen, 1967). In the French West Indies, the deceased's neighbors wash the body with rum, pour a liter or more of rum down the throat, and place the body on a bed (Horowitz, 1967).

In South Korea today, a small minority of people still choose to employ the services of a *mudang* (Korean "shaman") to conduct a lengthy ritual known as *Ogu Kut*, in which the *mudang* summons the deceased's spirit into the ritual space; expresses the deceased's feelings of unhappiness through song, dance, and the spoken word; and encourages the bereaved to express their own grievances within symbolic psychodrama. Once the emotional ties between the bereaved and the deceased have been loosened, prayers for protection are offered to various deities, and the *mudang* guides the spirit toward the Buddhist paradise. Finally, the deceased's earthly possessions are cremated and the bereaved are left better able to move on in their lives (Mills, 2012).

Death rituals vary among religions. Among Hindus, a good death is a holy death, one that is welcomed by the dying person, who rests on the ground and is surrounded by family and friends chanting prayers (Dennis, 2008). Buddhists believe that the dying person's task is to gain insight. Death is not an end, as the individual will be reincarnated in the hopes of reaching nirvana, an ultimate, perfect state of enlightenment. Among Jews, the dying person remains part of the community and is never left alone before or immediately after death. Christians generally believe that death is the entry to an eternity in heaven or hell and therefore is an event to be welcomed or feared. In Islam, death is united with life because it is believed that the achievements and concerns of this life are fleeting, and everyone should be mindful and ready for death. Muslim death rituals, such as saying prayers and washing the body, aid in the dying person's transition to the afterlife.

Many cultures express beliefs in **noncorporeal continuation**, the view that some form of life and personal continuity exists after the physical body has died (Kenyon, 2001). A spirit may endure, life may persist in heaven, or a soul may be reincarnated into another body. These beliefs are consistent with the doctrine of many religions and can coexist with mature understandings of death as the irreversible and inevitable ceasing of biological functioning (Corr & Corr, 2013).

The Cremation Ceremony held in Bali, Indonesia, is a ritual performed to send the deceased to the next life. The body is placed in a wood coffin inside a temple-like structure made of paper and wood. The structure and body are burned to release the deceased's spirit and enable reincarnation.

iStock/ laughingmango

Grief Process

Grief is sometimes described as progressing through phases or stages similar to the stages of emotional adjustment to death posited by Kübler-Ross (1969). People may traverse through several phases of mourning, from shock, to intense grieving, to establishing a sense of balance, accommodating the loss into one's sense of being (Buglass, 2010; Wright & Hogan, 2008). Phases of mourning are useful in describing common reactions to loss, but they represent a generalization and perhaps oversimplification of the process (Stroebe, Schut, et al., 2017). The expectation that bereaved persons will progress through predictable stages can be harmful to those who do not. The progression through grief is not linear. Steps do not always occur in sequence and there is no universal timeframe for processing grief (Maciejewski et al., 2007).

There are no rules to grieving. People vary in the intensity of their reactions to loss and in the timing of their reactions. People grieve differently, and the same person may react differently to different losses. Some might feel intense but short-lived grief. Other people may find that grief lingers for many months. Sometimes grief may seem to resolve only to resurface periodically and unexpectedly. Common physical responses to grief include tightness in the chest, feeling out of breath, stomach pains, and weakness. Grief may affect the immune response and manifest as health problems (O'Connor, 2019). Cognitive responses include reductions in attention, memory, processing speed, and verbal fluency (Rosnick et al., 2010). The stress that accompanies grief may influence function, including neurogenesis, the maintenance of dendrites, neurotransmission, and plasticity (Egeland et al., 2015; Schoenfeld & Gould, 2013). Behavioral responses including looking for the person in crowds and familiar places, absentmindedness, sleep problems, avoiding reminders of the deceased, and loss of interest are common (Lancel et al., 2020).

Grief is accompanied by many stressors that pose challenges to adaptation. According to the **dual-process model of grief**, bereavement is accompanied by two types of stressors (Stroebe, Schut, et al., 2017; Stroebe & Schut, 2016). The first is loss-oriented and comprises the emotional aspects of grief that accompany the loss of an attachment figure, such as managing emotions and breaking ties to the deceased. Restoration-oriented stressors represent secondary losses; these are the life changes that accompany the death, such as moving to a different residence, social isolation, establishing new roles, and managing practical details, such as paperwork. At any given time, the grieving person may focus on the loss-oriented stressors or the life changes that comprise the restoration-oriented stressors. Healthy adjustment is promoted by alternating focus between the two types. When the person is able, he or she confronts the losses, yet at other times the person may set that task aside to instead consider restoration (Stroebe, Boerner, et al., 2017; Stroebe & Schut, 2010). In this way, the grieving person adaptively copes as he or she is able, gradually moving forward. Some bereaved individuals experience *overload*, the feeling that he or she has too much to deal with—whether too many losses, too many stimuli, too many stressors—and this can interfere with the grieving process (Stroebe & Schut, 2016).

Ultimately the grieving person must confront the loss and come to terms with its effects on their physical world, interpersonal interactions, and sense of self (Buglass, 2010; Trevino et al., 2018). It was once believed that effective grieving required loosening emotional ties to the deceased, permitting the grieving person to "work through" the death (Buglass, 2010; Wright & Hogan, 2008). During a period of mourning, the survivor would sever attachments to the deceased and become ready for new relationships and attachments. Instead, in recent decades, theorists have come to view the bereaved person's continued attachment to the deceased as normative and adaptive in providing a sense of continuity despite loss (Sirrine et al., 2018; Stroebe et al., 2010). Attachment is illustrated in several behaviors common among the bereaved, such as feeling that the deceased is watching over them, keeping the deceased's possessions, and talking about the deceased to keep their memory alive. Successful adaptation entails moving toward abstract manifestations of attachment, such as thoughts and memories, and away from concrete manifestations such as possessions (Field et al., 2003). Most important, and most difficult, the grieving person must establish new patterns of behavior and redefine relationships with family and friends in light of the loss (Leming & Dickinson, 2020). The grieving person must construct a new sense of self that takes into account the loss of the deceased and how that loss has changed everyday life. Yet an enduring connection to the deceased remains. Grieving appears to involve learning to live with loss, rather than getting over loss.

Contextual Influences on the Grief Process

No two deaths are experienced in the same way. Deaths are interpreted and grieved differently based on a variety of factors, such as the age of the deceased, the nature of the death, and age of the bereaved. The death of a child or young adult is grieved more intensely and is viewed as more catastrophic than that of an older adult (Jecker, 2011). Younger and older adults judge a 19-year-old victim of a fatal car accident as a more tragic and unjust death than that of a 79-year-old victim (Chasteen & Madey, 2003). The young are grieved more intensely as they are viewed as robbed of the chance to experience significant life events such as falling in love or becoming a parent. They are not able to set and fulfill dreams. Generally, off-time deaths, especially those that occur much before our expectations, are particularly difficult (Moos, 1994).

Students embrace at a makeshift memorial for two peers killed in a car accident. Grieving the loss of a young person involves grieving for their lost future.

Jessica Rinaldi/The Boston Globe via Getty Images

The term **widowhood** refers to the status of a person who has lost a spouse through death and has not remarried. About one-third of U.S. older adults over the age of 65 are widowed. Women who have lost a spouse live longer than men and are less likely to remarry. Among adults 75 years or older, more than one-half of women and one in five men are widowed (Gurrentz & Mayol-Garcia, 2021). Compared with their functioning prior to the loss of a spouse, bereaved adults show increased levels of depression, anxiety, stress, as well as poorer performance on cognitive tests measuring attention, processing speed, and memory (King et al., 2019; Rosnick et al., 2010; Schmitz, 2021; Shin et al., 2018). The prevalence of depression may be especially elevated in the first year after the loss of a spouse, with about 20% of adults meeting the diagnostic criteria for major depression (Blanner Kristiansen et al., 2019).

Perhaps the most striking effect of widowhood is on adults' physical health. The increased likelihood for a recently widowed person to die, often called the **widowhood effect**, is one of the best-documented examples of the relationship between social relations and health (Elwert & Christakis, 2008; (Ennis & Majid, 2020). Widowed adults show maladaptive immune and hormone responses and poor health behaviors (Fagundes & Wu, 2020). The widowhood effect has been found among men and women of all ages throughout the world. Widowhood increases survivors' risk of dying from almost all causes but is especially linked with cardiovascular problems (Ennis & Majid, 2021; Fagundes et al., 2018; Subramanian et al., 2008). Interestingly, the widowhood effect persists into old age, stopping at about age 90 in women and 95 in men (Blanner et al., 2020).

The nature of the death influences how it is experienced and the grief process. When death is the result of a prolonged illness, it is no surprise, yet it is still a source of grief. Some theorists have posited the existence of anticipatory grief, feelings of loss that begin before a death occurs but are not fully realized (Coelho et al., 2018; Siegel & Weinstein, 2008). Although many people believe that having the time and opportunity to prepare for loss will make it less distressing, research suggests that this is not true (Coelho et al., 2018; Siegel & Weinstein, 2008). All deaths are stressful, just in different ways. Sudden, unexpected deaths are particularly challenging. Mourners are unprepared, with no support group in place. Many feel intense guilt and the need to assign blame and responsibility for accidental deaths. There often is no chance to say goodbye or mend relationships. Anger is a common reaction, especially if the deceased contributed to his or her demise through poor decisions. Sudden and traumatic deaths, such as from natural or man-made disasters, can leave losses that are difficult to make sense of. Feeling that a death is traumatic is associated with increased grief, depression, loneliness, and risk for mental health problems (Keyes et al., 2014; Kristensen et al., 2015; Tang & Chow, 2017).

The incidence of complicated grief, including long-lasting symptoms such as persistent intense yearning and disruptive preoccupation with thoughts of the deceased (De Stefano et al., 2020;

Nakajima, 2018), is thought to have increased during the COVID-19 pandemic (Mortazavi et al., 2020; Wallace et al., 2020). Fear, lockdown orders, and social distancing disrupted social connections at the same time as the deadly virus caused widespread illness and death. Sudden loss without the opportunity to say goodbye coupled with a lack of social support can disrupt the grief process (Nakajima, 2018;Otani et al., 2017). The unexpected nature of pandemic-related death, coupled with the lack of contact with the dying person and other mourners, can intensify feelings of guilt, helplessness, and anger and is associated with heightened grief reactions (Eisma et al., 2021;Mortazavi et al., 2020). Social disconnection is associated with heightened psychological distress (Smith et al., 2020). Adjusting to the death is difficult in the absence of rituals, connections, and a return to daily routines.

Death and loss are not easy topics to consider. We have seen that, regardless of age, both dying and grieving people have some common needs. All need to move past denial and accept the death, whether upcoming or past. Both the dying and grieving require help managing their emotional reactions to loss, including common physical reactions, such as stomach aches, headaches, and lethargy. People of all ages have a need to express their reactions to the loss and may need help identifying and articulating their reactions that may feel very strange and unfamiliar to them. Finally, the dying and the bereaved need to make some sense of the loss. The dying must connect to their loved ones and accept the loss. The bereaved, in turn, must find a way to maintain the connection to the deceased while moving on in their life, recognizing that in some ways they will never be the same.

Thinking in Context: Lifespan Development

1. How might the grief process be influenced by a person's prior socioemotional development, such as attachment experiences, emotional regulation, and psychosocial development? What role does development play in influencing how a person experiences and understands grief?
2. Grief itself is a developmental process. Agree or disagree? Why?
3. From your perspective, is the process of adjusting to the death of a loved one a continuous or discontinuous one? (Review these terms in Chapter 1.) Why?

Thinking in Context: Biological Influences

Considering what you know about stress and health over the lifespan, why is grief associated with health problems? How might grieving individuals minimize the negative health effects of grief? What do you suggest?

CHAPTER SUMMARY

16.1 Summarize patterns of psychosocial development in late adulthood.

Most older adults feel that they are younger than their years and this tendency is associated with health and well-being. Self-conceptions are more multifaceted, complex, and stable in old age than at other periods of life. Most older adults maintain a positive view of themselves by accepting their weaknesses and compensating by focusing on their strengths. Life review help adults find continuity in their lives, come to terms with choices, and develop ego integrity. Big 5 personality traits largely remain stable into late adulthood, but most adults experience subtle shifts with age. Sexual interest and activity persists into late life. Most adults become more religious as they age, which often provides support and a buffer against stress.

16.2 Discuss features of older adults' relationships with others, including friends, spouses, children, and grandchildren.

In older adulthood, friendships become more important and more fulfilling. Marital satisfaction increases in older adulthood. Older adult cohabiters do not differ from marrieds in their reports of emotional satisfaction, pleasure, openness, time spent together, criticism, and demands. The nature of the relationship and the exchange of help between elderly parents and their adult children increasingly emphasizes children-to-parent assistance, most often taking the form of emotional support. Regardless of distance and contact, affection between grandchildren and grandparents tends to remain strong.

16.3 Describe the social contexts in which older adults live and their influence on development.

Social networks tend to become smaller in older adulthood, focused more on family and less on peripheral relationships. Adults strive to remain active and sustain continuity in their relationships and sense of self. Socioemotional selectivity theory explains that a shrinking time horizon causes adults to change their priorities to emphasize the emotional aspects of relationships. Most older adults prefer to age in place. There are a variety of different types of residential communities for older adults, but only a small number live in nursing homes, which offer the greatest amount of care but also the greatest restriction of adults' autonomy. Factors that influence the quality of living environments for older adults include freedom of choice, involvement in decision making, right to privacy, stimulating environment, and sense of connectedness.

16.4 Examine influences on the timing of retirement and adaptation to retirement.

The period of retirement has lengthened in all Western nations. The decision of when to retire is influenced by job conditions, health, finances, and personal preferences. Health status and financial resources are often determining factors on whether and when an older adult retires. Workers in high stress, demanding jobs, or those that provide little satisfaction, tend to show positive adaptation to retirement. Research suggests the worker's sense of control influences the transition to retirement. Continuity in other social roles and the ability to adapt to role changes leads to few changes in life satisfaction after retirement. Engagement in leisure activities and volunteer work increases retirement satisfaction.

16.5 Consider definitions of death and end-of-life considerations.

Clinical death occurs when the heart stops beating. Advances in medicine have led to a definition of death as entailing whole brain death. Cortical death, but survival of the brain stem, is known as a persistent vegetative state. People tend to show a range of emotional reactions to the knowledge that they are dying, including denial, anger, bargaining, depression, and acceptance. Although described as stages, not everyone experiences all of them or proceeds through them at the same pace or in the same order. Advance directives, including a living will and durable power of attorney, permit individuals to make their wishes regarding end-of-life care known. Euthanasia refers to the practice of assisting terminally ill people in dying naturally. Physician-assisted suicide occurs when the terminally ill patient makes the conscious decision that they want their life to end and seeks assistance from a physician. Hospice emphasizes prolonging quality of life by meeting dying patients' needs for pain management; psychological, spiritual, and social support; and to die with dignity.

16.6 Analyze typical grief reactions to the loss of loved ones and influences on the grief process.

Grief is associated with physical and cognitive changes and health problems. Some theorists suggest phases or stages in grieving that are similar to the stages of emotional adjustment to death. Other theorists view mourning as a set of tasks to accomplish. According to the dual-process model, bereavement is accompanied by loss-oriented stressors and restoration-oriented stressors. Healthy adjustment is promoted by alternating focus between the two types of stressors. Deaths are interpreted and grieved differently based on a variety of factors, such as the age of the deceased, the nature of the death, and age of the bereaved. Bereavement is associated with increased levels of depression, anxiety, stress, and poor performance on cognitive tests and poor health.

KEYWORDS

active euthanasia (p. 505)
activity theory (p. 492)
bereavement (p. 506)
clinical death (p. 501)
continuity theory (p. 493)
disengagement theory (p. 492)
dual-process model of grief (p. 508)
durable power of attorney (p. 504)
dying trajectory (p. 502)
death with dignity (p. 504)
ego integrity vs. despair (p. 485)
euthanasia (p. 505)
grief (p. 506)
hospice (p. 505)
life review (p. 485)
living will (p. 504)
mourning (p. 506)
noncorporeal continuation (p. 507)
palliative care (p. 505)
passive euthanasia (p. 505)
persistent vegetative state (PVS) (p. 502)
physician-assisted suicide (p. 505)
socioemotional selectivity theory (p. 493)
whole brain death (p. 502)
widowhood (p. 509)
widowhood effect (p. 509)

PART 8 LIFESPAN DEVELOPMENT AT WORK: LATE ADULTHOOD

Over the course of late adulthood, older adults develop specialized physical and mental health care needs. Many of the professions we have described thus far, such as social workers, counselors, psychologists, and physical and occupational therapists, work with older adults. Here we examine several professions that specialize in aging.

Audiologist

Audiologists are health professionals who diagnose and treat hearing and balance disorders for people of all ages. They screen and test older adults' hearing and evaluate and treat dizziness, tinnitus (ringing in the ears), and balance problems. They help older adults select hearing aids and customize them to the adults' needs. Hearing aids are not one size fits all, so customization and helping the adult adjust to a hearing aid can take time and multiple visits. Audiologists also counsel and educate patients and their families on how to manage hearing impairments and balance problems. Audiologists work in hospitals, schools, physicians' offices, rehabilitation centers, residential health care facilities, and private practice.

Becoming an audiologist requires a doctorate in audiology, a 4-year program. About 375 hours of supervised experience and a passing grade on a state licensure exam is needed to practice. The median annual wage for audiologists was $81,030 in May 2020 (U.S. Bureau of Labor Statistics, 2021).

Geriatric Nurse

A geriatric nurse specializes in working with older adults. In addition to the nurse duties that we have discussed in previous chapters, geriatric nurses assist patients who are experiencing terminal illnesses, other illnesses, and neurocognitive disorders (such as Alzheimer's). They help monitor and assess the cognitive skills and mental status of their patients. Geriatric nurses assist patients who are bedridden and may help feed, clothe, administer drugs, and offer moral support and therapy to older adult patients. Understanding patients' medications and how medications interact is important because many older adults take several medications that may conflict.

In addition to the qualifications required to become a nurse, becoming a geriatric nurse entails specializing in working with older adults. Although nurses often gain experience with geriatric patients, Gerontological Nursing Certification documents experience and certifies competence. It requires 30 hours of continuing education in geriatrics, 2000 hours of experience, and completing an exam. The median salary for a registered nurse was $75,330 in May 2020, but geriatric nursing is a specialized field and likely earns a higher salary (U.S. Bureau of Labor Statistics, 2021).

Geriatrician

A geriatrician is a physician who specializes in the care of older adults. They are trained to manage the unique health care needs of older people and diagnose and treat illnesses, injuries, and conditions that commonly occur with age. Like other physicians, geriatricians provide medical and lifestyle advice. Geriatricians must be keenly aware of the risks of various medications and their interactions because older adults are often prescribed multiple medications and medications may have different effects with age. Geriatricians collaborate with many other health care professionals.

Becoming a geriatrician requires completing medical school and residency, then specializing in a geriatrics fellowship program to get experience. In 2020, physicians earned a median wage of about $208,000 (U.S. Bureau of Labor Statistics, 2021).

Geropsychologist

A geropsychologist is a psychologist who specializes in older adults. Geropsychologists must understand normative adult development and aging, behavioral and mental health issues that may arise in late life, and how to assess older adults. They treat problems including mental disorders such depression and anxiety (which sometimes manifest differently in older adults), dementia, changes in decision making and living abilities, coping with chronic illness, grief and loss, family caregiving, and end-of-life care.

Becoming a geropsychologist requires a doctoral degree in clinical or counseling psychology, supervised experience, and state licensure. The American Board of Professional Psychology certifies geropsychologists with a year of full-time supervised training in geropsychology or 2000 hours equivalent experience and the completion of a certification exam. In 2020, psychologists earned a median salary of about $80,000 (U.S. Bureau of Labor Statistics, 2021).

User Design and Usability

Products that are designed for older adults often have special features, such as large buttons, easy to read font, and a simple layout. A variety of professionals work to create products that older adults perceive as accessible, functional, and attractive. Positions in user design carry many titles, such as usability specialist, user experience strategist, and user interface designer. What all of these "user-oriented" titles have in common is an emphasis on understanding how people use and interact with a product and improving their experience.

User experience designers work with all kinds of products, such as toys, computer hardware and software, electronic equipment, and cars. Some work on teams to create product prototypes and test and modify them based on input from potential users. Knowledge about human development can help in creating websites, apps, and video games with users' development in mind. For example, an understanding of how attention, perception, and cognition changes with age can help user experience designers create software that is easily understood, meaningful, and engaging for older adults. This might include creating software layouts and backgrounds that are sensitive to older adults' needs by including larger text and icons, contrasting colors that are easily distinguished, and slower movements. They might record and analyze users' behaviors when they try to accomplish a task using a software product. They interview users about their experience with the product: Was it easy to use? What confused them about the interface? The resulting knowledge is used to improve the design.

Preparation for user experience careers emphasizes experience over a specific major or degree. Web design, graphic design, computer programming, and an understanding of human behavior are helpful. Some colleges offer bachelor's and master's degrees in user design, as well as one- or two-semester programs and certifications in user design. Generally, median salaries in these fields range from $65,000–$75,000 depending on data source (Payscale, 2021).

Grief Counselor

Also known as bereavement counselors, grief counselors specialize in working with the bereaved. They help individuals who are grieving the death of a loved one as well as those who are grieving personal losses or transitions, such as a pet, miscarriage, or a career. Grief counselors provide support and therapy to help individuals process their grief, accept their loss, and find a way to continue their lives.

Like other counselors, grief counselors consult and interview clients, record observations, determine clients' intervention needs and develop treatment plans, and monitor clients' progress and adjust treatment plans if necessary. They facilitate individual and group therapy sessions and collaborate with other health professionals as needed. They work with individuals, couples, families, and groups in hospitals, mental health clinics, community centers, funeral homes, and private practice.

Becoming a grief counselor requires a master's degree in counseling. Grief counselors must seek state licensure or certification, usually as a licensed professional counselor (LPC), to practice. Licensure requirements include post-graduate supervised experience (3,000 hours in many states) and a passing grade on the National Counselor Examination. Some grief counselors are licensed clinical social workers (LCSW), who have obtained master's degrees, supervised experience (often 3,000 hours), and licensure. Grief counseling is a specialty field. Additional certification is desirable, which typically includes additional coursework and perhaps supervised experience and/or exams in grief counseling.

Counselors earned a median salary of about $48,000 in 2020 (U.S. Bureau of Labor Statistics, 2021).

Hospice Services

Hospice services are designed to help terminally ill people retain their quality of life by providing physical, emotional, and spiritual support to dying people and their families. Similar to a medical team in a hospital, hospice services are provided by a team of health care professionals. Hospice services are provided in residential settings and at home.

Hospice services include providing palliative care designed to ease pain and prolong quality of life as well as helping dying people and their loved ones have meaningful interactions, prepare for the time before and after death, and manage their grief. These difficult tasks are eased with the assistance of many of the health and mental health professionals we have discussed, including nurses, nurse practitioners, physicians, social workers, counselors, occupational therapists, and physical therapists.

Nursing assistants, hospice aides, and home health aides are tasked with providing basic care and helping patients with activities of daily living. They help patients with bathing, grooming, and assist with movement. They monitor patients' condition and report information to nurses and other health care professionals. Typically, becoming a home health aide does not require a college degree, but some states or employers may require training or completing an exam. Nursing assistants must be certified by the state (certified nursing assistant), which requires completing about 8 weeks of coursework at a community college, vocational school, or hospital and completing an exam. Nursing assistants earned a median salary of about $31,000 and home health aides earned $27,000 in 2021 (U.S. Bureau of Labor Statistics, 2021).

GLOSSARY

academically centered preschool programs. An approach to early childhood education that emphasizes providing children with structured learning environments in which teachers deliver direct instruction on letters, numbers, shapes, and academic skills.

accommodation. In Piaget's theory, the process by which schemas are modified or new schemas created in light of experience.

achievement motivation. The willingness to persist at challenging tasks and meet high standards of accomplishment.

active euthanasia. The practice of assisting terminally ill people in dying more quickly by deliberate means, such as by administering a fatal dose of pain medication.

activity theory. The view that older adults want to remain active and that declines in social interaction are not a result of elders' desires but are a function of social barriers to engagement.

adolescent egocentrism. A characteristic of adolescents' thinking in which they have difficulty separating others' perspectives from their own; composed of the imaginary audience and personal fable.

adolescent growth spurt. The first outward sign of puberty, it refers to a rapid gain in height and weight that generally begins in girls at about age 10 and in boys about age 12.

advance directive. A document or order that allows patients to make decisions about their health care, death, and what happens to their bodies and possessions after death.

affordances. Refers to the actional properties of objects—their nature, opportunities, and limits.

aggressive behavior. Behavior that harms or violates the rights of others; can be physical or relational.

aggressive-rejected children. Children who are confrontational and hostile toward peers and are shunned by peers.

alcohol dependence. A maladaptive pattern of alcohol use that leads to clinically significant impairment or distress, as indicated by tolerance, withdrawal, and inability to reduce drinking; also known as alcohol use disorder.

allele. A variation of a gene that influences an individual's characteristics.

Alzheimer's disease. A neurodegenerative disorder characterized by dementia and the deterioration of memory and personality; it is marked by the presence of amyloid plaques and neurofibrillary tangles in the cerebral cortex.

amnion. A membrane that holds amniotic fluid.

amniocentesis. A prenatal diagnostic procedure in which a small sample of the amniotic fluid is extracted from the mother's uterus and subject to genetic analysis.

amygdala. A brain structure that is part of the limbic system and plays a role in emotion, especially fear and anger.

amyloid plaque. Found in the brains of patients with Alzheimer's disease, deposits of beta-amyloid accumulate along with clumps of dead neurons and glial cells.

androgyny. The gender identity of those who score high on both instrumental and expressive traits.

anencephaly. A neural tube defect that results in the failure of all or part of the brain to develop, resulting in death prior to or shortly after birth.

animism. The belief that inanimate objects are alive and have feelings and intentions; a characteristic of preoperational reasoning.

anorexia nervosa. An eating disorder characterized by compulsive starvation and extreme weight loss and accompanied by a distorted body image.

Apgar scale. A quick overall assessment of a baby's immediate health at birth, including appearance, pulse, grimace, activity, and respiration.

appearance-reality distinction. The ability to distinguish between what something appears to be and what it really is.

applied developmental science. A field that studies lifespan interactions between individuals and the contexts in which they live and applies research findings to real-world settings; findings can be used to influence social policy and create interventions.

assimilation. In Piaget's theory, the process by which new experiences are interpreted and integrated into preexisting schemas.

attachment. A lasting emotional tie between two individuals.

attention. The ability to direct one's awareness.

attention-deficit/hyperactivity disorder. A condition characterized by persistent difficulties with attention and/or impulsivity that interfere with performance and behavior in school and daily life.

authoritarian parenting style. An approach to childrearing that emphasizes high behavioral control and low levels of warmth and autonomy granting.

authoritative parenting style. An approach to childrearing in which parents are warm and sensitive to children's needs, grant appropriate autonomy, and exert firm control.

autistic spectrum disorder. Refers to a family of disorders that range in severity and are marked by social and communication deficits, often accompanied by restrictive and repetitive behaviors.

autobiographical memory. The recollection of a personally meaningful event that took place at a specific time and place in one's past.

autonomous morality. Piaget's second stage of morality in which children have a more flexible view of rules as they begin to value fairness and equality and account for factors like act, intent, and situation.

autonomy. The ability to make and carry out decisions independently.

autonomy versus shame and doubt. In Erikson's theory, the psychosocial crisis of toddlerhood in which individuals must establish the sense that they can make choices and guide their actions and bodies.

babbling. An infant's repetition of syllables such as "ba-ba-ba-ba" and "ma-ma-ma," which begins at about 6 months of age.

basic emotions. Emotions that are universal in humans, appear early in life, and are thought to have a long evolutional history; includes happiness, interest, surprise, fear, anger, sadness, and disgust.

behavioral genetics. The field of study that examines how genes and environment combine to influence the diversity of human traits, abilities, and behaviors.

behaviorism. A theoretical approach that studies how observable behavior is controlled by the physical and social environment through conditioning.

bereavement. The process of coping with the sense of loss that follows a loved one's death.

Big 5 personality traits. Five clusters of personality traits that reflect an inherited predisposition that is stable throughout life; the five traits are openness, conscientiousness, extroversion, agreeableness, and neuroticism.

binge drinking. Heavy episodic drinking; consuming five or more alcoholic beverages in one sitting for men and four drinks in one sitting for women.

binge eating disorder. An eating disorder characterized by binges, consuming an abnormally large amount of food (thousands of calories) in a single sitting coupled with a feeling of being out of control.

biological gender transition. A medical process by which transgender individuals can undergo body changes to match their gender identity. Typically involves body changes that are induced by hormone therapy and permanent changes to the external genitals, accomplished by means of gender reassignment surgery.

bioecological systems theory. A theory introduced by Bronfenbrenner that emphasizes the role of context in development, positing that contexts are organized into a series of systems in which individuals are embedded and that interact with one another and the person to influence development.

blastocyst. A thin-walled, fluid-filled sphere containing an inner mass of cells from which the embryo will develop; it is implanted into the uterine wall during the germinal period.

body mass index (BMI). A measure of body fat based on weight in kilograms divided by height in meters squared (kg/m^2).

Broca's area. The region in the brain that controls the ability to use language for expression; damage to the area inhibits fluent speech.

bulimia nervosa. An eating disorder characterized by recurrent episodes of binge eating and subsequent purging, usually by induced vomiting and the use of laxatives.

bullying. Refers to an ongoing interaction in which a child repeatedly attempts to inflict physical, verbal, or social harm on another child; also known as *peer victimization*.

bully-victim. An individual who attacks or inflicts harm on others and who is also attacked or harmed by others; the child is both bully and victim.

cardiovascular disease. A disease marked by high blood pressure, high blood cholesterol, plaque buildup in the arteries, irregular heartbeat, and risk factor for heart attack and stroke.

care orientation. Gilligan's feminine mode of moral reasoning, characterized by a desire to maintain relationships and a responsibility to avoid hurting others.

carrier. An individual who is heterozygous for a particular trait, in which a recessive gene is not expressed in the phenotype yet may be passed on to the carrier's offspring.

case study. An in-depth examination of a single individual (or small group of individuals).

cataract. A clouding of the lens of the eye resulting in blurred, foggy vision that can lead to blindness.

categorical self. A classification of the self children use to guide their behavior; based on broad ways in which people differ, such as sex, age, and physical characteristics.

categorization. An adaptive mental process in which objects are grouped into conceptual categories, allowing for organized storage of information in memory, efficient retrieval of that information, and the capacity to respond with familiarity to new stimuli from a common class.

central executive. In information processing, the part of our mental system that directs the flow of information and regulates cognitive activities such as attention, action, and problem solving.

centration. The tendency to focus on one part of a stimulus, situation, or idea and exclude all others; a characteristic of preoperational reasoning.

cephalocaudal development. The principle that growth proceeds from the head downward; the head and upper regions of the body develop before the lower regions.

cerebellum. Part of the brain at the back of the skull that is responsible for body movements, balance, and coordination.

Cesarean section. Also known as a C-section; a surgical procedure that removes the fetus from the uterus through the abdomen.

child assent. A child's agreement to participate in a study.

child-centered preschool programs. A constructivist approach to early childhood education that encourages children to actively build their own understanding of the world through observing, interacting with objects and people, and engaging in a variety of activities that allow them to manipulate materials and interact with teachers and peers.

child maltreatment. Also known as child abuse; any intentional harm to a minor, including actions that harm the child physically, emotionally, sexually, or through neglect.

cisgender. An individual who identifies with his or her chromosomal sex.

chorionic villus sampling (CVS). Prenatal diagnostic test that is conducted on cells sampled from the chorion to detect chromosomal abnormalities.

chromosome. One of 46 rod-like molecules that contain 23 pairs of DNA found in every body cell; they collectively contain all of the genes.

chronosystem. In bioecological systems theory, refers to how people and contexts change over time.

classical conditioning. A form of learning in which an environmental stimulus becomes associated with stimuli that elicit reflex responses.

classification. The ability to organize things into groups based on similar characteristics.

class inclusion. Involves understanding hierarchical relationships among items.

clinical death. Defines death as the moment the heart stops beating.

clique. A tightly knit peer group of about three to eight close friends who share similarities such as demographics and attitudes.

cognitive development. Maturation of mental processes and tools individuals use to obtain knowledge, think, and solve problems.

cognitive disequilibrium. A mismatch between an individual's schemas and the world.

cognitive reserve. The ability to make flexible and efficient use of available brain resources that permits cognitive efficiency, flexibility, and adaptability; it is cultivated throughout life from experience and environmental factors.

cognitive-affective complexity. A form of mature thinking that involves emotional awareness, the ability to integrate and regulate intense emotions, and the recognition and appreciation of individual experience.

cognitive-developmental theory. A perspective posited by Piaget that views individuals as active explorers of their world, learning by interacting with the world around them, and describes cognitive development as progressing through stages.

cognitive equilibrium. A balance between the processes of assimilation and accommodation such that an individual's schemas match the world.

cognitive schema. A mental representation, such as concepts, ideas, and ways of interacting with the world.

cohabitation. An arrangement in which a committed, unmarried couple lives together in the same home.

cohort. A generation of people born at the same time, influenced by the same historical and cultural conditions.

computerized tomography (CT scan). A scan that compiles multiple x-ray images to create a 3-D picture of a person's brain, providing images of brain structures, bone, brain vasculature, and tissue.

concrete operational stage of reasoning. Piaget's third stage of reasoning, from about 6 to 11, in which thought becomes logical and is applied to direct tangible experiences but not to abstract problems.

confidentiality. Researchers generally promise participants that their responses will not be disclosed to others.

conservation. The principle that a physical quantity, such as number, mass, or volume, remains the same even when its appearance changes.

context. Unique conditions in which a person develops, including aspects of the physical and social environment such as family, neighborhood, culture, and historical time period.

continuity theory. The perspective that older adults strive to maintain continuity and consistency in self across the past and into the future; successful elders retain a sense that they are the same person they have always been despite physical, cognitive, emotional, and social changes.

continuous change. An aspect of development that unfolds slowly and gradually over time.

conventional moral reasoning. The second level of Kohlberg's theory in which moral decisions are based on conforming to social rules.

cooing. An infant's repetition of sounds, such as "ahhhh," "ohhh," and "eeee," that begins between 2 and 3 months of age.

core knowledge theory. A framework explaining that infants are born with several innate knowledge systems or core domains of thought that enable early rapid learning and adaptation.

correlational research. A research design that measures relationships among participants' measured characteristics, behaviors, and development.

cortex. The outermost part of the brain containing the greatest numbers of neurons and accounting for thought and consciousness.

cross-sectional research study. A developmental research design that compares people of different ages at a single point in time to infer age differences.

crowd. A large group of adolescents grouped based on perceived shared characteristics, interests, and reputation.

crystallized intelligence. Intellectual ability that reflects accumulated knowledge acquired through experience and learning.

cyberbullying. Bullying, or repeated acts intended to hurt a victim, carried out via electronic means such as text messaging, posting in chat rooms and discussion boards, and creating websites and blogs.

culture. A set of customs, knowledge, attitudes, and values shared by a group of people and learned through interactions with group members.

dating violence. The actual or threatened physical or sexual violence or psychological abuse directed toward a current or former boyfriend, girlfriend, or dating partner.

deferred imitation. Imitating the behavior of an absent model; illustrates infants' capacity for mental representation.

delayed phase preference. Change in pubertal hormone levels that causes adolescents' sleep patterns to shift such that they tend to remain awake late at night and groggy early in the morning.

dementia. A progressive deterioration in mental abilities due to changes in the brain that influence higher cortical functions such as thinking, memory, comprehension, and emotional control and are reflected in impaired thought and behavior, interfering with the older adult's ability to engage in everyday activities.

deoxyribonucleic acid (DNA). The chemical structure, shaped like a twisted ladder, that contains all of the genes.

dependent variable. The behavior under study in an experiment; it is expected to be affected by changes in the independent variable.

dermis. Middle layer of skin consisting of connective tissue that gives skin its flexibility.

depth perception. The ability to perceive the distance of objects from each other and from ourselves.

development. The processes by which individuals grow and change, as well as the ways in which they stay the same over time.

developmental dyscalculia. A specific learning disorder that affects mathematics ability.

developmental dysgraphia. A specific learning disorder that affects writing abilities.

developmental dyslexia. The most commonly diagnosed learning disability, characterized by unusual difficulty in matching letters to sounds and difficulty with word recognition and spelling despite adequate instruction and intelligence and intact sensory abilities.

developmentally appropriate practice. An educational approach that tailors instruction to the age of the child, recognizing individual differences and the need for hands-on active teaching methods.

developmental science. The study of human development at all points in life, from conception to death.

diabetes. A disease marked by high levels of blood glucose that occurs when the body is unable to regulate the amount of glucose in the bloodstream because there is not enough insulin produced (Type 1 diabetes) or the body shows insulin resistance and becomes less sensitive to it, failing to respond to it (Type 2 diabetes); symptoms include fatigue, great thirst, blurred vision, frequent infections, and slow healing.

difficult temperament. A temperament characterized by irregularity in biological rhythms, slow adaptation to change, and a tendency for intense negative reactions.

diffusion tensor imaging (DTI). Uses an MRI machine to track how water molecules move in and around the fibers connecting different parts of the brain, measure the brain's white matter, and determine changes that occur with development.

discipline. The methods a parent uses to teach and socialize children.

discontinuous change. An aspect of development that is characterized by abrupt change.

dishabituation. The recovery of attention after habituation; signifies that a person recognizes a new stimulus.

disengagement theory. The view that declines in social interaction in older age are due to mutual withdrawal between older adults and society as they anticipate death.

divided attention. Attending to two stimuli at once.

domains of development. A type or area of development, such as physical, cognitive, or socioemotional.

dominant-recessive inheritance. A form of genetic inheritance in which the phenotype reflects only the dominant allele of a heterozygous pair.

doula. A caregiver who provides support to an expectant mother and her partner throughout the birth process.

Down syndrome. A condition in which a third, extra chromosome appears at the 21st site; also known as *trisomy 21.* Down syndrome is associated with distinctive physical characteristics accompanied by developmental disability.

dualistic thinking. Polar reasoning in which knowledge and accounts of phenomena are viewed as absolute facts, either right or wrong with no in-between.

dual-language learning. Also known as two-way immersion; an approach in which children are taught and develop skills in two languages.

dual-process model of grief. Posits that bereavement is accompanied by loss-oriented stressors (emotional attachment) and restoration-oriented stressors (life changes); healthy adjustment is promoted by alternating focus between the two types.

dual-systems model. A model of the brain consisting of two systems, one emotional and the other rational, that develop on different timeframes, accounting for typical adolescent behavior.

durable power of attorney. A document in which individuals legally authorize a trusted relative or friend to make legal, financial, or health care decisions on their behalf if they are unable to do so.

dying trajectory. Refers to the variability in the rate of decline that people show prior to death.

death with dignity. Ending one's life in a way that is true to one's preferences and controlling end-of-life care.

dynamic systems theory. A framework describing motor skills as resulting from ongoing interactions among physical, cognitive, and socioemotional influences and environmental supports; previously mastered skills are combined to provide more complex and effective ways of exploring and controlling the environment.

easy temperament. A temperament characterized by regularity in biological rhythms, the tendency to adapt easily to new experiences, and a general cheerfulness.

eating disorders. Mental disorders that are characterized by extreme over- or undercontrol of eating and behaviors intended to control weight such as compulsive exercise, dieting, or purging.

egocentrism. Piaget's term for children's inability to take another person's point of view or perspective and to assume that others share the same feelings, knowledge, and physical view of the world.

ego integrity versus despair. The final stage in Erikson's psychosocial theory, in which older adults find a sense of coherence in life experiences and conclude that their lives are meaningful and valuable.

elaboration. A memory strategy in which one imagines a scene or story to link the material to be remembered.

embryo. Prenatal organism between about 2 and 8 weeks after conception; a period of major structural development.

embryonic period. Occurs from about 2 to 8 weeks after pregnancy, in which rapid structural development takes place.

emerging adulthood. A developmental period between adolescence and early adulthood, extending from the completion of secondary education to the adoption of adult roles.

emotional display rule. Unstated cultural guidelines for acceptable emotions and emotional expression that are communicated to children via parents' emotional behavior, expressions, and socialization.

emotion regulation. The ability to adjust and control one's emotional state to influence how and when emotions are expressed.

empathy. The capacity to understand another person's emotions and concerns.

empty nest. A transitional time of parenting when the youngest child leaves home.

epidermis. The outer protective layer of the skin that produces new skin cells.

epidural. A method of pain management often used during labor in which a regional anesthetic drug is administered to a small space between the vertebrae of the lower spine to numb the woman's lower body.

epigenetics. A perspective that development results from dynamic interactions between genetics and the environment such that the expression of genetic inheritance is influenced by environmental forces.

episodic memory. Memory for everyday experiences.

epistemic cognition. The ways in which an individual understands how theyarrived at ideas, beliefs, and conclusions.

estrogen. The primary female sex hormone responsible for development and regulation of the female reproductive system and secondary sex characteristics.

ethnic-racial identity. A sense of membership in an ethnic or racial group and viewing the attitudes and practices associated with that group as an enduring part of the self.

ethology. Emphasizes the evolutionary basis of behavior and its adaptive value in ensuring survival of a species.

euthanasia. Refers to the practice of assisting terminally ill people in dying more quickly.

evolutionary developmental theory. A perspective that applies principles of evolution and scientific knowledge about the interactive influence of genetic and environmental mechanisms to understand the adaptive value of developmental changes that are experienced with age.

executive function. The set of cognitive operations that support planning, decision making, and goal-setting abilities, such as the ability to control attention, coordinate information in working memory, and inhibit impulses.

exosystem. In bioecological systems theory, social settings in which an individual does not participate but has an indirect influence on development.

experience-dependent brain development. Brain growth and development in response-specific learning experiences.

experience-expectant brain development. Brain growth and development that are dependent on basic environmental experiences, such as visual and auditory stimulation, in order to develop normally.

experimental research. A research design that permits inferences about cause and effect by exerting control, systematically manipulating a variable, and studying the effects on measured variables.

expertise. An elaborate and integrated knowledge base that underlies extraordinary proficiency in given area.

external attributions. Emphasizing external factors that cannot be controlled as causes of an outcome.

externality effect. Refers to a particular pattern of infant visual processing.

extremely low birthweight. Refers to a birthweight of less than 750 grams (1 lb., 10 oz.); poses serious risks for survival, developmental challenges, and handicaps.

false-belief task. A task that requires children to understand that someone does not share their knowledge.

fast mapping. A process by which children learn new words after only a brief encounter, connecting it with their own mental categories.

fetal alcohol spectrum disorders. The continuum of physical, mental, and behavioral outcomes caused by prenatal exposure to alcohol.

fetal alcohol syndrome (FAS). The most severe form of fetal alcohol spectrum disorder accompanying heavy prenatal exposure to alcohol, including a distinct pattern of facial characteristics, growth deficiencies, and deficits in intellectual development.

fetal MRI. Applies MRI technology to image the fetus's body and diagnose malformations.

fetal period. Occurs during the ninth week of prenatal development to birth, in which the fetus grows rapidly, and its organs become more complex and begin to function.

fetus. The prenatal organism from about the ninth week of pregnancy to delivery; a period of rapid growth and maturation of body structures.

fine motor development. The ability to control small movements of the fingers such as reaching and grasping.

fixed mindset. Viewing one's characteristics as enduring and unchangeable.

fluid intelligence. Intellectual ability that reflects basic information processing skills, including working memory, processing speed, and the ability to detect relations among stimuli and draw inferences;underlies learning, is not influenced by culture, and reflects brain functioning.

Flynn effect. The rise in IQ scores over generations in many nations.

formal operational reasoning. Piaget's fourth stage of cognitive development, characterized by abstract, logical, and systematic thinking.

fragile X syndrome. An example of a dominant–recessive disorder carried on the X chromosome characterized by intellectual disability, cardiac defects, and behavioral mannerisms common in individuals with autistic spectrum disorders; occurs in both males and females but is more severe in males.

free radical. A highly reactive, corrosive substance that forms when a cell is exposed to oxygen; through chemical reactions, free radicals destroy DNA, proteins, and other cellular materials.

functional magnetic resonance imaging (fMRI). A test that measures brain activity with a powerful magnet that uses radio waves and to measure blood oxygen level, an indicator of brain activity

gamete. A reproductive cell; sperm in males and ovum in females.

gender. The adoption of characteristics associated with men and women, acquired through socialization.

gender constancy. A child's understanding of the biological permanence of gender and that it does not change regardless of appearance, activities, or attitudes.

gender contentedness. Children's satisfaction with their gender assignment at birth (girl or boy).

gender identity. Awareness of one's gender.

gender intensification. The hypothesis that young adolescents become sensitive to gender stereotypes and are increasingly likely to adhere to gender stereotypes.

gender schema. A concept or a mental structure that organizes gender-related information and embodies a person's understanding of what it means to be a male or female and is used as a guide to attitudes and behaviors.

gender stereotypes. Broad generalized judgments of the activities, attitudes, skills, and characteristics deemed appropriate for males or females in a given culture.

gender typing. The process in which young children acquire the characteristics and attitudes that are considered appropriate for their gender.

gene. The basic unit of heredity; a small section of a chromosome that contains the string of chemicals (DNA) that provide instructions for the cell to manufacture proteins.

gene-environment correlation. The idea that many of an individual's traits are supported by his or her genes and environment; there are three types of correlations: passive, reactive, and active.

gene-environment interactions. Refer to the dynamic interplay between genes and our environment in determining characteristics, behavior, physical, cognitive, and social development as well as health.

generativity versus stagnation. The seventh stage in Erikson's theory in which adults seek to move beyond a concern for their own personal goals and welfare in order to guide future generations and give back to society.

genotype. An individual's collection of genes that contain instructions for all physical and psychological characteristics, including hair, eye color, personality, health, and behavior.

germinal period. Also referred to as the period of the zygote; refers to the first 2 weeks after conception.

glass ceiling. Metaphor for the invisible barrier that prevents women and people of color from advancing to the highest levels of the career ladder.

goodness of fit. The compatibility between a child's temperament and their environment, especially the parent's temperament and childrearing methods; the greater the degree of match, the more favorable the child's adjustment.

grammar. The rules of language.

gray matter. Unmyelinated neurons.

grief. The affective response to bereavement that includes distress and an intense array of emotions such as hurt, anger, and guilt.

gross motor development. The ability to control large movements of the body, such as walking and jumping.

growth faltering. A condition in which growth and weight are substantially lower than the norm expected for a child's age; also known as *failure to thrive*.

growth mindset. Viewing one's skills and characteristics as malleable or changeable.

growth norm. The expectation for typical gains and variations in height and weight for children based on their chronological age and ethnic background.

growth stunting. A reduced growth rate.

guided participation. Also known as apprenticeship in thinking; the process by which people learn from others who guide them, providing a scaffold to help them accomplish more than the child could do alone.

habituation. The gradual decline in the intensity, frequency, or duration of a response when repeatedly exposed to a stimulus; indicates learning.

hardiness. Personal qualities, including a sense of control, orientation toward personal growth, and commitment to life choices, that influence adults' ability to adapt to changes and life circumstances.

hemophilia. An X-linked chromosomal disorder involving abnormal blood clotting.

heteronomous morality. Piaget's first stage of morality when children become aware of rules and view them as absolute and unalterable.

heterozygous. Refers to a chromosomal pair consisting of two different alleles.

hippocampus. A structure located in the inner region of the temporal lobe.

holophrase. A one-word expression used to convey a complete thought.

homozygous. Refers to a chromosomal pair consisting of two identical alleles.

hormone. A chemical that is produced and secreted into the bloodstream to affect and influence physiological functions.

hormone replacement therapy. Compensating for reductions in hormones, such as in menopause, by taking hormones.

hospice. An approach to end-of-life care that emphasizes a dying patient's need for pain management; psychological, spiritual, and social support; and death with dignity.

human immunodeficiency virus (HIV). Infection most commonly passed through sexual activity and intravenous drug use, which causes acquired immune deficiency syndrome (AIDS).

human papillomavirus (HPV). The most common type of sexually transmitted infection diagnosed in people of all ages; comprises several types, some of which can cause cancer in different areas of the body (e.g., cervical cancer in women).

hypodermis. Innermost layer of skin composed of fat.

hypothesis. A proposed explanation for a phenomenon that can be tested.

hypothetical-deductive reasoning. The ability to consider propositions and probabilities, generate and systematically test hypotheses, and draw conclusions.

identity. A coherent organized sense of self that includes values, attitudes, and goals to which one is committed.

identity achievement. The identity state in which, after undergoing a period of exploration, a person commits to self-chosen values and goals.

identity diffusion. The identity state in which an individual has not undergone exploration or committed to self- chosen values and goals.

identity foreclosure. The identity state in which an individual has not undergone exploration but has committed to values and goals chosen by an authority figure.

identity moratorium. The identity state in which an individual actively explores identity alternatives without having committed to an identity; it embodies Erikson's psychosocial moratorium.

identity status. The degree to which individuals have explored possible selves and whether they have committed to specific beliefs and goals, assessed by administering interview and survey measures, and categorized into four identity statuses.

imaginary audience. A manifestation of adolescent egocentrism in which they assume that they are the focus of others' attention.

imaginary companion. A make-believe friend or companion a child comes up with during early childhood.

implantation. The process by which the blastocyst becomes attached to the uterine wall, completed by about 10 days after fertilization.

incomplete dominance. A genetic inheritance pattern in which both genes are expressed in the phenotype.

independent variable. The factor proposed to change the behavior under study in an experiment; it is systematically manipulated during an experiment.

indifferent gonad. A gonad in an embryo that has not yet differentiated into testes or ovaries.

inductive discipline. Strategy to control children's behavior that relies on reasoning and discussion.

industry versus inferiority. Erikson's fourth stage in which children attempt new skills, developing feelings of competence in their success or feeling inferior or incompetent.

infant-directed speech. Uses shorter words and sentences, higher and more varied pitch, repetitions, a slower rate, and longer pauses; also known as motherese.

information processing theory. A perspective that uses a computer analogy to describe how the mind receives information and manipulates, stores, recalls, and uses it to solve problems.

informed consent. A participant's informed (knowledge of the scope of the research and potential harm and benefits of participating), rational, and voluntary agreement to participate in a study.

initiative versus guilt. Erikson's third psychosocial stage in which young children develop a sense of purposefulness, trying new skills and activities, and take pride in their accomplishments, as well as feel guilt if they are unsuccessful.

insecure-avoidant attachment. An attachment pattern in which an infant avoids connecting with the caregiver, showing no distress when separated from a caregiver, such as during the Strange Situation, and does not seem to care about the caregiver's return.

insecure-disorganized attachment. An attachment in which an infant shows inconsistent, contradictory behavior in the Strange Situation, suggesting a conflict between approaching and fleeing the caregiver and perhaps fear.

insecure-resistant attachment. An attachment pattern in which an infant shows anxiety and uncertainty, showing great distress at separation from the caregiver during the Strange Situation and simultaneously seeks and avoids contact upon the caregiver's return.

instrumental aggression. Behavior that hurts someone else in order to achieve a goal such as gaining a possession.

instrumental assistance. Tangible help.

intelligence. An individual's ability to adapt to the environment.

intelligence test (IQ test). A test designed to measure the aptitude to learn at school;intellectual aptitude.

intermodal perception. The process of combining information from more than one sensory system such as visual and auditory senses.

internal attributions. Emphasizing one's own role influence as the cause of an outcome.

internal working model. A set of expectations about one's worthiness of love and the availability of attachment figures during times of distress.

intersectionality. The dynamic interrelations of social categories, such as gender, race and ethnicity, sexual orientation, socioeconomic status, immigration status, age, and disabilities, and the interwoven systems of power and privilege that accompany social category membership.

intimacy versus isolation. Erikson's sixth psychosocial stage in which individuals demonstrate the capacity to feel closeness and bond with another individual to make a permanent commitment to a romantic partner.

intimate partner violence. Physical, sexual, and psychological abuse within a romantic relationship.

irreversibility. A characteristic of preoperational reasoning in which a child does not understand that an action can be reversed and a thing restored to its original state.

isometric strength. Subtle contractions in which the length of the muscle does not change, is maintained through adulthood.

Jacob's syndrome. A sex chromosome abnormality experienced by men in which they produce high levels of testosterone; also known as XYY syndrome.

job burnout. Refers to a sense of mental exhaustion that accompanies long-term job stress, excessive workloads, and reduced feelings of control; relatively frequent in professions that are interpersonally demanding and whose demands may exceed workers' coping skills.

justice. The ethical principle that requires that risks and benefits of research participation must be spread equitably across individuals and groups.

kangaroo care. An intervention for low-birthweight babies in which the infant is placed vertically against the parent's chest, under the shirt, providing skin-to-skin contact.

Klinefelter syndrome. Sex chromosome abnormality in which a male has an extra X chromosome (XXY).

labor. Occurs at about 40 weeks of pregnancy, or 38 weeks after conception; also known as *childbirth*.

language acquisition device (LAD). In Chomsky's theory, an innate facilitator of language that allows infants to quickly and efficiently analyze everyday speech and determine its rules, regardless of their native language.

lateralization. The process by which the two hemispheres of the brain become specialized to carry out different functions.

learned helplessness orientation. An orientation characterized by a fixed mind-set and the attribution of poor performance to internal factors.

Lewy body dementia. Common form of dementia characterized by the formation of spherical protein deposits known as Lewy bodies.

life review. The reflection on past experiences and one's life, permitting greater self-understanding and the assignment of meaning to their lives.

lifespan human development. An approach to studying human development that examines ways in which individuals grow, change, and stay the same throughout their lives, from conception to death.

life structure. In Levenson's theory, a person's overall organization of their life, particularly dreams, goals, and relationships with significant others as well as institutions, such as marriage, family, and vocation.

limbic system. A collection of brain structures responsible for emotion.

living will. A legal document that permits a person to make his or her wishes known regarding medical care in the event that the person is incapacitated by an illness or accident and is unable to speak for himself or herself.

logical extension. A strategy children use to increase their vocabulary in which they extend a new word to other objects in the same category.

longitudinal research study. A developmental study in which one group of participants is studied repeatedly to infer age changes.

long-term memory. The component of the information processing system that is an unlimited store that holds information indefinitely, until it is retrieved to manipulate working memory.

low birthweight. Classifies infants who weigh less than 2,500 grams (5.5 pounds) at birth.

macrosystem. In bioecological systems theory, the sociohistorical context—cultural values, laws, and societal norms and values—in which the microsystem, mesosystem, and exosystem are embedded, posing indirect influences on individuals.

macular degeneration. A substantial loss of cells in the center area of the retina (the macula), causing blurring and eventual loss of central vision; its onset is influenced by heredity and environmental factors.

mandated reporter. A professional who is legally obligated to report suspected child maltreatment to law enforcement.

mastery orientation. A belief that success stems from trying hard and that failures are influenced by factors that can be controlled, like effort.

meiosis. The process by which a gamete is formed, containing one half of the cell's chromosomes, producing ova and sperm with 23 single, unpaired chromosomes.

melatonin. A hormone that influences sleep.

memory strategy. Deliberate cognitive activities that make an individual more likely to remember information.

menarche. A girl's first menstrual period.

menopause. The end of menstruation and a woman's reproductive capacity.

menstruation. The monthly shedding of the uterine lining, which has thickened in preparation for the implantation of a fertilized egg.

mental representation. An internal depiction of an object; thinking of an object using mental pictures.

mesosystem. In bioecological systems theory, the relations and interactions among microsystems.

metacognition. The ability to think about thinking; knowledge of how the mind works.

metamemory. An aspect of metacognition that refers to the understanding of memory and how to use strategies to enhance memory.

microsystem. In bioecological systems theory, the innermost level of context, which includes an individual's immediate physical and social environment.

midlife crisis. A period of self-doubt and stress attributed to entering midlife once thought to contribute to a major reorganization of personality in midlife;now thought to occur in a small minority of adults and to be related to history more than age.

midwife. A health care professional, usually a nurse, who specializes in childbirth;midwives provide health care throughout pregnancy and supervise home births.

mitosis. The process of cell duplication in which DNA is replicated and the resulting cell is genetically identical to the original.

Montessori school. A child-centered educational approach, first created in the early 1900s by the Italian physician and educator Maria Montessori (1870–1952), in which children are viewed as active constructors of their own development and are given freedom in choosing their activities.

moral reasoning. A person's understanding of moral issues and judgments of right and wrong; relates to Kohlberg's theory or moral reasoning.

mourning. The ceremonies and rituals a culture prescribes for expressing bereavement.

multiple intelligence theory. Gardner's proposition that human intelligence is composed of a varied set of abilities.

mutation. A sudden permanent change in the structure of genes.

mutual exclusivity assumption. When learning new words, young children assume that objects have only one label or name.

myelin. The fatty substance that coats the axons, which speeds the transmission of electrical impulses and neurological function.

myelination. The process in which neurons are coated in a fatty substance, myelin, which contributes to faster neural communication.

natural childbirth. An approach to birth that reduces pain through the use of breathing and relaxation exercises.

naturalistic observation. A research method in which a researcher views and records an individual's behavior in natural, real-world settings.

nature-nurture debate. A debate within the field of human development regarding whether development is caused by nature (genetics or heredity) or nurture (the physical and social environment).

neonate. A newborn human.

neural tube. Forms during the third week after conception and will develop into the central nervous system (brain and spinal cord).

neurofibrillary tangle. A twisted bundle of threads of a protein called tau that occur in the brain when neurons collapse; found in individuals with Alzheimer's disease.

neurogenesis. The production of new neurons.

neuron. A nerve cell that stores and transmits information; billions of neurons comprise the brain.

niche picking. An active gene-environment correlation in which individuals seek out experiences and environments that complement their genetic tendencies.

noncorporeal continuation. The view that some form of life and personal continuity exists after the physical body has died.

noninvasive prenatal testing (NIPT). A prenatal diagnostic that samples cell- free fetal DNA from the mother's blood for chromosomal abnormalities.

obesity. In children, defined as having a body mass index at or above the 95th percentile for height and age.

object permanence. The understanding that objects continue to exist outside of sight.

observational learning. Learning that occurs by watching and imitating models, as posited by social learning theory.

oldest-old. Adults aged 85 and older, who are most likely to depend on others for physical and social support to complete daily tasks.

old-old. Adults aged 75 to 84, who typically live independently but often experience some physical and mental impairment.

ontogenetic development. Developmental changes within the individual, including interacting biological, cognitive, and socioemotional traits.

open-ended interview. A research method in which a researcher asks a participant questions using a flexible, conversational style and may vary the order of questions, probe, and ask follow-up questions based on the participant's responses.

osteoarthritis. The most common type of arthritis; it affects joints that are injured by overuse, most commonly the hips, knees, lower back, and hands, in which the cartilage protecting the ends of the bones where they meet at the joints wears away, and joints become less flexible and swell.

osteoporosis. A condition characterized by severe loss of bone mass, leading to increased risk of fractures.

overregularization errors. Grammatical mistakes that children make because they apply grammatical rules too stringently to words that are exceptions.

palliative care. An alternative to medical treatment in which dying patients receive medications to control pain and related symptoms.

parental monitoring. Parents' awareness of their children's activities, whereabouts, and companions.

parenting style. Sets of childrearing behaviors a parent uses across situations to form a childrearing climate.

Parkinson's disease. A chronic progressive brain disorder caused by deterioration of neurons in the substantia nigra; characterized by muscle rigidity, tremors, and sometimes dementia.

passive consent. a type of consent procedure in which parents are notified about the research and must reply if they do not want their child to participate.

passive euthanasia. Occurs when life-sustaining treatment, such as a ventilator, is withheld or withdrawn, allowing a person to die naturally.

peer acceptance. Likeability or the degree to which a child is viewed as a worthy social partner by his or her peers.

peer rejection. An ongoing interaction in which a child is deliberately excluded by peers.

perception. The mental processing of sensory information, which is interpreted as sight, sound, and smell, for example.

perceived other-gender typicality. Children's beliefs about their similarity to peers of the other gender.

perceived pressure to conform to gender roles. The degree to which children feel pressure to avoid other-gender behavior, including anticipating negative consequences such as ridicule, criticism, and shaming, from parents, peers, and oneself self for engaging in behavior characteristic of the other gender.

perceived same-gender typicality. Children's beliefs about their similarity to their gender and same-gender peers.

perimenopause. Transition to menopause in which the production of reproductive hormones declines and symptoms associated with menopause first appear, such as hot flashes.

permissive parenting style. A childrearing approach characterized by high levels of warmth and low levels of control or discipline.

persistent vegetative state (PVS). Cortical death when the person appears awake but is not aware, due to permanent loss of all activity in the cortex.

personal fable. A manifestation of adolescent egocentrism in which adolescents believe their thoughts, feelings, and experiences are more special and unique than anyone else's, as well as the sense that they are invulnerable.

phenotype. A person's observable physical traits, such as eye color, hair color, or height.

phenylketonuria (PKU). A recessive disorder that prevents the body from producing an enzyme that breaks down phenylalanine (an amino acid) from proteins that, without treatment, leads to buildup that damages the central nervous system.

phonics instruction. An approach to reading instruction that emphasizes teaching children to sound out words and connect sounds to written symbols.

physical development. Body maturation, including body size, proportion, appearance, health, and perceptual abilities.

physician-assisted suicide. A type of voluntary active euthanasia in which terminally ill patients make the conscious decision that they want their life to end before dying becomes a protracted process.

placenta. The principal organ of exchange between the mother and the developing organism, enabling the exchange of nutrients, oxygen, and wastes via the umbilical cord.

plasticity. A characteristic of development refers to malleability or openness to change in response to experience.

polygenic inheritance. Occurs when a trait is a function of the interaction of many genes, such as with height, intelligence, and temperament.

popular children. Children who receive many positive ratings from peers indicating that they are accepted and valued by peers.

positivity effect. An age-related shift in attention preferences prioritizing positive information in late adulthood.

positron emission tomography (PET). Technique to examine brain activity by injecting a small dose of radioactive material into the participant's blood stream.

possible selves. Future-oriented representations of self-concept into the future; who an individual might become, both hoped for and feared, that guides and motivates choices and behaviors.

postconventional moral reasoning. Kohlberg's third level of moral reasoning emphasizing autonomous decision making based on principles such as valuing human dignity.

postformal reasoning. A stage of cognitive development proposed to follow Piaget's formal operational stage;thinking and problem solving are restructured in adulthood to integrate abstract reasoning with practical considerations.

pragmatics. The practical application of language for everyday communication.

pragmatic thought. In Labouvie-Vief's theory, a type of thinking where logic is used as a tool to address everyday problems and contradictions are viewed as part of life.

preconventional reasoning. Kohlberg's first level of reasoning in which young children's behavior is governed by punishment and gaining rewards.

prefrontal cortex. Located in the front of the brain, responsible for higher thought, such as planning, goal setting, controlling impulses, and using cognitive skills and memory to solve problems.

prenatal care. A set of services provided to improve pregnancy outcomes and engage the expectant mother, family members, and friends in pregnancy-related health care decisions.

prenatal development. The process by which a single cell develops into a newborn.

Preoperational reasoning. Piaget's second stage of cognitive development, between about ages 2 and 6, characterized by advances in symbolic thought, but thought is not yet logical.

presbycusis. Age-related hearing loss, first to high-frequency sounds, gradually spreading.

presbyopia. An age-related condition in which the lens of the eye becomes less able to adjust its focus on objects at a close range.

preterm. A birth that occurs 35 or fewer weeks after conception.

primary sex characteristic. The reproductive organs; in females, this includes the ovaries, fallopian tubes, uterus, and vagina, and in males, this includes the penis, testes, scrotum, seminal vesicles, and prostate gland.

private speech. Self-directed speech that children use to guide their behavior.

proactive interference. A phenomenon that occurs when information that has previously been remembered interferes with memory for new information.

productive language. Language individuals can produce for themselves.

Project Head Start. Early childhood intervention program funded by the U.S. federal government that provides low-income children with nutritional, health, and educational services, as well as helps parents become involved in their children's development.

prosocial behavior. Actions that are oriented toward others for the pure sake of helping, without a reward.

protective factor. Variable that is thought to reduce the poor outcomes associated with adverse circumstances.

proximodistal development. The principle that growth and development proceed from the center of the body outward.

psychoanalytic theory. A perspective introduced by Freud that development and behavior are stage-like and influenced by inner drives, memories, and conflicts of which an individual is unaware and cannot control.

psychosocial moratorium. In Erikson's theory, a period in which the individual is free to explore identity possibilities before committing to an identity.

puberty. The biological transition to adulthood, in which hormones cause the body to physically mature and permit sexual reproduction.

punishment. In operant conditioning, the process in which a behavior is followed by an aversive or unpleasant outcome that decreases the likelihood of a response.

questionnaire. A research method in which researchers use a survey or set of questions to collect data from large samples of people.

recall memory. The ability to generate a memory of a stimulus encountered before without seeing it again.

recast. When an adult repeats a child's sentence back to him or her in a new grammatical form, helping the child to acquire grammatical rules more quickly.

receptive language. Language that one can understand.

reciprocal determinism. A perspective positing that individuals and their environment interact and influence each other.

recognition memory. The ability to identify a previously encountered stimulus.

reflective judgment. Mature type of reasoning that synthesizes contradictions among perspectives.

reflex. Involuntary and automatic responses to stimuli such as touch, light, and sound.

rehearsal. A mnemonic strategy that involves systematically repeating information to retain it in working memory.

reinforcement. In operant conditioning, the process by which a behavior is followed by a desirable outcome increases the likelihood of a response.

relational aggression. Nonphysical acts aimed at harming a person's connections with others, such as by exclusion and rumor spreading.

relativistic thinking. Type of reasoning in which knowledge is viewed as subjective and dependent on the situation.

reminiscence. The process of telling stories from one's past, to oneself or others.

representational play. Make-believe play in which children often pretend that one object is something else.

resilience. The ability to adapt to serious adversity.

respect for autonomy. The ethical principle that states researchers have a special obligation to respect participants' autonomy, their ability to make and implement decisions.

response inhibition. Part of executive function, the ability to control and stop responding to a stimulus.

responsibility. The ethical principle that requires researchers to act responsibly by adhering to professional standards of conduct and clarifying their obligations and roles to others.

rheumatoid arthritis. An autoimmune illness in which the connective tissues, the membranes that line the joints, become inflamed and stiff.

risk factors. Individual or contextual challenges that tax an individual's coping capacities and can evoke psychological stress.

rough-and-tumble play. Social interaction involving chasing and play fighting with no intent to harm.

scaffolding. Temporary support that permits a child to bridge the gap between his or her current competence level and the task at hand.

seasons of life. A set of life phases that Levinson concluded adults progress through in which life structures are constructed, tested, and modified, based on experiences and opportunities.

secondary sex characteristic. Physical traits that indicate sexual maturity but are not directly related to fertility, such as breast development and the growth of body hair.

secular trend. The change from one generation to the next in an aspect of development, such as body size or in the timing of puberty.

secure attachment. The attachment pattern in which an infant uses the caregiver as a secure base from which to explore, seeks contact during reunions, and is easily comforted by the caregiver.

secure base. The use of a caregiver as a foundation from which to explore and return to for emotional support.

security of attachment. The extent to which an individual feels that an attachment object, such as a caregiver, can reliably meet their needs; measured by the Strange Situation.

selective attention. The ability to focus on relevant stimuli and ignore others.

selective optimization with compensation. The ability to adapt to changes over time, optimize current functioning, and compensate for losses in order to preserve performance despite declines in fluid abilities.

self-concept. The set of attributes, abilities, and characteristics that a person describes themselves with.

self-conscious emotion. Emotion that requires cognitive development and an awareness of self, such as empathy, embarrassment, shame, and guilt.

self-esteem. The emotional evaluation of one's own worth.

self-recognition. The ability to identify the self, typically measured as mirror recognition.

semen. The fluid that contains sperm.

senescence. A pattern of gradual age-related declines in physical functioning.

sensation. The physical response of sensory receptors when a stimulus is detected (e.g., activity of the sensory receptors in the eye in response to light); awareness of stimuli in the senses.

sensitive period. A period during which experience has a particularly powerful role in shaping developmental outcomes.

separation anxiety. Also known as separation protest; occurs when infants respond to the departure of an attachment figure with distress and crying.

seriation. A type of classification that involves ordering objects in a series according to a physical dimension such as height, weight, or color.

sex. Generally the gender assigned at birth, biological and determined by the presence of a Y chromosome in the 23rd pair of chromosomes, and usually indicated by the genitals.

sexual orientation. A term that refers to whether someone is sexually attracted to others of the same sex, opposite sex, or both.

sickle cell trait. A recessive trait, most often affecting African Americans, that causes red blood cells to becomecrescent or sickle shaped, resulting in difficulty distributing oxygen throughout the circulatory system.

singlehood. Refers to not living with a romantic partner.

slow-to-warm-up temperament. A temperament characterized by mild irregularity in biological rhythms, slow adaptation to change, and mildly negative mood.

small for date. Describes an infant who is full term but who has significantly lower weight than expected for the gestational age.

social comparison. The tendency to compare and judge one's abilities, achievements, and behaviors in relation to others.

social gender transition. A process by which transgender individuals adopt social changes to match their gender identity, such as by changing pronouns and appearance.

social learning theory. An approach that emphasizes the role of modeling and observational learning over people's behavior in addition to reinforcement and punishment.

social perspective taking. The ability to understand different viewpoints.

social referencing. Seeking information from caregivers about how to interpret unfamiliar or ambiguous events by observing their emotional expressions and reactions.

social smile. A smile that emerges in response to seeing familiar people; occurs in an infant between 6 and 10 weeks after birth.

sociocultural theory. Vygotsky's theory that individuals acquire culturally relevant ways of thinking through social interactions with members of their culture.

sociodramatic play. Make-believe play in which children act out roles and themes.

socioemotional development. Maturation of social and emotional functioning, which includes changes in personality, emotions, personal perceptions, social skills, and interpersonal relationships.

socioemotional selectivity theory. The perspective that as the emotional regulation function of social interaction becomes increasingly important to older adults, they prefer to interact with familiar social partners, accounting for the narrowing of the social network with age.

special education. Education tailored to meet the needs of a child with special needs, such as a specific learning disability.

specific learning disorder (SLD). Diagnosed in children who demonstrate a measurable discrepancy between aptitude and achievement in a particular academic area given their age, intelligence, and amount of schooling.

spermarche. A boy's first ejaculation of sperm.

spina bifida. A neural tube that results in spinal nerves growing outside of the vertebrae, often resulting in paralysis and developmental disability.

stage-environment fit. Refers to the match between the characteristics and supports of the school environment and the developing person's needs and capacities; influences well-being.

states of arousal. Degrees of wakefulness; newborns shift among six states of arousal ranging from regular sleep to waking activity.

stereotype threat. Phenomenon in which individuals' awareness of negative stereotypes influences their performance on intelligence and other tests.

Strange Situation. A structured laboratory procedure that measures the security of attachment by observing infants' reactions to being separated from the caregiver in an unfamiliar environment.

stranger wariness. Also known as stranger anxiety; an infant's expression of fear of unfamiliar people.

structured interview. A research method in which each participant is asked the same set of questions in the same way.

structured observation. An observational measure in which an individual's behavior is viewed and recorded in a controlled environment; a situation created by the experimenter.

successful aging. Demonstrating high levels of physical, social, and psychological well-being in advanced age.

sudden infant death syndrome (SIDS). The sudden unexpected death of an infant less than 1 year of age that occurs seemingly during sleep and remains unexplained after a thorough investigation.

surrogacy. An alternative form of reproduction known in which a woman (the surrogate) is impregnated and carries a fetus to term and agrees to turn the baby over to a woman, man, or couple who will raise it.

suicide. Death caused by self-directed injuries with the intent to die.

sustained attention. The ability to remain focused on a stimulus for an extended period of time.

synapse. The intersection or gap between the axon of one neuron and the dendrites of other neurons; the gap that neurotransmitters must cross.

synaptic pruning. The process by which synapses, neural connections that are seldom used, disappear.

synaptogenesis. The process in which neurons form synapses and increase connections between neurons.

telegraphic speech. Two-word utterances produced by toddlers that communicate only the essential words.

temperament. Characteristic differences among individuals in emotional reactivity, self-regulation, and activity that influence reactions to the environment and are stable and appear early in life.

teratogen. An environmental factor that causes damage to prenatal development.

testes. The glands that produce sperm.

testosterone. The primary male sex hormone responsible for development and regulation of the male reproductive system and secondary sex characteristics.

theory. An organized set of observations to describe, explain, and predict a phenomenon.

theory of mind. Children's awareness of their own and other people's mental processes and realization that other people do not share their thoughts.

three-mountains task. A classic Piagetian task used to illustrate preoperational children's egocentrism.

transgender. Denotes when a person's sense of identity and gender do not correspond to that person's chromosomal sex.

transfer deficit. Sometimes called the video deficit; when infants are less able to transfer or generalize what they see on a screen to their own behavior than what they learn through active interactions with adults.

transitive inference. A classification skill in which a child can infer the relationship between two objects by understanding each object's relationship to a third object.

triarchic theory of intelligence. Sternberg's theory positing three independent forms of intelligence: analytical, creative, and applied.

triple X syndrome. Chromosomal disorder in which an individual is born with three X chromosomes. Often unnoticed.

trust versus mistrust. The first psychosocial crisis in Erikson's theory in which infants must develop a basic sense of trust of the world as a safe place where their basic needs will be met.

Turner syndrome. Sex chromosome abnormality in which a female is born with only one X chromosome; girls with Turner syndrome show abnormal growth patterns, abnormalities in primary and secondary sex characteristics, and other disorders.

ultrasound. Prenatal diagnostic procedure in which high-frequency sound waves are directed at the mother's abdomen to provide clear images of the womb projected onto a video monitor.

underextension. A vocabulary error in which the infant applies a word too narrowly to a single object rather than the more appropriate, wider class of objects.

uninvolved parenting style. A childrearing style characterized by low levels of warmth and acceptance coupled with little control or discipline.

universal grammar. In Chomsky's theory, rules that apply to all human languages.

vascular dementia. Neurocognitive disorder in which sporadic and progressive losses occur, caused by small blockages of blood vessels in the brain.

verbal aggression. A form of relational aggression, intended to harm others' social relationships.

very low birthweight. Refers to a birthweight less than 1,500 grams (3.5 lbs.); poses risks for developmental disabilities and handicaps.

visual acuity. Sharpness of vision.

vocabulary spurt. Also known as a naming explosion; a period of rapid vocabulary learning that occurs from about 16 to 24 months of age.

Wernicke's area. The region of the brain that is responsible for language comprehension; damage to this area impairs the ability to understand others' speech and sometimes the ability to speak coherently.

white matter. Myelinated brain tissue.

whole brain death. Refers to the irreversible loss of functioning in the entire brain that may occur prior to clinical death.

widowhood. Refers to the status of a person who has lost a spouse through death and has not remarried.

widowhood effect. Refers to the increased likelihood for a widowed person to die, illustrating the relationship between social relations and health.

wisdom. Expertise in the conduct and meanings of life, characterized by emotional maturity and the ability to show insight and apply it to problems.

withdrawn-rejected children. Children who are withdrawn and passive and are shunned by peers.

working memory. The component of the information processing system that holds and processes information that is being manipulated, encoded, or retrieved and is responsible for maintaining and processing information used in cognitive tasks.

work-life balance. The challenge of finding time and energy for both a career and personal pursuits, such as family.

young-old. Older adults aged 65 to 74, who tend to be active, healthy, and financially and physically independent.

zone of proximal development. Vygotsky's term for the tasks that children cannot do alone but can exercise with the aid of more skilled partners.

zygote. A fertilized ovum.

REFERENCES

CHAPTER 1

Abrams, J. A., Tabaac, A., Jung, S., & Else-Quest, N. M. (2020). Considerations for employing intersectionality in qualitative health research. *Social Science & Medicine*, *258*, 113–138. https://doi.org/10.1016/j.socscimed.2020.113138

Aizer, A. (2017). The role of children's health in the intergenerational transmission of economic status. *Child Development Perspectives*, *11*(3), 167–172. https://doi.org/10.1111/cdep.12231

American Psychological Association. (2010). *Ethical principles of psychologists and code of conduct*. http://www.apa.org/ethics/code/principles.pdf

Anjos, T., Altmäe, S., Emmett, P., Tiemeier, H., Closa-Monasterolo, R., Luque, V., Wiseman, S., Pérez-García, M., Lattka, E., Demmelmair, H., Egan, B., Straub, N., Szajewska, H., Evans, J., Horton, C., Paus, T., Isaacs, E., van Klinken, J. W., Koletzko, B., & NUTRIMENTHE Research Group. (2013). Nutrition and neurodevelopment in children: Focus on NUTRIMENTHE project. *European Journal of Nutrition*, *52*(8), 1825–1842. https://doi.org/10.1007/s00394-013-0560-4

Baltes, P. B. (1987). Theoretical propositions of life-span developmental psychology: On the dynamics between growth and decline. *Developmental Psychology*, *23*, 611–626.

Baltes, P. B., Lindenberger, U., & Staudinger, U. M. (2006). Life span theory in developmental psychology. In R. M. Lerner (Ed.), *Handbook of child psychology: Vol. 1. Theoretical models of human development* (6th ed., pp. 569–664). Wiley.

Bandura, A. (2010). Vicarious learning. In D. Matsumoto (Ed.), *Cambridge dictionary of psychology* (p. 344). Cambridge University Press.

Bandura, A. (2011). But what about that gigantic elephant in the room? In R. M. Arkin (Ed.), *Most underappreciated: 50 prominent social psychologists describe their most unloved work. Arkin* (pp. 51–59). Oxford University Press.

Bandura, A. (2012). Social cognitive theory. In P. A. M. Van Lange, A. W. Kruglanski, & E. T. Higgins (Eds.), *Handbook of theories of social psychology (Vol 1). Van Lange* (pp. 349–373). SAGE.

Bandura, A. (2018). Toward a psychology of human agency: Pathways and reflections. *Perspectives on Psychological Science*, *13*(2), 130–136. https://doi.org/10.1177/1745691617699280

Bass, R. W., Brown, D. D., Laurson, K. R., & Coleman, M. M. (2013). Physical fitness and academic performance in middle school students. *Acta Paediatrica*, *102*(8), 832–837. https://doi.org/10.1111/apa.12278

Bateson, P. (2015). Human evolution and development: An ethological perspective. In W. F. Overton & P. C. M. Molenaar (Eds.), *Handbook of child psychology and developmental science. Vol. 1. Theory and method* (7th ed., pp. 208–243). Wiley.

Beran, T. N., Ramirez-Serrano, A., Kuzyk, R., Fior, M., & Nugent, S. (2011). Understanding how children understand robots: Perceived animism in child–robot interaction. *International Journal of Human-Computer Studies*, *69*(7–8), 539–550.

Biddle, S. J. H., Ciaccioni, S., Thomas, G., & Vergeer, I. (2019, May 1). Physical activity and mental health in children and adolescents: An updated review of reviews and an analysis of causality. *Psychology of Sport and Exercise*, *42*, 146–155. https://doi.org/10.1016/j.psychsport.2018.08.011

Bjorklund, D. F. (2018a). A metatheory for cognitive development (or "Piaget is dead" revisited). *Child Development*. https://doi.org/10.1111/cdev.13019

Bjorklund, D. F. (2018b). Behavioral epigenetics: The last nail in the coffin of genetic determinism. *Human Development*, *61*(1), 54–59. https://doi.org/10.1159/000481747

Boker, S. M. (2013). Selection, optimization, compensation, and equilibrium dynamics. *GeroPsych: The Journal of Gerontopsychology and Geriatric Psychiatry*, *26*(1), 61–73. https://doi.org/10.1024/1662-9647/a000081

Bowlby, J. (1969). *Attachment and loss: Vol. 1. Attachment*. Basic Books.

Bowlby, J. (1973). *Attachment and loss: Vol. 2. Separation: Anxiety and anger.* Basic Books.

Brawner, B. M., Volpe, E. M., Stewart, J. M., & Gomes, M. M. (2013). Attitudes and beliefs toward biobehavioural research participation: Voices and concerns of urban adolescent females receiving outpatient mental health treatment. *Annals of Human Biology*, *40*(6), 485–495. https://doi.org/10.3109/03014460.2013.806590

Bronfenbrenner, U., & Morris, P. A. (2006). The bioecological model of human development. In R. M. Lerner & W. Damon (Eds.), *Handbook of child psychology:* (Vol. 1, pp. 793–828). Wiley.

Brown, C. S., Mistry, R. S., & Yip, T. (2019). Moving from the margins to the mainstream: Equity and justice as key considerations for developmental science. *Child Development Perspectives*, *13*(4), 235–240. https://doi.org/10.1111/cdep.12340

Brown, H. R., Harvey, E. A., Griffith, S. F., Arnold, D. H., & Halgin, R. P. (2017). Assent and dissent: Ethical considerations in research with toddlers. *Ethics & Behavior*, *27*(8), 651–664. https://doi.org/10.1080/10508422.2016.1277356

Callaghan, T., & Corbit, J. (2015). The development of symbolic representation. In *Handbook of child psychology and developmental science* (pp. 1–46). https://doi.org/10.1002/9781118963418.childpsy207

Coplan, R. J., Ooi, L. L., & Nocita, G. (2015). When one is company and two is a crowd: Why some children prefer solitude. *Child Development Perspectives*, *9*(3), 133–137. https://doi.org/10.1111/cdep.12131

Crain, T. (2016). *The unity of unconsciousness*. Proceedings of the Aristotelian Society.

Crane, S., & Broome, M. E. (2017). Understanding ethical issues of research participation from the perspective of participating children and adolescents: A systematic review. *Worldviews on Evidence-Based Nursing*, *14*(3), 200–209. https://doi.org/10.1111/wvn.12209

Crenshaw, K. (1989). *Demarginalizing the intersection of race and sex: A black feminist critique of antidiscrimination doctrine, feminist theory and antiracist politics*. University of Chicago Legal Forum. https://heinonline.org/HOL/Page?handle=hein.journals/uchclf1989&id=143&div=&collection=

DelGiudice, M. (2018). Middle childhood: An evolutionary-developmental synthesis. In N. Halfon, C. B. Forrest, R. M. Lerner, & E. M. Faustman (Eds.), *Handbook of life course health development* (pp. 95–107). Springer. https://doi.org/10.1007/978-3-319-47143-3_5

Elder, G. H., & George, L. K. (2016). Age, cohorts, and the life course. In M. J. Shanahan, J. T. Mortimer, & M. K. Johnson (Eds.), *Handbook of the life course* (pp. 59–85). Springer. https://doi.org/10.1007/978-3-319-20880-0_3

Elder, G. H., Shanahan, M. J., & Jennings, J. A. (2015). Human development in time and place. In W. Damon (Ed.), *Handbook of child psychology and developmental science* (pp. 1–49). Wiley. https://doi.org/10.1002/9781118963418.childpsy402

Elder, G. H., Shanahan, M. J., & Jennings, J. A. (2016). Human development in time and place. In M. H. Bornstein & T. Leventhal (Eds.), *Handbook of child psychology: Vol. 4. Ecological settings and processes* (7th ed., pp. 6–54). Wiley.

Else-Quest, N. M., & Hyde, J. S. (2016). Intersectionality in quantitative psychological research. *Psychology of Women Quarterly*, *40*(2), 155–170. https://doi.org/10.1177/0361684316629797

Erikson, E. H. (1950). *Childhood and society* (2nd ed.). Norton.

Feurer, C., Burkhouse, K. L., Siegle, G., & Gibb, B. E. (2017). Increased pupil dilation to angry faces predicts interpersonal stress generation in offspring of depressed mothers. *Journal of Child Psychology and Psychiatry*, *58*(8), 950–957. https://doi.org/10.1111/jcpp.12739

Fisher, C. B., Busch-Rossnagel, N. A., Jopp, D. S., & Brown, J. (2013). Applied developmental science: Contributions and challenges for the 21st century. In I. B. Weiner (Ed.), *Handbook of psychology* (Vol. 6, pp. 517–546). Wiley.

Fisher, C. B., Busch-Rossnagel, N. A., Jopp, D. S., & Brown, J. L. (2012). Applied dDevelopmental science, social justice, and socio-political well-being. *Applied Developmental Science*, *16*(1), 54–64. https://doi.org/10.1080/10888691.2012.642786

Fisher, C. B., Higgins-D'Alessandro, A., Rau, J. M., Kuther, T. L., & Belanger, S. (1996). Referring and reporting research participants at risk: Views from urban adolescents. *Child Development*, *67*(5), 2086–2100. http://www.ncbi.nlm.nih.gov/pubmed/9022231

Flavell, J. H. (1992). Cognitive development: Past, present, and future. *Developmental Psychology*, *28*, 998–1005.

Frankenhuis, W. E., & Tiokhin, L. (2018). Bridging evolutionary biology and developmental psychology: Toward an enduring theoretical infrastructure. *Child Development*, *89*, 2303–2306. https://doi.org/10.1111/cdev.13021

Gabbard, C. P. (2018). *Lifelong motor development* (6th ed.). Pearson.

Gauvain, M. (2018). From developmental psychologist to water scientist and back again: The role of interdisciplinary research in developmental science. *Child Development Perspectives*, *12*(1), 45–50. https://doi.org/10.1111/cdep.12255

Gentile, D. A., Bender, P. K., & Anderson, C. A. (2017). Violent video game effects on salivary cortisol, arousal, and aggressive thoughts in children.. *Computers in Human Behavior*, *70*, 39–43, .

Ghavami, N., Katsiaficas, D., & Rogers, L. O. (2016). Toward an intersectional approach in developmental science: The role of race, gender, sexual orientation, and immigrant status. *Advances in Child Development and Behavior*, *50*, 31–73. https://doi.org/10.1016/BS.ACDB.2015.12.001

Ginsburg, H. P. (1997). *Entering the child's mind: The clinical interview in psychological research and practice*. Cambridge University Press.

Godfrey, E. B., & Burson, E. (2018). Interrogating the intersections: How intersectional perspectives can inform developmental scholarship on critical consciousness. *New Directions for Child and Adolescent Development*, *2018*(161), 17–38. https://doi.org/10.1002/cad.20246

Golberstein, E., Wen, H., & Miller, B. F. (2020). Coronavirus disease 2019 (COVID-19) and mental health for children and adolescents. *JAMA Pediatrics*. https://doi.org/10.1001/jamapediatrics.2020.1456

Golinkoff, R. M., Hirsh-Pasek, K., Grob, R., & Schlesinger, M. (2017). "Oh, the places you'll go" by bringing developmental science into the world! *Child Development*, *88*(5), 1403–1408. https://doi.org/10.1111/cdev.12929

Grzanka, P. R. (2020). From buzzword to critical psychology: An invitation to take intersectionality seriously. *Women and Therapy*, *43*, 244–261. https://doi.org/10.1080/02703149.2020.1729473

Halford, G. S., & Andrews, G. (2011). Information-processing models of cognitive development. In U. Goswami (Ed.), *The Wiley-Blackwell handbook of childhood cognitive development* (2nd ed., pp. 697–721). Wiley.

Hiriscau, I. E., Stingelin-Giles, N., Stadler, C., Schmeck, K., & Reiter-Theil, S. (2014). A right to confidentiality or a duty to disclose? Ethical guidance for conducting prevention research with children and adolescents. *European Child & Adolescent Psychiatry*, *23*(6), 409–416. https://doi.org/10.1007/s00787-014-0526-y

Holmes, C. J., Kim-Spoon, J., & Deater-Deckard, K. (2016). Linking executive function and peer problems from early childhood through middle adolescence. *Journal of Abnormal Child Psychology*, *44*(1), 31–42. https://doi.org/10.1007/s10802-015-0044-5

Hopkins, B., & Westra, T. (1989). Maternal expectations of their infants' development: Some cultural differences. *Developmental Medicine & Child Neurology*, *31*(3), 384–390.

Huston, A. C. (2018). A life at the intersection of science and social issues. *Child Development Perspectives*, *12*, 75–79. https://doi.org/10.1111/cdep.12265

Keller, H. (2017). Culture and development: A systematic relationship. *Perspectives on Psychological Science*, *12*(5), 833–840. https://doi.org/10.1177/1745691617704097

Keller, K., & Engelhardt, M. (2013). Strength and muscle mass loss with aging process. Age and strength loss. *Muscles, Ligaments and Tendons Journal*, *3*(4), 346–350. http://europepmc.org/articles/PMC3940510/?report=abstract

Krampe, R. T., & Charness, N. (2018). Aging and expertise. In K. A. Ericsson, R. R. Hoffman, A. Kozbelt, & A. M. Williams (Eds.), *The Cambridge handbook of expertise and expert performance* (pp. 835–856). Cambridge University Press. https://doi.org/10.1017/9781316480748.042

Lampl, M., Johnson, M. L., & Frongillo, E. A. (2001). Mixed distribution analysis identifies saltation and stasis growth. *Annals of Human Biology, 28*(4), 403–411.

Lampl, M., Veldhuis, J. D., & Johnson, M. L. (1992). Saltation and stasis: A model of human growth. *Science, 258*, 801–803. Figure 1

Lee, J. (2020). Mental health effects of school closures during COVID-19. *The Lancet Child and Adolescent Health, 4*(6), 421. https://doi.org/10.1016/S2352-4642(20)30109-7

Legare, C. H., Clegg, J. M., & Wen, N. J. (2018). Evolutionary developmental psychology: 2017 redux. *Child Development, 89*, 2282–2287. https://doi.org/10.1111/cdev.13018

Lerner, R. M. (2012). Developmental science: Past, present, and future. *International Journal of Developmental Science, 6*(1-2), 29–36. https://doi.org/10.3233/DEV-2012-12102

Lerner, R. M., Agans, J. P., DeSouza, L. M., & Hershberg, R. M. (2014). Developmental science in 2025: A predictive review. *Research in Human Development, 11*(4), 255–272. https://doi.org/10.1080/15427609.2014.967046

Lerner, R. M., Johnson, S. K., & Buckingham, M. H. (2015). Relational developmental systems-based theories and the study of children and families: Lerner and Spanier (1978) revisited. *Journal of Family Theory & Review, 7*(2), 83–104. https://doi.org/10.1111/jftr.12067

Lickliter, R., & Witherington, D. C. (2017). Towards a truly developmental epigenetics. *Human Development, 60*(2-3), 124–138. https://doi.org/10.1159/000477996

Lilienfeld, S. O. (2002). When worlds collide. Social science, politics, and the Rind et al. (1998). Child sexual abuse meta-analysis. *The American Psychologist, 57*(3), 176–188. http://www.ncbi.nlm.nih.gov/pubmed/11905116

Liu, C., Cox, R. B., Washburn, I. J., Croff, J. M., & Crethar, H. C. (2017). The effects of requiring parental consent for research on adolescents' risk behaviors: A meta-analysis. *Journal of Adolescent Health, 61*(1), 45–52. https://doi.org/10.1016/j.jadohealth.2017.01.015

Lorenz, K. (1952). *King Solomon's ring*. Crowell.

Luna, B., Marek, S., Larsen, B., Tervo-Clemmens, B., & Chahal, R. (2015). An integrative model of the maturation of cognitive control. *Annual Review of Neuroscience, 38*(1), 151–170. https://doi.org/10.1146/annurev-neuro-071714-034054

Luthar, S. S., Crossman, E. J., Small, P. J., Luthar, S. S., Crossman, E. J., & Small, P. J. (2015). Resilience and adversity. In M. E. Lamb (Ed.), *Handbook of child psychology and developmental science* (pp. 1–40). Wiley. https://doi.org/10.1002/9781118963418.childpsy307

Macapagal, K., Coventry, R., Arbeit, M. R., Fisher, C. B., & Mustanski, B. (2017). 'I won't out myself just to do a survey': Sexual and gender minority adolescents' perspectives on the risks and benefits of sex research. *Archives of Sexual Behavior, 46*(5), 1393–1409. https://doi.org/10.1007/s10508-016-0784-5

Margrett, J. A., Allaire, J. C., Johnson, T. L., Daugherty, K. E., & Weatherbee, S. R. (2010). Everyday problem solving. In J. C. Cavanaugh, C. K. Cavanaugh, J. Berry, & R. West (Eds.), *Aging in America, Vol 1: Psychological aspects* (pp. 80–101). Praeger/ABC-CLIO.

Markus, H. R., & Kitayama, S. (1991). Culture and the self: Implications for cognition, emotion, and motivation. *Psychological Review, 98*(2), 224–253. https://doi.org/10.1037/0033-295X.98.2.224

Markus, H. R., & Kitayama, S. (2010). Cultures and selves: A cycle of mutual constitution. *Perspectives on Psychological Science, 5*(4), 420–430. https://doi.org/10.1177/1745691610375557

Masten, A. S. (2016). Resilience in developing systems: The promise of integrated approaches. *European Journal of Developmental Psychology, 13*(3), 297–312. https://doi.org/10.1080/17405629.2016.1147344

McAuley, E., Wójcicki, T. R., Gothe, N. P., Mailey, E. L., Szabo, A. N., Fanning, J., Olson, E. A., Phillips, S. M., Motl, R. W., & Mullen, S. P. (2013). Effects of a DVD-delivered exercise intervention on physical function in older adults. *Journals of Gerontology Series A: Biological Sciences & Medical Sciences, 68*(9), 1076–1082.

Meaney, M. J. (2017). Epigenetics and the biology of gene × environment interactions. In P. H. Tolan & B. L. Leventhal (Eds.), *Gene-environment transactions in developmental psychopathology* (pp. 59–94). Springer. https://doi.org/10.1007/978-3-319-49227-8_4

Miech, R. A., Johnston, L. D., O'Malley, P. M., Bachman, J. G., Schulenberg, J. E., & Patrick, M. E. (2017). *Monitoring the future national survey results on drug use, 1975–2016: Volume I, Secondary school students*. http://www.monitoringthefuture.org/pubs/monographs/mtf-vol1_2016.pdf

Miller, P. H. (2016). *Theories of developmental psychology* (6th ed.). Worth.

Mistry, J. (2013). Integration of culture and biology in human development. *Advances in Child Development and Behavior, 45*, 287–314. http://www.ncbi.nlm.nih.gov/pubmed/23865120

Mistry, J., & Dutta, R. (2015). Human development and culture. *Handbook of Child Psychology and Developmental Science, 1*(10), 1–38. https://doi.org/10.1002/9781118963418.childpsy110

Mistry, J., Li, J., Yoshikawa, H., Tseng, V., Tirrell, J., Kiang, L., Mistry, R., & Wang, Y. (2016). An integrated conceptual framework for the development of Asian American children and youth. *Child Development, 87*(4), 1014–1032. https://doi.org/10.1111/cdev.12577

Müller, U., Kerns, K., Müller, U., & Kerns, K. (2015). The development of executive function. In R. M. Lerner (Ed.), *Handbook of child psychology and developmental science* (7th ed., pp. 1–53). Wiley. https://doi.org/10.1002/9781118963418.childpsy214

Newell, B. R., & Shanks, D. R. (2014). Unconscious influences on decision making: A critical review. *Behavioral and Brain Sciences, 38*(01), 1–19. https://doi.org/10.1017/S0140525X12003214

Nielsen, M., Haun, D., Kärtner, J., & Legare, C. H. (2017). The persistent sampling bias in developmental psychology: A call to action. *Journal of Experimental Child Psychology, 162*, 31–38. https://doi.org/10.1016/J.JECP.2017.04.017

Overton, W. F. (2015). Processes, relations, and relational-developmental-systems. In W. F. Overton & P. C. M. Molenaar (Eds.), *Handbook of child psychology and developmental science* (pp. 1–54). Wiley. https://doi.org/10.1002/9781118963418.childpsy102

Overton, W. F., & Molenaar, P. C. M. (2015). Concepts, theory, and method in developmental science: A view of the issues. In W. F. Overton & P. C. M. Molenaar (Eds.), *Handbook of child psychology and developmental science: Vol. 1. Theory and method* (pp. 1–8). Wiley.

Oyserman, D. (2016). What does a priming persepctive reveal about culture: Culture-as-situated cognition. *Current Opinion in Psychology, 12,* 94–99. https://doi.org/doi.org/10.1016/j.copsyc.2016.10.002

Oyserman, D. (2017). Culture three ways: Cultures and subcultures within countries. *Annual Review of Psychology, 68*(15), 1–29.

Payne, V. G., & Isaacs, L. D. (2016). *Human motor development : A lifespan approach.* http://dl.acm.org/citation.cfm?id=1214267

Petranovich, C. L., Smith-Paine, J., Wade, S. L., Yeates, K. O., Taylor, H. G., Stancin, T., & Kurowski, B. G. (2020). From early childhood to adolescence: Lessons about traumatic brain injury from the Ohio head injury outcomes study. *Journal of Head Trauma Rehabilitation, 35*(3), 226–239. https://doi.org/10.1097/HTR.0000000000000555

Pezaro, N., Doody, J. S., & Thompson, M. B. (2017). The ecology and evolution of temperature-dependent reaction norms for sex determination in reptiles: A mechanistic conceptual model. *Biological Reviews, 92*(3), 1348–1364. https://doi.org/10.1111/brv.12285

Pfefferbaum, B., & North, C. S. (2020). Mental health and the Covid-19 pandemic. *New England Journal of Medicine, 383,* 510–512. https://doi.org/10.1056/nejmp2008017

Prusaczyk, B., Cherney, S. M., Carpenter, C. R., & DuBois, J. M. (2017). Informed consent to research with cognitively impaired adults: Transdisciplinary challenges and opportunities. *Clinical Gerontologist, 40*(1), 63–73. https://doi.org/10.1080/07317115.2016.1201714

Ristic, J., & Enns, J. T. (2015). Attentional development. In L. S. Liben & U. Muller (Eds.), *Handbook of child psychology and developmental science* (pp. 1–45). Wiley. https://doi.org/10.1002/9781118963418.childpsy205

Roberts, S. O., Bareket-Shavit, C., Dollins, F. A., Goldie, P. D., & Mortenson, E. (2020). Racial inequality in psychological research: Trends of the past and recommendations for the future. *Perspectives on Psychological Science, 15*(6), 1295–1309. https://doi.org/10.1177/1745691620927709

Rogler, L. H. (2002). Historical generations and psychology: The case of the Great Depression and World War II. *American Psychologist, 57,* 1013–1023.

Rogoff, B. (2016). Culture and participation: A paradigm shift. *Current Opinion in Psychology, 8,* 182–189. https://doi.org/10.1016/j.copsyc.2015.12.002

Rogoff, B., Moore, L. C., Correa-Chavez, M., & Dexter, A. L. (2014). Children develop cultural repertoires through engaging in everyday routines and practices. In J. Grusec & P. Hastings (Eds.), *Handbook of socialization: Theory and research* (pp. 472–498). Guilford.

Rosenthal, L. (2016). Incorporating intersectionality into psychology: An opportunity to promote social justice and equity. *American Psychologist, 71*(6), 474–485. https://doi.org/10.1037/a0040323

Roth-Cline, M., & Nelson, R. M. (2013). Parental permission and child assent in research on children. *The Yale Journal of Biology and Medicine, 86*(3), 291–301. http://www.ncbi.nlm.nih.gov/pubmed/24058304

Roy, A. L. (2018). Intersectional ecologies: Positioning intersectionality in settings-level research. *New Directions for Child and Adolescent Development, 2018*(161), 57–74. https://doi.org/10.1002/cad.20248

Rudman, R., & Titjen, F. (2018). *Language development.* Cambridge University Press.

Rutter, M. (2014). Nature–nurture integration. In M. Lewis & K. D. Rudolph (Eds.), *Handbook of developmental psychopathology* (pp. 45–65). Springer. https://doi.org/10.1007/978-1-4614-9608-3_3

Santos, C. E., & Toomey, R. B. (2018). Integrating an intersectionality lens in theory and research in developmental science. *New Directions for Child and Adolescent Development, 2018*(161), 7–15. https://doi.org/10.1002/cad.20245

Sañudo, B., González-Navarrete, Á., Álvarez-Barbosa, F., de Hoyo, M., Del Pozo, J., & Rogers, M. E. (2019). Effect of flywheel resistance training on balance performance in older adults. A randomized controlled trial. *Journal of Sports Science and Medicine, 18*(2), 344–350. /pmc/articles/PMC6543991/?report=abstract

Sasaki, J. Y., & Kim, H. S. (2017). Nature, nurture, and their interplay. *Journal of Cross-Cultural Psychology, 48*(1), 4–22. https://doi.org/10.1177/0022022116680481

Schwaba, T., & Bleidorn, W. (2018). Individual differences in personality change across the adult life span. *Journal of Personality, 86*(3), 450–484. https://doi.org/10.1111/jopy.12327

Sharkey, J. D., Reed, L. A., & Felix, E. D. (2017). Dating and sexual violence research in the schools: Balancing protection of confidentiality with supporting the welfare of survivors. *American Journal of Community Psychology, 60*(3–4), 361–367. https://doi.org/10.1002/ajcp.12186

Siegler, R. S. (2016). Continuity and change in the field of cognitive development and in the perspectives of one cognitive developmentalist. *Child Development Perspectives, 10*(2), 128–133. https://doi.org/10.1111/cdep.12173

Siekerman, K., Barbu-Roth, M., Anderson, D. I., Donnelly, A., Goffinet, F., & Teulier, C. (2015). Treadmill stimulation improves newborn stepping. *Developmental Psychobiology, 57*(2), 247–254. https://doi.org/10.1002/dev.21270

Simons, S. S. H., Cillessen, A. H. N., & de Weerth, C. (2017). Cortisol stress responses and children's behavioral functioning at school. *Developmental Psychobiology, 59*(2), 217–224. https://doi.org/10.1002/dev.21484

Smith, C. D., & Smith Lee, J. R. (2019). Advancing social justice and affirming humanity in developmental science research with African American boys and young men. *Applied Developmental Science, 24,* 208–214. https://doi.org/10.1080/10888691.2019.1630277

Society for Research in Child Development. (2007). *Ethical standards in research.* http://www.srcd.org/about-us/ethical-standards-research

Society for Research in Child Development. (2021). *Ethical standards in research.* http://www.srcd.org/about-us/ethical-standards-research

Stiles, J., Brown, T. T., Haist, F., & Jernigan, T. L. (2015). Brain and cognitive development. In L. S. Liben & U. Muller (Eds.), *Handbook of child psychology and developmental science* (pp. 1–54). Wiley. https://doi.org/10.1002/9781118963418.childpsy202

Super, C. M. (1981). Cross-cultural research on infancy. In H. C. Triandis & A. Heron (Eds.), *Handbook of cross-cultural psychology: Vol. 4. developmental psychology*. Allyn & Bacon.

Syed, M., & Ajayi, A. A. (2018). Promises and pitfalls in the integration of intersectionality with development science. *New Directions for Child and Adolescent Development, 2018*(161), 109–117. https://doi.org/10.1002/cad.20250

Syed, M., Santos, C., Yoo, H. C., & Juang, L. P. (2018). Invisibility of racial/ethnic minorities in developmental science: Implications for research and institutional practices. *American Psychologist, 73*(6), 812–826. https://doi.org/10.1037/amp0000294

Tait, A. R., & Geisser, M. E. (2017). Development of a consensus operational definition of child assent for research. *BMC Medical Ethics, 18*(1), 41. https://doi.org/10.1186/s12910-017-0199-4

Tamnes, C. K., Overbye, K., Ferschmann, L., Fjell, A. M., Walhovd, K. B., Blakemore, S. J., & Dumontheil, I. (2018). Social perspective taking is associated with self-reported prosocial behavior and regional cortical thickness across adolescence. *Developmental Psychology, 54*(9), 1745–1757. https://doi.org/10.1037/dev0000541

Triebel, K. L., Martin, R. C., Novack, T. A., Dreer, L. E., Turner, C., Kennedy, R., & Marson, D. C. (2014). Recovery over 6 months of medical decision-making capacity after traumatic brain injury. *Archives of Physical Medicine and Rehabilitation, 95*(12), 2296–2303. https://doi.org/10.1016/j.apmr.2014.07.413

Varnum, M. E. W., & Grossmann, I. (2017). Cultural change: The how and the why. *Perspectives on Psychological Science, 12*(6), 956–972. https://doi.org/10.1177/1745691617699971

Vélez-Agosto, N. M., Soto-Crespo, J. G., Vizcarrondo-Oppenheimer, M., Vega-Molina, S., & García Coll, C. (2017). Bronfenbrenner's bioecological theory revision: Moving culture from the macro into the micro. *Perspectives on Psychological Science, 12*(5), 900–910. https://doi.org/10.1177/1745691617704397

Vygotsky, L. S. (1978). *Mind in society: The development of higher psychological processes*. Harvard University Press.

Watson, J. (1925). *Behaviorism*. Norton . Watson *Behaviorism Behaviorism* Norton

Westen, D. (1998). The scientific legacy of Sigmund Freud: Toward a psychodynamically informed psychological science. *Psychological Bulletin, 124*, 333–371.

Wetzel, N., Buttelmann, D., Schieler, A., & Widmann, A. (2016). Infant and adult pupil dilation in response to unexpected sounds. *Developmental Psychobiology, 58*(3), 382–392. https://doi.org/10.1002/dev.21377

Witherington, D. C., & Lickliter, R. (2016). Integrating development and evolution in psychological science: Evolutionary developmental psychology, developmental systems, and explanatory pluralism. *Human Development, 59*(4), 200–234. https://doi.org/10.1159/000450715

Wolf, R. M., & Long, D. (2016). Pubertal development. *Pediatrics in Review, 37*(7), 292–300. https://doi.org/10.1542/pir.2015-0065

Worobey, J. (2014). Physical activity in infancy: Developmental aspects, measurement, and importance. *American Journal of Clinical Nutrition, 99*(3), 729S–733S. https://doi.org/10.3945/ajcn.113.072397

Wortman, J., Lucas, R. E., & Donnellan, M. B. (2012). Stability and change in the big five personality domains: Evidence from a longitudinal study of Australians. *Psychology and Aging, 27*(4), 867–874. https://doi.org/10.1037/a0029322

Yoshikawa, H., Mistry, R., & Wang, Y. (2016). Advancing methods in research on Asian American children and youth. *Child Development, 87*(4), 1033–1050. https://doi.org/10.1111/cdev.12576

Zacher, H., Rudolph, C. W., & Baltes, B. B. (2019). An invitation to lifespan thinking. In B. B. Baltes, C. W. Rudolph, & H. Zacher (Eds.), *Work across the lifespan* (pp. 1–14). Elsevier. https://doi.org/10.1016/B978-0-12-812756-8.00001-3

Zaitchik, D., Iqbal, Y., & Carey, S. (2014). The effect of executive function on biological reasoning in young children: An individual differences study. *Child Development, 85*(1), 160–175. https://doi.org/10.1111/cdev.12145

CHAPTER 2

Abramowicz, J. S. (2019). Ultrasound in reproductive medicine: Is it safe? In L. A. Stadtmauer & I. Tur-Kaspa (Eds.), *Ultrasound imaging in reproductive medicine* (pp. 3–17). Springer International Publishing. https://doi.org/10.1007/978-3-030-16699-1_1

Adams-Chapman, I., Hansen, N. I., Shankaran, S., Bell, E. F., Boghossian, N. S., Murray, J. C., Laptook, A. R., Walsh, M. C., Carlo, W. A., Sánchez, P. J., Van Meurs, K. P., Das, A., Hale, E. C., Newman, N. S., Ball, M. B., Higgins, R. D., & Stoll, B. J. (2013). Ten-year review of major birth defects in VLBW infants. *Pediatrics, 132*(1), 49–61. https://doi.org/10.1542/peds.2012-3111

Aertsen, M., Diogo, M. C., Dymarkowski, S., Deprest, J., & Prayer, D. (2020). Fetal MRI for dummies: What the fetal medicine specialist should know about acquisitions and sequences. *Prenatal Diagnosis, 40*(1), 6–17. https://doi.org/10.1002/pd.5579

Agrawal, A., Rogers, C. E., Lessov-Schlaggar, C. N., Carter, E. B., Lenze, S. N., & Grucza, R. A. (2019). Alcohol, cigarette, and cannabis use between 2002 and 2016 in pregnant women from a nationally representative sample. In *JAMA Pediatrics* (Vol. 173, pp. 95–96). American Medical Association. https://doi.org/10.1001/jamapediatrics.2018.3096

Akolekar, R., Beta, J., Picciarelli, G., Ogilvie, C., & D'Antonio, F. (2015). Procedure-related risk of miscarriage following amniocentesis and chorionic villus sampling: a systematic review and meta-analysis. *Ultrasound in Obstetrics & Gynecology, 45*(1), 16–26. https://doi.org/10.1002/uog.14636

Almeida, J., Bécares, L., Erbetta, K., Bettegowda, V. R., & Ahluwalia, I. B. (2018). Racial/ethnic inequities in low birth weight and preterm birth: The role of multiple forms of stress. *Maternal and Child Health Journal, 22*(8), 1154–1163. https://doi.org/10.1007/s10995-018-2500-7

Alshaarawy, O., Breslau, N., & Anthony, J. C. (2016). Monthly estimates of alcohol drinking during pregnancy: United States, 2002-2011. *Journal of Studies on Alcohol and Drugs, 77*(2), 272–276. https://doi.org/10.15288/JSAD.2016.77.272

Alvarez, A. V. G., Rubin, D., Pina, P., & Velasquez, M. S. (2018). Neurodevelopmental outcomes and prenatal exposure to marijuana. *Pediatrics*, *142*(1 MeetingAbstract), 787–787. https://doi.org/10.1542/PEDS.142.1_MEETINGABSTRACT.787

American College of Obstetricians and Gynecologists. (2011). *Substance abuse reporting and pregnancy: The role of the obstetrician-gynecologist*. http://www.acog.org/~/media/CommitteeOpinions/CommitteeonHealthCarefor UnderservedWomen/co473.pdf?dmc=1&ts=20140604T1051541013

American College of Obstetricians and Gynecologists. (2017). Obstetric analgesia and anesthesia: Practice bulletin no. 177. *Obstetrics & Gynecology*, *129*(4), e73–e89. https://doi.org/10.1097/AOG.0000000000002018

American Medical Association. (2014). *Pregnant women's rights*. http://www.ama-assn.org//ama/pub/physician-resources/legal-topics/litigation-center/case-summaries-topic/pregnant-women s-rights.page

Andescavage, N. N., du Plessis, A., McCarter, R., Serag, A., Evangelou, I., Vezina, G., Robertson, R., & Limperopoulos, C. (2016). Complex Trajectories of brain development in the healthy human fetus. *Cerebral Cortex*, *27*(11), 5274–5283. https://doi.org/10.1093/cercor/bhw306

Antonarakis, S. E., Skotko, B. G., Rafii, M. S., Strydom, A., Pape, S. E., Bianchi, D. W., Sherman, S. L., & Reeves, R. H. (2020). Down syndrome. *Nature Reviews Disease Primers*, *6*(1), 1–20. https://doi.org/10.1038/s41572-019-0143-7

Antonucci, R., Zaffanello, M., Puxeddu, E., Porcella, A., Cuzzolin, L., Dolores Pilloni, M., & Fanos, V. (2012). Use of non-steroidal anti-inflammatory drugs in pregnancy: Impact on the fetus and newborn. *Current Drug Metabolism*, *13*(4), 474–490. https://doi.org/10.2174/138920012800166607

Apgar, V. (1953). A proposal for a new method of evaluation in the newborn infant. *Current Research in Anesthesia and Analgesia*, *32*, 260–267.

Atkins, D. N., & Durrance, C. P. (2020). State policies that treat prenatal substance use as child abuse or neglect fail to achieve their intended goals. *Health Affairs (Project Hope)*, *39*(5), 756–763. https://doi.org/10.1377/hlthaff.2019.00785

Avagliano, L., Massa, V., George, T. M., Qureshy, S., Bulfamante, G. P., & Finnell, R. H. (2019). Overview on neural tube defects: From development to physical characteristics. *Birth Defects Research*, *111*(19), 1455–1467. https://doi.org/10.1002/bdr2.1380

Azuine, R. E., Ji, Y., Chang, H. Y., Kim, Y., Ji, H., Dibari, J., Hong, X., Wang, G., Singh, G. K., Pearson, C., Zuckerman, B., Surkan, P. J., & Wang, X. (2019). Prenatal risk factors and perinatal and postnatal outcomes associated with maternal opioid exposure in an urban, low-income, multiethnic US population. *JAMA Network Open*, *2*(6), e196405–e196405. https://doi.org/10.1001/jamanetworkopen.2019.6405

Bada, H. S., Bann, C. M., Whitaker, T. M., Bauer, C. R., Shankaran, S., Lagasse, L., Lester, B. M., Hammond, J., & Higgins, R. (2012). Protective factors can mitigate behavior problems after prenatal cocaine and other drug exposures. *Pediatrics*, *130*(6), e1479–88. https://doi.org/10.1542/peds.2011-3306

Baer, R. J., Altman, M. R., Oltman, S. P., Ryckman, K. K., Chambers, C. D., Rand, L., & Jelliffe-Pawlowski, L. L. (2018). Maternal factors influencing late entry into prenatal care: A stratified analysis by race or ethnicity and insurance status. *The Journal of Maternal-Fetal & Neonatal Medicine*, *32*, 1–7. https://doi.org/10.1080/14767058.2018.1463366

Bagni, C., & Zukin, R. S. (2019). A Synaptic perspective of fragile X syndrome and autism spectrum disorders. *Neuron*, *101*, 1070–1088. https://doi.org/10.1016/j.neuron.2019.02.041

Baião, R., Fearon, P., Belsky, J., Teixeira, P., Soares, I., & Mesquita, A. (2020). Does 5-HTTLPR moderate the effect of the quality of environmental context on maternal sensitivity? Testing the differential susceptibility hypothesis. *Psychiatric Genetics*, *30*(2), 49–56. https://doi.org/10.1097/YPG.0000000000000247

Bandoli, G., Coles, C. D., Kable, J. A., Wertelecki, W., Yevtushok, L., Zymak-Zakutnya, N., Wells, A., Granovska, I. V., Pashtepa, A. O., & Chambers, C. D. (2019). Patterns of prenatal alcohol use that predict infant growth and development. *Pediatrics*, *143*(2), e20182399. https://doi.org/10.1542/peds.2018-2399

Bazinet, A. D., Squeglia, L., Riley, E., & Tapert, S. F. (2016). In K. J. Sher (Ed.), *Effects of drug exposure on development* (Vol. 1). Oxford University Press. https://doi.org/10.1093/oxfordhb/9780199381708.013.21

Beach, S. R. H., Brody, G. H., Gunter, T. D., Packer, H., Wernett, P., & Philibert, R. A. (2010). Child maltreatment moderates the association of MAOA with symptoms of depression and antisocial personality disorder. *Journal of Family Psychology*, *24*(1), 12–20. https://doi.org/doi: 10.1037/a0018074

Beal, M. A., Yauk, C. L., & Marchetti, F. (2017). From sperm to offspring: Assessing the heritable genetic consequences of paternal smoking and potential public health impacts. *Mutation Research/Reviews in Mutation Research*, *773*, 26–50. https://doi.org/10.1016/J.MRREV.2017.04.001

Benasich, A. A., & Brooks-Gunn, J. (1996). Maternal attitudes and knowledge of child-rearing: Associations with family and child outcomes. *Child Development*, *67*, 1186–1205.

Berlin, I., Golmard, J.-L., Jacob, N., Tanguy, M.-L., & Heishman, S. J. (2017). Cigarette smoking during pregnancy: Do complete abstinence and low level cigarette smoking have similar impact on birth weight? *Nicotine & Tobacco Research*, *19*(5), 518–524. https://doi.org/10.1093/ntr/ntx033

Bibbins-Domingo, K., Grossman, D. C., Curry, S. J., Davidson, K. W., Epling, J. W., Garcia, F. A. R., Kemper, A. R., Krist, A. H., Kurth, A. E., Landefeld, C. S., Mangione, C. M., Phillips, W. R., Phipps, M. G., Pignone, M. P., Silverstein, M., & Tseng, C. W. (2017). Folic acid supplementation for the prevention of neural tube defects US preventive services task force recommendation statement. *JAMA - Journal of the American Medical Association*, *317*, 183–189. https://doi.org/10.1001/jama.2016.19438

Bird, R. J., & Hurren, B. J. (2016). Anatomical and clinical aspects of Klinefelter's syndrome. *Clinical Anatomy*, *29*(5), 606–619. https://doi.org/10.1002/ca.22695

Black, S. E., Bütikofer, A., Devereux, P. J., & Salvanes, K. G. (2019). This is only a test? Long-run and intergenerational impacts of prenatal exposure to radioactive fallout. *Review of Economics and Statistics*, *101*(3), 531–546. https://doi.org/10.1162/rest_a_00815

Blakeney, E. L., Herting, J. R., Bekemeier, B., & Zierler, B. K. (2019). Social determinants of health and disparities in prenatal care utilization during the Great Recession period 2005-2010. *BMC Pregnancy and Childbirth*, *19*(1), 1–20. https://doi.org/10.1186/s12884-019-2486-1

Blau, N. (2016). Genetics of phenylketonuria: Then and now. *Human Mutation*, *37*(6), 508–515. https://doi.org/10.1002/humu.22980

Bonomi, M., Rochira, V., Pasquali, D., Balercia, G., Jannini, E. A., Ferlin, A., & (KING), O. behalf of the K. I. G, . (2017). Klinefelter syndrome (KS): Genetics, clinical phenotype and hypogonadism. *Journal of Endocrinological Investigation*, *40*(2), 123–134. https://doi.org/10.1007/s40618-016-0541-6

Borges, E., Braga, D. P. de A. F., Provenza, R. R., Figueira, R. de C. S., Iaconelli, A., & Setti, A. S. (2018). Paternal lifestyle factors in relation to semen quality and in vitro reproductive outcomes. *Andrologia*, *50*(9), e13090. https://doi.org/10.1111/and.13090

Bošković, A., & Rando, O. J. (2018). Transgenerational epigenetic inheritance. *Annual Review of Genetics*, *52*(1), 21–41. https://doi.org/10.1146/annurev-genet-120417-031404

Bouchard, T. J. (2014). Genes, evolution and intelligence. *Behavior Genetics*, *44*(6), 549–577. https://doi.org/10.1007/s10519-014-9646-x

Boundy, E. O., Dastjerdi, R., Spiegelman, D., Fawzi, W. W., Missmer, S. A. Lieberman, E., Kajeepeta, S., Wall, S., Chan, G. J., Lawn, J., Cousens, S., Zupan, J., Bryce, J., Black, R., Victora, C., Charpak, N., Ruiz, J., Zupan, J., Lawn, J., & ... Guedes, Z. (2015). Kangaroo mother care and neonatal outcomes: A meta-analysis. *Pediatrics*, *365*(9462), 891–900. https://doi.org/10.1542/peds.2015-2238

Bouthry, E., Picone, O., Hamdi, G., Grangeot-Keros, L., Ayoubi, J.-M., & Vauloup-Fellous, C. (2014). Rubella and pregnancy: Diagnosis, management and outcomes. *Prenatal Diagnosis*, *34*(13), 1246–1253. https://doi.org/10.1002/pd.4467

Bralten, J., Klemann, C., Mota, N., Witte, W. D., Arango, C., Fabbri, C., Kas, M., Wee, N., van der Penninx, B., Serretti, A., Franke, B., & Poelmans, G. (2019). Genetic underpinnings of sociability in the UK Biobank. *BioRxiv*, *46*, 1627–1634. https://doi.org/10.1101/781195

Brand, J. S., Gaillard, R., West, J., McEachan, R. R. C., Wright, J., Voerman, E., Felix, J. F., Tilling, K., & Lawlor, D. A. (2019). Associations of maternal quitting, reducing, and continuing smoking during pregnancy with longitudinal fetal growth: Findings from Mendelian randomization and parental negative control studies. *PLOS Medicine*, *16*(11), e1002972. https://doi.org/10.1371/journal.pmed.1002972

Brandt, J. S., Cruz Ithier, M. A., Rosen, T., & Ashkinadze, E. (2019). Advanced paternal age, infertility, and reproductive risks: A review of the literature. *Prenatal Diagnosis*, *39*(2), 81–87. https://doi.org/10.1002/pd.5402

Braun, M., Klingelhöfer, D., Oremek, G. M., Quarcoo, D., & Groneberg, D. A. (2020). Influence of second-hand smoke and prenatal tobacco smoke exposure on biomarkers, genetics and physiological processes in children—an overview in research insights of the last few years. *International Journal of Environmental Research and Public Health*, *17*(9), 3212. https://doi.org/10.3390/ijerph17093212

Braveman, P. A., Heck, K., Egerter, S., Marchi, K. S., Dominguez, T. P., Cubbin, C., Fingar, K., Pearson, J. A., & Curtis, M. (2015). The role of socioeconomic factors in Black-White disparities in preterm birth. *American Journal of Public Health*, *105*(4), 694–702. https://doi.org/10.2105/AJPH.2014.302008

Briley, D. A., Livengood, J., Derringer, J., Tucker-Drob, E. M., Fraley, R. C., & Roberts, B. W. (2019). Interpreting behavior genetic models: seven developmental processes to understand. *Behavior Genetics*, *49*(2), 196–210. https://doi.org/10.1007/s10519-018-9939-6

Brocklehurst, P., Hardy, P., Hollowell, J., Linsell, L., Macfarlane, A., McCourt, C., Marlow, N., Miller, A., Newburn, M., Petrou, S., Puddicombe, D., Redshaw, M., Rowe, R., Sandall, J., Silverton, L., & Stewart, M. (2011). Perinatal and maternal outcomes by planned place of birth for healthy women with low risk pregnancies: The Birthplace in England national prospective cohort study. *BMJ (Clinical Research Ed.)*, *343*, d7400. https://doi.org/10.1136/BMJ.D7400

Brodie, N., Keim, J. L., Silberholz, E. A., Spector, N. D., & Pattishall, A. E. (2019). Promoting resilience in vulnerable populations. *Current Opinion in Pediatrics*, *31*(1), 157–165. https://doi.org/10.1097/MOP.0000000000000722

Brown, Q. L., Sarvet, A. L., Shmulewitz, D., Martins, S. S., Wall, M. M., & Hasin, D. S. (2017). Trends in marijuana use among pregnant and nonpregnant reproductive-aged women, 2002-2014. *JAMA -Jjournal of the American Medical Association*, *317*, 207–209. https://doi.org/10.1001/jama.2016.17383

Bubac, C. M., Miller, J. M., & Coltman, D. W. (2020). The genetic basis of animal behavioural diversity in natural populations. *Molecular Ecology*, *29*(11), 1957–1971. https://doi.org/10.1111/mec.15461

Buckingham-Howes, S., Berger, S. S., Scaletti, L. A., & Black, M. M. (2013). Systematic review of prenatal cocaine exposure and adolescent development. *Pediatrics*, *131*(6), e1917–36. https://doi.org/10.1542/peds.2012-0945

Bull, M. J. (2020). Down syndrome. In A. H. Ropper (Ed.), *New England journal of medicine* (Vol. 382, pp. 2344–2352). Massachussetts Medical Society. https://doi.org/10.1056/NEJMra1706537

Byrd, A. L., & Manuck, S. B. (2014). MAOA, childhood maltreatment, and antisocial behavior: meta-analysis of a gene-environment interaction. *Biological Psychiatry*, *75*(1), 9–17. https://doi.org/10.1016/j.biopsych.2013.05.004

Calhoun, S., Conner, E., Miller, M., & Messina, N. (2015). Improving the outcomes of children affected by parental substance abuse: a review of randomized controlled trials. *Substance Abuse and Rehabilitation*, *6*, 15–24. https://doi.org/10.2147/SAR.S46439

Camerota, M., Willoughby, M. T., Cox, M., & Greenberg, M. (2015). Executive function in low birth weight preschoolers: The moderating effect of parenting. *Journal of Abnormal Child Psychology*, *43*(8), 1551–1562. https://doi.org/10.1007/s10802-015-0032-9

Camp, K. M., Parisi, M. A., Acosta, P. B., Berry, G. T., Bilder, D. A., Blau, N., Bodamer, O. A., Brosco, J. P., Brown, C. S., Burlina, A. B., Burton, B. K., Chang, C. S., Coates, P. M., Cunningham, A. C., Dobrowolski, S. F., Ferguson, J. H., Franklin, T. D., Frazier, D. M., Grange, D. K., & Young, J. M. (2014). Phenylketonuria scientific review conference: State of the science and future research needs. *Molecular Genetics and Metabolism*, *112*(2), 87–122. https://doi.org/10.1016/j.ymgme.2014.02.013

Carlberg, C., & Molnar, F. (2019). *Human epigenetics: How science works*. Springer Publishing Company.

Centers for Disease Control and Prevention. (2019). *Data and statistics on down syndrome | CDC*. https://www.cdc.gov/ncbddd/birthdefects/downsyndrome/data.html

Chakravorty, S., & Williams, T. N. (2015). Sickle cell disease: A neglected chronic disease of increasing global health importance. *Archives of Disease in Childhood*, *100*(1), 48–53. https://doi.org/10.1136/archdischild-2013-303773

Chan, W., Kwok, Y., Choy, K., Leung, T., & Wang, C. (2013). Single fetal cells for non-invasive prenatal genetic diagnosis: Old myths new prospective. *Medical Journal of Obstetrics and Gynecology*, *1*(1), 1004.

Chang, D. S., Lasley, F. D., Das, I. J., Mendonca, M. S., & Dynlacht, J. R. (2014). Radiation effects in the embryo and fetus. In *Basic radiotherapy physics and biology* (pp. 313–316). Springer International Publishing. https://doi.org/10.1007/978-3-319-06841-1_32

Chang, S. M., Grantham-McGregor, S. M., Powell, C. A., Vera-Hernández, M., Lopez-Boo, F., Baker-Henningham, H., Walker, S. P., Hackman, D., Farah, M., Meaney, M., Hertzman, C., Boyce, T., Grantham-McGregor, S., Cheung, Y., Cueto, S., Glewwe, P., Richter, L., Strupp, B., Walker, S., & Aboud, F. (2015). Integrating a parenting intervention with routine primary health care: A cluster randomized trial. *Pediatrics*, *136*(2), 272–280. https://doi.org/10.1542/peds.2015-0119

Charles, E., Hunt, K. A., Harris, C., Hickey, A., & Greenough, A. (2018). Small for gestational age and extremely low birth weight infant outcomes. *Journal of Perinatal Medicine*, *47*(2), 247–251. https://doi.org/10.1515/jpm-2018-0295

Charpak, N., Gabriel Ruiz, J., Zupan, J., Cattaneo, A., Figueroa, Z., Tessier, R., Cristo, M., Anderson, G., Ludington, S., Mendoza, S., Mokhachane, M., & Worku, B. (2005). Kangaroo mother care: 25 years after. *Acta Paediatrica*, *94*(5), 514–522. https://doi.org/10.1111/j.1651-2227.2005.tb01930.x

Chasan-Taber, L., Kini, N., Harvey, M. W., Pekow, P., & Dole, N. (2020). The association between acculturation and prenatal psychosocial stress among latinas. *Journal of Immigrant and Minority Health*, *22*(3), 534–544. https://doi.org/10.1007/s10903-019-00909-2

Chen, L.-W., Wu, Y., Neelakantan, N., Chong, M. F.-F., Pan, A., & van Dam, R. M. (2014). Maternal caffeine intake during pregnancy is associated with risk of low birth weight: A systematic review and dose-response meta-analysis. *BMC Medicine*, *12*(1), 174. https://doi.org/10.1186/s12916-014-0174-6

Chen, L.-W., Wu, Y., Neelakantan, N., Chong, M. F.-F., Pan, A., & van Dam, R. M. (2016). Maternal caffeine intake during pregnancy and risk of pregnancy loss: A categorical and dose–response meta-analysis of prospective studies. *Public Health Nutrition*, *19*(07), 1233–1244. https://doi.org/10.1017/S1368980015002463

Chen, L.-W., Wu, Y., Neelakantan, N., Chong, M. F.-F., Pan, A., van Dam, R. M., Wardlaw, T., Lawn, J., Cousens, S., Zupan, J., Mcmillen, I., Maslova, E., Bhattacharya, S., Lin, S., Michels, K., Eteng, M., Eyong, E., Akpanyung, E., Agiang, M., & Rehm, J. (2014). Maternal caffeine intake during pregnancy is associated with risk of low birth weight: A systematic review and dose-response meta-analysis. *BMC Medicine*, *12*(1), 174. https://doi.org/10.1186/s12916-014-0174-6

Chou, B., Bienstock, J. L., & Satin, A. J. (2020). *The Johns Hopkins manual of gynecology and obstetrics* (B. Chou, Trans.). Wolters Kluwer.

Christ, S. E., Clocksin, H. E., Burton, B. K., Grant, M. L., Waisbren, S., Paulin, M. C., Bilder, D. A., White, D. A., & Saville, C. (2020). Executive function in phenylketonuria (PKU): Insights from the behavior rating inventory of executive function (BRIEF) and a large sample of individuals with PKU. *Neuropsychology*. https://doi.org/10.1037/neu0000625

Church, J. S., Chace-Donahue, F., Blum, J. L., Ratner, J. R., Zelikoff, J. T., & Schwartzer, J. J. (2020). Neuroinflammatory and behavioral outcomes measured in adult offspring of mice exposed prenatally to E-cigarette aerosols. *Environmental Health Perspectives*, *128*(4), 047006. https://doi.org/10.1289/EHP6067

Cicchetti, D., Rogosch, F. A., & Sturge-Apple, M. L. (2007). Interactions of child maltreatment and serotonin transporter and monoamine oxidase a polymorphisms: Depressive symptomatology among adolescents from low socioeconomic status backgrounds. *Development and Psychopathology*, *19*(4), 1161–1180. https://doi.org/10.1017/S0954579407000600

Cicchetti, D., & Toth, S. L. (2015). Child maltreatment. In M. E. Lamb (Ed.), *Handbook of child psychology and developmental science* (Vol. 3, pp. 1–51). John Wiley & Sons, Inc. https://doi.org/10.1002/9781118963418.childpsy313

Conradt, E., Flannery, T., Aschner, J. L., Annett, R. D., Croen, L. A., Duarte, C. S., Friedman, A. M., Guille, C., Hedderson, M. M., Hofheimer, J. A., Jones, M. R., Ladd-Acosta, C., McGrath, M., Moreland, A., Neiderhiser, J. M., Nguyen, R. H. N., Posner, J., Ross, J. L., Savitz, D. A., & Lester, B. M. (2019). Prenatal opioid exposure: Neurodevelopmental consequences and future research priorities. *Pediatrics*, *144*(3), e20190128. https://doi.org/10.1542/peds.2019-0128

Corrigall, K. A., & Schellenberg, E. G. (2015). Predicting who takes music lessons: parent and child characteristics. *Frontiers in Psychology*, *6*, 282. https://doi.org/10.3389/fpsyg.2015.00282

Croke, K., Ishengoma, D. S., Francis, F., Makani, J., Kamugisha, M. L., Lusingu, J., Lemnge, M., Larreguy, H., Fink, G., & Mmbando, B. P. (2017). Relationships between sickle cell trait, malaria, and educational outcomes in Tanzania. *BMC Infectious Diseases*, *17*(1), 568. https://doi.org/10.1186/s12879-017-2644-x

Culen, C., Ertl, D.-A., Schubert, K., Bartha-Doering, L., & Haeusler, G. (2017). Care of girls and women with Turner syndrome: beyond growth and hormones. *Endocrine Connections*, *6*(4), R39–R51. https://doi.org/10.1530/EC-17-0036

Daniels, P., Noe, G. F., & Mayberry, R. (2006). Barriers to prenatal care among black women of low socioeconomic status. *American Journal of Health Behavior*, *30*(2), 188–198.

Davis, S. M., Soares, K., Howell, S., Cree-Green, M., Buyers, E., Johnson, J., & Tartaglia, N. R. (2020). Diminished ovarian reserve in girls and adolescents with trisomy x syndrome. *Reproductive Sciences*, *27*, 1–7. https://doi.org/10.1007/s43032-020-00216-4

Deaton, A. E., Sheiner, E., Wainstock, T., Landau, D., & Walfisch, A. (2017). 613: Does lack of prenatal care predict later lack of child care? *American Journal of Obstetrics and Gynecology*, *216*(1), S359–S360. https://doi.org/10.1016/j.ajog.2016.11.347

Declercq, E. R., Sakala, C., Corry, M. P., Applebaum, S., & Herrlich, A. (2014). Major survey findings of listening to mothers(SM) III: Pregnancy and birth: Report of the third national U.S. survey of women's childbearing experiences. *The Journal of Perinatal Education*, *23*(1), 9–16. https://doi.org/10.1891/1058-1243.23.1.9

de Graaf, G., Buckley, F., Dever, J., & Skotko, B. G. (2017). Estimation of live birth and population prevalence of Down syndrome in nine U.S. states. *American Journal of Medical Genetics Part A*, *173*(10), 2710–2719. https://doi.org/10.1002/ajmg.a.38402

Dejong, K., Olyaei, A., & Lo, J. O. (2019). Alcohol use in pregnancy. *Clinical Obstetrics and Gynecology*, *62*(1), 142–155. https://doi.org/10.1097/GRF.0000000000000414

de Jonge, A., Geerts, C., van der Goes, B., Mol, B., Buitendijk, S., & Nijhuis, J. (2015). Perinatal mortality and morbidity up to 28days after birth among 743070 low-risk planned home and hospital births: a cohort study based on three merged national perinatal databases. *BJOG: An International Journal of Obstetrics & Gynaecology*, *122*(5), 720–728. https://doi.org/10.1111/1471-0528.13084

DeSocio, J. E. (2018). Epigenetics, maternal prenatal psychosocial stress, and infant mental health. *Archives of Psychiatric Nursing*, *32*(6), 901–906. https://doi.org/10.1016/j.apnu.2018.09.001

Diamandopoulos, K., & Green, J. (2018). Down syndrome: An integrative review. *Journal of Neonatal Nursing*, *24*(5), 235–241. https://doi.org/10.1016/J.JNN.2018.01.001

Dodge, K. A., & Rutter, M. (2011). Gene–environment interactions in developmental psychopathology. In K. A. Dodge & M. Rutter (Eds.), *Gene–environment interactions in developmental psychopathology*. Guilford Press.

Doherty, B. R., & Scerif, G. (2017). Genetic syndromes and developmental risk for autism spectrum and attention deficit hyperactivity disorders: Insights from fragile X syndrome. *Child Development Perspectives*, *11*(3), 161–166. https://doi.org/10.1111/cdep.12227

d'Oiron, R. (2019). Carriers of hemophilia A and hemophilia B. In R. A. Kadir, P. D. James, & C. A. Lee (Eds.), *Inherited bleeding disorders in women 2e* (pp. 65–82). : John Wiley & Sons, Ltd. https://doi.org/10.1002/9781119426080.ch5

Donnan, J., Walsh, S., Sikora, L., Morrissey, A., Collins, K., & MacDonald, D. (2017). A systematic review of the risks factors associated with the onset and natural progression of spina bifida. *NeuroToxicology*, *61*, 20–31. https://doi.org/10.1016/J.NEURO.2016.03.008

dos Santos, J. F., de Melo Bastos Cavalcante, C., Barbosa, F. T., Gitaí, D. L. G., Duzzioni, M., Tilelli, C. Q., Shetty, A. K., & de Castro, O. W. (2018). Maternal, fetal and neonatal consequences associated with the use of crack cocaine during the gestational period: a systematic review and meta-analysis. *Archives of Gynecology and Obstetrics*, *298*, 487–503. https://doi.org/10.1007/s00404-018-4833-2

Dubois, L., Ohm Kyvik, K., Girard, M., Tatone-Tokuda, F., Pérusse, D., Hjelmborg, J., Skytthe, A., Rasmussen, F., Wright, M. J., Lichtenstein, P., & Martin, N. G. (2012). Genetic and environmental contributions to weight, height, and BMI from birth to 19 years of age: an international study of over 12,000 twin pairs. *PloS One*, *7*(2), e30153. https://doi.org/10.1371/journal.pone.0030153

Durkin, M. S., Benedict, R. E., Christensen, D., Dubois, L. A., Fitzgerald, R. T., Kirby, R. S., Maenner, M. J., Van Naarden Braun, K., Wingate, M. S., & Yeargin-Allsopp, M. (2016). Prevalence of cerebral palsy among 8-year-old children in 2010 and preliminary evidence of trends in its relationship to low birthweight. *Paediatric and Perinatal Epidemiology*, *30*(5), 496–510. https://doi.org/10.1111/ppe.12299

Eckerman, C. O., Hsu, H. C., Molitor, A., Leung, E. H. L., & Goldstein, R. F. (1999). Infant arousal as an en-face exchange with a new partner: Effects of prematurity and perinatal biological risk. *Developmental Psychology*, *35*, 282–293.

El Marroun, H., Brown, Q. L., Lund, I. O., Coleman-Cowger, V. H., Loree, A. M., Chawla, D., & Washio, Y. (2018). An epidemiological, developmental and clinical overview of cannabis use during pregnancy. *Preventive Medicine*, *116*, 1–5. https://doi.org/10.1016/J.YPMED.2018.08.036

Erlich, K. J. (2019). Case report: Neuropsychiatric symptoms in PKU disease. *Journal of Pediatric Health Care*, *33*(6), 718–721. https://doi.org/10.1016/j.pedhc.2019.02.007

Eryigit Madzwamuse, S., Baumann, N., Jaekel, J., Bartmann, P., & Wolke, D. (2015). Neuro-cognitive performance of very preterm or very low birth weight adults at 26 years. *Journal of Child Psychology and Psychiatry*, *56*(8), 857–864. https://doi.org/10.1111/jcpp.12358

Estill, M. S., & Krawetz, S. A. (2016). The epigenetic consequences of paternal exposure to environmental contaminants and reproductive toxicants. *Current Environmental Health Reports*, *3*(3), 202–213. https://doi.org/10.1007/s40572-016-0101-4

Fergusson, D. M., Boden, J. M., Horwood, L. J., Miller, A. L., & Kennedy, M. A. (2011). MAOA, abuse exposure and antisocial behaviour: 30-year longitudinal study. *The British Journal of Psychiatry : The Journal of Mental Science*, *198*(6), 457–463. https://doi.org/10.1192/bjp.bp.110.086991

Finegold, D. N. (2019). Overview of genetics - special subjects - merck manuals professional edition. In *Merck manual*. Merck. https://www.merckmanuals.com/professional/special-subjects/general-principles-of-medical-genetics/overview-of-genetics

Flint, J., Greenspan, R. J., & Kendler, K. S. (2020). *How genes influence behavior 2e* (J. Flint, R. J. Greenspan, & K. S. Kendler, Trans.). Oxford University Press. https://global.oup.com/academic/product/how-genes-influence-behavior-2e-9780198716877?cc=us&lang=en&

Ford, S., O'Driscoll, M., & MacDonald, A. (2018). Living with phenylketonuria: Lessons from the PKU community. *Molecular Genetics and Metabolism Reports*, *17*, 57–63. https://doi.org/10.1016/j.ymgmr.2018.10.002

Fowler-Finn, K. D., & Boutwell, B. (2019). Using variation in heritability estimates as a test of G × E in behavioral research: A brief research note. *Behavior Genetics*, *49*(3), 340–346. https://doi.org/10.1007/s10519-019-09948-9

Fracasso, M. P., & Busch-Rossnagel, N. A. (1992). Children and parents of Hispanic origin. In M. E. Procidano & C. B. Fisher (Eds.), *Families: A handbook for school professionals* (pp. 83–98). Teachers College Press.

Franz, A. P., Bolat, G. U., Bolat, H., Matijasevich, A., Santos, I. S., Silveira, R. C., Procianoy, R. S., Rohde, L. A., & Moreira-Maia, C. R. (2018). Attention-deficit/hyperactivity disorder and very preterm/very low birth weight: A meta-analysis. *Pediatrics*, *141*, 20171645. https://doi.org/10.1542/peds.2017-1645

Frederiksen, L. E., Ernst, A., Brix, N., Braskhøj Lauridsen, L. L., Roos, L., Ramlau-Hansen, C. H., & Ekelund, C. K. (2018). Risk of adverse pregnancy outcomes at advanced maternal age. *Obstetrics & Gynecology*, *131*(3), 457–463. https://doi.org/10.1097/AOG.0000000000002504

Froggatt, S., Covey, J., & Reissland, N. (2020). Infant neurobehavioural consequences of prenatal cigarette exposure: A systematic review and meta-analysis. *Acta Paediatrica*, *109*(6), 1112–1124. https://doi.org/10.1111/apa.15132

Fryer, K., Munoz, M. C., Rahangdale, L., & Stuebe, A. M. (2021). Multiparous black and latinx women face more barriers to prenatal care than white women. *Journal of Racial and Ethnic Health Disparities*, *8*, 80–87. https://doi.org/10.1007/s40615-020-00759-x

Gabbe, S. G., Niebyl, J., Simpson, J., Landon, M., Galan, H., Jauniaux, E., Driscoll, D., Berghella, V., & Grobman, W. (2016). *Obstetrics : Normal and problem pregnancies*. Elsevier.

Gardon, L., Picciolini, O., Squarza, C., Frigerio, A., Giannì, M. L., Gangi, S., Fumagalli, M., & Mosca, F. (2019). Neurodevelopmental outcome and adaptive behaviour in extremely low birth weight infants at 2 years of corrected age. *Early Human Development*, *128*, 81–85. https://doi.org/10.1016/j.earlhumdev.2018.12.013

Georgsdottir, I., Haraldsson, A., & Dagbjartsson, A. (2013). Behavior and well-being of extremely low birth weight teenagers in Iceland. *Early Human Development*, *89*(12), 999–1003. https://doi.org/10.1016/j.earlhumdev.2013.08.018

Ghosh, R., & Tabrizi, S. J. (2018). Huntington disease. In *Handbook of clinical neurology* (Vol. 147, pp. 255–278). Elsevier B.V. https://doi.org/10.1016/B978-0-444-63233-3.00017-8

Glover, V., & Capron, L. (2017). Prenatal parenting. *Current Opinion in Psychology*, *15*, 66–70. https://doi.org/10.1016/j.copsyc.2017.02.007

Gong, L., Parikh, S., Rosenthal, P. J., & Greenhouse, B. (2013). Biochemical and immunological mechanisms by which sickle cell trait protects against malaria. *Malaria Journal*, *12*, 317. https://doi.org/10.1186/1475-2875-12-317

Goodarzi, M. O. (2018). Genetics of obesity: What genetic association studies have taught us about the biology of obesity and its complications. *The Lancet Diabetes & Endocrinology*, *6*(3), 223–236. https://doi.org/10.1016/S2213-8587(17)30200-0

Grant, K. S., Petroff, R., Isoherranen, N., Stella, N., & Burbacher, T. M. (2018). Cannabis use during pregnancy: Pharmacokinetics and effects on child development. *Pharmacology & Therapeutics*, *182*, 133–151. https://doi.org/10.1016/J.PHARMTHERA.2017.08.014

Gravholt, C. H., Chang, S., Wallentin, M., Fedder, J., Moore, P., & Skakkebæk, A. (2018). Klinefelter syndrome: Integrating genetics, neuropsychology, and endocrinology. *Endocrine Reviews*, *39*(4), 389–423. https://doi.org/10.1210/er.2017-00212

Gravholt, C. H., Viuff, M. H., Brun, S., Stochholm, K., & Andersen, N. H. (2019). Turner syndrome: mechanisms andmanagement. In *Nature reviews endocrinology* (Vol. 15, pp. 601–614). Nature Publishing Group. https://doi.org/10.1038/s41574-019-0224-4

Greene, R. M., & Pisano, M. M. (2019). Developmental toxicity of e-cigarette aerosols. *Birth Defects Research*, *111*(17), 1294–1301. https://doi.org/10.1002/bdr2.1571

Gregg, A. R., Gross, S. J., Best, R. G., Monaghan, K. G., Bajaj, K., Skotko, B. G., Thompson, B. H., & Watson, M. S. (2013). ACMG statement on noninvasive prenatal screening for fetal aneuploidy. *Genetics in Medicine*, *15*(5), 395–398. https://doi.org/10.1038/gim.2013.29

Grewen, K., Burchinal, M., Vachet, C., Gouttard, S., Gilmore, J. H., Lin, W., Johns, J., Elam, M., & Gerig, G. (2014). Prenatal cocaine effects on brain structure in early infancy. *NeuroImage*, *101*, 114–123. https://doi.org/10.1016/J.NEUROIMAGE.2014.06.070

Griffiths, P. D., Bradburn, M., Campbell, M. J., Cooper, C. L., Graham, R., Jarvis, D., Kilby, M. D., Mason, G., Mooney, C., Robson, S. C., & Wailoo, A. (2017). Use of MRI in the diagnosis of fetal brain abnormalities in utero (MERIDIAN): a multicentre, prospective cohort study. *The Lancet*, *389*(10068), 538–546. https://doi.org/10.1016/S0140-6736(16)31723-8

Grotegut, C. A., Chisholm, C. A., Johnson, L. N. C., Brown, H. L., Heine, R. P., & James, A. H. (2014). Medical and obstetric complications among pregnant women aged 45 and older. *PloS One*, *9*(4), e96237. https://doi.org/10.1371/journal.pone.0096237

Grover, M. M., & Jenkins, T. G. (2020). Transgenerational epigenetics: A window into paternal health influences on offspring. In *Urologic clinics of North America* (Vol. 47, pp. 219–225). W.B. Saunders. https://doi.org/10.1016/j.ucl.2019.12.010

Gupta, K. K., Gupta, V. K., & Shirasaka, T. (2016). An update on fetal alcohol syndrome-pathogenesis, risks, and treatment. *Alcoholism: Clinical and Experimental Research*, *40*(8), 1594–1602. https://doi.org/10.1111/acer.13135

Guttmacher Institute. (2020). *Substance use during pregnancy*. https://www.guttmacher.org/state-policy/explore/substance-use-during-pregnancy

Hacker, N. F., Gambone, J. C., & Hobel, C. J. (2016). *Hacker & Moore's essentials of obstetrics and gynecology*. Elsevier.

Hagerman, R. J., Berry-Kravis, E., Hazlett, H. C., Bailey, D. B., Moine, H., Kooy, R. F., Tassone, F., Gantois, I., Sonenberg, N., Mandel, J. L., & Hagerman, P. J. (2017). Fragile X syndrome. *Nature Reviews Disease Primers*, *3*, 17065. https://doi.org/10.1038/nrdp.2017.65

Hamilton, B. E., Martin, J. A., Osterman, M. J. K., & Rossen, L. M. (2018). *Births: Provisional data for 2018*. https://www.cdc.gov/nchs/products/index.htm.

Hamilton, B. E., Martin, J. A., Osterman, M. J. K. S., Driscoll, A. K., & Rossen, L. M. (2017). *Vital statistics rapid release births: Provisional data for 2016*. Vital Statistics Rapid Release. https://www.cdc.gov/nchs/data/vsrr/report002.pdf

Han, C., & Hong, Y. C. (2019). Fetal and childhood malnutrition during the Korean War and metabolic syndrome in adulthood. *Nutrition*, *62*, 186–193. https://doi.org/10.1016/j.nut.2019.01.003

Hartman, S., Eilertsen, E. M., Ystrom, E., Belsky, J., & Gjerde, L. C. (2020). Does prenatal stress amplify effects of postnatal maternal depressive and anxiety symptoms on child problem behavior? *Developmental Psychology*, *56*(1), 128–137. https://doi.org/10.1037/dev0000850

Hartwig, T. S., Ambye, L., Sørensen, S., & Jørgensen, F. S. (2017). Discordant non-invasive prenatal testing (NIPT) - a systematic review. *Prenatal Diagnosis*, *37*(6), 527–539. https://doi.org/10.1002/pd.5049

Hawks, Z. W., Strube, M. J., Johnson, N. X., Grange, D. K., & White, D. A. (2018). Developmental trajectories of executive and verbal processes in children with phenylketonuria. *Developmental Neuropsychology, 43*(3), 207–218. https://doi.org/10.1080/87565641.2018.1438439

Hazlett, H. C., Hammer, J., Hooper, S. R., & Kamphaus, R. W. (2011). Down syndrome. In S. Goldstein & C. R. Reynolds (Eds.), *Handbook of neurodevelopmental and genetic disorders in children* (2nd ed., pp. 362–381). Guilford Press.

He, Y., Chen, J., Zhu, L.-H., Hua, L.-L., & Ke, F.-F. (2017). Maternal smoking during pregnancy and ADHD. *Journal of Attention Disorders*, 108705471769676. https://doi.org/10.1177/1087054717696766

Heaman, M. I., Sword, W., Elliott, L., Moffatt, M., Helewa, M. E., Morris, H., Gregory, P., Tjaden, L., Cook, C., Chalmers, B., Mangiaterra, V., Porter, R., D'Ascoli, P., Alexander, G., Petersen, D., Kogan, M., Heaman, M., Green, C., Newburn-Cook, C., & Brown, J. (2015). Barriers and facilitators related to use of prenatal care by inner-city women: perceptions of health care providers. *BMC Pregnancy and Childbirth, 15*(1), 2. https://doi.org/10.1186/s12884-015-0431-5

Hentges, R. F., Graham, S. A., Plamondon, A., Tough, S., & Madigan, S. (2019). A developmental cascade from prenatal stress to child internalizing and externalizing problems. *Journal of Pediatric Psychology, 44*(9), 1057–1067. https://doi.org/10.1093/JPEPSY/JSZ044

Hepper, P. (2015). Behavior during the prenatal period: Adaptive for development and survival. *Child Development Perspectives, 9*(1), 38–43. https://doi.org/10.1111/cdep.12104

Herati, A. S., Zhelyazkova, B. H., Butler, P. R., & Lamb, D. J. (2017). Age-related alterations in the genetics and genomics of the male germ line. *Fertility and Sterility, 107*(2), 319–323. https://doi.org/10.1016/J.FERTNSTERT.2016.12.021

Herrera-Gómez, A., Luna-Bertos, E. De., Ramos-Torrecillas, J., Ocaña-Peinado, F. M., García-Martínez, O., & Ruiz, C. (2017). The effect of epidural analgesia alone and in association with other variables on the risk of cesarean section. *Biological Research For Nursing, 19*(4), 393–398. https://doi.org/10.1177/1099800417706023

Hoerr, J. J., Heard, A. M., Baker, M. M., Fogel, J., Glassgow, A. E., Kling, W. C., Clark, M. D., & Ronayne, J. P. (2018). Substance-exposed newborn infants and public health law: Differences in addressing the legal mandate to report. *Child Abuse and Neglect, 81*, 206–213. https://doi.org/10.1016/j.chiabu.2018.04.021

Hofman, D. L., Champ, C. L., Lawton, C. L., Henderson, M., & Dye, L. (2018). A systematic review of cognitive functioning in early treated adults with phenylketonuria. In *Orphanet journal of rare diseases* (Vol. 13, pp. 1–19). BioMed Central Ltd. https://doi.org/10.1186/s13023-018-0893-4

Hoggatt, K. J., Flores, M., Solorio, R., Wilhelm, M., & Ritz, B. (2012). The "Latina Epidemiologic Paradox" revisited: The role of birthplace and acculturation in predicting infant low birth weight for latinas in Los Angeles, CA. *Journal of Immigrant and Minority Health, 14*(5), 875–884. https://doi.org/10.1007/s10903-011-9556-4

Homola, W., & Zimmer, M. (2019). Safety of amniocentesis in normal pregnancies and pregnancies considered high-risk due to fetal genetic anomalies – an observational study. *Clinical and Experimental Obstetrics and Gynecology, 46*(3), 403–407. https://doi.org/10.12891/ceog4713.2019

Howe, T.-H., Sheu, C.-F., Wang, T.-N., & Hsu, Y.-W. (2014). Parenting stress in families with very low birth weight preterm infants in early infancy. *Research in Developmental Disabilities, 35*(7), 1748–1756. https://doi.org/10.1016/j.ridd.2014.02.015

Hoyme, H. E., Kalberg, W. O., Elliott, A. J., Blankenship, J., Buckley, D., Marais, A.-S., Manning, M. A., Robinson, L. K., Adam, M. P., Abdul-Rahman, O., Jewett, T., Coles, C. D., Chambers, C., Jones, K. L., Adnams, C. M., Shah, P. E., Riley, E. P., Charness, M. E., Warren, K. R., & May, P. A. (2016). Updated clinical guidelines for diagnosing fetal alcohol spectrum disorders. *Pediatrics, 138*(2), e20154256. https://doi.org/10.1542/peds.2015-4256

Hui, K., Angelotta, C., & Fisher, C. E. (2017). Criminalizing substance use in pregnancy: misplaced priorities. *Addiction, 112*(7), 1123–1125. https://doi.org/10.1111/add.13776

Hutchinson, E. A., De Luca, C. R., Doyle, L. W., Roberts, G., Anderson, P. J., & Victorian Infant Collaborative Study Group, for the V. I. C. S. (2013). School-age outcomes of extremely preterm or extremely low birth weight children. *Pediatrics, 131*(4), e1053–1061. https://doi.org/10.1542/peds.2012-2311

Jaekel, J., Baumann, N., Bartmann, P., & Wolke, D. (2018). Mood and anxiety disorders in very preterm/very low-birth weight individuals from 6 to 26 years. *Journal of Child Psychology and Psychiatry, 59*(1), 88–95. https://doi.org/10.1111/jcpp.12787

Jahja, R., Huijbregts, S. C. J., de Sonneville, L. M. J., van der Meere, J. J., Legemaat, A. M., Bosch, A. M., Hollak, C. E. M., Rubio-Gozalbo, M. E., Brouwers, M. C. G. J., Hofstede, F. C., de Vries, M. C., Janssen, M. C. H., van der Ploeg, A. T., Langendonk, J. G., & van Spronsen, F. J. (2017). Cognitive profile and mental health in adult phenylketonuria: A PKU-COBESO study. *Neuropsychology, 31*(4), 437–447. https://doi.org/10.1037/neu0000358

Jean, A. D. L., & Stack, D. M. (2012). Full-term and very-low-birth-weight preterm infants' self-regulating behaviors during a still-face interaction: Influences of maternal touch. *Infant Behavior and Development, 35*(4), 779–791. https://doi.org/10.1016/j.infbeh.2012.07.023

Jefferies, A. L. (2012). Kangaroo care for the preterm infant and family. *Paediatrics & Child Health, 17*(3), 141–146. http://www.pubmedcentral.nih.gov/articlerender.fcgi?artid=3287094&tool=pmcentrez&rendertype=abstract

Jelenkovic, A., Sund, R., Hur, Y.-M., Yokoyama, Y., Hjelmborg, J. v. B., Möller, S., Honda, C., Magnusson, P. K. E., Pedersen, N. L., Ooki, S., Aaltonen, S., Stazi, M. A., Fagnani, C., D'Ippolito, C., Freitas, D. L., Maia, J. A., Ji, F., Ning, F., Pang, Z., & Silventoinen, K. (2016). Genetic and environmental influences on height from infancy to early adulthood: An individual-based pooled analysis of 45 twin cohorts. *Scientific Reports, 6*(1), 28496, . https://doi.org/10.1038/srep28496

Jha, A. K., Baliga, S., Kumar, H. H., Rangnekar, A., & Baliga, B. S. (2015). Is there a preventive role for vernix caseosa? An invitro study. *Journal of Clinical and Diagnostic Research : JCDR, 9*(11), SC13–6. https://doi.org/10.7860/JCDR/2015/14740.6784

Jones, L., Rowe, J., & Becker, T. (2009). Appraisal, coping, and social support as predictors of psychological distress and parenting efficacy in parents of premature infants. *Children's Health Care, 38*(4), 245–262. https://doi.org/10.1080/02739610903235976

Joubert, B. R., Felix, J. F., Yousefi, P., Bakulski, K. M., Just, A. C., Breton, C., Reese, S. E., Markunas, C. A., Richmond, R. C., Xu, C.-J., Küpers, L. K., Oh, S. S., Hoyo, C., Gruzieva, O., Söderhäll, C., Salas, L. A., Baïz, N., Zhang, H., Lepeule, J., & London, S. J. (2016). DNA methylation in newborns and maternal smoking in pregnancy: Genome-wide consortium meta-analysis. *The American Journal of Human Genetics*, *98*(4), 680–696. https://doi.org/10.1016/J.AJHG.2016.02.019

Jouhki, M.-R., Suominen, T., & Åstedt-Kurki, P. (2017). Giving birth on our own terms-Women's experience of childbirth at home. *Midwifery*, *53*, 35–41. https://doi.org/10.1016/j.midw.2017.07.008

Juárez, S. P., & Merlo, J. (2013). Revisiting the effect of maternal smoking during pregnancy on offspring birthweight: A quasi-experimental sibling analysis in Sweden. *PloS One*, *8*(4), e61734. https://doi.org/10.1371/journal.pone.0061734

Juul, A., Aksglaede, L., Bay, K., Grigor, K. M., & Skakkebæk, N. E. (2011). Klinefelter syndrome: The forgotten syndrome. *Acta Paediatrica*, *100*(6), 791–792. https://doi.org/10.1111/j.1651-2227.2011.02283.x

Kaiser, L., Allen, L., & American Dietetic Association. (2008). Position of the American Dietetic association: Nutrition and lifestyle for a healthy pregnancy outcome. *Journal of the American Dietetic Association*, *108*(3), 553–561. https://doi.org/10.1016/j.jada.2008.01.030

Kaminen-Ahola, N. (2020). Fetal alcohol spectrum disorders: Genetic and epigenetic mechanisms. *Prenatal Diagnosis*, *40*, d.5731. https://doi.org/10.1002/pd.5731

Kang, H.-K. (2014). Influence of culture and community perceptions on birth and perinatal care of immigrant women: doulas' perspective. *The Journal of Perinatal Education*, *23*(1), 25–32. https://doi.org/10.1891/1058-1243.23.1.25

Kapoor, A., Lubach, G. R., Ziegler, T. E., & Coe, C. L. (2016). Hormone levels in neonatal hair reflect prior maternal stress exposure during pregnancy. *Psychoneuroendocrinology*, *66*, 111–117. https://doi.org/10.1016/j.psyneuen.2016.01.010

Kaufmann, W. E., Kidd, S. A., Andrews, H. F., Budimirovic, D. B., Esler, A., Haas-Givler, B., Stackhouse, T., Riley, C., Peacock, G., Sherman, S. L., Brown, W. T., & Berry-Kravis, E. (2017). Autism spectrum disorder in fragile X syndrome: Cooccurring conditions and current treatment. *Pediatrics*, *139*(Suppl 3), S194–S206. https://doi.org/10.1542/peds.2016-1159F

Kaur, G., Begum, R., Thota, S., & Batra, S. (2019). A systematic review of smoking-related epigenetic alterations. *Archives of Toxicology*, *93*, 2715–2740. https://doi.org/10.1007/s00204-019-02562-y

Kenny, L. C., Lavender, T., McNamee, R., O'Neill, S. M., Mills, T., & Khashan, A. S. (2013). Advanced maternal age and adverse pregnancy outcome: evidence from a large contemporary cohort. *PloS One*, *8*(2), e56583. https://doi.org/10.1371/journal.pone.0056583

Khalil, A., Syngelaki, A., Maiz, N., Zinevich, Y., & Nicolaides, K. H. (2013). Maternal age and adverse pregnancy outcome: A cohort study. *Ultrasound in Obstetrics & Gynecology: The Official Journal of the International Society of Ultrasound in Obstetrics and Gynecology*, *42*(6), 634–643. https://doi.org/10.1002/uog.12494

Kim, S., Fleisher, B., & Sun, J. Y. (2017). The long-term health effects of fetal malnutrition: Evidence from the 1959-1961 China great leap forward famine. *Health Economics*, *26*(10), 1264–1277. https://doi.org/10.1002/hec.3397

Klein, K. O., Rosenfield, R. L., Santen, R. J., Gawlik, A. M., Backeljauw, P., Gravholt, C. H., Sas, T. C. J., & Mauras, N. (2020). Estrogen replacement in turner syndrome. In P. Y. Fechner (Ed.), *Turner syndrome* (pp. 93–122). Springer International Publishing. https://doi.org/10.1007/978-3-030-34150-3_5

Knafo, A., & Jaffee, S. R. (2013). Gene–environment correlation in developmental psychopathology. *Development and Psychopathology*, *25*(01), 1–6. https://doi.org/10.1017/S0954579412000855

Knopik, V. S., Neiderhiser, J. M., DeFries, J. C., & Plomin, R. (2017). *Behavioral genetics*. Macmillan Higher Education.

Kondracki, A. J. (2019). Prevalence and patterns of cigarette smoking before and during early and late pregnancy according to maternal characteristics: The first national data based on the 2003 birth certificate revision, United States, 2016. *Reproductive Health*, *16*(1), 142. https://doi.org/10.1186/s12978-019-0807-5

Kozhimannil, K. B., Dowd, W. N., Ali, M. M., Novak, P., & Chen, J. (2019). Substance use disorder treatment admissions and state-level prenatal substance use policies: Evidence from a national treatment database. *Addictive Behaviors*, *90*, 272–277. https://doi.org/10.1016/j.addbeh.2018.11.019

Kozhimannil, K. B., Hardeman, R. R., Alarid-Escudero, F., Vogelsang, C. A., Blauer-Peterson, C., & Howell, E. A. (2016). Modeling the cost-effectiveness of doula care associated with reductions in preterm birth and cesarean delivery. *Birth*, *43*(1), 20–27. https://doi.org/10.1111/birt.12218

Lau, R., & Morse, C. A. (2003). Stress experiences of parents with premature infants in a special care nursery. *Stress and Health*, *19*, 69–78.

Lee, S. J., Bora, S., Austin, N. C., Westerman, A., & Henderson, J. M. T. (2020). Neurodevelopmental outcomes of children born to opioid-dependent mothers: A systematic review and meta-analysis. *Academic Pediatrics*, *20*, 308–318. https://doi.org/10.1016/j.acap.2019.11.005

Legoff, L., D'Cruz, S. C., Tevosian, S., Primig, M., & Smagulova, F. (2019). Transgenerational inheritance of environmentally induced epigenetic alterations during mammalian development. *Cells*, *8*(12), 1559. https://doi.org/10.3390/cells8121559

Lerner, R. M., & Overton, W. F. (2017). Reduction to absurdity: Why epigenetics invalidates all models involving genetic reduction. *Human Development*, *60*(2–3), 107–123. https://doi.org/10.1159/000477995

Lester, B. M., Conradt, E., & Marsit, C. (2016). Introduction to the special section on epigenetics. *Child Development*, *87*(1), 29–37. https://doi.org/10.1111/cdev.12489

Levine, T. A., & Woodward, L. J. (2018). Early inhibitory control and working memory abilities of children prenatally exposed to methadone. *Early Human Development*, *116*, 68–75. https://doi.org/10.1016/j.earlhumdev.2017.11.010

Lewis, R. (2017). *Human genetics*. Mcgraw-Hill Education.

Li, J. J., Berk, M. S., & Lee, S. S. (2013). Differential susceptibility in longitudinal models of gene-environment interaction for adolescent depression. *Development and Psychopathology*, *25*, 991–1003. https://doi.org/10.1017/S0954579413000321

Lickliter, R., & Witherington, D. C. (2017). Towards a truly developmental epigenetics. *Human Development*, *60*(2–3), 124–138. https://doi.org/10.1159/000477996

Lima, S. A. M., El Dib, R. P., Rodrigues, M. R. K., Ferraz, G. A. R., Molina, A. C., Neto, C. A. P., de Lima, M. A. F., & Rudge, M. V. C. (2018). Is the risk of low birth weight or preterm labor greater when maternal stress is experienced during pregnancy? A systematic review and meta-analysis of cohort studies. *PLOS ONE*, *13*(7), e0200594. https://doi.org/10.1371/journal.pone.0200594

Lin, Y., Xu, J., Huang, J., Jia, Y., Zhang, J., Yan, C., & Zhang, J. (2017). Effects of prenatal and postnatal maternal emotional stress on toddlers' cognitive and temperamental development. *Journal of Affective Disorders*, *207*, 9–17. https://doi.org/10.1016/j.jad.2016.09.010

Londero, A. P., Rossetti, E., Pittini, C., Cagnacci, A., & Driul, L. (2019). Maternal age and the risk of adverse pregnancy outcomes: A retrospective cohort study. *BMC Pregnancy and Childbirth*, *19*(1), 1–10. https://doi.org/10.1186/s12884-019-2400-x

Loock, C., Elliott, E., & Social, L. C. (2020). Fetal alcohol spectrum disorder. In A. L. Begun & M. M. Murray (Eds.), *The Routledge handbook of social work and addictive behaviors*. Routledge.

Loussert, L., Vidal, F., Parant, O., Hamdi, S. M., Vayssiere, C., & Guerby, P. (2020). Aspirin for prevention of preeclampsia and fetal growth restriction. *Prenatal Diagnosis*, *40*(5), 519–527. https://doi.org/10.1002/pd.5645

Lynch, J. L., & Gibbs, B. G. (2017). Birth weight and early cognitive skills: Can parenting offset the link? *Maternal and Child Health Journal*, *21*(1), 156–167. https://doi.org/10.1007/s10995-016-2104-z

Lynch, K. (2016). Gene-environment correlation. In V. Zeigler-Hill & T. K. Shackelford (Eds.), *Encyclopedia of personality and individual differences* (pp. 1–4). Springer International Publishing. https://doi.org/10.1007/978-3-319-28099-8_1470-1

MacDorman, M. F., & Declercq, E. (2016). Trends and characteristics of United States out-of-hospital births 2004-2014: New information on risk status and access to care. *Birth*, *43*(2), 116–124. https://doi.org/10.1111/birt.12228

MacKay, D. F., Smith, G. C. S., Dobbie, R., & Pell, J. P. (2010). Gestational age at delivery and special educational need: Retrospective cohort study of 407,503 schoolchildren. *PLoS Medicine*, *7*(6), e1000289. https://doi.org/10.1371/journal.pmed.1000289

MacKinnon, N., Kingsbury, M., Mahedy, L., Evans, J., & Colman, I. (2018). The association between prenatal stress and externalizing symptoms in childhood: Evidence from the avon longitudinal study of parents and children. *Biological Psychiatry*, *83*(2), 100–108. https://doi.org/10.1016/j.biopsych.2017.07.010

Madigan, S., Oatley, H., Racine, N., Fearon, R. M. P., Schumacher, L., Akbari, E., Cooke, J. E., & Tarabulsy, G. M. (2018). A meta-analysis of maternal prenatal depression and anxiety on child socioemotional development. *Journal of the American Academy of Child and Adolescent Psychiatry*, *57*, 645–657. https://doi.org/10.1016/j.jaac.2018.06.012

Magnus, M. C., Wilcox, A. J., Morken, N. H., Weinberg, C. R., & Håberg, S. E. (2019). Role of maternal age and pregnancy history in risk of miscarriage: Prospective register based study. *BMJ (Online)*, *364*, 869. https://doi.org/10.1136/bmj.l869

Mamluk, L., Edwards, H. B., Savović, J., Leach, V., Jones, T., Moore, T. H. M., Ijaz, S., Lewis, S. J., Donovan, J. L., Lawlor, D., Smith, G. D., Fraser, A., & Zuccolo, L. (2017). Low alcohol consumption and pregnancy and childhood outcomes: Time to change guidelines indicating apparently "safe" levels of alcohol during pregnancy? A systematic review and meta-analyses. *BMJ Open*, *7*(7), e015410. https://doi.org/10.1136/bmjopen-2016-015410

Manuck, S. B., & McCaffery, J. M. (2014). Gene-environment interaction. *Annual Review of Psychology*, *65*, 41–70.

Manzari, N., Matvienko-Sikar, K., Baldoni, F., O'Keeffe, G. W., & Khashan, A. S. (2019). Prenatal maternal stress and risk of neurodevelopmental disorders in the offspring: A systematic review and meta-analysis. *Social Psychiatry and Psychiatric Epidemiology*, *54*, 1299–1309. https://doi.org/10.1007/s00127-019-01745-3

Marozio, L., Picardo, E., Filippini, C., Mainolfi, E., Berchialla, P., Cavallo, F., Tancredi, A., & Benedetto, C. (2019). Maternal age over 40 years and pregnancy outcome: A hospital-based survey. *Journal of Maternal-Fetal and Neonatal Medicine*, *32*(10), 1602–1608. https://doi.org/10.1080/14767058.2017.1410793

Martin, J. A., Hamilton, B. E., Osterman, M. J., Driscoll, A. K., & Drake, P. (2018). *Births: Final data for 2016. National Vital Statistics Reports*, *67*(1), 1–55. https://stacks.cdc.gov/view/cdc/51199

Martin, J. A., Hamilton, B. E., Osterman, M. J. K., Curtin, S. C., & Mathews, T. J. (2013). *Births: Final data for 201 2. National Vital Statistics Reports*, *62*(9), 1–68. http://www.cdc.gov/nchs/data/nvsr/nvsr62/nvsr62_09.pdf#table21

Martinson, M. L., & Reichman, N. E. (2016). Socioeconomic inequalities in low birth weight in the United States, the United Kingdom, Canada, and Australia. *American Journal of Public Health*, *106*(4), 748–754. https://doi.org/10.2105/AJPH.2015.303007

Masselli, G., Vaccaro Notte, M. R., Zacharzewska-Gondek, A., Laghi, F., Manganaro, L., & Brunelli, R. (2020). Fetal MRI of CNS abnormalities. *Clinical Radiology*, *75*, P640.E1–640.E11. https://doi.org/10.1016/j.crad.2020.03.035

Mathews, T. J., & MacDorman, M. F. (2013). Infant mortality statistics from the 2010 period linked birth/infant death data set. *National Vital Statistics Reports*, *62*(8), 1–26. http://www.cdc.gov/nchs/data/nvsr/nvsr62/nvsr62_08.pdf

Mathewson, K. J., Chow, C. H. T., Dobson, K. G., Pope, E. I., Schmidt, L. A., & Van Lieshout, R. J. (2017). Mental health of extremely low birth weight survivors: A systematic review and meta-analysis. *Psychological Bulletin*, *143*(4), 347–383. https://doi.org/10.1037/bul0000091

Mattson, S. N., Bernes, G. A., & Doyle, L. R. (2019). Fetal alcohol spectrum disorders: A review of the neurobehavioral deficits associated with prenatal alcohol exposure. *Alcoholism: Clinical and Experimental Research*, *43*(6), acer.14040. https://doi.org/10.1111/acer.14040

May, P. A., Baete, A., Russo, J., Elliott, A. J., Blankenship, J., Kalberg, W. O. W., Buckley, D., Brooks, M., Hasken, J., Abdul-Rahman, O., Adam, M. P., Robinson, L. K., Manning, M., Hoyme, H. E., Jones, K., Smith, D., Robinson, G., Conry, J., Conry, R., & Vagnarelli, F. (2014). Prevalence and characteristics of fetal alcohol spectrum disorders. *Pediatrics*, *134*(5), 855–866. https://doi.org/10.1542/peds.2013-3319

May, P. A., Chambers, C. D., Kalberg, W. O., Zellner, J., Feldman, H., Buckley, D., Kopald, D., Hasken, J. M., Xu, R., Honerkamp-Smith, G., Taras, H., Manning, M. A., Robinson, L. K., Adam, M. P., Abdul-Rahman, O., Vaux, K., Jewett, T., Elliott, A. J., Kable, J. A., & Hoyme, H. (2018). Prevalence of fetal alcohol spectrum disorders in 4 US communities. *JAMA*, *319*(5), 474. https://doi.org/10.1001/jama.2017.21896

Mazul, M. C., Salm Ward, T. C., & Ngui, E. M. (2017). Anatomy of good prenatal care: Perspectives of low income African-American women on barriers and facilitators to prenatal care. *Journal of Racial and Ethnic Health Disparities*, *4*(1), 79–86. https://doi.org/10.1007/s40615-015-0204-x

McGlade, M. S., Saha, S., & Dahlstrom, M. E. (2004). The latina paradox: An opportunity for restructuring prenatal care delivery. *American Journal of Public Health*, *94*(12), 2062–2065.

McGowan, P. O., & Matthews, S. G. (2018). Prenatal stress, glucocorticoids, and developmental programming of the stress response. *Endocrinology*, *159*, 69–82. https://doi.org/10.1210/en.2017-00896

McKusick-Nathans Institute of Genetic Medicine. (2017). *OMIM - online mendelian inheritance in man. OMIM - Online mendelian inheritance in man.* http://www.omim.org/about

McKusick-Nathans Institute of Genetic Medicine. (2020). *OMIM - online mendelian inheritance in man. OMIM - Online mendelian inheritance in man.* http://www.omim.org/about

Meaney, M. J. (2017). Epigenetics and the biology of gene × Environment interactions. In P. H. Tolan & B. L. Leventhal (Eds.), *Gene-environment transactions in developmental psychopathology* (pp. 59–94). Springer International Publishing. https://doi.org/10.1007/978-3-319-49227-8_4

Medford, E., Hare, D. J., & Wittkowski, A. (2017). *Demographic and psychosocial influences on treatment adherence for children and adolescents with PKU: A systematic review* (pp. 1–10). Springer Publishing Company. https://doi.org/10.1007/8904_2017_52

Mehta, P. K. (2016). Pregnancy with chicken pox. In A. Gandhi, N. Malhotra, J. Malhotra, N. Gupta, & N. M. Bora (Eds.), *Principles of critical care in obstetrics* (pp. 21–30). Springer India. https://doi.org/10.1007/978-81-322-2686-4_4

Milani, H. J., Araujo Júnior, E., Cavalheiro, S., Oliveira, P. S., Hisaba, W. J., Barreto, E. Q. S., Barbosa, M. M., Nardozza, L. M., & Moron, A. F. (2015). Fetal brain tumors: Prenatal diagnosis by ultrasound and magnetic resonance imaging. *World Journal of Radiology*, *7*(1), 17–21. https://doi.org/10.4329/wjr.v7.i1.17

Miller, J. E., Hammond, G. C., Strunk, T., Moore, H. C., Leonard, H., Carter, K. W., Bhutta, Z., Stanley, F., de Klerk, N., & Burgner, D. P. (2016). Association of gestational age and growth measures at birth with infection-related admissions to hospital throughout childhood: A population-based, data-linkage study from Western Australia. *The Lancet Infectious Diseases*, *16*(8), 952–961. https://doi.org/10.1016/S1473-3099(16)00150-X

Min, M. O., Minnes, S., Yoon, S., Short, E. J., & Singer, L. T. (2014). Self-reported adolescent behavioral adjustment: Effects of prenatal cocaine exposure. *The Journal of Adolescent Health : Official Publication of the Society for Adolescent Medicine*, *55*(2), 167–174. https://doi.org/10.1016/j.jadohealth.2013.12.032

Modzelewska, D., Bellocco, R., Elfvin, A., Brantsæter, A. L., Meltzer, H. M., Jacobsson, B., & Sengpiel, V. (2019). Caffeine exposure during pregnancy, small for gestational age birth and neonatal outcome - results from the Norwegian mother and child cohort study. *BMC Pregnancy and Childbirth*, *19*(1), 80. https://doi.org/10.1186/s12884-019-2215-9

Monnelly, V. J., Anblagan, D., Quigley, A., Cabez, M. B., Cooper, E. S., Mactier, H., Semple, S. I., Bastin, M. E., & Boardman, J. P. (2018). Prenatal methadone exposure is associated with altered neonatal brain development. *NeuroImage: Clinical*, *18*, 9–14. https://doi.org/10.1016/J.NICL.2017.12.033

Moore, D. S. (2017). Behavioral epigenetics. *Wiley Interdisciplinary Reviews: Systems Biology and Medicine*, *9*(1), e1333. https://doi.org/10.1002/wsbm.1333

Moore, K. L., Persaud, T. V. N., & Torchia, M. G. (2019). *Before we are born: Essentials of embryology and birth defects* (10th ed.). Saunders.

Morgan, C., Forti, M. Di., & Fisher, H. L. (2020). Gene–environment interaction. In J. Das-Munshi, T. Ford, M. Hotopf, M. Prince, & R. Stewart (Eds.), *Practical psychiatric epidemiology* (pp. 343–358). Oxford.

Morneau-Vaillancourt, G., Dionne, G., Brendgen, M., Vitaro, F., Feng, B., Henry, J., Forget-Dubois, N., Tremblay, R., & Boivin, M. (2019). The genetic and environmental etiology of shyness through childhood. *Behavior Genetics*, *49*(4), 376–385. https://doi.org/10.1007/s10519-019-09955-w

Morrison, M. L., & McMahon, C. J. (2018). Congenital heart disease in down syndrome. In S. Dey (Ed.), *Advances in research on down syndrome* (pp. 128–144). InTech. https://doi.org/10.5772/intechopen.71060

Murphy, S. L., Xu, J., Kochanek, K. D., & Arias, E. (2018). *Mortality in the United States, 2017.* https://www.cdc.gov/nchs/data/databriefs/db328_tables-508.pdf#1.

Næss, K.-A. B., Nygaard, E., Ostad, J., Dolva, A.-S., & Lyster, S.-A. H. (2017). The profile of social functioning in children with Down syndrome. *Disability and Rehabilitation*, *39*(13), 1320–1331. https://doi.org/10.1080/09638288.2016.1194901

National Human Genome Research Institute. (2018). *Genetics vs. genomics fact sheet.* https://www.genome.gov/about-genomics/fact-sheets/Genetics-vs-Genomics

National Library of Medicine. (2019). Home reference handbook - help me understand genetics. In *Genetics home reference*. US National Library of Medicine. http://ghr.nlm.nih.gov/handbook

Nazzari, S., Fearon, P., Rice, F., Dottori, N., Ciceri, F., Molteni, M., & Frigerio, A. (2019). Beyond the HPA-axis: Exploring maternal prenatal influences on birth outcomes and stress reactivity. *Psychoneuroendocrinology*, *101*, 253–262. https://doi.org/10.1016/j.psyneuen.2018.11.018

Ncube, C. N., Enquobahrie, D. A., Albert, S. M., Herrick, A. L., & Burke, J. G. (2016). Association of neighborhood context with offspring risk of preterm birth and low birthweight: A systematic review and meta-analysis of population-based studies. *Social Science & Medicine*, *153*, 156–164. https://doi.org/10.1016/J.SOCSCIMED.2016.02.014

Nelson, C. A., & Gabard-Durnam, L. J. (2020). Early adversity and critical periods: Neurodevelopmental consequences of violating the expectable environment. *Trends in Neurosciences*, *43*, 133–143. https://doi.org/10.1016/j.tins.2020.01.002

Nguyen, T., Li, G. E., Chen, H., Cranfield, C. G., McGrath, K. C., & Gorrie, C. A. (2018). Maternal E-cigarette exposure results in cognitive and epigenetic alterations in offspring in a mouse model. *Chemical Research in Toxicology*, *31*(7), 601–611. https://doi.org/10.1021/acs.chemrestox.8b00084

Nikulina, V., Widom, C. S., & Brzustowicz, L. M. (2012). Child abuse and neglect, MAOA, and mental health outcomes: A prospective examination. *Biological Psychiatry*, *71*(4), 350–357. https://doi.org/10.1016/j.biopsych.2011.09.008

Nygaard, E., Slinning, K., Moe, V., Due-Tønnessen, P., Fjell, A., & Walhovd, K. B. (2018). Neuroanatomical characteristics of youths with prenatal opioid and poly-drug exposure. *Neurotoxicology and Teratology*, *68*, 13–26. https://doi.org/10.1016/J.NTT.2018.04.004

Odibo, A. O. (2015). Amniocentesis, chorionic villus sampling, and fetal blood sampling. In A. Milunsky & J. M. Milunsky (Eds.), *Genetic disorders and the fetus* (pp. 68–97). John Wiley & Sons, Inc. https://doi.org/10.1002/9781118981559.ch2

O'Donnell, K. J., & Meaney, M. J. (2020). Epigenetics, development, and psychopathology. *Annual Review of Clinical Psychology*, *16*(1), 327–350. https://doi.org/10.1146/annurev-clinpsy-050718-095530

Ojodu, J., Hulihan, M. M., Pope, S. N., & Grant, A. M. (2014). Incidence of sickle cell trait — United States, 2010. *Morbidity and Mortality Weekly Report*, *63*(49), 1155–1158. https://www.cdc.gov/mmwr/preview/mmwrhtml/mm6349a3.htm

Paltrow, L. M., & Flavin, J. (2013). Arrests of and forced interventions on pregnant women in the United States, 1973–2005: Implications for women's legal status and public health. *Journal of Health Politics, Policy and Law*, *38*(2), 299–343. https://doi.org/10.1215/03616878-1966324

Pappas, K. B., Migeon, C. J., Pappas, K. B., & Migeon, C. J. (2017). Sex chromosome abnormalities. In *eLS* (pp. 1–9). John Wiley & Sons, Ltd. https://doi.org/10.1002/9780470015902.a0005943.pub2

Partridge, S., Balayla, J., Holcroft, C., & Abenhaim, H. (2012). Inadequate prenatal care utilization and risks of infant mortality and poor birth outcome: A retrospective analysis of 28,729,765 U.S. deliveries over 8 Years. *American Journal of Perinatology*, *29*(10), 787–794. https://doi.org/10.1055/s-0032-1316439

Patenaude, Y., Pugash, D., Lim, K., Morin, L., Lim, K., Bly, S., Butt, K., Cargill, Y., Davies, G., Denis, N., Hazlitt, G., Morin, L., Naud, K., Ouellet, A., & Salem, S. (2014). The use of magnetic resonance imaging in the obstetric patient. *Journal of Obstetrics and Gynaecology Canada*, *36*(4), 349–355. https://doi.org/10.1016/S1701-2163(15)30612-5

Penke, L., & Jokela, M. (2016). The evolutionary genetics of personality revisited. *Current Opinion in Psychology*, *7*, 104–109. https://doi.org/10.1016/J.COPSYC.2015.08.021

Pierrehumbert, B., Nicole, A., Muller-Nix, C., Forcada-Guex, M., & Ansermet, F. (2003). Parental post-traumatic reactions after premature birth: Implications for sleeping and eating problems in the infant. *Archives of Disease in Childhood - Fetal and Neonatal Edition*, *88*(5), 400–404. https://doi.org/10.1136/fn.88.5.F400

Pieters, S., Burk, W. J., Van der Vorst, H., Dahl, R. E., Wiers, R. W., & Engels, R. C. M. E. (2015). Prospective relationships between sleep problems and substance use, internalizing and externalizing problems. *Journal of Youth and Adolescence*, *44*(2), 379–388. https://doi.org/10.1007/s10964-014-0213-9

Pinel, C., Prainsack, B., & McKevitt, C. (2018). Markers as mediators: A review and synthesis of epigenetics literature. *BioSocieties*, *13*, 276–303. https://doi.org/10.1057/s41292-017-0068-x

Plomin, R. (2019). *Blueprint: How DNA makes us who we are*. MIT Press. https://mitpress.mit.edu/books/blueprint

Popova, S., Lange, S., Probst, C., Parunashvili, N., & Rehm, J. (2017). Prevalence of alcohol consumption during pregnancy and fetal alcohol spectrum disorders among the general and Aboriginal populations in Canada and the United States. *European Journal of Medical Genetics*, *60*(1), 32–48. https://www.sciencedirect.com/science/article/pii/S1769721216303159

Provasi, J. (2019). Parent-preterm infant interaction. In G. Apter, E. Devouche, & M. Gratier (Eds.), *Early interaction and developmental psychopathology* (pp. 123–149). Springer International Publishing. https://doi.org/10.1007/978-3-030-04769-6_7

Puls, H. T., Anderst, J. D., Bettenhausen, J. L., Clark, N., Krager, M., Markham, J. L., & Hall, M. (2019). Newborn risk factors for subsequent physical abuse hospitalizations. *Pediatrics*, *143*(2), e20182108. https://doi.org/10.1542/peds.2018-2108

Purves, K. L., Coleman, J. R. I., Meier, S. M., Rayner, C., Davis, K. A. S., Cheesman, R., Bækvad-Hansen, M., Børglum, A. D., Wan Cho, S., Jürgen Deckert, J., Gaspar, H. A., Bybjerg-Grauholm, J., Hettema, J. M., Hotopf, M., Hougaard, D., Hübel, C., Kan, C., McIntosh, A. M., Mors, O., & Eley, T. C. (2019). A major role for common genetic variation in anxiety disorders. *Molecular Psychiatry*, *25*, 1–12. https://doi.org/10.1038/s41380-019-0559-1

Qian, J., Chen, Q., Ward, S. M., Duan, E., & Zhang, Y. (2020). Impacts of caffeine during pregnancy. *Trends in Endocrinology and Metabolism*, *31*, 218–227. https://doi.org/10.1016/j.tem.2019.11.004

Raffaeli, G., Cavallaro, G., Allegaert, K., Wildschut, E. D., Fumagalli, M., Agosti, M., Tibboel, D., & Mosca, F. (2017). Neonatal abstinence syndrome: Update on diagnostic and therapeutic strategies. *Pharmacotherapy: The Journal of Human Pharmacology and Drug Therapy*, *37*(7), 814–823. https://doi.org/10.1002/phar.1954

Ramraj, C., Pulver, A., O'Campo, P., Urquia, M. L., Hildebrand, V., & Siddiqi, A. (2020). A scoping review of socioeconomic inequalities in distributions of birth outcomes: Through a conceptual and methodological lens. *Maternal and Child Health Journal*, *24*, 144–152. https://doi.org/10.1007/s10995-019-02838-w

Raspa, M., Wheeler, A. C., & Riley, C. (2017). Public health literature review of fragile X syndrome. *Pediatrics*, *139*(Suppl 3), S153–S171. https://doi.org/10.1542/peds.2016-1159C

Rebbe, R., Mienko, J. A., Brown, E., & Rowhani-Rahbar, A. (2019). Child protection reports and removals of infants diagnosed with prenatal substance exposure. *Child Abuse and Neglect*, *88*, 28–36. https://doi.org/10.1016/j.chiabu.2018.11.001

Richardson, G. A., De Genna, N. M., Goldschmidt, L., Larkby, C., & Donovan, J. E. (2019). Prenatal cocaine exposure: Direct and indirect associations with 21-year-old offspring substance use and behavior problems. *Drug and Alcohol Dependence*, *195*, 121–131. https://doi.org/10.1016/j.drugalcdep.2018.10.033

Richardson, G. A., Goldschmidt, L., Larkby, C., & Day, N. L. (2015). Effects of prenatal cocaine exposure on adolescent development. *Neurotoxicology and Teratology*, *49*, 41–48. https://doi.org/10.1016/J.NTT.2015.03.002

Ritchie, K., Bora, S., & Woodward, L. J. (2015). Social development of children born very preterm: A systematic review. *Developmental Medicine & Child Neurology*, *57*(10), 899–918. https://doi.org/10.1111/dmcn.12783

Ritz, B. R., Chatterjee, N., Garcia-Closas, M., Gauderman, W. J., Pierce, B. L., Kraft, P., Tanner, C. M., Mechanic, L. E., & McAllister, K. (2017). Lessons learned from past gene-environment interaction successes. *American Journal of Epidemiology*, *186*(7), 778–786. https://doi.org/10.1093/aje/kwx230

Roberge, S., Bujold, E., & Nicolaides, K. H. (2017). Aspirin for the prevention of preterm and term preeclampsia: Systematic review and meta-analysis. *American Journal of Obstetrics and Gynecology*, *218*(3), 287–293. https://doi.org/10.1016/J.AJOG.2017.11.561

Roizen, N. J., Magyar, C. I., Kuschner, E. S., Sulkes, S. B., Druschel, C., van Wijngaarden, E., Rodgers, L., Diehl, A., Lowry, R., & Hyman, S. L. (2014). A community cross-sectional survey of medical problems in 440 children with down syndrome in New York State. *The Journal of Pediatrics*, *164*(4), 871–875. https://doi.org/10.1016/j.jpeds.2013.11.032

Romani, C., Palermo, L., MacDonald, A., Limback, E., Hall, S. K., & Geberhiwot, T. (2017). The impact of phenylalanine levels on cognitive outcomes in adults with phenylketonuria: Effects across tasks and developmental stages. *Neuropsychology*, *31*(3), 242–254. https://doi.org/10.1037/neu0000336

Rosiak-Gill, A., Gill, K., Jakubik, J., Fraczek, M., Patorski, L., Gaczarzewicz, D., Kurzawa, R., Kurpisz, M., & Piasecka, M. (2019). Age-related changes in human sperm DNA integrity. *Aging*, *11*(15), 5399–5411. https://doi.org/10.18632/aging.102120

Ruiz, J. M., Hamann, H. A., Mehl, M. R., & OConnor, M.-F. (2016). The Hispanic health paradox: From epidemiological phenomenon to contribution opportunities for psychological science. *Group Processes & Intergroup Relations*, *19*(4), 462–476. https://doi.org/10.1177/1368430216638540

Sadler, T. L. (2018). *Langman's medical embryology* (14th ed.). Lippincott Williams & Wilkins.

Salcedo-Arellano, M. J., Dufour, B., McLennan, Y., Martinez-Cerdeno, V., & Hagerman, R. (2020). Fragile X syndrome and associated disorders: Clinical aspects and pathology. *Neurobiology of Disease*, *136*, 104740, . https://doi.org/10.1016/j.nbd.2020.104740

Salomon, L. J., Sotiriadis, A., Wulff, C. B., Odibo, A., & Akolekar, R. (2019). Risk of miscarriage following amniocentesis or chorionic villus sampling: systematic review of literature and updated meta-analysis. *Ultrasound in Obstetrics & Gynecology*, *54*(4), 442–451. https://doi.org/10.1002/uog.20353

Saltz, J. B. (2019). Gene-environment correlation in humans: Lessons from psychology for quantitative genetics. *Journal of Heredity*, *110*(4), 455–466. https://doi.org/10.1093/jhered/esz027

Sanchez-Vaznaugh, E. V., Braveman, P. A., Egerter, S., Marchi, K. S., Heck, K., & Curtis, M. (2016). Latina birth outcomes in California: Not so paradoxical. *Maternal and Child Health Journal*, *20*(9), 1849–1860. https://doi.org/10.1007/s10995-016-1988-y

Sarman, I. (2018). Review shows that early foetal alcohol exposure may cause adverse effects even when the mother consumes low levels. *Acta Paediatrica*, *107*(6), 938–941. https://doi.org/10.1111/apa.14221

Scarr, S., & McCartney, K. (1983). How people make their own environments: A theory of genotype environment effects. *Child Development*, *54*(2), 424. https://doi.org/10.1111/1467-8624.ep8877295

Schetter, C. D., & Tanner, L. (2012). Anxiety, depression and stress in pregnancy: Implications for mothers, children, research, and practice. *Current Opinion in Psychiatry*, *25*(2), 141–148. https://doi.org/10.1097/YCO.0b013e3283503680

Schmitt, L.., Shaffer, R.., Hessl, D.., & Erickson, C.. (2019). Executive function in fragile X syndrome: A systematic review. *Brain Sciences*, *9*(1), 15. http://dx.doi.org/10.3390/brainsci9010015

Schwartz, N. L., Patel, B. A., Garland, T., & Horner, A. M. (2018). Effects of selective breeding for high voluntary wheel-running behavior on femoral nutrient canal size and abundance in house mice. *Journal of Anatomy*, *233*(2), 193–203. https://doi.org/10.1111/joa.12830

Seiler, N. K. (2016). Alcohol and pregnancy: CDC's health advice and the legal rights of pregnant women. *Public Health Reports (Washington, D.C. : 1974)*, *131*(4), 623–627. https://doi.org/10.1177/0033354916662222

Servey, J., & Chang, J. (2014). Over-the-counter medications in pregnancy. *American Family Physician*, *90*(8), 548–555. http://www.ncbi.nlm.nih.gov/pubmed/25369643

Shah, K., DeRemigis, A., Hageman, J. R., Sriram, S., & Waggoner, D. (2017). Unique characteristics of the X chromosome and related disorders. *NeoReviews*, *18*(4), e209–e216. https://doi.org/10.1542/neo.18-4-e209

Shahbazian, N., Barati, M., Arian, P., & Saadati, N. (2012). Comparison of complications of chorionic villus sampling and amniocentesis. *International Journal of Fertility & Sterility*, *5*(4), 241–244.

Sharapova, S. R., Phillips, E., Sirocco, K., Kaminski, J. W., Leeb, R. T., & Rolle, I. (2018). Effects of prenatal marijuana exposure on neuropsychological outcomes in children aged 1-11 years: A systematic review. *Paediatric and Perinatal Epidemiology*, *32*(6), 512–532. https://doi.org/10.1111/ppe.12505

Sharma, D., Farahbakhsh, N., Sharma, S., Sharma, P., & Sharma, A. (2019). Role of kangaroo mother care in growth and breast feeding rates in very low birth weight (VLBW) neonates: A systematic review. *Journal of Maternal-Fetal and Neonatal Medicine*, *32*, 129–142. https://doi.org/10.1080/14767058.2017.1304535

Shim, S.-S., Malone, F., Canick, J., Ball, R., Nyberg, D., Comstock, C., Bukowski, R., Norwitz, E., Levy, B., Brambati, B., Guercilena, S., Bonacchi, I., Oldrini, A., Lanzani, A., Piceni, L., South, S., Chen, Z., Brothman, A., Hsu, L., & Abuhamad, A. (2014). Chorionic villus sampling. *Journal of Genetic Medicine*, *11*(2), 43–48. https://doi.org/10.5734/JGM.2014.11.2.43

Shuffrey, L. C., Myers, M. M., Isler, J. R., Lucchini, M., Sania, A., Pini, N., Nugent, J. D., Condon, C., Ochoa, T., Brink, L., du Plessis, C., Odendaal, H. J., Nelson, M. E., Friedrich, C., Angal, J., Elliott, A. J., Groenewald, C., Burd, L., & Fifer, W. P. (2020). Association between prenatal exposure to alcohol and tobacco and neonatal brain activity: Results from the safe passage study. *JAMA Network Open*, *3*(5), e204714, . https://doi.org/10.1001/jamanetworkopen.2020.4714

Singer, L. T., Minnes, S., Min, M. O., Lewis, B. A., & Short, E. J. (2015). Prenatal cocaine exposure and child outcomes: A conference report based on a prospective study from Cleveland. *Human Psychopharmacology: Clinical and Experimental*, *30*(4), 285–289. https://doi.org/10.1002/hup.2454

Singh, C. (2020). Rubella in pregnancy. *Journal of Fetal Medicine*, *7*(1), 37–41. https://doi.org/10.1007/s40556-019-00238-2

Sirnes, E., Oltedal, L., Bartsch, H., Eide, G. E., Elgen, I. B., & Aukland, S. M. (2017). Brain morphology in school-aged children with prenatal opioid exposure: A structural MRI study. *Early Human Development*, *106–107*, 33–39. https://doi.org/10.1016/J.EARLHUMDEV.2017.01.009

Smith, A. M., Mioduszewski, O., Hatchard, T., Byron-Alhassan, A., Fall, C., & Fried, P. A. (2016). Prenatal marijuana exposure impacts executive functioning into young adulthood: An fMRI study. *Neurotoxicology and Teratology*, *58*, 53–59. https://doi.org/10.1016/J.NTT.2016.05.010

Soneji, S., & Beltrán-Sánchez, H. (2019). Association of maternal cigarette smoking and smoking cessation with preterm birth. *JAMA Network Open*, *2*(4), e192514. https://doi.org/10.1001/jamanetworkopen.2019.2514

Stanley, A. Y., Durham, C. O., Sterrett, J. J., & Wallace, J. B. (2019). Safety of over-the-counter medications in pregnancy. *MCN, The American Journal of Maternal/Child Nursing*, *44*(4), 196–205. https://doi.org/10.1097/NMC.0000000000000537

Stephenson, J. (2005). Fetal ultrasound safety. *JAMA: Journal of the American Medical Association*, *293*(3), 286.

Sutin, A. R., Flynn, H. A., & Terracciano, A. (2017). Maternal cigarette smoking during pregnancy and the trajectory of externalizing and internalizing symptoms across childhood: Similarities and differences across parent, teacher, and self reports. *Journal of Psychiatric Research*, *91*, 145–148. https://doi.org/10.1016/J.JPSYCHIRES.2017.03.003

Szyf, M. (2015). Nongenetic inheritance and transgenerational epigenetics. *Trends in Molecular Medicine*, *21*(2), 134–144. https://doi.org/10.1016/j.molmed.2014.12.004

Taneri, B., Asilmaz, E., Delikurt, T., Savas, P., & Targen, S. (2020). *Human genetics and genomics: A practical guide*. Wiley.

Taylor, H. G., Klein, N., Minich, N. M., & Hack, M. (2001). Long-term family outcomes for children with very low birth weights. *Archives of Pediatrics & Adolescent Medicine*, *155*(2), 155–161.

Theodora, M., Antsaklis, A., Antsaklis, P., Blanas, K., Daskalakis, G., Sindos, M., Mesogitis, S., & Papantoniou, N. (2016). Fetal loss following second trimester amniocentesis. Who is at greater risk? How to counsel pregnant women? *The Journal of Maternal-Fetal & Neonatal Medicine*, *29*(4), 590–595. https://doi.org/10.3109/14767058.2015.1012061

Tong, V. T., England, L. J., Rockhill, K. M., & D'Angelo, D. V. (2017). Risks of preterm delivery and small for gestational age infants: Effects of nondaily and low-intensity daily smoking during pregnancy. *Paediatric and Perinatal Epidemiology*, *31*(2), 144–148. https://doi.org/10.1111/ppe.12343

Towers, C. V., Hyatt, B. W., Visconti, K. C., Chernicky, L., Chattin, K., & Fortner, K. B. (2019). Neonatal head circumference in newborns with neonatal abstinence syndrome. *Pediatrics*, *143*(1), e20180541. https://doi.org/10.1542/peds.2018-0541

Trucco, E. M., Cope, L. M., Burmeister, M., Zucker, R. A., & Heitzeg, M. M. (2018). Pathways to youth behavior: The Role of genetic, neural, and behavioral markers. *Journal of Research on Adolescence*, *28*(1), 26–39. https://doi.org/10.1111/jora.12341

Tsamantioti, E. S., & Hashmi, M. F. (2020). Teratogenic medications. In *StatPearls*. StatPearls Publishing. http://www.ncbi.nlm.nih.gov/pubmed/31971726

Tsimis, M. E., & Sheffield, J. S. (2017). Update on syphilis and pregnancy. *Birth Defects Research*, *109*(5), 347–352. https://doi.org/10.1002/bdra.23562

United States Department of Agriculture. (2019). *Food security status of Us households in 2018. Food security in the US*. https://www.ers.usda.gov/topics/food-nutrition-assistance/food-security-in-the-us/key-statistics-graphics.aspx

U.S. Bureau of Labor Statistics, 2021. (2021). *Occupational outlook handbook: 2021*. https://www.bls.gov/ooh/

U.S. Department of Health and Human Services. (2013). Maternal and Child Health Bureau USA, 2013.

U.S. Department of Health and Human Services. (2014). Maternal and Child Health Bureau USA, 2014.

U.S. Department of Health and Human Services. (2015). Maternal and Child Health Bureau USA, 2015.

U.S. National Library of Medicine. (2020). *Help me understand genetics - genetics home reference - NIH*. https://ghr.nlm.nih.gov/primer

Uyoga, S., Macharia, A. W., Ndila, C. M., Nyutu, G., Shebe, M., Awuondo, K. O., Mturi, N., Peshu, N., Tsofa, B., Scott, J. A. G., Maitland, K., & Williams, T. N. (2019). The indirect health effects of malaria estimated from health advantages of the sickle cell trait. *Nature Communications*, *10*(1), 1–7. https://doi.org/10.1038/s41467-019-08775-0

Vanhees, K., Vonhögen, I. G. C., van Schooten, F. J., & Godschalk, R. W. L. (2014). You are what you eat, and so are your children: The impact of micronutrients on the epigenetic programming of offspring. *Cellular and Molecular Life Sciences : CMLS*, *71*(2), 271–285. https://doi.org/10.1007/s00018-013-1427-9

Vigeh, M., Yokoyama, K., Matsukawa, T., Shinohara, A., & Ohtani, K. (2014). Low level prenatal blood lead adversely affects early childhood mental development. *Journal of Child Neurology*, *29*(10), 1305–1311. https://doi.org/10.1177/0883073813516999

Villela, D., Che, H., Van Ghelue, M., Dehaspe, L., Brison, N., Van Den Bogaert, K., Devriendt, K., Lewi, L., Bayindir, B., & Vermeesch, J. R. (2019). Fetal sex determination in twin pregnancies using non-invasive prenatal testing. *Npj Genomic Medicine*, *4*(1), 1–6. https://doi.org/10.1038/s41525-019-0089-4

Vink, J., & Quinn, M. (2018a). Amniocentesis. In J. Copel, M. E. D'Alton, H. Feltovich, E. Gratacos, A. O. Odibo, L. Platt, & B. Tutschek (Eds.), *Obstetric imaging: Fetal diagnosis and care* (pp. 473–475). Elsevier. https://doi.org/10.1016/B978-0-323-44548-1.00111-X

Vink, J., & Quinn, M. (2018b). Chorionic villus sampling. In J. D. Copel, M. E. Feltovich, H. Gratacos, E. Odibo, A. O. Platt, & L. Tutschek (Eds.), *Obstetric imaging: Fetal diagnosis and care* (pp. 479–481). Elsevier. https://doi.org/10.1016/B978-0-323-44548-1.00113-3

Visscher, M., & Narendran, V. (2014). Vernix caseosa: Formation and functions. *Newborn and Infant Nursing Reviews*, *14*(4), 142–146. https://doi.org/10.1053/j.nainr.2014.10.005

Vissers, L. E. L. M., Gilissen, C., & Veltman, J. A. (2016). Genetic studies in intellectual disability and related disorders. *Nature Reviews Genetics*, *17*(1), 9–18. https://doi.org/10.1038/nrg3999

Wagner, N. J., Camerota, M., & Propper, C. (2017). Prevalence and perceptions of electronic cigarette use during pregnancy. *Maternal and Child Health Journal*, *21*(8), 1655–1661. https://doi.org/10.1007/s10995-016-2257-9

Wang, Q., Zheng, S.-X., Ni, Y.-F., Lu, Y.-Y., Zhang, B., Lian, Q.-Q., & Hu, M.-P. (2018). The effect of labor epidural analgesia on maternal–fetal outcomes: A retrospective cohort study. *Archives of Gynecology and Obstetrics*, *298*(1), 89–96. https://doi.org/10.1007/s00404-018-4777-6

Ware, R. E., de Montalembert, M., Tshilolo, L., & Abboud, M. R. (2017). Sickle cell disease. *The Lancet*, *390*(10091), 311–323. http://www.ncbi.nlm.nih.gov/pubmed/28159390

Warsof, S. L., Larion, S., & Abuhamad, A. Z. (2015). Overview of the impact of noninvasive prenatal testing on diagnostic procedures. *Prenatal Diagnosis*, *35*(10), 972–979. https://doi.org/10.1002/pd.4601

Webster, S., Morris, G., & Kevelighan, E. (2018). *Essential human development*. Wiley.

Wentz, E. E. (2017). Importance of initiating a "Tummy Time" intervention early in infants with down syndrome. *Pediatric Physical Therapy*, *29*(1), 68–75. https://doi.org/10.1097/PEP.0000000000000335

Whittington, J. R., Simmons, P. M., Phillips, A. M., Gammill, S. K., Cen, R., Magann, E. F., & Cardenas, V. M. (2018). The use of electronic cigarettes in pregnancy. *Obstetrical & Gynecological Survey*, *73*(9), 544–549. https://doi.org/10.1097/OGX.0000000000000595

Wigby, K., D'Epagnier, C., Howell, S., Reicks, A., Wilson, R., Cordeiro, L., & Tartaglia, N. (2016). Expanding the phenotype of triple X syndrome: A comparison of prenatal versus postnatal diagnosis. *American Journal of Medical Genetics Part A*, *170*(11), 2870–2881. https://doi.org/10.1002/ajmg.a.37688

Wilbur, M. B., Little, S., & Szymanski, L. M. (2015). Is home birth safe? *New England Journal of Medicine*, *373*(27), 2683–2685. https://doi.org/10.1056/NEJMclde1513623

Wilkinson, P. O., Trzaskowski, M., Haworth, C. M. A., & Eley, T. C. (2013). The role of gene–environment correlations and interactions in middle childhood depressive symptoms. *Development and Psychopathology*, *25*(01), 93–104. https://doi.org/10.1017/S0954579412000922

Wistuba, J., Brand, C., Zitzmann, M., & Damm, O. S. (2017). Genetics of klinefelter syndrome: Experimental exploration. In P. H. Vogt (Ed.), *Genetics of human infertility* (Vol. 21, pp. 40–56). Karger Publishers. https://doi.org/10.1159/000477277

Wolke, D., Eryigit-Madzwamuse, S., & Gutbrod, T. (2014). Very preterm/very low birthweight infants' attachment: Infant and maternal characteristics. Archives of disease in childhood. *Fetal and Neonatal Edition*, *99*(1), F70–5. https://doi.org/10.1136/archdischild-2013-303788

Womack, L. S., Rossen, L. M., & Martin, J. A. (2018). Singleton Low Birthweight Rates, by Race and Hispanic Origin: United States, 2006-2016. *NCHS Data Brief*, *306*, 1–8. http://www.ncbi.nlm.nih.gov/pubmed/29616897

Wozniak, J. R., Riley, E. P., & Charness, M. E. (2019). Clinical presentation, diagnosis, and management of fetal alcohol spectrum disorder. *The Lancet Neurology*, *18*, 760–770. https://doi.org/10.1016/S1474-4422(19)30150-4

Xaverius, P., Alman, C., Holtz, L., & Yarber, L. (2016). Risk factors associated with very low birth weight in a large urban area, stratified by adequacy of prenatal care. *Maternal and Child Health Journal*, *20*(3), 623–629. https://doi.org/10.1007/s10995-015-1861-4

Xie, X., Ding, G., Cui, C., Chen, L., Gao, Y., Zhou, Y., Shi, R., & Tian, Y. (2013). The effects of low-level prenatal lead exposure on birth outcomes. *Environmental Pollution*, *175*, 30–34. https://doi.org/10.1016/j.envpol.2012.12.013

Xu, J. Z., & Thein, S. L. (2019). The carrier state for sickle cell disease is not completely harmless. *Haematologica*, *104*(6), 1106–1111. https://doi.org/10.3324/haematol.2018.206060

Yaniv, S. S., Levy, A., Wiznitzer, A., Holcberg, G., Mazor, M., & Sheiner, E. (2011). A significant linear association exists between advanced maternal age and adverse perinatal outcome. *Archives of Gynecology and Obstetrics*, *283*(4), 755–759. https://doi.org/10.1007/s00404-010-1459-4

Yau, G., Schluchter, M., Taylor, H. G., Margevicius, S., Forrest, C. B., Andreias, L., Drotar, D., Youngstrom, E., & Hack, M. (2013). Bullying of extremely low birth weight children: associated risk factors during adolescence. *Early Human Development*, *89*(5), 333–338. https://doi.org/10.1016/j.earlhumdev.2012.11.004

Yeoh, S. L., Eastwood, J., Wright, I. M., Morton, R., Melhuish, E., Ward, M., & Oei, J. L. (2019). Cognitive and motor outcomes of children with prenatal opioid exposure: A systematic review and meta-analysis. *JAMA Network Open*, *2*(7), 197025. https://doi.org/10.1001/jamanetworkopen.2019.7025

York, C. (2020). Behavior genetics and twin studies. In K. Floyd & R. Weber (Eds.), *The handbook of communication science and biologu*. Routledge.

Young-Wolff, K. C., Sarovar, V., Tucker, L. Y., Avalos, L. A., Alexeeff, S., Conway, A., Armstrong, M. A., Weisner, C., Campbell, C. I., & Goler, N. (2019). Trends in marijuana use among pregnant women with and without nausea and vomiting in pregnancy, 2009–2016. *Drug and Alcohol Dependence*, *196*, 66–70. https://doi.org/10.1016/j.drugalcdep.2018.12.009

Zampieri, B. L., Biselli-Périco, J. M., de Souza, J. E. S., Bürger, M. C., Silva Júnior, W. A., Goloni-Bertollo, E. M., Pavarino, É. C., Chistiakov, D., Xavier, A., Ge, Y., Taub, J., Ram, G., Chinen, J., Broers, C., Gemke, R., Weijerman, M., Kuik, D., Hoogstraten, I., & Flavell, R. (2014). Altered expression of immune-related genes in children with down syndrome. *PLoS ONE*, *9*(9), e107218. https://doi.org/10.1371/journal.pone.0107218

Zielinski, R., Ackerson, K., & Kane Low, L. (2015). Planned home birth: benefits, risks, and opportunities. *International Journal of Women's Health*, *7*, 361–377. https://doi.org/10.2147/IJWH.S55561

CHAPTER 3

Abraham, L. M., Crais, E., & Vernon-Feagans, L. (2013). Early maternal language use during book sharing in families from low-income environments. *American Journal of Speech-Language Pathology / American Speech-Language-Hearing Association*, *22*(1), 71–83. https://doi.org/10.1044/1058-0360(2012/11-0153)

Adolph, K. E., & Franchak, J. M. (2017). The development of motor behavior. *Wiley Interdisciplinary Reviews: Cognitive Science*, *8*(1–2), e1430. https://doi.org/10.1002/wcs.1430

Adolph, K. E., Hoch, J. E., & Cole, W. G. (2018). Development (of walking): 15 suggestions. *Trends in Cognitive Sciences*, *22*, 699–711. https://doi.org/10.1016/j.tics.2018.05.010

Adolph, K. E., Kretch, K. S., & LoBue, V. (2014). Fear of heights in infants? *Current Directions in Psychological Science*, *23*(1), 60–66. https://doi.org/10.1177/0963721413498895

Adolph, K. E., & Robinson, S. R. (2015). Motor development. In L. S. Liben & U. Müller (Eds.), *Handbook of child psychology and developmental science* (pp. 1–45). John Wiley & Sons, Inc. https://doi.org/10.1002/9781118963418.childpsy204

Adolph, K., & Kretch, K. S. (2015). Gibson's theory of perceptual learning. *International Encyclopedia of Social and Behavioral Sciences*. https://nyuscholars.nyu.edu/en/publications/gibsons-theory-of-perceptual-learning

Agyei, S. B., van der Weel, F. R. R., & van der Meer, A. L. H. (2016). Development of visual motion perception for prospective control: Brain and behavioral studies in infants. *Frontiers in Psychology*, *7*, 100. https://doi.org/10.3389/fpsyg.2016.00100

Akhtar, N., Jipson, J., & Callanan, M. A. (2001). Learning words through overhearing. *Child Development*, *72*, 416–430.

Álvarez, M. J., Fernández, D., Gómez-Salgado, J., Rodríguez-González, D., Rosón, M., & Lapeña, S. (2017). The effects of massage therapy in hospitalized preterm neonates: A systematic review. *International Journal of Nursing Studies*, *69*, 119–136. https://doi.org/10.1016/J.IJNURSTU.2017.02.009

American Academy of Pediatrics. (1992). American academy of pediatrics AAP task force on infant positioning and SIDS: Positioning and SIDS. *Pediatrics*, *89*(6 Pt 1), 1120–1126. http://www.ncbi.nlm.nih.gov/pubmed/1503575

American Academy of Pediatrics. (2012). Breastfeeding and the use of human milk. *Pediatrics*, *129*, e827–e841. https://doi.org/10.1542/peds.2011-3552

American Academy of Pediatrics Council on Communications and Media. (2016). Media and young minds. *Pediatrics*, *138*(5), e20162591. http://pediatrics.aappublications.org/content/138/5/e20162591

Anderson, D. R., & Subrahmanyam, K. (2017). Digital screen media and cognitive development. *Pediatrics*, *140*(Supplement 2), S57–S61. https://doi.org/10.1542/peds.2016-1758C

Andruski, J. E., Casielles, E., & Nathan, G. (2013). Is bilingual babbling language-specific? Some evidence from a case study of Spanish–English dual acquisition. *Bilingualism: Language and Cognition*, *17*(03), 660–672. https://doi.org/10.1017/S1366728913000655

Axe, J. B.. (2007). Child care and child development: Results from the NICHD Study of Early Child Care and Youth Development. *Education & Treatment of Children* , *30*(3), 129–136.

Baddeley, A. D., Hitch, G. J., & Allen, R. J. (2019). From short-term store to multicomponent working memory: The role of the modal model. *Memory and Cognition*, *47*(4), 575–588. https://doi.org/10.3758/s13421-018-0878-5

Baillargeon, R. (2004). Infants' reasoning about hidden objects: Evidence for event-general and event-specific expectations. *Developmental Science*, *7*(4), 391–414. http://www.ncbi.nlm.nih.gov/pubmed/15484586

Baillargeon, R., Scott, R. M., & Bian, L. (2016). Psychological Reasoning in Infancy. *Annual Review of Psychology*, *67*(1), 159–186. https://doi.org/10.1146/annurev-psych-010213-115033

Bajanowski, T., & Vennemann, M. (2017). Sudden Infant Death Syndrome (SIDS). In M. M. Houck (Ed.), *Forensic Pathology* (pp. 259-). Elsevier.

Baldwin, D. A., Markman, E. M., Bill, B., Desjardins, R. N., Irwin, J. M., & Tidball, G. (1996). Infants' reliance on social criteria for establishing word-object relations. *Child Development*, *67*, 3135–3153.

Banghart, P.., Halle, T.., Bamdad, T.., Cook, M.., Redd, Z.., Cox, A.., & Carlson, J.. (2020). *A review of the literature on access to high-quality care for infants and toddlers*. Retrieved from https://www.childtrends.org/wp-content/uploads/2020/05/HighQualityCareLitReview_ChildTrends_May2020.pdf

Barr, R. (2010). Transfer of learning between 2D and 3D sources during infancy: Informing theory and practice. *Developmental Review*, *30*(2), 128–154. https://doi.org/10.1016/j.dr.2010.03.001

Barr, R. (2013). Memory constraints on infant Learning from picture books, television, and touchscreens. *Child Development Perspectives*, *7*(4), 205–210. https://doi.org/10.1111/cdep.12041

Barr, R. (2019). Growing up in the digital age: Early learning and family media ecology. *Current Directions in Psychological Science*, *28*(4), 341–346. https://doi.org/10.1177/0963721419838245

Barros, M. C. M., Mitsuhiro, S., Chalem, E., Laranjeira, R. R., & Guinsburg, R. (2011). Neurobehavior of late preterm infants of adolescent mothers. *Neonatology*, *99*(2), 133–139. https://doi.org/10.1159/000313590

Bates, E., Bretherton, I., & Snyder, L. (1988). *From first words to grammar*. Cambridge University Press.

Bauer, P. J., Burch, M. M., & Kleinknecht, E. E. (2002). Developments in early recall memory: normative trends and individual differences. *Advances in Child Development and Behavior*, *30*, 103–152. http://www.ncbi.nlm.nih.gov/pubmed/12402673

Bauer, P. J., Wenner, J. A., Dropik, P. L., & Wewerka, S. S. (2000). Parameters of remembering and forgetting in the transition from infancy to early childhood. *Monographs of the Society for Research in Child Development*, *65*(4), 1–204. http://www.ncbi.nlm.nih.gov/pubmed/12467092

Beauchamp, G. K., & Mennella, J. A. (2011). Flavor perception in human infants: Development and functional significance. *Digestion*, *83*(Suppl 1), 1–6. https://doi.org/10.1159/000323397

Beauregard, J. L., Hamner, H. C., Chen, J., Avila-Rodriguez, W., Elam-Evans, L. D., & Perrine, C. G. (2019). Racial disparities in breastfeeding initiation and duration among U.S. Infants born in 2015. *MMWR. Morbidity and Mortality Weekly Report*, *68*(34), 745–748. https://doi.org/10.15585/mmwr.mm6834a3

Bergelson, E., & Swingley, D. (2012). At 6-9 months, human infants know the meanings of many common nouns. *Proceedings of the National Academy of Sciences of the United States of America*, *109*(9), 3253–3258. https://doi.org/10.1073/pnas.1113380109

Berger, S. E., Theuring, C., & Adolph, K. E. (2007). How and when infants learn to climb stairs. *Infant Behavior & Development, 30*(1), 36–49. https://doi.org/10.1016/j.infbeh.2006.11.002

Bergman, N. J. (2015). Proposal for mechanisms of protection of supine sleep against sudden infant death syndrome: An integrated mechanism review. *Pediatric Research, 77*(1-1), 10–19. https://doi.org/10.1038/pr.2014.140

Bernier, A., Calkins, S. D., & Bell, M. A. (2016). Longitudinal associations between the quality of mother-infant interactions and brain development across infancy. *Child Development, 87*(4), 1159–1174. https://doi.org/10.1111/cdev.12518

Berry, D.., Blair, C.., Willoughby, M.., Garrett-Peters, P.., Vernon-Feagans, L.., & Mills-Koonce, W. R.. (2016). Household chaos and children's cognitive and socio-emotional development in early childhood: Does childcare play a buffering role? *Early Childhood Research Quarterly, 34*, 115–127. doi:10.1016/J.ECRESQ.2015.09.003

Bertenthal, B. I., Campos, J. J., & Barrett, K. (1984). Self-produced locomotion: An organizer of emotional, cognitive, and social development in infancy. In R. Emde & R. Harmon (Eds.), *Continuities and discontinuities in development* (pp. 174–210). Plenum.

Bick, J., & Nelson, C. A. (2017). Early experience and brain development. *Wiley Interdisciplinary Reviews: Cognitive Science, 8*(1-2), e1387. https://doi.org/10.1002/wcs.1387

Bjorklund, D. F., & Myers, A. (2015). The development of cognitive abilities. In M. H. Bornstein & M. E. Lamb (Eds.), *Developmental science: An advanced textbook* (pp. 391–441). Psychology Press.

Bloomfield, F. H., Alexander, T., Muelbert, M., & Beker, F. (2017). Smell and taste in the preterm infant. *Early Human Development, 114*, 31–34. https://doi.org/10.1016/J.EARLHUMDEV.2017.09.012

Bohannon, J. N., Padgett, R. J., Nelson, K. E., & Mark, M. (1996). Useful evidence on negative evidence. *Developmental Psychology, 32*, 551–555.

Bohannon, J. N., & Stanowicz, L. (1988). The issue of negative evidence: Adult responses to children's language errors. *Developmental Psychology, 24*, 684–689.

Bornstein, M. H., & Arterberry, M. E. (2010). The development of object categorization in young children: Hierarchical inclusiveness, age, perceptual attribute, and group versus individual analyses. *Developmental Psychology, 46*(2), 350–365. https://doi.org/10.1037/a0018411

Bornstein, M. H., & Lamb, M. E. (1992). *Development in infancy* (3rd ed.). McGraw-Hill.

Bremner, J. G., Slater, A. M., & Johnson, S. P. (2015). Perception of object persistence: The origins of object permanence in infancy. *Child Development Perspectives, 9*(1), 7–13. https://doi.org/10.1111/cdep.12098

Broesch, T. L., & Bryant, G. A. (2015). Prosody in infant-directed speech is similar across western and traditional cultures. *Journal of Cognition and Development, 16*(1), 31–43. https://doi.org/10.1080/15248372.2013.833923

Bryant, G. A., Liénard, P., & Barrett, H. C. (2012). Recognizing infant-directed speech across distant cultures: Evidence from Africa. *Journal of Evolutionary Psychology, 10*(2).

Cabinian, A., Sinsimer, D., Tang, M., Zumba, O., Mehta, H., Toma, A., Sant'Angelo, D., Laouar, Y., Laouar, A., Nguyen, T., Vieira-Silva, S., Liston, A., Raes, J., Ouellette, A., Selsted, M., Cunliffe, R., Rose, F., Keyte, J., Abberley, L., & Richardson, B. (2016). Transfer of maternal immune cells by breastfeeding: Maternal cytotoxic t lymphocytes present in breast milk localize in the peyer's patches of the nursed infant. *PLOS ONE, 11*(6), e0156762. https://doi.org/10.1371/journal.pone.0156762

Carey, S., Zaitchik, D., & Bascandziev, I. (2015). Theories of development: In dialog with Jean Piaget. *Developmental Review, 38*, 36–54. https://doi.org/10.1016/J.DR.2015.07.003

Carlin, R. F., & Moon, R. Y. (2017). Risk factors, protective factors, and current recommendations to reduce sudden infant death syndrome. *JAMA Pediatrics, 171*(2), 175. https://doi.org/10.1001/jamapediatrics.2016.3345

Carson, N. (2014). *foundations of behavioral neuroscience*. Pearson.

Centers for Disease Control. (2019). *Breastfeeding report card | Breastfeeding*. https://www.cdc.gov/breastfeeding/data/reportcard.htm

Centers for Disease Control and Prevention. (2013). Progress in increasing breastfeeding and reducing racial/ethnic differences - United States, 2000-2008 births. *MMWR. Morbidity and Mortality Weekly Report, 62*(5), 77–80. http://www.ncbi.nlm.nih.gov/pubmed/23388550

Centers for Disease Control and Prevention. (2017). *Breastfeeding Among U.S. Children Born 2002–2014, CDC National Immunization Survey*. https://www.cdc.gov/breastfeeding/data/nis_data/results.html

Chaibal, S., Bennett, S., Rattanathanthong, K., & Siritaratiwat, W. (2016). Early developmental milestones and age of independent walking in orphans compared with typical home-raised infants. *Early Human Development, 101*, 23–26. https://doi.org/10.1016/j.earlhumdev.2016.06.008

Chen, L.-M., & Kent, R. D. (2010). Segmental production in mandarin-learning infants. *Journal of Child Language, 37*(2), 341–371. https://doi.org/10.1017/s0305000909009581

Cheung, C. H. M., Bedford, R., Saez De Urabain, I. R., Karmiloff-Smith, A., & Smith, T. J. (2017). Daily touchscreen use in infants and toddlers is associated with reduced sleep and delayed sleep onset. *Scientific Reports, 7*(1), 1–7. https://doi.org/10.1038/srep46104

Cheung, P., & Ansari, D. (2020). Early understanding of number. In S. Hupp & J. D. Jewell (Eds.), *The Encyclopedia of Child and Adolescent Development* (pp. 1–12). Wiley. https://doi.org/10.1002/9781119171492.wecad133

Chevalier, N., Kurth, S., Doucette, M. R., Wiseheart, M., Deoni, S. C. L. S., Dean, D. C. D., O'Muircheartaigh, J., Blackwell, K. A., Munakata, Y., LeBourgeois, M. K., Kail, R., Fry, A., Hale, S., Fry, A., Hale, S., Salthouse, T., McAuley, T., White, D., Nettelbeck, T., & Greenstein, D. (2015). Myelination is associated with processing speed in early childhood: Preliminary insights. *PLOS ONE, 10*(10), e0139897. https://doi.org/10.1371/journal.pone.0139897

Child Care Aware of America. (2014). *Parents and the high cost of child care: 2013 report* . Retrieved from http://usa.childcareaware.org/sites/default/files/cost_of_care_2013_103113_0.pdf

Chomsky, N. (1959). Review of B. F. Skinner's verbal behavior. *Language, 35*, 26–58.

Chomsky, N. (2017). Language architecture and its import for evolution. *Neuroscience & Biobehavioral Reviews*, *81*, 295–300. https://doi.org/10.1016/J.NEUBIOREV.2017.01.053

Christodoulou, J., Lac, A., & Moore, D. S. (2017). Babies and math: A meta-analysis of infants' simple arithmetic competence. *Developmental Psychology*, *53*(8), 1405–1417. https://doi.org/10.1037/dev0000330

Clifford, A., Franklin, A., Davies, I. R. L., & Holmes, A. (2009). Electrophysiological markers of categorical perception of color in 7-month old infants. *Brain & Cognition*, *71*(2), 165–172. https://doi.org/10.1016/j.bandc.2009.05.002

Clifton, R. K., Rochat, P., Robin, D. J., & Berthier, N. E. (1994). Multimodal perception in the control of infant reaching. *Journal of Experimental Psychology: Human Perception and Performance*, *20*, 876–886.

Cloney, D.., Cleveland, G.., Hattie, J.., & Tayler, C.. (2016). Variations in the Availability and Quality of Early Childhood Education and Care by Socioeconomic Status of Neighborhoods. *Early Education and Development*, *27*(3), 384–401. http://dx.doi.org/10.1080/10409289.2015.1076674

Cole, W. G., Lingeman, J. M., & Adolph, K. E. (2012). Go naked: Diapers affect infant walking. *Developmental Science*, *15*(6), 783–790. https://doi.org/10.1111/j.1467-7687.2012.01169.x

Cole, W. G., Robinson, S. R., & Adolph, K. E. (2016). Bouts of steps: The organization of infant exploration. *Developmental Psychobiology*, *58*(3), 341–354. https://doi.org/10.1002/dev.21374

Coleman-Jensen, A., Rabbitt, M. P., Gregory, C. A., & Singh, A. (2018). *Household food security in the United States in 2017.* Economic Research report ERR-256. https://www.ers.usda.gov/publications/pub-details/?pubid=90022

Colombo, J., Brez, C. C., & Curtindale, L. M. (2015). Infant perception and cognition. In I. B. Weiner, R. M. Lerner, M. A. Easterbrooks, & J. Mistry (Eds.), *Handbook of psychology: Developmental psychology* (pp. 61–90). Wiley.

Colson, E. R., Willinger, M., Rybin, D., Heeren, T., Smith, L. A., Lister, G., & Corwin, M. J. (2013). Trends and factors associated with infant bed sharing, 1993-2010. *JAMA Pediatrics*, *167*(11), 1032. https://doi.org/10.1001/jamapediatrics.2013.2560

Corbetta, D., & Snapp-Childs, W. (2009). Seeing and touching: The role of sensory-motor experience on the development of infant reaching. *Infant Behavior & Development*, *32*(1), 44–58. https://doi.org/10.1016/j.infbeh.2008.10.004

Courage, M. L. (2017). Screen media and the youngest viewers: Implications for attention and learning. In F. C. Blumberg & P. J. Brooks (Eds.), *Cognitive development in digital contexts* (pp. 3–28). Elsevier. https://doi.org/10.1016/B978-0-12-809481-5.00001-8

Courage, M. L., Reynolds, G. D., & Richards, J. E. (2006). Infants' attention to patterned stimuli: Developmental change From 3 to 12 months of age. *Child Development*, *77*(3), 680–695. https://doi.org/10.1111/j.1467-8624.2006.00897.x

Cuevas, K., & Sheya, A. (2019). Ontogenesis of learning and memory: Biopsychosocial and dynamical systems perspectives. *Developmental Psychobiology*, *61*(3), 402–415. https://doi.org/10.1002/dev.21817

Dąbrowska, E. (2015). What exactly is universal grammar, and has anyone seen it? *Frontiers in Psychology*, *6*, 852. https://doi.org/10.3389/fpsyg.2015.00852

Dahl, A., Campos, J. J., Anderson, D. I., Uchiyama, I., Witherington, D. C., Ueno, M., & Barbu-roth, M. (2013). The epigenesis of wariness of heights. *Psychological Science*, *24*, 1361–1367. https://doi.org/10.1177/0956797613476047

Dediu, D., & Christiansen, M. H. (2016). Language evolution: Constraints and opportunities from modern genetics. *Topics in Cognitive Science*, *8*(2), 361–370. https://doi.org/10.1111/tops.12195

DeHaan, L.. (2006). Child Care and Development: Results From the NICHD Study of Early Child Care and Youth Development. The NICHD Early Child Care Research Network. *J Marriage and Family*, *68*(1), 252–253. http://dx.doi.org/10.1111/j.1741-3737.2006.00245.x

Dehaene-Lambertz, G. (2017). The human infant brain: A neural architecture able to learn language. *Psychonomic Bulletin & Review*, *24*(1), 48–55. https://doi.org/10.3758/s13423-016-1156-9

Dehaene-Lambertz, G., & Spelke, E. S. (2015). The infancy of the human brain. *Neuron*, *88*(1), 93–109. https://doi.org/10.1016/j.neuron.2015.09.026

DeLoache, J. S., Chiong, C., Sherman, K., Islam, N., Vanderborght, M., Troseth, G. L., Strouse, G. A., & O'Doherty, K. (2010). Do babies learn from baby media? *Psychological Science*, *21*(11), 1570–1574. https://doi.org/10.1177/0956797610384145

Dennis, W. (1960). Causes of retardation among institutional children: Iran. *Journal of Genetic Psychology*, *96*, 47–59.

Dennis, W., & Dennis, M. G. (1991). The effect of cradling practices upon the onset of walking in Hopi children. *Journal of Genetic Psychology*, *152*(4), 563–572.

de Onis, M.., & Branca, F.. (2016). Childhood stunting: A global perspective. *Maternal & Child Nutrition*, *12*, 12–26. doi:10.1111/mcn.12231

Dinour, L. M., Rivera Rodas, E. I., Amutah-Onukagha, N. N., & Doamekpor, L. A. (2020). The role of prenatal food insecurity on breastfeeding behaviors: Findings from the United States pregnancy risk assessment monitoring system. *International Breastfeeding Journal*, *15*(1). https://doi.org/10.1186/s13006-020-00276-x

Domingues-Montanari, S. (2017). Clinical and psychological effects of excessive screen time on children. *Journal of Paediatrics and Child Health*, *53*(4), 333–338. https://doi.org/10.1111/jpc.13462

Dowe, K. N., Planalp, E. M., Dean, D. C., Alexander, A. L., Davidson, R. J., & Goldsmith, H. H. (2020). Early microstructure of white matter associated with infant attention. *Developmental Cognitive Neuroscience*, *45*, 100815. https://doi.org/10.1016/j.dcn.2020.100815

D'Souza, H., Cowie, D., Karmiloff-Smith, A., & Bremner, A. J. (2017). Specialization of the motor system in infancy: From broad tuning to selectively specialized purposeful actions. *Developmental Science*, *20*(4), e12409. https://doi.org/10.1111/desc.12409

Elsabbagh, M., Hohenberger, A., Campos, R., Van Herwegen, J., Serres, J., de Schonen, S., Aschersleben, G., & Karmiloff-Smith, A. (2013). Narrowing perceptual sensitivity to the native language in infancy: Exogenous influences on developmental timing. *Behavioral Sciences*, *3*(1), 120–132. https://doi.org/10.3390/bs3010120

Ely, D. M.., & Hoyert, D. L.. (2018). *Differences between rural and urban areas in mortality rates for the leading causes of infant death: United States, 2013–2015. NCHS Data Brief No 300* . https://www.cdc.gov/nchs/products/databriefs/db300.htm

Ennouri, K., & Bloch, H. (1996). Visual control of hand approach movements in new-borns. *British Journal of Developmental Psychology*, *14*(3), 327–338. https://doi.org/10.1111/j.2044-835X.1996.tb00709.x

Estes, K. G., & Hurley, K. (2013). Infant-directed prosody helps infants map sounds to meanings. *Infancy*, *18*(5), 10.1111/infa.12006.

Evans, A., Bagnall, R. D., Duflou, J., & Semsarian, C. (2013). Postmortem review and genetic analysis in sudden infant death syndrome: an 11-year review. *Human Pathology*, *44*(9), 1730–1736. https://doi.org/10.1016/j.humpath.2013.01.024

Fagard, J., Spelke, E., & von Hofsten, C. (2009). Reaching and grasping a moving object in 6-, 8-, and 10-month-old infants: Laterality and performance. *Infant Behavior & Development*, *32*(2), 137–146. https://doi.org/10.1016/j.infbeh.2008.12.002

Fantz, R. L. (1961). The origin of form perception. *Scientific American*, *204*, 66–72.

Farroni, T., & Menon, E. (2008). Visual perception and early brain development. In R. E. Tremblay, R. G. Barr, RDeV. Peters, & M. Boivin (Eds.), *Encyclopedia on early childhood development* (pp. 1–6). Centre of Excellence for Early Childhood Development. http://www.child-encyclopedia.com/documents/Farroni-MenonANGxp.pdf

Federal Interagency Forum on Child and Family Statistics. (2014). *America's children: Key national indicators of well-being, 2013* . http://www.childstats.gov/americaschildren Federal Interagency Forum on Child and Family Statistics

Fenstermacher, S. K., Barr, R., Salerno, K., Garcia, A., Shwery, C. E., Calvert, S. L., & Linebarger, D. L. (2010). Infant-directed media: an analysis of product information and claims. *Infant & Child Development*, *19*(6), 556–557. https://doi.org/10.1002/icd.718

Ferguson, C. J., & Donnellan, M. B. (2014). Is the association between children's baby video viewing and poor language development robust? A reanalysis of Zimmerman, Christakis, and Meltzoff (2007). *Developmental Psychology*, *50*(1), 129–137. https://doi.org/10.1037/a0033628

Filiano, J. J., & Kinney, H. C. (1994). A Perspective on neuropathologic findings in victims of the sudden infant death syndrome: The triple-risk model. *Neonatology*, *65*(3–4), 194–197. https://doi.org/10.1159/000244052

Fisher, A. V. (2019). Selective sustained attention: A developmental foundation for cognition. *Current Opinion in Psychology*, *29*, 248–253. https://doi.org/10.1016/j.copsyc.2019.06.002

Fisher, S. E. (2017). Evolution of language: Lessons from the genome. *Psychonomic Bulletin & Review*, *24*(1), 34–40. https://doi.org/10.3758/s13423-016-1112-8

Fitneva, S. A., & Matsui, T. (2015). The Emergence and development of language across cultures. In L. A. Jensen (Ed.), *The oxford handbook of human development and culture*. Oxford University Press. https://doi.org/10.1093/oxfordhb/9780199948550.013.8

Forestell, C. A. (2016). The development of flavor perception and acceptance: The roles of nature and nurture. *Nestle Nutrition Institute Workshop Series*, *85*, 135–143. https://doi.org/10.1159/000439504

Forestell, C. A. (2017). Flavor perception and preference development in human infants. *Annals of Nutrition and Metabolism*, *70*(3), 17–25. https://doi.org/10.1159/000478759

Frank, M. C., Vul, E., & Johnson, S. P. (2009). Development of infants' attention to faces during the first year. *Cognition*, *110*(2), 160–170. https://doi.org/10.1016/j.cognition.2008.11.010

Friederici, A. D. (2017). Evolution of the neural language network. *Psychonomic Bulletin & Review*, *24*(1), 41–47. https://doi.org/10.3758/s13423-016-1090-x

Gabriel, M. A. M., Alonso, C. R. P., Bértolo, J. D. L. C., Carbonero, S. C., Maestro, M. L., Pumarega, M. M., Díaz, C. A., & Pablos, D. L. (2009). Age of sitting unsupported and independent walking in very low birth weight preterm infants with normal motor development at 2 years. *Acta Paediatrica*, *98*(11), 1815–1821. https://doi.org/10.1111/j.1651-2227.2009.01475.x

Galler, J. R., Bryce, C. P., Zichlin, M. L., Fitzmaurice, G., Eaglesfield, G. D., & Waber, D. P. (2012). Infant malnutrition is associated with persisting attention deficits in middle adulthood. *The Journal of Nutrition*, *142*(4), 788–794. https://doi.org/10.3945/jn.111.145441

Garcia-Sierra, A., Rivera-Gaxiola, M., Percaccio, C. R., Conboy, B. T., Romo, H., Klarman, L., Ortiz, S., & Kuhl, P. K. (2011). Bilingual language learning: An ERP study relating early brain responses to speech, language input, and later word production. *Journal of Phonetics*, *39*(4), 546–557. https://doi.org/10.1016/J.WOCN.2011.07.002

Gaskins, S., & Paradise, R. (2010). Learning through observation in daily life. In D. F. Lancy, J. Bock, & S. Gaskins (Eds.), *The anthropology of learning in childhood* (pp. 85–117). AltaMira Press. https://psycnet.apa.org/record/2010-03678-005

Gervain, J., Macagno, F., Cogoi, S., Peña, M., & Mehler, J. (2008). The neonate brain detects speech structure. *Proceedings of the National Academy of Sciences of the United States of America*, *105*(37), 14222–14227. https://doi.org/10.1073/pnas.0806530105

Gervain, J., & Mehler, J. (2010). Speech perception and language acquisition in the first year of life. *Annual Review of Psychology*, *61*, 191–218. https://doi.org/10.1146/annurev.psych.093008.100408

Gialamas, A.., Mittinty, M. N.., Sawyer, M. G.., Zubrick, S. R.., & Lynch, J.. (2014). Child care quality and children\'s cognitive and socio-emotional development: an Australian longitudinal study. *Early Child Development and Care*, *184*(7), 977–997. http://dx.doi.org/10.1080/03004430.2013.847835

Gibb, R., & Kovalchuk, A. (2018). Brain development. In R. Gibb & B. Kolb (Eds.), *The neurobiology of brain and behavioral development* (pp. 3–27). Academic Press. https://doi.org/10.1016/B978-0-12-804036-2.00001-7

Gibson, E. J., & Pick, A. D. (2000). *An ecological approach to perceptual learning and development*. Oxford University Press. http://psycnet.apa.org/psycinfo/2001-18056-000

Gibson, E J., & Walk, R. D. (1960). The "visual cliff". *Scientific American*, *202*, 64–71.

Gibson, J. (1979). *The ecological approach to visual perception*. Houghton, Mifflin and Company. http://psycnet.apa.org/psycinfo/2003-00063-000

Gilmore, J. H., Knickmeyer, R. C., & Gao, W. (2018). Imaging structural and functional brain development in early childhood. *Nature Reviews Neuroscience*, *19*(3), 123–137. https://doi.org/10.1038/nrn.2018.1

Goldstein, M. H., & Schwade, J. A. (2008). Social feedback to infants' babbling facilitates rapid phonological learning. *Psychological Science, 19*(5), 515–523. https://doi.org/10.1111/j.1467-9280.2008.02117.x

Hadley, P. A., Rispoli, M., Fitzgerald, C., & Bahnsen, A. (2011). Predictors of morphosyntactic growth in typically developing toddlers: Contributions of parent input and child sex. *Journal of Speech Language and Hearing Research, 54*(2), 549. https://doi.org/10.1044/1092-4388(2010/09-0216)

Haith, M. M. (1993). Preparing for the 21st century: Some goals and challenges for studies of infant sensory and perceptual development. *Developmental Review, 13*, 354–371.

Harker, A. (2018). Social dysfunction. In R. Gibb & B. Kolb (Eds.), *The neurobiology of brain and behavioral development* (pp. 439–467). Elsevier. https://doi.org/10.1016/B978-0-12-804036-2.00016-9

Harriman, A. E., & Lukosius, P. A. (1982). On why wayne dennis found hopi infants retarded in age at onset of walking. *Perceptual & Motor Skills, 55*(1), 79–86.

Hauck, Y. L., Fenwick, J., Dhaliwal, S. S., & Butt, J. (2011). A western Australian survey of breastfeeding initiation, prevalence and early cessation patterns. *Maternal & Child Health Journal, 15*(2), 260–268. https://doi.org/10.1007/s10995-009-0554-2

Hensch, T. K. (2018). Critical periods in cortical development. In R. Gibb & B. Kolb (Eds.), *The Neurobiology of brain and behavioral development* (pp. 133–151). Elsevier. https://doi.org/10.1016/B978-0-12-804036-2.00006-6

Hernandez-Pavon, J. C., Sosa, M., Lutter, W. J., Maier, M., & Wakai, R. T. (2008). Auditory evoked responses in neonates by MEG. *AIP Conference Proceedings, 1032*(1), 114–117. https://doi.org/10.1063/1.2979244

Hewitt, L., Kerr, E., Stanley, R. M., & Okely, A. D. (2020). Tummy time and infant health outcomes: A systematic review. *Pediatrics, 145*(6). https://doi.org/10.1542/peds.2019-2168

Hodel, A. S. (2018). Rapid infant prefrontal cortex development and sensitivity to early environmental experience. *Developmental Review, 48*, 113–144. https://doi.org/10.1016/J.DR.2018.02.003

Hoff, E. (2015). Language development. In M. H. Bornstein & M. E. Lamb (Eds.), *Developmental science: An advanced textbook* (5th ed.). Psychology Press.

Hoff, E., & Core, C. (2015). What clinicians need to know about bilingual development. *Seminars in Speech and Language, 36*(02), 089–099. https://doi.org/10.1055/s-0035-1549104

Hoff, E., Core, C., Place, S., & Rumiche, R. (2012). Dual language exposure and early bilingual development. *Journal of Child Language, 39*(01), 1–27. https://doi.org/10.1017/S0305000910000759

Horne, R. S. C. (2019). Sudden infant death syndrome: current perspectives. *Internal Medicine Journal, 49*(4), 433–438. https://doi.org/10.1111/imj.14248

Howe, M. L. (2015). Memory development. In L. S. Liben & U. Mueller (Eds.), *Handbook of child psychology and developmental science* (pp. 1–47). John Wiley & Sons, Inc. https://doi.org/10.1002/9781118963418.childpsy206

Hunnius, S., & Geuze, R. H. (2004). Developmental changes in visual scanning of dynamic faces and abstract stimuli in infants: A longitudinal study. *Infancy, 6*(2), 231–255.

Hurtado, N., Marchman, V. A., & Fernald, A. (2008). Does input influence uptake? Links between maternal talk, processing speed and vocabulary size in Spanish-learning children. *Developmental Science, 11*(6), F31–F39. https://doi.org/10.1111/j.1467-7687.2008.00768.x

Huttenlocher, J., Waterfall, H., Vasilyeva, M., Vevea, J., & Hedges, L. V. (2010). Sources of variability in children's language growth. *Cognitive Psychology, 61*(4), 343–365. https://doi.org/10.1016/j.cogpsych.2010.08.002

Ibbotson, P., & Tomasello, M. (2016). Evidence rebuts Chomsky's theory of language learinng. *Scientific American, 315*(5), 70–75. https://doi.org/10.1038/scientificamerican1116-70

Jenkins, J. M., & Foster, E. M. (2014). The effects of breastfeeding exclusivity on early childhood outcomes. *American Journal of Public Health, 104*, S128–135. https://doi.org/10.2105/AJPH.2013.301713

Johnson, S. P., & Hannon, E. E. (2015). Perceptual development. In L. S. Liben & U. Müller (Eds.), *Handbook of child psychology and developmental science* (pp. 1–50). John Wiley & Sons, Inc. https://doi.org/10.1002/9781118963418.childpsy203

Jones, K. M., Power, M. L., Queenan, J. T., & Schulkin, J. (2015). Racial and ethnic disparities in breastfeeding. *Breastfeeding Medicine, 10*, 186–196. https://doi.org/10.1089/bfm.2014.0152

Juett, J., & Kuipers, B. (2019). Learning and acting in peripersonal space: Moving, reaching, and grasping. *Frontiers in Neurorobotics, 13*, 4. https://doi.org/10.3389/fnbot.2019.00004

Kaldy, Z., & Blaser, E. (2020). Putting effort into infant cognition. *Current Directions in Psychological Science, 29*(2), 180–185. https://doi.org/10.1177/0963721420903015

Kan, P. F., & Kohnert, K. (2008). Fast mapping by bilingual preschool children. *Journal of Child Language, 35*(3), 495–514. https://doi.org/10.1017/S0305000907008604

Kärtner, J., Schuhmacher, N., & Giner Torréns, M. (2020). Culture and early social-cognitive development. In S. Hunnius & M. Meyer (Eds.), *Progress in brain research* (Vol. 254, pp. 225–246). Elsevier B.V. https://doi.org/10.1016/bs.pbr.2020.06.011

Kayed, N. S., Farstad, H., & van der Meer, A. L. H. (2008). Preterm infants' timing strategies to optical collisions. *Early Human Development, 84*(6), 381–388. https://doi.org/10.1016/j.earlhumdev.2007.10.006

Keller, H. (2003). Socialization for competence: Cultural models of infancy. *Human Development, 46*(5), 288–311.

Keller, H., Borke, J., Staufenbiel, T., Yovsi, R. D., Abels, M., Papaligoura, Z., Jensen, H., Lohaus, A., Chaudhary, N., Lo, W., & Su, Y. (2009). Distal and proximal parenting as alternative parenting strategies during infants' early months of life: A cross-cultural study. *International Journal of Behavioral Development, 33*(5), 412–420. https://doi.org/10.1177/0165025409338441

Kibbe, M. M. (2015). Varieties of visual working memory representation in infancy and beyond. *Current Directions in Psychological Science, 24*(6), 433–439. https://doi.org/10.1177/0963721415605831

Kim, K. M., & Choi, J.-W. (2020). Associations between breastfeeding and cognitive function in children from early childhood to school age: A prospective birth cohort study. *International Breastfeeding Journal, 15*(1), 1–9. https://doi.org/10.1186/S13006-020-00326-4

Kisilevsky, B. S. (2016). Fetal auditory processing: implications for language development? In N. Reissland & B. S. Kisilevsky (Eds.), *Fetal development* (pp. 133–152). Springer International Publishing. https://doi.org/10.1007/978-3-319-22023-9_8

Kit, B. K., Akinbami, L. J., Isfahani, N. S., & Ulrich, D. A. (2017). Gross motor development in children aged 3–5 Years, United States 2012. *Maternal and Child Health Journal, 21*(7), 1–8. https://doi.org/10.1007/s10995-017-2289-9

Kitamura, C., & Burnham, D. (2003). Pitch and communicative intent in mother's speech: Adjustments for age and sex in the first year. *Infancy, 4*(1), 85–110.

Kliegman, R. M., & Geme, J, St. (2020). *Nelson textbook of pediatrics* (21st ed.). Elsevier. https://www.us.elsevierhealth.com/nelson-textbook-of-pediatrics-2-volume-set-9780323529501.html#additional

Kolb, B. (2018). Overview of factors influencing brain development. In R. Gibb & B. Kolb (Eds.), *The neurobiology of brain and behavioral development* (pp. 51–79). Elsevier. https://doi.org/10.1016/B978-0-12-804036-2.00003-0

Kolb, B. (2020). Brain development during early childhood. In D. Güngör (Ed.), *The encyclopedia of child and adolescent development* (pp. 1–14). Wiley. https://doi.org/10.1002/9781119171492.wecad015

Kolb, B., Mychasiuk, R., & Gibb, R. (2014). Brain development, experience, and behavior. *Pediatric Blood & Cancer, 61*(10), 1720–1723. https://doi.org/10.1002/pbc.24908

Kolb, B., Whishaw, I., & Teskey, G. C. (2016). *An introduction to brain and behavior.* Worth.

Konner, M. (2017). Hunter-Gatherer infancy and childhood. In B. S. Hewlett (Ed.), *Hunter-gatherer childhoods* (pp. 19–64). Routledge. https://doi.org/10.4324/9780203789445-3

Köster, M., Kayhan, E., Langeloh, M., & Hoehl, S. (2020). Making sense of the world: Infant learning from a predictive processing perspective. *Perspectives on Psychological Science, 15*(3), 562–571. https://doi.org/10.1177/1745691619895071

Kothari, C. L.., Romph, C.., Bautista, T.., & Lenz, D.. (2017). Perinatal Periods of Risk Analysis: Disentangling Race and Socioeconomic Status to Inform a Black Infant Mortality Community Action Initiative. *Matern Child Health J, 21*, 49–58. doi:10.1007/s10995-017-2383-z

Kretch, K. S., Franchak, J. M., & Adolph, K. E. (2014). Crawling and walking infants see the world differently. *Child Development, 85*(4), 1503–1518. https://doi.org/10.1111/cdev.12206

Kuhl, P. K. (2015). Baby talk. *Scientific American, 313*(5), 64–69. https://doi.org/10.1038/scientificamerican1115-64

Kuhl, P. K. (2016). Language and the social brain: The power of surprise in science. In R. J. Sternberg, S. T. Fiske, & D. J. Foss (Eds.), *Scientists making a difference: One hundred eminent behavioral and brain scientists talk about their most important contributions* (pp. 206–209). Cambridge Univ Press.

Kuhl, P. K., Andruski, J. E., Christovich, I. A., Christovich, L. A., Kozhevnikova, E. V., Ryskina, V. L., Stolyarova, E. I., Sundberg, U., & Lacerda, F. (1997). Cross-language analysis of phonetic units in language addressed to infants. *Science, 277*, 684–686.

Kuhl, P. K., & Ramirez, N. F. (2016). *Bilingual language learning in children.* http://ilabs.washington.edu/sites/default/files/Ramirez_WhiteHouse_Paper.pdf

Kuo, Y.-L., Liao, H.-F., Chen, P.-C., Hsieh, W.-S., & Hwang, A.-W. (2008). The influence of wakeful prone positioning on motor development during the early life. *Journal of Developmental and Behavioral Pediatrics, 29*(5), 367–376. https://doi.org/10.1097/DBP.0b013e3181856d54

Lampl, M., Johnson, M. L., & Frongillo, E. A. (2001). Mixed distribution analysis identifies saltation and stasis growth. *Annals of Human Biology, 28*(4), 403–411.

Learmonth, A. E., Lamberth, R., & Rovee-Collier, C. (2004). Generalizations of deferred imitation during the first year of life. *Journal of Experimental Child Psychology, 88*(4), 297–318.

Leat, S. J.., Yadav, N. K.., & Irving, E. L.. (2009). Development of Visual Acuity and Contrast Sensitivity in Children. *Journal of Optometry, 2*(1), 19–26. http://dx.doi.org/10.3921/joptom.2009.19

Lebel, C., & Deoni, S. (2018). The development of brain white matter microstructure. *NeuroImage.* https://doi.org/10.1016/J.NEUROIMAGE.2017.12.097

Legare, C. H., Wen, N. J., Herrmann, P. A., & Whitehouse, H. (2015). Imitative flexibility and the development of cultural learning. *Cognition, 142*, 351–361. https://doi.org/10.1016/J.COGNITION.2015.05.020

Lenehan, S. M., Boylan, G. B., Livingstone, V., Fogarty, L., Twomey, D. M., Nikolovski, J., Irvine, A. D., Kiely, M., Kenny, L. C., Hourihane, J. O. B., & Murray, D. M. (2020). The impact of short-term predominate breastfeeding on cognitive outcome at 5 years. *Acta Paediatrica, 109*(5), 982–988. https://doi.org/10.1111/apa.15014

Lewkowicz, D. J., Leo, I., & Simion, F. (2010). Intersensory perception at Birth: Newborns match nonhuman primate faces and voices. *Infancy, 15*(1), 46–60. https://doi.org/10.1111/j.1532-7078.2009.00005.x

Libertus, K., Gibson, J., Hidayatallah, N. Z., Hirtle, J., Adcock, R. A., & Needham, A. (2013). Size matters: How age and reaching experiences shape infants' preferences for different sized objects. *Infant Behavior & Development, 36*(2), 189–198. https://doi.org/10.1016/j.infbeh.2013.01.006

Libertus, K., Joh, A. S., & Needham, A. W. (2016). Motor training at 3 months affects object exploration 12 months later. *Developmental Science, 19*(6), 1058–1066. https://doi.org/10.1111/desc.12370

Lieven, E., & Stoll, S. (2010). Language. In M. H. Bornstein (Ed.), *Handbook of cultural developmental science* (pp. 143–160). Psychology Press.

Lind, J. N., Perrine, C. G., Li, R., Scanlon, K. S., Grummer-Strawn, L. M., & Centers for Disease Control and Prevention. (2014). Racial disparities in access to maternity care practices that support breastfeeding - United States, 2011. *MMWR. Morbidity and Mortality Weekly Report, 63*(33), 725–728. 2011

Linebarger, D. L., & Vaala, S. E. (2010). Screen media and language development in infants and toddlers: An ecological perspective. *Developmental Review, 30*(2), 176–202. https://doi.org/10.1016/j.dr.2010.03.006

Litovsky, R. Y., & Ashmead, D. H. (1997). Developmental of binaural and spatial hearing in infants and children. In R. H. Gilkey & T. R. Anderson (Eds.), *Binaural and special hearing in real and virtual environments* (pp. 571–592). Erlbaum.

Lobo, M. A., & Galloway, J. C. (2012). Enhanced handling and positioning in early infancy advances development throughout the first year. *Child Development*, *83*(4), 1290–1302. https://doi.org/10.1111/j.1467-8624.2012.01772.x

LoBue, V., & Adolph, K. E. (2019). Fear in infancy: Lessons from snakes, spiders, heights, and strangers. *Developmental Psychology*, *55*, 1889–1907. https://doi.org/10.1037/dev0000675

Lohaus, A., Keller, H., Lamm, B., Teubert, M., Fassbender, I., Freitag, C., Goertz, C., Graf, F., Kolling, T., Spangler, S., Vierhaus, M., Knopf, M., & Schwarzer, G. (2011). Infant development in two cultural contexts: Cameroonian Nso farmer and German middle-class infants. *Journal of Reproductive and Infant Psychology*, *29*(2), 148–161. https://doi.org/10.1080/02646838.2011.558074

Louis-Jacques, A., & Stuebe, A. (2018). Long-term maternal benefits of breastfeeding: Longer durations of breastfeeding are associated with improved health outcomes for mothers and should be supported by ob/gyns. *Contemporary OB/GYN*, *63*(7), 26–30.

Lyall, A. E., Shi, F., Geng, X., Woolson, S., Li, G., Wang, L., Hamer, R. M., Shen, D., & Gilmore, J. H. (2015). Dynamic development of regional cortical thickness and surface area in early childhood. *Cerebral Cortex*, *25*(8), 2204–2212. https://doi.org/10.1093/cercor/bhu027

Lynch, A., Lee, H. M., Bhat, A., & Galloway, J. C. (2008). No stable arm preference during the pre-reaching period: A comparison of right and left hand kinematics with and without a toy present. *Developmental Psychobiology*, *50*(4), 390–398. https://doi.org/10.1002/dev.20297

Macfarlane, A. J. (1975). Olfaction in the development of social preferences in the human neonate. *Ciba Foundation Symposia*, *33*, 103–117.

Mandler, J. M. (2004). . In *The foundations of mind: Origins of conceptual thought*. Oxford University Press.

Mandler, J. M., & McDonough, L. (1998). On developing a knowledge base in infancy. *Developmental Psychology*, *34*, 1274–1288.

Mani, N., & Ackermann, L. (2018). Why do children learn the words they do? *Child Development Perspectives*, *12*(4), 253–257. https://doi.org/10.1111/cdep.12295

Marin, M. M., Rapisardi, G., & Tani, F. (2015). Two-day-old newborn infants recognise their mother by her axillary odour. *Acta Paediatrica*, *104*(3), 237–240. https://doi.org/10.1111/apa.12905

Marinellie, S. A., & Kneile, L. A. (2012). Acquiring knowledge of derived nominals and derived adjectives in context. *Language Speech and Hearing Services in Schools*, *43*(1), 53. https://doi.org/10.1044/0161-1461(2011/10-0053)

Marlier, L., & Schaal, B. (2005). Human newborns prefer human milk: Conspecific milk odor is attractive without postnatal exposure. *Child Development*, *76*(1), 155–168.

Matlin, M. W., & Foley, H. J. (1997). *Sensation and perception* (4th ed.). : Allyn &amp.

Maurer, D. (2017). Critical periods re-examined: Evidence from children treated for dense cataracts. *Cognitive Development*, *42*, 27–36. https://doi.org/10.1016/j.cogdev.2017.02.006

May, L., Gervain, J., Carreiras, M., & Werker, J. F. (2018). The specificity of the neural response to speech at birth. *Developmental Science*, *21*(3), e12564. https://doi.org/10.1111/desc.12564

McKinney, C. O., Hahn-Holbrook, J., Chase-Lansdale, P. L., Ramey, S. L., Krohn, J., Reed-Vance, M., Raju, T. N. K., & Shalowitz, M. U. (2016). Racial and ethnic differences in breastfeeding. *Pediatrics*, *138*(2). https://doi.org/10.1542/peds.2015-2388

McLaughlin, K. A., Sheridan, M. A., & Nelson, C. A. (2017). Neglect as a violation of species-expectant experience: Neurodevelopmental consequences. *Biological Psychiatry*, *82*(7), 462–471. https://doi.org/10.1016/J.BIOPSYCH.2017.02.1096

McMurray, B. (2007). Defusing the childhood vocabulary explosion. *Science*, *317*(5838), 631. https://doi.org/10.1126/science.1144073

Meltzoff, A. N., & Borton, R. W. (1979). Intermodal matching by human neonates. *Nature*, *282*, 403–404.

Mennella, J. A., & Beauchamp, G. K. (2002). Flavor experiences during formula feeding are related to preferences during childhood. *Early Human Development*, *68*(2), 71–82.

Mercuri, E., Baranello, G., Romeo, D. M. M., Cesarini, L., & Ricci, D. (2007). The development of vision. *Early Human Development*, *83*(12), 795–800. https://doi.org/10.1016/j.earlhumdev.2007.09.014

Moon, R. Y., & Task Force on Sudden Infant Death Syndrome, . (2016a). SIDS and other sleep-related infant Deaths: Evidence Base for 2016 updated recommendations for a safe infant sleeping environment. *Pediatrics*, *138*(5), e20162940–e20162940. https://doi.org/10.1542/peds.2016-2940

Moon, R. Y., & Task Force on Sudden Infant Death Syndrome. (2016b). SIDS and other sleep-related infant deaths: Updated 2016 recommendations for a safe infant sleeping environment. *Pediatrics*, *138*(5), e20162938–e20162938. https://doi.org/10.1542/peds.2016-2938

Moore, C., Angelopoulos, M., & Bennett, P. (1999). Word learning in the context of referential and salience cues. *Developmental Psychology*, *35*, 60–68.

Mortensen, J. A.., & Barnett, M. A.. (2015). Teacher–Child Interactions in Infant\/Toddler Child Care and Socioemotional Development. *Early Education and Development*, *26*(2), 209–229. doi: 10.1080/10409289.2015.985878

Muenssinger, J., Matuz, T., Schleger, F., Kiefer-Schmidt, I., Goelz, R., Wacker-Gussmann, A., Birbaumer, N., & Preissl, H. (2013). Auditory habituation in the fetus and neonate: an fMEG study. *Developmental Science*, *16*(2), 287–295. https://doi.org/10.1111/desc.12025

Mummert, A., Schoen, M., & Lampl, M. (2018). Growth and life course health development. In N. Halfon, C. B. Forrest, R. M. Lerner, & E. M. Faustman (Eds.), *Handbook of life course health development* (pp. 405–429). Springer International Publishing. https://doi.org/10.1007/978-3-319-47143-3_17

Náñez, J. E., & Yonas, A. (1994). Effects of luminance and texture motion on infant defensive reactions to optical collision. *Infant Behavior & Development*, *17*, 165–174.

Nelson, C., Zeanah, C. H., & Fox, N. A. (2019). How early experience shapes human development: The case of psychosocial deprivation. *Neural Plasticity*, *2019*, 1676285. https://doi.org/10.1155/2019/1676285

Neshat, H., Jebreili, M., Seyyedrasouli, A., Ghojazade, M., Hosseini, M. B., & Hamishehkar, H. (2016). Effects of breast milk and vanilla odors on premature neonate's heart rate and blood oxygen saturation during and after venipuncture. *Pediatrics & Neonatology, 57*(3), 225–231. https://doi.org/10.1016/J.PEDNEO.2015.09.004

Newell, F. N. (2004). Cross-modal object recognition. In G. A. Calvert, C. Spence, & B. E. Stein (Eds.), *The handbook of multisensory processes* (pp. 123–139). MIT Press.

Ngandu, C. B., Momberg, D., Magan, A., Chola, L., Norris, S. A., & Said-Mohamed, R. (2019). The association between household socio-economic status, maternal socio-demographic characteristics and adverse birth and infant growth outcomes in sub-Saharan Africa: A systematic review. *Journal of Developmental Origins of Health and Disease, 11*, 317–334. https://doi.org/10.1017/S2040174419000680

NICHD Early Child Care Research Network. (2005). Early Child Care and Children's Development in the Primary Grades: Follow-Up Results From the NICHD Study of Early Child Care. *American Educational Research Journal, 42*(3), 537–570. doi:10.3102/00028312042003537

Northern, J. L., & Downs, M. P. (2014). *Hearing in children* (6th ed.). Plural Publishing.

Oakes, L. M. (2010). Using habituation of looking time to assess mental processes in infancy. *Journal of Cognition & Development, 11*(3), 255–268. https://doi.org/10.1080/15248371003699977

Oakes, L. M., & Luck, S. J. (2013). Short-term memory in infancy. In P. J. Bauer & R. Fivush (Eds.), *The wiley handbook on the development of children's memory* (pp. 151–180). John Wiley & Sons Ltd. https://doi.org/10.1002/9781118597705.ch8

Oberauer, K. (2019). Working memory and attention – A conceptual analysis and review. *Journal of Cognition, 2*(1), 1–23. https://doi.org/10.5334/joc.58

Ochs, E., & Schieffein, B. (1984). Language acquisition and socialization: Three developmental stories and their implications. In R. A. Shweder & R. A. LeVine (Eds.), *Culture theory: Essays on mind, self, and emotion* (pp. 276–320). Cambridge University Press.

Ohta, H. (2019). Growth spurts of the bone from infancy to puberty. *Clinical Calcium, 29*(1), 9–17. https://doi.org/clica1901917

Owen, K., & Barnes, C. (2021). The development of categorization in early childhood: A review. *Early Child Development and Care*. https://doi.org/10.1080/03004430.2019.1608193

Owens, R. E. (2019). *Language development: An introduction*. Pearson.

Pandita, A., Panghal, A., Gupta, G., Verma, A., Pillai, A., Singh, A., & Naranje, K. (2018). Is kangaroo mother care effective in alleviating vaccination associated pain in early infantile period? A RCT. *Early Human Development, 127*, 69–73. https://doi.org/10.1016/J.EARLHUMDEV.2018.10.001

Parks, S. E., Erck Lambert, A. B., & Shapiro-Mendoza, C. K. (2017). Racial and ethnic trends in sudden unexpected infant deaths: United States, 1995–2013. *Pediatrics, 139*(6), e20163844.

Pascalis, O., Dechonen, S., Morton, J., Duruelle, C., & Grenet, F. (1995). Mother's face recognition in neonates: A replication and an extension. *Infant Behavior and Development, 18*, 79–85.

Payne, G., & Isaacs, L. (2020). *Human motor development: A lifespan approach* (10th ed.). Routledge. https://www.routledge.com/Human-Motor-Development-A-Lifespan-Approach/Payne-Isaacs/p/book/9780367347376

Pérez-Escamilla, R., Martinez, J. L., & Segura-Pérez, S. (2016). Impact of the Baby-friendly Hospital Initiative on breastfeeding and child health outcomes: A systematic review. *Maternal and Child Nutrition, 12*, 402–417. https://doi.org/10.1111/mcn.12294

Perry, L. K. (2015). To have and to hold: Looking vs. touching in the study of categorization. *Frontiers in Psychology, 6*, 178. https://doi.org/10.3389/fpsyg.2015.00178

Peter, C. J., Fischer, L. K., Kundakovic, M., Garg, P., Jakovcevski, M., Dincer, A., Amaral, A. C., Ginns, E. I., Galdzicka, M., Bryce, C. P., Ratner, C., Waber, D. P., Mokler, D., Medford, G., Champagne, F. A., Rosene, D. L., McGaughy, J. A., Sharp, A. J., Galler, J. R., & Akbarian, S. (2016). DNA methylation signatures of early childhood malnutrition associated with impairments in attention and cognition. *Biological Psychiatry, 80*(10), 765–774. https://doi.org/10.1016/J.BIOPSYCH.2016.03.2100

Petitto, L. A., Berens, M. S., Kovelman, I., Dubins, M. H., Jasinska, K., & Shalinsky, M. (2012). The "Perceptual wedge hypothesis" as the basis for bilingual babies' phonetic processing advantage: New insights from fNIRS brain imaging. *Brain and Language, 121*(2), 130–143. https://doi.org/10.1016/j.bandl.2011.05.003

Piaget, J. (1952). *The origins of intelligence in children*. International Universities Press. (Original work published in 1936)

Qiao, J., Dai, L. J., Zhang, Q., & Ouyang, Y. Q. (2020). A meta-analysis of the association between breastfeeding and early childhood obesity. *Journal of Pediatric Nursing, 53*, 57–66. https://doi.org/10.1016/j.pedn.2020.04.024

Qiu, A., Mori, S., & Miller, M. I. (2015). Diffusion tensor imaging for understanding brain development in early life. *Annual Review of Psychology, 66*(1), 853–876. https://doi.org/10.1146/annurev-psych-010814-015340

Quinn, P. C. (2016). Establishing cognitive organization in infancy. In L. Balter & C. S. Tamis-LeMonda (Eds.), *Child psychology: A handbook of contemporary issues*. Psychology Press.

Quinn, P C., Eimas, P. D., & Rosenkrantz, S. L. (1993). Evidence for representations of perceptual similar natural categories by 3 and 4 month old infants. *Perception, 22*, 463–475.

Quinn, P. C., Lee, K., & Pascalis, O. (2018). Perception of face race by infants: Five developmental changes. *Child Development Perspectives, 12*(3), 204–209. https://doi.org/10.1111/cdep.12286

Radvansky, G. A. (2017). *Human memory*. Routledge. https://doi.org/10.4324/9781315542768

Rakison, D. H., & Butterworth, G. E. (1998). Infants' use of object parts in early categorization. *Developmental Psychology, 34*, 49–62.

Ramírez-Esparza, N., García-Sierra, A., & Kuhl, P. K. (2017). The impact of early social interactions on later language development in spanish-english bilingual infants. *Child Development, 88*(4), 1216–1234. https://doi.org/10.1111/cdev.12648

Rattaz, C., Goubet, N., & Bullinger, A. (2005). The calming effect of a familiar odor on full-term newborns. *Journal of Developmental and Behavioral Pediatrics, 26*(2), 86–92.

Reissland, N., Francis, B., & Mason, J. (2013). Can healthy fetuses show facial expressions of "pain" or "distress"? *PLoS ONE, 8*(6), e65530. https://doi.org/10.1371/journal.pone.0065530

Rekow, D., Leleu, A., Poncet, F., Damon, F., Rossion, B., Durand, K., Schaal, B., & Baudouin, J. Y. (2020). Categorization of objects and faces in the infant brain and its sensitivity to maternal odor: Further evidence for the role of intersensory congruency in perceptual development. *Cognitive Development*, *55*, 100930. https://doi.org/10.1016/j.cogdev.2020.100930

Remer, J., Croteau-Chonka, E., Dean, D. C., D'Arpino, S., Dirks, H., Whiley, D., & Deoni, S. C. L. (2017). Quantifying cortical development in typically developing toddlers and young children, 1–6 years of age. *NeuroImage*, *153*, 246–261. https://doi.org/10.1016/J.NEUROIMAGE.2017.04.010

Reynolds, G. D., & Romano, A. C. (2016). The development of attention systems and working memory in infancy. *Frontiers in Systems Neuroscience*, *10*, 15. https://doi.org/10.3389/fnsys.2016.00015

Reynolds, G. D., Zhang, D., & Guy, M. W. (2013). Infant attention to dynamic audiovisual stimuli: Look duration From 3 to 9 Months of Age. *Infancy*, *18*(4), 554–577. https://doi.org/10.1111/j.1532-7078.2012.00134.x

Reznick, J. S. (2009). Working memory in infants and toddlers. In M. Courage & N. Cowan (Eds.), *The development of memory in infancy and childhood* (pp. 355–378). Psychology Press. https://doi.org/10.4324/9780203934654-17

Richards, J. E., & Holley, F. B. (1999). Infant attention and the development of smooth pursuit tracking. *Developmental Psychology*, *35*, 856–867.

Rodriguez, E. T., & Tamis-LeMonda, C. S. (2011). Trajectories of the home learning environment across the first 5 years: Associations with children's vocabulary and literacy skills at prekindergarten. *Child Development*, *82*(4), 1058–1075. https://doi.org/10.1111/j.1467-8624.2011.01614.x

Rose, S. A., Feldman, J. F., Jankowski, J. J., & Van Rossem, R. (2011). The structure of memory in infants and toddlers: An SEM study with full-terms and preterms. *Developmental Science*, *14*(1), 83–91. https://doi.org/10.1111/j.1467-7687.2010.00959.x

Rosenberg, R. D., & Feigenson, L. (2013). Infants hierarchically organize memory representations. *Developmental Science*, *16*(4), 610–621. https://doi.org/10.1111/desc.12055

Ross, E. S. (2017). Flavor and taste development in the first years of life. *Nestle Nutrition Institute Workshop Series*, *87*, 49–58. https://doi.org/10.1159/000448937

Saffran, J. R., & Kirkham, N. Z. (2018). Infant statistical learning. *Annual Review of Psychology*, *69*(1), 181–203. https://doi.org/10.1146/annurev-psych-122216-011805

Sai, F. Z. (2005). The role of the mother's voice in developing mother's face preference: Evidence for intermodal perception at birth. *Infant & Child Development*, *14*, 29–50.

Samuelson, L. K., & McMurray, B. (2017). What does it take to learn a word? *Wiley Interdisciplinary Reviews: Cognitive Science*, *8*(1–2), e1421. https://doi.org/10.1002/wcs.1421

Sann, C., & Streri, A. (2007). Perception of object shape and texture in human newborns: Evidence from cross-modal transfer tasks. *Developmental Science*, *10*(3), 399–410. https://doi.org/10.1111/j.1467-7687.2007.00593.x

Sattari, M., Serwint, J. R., & Levine, D. M. (2019). Maternal implications of breastfeeding: A review for the internist. *American Journal of Medicine*, *132*, 912–920. https://doi.org/10.1016/j.amjmed.2019.02.021

Savelsbergh, G., van der Kamp, J., & van Wermeskerken, M. (2013). The development of reaching actions. In P. D. Zelazo (Ed.), *The oxford handbook of developmental psychology* (Vol. 1). Oxford University Press. https://doi.org/10.1093/oxfordhb/9780199958450.013.0014

Saxton, M. (1997). The contrast theory of negative input. *Journal of Child Language*, *24*, 139–161.

Schaal, B. (2017). Infants and children making sense of scents. In A. Buettner (Ed.), *Springer handbook of odor* (pp. 107–108). Springer International Publishing. https://doi.org/10.1007/978-3-319-26932-0_43

Schachner, A., & Hannon, E. E. (2011). Infant-directed speech drives social preferences in 5-month-old infants. *Developmental Psychology*, *47*(1), 19–25. https://doi.org/10.1037/a0020740

Schoenmaker, C., Juffer, F., van IJzendoorn, M. H., van den Dries, L., Linting, M., van der Voort, A., & Bakermans-Kranenburg, M. J. (2015). Cognitive and health-related outcomes after exposure to early malnutrition: The Leiden longitudinal study of international adoptees. *Children and Youth Services Review*, *48*, 80–86. https://doi.org/10.1016/j.childyouth.2014.12.010

Schuldiner, O., & Yaron, A. (2015). Mechanisms of developmental neurite pruning. *Cellular and Molecular Life Sciences : CMLS*, *72*(1), 101–119. https://doi.org/10.1007/s00018-014-1729-6

Schulte, B.., & Durana, A.. (2016). *The New America Care Report* . Retrieved from https://www.newamerica.org/better-life-lab/policy-papers/new-america-care-report/

Semega, J.., Kollar, M.., Shrider, E. A.., & Creamter, J.. (2020). *Income and poverty in the United States: 2019* . Retrieved from https://www.census.gov/library/publications/2020/demo/p60-270.html

Shankar, P., Chung, R., & Frank, D. A. (2017). Association of food insecurity with children's behavioral, emotional, and academic outcomes: A systematic review. *Journal of Developmental and Behavioral Pediatrics : JDBP*, *38*(2), 135–150. https://doi.org/10.1097/DBP.0000000000000383

Shapiro-Mendoza, C. K., Colson, E. R., Willinger, M., Rybin, D. V., Camperlengo, L., & Corwin, M. J. (2014). Trends in infant bedding use: National infant sleep position study, 1993–2010. *Pediatrics*, *135*(1), 10–17. http://pediatrics.aappublications.org/content/early/2014/11/25/peds.2014-1793

Siekerman, K., Barbu-Roth, M., Anderson, D. I., Donnelly, A., Goffinet, F., & Teulier, C. (2015). Treadmill stimulation improves newborn stepping. *Developmental Psychobiology*, *57*(2), 247–254. https://doi.org/10.1002/dev.21270

Sim, Z. L., & Xu, F. (2019). Another look at looking time: Surprise as rational statistical inference. *Topics in Cognitive Science*, *11*(1), 154–163. https://doi.org/10.1111/tops.12393

Singh, G. K.., & Yu, S. M.. (2019). Infant Mortality in the United States, 1915-2017: Large Social Inequalities have Persisted for Over a Century. *Int J MCH AIDS*, *8*(1), 19–31. http://dx.doi.org/10.21106/ijma.271

Singh, L., Fu, C. S. L., Tay, Z. W., & Golinkoff, R. M. (2018). Novel word learning in bilingual and monolingual infants: Evidence for a bilingual advantage. *Child Development*, *89*(3), e183–e198. https://doi.org/10.1111/cdev.12747

Slater, A., Rose, D., & Morison, V. (1984). New-born infants' perception of similarities and differences between two- and three-dimensional stimuli. *British Journal of Developmental Psychology*, *3*, 211–220.

Smith, L., van Jaarsveld, C. H. M., Llewellyn, C. H., Fildes, A., López Sánchez, G. F., Wardle, J., & Fisher, A. (2017). Genetic and environmental influences on developmental milestones and movement: Results from the gemini cohort study. *Research Quarterly for Exercise and Sport*, *88*(4), 401–407. https://doi.org/10.1080/02701367.2017.1373268

Spelke, E. S. (2016). Core knowledge and conceptual change. In D. Barner & A. S. Baron (Eds.), *Core knowledge and conceptual change* (pp. 279–300). Oxford University Press.

Spelke, E. S. (2017). Core knowledge, language, and number. *Language Learning and Development*, *13*(2), 147–170. https://doi.org/10.1080/15475441.2016.1263572

Spencer, J. P., Vereijken, B., Diedrich, F. J., & Thelen, E. (2000). Posture and the emergence of manual skills. *Developmental Science*, *3*(2), 216–217.

Spiegel, C., & Halberda, J. (2011). Rapid fast-mapping abilities in 2-year-olds. *Journal of Experimental Child Psychology*, *109*(1), 132–140. https://doi.org/10.1016/j.jecp.2010.10.013

Spinelli, J., Collins-Praino, L., Van Den Heuvel, C., & Byard, R. W. (2017). Evolution and significance of the triple risk model in sudden infant death syndrome. *Journal of Paediatrics and Child Health*, *53*(2), 112–115. https://doi.org/10.1111/jpc.13429

Stahl, A. E., & Feigenson, L. (2019). Violations of core knowledge shape early learning. *Topics in Cognitive Science*, *11*(1), 136–153. https://doi.org/10.1111/tops.12389

Steiner, J. E. (1979). Human facial expressions in response to taste and smell stimulations. In L. P. Lipsitt & H. W. Reese (Eds.), *Advances in child development:* (Vol. 13, pp. 257–295). Academic Press.

Stiles, J. (2017). Principles of brain development. *Wiley Interdisciplinary Reviews: Cognitive Science*, *8*(1–2), e1402. https://doi.org/10.1002/wcs.1402

Streri, A., Hevia, M., Izard, V., & Coubart, A. (2013). What do we know about neonatal cognition? *Behavioral Sciences*, *3*(1), 154–169. https://doi.org/10.3390/bs3010154

Sugita, Y. (2004). Experience in early infancy is indispensable for color perception. *American Journal of Ophthalmology*, *138*(5), 902.

Super, C. M., & Harkness, S. (2015). Charting infant development. In L. A. Jensen (Ed.), *The oxford handbook of human development and culture*. Oxford University Press. https://doi.org/10.1093/oxfordhb/9780199948550.013.6

Tamis-Lemonda, C. S., & Bornstein, M. (2015). Infant word learning in biopsychosocial perspective. In S. Calkins (Ed.), *Handbook of infant development: A biopsychosocial perspective*. Guilford. https://nyuscholars.nyu.edu/en/publications/infant-word-learning-in-biopsychosocial-perspective

Tamis-LeMonda, C. S., Kuchirko, Y., & Song, L. (2014). Why is infant language learning facilitated by parental responsiveness? *Current Directions in Psychological Science*, *23*(2), 121–126. https://doi.org/10.1177/0963721414522813

Tamnes, C. K., Herting, M. M., Goddings, A.-L., Meuwese, R., Blakemore, S.-J., Dahl, R. E., Güroğlu, B., Raznahan, A., Sowell, E. R., Crone, E. A., & Mills, K. L. (2017a). Development of the cerebral cortex across adolescence: A multisample study of inter-related longitudinal changes in cortical volume, surface area, and thickness. *The Journal of Neuroscience : The Official Journal of the Society for Neuroscience*, *37*(12), 3402–3412. https://doi.org/10.1523/JNEUROSCI.3302-16.2017

Tamnes, C. K., Herting, M. M., Goddings, A.-L., Meuwese, R., Blakemore, S.-J., Dahl, R. E., Güroğlu, B., Raznahan, A., Sowell, E. R., Crone, E. A., & Mills, K. L. (2017b). Development of the cerebral cortex across adolescence: A multisample study of inter-related longitudinal changes in cortical volume, surface area, and thickness. *The Journal of Neuroscience : The Official Journal of the Society for Neuroscience*, *37*(12), 3402–3412. https://doi.org/10.1523/JNEUROSCI.3302-16.2017

Teller, D. Y. (1997). First glances: The vision of infants. *Investigative Ophthalmology & Visual Science*, *38*, 2183–2203.

Teller, D. Y. (1998). Spatial and temporal aspects of infant color vision. *Vision Research*, *38*, 3275–3282.

Thelen, E. (1995). Motor development: A new synthesis. *American Psychologist*, *50*(2), 79–95. https://doi.org/10.1037/0003-066X.50.2.79

Thelen, E. (2000). Motor development as foundation and future of developmental psychology. *International Journal of Behavioral Development*, *24*(4), 385–397.

Thiessen, E. D., Hill, E. A., & Saffran, J. R. (2005). Infant-directed speech facilitates word segmentation. *Infancy*, *7*(1), 53–71.

Tomasello, M. (2012). A usage-based approach to child language acquisition. *Proceedings of the Annual Meeting of the Berkeley Linguistics Society*, *26*(1), 305–319.

Trettien, A. W. (1990). Creeping and walking. *American Journal of Psychology*, *12*, 1–57.

Turfkruyer, M., & Verhasselt, V. (2015). Breast milk and its impact on maturation of the neonatal immune system. *Current Opinion in Infectious Diseases*, *28*(3), 199–206. https://doi.org/10.1097/QCO.0000000000000165

U.S. Bureau of Labor Statistics. (2016). Retrieved from https://www.bls.gov/news.release/pdf/famee.pdf

Vaala, S. E., & LaPierre, M. A. (2014). Marketing genius: The impact of educational claims and cues on parents' reactions to infant/toddler DVDs. *Journal of Consumer Affairs*, *48*(2), 323–350. https://doi.org/10.1111/joca.12023

Vandell, D. L.., Belsky, J.., Burchinal, M.., Steinberg, L.., & Vandergrift, N.. (2010). Do Effects of Early Child Care Extend to Age 15 Years? Results From the NICHD Study of Early Child Care and Youth Development. *81*(3), 737–756. http://dx.doi.org/10.1111/j.1467-8624.2010.01431.x

Vandell, D. L.., Burchinal, M.., & Pierce, K. M.. (2016). Early child care and adolescent functioning at the end of high school: Results from the NICHD Study of Early Child Care and Youth Development. *Developmental Psychology*, *52*(10), 1634–1645. http://dx.doi.org/10.1037/dev0000169

Vannasing, P., Florea, O., González-Frankenberger, B., Tremblay, J., Paquette, N., Safi, D., Wallois, F., Lepore, F., Béland, R., Lassonde, M., & Gallagher, A. (2016). Distinct hemispheric specializations for native and non-native languages in one-day-old newborns identified by fNIRS. *Neuropsychologia*, *84*, 63–69. https://doi.org/10.1016/j.neuropsychologia.2016.01.038

Veissière, S. P. L., Constant, A., Ramstead, M. J. D., Friston, K. J., & Kirmayer, L. J. (2019). Thinking through other minds: A variational approach to cognition and culture. *Behavioral and Brain Sciences*, *43*. https://doi.org/10.1017/S0140525X19001213

Vereijken, B., & Thelen, E. (1997). Training infant treadmill stepping: The role of individual pattern stability. *Developmental Psychobiology*, *30*, 89–102.

Victora, C. G., Bahl, R., Barros, A. J. D., França, G. V. A., Horton, S., Krasevec, J., Murch, S., Sankar, M. J., Walker, N., & Rollins, N. C. (2016). Breastfeeding in the 21st century: Epidemiology, mechanisms, and lifelong effect. *The Lancet*, *387*(10017), 475–490. https://doi.org/10.1016/S0140-6736(15)01024-7

von Hofsten, C., & Rönnqvist, L. (1993). The structuring of neonatal arm movements. *Child Development*, *64*(4), 1046–1057. http://www.ncbi.nlm.nih.gov/pubmed/8404256

Von Holle, A., North, K. E., Gahagan, S., Burrows, R. A., Blanco, E., Lozoff, B., Howard, A. G., Justice, A., Graff, M., & Voruganti, V. S. (2020). Sociodemographic predictors of early postnatal growth: Evidence from a chilean infancy cohort. *BMJ Open*, *10*, 33695. https://doi.org/10.1136/bmjopen-2019-033695

Waber, D. P., Bryce, C. P., Fitzmaurice, G. M., Zichlin, M. L., McGaughy, J., Girard, J. M., & Galler, J. R. (2014). Neuropsychological outcomes at midlife following moderate to severe malnutrition in infancy. *Neuropsychology*, *28*(4), 530–540. https://doi.org/10.1037/neu0000058

Walk, R. D. (1968). Monocular compared to binocular depth perception in human infants. *Science*, *162*, 473–475.

Watamura, S. E.., Phillips, D. A.., Morrissey, T. W.., McCartney, K.., & Bub, K.. (2011). Double Jeopardy: Poorer Social-Emotional Outcomes for Children in the NICHD SECCYD Experiencing Home and Child-Care Environments That Confer Risk. *82*(1), 48–65. http://dx.doi.org/10.1111/j.1467-8624.2010.01540.x

Waxman, S., Fu, X., Arunachalam, S., Leddon, E., Geraghty, K., & Song, H. (2013). Are nouns learned before verbs? Infants provide insight into a long-standing debate. *Child Development Perspectives*, *7*(3), 155–159. https://doi.org/10.1111/cdep.12032

Weaver, J., Crespi, S., Tosetti, M., & Morrone, M. (2015). Map of visual activity in the infant brain sheds light on neural development. *PLOS Biology*, *13*(9), e1002261. https://doi.org/10.1371/journal.pbio.1002261

Weisleder, A., & Fernald, A. (2013). Talking to children matters: Early language experience strengthens processing and builds vocabulary. *Psychological Science*, *24*(11), 2143–2152. https://doi.org/10.1177/0956797613488145

Werker, J. F., Yeung, H. H., & Yoshida, K. A. (2012). How do infants become experts at native-speech perception? *Current Directions in Psychological Science*, *21*(4), 221–226. https://doi.org/10.1177/0963721412449459

Wetzel, N., Buttelmann, D., Schieler, A., & Widmann, A. (2016). Infant and adult pupil dilation in response to unexpected sounds. *Developmental Psychobiology*, *58*(3), 382–392. https://doi.org/10.1002/dev.21377

Witherington, D. C., Campos, J. J., Anderson, D. I., Lejeune, L., & Seah, E. (2005). Avoidance of heights on the visual cliff in newly walking infants. *Infancy*, *7*(3), 285–298. https://doi.org/10.1207/s15327078in0703_4

Woodward, A. L., Markman, E. M., & Fitzsimmons, C. M. (1994). Rapid word learning in 13- and 18-month-olds. *Developmental Psychology*, *30*, 553–556.

Yang, C., Crain, S., Berwick, R. C., Chomsky, N., & Bolhuis, J. J. (2017). The growth of language: Universal Grammar, experience, and principles of computation. *Neuroscience & Biobehavioral Reviews*, *81*, 103–119. https://doi.org/10.1016/J.NEUBIOREV.2016.12.023

Zelazo, N. A., Zelazo, P. R. D. R., Cohen, K. M., & Zelazo, P. R. D. R. (1993). Specificity of practice effects on elementary neuromotor patterns. *Developmental Psychology*, *29*(4), 686–691. https://doi.org/10.1037/0012-1649.29.4.686

Zelazo, P. R. (1983). The development of walking: New findings on old assumptions. *Journal of Motor Behavior*, *2*, 99–137.

Zhu, Y., Mangini, L., Dong, Y., Journal, M. F.-T. F., & &. (2017). Episodes of food insecurity and linear growth in childhood: a prospective cohort study. *FAESB Journal*, *31*(1), 297. https://www.fasebj.org/doi/abs/10.1096/fasebj.31.1_supplement.297.1

CHAPTER 4

Addabbo, M., Longhi, E., Marchis, I. C., Tagliabue, P., & Turati, C. (2018). Dynamic facial expressions of emotions are discriminated at birth. *PLoS One*, *13*(3), e0193868. https://doi.org/10.1371/journal.pone.0193868

Adolph, K. E., & Franchak, J. M. (2017). The development of motor behavior. *Wiley Interdisciplinary Reviews: Cognitive Science*, *8*(1–2), e1430. https://doi.org/10.1002/wcs.1430

Agorastos, A., Pervanidou, P., Chrousos, G. P., & Baker, D. G. (2019). Developmental trajectories of early life stress and trauma: A narrative review on neurobiological aspects beyond stress system dysregulation. In *Frontiers in psychiatry* (Vol. 10, p. 118). Frontiers Media S.A. https://doi.org/10.3389/fpsyt.2019.00118

Ainsworth, M. D. S., Blehar, M. C., Waters, E., & Wall, S. (1978). *Patterns of attachment*. Erlbaum.

Andreadakis, E., Joussemet, M., & Mageau, G. A. (2019). How to support toddlers' autonomy: Socialization practices reported by parents. *Early Education and Development*, *30*(3), 297–314. https://doi.org/10.1080/10409289.2018.1548811

Axia, V. D., & Weisner, T. S. (2002). Infant stress reactivity and home cultural ecology of Italian infants and families. *Infant Behavior & Development*, *25*(3), 255.

Baker, S. (2018). The effects of parenting on emotion and self-regulation. In M. R. Sanders & A. Morawska (Eds.), *Handbook of parenting and child development across the lifespan* (pp. 217–240). Springer International Publishing. https://doi.org/10.1007/978-3-319-94598-9_10

Bard, K. A., Todd, B. K., Bernier, C., Love, J., & Leavens, D. A. (2006). Self-awareness in human and chimpanzee infants: What is measured and what is meant by the mark and mirror test? *Infancy*, *9*(2), 191–219. https://doi.org/10.1207/s15327078in0902_6

Barnes, J., & Theule, J. (2019). Maternal depression and infant attachment security: A meta-analysis. *Infant Mental Health Journal*, *40*(6), 817–834. https://doi.org/10.1002/imhj.21812

Barr, R. G., Konner, M., Bakeman, R., & Adamson, L. (1991). Crying in pKung San infants: A test of the cultural specificity hypothesis. *Developmental Medicine & Child Neurology*, *33*(7), 601–610.

Bates, E. (1990). Language about me and you: Pronominal reference and the emerging concept of self. In D. Cicchetti & M. Beeghly (Eds.), *The self in transition: Infancy to childhood* (pp. 165–182). University of Chicago Press.

Bates, J., Pettit, G., Dodge, K., & Ridge, B. (1998). Interaction of temperamental resistance to control and restrictive parenting in the development of externalizing behavior. *Developmental Psychology, 34*, 982–995.

Beebe, B., Jaffe, J., Markese, S., Buck, K., Chen, H., Cohen, P., Bahrick, L., Andrews, H., & Feldstein, S. (2010). The origins of 12-month attachment: A microanalysis of 4-month mother-infant interaction. *Attachment & Human Development, 12*(1/2), 3–141. https://doi.org/10.1080/14616730903338985

Beebe, B., Messinger, D., Bahrick, L. E., Margolis, A., Buck, K. A., & Chen, H. (2016). A systems view of mother–infant face-to-face communication. *Developmental Psychology, 52*(4), 556–571. https://doi.org/10.1037/a0040085

Behrens, K. Y., Parker, A. C., & Haltigan, J. D. (2011). Maternal sensitivity assessed during the strange situation procedure predicts child's attachment quality and reunion behaviors. *Infant Behavior & Development, 34*(2), 378–381. https://doi.org/10.1016/j.infbeh.2011.02.007

Best, D. L., House, A. S., Barnard, A. E., & Spicker, B. S. (1994). Parent-child interactions in France, Germany, and Italy: The effects of gender and culture. *Journal of Cross-Cultural Psychology, 25*(2), 181–193. https://doi.org/10.1177/0022022194252002

Białecka-Pikul, M., Byczewska-Konieczny, K., Kosno, M., Białek, A., & Stępień-Nycz, M. (2018). Waiting for a treat. Studying behaviors related to self-regulation in 18- and 24-month-olds. *Infant Behavior and Development, 50*, 12–21. https://doi.org/10.1016/J.INFBEH.2017.10.004

Bigelow, A. E. (2017). Self knowledge ☆. In J. B. Benson (Ed.), *Reference module in neuroscience and biobehavioral psychology*. Elsevier. https://doi.org/10.1016/B978-0-12-809324-5.05882-X

Biro, S., Alink, L. R. A., van IJzendoorn, M. H., & Bakermans-Kranenburg, M. J. (2014). Infants' monitoring of social interactions: The effect of emotional cues. *Emotion, 14*(2), 263–271.

Blair, C. (2010). Stress and the development of self-regulation in context. *Child Development Perspectives, 4*(3), 181–188. https://doi.org/10.1111/j.1750-8606.2010.00145.x

Bleah, D. A., & Ellett, M. L. (2010). Infant crying among recent African immigrants. *Health Care for Women International, 31*(7), 652–663. https://doi.org/10.1080/07399331003628446

Boldt, L. J., Kochanska, G., Yoon, J. E., & Koenig Nordling, J. (2014). Children's attachment to both parents from toddler age to middle childhood: Links to adaptive and maladaptive outcomes. *Attachment & Human Development, 16*(3), 211–229. https://doi.org/10.1080/14616734.2014.889181

Booth-LaForce, C., Groh, A. M., Burchinal, M. R., Roisman, G. I., Owen, M. T., & Cox, M. J. (2014). V. Caregiving and contextual sources of continuity and change in attachment security from infancy to late adolescence. *Monographs of the Society for Research in Child Development, 79*(3), 67–84. https://doi.org/10.1111/mono.12114

Bornstein, M. H., Arterberry, M. E., & Lamb, M. E. (2013). *Development in infancy: A contemporary introduction*. Psychology Press.

Bornstein, M. H., Hahn, C. -S., Suwalsky, J. T. D., & Haynes, O. M. (2011). Maternal and infant behavior and context associations with mutual emotion availability. *Infant Mental Health Journal, 32*(1), 70–94. https://doi.org/10.1002/imhj.20284

Bornstein, M. H., Hahn, C.-S., Putnick, D. L., & Pearson, R. (2019). Stability of child temperament: Multiple moderation by child and mother characteristics. *British Journal of Developmental Psychology, 37*(1), 51–67. https://doi.org/10.1111/bjdp.12253

Bornstein, M. H., Putnick, D. L., Gartstein, M. A., Hahn, C. -S., Auestad, N., & O'Connor, D. L. (2015). Infant temperament: Stability by age, gender, birth order, term status, and socioeconomic status. *Child Development, 86*(3), 844–863. https://doi.org/10.1111/cdev.12367

Bornstein, M. H., Putnick, D. L., Rigo, P., Esposito, G., Swain, J. E., Suwalsky, J. T. D., Su, X., Du, X., Zhang, K., Cote, L. R., De Pisapia, N., & Venuti, P. (2017). Neurobiology of culturally common maternal responses to infant cry. *Proceedings of the National Academy of Sciences of the United States of America, 114*(45), E9465–E9473. https://doi.org/10.1073/pnas.1712022114

Bornstein, M. H., Suwalsky, J. T. D., & Breakstone, D. A. (2012). Emotional relationships between mothers and infants: Knowns, unknowns, and unknown unknowns. *Development and Psychopathology, 24*(1), 113–123. https://doi.org/10.1017/S0954579411000708

Bowlby, J. (1969). Attachment and loss. In *Attachment* (Vol. 1). Basic Books.

Bowlby, J. (1988). *A secure base : Clinical applications of attachment theory*. Routledge.

Brand, R. J., Escobar, K., & Patrick, A. M. (2020). Coincidence or cascade? The temporal relation between locomotor behaviors and the emergence of stranger anxiety. *Infant Behavior and Development, 58*, 101423. https://doi.org/10.1016/j.infbeh.2020.101423

Brandl, J. L. (2018). The puzzle of mirror self-recognition. *Phenomenology and the Cognitive Sciences, 17*(2), 1–26. https://doi.org/10.1007/s11097-016-9486-7

Braungart-Rieker, J. M., Hill-Soderlund, A. L., & Karrass, J. (2010). Fear and anger reactivity trajectories from 4 to 16 months: The roles of temperament, regulation, and maternal sensitivity. *Developmental Psychology, 46*(4), 791–804. https://doi.org/10.1037/a0019673

Bretherton, I., & Munholland, K. (2016). The internal working model construct in light of contemporary neuroimaging research. In J. Cassidy & P. R. Shaver (Eds.), *Handbook of attachment: Theory, research, and clinical applications* (pp. 63–88). Guilford.

Broesch, T., Rochat, P., Olah, K., Broesch, J., & Henrich, J. (2016). Similarities and differences in maternal responsiveness in three societies: Evidence from Fiji, Kenya, and the United States. *Child Development, 87*(3), 700–711. https://doi.org/10.1111/cdev.12501

Brooker, R. J., Buss, K. A., Lemery-Chalfant, K., Aksan, N., Davidson, R. J., & Goldsmith, H. H. (2013). The development of stranger fear in infancy and toddlerhood: Normative development, individual differences, antecedents, and outcomes. *Developmental Science, 16*(6), 864–878. https://doi.org/10.1111/desc.12058

Brooks, R., & Meltzoff, A. N. (2008). Infant gaze following and pointing predict accelerated vocabulary growth through two years of age: A longitudinal, growth curve modeling study. *Journal of Child Language*, *35*(1), 207–220. https://doi.org/10.1017/s030500090700829x

Brown, G. L., Mangelsdorf, S. C., & Neff, C. (2012). Father involvement, paternal sensitivity, and father-child attachment security in the first 3 years. *Journal of Family Psychology : JFP : Journal of the Division of Family Psychology of the American Psychological Association (Division 43)*, *26*(3), 421–430. https://doi.org/10.1037/a0027836

Bulgarelli, C., Blasi, A., de Klerk, C. C. J. M., Richards, J. E., Hamilton, A., & Southgate, V. (2019). Fronto-temporoparietal connectivity and self-awareness in 18-month-olds: A resting state fNIRS study. *Developmental Cognitive Neuroscience*, *38*, 100676. https://doi.org/10.1016/j.dcn.2019.100676

Bullock, M., & Lutkenhaus, P. (1990). Who am I? Self-understanding in toddlers. *Merrill-Palmer Quarterly*, *36*, 217–238.

Buss, A. H., & Plomin, R. (1984). *Temperament: Early developing personality traits*. Erlbaum.

Butterworth, G. (1992). Origins of self-perception in infancy. *Psychological Inquiry*, *3*(2), 103–111. https://doi.org/10.1207/s15327965pli0302_1

Cabrera, N. J., Fitzgerald, H. E., Bradley, R. H., & Roggman, L. (2014). The ecology of father-child relationships: An expanded model. *Journal of Family Theory & Review*, *6*(4), 336–354. https://doi.org/10.1111/jftr.12054

Cabrera, N. J., Volling, B. L., & Barr, R. (2018). Fathers are parents, too! Widening the lens on parenting for children's development. *Child Development Perspectives*, *12*(3), 152–157. https://doi.org/10.1111/cdep.12275

Camras, L. A. (2019). Facial expressions across the life span. In V. LoBue, K. Pérez-Edgar, & K. A. Buss (Eds.), *Handbook of emotional development* (pp. 83–103). Springer International Publishing. https://doi.org/10.1007/978-3-030-17332-6_5

Carlson, V. J., & Harwood, R. L. (2003). Attachment, culture, and the caregiving system: The cultural patterning of everyday experiences among Anglo and Puerto Rican mother-infant pairs. *Infant Mental Health Journal*, *24*, 53–73.

Cassiano, R. G. M., Provenzi, L., Linhares, M. B. M., Gaspardo, C. M., & Montirosso, R. (2020). Does preterm birth affect child temperament? A meta-analytic study. *Infant Behavior and Development*, *58*, 101417. https://doi.org/10.1016/j.infbeh.2019.101417

Cassibba, R., Sette, G., Bakermans-Kranenburg, M. J., & van IJzendoorn, M. H. (2013). Attachment the Italian way: In search of specific patterns of infant and adult attachments in Italian typical and atypical samples. *European Psychologist*, *18*(1), 47–58.

Cassidy, J., Woodhouse, S. S., Cooper, G., Hoffman, K., Powell, B., & Rodenberg, M. (2005). Examination of the precursors of infant attachment security: Implications for early intervention and intervention research. In L. J. Berlin, Y. Ziv, L. Amaya-Jackson, & M. T. Greenberg (Eds.), *Enhancing early attachments: Theory, research, intervention, and policy* (pp. 34–60). Guilford Press. https://psycnet.apa.org/record/2005-08750-002

Celeghin, A., Diano, M., Bagnis, A., Viola, M., & Tamietto, M. (2017). Basic emotions in human neuroscience: Neuroimaging and beyond. *Frontiers in Psychology*, *8*, 1432. https://doi.org/10.3389/fpsyg.2017.01432

Challamel, M.-J., Hartley, S., Debilly, G., Lahlou, S., & Franco, P. (2020). A video polysomnographic study of spontaneous smiling during sleep in newborns. *Journal of Sleep Research*, *e131*(29). https://doi.org/10.1111/jsr.13129

Chen, S. H., Zhou, Q., Main, A., & Lee, E. H. (2015). Chinese American immigrant parents' emotional expression in the family: Relations with parents' cultural orientations and children's emotion-related regulation. *Cultural Diversity and Ethnic Minority Psychology*, *21*(4), 619–629. https://doi.org/10.1037/cdp0000013

Chen, X., & Schmidt, L. A. (2015). Temperament and personality. In R. Lerner (Ed.), *Handbook of child psychology and developmental science* (pp. 1–49). John Wiley & Sons, Inc. https://doi.org/10.1002/9781118963418.childpsy305

Cheng, N., Lu, S., Archer, M., & Wang, Z. (2018). Quality of maternal parenting of 9-month-old infants predicts executive function performance at 2 and 3 years of age. *Frontiers in Psychology*, *8*, 2293. https://doi.org/10.3389/fpsyg.2017.02293

Chess, S., & Thomas, A. (1991). Temperament and the concept of goodness of fit. In J. Strelau & A. Angleitner (Eds.), *Explorations in temperament: International perspectives on theory and measurement* (pp. 15–28). Plenum.

Cicchetti, D., Rogosch, F. A., Toth, S. L., & Spagnola, M. (1997). Affect, cognition, and the emergence of self-knowledge in the toddler offspring of. *Journal of Experimental Child Psychology*, *67*(3), 338.

Clearfield, M. W. (2011). Learning to walk changes infants' social interactions. *Infant Behavior & Development*, *34*(1), 15–25. https://doi.org/10.1016/j.infbeh.2010.04.008

Combs-Orme, T., & Renkert, L. E. (2009). Fathers and their infants: Caregiving and affection in the modern family. *Journal of Human Behavior in the Social Environment*, *19*(4), 394–418. https://doi.org/10.1080/10911350902790753

Conradt, E. (2017). Using principles of behavioral epigenetics to advance research on early-life stress. *Child Development Perspectives*, *11*(2), 107–112. https://doi.org/10.1111/cdep.12219

Cooke, J. E., Kochendorfer, L. B., Stuart-Parrigon, K. L., Koehn, A. J., & Kerns, K. A. (2019). Parent-child attachment and children's experience and regulation of emotion: A meta-analytic review. *Emotion*, *19*(6), 1103–1126. https://doi.org/10.1037/emo0000504

Cordaro, D. T., Sun, R., Keltner, D., Kamble, S., Huddar, N., & McNeil, G. (2018). Universals and cultural variations in 22 emotional expressions across five cultures. *Emotion*, *18*(1), 75–93. https://doi.org/10.1037/emo0000302

Courage, M. L., Edison, S. C., & Howe, M. L. (2004). Variability in the early development of visual self-recognition. *Infant Behavior & Development*, *27*(4), 509–532. https://doi.org/10.1016/j.infbeh.2004.06.001

Crockenberg, S. C., & Leerkes, E. M. (2004). Infant and maternal behaviors regulate infant reactivity to novelty at 6 months. *Developmental Psychology*, *40*(6), 1123–1132.

Dagan, O., & Sagi-Schwartz, A. (2018). Early attachment network with mother and father: An unsettled issue. *Child Development Perspectives*, *12*(2), 115–121. https://doi.org/10.1111/cdep.12272

Ding, Y., Xu, X., Wang, Z., Li, H., & Wang, W. (2014). The relation of infant attachment to attachment and cognitive and behavioural outcomes in early childhood. *Early Human Development*, *90*(9), 459–464. https://doi.org/10.1016/J.EARLHUMDEV.2014.06.004

Dollar, J. M., & Calkins, S. D. (2019). The development of anger. In V. LoBue, K. Pérez-Edgar, & K. A. Buss (Eds.), *Handbook of emotional development* (pp. 199–225). Springer International Publishing. https://doi.org/10.1007/978-3-030-17332-6_9

Dondi, M., Simion, F., & Caltran, G. (1999). Can newborns discriminate between their own cry and the cry of another newborn infant? *Developmental Psychology*, *35*, 418–426.

Duschinsky, R. (2015). The emergence of the disorganized/disoriented (D) attachment classification, 1979-1982. *History of Psychology*, *18*(1), 32–46. https://doi.org/10.1037/a0038524

Dyson, M. W., Olino, T. M., Durbin, C. E., Goldsmith, H. H., Bufferd, S. J., Miller, A. R., & Klein, D. N. (2015). The structural and rank-order stability of temperament in young children based on a laboratory-observational measure. *Psychological Assessment*, *27*(4), 1388–1401. https://doi.org/10.1037/pas0000104

Easterbrooks, M. A., Bartlett, J. D., Beeghly, M., & Thompson, R. A. (2012). Social and emotional development in infancy. In I. B. Weiner, R. M. Lerner, M. A. Easterbrooks, & J. Mistry (Eds.), *Handbook of psychology, developmental psychology* (p. 752). John Wiley & Sons.

Enlow, M. B., King, L., Schreier, H. M., Howard, J. M., Rosenfield, D., Ritz, T., & Wright, R. J. (2014). Maternal sensitivity and infant autonomic and endocrine stress responses. *Early Human Development*, *90*(7), 377–385. https://doi.org/10.1016/J.EARLHUMDEV.2014.04.007

Erikson, E. H. (1950). *Childhood and society* (2nd ed.). Norton.

Farroni, T., Menon, E., Rigato, S., & Johnson, M. H. (2007). The perception of facial expressions in newborns. *European Journal of Developmental Psychology*, *4*(1), 2–13. https://doi.org/10.1080/17405620601046832

Feeney, B. C., & Monin, J. K. (2016). Divorce through the lens of attachment theory. In J. Shaver & P. R. Cassidy (Eds.), *Handbook of attachment: Theory, research, and clinical applications* (pp. 941–965). Guilford.

Feldman, R. (2003). Infant–mother and infant–father synchrony: The coregulation of positive arousal. *Infant Mental Health Journal*, *24*(1), 1–23. https://doi.org/10.1002/imhj.10041

Feldman, R., Dollberg, D., & Nadam, R. (2011). The expression and regulation of anger in toddlers: Relations to maternal behavior and mental representations. *Infant Behavior & Development*, *34*(2), 310–320. https://doi.org/10.1016/j.infbeh.2011.02.001

Flanders, J. L., Leo, V., Paquette, D., Pihl, R. O., & Séguin, J. R. (2009). Rough-and-tumble play and the regulation of aggression: An observational study of father–child play dyads. *Aggressive Behavior*, *35*(4), 285–295. https://doi.org/10.1002/ab.20309

Frick, M. A., Forslund, T., Fransson, M., Johansson, M., Bohlin, G., & Brocki, K. C. (2018). The role of sustained attention, maternal sensitivity, and infant temperament in the development of early self-regulation. *British Journal of Psychology*, *109*(2), 277–298. https://doi.org/10.1111/bjop.12266

Friedlmeier, W., Çorapçi, F., & Benga, O. (2015). Early emotional development in cultural perspective. In L. A. Jensen (Ed.), *The oxford handbook of human development and culture* (pp. 127–148). Oxford University Press. https://doi.org/10.1093/oxfordhb/9780199948550.013.9

Frodi, A. M., Lamb, M. E., Hwang, C.-P., & Frodi, M. (1983). Father-mother infant interaction in traditional and nontraditional Swedish families: A longitudinal study. *Alternative Lifestyles*, *5*(3), 142–163. https://doi.org/10.1007/bf01091325

Gardiner, H. W., & Kosmitzki, C. (2018). *Lives across cultures: Cross-cultural human development* (6th ed.). Pearson.

Gartstein, M. A., & Iverson, S. (2014). Attachment security: The role of infant, maternal, and contextual factors. *International Journal of Psychology & Psychological Therapy*, *14*(2), 261–276.

Gartstein, M. A., Putnam, S. P., Aron, E. N., & Rothbart, M. K. (2016). Temperament and personality. *Psychology*, *1*. https://doi.org/10.1093/oxfordhb/9780199739134.013.2

Gedge, E., & Abell, S. (2020). Trust versus mistrust. In V. Zeigler-Hill & T. K. Shackelford (Eds.), *Encyclopedia of personality and individual differences* (pp. 5585–5588). Springer International Publishing. https://doi.org/10.1007/978-3-319-24612-3_639

Goldsmith, H. H., Buss, A. H., Plomin, R., Rothbart, M. K., Thomas, A., Chess, S., Hinde, R. A., & McCall, R. B. (1987). Roundtable: What is temperament? Four approaches. *Child Development*, *58*, 505–529.

Goodvin, R., Thompson, R. A., & Winer, A. C. (2015). The individual child: Temperament, emotion, self, and personality. In M. Bornstein & M. Lamb (Eds.), *Developmental psychology: An advanced textbook* (pp. 491–533). Psychology Press.

Goodvin, R., Thompson, R. A., Winer, A. C., & Goodvin, R. (2013). The individual child: Temperament, emotion, self, and personality. In M. H. Bornstein & M. E. Lamb (Eds.), *Developmental science: An advanced textbook* (5th ed., pp. 377–409). Psychology Press.

Grady, J. S., & Karraker, K. (2017). Mother and child temperament as interacting correlates of parenting sense of competence in toddlerhood. *Infant and Child Development*, *26*(4), e1997. https://doi.org/10.1002/icd.1997

Granat, A., Gadassi, R., Gilboa-Schechtman, E., & Feldman, R. (2017). Maternal depression and anxiety, social synchrony, and infant regulation of negative and positive emotions. *Emotion*, *17*(1), 11–27. https://doi.org/10.1037/emo0000204

Granqvist, P., Sroufe, L. A., Dozier, M., Hesse, E., Steele, M., van Ijzendoorn, M., Solomon, J., Schuengel, C., Fearon, P., Bakermans-Kranenburg, M., Steele, H., Cassidy, J., Carlson, E., Madigan, S., Jacobvitz, D., Foster, S., Behrens, K., Rifkin-Graboi, A., Gribneau, N., & Duschinsky, R. (2017). Disorganized attachment in infancy: A review of the phenomenon and its implications for clinicians and policy-makers. *Attachment & Human Development*, *19*(6), 534–558. https://doi.org/10.1080/14616734.2017.1354040

Graves, J. A.. (2020). *Clinical social worker.* US News and World Report. https://money.usnews.com/careers/best-jobs/clinical-social-worker

Groh, A. M., Fearon, R. M. P., van IJzendoorn, M. H., Bakermans-Kranenburg, M. J., & Roisman, G. I. (2017). Attachment in the early life course: Meta-analytic evidence for its role in socioemotional development. *Child Development Perspectives*, *11*(1), 70–76. https://doi.org/10.1111/cdep.12213

Groh, A. M., & Narayan, A. J. (2019). Infant attachment insecurity and baseline physiological activity and physiological reactivity to interpersonal stress: A meta-analytic review. *Child Development*, *90*(3), 679–693. https://doi.org/10.1111/cdev.13205

Grossmann, K. E., Grossman, K. E., Fremmer-Bombik, E., Kindler, H., Scheuerer-Englisch, H., & Zimmermann, P. (2002). The uniqueness of the child–father attachment relationship: Fathers' sensitive and challenging play as a pivotal variable in a 16-year longitudinal study. *Social Development*, *11*(3), 301–337.

Grossmann, K. E., Spangler, G., Suess, G., & Unzner, L. (1985). Maternal sensitivity and newborns' orientation responses as related to quality of attachment in Northern Germany. In I. Bretherton & E. Waters (Eds.), *Growing points of attachment theory and research* (Vol. 50, pp. 233–256). Monographs of the Society for Research in Child Development.

Guo, Y., Leu, S. -Y., Barnard, K. E., Thompson, E. A., & Spieker, S. J. (2015). An examination of changes in emotion co-regulation among mother and child dyads during the strange situation. *Infant and Child Development*, *24*(3), 256–273. https://doi.org/10.1002/icd.1917

Hahn-Holbrock, J., Holbrook, C., & Bering, J. (2010). Snakes, spiders, strangers: How the evolved fear of strangers may misdirect efforts to protect children from harm. In J. M. Lampinen & K. Sexton-Radek (Eds.), *Protecting children from violence: Evidence based interventions*. Psychology Press. https://digitalcommons.chapman.edu/psychology_books/4

Halberstadt, A. G., & Lozada, F. T. (2011). Emotion development in infancy through the lens of culture. *Emotion Review*, *3*(2), 158–168. https://doi.org/10.1177/1754073910387946

Harlow, H. F.. (1958). The nature of love. *American Psychologist* , *13*(12).

Harlow, H. F., & Zimmerman, R. (1959). Affectional responses in the infant monkey. *Science*, *130*, 421–432.

Harwood, R. L., Scholmerich, A., Schulze, P. A., & Gonzalez, Z. (1999). Cultural differences in maternal beliefs and behaviors: A study of middle class Anglo and Puerto Rican mother-infant pairs in four everyday situations. *Child Development*, *70*, 1005–1016.

Hewlett, B. S. (2008). Fathers and infants among Aka pygmies. In R. A. LeVine & R. S. New (Eds.), *Anthropology and child development: A cross-cultural reader* (pp. 84–99). Blackwell Publishing.

Hewlett, B. S., Lamb, M. E., Shannon, D., Leyendecker, B., & Scholmerich, A. (1998). Culture and early infancy among central African foragers and farmers. *Developmental Psychology*, *34*, 653–661.

Hewlett, B. S., & MacFarlan, S. J. (2010). Fathers, roles in hunter-gatherer and other small-scale cultures. In M. E. Lamb (Ed.), *The roles of the father in child development* (5th ed., pp. 413–434). Wiley.

Hock, A., Oberst, L., Jubran, R., White, H., Heck, A., & Bhatt, R. S. (2017). Integrated emotion processing in infancy: Matching of faces and bodies. *Infancy*, *22*(5), 608–625. https://doi.org/10.1111/infa.12177

Hossain, Z., Field, T., Pickens, J., Malphurs, J., & Del Valle, C. (1997). Fathers' caregiving in low-income African-American and Hispanic-American families. *Early Development & Parenting*, *6*(2), 73–82. https://doi.org/10.1002/(sici)1099-0917(199706)6:2<73::aid-edp145>3.0.co;2-o

Hossain, Z., Roopnarine, J. L., Ismail, R., Hashmi, S. I., & Sombuling, A. (2007). Fathers' and mothers' reports of involvement in caring for infants in Kadazan families in Sabah, Malaysia. *Fathering: A Journal of Theory, Research, & Practice about Men as Fathers*, *5*(1), 58–72. https://doi.org/10.3149/fth.0501.58

Howell, B. R., McMurray, M. S., Guzman, D. B., Nair, G., Shi, Y., McCormack, K. M., Hu, X., Styner, M. A., & Sanchez, M. M. (2017). Maternal buffering beyond glucocorticoids: Impact of early life stress on corticolimbic circuits that control infant responses to novelty. *Social Neuroscience*, *12*(1), 50–64. https://doi.org/10.1080/17470919.2016.1200481

Huang, Z. J., Lewin, A., Mitchell, S. J., & Zhang, J. (2012). Variations in the relationship between maternal depression, maternal sensitivity, and child attachment by race/ethnicity and nativity: Findings from a nationally representative cohort study. *Maternal and Child Health Journal*, *16*(1), 40–50. https://doi.org/10.1007/s10995-010-0716-2

Hughes, C., Lindberg, A., & Devine, R. T. (2018). Autonomy support in toddlerhood: Similarities and contrasts between mothers and fathers. *Journal of Family Psychology*, *32*(7), 915–925. https://doi.org/10.1037/fam0000450

Izard, C. E., Woodburn, E. M., & Finlon, K. J. (2010). Extending emotion science to the study of discrete emotions in infants. *Emotion Review*, *2*(2), 134–136. https://doi.org/10.1177/1754073909355003

Jahromi, L. B., & Stifter, C. A. (2007). Individual differences in the contribution of maternal soothing to infant distress reduction. *Infancy*, *11*(3), 255–269. https://doi.org/10.1080/15250000701310371

Janusek, L. W., Tell, D., & Mathews, H. L. (2019). Epigenetic perpetuation of the impact of early life stress on behavior. *Current Opinion in Behavioral Sciences*, *28*, 1–7. https://doi.org/10.1016/j.cobeha.2019.01.004

Jennings, K. D., Sandberg, I., Kelley, S. A., Valdes, L., Yaggi, K., Abrew, A., & Macey-Kalcevic, M. (2008). Understanding of self and maternal warmth predict later self-regulation in toddlers. *International Journal of Behavioral Development*, *32*(2), 108–118. https://doi.org/10.1177/0165025407087209

Jin, M. K., Jacobvitz, D., Hazen, N., & Jung, S. H. (2012). Maternal sensitivity and infant attachment security in Korea: Cross-cultural validation of the strange situation. *Attachment & Human Development*, *14*(1), 33–44. https://doi.org/10.1080/14616734.2012.636656

Jonas, W., Atkinson, L., Steiner, M., Meaney, M. J., Wazana, A., & Fleming, A. S. (2015). Breastfeeding and maternal sensitivity predict early infant temperament. *Acta Paediatrica*, *104*(7), 678–686. https://doi.org/10.1111/apa.12987

Juruena, M. F., Eror, F., Cleare, A. J., & Young, A. H. (2020). The role of early life stress in HPA axis and anxiety. In *Advances in experimental medicine and biology* (Vol. 1191, pp. 141–153). Springer Publishing Company. https://doi.org/10.1007/978-981-32-9705-0_9

Kagan, J. (2013). Temperamental contributions to inhibited and uninhibited profiles. In P. D. Zelazo (Ed.), *The oxford handbook of developmental psychology, Vol. 2: Self and other* (Vol. 1, pp. 142–165). Oxford University Press. https://doi.org/10.1093/oxfordhb/9780199958474.013.0007

Kagan, J., Arcus, D., Snidman, N., Feng, W., Handler, J., & Greene, S. (1994). Reactivity in infants: A cross national comparison. *Developmental Psychology, 30*, 342–345.

Kaler, S. B., & Kopp, C. B. (1990). Compliance and comprehension in very young toddlers. *Child Development, 61*, 1997–2003.

Kawakami, K., Takai-Kawakami, K., Kawakami, F., Tomonaga, M., Suzuki, M., & Shimizu, Y. (2008). Roots of smile: A preterm neonates' study. *Infant Behavior & Development, 31*(3), 518–522. https://doi.org/10.1016/j.infbeh.2008.03.002

Keller, H. (2018). Parenting and socioemotional development in infancy and early childhood. *Developmental Review, 50*, 31–41. https://doi.org/10.1016/j.dr.2018.03.001

Keller, H. (2019). The role of emotions in socialization processes across cultures. Implications for theory and practice. In D. Matsumoto & H. Hwang (Eds.), *Oxford handbook of culture and psycholog*. Oxford University Press.

Keller, H.., & Otto, H.. (2009). The cultural socialization of emotion regulation during infancy. *Journal of Cross-Cultural Psychology, 40*(6), 996–1011. http://dx.doi.org/10.1177/0022022109348576

Kim, B. -R., & Teti, D. M. (2014). Maternal emotional availability during infant bedtime: An ecological framework. *Journal of Family Psychology : JFP : Journal of the Division of Family Psychology of the American Psychological Association (Division 43), 28*, 1–11. https://doi.org/10.1037/a0035157

Kochanska, G. (2000). Mother-child mutually responsive orientation and conscience development: From toddler to early school age. *Child Development, 71*(2), 417.

Kochanska, G., & Kim, S. (2013). Early attachment organization with both parents and future behavior problems: From infancy to middle childhood. *Child Development, 84*(1), 283–296. https://doi.org/10.1111/j.1467-8624.2012.01852.x

Kojima, H. (1986). Becoming nurturant in Japan: Past and present. In A. Fogel & G. F. Melson (Eds.), *Origins of nurturance: Developmental, biological, and cultural perspectives on caregiving* (pp. 359–376). Erlbaum.

Kragel, P. A., & LaBar, K. S. (2016). Decoding the nature of emotion in the brain. *Trends in Cognitive Sciences, 20*(6), 444–455. https://doi.org/10.1016/J.TICS.2016.03.011

Krassner, A. M., Gartstein, M. A., Park, C., Dragan, W. Ł., Lecannelier, F., & Putnam, S. P. (2017). East–west, collectivist-individualist: A cross-cultural examination of temperament in toddlers from Chile, Poland, South Korea, and the U.S. *. *European Journal of Developmental Psychology, 14*(4), 449–464. https://doi.org/10.1080/17405629.2016.1236722

Kringelbach, M. L., Stark, E. A., Alexander, C., Bornstein, M. H., & Stein, A. (2016). On cuteness: Unlocking the parental brain and beyond. *Trends in Cognitive Sciences, 20*(7), 545–558. https://doi.org/10.1016/J.TICS.2016.05.003

Lamb, M. E., & Lewis, C. (2015). The role of parent-child relationships in child development. In M. H. Bornstein & M. E. Lamb (Eds.), *Developmental science: An advanced textbook* (7th ed., pp. 469–517). Psychology Press.

Lamb, M. E., & Lewis, C. (2016). The role of parent-child relationships in development. In M. H. Bornstein & M. E. Lamb (Eds.), *Developmental science: An advanced textbook* (7th ed., pp. 535–585). Psychology Press.

Langfur, S. (2013). The You-I event: On the genesis of self-awareness. *Phenomenology and the Cognitive Sciences, 12*(4), 769–790. https://doi.org/10.1007/s11097-012-9282-y

Laurent, H. K., & Ablow, J. C. (2013). A face a mother could love: Depression-related maternal neural responses to infant emotion faces. *Social Neuroscience, 8*(3), 228–239. https://doi.org/10.1080/17470919.2012.762039

Laurent, H. K., Harold, G. T., Leve, L., Shelton, K. H., & Van Goozen, S. H. M. (2016). Understanding the unfolding of stress regulation in infants. *Development and Psychopathology, 28*(4pt2), 1431–1440. https://doi.org/10.1017/S0954579416000171

Laurin, J. C., & Joussemet, M. (2017). Parental autonomy-supportive practices and toddlers' rule internalization: A prospective observational study. *Motivation and Emotion, 41*(5), 562–575. https://doi.org/10.1007/s11031-017-9627-5

Lavelli, M., Carra, C., Rossi, G., & Keller, H. (2019). Culture-specific development of early mother-infant emotional co-regulation: Italian, Cameroonian, and West African immigrant dyads. *Developmental Psychology, 55*(9), 1850–1867. https://doi.org/10.1037/dev0000696

Le Bas, G. A., Youssef, G. J., Macdonald, J. A., Rossen, L., Teague, S. J., Kothe, E. J., McIntosh, J. E., Olsson, C. A., & Hutchinson, D. M. (2020). The role of antenatal and postnatal maternal bonding in infant development: A systematic review and meta-analysis. *Social Development, 29*(1), 3–20. https://doi.org/10.1111/sode.12392

Lemery-Chalfant, K., Kao, K., Swann, G., & Goldsmith, H. H. (2013). Childhood temperament: Passive gene–environment correlation, gene–environment interaction, and the hidden importance of the family environment. *Development and Psychopathology, 25*(01), 51–63. https://doi.org/10.1017/S0954579412000892

Lench, H. C., Baldwin, C. L., An, D., & Garrison, K. E. (2018). The emotional toolkit: Lessons from the science of emotion. In H. C. Lench (Ed.), *The function of emotions* (pp. 253–261). Springer International Publishing. https://doi.org/10.1007/978-3-319-77619-4_13

Leppanen, J. M. (2011). Neural and developmental bases of the ability to recognize social signals of emotions. *Emotion Review, 3*(2), 179–188. https://doi.org/10.1177/1754073910387942

Leventon, J. S., & Bauer, P. J. (2013). The sustained effect of emotional signals on neural processing in 12-month-olds. *Developmental Science, 16*(4), 485–498. https://doi.org/10.1111/desc.12041

Levine, L. E. (1983). Mine: Self-definition in 2-year-old boys. *Developmental Psychology, 19*, 544–549.

Levine, R. A., Levine, S., Dixon, S., Richman, A., Keefer, C. H., Leiderman, P. H., & Brazelton, T. B. (1994). *Child care and culture: Lessons from Africa*. Cambridge University Press.

Lewis, M. (2011). Inside and outside: The relation between emotional states and expressions. *Emotion Review, 3*(2), 189–196. https://doi.org/10.1177/1754073910387947

Lewis, M. (2016). Self-conscious emotions: Embarrassment, pride, shame, guilt, and hubris. In L. F. Barrett, M. Lewis, & J. M. Haviland-Jones (Eds.), *Handbook of emotions* (p. 928). Guilford.

Lewis, M. (2019). The self-conscious emotions and the role of shame in psychopathology. In V. LoBue, K. Pérez-Edgar, & K. A. Buss (Eds.), *Handbook of emotional development* (pp. 311–350). Springer International Publishing. https://doi.org/10.1007/978-3-030-17332-6_13

Lewis, M.., & Brooks-Gunn, J.. (1979). Toward a theory of social cognition: The development of self. *New Directions for Child and Adolescent Development , 1979*, 1–20.

Lewis, M., & Carmody, D. P. (2008). Self-representation and brain development. *Developmental Psychology, 44*(5), 1329–1334. 10.1037/a0012681

Lewis, M., Ramsay, D. S., & Kawakami, K. (1993a). Differences between Japanese infants and Caucasian American infants in behavioral and cortisol response to inoculation. *Child Development, 64*, 1722–1731.

Lewis, M., Ramsay, D. S., & Kawakami, K. (1993b). Differences between Japanese infants and Caucasian American infants in behavioral and cortisol response to inoculation. *Child Development, 64*(6), 1722–1731. https://doi.org/10.1111/j.1467-8624.1993.tb04209.x

Lewis, S., & Abell, S. (2020). Autonomy versus shame and doubt. In V. Zeigler-Hill & T. K. Shackelford (Eds.), *Encyclopedia of personality and individual differences* (pp. 338–341). Springer International Publishing. https://doi.org/10.1007/978-3-319-24612-3_570

Lickenbrock, D. M., & Braungart-Rieker, J. M. (2015). Examining antecedents of infant attachment security with mothers and fathers: An ecological systems perspective. *Infant Behavior and Development, 39*, 173–187. https://doi.org/10.1016/J.INFBEH.2015.03.003

Liu, C. H., Yang, Y., Fang, S., Snidman, N., & Tronick, E. (2013). Maternal regulating behaviors through face-to-face play in first- and second-generation Chinese American and European American mothers of infants. *Research in Human Development, 10*(4), 289–307. https://doi.org/10.1080/15427609.2013.846042

Liu, Y., Kaaya, S., Chai, J., McCoy, D. C., Surkan, P. J., Black, M. M., Sutter-Dallay, A.-L., Verdoux, H., & Smith-Fawzi, M. C. (2017). Maternal depressive symptoms and early childhood cognitive development: A meta-analysis. *Psychological Medicine, 47*(04), 680–689. https://doi.org/10.1017/S003329171600283X

LoBue, V., & Adolph, K. E. (2019). Fear in infancy: Lessons from snakes, spiders, heights, and strangers. *Developmental Psychology, 55*, 1889–1907. https://doi.org/10.1037/dev0000675

LoBue, V., Kim, E., & Delgado, M. (2019). Fear in development. In V. LoBue, K. Pérez-Edgar, & K. A. Buss (Eds.), *Handbook of emotional development* (pp. 257–282). Springer International Publishing. https://doi.org/10.1007/978-3-030-17332-6_11

Lucassen, N., Tharner, A., Van Ijzendoorn, M. H., Bakermans-Kranenburg, M. J., Volling, B. L., Verhulst, F. C., Lambregtse-Van den Berg, M. P., & Tiemeier, H. (2011). The association between paternal sensitivity and infant-father attachment security: A meta-analysis of three decades of research. *Journal of Family Psychology, 25*(6), 986–992. https://doi.org/10.1037/a0025855

Lyons-Ruth, K., & Jacobvitz, D. (2016). Attachment disorganization from infancy to adulthood: Neurobiological correlates, parenting contexts, and pathways to disorder. In J. Cassidy & P. R. Shaver (Eds.), *Handbook of attachment: Theory, research, and clinical applications* (pp. 667–695). Guilford.

MacNeill, L. A., & Pérez-Edgar, K. (2020). Temperament and emotion. In S. J. Hupp & J. D. Jewell (Eds.), *The encyclopedia of child and adolescent development* (pp. 1–12). Wiley. https://doi.org/10.1002/9781119171492.wecad180

Main, M., & Solomon, J. (1986). Discovery of an insecure, disorganized/disoriented attachment pattern: Procedures, findings, and implications for the classification of behavior. In M. Yogman & T. B. Brazelton (Eds.), *Affective development in infancy* (pp. 95–124). Ablex.

Malatesta, C. Z., & Haviland, J. M. (1982). Learning display rules: The socialization of emotion expression in infancy. *Child Development, 53*(4), 991–1003. http://www.ncbi.nlm.nih.gov/pubmed/7128264

Mangelsdorf, S. C. (1992). Developmental changes in infant-stranger interaction. *Infant Behavior & Development, 15*(2), 191–208. https://doi.org/10.1016/0163-6383(92)80023-n

Marvin, R. S., Britner, P. A., & Russell, B. S. (2016). Normative development: The ontogeny of attachment in childhood. In J. Cassidy & P. R. Shaver (Eds.), *Handbook of attachment third edition theory, research, and clinical applications* (pp. 273–289). Guilford.

McMahan True, M., Pisani, L., & Oumar, F. (2001). Infant – mother attachment among the Dogon of Mali. *Child Development, 72*(5), 1451.

Meehan, C. L., & Hawks, S. (2013). Cooperative breeding and attachment among the aka foragers. In N. Quinn & J. M. Mageo (Eds.), *Attachment reconsidered* (pp. 85–113). Palgrave Macmillan US. https://doi.org/10.1057/9781137386724_4

Meléndez, L. (2005). Parental beliefs and practices around early self-regulation: The impact of culture and immigration. *Infants & Young Children, 18*(2), 136–146.

Meltzoff, A. N. (1990). Towards a developmental cognitive science. *Annals of the New York Academy of Sciences, 608*, 1–37.

Meltzoff, A. N. (2007). 'Like me': A foundation for social cognition. *Developmental Science, 10*(1), 126–134. https://doi.org/10.1111/j.1467-7687.2007.00574.x

Mesman, J., van IJzendoorn, M. H., & Sagi-Schwartz, A. (2016). Cross-cultural patterns of attachment: Universal and contextual dimensions. In J. Cassidy & P. R. Shaver (Eds.), *Handbook of attachment third edition theory, research, and clinical applications* (pp. 852–876). Guilford.

Messinger, D., & Fogel, A. (2007). The interactive development of social smiling. In R. V Kail (Ed.), *Advances in child development and behavior* (Vol. 35, pp. 327–366). Elsevier Academic Press.

Messinger, D., Mitsven, S. G., Ahn, Y. A., Prince, E. B., Sun, L., & Rivero-Fernández, C. (2019). Happiness and joy. In V. LoBue, K. Pérez-Edgar, & K. A. Buss (Eds.), *Handbook of emotional development* (pp. 171–198). Springer International Publishing. https://doi.org/10.1007/978-3-030-17332-6_8

Meuwissen, A. S., & Carlson, S. M. (2019). An experimental study of the effects of autonomy support on preschoolers' self-regulation. *Journal of Applied Developmental Psychology, 60*, 11–23. https://doi.org/10.1016/j.appdev.2018.10.001

Montirosso, R., & McGlone, F. (2020). The body comes first. Embodied reparation and the co-creation of infant bodily-self. *Neuroscience and Biobehavioral Reviews, 113*, 77–87. https://doi.org/10.1016/j.neubiorev.2020.03.003

Morawska, A., Dittman, C. K., & Rusby, J. C. (2019). Promoting self-regulation in young children: The role of parenting interventions. *Clinical Child and Family Psychology Review, 22*, 43–51. https://doi.org/10.1007/s10567-019-00281-5

Morelli, G. (2015). The evolution of attachment theory and cultures of human attachment in infancy and early childhood. In L. A. Jensen (Ed.), *The oxford handbook of human development and culture* (pp. 149–164). Oxford University Press. https://doi.org/10.1093/oxfordhb/9780199948550.013.10

Mueller, I., & Tronick, E. (2019). Early life exposure to violence: Developmental consequences on brain and behavior. *Frontiers in Behavioral Neuroscience*, *13*, 156. https://doi.org/10.3389/fnbeh.2019.00156

Neisser, U. (1993). *The perceived self: Ecological and interpersonal sources of self-knowledge*. Cambridge University Press.

Newland, R. P., Parade, S. H., Dickstein, S., & Seifer, R. (2016). The association between maternal depression and sensitivity: Child-directed effects on parenting during infancy. *Infant Behavior and Development*, *45*, 47–50. https://doi.org/10.1016/J.INFBEH.2016.09.001

Oddi, K. B., Murdock, K. W., Vadnais, S., Bridgett, D. J., & Gartstein, M. A. (2013). Maternal and infant temperament characteristics as contributors to parenting stress in the first year postpartum. *Infant and Child Development*, *22*(6), 553–579. https://doi.org/10.1002/icd.1813

Olsavsky, A. L., Berrigan, M. N., Schoppe-Sullivan, S. J., Brown, G. L., & Kamp Dush, C. M. (2020). Paternal stimulation and father-infant attachment. *Attachment and Human Development*, *22*(1), 15–26. https://doi.org/10.1080/14616734.2019.1589057

Opendak, M., & Sullivan, R. M. (2019). Unique infant neurobiology produces distinctive trauma processing. *Developmental Cognitive Neuroscience*, *36*, 100637. https://doi.org/10.1016/j.dcn.2019.100637

Pallini, S., Chirumbolo, A., Morelli, M., Baiocco, R., Laghi, F., & Eisenberg, N. (2018). The relation of attachment security status to effortful self-regulation: A meta-analysis. *Psychological Bulletin*, *144*(5), 501–531. https://doi.org/10.1037/bul0000134

Papageorgiou, K. A., Smith, T. J., Wu, R., Johnson, M. H., Kirkham, N. Z., & Ronald, A. (2014). Individual differences in infant fixation duration relate to attention and behavioral control in childhood. *Psychological Science*, *25*(7), 1371–1379. https://doi.org/10.1177/0956797614531295

Papoušek, M., & Papoušek, H. (1990). Excessive infant crying and intuitive parental care: Buffering support and its failures in parent-infant interaction. *Early Child Development and Care*, *65*, 117–126. https://doi.org/10.1080/0300443900650114

Paulussen-Hoogeboom, M. C., Stams, G. J. J. M., Hermanns, J. M. A., & Peetsma, T. T. D. (2007). Child negative emotionality and parenting from infancy to preschool: A meta-analytic review. *Developmental Psychology*, *43*(2), 438–453. https://doi.org/10.1037/0012-1649.43.2.438

Pemberton Roben, C. K., Bass, A. J., Moore, G. A., Murray-Kolb, L., Tan, P. Z., Gilmore, R. O., Buss, K. A., Cole, P. M., & Teti, L. O. (2012). Let me go: The influences of crawling experience and temperament on the development of anger expression. *Infancy*, *17*(5), 558–577. https://doi.org/10.1111/j.1532-7078.2011.00092.x

Pinquart, M., Feußner, C., & Ahnert, L. (2013). Meta-analytic evidence for stability in attachments from infancy to early adulthood. *Attachment & Human Development*, *15*(2), 189–218. https://doi.org/10.1080/14616734.2013.746257

Planalp, E. M., & Goldsmith, H. H. (2020). Observed profiles of infant temperament: Stability, heritability, and associations with parenting. *Child Development*, *91*(3), e563–e580. https://doi.org/10.1111/cdev.13277

Planalp, E. M., Van Hulle, C., Lemery-Chalfant, K., & Goldsmith, H. H. (2017). Genetic and environmental contributions to the development of positive affect in infancy. *Emotion*, *17*(3), 412–420. https://doi.org/10.1037/emo0000238

Pluess, M., Birkbeck, J. B., & Belsky, J. (2010). Differential susceptibility to parenting and quality child care. *Developmental Psychology*, *46*(2), 379–390. https://doi.org/10.1037/a0015203

Poehlmann, J., Schwichtenberg, A. J. M., Shlafer, R. J., Hahn, E., Bianchi, J. -P., & Warner, R. (2011). Emerging self-regulation in toddlers born preterm or low birth weight: Differential susceptibility to parenting? *Development & Psychopathology*, *23*(1), 177–193. https://doi.org/10.1017/s0954579410000726

Posner, M. I., & Rothbart, M. K. (2018). Temperament and brain networks of attention. *Philosophical Transactions of the Royal Society of London. Series B, Biological Sciences*, *373*(1744), 20170254. https://doi.org/10.1098/rstb.2017.0254

Potegal, M., Robison, S., Anderson, F., Jordan, C., & Shapiro, E. (2007). Sequence and priming in 15 month-olds' reactions to brief arm restraint: Evidence for a hierarchy of anger responses. *Aggressive Behavior*, *33*(6), 508–518. https://doi.org/10.1002/ab.20207

Prady, S. L., Kiernan, K., Fairley, L., Wilson, S., & Wright, J. (2014). Self-reported maternal parenting style and confidence and infant temperament in a multi-ethnic community: Results from the Born in Bradford cohort. *Journal of Child Health Care : For Professionals Working with Children in the Hospital and Community*, *18*(1), 31–46. https://doi.org/10.1177/1367493512473855

Prenoveau, J. M., Craske, M. G., West, V., Giannakakis, A., Zioga, M., Lehtonen, A., Davies, B., Netsi, E., Cardy, J., Cooper, P., Murray, L., & Stein, A. (2017). Maternal postnatal depression and anxiety and their association with child emotional negativity and behavior problems at two years. *Developmental Psychology*, *53*(1), 50–62. https://doi.org/10.1037/dev0000221

Priel, B., & deSchonen, S. (1986). Self-recognition: A study of a population without mirrors. *Journal of Experimental Child Psychology*, *41*, 237–250.

Provenzi, L., Brambilla, M., Scotto di Minico, G., Montirosso, R., & Borgatti, R. (2020). Maternal caregiving and DNA methylation in human infants and children: Systematic review. *Genes, Brain and Behavior*, *19*(3). https://doi.org/10.1111/gbb.12616

Raby, K. L., Steele, R. D., Carlson, E. A., & Sroufe, L. A. (2015). Continuities and changes in infant attachment patterns across two generations. *Attachment & Human Development*, *17*(4), 414–428. https://doi.org/10.1080/14616734.2015.1067824

Reyes, L. M., Jaekel, J., Kreppner, J., Wolke, D., & Sonuga-Barke, E. (2019). A comparison of the effects of preterm birth and institutional deprivation on child temperament. *Development and Psychopathology*, 1–10. https://doi.org/10.1017/s0954579419001457

Roben, C. K. P., Moore, G. A., Cole, P. M., Molenaar, P., Leve, L. D., Shaw, D. S., Reiss, D., & Neiderhiser, J. M. (2015). Transactional patterns of maternal depressive symptoms and mother-child mutual negativity in an adoption sample. *Infant and Child Development*, *24*(3), 322–342. https://doi.org/10.1002/icd.1906

Rochat, P. (1998). Self-perception and action in infancy. *Experimental Brain Research, 123*(1–2), 102–109. https://doi.org/10.1007/s002210050550

Rochat, P. (2010). Emerging self-concept. In J. G. Bremner & T. D. Wachs (Eds.), *The Wiley-Blackwell handbook of infant development* (pp. 320–344). Wiley-Blackwell. https://doi.org/10.1002/9781444327564.ch10

Rochat, P. (2013). Self-conceptualizing in development. In P. D. Zelazo (Ed.), *The oxford handbook of developmental psychology, Vol. 2: Self and other* (Vol. 2, pp. 378–396). Oxford University Press. https://doi.org/10.1093/oxfordhb/9780199958474.013.0015

Rochat, P. (2018). The ontogeny of human self-consciousness. *Current Directions in Psychological Science, 27*(5), 345–350. https://doi.org/10.1177/0963721418760236

Rolls, E. T. (2017). Evolution of the emotional brain. In S. Watanabe, M. A. Hofman, & T. Shimizu (Eds.), *Evolution of the brain, cognition, and emotion in vertebrates* (pp. 251–272). Springer Publishing Company. https://doi.org/10.1007/978-4-431-56559-8_12

Roopnarine, J. L., Talukder, E., Jain, D., Joshi, P., & Srivastav, P. (1992). Personal well-being, kinship tie, and mother-infant and father-infant interactions in single-wage and dual-wage families in New Delhi, India. *Journal of Marriage & Family, 54*(2), 293–301.

Rothbart, M. K. (2011). *Becoming who we are: Temperament and personality in development.* Guilford Press.

Rothbart, M. K., & Bates, J. E. (1998). Temperament. In N. Eisenberg (Ed.), *Handbook of child psychology: Vol. 3. Social, emotional, and personality development* (5th ed., Vol. 3, pp. 105–176). Wiley.

Rothbart, M. K., & Bates, J. E. (2007). Temperament. In N. Eisenberg (Ed.), *Handbook of child psychology* (pp. 207–212). John Wiley & Sons, Inc. https://doi.org/10.1002/9780470147658.chpsy0303

Rothbaum, F., Weisz, J., Pott, M., Miyake, K., & Morelli, G. (2000). Attachment and culture: Security in the United States and Japan. *American Psychologist, 55*, 1093–1104.

Ruba, A. L., & Repacholi, B. M. (2019). Do preverbal infants understand discrete facial expressions of emotion? *Emotion Review, 12*, 235–250. https://doi.org/10.1177/1754073919871098

Rubin, K. H., Hastings, P., Chen, X., Stewart, S., & McNichol, K. (1998). Interpersonal and maternal correlates of aggression, conflict, and externalizing problems in toddlers. *Child Development, 69*, 1614–1629.

Saarni, C., Mumme, D. L., & Campos, J. J. (1998). Emotional development: Action, communication, and understanding. In N. Eisenberg & W. Damon (Eds.), *Handbook of child psychology, 5th ed.: Vol 3. Social, emotional, and personality development* (5th ed., Vol. 3, pp. 237–309). John Wiley & Sons Inc.

Safdar, S., Friedlmeier, W., Matsumoto, D., Yoo, S. H., Kwantes, C. T., Kakai, H., & Shigemasu, E. (2009). Variations of emotional display rules within and across cultures: A comparison between Canada, USA, and Japan. *Canadian Journal of Behavioural Science/Revue Canadienne Des Sciences Du Comportement, 41*(1), 1–10. https://doi.org/10.1037/a0014387

Sagi, A., Lamb, M. E., Lewkowicz, K. S., Shoham, R., Dvir, R., & Estes, D. (1985). Security of infant-mother, -father, and -metapelet attachments among kibbutz-reared israeli children. *Monographs of the Society for Research in Child Development, 50*(1/2), 257–275. https://doi.org/10.1111/1540-5834.ep11890146

Sagi, A., Van IJzendoorn, M. H., & Koren-Karie, N. (1991). Primary appraisal of the strange situation: A cross-cultural analysis of preseparation episodes. *Developmental Psychology, 27*(4), 587–596.

Salter, M. D. (1940). *An evaluation of adjustment based upon the concept of security.* University of Toronto Press.

Sarkadi, A., Kristiansson, R., Oberklaid, F., & Bremberg, S. (2008). Fathers' involvement and children's developmental outcomes: A systematic review of longitudinal studies. *Acta Paediatrica, 97*(2), 153–158. https://doi.org/10.1111/j.1651-2227.2007.00572.x

Saudino, K. J., & Micalizzi, L. (2015). Emerging trends in behavioral genetic studies of child temperament. *Child Development Perspectives, 9*(3), 144–148. https://doi.org/10.1111/cdep.12123

Schoppmann, J., Schneider, S., & Seehagen, S. (2019). Wait and see: Observational learning of distraction as an emotion regulation strategy in 22-month-old toddlers. *Journal of Abnormal Child Psychology, 47*(5), 851–863. https://doi.org/10.1007/s10802-018-0486-7

Seifer, R., Dickstein, S., Parade, S., Hayden, L. C., Magee, K. D., & Schiller, M. (2014). Mothers' appraisal of goodness of fit and children's social development. *International Journal of Behavioral Development, 38*(1), 86–97. https://doi.org/10.1177/0165025413507172

Sethna, V. F., Perry, E., Domoney, J., Iles, J., Psychogiou, L., Rowbotham, N. E. L., Stein, A., Murray, L., & Ramchandani, P. G. (2016). Father-child interactions at 3-months and 2 years: Contributions to children's cognitive development at 2 years. *Infant Mental Health Journal, 38*(3), 378–390.

Slobodskaya, H. R., Gartstein, M. A., Nakagawa, A., & Putnam, S. P. (2013). Early temperament in Japan, the United States, and Russia. *Journal of Cross-Cultural Psychology, 44*(3), 438–460. https://doi.org/10.1177/0022022112453316

Spinelli, M., & Mesman, J. (2018). The regulation of infant negative emotions: The role of maternal sensitivity and infant-directed speech prosody. *Infancy, 23*(4), 502–518. https://doi.org/10.1111/infa.12237

Sroufe, L. A. (1977). Wariness of strangers and the study of infant development. *Child Development, 48*(3), 731–746.

Sroufe, L. A. (1997). Psychopathology as an outcome of development. *Development and Psychopathology, 7*, 323–336.

Sroufe, L. A. (2016). The place of attachment in development. J. Cassidy & P. R. Shaver (Eds.), *Handbook of attachment : Theory, research, and clinical applications*, 997–1010. Guilford. https://www.guilford.com/books/Handbook-of-Attachment/Cassidy-Shaver/9781462525294/contents

Sroufe, L. A., & Waters, E. (1976). The ontogenesis of smiling and laughter: A perspective on the organization of development in infancy. *Psychological Review, 83*(3), 173–189. https://doi.org/10.1037/0033-295x.83.3.173

Stapel, J. C., van Wijk, I., Bekkering, H., & Hunnius, S. (2017). Eighteen-month-old infants show distinct electrophysiological responses to their own faces. *Developmental Science, 20*(5), e12437, . https://doi.org/10.1111/desc.12437

Stenberg, G. (2017). Does contingency in adults' responding influence 12-month-old infants' social referencing? *Infant Behavior and Development, 46*, 67–79. https://doi.org/10.1016/j.infbeh.2016.11.013

Stern, J. A., & Cassidy, J. (2018). Empathy from infancy to adolescence: An attachment perspective on the development of individual differences. *Developmental Review*, *47*, 1–22. https://doi.org/10.1016/J.DR.2017.09.002

Stifter, C., & Augustine, M. (2019). Emotion regulation. In V. LoBue, K. Pérez-Edgar, & K. A. Buss (Eds.), *Handbook of emotional development* (pp. 405–430). Springer International Publishing. https://doi.org/10.1007/978-3-030-17332-6_16

Stipek, D., Gralinski, J. H., & Kopp, C. B. (1990). Self-concept development in the toddler years. *Developmental Psychology*, *26*(6), 972–977. https://doi.org/10.1037/0012-1649.26.6.972

Strathearn, L., Jian, L., Fonagy, P., & Montague, P. R. (2008). What's in a smile? Maternal brain responses to infant facial cues. *Pediatrics*, *122*(1), 40–51. https://doi.org/10.1542/peds.2007-1566

Strelau, J. (2020). Temperament. In V. Zeigler-Hill & T. K. Shackelford (Eds.), *Encyclopedia of personality and individual differences* (pp. 5388–5407). Springer International Publishing. https://doi.org/10.1007/978-3-319-24612-3_446

Sullivan, M. W., & Lewis, M. (2003). Contextual determinants of anger and other negative expressions in young infants. *Developmental Psychology*, *39*(4), 693–705. https://doi.org/10.1037/0012-1649.39.4.693

Super, C. M., & Harkness, S. (2010). Culture and infancy. In J. G. Bremner & T. D. Wachs (Eds.), *The Wiley-Blackwell handbook of infant development* (pp. 623–649). Wiley-Blackwell. https://doi.org/10.1002/9781444327564.ch21

Suurland, J., van der Heijden, K. B., Smaling, H. J. A., Huijbregts, S. C. J., van Goozen, S. H. M., & Swaab, H. (2017). Infant autonomic nervous system response and recovery: Associations with maternal risk status and infant emotion regulation. *Development and Psychopathology*, *29*(03), 759–773. https://doi.org/10.1017/S0954579416000456

Takács, L., Smolík, F., Kaźmierczak, M., & Putnam, S. P. (2020). Early infant temperament shapes the nature of mother-infant bonding in the first postpartum year. *Infant Behavior and Development*, *58*, 101428. https://doi.org/10.1016/j.infbeh.2020.101428

Takács, L., Smolík, F., & Putnam, S. (2019). Assessing longitudinal pathways between maternal depressive symptoms, parenting self-esteem and infant temperament. *PLoS One*, *14*(8), e0220633. https://doi.org/10.1371/journal.pone.0220633

Takahashi, K. (1990). Are the key assumptions of the "Strange Situation" procedure universal? A view from Japanese research. *Human Development*, *33*, 23–30.

Tamis-LeMonda, C. S., Kahana-Kalman, R., & Yoshikawa, H. (2009). Father involvement in immigrant and ethnically diverse families from the prenatal period to the second year: Prediction and mediating mechanisms. *Sex Roles*, *60*(7), 496–509. https://doi.org/10.1007/s11199-009-9593-9

Tan, E. S., McIntosh, J. E., Kothe, E. J., Opie, J. E., & Olsson, C. A. (2018). Couple relationship quality and offspring attachment security: A systematic review with meta-analysis. *Attachment & Human Development*, *20*(4), 349–377. https://doi.org/10.1080/14616734.2017.1401651

Thomas, A., & Chess, S. (1977). *Temperament and development*. Brunner/Mazel.

Thomas, A., Chess, S., & Birch, H. G. (1970). The origin of personality. *Scientific American*, *223*, 102–109.

Thomas, J. C., Letourneau, N., Campbell, T. S., Tomfohr-Madsen, L., & Giesbrecht, G. F. (2017). Developmental origins of infant emotion regulation: Mediation by temperamental negativity and moderation by maternal sensitivity. *Developmental Psychology*, *53*(4), 611–628. https://doi.org/10.1037/dev0000279

Thompson, R. A. (2013). Attatchment theory and research: Précis and prospect. In P. D. Zelazo (Ed.), *The oxford handbook of developmental psychology, Volume 2: Self and Other* (2nd ed., pp. 191–216). Oxford University Press. https://doi.org/10.1093/oxfordhb/9780199958474.013.0009

Thompson, R. A. (2016). Early attachment and later development: Reframing the questions. In J. Cassidy & P. R. Shaver (Eds.), *Handbook of attachment third edition theory, research, and clinical applications* (pp. 330–347). Guilford.

Thompson, R. A., & Limber, S. (1991). "Social anxiety" in infancy: Stranger wariness and separation distress. In H. Leitenberg (Ed.), *Handbook of social and evaluation anxiety* (pp. 85–137). Plenum.

Thurman, S. L., & Corbetta, D. (2017). Spatial exploration and changes in infant–mother dyads around transitions in infant locomotion. *Developmental Psychology*, *53*(7), 1207–1221. https://doi.org/10.1037/dev0000328

Tronick, E. Z., Morelli, G. A., & Ivey, P. K. (1992). The Efe forager infant and toddler's pattern of social relationships: Multiple and simultaneous. *Developmental Psychology*, *28*, 568–577.

Turecki, G., & Meaney, M. J. (2016). Effects of the social environment and stress on glucocorticoid receptor gene methylation: A systematic review. *Biological Psychiatry*, *79*(2), 87–96. https://doi.org/10.1016/j.biopsych.2014.11.022

Turner, J. H. (2014). *The evolution of human emotions* (pp. 11–31). Springer Publishing Company. https://doi.org/10.1007/978-94-017-9130-4_2

U.S. Bureau of Labor Statistics. (2021). *Occupational outlook handbook: 2021* . https://www.bls.gov/ooh/

Vaish, A., Grossmann, T., & Woodward, A. (2008). Not all emotions are created equal: The negativity bias in social-emotional development. *Psychological Bulletin*, *134*(3), 383–403. https://doi.org/10.1037/0033-2909.134.3.383

Van Ijzendoorn, M. H., & Kroonenberg, P. M. (1988). Cross-cultural patterns of attachment: A meta-analysis of the strange situation. *Child Development*, *59*, 147–156.

Van Ryzin, M. J., Carlson, E. A., & Sroufe, L. A. (2011). Attachment discontinuity in a high-risk sample. *Attachment & Human Development*, *13*(4), 381–401. https://doi.org/10.1080/14616734.2011.584403

Verhage, M. L., Oosterman, M., & Schuengel, C. (2013). Parenting self-efficacy predicts perceptions of infant negative temperament characteristics, not vice versa. *Journal of Family Psychology : JFP : Journal of the Division of Family Psychology of the American Psychological Association (Division 43)*, *27*(5), 844–849. https://doi.org/10.1037/a0034263

Veríssimo, M. J., Santos, A. J., Fernandes, C., Shin, N., & Vaughn, B. E. (2014). Associations between attachment security and social competence in preschool children. *Merrill-Palmer Quarterly*, *60*(1), 80, . https://doi.org/10.13110/merrpalmquar1982.60.1.0080

Walle, E. A., Reschke, P. J., & Knothe, J. M. (2017). Social referencing: Defining and delineating a basic process of emotion. *Emotion Review*, *9*(3), 245–252. https://doi.org/10.1177/1754073916669594

Waters, S. F., West, T. V., Karnilowicz, H. R., & Mendes, W. B. (2017). Affect contagion between mothers and infants: Examining valence and touch. *Journal of Experimental Psychology: General, 146*(7), 1043–1051. https://doi.org/10.1037/xge0000322

Waters, S. F., West, T. V., & Mendes, W. B. (2014). Stress contagion: Physiological covariation between mothers and infants. *Psychological Science, 25*(4), 934–942. https://doi.org/10.1177/0956797613518352

Webb, R., & Ayers, S. (2015). Cognitive biases in processing infant emotion by women with depression, anxiety and post-traumatic stress disorder in pregnancy or after birth: A systematic review. *Cognition and Emotion, 29*(7), 1278–1294. https://doi.org/10.1080/02699931.2014.977849

Weinfield, N. S., Sroufe, L. A., Egeland, B., & Carlson, E. (2008). Individual differences in infant-caregiver attachment: Conceptual and empirical aspects of security. In J. Cassidy & P. R. Shaver (Eds.), *Handbook of attachment: Theory, research, and clinical applications* (pp. 78–101). Guilford Press.

Wittig, S. M. O., & Rodriguez, C. M. (2019). Emerging behavior problems: Bidirectional relations between maternal and paternal parenting styles with infant temperament. *Developmental Psychology, 55*(6), 1199–1210. https://doi.org/10.1037/dev0000707

Wolke, D., Eryigit-Madzwamuse, S., & Gutbrod, T. (2014). Very preterm/very low birthweight infants' attachment: infant and maternal characteristics. *Archives of Disease in Childhood. Fetal and Neonatal Edition, 99*(1), F70–F75. https://doi.org/10.1136/archdischild-2013-303788

Woodhouse, S. S., Scott, J. R., Hepworth, A. D., & Cassidy, J. (2020). Secure base provision: A new approach to examining links between maternal caregiving and infant attachment. *Child Development, 91*(1), e249–e265. https://doi.org/10.1111/cdev.13224

Yang, Y., & Wang, Q. (2019). Culture in emotional development. In V. LoBue, K. Pérez-Edgar, & K. A. Buss (Eds.), *Handbook of emotional development* (pp. 569–593). Springer International Publishing. https://doi.org/10.1007/978-3-030-17332-6_22

Zajac, L., Bookhout, M. K., Hubbard, J. A., Carlson, E. A., & Dozier, M. (2020). Attachment disorganization in infancy: A developmental precursor to maladaptive social information processing at age 8. *Child Development, 91*(1), 145–162. https://doi.org/10.1111/cdev.13140

Zimmer-Gembeck, M. J., Webb, H. J., Pepping, C. A., Swan, K., Merlo, O., Skinner, E. A., Avdagic, E., & Dunbar, M. (2017). Is parent–child attachment a correlate of children's emotion regulation and coping? *International Journal of Behavioral Development, 41*(1), 74–93.

CHAPTER 5

Ablewhite, J., Peel, I., McDaid, L., Hawkins, A., Goodenough, T., Deave, T., Stewart, J., & Kendrick, D. (2015). Parental perceptions of barriers and facilitators to preventing child unintentional injuries within the home: A qualitative study. *BMC Public Health, 15*(1), 280. https://doi.org/10.1186/s12889-015-1547-2

Acar, E., Dursun, O. B., Esin, İ. S., Öğütlü, H., Özcan, H., & Mutlu, M. (2015). Unintentional injuries in preschool age children: Is there a correlation with parenting style and parental attention deficit and hyperactivity symptoms. *Medicine, 94*(32), e1378. https://doi.org/10.1097/MD.0000000000001378

Ackerman, D. J. (2019). The Montessori preschool landscape in the United States: History, programmatic inputs, availability, and effects. *ETS Research Report Series, 2019*(1), 1–20. https://doi.org/10.1002/ets2.12252

Ackermann, L., Hepach, R., & Mani, N. (2020). Children learn words easier when they are interested in the category to which the word belongs. *Developmental Science, 23*(3), e12915. https://doi.org/10.1111/desc.12915

Al-Namlah, A. S., Meins, E., & Fernyhough, C. (2012). Self-regulatory private speech relates to children's recall and organization of autobiographical memories. *Early Childhood Research Quarterly, 27*(3), 441–446. https://doi.org/10.1016/j.ecresq.2012.02.005

Alarcón-Rubio, D., Sánchez-Medina, J. A., & Prieto-García, J. R. (2014). Executive function and verbal self-regulation in childhood: Developmental linkages between partially internalized private speech and cognitive flexibility. *Early Childhood Research Quarterly, 29*(2), 95–105. https://doi.org/10.1016/j.ecresq.2013.11.002

Alderson-Day, B., & Fernyhough, C. (2015). Inner speech: Development, cognitive functions, phenomenology, and neurobiology. *Psychological Bulletin, 141*(5), 931–965. https://doi.org/10.1037/bul0000021

Anderson, S., & Phillips, D. (2017). Is Pre-K Classroom quality associated with kindergarten and middle-school academic skills? *Developmental Psychology, 53*(6), 1063–1078. https://doi.org/10.1037/dev0000312

Anderson-Yockel, J., & Haynes, W. O. (1994). Joint book-reading strategies in working-class African American and white mother-toddler dyads. *Journal of Speech, Language, and Hearing Research, 37*(3), 583–593. https://doi.org/10.1044/jshr.3703.583

Aslan, A., & Bäuml, K.-H. T. (2010). Retrieval-induced forgetting in young children. *Psychonomic Bulletin & Review, 17*(5), 704–709. https://doi.org/10.3758/pbr.17.5.704

Astington, J. W. (1993). *The child's discovery of the mind.* Harvard University Press.

Backschneider, A. G., Shatz, M., & Gelman, S. A. (1993). Preschoolers' ability to distinguish living kinds as a function of regrowth. *Child Development, 64*, 1242–1257.

Baddeley, A. (2016). Working memory. In R. J. Sternberg, S. T. Fiske, & D. J. Foss (Eds.), *Scientists making a difference: One hundred eminent behavioral and brain scientist talk about their most important contributions* (pp. 119–122). Cambridge University Press.

Ball, J. W., Bindler, R. C., Cowen, K., & Shaw, M. R. (2017). *Principles of pediatric nursing + mynuringlab with pearson etext access card caring for children.* Pearson College Div.

Bauer, P. J. (2015). Development of episodic and autobiographical memory: The importance of remembering forgetting. *Developmental Review, 38*, 146–166. https://doi.org/10.1016/J.DR.2015.07.011

Benigno, J. P., Byrd, D. L., McNamara, J. P., Berg, W. K., & Farrar, M. J. (2011). Talking through transitions: Microgenetic changes in preschoolers' private speech and executive functioning. *Child Language Teaching and Therapy, 27*(3), 269–285. https://doi.org/10.1177/0265659010394385

Benjamin Neelon, S. E., Vaughn, A., Ball, S. C., McWilliams, C., & Ward, D. S. (2012). Nutrition practices and mealtime environments of North Carolina child care centers. *Childhood Obesity, 8*(3), 216–223. https://doi.org/10.1089/chi.2011.0065

Benson, J. E., Sabbagh, M. A., Carlson, S. M., & Zelazo, P. D. (2013). Individual differences in executive functioning predict preschoolers' improvement from theory-of-mind training. *Developmental Psychology, 49*(9), 1615–1627. https://doi.org/10.1037/a0031056

Berger, R. H., Miller, A. L., Seifer, R., Cares, S. R., & Lebourgeois, M. K. (2012). Acute sleep restriction effects on emotion responses in 30- to 36-month-old children. *Journal of Sleep Research, 21*(3), 235–246. https://doi.org/10.1111/j.1365-2869.2011.00962.x

Berk, L. E. (1986). Development of private speech among preschool children. *Early Child Development and Care, 24*, 113–136.

Berk, L. E. (1992). The extracurriculum. In P. W. Jackson (Ed.), *Handbook of research on curriculum* (pp. 1003–1043). Macmillan.

Berk, L. E., & Garvin, R. A. (1984). Development of private speech among low-income Appalachian children. *Developmental Psychology, 20*, 271–286.

Bernard, S., & Deleau, M. (2007). Conversational perspective-taking and false belief attribution: A longitudinal study. *British Journal of Developmental Psychology, 25*(3), 443–460. https://doi.org/10.1348/026151006X171451

Bernstein, D. M., Atance, C., Meltzoff, A. N., & Loftus, G. R. (2007). Hindsight Bias and developing theories of mind. *Child Development, 78*(4), 1374–1394. https://doi.org/10.1111/j.1467-8624.2007.01071.x

Birch, S. A. J. (2005). When knowledge is a curse: Biases in mental state attribution. *Current Directions in Psychological Science, 14*, 25–29.

Bjorklund, D. F., & Myers, A. (2015). The Development of cognitive abilities. In M. H. Bornstein & M. E. Lamb (Eds.), *Developmental science: An advanced textbook* (pp. 391–441). Psychology Press.

Bodrova, E., & Leong, D. J. (2018). Tools of the mind: A Vygotskian early childhood curriculum. In M. Fleer & B. van Oers (Eds.), *International handbook of early childhood education* (pp. 1095–1111). Springer Publishing Comapny. https://doi.org/10.1007/978-94-024-0927-7_56

Bosch, L., & Ramon-Casas, M. (2014). First translation equivalents in bilingual toddlers' expressive vocabulary: Does form similarity matter? *International Journal of Behavioral Development, 38*(4), 317–322. https://doi.org/10.1177/0165025414532559

Bower, B. (1993). A child's theory of mind. *Science News, 144*, 40–42.

Brinums, M., Imuta, K., & Suddendorf, T. (2018). Practicing for the Future: Deliberate practice in early childhood. *Child Development, 89*, 2051–2058. https://doi.org/10.1111/cdev.12938

Bronfenbrenner, U. (1979). *The ecology of human development: Experiments by nature and design*. Harvard University Press.

Brooks-Gunn, J., & Markman, L. B. (2005). The contribution of parenting to ethnic and racial gaps in school readiness. *Future of Children, 15*, 139–168. https://doi.org/10.1353/foc.2005.0001

Brown, D. A., & Lamb, M. E. (2015). Can children be useful witnesses? It depends how they are Questioned. *Child Development Perspectives, 9*(4), 250–255. https://doi.org/10.1111/cdep.12142

Bryck, R. L., & Fisher, P. A. (2012). Training the brain: Practical applications of neural plasticity from the intersection of cognitive neuroscience, developmental psychology, and prevention science. *American Psychologist, 67*(2), 87–100.

Callaghan, T., Rochat, P., Lillard, A., Claux, M. L., Odden, H., Itakura, S., Tapanya, S., & Singh, S. (2005). Synchrony in the onset of mental-state reasoning. *Psychological Science, 16*(5), 378–384. https://doi.org/10.1111/j.0956-7976.2005.01544.x

Campbell, F. A., Pungello, E. P., Burchinal, M., Kainz, K., Pan, Y., Wasik, B. H., Barbarin, O. A., Sparling, J. J., & Ramey, C. T. (2012). Adult outcomes as a function of an early childhood educational program: An Abecedarian project follow-up. *Developmental Psychology, 48*(4), 1033–1043. https://doi.org/10.1037/a0026644

Campbell, F. A., & Ramey, C. T. (1994). Effects of early intervention on intellectual and academic achievement: A follow-up study of children from low-income families. *Child Development, 65*(2), 684–698. https://doi.org/10.1111/j.1467-8624.1994.tb00777.x

Campbell, F. A., Ramey, C. T., Pungello, E., Sparling, J., & Miller-Johnson, S. (2002). Early childhood education: Young adult outcomes from the abecedarian project. *Applied Developmental Science, 6*(1), 42–57. http://www.safetylit.org/citations/index.php?fuseaction=citations.viewdetails&citationIds%255B%255D=citjournalarticle_416815_38

Caporaso, J. S., Boseovski, J. J., & Marcovitch, S. (2019). The individual contributions of three executive function components to preschool social competence. *Infant and Child Development, 28*(4), e2132. https://doi.org/10.1002/icd.2132

Carlson, S. M., Zelazo, P. D., & Faja, S. (2013). P. D. Zelazo (Ed.), *Executive function*. Oxford University Press. https://doi.org/10.1093/oxfordhb/9780199958450.013.0025

Carson, V., Lee, E.-Y., Hewitt, L., Jennings, C., Hunter, S., Kuzik, N., Stearns, J. A., Unrau, S. P., Poitras, V. J., Gray, C., Adamo, K. B., Janssen, I., Okely, A. D., Spence, J. C., Timmons, B. W., Sampson, M., & Tremblay, M. S. (2017). Systematic review of the relationships between physical activity and health indicators in the early years (0-4years. *BMC Public Health, 17*(S5), 854, . https://doi.org/10.1186/s12889-017-4860-0

Ceci, S. J., & Bruck, M. (1998). The ontogeny and durability of true and false memories: A fuzzy trace account. *Journal of Experimental Child Psychology, 71*, 165–169.

Ceci, S. J., Huffman, M. L., Smith, E., & Loftus, E. F. (1994). Repeatedly thinking about a non-event: Source misattributions among preschoolers. *Consciousness and Cognition, 3*, 388–407.

Centers for Disease Control. (2019). *Measles | cases and outbreaks | CDC*. https://www.cdc.gov/measles/cases-outbreaks.html

Centers for Disease Control and Prevention. (2017). *10 Leading causes of injury deaths by age group highlighting unintentional injury deaths, United States – 2015*. https://www.cdc.gov/injury/images/lc-charts/leading_causes_of_death_age_group_2015_1050w740h.gif

Centers for Disease Control and Prevention. (2018). *National estimates of the 10 leading causes of nonfatal injuries treated in hospital emergency departments - 2017*. https://www.cdc.gov/injury/wisqars/pdf//leading_causes_of_nonfatal_injury_2017-508.pdf

Chandler, M. J., & Carpendale, J. I. (1998). Inching toward a mature theory of mind. In M. Ferrari & R. J. Sternberg (Eds.), *Self-awareness: Its nature and development* (pp. 148–190). Guilford.

Chevalier, N., Kurth, S., Doucette, M. R., Wiseheart, M., Deoni, S. C. L. S., Dean, D. C. D., O'Muircheartaigh, J., Blackwell, K. A., Munakata, Y., & LeBourgeois, M. K. (2015). Myelination is associated with processing speed in early childhood: Preliminary insights. *PLoS One*, *10*(10), e0139897. https://doi.org/10.1371/journal.pone.0139897

Conboy, B. T., & Thal, D. J. (2006). Ties between the Lexicon and grammar: Cross-sectional and longitudinal studies of bilingual toddlers. *Child Development*, *77*(3), 712–735. https://doi.org/10.1111/j.1467-8624.2006.00899.x

Copeland, K. A., Khoury, J. C., & Kalkwarf, H. J. (2016). Child care center characteristics associated with preschoolers' Physical activity. *American Journal of Preventive Medicine*, *50*(4), 470–479. https://doi.org/10.1016/j.amepre.2015.08.028

Deák, G. O. (2006). Do children really confuse appearance and reality? *Trends in Cognitive Sciences*, *10*(12), 546–550.

Dean, D. C., O'Muircheartaigh, J., Dirks, H., Waskiewicz, N., Walker, L., Doernberg, E., Piryatinsky, I., & Deoni, S. C. L. (2014). Characterizing longitudinal white matter development during early childhood. *Brain Structure & Function*, *220*(4), 1921–1933. https://doi.org/10.1007/s00429-014-0763-3

de Onis, M., & Branca, F. (2016). Childhood stunting: A global perspective. *Maternal & Child Nutrition*, *12*(S1), 12–26. https://doi.org/10.1111/mcn.12231

de Villiers, J. G., & de Villiers, P. A. (2014). The Role of language in theory of mind development. *Topics in Language Disorders*, *34*(4), 313–328. https://doi.org/10.1097/TLD.0000000000000037

Devine, R. T., & Hughes, C. H. (2019). Let's talk: Parents' mental talk (Not mind-mindedness or mindreading capacity) predicts children's false belief understanding. *Child Development*, *90*(4), 1236–1253. https://doi.org/10.1111/cdev.12990

Devine, R. T., & Hughes, C. H. (2019). Let's talk: Parents' mental talk (Not Mind-Mindedness or Mindreading Capacity) predicts children's false belief understanding. *Child Development*, *90*(4), 1236–1253. https://doi.org/10.1111/cdev.12990

DeVries, R. (1969). Constancy of generic identity in the years three to six. *Monographs of the Society for Research in Child Development*, *34*, iii-iv+1-67.

Di Cristo, G., & Chattopadhyaya, B. (2020). Development of neuronal circuits: From synaptogenesis to synapse plasticity. In A. Gallagher, C. Bulteau, D. Cohen, & J. L. Michaud (Eds.), *Handbook of clinical neurology* (Vol. 173, pp. 43–53). Elsevier B.V. https://doi.org/10.1016/B978-0-444-64150-2.00005-8

Doebel, S. (2020). Rethinking executive function and its development. *Perspectives on Psychological Science*, *15*(4), 942–956. https://doi.org/10.1177/1745691620904771

Doenyas, C., Yavuz, H. M., & Selcuk, B. (2018). Not just a sum of its parts: How tasks of the theory of mind scale relate to executive function across time. *Journal of Experimental Child Psychology*, *166*, 485–501. https://doi.org/10.1016/J.JECP.2017.09.014

Dowdall, N., Melendez-Torres, G. J., Murray, L., Gardner, F., Hartford, L., & Cooper, P. J. (2020). Shared picture book reading interventions for child language development: A systematic review and meta-analysis. *Child Development*, *91*(2), e383–e399. https://doi.org/10.1111/cdev.13225

Duboc, V., Dufourcq, P., Blader, P., & Roussigné, M. (2015). Asymmetry of the brain: Development and implications. *Annual Review of Genetics*, *49*(1), 647–672. https://doi.org/10.1146/annurev-genet-112414-055322

Dubois, J., Dehaene-Lambertz, G., Kulikova, S., Poupon, C., Hüppi, P. S., & Hertz-Pannier, L. (2013). The early development of brain white matter: A review of imaging studies in fetuses, newborns and infants. *Neuroscience*, *276*, 48–71. https://doi.org/10.1016/j.neuroscience.2013.12.044

Duncan, G. J., Ludwig, J., & Magnuson, K. A. (2007). Reducing poverty through preschool interventions. *The Future of Children*, *17*(2), 143–160.

Duncan, G. J., & Magnuson, K. (2013). Investing in preschool programs. *The Journal of Economic Perspectives: A Journal of the American Economic Association*, *27*(2), 109–132. https://doi.org/10.1257/jep.27.2.109

Education Commission of the States. (2014). *Child must attend kindergarten*. http://ecs.force.com/mbdata/mbquestRT?rep=Kq1403

Eisbach, A. O. (2004). Children's developing awareness of diversity in people's trains of thoughts. *Child Development*, *75*(6), 1694–1707.

Eisenberg, S. L., Guo, L.-Y., & Germezia, M. (2012). How grammatical are 3-year-olds?. *Language, Speech, and Hearing Services in Schools*, *43*(1), 36–52. https://doi.org/10.1044/0161-1461(2011/10-0093)

Etel, E., & Slaughter, V. (2019). Theory of mind and peer cooperation in two play contexts. *Journal of Applied Developmental Psychology*, *60*, 87–95. https://doi.org/10.1016/j.appdev.2018.11.004

Fischer, U., Suggate, S. P., Schmirl, J., & Stoeger, H. (2018). Counting on fine motor skills: links between preschool finger dexterity and numerical skills. *Developmental Science*, *21*(4), e12623. https://doi.org/10.1111/desc.12623

Fischer, U., Suggate, S. P., & Stoeger, H. (2020). The implicit contribution of fine motor skills to mathematical insight in early childhood. *Frontiers in Psychology*, *11*, 1143. https://doi.org/10.3389/fpsyg.2020.01143

Fivush, R. (2011). The development of autobiographical memory. *Annual Review of Psychology*, *62*, 559–582. https://doi.org/10.1146/annurev.psych.121208.131702

Fivush, R. (2019). Sociocultural developmental approaches to autobiographical memory. *Applied Cognitive Psychology*, *33*(4), 489–497. https://doi.org/10.1002/acp.3512

Fivush, R., Hudson, J., & Nelson, K. (1983). Children's long-term memory for a novel event: An exploratory study. *Merrill-Palmer Quarterly*, *30*, 303–316.

Flavell, J. H. (1993). The development of children's understanding of false belief and the appearance-reality distinction. *International Journal of Psychology*, *28*, 595–604.

Flavell, J. H. (1999). Cognitive development: Children's knowledge about the mind. *Annual Review of Psychology*, *50*, 21–45.

Flavell, J. H., Everett, B. H., Croft, K., & Flavell, E. R. (1981). Young children's knowledge about visual perception: Further evidence for the level 1-level 2 distinction. *Developmental Psychology*, *17*, 99–103.

Flavell, J. H., Green, F. L., & Flavell, E. R. (1995). Young children's knowledge about thinking. *Monographs of the Society for Research in Child Development*, *60*(1, Serial No. 243), 1–96.

Flavell, J. H., Green, F. L., Flavell, E. R., Watson, M. W., & Campione, J. C. (1986). Development of knowledge about the appearance-reality distinction. *Monographs of the Society for Research in Child Development, 51*, 1–87, .

Friedman-Krauss, A. H., Barnett, W. S. K. A., Hodges, K. S., Weisenfeld, G. G., & DiCrecchio, N. (2019). *The state of preschool 2018: State preschool yearbook*. National Institute for Early Education Research.

Gabbard, C. P. (2018). *Lifelong motor development* (6th ed.). Pearson.

Gallagher, A. (2008). *Developing thinking with four and five year old pupils: The impact of a cognitive acceleration programme through early science skill development*. Education department and school of chemical sciences: Vol. Master of, Dublin City University.

Gathercole, V. C. M., & Thomas, E. M. (2009). Bilingual first-language development: Dominant language takeover, threatened minority language take-up. *Bilingualism: Language and Cognition, 12*(2), 213–237. https://doi.org/10.1017/S1366728909004015

Genesee, F., & Nicoladis, E. (2007). Bilingual first language acquisition. In E. Hoff & M. Shatz (Eds.), *Blackwell handbook of language development* (pp. 324–344). Blackwell.

Gilliard, J. L., & Moore, R. A. (2007). An investigation of how culture shapes curriculum in early care and education programs on a Native American Indian reservation. *Early Childhood Education Journal, 34*(4), 251–258. https://doi.org/10.1007/s10643-006-0136-5

Gilmore, J. H., Knickmeyer, R. C., & Gao, W. (2018). Imaging structural and functional brain development in early childhood. *Nature Reviews Neuroscience, 19*(3), 123–137. https://doi.org/10.1038/nrn.2018.1

Gjersoe, N. L., Hall, E. L., & Hood, B. (2015). Children attribute mental lives to toys when they are emotionally attached to them. *Cognitive Development, 34*, 28–38. https://doi.org/10.1016/j.cogdev.2014.12.002

Goldizen, F. C., Sly, P. D., & Knibbs, L. D. (2016). Respiratory effects of air pollution on children. *Pediatric Pulmonology, 51*(1), 94–108. https://doi.org/10.1002/ppul.23262

Golinkoff, R. M., Hoff, E., Rowe, M. L., Tamis-LeMonda, C. S., & Hirsh-Pasek, K. (2019). Language matters: Denying the existence of the 30-million-word gap has serious consequences. *Child Development, 90*(3), 985–992. https://doi.org/10.1111/cdev.13128

Göncü, A., & Gauvain, M. (2012). Sociocultural approaches to educational psychology: Theory, research, and application. In J. Harris, K. R. Graham, S. Urdan, T. McCormick, C. B. Sinatra, & G. M. Sweller (Eds.), *APA educational psychology handbook, Vol 1: Theories, constructs, and critical issues* (pp. 125–154). American Psychological Association. https://doi.org/10.1037/13273-006

Goodman, G. S., & Aman, C. J. (1990). Children's use of anatomically detailed dolls to recount an event. *Child Development, 61*, 1859–1871.

Goodman, G. S., Rudy, L., Bottoms, B. L., & Aman, C. (1990). Children's concerns and memory: Issues of ecological validity in the study of children's eyewitness testimony. In R. Fivush & J. A. Hudson (Eds.), *Knowing and remembering in young children* (pp. 249–284). Cambridge University Press.

Gordon, A. M., & Browne, K. W. (2016). *Beginning essentials in early childhood education*. Cengage Learning.

Gormley Jr, W. T., Phillips, D., Adelstein, S., & Shaw, C. (2010). Head start's comparative advantage: Myth or reality? *Policy Studies Journal, 38*(3), 397–418. https://doi.org/10.1111/j.1541-0072.2010.00367.x

Grosse Wiesmann, C., Friederici, A. D., Singer, T., & Steinbeis, N. (2017). Implicit and explicit false belief development in preschool children. *Developmental Science, 20*(5), e12445. https://doi.org/10.1111/desc.12445

Haden, C. A., & Fivush, F. (1996). Contextual variation in maternal conversational styles. *Merrill-Palmer Quarterly, 42*, 200–227.

Hanania, R., & Smith, L. B. (2010). Selective attention and attention switching: Towards a unified developmental approach. *Developmental Science, 13*(4), 622–635. https://doi.org/10.1111/j.1467-7687.2009.00921.x

Hart, B., & Risley, T. R. (1995). *Meaningful differences in the everyday experience of young American children*. Paul H. Brookes.

Hesketh, K. R., Lakshman, R., & van Sluijs, E. M. F. (2017). Barriers and facilitators to young children's physical activity and sedentary behaviour: A systematic review and synthesis of qualitative literature. *Obesity Reviews, 18*(9), 987–1017. https://doi.org/10.1111/obr.12562

Hess, J., & Slavin, J. (2014). Snacking for a cause: Nutritional insufficiencies and excesses of U.S. children, a critical review of food consumption patterns and macronutrient and micronutrient intake of U.S. Children. *Nutrients, 6*(11), 4750–4759. https://doi.org/10.3390/nu6114750

Hindman, A. H., Skibbe, L. E., & Foster, T. D. (2014). Exploring the variety of parental talk during shared book reading and its contributions to preschool language and literacy: Evidence from the early childhood longitudinal study-birth cohort. *Reading and Writing, 27*(2), 287–313. https://doi.org/10.1007/s11145-013-9445-4

Hindman, A. H., & Wasik, B. A. (2015). Building vocabulary in two languages: An examination of Spanish-speaking dual language learners in head start. *Early Childhood Research Quarterly, 31*, 19–33. https://doi.org/10.1016/j.ecresq.2014.12.006

Hindman, A. H., Wasik, B. A., & Snell, E. K. (2016). Closing the 30 million word gap: Next steps in designing research to inform practice. *Child Development Perspectives, 10*(2), 134–139. https://doi.org/10.1111/cdep.12177

Hoff, E. (2020). Lessons from the study of input effects on bilingual development. *International Journal of Bilingualism, 24*(1), 82–88. https://doi.org/10.1177/1367006918768370

Hoff, E., & Core, C. (2015). What clinicians need to know about bilingual development. *Seminars in Speech and Language, 36*(02), 089–099. https://doi.org/10.1055/s-0035-1549104

Hoff, E., Core, C., Place, S., & Rumiche, R. (2012). Dual language exposure and early bilingual development. *Journal of Child Language, 39*(01), 1–27. https://doi.org/10.1017/S0305000910000759

Hoff, E., Rumiche, R., Burridge, A., Ribot, K. M., & Welsh, S. N. (2014). Expressive vocabulary development in children from bilingual and monolingual homes: A longitudinal study from two to four years. *Early Childhood Research Quarterly, 29*(4), 433–444. https://doi.org/10.1016/j.ecresq.2014.04.012

Holloway, S. D. (1999). Divergent cultural models of child rearing and pedagogy in Japanese preschools. *New Directions for Child and Adolescent Development, 83*, 61–75.

Honaker, S. M., & Meltzer, L. J. (2014). Bedtime problems and night wakings in young children: An update of the evidence. *Paediatric Respiratory Reviews*, *15*(4), 333–339. https://doi.org/10.1016/j.prrv.2014.04.011

Honomichl, R. D., & Zhe, C. (2011). Relations as rules: The role of attention in the dimensional change card sort task. *Developmental Psychology*, *47*(1), 50–60. https://doi.org/10.1037/a0021025

Hughes, C. H., & Devine, R. T. (2015). A Social perspective on theory of mind. In M. E. Lamb (Ed.), *Handbook of child psychology and developmental science* (pp. 1–46). John Wiley & Sons, Inc. https://doi.org/10.1002/9781118963418.childpsy314

Huston, A. C. (2008). From research to policy and back. *Child Development*, *79*(1), 1–12. https://doi.org/10.1111/j.1467-8624.2007.01107.x

Huttenlocher, J., Vasilyeva, M., Cymerman, E., & Levine, S. (2002). Language input and child syntax. *Cognitive Psychology*, *45*(3), 337.

Hyde, K. L., Lerch, J., Norton, A., Forgeard, M., Winner, E., Evans, A. C., & Schlaug, G. (2009). Musical training shapes structural brain development. *Journal of Neuroscience*, *29*(10), 3019–3025. https://doi.org/10.1523/JNEUROSCI.5118-08.2009

Jernigan, T. L., & Stiles, J. (2017). Construction of the human forebrain. *Wiley Interdisciplinary Reviews: Cognitive Science*, *8*(1–2), e1409. https://doi.org/10.1002/wcs.1409

Jipson, J. L., Gülgöz, S., & Gelman, S. A. (2016). Parent–child conversations regarding the ontological status of a robotic dog. *Cognitive Development*, *39*, 21–35. https://doi.org/10.1016/j.cogdev.2016.03.001

Joo, M. (2010). Long-term effects of head start on academic and school outcomes of children in persistent poverty: Girls vs. boys. *Children & Youth Services Review*, *32*(6), 807–814. https://doi.org/10.1016/j.childyouth.2010.01.018

Kalashnikova, M., Mattock, K., & Monaghan, P. (2016). Flexible use of mutual exclusivity in word learning. *Language Learning and Development*, *12*(1), 79–91. https://doi.org/10.1080/15475441.2015.1023443

Keefe-Cooperman, K., & Brady-Amoon, P. (2014). Preschooler sleep patterns related to cognitive and adaptive functioning. *Early Education and Development*, *25*(6), 859–874. https://doi.org/10.1080/10409289.2014.876701

Király, I., Takács, S., Kaldy, Z., & Blaser, E. (2017). Preschoolers have better long-term memory for rhyming text than adults. *Developmental Science*, *20*(3), e12398. https://doi.org/10.1111/desc.12398

Klemfuss, J. Z., & Olaguez, A. P. (2018). Individual differences in children's suggestibility: An updated review. *Journal of Child Sexual Abuse*, *29*, 158–182. https://doi.org/10.1080/10538712.2018.1508108

Kliegman, R., Stanton, B., St. Geme, J. W., Schor, N. F., Behrman, R. E., & Nelson, W. E. (2016). *Nelson textbook of pediatrics*. Elsevier.

Kolb, B. (2020). Brain development during early childhood. In D. Güngör (Ed.), *The encyclopedia of child and adolescent development* (pp. 1–14). Wiley. https://doi.org/10.1002/9781119171492.wecad015

Kolb, B., Whishaw, I. Q., & Teskey, G. C. (2019). *Introduction to brain and behavior*. MacMillan.

Kostelnik, M. J., Soderman, A. K., Whiren, A. P., & Rupiper, M. Q. (2015). *Developmentally appropriate curriculum: Best practices in early childhood education*. Pearson.

Kucker, S. C., McMurray, B., & Samuelson, L. K. (2015). Slowing down fast mapping: Redefining the dynamics of word learning. *Child Development Perspectives*, *9*(2), 74–78. https://doi.org/10.1111/cdep.12110

La Rooy, D., Lamb, M. E., & Pipe, M. (2011). Repeated interviewing: A critical evaluation of the risks and potential benefits. In K. Kuehnle & M. Connell (Eds.), *The evaluation of child sexual abuse allegations: A comprehensive guide to assessment and testimony* (pp. 327–361). Wiley-Blackwell.

Landrigan, P. J., Fuller, R., Fisher, S., Suk, W. A., Sly, P., Chiles, T. C., & Bose-O'Reilly, S. (2019). Pollution and children's health. *Science of The Total Environment*, *650*, 2389–2394. https://doi.org/10.1016/J.SCITOTENV.2018.09.375

Lange, H., Buse, J., Bender, S., Siegert, J., Knopf, H., & Roessner, V. (2016). Accident proneness in children and adolescents affected by ADHD and the impact of medication. *Journal of Attention Disorders*, *20*(6), 501–509. https://doi.org/10.1177/1087054713518237

Lecce, S., Demicheli, P., Zocchi, S., & Palladino, P. (2015). The origins of children's metamemory: The role of theory of mind. *Journal of Experimental Child Psychology*, *131*, 56–72. https://doi.org/10.1016/j.jecp.2014.11.005

Leow, C., & Wen, X. (2017). Is full day better than half day? A propensity score analysis of the association between head start program intensity and children's school performance in Kindergarten. *Early Education and Development*, *28*(2), 224–239. https://doi.org/10.1080/10409289.2016.1208600

Lerkkanen, M.-K., Kiuru, N., Pakarinen, E., Poikkeus, A.-M., Rasku-Puttonen, H., Siekkinen, M., & Nurmi, J.-E. (2016). Child-centered versus teacher-directed teaching practices: Associations with the development of academic skills in the first grade at school. *Early Childhood Research Quarterly*, *36*, 145–156. https://doi.org/10.1016/j.ecresq.2015.12.023

Li, Q., Liu, P., Yan, N., & Feng, T. (2020). Executive function training improves emotional competence for preschool children: The roles of inhibition control and working memory. *Frontiers in Psychology*, *11*, 347. https://doi.org/10.3389/fpsyg.2020.00347

Lillard, A. S. (2021). Montessori as an alternative early childhood education. *Early Child Development and Care*, *191*, 1196–1206. https://doi.org/10.1080/03004430.2020.1832998

Lindsay, A. C., Greaney, M. L., Wallington, S. F., Mesa, T., & Salas, C. F. (2017). A review of early influences on physical activity and sedentary behaviors of preschool-age children in high-income countries. *Journal for Specialists in Pediatric Nursing*, *22*(3), e12182. https://doi.org/10.1111/jspn.12182

Littschwager, J. C., & Markman, E. M. (1994). Sixteen- and 24-month-olds' use of mutual exclusivity as a default assumption in second-label learning. *Developmental Psychology*, *30*, 955–968.

Liu, D., Wellman, H. M., Tardif, T., & Sabbagh, M. A. (2008). Theory of mind development in Chinese children: A meta-analysis of false-belief understanding across cultures and languages. *Developmental Psychology*, *44*(2), 523–531. https://doi.org/10.1037/0012-1649.44.2.523

Lloyd, B. J., Coller, R., & Miller, L. T. (2019). *BRS pediatrics*. Wolters Kluwer. https://books.google.com/books?id=Mi53DwAAQBAJ&dq=pediatrics+brown+wolters+kluwer&source=gbs_navlinks_s

Lockl, K., & Schneider, W. (2007). Knowledge about the mind: Links between theory of mind and later metamemory. *Child Development*, *78*(1), 148–167. https://doi.org/10.1111/j.1467-8624.2007.00990.x

Lohmann, H., & Tomasello, M. (2003). The role of language in the development of false belief understanding: A training study. *Child Development*, *74*(4), 1130–1144. https://doi.org/10.1111/1467-8624.00597

Lyons, R. A., Delahunty, A. M., Heaven, M., McCabe, M., Allen, H., & Nash, P. (2000). Incidence of childhood fractures in affluent and deprived areas: Population based study. *BMJ (Clinical Research Ed.)*, *320*(7228), 149. http://www.ncbi.nlm.nih.gov/pubmed/10634734

MacConnell, A., & Daehler, M. W. (2004). The development of representational insight: Beyond the model/room paradigm. *Cognitive Development*, *19*(3), 345–362.

MacWhinney, B. (2015). Language development. In L. S. Liben & U. Müller (Eds.), *Handbook of child psychology and developmental science* (pp. 296–338). John Wiley & Sons. https://doi.org/10.1002/9781118963418.childpsy208

Magee, C. A., Gordon, R., & Caputi, P. (2014). Distinct developmental trends in sleep duration during early childhood. *Pediatrics*, *133*(6), 1561–1567. https://doi.org/10.1542/peds.2013-3806

Manfra, L., & Winsler, A. (2006). Preschool children's awareness of private speech. *International Journal of Behavioral Development*, *30*(6), 537–549.

Mani, N., & Ackermann, L. (2018). Why do children learn the words they do? *Child Development Perspectives*, *12*(4), 253–257. https://doi.org/10.1111/cdep.12295

Marcon, R. A. (1999). Positive relationships between parent-school involvement and public school inner-city preschoolers' development and academic performance. *School Psychology Review*, *28*, 395–412.

Markman, E. M., & Wachtel, G. F. (1988). Children's use of mutual exclusivity to constrain the meaning of words. *Cognitive Psychology*, *20*(2), 121–157. https://doi.org/10.1016/0010-0285(88)90017-5

Markman, E. M., Wasow, J. L., & Hansen, M. B. (2003). Use of the mutual exclusivity assumption by young word learners. *Cognitive Psychology*, *47*(3), 241–275. https://doi.org/10.1016/S0010-0285(03)00034-3

Markowitz, A. J., Bassok, D., & Hamre, B. (2018). Leveraging developmental insights to improve early childhood education. *Child Development Perspectives*, *12*(2), 87–92. https://doi.org/10.1111/cdep.12266

Marotz, L. R. (2015). *Health, safety, and nutrition for the young child*. Cengage. https://www.cengage.com/c/health-safety-and-nutrition-for-the-young-child-9e-marotz/9781285427331

Martzog, P., Stoeger, H., & Suggate, S. (2019). Relations between preschool children's fine motor skills and general cognitive abilities. *Journal of Cognition and Development*, *20*(4), 443–465. https://doi.org/10.1080/15248372.2019.1607862

McAlister, A. R., & Peterson, C. C. (2013). Siblings, theory of mind, and executive functioning in children aged 3-6 years: New longitudinal evidence. *Child Development*, *84*(4), 1442–1458. https://doi.org/10.1111/cdev.12043

McClure, R., Kegler, S., Davey, T., & Clay, F. (2015). Contextual determinants of childhood injury: A systematic review of studies with multilevel analytic methods. *American Journal of Public Health*, *105*(12), e37–e43. https://doi.org/10.2105/AJPH.2015.302883

McGonigle-Chalmers, M., Slater, H., & Smith, A. (2014). Rethinking private speech in preschoolers: The effects of social presence. *Developmental Psychology*, *50*(3), 829–836. https://doi.org/10.1037/a0033909

Meisel, J. M. (1989). Early differentiation of languages in bilingual children. In K. Hyltenstam & L. K. Obler (Eds.), *Bilingualism across the lifespan: Aspects of acquisition, maturity and loss* (pp. 13–40). Cambridge University Press.

Mermelshtine, R. (2017). Parent-child learning interactions: A review of the literature on scaffolding. *British Journal of Educational Psychology*, *87*(2), 241–254. https://doi.org/10.1111/bjep.12147

Miller, A. L., Seifer, R., Crossin, R., & Lebourgeois, M. K. (2015). Toddler's self-regulation strategies in a challenge context are nap-dependent. *Journal of Sleep Research*, *24*(3), 279–287. https://doi.org/10.1111/jsr.12260

Miller, J. M., Fan, Y., Sherwood, N. E., Osypuk, T., & French, S. (2020). Are low income children more physically active when they live in homes with bigger yards? A longitudinal analysis of the NET-works Study. *Health and Place*, *63*, 102330. https://doi.org/10.1016/j.healthplace.2020.102330

Milligan, K., Astington, J. W., & Dack, L. A. (2007). Language and theory of mind: Meta-analysis of the relation between language ability and false-belief understanding. *Child Development*, *78*(2), 622–646.

Miyake, A., & Friedman, N. P. (2012). The nature and organization of individual differences in executive functions. *Current Directions in Psychological Science*, *21*(1), 8–14. https://doi.org/10.1177/0963721411429458

Mori, A., & Cigala, A. (2016). Perspective taking: Training procedures in developmentally typical preschoolers. Different intervention methods and their effectiveness. *Educational Psychology Review*, *28*(2), 267–294. https://doi.org/10.1007/s10648-015-9306-6

Moriguchi, Y. (2014). The early development of executive function and its relation to social interaction: A brief review. *Frontiers in Psychology*, *5*, 388. https://doi.org/10.3389/fpsyg.2014.00388

Moriguchi, Y., Kanda, T., Ishiguro, H., Shimada, Y., & Itakura, S. (2011). Can young children learn words from a robot? *Interaction Studies: Social Behaviour and Communication in Biological and Artificial Systems*, *12*(1), 107–118.

Morrongiello, B. A., Corbett, M., McCourt, M., & Johnston, N. (2006). Understanding unintentional injury risk in young children II. The contribution of caregiver supervision, child attributes, and parent attributes. *Journal of Pediatric Psychology*, *31*(6), 540–551. https://doi.org/10.1093/jpepsy/jsj073

Moses, L. J., Coon, J. A., & Wusinich, N. (2000). Young children's understanding of desire information. *Developmental Psychology*, *36*, 77–90.

Muennig, P., Robertson, D., Johnson, G., Campbell, F., Pungello, E. P., & Neidell, M. (2011). The effect of an early education program on adult health: The Carolina Abecedarian project randomized controlled trial. *American Journal of Public Health*, *101*(3), 512–516. https://doi.org/10.2105/AJPH.2010.200063

Myers, N. A., & Perlmutter, M. (2014). Memory in the years from two to five. In P. A. Ornstein (Ed.), *Memory development in children* (pp. 191–218). Psychology Press.

Nagayama, M., & Gilliard, J. L. (2005). An Investigation of Japanese and American early care and education. *Early Childhood Education Journal*, *33*(3), 137–143.

Natale, V., & Rajagopalan, A. (2014). Worldwide variation in human growth and the world health organization growth standards: A systematic review. *BMJ Open*, *4*(1), e003735. https://doi.org/10.1136/bmjopen-2013-003735

Newcombe, N., & Huttenlocher, J. (1992). Children's early ability to solve perspective-taking problems. *Developmental Psychology*, *28*, 635–643.

New York City Department of Health. (2019). *Measles*. https://www1.nyc.gov/site/doh/health/health-topics/measles.page

Nieto, M., Ros, L., Ricarte, J. J., & Latorre, J. M. (2018). The role of executive functions in accessing specific autobiographical memories in 3- to 6- year-olds. *Early Childhood Research Quarterly*, *43*, 23–32. https://doi.org/10.1016/j.ecresq.2017.11.004

Nuttall, A. K., Valentino, K., Comas, M., McNeill, A. T., & Stey, P. C. (2014). Autobiographical memory specificity among preschool-aged children. *Developmental Psychology*, *50*, 1963–1972.

Otgaar, H., Howe, M. L., Merckelbach, H., & Muris, P. (2018). Who is the better eyewitness? Adults and children - City research online. *Current Directions in Psychological Science*, *27*, 378–385. http://openaccess.city.ac.uk/19272/

Owens, R. E. (2020). *Language development : An introduction* (10th ed.). Pearson.

Pace, A., Luo, R., Levine, D., Iglesias, A., Villiers, J., Golinkoff, R. M., Wilson, M. S., & Hirsh-Pasek, K. (2020). Within and across language predictors of word learning processes in dual language learners. *Child Development*, cdev.13418. https://doi.org/10.1111/cdev.13418

Page, J., Cock, M. L., Murray, L., Eadie, T., Niklas, F., Scull, J., & Sparling, J. (2019). An abecedarian approach with aboriginal families and their young children in Australia: Playgroup participation and developmental outcomes. *International Journal of Early Childhood*, *51*(2), 233–250. https://doi.org/10.1007/s13158-019-00246-3

Pantell, R. H., & Committee on Psychosocial Aspects of Child and Family Health. (2017). The child witness in the courtroom. *Pediatrics*, *139*(3), e20164008, . https://doi.org/10.1542/peds.2016-4008

Park, C. J., Yelland, G. W., Taffe, J. R., & Gray, K. M. (2012). Brief report: The relationship between language skills, adaptive behavior, and emotional and behavior problems in Pre-schoolers with Autism. *Journal of Autism and Developmental Disorders*, *42*(12), 2761–2766. https://doi.org/10.1007/s10803-012-1534-8

Parra, M., Hoff, E., & Core, C. (2011). Relations among language exposure, phonological memory, and language development in Spanish–English bilingually developing 2-year-olds. *Journal of Experimental Child Psychology*, *108*(1), 113–125. https://doi.org/10.1016/j.jecp.2010.07.011

Paruthi, S., Brooks, L. J., D'Ambrosio, C., Hall, W. A., Kotagal, S., Lloyd, R. M., Malow, B. A., Maski, K., Nichols, C., Quan, S. F., Rosen, C. L., Troester, M. M., & Wise, M. S. (2016). Recommended amount of sleep for pediatric populations: A Consensus statement of the American academy of sleep medicine. *Journal of Clinical Sleep Medicine*, *12*(06), 785–786. https://doi.org/10.5664/jcsm.5866

Pate, R. R., O'Neill, J. R., Brown, W. H., Pfeiffer, K. A., Dowda, M., & Addy, C. L. (2015). Prevalence of compliance with a new physical activity guideline for preschool-age children. *Childhood Obesity (Print)*, *11*(4), 415–420. https://doi.org/10.1089/chi.2014.0143

Payne, V. G., Isaacs, L. D., & Larry, D. (2016). *Human motor development : A lifespan approach*. McGraw-Hill. http://dl.acm.org/citation.cfm?id=1214267

Petitto, L. A., Berens, M. S., Kovelman, I., Dubins, M. H., Jasinska, K., & Shalinsky, M. (2012). The "Perceptual wedge hypothesis" as the basis for bilingual babies' phonetic processing advantage: New insights from fNIRS brain imaging. *Brain and Language*, *121*(2), 130–143. https://doi.org/10.1016/j.bandl.2011.05.003

Phillips, D., Gormley, W., & Anderson, S. (2016). The effects of Tulsa's CAP head start program on middle-school academic outcomes and progress. *Developmental Psychology*, *52*(8), 1247–1261. https://doi.org/10.1037/dev0000151

Piaget, J., & Inhelder, B. (1967). *The child's conception of space*. Norton.

Pillow, B. H. (2008). Development of children's understanding of cognitive activities. *Journal of Genetic Psychology*, *169*(4), 297–321.

Plebanek, D. J., & Sloutsky, V. M. (2019). Selective attention, filtering, and the development of working memory. *Developmental Science*, *22*(1), e12727. https://doi.org/10.1111/desc.12727

Poole, D. A., & White, L. T. (1991). Effects of question repetition on the eyewitness testimony of children and adults. *Developmental Psychology*, *27*, 975–986.

Poole, D. A., & White, L. T. (1993). Two years later: Effects of question repetition and retention interval on the eyewitness testimony of children and adults. *Developmental Psychology*, *29*, 844–853.

Qiu, A., Mori, S., & Miller, M. I. (2015). Diffusion tensor imaging for understanding brain development in early life. *Annual Review of Psychology*, *66*(1), 853–876. https://doi.org/10.1146/annurev-psych-010814-015340

Racy, F., Morin, A., & Duhnych, C. (2020). Using a thought listing procedure to construct the general inner speech questionnaire: An ecological approach. *Journal of Constructivist Psychology*, *33*(4), 385–405. https://doi.org/10.1080/10720537.2019.1633572

Rakoczy, H., Warneken, F., & Tomasello, M. (2007). "This way!" "No! That way!" 3-year olds know that two people can have mutually incompatible desires. *Cognitive Development*, *22*(1), 47–68.

Ramey, C. T., & Ramey, S. L. (1998). Early intervention and early experience. *American Psychologist*, *53*(2), 109–120. https://doi.org/10.1037/0003-066X.53.2.109

Rees, C. A., Monuteaux, M. C., Raphael, J. L., & Michelson, K. A. (2020). Disparities in pediatric mortality by neighborhood income in united states emergency departments. *Journal of Pediatrics*, *219*, 209–215. e3. https://doi.org/10.1016/j.jpeds.2019.09.016

Remington, A., An˜ñez, E., Croker, H., Wardle, J., & Cooke, L. (2012). Increasing food acceptance in the home setting: A randomized controlled trial of parent-administered taste exposure with incentives. *The American Journal of Clinical Nutrition*, *95*(1), 72–77. https://doi.org/10.3945/ajcn.111.024596

Reuben, A., Caspi, A., Belsky, D. W., Broadbent, J., Harrington, H., Sugden, K., Houts, R. M., Ramrakha, S., Poulton, R., & Moffitt, T. E. (2017). Association of childhood blood lead levels with cognitive function and socioeconomic status at Age 38 Years and With IQ change and socioeconomic mobility between childhood and adulthood. *JAMA*, *317*(12), 1244. https://doi.org/10.1001/jama.2017.1712

Reynolds, J. E., Grohs, M. N., Dewey, D., & Lebel, C. (2019). Global and regional white matter development in early childhood. *NeuroImage*, *196*, 49–58. https://doi.org/10.1016/j.neuroimage.2019.04.004

Ristic, J., & Enns, J. T. (2015). Attentional development. In L. S. Liben & U. Muller (Eds.), *Handbook of child psychology and developmental science* (pp. 1–45). John Wiley & Sons, Inc. https://doi.org/10.1002/9781118963418.childpsy205

Robbins, J. (2005). Contexts, collaboration, and cultural tools: A sociocultural perspective on researching children's thinking. *Contemporary Issues in Early Childhood*, *6*(2), 140. https://doi.org/10.2304/ciec.2005.6.2.4

Robinson, J. B., Burns, B. M., & Davis, D. W. (2009). Maternal scaffolding and attention regulation in children living in poverty. *Journal of Applied Developmental Psychology*, *30*(2), 82–91. 10.1016/j.appdev.2008.10.013

Roediger, H. L., & Marsh, E. J. (2003). Episodic and autobiographical memory. In I. B. Weiner (Ed.), *Handbook of psychology, part six. Complex learning and memory processes*. John Wiley & Sons, Inc.

Rogoff, B. (2014). Learning by observing and pitching in to family and community endeavors: An orientation. *Human Development*, *57*(2–3), 69–81. https://doi.org/10.1159/000356757

Rogoff, B., Callanan, M., Gutiérrez, K. D., & Erickson, F. (2016). The organization of informal learning. *Review of Research in Education*, *40*(1), 356–401. https://doi.org/10.3102/0091732X16680994

Rogoff, B., Dahl, A., & Callanan, M. (2018). The importance of understanding children's lived experience. *Developmental Review*, *50*, 5–15. https://doi.org/10.1016/j.dr.2018.05.006

Roseberry, S., Hirsh-Pasek, K., & Golinkoff, R. M. (2014). Skype me! Socially contingent interactions help toddlers learn language. *Child Development*, *85*(3), 956–970. https://doi.org/10.1111/cdev.12166

Rowe, M. L. (2018). Understanding socioeconomic differences in parents' speech to children. *Child Development Perspectives*, *12*(2), 122–127. https://doi.org/10.1111/cdep.12271

Rueda, M. R. (2013). Developement of attention. In K. Ochsner & S. M. Kosslyn (Eds.), *The oxford handbook of cognitive neuroscience, Volume 1: Core topics* (p. 656). Oxford University Press.

Ryalls, B. O. (2000). Dimensional adjectives: Factors affecting children's ability to compare objects using novel words. *Journal of Experimental Child Psychology*, *76*(1), 26–49.

Sabbagh, M. A., Xu, F., Carlson, S. M., Moses, L. J., & Lee, K. (2006). The development of executive functioning and theory of mind. *Psychological Science*, *17*(1), 74–81.

Sapp, F., Lee, K., & Muir, D. (2000). Three-year-olds' difficulty with the appearance-reality distinction: Is it real or is it apparent? *Developmental Psychology*, *36*, 547–560.

Savina, E. (2020). Self-regulation in preschool and early elementary classrooms: Why it is important and how to promote it. In *Early childhood education journal* (pp. 1–9). Springer Publishing Comapny. https://doi.org/10.1007/s10643-020-01094-w

Schnur, E., & Belanger, S. (2000). What works in head start. In M. P. Kluger, G. Alexander, & P. A. Curtis (Eds.), *What works in child welfare* (pp. 277–284). Child Welfare League of America.

Schumacher, A. M., Miller, A. L., Watamura, S. E., Kurth, S., Lassonde, J. M., & LeBourgeois, M. K. (2017). Sleep moderates the association between response inhibition and self-regulation in early childhood. *Journal of Clinical Child & Adolescent Psychology*, *46*(2), 222–235. https://doi.org/10.1080/15374416.2016.1204921

Schwab, J. F., & Lew-Williams, C. (2016). Language learning, socioeconomic status, and child-directed speech. *Wiley Interdisciplinary Reviews: Cognitive Science*, *7*(4), 264–275. https://doi.org/10.1002/wcs.1393

Schwartz, B. L. (2018). *Memory*. Sage. https://us.sagepub.com/en-us/nam/memory/book248685

Schwebel, D. C., Rosen, C. S., & Singer, J. L. (1999). Preschoolers' pretend play and theory of mind: The role of jointly constructed pretence. *British Journal of Developmental Psychology*, *17*(3), 333–348. 10.1348/026151099165320

Schweinhart, L. J., Montie, J., lang, Z., Barnett, W. S., Belfield, C. R., & Nores, M. (2005). *Lifetime effects: The high/scope perry preschool study through age 40*. High/Scope Press.

Shannon, K. A., Scerif, G., & Raver, C. C. (2020). Using a multidimensional model of attention to predict low-income preschoolers' early academic skills across time. *Developmental Science*. https://doi.org/10.1111/desc.13025

Sills, J., Rowse, G., & Emerson, L.-M. (2016). The role of collaboration in the cognitive development of young children: A systematic review. *Child: Care, Health and Development*, *42*(3), 313–324. https://doi.org/10.1111/cch.12330

Silva, M., Strasser, K., & Cain, K. (2014). Early narrative skills in Chilean preschool: Questions scaffold the production of coherent narratives. *Early Childhood Research Quarterly*, *29*(2), 205–213. https://doi.org/10.1016/j.ecresq.2014.02.002

Silva-Santos, S., Santos, A., Duncan, M., Vale, S., & Mota, J. (2019). Association between moderate and vigorous physical activity and gross motor coordination in preschool children. *Journal of Motor Learning and Development*, *7*(2), 273–285. https://doi.org/10.1123/jmld.2017-0056

Slaughter, V., & Perez-Zapata, D. (2014). Cultural variations in the development of mind reading. *Child Development Perspectives*, *8*(4), 237–241. https://doi.org/10.1111/cdep.12091

Slicker, G., & Hustedt, J. T. (2019). Children's school readiness in socioeconomically diverse pre-K classrooms. *Early Child Development and Care*, *190*, 1–14. https://doi.org/10.1080/03004430.2019.1582527

Sodian, B., Kristen-Antonow, S., & Kloo, D. (2020). How does children's theory of mind become explicit? A review of longitudinal findings. *Child Development Perspectives*, *14*(3), 171–177. https://doi.org/10.1111/cdep.12381

Sparling, J., & Meunier, K. (2019). Abecedarian: An early childhood education approach that has a rich history and a vibrant present. *International Journal of Early Childhood*, *51*(2), 207–216. https://doi.org/10.1007/s13158-019-00247-2

Stark, A. D., Bennet, G. C., Stone, D. H., & Chishti, P. (2002). Association between childhood fractures and poverty: Population based study. *BMJ (Clinical Research Ed.)*, *324*(7335), 457. http://www.ncbi.nlm.nih.gov/pubmed/11859047

Stiles, J. (2017). Principles of brain development. *Wiley Interdisciplinary Reviews: Cognitive Science*, *8*(1–2), e1402. https://doi.org/10.1002/wcs.1402

Stipek, D., Feiler, R., Daniels, D., & Milburn, S. (1995). Effects of different instructional approaches on young children's achievement and motivation. *Child Development*, *66*, 209–223.

Stone, M. M., Blumberg, F. C., Blair, C., & Cancelli, A. A. (2016). The "EF" in deficiency: Examining the linkages between executive function and the utilization deficiency observed in preschoolers. *Journal of Experimental Child Psychology*, *152*, 367–375. https://doi.org/10.1016/j.jecp.2016.07.003

Stulp, G., & Barrett, L. (2016). Evolutionary perspectives on human height variation. *Biological Reviews*, *91*(1), 206–234. https://doi.org/10.1111/brv.12165

Suk, W. A., Ahanchian, H., Asante, K. A., Carpenter, D. O., Diaz-Barriga, F., Ha, E.-H., Huo, X., King, M., Ruchirawat, M., da Silva, E. R., Sly, L., Sly, P. D., Stein, R. T., van den Berg, M., Zar, H., & Landrigan, P. J. (2016). Environmental pollution: An under-recognized threat to children's health, especially in low- and middle-income countries. *Environmental Health Perspectives*, *124*(3), 41–45. https://doi.org/10.1289/ehp.1510517

Szpak, M., & Białecka-Pikul, M. (2020). Links between attachment and theory of mind in childhood: Meta-analytic review. *Social Development*, *29*(3), 653–673. https://doi.org/10.1111/sode.12432

Taber, K. S. (2020). *Mediated learning leading development—The social development theory of Lev Vygotsky* (pp. 277–291). Springer Publishing Company. https://doi.org/10.1007/978-3-030-43620-9_19

Taylor, K. (2017, April 24). New York City will offer free preschool for All 3-year-olds. *New York Times*. https://www.nytimes.com/2017/04/24/nyregion/de-blasio-pre-k-expansion.html?_r=0

Thapar, A., Cooper, M., Eyre, O., & Langley, K. (2013). What have we learnt about the causes of ADHD? *Journal of Child Psychology and Psychiatry, and Allied Disciplines*, *54*(1), 3–16. https://doi.org/10.1111/j.1469-7610.2012.02611.x

Titz, C., & Karbach, J. (2014). Working memory and executive functions: Effects of training on academic achievement. *Psychological Research*, *78*(6), 852–868. https://doi.org/10.1007/s00426-013-0537-1

Trawick-Smith, J., & Dziurgot, T. (2011). 'Good-fit' teacher–child play interactions and the subsequent autonomous play of preschool children. *Early Childhood Research Quarterly*, *26*(1), 110–123. https://doi.org/10.1016/j.ecresq.2010.04.005

Tulving, E. (2002). Episodic memory: From mind to brain. *Annual Review of Psychology*, *53*, 1–25.

Turnbull, K., & Justice, L. M. (2016). *Language development from theory to practice*. Pearson.

Uhl, E. R., Camilletti, C. R., Scullin, M. H., & Wood, J. M. (2016). Under pressure: Individual differences in children's suggestibility in response to intense social influence. *Social Development*, *25*(2), 422–434. https://doi.org/10.1111/sode.12156

U.S. Department of Health and Human Services. (2018). . In *The physical activity guidelines for Americans* (2nd ed.). Author. https://doi.org/10.1001/jama.2018.14854

U.S. Department of Health and Human Services, & Administration for Children and Families. (2010). *Head start impact study: Final report*. Author.

Vandermaas-Peeler, M., Massey, K., & Kendall, A. (2016). Parent guidance of young children's scientific and mathematical reasoning in a science Museum. *Early Childhood Education Journal*, *44*(3), 217–224. https://doi.org/10.1007/s10643-015-0714-5

Vaughn, B. E., Elmore-Staton, L., Shin, N., & El-Sheikh, M. (2015). Sleep as a support for social competence, peer relations, and cognitive functioning in preschool children. *Behavioral Sleep Medicine*, *13*(2), 92–106. https://doi.org/10.1080/15402002.2013.845778

Veer, I. M., Luyten, H., Mulder, H., van Tuijl, C., & Sleegers, P. J. C. (2017). Selective attention relates to the development of executive functions in 2,5- to 3-year-olds: A longitudinal study. *Early Childhood Research Quarterly*, *41*, 84–94. https://doi.org/10.1016/J.ECRESQ.2017.06.005

Vernon-Feagans, L., Bratsch-Hines, M., Reynolds, E., & Willoughby, M. (2020). How early maternal language input varies by race and education and predicts later child language. *Child Development*, *91*(4), 1098–1115. https://doi.org/10.1111/cdev.13281

Vissers, C. T. W. M., Tomas, E., & Law, J. (2020). The emergence of inner speech and its measurement in atypically developing children. *Frontiers in Psychology*, *11*, 279. https://doi.org/10.3389/fpsyg.2020.00279

Vonk, J., Jett, S. E., Tomeny, T. S., Mercer, S. H., & Cwikla, J. (2020). Young children's theory of mind predicts more sharing with friends over time. *Child Development*, *91*(1), 63–77. https://doi.org/10.1111/cdev.13112

Vygotsky, L.. (1962). *Thought and language* . Cambridge, MA: MIT Press. (Original work published 1934)

Vygotsky, L. S. (1978). *Mind in society: The development of higher psychological processes*. Harvard University Press.

Vygotsky, L. S., & Minick, N. (1987). In T. N. Minick (Ed.), *Thinking and speech*. Plenum Press.

Walton, M., Dewey, D., & Lebel, C. (2018). Brain white matter structure and language ability in preschool-aged children. *Brain and Language*, *176*, 19–25. https://doi.org/10.1016/J.BANDL.2017.10.008

Wass, R., & Golding, C. (2014). Sharpening a tool for teaching: The zone of proximal development. *Teaching in Higher Education*, *19*(6), 671–684. https://doi.org/10.1080/13562517.2014.901958

Wellman, H. M. (2017). The Development of theory of mind: Historical reflections. *Child Development Perspectives*, *11*(3), 207–214. https://doi.org/10.1111/cdep.12236

Wellman, H. M., & Banerjee, M. (1991). Mind and emotion: Children's understanding of the emotional consequences of beliefs and desires. *British Journal of Developmental Psychology*, *9*, 191–214.

Wellman, H. M., Fang, F., & Peterson, C. C. (2011). Sequential progressions in a theory-of-mind scale: Longitudinal perspectives. *Child Development*, *82*(3), 780–792. https://doi.org/10.1111/j.1467-8624.2011.01583.x

Wellman, H. M., Somerville, S. C., & Haake, R. J. (1979). Development of search procedures in real-life spatial environments. *Developmental Psychology*, *15*, 530–542.

Welshman, J. (2010). From head start to sure start: Reflections on policy transfer. *Children & Society*, *24*(2), 89–99. https://doi.org/10.1111/j.1099-0860.2008.00201.x

Werker, J. (2012). Perceptual foundations of bilingual acquisition in infancy. *Annals of the New York Academy of Sciences*, *1251*(1), 50–61. https://doi.org/10.1111/j.1749-6632.2012.06484.x

Wertsch, J. V. (1998). *Mind as action*. Oxford University Press.

Williams, E. (2015). *Pre-kindergarten across states*. New America Ed Central. http://www.edcentral.org/prekstatefunding/

Winsler, A., Fernyhough, C., & Montero, I. (2009). *Private speech, executive functioning, and the development of verbal self-regulation*. Cambridge University Press.

Woolley, J. D., & E Ghossainy, M. (2013). Revisiting the fantasy-reality distinction: Children as naïve skeptics. *Child Development*, *84*(5), 1496–1510. https://doi.org/10.1111/cdev.12081

Wu, Y., & Jobson, L. (2019). Maternal reminiscing and child autobiographical memory elaboration: A meta-analytic review. *Developmental Psychology*, *55*, 2505. https://doi.org/10.1037/dev0000821

Wysman, L., Scoboria, A., Gawrylowicz, J., & Memon, A. (2014). The cognitive interview buffers the effects of subsequent repeated questioning in the absence of negative feedback. *Behavioral Sciences & the Law*, *32*(2), 207–219. https://doi.org/10.1002/bsl.2115

Zaitchik, D., Iqbal, Y., & Carey, S. (2014). The effect of executive function on biological reasoning in young children: an individual differences study. *Child Development*, *85*(1), 160–175. https://doi.org/10.1111/cdev.12145

Zhai, F., Brooks-Gunn, J., & Waldfogel, J. (2011). Head start and urban children's school readiness: A birth cohort study in 18 cities. *Developmental Psychology*, *47*(1), 134–152. https://doi.org/10.1037/a0020784

Zhang, N., Baker, HW., Tufts, M., Raymond, RE., Salihu, H., & Elliott, MR. (2013). Early childhood lead exposure and academic achievement: Evidence from detroit public schools, 2008-2010. *American Journal of Public Health*, *103*, 72–77.

Zigler, E., & Styfco, S. J. (2004). Moving head start to the states: One experiment too many. *Applied Developmental Science*, *8*(1), 51–55.

Zosh, J. M., Brinster, M., & Halberda, J. (2013). Optimal contrast: Competition between two referents improves word learning. *Applied Developmental Science*, *17*(1), 20–28. https://doi.org/10.1080/10888691.2013.748420

Zuckerman, G. (2007). Child-adult interaction that creates a zone of proximal development. *Journal of Russian & East European Psychology*, *45*(3), 43–69. https://doi.org/10.2753/RPO1061-0405450302

CHAPTER 6

AAP Committee on Psychosocial Aspects of Child and Family Health. (1998). Guidance for effective discipline. *Pediatrics*, *101*, 723–728.

Aboud, F. E., & Steele, J. R. (2017). Theoretical perspectives on the development of implicit and explicit prejudice. In A. Rutland, D. Nesdale, & C. S. Brown (Eds.), *The Wiley handbook of group processes in children and adolescents* (pp. 165–183). John Wiley & Sons, Ltd. https://doi.org/10.1002/9781118773123.ch8

Arthur, A. E., Bigler, R. S., & Ruble, D. N. (2009). An experimental test of the effects of gender constancy on sex typing. *Journal of Experimental Child Psychology*, *104*(4), 427–446. https://doi.org/10.1016/j.jecp.2009.08.002

Baker, E. R., Tisak, M. S., & Tisak, J. (2016). What can boys and girls do? Preschoolers' perspectives regarding gender roles across domains of behavior. *Social Psychology of Education*, *19*(1), 23–39. https://doi.org/10.1007/s11218-015-9320-z

Balan, R., Dobrean, A., Roman, G. D., & Balazsi, R. (2017). Indirect effects of parenting practices on internalizing problems among adolescents: The role of expressive suppression. *Journal of Child and Family Studies*, *26*(1), 40–47. https://doi.org/10.1007/s10826-016-0532-4

Ball, C. L., Smetana, J. G., & Sturge-Apple, M. L. (2017). Following my head and my heart: Integrating preschoolers' empathy, theory of mind, and moral judgments. *Child Development*, *88*(2), 597–611. https://doi.org/10.1111/cdev.12605

Bandura, A. (1977). *Social learning theory*. Prentice Hall.

Bandura, A. (1986). *Social foundations of thought and action: A social cognitive theory*. Prentice Hall.

Bandura, A., & Bussey, K. (2004). On Broadening the cognitive, motivational, and sociostructural scope of theorizing about gender development and functioning: Comment on Martin, Ruble, and Szkrybalo (2002). *Psychological Bulletin*, *130*(5), 691–701.

Bandura, A., & McDonald, F. J. (1963). The influence of social reinforcement and the behavior of models in shaping children's moral judgments. *Journal of Abnormal and Social Psychology*, *67*, 274–281.

Barth, R. P., Scarborough, A., Lloyd, E. C., Losby, J., Casanueva, C., & Mann, T. (2007). *Developmental status and early intervention service needs of maltreated children*. U.S. Department of Health and Human Services, Office of the Assistant Secretary for Planning and Evaluation.

Basow, S. (2008). Gender socialization, or how long a way has baby come? In J. C. Chrisler, C. Golden, & P. D. Rozee (Eds.), *Lectures on the psychology of women* (4th ed., pp. 81–95). McGraw-Hill.

Baumrind, D. (1971). Current patterns of parental authority. *Developmental Psychology*, *4*(Monograph 1), 1–103.

Baumrind, D. (2012). Differentiating between confrontive and coercive kinds of parental power-assertive disciplinary practices. *Human Development*, *55*(2), 35–51. https://doi.org/10.1159/000337962

Baumrind, D. (2013). Authoritative parenting revisited: History and current status. In R. E. Larzelere, A. S. Morris, & A. W. Harrist (Eds.), *Authoritative parenting: Synthesizing nurturance and discipline for optimal child development* (pp. 11–34). APA. http://psycnet.apa.org/buy/2012-15622-002

Baumrind, D., Larzelere, R. E., & Owens, E. B. (2010). Effects of preschool parents' power assertive patterns and practices on adolescent development. *Parenting: Science & Practice, 10*(3), 157–201. https://doi.org/10.1080/15295190903290790

Beier, J. S., Gross, J. T., Brett, B. E., Stern, J. A., Martin, D. R., & Cassidy, J. (2019). Helping, sharing, and comforting in young children: Links to individual differences in attachment. *Child Development, 90*(2), e273–e289. https://doi.org/10.1111/cdev.13100

Beneke, M. R., Park, C. C., & Taitingfong, J. (2019). An inclusive, anti-bias framework for teaching and learning about race with young children. *Young Exceptional Children, 22*(2), 74–86. https://doi.org/10.1177/1096250618811842

Berenbaum, S. A. (2018). Beyond pink and blue: The complexity of early androgen effects on gender development. *Child Development Perspectives, 12*(1), 58–64. https://doi.org/10.1111/cdep.12261

Berk, L. E., & Winsler, A. (1995). *Scaffolding children's learning: Vygotsky and early childhood education. NAEYC research into practice series.* National Association for the Education of Young Children. 1509 16th Street, NW, Washington, DC 20036-1426 (NAEYC catalog# 146)

Bigler, R. S., & Pahlke, E. (2019). "I disagree! Sexism is silly to me!" Teaching children to recognize and confront gender biases. In M. J. Monteith & R. K. Mallett (Eds.), *Confronting prejudice and discrimination* (pp. 299–318). Elsevier. https://doi.org/10.1016/B978-0-12-814715-3.00012-6

Blakemore, J. E. O., Berenbaum, S. A., & Liben, L. S. (2009). *Gender development*. Psychology Press.

Boseovski, J. J. (2010). Evidence for "rose-colored glasses": An examination of the positivity bias in young children's personality judgments. *Child Development Perspectives, 4*(3), 212–218. https://doi.org/10.1111/j.1750-8606.2010.00149.x

Brownell, C. A. (2016). Prosocial behavior in infancy: The role of socialization. *Child Development Perspectives, 10*(4), 222–227. https://doi.org/10.1111/cdep.12189

Burgdorf, J., Kroes, R. A., & Moskal, J. R. (2017). Rough-and-tumble play induces resilience to stress in rats. *NeuroReport, 28*(17), 1122–1126. https://doi.org/10.1097/WNR.0000000000000864

Bussey, K. (1992). Lying and truthfulness: Children's definitions, standards, and evaluative reactions. *Child Development, 63*, 129–137.

Bussey, K. (2013). Gender development. In M. K. Ryan & N. R. Branscombe (Eds.), *The SAGE handbook of gender and psychology* (pp. 81–100). SAGE.

Cabrera, C., Torres, H., & Harcourt, S. (2020). The neurological and neuropsychological effects of child maltreatment. *Aggression and Violent Behavior, 54*, 101408. https://doi.org/10.1016/j.avb.2020.101408

Camras, L. A., & Halberstadt, A. G. (2017). Emotional development through the lens of affective social competence. *Current Opinion in Psychology, 17*, 113–117. https://doi.org/10.1016/J.COPSYC.2017.07.003

Canevello, A. (2016). Gender schema theory. In V. Zeigler-Hill & T. K. Shackelford (Eds.), *Encyclopedia of personality and individual differences* (pp. 1–3). Springer International Publishing. https://doi.org/10.1007/978-3-319-28099-8_978-1

Carlson, M., Oshri, A., & Kwon, J. (2015). Child maltreatment and risk behaviors: The roles of callous/unemotional traits and conscientiousness. *Child Abuse & Neglect, 50*, 234–243. https://doi.org/10.1016/j.chiabu.2015.07.003

Carson, A. S., & Banuazizi, A. (2008). "That's not fair": Similarities and differences in distributive justice reasoning between American and Filipino children. *Journal of Cross-Cultural Psychology, 39*(4), 493–514. carsona@mville.edu.

Casanueva, C., Goldman-Fraser, J., Ringeisen, H., Lederman, C., Katz, L., & Osofsky, J. (2010). Maternal perceptions of temperament among infants and toddlers investigated for maltreatment: Implications for services need and referral. *Journal of Family Violence, 25*(6), 557–574. https://doi.org/10.1007/s10896-010-9316-6

Cauce, A. M. (2008). Parenting, culture, and context: Reflections on excavating culture. *Applied Developmental Science, 12*(4), 227–229. https://doi.org/10.1080/10888690802388177

Cecil, C. A. M., Viding, E., Fearon, P., Glaser, D., & McCrory, E. J. (2017). Disentangling the mental health impact of childhood abuse and neglect. *Child Abuse & Neglect, 63*, 106–119. https://doi.org/10.1016/j.chiabu.2016.11.024

Chao, R. K. (2001). Extending research on the consequences of parenting style for Chinese Americans and European Americans. *Child Development, 72*, 1832–1843.

Cheah, C. S. L., Leung, C. Y. Y., Tahseen, M., & Schultz, D. (2009). Authoritative parenting among immigrant Chinese mothers of preschoolers. *Journal of Family Psychology, 23*(3), 311–320. https://doi.org/10.1037/a0015076

Child Welfare Information Gateway. (2013). *What is child abuse and neglect? Recognizing the signs and symptoms.* https://www.childwelfare.gov/pubpdfs/whatiscan.pdf

Child Welfare Information Gateway. (2019). *What is child abuse and neglect? Recognizing the signs and symptoms.* https://www.childwelfare.gov/topics/

Choe, D. E., Olson, S. L., & Sameroff, A. J. (2013). The interplay of externalizing problems and physical and inductive discipline during childhood. *Developmental Psychology, 49*(11), 2029–2039. https://doi.org/10.1037/a0032054

Cicchetti, D. (2016). Socioemotional, personality, and biological development: Illustrations from a multilevel developmental psychopathology perspective on child maltreatment. *Annual Review of Psychology, 67*(1), 187–211. https://doi.org/10.1146/annurev-psych-122414-033259

Cicchetti, D., & Banny, A. (2014). A developmental psychopathology perspective on child maltreatment. In M. Lewis & K. D. Rudolph (Eds.), *Handbook of developmental psychopathology* (pp. 723–741). Springer US. https://doi.org/10.1007/978-1-4614-9608-3

Cicchetti, D., & Toth, S. L. (2015). Child maltreatment. In M. E. Lamb (Ed.), *Handbook of child psychology and developmental science* (Vol. 3, pp. 1–51). John Wiley & Sons, Inc. https://doi.org/10.1002/9781118963418.childpsy313

Cimpian, A., Hammond, M. D., Mazza, G., & Corry, G. (2017). Young children's self-concepts include representations of abstract traits and the global self. *Child Development, 88*(6), 1786–1798. https://doi.org/10.1111/cdev.12925

Coley, R. L., Kull, M. A., & Carrano, J. (2014). Parental endorsement of spanking and children's internalizing and externalizing problems in African American and Hispanic families. *Journal of Family Psychology : JFP : Journal of the Division of Family Psychology of the American Psychological Association (Division 43)*, *28*(1), 22–31. https://doi.org/10.1037/a0035272

Conron, K. J., Scott, G., Stowell, G. S., & Landers, S. J. (2012). Transgender health in Massachusetts: Results from a household probability sample of adults. *American Journal of Public Health*, *102*(1), 118–122. https://doi.org/10.2105/AJPH.2011.300315

Coplan, R. J., & Arbeau, K. A. (2009). Peer interactions and play in early childhood. In K. H. Rubin, W. M. Bukowski, & B. Laursen (Eds.), *Handbook of peer interactions, relationships, and groups* (pp. 143–161). Guilford Press.

Côté, S. M. (2009). A developmental perspective on sex differences in aggressive behaviours. In R. E. Tremblay, M. A. G. van Aken, & W. Koops (Eds.), *Development and prevention of behaviour problems: From genes to social policy* (pp. 143–163). Psychology Press.

Coyne, S. M., Linder, J. R., Rasmussen, E. E., Nelson, D. A., & Birkbeck, V. (2016). Pretty as a Princess: Longitudinal effects of engagement With Disney Princesses on gender stereotypes, body esteem, and prosocial behavior in children. *Child Development*, *87*(6), 1909–1925. https://doi.org/10.1111/cdev.12569

Crespo, L. M., Trentacosta, C. J., Aikins, D., & Wargo-Aikins, J. (2017). Maternal emotion regulation and children's behavior problems: The mediating role of child emotion regulation. *Journal of Child and Family Studies*, *26*(10), 2797–2809. https://doi.org/10.1007/s10826-017-0791-8

Cuartas, J. (2018). Neighborhood crime undermines parenting: Violence in the vicinity of households as a predictor of aggressive discipline. *Child Abuse & Neglect*, *76*, 388–399. https://doi.org/10.1016/J.CHIABU.2017.12.006

Cuellar, J., Jones, D. J., & Sterrett, E. (2013). Examining parenting in the neighborhood context: A review. *Journal of Child and Family Studies*, *24*(1), 195–219. https://doi.org/10.1007/s10826-013-9826-y

Dadds, M. R., & Tully, L. A. (2019). What is it to discipline a child: What should it be? A reanalysis of time-out from the perspective of child mental health, attachment, and trauma. *American Psychologist*, *74*(7), 794–808. https://doi.org/10.1037/amp0000449

Dahl, A. (2015). The developing social context of infant helping in two U.S. samples. *Child Development*, *86*(4), 1080–1093. https://doi.org/10.1111/cdev.12361

Dahl, A. (2018). New beginnings: An interactionist and constructivist approach to early moral development. *Human Development*, *61*(4–5), 232–247. https://doi.org/10.1159/000492801

Dahl, A. (2019). The science of early moral development: On defining, constructing, and studying morality from birth. *Advances in Child Development and Behavior*, *56*, 1–35. https://doi.org/10.1016/bs.acdb.2018.11.001

Dahl, A., & Brownell, C. A. (2019). The social origins of human prosociality. *Current Directions in Psychological Science*, *28*(3), 274–279. https://doi.org/10.1177/0963721419830386

Dahl, A., & Paulus, M. (2019). From interest to obligation: The gradual development of human altruism. *Child Development Perspectives*, *13*(1), 10–14. https://doi.org/10.1111/cdep.12298

Damon, W. (1977). *The social world of the child*. Jossey-Bass.

Davis, P. E., Meins, E., & Fernyhough, C. (2014). Children with imaginary companions focus on mental characteristics when describing their real-life friends. *Infant and Child Development*, *23*(6), 622–633. https://doi.org/10.1002/icd.1869

Dede Yildirim, E., Roopnarine, J. L., & Abolhassani, A. (2020). Maternal use of physical and non-physical forms of discipline and preschoolers' social and literacy skills in 25 African countries. *Child Abuse & Neglect*, *106*, 104513. https://doi.org/10.1016/j.chiabu.2020.104513

Deneault, J., & Ricard, M. (2013). Are emotion and mind understanding differently linked to young children's social adjustment? Relationships between behavioral consequences of emotions, false belief, and SCBE. *The Journal of Genetic Psychology*, *174*(1), 88–116. https://doi.org/10.1080/00221325.2011.642028

Dennis, T. A., Cole, P. M., Zahn-Waxler, C., & Mizuta, I. (2002). Self in context: Autonomy and relatedness in Japanese and U. S. mother-preschooler dyads. *Child Development*, *73*, 1803–1817.

DeVries, R., & Zan, B. (2003). When children make rules. *Educational Leadership*, *61*(1), 64–67.

D'Souza, A. J., Russell, M., Wood, B., Signal, L., & Elder, D. (2016). Attitudes to physical punishment of children are changing. *Archives of Disease in Childhood*, *101*(8), 690–693. https://doi.org/10.1136/archdischild-2015-310119

Durwood, L., McLaughlin, K. A., & Olson, K. R. (2017). Mental health and self-worth in socially transitioned transgender youth. *Journal of the American Academy of Child and Adolescent Psychiatry*, *56*(2), 116–123. https://doi.org/10.1016/j.jaac.2016.10.016

Dyer, S., & Moneta, G. B. (2006). Frequency of parallel, associative, and cooperative play in British children of different socioeconomic status. *Social Behavior and Personality: An International Journal*, *34*(5), 587–592.

Eisenberg, N., Spinrad, T. L., & Knafo-Noam, A. (2015). Prosocial development. In P. D. Zelazo (Ed.), *Handbook of child psychology and developmental science* (pp. 1–47). John Wiley & Sons, Inc. https://doi.org/10.1002/9781118963418.childpsy315

Eisenberg, N., Spinrad, T. L., & Morris, A. S. (2013). Prosocial development. In P. D. Zelazo (Ed.), *The Oxford handbook of developmental psychology, Vol. 2: Self and other* (Vol. 1, pp. 300–324). Oxford University Press. https://doi.org/10.1093/oxfordhb/9780199958474.013.0013

Eisner, M. P., & Malti, T. (2015). Aggressive and violent behavior. In M. E. Lamb (Ed.), *Handbook of child psychology and developmental science* (pp. 1–48). John Wiley & Sons, Inc. https://doi.org/10.1002/9781118963418.childpsy319

Elenbaas, L. (2019). Interwealth contact and young children's concern for equity. *Child Development*, *90*(1), 108–116. https://doi.org/10.1111/cdev.13157

Else-Quest, N. M., Higgins, A., Allison, C., & Morton, L. C. (2012). Gender differences in self-conscious emotional experience: A meta-analysis. *Psychological Bulletin*, *138*(5), 947–981. https://doi.org/10.1037/a0027930

Endendijk, J. J., Groeneveld, M. G., van der Pol, L. D., van Berkel, S. R., Hallers-Haalboom, E. T., Bakermans-Kranenburg, M. J., & Mesman, J. (2017). Gender differences in child aggression: Relations with gender-differentiated parenting and parents' gender-role stereotypes. *Child Development*, *88*(1), 299–316. https://doi.org/10.1111/cdev.12589

England, D. E., Descartes, L., & Collier-Meek, M. A. (2011). Gender role portrayal and the disney princesses. *Sex Roles*, *64*(7–8), 555–567. https://doi.org/10.1007/s11199-011-9930-7

Enright, R. D., Bjerstedt, Å., Enright, W. F., Levy, V. M., Lapsley, D. K., Buss, R. R., Harwell, M., & Zindler, M. (1984). Distributive justice development: Cross-cultural, contextual, and longitudinal evaluations. *Child Development*, *55*(5), 1737. https://doi.org/10.1111/1467-8624.ep7304494

Erikson, E. H. (1950). *Childhood and society* (2nd ed.). : Norton.

Evans, J. (1998). "Princesses are not into war 'n things, they always scream and run off": Exploring gender stereotypes in picture books. *Reading*, *32*(3), 5–11.

Fast, A. A., & Olson, K. R. (2018). Gender development in transgender preschool children. *Child Development*, *89*(2), 620–637. https://doi.org/10.1111/cdev.12758

Fehr, K. K., Boog, K. E., & Leraas, B. C. (2020). Play behaviors: Definition and typology. In S. Hupp & J. D. Jewell (Eds.), *The encyclopedia of child and adolescent development* (pp. 1–10). Wiley. https://doi.org/10.1002/9781119171492.wecad272

Filipović, K. (2018). Gender representation in children's books: Case of an early childhood setting. *Journal of Research in Childhood Education*, *32*(3), 310–325. https://doi.org/10.1080/02568543.2018.1464086

Fitzpatrick, M., & McPherson, B. (2010). Coloring within the lines: Gender stereotypes in contemporary coloring books. *Sex Roles*, *62*(1/2), 127–137. https://doi.org/10.1007/s11199-009-9703-8

Font, S. A., & Berger, L. M. (2014). Child maltreatment and children's developmental trajectories in early to middle childhood. *Child Development*, *86*(2), 536–556. https://doi.org/10.1111/cdev.12322

Frawley, T. J. (2008). Gender schema and prejudicial recall: How children misremember, fabricate, and distort gendered picture book information. *Journal of Research in Childhood Education*, *22*(3), 291–303.

Freeman, N. (2007). Preschoolers' perceptions of gender appropriate toys and their parents' beliefs about genderized behaviors: Miscommunication, mixed messages, or hidden truths? *Early Childhood Education Journal*, *34*(5), 357–366. https://doi.org/10.1007/s10643-006-0123-x

Frost, J. L., Wortham, S. C., & Reifel, S. C. (2012). *Play and child development*. Pearson. https://www.pearson.com/us/higher-education/program/Frost-Play-and-Child-Development-4th-Edition/PGM141867.html

Fuss, J., Auer, M. K., & Briken, P. (2015). Gender dysphoria in children and adolescents. *Current Opinion in Psychiatry*, *28*(6), 430–434. https://doi.org/10.1097/YCO.0000000000000203

Gagnon, S. G., Huelsman, T. J., Reichard, A. E., Kidder-Ashley, P., Griggs, M. S., Struby, J., & Bollinger, J. (2013). Help me play! Parental behaviors, child temperament, and preschool peer play. *Journal of Child and Family* Studies, *23*(5), 872–884. https://doi.org/10.1007/s10826-013-9743-0

Gaskins, S. (2014). Children's play as cultural activity. In E. Brooker, M. Blaise, & S. Edwards (Eds.), *SAGE handbook of play and learning in early childhood* (pp. 31–42). SAGE.

Gates, G. J. (2011). *How many people are lesbian, gay, bisexual and transgender?* https://escholarship.org/uc/item/09h684x2

Gershoff, E. T., Goodman, G. S., Miller-Perrin, C. L., Holden, G. W., Jackson, Y., & Kazdin, A. E. (2018). The strength of the causal evidence against physical punishment of children and its implications for parents, psychologists, and policymakers. *American Psychologist*, *73*(5), 626–638. https://doi.org/10.1037/amp0000327

Gershoff, E. T., & Grogan-Kaylor, A. (2016). Spanking and child outcomes: Old controversies and new meta-analyses. *Journal of Family Psychology*, *30*(4), 453–469. https://doi.org/10.1037/fam0000191

Gibbs, J. C. (2003). *Moral development and reality: Beyond the theories of Kohlberg and Hoffman*. Sage.

Giménez-Dasí, M., Pons, F., & Bender, P. K. (2016). Imaginary companions, theory of mind and emotion understanding in young children. *European Early Childhood Education Research Journal*, *24*(2), 186–197. https://doi.org/10.1080/1350293X.2014.919778

Ginsburg, K. R. (2007). The importance of play in promoting healthy child development and maintaining strong parent-child bonds. *Pediatrics*, *119*(1), 182–191.

Gioia, K. A., & Tobin, R. M. (2010). Role of sociodramatic play in promoting self-regulation. In C. E. Schaefer (Ed.), *Play therapy for preschool children* (pp. 181–198). American Psychological Association. https://doi.org/10.1037/12060-009

Gleason, T. R. (2017). The psychological significance of play with imaginary companions in early childhood. *Learning & Behavior*, *45*(4), 432–440. https://doi.org/10.3758/s13420-017-0284-z

Gleason, T. R., & Kalpidou, M. (2014). Imaginary companions and young children's coping and competence. *Social Development*, *23*(4), 820–839. https://doi.org/10.1111/sode.12078

Gleason, T. R., Sebanc, A. M., & Hartup, W. W. (2000). Imaginary companions of preschool children. *Developmental Psychology*, *36*, 419–428.

Golden, J. C., & Jacoby, J. W. (2018). Playing princess: Preschool girls' interpretations of gender stereotypes in disney princess media. *Sex Roles*, *79*(5–6), 299–313. https://doi.org/10.1007/s11199-017-0773-8

Goldstein, T. R., & Lerner, M. D. (2018). Dramatic pretend play games uniquely improve emotional control in young children. *Developmental Science*, *21*(4), e12603. https://doi.org/10.1111/desc.12603

Goodvin, R., Meyer, S., Thompson, R. A., & Hayes, R. (2008). Self-understanding in early childhood: Associations with child attachment security and maternal negative affect. *Attachment & Human Development*, *10*(4), 433–450. https://doi.org/10.1080/14616730802461466

Goodvin, R., Thompson, R. A., & Winer, A. C. (2015). The individual child: Temperament, emotion, self, and personality. In M. Bornstein & M. Lamb (Eds.), *Developmental psychology: An advanced textbook* (pp. 491–533). Psychology Press.

Gower, A. L., Lingras, K. A., Mathieson, L. C., Kawabata, Y., & Crick, N. R. (2014). The role of preschool relational and physical aggression in the transition to kindergarten: Links with social-psychological adjustment. *Early Education and Development*, *25*(5), 619–640. https://doi.org/10.1080/10409289.2014.844058

Griffith, A. K. (2020). Parental burnout and child maltreatment during the COVID-19 pandemic. *Journal of Family Violence*, 1–7. https://doi.org/10.1007/s10896-020-00172-2

Grogan-Kaylor, A., Ma, J., & Graham-Bermann, S. A. (2018). The case against physical punishment. *Current Opinion in Psychology, 19,* 22–27. http://www.sciencedirect.com/science/article/pii/S2352250X17300519

Grusec, J. E. (1992). Social learning theory and developmental psychology: The legacies of Robert Sears and Albert Bandura. *Developmental Psychology, 28*(5), 776–786.

Grusec, J. E., & Goodnow, J. J. (1994). Impact of parental discipline methods on the child's internalization of values: A reconceptualization of current points of view. *Developmental Psychology, 30,* 4–19.

Gu, M., & Kwok, S. Y. C. L. (2020). A longitudinal study of power-assertive discipline, inductive discipline and preschoolers' anxiety: Preschoolers' forgiveness as a moderator. *Child Indicators Research, 13*(1), 85–103. https://doi.org/10.1007/s12187-019-09654-2

Guimond, S., Chatard, A., & Lorenzi-Cioldi, F. (2013). The social psychology of gender across cultures. In M. K. Ryan (Ed.), *The SAGE handbook of gender and psychology* (pp. 216–233). SAGE Publications. https://doi.org/10.4135/9781446269930.n14

Gülgöz, S., DeMeules, M., Gelman, S. A., & Olson, K. R. (2019). Gender essentialism in transgender and cisgender children. *PLoS One, 14*(11), e0224321, . https://doi.org/10.1371/journal.pone.0224321

Halim, M. L. D. (2016). Princesses and superheroes: Social-cognitive influences on early gender rigidity. *Child Development Perspectives, 10*(3), 155–160. https://doi.org/10.1111/cdep.12176

Halim, M. L. D., Gutierrez, B. C., Bryant, D. N., Arredondo, M., & Takesako, K. (2018). Gender is what you look like: Emerging gender identities in young children and preoccupation with appearance. *Self and Identity, 17*(4), 455–466. https://doi.org/10.1080/15298868.2017.1412344

Halim, M. L. D., Ruble, D. N., Tamis-LeMonda, C. S., & Shrout, P. E. (2013). Rigidity in gender-typed behaviors in early childhood: A longitudinal study of ethnic minority children. *Child Development, 84*(4), 1269–1284. https://doi.org/10.1111/cdev.12057

Halim, M. L. D., Ruble, D. N., Tamis-LeMonda, C. S., Shrout, P. E., & Amodio, D. M. (2017). Gender attitudes in early childhood: Behavioral consequences and cognitive antecedents. *Child Development, 88*(3), 882–899. https://doi.org/10.1111/cdev.12642

Halim, M. L. D., Ruble, D. N., Tamis-LeMonda, C. S., Zosuls, K. M., Lurye, L. E., & Greulich, F. K. (2014). Pink frilly dresses and the avoidance of all things "girly": Children's appearance rigidity and cognitive theories of gender development. *Developmental Psychology, 50*(4), 1091–1101. https://doi.org/10.1037/a0034906

Hammond, S. I., & Carpendale, J. I. M. (2015). Helping children help: The relation between maternal scaffolding and children's early help. *Social Development, 24*(2), 367–383. https://doi.org/10.1111/sode.12104

Hanish, L. D., Fabes, R. A., Leaper, C., Bigler, R., Hayes, A. R., Hamilton, V., & Beltz, A. M. (2013). Gender: Early socialization. In D. A. Crosby, E. T. Gershoff, & R. S. Mistry (Eds.), *Societal contexts of child development: Pathways of influence and implications for practice and policy.* Oxford University Press.

Harrington, E. M., Trevino, S. D., Lopez, S., & Giuliani, N. R. (2020). Emotion regulation in early childhood: Implications for socioemotional and academic components of school readiness. *Emotion, 20,* 48–53. https://doi.org/10.1037/emo0000667

Harter, S. (2012). Emerging self-processes during childhood and adolescence. In M. R. Leary & J. P. Tangney (Eds.), *Handbook of self and identity* (pp. 680–715). Guilford.

Haslam, D., Poniman, C., Filus, A., Sumargi, A., & Boediman, L. (2020). Parenting style, child emotion regulation and behavioral problems: The moderating role of cultural values in Australia and Indonesia. *Marriage and Family Review, 56*(4), 320–342. https://doi.org/10.1080/01494929.2020.1712573

Hay, D. F., Hurst, S.-L., Waters, C. S., & Chadwick, A. (2011). Infants' use of force to defend toys: The origins of instrumental aggression. *Infancy, 16*(5), 471–489. https://doi.org/10.1111/j.1532-7078.2011.00069.x

Hein, T. C., & Monk, C. S. (2017). Research review: Neural response to threat in children, adolescents, and adults after child maltreatment - a quantitative meta-analysis. *Journal of Child Psychology and Psychiatry, 58*(3), 222–230. https://doi.org/10.1111/jcpp.12651

Helm, A. F., McCormick, S. A., Deater-Deckard, K., Smith, C. L., Calkins, S. D., & Bell, M. A. (2020). Parenting and children's executive function stability across the transition to school. *Infant and Child Development, 29*(1), e2171. https://doi.org/10.1002/icd.2171

Hepach, R., Vaish, A., & Tomasello, M. (2012). Young children are intrinsically motivated to see others helped. *Psychological Science, 23*(9), 967–972. https://doi.org/10.1177/0956797612440571

Hicks-Pass, S. (2009). Corporal punishment in America today: Spare the rod, spoil the child? A systematic review of the literature. *Best Practice in Mental Health: An International Journal, 5*(2), 71–88.

Hines, M. (2015). Gendered development. In M. Lewis (Ed.), *Handbook of child psychology and developmental science* (pp. 1–46). John Wiley & Sons, Inc. https://doi.org/10.1002/9781118963418.childpsy320

Hines, M., Pasterski, V., Spencer, D., Neufeld, S., Patalay, P., Hindmarsh, P. C., Hughes, I. A., & Acerini, C. L. (2016). Prenatal androgen exposure alters girls' responses to information indicating gender-appropriate behaviour. *Philosophical Transactions of the Royal Society of London B: Biological Sciences, 371*(1688), 20150125. http://rstb.royalsocietypublishing.org/content/371/1688/20150125

Hinkelman, L., & Bruno, M. (2008). Identification and reporting of child sexual abuse: The role of elementary school professionals. *Elementary School Journal, 108*(5), 376–391.

Hoeve, M., Dubas, J. S., Gerris, J. R. M., van der Laan, P. H., & Smeenk, W. (2011). Maternal and paternal parenting styles: Unique and combined links to adolescent and early adult delinquency. *Journal of Adolescence, 34*(5), 813–827. https://doi.org/10.1016/j.adolescence.2011.02.004

Hoffmann, J., & Russ, S. (2012). Pretend play, creativity, and emotion regulation in children. *Psychology of Aesthetics, Creativity, and the Arts, 6*(2), 175–184.

Hu, Y., Emery, H. T., Ravindran, N., & McElwain, N. L. (2020). Direct and indirect pathways from maternal and paternal empathy to young children's socioemotional functioning. *Journal of Family Psychology, 34*(7), 825–835. https://doi.org/10.1037/fam0000745

Hughes, C., McHarg, G., & White, N. (2018). Sibling influences on prosocial behavior. *Current Opinion in Psychology, 20,* 96–101. https://doi.org/10.1016/J.COPSYC.2017.08.015

Huntsinger, C. S., Jose, P. E., & Larson, S. L. (1998). Do parent practices to encourage academic competence influence the social adjustment of young European American and Chinese American children? *Developmental Psychology, 34*, 747–756.

Hyde, J. S. (2014). Gender similarities and differences. *Annual Review of Psychology, 65*, 373–398. https://doi.org/10.1146/annurev-psych-010213-115057

Imuta, K., Henry, J. D., Slaughter, V., Selcuk, B., & Ruffman, T. (2016). Theory of mind and prosocial behavior in childhood: A meta-analytic review. *Developmental Psychology, 52*(8), 1192–1205. https://doi.org/10.1037/dev0000140

Janssens, J. M. A. M., & Dekovic, M. (1997). Child rearing, prosocial moral reasoning, and prosocial behaviour. *International Journal of Behavioral Development, 20*, 509–527.

Jewell, J. D., Krohn, E. J., Scott, V. G., Carlton, M., & Meinz, E. (2008). The differential impact of mothers' and fathers' discipline on preschool children's home and classroom behavior. *North American Journal of Psychology, 10*(1), 173–188.

Jones, D. J., Lewis, T., Litrownik, A., Thompson, R., Proctor, L. J., Isbell, P., Dubowitz, H., English, D., Jones, B., Nagin, D., & Runyan, D. (2013). Linking childhood sexual abuse and early adolescent risk behavior: The intervening role of internalizing and externalizing problems. *Journal of Abnormal Child Psychology, 41*(1), 139–150. https://doi.org/10.1007/s10802-012-9656-1

Jordan, P., & Hernandez-Reif, M. (2009). Reexamination of young children's racial attitudes and skin tone preferences. *Journal of Black Psychology, 35*(3), 388–403. https://doi.org/10.1177/0095798409333621

Kaufman, E. A., & Wiese, D. L. (2012). Skin-tone preferences and self-representation in Hispanic children. *Early Child Development and Care, 182*(2), 277–290. https://doi.org/10.1080/03004430.2011.556250

Killen, M., Smetana, J. G., Killen, M., & Smetana, J. G. (2015). Origins and development of morality. In M. Lamb (Ed.), *Handbook of child psychology and developmental science* (Vol. 3, pp. 701–749). John Wiley & Sons, Inc. https://doi.org/10.1002/9781118963418.childpsy317

Kochanska, G., Casey, R. J., & Fukumoto, A. (1995). Toddlers' sensitivity to standard violations. *Child Development, 66*, 643–656.

Kohlberg, L. (1966). A cognitive-developmental analysis of children's sex-role concepts and attitudes. In E. E. Maccoby (Ed.), *The development of sex differences* (pp. 82–173). Stanford University Press.

Kohlberg, L. (1969). Stage and sequence: The cognitive-developmental approach to socialization. In D. A. Goslin (Ed.), *Handbook of socialization* (pp. 347–480). Rand McNally.

Kohlberg, L. (1976). Moral stages and moralization: The cognitive developmental approach. In T. Lickona (Ed.), *Moral development and moral behavior: Theory, research, and social issues* (pp. 31–53). Holt, Rinehart & Winston.

Kramer, L. (2014). Learning emotional understanding and emotion regulation through sibling interaction. *Early Education and Development, 25*(2), 160–184. https://doi.org/10.1080/10409289.2014.838824

Kuhlmeier, V., Dunfield, K., & O'Neill, A. (2014). Selectivity in early prosocial behavior. *Frontiers in Psychology, 5*(00836), 836. https://doi.org/10.3389/fpsyg.2014.00836

Laible, D., Davis, A., Karahuta, E., & Van Norden, C. (2020). Does corporal punishment erode the quality of the mother–child interaction in early childhood? *Social Development, 29*(3), 674–688. https://doi.org/10.1111/sode.12427

Lambert, M. C., & Kelley, H. M. (2011). Initiative versus guilt. In S. Goldstein & J. A. Naglieri (Eds.), *Encyclopedia of child behavior and development* (pp. 816–817). Springer US. https://doi.org/10.1007/978-0-387-79061-9_1499

Lansford, J. E., Deater-Deckard, K., Dodge, K. A., Bates, J. E., & Pettit, G. S. (2004). Ethnic differences in the link between physical discipline and later adolescent externalizing behaviors. *Journal of Child Psychology & Psychiatry, 45*(4), 801–812. https://doi.org/10.1111/j.1469-7610.2004.00273.x

Lauer, J. E., Yhang, E., & Lourenco, S. F. (2019). The development of gender differences in spatial reasoning: A meta-analytic review. *Psychological Bulletin, 145*(6), 537–565. https://doi.org/10.1037/bul0000191

Lawrence, J., Haszard, J. J., Taylor, B., Galland, B., Gray, A., Sayers, R., Hanna, M., & Taylor, R. (2021). A longitudinal study of parental discipline up to 5 years. *Journal of Family Studies, 100*(5). https://doi.org/10.1080/13229400.2019.1665570

Leaper, C. (2013). Gender development during childhood. In P. D. Zelaz (Ed.), *The Oxford handbook of developmental psychology, Vol. 2: Self and other (p. Gender development during childhood.)*. Oxford.

Lee, E. H., Zhou, Q., Eisenberg, N., & Wang, Y. (2013). Bidirectional relations between temperament and parenting styles in Chinese children. *International Journal of Behavioral Development, 37*(1), 57–67. https://doi.org/10.1177/0165025412460795

Lee, Y.-E., Brophy-Herb, H. E., Vallotton, C. D., Griffore, R. J., Carlson, J. S., & Robinson, J. L. (2016). Do young children's representations of discipline and empathy moderate the effects of punishment on emotion regulation? *Social Development, 25*(1), 120–138. https://doi.org/10.1111/sode.12141

Lewis, M., Takai-Kawakami, K., Kawakami, K., & Sullivan, M. W. (2010). Cultural differences in emotional responses to success and failure. *International Journal of Behavioral Development, 34*(1), 53–61. https://doi.org/10.1177/0165025409348559

Liben, L. S., Bigler, R. S., & Hilliard, L. J. (2013). Gender development. In D. A. Crosby, E. T. Gershoff, & R. S. Mistry (Eds.), *Societal contexts of child development: Pathways of influence and implications for practice and policy* (pp. 3–18). Oxford Univ Press.

Lillard, A. S. (2015). The development of play. In M. Lewis (Ed.), *Handbook of child psychology and developmental science* (pp. 1–44). John Wiley & Sons, Inc. https://doi.org/10.1002/9781118963418.childpsy211

Lindsey, E. W., & Colwell, M. J. (2013). Pretend and physical play: Links to preschoolers' affective social competence. *Merrill-Palmer Quarterly, 59*(3), 330–360. https://doi.org/10.1353/mpq.2013.0015

Lockenhoff, C. E., Chan, W., McCrae, R. R., De Fruyt, F., Jussim, L., De Bolle, M., Costa, P. T., Sutin, A. R., Realo, A., Allik, J., Nakazato, K., Shimonaka, Y., H ebi kova, M., Graf, S., Yik, M., Fickova, E., Brunner-Sciarra, M., Leibovich de Figueora, N., Schmidt, V., & Terracciano, A. (2014). Gender stereotypes of personality: Universal and accurate? *Journal of Cross-Cultural Psychology, 45*(5), 675–694. https://doi.org/10.1177/0022022113520075

MacPhee, D., & Prendergast, S. (2019). Room for improvement: Girls' and boys' home environments are still gendered. *Sex Roles, 80*(5–6), 332–346. https://doi.org/10.1007/s11199-018-0936-2

Main, A., & Kho, C. (2020). A relational framework for integrating the study of empathy in children and adults. *Emotion Review, 12*(4), 280–290. https://doi.org/10.1177/1754073919868755

Malti, T., & Dys, S. P. (2018). From being nice to being kind: Development of prosocial behaviors. *Current Opinion in Psychology, 20*, 45–49. https://doi.org/10.1016/J.COPSYC.2017.07.036

Martin, C. L., Fabes, R., Hanish, L., Leonard, S., & Dinella, L. (2011). Experienced and expected similarity to same-gender peers: Moving toward a comprehensive model of gender segregation. *Sex Roles, 65*(5/6), 421–434. https://doi.org/10.1007/s11199-011-0029-y

Martin, C. L., Kornienko, O., Schaefer, D. R., Hanish, L. D., Fabes, R. A., & Goble, P. (2013). The role of sex of peers and gender-typed activities in young children's peer affiliative networks: a longitudinal analysis of selection and influence. *Child Development, 84*(3), 921–937. https://doi.org/10.1111/cdev.12032

Martin, C. L., & Ruble, D. N. (2010). Patterns of gender development. *Annual Review of Psychology, 61*, 353–381. https://doi.org/10.1146/annurev.psych.093008.100511

McAnally, H. M., Forsyth, B. J., Taylor, M., & Reese, E. (2020). Imaginary companions in childhood: What can prospective longitudinal research tell us about their fate by adolescence? *The Journal of Creative Behavior, 55*, 276–283. https://doi.org/10.1002/jocb.468

McClelland, M. M., & Cameron, C. E. (2011). Self-regulation and academic achievement in elementary school children. *New Directions for Child and Adolescent Development, 2011*(133), 29–44. https://doi.org/10.1002/cd.302

McKinney, C., & Renk, K. (2011). A multivariate model of parent-adolescent relationship variables in early adolescence. *Child Psychiatry and Human Development, 42*(4), 442–462. https://doi.org/10.1007/s10578-011-0228-3

McLoyd, V. C., & Smith, J. (2002). Physical discipline and behavior problems in African American, European American, and Hispanic children: Emotional support as a moderator. *Journal of Marriage and Family, 64*, 40–53.

Mehus, C. J., & Patrick, M. E. (2020). Prevalence of spanking in US national samples of 35-year-old parents from 1993 to 2017. *JAMA Pediatrics*. https://doi.org/10.1001/jamapediatrics.2020.2197

Mendez, M., Durtschi, J., Neppl, T. K., & Stith, S. M. (2016). Corporal punishment and externalizing behaviors in toddlers: The moderating role of positive and harsh parenting. *Journal of Family Psychology, 30*(8), 887–895.

Miller, C. F., Trautner, H. M., & Ruble, D. N. (2006). The role of gender stereotypes in children's preferences and behavior. In L. Balter & C. S. Tamis-LeMonda (Eds.), *Child psychology: A handbook of contemporary issues* (2nd ed., pp. 293–323). Psychology Press.

Miller, D. I., & Halpern, D. F. (2014). The new science of cognitive sex differences. *Trends in Cognitive Sciences, 18*(1), 37–45. https://doi.org/10.1016/j.tics.2013.10.011

Miller, J. G., & Hastings, P. D. (2020). Prosocial behaviors in children. In S. Hupp & J. D. Jewell (Eds.), *The encyclopedia of child and adolescent development* (pp. 1–10). Wiley. https://doi.org/10.1002/9781119171492.wecad277

Molnar, B. E., Goerge, R. M., Gilsanz, P., Hill, A., Subramanian, S. V., Holton, J. K., Duncan, D. T., Beatriz, E. D., & Beardslee, W. R. (2016). Neighborhood-level social processes and substantiated cases of child maltreatment. *Child Abuse & Neglect, 51*, 41–53. https://doi.org/10.1016/j.chiabu.2015.11.007

Morawska, A., & Sanders, M. (2011). Parental use of time out revisited: A useful or harmful parenting strategy? *Journal of Child & Family Studies, 20*(1), 1–8. https://doi.org/10.1007/s10826-010-9371-x

Mounts, N. S., & Allen, C. (2019). Parenting styles and practices. In D. J. Laible, G. Carlo, & L. M. Padilla-Walker (Eds.), *The Oxford handbook of parenting and moral development* (pp. 40–56). Oxford University Press. https://doi.org/10.1093/oxfordhb/9780190638696.013.4

Muris, P., & Meesters, C. (2014). Small or big in the eyes of the other: On the developmental psychopathology of self-conscious emotions as shame, guilt, and pride. *Clinical Child and Family Psychology Review, 17*(1), 19–40. https://doi.org/10.1007/s10567-013-0137-z

Murry, V. M., Brody, G. H., Simons, R. L., Cutrona, C. E., & Gibbons, F. X. (2008). Disentangling ethnicity and context as predictors of parenting within rural African American families. *Applied Developmental Science, 12*(4), 202–210. https://doi.org/10.1080/10888690802388144

Mussen, P., & Eisenberg-Berg, N. (1977). *Roots of caring, sharing, and helping*. Freeman.

Newton, E., & Jenvey, V. (2011). Play and theory of mind: Associations with social competence in young children. *Early Child Development & Care, 181*(6), 761–773. https://doi.org/10.1080/03004430.2010.486898

Nobes, G., & Pawson, C. (2003). Children's understanding of social rules and social status. *Merrill-Palmer Quarterly, 49*, 77–99.

Olson, K. R., Durwood, L., DeMeules, M., & McLaughlin, K. A. (2016). Mental health of transgender children who are supported in their identities. *Pediatrics, 137*(3), e20153223. https://doi.org/10.1542/peds.2015-3223

Olson, K. R., & Gülgöz, S. (2018). Early findings from the transyouth project: Gender development in transgender children. *Child Development Perspectives, 12*(2), 93–97. https://doi.org/10.1111/cdep.12268

Olson, K. R., Key, A. C., & Eaton, N. R. (2015). Gender cognition in transgender children. *Psychological Science, 26*(4), 467–474. https://doi.org/10.1177/0956797614568156

Ostrov, J. M., & Godleski, S. A. (2010). Toward an integrated gender-linked model of aggression subtypes in early and middle childhood. *Psychological Review, 117*(1), 233–242. https://doi.org/10.1037/a0018070

Oveisi, S., Eftekhare Ardabili, H., Majdzadeh, R., Mohammadkhani, P., Alaqband Rad, J., & Loo, J. (2010). Mothers' attitudes toward corporal punishment of children in Qazvin-Iran. *Journal of Family Violence, 25*(2), 159–164. https://doi.org/10.1007/s10896-009-9279-7

Padilla-Walker, L. M., & Memmott-Elison, M. K. (2020). Family and moral development. In L. A. Jensen (Ed.), *The Oxford handbook of moral development: An interdisciplinary perspective* (pp. 461). Oxford.

Parten, M. (1932). Social participation among preschool children. *Journal of Abnormal and Social Psychology, 27*, 243–269.

Paulus, M. (2020). How do young children become moral agents? A developmental perspective. In J. Decety (Ed.), *The social brain: A developmental perspective*. MIT Press.

Paulus, M., & Moore, C. (2014). The development of recipient-dependent sharing behavior and sharing expectations in preschool children. *Developmental Psychology, 50*(3), 914–921. https://doi.org/10.1037/a0034169

Paulus, M., Nöth, A., & Wörle, M. (2018). Preschoolers' resource allocations align with their normative judgments. *Journal of Experimental Child Psychology, 175*, 117–126. https://doi.org/10.1016/j.jecp.2018.05.001

Paulus, M., Wörle, M., & Christner, N. (2020). The emergence of human altruism: Preschool children develop a norm for empathy-based comforting. *Journal of Cognition and Development, 21*(1), 104–124. https://doi.org/10.1080/15248372.2019.1693375

Pellegrini, A. D. (2013). Play. In P. D. Zelazo (Ed.), *The Oxford handbook of developmental psychology, Vol. 2: Self and other* (pp. 276–299). Oxford University Press. https://doi.org/10.1093/oxfordhb/9780199958474.013.0012

Pellegrini, A. D., & Roseth, C. J. (2006). Relational aggression and relationships in preschoolers: A discussion of methods, gender differences, and function. *Journal of Applied Developmental Psychology, 27*(3), 269–276.

Perszyk, D. R., Lei, R. F., Bodenhausen, G. V., Richeson, J. A., & Waxman, S. R. (2019). Bias at the intersection of race and gender: Evidence from preschool-aged children. *Developmental Science, 22*(3), e12788. https://doi.org/10.1111/desc.12788

Piaget, J. (1932). *The moral judgment of the child*. Harcourt Brace.

Pinquart, M. (2017). Associations of parenting dimensions and styles with externalizing problems of children and adolescents: An updated meta-analysis. *Developmental Psychology, 53*(5), 873–932. https://doi.org/10.1037/dev0000295

Pinquart, M., & Gerke, D. C. (2019). Associations of parenting styles with self-esteem in children and adolescents: A meta-analysis. *Journal of Child and Family Studies, 28*, 2017–2035. https://doi.org/10.1007/s10826-019-01417-5

Piotrowski, J. T., Lapierre, M. A., & Linebarger, D. L. (2013). Investigating correlates of self-regulation in early childhood with a representative sample of english-speaking American families. *Journal of Child and Family Studies, 22*(3), 423–436. https://doi.org/10.1007/s10826-012-9595-z

Pirchio, S., Passiatore, Y., Panno, A., Maricchiolo, F., & Carrus, G. (2018). A chip off the old block: Parents' subtle ethnic prejudice predicts children's implicit prejudice. *Frontiers in Psychology, 9*, 1–9. https://doi.org/10.3389/fpsyg.2018.00110

Pons, F., Giménez-Dasí, M., Daniel, M. F., Auriac-Slusarczyk, E., Businaro, N., & Viana, K. (2019). Impact of a low-cost classroom dialogue-based intervention on preschool children's emotion understanding. *European Early Childhood Education Research Journal, 27*(5), 630–646. https://doi.org/10.1080/1350293X.2019.1651961

Quinn, M., & Hennessy, E. (2010). Peer relationships across the preschool to school transition. *Early Education & Development, 21*(6), 825–842. https://doi.org/10.1080/10409280903329013

Rochat, P. (2013). Self-conceptualizing in development. In P. D. Zelazo (Ed.), *The Oxford handbook of developmental psychology, Vol. 2: Self and other* (Vol. 1, pp. 378–396). Oxford University Press. https://doi.org/10.1093/oxfordhb/9780199958474.013.0015

Roopnarine, J. L., Hossain, Z., Gill, P., & Brophy, H. (1994). Play in the East Indian context. In J. L. Roopnarine, J. E. Johnson, & F. H. Hooper (Eds.), *Children's play in diverse cultures* (pp. 9–30). State University of New York Press.

Roopnarine, J. L., Lasker, J., Sacks, M., & Stores, M. (1998). The cultural contexts of children's play. In O. N. Saracho & B. Spodek (Eds.), *Multiple perspectives on play in early childhood education* (pp. 194–219). State University of New York Press.

Rose, J., Roman, N., Mwaba, K., & Ismail, K. (2018). The relationship between parenting and internalizing behaviours of children: A systematic review. *Early Child Development and Care, 188*(10), 1468–1486. https://doi.org/10.1080/03004430.2016.1269762

Rosenkoetter, L. I. (1973). Resistance to temptation: Inhibitory and disinhibitory effects of models. *Developmental Psychology, 8*, 80–84.

Ross, J. (2017). You and me: Investigating the role of self-evaluative emotion in preschool prosociality. *Journal of Experimental Child Psychology, 155*, 67–83. https://doi.org/10.1016/J.JECP.2016.11.001

Rubin, K. H., Bukowski, W. M., & Bowker, J. C. (2015). Children in peer groups. In M. H. Bornstein & T. Leventhal (Eds.), *Handbook of child psychology and developmental science* (pp. 1–48). John Wiley & Sons, Inc. https://doi.org/10.1002/9781118963418.childpsy405

Ryan, C., Russell, S. T., Huebner, D., Diaz, R., & Sanchez, J. (2010). Family acceptance in adolescence and the health of LGBT young adults. *Journal of Child and Adolescent Psychiatric Nursing, 23*(4), 205–213. https://doi.org/10.1111/j.1744-6171.2010.00246.x

Ryan, J. P., Jacob, B. A., Gross, M., Perron, B. E., Moore, A., & Ferguson, S. (2018). Early exposure to child maltreatment and academic outcomes. *Child Maltreatment, 23*(4), 365–375. https://doi.org/10.1177/1077559518786815

Sala, M. N., Pons, F., & Molina, P. (2014). Emotion regulation strategies in preschool children. *British Journal of Developmental Psychology, 32*(4), 440–453. https://doi.org/10.1111/bjdp.12055

Schapira, R., & Aram, D. (2020). Shared book reading at home and preschoolers' socio-emotional competence. *Early Education and Development, 31*(6), 819–837. https://doi.org/10.1080/10409289.2019.1692624

Schenck-Fontaine, A., & Gassman-Pines, A. (2020). Income inequality and child maltreatment risk during economic recession. *Children and Youth Services Review, 112*, 104926. https://doi.org/10.1016/j.childyouth.2020.104926

Schlesinger, M. A., Hassinger-Das, B., Zosh, J. M., Sawyer, J., Evans, N., & Hirsh-Pasek, K. (2020). Cognitive behavioral science behind the value of play: Leveraging everyday experiences to promote play, learning, and positive interactions. *Journal of Infant, Child, and Adolescent Psychotherapy, 19*(2), 202–216. https://doi.org/10.1080/15289168.2020.1755084

Sebanc, A. M., Kearns, K. T., Hernandez, M. D., & Galvin, K. B. (2007). Predicting having a best friend in young children: Individual characteristics and friendship features. *The Journal of Genetic Psychology, 168*(1), 81–96. https://doi.org/10.3200/GNTP.168.1.81-96

Sege, R. D., & Siegel, B. S. (2018). Effective discipline to raise healthy children. *Pediatrics, 142*(6). https://doi.org/10.1542/peds.2018-3112

Shutts, K., Kenward, B., Falk, H., Ivegran, A., & Fawcett, C. (2017). Early preschool environments and gender: Effects of gender pedagogy in Sweden. *Journal of Experimental Child Psychology, 162*, 1–17. https://doi.org/10.1016/J.JECP.2017.04.014

Signorella, M., & Liben, L. S. (1984). Recall and reconstruction of gender-related pictures: Effects of attitude, task difficulty, and age. *Child Development, 55*, 393–405.

Silkenbeumer, J. R., Schiller, E.-M., & Kärtner, J. (2018). Co- and self-regulation of emotions in the preschool setting. *Early Childhood Research Quarterly, 44*, 72–81.

Silva, R. L., & Alves, S. G. (2020a). Contemporary theories of gender identity. In B. J. Carducci, C. S. Nave, J. S. Mio, & R. E. Riggio (Eds.), *The Wiley encyclopedia of personality and individual differences* (pp. 215–219). Wiley. https://doi.org/10.1002/9781118970843.ch36

Silva, R. L., & Alves, S. G. (2020b). Contemporary theories of gender identity. In B. J. Carducci, C. S. Nave, J. S. Mio, & R. E. Riggio (Eds.), *The Wiley encyclopedia of personality and individual differences* (pp. 215–219). Wiley. https://doi.org/10.1002/9781118970843.ch36

Simons, L., Schrager, S. M., Clark, L. F., Belzer, M., & Olson, J. (2013). Parental support and mental health among transgender adolescents. *Journal of Adolescent Health, 53*(6), 791–793. https://doi.org/10.1016/j.jadohealth.2013.07.019

Skitka, L. J., Bauman, C. W., & Mullen, E. (2016). Morality and justice. In C. Sabbagh & M. Schmitt (Eds.), *Handbook of social justice theory and research* (pp. 407–423). Springer Publishing Company. https://doi.org/10.1007/978-1-4939-3216-0_22

Smith, C. E., Blake, P. R., & Harris, P. L. (2013). I should but I won't: Why young children endorse norms of fair sharing but do not follow them. *PLoS One, 8*(3), e59510. https://doi.org/10.1371/journal.pone.0059510

Sorkhabi, N. (2005). Applicability of Baumrind's parent typology to collective cultures: Analysis of cultural explanations of parent socialization effects. *International Journal of Behavioral Development, 29*(6), 552–563.

Sosic-Vasic, Z., Kröner, J., Schneider, S., Vasic, N., Spitzer, M., & Streb, J. (2017). The association between parenting behavior and executive functioning in children and young adolescents. *Frontiers in Psychology, 8*, 472. https://doi.org/10.3389/fpsyg.2017.00472

Spinrad, T. L., & Gal, D. E. (2018). Fostering prosocial behavior and empathy in young children. *Current Opinion in Psychology, 20*, 40–44. https://doi.org/10.1016/J.COPSYC.2017.08.004

Spivey, L. A., Huebner, D. M., & Diamond, L. M. (2018). Parent responses to childhood gender nonconformity: Effects of parent and child characteristics. *Psychology of Sexual Orientation and Gender Diversity, 5*(3), 360–370. https://doi.org/10.1037/sgd0000279

St. George, J., & Fletcher, R. (2020). Rough-and-tumble play. In S. Hupp & J. D. Jewell (Eds.), *The encyclopedia of child and adolescent development* (pp. 1–14). Wiley. https://doi.org/10.1002/9781119171492.wecad276

Stacks, A. M., Oshio, T., Gerard, J., & Roe, J. (2009). The moderating effect of parental warmth on the association between spanking and child aggression: A longitudinal approach. *Infant & Child Development, 18*(2), 178–194. https://doi.org/10.1002/icd.596

Steensma, T. D., & Cohen-Kettenis, P. T. (2011). Gender transitioning before puberty? *Archives of Sexual Behavior, 40*(4), 649–650. https://doi.org/10.1007/s10508-011-9752-2

Ştefan, C. A., & Avram, J. (2018). The multifaceted role of attachment during preschool: Moderator of its indirect effect on empathy through emotion regulation. *Early Child Development and Care, 188*(1), 62–76. https://doi.org/10.1080/03004430.2016.1246447

Stern, J. A., & Cassidy, J. (2018). Empathy from infancy to adolescence: An attachment perspective on the development of individual differences. *Developmental Review, 47*, 1–22. https://doi.org/10.1016/J.DR.2017.09.002

Sullivan, J., Wilton, L., & Apfelbaum, E. P. (2021). Adults delay conversations about race because they underestimate children's processing of race. *Journal of Experimental Psychology: General, 150*, 395–400. https://doi.org/10.1037/xge0000851

Sullivan, M. W., Carmody, D. P., & Lewis, M. (2010). How neglect and punitiveness influence emotion knowledge. *Child Psychiatry and Human Development, 41*(3), 285–298. https://doi.org/10.1007/s10578-009-0168-3

Svetlova, M., Nichols, S. R., & Brownell, C. A. (2010). Toddlers prosocial behavior: From instrumental to empathic to altruistic helping. *Child Development, 81*(6), 1814–1827. https://doi.org/10.1111/j.1467-8624.2010.01512.x

Syed, M., & McLean, K. C. (2018). Erikson's theory of psychosocial development. In E. Braaten & B. Willoughby (Eds.), *The SAGE encyclopedia of intellectual and developmental disorders* (pp. 577–581). PsyArXiv. https://doi.org/10.17605/OSF.IO/ZF35D

Tamis-LeMonda, C. S., Briggs, R. D., McClowry, S. G., & Snow, D. L. (2009). Maternal control and sensitivity, child gender, and maternal education in relation to children's behavioral outcomes in African American families. *Journal of Applied Developmental Psychology, 30*(3), 321–331. https://doi.org/10.1016/j.appdev.2008.12.018

Tannock, M. (2011). Observing young children's rough-and-tumble play. *Australasian Journal of Early Childhood, 36*(2), 13–20.

Taylor, M. (1999). *Imaginary companions and the children who create them*. Oxford University Press.

Taylor, M., Shawber, A. B., & Mannering, A. M. (2009). Children's imaginary companions: What is it like to have an invisible friend? In K. D. Markman, W. M. P. Klein, & J. A. Suhr (Eds.), *Handbook of imagination and mental simulation* (pp. 211–224). Psychology Press.

Taylor, Z. E., Eisenberg, N., Spinrad, T. L., Eggum, N. D., & Sulik, M. J. (2013). The relations of ego-resiliency and emotion socialization to the development of empathy and prosocial behavior across early childhood. *Emotion, 13*(5), 822–831.

Thompson, A. E., & Voyer, D. (2014). Sex differences in the ability to recognise non-verbal displays of emotion: A meta-analysis. *Cognition and Emotion, 28*(7), 1164–1195. https://doi.org/10.1080/02699931.2013.875889

Thompson, R. A., & Goodvin, R. (2007). Taming the tempest in the teapot: Emotion regulation in toddlers. In C. A. Brownell & C. B. Kopp (Eds.), *Transitions in early socioemotional development: The toddler years* (pp. 320–341). Guilford.

Thompson, R. A., Kaczor, K., Lorenz, D. J., Bennett, B. L., Meyers, G., & Pierce, M. C. (2017). Is the use of physical discipline associated with aggressive behaviors in young children? *Academic Pediatrics, 17*(1), 34–44. https://doi.org/10.1016/J.ACAP.2016.02.014

Thompson, R. A., & Newton, E. K. (2013). Baby altruists? Examining the complexity of prosocial motivation in young children. *Infancy, 18*(1), 120–133. https://doi.org/10.1111/j.1532-7078.2012.00139.x

Thompson, R. A., & Virmani, E. A. (2010). Self and personality. In M. H. Bornstein (Ed.), *Handbook of cultural developmental science* (pp. 195–207). Psychology Press.

Thompson, S. F., Zalewski, M., Kiff, C. J., Moran, L., Cortes, R., & Lengua, L. J. (2020). An empirical test of the model of socialization of emotion: Maternal and child contributors to preschoolers' emotion knowledge and adjustment. *Developmental Psychology, 56*(3), 418–430. https://doi.org/10.1037/dev0000860

Todd, B. K., Fischer, R. A., Di Costa, S., Roestorf, A., Harbour, K., Hardiman, P., & Barry, J. A. (2018). Sex differences in children's toy preferences: A systematic review, meta-regression, and meta-analysis. *Infant and Child Development, 27*(2), e2064. https://doi.org/10.1002/icd.2064

Tomasello, M. (2018). The normative turn in early moral development. *Human Development, 61*(4–5), 248–263. https://doi.org/10.1159/000492802

Tompkins, V., & Villaruel, E. (2021). Parent discipline and preschoolers' social skills. *Early Child Development and Care*. https://doi.org/10.1080/03004430.2020.1763978

Tremblay, R. E. (2014). Early development of physical aggression and early risk factors for chronic physical aggression in humans. *Current Topics in Behavioral Neurosciences, 17*, 315–327. https://doi.org/10.1007/7854_2013_262

Tremblay, R. E., Nagin, D. S., Séguin, J. R., Zoccolillo, M., Zelazo, P. D., Boivin, M., Pérusse, D., & Japel, C. (2004). Physical aggression during early childhood: Trajectories and predictors. *Pediatrics, 114*(1), e43–e50.

Tsao, Y.-L. (2020). Gender issues in young children’s literature. *Reading Improvement, 57*(1), 16–21.

Tzeng, O., Jackson, J., & Karlson, H. (1991). *Theories of child abuse and neglect: Differential perspectives, summaries, and evaluations*. Praeger Publishers.

U.S. Bureau of Labor Statistics. (2021). *Occupational outlook handbook: 2021*. https://www.bls.gov/ooh/

U.S. Department of Health and Human Services. (2016). *Child maltreatment, 2014*. http://www.acf.hhs.gov/sites/default/files/cb/cm2014.pdf

U.S. Department of Health and Human Services. (2020). *Child maltreatment, 2018*. https://www.acf.hhs.gov/cb/research-data-technology/statistics-research/child-maltreatment

Vaish, A. (2018). The prosocial functions of early social emotions: The case of guilt. *Current Opinion in Psychology, 20*, 25–29. https://doi.org/10.1016/J.COPSYC.2017.08.008

Vaish, A., & Hepach, R. (2020). The development of prosocial emotions. *Emotion Review, 12*(4), 259–273. https://doi.org/10.1177/1754073919885014

Valiente, C., Swanson, J., DeLay, D., Fraser, A. M., & Parker, J. H. (2020). Emotion-related socialization in the classroom: Considering the roles of teachers, peers, and the classroom context. *Developmental Psychology, 56*(3), 578–594. https://doi.org/10.1037/dev0000863

Vally, Z., & El Hichami, F. (2020). Knowledge about parenting as a predictor of behavioral discipline practices between mothers and fathers. *Psychological Studies, 65*(1), 40–50. https://doi.org/10.1007/s12646-019-00497-z

van Dijken, M. W., Stams, G. J. J. M., & de Winter, M. (2016). Can community-based interventions prevent child maltreatment? *Children and Youth Services Review, 61*, 149–158. https://doi.org/10.1016/j.childyouth.2015.12.007

van Hoogdalem, A. G., Singer, E., Eek, A., & Heesbeen, D. (2013). Friendship in young children: Construction of a behavioural sociometric method. *Journal of Early Childhood Research, 11*(3), 236–247. https://doi.org/10.1177/1476718X13488337

Vasc, D., & Lillard, A. (2020). Pretend and sociodramatic play. In S. Hupp & J. D. Jewell (Eds.), *The encyclopedia of child and adolescent development* (pp. 1–9). Wiley. https://doi.org/10.1002/9781119171492.wecad274

Verschueren, K. (2020). Attachment, self-esteem, and socio-emotional adjustment: There is more than just the mother. *Attachment and Human Development, 22*(1), 105–109. https://doi.org/10.1080/14616734.2019.1589066

Vial, A., van der Put, C., Stams, G. J. J. M., Kossakowski, J., & Assink, M. (2020). Exploring the interrelatedness of risk factors for child maltreatment: A network approach. *Child Abuse and Neglect, 107*, 104622. https://doi.org/10.1016/j.chiabu.2020.104622

Vygotsky, L. S. (1978). *Mind in society: The development of higher psychological processes*. Harvard University Press.

Vygotsky, L. S. (1986). *Thought and language*. MIT Press.

Wagner, M. F., Milner, J. S., McCarthy, R. J., Crouch, J. L., McCanne, T. R., & Skowronski, J. J. (2015). Facial emotion recognition accuracy and child physical abuse: An experiment and a meta-analysis. *Psychology of Violence, 5*(2), 154–162. https://doi.org/10.1037/a0036014

Wang, F., Christ, S. L., Mills-Koonce, W. R., Garrett-Peters, P., & Cox, M. J. (2013). Association between maternal sensitivity and externalizing behavior from preschool to preadolescence. *Journal of Applied Developmental Psychology, 34*(2), 89–100. https://doi.org/10.1016/j.appdev.2012.11.003

Wang, Q. (2004). The emergence of cultural self-constructs: Autobiographical memory and self-description in European American and Chinese children. *Developmental Psychology, 40*, 3–15.

Wang, Y., Palonen, T., Hurme, T. R., & Kinos, J. (2019). Do you want to play with me today? Friendship stability among preschool children. *European Early Childhood Education Research Journal, 27*(2), 170–184. https://doi.org/10.1080/1350293X.2019.1579545

Ward, L. M., & Grower, P. (2020). Media and the development of gender role stereotypes. *Annual Review of Developmental Psychology, 2*(1), 177–199. https://doi.org/10.1146/annurev-devpsych-051120-010630

Weis, R., & Toolis, E. E. (2010). Parenting across cultural contexts in the USA: Assessing parenting behaviour in an ethnically and socioeconomically diverse sample. *Early Child Development & Care, 180*(7), 849–867. https://doi.org/10.1080/03004430802472083

Weisgram, E. S. (2016). The cognitive construction of gender stereotypes: Evidence for the dual pathways model of gender differentiation. *Sex Roles, 75*(7–8), 301–313. https://doi.org/10.1007/s11199-016-0624-z

Wellman, H. M. (2017). The development of theory of mind: Historical reflections. *Child Development Perspectives*, *11*(3), 207–214. https://doi.org/10.1111/cdep.12236

Widom, C. S. (2014). Handbook of child maltreatment. In J. E. Korbin & R. D. Krugman (Eds.), *Handbook of child maltreatment* (Vol. 2, pp. 225–247). Springer Publishing Company. https://doi.org/10.1007/978-94-007-7208-3

Williams, A., & Steele, J. R. (2019). Examining children's implicit racial attitudes using exemplar and category-based measures. *Child Development*, *90*(3), e322–e338. https://doi.org/10.1111/cdev.12991

Wong, T. K. Y., Konishi, C., & Kong, X. (2021). Parenting and prosocial behaviors: A meta-analysis. *Social Development*, *30*, 343–373. https://doi.org/10.1111/sode.12481

Xiao, S. X., Cook, R. E., Martin, C. L., & Nielson, M. G. (2019). Characteristics of preschool gender enforcers and peers who associate with them. *Sex Roles*, *81*(11–12), 671–685. https://doi.org/10.1007/s11199-019-01026-y

Xu, Y., Farver, J. A. M., Zhang, Z., Zeng, Q., Yu, L., & Cai, B. (2005). Mainland Chinese parenting styles and parent-child interaction. *International Journal of Behavioral Development*, *29*(6), 524–531.

Yang, M. -Y., & Maguire-Jack, K. (2018). Individual and cumulative risks for child abuse and neglect. *Family Relations*, *67*(2), 287–301. https://doi.org/10.1111/fare.12310

Yaoying, X., & Xu, Y. (2010). Children's social play sequence: Parten's classic theory revisited. *Early Child Development and Care*, *180*(4), 489–498. https://doi.org/10.1080/03004430802090430

Yarrow, M. R., Scott, P. M., & Waxler, C. Z. (1973). Learning concern for others. *Developmental Psychology*, *8*, 240–260.

Yelinek, J., & Grady, J. S. (2019). 'Show me your mad faces!' preschool teachers' emotion talk in the classroom. *Early Child Development and Care*, *189*(7), 1063–1071. https://doi.org/10.1080/03004430.2017.1363740

Yuill, N., & Perner, J. (1988). Intentionality and knowledge in children's judgments of actor's responsibility and recipient's emotional reaction. *Developmental Psychology*, *24*, 358–365.

Zeman, J., Cassano, M., & Adrian, M. C. (2013). Socialization influences on children's and adolescents' emotional self-regulation processes. In L. A. Daunhauer, K. C. Barrett, N. A. Fox, G. A. Morgan, & D. J. Fidler (Eds.), *Handbook of self-regulatory processes in development* (pp. 79–107). Psychology Press. https://doi.org/10.4324/9780203080719.ch5

Zosuls, K. M., Ruble, D. N., Tamis-LeMonda, C. S., Shrout, P. E., Bornstein, M. H., & Greulich, F. K. (2009). The acquisition of gender labels in infancy: Implications for gender-typed play. *Developmental Psychology*, *45*(3), 688–701. https://doi.org/10.1037/a0014053

Zucker, K. J., Wood, H., Singh, D., & Bradley, S. J. (2012). A developmental, biopsychosocial model for the treatment of children with gender identity disorder. *Journal of Homosexuality*, *59*(3), 369–397. https://doi.org/10.1080/00918369.2012.653309

CHAPTER 7

Afshin, A., Reitsma, M. B., & Murray, C. J. L. (2017). Health effects of overweight and obesity in 195 countries. *The New England Journal of Medicine*, *377*(15), 1496–1497. https://doi.org/10.1056/NEJMc1710026

Agrawal, S., Rao, S. C., Bulsara, M. K., & Patole, S. K. (2018). Prevalence of autism spectrum disorder in preterm infants: A meta-Analysis. *Pediatrics*, *142*(3), 20180134. https://doi.org/10.1542/peds.2018-0134

Aguiar, A., Eubig, P. A., & Schantz, S. L. (2010). Attention deficit/hyperactivity disorder: A focused overview for children's environmental health researchers. *Environmental Health Perspectives*, *118*(12), 1646–1653. https://doi.org/10.1289/ehp.1002326

Albuquerque, D., Nóbrega, C., Manco, L., & Padez, C. (2017). The contribution of genetics and environment to obesity. *British Medical Bulletin*, *123*(1), 159–173. https://doi.org/10.1093/bmb/ldx022

Alexander, P. A. (2020). What research has revealed about readers' struggles with comprehension in the digital age: Moving beyond the phonics versus whole language debate. *Reading Research Quarterly*, *55*(S1), S89–S97. https://doi.org/10.1002/rrq.331

Allen, K., Higgins, S., & Adams, J. (2019). The relationship between visuospatial working memory and mathematical performance in school-aged children: A systematic review. *Educational Psychology Review*, *31*(3), 509–531. https://doi.org/10.1007/s10648-019-09470-8

Allen, S. E. M., & Crago, M. B. (1996). Early passive acquisition in Inukitut. *Journal of Child Language*, *23*, 129–156.

Alviola, P. A., Nayga, R. M., Thomsen, M. R., Danforth, D., & Smartt, J. (2014). The effect of fast-food restaurants on childhood obesity: A school level analysis. *Economics & Human Biology*, *12*, 110–119. https://doi.org/10.1016/j.ehb.2013.05.001

American Psychiatric Association. (2013). *Diagnostic and statistical manual of mental disorders DSM-V* (5th ed.).

Anderson, M. (2018). *About a quarter of rural Americans say access to high-speed internet is a major problem*. Fact Tank - Pew Research Center. https://www.pewresearch.org/fact-tank/2018/09/10/about-a-quarter-of-rural-americans-say-access-to-high-speed-internet-is-a-major-problem/

Antshel, K. M. (2020). Attention-deficit/hyperactivity disorder in childhood. In S. Hupp & J. D. Jewell (Eds.), *The encyclopedia of child and adolescent development* (pp. 1–11). Wiley. https://doi.org/10.1002/9781119171492.wecad504

Aranda, M. P. (2008). Relationship between religious involvement and psychological well-being: A social justice perspective. *Health & Social Work*, *33*(1), 9–21.

Ardila, A. (2013). Development of metacognitive and emotional executive functions in children. *Applied Neuropsychology. Child*, *2*(2), 82–87. https://doi.org/10.1080/21622965.2013.748388

Armon-Lotem, S., Haman, E., Jensen de López, K., Smoczynska, M., Yatsushiro, K., Szczerbinski, M., van Hout, A., Dabašinskienė, I., Gavarró, A., Hobbs, E., Kamandulytė-Merfeldienė, L., Katsos, N., Kunnari, S., Nitsiou, C., Sundahl Olsen, L., Parramon, X., Sauerland, U., Torn-Leesik, R., & van der Lely, H. (2016). A large-scale cross-linguistic investigation of the acquisition of passive. *Language Acquisition*, *23*(1), 27–56. https://doi.org/10.1080/10489223.2015.1047095

Artman, L., & Cahan, S. (1993). Schooling and the development of transitive inference. *Developmental Psychology*, *29*(4), 753–759.

Atkinson, A. L., Waterman, A. H., & Allen, R. J. (2019). Can children prioritize more valuable information in working memory? An exploration into the effects of motivation and memory load. *Developmental Psychology*, *55*(5), 967–980. https://doi.org/10.1037/dev0000692

Bangsbo, J., Krustrup, P., Duda, J., Hillman, C., Andersen, L. B., Weiss, M., Williams, C. A., Lintunen, T., Green, K., Hansen, P. R., Naylor, P.-J., Ericsson, I., Nielsen, G., Froberg, K., Bugge, A., Lundbye-Jensen, J., Schipperijn, J., Dagkas, S., Agergaard, S. ... Elbe, A. (2016). The copenhagen consensus conference 2016: Children, youth, and physical activity in schools and during leisure time. *British Journal of Sports Medicine*, *50*(19), 1177–1178. https://doi.org/10.1136/bjsports-2016-096325

Barac, R., Bialystok, E., Castro, D. C., & Sanchez, M. (2014). The cognitive development of young dual language learners: A critical review. *Early Childhood Research Quarterly*, *29*(4), 699–714. https://doi.org/10.1016/j.ecresq.2014.02.003

Barnett, S. M., Ceci, S. J., & Williams, W. M. (2006). Is the ability to make a bacon sandwich a mark of intelligence? and other issues: Some reflections on Gardner's theory of multiple intelligences. In J. A. Schaler (Ed.), *Howard Gardner under fire: The rebel psychologist faces his critics* (pp. 95–114). Open Court.

Baus, C., Costa, A., & Carreiras, M. (2013). On the effects of second language immersion on first language production. *Acta Psychologica*, *142*(3), 402–409. https://doi.org/10.1016/j.actpsy.2013.01.010

Bax, A. C., Bard, D. E., Cuffe, S. P., McKeown, R. E., & Wolraich, M. L. (2019). The association between race/ethnicity and socioeconomic factors and the diagnosis and treatment of children with attention-deficit hyperactivity disorder. *Journal of Developmental & Behavioral Pediatrics*, *40*(2), 81–91. https://doi.org/10.1097/DBP.0000000000000626

Beaujean, A. A., & Woodhouse, N. (2020). Wechsler Intelligence Scale for Children (WISC). In B. J. Carducci, C. S. Nave, J. S. Mio, & R. E. Riggio (Eds.), *The wiley encyclopedia of personality and individual differences* (pp. 465–471). Wiley. https://doi.org/10.1002/9781118970843.ch147

Benner, G. J., Nelson, J. R., & Epstein, M. H. (2002). The language skills of students with emotional and behavioral disorders: A literature review. *Journal of Emotional and Behavioral Disorders*, *10*, 43–59.

Berninger, V. W., Abbott, R., Cook, C. R., & Nagy, W. (2017). Relationships of attention and executive functions to oral language, reading, and writing skills and systems in middle childhood and early adolescence. *Journal of Learning Disabilities*, *50*(4), 434–449. https://doi.org/10.1177/0022219415617167

Berninger, V. W., & Wolf, B. J. (2009). *Teaching students with dyslexia and dysgraphia: Lessons from teaching and science*. Paul H Brookes Publishing. https://psycnet.apa.org/record/2009-08969-000

Best, R. M., Dockrell, J. E., & Braisby, N. R. (2006). Real-world word learning: Exploring children's developing semantic representations of a science term. *British Journal of Developmental Psychology*, *24*(2), 265–282. https://doi.org/10.1348/026151005X36128

Bialystok, E. (2015). Bilingualism and the development of executive function: The role of attention. *Child Development Perspectives*, *9*(2), 117–121. https://doi.org/10.1111/cdep.12116

Bialystok, E. (2020). Bilingual effects on cognition in children. In *Oxford research encyclopedia of education*. Oxford University Press. https://doi.org/10.1093/acrefore/9780190264093.013.962

Biddle, S. J. H., & Vergeer, I. (2020). Mental health benefits of physical activity for young people. In T. Brusseau, S. Fairclough, & D. Lubans (Eds.), *The routledge handbook of youth physical activity* (pp. 121–147). Routledge. https://doi.org/10.4324/9781003026426-8

Black, I. E., Menzel, N. N., & Bungum, T. J. (2015). The relationship among playground areas and physical activity levels in children. *Journal of Pediatric Health Care*, *29*(2), 156–168. https://doi.org/10.1016/j.pedhc.2014.10.001

Bölte, S., Girdler, S., & Marschik, P. B. (2019). The contribution of environmental exposure to the etiology of autism spectrum disorder. *Cellular and Molecular Life Sciences*, *76*(7), 1275–1297. https://doi.org/10.1007/s00018-018-2988-4

Borich, G. D. (2017). *Effective teaching methods: Research-based practice* (9th ed.). Pearson.

Borst, G., Poirel, N., Pineau, A., Cassotti, M., & Houdé, O. (2013). Inhibitory control efficiency in a Piaget-like class-inclusion task in school-age children and adults: A developmental negative priming study. *Developmental Psychology*, *49*(7), 1366–1374. https://doi.org/10.1037/a0029622

Bourgeron, T. (2015). From the genetic architecture to synaptic plasticity in autism spectrum disorder. *Nature Reviews Neuroscience*, *16*(9), 551–563. https://doi.org/10.1038/nrn3992

Brady, S. A. (2011). Efficacy of phonics teaching for reading outcomes: Indications from Post-NRP Research. In S. A. Brady, D. Braze, & C. A. Fowler (Eds.), *Explaining individual differences in reading: Theory and evidence* (pp. 69–96). Psychology Press.

Braudt, D. B., Lawrence, E. M., Tilstra, A. M., Rogers, R. G., & Hummer, R. A. (2019). Family socioeconomic status and early life mortality risk in the United States. *Maternal and Child Health Journal*, *23*(10), 1382–1391. https://doi.org/10.1007/s10995-019-02799-0

Bryant, B. R., Bryant, D. P., Porterfield, J., Dennis, M. S., Falcomata, T., Valentine, C., Brewer, C., & Bell, K. (2016). The effects of a tier 3 intervention on the mathematics performance of second grade students with severe mathematics difficulties. *Journal of Learning Disabilities*, *49*(2), 176–188. https://doi.org/10.1177/0022219414538516

Burden, P. R., & Byrd, D. M. (2019). *Methods for effective teaching: Meeting the needs of all students* (8th ed.). Pearson. https://www.pearson.com/us/higher-education/product/Burden-Methods-for-Effective-Teaching-Meeting-the-Needs-of-All-Students-8th-Edition/9780134695747.html

Bush, N. R., Allison, A. L., Miller, A. L., Deardorff, J., Adler, N. E., & Boyce, W. T. (2017). Socioeconomic disparities in childhood obesity risk: Association with an oxytocin receptor polymorphism. *JAMA Pediatrics*, *171*(1), 61. https://doi.org/10.1001/jamapediatrics.2016.2332

Cabral, M. D. I., Liu, S., & Soares, N. (2020). Attention-deficit/hyperactivity disorder: Diagnostic criteria, epidemiology, risk factors and evaluation in youth. *Translational Pediatrics*, *9*((S1)), S104–S113. https://doi.org/10.21037/tp.2019.09.08

Cafiero, R., Brauer, J., Anwander, A., & Friederici, A. D. (2019). The concurrence of cortical surface area expansion and white matter myelination in human brain development. *Cerebral Cortex*, *29*(2), 827–837. https://doi.org/10.1093/cercor/bhy277

Caldas, S. J., & Reilly, M. S. (2018). The influence of race–ethnicity and physical activity levels on elementary school achievement. *The Journal of Educational Research*, *111*(4), 473–486. https://doi.org/10.1080/00220671.2017.1297925

Calvert, H. G., Mahar, M. T., Flay, B., & Turner, L. (2018). Classroom-based physical activity: Minimizing disparities in school-day physical activity among elementary school students. *Journal of Physical Activity and Health*, *15*(3), 161–168. https://doi.org/10.1123/jpah.2017-0323

Carbonneau, K. J., Marley, S. C., & Selig, J. P. (2013). A meta-analysis of the efficacy of teaching mathematics with concrete manipulatives. *Journal of Educational Psychology*, *105*(2), 380–400. https://doi.org/10.1037/a0031084

Carson, V., Ridgers, N. D., Howard, B. J., Winkler, E. A. H., Healy, G. N., Owen, N., Dunstan, D. W., Salmon, J., Ridley, K., Ainsworth, B., Olds, T., Troiano, R., Berrigan, D., Dodd, K., Masse, L., Tilert, T., Colley, R., Garriguet, D., Janssen, I. ... Zheng, Y. (2013). Light-intensity physical activity and cardiometabolic biomarkers in US adolescents. *PLoS One*, *8*(8), e71417. https://doi.org/10.1371/journal.pone.0071417

Castaldi, E., Piazza, M., & Iuculano, T. (2020). Learning disabilities: Developmental dyscalculia. In A. Gallagher, C. Bulteau, D. Cohen, & J. L. Michaud (Eds.), *Handbook of Clinical Neurology* (Vol. 174, pp. 61–75). Elsevier B.V. https://doi.org/10.1016/B978-0-444-64148-9.00005-3

Castillo, J. C., Clark, B. R., Butler, C. E., & Racette, S. B. (2015). Support for physical education as a core subject in urban elementary schools. *American Journal of Preventive Medicine*, *49*(5), 753–756. https://doi.org/10.1016/j.amepre.2015.04.015

Castro, D. C., Páez, M. M., Dickinson, D. K., & Frede, E. (2011). Promoting language and literacy in young dual language learners: Research, practice, and policy. *Child Development Perspectives*, *5*(1), 15–21. https://doi.org/10.1111/j.1750-8606.2010.00142.x

Cavas, B., & Cavas, P. (2020). Multiple intelligences theory—Howard gardner. In B. Akpan & T. J. Kennedy (Eds.), *Science education in theory and practice* (pp. 405–418). Cham: Springer. https://doi.org/10.1007/978-3-030-43620-9_27

Centers for Disease Control and Prevention. (2019). *WISQARS leading causes of nonfatal injury reports. WISQARS*. https://webappa.cdc.gov/sasweb/ncipc/nfilead.html

Centers for Disease Control and Prevention. (2020). *WISQARS leading causes of nonfatal injury reports*. https://webappa.cdc.gov/sasweb/ncipc/nfilead.html

Chauhan, S. (2017). A meta-analysis of the impact of technology on learning effectiveness of elementary students. *Computers & Education*, *105*, 14–30. https://doi.org/10.1016/J.COMPEDU.2016.11.005

Chemin, A. (2014). *Handwriting vs typing: Is the pen still mightier than the keyboard. The Guardian*. https://www.theguardian.com/science/2014/dec/16/cognitive-benefits-handwriting-decline-typing

Cheng, W., Rolls, E. T., Gu, H., Zhang, J., & Feng, J. (2015). Autism: Reduced connectivity between cortical areas involved in face expression, theory of mind, and the sense of self. *Brain*, *138*(5), 1382–1393. https://doi.org/10.1093/brain/awv051

Cheroni, C., Caporale, N., & Testa, G. (2020). Autism spectrum disorder at the crossroad between genes and environment: Contributions, convergences, and interactions in ASD developmental pathophysiology. *Molecular Autism*, *11*(1), 69. https://doi.org/10.1186/s13229-020-00370-1

Child, A. E., Cirino, P. T., Fletcher, J. M., Willcutt, E. G., & Fuchs, L. S. (2019). A cognitive dimensional approach to understanding shared and unique contributions to reading, math, and attention skills. *Journal of Learning Disabilities*, *52*(1), 15–30. https://doi.org/10.1177/0022219418775115

Child Trends. (2019a). *Dual language learners*. https://www.childtrends.org/indicators/dual-language-learners

Child Trends. (2019b). *Infant, child, and teen mortality*. https://www.childtrends.org/indicators/infant-child-and-teen-mortality

Clark, E. V. (2017). *Language in children : A brief introduction. Routledge*. https://www.routledge.com/Language-in-Children/Clark/p/book/9781138906075

Cliffordson, C., & Gustafsson, J.-E. (2008). Effects of age and schooling on intellectual performance: Estimates obtained from analysis of continuous variation in age and length of schooling. *Intelligence*, *36*(2), 143–152. https://doi.org/10.1016/j.intell.2007.03.006

Collette, F., & Van der Linden, M. (2002). Brain imaging of the central executive component of working memory. *Neuroscience & Biobehavioral Reviews*, *26*(2), 105–125.

Cottini, M., Basso, D., & Palladino, P. (2018). The role of declarative and procedural metamemory in event-based prospective memory in school-aged children. *Journal of Experimental Child Psychology*, *166*, 17–33. https://doi.org/10.1016/J.JECP.2017.08.002

Coughlin, C., Leckey, S., & Ghetti, S. (2018). Development of episodic memory: Processes and implications. In S. Ghetti (Ed.), *Stevens' handbook of experimental psychology and cognitive neuroscience* (pp. 1–25). John Wiley & Sons, Inc. https://doi.org/10.1002/9781119170174.epcn404

Cowan, N., Hismjatullina, A., AuBuchon, A. M., Saults, J. S., Horton, N., Leadbitter, K., & Towse, J. (2010). With development, list recall includes more chunks, not just larger ones. *Developmental Psychology*, *46*(5), 1119–1131. https://doi.org/10.1037/a0020618

Crone, E. A., & Steinbeis, N. (2017). Neural perspectives on cognitive control development during childhood and adolescence. *Trends in Cognitive Sciences*, *21*(3), 205–215. https://doi.org/10.1016/J.TICS.2017.01.003

Cunningham, P. M. (2013). *Phonics they use : Words for reading and writing*. Pearson.

Dajani, D. R., & Uddin, L. Q. (2016). Local brain connectivity across development in autism spectrum disorder: A cross-sectional investigation. *Autism Research*, *9*(1), 43–54. https://doi.org/10.1002/aur.1494

Daley, C. E., & Onwuegbuzie, A. J. (2011). Race and intelligence. In R. J. Sternberg & S. B. Kaufman (Eds.), *The cambridge handbook of intelligence* (pp. 293–308). Cambridge University Press.

Daoud, R., Starkey, L., Eppel, E., Vo, T. D., & Sylvester, A. (2021). The educational value of internet use in the home for school children: A systematic review of literature. *Journal of Research on Technology in Education*, *53*(4), 353–374. https://doi.org/10.1080/15391523.2020.1783402

Dasen, P. R. (1994). Culture and cognitive development from a Piagetian perspective. In W. J. Lonner & R. Malpass (Eds.), *Psychology and culture* (pp. 145–149). Allyn & Bacon.

Dellinger, A., & Gilchrist, J. (2018). Leading causes of fatal and nonfatal unintentional injury for children and teens and the role of lifestyle clinicians. *American Journal of Lifestyle Medicine*, *13*(1), 155982761769629. https://doi.org/10.1177/1559827617696297

Deneault, J., & Ricard, M. (2006). The assessment of children's understanding of inclusion relations: Transitivity, asymmetry, and quantification. *Journal of Cognition & Development*, *7*(4), 551–570.

Di Cesare, M., Sorić, M., Bovet, P., Miranda, J. J., Bhutta, Z., Stevens, G. A., Laxmaiah, A., Kengne, A. P., & Bentham, J. (2019). The epidemiological burden of obesity in childhood: A worldwide epidemic requiring urgent action. *BMC Medicine*, *17*(1), 1–20. https://doi.org/10.1186/s12916-019-1449-8

Di Cristo, G., & Chattopadhyaya, B. (2020). Development of neuronal circuits: From synaptogenesis to synapse plasticity. *Handbook of Clinical Neurology*, *173*, 43–53. https://doi.org/10.1016/B978-0-444-64150-2.00005-8

Dick, A. S., Garcia, N. L., Pruden, S. M., Thompson, W. K., Hawes, S. W., Sutherland, M. T., Riedel, M. C., Laird, A. R., & Gonzalez, R. (2019). No evidence for a bilingual executive function advantage in the nationally representative ABCD study. *Nature Human Behaviour*, *3*(7), 692–701. https://doi.org/10.1038/s41562-019-0609-3

Dinehart, L. H. (2015). Handwriting in early childhood education: Current research and future implications. *Journal of Early Childhood Literacy*, *15*(1), 97–118. https://doi.org/10.1177/1468798414522825

Döhla, D., & Heim, S. (2016). Developmental dyslexia and dysgraphia: What can we learn from the one about the other? *Frontiers in Psychology*, *6*, 2045. https://doi.org/10.3389/fpsyg.2015.02045

Döhla, D., Willmes, K., & Heim, S. (2018). Cognitive profiles of developmental dysgraphia. *Frontiers in Psychology*, *9*(NOV), 2006. https://doi.org/10.3389/fpsyg.2018.02006

Drollette, E. S., & Hillman, C. H. (2020). Cognitive and academic benefits of physical activity for school-age children. In T. Brusseau, S. Fairclough, & D. Lubans (Eds.), *The Routledge handbook of youth physical activity* (pp. 148–169). Routledge. https://doi.org/10.4324/9781003026426-9

Dubois, L., Ohm Kyvik, K., Girard, M., Tatone-Tokuda, F., Pérusse, D., Hjelmborg, J., Skytthe, A., Rasmussen, F., Wright, M. J., Lichtenstein, P., & Martin, N. G. (2012). Genetic and environmental contributions to weight, height, and BMI from birth to 19 years of age: An international study of over 12,000 twin pairs. *PloS One*, *7*(2), e30153. https://doi.org/10.1371/journal.pone.0030153

Dunn, J., Gray, C., Moffett, P., & Mitchell, D. (2018). 'It's more funner than doing work': Children's perspectives on using tablet computers in the early years of school. *Early Child Development and Care*, *188*(6), 819–831. https://doi.org/10.1080/03004430.2016.1238824

Durante, F., & Fiske, S. T. (2017). How social-class stereotypes maintain inequality. *Current Opinion in Psychology*, *18*, 43–48. https://doi.org/10.1016/j.copsyc.2017.07.033

Durkin, M. S., Maenner, M. J., Baio, J., Christensen, D., Daniels, J., Fitzgerald, R., Imm, P., Lee, L. C., Schieve, L. A., Van Naarden Braun, K., Wingate, M. S., & Yeargin-Allsopp, M. (2017). Autism spectrum disorder among US children (2002-2010): Socioeconomic, racial, and ethnic disparities. *American Journal of Public Health*, *107*(11), 1818–1826. https://doi.org/10.2105/AJPH.2017.304032

Eather, N., Ridley, K., & Leahy, A. (2020). Physiological health benefits of physical activity for young people. In T. Brusseau, S. Fairclough, & D. Lubans (Eds.), *The Routledge handbook of youth physical activity* (pp. 103–120). Routledge.

Ehri, L. C. (2020). The science of learning to read words: A case for systematic phonics instruction. *Reading Research Quarterly*, *55*(S1), S45–S60. https://doi.org/10.1002/rrq.334

Ericsson, K. A., & Moxley, J. H. (2013). Experts' superior memory: From accumulation of chunks to building memory skills that mediate improved performance and learning. In D. S. Lindsay & T. J Perfect (Eds.), *The SAGE handbook of applied memory* (pp. 404–420). SAGE.

Evans, S. W., Owens, J. S., Wymbs, B. T., & Ray, A. R. (2018). Evidence-based psychosocial treatments for children and adolescents with attention deficit/hyperactivity disorder. *Journal of Clinical Child & Adolescent Psychology*, *47*(2), 157–198. https://doi.org/10.1080/15374416.2017.1390757

Fadus, M. C., Ginsburg, K. R., Sobowale, K., Halliday-Boykins, C. A., Bryant, B. E., Gray, K. M., & Squeglia, L. M. (2020). Unconscious bias and the diagnosis of disruptive behavior disorders and ADHD in African American and hispanic youth. *Academic Psychiatry*, *44*(1), 95–102. https://doi.org/10.1007/s40596-019-01127-6

Fan, M., & Jin, Y. (2014). Do neighborhood parks and playgrounds reduce childhood obesity? *American Journal of Agricultural Economics*, *96*(1), 26–42. https://doi.org/10.1093/ajae/aat047

Farber, D. A., & Beteleva, T. G. (2011). Development of the brain's organization of working memory in young schoolchildren. *Human Physiology*, *37*(1), 1–13. https://doi.org/10.1134/s0362119710061015

Farooq, M. A., Parkinson, K. N., Adamson, A. J., Pearce, M. S., Reilly, J. K., Hughes, A. R., Janssen, X., Basterfield, L., & Reilly, J. J. (2018). Timing of the decline in physical activity in childhood and adolescence: Gateshead Millennium Cohort Study. *British Journal of Sports Medicine*, *52*, 1002–1006. https://doi.org/10.1136/bjsports-2016-096933

Federal Interagency Forum on Child and Family Statistics. (2017). *America's children: Key national indicators of well-being, 2017*. https://www.childstats.gov/americaschildren/index.asp

Ferreira, L., Godinez, I., Gabbard, C., Vieira, J. L. L., & Caçola, P. (2018). Motor development in school-age children is associated with the home environment including socioeconomic status. *Child: Care, Health and Development*, *44*(6), 801–806. https://doi.org/10.1111/cch.12606

Filippova, E., & Astington, J. W. (2008). Further development in social reasoning revealed in discourse irony understanding. *Child Development*, *79*(1), 126–138. https://doi.org/10.1111/j.1467-8624.2007.01115.x

Finch, J. E. (2019). Do schools promote executive functions? Differential working memory growth across school-year and summer months. *AERA Open*, *5*(2), 233285841984844. https://doi.org/10.1177/2332858419848443

Fish, R. E. (2019). Standing out and sorting in: Exploring the role of racial composition in racial disparities in special education. *American Educational Research Journal*, *56*(6), 2573–2608. https://doi.org/10.3102/0002831219847966

Flanagan, D. P., & Alfonso, V. C. (2017). *Essentials of WISC-V assessment*. Wiley.

Flynn, J. R., & Sternberg, R. J. (2019). Environment and intelligence. In R. J. Sternberg (Ed.), *Human intelligence: An introduction*. Cambridge University Press. https://www.cambridge.org/us/academic/subjects/psychology/psychology-general-interest/human-intelligence-introduction?format=PB&isbn=9781108703864

Forbringer, L. (2020). Special education. In S. Hupp & J. D. Jewell (Eds.), *The encyclopedia of child and adolescent development* (pp. 1–12). Wiley. https://doi.org/10.1002/9781119171492.wecad379

Fry, A. F., & Hale, S. (1996). Processing speed, working memory, and fluid intelligence: Evidence for a developmental cascade. *Psychological Science*, *7*, 237–241.

Fuchs, L. S., Malone, A. S., Schumacher, R. F., Namkung, J., & Wang, A. (2017). Fraction intervention for students with mathematics difficulties: Lessons learned from five randomized controlled trials. *Journal of Learning Disabilities*, *50*(6), 631–639. https://doi.org/10.1177/0022219416677249

Gabbard, C. P. (2018). *Lifelong motor development* (6th ed.). Pearson.

Gardiner, H. W., & Kosmitzki, C. (2018). *Lives across cultures: Cross-cultural human development* (6th ed.). Pearson.

Gardner, H. (2017). Taking a multiple intelligences (MI) perspective. *Behavioral and Brain Sciences*, *40*, e203. https://doi.org/10.1017/S0140525X16001631

Gardner, H., Kornhaber, M., & Chen, J.-Q. (2018). The theory of multiple intelligences. In R. J. Sternberg (Ed.), *The nature of human intelligence* (pp. 116–129). Cambridge University Press. https://doi.org/10.1017/9781316817049.009

Garrido-Miguel, M., Cavero-Redondo, I., Álvarez-Bueno, C., Rodríguez-Artalejo, F., Moreno, L. A., Ruiz, J. R., Ahrens, W., & Martínez-Vizcaíno, V. (2019). Prevalence and trends of overweight and obesity in European children from 1999 to 2016: A systematic review and meta-analysis. *JAMA Pediatrics*, *173*(10), 192430. https://doi.org/10.1001/jamapediatrics.2019.2430

Gauvain, M., Perez, S., Gauvain, M., & Perez, S. (2015). Cognitive development and culture. In L. S. Liben & U. Müller (Eds.), *Handbook of child psychology and developmental science* (pp. 1–43). John Wiley & Sons, Inc. https://doi.org/10.1002/9781118963418.childpsy220

Georgas, J., Weiss, L. G., van de Vijver, F. J. R., & Saklofske, D. H. (2003). Cross-cultural psychology, intelligence, and cognitive processes. In J. Georgas, L. G. Weiss, F. J. Van de. Vijver, & D. H. Saklofske (Eds.), *Culture and children's intelligence: Cross-cultural analysis of the WISC-III* (pp. 23–37). Academic Press.

Gibb, R., & Kovalchuk, A. (2018). Brain development. In R. Gibb & B. Kolb (Eds.), *The neurobiology of brain and behavioral development* (pp. 3–27). Academic Press. https://doi.org/10.1016/B978-0-12-804036-2.00001-7

Gilmore, C. K., McCarthy, S. E., & Spelke, E. S. (2010). Non-symbolic arithmetic abilities and mathematics achievement in the first year of formal schooling. *Cognition*, *115*(3), 394–406. https://doi.org/10.1016/j.cognition.2010.02.002

Glenwright, M., & Pexman, P. M. (2010). Development of children's ability to distinguish sarcasm and verbal irony*. *Journal of Child Language*, *37*(02), 429. https://doi.org/10.1017/S0305000909009520

Goodarzi, M. O. (2018). Genetics of obesity: What genetic association studies have taught us about the biology of obesity and its complications. *The Lancet Diabetes & Endocrinology*, *6*(3), 223–236. https://doi.org/10.1016/S2213-8587(17)30200-0

Goodnow, J. J., Lawrence, J. A., Goodnow, J. J., & Lawrence, J. A. (2015). Children and cultural context. In M. H. Bornstein & T. Leventhal (Eds.), *Handbook of child psychology and developmental science* (Vol. 4, pp. 1–41). John Wiley & Sons, Inc. https://doi.org/10.1002/9781118963418.childpsy419

Goodwin, G. P., & Johnson-Laird, P. N. (2008). Transitive and pseudo-transitive inferences. *Cognition*, *108*(2), 320–352. https://doi.org/10.1016/j.cognition.2008.02.010

Graham, N., Schultz, L., Mitra, S., & Mont, D. (2017). Disability in middle childhood and adolescence. In D. A. P. Bundy, N. de Silva, S. Horton, D. T. Jamison, & G. C. Patton (Eds.), *Disease control priorities, Third edition (Volume 8): Child and adolescent health and development* (pp. 221–238). The World Bank. https://doi.org/10.1596/978-1-4648-0423-6_ch17

Grigorenko, E. L., Compton, D. L., Fuchs, L. S., Wagner, R. K., Willcutt, E. G., & Fletcher, J. M. (2020). Understanding, educating, and supporting children with specific learning disabilities: 50 years of science and practice. *American Psychologist*, *75*(1), 37. https://doi.org/10.1037/amp0000452

Grove, J., Ripke, S., Als, T. D., Mattheisen, M., Walters, R. K., Won, H., Pallesen, J., Agerbo, E., Andreassen, O. A., Anney, R., Awashti, S., Belliveau, R., Bettella, F., Buxbaum, J. D., Bybjerg-Grauholm, J., Bækvad-Hansen, M., Cerrato, F., Chambert, K., Christensen, J. H. ... Børglum, A. D. (2019). Identification of common genetic risk variants for autism spectrum disorder. *Nature Genetics*, *51*(3), 431–444. https://doi.org/10.1038/s41588-019-0344-8

Guo, Y., Sun, S., Breit-Smith, A., Morrison, F. J., & Connor, C. M. (2015). Behavioral engagement and reading achievement in elementary-school-age children: A longitudinal cross-lagged analysis. *Journal of Educational Psychology*, *107*(2), 332–347. https://doi.org/10.1037/a0037638

Haft, S. L., Myers, C. A., & Hoeft, F. (2016). Socio-emotional and cognitive resilience in children with reading disabilities. *Current Opinion in Behavioral Sciences*, *10*, 133–141. https://doi.org/10.1016/j.cobeha.2016.06.005

Hahamy, A., Behrmann, M., & Malach, R. (2015). The idiosyncratic brain: Distortion of spontaneous connectivity patterns in autism spectrum disorder. *Nature Neuroscience*, *18*(2), 302–309. https://doi.org/10.1038/nn.3919

Hales, C. M., Fryar, C. D., Carroll, M. D., Freedman, D. S., & Ogden, C. L. (2018). Trends in obesity and severe obesity prevalence in US youth and adults by sex and age, 2007-2008 to 2015-2016. *JAMA*, *319*(16), 1723. https://doi.org/10.1001/jama.2018.3060

Hall, L. J. (2018). *Autism spectrum disorders : From theory to practice*. Prentice Hall. https://www.vitalsource.com/educators/products/autism-spectrum-disorders-laura-j-hall-v9780134461168

Hanley, J. R., Cortis, C., Budd, M.-J., & Nozari, N. (2016). Did I say dog or cat? A study of semantic error detection and correction in children. *Journal of Experimental Child Psychology*, *142*, 36–47. https://doi.org/10.1016/j.jecp.2015.09.008

Harrist, A. W., Swindle, T. M., Hubbs-Tait, L., Topham, G. L., Shriver, L. H., & Page, M. C. (2016). The social and emotional lives of overweight, obese, and severely obese children. *Child Development*, *87*(5), 1564–1580. https://doi.org/10.1111/cdev.12548

Hartanto, A., Yang, H., & Yang, S. (2018). Bilingualism positively predicts mathematical competence: Evidence from two large-scale studies. *Learning and Individual Differences*, *61*, 216–227. https://doi.org/10.1016/j.lindif.2017.12.007

Hawk, L. W., Fosco, W. D., Colder, C. R., Waxmonsky, J. G., Pelham, W. E., & Rosch, K. S. (2018). How do stimulant treatments for ADHD work? Evidence for mediation by improved cognition. *Journal of Child Psychology and Psychiatry*, *59*(12), 1271–1281. https://doi.org/10.1111/jcpp.12917

Henry, D. A., Cortés, L. B., & Votruba-Drzal, E. (2020). Black-white achievement gaps differ by family socioeconomic status from early childhood through early adolescence. *Journal of Educational Psychology*, *112*(8), 1489–1489. https://doi.org/10.1037/edu0000439

Herts, J., Levine, S. C., Herts, J., & Levine, S. C. (2020). Gender and math development. In *Oxford research encyclopedia of education*. Oxford University Press. https://doi.org/10.1093/acrefore/9780190264093.013.1186

Heward, W. L. (2018). *Exceptional children : An introduction to special education* (11th ed.). Pearson. https://www.pearson.com/us/higher-education/program/Heward-Exceptional-Children-An-Introduction-to-Special-Education-Plus-Revel-Access-Card-Package-11th-Edition/PGM2019655.html

Hillman, C., Logan, N., & Shigeta, T. (2019). A review of acute physical activity effects on brain and cognition in children. *Translational Journal of the American College of Sports Medicine*, *4*(17), 132. https://doi.org/10.1249/TJX.0000000000000101

Hinshaw, S. P. (2018). Attention Deficit Hyperactivity Disorder (ADHD): Controversy, developmental mechanisms, and multiple levels of analysis. *Annual Review of Clinical Psychology*, *14*(1), 291–316. https://doi.org/10.1146/annurev-clinpsy-050817-084917

Hitch, G. J., Towse, J. N., & Hutton, U. (2001). What limits children's working memory span? Theoretical accounts and applications for scholastic development. *Journal of Experimental Psychology: General*, *130*(2), 184–198.

Hodges, H., Fealko, C., & Soares, N. (2020). Autism spectrum disorder: Definition, epidemiology, causes, and clinical evaluation. *Translational Pediatrics*, *9*(S1), S55–S65. https://doi.org/10.21037/tp.2019.09.09

Hoff, E. (2015). Language development. In M. H. Bornstein & M. E. Lamb (Eds.), *Developmental science: An advanced textbook* (5th ed.). Psychology Press.

Hollis, J. L., Williams, A. J., Sutherland, R., Campbell, E., Nathan, N., Wolfenden, L., Morgan, P. J., Lubans, D. R., & Wiggers, J. (2016). A systematic review and meta-analysis of moderate-to-vigorous physical activity levels in elementary school physical education lessons. *Preventive Medicine*, *86*, 34–54. https://doi.org/10.1016/J.YPMED.2015.11.018

Horowitz, S. H., Rawe, J., & Whittaker, M. C. (2017). *The state of learning disabilities: Understanding the 1 in 5*. National Center for Learning Disabilities.

Houtrow, A. J., Larson, K., Olson, L. M., Newacheck, P. W., & Halfon, N. (2014). Changing trends of childhood disability, 2001-2011. *Pediatrics*, *134*(3), 530–538. https://doi.org/10.1542/peds.2014-0594

Huang, L., Wang, Y., Zhang, L., Zheng, Z., Zhu, T., Qu, Y., & Mu, D. (2018). Maternal smoking and attention-deficit/hyperactivity disorder in offspring: A meta-analysis. *Pediatrics*, *141*(1), 20172465. https://doi.org/10.1542/peds.2017-2465

Hull, C. (2020). Prediction signals in the cerebellum: Beyond supervised motor learning. *eLife*, *9*, e54073. https://doi.org/10.7554/eLife.54073

Hull, J. V., Dokovna, L. B., Jacokes, Z. J., Torgerson, C. M., Irimia, A., & Van Horn, J. D. (2017). Resting-state functional connectivity in autism spectrum disorders: A review. *Frontiers in Psychiatry*, *7*, 205. https://doi.org/10.3389/fpsyt.2016.00205

Huttenlocher, J., Levine, S., & Vevea, J. (1998). Environmental input and cognitive growth: A study using time-period comparisons. *Child Development*, *69*, 1012–1029.

Hviid, A., Hansen, J. V., Frisch, M., & Melbye, M. (2019). Measles, mumps, rubella vaccination and autism. *Annals of Internal Medicine*, *170*(8), 513. https://doi.org/10.7326/M18-2101

Hwang, G.-J., Chiu, L.-Y., & Chen, C.-H. (2015). A contextual game-based learning approach to improving students' inquiry-based learning performance in social studies courses. *Computers & Education*, *81*, 13–25. https://doi.org/10.1016/J.COMPEDU.2014.09.006

Inhelder, B., & Piaget, J. (1964). *The early growth of logic in the child: Classification and seriation*. Harper and Row.

Jacobson, L. A., Crocetti, D., Dirlikov, B., Slifer, K., Denckla, M. B., Mostofsky, S. H., & Mahone, E. M. (2018). Anomalous brain development is evident in preschoolers with attention-deficit/hyperactivity disorder. *Journal of the International Neuropsychological Society : JINS*, *24*(6), 531–539. https://doi.org/10.1017/S1355617718000103

Janssen, I., LeBlanc, A. G., Janssen, I., Twisk, J., Tolfrey, K., Jones, A., Campbell, I., Kelley, G., Kelley, K., Reilly, J., McDowell, Z., Etnier, J., Nowell, P., Landers, D., Sibley, B., Cook, D., Mulrow, C., Haynes, R., Tremblay, M. ... Janssen, I. (2010). Systematic review of the health benefits of physical activity and fitness in school-aged children and youth. *International Journal of Behavioral Nutrition and Physical Activity*, *7*(1), 40. https://doi.org/10.1186/1479-5868-7-40

Jaxon, J., Lei, R. F., Shachnai, R., Chestnut, E. K., & Cimpian, A. (2019). The acquisition of gender stereotypes about intellectual ability: Intersections with race. *Journal of Social Issues*, *75*(4), 1192–1215. https://doi.org/10.1111/josi.12352

Kana, R. K., Maximo, J. O., Williams, D. L., Keller, T. A., Schipul, S. E., Cherkassky, V. L., Minshew, N. J., Just, M. A., Gallagher, H., Frith, C., Barch, D., Burgess, G., Harms, M., Petersen, S., Schlaggar, B., Corbetta, M., Overwalle, F., Dufour, N., Redcay, E. ... Müller, R. (2015). Aberrant functioning of the theory-of-mind network in children and adolescents with autism. *Molecular Autism*, *6*(1), 59. https://doi.org/10.1186/s13229-015-0052-x

Kann, L., Kinchen, S., Shanklin, S. L., Flint, K. H., Kawkins, J., Harris, W. A., Lowry, R., Olsen, E. O., McManus, T., Chyen, D., Whittle, L., Taylor, E., Demissie, Z., Brener, N., Thornton, J., Moore, J., & Zaza, S. (2014). Youth risk behavior surveillance--United States, 2013. *Morbidity and Mortality Weekly Report. Surveillance Summaries (Washington, D.C.: 2002)* , *63*(Suppl 4), 1–168.

Kantomaa, M. T., Stamatakis, E., Kankaanpää, A., Kaakinen, M., Rodriguez, A., Taanila, A., Ahonen, T., Järvelin, M.-R., & Tammelin, T. (2013). Physical activity and obesity mediate the association between childhood motor function and adolescents' academic achievement. *Proceedings of the National Academy of Sciences of the United States of America*, *110*(5), 1917–1922. https://doi.org/10.1073/pnas.1214574110

Katz, A. N. (2017). Psycholinguistic approaches to metaphor acquisition and use. In E. Semino & Z. Demjén (Eds.), *The Routledge handbook of metaphor and language* (pp. 490–503). Routledge.

Katz, V. S., Moran, M. B., & Gonzalez, C. (2018). Connecting with technology in lower-income US families. *New Media & Society*, *20*(7), 2509–2533. https://doi.org/10.1177/1461444817726319

Kaufman, J. C., Kaufman, S. B., & Plucker, J. A. (2013). Contemporary theories of intelligence. In D. Reisberg (Ed.), *Oxford handbook of cognitive psychology* (pp. 811–822). Oxford.

Kaufmann, L., Mazzocco, M. M., Dowker, A., von Aster, M., Göbel, S. M., Grabner, R. H., Henik, A., Jordan, N. C., Karmiloff-Smith, A. D., Kucian, K., Rubinsten, O., Szucs, D., Shalev, R., & Nuerk, H.-C. (2013). Dyscalculia from a developmental and differential perspective. *Frontiers in Psychology*, *4*, 516. https://doi.org/10.3389/fpsyg.2013.00516

Kent, C., Cordier, R., Joosten, A., Wilkes-Gillan, S., Bundy, A., & Speyer, R. (2020). A systematic review and meta-analysis of interventions to improve play skills in children with autism spectrum disorder. *Review Journal of Autism and Developmental Disorders*, *7*(1), 91–118. https://doi.org/10.1007/s40489-019-00181-y

Khan, A. J., Nair, A., Keown, C. L., Datko, M. C., Lincoln, A. J., & Müller, R.-A. (2015). Cerebro-cerebellar resting state functional connectivity in children and adolescents with autism spectrum disorder. *Biological Psychiatry*, *78*(9), 625. https://doi.org/10.1016/J.BIOPSYCH.2015.03.024

Kharitonova, M., Winter, W., & Sheridan, M. A. (2015). As working memory grows: A developmental account of neural bases of working memory capacity in 5- to 8-year old children and adults. *Journal of Cognitive Neuroscience*, *27*(9), 1775–1788. https://doi.org/10.1162/jocn_a_00824

Kliegman, R., Stanton, B., Geme, St., W, J., Schor, N. F., Behrman, R. E., & Nelson, W. E. (2016). *Nelson textbook of pediatrics*. Elsevier.

Kohnert, K. J., & Bates, E. (2002). Balancing bilinguals II. *Journal of Speech Language and Hearing Research*, *45*(2), 347. https://doi.org/10.1044/1092-4388(2002/027)

Kriegbaum, K., Becker, N., & Spinath, B. (2018). The relative importance of intelligence and motivation as predictors of school achievement: A meta-analysis. *Educational Research Review*, *25*, 120–148. https://doi.org/10.1016/j.edurev.2018.10.001

Kubota, M., Chevalier, N., & Sorace, A. (2020). Losing access to the second language and its effect on executive function development in childhood: The case of "returnees.". *Journal of Neurolinguistics*, *55*, 100906. https://doi.org/10.1016/j.jneuroling.2020.100906

Kucian, K., & von Aster, M. (2015). Developmental dyscalculia. *European Journal of Pediatrics*, *174*(1), 1–13. https://doi.org/10.1007/s00431-014-2455-7

Kumar, S., & Kelly, A. S. (2017). Review of childhood obesity: From epidemiology, etiology, and comorbidities to clinical assessment and treatment. *Mayo Clinic Proceedings*, *92*(2), 251–265. https://doi.org/10.1016/j.mayocp.2016.09.017

Lange, H., Buse, J., Bender, S., Siegert, J., Knopf, H., & Roessner, V. (2016). Accident proneness in children and adolescents affected by ADHD and the impact of medication. *Journal of Attention Disorders*, *20*(6), 501–509. https://doi.org/10.1177/1087054713518237

Laukkanen, A., Pesola, A., Havu, M., Sääkslahti, A., & Finni, T. (2014). Relationship between habitual physical activity and gross motor skills is multifaceted in 5- to 8-year-old children. *Scandinavian Journal of Medicine & Science in Sports*, *24*(2), e102–e110. https://doi.org/10.1111/sms.12116

Leather, C. V., & Henry, L. A. (1994). Working memory span and phonological awareness tasks as predictors of early reading ability. *Journal of Experimental Child Psychology*, *58*, 88–111.

Lewis, R. B., Wheeler, J. J., & Carter, S. L. (2017). *Teaching students with special needs in general education classrooms*. Pearson.

Li, D. b., Yao, J., Sun, L., Wu, B., Li, X., Liu, S. lei., Hou, J. m., Liu, H. l., Sui, J. f., & Wu, G. y. (2019). Reevaluating the ability of cerebellum in associative motor learning. *Scientific Reports*, *9*(1), 6029. https://doi.org/10.1038/s41598-019-42413-5

Lobstein, T., Jackson-Leach, R., Moodie, M. L., Hall, K. D., Gortmaker, S. L., Swinburn, B. A., James, W. P. T., Wang, Y., & McPherson, K. (2015). Child and adolescent obesity: Part of a bigger picture. *Lancet (London, England)*, (385), 2510–2520. https://doi.org/10.1016/S0140-6736(14)61746-3

Lord, C., Brugha, T. S., Charman, T., Cusack, J., Dumas, G., Frazier, T., Jones, E. J. H., Jones, R. M., Pickles, A., State, M. W., Taylor, J. L., & Veenstra-VanderWeele, J. (2020). Autism spectrum disorder. *Nature Reviews Disease Primers*, *6*(1), 1–23. https://doi.org/10.1038/s41572-019-0138-4

Lu, Y., Ma, M., Chen, G., & Zhou, X. (2020). Can abacus course eradicate developmental dyscalculia. *Psychology in the Schools*, *58*(2), 235–251. https://doi.org/10.1002/pits.22441 https://doi.org/10.1002/pits.22441

Luo, Y., Weibman, D., Halperin, J. M., & Li, X. (2019). A review of heterogeneity in attention deficit/hyperactivity disorder (ADHD). *Frontiers in Human Neuroscience*, *13*, 42. https://doi.org/10.3389/fnhum.2019.00042

Mackintosh, J. N. (2011). *IQ and human intelligence* (2nd ed.). Oxford University Press.

Macswan, J., Thompson, M. S., Rolstad, K., McAlister, K., & Lobo, G. (2017). Three theories of the effects of language education programs: An empirical evaluation of bilingual and English-only policies. *Annual Review of Applied Linguistics*, *37*, 218–240. https://doi.org/10.1017/S0267190517000137

Mahboob, A., Richmond, S. A., Harkins, J. P., & Macpherson, A. K. (2021). Childhood unintentional injury: The impact of family income, education level, occupation status, and other measures of socioeconomic status. A systematic review. *Paediatrics & Child Health*, *26*, e39–e45. https://doi.org/10.1093/pch/pxz145

Mancilla-Martinez, J., Hwang, J. K., Oh, M. H., & Mcclain, J. B. (2020). Early elementary grade dual language learners from Spanish-speaking homes struggling with english reading comprehension: The dormant role of language skills. *Journal of Educational Psychology*, *112*(5), 880–894. https://doi.org/10.1037/edu0000402

Manoach, D. S., Schlaug, G., Siewert, B., Darby, D. G., Bly, B. M., Benfield, A., Edelman, R R., & Warach, S. (1997). Prefrontal cortex fMRI signal changes are correlated with working memory load. *NeuroReport*, *8*, 545–549.

Masi, A., DeMayo, M. M., Glozier, N., & Guastella, A. J. (2017). An overview of autism spectrum disorder, heterogeneity and treatment options. *Neuroscience Bulletin*, *33*(2), 183–193. https://doi.org/10.1007/s12264-017-0100-y

Masonbrink, A. R., & Hurley, E. (2020). Advocating for children during the COVID-19 school closures. *Pediatrics*, *146*(3), 20201440. https://doi.org/10.1542/PEDS.2020-1440

Mastropieri, M. A., & Scruggs, T. E. (2017). *The inclusive classroom : Strategies for effective differentiated instruction*. Pearson.

Mavilidi, M. F., Drew, R., Morgan, P. J., Lubans, D. R., Schmidt, M., & Riley, N. (2020). Effects of different types of classroom physical activity breaks on children's on-task behaviour, academic achievement and cognition. *Acta Paediatrica*, *109*(1), 158–165. https://doi.org/10.1111/apa.14892

McCaskey, U., von Aster, O'Gorman, R., & Kucian, K. (2020). Persistent differences in brain structure in developmental dyscalculia: A longitudinal morphometry study. *Frontiers in Human Neuroscience*, *14*, 272. https://doi.org/10.3389/fnhum.2020.00272

McKown, C., & Strambler, M. J. (2009). Developmental antecedents and social and academic consequences of stereotype-Consciousness in middle childhood. *Child Development*, *80*(6), 1643–1659. https://doi.org/10.1111/j.1467-8624.2009.01359.x

McKown, C., & Weinstein, R. S. (2003). The development and consequences of stereotype consciousness in middle childhood. *Child Development*, *74*(2), 498–515. https://doi.org/10.1111/1467-8624.7402012

Menon, V. (2016). Working memory in children's math learning and its disruption in dyscalculia. *Current Opinion in Behavioral Sciences*, *10*, 125–132. https://doi.org/10.1016/j.cobeha.2016.05.014

Miller, S., McCulloch, S., & Jarrold, C. (2015). The development of memory maintenance strategies: Training cumulative rehearsal and interactive imagery in children aged between 5 and 9. *Frontiers in Psychology*, *06*, 524. https://doi.org/10.3389/fpsyg.2015.00524

Mills, K. L., Goddings, A.-L., Herting, M. M., Meuwese, R., Blakemore, S.-J., Crone, E. A., Dahl, R. E., Güroğlu, B., Raznahan, A., Sowell, E. R., & Tamnes, C. K. (2016). Structural brain development between childhood and adulthood: Convergence across four longitudinal samples. *NeuroImage*, *141*, 273–281. https://doi.org/10.1016/J.NEUROIMAGE.2016.07.044

Mirkovic, B., Chagraoui, A., Gerardin, P., & Cohen, D. (2020). Epigenetics and attention-deficit/hyperactivity disorder: New perspectives? *Frontiers in Psychiatry*, *11*, 579. https://doi.org/10.3389/fpsyt.2020.00579

Molitor, A., & Hsu, H.-C. (2019). Child development across cultures. In K. Keith (Ed.), *Cross-cultural psychology* (pp. 153–189). Ltd: John Wiley & Sons. https://doi.org/10.1002/9781119519348.ch8

Moore, R., Vitale, D., & Stawinoga, N. (2018). *The digital divide and educational equity: A look at students with very limited access to electronic devices at home*. https://equityinlearning.act.org/wp-content/themes/voltron/img/tech-briefs/the-digital-divide.pdf

Morey, C. C., Mareva, S., Lelonkiewicz, J. R., & Chevalier, N. (2018). Gaze-based rehearsal in children under 7: A developmental investigation of eye movements during a serial spatial memory task. *Developmental Science*, *21*(3), e12559. https://doi.org/10.1111/desc.12559

Morgan, P. L., Farkas, G., Hillemeier, M. M., & Maczuga, S. (2017). Replicated evidence of racial and ethnic disparities in disability identification in U.S. schools. *Educational Researcher*, *46*(6), 305–322. https://doi.org/10.3102/0013189X17726282

Mpofu, E., & van de Vijver, F. J. R. (2000). Taxonomic structure in early to middle childhood: A longitudinal study with Zimbabwean schoolchildren. *International Journal of Behavioral Development*, *24*(2), 204–212.

Nasir, N. S., McKinney de Royston, M., O'Connor, K., & Wischnia, S. (2017). Knowing about racial stereotypes versus believing them. *Urban Education*, *52*(4), 491–524. https://doi.org/10.1177/0042085916672290

National Center for Education Statistics. (2020a). *NAEP report card: 2019 NAEP mathematics assessment*. https://www.nationsreportcard.gov/highlights/mathematics/2019/

National Center for Education Statistics. (2020b). *NAEP report card: 2019 NAEP reading assessment*. https://www.nationsreportcard.gov/highlights/reading/2019/

National Science Foundation. (2018). Instructional technology and digital learning. In *Science and Engineering Indicators*. https://www.nsf.gov/statistics/2018/nsb20181/report/sections/elementary-and-secondary-mathematics-and-science-education/instructional-technology-and-digital-learning.

Neisser, U., Boodoo, G., Bouchard, Jr., J, T., Boykin, A. W., Brody, N., Ceci, S. J., Halpern, D. F., Loehlin, J. C., Perloff, R., Sternberg, R. J., & Urbina, S. (1996). Intelligence: Knowns and unknowns. *American Psychologist*, *51*(2), 77–101.

Niebaum, J., & Munakata, Y. (2020). Deciding what to do: Developments in children's spontaneous monitoring of cognitive demands. *Child Development Perspectives*, *14*(4), 202–207. https://doi.org/10.1111/cdep.12383

Ninio, A. (2014). Pragmatic development. In P. J. Brooks & V. Kempe (Eds.), *Encyclopedia of language development*. SAGE. https://doi.org/10.4135/9781483346441.n153

Nisbett, R. E., Aronson, J., Blair, C., Dickens, W., Flynn, J., Halpern, D. F., & Turkheimer, E. (2013). Intelligence: New findings and theoretical developments. *American Psychologist*, *67*(2), 130–159. https://doi.org/10.1037/a0026699

Oppenheim, G. M., Griffin, Z., Peña, E. D., & Bedore, L. M. (2020). Longitudinal evidence for simultaneous bilingual language development with shifting language dominance, and how to explain it. *Language Learning*, *70*(S2), 20–44. https://doi.org/10.1111/lang.12398

Ose Askvik, E., van der Weel, F. R. (Ruud)., & van der Meer, A. L. H. (2020). The importance of cursive handwriting over typewriting for learning in the classroom: A high-density EEG study of 12-year-old children and young adults. *Frontiers in Psychology*, *11*, 1810. https://doi.org/10.3389/fpsyg.2020.01810

Outhwaite, L. A., Gulliford, A., & Pitchford, N. J. (2017). Closing the gap: Efficacy of a tablet intervention to support the development of early mathematical skills in UK primary school children. *Computers & Education*, *108*, 43–58. https://doi.org/10.1016/J.COMPEDU.2017.01.011

Owens, R. E. (2015). *Language development: An introduction*. Pearson.

Owens, R. E. (2020). *Language development : An introduction* (10th ed.). Pearson.

Parasuraman, S. R., Ghandour, R. M., & Kogan, M. D. (2020). Epidemiological profile of health and behaviors in middle childhood. *Pediatrics*, *145*(6), e20192244. https://doi.org/10.1542/peds.2019-2244

Payne, G., & Isaacs, L. (2020). *Human motor development: A lifespan approach* (10th ed.). Routledge. https://www.routledge.com/Human-Motor-Development-A-Lifespan-Approach/Payne-Isaacs/p/book/9780367347376

Peng, P., Barnes, M., Wang, C., Wang, W., Li, S., Swanson, H. L., Dardick, W., & Tao, S. (2018). A meta-analysis on the relation between reading and working memory. *Psychological Bulletin*, *144*(1), 48–76. https://doi.org/10.1037/bul0000124

Perlman, S. B., Huppert, T. J., & Luna, B. (2016). Functional near-infrared spectroscopy evidence for development of prefrontal engagement in working memory in early through middle childhood. *Cerebral Cortex(New York, N.Y. : 1991)*, *26*(6), 2790–2799. https://doi.org/10.1093/cercor/bhv139

Perone, S., Almy, B., & Zelazo, P. D. (2018). Toward an understanding of the neural basis of executive function development. In R. Gibb & B. Kolb (Eds.), *The neurobiology of brain and behavioral development* (pp. 291–314). Elsevier. https://doi.org/10.1016/B978-0-12-804036-2.00011-X

Peterson, R. L., & Pennington, B. F. (2012). Developmental dyslexia. *Lancet*, *379*(9830), 1997–2007. https://doi.org/10.1016/S0140-6736(12)60198-6

Pexman, P. M. (2014). Nonliteral language use. In P. J. BrVooks & V. Kempe (Eds.), *Encyclopedia of language development*. SAGE. https://doi.org/10.4135/9781483346441.n132

Plomin, R. D., & Deary, I. J. (2015). Genetics and intelligence differences: Five special findings. *Molecular Psychiatry*, *20*(1), 98–108. https://doi.org/10.1038/mp.2014.105

Plomin, R. D., DeFries, J. C., Knopik, V. S., & Neiderhiser, J. M. (2016). Top 10 replicated findings from behavioral genetics. *Perspectives on Psychological Science*, *11*(1), 3–23. https://doi.org/10.1177/1745691615617439

Poitras, V. J., Gray, C. E., Borghese, M. M., Carson, V., Chaput, J.-P., Janssen, I., Katzmarzyk, P. T., Pate, R. R., Connor Gorber, S., Kho, M. E., Sampson, M., & Tremblay, M. S. (2016). Systematic review of the relationships between objectively measured physical activity and health indicators in school-aged children and youth. *Applied Physiology, Nutrition, and Metabolism*, *41*(6 (Suppl. 3), S197–S239. https://doi.org/10.1139/apnm-2015-0663

Powell, S. D. (2019). *Your introduction to education: Explorations in teaching*. Pearson. https://bookshelf.vitalsource.com/#/books/9780134737027/cfi/1!/4/4@0:0.00

Pulgarón, E. R. (2013). Childhood obesity: A review of increased risk for physical and psychological comorbidities. *Clinical Therapeutics*, *35*(1), A18–A32. https://doi.org/10.1016/j.clinthera.2012.12.014

Quek, Y.-H., Tam, W. W. S., Zhang, M. W. B., & Ho, R. C. M. (2017). Exploring the association between childhood and adolescent obesity and depression: A meta-analysis. *Obesity Reviews*, *18*(7), 742–754. https://doi.org/10.1111/obr.12535

Rabiner, D. L., Godwin, J., & Dodge, K. A. (2016). Predicting academic achievement and attainment: The contribution of early academic skills, attention difficulties, and social competence. *School Psychology Review*, *45*(2), 250–267. https://doi.org/10.17105/SPR45-2.250-267

Ramírez, P. C. (2020). Secondary dual language learners and emerging pedagogies. In C. J. Faltis & P. C. Ramírez (Eds.), *Dual language education in the US: Rethinking pedagogy, curricula, and teacher education to support dual language learning for all*. Taylor & Francis.

Ramos, D. K., & Melo, H. M. (2019). Can digital games in school improve attention? A study of Brazilian elementary school students. *Journal of Computers in Education*, *6*(1), 5–19. https://doi.org/10.1007/s40692-018-0111-3

Ramus, F. (2014). Neuroimaging sheds new light on the phonological deficit in dyslexia. *Trends in Cognitive Sciences*, *18*(6), 274–275. https://doi.org/10.1016/j.tics.2014.01.009

Rapin, I. (2016). Dyscalculia and the calculating brain. *Pediatric Neurology*, *61*, 11–20. https://doi.org/10.1016/j.pediatrneurol.2016.02.007

Reilly, J. J. (2007). Childhood obesity: An overview. *Children & Society*, *21*(5), 390–396.

Relji, G., Ferring, D., & Martin, R. (2015). A meta-analysis on the effectiveness of bilingual programs in Europe. *Review of Educational Research*, *85*(1), 92–128. https://doi.org/10.3102/0034654314548514

Richards, T. L., Grabowski, T. J., Boord, P., Yagle, K., Askren, M., Mestre, Z., Robinson, P., Welker, O., Gulliford, D., Nagy, W., & Berninger, V. (2015). Contrasting brain patterns of writing-related DTI parameters, fMRI connectivity, and DTI–fMRI connectivity correlations in children with and without dysgraphia or dyslexia. *NeuroImage: Clinical*, *8*, 408–421. https://doi.org/10.1016/J.NICL.2015.03.018

Richlan, F. (2019). The functional neuroanatomy of letter-speech sound integration and its relation to brain abnormalities in developmental dyslexia. *Frontiers in Human Neuroscience*, *13*, 21. https://doi.org/10.3389/fnhum.2019.00021

Rideout, V. J. (2015). *THE common sense census: Media use by tweens and teens 3.* https://static1.squarespace.com/static/5ba15befec4eb7899898240d/t/5ba261f24fa51a7fb2c19904/1537368577261/CSM_TeenTween_MediaCensus_FinalWebVersion_1%281%29.pdf

Rideout, V. J., & Katz, V. S. (2016). *Opportunity for all? Technology and learning in lower-income families. Joan Ganz Cooney Center at Sesame Workshop* https://eric.ed.gov/?id=ED574416

Rindermann, H., & Thompson, J. (2013). Ability rise in NAEP and narrowing ethnic gaps? *Intelligence*, *41*(6), 821–831. https://doi.org/10.1016/j.intell.2013.06.016

Ristic, J., & Enns, J. T. (2015). The changing face of attentional development. *Current Directions in Psychological Science*, *24*(1), 24–31. https://doi.org/10.1177/0963721414551165

Roberts, G., Quach, J., Spencer-Smith, M., Anderson, P. J., Gathercole, S., Gold, L., Sia, K.-L., Mensah, F., Rickards, F., Ainley, J., & Wake, M. (2016). Academic outcomes 2 years after working memory training for children with low working memory. *JAMA Pediatrics*, *170*(5), e154568. https://doi.org/10.1001/jamapediatrics.2015.4568

Robinson, T. N., Banda, J. A., Hale, L., Lu, A. S., Fleming-Milici, F., Calvert, S. L., & Wartella, E. (2017). Screen media exposure and obesity in children and adolescents. *Pediatrics*, *140*(Suppl 2), S97–S101. https://doi.org/10.1542/peds.2016-1758K

Rogoff, B. (2003). *The cultural nature of human development*. Oxford University Press.

Rogoff, B., & Chavajay, P. (1995). What's become of research on the cultural basis of cognitive development? *American Psychologist*, *50*, 859–877.

Rogoff, B., & Waddell, K. J. (1982). Memory for information organized in a scene by children from two cultures. *Child Development*, *53*(5), 1224–1228. http://www.ncbi.nlm.nih.gov/pubmed/7140428

Salend, S. J. (2015). *Creating Inclusive Classrooms: Effective, differentiated and reflective practices*. Pearson College Div.

Sato, W., & Uono, S. (2019). The atypical social brain network in autism. *Current Opinion in Neurology*, *32*(4), 617–621. https://doi.org/10.1097/WCO.0000000000000713

Sattler, J. M. (2014). *Foundations of behavioral, social and clinical assessment of children*. Jerome M. Sattler, Publisher, Incorporated.

Sauce, B., & Matzel, L. D. (2018). The paradox of intelligence: Heritability and malleability coexist in hidden gene-environment interplay. *Psychological Bulletin*, *144*(1), 26–47. https://doi.org/10.1037/bul0000131

Schachar, R. (2014). Genetics of Attention Deficit Hyperactivity Disorder (ADHD): Recent updates and future prospects. *Current Developmental Disorders Reports*, *1*(1), 41–49. https://doi.org/10.1007/s40474-013-0004-0

Schneider, W., & Bjorklund, D. F. (1992). Expertise, aptitude, and strategic remembering. *Child Development*, *63*(2), 461–473. https://doi.org/10.1111/j.1467-8624.1992.tb01640.x

Schneider, W., & Ornstein, P. A. (2015). The development of children's memory. *Child Development Perspectives*, *9*(3), 190–195. https://doi.org/10.1111/cdep.12129

Schneider, W., & Pressley, M. (2013). *Memory development between two and twenty* (3rd ed.). Erlbaum.

Schurz, M., Wimmer, H., Richlan, F., Ludersdorfer, P., Klackl, J., & Kronbichler, M. (2015). Resting-state and task-based functional brain connectivity in developmental dyslexia. *Cerebral Cortex*, *25*, 3502–3514. https://doi.org/10.1093/cercor/bhu184

Schwartz, F., Epinat-Duclos, J., Léone, J., Poisson, A., & Prado, J. (2020). Neural representations of transitive relations predict current and future math calculation skills in children. *Neuropsychologia*, *141*, 107410. https://doi.org/10.1016/j.neuropsychologia.2020.107410

Schwebel, D. C. (2019). Why "accidents" are not accidental: Using psychological science to understand and prevent unintentional child injuries. *American Psychologist*, *74*(9), 1137–1147. https://doi.org/10.1037/amp0000487

Semeraro, C., Coppola, G., Cassibba, R., & Lucangeli, D. (2019). Teaching of cursive writing in the first year of primary school: Effect on reading and writing skills. *PLoS One*, *14*(2), e0209978. https://doi.org/10.1371/journal.pone.0209978

Shayer, M., Demetriou, A., & Pervez, M. (1988). The structure and scaling of concrete operational thought: Three studies in four countries. *Genetic, Social, and General Psychology Monographs*, *114*(3), 307–375.

Shea, J. D. (1985). Studies of cognitive development in papua new guinea. *International Journal of Psychology*, *20*(1), 33–61. https://doi.org/10.1002/j.1464-066X.1985.tb00013.x

Shearer, C. B. (2020). A resting state functional connectivity analysis of human intelligence: Broad theoretical and practical implications for multiple intelligences theory. *Psychology and Neuroscience*, *13*(2), 127–148. https://doi.org/10.1037/pne0000200

Shearer, C. B., & Karanian, J. M. (2017). The neuroscience of intelligence: Empirical support for the theory of multiple intelligences? *Trends in Neuroscience and Education*, *6*, 211–223. https://doi.org/10.1016/J.TINE.2017.02.002

Simard, D., & Gutiérrez, X. (2018). The study of metalinguistic constructs in second language a cquisition research. In P. Garrett & J. M. Cots (Eds.), *The Routledge handbook of language awareness*. Routledge. https://www.routledge.com/The-Routledge-Handbook-of-Language-Awareness/Garrett-Cots/p/book/9781138937048

Simmonds, M., Llewellyn, A., Owen, C. G., & Woolacott, N. (2016). Predicting adult obesity from childhood obesity: A systematic review and meta-analysis. *Obesity Reviews*, *17*(2), 95–107. https://doi.org/10.1111/obr.12334

Slobodin, O., & Masalha, R. (2020). Challenges in ADHD care for ethnic minority children: A review of the current literature. *Transcultural Psychiatry*, *57*(3), 468–483. https://doi.org/10.1177/1363461520902885

Snowling, M. J. (2013). Early identification and interventions for dyslexia: A contemporary view. *Journal of Research in Special Educational Needs*, *13*(1), 7–14. https://doi.org/10.1111/j.1471-3802.2012.01262.x

Solity, J. E. (2020). Instructional psychology and teaching reading: Ending the reading wars. *Educational and Developmental Psychologist*, *37*(2), 123–132. https://doi.org/10.1017/edp.2020.18

Sparapani, N., Connor, C. M. D., McLean, L., Wood, T., Toste, J., & Day, S. (2018). Direct and reciprocal effects among social skills, vocabulary, and reading comprehension in first grade. *Contemporary Educational Psychology*, *53*, 159–167. https://doi.org/10.1016/j.cedpsych.2018.03.003

Spencer, S. J., Logel, C., & Davies, P. G. (2016). Stereotype threat. *Annual Review of Psychology*, *67*(1), 415–437. https://doi.org/10.1146/annurev-psych-073115-103235

Spinelli, A., Buoncristiano, M., Kovacs, V. A., Yngve, A., Spiroski, I., Obreja, G., Starc, G., Pérez, N., Rito, A. I., Kunešová, M., Sant'Angelo, V. F., Meisfjord, J., Bergh, I. H., Kelleher, C., Yardim, N., Pudule, I., Petrauskiene, A., Duleva, V., Sjöberg, A. ... Breda, J. (2019). Prevalence of severe obesity among primary school children in 21 European countries. *Obesity Facts*, *12*(2), 244–258. https://doi.org/10.1159/000500436

Steele, C. M., & Aronson, J. (1995). Stereotype threat and the intellectual test performance of African Americans. *Journal of Personality and Social Psychology*, *69*(5), 797–811. https://doi.org/10.1037/0022-3514.69.5.797

Sternberg, R. J. (1985). *Beyond IQ: A triarchic theory of human intelligence*. Cambridge University Press.

Sternberg, R. J. (2011). The theory of successful intelligence. In R. J. Sternberg & S. B. Kaufman (Eds.), *The Cambridge handbook of intelligence* (pp. 504–527). Cambridge University Press.

Sternberg, R. J. (2014). Teaching about the nature of intelligence. *Intelligence*, *42*, 176–179. https://doi.org/10.1016/j.intell.2013.08.010

Sternberg, R. J. (2018). The triarchic theory of successful intelligence. In D. P. Flanagan & E. M. McDonough (Eds.), *Contemporary intellectual assessment: Theories, tests, and issues* (pp. 174–194). Guilford. https://psycnet.apa.org/record/2018-36604-005

Sternberg, R. J. (2020). The nature of intelligence and its development in childhood. In *The Nature of Intelligence and Its Development in Childhood*. Cambridge University Press. https://doi.org/10.1017/9781108866217

Sternberg, R. J., Grigorenko, E. L., & Bundy, D. A. (2001). The predictive value of IQ. *Merrill-Palmer Quarterly*, *47*, 1–41.

Stiles, J. (2017). Principles of brain development. *Wiley Interdisciplinary Reviews: Cognitive Science*, *8*(1–2), e1402. https://doi.org/10.1002/wcs.1402

Stone, M. M., Blumberg, F. C., Blair, C., & Cancelli, A. A. (2016). The "EF" in deficiency: Examining the linkages between executive function and the utilization deficiency observed in preschoolers. *Journal of Experimental Child Psychology*, *152*, 367–375. https://doi.org/10.1016/j.jecp.2016.07.003

Tarver, J., Daley, D., & Sayal, K. (2014). Attention-deficit hyperactivity disorder (ADHD): An updated review of the essential facts. *Child: Care, Health and Development*, *40*(6), 762–774. https://doi.org/10.1111/cch.12139

Tiemeier, H., Lenroot, R. K., Greenstein, D. K., Tran, L., Pierson, R., & Giedd, J. N. (2010). Cerebellum development during childhood and adolescence: A longitudinal morphometric MRI study. *NeuroImage*, *49*(1), 63–70. https://doi.org/10.1016/j.neuroimage.2009.08.016

Tistarelli, N., Fagnani, C., Troianiello, M., Stazi, M. A., & Adriani, W. (2020). The nature and nurture of ADHD and its comorbidities: A narrative review on twin studies. *Neuroscience and Biobehavioral Reviews*, *109*, 63–77. https://doi.org/10.1016/j.neubiorev.2019.12.017

Tsujimoto, S., Kuwajima, M., & Sawaguchi, T. (2007). Developmental fractionation of working memory and response inhibition during childhood. *Experimental Psychology*, *54*(1), 30–37.

Turnbull, K., & Justice, L. M. (2016). *Language development from theory to practice*. Pearson.

Turunen, T., Kiuru, N., Poskiparta, E., Niemi, P., & Nurmi, J.-E. (2019). Word reading skills and externalizing and internalizing problems from grade 1 to grade 2—Developmental trajectories and bullying involvement in grade 3. *Scientific Studies of Reading*, *23*(2), 161–177. https://doi.org/10.1080/10888438.2018.1497036

Ullman, H., Almeida, R., & Klingberg, T. (2014). Structural maturation and brain activity predict future working memory capacity during childhood development. *Journal of Neuroscience*, *34*(5), 1592–1598. https://doi.org/10.1523/jneur0sci.0842-13.2014

U.S. Department of Health and Human Services. (2018). *The physical activity guidelines for Americans* (2nd ed.). https://doi.org/10.1001/jama.2018.14854

van der Niet, A. G., Smith, J., Scherder, E. J. A., Oosterlaan, J., Hartman, E., & Visscher, C. (2015). Associations between daily physical activity and executive functioning in primary school-aged children. *Journal of Science and Medicine in Sport*, *18*(6), 673–677. https://doi.org/10.1016/j.jsams.2014.09.006

Van de Vijver, F., Weiss, L., & Saklofske, D. (2019). Cross cultural issues in children's intelligence: An international perspective. L. Weiss, D. Saklofske, J. Holdnack, & A. Prifitera (Eds.), *WISC_V clinical use and interpretation*, Academic Press. 2nd https://www.elsevier.com/books/wisc-v/weiss/978-0-12-815744-2

Vanbinst, K., van Bergen, E., Ghesquière, P., & De Smedt, B. (2020). Cross-domain associations of key cognitive correlates of early reading and early arithmetic in 5-year-olds. *Early Childhood Research Quarterly*, *51*, 144–152. https://doi.org/10.1016/j.ecresq.2019.10.009

Visser, S. N., Danielson, M. L., Bitsko, R. H., Holbrook, J. R., Kogan, M. D., Ghandour, R. M., Perou, R., & Blumberg, S. J. (2014). Trends in the parent-report of health care provider-diagnosed and medicated attention-deficit/hyperactivity disorder: United States, 2003-2011. *Journal of the American Academy of Child and Adolescent Psychiatry*, *53*(1), 34–46.e2. https://doi.org/10.1016/j.jaac.2013.09.001

Voorhies, W., Dajani, D. R., Vij, S. G., Shankar, S., Turan, T. O., & Uddin, L. Q. (2018). Aberrant functional connectivity of inhibitory control networks in children with autism spectrum disorder. *Autism Research*, *11*(11), 1468–1478. https://doi.org/10.1002/aur.2014

Wang, C., Geng, H., Liu, W., & Zhang, G. (2017a). Prenatal, perinatal, and postnatal factors associated with autism: A meta-analysis. *Medicine (United States)*, *96*(18), e6696. https://doi.org/10.1097/MD.0000000000006696

Wang, Y., Zhang, Y., Liu, L., Cui, J., Wang, J., Shum, D. H. K., van, Amelsvoort T., & Chan, R. C. K. (2017b). A meta-analysis of working memory impairments in autism spectrum disorders. *Neuropsychology Review*, *27*(1), 46–61. https://doi.org/10.1007/s11065-016-9336-y

Wasik, B. A., Hindman, A. H., & Snell, E. K. (2016). Book reading and vocabulary development: A systematic review. *Early Childhood Research Quarterly*, *37*, 39–57. https://doi.org/10.1016/j.ecresq.2016.04.003

Wasserberg, M. J. (2014). Stereotype threat effects on African American children in an urban elementary school. *Journal of Experimental Education*, *82*(4), 502–517. https://doi.org/10.1080/00220973.2013.876224

Waterhouse, L. (2006). Multiple intelligences, the mozart effect, and emotional intelligence: A critical review. *Educational Psychologist*, *41*(4), 207–225. https://doi.org/10.1207/s15326985ep4104_1

Wechsler, D. (1944). *The measurement of adult intelligence* (3rd ed.). Williams & Wilkins.

Wechsler, D. (2014a). *Wechsler intelligence scale for children* (5th ed.). Bloomington, MN: NCS Pearson.

Wechsler, D.. (2014b). Toronto, ON: Pearson. Retrieved from https://www.pearsonclinical.ca/en/products/product-master/item-84.html

Wenger, Y. (2018). *Baltimore tries to close digital divide with free tablets, internet*. Government Technology. https://www.govtech.com/network/Baltimore-Tries-to-Close-Digital-Divide-with-Free-Tablets-Internet.html

Westrupp, E. M., Reilly, S., McKean, C., Law, J., Mensah, F., & Nicholson, J. M. (2020). Vocabulary development and trajectories of behavioral and emotional difficulties via academic ability and peer problems. *Child Development*, *91*(2), e365–e382. https://doi.org/10.1111/cdev.13219

Wigfield, A., & Eccles, J. S. (2020). 35 years of research on students' subjective task values and motivation: A look back and a look forward. *Advances in Motivation Science*, *7*, 161–198. https://doi.org/10.1016/bs.adms.2019.05.002

Wigfield, A., Gladstone, J. R., & Turci, L. (2016). Beyond cognition: Reading motivation and reading comprehension. *Child Development Perspectives*, *10*(3), 190–195. https://doi.org/10.1111/cdep.12184

World Health Organization. (2009). *BMI classification.* http://apps.who.int/bmi/index.jsp?introPage=intro_3.html

Wright, A. J. (2020). Equivalence of remote, digital administration and traditional, in-person administration of the wechsler intelligence scale for children, fifth edition (WISC-V). *Psychological Assessment*, *32*(9), 809–817. https://doi.org/10.1037/pas0000939

Wright, B. C., & Smailes, J. (2015). Factors and processes in children's transitive deductions. *Journal of Cognitive Psychology*, *27*(8), 967–978. https://doi.org/10.1080/20445911.2015.1063641

Xu, J., Hardy, L. L., Guo, C. Z., & Garnett, S. P. (2018). The trends and prevalence of obesity and morbid obesity among Australian school-aged children, 1985-2014. *Journal of Paediatrics and Child Health*, *54*(8), 907–912. https://doi.org/10.1111/jpc.13922

Xu, J., Murphy, S. L., Kochanek, K. D., & Bastian, B. A. (2016). *Deaths: Final data for 2013. National Vital and Statistics Reports,1, 64*(2). http://www.cdc.gov/nchs/data/nvsr/nvsr64/nvsr64_02.pdf

Yuma-Guerrero, P., Orsi, R., Lee, P.-T., & Cubbin, C. (2018). A systematic review of socioeconomic status measurement in 13 years of U.S. injury research. *Journal of Safety Research*, *64*, 55–72. https://doi.org/10.1016/J.JSR.2017.12.017

Zablotsky, B., & Black, L. I. (2020). *Prevalence of children aged 3-17 years with developmental disabilities, by urbanicity: United States, 2015-2018. National Health Statistics Reports. 139* https://www.cdc.gov/nchs/products/index.htm.

Zablotsky, B., Black, L. I., Maenner, M. J., Schieve, L. A., Danielson, M. L., Bitsko, R. H., Blumberg, S. J., Kogan, M. D., & Boyle, C. A. (2019). Prevalence and trends of developmental disabilities among children in the United States: 2009–2017. *Pediatrics*, *144*(4), e20190811. https://doi.org/10.1542/peds.2019-0811

Zablotsky, B., Bramlett, M. D., & Blumberg, S. J. (2020). The co-occurrence of autism spectrum disorder in children with ADHD. *Journal of Attention Disorders*, *24*(1), 94–103. https://doi.org/10.1177/1087054717713638

Zagel, A. L., Cutler, G. J., Linabery, A. M., Spaulding, A. B., & Kharbanda, A. B. (2019). Unintentional injuries in primary and secondary schools in the United States, 2001-2013. *Journal of School Health*, *89*(1), 38–47. https://doi.org/10.1111/josh.12711

Zhang, F., & Roeyers, H. (2019). Exploring brain functions in autism spectrum disorder: A systematic review on functional near-infrared spectroscopy (fNIRS) studies. *International Journal of Psychophysiology*, *137*, 41–53. https://doi.org/10.1016/j.ijpsycho.2019.01.003

CHAPTER 8

Afifi, T. O., & MacMillan, H. L. (2011). Resilience Following Child Maltreatment: A Review of Protective Factors. *La Résilience Aprés La Maltraitance Clans l'enfance :. Une Revue Des Facteurs Protecteurs*, *56*(5), 266–272.

Alaggia, R., Collin-Vézina, D., & Lateef, R. (2018). Facilitators and Barriers to Child Sexual Abuse (CSA) Disclosures. *Trauma, Violence, & Abuse*, *20*(2), 152483801769731. https://doi.org/10.1177/1524838017697312

Amato, P. R. (2010). Research on Divorce: Continuing Trends and New Developments. *Journal of Marriage & Family*, *72*(3), 650–666. https://doi.org/10.1111/j.1741-3737.2010.00723.x

Amato, P. R., & Anthony, C. J. (2014). Estimating the Effects of Parental Divorce and Death With Fixed Effects Models. *Journal of Marriage and Family*, *76*(2), 370–386. https://doi.org/10.1111/jomf.12100

Archer, L., DeWitt, J., Osborne, J., Dillon, J., Willis, B., & Wong, B. (2012). Science Aspirations, Capital, and Family Habitus: How Families Shape Children's Engagement and Identification With Science. *American Educational Research Journal*, *49*(5), 881–908. https://doi.org/10.3102/0002831211433290

Arditti, J. A., & Johnson, E. I. (2020). A family resilience agenda for understanding and responding to parental incarceration. *American Psychologist*. https://doi.org/10.1037/amp0000687

Arseneault, L. (2018). Annual Research Review: The persistent and pervasive impact of being bullied in childhood and adolescence: implications for policy and practice. *Journal of Child Psychology and Psychiatry*, *59*(4), 405–421. https://doi.org/10.1111/jcpp.12841

Asher, S. R., & Weeks, M. S. (2018). Friendships in Childhood. In A. L. Vangelisti & D. Perlman (Eds.), *The Cambridge Handbook of Personal Relationships* (pp. 119–134). Cambridge University Press. https://doi.org/10.1017/9781316417867.011

Assink, M., van der Put, C. E., Meeuwsen, M. W. C. M., de Jong, N. M., Oort, F. J., Stams, G. J. J. M., & Hoeve, M. (2019). Risk factors for child sexual abuse victimization: A meta-analytic review. *Psychological Bulletin, 145*(5), 459–489. https://doi.org/10.1037/bul0000188

Association of Child Life Professionals. (2021). https://www.childlife.org/

Bagwell, C. L. (2020). Friendship in Childhood. In *The Encyclopedia of Child and Adolescent Development* (pp. 1–14). Wiley. https://doi.org/10.1002/9781119171492.wecad278

Bagwell, C. L., & Bukowski, W. M. (2018). Friendship in childhood and adolescence: Features, effects, and processes. W. M. Bukowski, B. Laursen, & K. H. Rubin (Eds.), *Handbook of peer interactions, relationships, and groups*, 371–390. Guilford Press https://psycnet.apa.org/record/2018-00748-019

Baker, E. R., Tisak, M. S., & Tisak, J. (2016). What can boys and girls do? Preschoolers' perspectives regarding gender roles across domains of behavior. *Social Psychology of Education, 19*(1), 23–39. https://doi.org/10.1007/s11218-015-9320-z

Banneyer, K. N., Koenig, S. A., Wang, L. A., & Stark, K. D. (2017). A review of the effects of parental PTSD: A focus on military children. *Couple and Family Psychology: Research and Practice, 6*(4), 274–286. https://doi.org/10.1037/cfp0000093

Banse, R., Gawronski, B., Rebetez, C., Gutt, H., & Bruce Morton, J. (2010). The development of spontaneous gender stereotyping in childhood: relations to stereotype knowledge and stereotype flexibility. *Developmental Science, 13*(2), 298–306. https://doi.org/10.1111/j.1467-7687.2009.00880.x

Bastaits, K., & Mortelmans, D. (2016). Parenting as Mediator Between Post-divorce Family Structure and Children's Well-being. *Journal of Child and Family Studies, 25*(7), 2178–2188. https://doi.org/10.1007/s10826-016-0395-8

Berger, L. M., Cancian, M., Cuesta, L., & Noyes, J. L. (2016). Families at the Intersection of the Criminal Justice and Child Protective Services Systems. *The ANNALS of the American Academy of Political and Social Science, 665*(1), 171–194. https://doi.org/10.1177/0002716216633058

Bierman, K. L., Kalvin, C. B., & Heinrichs, B. S. (2014). Early Childhood Precursors and Adolescent Sequelae of Grade School Peer Rejection and Victimization. *Journal of Clinical Child and Adolescent Psychology, 44*(3), 367–379. https://doi.org/10.1080/15374416.2013.873983

Bing, N. M., Nelson, W. M., & Wesolowski, K. L. (2009). Comparing the Effects of Amount of Conflict on Children's Adjustment Following Parental Divorce. *Journal of Divorce & Remarriage, 50*(3), 159–171. 10.1080/10502550902717699

Birditt, K. S., & Fingerman, K. L. (2003). Age and Gender Differences in Adults' Descriptions of Emotional Reactions to Interpersonal Problems. *The Journals of Gerontology Series B: Psychological Sciences and Social Sciences, 58*(4), 237–P245. https://doi.org/10.1093/geronb/58.4.P237

Blakemore, J. E. O. (2003). Children's Beliefs About Violating Gender Norms: Boys Shouldn't Look Like Girls, and Girls Shouldn't Act Like Boys. *Sex Roles, 48*(9/10), 411–419. https://doi.org/10.1023/A:1023574427720

Blakemore, J. E. O., Berenbaum, S. A., & Liben, L. S. (2009). Gender development. *Gender Development.*

Blandon, A. Y., Calkins, S. D., Grimm, K. J., Keane, S. P., & O'Brien, M. (2010). Testing a developmental cascade model of emotional and social competence and early peer acceptance. *Development and Psychopathology, 22*(4), 737–748. https://doi.org/10.1017/S0954579410000428

Bos, H., & Gartrell, N. (2020). Lesbian-mother families formed through donor insemination. In A. E.. Goldberg & K. R.. Allen (Eds.), *LGBTQ-Parent Families: Innovations in Research and Implications for Practice* (pp. 25–44). Springer International Publishing. https://doi.org/10.1007/978-3-030-35610-1_2

Bos, H. M. W., Knox, J. R., van Rijn-van Gelderen, L., & Gartrell, N. K. (2016). Same-Sex and Different-Sex Parent Households and Child Health Outcomes. *Journal of Developmental & Behavioral Pediatrics, 37*(3), 179–187. https://doi.org/10.1097/DBP.0000000000000288

Boseovski, J. J. (2010). Evidence for "rose-colored glasses": An examination of the positivity bias in young children's personality judgments. *Child Development Perspectives, 4*(3), 212–218. https://doi.org/10.1111/j.1750-8606.2010.00149.x

Boutwell, B. B., Meldrum, R. C., & Petkovsek, M. A. (2017). General intelligence in friendship selection: A study of preadolescent best friend dyads. *Intelligence, 64*, 30–35. https://doi.org/10.1016/J.INTELL.2017.07.002

Bradley, R. H., & Corwyn, R. F. (2008). Infant temperament, parenting, and externalizing behavior in first grade: a test of the differential susceptibility hypothesis. *Journal of Child Psychology & Psychiatry, 49*(2), 124–131. 10.1111/j.1469-7610.2007.01829.x

Bradley, R. H., Iida, M., Pennar, A., Owen, M. T., & Vandell, D. L. (2017). The dialectics of parenting: Changes in the interplay of maternal behaviors during early and middle childhood. *Journal of Child and Family Studies, 26*(11), 3214–3225. https://doi.org/10.1007/s10826-017-0805-6

Brassard, M. R., & Fiorvanti, C. M. (2015). School-based child abuse prevention programs. *Psychology in the Schools, 52*(1), 40–60. https://doi.org/10.1002/pits.21811

Bratberg, E., & Tjøtta, S. (2008). Income effects of divorce in families with dependent children. *Journal of Population Economics, 21*(2), 439–461. 10.1007/s00148-005-0029-8

Brodie, N., Keim, J. L., Silberholz, E. A., Spector, N. D., & Pattishall, A. E. (2019). Promoting resilience in vulnerable populations. *Current Opinion in Pediatrics, 31*(1), 157–165. https://doi.org/10.1097/MOP.0000000000000722

Brown, S. L., Manning, W. D., & Stykes, J. B. (2015). Family Structure and Child Well-Being: Integrating Family Complexity. *Journal of Marriage and the Family, 77*(1), 177–190. https://doi.org/10.1111/jomf.12145

Brumariu, L. E. (2015). Parent-Child Attachment and Emotion Regulation. *New Directions for Child and Adolescent Development, 2015*(148), 31–45. https://doi.org/10.1002/cad.20098

Brumariu, L. E., Giuseppone, K. R., Kerns, K. A., Van de Walle, M., Bureau, J. F., Bosmans, G., & Lyons-Ruth, K. (2018). Middle Childhood Attachment Strategies: validation of an observational measure. *Attachment and Human Development, 20*(5), 491–513. https://doi.org/10.1080/14616734.2018.1433696

Brummelman, E.. (2017). The emergence of narcissism and self-esteem: A social-cognitive approach. *European Journal of Developmental Psychology, 15*(6), 756–767. http://dx.doi.org/10.1080/17405629.2017.1419953

Brummelman, E., & Sedikides, C. (2020). Raising Children With High Self-Esteem (But Not Narcissism). *Child Development Perspectives*, *14*(2), 83–89. https://doi.org/10.1111/cdep.12362

Bruns, A., & Lee, H. (2019). Racial/ethnic disparities. In J. Mark Eddy & J. Poehlmann-Tynan (Eds.), *Handbook on Children with Incarcerated Parents: Research, Policy, and Practice* (pp. 37–52). Springer International Publishing. https://doi.org/10.1007/978-3-030-16707-3_4

Bussey, K. (2013). Gender Development. In M. K. Ryan & N. R. Branscombe (Eds.), *The SAGE Handbook of Gender and Psychology* (pp. 81–100). SAGE.

Cancian, M., & Meyer, D. R. (2018). Reforming policy for single-parent families to reduce child poverty. *Russell Sage Foundation Journal of the Social Sciences*, *4*(2), 91–112. https://doi.org/10.7758/rsf.2018.4.2.05

Carver, P. R., Yunger, J. L., & Perry, D. G. (2003). Gender identity and adjustment in middle childhood. *Sex Roles*, *49*(3–4), 95–109. https://doi.org/10.1023/A:1024423012063

Cavanagh, S. E., & Fomby, P. (2019). Family Instability in the Lives of American Children. In *Annual Review of Sociology*, *45*(1), 493–513. https://doi.org/10.1146/annurev-soc-073018-022633

Ceci, S. J., Ginther, D. K., Kahn, S., & Williams, W. M. (2014). Women in Academic Science. *Psychological Science in the Public Interest*, *15*(3), 75–141. https://doi.org/10.1177/1529100614541236

Chaplin, T. M. (2015). Gender and Emotion Expression: A Developmental Contextual Perspective. *Emotion Review*, *7*(1), 14–21. https://doi.org/10.1177/1754073914544408

Child Trends. (2013). *Measures of Flourishing*. http://www.childtrends.org/?indicators=measures-of-flourishing#sthash.ODuubJhm.dpuf

Cicchetti, D. (2016). Socioemotional, Personality, and Biological Development: Illustrations from a Multilevel Developmental Psychopathology Perspective on Child Maltreatment. *Annual Review of Psychology*, *67*(1), 187–211. https://doi.org/10.1146/annurev-psych-122414-033259

Cimpian, J. R., Lubienski, S. T., Timmer, J. D., Makowski, M. B., & Miller, E. K. (2016). Have Gender Gaps in Math Closed? Achievement, Teacher Perceptions, and Learning Behaviors Across Two ECLS-K Cohorts. *AERA Open*, *2*(4), 233285841667361. https://doi.org/10.1177/2332858416673617

Cooley, J. L., Blossom, J. B., Tampke, E. C., & Fite, P. J. (2020). Emotion Regulation Attenuates the Prospective Links from Peer Victimization to Internalizing Symptoms during Middle Childhood. *Journal of Clinical Child and Adolescent Psychology*. https://doi.org/10.1080/15374416.2020.1731819

Cooley, J. L., & Fite, P. J. (2016). Peer Victimization and Forms of Aggression During Middle Childhood: The Role of Emotion Regulation. *Journal of Abnormal Child Psychology*, *44*(3), 535–546. https://doi.org/10.1007/s10802-015-0051-6

Cooper, P. J., Pauletti, R. E., Tobin, D. D., Menon, M., Menon, M., Spatta, B. C., Hodges, E. V. E., & Perry, D. G. (2013). Mother-Child Attachment and Gender Identity in Preadolescence. *Sex Roles*, *69*(11–12), 618–631. https://doi.org/10.1007/s11199-013-0310-3

Copen, C. E., Daniels, K., Vespa, J., & Mosher, W. D. (2012). First Marriages in the United States: Data From the 2006–2010 National Survey of Family Growth. *National Health Statistics Reports*, *49*(49), 1–21. http://www.ncbi.nlm.nih.gov/pubmed/22803221

Coplan, R. J., Rose-Krasnor, L., Weeks, M., Kingsbury, A., Kingsbury, M., & Bullock, A. (2013). Alone is a crowd: Social motivations, social withdrawal, and socioemotional functioning in later childhood. *Developmental Psychology*, *49*(5), 861–875.

Corby, B. C., Hodges, E. V. E., & Perry, D. G. (2007). Gender identity and adjustment in Black, Hispanic, and White preadolescents. *Developmental Psychology*, *43*(1), 261–266. https://doi.org/10.1037/0012-1649.43.1.261

Cortés-García, L., Wichstrøm, L., Viddal, K. R., & Senra, C. (2019). Prospective Bidirectional Associations between Attachment and Depressive Symptoms from Middle Childhood to Adolescence. *Journal of Youth and Adolescence*, *48*(11), 2099–2113. https://doi.org/10.1007/s10964-019-01081-4

Cramm, H., Mccoll, M. A., Aiken, A. B., & Williams, A. (2019). The Mental Health of Military-Connected Children: A Scoping Review. *Journal of Child and Family Studies*, *28*, 1725–1735. https://doi.org/10.1007/s10826-019-01402-y

Creech, S. K., Hadley, W., & Borsari, B. (2014). The impact of military deployment and reintegration on children and parenting: A systematic review. *Professional Psychology: Research and Practice*, *45*(6), 452–463. https://doi.org/10.1037/a0035055

Cunitz, K., Dölitzsch, C., Kösters, M., Willmund, G. D., Zimmermann, P., Bühler, A. H., Fegert, J. M., Ziegenhain, U., & Kölch, M. (2019). Parental military deployment as risk factor for children's mental health: A meta-analytical review. *Child and Adolescent Psychiatry and Mental Health*, *13*(1), 1–10. https://doi.org/10.1186/s13034-019-0287-y

Cutuli, J. J., Ahumada, S. M., Herbers, J. E., Lafavor, T. L., Masten, A. S., & Oberg, C. N. (2017). Adversity and children experiencing family homelessness: implications for health. *Journal of Children and Poverty*, *23*(1), 41–55. https://doi.org/10.1080/10796126.2016.1198753

Cutuli, J. J., Herbers, J. E., Masten, A. S., & Reed, M. G. J. (2021). Resilience in Development. In C. R. Snyder, S. J. Lopez, L. M. Edwards, & S. C. Marques (Eds.), *The Oxford Handbook of Positive Psychology*. Oxford.

Cvencek, D., Meltzoff, A. N., & Greenwald, A. G. (2011). Math-Gender Stereotypes in Elementary School Children. *Child Development*, *82*(3), 766–779. https://doi.org/10.1111/j.1467-8624.2010.01529.x

Dahl, A. (2018). New Beginnings: An Interactionist and Constructivist Approach to Early Moral Development. *Human Development*, *61*(4–5), 232–247. https://doi.org/10.1159/000492801

Dahl, A. (2019). The science of early moral development: On defining, constructing, and studying morality from birth. *Advances in Child Development and Behavior*, *56*, 1–35. https://doi.org/10.1016/bs.acdb.2018.11.001

Damaske, S., Bratter, J. L., & Frech, A. (2017). Single mother families and employment, race, and poverty in changing economic times. *Social Science Research*, *62*, 120–133. https://doi.org/10.1016/j.ssresearch.2016.08.008

Damon, W. (1977). *The social world of the child*. Jossey-Bass.

Damon, W. (1988). *The moral child*. Free Press.

Danovitch, J., & Bloom, P. (2009). Children's extension of disgust to physical and moral events. *Emotion (Washington, D.C.)*, *9*(1), 107–112. https://doi.org/10.1037/a0014113

Dasgupta, N., & Stout, J. G. (2014). Girls and Women in Science, Technology, Engineering, and Mathematics. *Policy Insights from the Behavioral and Brain Sciences*, *1*(1), 21–29. https://doi.org/10.1177/2372732214549471

Davidson, R. D., O'Hara, K. L., & Beck, C. J. A. (2014). Psychological and Biological Processes in Children Associated with High Conflict Parental Divorce. *Juvenile and Family Court Journal*, *65*(1), 29–44. https://doi.org/10.1111/jfcj.12015

Davies, P., & Martin, M. (2014). Children's Coping and Adjustment in High-Conflict Homes: The Reformulation of Emotional Security Theory. *Child Development Perspectives*, *8*(4), 242–249. https://doi.org/10.1111/cdep.12094

Davis-Kean, P. E., Jager, J., & Andrew Collins, W. (2009). The Self in Action: An Emerging Link Between Self-Beliefs and Behaviors in Middle Childhood. *Child Development Perspectives*, *3*(3), 184–188. https://doi.org/10.1111/j.1750-8606.2009.00104.x

de Haan, B., Mienko, J. A., & Eddy, J. M. (2019). The interface of child welfare and parental criminal justice involvement: Policy and practice implications for the children of incarcerated parents. In J. Mark Eddy & Poehlmann-Tynan. Julie (Eds.), *Handbook on Children with Incarcerated Parents: Research, Policy, and Practice* (pp. 279–294). Springer International Publishing. https://doi.org/10.1007/978-3-030-16707-3_19

Dempsey, J., McQuillin, S., Butler, A. M., & Axelrad, M. E. (2016). Maternal Depression and Parent Management Training Outcomes. *Journal of Clinical Psychology in Medical Settings*, *23*(3), 240–246. https://doi.org/10.1007/s10880-016-9461-z

Denissen, J. J. A., Zarrett, N. R., & Eccles, J. S. (2007). I Like to Do It, I'm Able, and I Know I Am: Longitudinal Couplings Between Domain-Specific Achievement, Self-Concept, and Interest. *Child Development*, *78*(2), 430–447.

Department of Defense. (2020). *ACTIVE DUTY FAMILIES Active Duty Spouses Active Duty Children*. https://download.militaryonesource.mil/12038/MOS/Reports/2019-demographics-report.pdf

DeVries, R., & Zan, B. (2003). When Children Make Rules. *Educational Leadership*, *61*(1), 64–67.

Domhardt, M., Münzer, A., Fegert, J. M., & Goldbeck, L. (2015). Resilience in Survivors of Child Sexual Abuse: A Systematic Review of the Literature. *Trauma, Violence & Abuse*, *16*(4), 476–493. https://doi.org/10.1177/1524838014557288

Doodson, L., & Morley, D. (2006). Understanding the Roles of Non-Residential Stepmothers. *Journal of Divorce & Remarriage*, *45*(3/4), 109–130. 10.1300/J087v45n03-06

Drapeau, S., Gagne, M.-H., Saint-Jacques, M.-C., Lepine, R., & Ivers, H. (2009). Post-Separation Conflict Trajectories: A Longitudinal Study. *Marriage & Family Review*, *45*(4), 353–373. 10.1080/01494920902821529

Duffy, A. L., Gardner, A. A., & J, Zimmer-Gembeck, M. (2020). Peer Rejection and Dislike. In Hupp. Stephen & D. Jewell. Jeremy (Eds.), *The Encyclopedia of Child and Adolescent Development* (pp. 1–13). Wiley. https://doi.org/10.1002/9781119171492.wecad191

Dweck, C. S. (2017). The Journey to Children's Mindsets-and Beyond. *Child Development Perspectives*, *11*(2), 139–144. https://doi.org/10.1111/cdep.12225

Dweck, C. S., & Yeager, D. S. (2019). Mindsets: A View From Two Eras. *Perspectives on Psychological Science*, *14*(3), 481–496. https://doi.org/10.1177/1745691618804166

Eccles, J. S., & Wang, M.-T. (2016). What motivates females and males to pursue careers in mathematics and science? *International Journal of Behavioral Development*, *40*(2), 100–106. https://doi.org/10.1177/0165025415616201

Egan, S. K., & Perry, D. G. (2001). Gender identity: A multidimensional analysis with implications for psychosocial adjustment. *Developmental Psychology*, *37*(4), 451–463. https://doi.org/10.1037/0012-1649.37.4.451

Ellemers, N. (2018). Gender Stereotypes. *Annual Review of Psychology*, *69*(1), 275–298. https://doi.org/10.1146/annurev-psych-122216-011719

Ellis, B. J., Bianchi, J., Griskevicius, V., & Frankenhuis, W. E. (2017). Beyond Risk and Protective Factors: An Adaptation-Based Approach to Resilience. *Perspectives on Psychological Science*, *12*(4), 561–587. https://doi.org/10.1177/1745691617693054

Erdley, C. A., & Day, H. J. (2017). Friendship in childhood and adolescence. In M. Hojjat & A. Moyer (Eds.), *The psychology of friendship* (pp. 3–19). Oxford Univ Press.

Erikson, E. H. (1950). *Childhood and society* (2nd ed.). Norton.

Espelage, D. L., Low, S. K., & Jimerson, S. R. (2014). Understanding school climate, aggression, peer victimization, and bully perpetration: Contemporary science, practice, and policy. *School Psychology Quarterly*, *29*(3), 233–237.

Ettekal, I., & Ladd, G. W. (2015). Developmental Pathways From Childhood Aggression-Disruptiveness, Chronic Peer Rejection, and Deviant Friendships to Early-Adolescent Rule Breaking. *Child Development*, *86*(2), 614–631. https://doi.org/10.1111/cdev.12321

Evans, G. W., Li, D., & Whipple, S. S. (2013). Cumulative risk and child development. *Psychological Bulletin*, *139*(6), 1342–1396. https://doi.org/10.1037/a0031808

Evans-Lacko, S., Takizawa, R., Brimblecombe, N., King, D., Knapp, M., Maughan, B., & Arseneault, L. (2017). Childhood bullying victimization is associated with use of mental health services over five decades: a longitudinal nationally representative cohort study. *Psychological Medicine*, *47*(01), 127–135. https://doi.org/10.1017/S0033291716001719

Falbo, T., Poston, D. L., Jr., Triscari, R. S., & Zhang, X. (1997). Self-enhancing illusions among Chinese schoolchildren. *Journal of Cross-Cultural Psychology*, *28*, 172–191.

Farr, R. H. (2017). Does parental sexual orientation matter? A longitudinal follow-up of adoptive families with school-age children. *Developmental Psychology*, *53*(2), 252–264. https://doi.org/10.1037/dev0000228

Farr, R. H., Bruun, S. T., & Patterson, C. J. (2019). Longitudinal Associations Between Coparenting and Child Adjustment Among Lesbian, Gay, and Heterosexual Adoptive Parent Families. *Developmental Psychology*, *55*(12), 2547–2560. https://doi.org/10.1037/dev0000828

Farver, J. A. M., Xu, Y., Eppe, S., Fernandez, A., & Schwartz, D. (2005). Community Violence, Family Conflict, and Preschoolers' Socioemotional Functioning. *Developmental Psychology*, *41*, 160–170.

Fedewa, A. L., Black, W. W., & Ahn, S. (2014). Children and Adolescents With Same-Gender Parents: A Meta-Analytic Approach in Assessing Outcomes. *Journal of GLBT Family Studies*, *11*(1), 1–34. https://doi.org/10.1080/1550428X.2013.869486

Fink, E., Patalay, P., Sharpe, H., & Wolpert, M. (2018). Child- and school-level predictors of children's bullying behavior: A multilevel analysis in 648 primary schools. *Journal of Educational Psychology, 110*(1), 17–26. https://doi.org/10.1037/edu0000204

Finkelhor, D., Ormrod, R. K., & Turner, H. A. (2009). The Developmental Epidemiology of Childhood Victimization. *Journal of Interpersonal Violence, 24*(5), 711–731.

Finkelhor, D., Shattuck, A., Turner, H. A., & Hamby, S. L. (2014). The lifetime prevalence of child sexual abuse and sexual assault assessed in late adolescence. *The Journal of Adolescent Health: Official Publication of the Society for Adolescent Medicine, 55*(3), 329–333. https://doi.org/10.1016/j.jadohealth.2013.12.026

Fite, P. J., Hendrickson, M., Rubens, S. L., Gabrielli, J., & Evans, S. (2013). The Role of Peer Rejection in the Link between Reactive Aggression and Academic Performance. *Child & Youth Care Forum, 42*(3), 193–205. https://doi.org/10.1007/s10566-013-9199-9

Foran, H. M., Eckford, R. D., Sinclair, R. R., & Wright, K. M. (2017). Child Mental Health Symptoms Following Parental Deployment: The Impact of Parental Posttraumatic Stress Disorder Symptoms, Marital Distress, and General Aggression. *SAGE Open, 7*(3), 215824401772048. https://doi.org/10.1177/2158244017720484

Fryda, C. M., & Hulme, P. A. (2015). School-Based Childhood Sexual Abuse Prevention Programs: An Integrative Review. *The Journal of School Nursing: The Official Publication of the National Association of School Nurses, 31*(3), 167–182. https://doi.org/10.1177/1059840514544125

Gagnier, C., & Collin-Vézina, D. (2016). The Disclosure Experiences of Male Child Sexual Abuse Survivors. *Journal of Child Sexual Abuse, 25*(2), 221–241. https://doi.org/10.1080/10538712.2016.1124308

Ganong, L., & Coleman, M. (2017). Siblings, Half-Siblings, and Stepsiblings. In *Stepfamily Relationships* (pp. 191–204). Springer US. https://doi.org/10.1007/978-1-4899-7702-1_10

Ganong, L.., Coleman, M.., & Russell, L. T.. (2015). Children in Diverse Families. 1–42. doi:10.1002/9781118963418.childpsy404

Gates, G. J. (2015). Marriage and Family: LGBT Individuals and Same-Sex Couples. *The Future of Children, 25*(2), 67–87. https://doi.org/10.1353/foc.2015.0013

Giff, S. T., Renshaw, K. D., & Allen, E. S. (2019). Post-deployment parenting in military couples: Associations with service members' PTSD symptoms. *Journal of Family Psychology, 33*(2), 166–175. https://doi.org/10.1037/fam0000477

Golombok, S. (2017). Parenting in new family forms. *Current Opinion in Psychology, 15*, 76–80. https://doi.org/10.1016/j.copsyc.2017.02.004

Golombok, S., Blake, L., Slutsky, J., Raffanello, E., Roman, G. D., & Ehrhardt, A. (2018). Parenting and the Adjustment of Children Born to Gay Fathers Through Surrogacy. *Child Development, 89*, 1223–1233. https://doi.org/10.1111/cdev.12728

Golombok, S., & Tasker, F. (2015). Socioemotional Development in Changing Families. In M. E.. Lamb (Ed.), *Handbook of Child Psychology and Developmental Science* (pp. 1–45). John Wiley & Sons, Inc. https://doi.org/10.1002/9781118963418.childpsy311

Gómez-Ortiz, O., Romera, E. M., & Ortega-Ruiz, R. (2016). Parenting styles and bullying. The mediating role of parental psychological aggression and physical punishment. *Child Abuse & Neglect, 51*, 132–143. https://doi.org/10.1016/j.chiabu.2015.10.025

Graham, S., Munniksma, A., & Juvonen, J. (2014). Psychosocial Benefits of Cross-Ethnic Friendships in Urban Middle Schools. *Child Development, 85*(2), 469–483. https://doi.org/10.1111/cdev.12159

Grassetti, S. N., Hubbard, J. A., Docimo, M. A., Bookhout, M. K., Swift, L. E., & Gawrysiak, M. J. (2020). Parental advice to preadolescent bystanders about how to intervene during bullying differs by form of bullying. *Social Development, 29*(1), 290–302. https://doi.org/10.1111/sode.12397

Grassetti, S. N., Hubbard, J. A., Smith, M. A., Bookhout, M. K., Swift, L. E., & Gawrysiak, M. J. (2018). Caregivers' Advice and Children's Bystander Behaviors During Bullying Incidents. *Journal of Clinical Child & Adolescent Psychology*, 1–12. https://doi.org/10.1080/15374416.2017.1295381

Guo, M., O'Connor Duffany, K., Shebl, F. M., Santilli, A., & Keene, D. E. (2018). The Effects of Length of Residence and Exposure to Violence on Perceptions of Neighborhood Safety in an Urban Sample. *Journal of Urban Health, 95*(2), 245–254. https://doi.org/10.1007/s11524-018-0229-7

Haimovitz, K., & Dweck, C. S. (2016). Parents' Views of Failure Predict Children's Fixed and Growth Intelligence Mind-Sets. *Psychological Science, 27*(6), 859–869. https://doi.org/10.1177/0956797616639727

Haimovitz, K., & Dweck, C. S. (2017). The Origins of Children's Growth and Fixed Mindsets: New Research and a New Proposal. *Child Development, 88*(6), 1849–1859. https://doi.org/10.1111/cdev.12955

Hakvoort, E. M., Bos, H. M. W., van Balen, F., & Hermanns, J. M. A. (2010). Family Relationships and the Psychosocial Adjustment of School-Aged Children in Intact Families. *Journal of Genetic Psychology, 171*(2), 182–201.

Halevi, G., Djalovski, A., Vengrober, A., & Feldman, R. (2016). Risk and resilience trajectories in war-exposed children across the first decade of life. *Journal of Child Psychology and Psychiatry, 57*(10), 1183–1193. https://doi.org/10.1111/jcpp.12622

Halim, M. L. D. (2016). Princesses and superheroes: Social-cognitive influences on early gender rigidity. *Child Development Perspectives, 10*(3), 155–160. https://doi.org/10.1111/cdep.12176

Halim, M. L. D.., Ruble, D. N.., Tamis-LeMonda, C. S.., Shrout, P. E.., & Amodio, D. M.. (2017). Gender Attitudes in Early Childhood: Behavioral Consequences and Cognitive Antecedents. *Child Dev, 88*(3), 882–899. doi:10.1111/cdev.12642

Halpern, D. F., & LaMay, M. L. (2000). The smarter sex: A critical review of sex differences in intelligence. *Educational Psychology Review, 12*(2), 229–246. https://doi.org/10.1023/A:1009027516424

Harper, S., & Ruicheva, I. (2010). Grandmothers as replacement parents and partners: The role of grandmotherhood in single parent families. *Journal of Intergenerational Relationships, 8*(3), 219–233. https://doi.org/10.1080/15350770.2010.498779

Harris, M. A., Donnellan, M. B., Guo, J., McAdams, D. P., Garnier-Villarreal, M., & Trzesniewski, K. H. (2017). Parental co-construction of 5- to 13-year-olds' global self-esteem through reminiscing about past events. *Child Development, 88*(6), 1810–1822. https://doi.org/10.1111/cdev.12944

Hart, D., Atkins, R., & Tursi, N. (2006). Origins and developmental influences on self-esteem. In M. H. Kernis (Ed.), *Self-esteem issues and answers: A sourcebook of current perspectives* (pp. 157–162). Psychology Press.

Harter, S. (2012a). Emerging self-processes during childhood and adolescence. In M. R. Leary & J. P. Tangney (Eds.), *Handbook of self and identity* (pp. 680–715). Guilford.

Harter, S. (2012b). *The construction of the self: Developmental and sociocultural foundations* (2nd ed.). Guilford Pubn.

Hartup, W. W. (2006). Relationships in early and middle childhood. In A. L. Vangelisti & D. Perlman (Eds.), *The Cambridge handbook of personal relationships* (pp. 177–190). Cambridge University Press. hartup@umn.edu

Hawes, D. J., & Tully, L. A. (2020). Parent discipline and socialization in middle childhood. In S. Hupp & J. D. Jewell (Eds.), *The encyclopedia of child and adolescent development* (pp. 1–10). Wiley. https://doi.org/10.1002/9781119171492.wecad236

Heatly, M. C., & Votruba-Drzal, E. (2019). Developmental precursors of engagement and motivation in fifth grade: Linkages with parent- and teacher-child relationships. *Journal of Applied Developmental Psychology, 60*, 144–156. https://doi.org/10.1016/j.appdev.2018.09.003

Hill, N. E., Bush, K. R., & Roosa, M. W. (2003). Parenting and socialization strategies and children's mental health: Low-income Mexican-American and Euro-American mothers and children. *Child Development, 74*, 189–204.

Hillis, S., Mercy, J., Amobi, A., & Kress, H. (2016). Global prevalence of past-year violence against children: A systematic review and minimum estimates. *Pediatrics, 137*(3), e20154079. https://doi.org/10.1542/peds.2015-4079

Hines, M. (2015). Gendered development. In M. Lewis (Ed.), *Handbook of child psychology and developmental science* (pp. 1–46). John Wiley & Sons, Inc. https://doi.org/10.1002/9781118963418.childpsy320

Hoffman, M. L. (1970). Conscience, personality, and socialization technique. *Human Development, 13*, 90–126.

Huesmann, L. R., Dubow, E. F., Boxer, P., Landau, S. F., Gvirsman, S. D., Shikaki, K., Abelson, R. P., Atran, S., Barber, B. K., Barber, B. K., Berkowitz, L., Boxer, P., Sloan-Power, E., Boxer, P., Sloan-Power, E., Mercado, I., Schappell, A., Bushman, B. J., Huesmann, L. R. ... Sapolsky, R. M. (2016). Children's exposure to violent political conflict stimulates aggression at peers by increasing emotional distress, aggressive script rehearsal, and normative beliefs favoring aggression. *Development and Psychopathology, 36*(7), 1–12. https://doi.org/10.1017/S0954579416001115

Huppert, E., Cowell, J. M., Cheng, Y., Contreras-Ibáñez, C., Gomez-Sicard, N., Gonzalez-Gadea, M. L., Huepe, D., Ibanez, A., Lee, K., Mahasneh, R., Malcolm-Smith, S., Salas, N., Selcuk, B., Tungodden, B., Wong, A., Zhou, X., & Decety, J. (2019). The development of children's preferences for equality and equity across 13 individualistic and collectivist cultures. *Developmental Science, 22*(2), e12729. https://doi.org/10.1111/desc.12729

Husky, M. M., Delbasty, E., Bitfoi, A., Carta, M. G., Goelitz, D., Koç, C., Lesinskiene, S., Mihova, Z., Otten, R., & Kovess-Masfety, V. (2020). Bullying involvement and self-reported mental health in elementary school children across Europe. *Child Abuse and Neglect, 107*, 104601. https://doi.org/10.1016/j.chiabu.2020.104601

Hutchison, J. E., Lyons, I. M., & Ansari, D. (2019). More Similar Than Different: Gender Differences in Children's Basic Numerical Skills Are the Exception Not the Rule. *Child Development, 90*(1), e66–e79. https://doi.org/10.1111/cdev.13044

Hutson, E., Kelly, S., & Militello, L. K. (2018). Systematic Review of Cyberbullying Interventions for Youth and Parents With Implications for Evidence-Based Practice. *Worldviews on Evidence-Based Nursing, 15*(1), 72–79. https://doi.org/10.1111/wvn.12257

Hyde, J. S. (2014). Gender similarities and differences. *Annual Review of Psychology, 65*, 373–398. https://doi.org/10.1146/annurev-psych-010213-115057

Hyde, J. S. (2016). Sex and cognition: gender and cognitive functions. *Current Opinion in Neurobiology, 38*, 53–56. https://doi.org/10.1016/j.conb.2016.02.007

Hymel, S., & Swearer, S. M. (2015). Four decades of research on school bullying: An introduction. *American Psychologist, 70*(4), 293–299. https://doi.org/10.1037/a0038928

Ilmarinen, V.-J., Vainikainen, M.-P., Verkasalo, M. J., & Lönnqvist, J.-E. (2017). Homophilous Friendship Assortment Based on Personality Traits and Cognitive Ability in Middle Childhood: The Moderating Effect of Peer Network Size. *European Journal of Personality, 31*(3), 208–219. https://doi.org/10.1002/per.2095

Imrie, S., & Golombok, S. (2020). Impact of New Family Forms on Parenting and Child Development. *Annual Review of Developmental Psychology, 2*(1), 295–316. https://doi.org/10.1146/annurev-devpsych-070220-122704

Iqbal, H., Neal, S., & Vincent, C. (2017). Children's friendships in super-diverse localities: Encounters with social and ethnic difference. *Childhood, 24*(1), 128–142. https://doi.org/10.1177/0907568216633741

Jacoby, S. F., Tach, L., Guerra, T., Wiebe, D. J., & Richmond, T. S. (2017). The health status and well-being of low-resource, housing-unstable, single-parent families living in violent neighbourhoods in Philadelphia, Pennsylvania. *Health & Social Care in the Community, 25*(2), 578–589. https://doi.org/10.1111/hsc.12345

Jaeger, M. M. (2012). The Extended Family and Children's Educational Success. *American Sociological Review, 77*(6), 903–922. https://doi.org/10.1177/0003122412464040

Jambon, M., & Smetana, J. G. (2014). Moral complexity in middle childhood: Children's evaluations of necessary harm. *Developmental Psychology, 50*(1), 22–33. https://doi.org/10.1037/a0032992

Jayakody, R., & Kalil, A. (2002). Social fathering in low-income, African American families with preschool children. *Journal of Marriage and Family, 64*, 504–516.

Jones, D. J., Lewis, T., Litrownik, A., Thompson, R., Proctor, L. J., Isbell, P., Dubowitz, H., English, D., Jones, B., Nagin, D., & Runyan, D. (2013). Linking childhood sexual abuse and early adolescent risk behavior: the intervening role of internalizing and externalizing problems. *Journal of Abnormal Child Psychology, 41*(1), 139–150. https://doi.org/10.1007/s10802-012-9656-1

Juvonen, J., & Graham, S. (2014). Bullying in schools: the power of bullies and the plight of victims. *Annual Review of Psychology, 65*, 159–185. https://doi.org/10.1146/annurev-psych-010213-115030

Kärnä, A., Voeten, M., Poskiparta, E., & Salmivalli, C. (2010). Vulnerable children in varying classroom contexts: Bystanders' behaviors moderate the effects of risk factors on victimization. *Merrill-Palmer Quarterly: Journal of Developmental Psychology, 56*(3), 261–282.

Kawabata, Y., & Crick, N. R. (2011). The significance of cross-racial/ethnic friendships: associations with peer victimization, peer support, sociometric status, and classroom diversity. *Developmental Psychology*, *47*(6), 1763–1775. https://doi.org/10.1037/a0025399

Keijsers, L., Loeber, R., Branje, S., & Meeus, W. H. J. (2011). Bidirectional links and concurrent development of parent-child relationships and boys' offending behavior. *Journal of Abnormal Psychology*, *120*(4), 878–889. https://doi.org/10.1037/a0024588

Kennedy, S., & Bumpass, L. (2008). Cohabitation and children's living arrangements: New estimates from the United State. *Demographic Research*, *19*, 1663–1692.

Kennedy, S., & Fitch, C. A. (2012). Measuring cohabitation and family structure in the United States: assessing the impact of new data from the Current Population Survey. *Demography*, *49*(4), 1479–1498. https://doi.org/10.1007/s13524-012-0126-8

Kenny, D. (2018). *Children, Sexuality and Child Sexual Abuse. Routledge*. https://www.routledge.com/Children-Sexuality-and-Child-Sexual-Abuse/Kenny/p/book/9781138089259

Kenny, M. C., & McEachern, A. (2009). Children's Self-Concept: A Multicultural Comparison. *Professional School Counseling*, *12*(3), 207–212.

Kenny, M. C., Wurtele, S. K., & Vázquez, A. L. (2020). Childhood Sexual Abuse. In *The Encyclopedia of Child and Adolescent Development* (pp. 1–12). Wiley. https://doi.org/10.1002/9781119171492.wecad232

Killen, M., Kelly, M., Richardson, C., Crystal, D., & Ruck, M. (2010). European-American Children's and Adolescents' Evaluations of Interracial Exclusion. *Group Processes & Intergroup Relations: GPIR*, *13*(3), 283–300. https://doi.org/10.1177/1368430209346700

Killen, M., & Smetana, J. G. (2015). Origins and Development of Morality. In M. Lamb (Ed.), *Handbook of Child Psychology and Developmental Science* (pp. 1–49). John Wiley & Sons, Inc. https://doi.org/10.1002/9781118963418.childpsy317

Kim, H., Drake, B., & Jonson-Reid, M. (2018). An examination of class-based visibility bias in national child maltreatment reporting. *Children and Youth Services Review*, *85*, 165–173. https://doi.org/10.1016/J.CHILDYOUTH.2017.12.019

Kjellstrand, J., Yu, G., Eddy, J. M., & Clark, M. (2020). Children with Incarcerated Parents and Developmental Trajectories of Internalizing Problems across Adolescence. *American Journal of Criminal Justice*, *45*(1), 48–69. https://doi.org/10.1007/s12103-019-09494-4

Koehn, A. J., & Kerns, K. A. (2018). Parent-child attachment: meta-analysis of associations with parenting behaviors in middle childhood and adolescence. *Attachment & Human Development*, *20*(4), 378–405. https://doi.org/10.1080/14616734.2017.1408131

Kohlberg, L. (1969). Stage and sequence: The cognitive-developmental approach to socialization. In D. A. Goslin (Ed.), *Handbook of socialization* (pp. 347–480). Rand McNally.

Kohlberg, L. (1976). Moral stages and moralization: The cognitive developmental approach. In T. Lickona (Ed.), *Moral development and moral behavior: Theory, research, and social issues* (pp. 31–53). Holt, Rinehart & Winston.

Kohlberg, L. (1981). *Essays on moral development*. Harper & Row.

Kornbluh, M., & Neal, J. W. (2016). Examining the many dimensions of children's popularity. *Journal of Social and Personal Relationships*, *33*(1), 62–80. https://doi.org/10.1177/0265407514562562

Kornienko, O., Santos, C. E., Martin, C. L., & Granger, K. L. (2016). Peer influence on gender identity development in adolescence. *Developmental Psychology*, *52*(10), 1578–1592. https://doi.org/10.1037/dev0000200

Krauss, S., Orth, U., & Robins, R. W. (2020). Family environment and self-esteem development: A longitudinal study from age 10 to 16. *Journal of Personality and Social Psychology*, *119*(2), 457–478. https://doi.org/10.1037/pspp0000263

Kurtz-Costes, B., Copping, K. E., Rowley, S. J., & Kinlaw, C. R. (2014). Gender and age differences in awareness and endorsement of gender stereotypes about academic abilities. *European Journal of Psychology of Education*, *29*(4), 603–618. https://doi.org/10.1007/s10212-014-0216-7

Labella, M. H., & Masten, A. S. (2018). Family influences on the development of aggression and violence. *Current Opinion in Psychology*, *19*, 11–16. https://doi.org/10.1016/J.COPSYC.2017.03.028

Ladd, G. W., & Kochenderfer-Ladd, B. (2016). Research in educational psychology: Social exclusion in school. In P. Riva & J. Eck (Eds.), *Social Exclusion* (pp. 109–132). Springer International Publishing. https://doi.org/10.1007/978-3-319-33033-4_6

LaFontana, K. M., & Cillessen, A. H. N. (2010). Developmental Changes in the Priority of Perceived Status in Childhood and Adolescence. *Social Development*, *19*(1), 130–147. https://doi.org/10.1111/j.1467-9507.2008.00522.x

Laible, D., McGinley, M., Carlo, G., Augustine, M., & Murphy, T. (2014). Does engaging in prosocial behavior make children see the world through rose-colored glasses? *Developmental Psychology*, *50*(3), 872–880.

Lamb, M. E. (2012). Mothers, Fathers, Families, and Circumstances: Factors Affecting Children's Adjustment. *Applied Developmental Science*, *16*(2), 98–111. https://doi.org/10.1080/10888691.2012.667344

Lamb, M. E., & Lewis, C. (2015). The role of parent-child relationships in child development. In M. H. Bornstein & M. E. Lamb (Eds.), *Developmental science: An advanced textbook (7th ed.)* (pp. 469–517). Psychology Press.

Lansford, J. E. (2014). Parenting Across Cultures. In H. Selin (Ed.), *Parenting Across Cultures* (Vol. 7, pp. 445–458). Springer Netherlands. https://doi.org/10.1007/978-94-007-7503-9

Lansford, J. E., Staples, A. D., Bates, J. E., Pettit, G. S., & Dodge, K. A. (2013). Trajectories of Mothers' Discipline Strategies and Interparental Conflict: Interrelated Change during Middle Childhood. *Journal of Family Communication*, *13*(3), 178–195. https://doi.org/10.1080/15267431.2013.796947

Laursen, B. (2017). Making and Keeping Friends: The Importance of Being Similar. *Child Development Perspectives*, *11*(4), 282–289. https://doi.org/10.1111/cdep.12246

Laursen, B., Altman, R. L., Bukowski, W. M., & Wei, L. (2020). Being fun: An overlooked indicator of childhood social status. *Journal of Personality*, *88*(5), 993–1006. https://doi.org/10.1111/jopy.12546

Leahey, E., & Guo, G. (2001). Gender Differences in Mathematical Trajectories. *Social Forces*, *80*(2), 713–732. https://doi.org/10.1353/sof.2001.0102

Leaper, C. (2013). Gender Development During Childhood. In P. D. Zelaz (Ed.), *The Oxford Handbook of Developmental Psychology, Vol. 2: Self and Other* (p. Gender development during childhood). Oxford.

Lease, A. M., Kwon, K., Lovelace, M., & Huang, H. chih. (2020). Peer Influence in Elementary School: The Importance of Assessing the Likeability of Popular Children. *Journal of Genetic Psychology*, *181*(2–3), 95–110. https://doi.org/10.1080/00221325.2020.1730744

Leclerc, B., & Wortley, R. (2015). Predictors of victim disclosure in child sexual abuse: Additional evidence from a sample of incarcerated adult sex offenders. *Child Abuse & Neglect*, *43*, 104–111. https://doi.org/10.1016/J.CHIABU.2015.03.003

Lee, L., Howes, C., & Chamberlain, B. (2007). Ethnic heterogeneity of social networks and cross-ethnic friendships of elementary school boys and girls. *Merrill-Palmer Quarterly*, *53*(3), 325–346. https://doi.org/10.1353/mpq.2007.0016

Lessard, L. M., & Juvonen, J. (2018). Losing and gaining friends: Does friendship instability compromise academic functioning in middle school? *Journal of School Psychology*, *69*, 143–153. https://doi.org/10.1016/j.jsp.2018.05.003

Lessard, L. M., Kogachi, K., & Juvonen, J. (2019). Quality and Stability of Cross-Ethnic Friendships: Effects of Classroom Diversity and Out-of-School Contact. *Journal of Youth and Adolescence*, *48*(3), 554–566. https://doi.org/10.1007/s10964-018-0964-9

Levy, G. D., Taylor, M. G., & Gelman, S. A. (1995). Traditional and evaluative aspects of flexibility in gender roles, social conventions, moral rules, and physical laws. *Child Development*, *66*(2), 515–531. http://www.ncbi.nlm.nih.gov/pubmed/7750381

Liben, L. S., Bigler, R. S., & Hilliard, L. J. (2013). Gender Development. In D. A. C.. Gershoff, T. Elizabeth, & R. S.. Mistry (Eds.), *Societal Contexts of Child Development: Pathways of Influence and Implications for Practice and Policy* (pp. 3–18). Oxford Univ Press.

Luthar, S. S., Crossman, E. J., Small, P. J., Luthar, S. S., Crossman, E. J., & Small, P. J. (2015). Resilience and Adversity. In M. E. Lamb (Ed.), *Handbook of Child Psychology and Developmental Science* (pp. 1–40). John Wiley & Sons, Inc. https://doi.org/10.1002/9781118963418.childpsy307

Maccoby, E. E., & Jacklin, C. N. (1987). *Gender Segregation in Childhood*. (pp. 239–287). https://doi.org/10.1016/S0065-2407(08)60404-8 https://doi.org/10.1016/S0065-2407(08)60404-8

Magro, S. W., Utesch, T., Dreiskämper, D., & Wagner, J. (2019). Self-esteem development in middle childhood: Support for sociometer theory. *International Journal of Behavioral Development*, *43*(2), 118–127. https://doi.org/10.1177/0165025418802462

Maholmes, V. (2012). Adjustment of Children and Youth in Military Families: Toward Developmental Understandings. *Child Development Perspectives*, *6*(4), 430–435. http://cat.inist.fr/?aModele=afficheN&cpsidt=26737497

Maikovich-Fong, A. K., & Jaffee, S. R. (2010). Sex differences in childhood sexual abuse characteristics and victims' emotional and behavioral problems: Findings from a national sample of youth. *Child Abuse & Neglect*, *34*(6), 429–437. https://doi.org/10.1016/j.chiabu.2009.10.006

Manning, W. D. (2015). Cohabitation and Child Wellbeing. *The Future of Children*, *25*(2), 51–66.

Manning, W. D., & Brown, S. (2006). Children's Economic Well-Being in Married and Cohabiting Parent Families. *Journal of Marriage & Family*, *68*(2), 345–362.

Marks, P. E. L. (2017). Introduction to the Special Issue: 20th-Century Origins and 21st-Century Developments of Peer Nomination Methodology. *New Directions for Child and Adolescent Development*, *2017*(157), 7–19. https://doi.org/10.1002/cad.20205

Martin, C. L., Andrews, N. C. Z., England, D. E., Zosuls, K., & Ruble, D. N. (2017). A Dual Identity Approach for Conceptualizing and Measuring Children's Gender Identity. *Child Development*, *88*(1), 167–182. https://doi.org/10.1111/cdev.12568

Martin, C. L., Ruble, D. N., & Szkrybalo, J. (2002). Cognitive theories of early gender development. *Psychological Bulletin*, *128*, 903–933.

Masten, A. S., Cicchetti, D., Masten, A. S., & Cicchetti, D. (2016). Resilience in Development: Progress and Transformation. In D. Cicchetti (Ed.), *Developmental Psychopathology* (pp. 1–63). John Wiley & Sons, Inc. https://doi.org/10.1002/9781119125556.devpsy406

Masten, A. S., & Monn, A. R. (2015). Child and Family Resilience: A Call for Integrated Science, Practice, and Professional Training. *Family Relations*, *64*(1), 5–21. https://doi.org/10.1111/fare.12103

Mathewson-Chapman, M., & Chapman, H. J. (2020). One Health and veterans' post-deployment health. *The Clinical Teacher*, tct.13244. https://doi.org/10.1111/tct.13244

Maunder, R., & Monks, C. P. (2019). Friendships in middle childhood: Links to peer and school identification, and general self-worth. *British Journal of Developmental Psychology*, *37*(2), 211–229. https://doi.org/10.1111/bjdp.12268

Mazrekaj, D., De Witte, K., & Cabus, S. (2020). School Outcomes of Children Raised by Same-Sex Parents: Evidence from Administrative Panel Data. *American Sociological Review*, *85*(5), 830–856. https://doi.org/10.1177/0003122420957249

McDonald, K. L., & Asher, S. R. (2018). Peer acceptance, peer rejection, and popularity: Social-cognitive and behavioral perspectives. W. M. Bukowski, B. Laursen, & K. H. Rubi (Eds.), *Handbook of peer interactions, relationships, and groups*, 429–446. Guilford. https://psycnet.apa.org/record/2018-00748-022

McDonald, K. L., Dashiell-Aje, E., Menzer, M. M., Rubin, K. H., Oh, W., & Bowker, J. C. (2013). Contributions of Racial and Sociobehavioral Homophily to Friendship Stability and Quality Among Same-Race and Cross-Race Friends. *The Journal of Early Adolescence*, *33*(7), 897–919. https://doi.org/10.1177/0272431612472259

McDougall, P., & Vaillancourt, T. (2015). Long-term adult outcomes of peer victimization in childhood and adolescence: Pathways to adjustment and maladjustment. *The American Psychologist*, *70*(4), 300–310. https://doi.org/10.1037/a0039174

McGuire, L., Mulvey, K. L., Goff, E., Irvin, M. J., Winterbottom, M., Fields, G. E., Hartstone-Rose, A., & Rutland, A. (2020). STEM gender stereotypes from early childhood through adolescence at informal science centers. *Journal of Applied Developmental Psychology, 67,* 101109. https://doi.org/10.1016/j.appdev.2020.101109

McMahon, S. D., Todd, N. R., Martinez, A., Coker, C., Sheu, C.-F., Washburn, J., & Shah, S. (2013). Aggressive and prosocial behavior: community violence, cognitive, and behavioral predictors among urban African American youth. *American Journal of Community Psychology, 51*(3–4), 407–421. https://doi.org/10.1007/s10464-012-9560-4

Meece, J. L., Anderman, E. M., & Anderman, L. H. (2006). Classroom Goal Structure, Student Motivation, and Academic Achievement. *Annual Review of Psychology, 57*(1), 487–503. https://doi.org/10.1146/annurev.psych.56.091103.070258

Menesini, E., & Salmivalli, C. (2017). Bullying in schools: the state of knowledge and effective interventions. *Psychology, Health & Medicine, 22*(sup1), 240–253. https://doi.org/10.1080/13548506.2017.1279740

Menon, M. (2011). Does Felt Gender Compatibility Mediate Influences of Self-Perceived Gender Nonconformity on Early Adolescents' Psychosocial Adjustment? *Child Development, 82*(4), 1152–1162. https://doi.org/10.1111/j.1467-8624.2011.01601.x

Menting, B., Koot, H., & van Lier, P. (2014). Peer acceptance and the development of emotional and behavioural problems: Results from a preventive intervention study. *International Journal of Behavioral Development, 39*(6), 530–540. https://doi.org/10.1177/0165025414558853

Menting, B., van Lier, P. A. C., & Koot, H. M. (2011). Language skills, peer rejection, and the development of externalizing behavior from kindergarten to fourth grade. *Journal of Child Psychology & Psychiatry, 52*(1), 72–79. https://doi.org/10.1111/j.1469-7610.2010.02279.x

Meter, D. J., & Card, N. A. (2016). Stability of children's and adolescents' friendships: A meta-analytic review. *Merrill-Palmer Quarterly, 62*(3), 252–284. https://doi.org/10.13110/merrpalmquar1982.62.3.0252

Miller, B. G., Kors, S., & Macfie, J. (2017). No differences? Meta-analytic comparisons of psychological adjustment in children of gay fathers and heterosexual parents. *Psychology of Sexual Orientation and Gender Diversity, 4*(1), 14–22. https://doi.org/10.1037/sgd0000203

Miller, D. I., & Halpern, D. F. (2014). The new science of cognitive sex differences. *Trends in Cognitive Sciences, 18*(1), 37–45. https://doi.org/10.1016/j.tics.2013.10.011

Moore, J. S. B., & Smith, M. (2018). Children's levels of contingent self-esteem and social and emotional outcomes. *Educational Psychology in Practice, 34*(2), 113–130. https://doi.org/10.1080/02667363.2017.1411786

Moore, S. E., Norman, R. E., Suetani, S., Thomas, H. J., Sly, P. D., & Scott, J. G. (2017). Consequences of bullying victimization in childhood and adolescence: A systematic review and meta-analysis. *World Journal of Psychiatry, 7*(1), 60–76. https://doi.org/10.5498/wjp.v7.i1.60

Muenks, K., Wigfield, A., & Eccles, J. S. (2018). I can do this! The development and calibration of children's expectations for success and competence beliefs. *Developmental Review, 48,* 24–39. https://doi.org/10.1016/J.DR.2018.04.001

Munniksma, A., & Juvonen, J. (2012). Cross-ethnic friendships and sense of social-emotional safety in a multiethnic middle school: An exploratory study. *Merrill-Palmer Quarterly, 58*(4), 489–506. https://doi.org/10.1353/mpq.2012.0023

Murray-Close, D.., Nelson, D. A.., Ostrov, J. M.., Casas, J. F.., & Crick, N. R.. (2016). Relational Aggression: A Developmental Psychopathology Perspective. 1–63. doi:10.1002/9781119125556.devpsy413

Mustillo, S., Wadsworth, S. M., & Lester, P. (2016). Parental deployment and well-being in children. *Journal of Emotional and Behavioral Disorders, 24*(2), 82–91. https://doi.org/10.1177/1063426615598766

National Center for Health Statistics. (2015). *National marriage and divorce rate trends.* National Center for Health Statistics.

National Center for Health Statistics. (2020). *FastStats - marriage and divorce.* https://www.cdc.gov/nchs/fastats/marriage-divorce.htm

Nese, R. N. T., Horner, R. H., Dickey, C. R., Stiller, B., & Tomlanovich, A. (2014). Decreasing bullying behaviors in middle school: Expect respect. *School Psychology Quarterly, 29*(3), 272–286.

Nixon, E., Hadfield, K., Nixon, E., & Hadfield, K. (2016). Blended families. In C. L. Shehan (Ed.), *Encyclopedia of family studies* (pp. 1–5). John Wiley & Sons, Inc. https://doi.org/10.1002/9781119085621.wbefs207

Nobes, G., & Pawson, C. (2003). Children's understanding of social rules and social status. *Merrill-Palmer Quarterly, 49,* 77–99.

Nocentini, A., Fiorentini, G., Di Paola, L., & Menesini, E. (2019). Parents, family characteristics and bullying behavior: A systematic review. *Aggression and Violent Behavior, 45,* 41–50. https://doi.org/10.1016/j.avb.2018.07.010

Olson, K. R., & Enright, E. A. (2018). Do transgender children (gender) stereotype less than their peers and siblings? *Developmental Science, 21*(4), e12606. https://doi.org/10.1111/desc.12606

Olson, K. R., & Gülgöz, S. (2018). Early Findings From the TransYouth Project: Gender Development in Transgender Children. *Child Development Perspectives, 12*(2), 93–97. https://doi.org/10.1111/cdep.12268

Olson, K. R., Key, A. C., & Eaton, N. R. (2015). Gender Cognition in Transgender Children. *Psychological Science, 26*(4), 467–474. https://doi.org/10.1177/0956797614568156

Olweus, D. (2013). School Bullying: Development and Some Important Challenges. *Annual Review of Clinical Psychology, 9*(1), 751–780. https://doi.org/10.1146/annurev-clinpsy-050212-185516

Olweus, D., & Limber, S. P. (2010). Bullying in School: Evaluation and Dissemination of the Olweus Bullying Prevention Program. *American Journal of Orthopsychiatry, 80*(1), 124–134. https://doi.org/10.1111/j.1939-0025.2010.01015.x

Orkin, M., May, S., & Wolf, M. (2017). How Parental Support During Homework Contributes to Helpless Behaviors Among Struggling Readers. *Reading Psychology, 38*(5), 506–541. https://doi.org/10.1080/02702711.2017.1299822

Orth, U. (2017). The Family Environment in Early Childhood Has a Long-Term Effect on Self-Esteem: A Longitudinal Study From Birth to Age 27 Years. *Journal of Personality and Social Psychology, 114*(4), 637–655. https://doi.org/10.1037/pspp0000143

Orth, U., Erol, R. Y., & Luciano, E. C. (2018). Development of self-esteem from age 4 to 94 Years: A meta-analysis of longitudinal studies. *Psychological Bulletin, 144*(10), 1045–1080. https://doi.org/10.1037/bul0000161

Osborne, C., Manning, W. D., & Smock, P. J. (2007). Married and Cohabiting Parentsâ€TM Relationship Stability: A Focus on Race and Ethnicity. *Journal of Marriage & Family, 69*(5), 1345–1366.

Padilla-Walker, L. M., & Memmott-Elison, M. K. (2020). Family and Moral Development. In L. A. Jensen (Ed.), *The Oxford Handbook of Moral Development: An Interdisciplinary Perspective* (pp. 461-). Oxford.

Park, N. (2011). Military Children and Families: Strengths and Challenges During Peace and War. *American Psychologist, 66*(1), 65–72. https://doi.org/10.1037/a0021249

Parra-Cardona, J. R., Cordova, D., Holtrop, K., Villarruel, F. A., & Wieling, E. (2008). Shared Ancestry, Evolving Stories: Similar and Contrasting Life Experiences Described by Foreign Born and U.S. Born Latino Parents. *Family Process, 47*(2), 157–172. https://doi.org/10.1111/j.1545-5300.2008.00246.x

Passolunghi, M. C., Rueda Ferreira, T. I., & Tomasetto, C. (2014). Math–gender stereotypes and math-related beliefs in childhood and early adolescence. *Learning and Individual Differences, 34*, 70–76. https://doi.org/10.1016/j.lindif.2014.05.005

Patterson, C. J. (2017). Parents' Sexual Orientation and Children's Development. *Child Development Perspectives, 11*(1), 45–49. https://doi.org/10.1111/cdep.12207

Pauletti, R. E., Cooper, P. J., & Perry, D. G. (2014). Influences of gender identity on children's maltreatment of gender-nonconforming peers: A person × target analysis of aggression. *Journal of Personality and Social Psychology, 106*(5), 843–866. https://doi.org/10.1037/a0036037

Pauletti, R. E., Menon, M., Cooper, P. J., Aults, C. D., & Perry, D. G. (2017). Psychological Androgyny and Children's Mental Health: A New Look with New Measures. *Sex Roles, 76*(11–12), 705–718. https://doi.org/10.1007/s11199-016-0627-9

Pérez-Fuentes, G., Olfson, M., Villegas, L., Morcillo, C., Wang, S., & Blanco, C. (2013). Prevalence and correlates of child sexual abuse: a national study. *Comprehensive Psychiatry, 54*(1), 16–27. https://doi.org/10.1016/j.comppsych.2012.05.010

Pérez-González, A., Guilera, G., Pereda, N., & Jarne, A. (2017). Protective factors promoting resilience in the relation between child sexual victimization and internalizing and externalizing symptoms. *Child Abuse & Neglect, 72*, 393–403. https://doi.org/10.1016/J.CHIABU.2017.09.006

Perren, S., Ettekal, I., & Ladd, G. (2013). The impact of peer victimization on later maladjustment: mediating and moderating effects of hostile and self-blaming attributions. *Journal of Child Psychology and Psychiatry, and Allied Disciplines, 54*(1), 46–55. https://doi.org/10.1111/j.1469-7610.2012.02618.x

Perrin, E. C., & Siegel, B. S. (2013). Promoting the well-being of children whose parents are gay or lesbian. *Pediatrics, 131*(4), e1374–83. https://doi.org/10.1542/peds.2013-0377

Perry, D. G., Pauletti, R. E., & Cooper, P. J. (2019). Gender identity in childhood: A review of the literature. *International Journal of Behavioral Development, 43*(4), 289–304. https://doi.org/10.1177/0165025418811129

Pesu, L., Viljaranta, J., & Aunola, K. (2016). The role of parents' and teachers' beliefs in children's self-concept development. *Journal of Applied Developmental Psychology, 44*(May-June), 63–71. https://doi.org/10.1016/j.appdev.2016.03.001

Petersen, J. (2018). Gender Difference in Verbal Performance: A Meta-analysis of United States State Performance Assessments. *Educational Psychology Review, 30*(4), 1269–1281. https://doi.org/10.1007/s10648-018-9450-x

Peverill, M., Dirks, M. A., Narvaja, T., Herts, K. L., Comer, J. S., & McLaughlin, K. A. (2021). Socioeconomic status and child psychopathology in the United States: A meta-analysis of population-based studies. *Clinical Psychology Review, 83*, 101933. https://doi.org/10.1016/j.cpr.2020.101933

Pew Research Center. (2015). *Parenting in America: The American family today.* http://www.pewsocialtrends.org/2015/12/17/1-the-american-family-today/

Piaget, J. (1932). *The moral judgment of the child.* Harcourt Brace.

Poehlmann-Tynan, J., & Turney, K. (2020). A Developmental Perspective on Children With Incarcerated Parents. *Child Development Perspectives*, cdep.12392. https://doi.org/10.1111/cdep.12392

Pomerantz, E. M., & Dong, W. (2006). Effects of mothers' perceptions of children's competence: The moderating role of mothers' theories of competence. *Developmental Psychology, 42*(5), 950–961. https://doi.org/10.1037/0012-1649.42.5.950

Potter, D. (2010). Psychosocial Well-Being and the Relationship Between Divorce and Children's Academic Achievement. *Journal of Marriage & Family, 72*(4), 933–946. https://doi.org/10.1111/j.1741-3737.2010.00740.x

Poulin, F., & Chan, A. (2010). Friendship stability and change in childhood and adolescence. *Developmental Review, 30*(3), 257–272. https://doi.org/10.1016/j.dr.2009.01.001

Pozzoli, T., Gini, G., & Vieno, A. (2012). The role of individual correlates and class norms in defending and passive bystanding behavior in bullying: a multilevel analysis. *Child Development, 83*(6), 1917–1931. https://doi.org/10.1111/j.1467-8624.2012.01831.x

Prabaharan, N., & Spadafora, N. (2020). Rejected Children. In T. K. Shackelford & V. A. Weekes-Shackelford (Eds.), *Encyclopedia of Evolutionary Psychological Science* (pp. 1–4). Springer International Publishing. https://doi.org/10.1007/978-3-319-16999-6_181-1

Qiu, X., Yu, J., Li, T., Cheng, N., & Zhu, L. (2017). Children's Inequity Aversion in Procedural Justice Context: A Comparison of Advantageous and Disadvantageous Inequity. *Frontiers in Psychology, 8*(OCT), 1855. https://doi.org/10.3389/fpsyg.2017.01855

Rajendran, K., Kruszewski, E., & Halperin, J. M. (2016). Parenting style influences bullying: a longitudinal study comparing children with and without behavioral problems. *Journal of Child Psychology and Psychiatry, 57*(2), 188–195. https://doi.org/10.1111/jcpp.12433

Reising, M. M., Watson, K. H., Hardcastle, E. J., Merchant, M. J., Roberts, L., Forehand, R., & Compas, B. E. (2013). Parental Depression and Economic Disadvantage: The Role of Parenting in Associations with Internalizing and Externalizing Symptoms in Children and Adolescents. *Journal of Child and Family Studies, 22*(3), 335–343. https://doi.org/10.1007/s10826-012-9582-4

Reiss, F., Meyrose, A.-K., Otto, C., Lampert, T., Klasen, F., & Ravens-Sieberer, U. (2019). Socioeconomic status, stressful life situations and mental health problems in children and adolescents: Results of the German BELLA cohort-study. *PLOS ONE*, *14*(3), e0213700. https://doi.org/10.1371/journal.pone.0213700

Roberts, J. E., & Bell, M. A. (2002). The effects of age and sex on mental rotation performance, verbal performance, and brain electrical activity. *Developmental Psychobiology*, *40*(4), 391–407. https://doi.org/10.1002/dev.10039

Romera, E. M., Bravo, A., Ortega-Ruiz, R., & Veenstra, R. (2019). Differences in perceived popularity and social preference between bullying roles and class norms. *PLOS ONE*, *14*(10), e0223499. https://doi.org/10.1371/journal.pone.0223499

Rose-Greenland, F., & Smock, P. J. (2013). Living Together Unmarried: What Do We Know About Cohabiting Families? In G. W. Peterson & K. R. Bush (Eds.), *Handbook of Marriage and the Family* (pp. 255–273). Springer.

Rubin, K. H., Bukowski, W. M., & Bowker, J. C. (2015a). Children in Peer Groups. In M. H. Bornstein & T. Leventhal (Eds.), *Handbook of Child Psychology and Developmental Science* (pp. 1–48). John Wiley & Sons, Inc. https://doi.org/10.1002/9781118963418.childpsy405

Rubin, K. H., Coplan, R. J., & Bowker, J. C. (2009). Social Withdrawal in Childhood. *Annual Review of Psychology*, *60*(1), 141–171. 10.1146/annurev.psych.60110707.163642

Rubin, K. H., Coplan, R. J., Chen, X., Bowker, J. C., McDonald, K. L., & Heverly-Fitt, S. (2015b). Peer relationships. In *Developmental science: An advanced textbook* (pp. 587–644). Psychology Press.

Rubin, K. H., Wojslawowicz, J. C., Rose-Krasnor, L., Booth-LaForce, C., & Burgess, K. B. (2006). The best friendships of shy/withdrawn children: prevalence, stability, and relationship quality. *Journal of Abnormal Child Psychology*, *34*(2), 143–157. https://doi.org/10.1007/s10802-005-9017-4

Ruble, D. N., Taylor, L. J., Cyphers, L., Greulich, F. K., Lurye, L. E., & Shrout, P. E. (2007). The Role of Gender Constancy in Early Gender Development. *Child Development*, *78*(4), 1121–1136. https://doi.org/10.1111/j.1467-8624.2007.01056.x

Russell, D. W., & Russell, C. A. (2019). The evolution of mental health outcomes across a combat deployment cycle: A longitudinal study of the Guam Army National Guard. *PLOS ONE*, *14*(10), e0223855. https://doi.org/10.1371/journal.pone.0223855

Ryan, R. M., Claessens, A., & Markowitz, A. J. (2015). Associations Between Family Structure Change and Child Behavior Problems: The Moderating Effect of Family Income. *Child Development*, *86*, 112–127. https://doi.org/10.1111/cdev.12283

Salary.com. (2021). Retrieved from https://www.salary.com/tools/salary-calculator/board-certified-behavior-analyst

Salmivalli, C. (2014). Participant Roles in Bullying: How Can Peer Bystanders Be Utilized in Interventions? *Theory Into Practice*, *53*(4), 286–292. https://doi.org/10.1080/00405841.2014.947222

Sanders, M. R., & Kirby, J. N. (2014). A Public-Health Approach to Improving Parenting and Promoting Children's Well-Being. *Child Development Perspectives*, *8*(4), 250–257. https://doi.org/10.1111/cdep.12086

Saraiya, A., Garakani, A., & Billick, S. B. (2013). Mental health approaches to child victims of acts of terrorism. *The Psychiatric Quarterly*, *84*(1), 115–124. https://doi.org/10.1007/s11126-012-9232-4

Schneider, B. H. (2016). *Childhood friendships and peer relations: friends and enemies*. Routledge.

Schroeder, K. M., & Liben, L. S. (2020). Felt Pressure to Conform to Cultural Gender Roles: Correlates and Consequences. *Sex Roles*, 1–14. https://doi.org/10.1007/s11199-020-01155-9

Schumm, W., & Crawford, D. (2019). Scientific Consensus on Whether LGBTQ Parents Are More Likely (or Not) to Have LGBTQ Children: An Analysis of 72 Social Science Reviews of the Literature Published Between 2001 and 2017. *Journal of International Women's Studies*, *20*(7). https://vc.bridgew.edu/jiws/vol20/iss7/1

Schwartz, D., Lansford, J. E., Dodge, K. A., Pettit, G. S., & Bates, J. E. (2015). Peer victimization during middle childhood as a lead indicator of internalizing problems and diagnostic outcomes in late adolescence. *Journal of Clinical Child and Adolescent Psychology: The Official Journal for the Society of Clinical Child and Adolescent Psychology, American Psychological Association, Division, 53*, *44*(3), 393–404. https://doi.org/10.1080/15374416.2014.881293

Schwartz-Mette, R. A., Shankman, J., Dueweke, A. R., Borowski, S., & Rose, A. J. (2020). Relations of friendship experiences with depressive symptoms and loneliness in childhood and adolescence: A meta-analytic review. *Psychological Bulletin*, *146*(8), 664–700. https://doi.org/10.1037/bul0000239

Scott, E., & Panksepp, J. (2003). Rough-and-tumble play in human children. *Aggressive Behavior*, *29*(6), 539–551. https://doi.org/10.1002/ab.10062

Serbin, L. A., Powlishta, K. K., & Gulko, J. (1993). The development of sex typing in middle childhood. *Monographs of the Society for Research in Child Development*, *58*(2), 1–99. http://www.ncbi.nlm.nih.gov/pubmed/8474512

Shi, B., & Xie, H. (2012). Popular and Nonpopular Subtypes of Physically Aggressive Preadolescents: Continuity of Aggression and Peer Mechanisms During the Transition to Middle School. *Merrill-Palmer Quarterly*, *58*(4), 530–553. https://doi.org/10.1353/mpq.2012.0025

Sim, A., Fazel, M., Bowes, L., & Gardner, F. (2018). Pathways linking war and displacement to parenting and child adjustment: A qualitative study with Syrian refugees in Lebanon. *Social Science & Medicine*, *200*, 19–26. https://doi.org/10.1016/J.SOCSCIMED.2018.01.009

Simpkins, S. D., Delgado, M. Y., Price, C. D., Quach, A., & Starbuck, E. (2013). Socioeconomic status, ethnicity, culture, and immigration: Examining the potential mechanisms underlying Mexican-origin adolescents' organized activity participation. *Developmental Psychology*, *49*(4), 706–721. https://doi.org/10.1037/a0028399

Slone, M., & Mann, S. (2016). Effects of War, Terrorism and Armed Conflict on Young Children: A Systematic Review. *Child Psychiatry & Human Development*, *47*(6), 950–965. https://doi.org/10.1007/s10578-016-0626-7

Smetana, J. G., & Ball, C. L. (2019). Heterogeneity in children's developing moral judgments about different types of harm. *Developmental Psychology*, *55*(6), 1150–1163. https://doi.org/10.1037/dev0000718

Smetana, J. G., & Braeges, J. L. (1990). The development of toddler's moral and conventional judgments. *Merrill-Palmer Quarterly*, *36*, 329–346.

Smetana, J. G., Jambon, M., & Ball, C. (2014). The Social Domain Approach to Children's Moral and Social Judgments. In M. Killen & J. G. Smetana (Eds.), *Handbook of Moral Development* (pp. 23–44). Psychology Press. https://doi.org/10.4324/9780203581957

Smetana, J. G., Jambon, M., & Ball, C. L. (2018). Normative Changes and Individual Differences in Early Moral Judgments: A Constructivist Developmental Perspective. *Human Development, 61*(4–5), 264–280. https://doi.org/10.1159/000492803

Smith, C. E., & Warneken, F. (2016). Children's reasoning about distributive and retributive justice across development. *Developmental Psychology, 52*(4), 613–628. https://doi.org/10.1037/a0040069

Smith, P. S. (2019). From research to reform: Improving the experiences of the children and families of incarcerated parents in Europe. In J. Mark Eddy & Poehlmann-Tynan. Julie (Eds.), *Handbook on Children with Incarcerated Parents: Research, Policy, and Practice* (pp. 267–277). Springer International Publishing. https://doi.org/10.1007/978-3-030-16707-3_18

Smock, P. J., & Schwartz, C. R. (2020). The Demography of Families: A Review of Patterns and Change. *Journal of Marriage and Family, 82*(1), 9–34. https://doi.org/10.1111/jomf.12612

Sravanti, L., & Kommu, J. V. S. (2020). Gender Identity in Middle Childhood. *Journal of Psychosexual Health, 2*(2), 192–193. https://doi.org/10.1177/2631831820924596

Stevenson, H. W., Lee, S., & Mu, X. (2000). Successful achievement in mathematics: China and the United States. In C. F. M. van. Lieshout & P. G. Heymans (Eds.), *Developing talent across the life span* (pp. 167–183). Psychology Press.

Strohschein, L. (2005). Parental divorce and child mental health trajectories. *Journal of Marriage and Family, 67*(5), 1286–1300.

Swearer, S. M., & Hymel, S. (2015). Understanding the psychology of bullying: Moving toward a social-ecological diathesis-stress model. *The American Psychologist, 70*(4), 344–353. https://doi.org/10.1037/a0038929

Taylor, D. (2020). Fifteen Percent of Same-Sex Couples Have Children in Their Household. *America Counts: Stories Behind the Numbers*. https://www.census.gov/library/stories/2020/09/fifteen-percent-of-same-sex-couples-have-children-in-their-household.html

Taylor, Z. E., & Conger, R. D. (2017). Promoting Strengths and Resilience in Single-Mother Families. *Child Development, 88*(2), 350–358. https://doi.org/10.1111/cdev.12741

Thomaes, S., Reijntjes, A., Orobio de Castro, B., Bushman, B. J., Poorthuis, A., & Telch, M. J. (2010). I Like Me If You Like Me: On the Interpersonal Modulation and Regulation of Preadolescents' State Self-Esteem. *Child Development, 81*(3), 811–825. https://doi.org/10.1111/j.1467-8624.2010.01435.x

Thomas, H. J., Connor, J. P., & Scott, J. G. (2017). Why do children and adolescents bully their peers? A critical review of key theoretical frameworks. *Social Psychiatry and Psychiatric Epidemiology, 53*(5), 437–451. https://doi.org/10.1007/s00127-017-1462-1

Thornberg, R., Thornberg, U. B., Alamaa, R., & Daud, N. (2016). Children's conceptions of bullying and repeated conventional transgressions: moral, conventional, structuring and personal-choice reasoning. *Educational Psychology, 36*(1), 95–111. https://doi.org/10.1080/01443410.2014.915929

Toyama, M. (2001). Developmental changes in social comparison in pre-school and elementary school children: Perceptions, feelings, and behavior. *Japanese Journal of Educational Psychology, 49*, 500–507.

Traub, F., & Boynton-Jarrett, R. (2017). Modifiable Resilience Factors to Childhood Adversity for Clinical Pediatric Practice. *Pediatrics, 139*(5), e20162569. https://doi.org/10.1542/peds.2016-2569

Trautner, H. M., Ruble, D. N., Cyphers, L., Kirsten, B., Behrendt, R., & Hartmann, P. (2005). Rigidity and flexibility of gender stereotypes in childhood: developmental or differential? *Infant and Child Development, 14*(4), 365–381. https://doi.org/10.1002/icd.399

Troop-Gordon, W., MacDonald, A. P., & Corbitt-Hall, D. J. (2019). Children's peer beliefs, friendlessness, and friendship quality: Reciprocal influences and contributions to internalizing symptoms. *Developmental Psychology, 55*(11), 2428–2439. https://doi.org/10.1037/dev0000812

Troutman, D. R., & Fletcher, A. C. (2010). Context and companionship in children's short-term versus long-term friendships. *Journal of Social & Personal Relationships, 27*(8), 1060–1074. https://doi.org/10.1177/0265407510381253

Turiel, E., & Nucci, L. (2017). Moral development in context. In A. Dick & U. Muller (Eds.), *Advancing Developmental Science: Philosophy, Theory, and Method* (pp. 107–121). Routledge.

Turney, K., & Goodsell, R. (2018). Parental Incarceration and Children's Wellbeing. *Future of Children, 28*(1), 147–164. https://doi.org/10.1353/foc.2018.0007

Twum-Antwi, A., Jefferies, P., & Ungar, M. (2020). Promoting child and youth resilience by strengthening home and school environments: A literature review. *International Journal of School and Educational Psychology, 8*(2), 78–89. https://doi.org/10.1080/21683603.2019.1660284

Ungar, M. (2015). Practitioner Review: Diagnosing childhood resilience - a systemic approach to the diagnosis of adaptation in adverse social and physical ecologies. *Journal of Child Psychology and Psychiatry, 56*(1), 4–17. https://doi.org/10.1111/jcpp.12306

U.S. Bureau of Labor Statistics. (2021). *Occupational outlook handbook: 2021.* Retrieved from https://www.bls.gov/ooh/ U.S. Bureau of Labor Statistics

U.S. Bureau of the Census. (2018). *America's Families and Living Arrangements: 2017.* https://www.census.gov/data/tables/2017/demo/families/cps-2017.html

U.S. Bureau of the Census. (2018). *America's families and living arrangements: 2017.* Retrieved from https://www.census.gov/data/tables/2017/demo/families/cps-2017.html

U.S. Department of Health and Human Services. (2018). *Child Maltreatment, 2016.* https://www.acf.hhs.gov/cb/resource/child-maltreatment-2016

U.S. News & World Report. (2020). *School psychologist salary.* Retrieved from https://money.usnews.com/careers/best-jobs/school-psychologist/salary

Vaillancourt, T., Faris, R., & Mishna, F. (2017). Cyberbullying in Children and Youth: Implications for Health and Clinical Practice. *The Canadian Journal of Psychiatry, 62*(6), 368–373. https://doi.org/10.1177/0706743716684791

van den Berg, Y. H. M., Deutz, M. H. F., Smeekens, S., & Cillessen, A. H. N. (2017). Developmental Pathways to Preference and Popularity in Middle Childhood. *Child Development*, *88*(5), 1629–1641. https://doi.org/10.1111/cdev.12706

van der Ploeg, R., Steglich, C., & Veenstra, R. (2020). The way bullying works: How new ties facilitate the mutual reinforcement of status and bullying in elementary schools. *Social Networks*, *60*, 71–82. https://doi.org/10.1016/j.socnet.2018.12.006

van der Wilt, F., van der Veen, C., van Kruistum, C., & van Oers, B. (2019). Why Do Children Become Rejected by Their Peers? A Review of Studies into the Relationship Between Oral Communicative Competence and Sociometric Status in Childhood. *Educational Psychology Review*, *31*(3), 699–724. https://doi.org/10.1007/s10648-019-09479-z

Van Dijk, A., Poorthuis, A. M. G., & Malti, T. (2017). Psychological processes in young bullies versus bully-victims. *Aggressive Behavior*, *43*(5), 430–439. https://doi.org/10.1002/ab.21701

Van Eldik, W. M., de Haan, A. D., Parry, L. Q., Davies, P. T., Luijk, M. P. C. M., Arends, L. R., & Prinzie, P. (2020). The Interparental Relationship: Meta-Analytic Associations With Children's Maladjustment and Responses to Interparental Conflict. *Psychological Bulletin*. https://doi.org/10.1037/bul0000233

van Tetering, M., van der Donk, M., de Groot, R. H. M., & Jolles, J. (2019). Sex Differences in the Performance of 7–12 Year Olds on a Mental Rotation Task and the Relation With Arithmetic Performance. *Frontiers in Psychology*, *10*(JAN), 107. https://doi.org/10.3389/fpsyg.2019.00107

Waasdorp, T. E., & Bradshaw, C. P. (2011). Examining student responses to frequent bullying: A latent class approach. *Journal of Educational Psychology*, *103*(2), 336–352. https://doi.org/10.1037/a0022747

Waasdorp, T. E., & Bradshaw, C. P. (2015). The overlap between cyberbullying and traditional bullying. *The Journal of Adolescent Health : Official Publication of the Society for Adolescent Medicine*, *56*(5), 483–488. https://doi.org/10.1016/j.jadohealth.2014.12.002

Waid-Lindberg, C. A., & Mohr, N. L. (2019). Child Sexual Abuse. In F. P. Bernat & K. Frailing (Eds.), *The Encyclopedia of Women and Crime* (pp. 1–7). John Wiley & Sons, Inc. https://doi.org/10.1002/9781118929803.ewac0051

Waldfogel, J., Craigie, T.-A., & Brooks-Gunn, J. (2010). Fragile families and child wellbeing. *The Future of Children*, *20*(2), 87–112. http://www.pubmedcentral.nih.gov/articlerender.fcgi?artid=3074431&tool=pmcentrez&rendertype=abstract

Walters, G. D. (2021). School-Age Bullying Victimization and Perpetration: A Meta-Analysis of Prospective Studies and Research. *Trauma, Violence, & Abuse*, 152483802090651. https://doi.org/10.1177/1524838020906513

Wang, M., Wang, J., Deng, X., & Chen, W. (2019). Why are empathic children more liked by peers? The mediating roles of prosocial and aggressive behaviors. *Personality and Individual Differences*, *144*, 19–23. https://doi.org/10.1016/j.paid.2019.02.029

Weaver, J. M., & Schofield, T. J. (2015). Mediation and Moderation of Divorce Effects on Children's Behavior Problems. *Journal of Family Psychology*, *29*(1), 39–48. http://dx.doi.org/10.1037/fam0000043

Weaver, J. M.., & Schofield, T. J.. (2015). Mediation and moderation of divorce effects on children's behavior problems. *Journal of Family Psychology*, *29*(1), 39–48. http://dx.doi.org/10.1037/fam0000043

Wei, W., Lu, H., Zhao, H., Chen, C., Dong, Q., & Zhou, X. (2012). Gender Differences in Children's Arithmetic Performance Are Accounted for by Gender Differences in Language Abilities. *Psychological Science*, *23*(3), 320–330. https://doi.org/10.1177/0956797611427168

Wentzel, K. R. (2002). Are effective teachers like good parents? Teaching styles and student adjustment in early adolescence. *Child Development*, *73*(1), 287–301. http://www.ncbi.nlm.nih.gov/pubmed/14717258

Wigfield, A., Eccles, J. S., Fredricks, J. A., Simpkins, S., Roeser, R. W., & Schiefele, U. (2015). Development of Achievement Motivation and Engagement. In M. Lamb (Ed.), *Handbook of Child Psychology and Developmental Science* (pp. 1–44). John Wiley & Sons, Inc. https://doi.org/10.1002/9781118963418.childpsy316

Wildeman, C., Goldman, A. W., & Turney, K. (2018). Parental Incarceration and Child Health in the United States. *Epidemiologic Reviews*, *40*(1), 146–156. https://doi.org/10.1093/epirev/mxx013

Williamson, V., Stevelink, S. A. M., Da Silva, E., & Fear, N. T. (2018). A systematic review of wellbeing in children: A comparison of military and civilian families. *Child and Adolescent Psychiatry and Mental Health*, *12*(1), 1–11. https://doi.org/10.1186/s13034-018-0252-1

Wojslawowicz Bowker, J. C., Rubin, K. H., Burgess, K. B., Booth-Laforce, C., & Rose-Krasnor, L. (2006). Behavioral characteristics associated with stable and fluid best friendship patterns in middle childhood. *Merrill-Palmer Quarterly*, *52*(4), 671–693. jcbowker@buffalo.edu.

Wright, K. M., Riviere, L. A., Merrill, J. C., & Cabrera, O. A. (2013). Resilience in military families: A review of programs and empirical evidence. In R. R. Sinclair & T. W. Britt (Eds.), *Building psychological resilience in military personnel: Theory and practice* (pp. 167–191). American Psychological Association. https://doi.org/10.1037/14190-008

Yeager, D. S., & Dweck, C. S. (2012). Mindsets That Promote Resilience: When Students Believe That Personal Characteristics Can Be Developed. *Educational Psychologist*, *47*(4), 302–314. https://doi.org/10.1080/00461520.2012.722805

Zadeh, S. (2020). Single Motherhood via Sperm Donation: Empirical Insights from a Longitudinal Study of Solo Mother Families in the UK. In K. Beier, B. Claudia, P. Thorn, & C. Wiesemann (Eds.), *Assistierte Reproduktion mit Hilfe Dritter* (pp. 389–399). Springer Berlin Heidelberg. https://doi.org/10.1007/978-3-662-60298-0_25

Zemp, M., & Bodenmann, G. (2018). Family structure and the nature of couple relationships: Relationship distress, separation, divorce, and repartnering. In M. R. Sanders & A. Morawska (Eds.), *Handbook of Parenting and Child Development Across the Lifespan* (pp. 415–440). Springer International Publishing. https://doi.org/10.1007/978-3-319-94598-9_18

Zimmermann, P., & Iwanski, A. (2014). Emotion regulation from early adolescence to emerging adulthood and middle adulthood: Age differences, gender differences, and emotion-specific developmental variations. *International Journal of Behavioral Development*, *38*(2), 182–194. https://doi.org/10.1177/0165025413515405

Zosuls, K. M., Andrews, N. C. Z., Martin, C. L., England, D. E., & Field, R. D. (2016). Developmental Changes in the Link Between Gender Typicality and Peer Victimization and Exclusion. *Sex Roles*, *75*(5–6), 243–256. https://doi.org/10.1007/s11199-016-0608-z

Zych, I., Farrington, D. P., Llorent, V. J., & Ttofi, M. M. (2017). *Protecting Children Against Bullying and Its Consequences*. Springer International Publishing. https://doi.org/10.1007/978-3-319-53028-4

CHAPTER 9

Aïte, A., Cassotti, M., Linzarini, A., Osmont, A., Houdé, O., & Borst, G. (2018). Adolescents' inhibitory control: keep it cool or lose control. *Developmental Science*, *21*(1), e12491. https://doi.org/10.1111/desc.12491

Akos, P., Rose, R. A., & Orthner, D. (2014). Sociodemographic moderators of middle school transition effects on academic achievement. *The Journal of Early Adolescence*, *35*(2), 170–198. https://doi.org/10.1177/0272431614529367

Albert, D., Chein, J., & Steinberg, L. (2013). The teenage brain: Peer influences on adolescent decision making. *Current Directions in Psychological Science*, *22*(2), 114–120. https://doi.org/10.1177/0963721412471347

Alberts, A., Elkind, D., & Ginsberg, S. (2007). The personal fable and risk-taking in early adolescence. *Journal of Youth & Adolescence*, *36*(1), 71–76.

Alivernini, F., & Lucidi, F. (2011). Relationship between social context, self-efficacy, motivation, academic achievement, and intention to drop out of high school: A longitudinal study. *The Journal of Educational Research*, *104*(4), 241–252. https://doi.org/10.1080/00220671003728062

Alley, K. M. (2019). Fostering middle school students' autonomy to support motivation and engagement. *Middle School Journal*, *50*(3), 5–14. https://doi.org/10.1080/00940771.2019.1603801

Andersson, U. (2008). Working memory as a predictor of written arithmetical skills in children: The importance of central executive functions. *British Journal of Educational Psychology*, *78*(2), 181–203.

Ardila, A. (2013). Development of metacognitive and emotional executive functions in children. *Applied Neuropsychology. Child*, *2*(2), 82–87. https://doi.org/10.1080/21622965.2013.748388

Arnett, J. J. (Ed.). (2016). *The oxford handbook of emerging adulthood* (Vol. 1). Oxford University Press. https://doi.org/10.1093/oxfordhb/9780199795574.001.0001

Asato, M. R., Terwilliger, R., Woo, J., & Luna, B. (2010). White matter development in adolescence: A DTI study. *Cerebral Cortex (New York, N.Y.: 1991)*, *20*(9), 2122–2131. https://doi.org/10.1093/cercor/bhp282

Assadi, S. M., Zokaei, N., Kaviani, H., Mohammadi, M. R., Ghaeli, P., Gohari, M. R., & van de Vijver, F. J. R. (2007). Effect of sociocultural context and parenting style on scholastic achievement among Iranian adolescents. *Social Development*, *16*, 169–180.

Baams, L., Dubas, J. S., Overbeek, G., & van Aken, M. A. G. (2015). Transitions in body and behavior: a meta-analytic study on the relationship between pubertal development and adolescent sexual behavior. *The Journal of Adolescent Health : Official Publication of the Society for Adolescent Medicine*, *56*(6), 586–598. https://doi.org/10.1016/j.jadohealth.2014.11.019

Baddeley, A. (2016). Working memory. In R. J. Sternberg, S. T. Fiske, & D. J. Foss (Eds.), *Scientists making a difference: One hundred eminent behavioral and brain scientist talk about their most important contributions* (pp. 119–122). Cambridge University Press.

Ballesteros, M. F., Williams, D. D., Mack, K. A., Simon, T. R., & Sleet, D. A. (2018). The epidemiology of unintentional and violence-related injury morbidity and mortality among children and adolescents in the United States. *International Journal of Environmental Research and Public Health*, *15*(4). https://doi.org/10.3390/ijerph15040616

Banfield, E. C., Liu, Y., Davis, J. S., Chang, S., & Frazier-Wood, A. C. (2016). Poor adherence to US dietary guidelines for children and adolescents in the national health and nutrition examination survey population. *Journal of the Academy of Nutrition and Dietetics*, *116*(1), 21–27. https://doi.org/10.1016/j.jand.2015.08.010

Barber, B. K., & Olsen, J. A. (2004). Assessing the transitions to middle and high school. *Journal of Adolescent Research*, *19*(1), 3–30.

Barrouillet, P., Gavens, N., Vergauwe, E., Gaillard, V., & Camos, V. (2009). Working memory span development: A time-based resource-sharing model account. *Developmental Psychology*, *45*(2), 477–490. https://doi.org/10.1037/a0014615

Bartel, K. A., Gradisar, M., & Williamson, P. (2015). Protective and risk factors for adolescent sleep: A meta-analytic review. *Sleep Medicine Reviews*, *21*, 72–85. https://doi.org/10.1016/j.smrv.2014.08.002

Battin-Pearson, S., & Newcomb, M. D. (2000). Predictors of early high school dropout: A test of five theories. *Journal of Educational Psychology*, *92*(3), 15p.

Battistella, G., Fornari, E., Annoni, J.-M., Chtioui, H., Dao, K., Fabritius, M., Favrat, B., Mall, J.-F., Maeder, P., & Giroud, C. (2014). Long-term effects of Cannabis on brain structure. *Neuropsychopharmacology*, *39*(9), 2041–2048. https://doi.org/10.1038/npp.2014.67

Bava, S., & Tapert, S. F. (2010). Adolescent brain development and the risk for alcohol and other drug problems. *Neuropsychology Review*, *20*(4), 398–413. https://doi.org/10.1007/s11065-010-9146-6

Behera, D., Sivakami, M., & Behera, M. R. (2015). Menarche and menstruation in rural adolescent girls in Maharashtra, India. *Journal of Health Management*, *17*(4), 510–519. https://doi.org/10.1177/0972063415612581

Belcher, B. R., Zink, J., Azad, A., Campbell, C. E., Chakravartti, S. P., & Herting, M. M. (2020). The roles of physical activity, exercise, and fitness in promoting resilience during adolescence: Effects on mental well-being and brain development. In *Biological Psychiatry: Cognitive Neuroscience and Neuroimaging*. *Elsevier Inc*. https://doi.org/10.1016/j.bpsc.2020.08.005

Benner, A. D. (2011). The transition to high school: Current knowledge, future directions. *Educational Psychology Review*, *23*(3), 299–328. https://doi.org/10.1007/s10648-011-9152-0

Benner, A. D., Boyle, A. E., & Bakhtiari, F. (2017). Understanding students' transition to high school: Demographic variation and the role of supportive relationships. *Journal of Youth and Adolescence*, *46*(10), 2129–2142. https://doi.org/10.1007/s10964-017-0716-2

Benner, A. D., Boyle, A. E., & Sadler, S. (2016). Parental involvement and adolescents' educational success: The roles of prior achievement and socioeconomic status. *Journal of Youth and Adolescence*, *45*(6), 1053–1064. https://doi.org/10.1007/s10964-016-0431-4

Benner, A. D., & Graham, S. (2009). The transition to high school as a developmental process among multiethnic urban youth. *Child Development*, *80*(2), 356–376. https://doi.org/10.1111/j.1467-8624.2009.01265.x

Berenbaum, S. A., Beltz, A. M., & Corley, R. (2015). The importance of puberty for adolescent development: Conceptualization and measurement. *Advances in Child Development and Behavior*, *48*, 53–92. https://doi.org/10.1016/BS.ACDB.2014.11.002

Berger, T., Peschel, T., Vogel, M., Pietzner, D., Poulain, T., Jurkutat, A., Meuret, S., Engel, C., Kiess, W., & Fuchs, M. (2019). Speaking voice in children and adolescents: Normative data and associations with BMI, tanner stage, and singing activity. *Journal of Voice*, *33*(4), 580.e21 –580.e30, . https://doi.org/10.1016/j.jvoice.2018.01.006

Biddle, S. J. H., Ciaccioni, S., Thomas, G., & Vergeer, I. (2019). Physical activity and mental health in children and adolescents: An updated review of reviews and an analysis of causality. *Psychology of Sport and Exercise*, *42*, 146–155. https://doi.org/10.1016/j.psychsport.2018.08.011

Biehl, M., Natsuaki, M., & Ge, X. (2007). The influence of pubertal timing on alcohol use and heavy drinking trajectories. *Journal of Youth & Adolescence*, *36*(2), 153–167.

Birney, D. P., & Sternberg, R. J. (2011). The development of cognitive abilities. Developmental science: An advanced textbook. In M. H. Bornstein & M. E. Lamb (Eds.), *Developmental science: An advanced textbook* (6th ed., pp. 353–388). Psychology Press.

Biro, F. M., Greenspan, L. C., & Galvez, M. P. (2012). Puberty in girls of the 21st century. *Journal of Pediatric and Adolescent Gynecology*, *25*(5), 289–294. https://doi.org/10.1016/j.jpag.2012.05.009

Biro, F. M., Pajak, A., Wolff, M. S., Pinney, S. M., Windham, G. C., Galvez, M. P., Greenspan, L. C., Kushi, L. H., & Teitelbaum, S. L. (2018). Age of menarche in a longitudinal US cohort. *Journal of Pediatric and Adolescent Gynecology*, *31*(4), 339–345. https://doi.org/10.1016/j.jpag.2018.05.002

Blake, M. J., Latham, M. D., Blake, L. M., & Allen, N. B. (2019). Adolescent-sleep-intervention research: Current state and future directions. *Current Directions in Psychological Science*, *28*(5), 475–482. https://doi.org/10.1177/0963721419850169

Blakemore, S.-J., & Mills, K. L. (2014). Is adolescence a sensitive period for sociocultural processing? *Annual Review of Psychology*, *65*, 187–207. https://doi.org/10.1146/annurev-psych-010213-115202

Boonk, L., Gijselaers, H. J. M., Ritzen, H., & Brand-Gruwel, S. (2018). A review of the relationship between parental involvement indicators and academic achievement. *Educational Research Review*, *24*, 10–30. https://doi.org/10.1016/j.edurev.2018.02.001

Booth, M. Z., & Gerard, J. M. (2014). Adolescents' stage-environment fit in middle and high school: The relationship between students' perceptions of their schools and themselves. *Youth & Society*, *46*(6), 735–755. https://doi.org/10.1177/0044118X12451276

Bowers, A. J., & Sprott, R. (2012). Examining the multiple trajectories associated with dropping out of high school: A growth mixture model analysis. *The Journal of Educational Research*, *105*(3), 176–195. https://doi.org/10.1080/00220671.2011.552075

Brain Development Cooperative Group. (2012). Total and Regional Brain Volumes in a Population-Based Normative Sample from 4 to 18 Years: The NIH MRI Study of Normal Brain Development. *Cerebral Cortex*, *22*(1), 1–12. doi:10.1093/cercor/bhr018

Breiner, K., Li, A., Cohen, A. O., Steinberg, L., Bonnie, R. J., Scott, E. S., Taylor-Thompson, K., Rudolph, M. D., Chein, J., Richeson, J. A., Dellarco, D. V., Fair, D. A., Casey, B. J., & Galván, A. (2018). Combined effects of peer presence, social cues, and rewards on cognitive control in adolescents. *Developmental Psychobiology*, *60*(3), 292–302. https://doi.org/10.1002/dev.21599

Brooks-Gunn, J., & Ruble, D. N. (2013). Developmental processes in the experience of menarche. In J. E. S. A. Baum & J. E. SinA. Baum (Eds.), *Issues in child health and adolescent health: Handbook of psychology and health* (pp. 117–148). Psychology Press.

Brown, S. L., Teufel, J., Birch, D. A., & Abrams, T. E. (2019). Family meals and adolescent perceptions of parent–child connectedness. *Journal of Family Studies*, *25*(1), 34–45. https://doi.org/10.1080/13229400.2016.1200115

Bucci, R., & Staff, J. (2020). Pubertal timing and adolescent delinquency †. *Criminology*, *58*(3), 537–567. https://doi.org/10.1111/1745-9125.12245

Burchinal, M., Roberts, J. E., Zeisel, S. A., Hennon, E. A., & Hooper, S. (2006). Social risk and protective child, parenting, and child care factors in early elementary school years. *Parenting: Science & Practice*, *6*(1), 79–113.

Burns, E. C. (2020). Factors that support high school completion: A longitudinal examination of quality teacher-student relationships and intentions to graduate. *Journal of Adolescence*, *84*, 180–189. https://doi.org/10.1016/j.adolescence.2020.09.005

Busch, A. S., Højgaard, B., Hagen, C. P., & Teilmann, G. (2020). Obesity is associated with earlier pubertal onset in boys. *The Journal of Clinical Endocrinology & Metabolism*, *105*(4), e1667–e1672. https://doi.org/10.1210/clinem/dgz222

Busch, A. S., Hollis, B., Day, F. R., Sørensen, K., Aksglaede, L., Perry, J. R. B., Ong, K. K., Juul, A., & Hagen, C. P. (2019). Voice break in boys-temporal relations with other pubertal milestones and likely causal effects of BMI. *Human Reproduction (Oxford, England)*, *34*(8), 1514–1522. https://doi.org/10.1093/humrep/dez118

Bygdell, M., Vandenput, L., Ohlsson, C., & Kindblom, J. M. (2014). A Secular Trend for Pubertal Timing in Swedish Men Born 1946-1991 – the Best Cohort : Puberty: From Bench to Bedside. *ENDO Meetings*. http://press.endocrine.org/doi/abs/10.1210/endo-meetings.2014.PE.10.OR11-3

Byrnes, V., & Ruby, A. (2007). Comparing achievement between K--8 and middle schools: A large-scale empirical study. *American Journal of Education*, *114*(1), 101–135.

Camos, V., Barrouillet, P., & Barrouillet, P. (2018). *Working memory in development*. Routledge. https://doi.org/10.4324/9781315660851

Campbell, C. E., Mezher, A. F., Eckel, S. P., Tyszka, J. M., Pauli, W. M., Nagel, B. J., & Herting, M. M. (2021). Restructuring of amygdala subregion apportion across adolescence. *Developmental Cognitive Neuroscience, 100883*. https://doi.org/10.1016/j.dcn.2020.100883

Carlson, S. M., Zelazo, P. D., & Faja, S. (2013). Executive funtion. In D. Zelazo (Ed.), *The Oxford handbook of developmental psychology, Vol. 1: Body and mind*. Oxford University Press. https://doi.org/10.1093/oxfordhb/9780199958450.013.0025

Carpendale, J. I. M., & Lewis, C. (2015). The development of Social understanding. In *Handbook of child psychology and developmental science* (pp. 1–44). John Wiley & Sons, Inc. https://doi.org/10.1002/9781118963418.childpsy210

Carskadon, M. A., & Tarokh, L. (2014). Developmental changes in sleep biology and potential effects on adolescent behavior and caffeine use. *Nutrition Reviews, 72*(suppl 1), 60–64. https://doi.org/10.1111/nure.12147

Carter, R. (2015). Anxiety symptoms in African American youth. *The Journal of Early Adolescence, 35*(3), 281–307. https://doi.org/10.1177/0272431614530809

Carter, R., Halawah, A., & Trinh, S. L. (2018). Peer exclusion during the pubertal transition: The role of social competence. *Journal of Youth and Adolescence, 47*(1), 121–134. https://doi.org/10.1007/s10964-017-0682-8

Carter, R., Mustafaa, F. N., & Leath, S. (2018). Teachers' expectations of girls' classroom performance and behavior. *The Journal of Early Adolescence, 38*(7), 885–907. https://doi.org/10.1177/0272431617699947

Casey, B. J. (2015). Beyond simple models of self-control to circuit-based accounts of adolescent behavior. *Annual Review of Psychology, 66*, 295–319. https://doi.org/10.1146/annurev-psych-010814-015156

Castro, M., Expósito-Casas, E., López-Martín, E., Lizasoain, L., Navarro-Asencio, E., & Gaviria, J. L. (2015). Parental involvement on student academic achievement: A meta-analysis. *In Educational Research Review, 14*, 33–46. Elsevier Ltd. https://doi.org/10.1016/j.edurev.2015.01.002

Chad, J. A. (2020). The first ejaculation: A male pubertal milestone comparable to Menarche? *Journal of Sex Research, 57*(2), 213–221. https://doi.org/10.1080/00224499.2018.1543643

Chandra-Mouli, V., & Patel, S. V. (2017). Mapping the knowledge and understanding of menarche, menstrual hygiene and menstrual health among adolescent girls in low- and middle-income countries. *Reproductive Health, 14*(1), 30. https://doi.org/10.1186/s12978-017-0293-6

Chen, F. R., Rothman, E. F., & Jaffee, S. R. (2017). Early puberty, friendship group characteristics, and dating abuse in US girls. *Pediatrics, 139*(6), e20162847. https://doi.org/10.1542/peds.2016-2847

Christenson, S. L., & Thurlow, M. L. (2004). School dropouts: Prevention considerations, interventions, and challenges. *Current Directions in Psychological Science, 13*(1), 36–39. https://doi.org/10.1111/j.0963-7214.2004.01301010.x

Chye, Y., Christensen, E., & Yücel, M. (2020). Cannabis use in adolescence: A review of neuroimaging findings. *Journal of Dual Diagnosis, 16*(1), 83–105. https://doi.org/10.1080/15504263.2019.1636171

Coelho, V. A., Marchante, M., & Jimerson, S. R. (2017). Promoting a positive middle school transition: A randomized-controlled treatment study examining self-concept and self-eEsteem. *Journal of Youth and Adolescence, 46*(3), 558–569. https://doi.org/10.1007/s10964-016-0510-6

Cohen, A. O., & Casey, B. J. (2017). The neurobiology of adolescent self-control. In T. Egner (Ed.), *The Wiley Handbook of Cognitive Control* (pp. 455–475). Ltd: John Wiley & Sons. https://doi.org/10.1002/9781118920497.ch26

Cohen Kadosh, K., Johnson, M. H., Dick, F., Cohen Kadosh, R., & Blakemore, S.-J. (2013). Effects of age, task performance, and structural brain development on face processing. *Cerebral Cortex (New York, N.Y.: 1991), 23*(7), 1630–1642. https://doi.org/10.1093/cercor/bhs150

Cooper, S. M., Kurtz-Costes, B., & Rowley, S. J. (2010). The schooling of African American children. In J. L. Meece & J. S. Eccles (Eds.), *Handbook of research on schools, schooling and human development* (pp. 275–292). Routledge.

Copeland, W. E., Worthman, C., Shanahan, L., Costello, E. J., & Angold, A. (2019). Early pubertal timing and testosterone associated With higher levels of adolescent depression in girls. *Journal of the American Academy of Child and Adolescent Psychiatry, 58*(12), 1197–1206. https://doi.org/10.1016/j.jaac.2019.02.007

Cornell, D., Gregory, A., Huang, F., & Fan, X. (2013). Perceived prevalence of teasing and bullying predicts high school dropout rates. *Journal of Educational Psychology, 105*(1), 138–149.

Costos, D., Ackerman, R., & Paradis, L. (2002). Recollections of menarche: Communication between mothers and daughters regarding menstruation. *Sex Roles, 46*(1–2), 49–59. https://doi.org/10.1023/A:1016037618567

Cowan, N., Hismjatullina, A., AuBuchon, A. M., Saults, J. S., Horton, N., Leadbitter, K., & Towse, J. (2010). With development, list recall includes more chunks, not just larger ones. *Developmental Psychology, 46*(5), 1119–1131. https://doi.org/10.1037/a0020618

Coyle, T. R., Pillow, D. R., Snyder, A. C., & Kochunov, P. (2011). Processing speed mediates the development of general intelligence (g) in adolescence. *Psychological Science, 22*(10), 1265–1269. https://doi.org/10.1177/0956797611418243

Crockett, L. J., Petersen, A. C., Graber, J. A., Schulenberg, J. E., & Ebata, A. (1989). School transitions and adjustment during early adolescence. *The Journal of Early Adolescence, 9*(3), 181–210. https://doi.org/10.1177/0272431689093002

Crone, E. A., Peters, S., & Steinbeis, N. (2018). Executive function: development in adolescence. In S. A. Wiebe & J. Karbach (Eds.), *Executive function: Development across the life span* (pp. 58–72). Routledge.

Croninger, R. G., & Lee, V. E. (2001). Social capital and dropping out of high school: Benefits to at-risk students of teachers' support and guidance. *Teachers College Record, 103*(4), 548–582.

Crosnoe, R., Benner, A. D., Crosnoe, R., & Benner, A. D. (2015). Children at school. In M. H. Bornstein & T. Leventhal (Eds.), *Handbook of child psychology and developmental science* (pp. 1–37). John Wiley & Sons, Inc. https://doi.org/10.1002/9781118963418.childpsy407

Cservenka, A., & Brumback, T. (2017). The burden of binge and heavy drinking on the brain: Effects on adolescent and young adult neural structure and function. *Frontiers in Psychology, 8*, 1111. https://doi.org/10.3389/fpsyg.2017.01111

Currie, C., Ahluwalia, N., Godeau, E., Nic Gabhainn, S., Due, P., & Currie, D. B. (2012). Is obesity at individual and national level associated with lower age at menarche? Evidence from 34 countries in the Health Behaviour in School-aged Children Study. *The Journal of Adolescent Health : Official Publication of the Society for Adolescent Medicine, 50*(6), 621–626. https://doi.org/10.1016/j.jadohealth.2011.10.254

Curtin, S. C., Heron, M., Miniño, A. M., & Warner, M. (2018). Recent increases in injury mortality among children and adolescents aged 10-19 years in the United States: 1999-2016. National vital statistics reports : From the centers for disease control and prevention. *National Center for Health Statistics, National Vital Statistics System, 67*(4), 1–16. http://www.ncbi.nlm.nih.gov/pubmed/29874162

Cyrus, E., Coudray, M. S., Kiplagat, S., Mariano, Y., Noel, I., Galea, J. T., Hadley, D., Dévieux, J. G., & Wagner, E. (2021). A review investigating the relationship between cannabis use and adolescent cognitive functioning. In *Current Opinion in Psychology* (Vol. 38, pp. 38–48). Elsevier B.V. https://doi.org/10.1016/j.copsyc.2020.07.006

Dallacker, M., Hertwig, R., & Mata, J. (2019). Quality matters: A meta-analysis on components of healthy family meals. *Health Psychology, 38*(12), 1137–1149. https://doi.org/10.1037/hea0000801

Das, J. K., Salam, R. A., Thornburg, K. L., Prentice, A. M., Campisi, S., Lassi, Z. S., Koletzko, B., & Bhutta, Z. A. (2017). Nutrition in adolescents: Physiology, metabolism, and nutritional needs. *Annals of the New York Academy of Sciences, 1393*(1), 21–33. https://doi.org/10.1111/nyas.13330

Deardorff, J., Abrams, B., Ekwaru, J. P., & Rehkopf, D. H. (2014). Socioeconomic status and age at menarche: An examination of multiple indicators in an ethnically diverse cohort. *Annals of Epidemiology, 24*(10), 727–733. https://doi.org/10.1016/j.annepidem.2014.07.002

Deardorff, J., Ekwaru, J. P., Kushi, L. H., Ellis, B. J., Greenspan, L. C., Mirabedi, A., Landaverde, E. G., & Hiatt, R. A. (2011). Father absence, body mass index, and pubertal timing in girls: Differential effects by family income and ethnicity. *The Journal of Adolescent Health : Official Publication of the Society for Adolescent Medicine, 48*(5), 441–447. https://doi.org/10.1016/j.jadohealth.2010.07.032

Deardorff, J., Hoyt, L. T., Carter, R., & Shirtcliff, E. A. (2019). Next steps in puberty research: Broadening the lens toward under-studied populations. *Journal of Research on Adolescence, 29*(1), 133–154. https://doi.org/10.1111/jora.12402

Demanet, J., & van Houtte, M. (2012). School belonging and school misconduct: The differing role of teacher and peer attachment. *Journal of Youth and Adolescence, 41*(4), 499–514. https://doi.org/10.1007/s10964-011-9674-2

Demissie, Z., Eaton, D. K., Lowry, R., Nihiser, A. J., & Foltz, J. L. (2018). Prevalence and correlates of missing meals among high school students—United States, 2010. *American Journal of Health Promotion, 32*(1), 89–95. https://doi.org/10.1177/0890117116667348

DeRose, L. M., & Brooks-Gunn, J. (2006). Transition into adolescence: The role of pubertal processes. In L. Balter & C. S. Tamis-LeMonda (Eds.), *Child psychology: A handbook of contemporary issues* (2nd ed., pp. 385–414). Psychology Press.

de Wit, J. B. F., Stok, F. M., Smolenski, D. J., de Ridder, D. D. T., de Vet, E., Gaspar, T., Johnson, F., Nureeva, L., & Luszczynska, A. (2015). Food culture in the home environment: family meal practices and values can support healthy eating and self-regulation in young people in four European countries. *Applied Psychology. Health and Well-Being, 7*(1), 22–40. https://doi.org/10.1111/aphw.12034

Dimler, L. M., & Natsuaki, M. N. (2021). Trajectories of violent and nonviolent behaviors from adolescence to early adulthood: Does early puberty matter, and, if so, How long? *Journal of Adolescent Health, 68*(3), 523–531. https://doi.org/10.1016/j.jadohealth.2020.06.034

Dosenbach, N. U. F., Nardos, B., Cohen, A. L., Fair, D. A., Power, J. D., Church, J. A., Nelson, S. M., Wig, G. S., Vogel, A. C., Lessov-Schlaggar, C. N., Barnes, K. A., Dubis, J. W., Feczko, E., Coalson, R. S., Pruett, J. R., Barch, D. M., Petersen, S. E., Schlaggar, B. L., & Schlaggar, B. L. (2010). Prediction of individual brain maturity using fMRI. *Science (New York, N.Y), 329*(5997), 1358–1361. https://doi.org/10.1126/science.1194144

Dotterer, A. M., Lowe, K., & McHale, S. M. (2014). Academic growth trajectories and family relationships among African American youth. *Journal of Research on Adolescence, 24*(4), 734–747. https://doi.org/10.1111/jora.12080

Douglass, S., Yip, T., & Shelton, J. N. (2014). Intragroup contact and anxiety among ethnic minority adolescents: considering ethnic identity and school diversity transitions. *Journal of Youth and Adolescence, 43*(10), 1628–1641. https://doi.org/10.1007/s10964-014-0144-5

Duchesne, S., Larose, S., & Feng, B. (2019). Achievement goals and engagement with academic work in early high school: Does seeking help from teachers matter? *Journal of Early Adolescence, 39*(2), 222–252. https://doi.org/10.1177/0272431617737626

Duell, N., Steinberg, L., Icenogle, G., Chein, J., Chaudhary, N., Di Giunta, L., Dodge, K. A., Fanti, K. A., Lansford, J. E., Oburu, P., Pastorelli, C., Skinner, A. T., Sorbring, E., Tapanya, S., Uribe Tirado, L. M., Alampay, L. P., Al-Hassan, S. M., Takash, H. M. S., Bacchini, D., & Chang, L. (2018). Age patterns in risk taking across the world. *Journal of Youth and Adolescence, 47*(5), 1052–1072. https://doi.org/10.1007/s10964-017-0752-y

Dumith, S. C., Gigante, D. P., Domingues, M. R., & Kohl, H. W. (2011). Physical activity change during adolescence: a systematic review and a pooled analysis. *International Journal of Epidemiology, 40*(3), 685–698. https://doi.org/10.1093/ije/dyq272

Dumontheil, I. (2016). Adolescent brain development. *Current Opinion in Behavioral Sciences, 10*, 39–44. https://doi.org/10.1016/j.cobeha.2016.04.012

Dupéré, V., Dion, E., Leventhal, T., Archambault, I., Crosnoe, R., & Janosz, M. (2018). High school dropout in proximal context: The triggering role of stressful life events. *Child Development, 89*(2), e107–e122. https://doi.org/10.1111/cdev.12792

Dupere, V., Leventhal, T., Dion, E., Crosnoe, R., Archambault, I., & Janosz, M. (2015). Stressors and turning points in high school and dropout: A stress process, life course framework. *Review of Educational Research, 85*(4), 591–629. https://doi.org/10.3102/0034654314559845

Eccles, J. S., & Roeser, R. W. (2011). Schools as developmental contexts during adolescence. *Journal of Research on Adolescence, 21*(1), 225–241. https://doi.org/10.1111/j.1532-7795.2010.00725.x

Eccles, J. S., & Roeser, R. W. (2015). School and community influences on human development. In H. Bornstein. Marc & M. E. Lamb (Eds.), *Developmental science: An advanced textbook* (7th ed., pp. 645–727). Psychology Press.

Eckert-Lind, C., Busch, A. S., Petersen, J. H., Biro, F. M., Butler, G., Bräuner, E. V., & Juul, A. (2020). Worldwideseculartrends inage atpubertalonsetassessed bybreastdevelopment amonggirls: Asystematicreview andmeta-analysis. *JAMA Pediatrics*, *174*(4), e195881–e195881. https://doi.org/10.1001/jamapediatrics.2019.5881

Elkind, D., & Bowen, R. (1979). Imaginary audience behavior in children and adolescents. *Developmental Psychology*, *15*(1), 38–44.

Embury, C. M., Wiesman, A. I., Proskovec, A. L., Mills, M. S., Heinrichs-Graham, E., Wang, Y. P., Calhoun, V. D., Stephen, J. M., & Wilson, T. W. (2019). Neural dynamics of verbal working memory processing in children and adolescents. *NeuroImage*, *185*, 191–197. https://doi.org/10.1016/j.neuroimage.2018.10.038

Emmanuel, M., & Bokor, B. R. (2017). Tanner Stages. In *StatPearls*. StatPearls Publishing. http://www.ncbi.nlm.nih.gov/pubmed/29262142

Espinoza, G., & Juvonen, J. (2011). Perceptions of the school social context across the transition to middle school: Heightened sensitivity among Latino students? *Journal of Educational Psychology*, *103*(3), 749–758. https://doi.org/10.1037/a0023811

Esteban-Cornejo, I., Tejero-Gonzalez, C. M., Sallis, J. F., & Veiga, O. L. (2015). Physical activity and cognition in adolescents: A systematic review. *Journal of Science and Medicine in Sport*, *18*(5), 534–539. https://doi.org/10.1016/J.JSAMS.2014.07.007

Farooq, M. A., Parkinson, K. N., Adamson, A. J., Pearce, M. S., Reilly, J. K., Hughes, A. R., Janssen, X., Basterfield, L., & Reilly, J. J. (2018). Timing of the decline in physical activity in childhood and adolescence: Gateshead Millennium Cohort Study. *British Journal of Sports Medicine*, *52*, 1002–1006. https://doi.org/10.1136/bjsports-2016-096933

Felmlee, D., McMillan, C., Inara Rodis, P., & Osgood, D. W. (2018). Falling Behind: Lingering Costs of the High School Transition for Youth Friendships and Grades. *Sociology of Education*, *91*(2), 159–182. https://doi.org/10.1177/0038040718762136

Figner, B., Mackinlay, R. J., Wilkening, F., & Weber, E. U. (2009). Affective and deliberative processes in risky choice: Age differences in risk taking in the Columbia Card Task. *Journal of Experimental Psychology: Learning, Memory, and Cognition*, *35*(3), 709–730. https://doi.org/10.1037/a0014983

Finn, A. S., Minas, J. E., Leonard, J. A., Mackey, A. P., Salvatore, J., Goetz, C., West, M. R., Gabrieli, C. F. O., & Gabrieli, J. D. E. (2017). Functional brain organization of working memory in adolescents varies in relation to family income and academic achievement. *Developmental Science*, *20*(5), e12450. https://doi.org/10.1111/desc.12450

Flannery, K. M., & Smith, R. L. (2017). The effects of age, gender, and gender role ideology on adolescents' social perspective-taking ability and tendency in friendships. *Journal of Social and Personal Relationships*, *34*(5), 617–635. https://doi.org/10.1177/0265407516650942

Fontanellaz-Castiglione, C. E., Markovic, A., & Tarokh, L. (2020). Sleep and the adolescent brain. In *Current Opinion in Physiology* (Vol. 15, pp. 167–171). Elsevier Ltd. https://doi.org/10.1016/j.cophys.2020.01.008

Frankel, L. L. (2002). I've never thought about it: Contradictions and taboos surrounding American males' experiences of first ejaculation (Semenarche). *Journal of Men's Studies*, *11*(1), 37–54.

Frazier-Wood, A. C., Banfield, E. C., Liu, Y., Davis, J. S., & Chang, S. (2015). Abstract 27: Poor adherence to US dietary guidelines for children and adolescents in the national health and nutrition examination survey (NHANES) 2005-2010 Population. *Circulation*, *131*(Suppl 1). http://circ.ahajournals.org/content/131/Suppl_1/A27.short

Frederick, C. B., Snellman, K., & Putnam, R. D. (2014). Increasing socioeconomic disparities in adolescent obesity. *Proceedings of the National Academy of Sciences of the United States of America*, *111*(4), 1338–1342. https://doi.org/10.1073/pnas.1321355110

Freeman, J., & Simonsen, B. (2015). Examining the impact of policy and practice interventions on high school dropout and school completion rates: A systematic review of the literature. *Review of Educational Research*, *85*(2), 205–248. https://doi.org/10.3102/0034654314554431

Frostad, P., Pijl, S. J., & Mjaavatn, P. E. (2014). Losing all interest in school: Social participation as a predictor of the intention to leave upper secondary school early. *Scandinavian Journal of Educational Research*, *59*(1), 110–122. https://doi.org/10.1080/00313831.2014.904420

Fuhrmann, D., Knoll, L. J., & Blakemore, S.-J. (2015). Adolescence as a sensitive period of brain development. *Trends in Cognitive Sciences*, *19*(10), 558–566. https://doi.org/10.1016/j.tics.2015.07.008

Fuligni, A. J., Arruda, E. H., Krull, J. L., & Gonzales, N. A. (2018). Adolescent sleep duration, variability, and peak levels of achievement and mental health. *Child Development*, *89*(2), e18–e28. https://doi.org/10.1111/cdev.12729

Gaddis, A., & Brooks-Gunn, J. (1985). The male experience of pubertal change. *Journal of Youth and Adolescence*, *14*(1), 61–69.

Gaillard, V., Barrouillet, P., Jarrold, C., & Camos, V. (2011). Developmental differences in working memory: Where do they come from? *Journal of Experimental Child Psychology*, *110*(3), 469–479. https://doi.org/10.1016/j.jecp.2011.05.004

Galván, A. (2019). The unrested adolescent brain. *Child Development Perspectives*, *13*(3), 141–146. https://doi.org/10.1111/cdep.12332

Galván, A. (2020). The need for sleep in the adolescent brain. *Trends in Cognitive Sciences*, *24*(1), 79–89. https://doi.org/10.1016/j.tics.2019.11.002

Gavand, K. A., Cain, K. L., Conway, T. L., Saelens, B. E., Frank, L. D., Kerr, J., Glanz, K., & Sallis, J. F. (2019). Associations between neighborhood recreation environments and adolescent physical activity. *Journal of Physical Activity and Health*, *16*(10), 880–885. https://doi.org/10.1123/jpah.2018-0556

Geeraert, B. L., Lebel, R. M., & Lebel, C. (2019). A multiparametric analysis of white matter maturation during late childhood and adolescence. *Human Brain Mapping*, *40*(15), 4345–4356. https://doi.org/10.1002/hbm.24706

Geier, C. F. (2013). Adolescent cognitive control and reward processing: implications for risk taking and substance use. *Hormones and Behavior*, *64*(2), 333–342. https://doi.org/10.1016/j.yhbeh.2013.02.008

Gentle-Genitty, C. (2009). Best practice program for low-income African American students transitioning from middle to high school. *Children & Schools*, *31*(2), 109–117.

Giedd, J. N. (2018). A ripe time for adolescent research. *Journal of Research on Adolescence*, *28*(1), 157–159. https://doi.org/10.1111/jora.12378

Giedd, J. N., Lalonde, F. M., Celano, M. J., White, S. L., Wallace, G. L., Lee, N. R., & Lenroot, R. K. (2009). Anatomical brain magnetic resonance imaging of typically developing children and adolescents. *Journal of the American Academy of Child & Adolescent Psychiatry*, *48*(5), 465–470. https://doi.org/10.1097/CHI.0b013e31819f215

Goddings, A.-L., Beltz, A., Peper, J. S., Crone, E. A., & Braams, B. R. (2019). Understanding the role of puberty in structural and functional development of the adolescent brain. *Journal of Research on Adolescence*, *29*(1), 32–53. https://doi.org/10.1111/jora.12408

Golden, A. R., Griffin, C. B., Metzger, I. W., & Cooper, S. M. (2018). School racial climate and academic outcomes in African American adolescents: The protective role of peers. *Journal of Black Psychology*, *44*(1), 47–73. https://doi.org/10.1177/0095798417736685

Goldstein, S. E., Boxer, P., & Rudolph, E. (2015). Middle school transition stress: Links with academic performance, motivation, and school eExperiences. *Contemporary School Psychology*, *19*(1), 21–29. https://doi.org/10.1007/s40688-014-0044-4

Gonzalez, A.-L., & Wolters, C. A. (2006). The relation between perceived parenting practices and achievement motivation in mathematics. *Journal of Research in Childhood Education*, *21*(2), 203–217.

Gopinath, B., Flood, V. M., Burlutsky, G., Louie, J. C. Y., Baur, L. A., & Mitchell, P. (2016). Frequency of takeaway food consumption and its association with major food group consumption, anthropometric measures and blood pressure during adolescence. *British Journal of Nutrition*, *115*(11), 2025–2030. https://doi.org/10.1017/S000711451600101X

Gorey, C., Kuhns, L., Smaragdi, E., Kroon, E., & Cousijn, J. (2019). Age-related differences in the impact of cannabis use on the brain and cognition: A systematic review. *European Archives of Psychiatry and Clinical Neuroscience*, *269*(1), 37–58. https://doi.org/10.1007/s00406-019-00981-7

Graber, J. A., Nichols, T. R., & Brooks-Gunn, J. (2010). Putting pubertal timing in developmental context: Implications for prevention. *Developmental Psychobiology*, *52*(3), 254–262. https://doi.org/10.1002/dev.20438

Gremmen, M. C., Berger, C., Ryan, A. M., Steglich, C. E. G., Veenstra, R., & Dijkstra, J. K. (2019). Adolescents' friendships, academic achievement, and risk behaviors: Same-behavior and cross-behavior selection and influence Processes. *Child Development*, *90*(2), e192–e211. https://doi.org/10.1111/cdev.13045

Gremmen, M. C., Dijkstra, J. K., Steglich, C., & Veenstra, R. (2017). First selection, then influence: Developmental differences in friendship dynamics regarding academic achievement. *Developmental Psychology*, *53*(7), 1356–1370. https://doi.org/10.1037/devC000314

Guerri, C., & Pascual, M. (2019). Impact of neuroimmune activation induced by alcohol or drug abuse on adolescent brain development. *International Journal of Developmental Neuroscience*, *77*, 89–98. https://doi.org/10.1016/j.ijdevneu.2018.11.006

Gyurkovics, M., Stafford, T., & Levita, L. (2020). Cognitive control across adolescence: Dynamic adjustments and mind-wandering. *Journal of Experimental Psychology: General*, *149*(6), 1017–1031. https://doi.org/10.1037/xge0000698

Hamlat, E. J., Snyder, H. R., Young, J. F., & Hankin, B. L. (2019). Pubertal timing as a transdiagnostic risk for psychopathology in youth. *Clinical Psychological Science*, *7*(3), 411–429. https://doi.org/10.1177/2167702618810518

Hanania, R., & Smith, L. B. (2010). Selective attention and attention switching: Towards a unified developmental approach. *Developmental Science*, *13*(4), 622–635. https://doi.org/10.1111/j.1467-7687.2009.00921.x

Hansen, A., Turpyn, C. C., Mauro, K., Thompson, J. C., & Chaplin, T. M. (2019). Adolescent brain response to reward is associated with a bias toward immediate reward. *Developmental Neuropsychology*, *44*(5), 417–428. https://doi.org/10.1080/87565641.2019.1636798

Heaven, P. C. L., & Ciarrochi, J. (2008). Parental styles, conscientiousness, and academic performance in high school: A three-wave longitudinal study. *Personality and Social Psychology Bulletin*, *34*(4), 451–461. https://doi.org/10.1177/0146167207311909

Henry, K. L., Knight, K. E., & Thornberry, T. P. (2012). School disengagement as a predictor of dropout, delinquency, and problem substance use during adolescence and early adulthood. *Journal of Youth and Adolescence*, *41*(2), 156–166. https://doi.org/10.1007/s10964-011-9665-3

Herman-Giddens, M. E. (2006). Recent data on pubertal milestones in United States children: the secular trend toward earlier development. *International Journal of Andrology*, *29*(1), 241–246.

Herman-Giddens, M. E., Steffes, J., Harris, D., Slora, E., Hussey, M., Dowshen, S. A., Wasserman, R., Serwint, J. R., Smitherman, L., & Reiter, E. O. (2012). Secondary sexual characteristics in boys: data from the Pediatric Research in Office Settings Network. *Pediatrics*, *130*(5), e1058–68. https://doi.org/10.1542/peds.2011-3291

Hodges-Simeon, C. R., Gurven, M., Cárdenas, R. A., & Gaulin, S. J. C. (2013). Voice change as a new measure of male pubertal timing: A study among Bolivian adolescents. *Annals of Human Biology*, *40*(3), 209–219. https://doi.org/10.3109/03014460.2012.759622

Horvath, G., Knopik, V. S., & Marceau, K. (2020). Polygenic influences on pubertal timing and tempo and depressive symptoms in boys and girls. *Journal of Research on Adolescence*, *30*(1), 78–94. https://doi.org/10.1111/jora.12502

Hueston, C. M., Cryan, J. F., & Nolan, Y. M. (2017). Stress and adolescent hippocampal neurogenesis: Diet and exercise as cognitive modulators. *Translational Psychiatry*, *7*(4), e1081. https://doi.org/10.1038/tp.2017.48

Inhelder, B., & Piaget, J. (1958). *The growth of logical thinking: From childhood to adolescence*. Basic Books.

Jacobus, J., Squeglia, L. M., Infante, M. A., Castro, N., Brumback, T., Meruelo, A. D., & Tapert, S. F. (2015). Neuropsychological performance in adolescent marijuana users with co-occurring alcohol use: A three-year longitudinal study. *Neuropsychology*, *29*(6), 829–843. https://doi.org/10.1037/neu0000203

Jahns, L., Siega-Riz, A. M., & Popkin, B. M. (2001). The increasing prevalence of snacking among US children from 1977 to 1996. *Journal of Pediatrics*, *138*, 493–498.

Jamieson, D., Broadhouse, K. M., Lagopoulos, J., & Hermens, D. F. (2020). Investigating the links between adolescent sleep deprivation, fronto-limbic connectivity and the Onset of Mental Disorders: a review of the literature. In *In Sleep Medicine* (Vol. 66, pp. 61–67). Elsevier B.V. https://doi.org/10.1016/j.sleep.2019.08.013

Janosz, M., Archambault, I., Morizot, J., & Pagani, L. S. (2008). School engagement trajectories and their differential predictive relations to dropout. *Journal of Social Issues*, *64*(1), 21–40. https://doi.org/10.1111/j.1540-4560.2008.00546.x

Janssen, H. G., Davies, I. G., Richardson, L. D., & Stevenson, L. (2018). Determinants of takeaway and fast food consumption: A narrative review. *Nutrition Research Reviews*, *31*(1), 16–34. https://doi.org/10.1017/S0954422417000178

Jaramillo, J., Mello, Z. R., & Worrell, F. C. (2016). Ethnic identity, stereotype threat, and perceived discrimination among native American adolescents. *Journal of Research on Adolescence*, *26*(4), 769–775. https://doi.org/10.1111/jora.12228

Javadi, A. H., Schmidt, D. H. K., & Smolka, M. N. (2014). Differential representation of feedback and decision in adolescents and adults. *Neuropsychologia*, *56*, 280–288. https://doi.org/10.1016/j.neuropsychologia.2014.01.021

Jia, Y., Konold, T. R., & Cornell, D. (2016). Authoritative school climate and high school dropout rates. *School Psychology Quarterly*, *31*(2), 289–303. https://doi.org/10.1037/spq0000139

Joos, C. M., Wodzinski, A. M., Wadsworth, M. E., & Dorn, L. D. (2018). Neither antecedent nor consequence: Developmental integration of chronic stress, pubertal timing, and conditionally adapted stress response. *Developmental Review*, *48*, 1–23. https://doi.org/10.1016/J.DR.2018.05.001

Juvonen, J., Kogachi, K., & Graham, S. (2018). When and how do students benefit from ethnic diversity in middle chool? *Child Development*, *89*(4), 1268–1282. https://doi.org/10.1111/cdev.12834

Kail, R. V. (2008). Speed of processing in childhood and adolescence: Nature, consequences, and implications for understanding atypical development. In J. DeLuca & J. H. Kalmar (Eds.), *Information processing speed in clinical populations* (pp. 101–123). Taylor & Francis.

Kann, L., Kinchen, S., Shanklin, S. L., Flint, K. H., Kawkins, J., Harris, W. A., Lowry, R., Olsen, E. O., McManus, T., Chyen, D., Whittle, L., Taylor, E., Demissie, Z., Brener, N., Thornton, J., Moore, J., & Zaza, S. (2014). Youth risk behavior surveillance--United States, 2013. *Morbidity and Mortality Weekly Report. Surveillance Summaries (Washington, D.C.: 2002)*, *63*(4 Suppl. 4), 1–168. http://www.ncbi.nlm.nih.gov/pubmed/24918634

Karbach, J., Gottschling, J., Spengler, M., Hegewald, K., & Spinath, F. M. (2013). Parental involvement and general cognitive ability as predictors of domain-specific academic achievement in early adolescence. *Learning and Instruction*, *23*, 43–51. https://doi.org/10.1016/j.learninstruc.2012.09.004

Karim, A., Qaisar, R., & Hussain, M. A. (2021). Growth and socio-economic status, influence on the age at menarche in school going girls. *Journal of Adolescence*, *86*, 40–53. https://doi.org/10.1016/j.adolescence.2020.12.001

Kazi, S., & Galanaki, E. (2020). Piagetian theory of cognitive development. In S. J. Hupp & D. Jeremy (Eds.), *The Encyclopedia of Child and Adolescent Development* (pp. 1–11). Wiley. https://doi.org/10.1002/9781119171492.wecad364

Keating, D. P. (2012). Cognitive and brain development in adolescence. *Enfance*, *2012*(03), 267–279. https://doi.org/10.4074/S0013754512003035

Kelly, Y., Zilanawala, A., Sacker, A., Hiatt, R., & Viner, R. (2017). Early puberty in 11-year-old girls: Millennium Cohort Study findings. *Archives of Disease in Childhood*, *102*(3), 232–237. https://doi.org/10.1136/archdischild-2016-310475

Kidger, J., Araya, R., Donovan, J., & Gunnell, D. (2012). The effect of the school environment on the emotional health of adolescents: A systematic review. *Pediatrics*, *129*(5), 925–949. https://doi.org/10.1542/peds.2011-2248

Kilford, E. J., Garrett, E., & Blakemore, S.-J. (2016). The development of social cognition in adolescence: An integrated perspective. *Neuroscience & Biobehavioral Reviews*, *70*, 106–120. https://doi.org/10.1016/J.NEUBIOREV.2016.08.016

Kleanthous, K., Dermitzaki, E., Papadimitriou, D. T., Papaevangelou, V., & Papadimitriou, A. (2017). Secular changes in the final height of Greek girls are levelling off. *Acta Paediatrica*, *106*(2), 341–343. https://doi.org/10.1111/apa.13677

Kochanek, K. D., Murphy, S. L., Xu, J., & Arias, E. (2017). *Mortality in the United States, 2016 key findings data from the national vital statistics system*. https://www.cdc.gov/nchs/data/databriefs/db293.pdf NCHS Data Brief, 293

Kretsch, N., Mendle, J., Cance, J. D., & Harden, K. P. (2016). Peer group similarity in perceptions of pubertal timing. *Journal of Youth and Adolescence*, *45*(8), 1696–1710. https://doi.org/10.1007/s10964-015-0275-3

Kretsch, N., Mendle, J., & Harden, K. P. (2016). A twin study of objective and subjective pubertal timing and peer influence on risk-taking. *Journal of Research on Adolescence: The Official Journal of the Society for Research on Adolescence*, *26*(1), 45–59. https://doi.org/10.1111/jora.12160

Kuhn, D. (2012). The development of causal reasoning. *Wiley Interdisciplinary Reviews: Cognitive Science*, *3*(3), 327–335. https://doi.org/10.1002/wcs.1160

Kuhn, D. (2013). Reasoning. In P. D. Zelazo (Ed.), *The oxford handbook of developmental psychology body and mind* (Vol. 1, pp. 744–764). Oxford University Press. https://doi.org/10.1093/oxfordhb/9780199958450.013.0026

Kundu, P., Benson, B. E., Rosen, D., Frangou, S., Leibenluft, E., Luh, W.-M., Bandettini, P. A., Pine, D. S., & Ernst, M. (2018). The integration of functional brain activity from adolescence to adulthood. *The Journal of Neuroscience*, *38*(14), 3559–3570. https://doi.org/10.1523/JNEUROSCI.1864-17.2018

Labouvie-Vief, G. (2015). *Integrating emotions and cognition throughout the lifespan*. Springer. https://doi.org/10.1007/978-3-319-09822-7

Lacroix, A. E., & Whitten, R. A. (2017). Menarche. In *StatPearls*. *StatPearls Publishing*. http://www.ncbi.nlm.nih.gov/pubmed/29261991

Last, B. S., Lawson, G. M., Breiner, K., Steinberg, L., & Farah, M. J. (2018). Childhood socioeconomic status and executive function in childhood and beyond. *PLOS ONE*, *13*(8), e0202964. https://doi.org/10.1371/journal.pone.0202964

Lawson, G. M., Hook, C. J., & Farah, M. J. (2018). A meta-analysis of the relationship between socioeconomic status and executive function performance among children. *Developmental Science*, *21*(2), e12529. https://doi.org/10.1111/desc.12529

Lebel, C., & Deoni, S. (2018). The development of brain white matter microstructure. *NeuroImage*. https://doi.org/10.1016/J.NEUROIMAGE.2017.12.097

Lee, J. M., Wasserman, R., Kaciroti, N., Gebremariam, A., Steffes, J., Dowshen, S., Harris, D., Serwint, J., Abney, D., Smitherman, L., Reiter, E., & Herman-Giddens, M. E. (2016). Timing of puberty in overweight versus obese boys. *Pediatrics*, *137*(2), e20150164–e20150164. https://doi.org/10.1542/peds.2015-0164

Lee, T. H., Perino, M. T., McElwain, N. L., & Telzer, E. H. (2019). Perceiving facial affective ambiguity: A behavioral and neural comparison of adolescents and adults. *Emotion*. https://doi.org/10.1037/emo0000558

Lees, B., Meredith, L. R., Kirkland, A. E., Bryant, B. E., & Squeglia, L. M. (2020). Effect of alcohol use on the adolescent brain and behavior. In *Pharmacology Biochemistry and Behavior* (Vol. 192, p. 172906). Elsevier Inc. https://doi.org/10.1016/j.pbb.2020.172906

Lehman, D. R., & Nisbett, R. E. (1990). A longitudinal study of the effects of undergraduate training on reasoning. *Developmental Psychology*, *26*, 952–960.

Luna, B., Marek, S., Larsen, B., Tervo-Clemmens, B., & Chahal, R. (2015). An integrative model of the maturation of cognitive control. *Annual Review of Neuroscience*, *38*(1), 151–170. https://doi.org/10.1146/annurev-neuro-071714-034054

Madjar, N., & Cohen-Malayev, M. (2016). Perceived school climate across the transition from elementary to middle school. *School Psychology Quarterly*, *31*(2), 270–288. https://doi.org/10.1037/spq0000129

Mahoney, J. L. (2014). School extracurricular activity participation and early school dropout: A mixed-method study of the role of peer social networks. *Journal of Educational and Developmental Psychology*, *4*(1), 143. https://doi.org/10.5539/jedp.v4n1p143

Malagoli, C., & Usai, M. C. (2018). The effects of gender and age on inhibition and working memory organization in 14- to 19-year-old adolescents and young adults. *Cognitive Development*, *45*, 10–23. https://doi.org/10.1016/j.cogdev.2017.10.005

Marti, E., & Rodríguez, C. (2012). *After piaget*. Transaction Publishers.

Marusak, H. A., Zundel, C. G., Brown, S., Rabinak, C. A., & Thomason, M. E. (2017). Convergent behavioral and corticolimbic connectivity evidence of a negativity bias in children and adolescents. *Social Cognitive and Affective Neuroscience*, *12*(4), 517–525. https://doi.org/10.1093/scan/nsw182

Marván, M. L., Chrisler, J. C., Gorman, J. A., & Barney, A. (2017). The meaning of menarche: A cross-cultural semantic network analysis. *Health Care for Women International*, *38*(9), 971–982. https://doi.org/10.1080/07399332.2017.1338706

McIlvain, G., Clements, R. G., Magoon, E. M., Spielberg, J. M., Telzer, E. H., & Johnson, C. L. (2020). Viscoelasticity of reward and control systems in adolescent risk taking. *NeuroImage*, *215*, 116850. https://doi.org/10.1016/j.neuroimage.2020.116850

McMahon, E. M., Corcoran, P., O'Regan, G., Keeley, H., Cannon, M., Carli, V., Wasserman, C., Hadlaczky, G., Sarchiapone, M., Apter, A., Balazs, J., Balint, M., Bobes, J., Brunner, R., Cozman, D., Haring, C., Iosue, M., Kaess, M., Kahn, J.-P., & Wasserman, D. (2017). Physical activity in European adolescents and associations with anxiety, depression and well-being. *European Child & Adolescent Psychiatry*, *26*(1), 111–122. https://doi.org/10.1007/s00787-016-0875-9

Memmert, D. (2014). Inattentional blindness to unexpected events in 8–15-year-olds. *Cognitive Development*, *32*, 103–109. https://doi.org/10.1016/J.COGDEV.2014.09.002

Mendle, J. (2014). Beyond pubertal timing: New directions for studying lidividual differences in development. *Current Directions in Psychological Science*, *23*(3), 215–219. https://doi.org/10.1177/0963721414530144

Mendle, J., & Ferrero, J. (2012). Detrimental psychological outcomes associated with pubertal timing in adolescent boys. *Developmental Review*, *32*(1), 49–66. https://doi.org/10.1016/j.dr.2011.11.001

Mendle, J., Turkheimer, E., D'Onofrio, B. M., Lynch, S. K., Emery, R. E., Slutske, W. S., & Martin, N. G. (2006). Family structure and age at menarche: A children-of-twins approach. *Developmental Psychology*, *42*, 533–542.

Meng, J., Martinez, L., Holmstrom, A., Chung, M., & Cox, J. (2017). Research on social networking sites and social support from 2004 to 2015: A narrative review and directions for future research. *Cyberpsychology, Behavior, and Social Networking*, *20*(1), 44–51. https://doi.org/10.1089/cyber.2016.0325

Metcalf, B. S., Hosking, J., Jeffery, A. N., Henley, W. E., & Wilkin, T. J. (2015). Exploring the adolescent fall in physical activity: A 10-yr cohort study (EarlyBird 41). *Medicine and Science in Sports and Exercise*, *47*(10), 2084–2092. https://doi.org/10.1249/MSS.0000000000000644

Midgley, C., Anderman, E., & Hicks, L. (1995). Differences between elementary and middle school teachers and students: A goal theory approach. *The Journal of Early Adolescence*, *15*(1), 90–113. https://doi.org/10.1177/0272431695015001006

Mielke, G. I., Brown, W. J., Nunes, B. P., Silva, I. C. M., & Hallal, P. C. (2017). Socioeconomic correlates of sedentary behavior in adolescents:. *Systematic Review and Meta-Analysis. Sports Medicine*, *47*(1), 61–75. https://doi.org/10.1007/s40279-016-0555-4

Miller, M. B., Janssen, T., & Jackson, K. M. (2017). The prospective association between sleep and initiation of substance use in young adolescents. *The Journal of Adolescent Health: Official Publication of the Society for Adolescent Medicine*, *60*(2), 154–160. https://doi.org/10.1016/j.jadohealth.2016.08.019

Mills, K. L., Goddings, A.-L., Clasen, L. S., Giedd, J. N., & Blakemore, S.-J. (2014). The developmental mismatch in structural brain maturation during adolescence. *Developmental Neuroscience*, *36*(3–4), 147–160. https://doi.org/10.1159/000362328

Mills, K. L., Goddings, A.-L., Herting, M. M., Meuwese, R., Blakemore, S.-J., Crone, E. A., Dahl, R. E., Güroğlu, B., Raznahan, A., Sowell, E. R., & Tamnes, C. K. (2016). Structural brain development between childhood and adulthood: Convergence across four longitudinal samples. *NeuroImage*, *141*, 273–281. https://doi.org/10.1016/J.NEUROIMAGE.2016.07.044

Mills, K. L., & Tamnes, C. K. (2018). Longitudinal structural and functional brain development in childhood and adolescence. *Preprint*. https://doi.org/10.31234/OSF.IO/87KFT

Minges, K. E., & Redeker, N. S. (2016). Delayed school start times and adolescent sleep: A systematic review of the experimental evidence. *Sleep Medicine Reviews*, *28*, 86–95. https://doi.org/10.1016/j.smrv.2015.06.002

Moore, S. A., Cumming, S. P., Balletta, G., Ramage, K., Eisenmann, J. C., Baxter-Jones, A. D. G., Jackowski, S. A., & Sherar, L. B. (2020). Exploring the relationship between adolescent biological maturation, physical activity, and sedentary behaviour: A systematic review and narrative synthesis. *Annals of Human Biology, 47*(4), 365–383. https://doi.org/10.1080/03014460.2020.1805006

Moore, S. R., Harden, K. P., & Mendle, J. (2014). Pubertal timing and adolescent sexual behavior in girls. *Developmental Psychology, 50*(6), 1734–1745. https://doi.org/10.1037/a0036027

Morris, A. S., Squeglia, L. M., Jacobus, J., & Silk, J. S. (2018). Adolescent brain development: Implications for understanding risk and resilience processes through neuroimaging research. *Journal of Research on Adolescence, 28*(1), 4–9. https://doi.org/10.1111/jora.12379

Moshman, D. (2021). Adolescent reasoning and rationality. In D. Fasko & F. Fair (Eds.), *Critical thinking and reasoning* (pp. 99–113). Brill | Sense. https://doi.org/10.1163/9789004444591_007

Motta-Mena, N. V., & Scherf, K. S. (2017). Pubertal development shapes perception of complex facial expressions. *Developmental Science, 20*(4), e12451. https://doi.org/10.1111/desc.12451

Mueller, C. E., & Anderman, E. M. (2010). Middle school transitions and adolescent development. In J. L. Meece & J. S. Eccles (Eds.), *Handbook of research on schools, schooling and human development* (pp. 216–233). Routledge. https://doi.org/10.4324/9780203874844-24

Mueller, S. C., Maheu, F. S., Dozier, M., Peloso, E., Mandell, D., Leibenluft, E., Pine, D. S., & Ernst, M. (2010). Early-life stress is associated with impairment in cognitive control in adolescence: an fMRI study. *Neuropsychologia, 48*(10), 3037–3044. https://doi.org/10.1016/j.neuropsychologia.2010.06.013

Müller, U., & Kerns, K. (2015). The development of executive function. In L. Liben & U. Müller (Eds.), *Handbook of child psychology and developmental science* (pp. 1–53). John Wiley & Sons, Inc. https://doi.org/10.1002/9781118963418.childpsy214

Nasiri, S., Dolatian, M., Tehrani, F. R., Majd, H. A., Bagheri, A., & Malekifar, P. (2020). Factors related to the age at menarche in Iran: A systematic review and meta-analysis. *Original Article, 8*(9), 12091–12104. https://doi.org/10.22038/ijp.2020.49222.3939

National Center for Educational Statistics. (2017). *Dropout rates. The condition of education 2017.* https://nces.ed.gov/programs/coe/indicator_coj.asp

National Middle School Association. (2003). *This we believe: Successful schools for young adolescents.* Author.

Natsuaki, M. N., Samuels, D., & Leve, L. D. (2015). Puberty, identity, and context. In K. C. McLean & M. Syed (Eds.), *The oxford handbook of identity development* (pp. 389–405). Oxford University Press. https://doi.org/10.1093/oxfordhb/9780199936564.013.005

Neel, C. G. O., & Fuligni, A. (2013). A longitudinal study of school belonging and academic motivation across high school. *Child Development, 84*(2), 678–692. https://doi.org/10.1111/j.1467-8624.2012.01862.x

Negriff, S., Blankson, A. N., & Trickett, P. K. (2015). Pubertal timing and tempo: Associations with childhood maltreatment. *Journal of Research on Adolescence, 25*(2), 201–213. https://doi.org/10.1111/jora.12128

Negriff, S., & Susman, E. J. (2011). Pubertal timing, depression, and externalizing problems: A framework, review, and examination of gender differences. *Journal of Research on Adolescence, 21*(3), 717–746. https://doi.org/10.1111/j.1532-7795.2010.00708.x

Nelson, C. A. (2011). Neural development and lifelong plasticity. In D. P. Keating (Ed.), *Nature and nurture in early child development* (pp. 45–69). Cambridge University Press.

Nguyen-Louie, T. T., Brumback, T., Worley, M. J., Colrain, I. M., Matt, G. E., Squeglia, L. M., & Tapert, S. F. (2018). Effects of sleep on substance use in adolescents: a longitudinal perspective. *Addiction Biology, 23*(2), 750–760. https://doi.org/10.1111/adb.12519

Nilsen, E. S., & Bacso, S. A. (2017). Cognitive and behavioural predictors of adolescents' communicative perspective-taking and social relationships. *Journal of Adolescence, 56*, 52–63. https://doi.org/10.1016/J.ADOLESCENCE.2017.01.004

Noble, K. G., Houston, S. M., Brito, N. H., Bartsch, H., Kan, E., Kuperman, J. M., Akshoomoff, N., Amaral, D. G., Bloss, C. S., Libiger, O., Schork, N. J., Murray, S. S., Casey, B. J., Chang, L., Ernst, T. M., Frazier, J. A., Gruen, J. R., Kennedy, D. N., Van Zijl, P., & ... Sowell, E. R. (2015). Family income, parental education and brain structure in children and adolescents. *Nature Neuroscience, 18*(5), 773–778. https://doi.org/10.1038/nn.3983

Noll, J. G., Trickett, P. K., Long, J. D., Negriff, S., Susman, E. J., Shalev, I., Li, J. C., & Putnam, F. W. (2017). Childhood sexual abuse and early timing of puberty. *Journal of Adolescent Health, 60*(1), 65–71. https://doi.org/10.1016/j.jadohealth.2016.09.008

Obeidallah, D. A., Brennan, R. T., Brooks-Gunn, J., Kindlon, D., & Earls, F. (2000). Socioeconomic status, race, and girls' pubertal maturation: Results from the project on human development in Chicago neighborhoods. *Journal of Research on Adolescence (Lawrence Erlbaum), 10*(4), 443–464.

Ohlsson, C., Bygdell, M., Celind, J., Sondén, A., Tidblad, A., Sävendahl, L., & Kindblom, J. M. (2019). Secular trends in pubertal growth acceleration in Swedish boys born from 1947 to 1996. *JAMA Pediatrics, 173*(9), 860–865. https://doi.org/10.1001/jamapediatrics.2019.2315

Omar, H., McElderry, D., & Zakharia, R. (2003). Educating adolescents about puberty: What are we missing? *International Journal of Adolescent Medicine and Health, 15*, 79–83.

Owens, J. A., Dearth-Wesley, T., Herman, A. N., Oakes, J. M., & Whitaker, R. C. (2017). A quasi-experimental study of the impact of school start time changes on adolescent sleep. *Sleep Health, 3*(6), 437–443. https://doi.org/10.1016/j.sleh.2017.09.001

Öztürk, R., & Güneri, S. E. (2020). Symptoms experiences and attitudes towards menstruation among adolescent girls. *Journal of Obstetrics and Gynaecology.* https://doi.org/10.1080/01443615.2020.1789962

Papadimitriou, A. (2016a). Timing of puberty and secular trend in human maturation. In P. Kumanov & A. Agarwal (Eds.), *Puberty* (pp. 121–136). Springer International Publishing. https://doi.org/10.1007/978-3-319-32122-6_9

Papadimitriou, A. (2016b). The evolution of the age at menarche from prehistorical to modern times. *Journal of Pediatric and Adolescent Gynecology, 29*(6), 527–530. https://doi.org/10.1016/j.jpag.2015.12.002

Paulsen, D. J., Hallquist, M. N., Geier, C. F., & Luna, B. (2014). Effects of incentives, age, and behavior on brain activation during inhibitory control: A longitudinal fMRI study. *Developmental Cognitive Neuroscience, 11*, 105–115. https://doi.org/10.1016/j.dcn.2014.09.003

Payne, G.., & Isaacs, L.. (2020). *Human motor development: A lifespan approach* (10th ed.). Routledge.

Payne, V. G., & Isaacs, L. D. (2016). *Human motor development: A lifespan approach*. McGraw-Hill. http://dl.acm.org/citation.cfm?id=1214267

Peeters, M., Janssen, T., Monshouwer, K., Boendermaker, W., Pronk, T., Wiers, R., & Vollebergh, W. (2015). Weaknesses in executive functioning predict the initiating of adolescents' alcohol use. *Developmental Cognitive Neuroscience, 16*, 139–146. https://doi.org/10.1016/j.dcn.2015.04.003

Peltz, J. S., Rogge, R. D., & O'Connor, T. G. (2019). Adolescent sleep quality mediates family chaos and adolescent mental health: A daily diary-based study. *Journal of Family Psychology, 33*(3), 259–269. https://doi.org/10.1037/fam0000491

Piaget, J. (1972). Intellectual evolution from adolescence to adulthood. *Human Development, 51*(1), 40–47. https://doi.org/10.1159/000112531

Picci, G., & Scherf, K. S. (2016). From caregivers to peers. *Psychological Science, 27*(11), 1461–1473. https://doi.org/10.1177/0956797616663142

Piccolo, L. R., Merz, E. C., & Noble, K. G. (2018). School climate is associated with cortical thickness and executive function in children and adolescents. *Developmental Science, e127*(19). https://doi.org/10.1111/desc.12719

Pieters, S., Burk, W. J., Van der Vorst, H., Dahl, R. E., Wiers, R. W., & Engels, R. C. M. E. (2015). Prospective relationships between sleep problems and substance use, internalizing and externalizing problems. *Journal of Youth and Adolescence, 44*(2), 379–388. https://doi.org/10.1007/s10964-014-0213-9

Pinquart, M. (2017). Associations of parenting dimensions and styles with externalizing problems of children and adolescents: An updated meta-analysis. *Developmental Psychology, 53*(5), 873–932. https://doi.org/10.1037/dev0000295

Piras, G. N., Bozzola, M., Bianchin, L., Bernasconi, S., Bona, G., Lorenzoni, G., Buzi, F., Rigon, F., Tonini, G., De Sanctis, V., & Perissinotto, E. (2020). The levelling-off of the secular trend of age at menarche among Italian girls. *Heliyon, 6*(6), e04222. https://doi.org/10.1016/j.heliyon.2020.e04222

Prewett, S. L., Bergin, D. A., & Huang, F. L. (2019). Student and teacher perceptions on student-teacher relationship quality: A middle school perspective. *School Psychology International, 40*(1), 66–87. https://doi.org/10.1177/0143034318807743

Pyra, E., & Schwarz, W. (2019). Puberty: Normal, delayed, and precocious. In A. Grossman, C. Follin, C. Yedinak, & S. Llahana (Eds.), *Advanced practice in endocrinology nursing* (pp. 63–84). Springer International Publishing. https://doi.org/10.1007/978-3-319-99817-6_4

Rai, R., Mitchell, P., Kadar, T., & Mackenzie, L. (2016). Adolescent egocentrism and the illusion of transparency: Are adolescents as egocentric as we might think? *Current Psychology, 35*(3), 285–294. https://doi.org/10.1007/s12144-014-9293-7

Rambaran, J. A., Hopmeyer, A., Schwartz, D., Steglich, C., Badaly, D., & Veenstra, R. (2017). Academic functioning and peer influences: A short-term longitudinal study of network-behavior dynamics in middle adolescence. *Child Development, 88*(2), 523–543. https://doi.org/10.1111/cdev.12611

Reigal, R. E., Moral-Campillo, L., Morillo-Baro, J. P., Juárez-Ruiz de Mier, R., Hernández-Mendo, A., & Morales-Sánchez, V. (2020). Physical exercise, fitness, cognitive functioning, and psychosocial variables in an adolescent sample. *International Journal of Environmental Research and Public Health, 17*(3), 1100. https://doi.org/10.3390/ijerph17031100

Rembeck, G., Möller, M., & Gunnarsson, R. (2006). Attitudes and feelings towards menstruation and womanhood in girls at menarche. *Acta Paediatrica, 95*(6), 707–714.

Reyna, V. F., & Farley, F. (2006). Risk and rationality in adolescent decision making: Implications for theory, practice, and public Policy. *Psychological Science in the Public Interest, 7*(1), 1–44.

Reyna, V. F., & Rivers, S. E. (2008). Current theories of risk and rational decision making. *Developmental Review, 28*(1), 1–11. https://doi.org/10.1016/j.dr.2008.01.002

Rickard, I. J., Frankenhuis, W. E., & Nettle, D. (2014). Why are childhood family factors associated with timing of maturation? A role for internal prediction. *Perspectives on Psychological Science, 9*(1), 3–15. https://doi.org/10.1177/1745691613513467

Roeser, R. W., Eccles, J. S., & Sameroff, A. J. (2000). School as a context of early adolescents' academic and social-emotional development: A summary of research findings. *Elementary School Journal, 100*(5), 443–471. http://eric.ed.gov/?id=EJ610301

Rojas-Gaona, C. E., Hong, J. S., & Peguero, A. A. (2016). The significance of race/ethnicity in adolescent violence: A decade of review, 2005–2015. *Journal of Criminal Justice, 46*, 137–147. https://doi.org/10.1016/J.JCRIMJUS.2016.05.001

Romeo, R. D. (2017). The impact of stress on the structure of the adolescent brain: Implications for adolescent mental health. *Brain Research, 1654*, 185–191. https://doi.org/10.1016/J.BRAINRES.2016.03.021

Rudolph, K. D., Lambert, S. F., Clark, A. G., & Kurlakowsky, K. D. (2001). Negotiating the transition to middle school: The role of self-regulatory processes. *Child Development, 72*(3), 929–947.

Rudolph, K. D., Troop-Gordon, W., Lambert, S. F., & Natsuaki, M. N. (2014). Long-term consequences of pubertal timing for youth depression: Identifying personal and contextual pathways of risk. *Development and Psychopathology, 26*(4pt2), 1423–1444. http://journals.cambridge.org/abstract_S0954579414001126

Sadler, K. (2017). Pubertal development. In M. A. Goldstein (Ed.), *The massGeneral hospital for children adolescent medicine handbook* (pp. 19–26). Springer International Publishing. https://doi.org/10.1007/978-3-319-45778-9_3

Sanders, J. O., Qiu, X., Lu, X., Duren, D. L., Liu, R. W., Dang, D., Menendez, M. E., Hans, S. D., Weber, D. R., & Cooperman, D. R. (2017). The uniform pattern of growth and skeletal maturation during the human adolescent growth spurt. *Scientific Reports, 7*(1), 16705. https://doi.org/10.1038/s41598-017-16996-w

Schelleman-Offermans, K., Knibbe, R. A., & Kuntsche, E. (2013). Are the effects of early pubertal timing on the initiation of weekly alcohol use mediated by peers and/or parents? A longitudinal study. *Developmental Psychology, 49*(7), 1277–1285.

Schlegel, A. (2008). A cross-cultural approach to adolescence. In D. L. Browning (Ed.), *Adolescent identities: A collection of readings* (pp. 31–44). The Analytic Press/Taylor & Francis Group.

Schwartz, P. D., Maynard, A. M., & Uzelac, S. M. (2008). Adolescent egocentrism: A contemporary view. *Adolescence, 43*(171), 441–448.

Scott, H., Biello, S. M., & Woods, H. C. (2019). Social media use and adolescent sleep patterns: Cross-sectional findings from the UK millennium cohort study. *BMJ Open, 9*(9), e031161. https://doi.org/10.1136/bmjopen-2019-031161

Scully, M., Morley, B., Niven, P., Crawford, D., Pratt, I. S., & Wakefield, M. (2020). Factors associated with frequent consumption of fast food among Australian secondary school students. *Public Health Nutrition, 23*(8), 1340–1349. https://doi.org/10.1017/S1368980019004208

Seaton, E. K., & Carter, R. (2018). Pubertal timing, racial identity, neighborhood, and school context among Black adolescent females. *Cultural Diversity and Ethnic Minority Psychology, 24*(1), 40–50. https://doi.org/10.1037/cdp0000162

Seaton, E. K., & Carter, R. (2019). Perceptions of pubertal timing and discrimination among African American and Caribbean black girls. *Child Development, 90*(2), 480–488. https://doi.org/10.1111/cdev.13221

Seaton, E. K., & Carter, R. (2020). Pubertal timing as a moderator between general discrimination experiences and self-esteem among African American and Caribbean black youth. *Cultural Diversity and Ethnic Minority Psychology, 26*(3), 390–398. https://doi.org/10.1037/cdp0000305

Seidman, E., Aber, J. L., & French, S. E. (2004). The organization of schooling and adolescent development. In K. I. Maton, C. J. Schellenbach, B. J. Leadbeater, & A. L. Solarz (Eds.), *Investing in children, youth, families, and communities: Strengths-based research and policy* (pp. 233–250). American Psychological Association.

Seidman, E., Lambert, L. E., Allen, L., & Aber, J. L. (2003). Urban adolescents' transition to junior high school and protective family transactions. *Journal of Early Adolescence, 23*(2), 166–194.

Servant, M., Cassey, P., Woodman, G. F., & Logan, G. D. (2018). Neural bases of automaticity. *Journal of Experimental Psychology: Learning, Memory, and Cognition, 44*(3), 440–464. https://doi.org/10.1037/xlm0000454

Sharman, R., & Illingworth, G. (2020). Adolescent sleep and school performance — the problem of sleepy teenagers. In *Current Opinion in Physiology* (Vol. 15, pp. 23–28). Elsevier Ltd. https://doi.org/10.1016/j.cophys.2019.11.006

Sherman, L. E., Rudie, J. D., Pfeifer, J. H., Masten, C. L., McNealy, K., & Dapretto, M. (2014). Development of the default mode and central executive networks across early adolescence: A longitudinal study. *Developmental Cognitive Neuroscience, 10*, 148–159. https://doi.org/10.1016/J.DCN.2014.08.002

Shimizu, M., Gillis, B. T., Buckhalt, J. A., & El-Sheikh, M. (2020). Linear and nonlinear associations between sleep and adjustment in adolescence. *Behavioral Sleep Medicine, 18*(5), 690–704. https://doi.org/10.1080/15402002.2019.1665049

Shubert, J., Wray-Lake, L., & McKay, B. (2020). Looking ahead and working hard: How school experiences foster adolescents' future orientation and perseverance. *Journal of Research on Adolescence, 30*(4), 989–1007. https://doi.org/10.1111/jora.12575

Shulman, E. P., & Cauffman, E. (2013). Reward-biased risk appraisal and its relation to juvenile versus adult crime. *Law and Human Behavior, 37*(6), 412–423. https://doi.org/10.1037/lhb0000033

Shulman, E. P., Smith, A. R., Silva, K., Icenogle, G., Duell, N., Chein, J., & Steinberg, L. (2016). The dual systems model: Review, reappraisal, and reaffirmation. *Developmental Cognitive Neuroscience, 17*, 103–117. https://doi.org/10.1016/j.dcn.2015.12.010

Silveri, M. M., Tzilos, G. K., & Yurgelun-Todd, D. A. (2008). Relationship between white matter volume and cognitive performance during adolescence: effects of age, sex and risk for drug use. *Addiction, 103*(9), 1509–1520. https://doi.org/10.1111/j.1360-0443.2008.02272.x

Simmonds, D., & Luna, B. (2015). Protracted development of brain systems underlying working memory in adolescence: a longitudinal study.

Singh, N., & Singh, S. (2020). Determination of age at menarche and its association with socio-economic status and physical activity: A study among Tibetan adolescent girls of Kangra district. *Online J Health Allied Scs, 19*(1), 2. https://www.researchgate.net/publication/342815215

Sisk, C. L. (2017). Development: Pubertal hormones meet the adolescent brain. *Current Biology, 27*(14), R706–R708. https://doi.org/10.1016/J.CUB.2017.05.092

Skoog, T., & Bayram Özdemir, S. (2016). Explaining why early-maturing girls are more exposed to sexual harassment in early adolescence. *The Journal of Early Adolescence, 36*(4), 490–509. https://doi.org/10.1177/0272431614568198

Skoog, T., Özdemir, S. B., & Stattin, H. (2016). Understanding the link between pubertal timing in girls and the development of depressive symptoms: The role of sexual harassment. *Journal of Youth and Adolescence, 45*(2), 316–327. https://doi.org/10.1007/s10964-015-0292-2

Smith, A. R., Steinberg, L., Strang, N., & Chein, J. (2015). Age differences in the impact of peers on adolescents' and adults' neural response to reward. *Developmental Cognitive Neuroscience, 11*, 75–82. https://doi.org/10.1016/j.dcn.2014.08.010

Sørensen, K.., Mouritsen, A.., Aksglaede, L.., Hagen, C. P.., Mogensen, S. S.., & Juul, A.. (2012). Recent secular trends in pubertal timing: Implications for evaluation and diagnosis of precocious puberty. *Hormone Research in Paediatrics, 77*(3), 137–145. https://doi.org/10.1159/000336325

Spear, L. P. (2018). Effects of adolescent alcohol consumption on the brain and behaviour. *Nature Reviews Neuroscience, 19*(4), 197–214. https://doi.org/10.1038/nrn.2018.10

Spera, C. (2005). A review of the relationship among parenting practices, parenting styles, and adolescent school achievement. *Educational Psychology Review, 17*(2), 125–146.

Spielberg, J. M., Olino, T. M., Forbes, E. E., & Dahl, R. E. (2014). Exciting fear in adolescence: Does pubertal development alter threat processing? *Developmental Cognitive Neuroscience, 8*, 86–95. https://doi.org/10.1016/j.dcn.2014.01.004

Squeglia, L. M., & Gray, K. M. (2016). Alcohol and drug use and the developing brain. *Current Psychiatry Reports, 18*(5), 46. https://doi.org/10.1007/s11920-016-0689-y

Squeglia, L. M., Tapert, S. F., Sullivan, E. V., Jacobus, J., Meloy, M. J., Rohlfing, T., & Pfefferbaum, A. (2015). Brain development in heavy-drinking adolescents. *American Journal of Psychiatry, 172*(6), 531–542. https://doi.org/10.1176/appi.ajp.2015.14101249

Stang, J. S., & Stotmeister, B. (2017). Nutrition in adolescence. In N. J. Temple, T. Wilson, & G. A. Bray (Eds.), *Nutrition guide for physicians and related healthcare professionals* (pp. 29–39). Springer International Publishing. https://doi.org/10.1007/978-3-319-49929-1_4

Stansfield, R., Williams, K. R., & Parker, K. F. (2017). Economic disadvantage and homicide. *Homicide Studies, 21*(1), 59–81. https://doi.org/10.1177/1088767916647990

Stein, J. H., & Reiser, L. W. (1994). A study of white middle-class adolescent boys' responses to ? semenarche? (the first ejaculation). *Journal of Youth and Adolescence, 23*(3), 373–384. https://doi.org/10.1007/BF01536725

Steinberg, L. (2008). A social neuroscience perspective on adolescent risk-taking. *Developmental Review, 28*(1), 78–106. https://doi.org/10.1016/j.dr.2007.08.002

Steinberg, L., Icenogle, G., Shulman, E. P., Breiner, K., Chein, J., Bacchini, D., Chang, L., Chaudhary, N., Giunta, L. Di., Dodge, K. A., Fanti, K. A., Lansford, J. E., Malone, P. S., Oburu, P., Pastorelli, C., Skinner, A. T., Sorbring, E., Tapanya, S., Tirado, L. M. U., . . . Takash, H. M. S. (2018). Around the world, adolescence is a time of heightened sensation seeking and immature self-regulation. *Developmental Science, 21*(2), e12532. https://doi.org/10.1111/desc.12532

Steinberg, L., & Lerner, R. M. (2004). The scientific study of adolescence: A brief history. *Journal of Early Adolescence, 24*(1), 45–54. https://doi.org/10.1177/0272431603260879

Stidham-Hall, K., Moreau, C., & Trussell, J. (2012). Patterns and correlates of parental and formal sexual and reproductive health communication for adolescent women in the United States, 2002-2008. *The Journal of Adolescent Health : Official Publication of the Society for Adolescent Medicine, 50*(4), 410–413. https://doi.org/10.1016/j.jadohealth.2011.06.007

Stojković, I. (2013). Pubertal timing and self-esteem in adolescents: The mediating role of body-image and social relations. *European Journal of Developmental Psychology, 10*(3), 359–377. https://doi.org/10.1080/17405629.2012.682145

Su, Q., Chen, Z., Li, R., Elgar, F. J., Liu, Z., & Lian, Q. (2018). Association between early menarche and school bullying. *Journal of Adolescent Health, 63*(2), 213–218. https://doi.org/10.1016/j.jadohealth.2018.02.008

Sun, Y., Mensah, F. K., Azzopardi, P., Patton, G. C., & Wake, M. (2017b). Childhood social disadvantage and pubertal timing: A national birth cohort from Australia. *Pediatrics, 139*(6), e20164099. https://doi.org/10.1542/peds.2016-4099

Sutton, A., Langenkamp, A. G., Muller, C., & Schiller, K. S. (2018). Who gets ahead and who falls behind during the transition to high school? Academic performance at the intersection of race/ethnicity and gender. *Social Problems, 65*(2), 154–173. https://doi.org/10.1093/socpro/spx044

Swartz, J. R., Weissman, D. G., Ferrer, E., Beard, S. J., Fassbender, C., Robins, R. W., Hastings, P. D., & Guyer, A. E. (2020). Reward-related brain activity prospectively predicts increases in alcohol use in adolescents. *Journal of the American Academy of Child and Adolescent Psychiatry, 59*(3), 391–400. https://doi.org/10.1016/j.jaac.2019.05.022

Takagi, M., Youssef, G., & Lorenzetti, V. (2016). Neuroimaging of the human brain in adolescent substance users. In D. De Micheli, A. L. Monezi Andrade, E. A. da Silva, & Maria Lucia Oliveira. de Souza Formigoni (Eds.), *Drug abuse in adolescence* (pp. 69–99). Springer International Publishing. https://doi.org/10.1007/978-3-319-17795-3_6

Tamnes, C., & Mills, K. (2020). Imaging structural brain development in childhood and adolescence. In D. Poeppel, G. Mangun, & M. Gazzaniga (Eds.), *The cognitive neurosciences VI* (pp. 17–25).

Tanner, J. M. (1990). *Foetus into man: Physical growth from conception to maturity.* Harvard University Press.

Taylor, R. L., Cooper, S. R., Jackson, J. J., & Barch, D. M. (2020). Assessment of neighborhood poverty, cognitive function, and prefrontal and hippocampal volumes in children. *JAMA Network Open, 3*(11), e2023774. https://doi.org/10.1001/jamanetworkopen.2020.23774

Theodoraki, T. E., McGeown, S. P., Rhodes, S. M., & MacPherson, S. E. (2020). Developmental changes in executive functions during adolescence: A study of inhibition, shifting, and working memory. *British Journal of Developmental Psychology, 38*(1), 74–89. https://doi.org/10.1111/bjdp.12307

Tinggaard, J., Mieritz, M. G., Sørensen, K., Mouritsen, A., Hagen, C. P., Aksglaede, L., Wohlfahrt-Veje, C., & Juul, A. (2012). The physiology and timing of male puberty. *Current Opinion in Endocrinology, Diabetes, and Obesity, 19*(3), 197–203. https://doi.org/10.1097/MED.0b013e3283535614

Tomlinson, R. C., Burt, S. A., Waller, R., Jonides, J., Miller, A. L., Gearhardt, A. N., Peltier, S. J., Klump, K. L., Lumeng, J. C., & Hyde, L. W. (2020). Neighborhood poverty predicts altered neural and behavioral response inhibition. *NeuroImage, 209*, 116536. https://doi.org/10.1016/j.neuroimage.2020.116536

Tomova, A. (2016). Body weight and puberty. In P. Kumanov & A. Agarwal (Eds.), *Puberty* (pp. 95–108). Springer International Publishing. https://doi.org/10.1007/978-3-319-32122-6_7

Tomova, A., Lalabonova, C., Robeva, R. N., & Kumanov, P. T. (2011). Timing of pubertal maturation according to the age at first conscious ejaculation. *Andrologia, 43*(3), 163–166. https://doi.org/10.1111/j.1439-0272.2009.01037.x

Tønnessen, E., Svendsen, I. S., Olsen, I. C., Guttormsen, A., & Haugen, T. (2015). Performance development in adolescent track and field athletes according to age, sex and sport discipline. *PLOS ONE, 10*(6), e0129014. https://doi.org/10.1371/journal.pone.0129014

Tottenham, N., & Galván, A. (2016). Stress and the adolescent brain: Amygdala-prefrontal cortex circuitry and ventral striatum as developmental targets. *Neuroscience & Biobehavioral Reviews, 70*, 217–227. https://doi.org/10.1016/J.NEUBIOREV.2016.07.030

Tremblay, L., & Larivière, M. (2020). Predictors of puberty onset. In S. J. Hupp & D. Jeremy (Eds.), *The encyclopedia of child and adolescent development* (pp. 1–10). Wiley. https://doi.org/10.1002/9781119171492.wecad352

Tsai, K. M., Dahl, R. E., Irwin, M. R., Bower, J. E., McCreath, H., Seeman, T. E., Almeida, D. M., & Fuligni, A. J. (2018). The roles of parental support and family stress in adolescent sleep. *Child Development, 89*(5), 1577–1588. https://doi.org/10.1111/cdev.12917

Tunau, K., Adamu, A., Hassan, M., Ahmed, Y., & Ekele, B. (2012). Age at menarche among school girls in Sokoto, Northern Nigeria. *Annals of African Medicine*, *11*, 103–107. http://www.ajol.info/index.php/aam/article/view/75230

Tyler, J. H., & Lofstrom, M. (2009). Finishing high school: Alternative pathways and dropout recovery. *The Future of Children / Center for the Future of Children , The David and Lucile Packard Foundation*, *19*(1), 77–103. http://europepmc.org/abstract/med/21141706

Ullsperger, J. M., & Nikolas, M. A. (2017). A meta-analytic review of the association between pubertal timing and psychopathology in adolescence: Are there sex differences in risk? *Psychological Bulletin*, *143*(9), 903–938. https://doi.org/10.1037/bul0000106

U.S. Department of Health and Human Services. (2017). *United States adolescent physical health facts | HHS.gov*. https://www.hhs.gov/ash/oah/facts-and-stats/national-and-state-data-sheets/adolescent-physical-health-and-nutrition/united-states/index.html

Utter, J., Denny, S., Peiris-John, R., Moselen, E., Dyson, B., & Clark, T. (2017). Family meals and adolescent emotional well-being: Findings from a national study. *Journal of Nutrition Education and Behavior*, *49*(1), 67-72.e1. https://doi.org/10.1016/j.jneb.2016.09.002

Utter, J., Larson, N., Berge, J. M., Eisenberg, M. E., Fulkerson, J. A., & Neumark-Sztainer, D. (2018). Family meals among parents: Associations with nutritional, social and emotional well-being. *Preventive Medicine*, *113*, 7–12. https://doi.org/10.1016/j.ypmed.2018.05.006

Valkenborghs, S. R., Noetel, M., Hillman, C. H., Nilsson, M., Smith, J. J., Ortega, F. B., & Lubans, D. R. (2019). The impact of physical activity on brain structure and function in youth: A systematic review. *Pediatrics: American Academy of Pediatrics*, *144*(4), 20184032. https://doi.org/10.1542/peds.2018-4032

van der Stel, M.., & Veenman, M. V. J.. (2013). Metacognitive skills and intellectual ability of young adolescents: A longitudinal study from a developmental perspective. *European Journal of Psychology Education*, *29*(1), 117–137. https://doi.org/10.1007/s10212-013-0190-5

van Duijvenvoorde, A. C. K., Peters, S., Braams, B. R., & Crone, E. A. (2016). What motivates adolescents? Neural responses to rewards and their influence on adolescents' risk taking, learning, and cognitive control. *Neuroscience & Biobehavioral Reviews*, *70*, 135–147. https://doi.org/10.1016/J.NEUBIOREV.2016.06.037

Vargas, T., Damme, K. S. F., & Mittal, V. A. (2020). Neighborhood deprivation, prefrontal morphology and neurocognition in late childhood to early adolescence. *NeuroImage*, *220*, 117086. https://doi.org/10.1016/j.neuroimage.2020.117086

Vermeulen, M. C. M., Heijden, K. B., Kocevska, D., Treur, J. L., Huppertz, C., Beijsterveldt, C. E. M., Boomsma, D. I., Swaab, H., Someren, E. J. W., & Bartels, M. (2021). Associations of sleep with psychological problems and well-being in adolescence: causality or common genetic predispositions? *Journal of Child Psychology and Psychiatry*, *62*(1), 28–39. https://doi.org/10.1111/jcpp.13238

Véronneau, M. H., Vitaro, F., Brendgen, M., Dishion, T. J., & Tremblay, R. E. (2010). Transactional analysis of the reciprocal links between peer experiences and academic achievement from middle childhood to early adolescence. *Developmental Psychology*, *46*(4), 773–790. https://doi.org/10.1037/a0019816

Vijayakumar, N., Allen, N. B., Youssef, G., Dennison, M., Yücel, M., Simmons, J. G., & Whittle, S. (2016). Brain development during adolescence: A mixed-longitudinal investigation of cortical thickness, surface area, and volume. *Human Brain Mapping*, *37*(6), 2027–2038. https://doi.org/10.1002/hbm.23154

Virtanen, M., Kivimäki, H., Ervasti, J., Oksanen, T., Pentti, J., Kouvonen, A., Halonen, J. I., Kivimäki, M., & Vahtera, J. (2015). Fast-food outlets and grocery stores near school and adolescents' eating habits and overweight in Finland. *The European Journal of Public Health*, *25*(4), 650–655. https://doi.org/10.1093/eurpub/ckv045

Walton, G. M., & Spencer, S. J. (2009). Latent ability: Grades and test scores systematically underestimate the intellectual ability of negatively stereotyped students. *Psychological Science*, *20*(9), 1132–1139. https://doi.org/10.1111/j.1467-9280.2009.02417.x

Wang, M.-T., & Fredricks, J. A. (2014). The reciprocal links between school engagement, youth problem behaviors, and school dropout during adolescence. *Child Development*, *85*(2), 722–737. https://doi.org/10.1111/cdev.12138

Wang, Y., & Lim, H. (2012). The global childhood obesity epidemic and the association between socio-economic status and childhood obesity. *International Review of Psychiatry (Abingdon, England)*, *24*(3), 176–188. https://doi.org/10.3109/09540261.2012.688195

Watson, N. F., Martin, J. L., Wise, M. S., Carden, K. A., Kirsch, D. B., Kristo, D. A., Malhotra, R. K., Olson, E. J., Ramar, K., Rosen, I. M., Rowley, J. A., Weaver, T. E., Chervin, R. D., & American Academy of Sleep Medicine Board of Director. (2017). Delaying middle school and high school start times promotes student health and performance: An American academy of sleep medicine position statement. *Journal of Clinical Sleep Medicine*, *13*(04), 623–625. https://doi.org/10.5664/jcsm.6558

Watts, A. W., Loth, K., Berge, J. M., Larson, N., & Neumark-Sztainer, D. (2017). No time for family meals? Parenting practices associated with adolescent fruit and vegetable intake when family meals are not an option. *Journal of the Academy of Nutrition and Dietetics*, *117*(5), 707–714. https://doi.org/10.1016/j.jand.2016.10.026

Watts, A. W., Mason, S. M., Loth, K., Larson, N., & Neumark-Sztainer, D. (2016). Socioeconomic differences in overweight and weight-related behaviors across adolescence and young adulthood: 10-year longitudinal findings from Project EAT. *Preventive Medicine*, *87*, 194–199. https://doi.org/10.1016/j.ypmed.2016.03.007

Way, N., Reddy, R., & Rhodes, J. (2007). Students' perceptions of school climate during the middle school years: Associations with trajectories of psychological and behavioral adjustment. *American Journal of Community Psychology*, *40*(3–4), 194–213. https://doi.org/10.1007/s10464-007-9143-y

Webster, G. D., Graber, J. A., Gesselman, A. N., Crosier, B. S., & Schember, T. O. (2014). A life history theory of father absence and menarche: A meta-analysis. *Evolutionary Psychology*, *12*(2), 147470491401200. https://doi.org/10.1177/147470491401200202

Weil, L. G., Fleming, S. M., Dumontheil, I., Kilford, E. J., Weil, R. S., Rees, G., Dolan, R. J., & Blakemore, S.-J. (2013). The development of metacognitive ability in adolescence. *Consciousness and Cognition*, *22*(1), 264–271. https://doi.org/10.1016/J.CONCOG.2013.01.004

Whittle, S., Vijayakumar, N., Simmons, J. G., Dennison, M., Schwartz, O., Pantelis, C., Sheeber, L., Byrne, M. L., & Allen, N. B. (2017). Role of positive parenting in the association between neighborhood social disadvantage and brain development across adolescence. *JAMA Psychiatry*, *74*(8), 824. https://doi.org/10.1001/jamapsychiatry.2017.1558

Wigmore-Sykes, M., Ferris, M., & Singh, S. (2020). Contemporary beliefs surrounding the menarche: a pilot study of adolescent girls at a school in middle England. *Education for Primary Care*. https://doi.org/10.1080/14739879.2020.1836678

Wohlfahrt-Veje, C., Mouritsen, A., Hagen, C. P., Tinggaard, J., Mieritz, M. G., Boas, M., Petersen, J. H., Skakkebæk, N. E., & Main, K. M. (2016). Pubertal onset in boys and girls is influenced by pubertal timing of both parents. *Journal of Clinical Endocrinology and Metabolism*, *101*(7), 2667–2674. https://doi.org/10.1210/jc.2016-1073

Wyatt, L. C., Ung, T., Park, R., Kwon, S. C., & Trinh-Shevrin, C. (2015). Risk factors of suicide and depression among Asian American, native Hawaiian, and pacific Islander youth: A systematic literature review. *Journal of Health Care for the Poor and Underserved*, *26*((2 Suppl)), 191–237. https://doi.org/10.1353/hpu.2015.0059

Yau, J. C., & Reich, S. M. (2018). "It's just a lot of work": Adolescents' self-presentation norms and practices on facebook and instagram. *Journal of Research on Adolescence*. https://doi.org/10.1111/jora.12376

Yousefi, M., Karmaus, W., Zhang, H., Roberts, G., Matthews, S., Clayton, B., & Arshad, S. H. (2013). Relationships between age of puberty onset and height at age 18 years in girls and boys. *World Journal of Pediatrics*, *9*(3), 230–238. https://doi.org/10.1007/s12519-013-0399-z

Yu, C., Li, X., Wang, S., & Zhang, W. (2016). Teacher autonomy support reduces adolescent anxiety and depression: An 18-month longitudinal study. *Journal of Adolescence*, *49*, 115–123. https://doi.org/10.1016/j.adolescence.2016.03.001

Yurgelun-Todd, D. (2007). Emotional and cognitive changes during adolescence. *Current Opinion in Neurobiology*, *17*(2), 251–257.

Zhou, D., Lebel, C., Treit, S., Evans, A., & Beaulieu, C. (2015). Accelerated longitudinal cortical thinning in adolescence. *NeuroImage*, *104*, 138–145. https://doi.org/10.1016/j.neuroimage.2014.10.005

Zhu, J., Kusa, T. O., & Chan, Y.-M. (2018). Genetics of pubertal timing. *Current Opinion in Pediatrics*, *30*(4), 532–540. https://doi.org/10.1097/MOP.0000000000000642

Zimmer-Gembeck, M. J., Webb, H. J., Farrell, L. J., & Waters, A. M. (2018). Girls' and boys' trajectories of appearance anxiety from age 10 to 15 years are associated with earlier maturation and appearance-related teasing. *Development and Psychopathology*, *30*(01), 337–350. https://doi.org/10.1017/S0954579417000657

CHAPTER 10

Ackard, D. M., Fulkerson, J. A., & Neumark-Sztainer, D. (2011). Stability of eating disorder diagnostic classifications in adolescents: Five-year longitudinal findings from a population-based study. *Eating Disorders*, *19*(4), 308–322. https://doi.org/10.1080/10640266.2011.584804

Adams, R. E., & Laursen, B. (2007). The correlates of conflict: Disagreement is not necessarily detrimental. *Journal of Family Psychology*, *21*(3), 445–458.

Ágh, T., Kovács, G., Supina, D., Pawaskar, M., Herman, B. K., Vokó, Z., & Sheehan, D. V. (2016). A systematic review of the health-related quality of life and economic burdens of anorexia nervosa, bulimia nervosa, and binge eating disorder. *Eating and Weight Disorders - Studies on Anorexia, Bulimia and Obesity*, *21*(3), 353–364. https://doi.org/10.1007/s40519-016-0264-x

Al-Owidha, A., Green, K. E., & Kroger, J. (2009). On the question of an identity status category order: Rasch model step and scale statistics used to identify category order. *International Journal of Behavioral Development*, *33*(1), 88–96. https://doi.org/10.1177/0165025408100110

Alaie, I., Låftman, S. B., Jonsson, U., & Bohman, H. (2020). Parent-youth conflict as a predictor of depression in adulthood: A 15-year follow-up of a community-based cohort. *European Child and Adolescent Psychiatry*, *29*(4), 527–536. https://doi.org/10.1007/s00787-019-01368-8

American Academy of Child and Adolescent Psychiatry. (2008). *Teen suicide. Facts for families*. http://www.aacap.org/galleries/FactsForFamilies/10_teen_suicide.pdf

American College of Obstetricians and Gynecologists. (2016). *ACOG committee opinion. Comprehensive sexuality education*. Author. https://www.acog.org/Clinical-Guidance-and-Publications/Committee-Opinions/Committee-on-Adolescent-Health-Care/Comprehensive-Sexuality-Education

American Psychiatric Association. (2013). *Diagnostic and statistical manual of mental disorders DSM-V* (5th ed.). Author.

American Public Health Association. American Public Health Association. American Public Health Association. (2014). *Sexuality education as part of a comprehensive health education program in K to 12 schools*. https://www.apha.org/policies-and-advocacy/public-health-policy-statements/policy-database/2015/01/23/09/37/sexuality-education-as-part-of-a-comprehensive-health-education-program-in-k-to-12-schools

Andersen, T. S. (2015). Race, ethnicity, and structural variations in youth risk of arrest: Evidence from a national longitudinal sample. *Criminal Justice and Behavior*, *42*, 900–916. https://doi.org/10.1177/0093854815570963

Angley, M., Divney, A., Magriples, U., & Kershaw, T. (2015). Social support, family functioning and parenting competence in adolescent parents. *Maternal and Child Health Journal*, *19*(1), 67–73. https://doi.org/10.1007/s10995-014-1496-x

Arnett, J. J. (2016). Identity Development from adolescence to emerging adulthood. In K. C. McLean & M. Syed (Eds.), *The Oxford handbook of identity development* (pp. 53–64). Oxford University Press. https://doi.org/10.1093/oxfordhb/9780199936564.013.009

Australian Institute of Health and Welfare. (2016). *Leading causes of death*. http://www.aihw.gov.au/deaths/leading-causes-of-death/

Babore, A., Carlucci, L., Cataldi, F., Phares, V., & Trumello, C. (2017). Aggressive behaviour in adolescence: Links with self-esteem and parental emotional availability. *Social Development*, *26*(4), 740–752. https://doi.org/10.1111/sode.12236

Bachman, J. G., O'Malley, P. M., Freedman-Doan, P., Trzesniewski, K. H., & Donnellan, M. B. (2011). Adolescent self-esteem: Differences by race/ethnicity, gender, and age. *Self and Identity: The Journal of the International Society for Self and Identity, 10*(4), 445–473. https://doi.org/10.1080/15298861003794538

Bagci, S. C., Rutland, A., Kumashiro, M., Smith, P. K., & Blumberg, H. (2014). Are minority status children's cross-ethnic friendships beneficial in a multiethnic context? *The British Journal of Developmental Psychology, 32*(1), 107–115. https://doi.org/10.1111/bjdp.12028

Baglivio, M. T., Jackowski, K., Greenwald, M. A., & Howell, J. C. (2014). Serious, violent, and chronic juvenile offenders. *Criminology & Public Policy, 13*(1), 83–116. https://doi.org/10.1111/1745-9133.12064

Bailey, J. M., Vasey, P. L., Diamond, L. M., Breedlove, S. M., Vilain, E., & Epprecht, M. (2016). Sexual orientation, controversy, and science. *Psychological Science in the Public Interest, 17*(2), 45–101. https://doi.org/10.1177/1529100616637616

Balakrishnan, A. (2020). Self-concept, expressions of the. In B. J. Carducci, C. S. Nave, A. D. Fabio, D. H. Saklofske, & C. Stough (Eds.), *The Wiley encyclopedia of personality and individual differences* (pp. 369–373). Wiley. https://doi.org/10.1002/9781119547174.ch240

Barnett, A. P., Molock, S. D., Nieves-Lugo, K., & Zea, M. C. (2019). Anti-LGBT victimization, fear of violence at school, and suicide risk among adolescents. *Psychology of Sexual Orientation and Gender Diversity, 6*(1), 88–95. https://doi.org/10.1037/sgd0000309

Barry, C. T., Loflin, D. C., & Doucette, H. (2015). Adolescent self-compassion: Associations with narcissism, self-esteem, aggression, and internalizing symptoms in at-risk males. *Personality and Individual Differences, 77*, 118–123. https://doi.org/10.1016/J.PAID.2014.12.036

Baudat, S., Van Petegem, S., Antonietti, J. P., & Zimmermann, G. (2020). Parental solicitation and adolescents' information management: The moderating role of autonomy-supportive parenting. *Journal of Child and Family Studies, 29*(2), 426–441. https://doi.org/10.1007/s10826-019-01687-z

Baudry, C., Tarabulsy, G. M., Atkinson, L., Pearson, J., & St-Pierre, A. (2017). Intervention with adolescent mother–child dyads and cognitive development in early childhood: A meta-analysis. *Prevention Science, 18*(1), 116–130. https://doi.org/10.1007/s11121-016-0731-7

Baumeister, R. F., & Vohs, K. D. (2018). Revisiting our reappraisal of the (surprisingly few) benefits of high self-esteem. *Perspectives on Psychological Science, 13*(2), 137–140. https://doi.org/10.1177/1745691617701185

Becerra-Culqui, T. A., Liu, Y., Nash, R., Cromwell, L., Flanders, W. D., Getahun, D., Giammattei, S. V., Hunkeler, E. M., Lash, T. L., Millman, A., Quinn, V. P., Robinson, B., Roblin, D., Sandberg, D. E., Silverberg, M. J., Tangpricha, V., & Goodman, M. (2018). Mental health of transgender and gender nonconforming youth compared with their peers. *Pediatrics, 141*(5), e20173845. https://doi.org/10.1542/PEDS.2017-3845

Becht, A. I., Nelemans, S. A., Branje, S. J. T., Vollebergh, W. A. M., Koot, H. M., & Meeus, W. H. J. (2017). Identity uncertainty and commitment making across adolescence: Five-year within-person associations using daily identity reports. *Developmental Psychology, 53*(11), 2103–2112. https://doi.org/10.1037/dev0000374

Beckmeyer, J. J., & Weybright, E. H. (2020). Exploring the associations between middle adolescent romantic activity and positive youth development. *Journal of Adolescence, 80*, 214–219. https://doi.org/10.1016/j.adolescence.2020.03.002

Bendezú, J. J., Pinderhughes, E. E., Hurley, S. M., McMahon, R. J., & Racz, S. J. (2018). Longitudinal relations among parental monitoring strategies, knowledge, and adolescent delinquency in a racially diverse at-risk sample. *Journal of Clinical Child and Adolescent Psychology, 47*(Suppl 1), S21–S34. https://doi.org/10.1080/15374416.2016.1141358

Benowitz-Fredericks, C. A., Garcia, K., Massey, M., Vasagar, B., & Borzekowski, D. L. G. (2012). Body image, eating disorders, and the relationship to adolescent media use. *Pediatric Clinics of North America, 59*(3), 693–704. https://doi.org/10.1016/j.pcl.2012.03.017

Berkman, N. D., Brownley, K. A., Peat, C. M., Lohr, K. N., Cullen, K. E., Morgan, L. C., Bann, C. M., Wallace, I. F., & Bulik, C. M. (2015). Management and outcomes of binge-eating disorder. *Management and outcomes of binge-eating disorder.* Agency for Healthcare Research and Quality (US. http://www.ncbi.nlm.nih.gov/pubmed/26764442

Berkman, N. D., Lohr, K. N., & Bulik, C. M. (2007). Outcomes of eating disorders: A systematic review of the literature. *International Journal of Eating Disorders, 40*(4), 293–309.

Berkowitz, M. W., & Begun, A. L. (1994). Assessing how adolescents think about the morality of substance use. *Drugs & Society, 8*(3/4), 111.

Berzonsky, M. D., & Kuk, L. S. (2000). Identity status, identity processing style, and the transition to university. *Journal of Adolescent Research, 15*, 81–99.

Birkeland, M. S., Breivik, K., & Wold, B. (2014). Peer acceptance protects global self-esteem from negative effects of low closeness to parents during adolescence and early adulthood. *Journal of Youth and Adolescence, 43*(1), 70–80. https://doi.org/10.1007/s10964-013-9929-1

Birkett, M., Newcomb, M. E., & Mustanski, B. (2015). Does it get better? A longitudinal analysis of psychological distress and victimization in Lesbian, Gay, Bisexual, Transgender, and questioning youth. *Journal of Adolescent Health, 56*(3), 280–285. https://doi.org/10.1016/j.jadohealth.2014.10.275

Bleidorn, W., Arslan, R. C., Denissen, J. J. A., Rentfrow, P. J., Gebauer, J. E., Potter, J., & Gosling, S. D. (2016). Age and gender differences in self-esteem—A cross-cultural window. *Journal of Personality and Social Psychology, 111*(3), 396–410. https://doi.org/10.1037/pspp0000078

Bonifacio, J. H., Maser, C., Stadelman, K., & Palmert, M. (2019). Management of gender dysphoria in adolescents in primary care. *Canadian Medical Association Journal, 191*(3), E69–E75. https://doi.org/10.1503/cmaj.180672

Boom, J. J., Wouters, H., & Keller, M. (2007). A cross-cultural validation of stage development: A Rasch re-analysis of longitudinal socio-moral reasoning data. *Ognitive Development, 22*(2), 213–229.

Bornstein, M. H., & Putnick, D. L. (2018). Parent—Adolescent relationships in global perspective. In J. E. Lansford & P. Banati (Eds.), *Handbook of adolescent development research and its impact on global policy.* Oxford.

Bowker, A., & Ramsay, K. (2018). Friendship characteristics. In R. J. R. Levesque (Ed.), *Encyclopedia of adolescence* (pp. 1–8). Springer Publishing Company. https://doi.org/10.1007/978-3-319-32132-5_49-2

Branje, S. (2018). Development of parent-adolescent relationships: Conflict interactions as a mechanism of change. *Child Development Perspectives*, *12*(3), 171–176. https://doi.org/10.1111/cdep.12278

Brechwald, W. A., & Prinstein, M. J. (2011). Beyond homophily: A decade of advances in understanding peer influence processes. *Journal of Research on Adolescence : The Official Journal of the Society for Research on Adolescence*, *21*(1), 166–179. https://doi.org/10.1111/j.1532-7795.2010.00721.x

Breuner, C. C., Mattson, G., & Commitee on Psychosocial Aspects of Child and Family Health. (2016). Sexuality education for children and adolescents. *Pediatrics*, *138*(2), e20161348. https://pediatrics.aappublications.org/content/pediatrics/138/2/e20161348.full.pdf

Brittian, A. S., Kim, S. Y., Armenta, B. E., Lee, R. M., Umaña-Taylor, A. J., Schwartz, S. J., Villalta, I. K., Zamboanga, B. L., Weisskirch, R. S., Juang, L. P., Castillo, L. G., & Hudson, M. L. (2015). Do dimensions of ethnic identity mediate the association between perceived ethnic group discrimination and depressive symptoms? *Cultural Diversity and Ethnic Minority Psychology*, *21*(1), 41–53. https://doi.org/10.1037/a0037531

Brooks-Russell, A., Simons-Morton, B., Haynie, D., Farhat, T., & Wang, J. (2014). Longitudinal relationship between drinking with peers, descriptive norms, and adolescent alcohol use. *Prevention Science : The Official Journal of the Society for Prevention Research*, *15*(4), 497–505. https://doi.org/10.1007/s11121-013-0391-9

Brown, B., Bank, H., & Steinberg, L. (2008). Smoke in the looking glass: Effects of discordance between self- and peer rated crowd affiliation on adolescent anxiety, depression and self-feelings. *Journal of Youth & Adolescence*, *37*(10), 1163–1177. https://doi.org/10.1007/s10964-007-9198-y

Brugman, D. (2010). Moral reasoning competence and the moral judgment-action discrepancy in young adolescents. In A. F. S. W. Koops, D. Brugman, & T. J. Ferguson (Eds.), *The development and structure of conscience* (pp. 119–133). Psychology Press.

Bruni, V., & Dei, M. (2018). Eating disorders in adolescence. In A. M. Fulghesu (Ed.), *Good practice in pediatric and adolescent gynecology* (pp. 131–141). Springer International Publishing. https://doi.org/10.1007/978-3-319-57162-1_8

Bukowski, W. M., Bagwell, C., Castellanos, M., & Persram, R. J. (2020). Friendship in adolescence. In S. Hupp & J. D. Jewell (Eds.), *The encyclopedia of child and adolescent development* (pp. 1–11). Wiley. https://doi.org/10.1002/9781119171492.wecad403

Burrow, A. L., & Ong, A. D. (2010). Racial identity as a moderator of daily exposure and reactivity to racial discrimination. *Self and Identity*, *9*(4), 383–402. https://doi.org/10.1080/15298860903192496

Burrus, B. B. (2018). Decline in adolescent pregnancy in the United States: A success not shared by all. *American Journal of Public Health*, *108*(S1), S5–S6. https://doi.org/10.2105/AJPH.2017.304273

Burton, L. M., & Jarrett, R. L. (2000). In the mix, yet on the margins: The Place of families in urban neighborhood and child development research. *Journal of Marriage and Family*, *62*(4), 1114–1135. https://doi.org/10.1111/j.1741-3737.2000.01114.x

Calzo, J. P., Antonucci, T. C., Mays, V. M., & Cochran, S. D. (2011). Retrospective recall of sexual orientation identity development among gay, lesbian, and bisexual adults. *Developmental Psychology*, *47*(6), 1658–1673. https://doi.org/10.1037/a0025508

Calzo, J. P., Masyn, K. E., Austin, S. B., Jun, H.-J., & Corliss, H. L. (2017). Developmental latent patterns of identification as mostly heterosexual versus Lesbian, Gay, or Bisexual. *Journal of Research on Adolescence*, *27*(1), 246–253. https://doi.org/10.1111/jora.12266

Campbell, K., & Peebles, R. (2014). Eating disorders in children and adolescents: State of the art review. *Pediatrics*, *134*(3), 582–592. https://doi.org/10.1542/peds.2014-0194

Carlo, G., Mestre, M. V., Samper, P., Tur, A., & Armenta, B. E. (2011). The longitudinal relations among dimensions of parenting styles, sympathy, prosocial moral reasoning, and prosocial behaviors. *International Journal of Behavioral Development*, *35*(2), 116–124. https://doi.org/10.1177/0165025410375921

Carlson, D. L., McNulty, T. L., Bellair, P. E., & Watts, S. (2014). Neighborhoods and racial/ethnic disparities in adolescent sexual risk behavior. *Journal of Youth and Adolescence*, *43*(9), 1536–1549. https://doi.org/10.1007/s10964-013-0052-0

Carlsson, J., Wängqvist, M., & Frisén, A. (2015). Identity development in the late twenties: A never ending story. *Developmental Psychology*, *51*(3), 334–345. https://doi.org/10.1037/a0038745

Carlsson, J., Wängqvist, M., & Frisén, A. (2016). Life on hold: Staying in identity diffusion in the late twenties. *Journal of Adolescence*, *47*, 220–229. https://doi.org/10.1016/j.adolescence.2015.10.023

Casares, W. N., Lahiff, M., Eskenazi, B., & Halpern-Felsher, B. L. (2010). Unpredicted trajectories: The relationship between race/ethnicity, pregnancy during adolescence, and young women's outcomes. *Journal of Adolescent Health*, *47*(2), 143–150. https://doi.org/10.1016/j.jadohealth.2010.01.013

Centers for Disease Control. (2018a). *HIV surveillance report, 2017; vol. 29.* https://www.cdc.gov/hiv/pdf/library/reports/surveillance/cdc-hiv-surveillance-report-2017-vol-29.pdf

Centers for Disease Control. (2018b). *New CDC analysis shows steep and sustained increases in STDs in recent years.* https://www.cdc.gov/nchhstp/newsroom/2018/press-release-2018-std-prevention-conference.html

Centers for Disease Control and Prevention. (2017). *10 leading causes of death, by age group, United States - 2015.* https://www.cdc.gov/injury/images/lc-charts/leading_causes_of_death_age_group_2015_1050w740h.gif

Chaplin, T. M., Sinha, R., Simmons, J. A., Healy, S. M., Mayes, L. C., Hommer, R. E., & Crowley, M. J. (2012). Parent-adolescent conflict interactions and adolescent alcohol use. *Addictive Behaviors*, *37*(5), 605–612. https://doi.org/10.1016/j.addbeh.2012.01.004

Chen, P., Voisin, D. R., & Jacobson, K. C. (2013). Community violence exposure and adolescent delinquency: Examining a spectrum of promotive factors. *Youth & Society*, *48*, 33–57. https://doi.org/10.1177/0044118X13475827

Child Trends. (2019a). *Dating among teens.* https://www.childtrends.org/indicators/dating.

Child Trends. (2019b). *Key facts about teen births.* https://www.childtrends.org/indicators/teen-births

Child Trends Databank. (2017). *Sexually active teens - child trends.* https://www.childtrends.org/indicators/sexually-active-teens/

Child Trends Databank. (2019). *Teen suicide - child trends*. https://www.childtrends.org/indicators/suicidal-teens

Choi, J. K., Teshome, T., & Smith, J. (2021). Neighborhood disadvantage, childhood adversity, bullying victimization, and adolescent depression: A multiple mediational analysis. *Journal of Affective Disorders, 279*, 554–562. https://doi.org/10.1016/j.jad.2020.10.041

Choukas-Bradley, S., Giletta, M., Cohen, G. L., & Prinstein, M. J. (2015). Peer influence, peer status, and prosocial behavior: An experimental investigation of peer socialization of adolescents' intentions to volunteer. *Journal of Youth and Adolescence, 44*(12), 2197–2210. https://doi.org/10.1007/s10964-015-0373-2

Choukas-Bradley, S., Giletta, M., Widman, L., Cohen, G. L., & Prinstein, M. J. (2014). Experimentally measured susceptibility to peer influence and adolescent sexual behavior trajectories: A Preliminary study. *Developmental Psychology, 50*(9), 2221–2227. https://doi.org/10.1037/a0037300

Chung, G. H., Flook, L., & Fuligni, A. J. (2009). Daily family conflict and emotional distress among adolescents from Latin American, Asian, and European backgrounds. *Developmental Psychology, 45*(5), 1406–1415. https://doi.org/10.1037/a0014163

Claus, R. E., Vidal, S., & Harmon, M. (2017). *Racial and ethnic disparities in the police handling of juvenile arrests*. https://www.ncjrs.gov/App/Publications/abstract.aspx? ID=272982

Coffey, C., & Patton, G. C. (2016). Cannabis use in adolescence and young adulthood. *The Canadian Journal of Psychiatry, 61*(6), 318–327. https://doi.org/10.1177/0706743716645289

Coley, R. L., Lombardi, C. M., Lynch, A. D., Mahalik, J. R., & Sims, J. (2013). Sexual partner accumulation from adolescence through early adulthood: The role of family, peer, and school social norms. *The Journal of Adolescent Health : Official Publication of the Society for Adolescent Medicine, 53*(1), 91–7.e1-2, . https://doi.org/10.1016/j.jadohealth.2013.01.005

Collibee, C., Furman, W., & Shoop, J. (2019). Risky interactions: Relational and developmental moderators of substance use and dating aggression. *Journal of Youth and Adolescence, 48*(1), 102–113. https://doi.org/10.1007/s10964-018-0950-2

Collier, K. L., van Beusekom, G., Bos, H. M. W., & Sandfort, T. G. M. (2013). Sexual orientation and gender identity/expression related peer victimization in adolescence: A systematic review of associated psychosocial and health outcomes. *Journal of Sex Research, 50*(3–4), 299–317. https://doi.org/10.1080/00224499.2012.750639

Collins, W. A., Welsh, D. P., & Furman, W. (2009). Adolescent romantic relationships. *Annual Review of Psychology, 60*, 631–652. https://doi.org/10.1146/annurev.psych.60.110707.163459

Comunian, A. L., & Gielen, U. P. (2000). Sociomoral reflection and prosocial and antisocial behavior: Two Italian studies. *Psychological Reports, 87*(1), 161–176.

Connolly, J., & McIsaac, C. (2011). Romantic relationships in adolescence. In M. K. Underwood & L. H. Rosen (Eds.), *Social development: Relationships in infancy, childhood, and adolescence* (p. 18). Guilford.

Connolly, J., Nguyen, H. N. T., Pepler, D., Craig, W., & Jiang, D. (2013). Developmental trajectories of romantic stages and associations with problem behaviours during adolescence. *Journal of Adolescence, 36*(6), 1013–1024. https://doi.org/10.1016/j.adolescence.2013.08.006

Coyle, K. K.., Guinosso, S. A.., Glassman, J. R.., Anderson, P. M.., & Wilson, H. W.. (2017). Exposure to Violence and Sexual Risk Among Early Adolescents in Urban Middle Schools. *The Journal of Early Adolescence, 37*(7), 889–909. http://dx.doi.org/10.1177/0272431616642324

Crissman, H. P., Berger, M. B., Graham, L. F., & Dalton, V. K. (2017). Transgender demographics: A Household probability sample of US Adults, 2014. *American Journal of Public Health, 107*(2), 213–215. https://doi.org/10.2105/AJPH.2016.303571

Crocetti, E. (2017a). Identity formation in adolescence: The Dynamic of forming and consolidating identity commitments. *Child Development Perspectives, 11*(2), 145–150. https://doi.org/10.1111/cdep.12226

Crocetti, E. (2017b). Identity formation in adolescence: The dynamic of forming and consolidating identity commitments. *Child Development Perspectives, 11*(2), 145–150. https://doi.org/10.1111/cdep.12226

Crocetti, E., Branje, S., Rubini, M., Koot, H. M., & Meeus, W. (2017). Identity processes and parent-child and sibling relationships in adolescence: A five-wave multi-informant longitudinal study. *Child Development, 88*(1), 210–228. https://doi.org/10.1111/cdev.12547

Crocetti, E., Klimstra, T., Keijsers, L., Hale Iii, W. W., & Meeus, W. H. J. (2009). Anxiety trajectories and identity development in adolescence: A five-wave longitudinal study. *Journal of Youth & Adolescence, 38*(6), 839–849. https://doi.org/10.1007/s10964-008-9302-y

Cross, J. R. (2018). Crowds. In R. J. R. Levesque (Ed.), *Encyclopedia of adolescence* (pp. 573–580). Springer Publishing Company. https://doi.org/10.1007/978-1-4419-1695-2_44

Cservenka, A., & Brumback, T. (2017). The burden of binge and heavy drinking on the brain: Effects on adolescent and young adult neural structure and function. *Frontiers in Psychology, 8*, 1111. https://doi.org/10.3389/fpsyg.2017.01111

Curtin, S. C., & Heron, M. (2019). Death rates due to suicide and homicide among persons aged 10-24: United States, 2000-2017. *NCHS Data Brief, 352*, 1–8. http://www.ncbi.nlm.nih.gov/pubmed/31751202

Cvencek, D., & Greenwald, A. G. (2020). Self-esteem, expressions of. In B. J. Carducci, C. S. Nave, A. D. Fabio, D. H. Saklofske, & C. Stough (Eds.), *The Wiley encyclopedia of personality and individual differences* (pp. 399–404). Wiley. https://doi.org/10.1002/9781119547174.ch245

Daspe, M., Arbel, R., Ramos, M. C., Shapiro, L. A. S., & Margolin, G. (2019). Deviant peers and adolescent risky behaviors: The protective effect of nonverbal display of parental Warmth. *Journal of Research on Adolescence, 29*(4), 863–878. https://doi.org/10.1111/jora.12418

Dawson, T. L. (2002). New tools, new insights: Kohlberg's moral judgement stages revisited. *International Journal of Behavioral Development, 26*(2), 154–166.

De Genna, N., Larkby, C., & Cornelius, M. (2011). Pubertal timing and early sexual intercourse in the offspring of teenage mothers. *Journal of Youth & Adolescence, 40*(10), 1315–1328. https://doi.org/10.1007/s10964-010-9609-3

De Los Reyes, A., Ohannessian, C. M., & Racz, S. J. (2019). Discrepancies between adolescent and parent reports about family relationships. *Child Development Perspectives*, *13*(1), 53–58. https://doi.org/10.1111/cdep.12306

de Graaf, H., Vanwesenbeeck, I., Meijer, S., Woertman, L., & Meeus, W. (2009). Sexual trajectories during adolescence: Relation to demographic characteristics and sexual risk. *Archives of Sexual Behavior*, *38*(2), 276–282. https://doi.org/10.1007/s10508-007-9281-1

Demissie, Z., Clayton, H. B., & Dunville, R. L. (2019). Association between receipt of school-based HIV education and contraceptive use among sexually active high school students — United States, 2011–2013. *Sex Education*, *19*(2), 237–246. https://doi.org/10.1080/14681811.2018.1501358

de Moor, E. L., Sijtsema, J. J., Weller, J. A., & Klimstra, T. A. (2021). Longitudinal links between identity and substance use in adolescence. *Self and Identity*, 1–24. https://doi.org/10.1080/15298868.2020.1818615

Department of Health and Human Services. (2019). *United States adolescent mental health facts | HHS.gov*. https://www.hhs.gov/ash/oah/facts-and-stats/national-and-state-data-sheets/adolescent-mental-health-fact-sheets/united-states/index.html

Desjardins, T., & Leadbeater, B. J. (2017). Changes in parental emotional support and psychological control in early adulthood. *Emerging Adulthood*, *5*(3), 177–190. https://doi.org/10.1177/2167696816666974

de Water, E., Burk, W. J., Cillessen, A. H. N., & Scheres, A. (2017). Substance use and decision-making in adolescent best friendship dyads: The Role of popularity. *Social Development*, *26*(4), 860–875. https://doi.org/10.1111/sode.12227

Diamond, L. M., & Savin-Williams, R. C. (2009). Adolescent sexuality. In R. M. Lerner & L. Steinberg (Eds.), *Handbook of adolescent psychology* (p. 479). John Wiley & Sons, Inc.

Dittus, P. J., Michael, S. L., Becasen, J. S., Gloppen, K. M., McCarthy, K., & Guilamo-Ramos, V. (2015). Parental monitoring and its associations with adolescent sexual risk behavior: A meta-analysis. *Pediatrics*, *136*(6), e1587–e1599. http://pediatrics.aappublications.org/content/136/6/e1587? sso=1&sso_redirect_count=2&nfstatus=401&nftoken=00000000-0000-0000-0000-000000000000&nfstatusdescription=ERROR%253A No local token&nfstatus=401&nftoken=00000000-0000-0000-0000-000000000000&nfstatus

Douglass, S., & Umaña-Taylor, A. J. (2016). Time-varying effects of family ethnic socialization on ethnic-racial identity development among Latino adolescents. *Developmental Psychology*, *52*(11), 1904–1912. https://doi.org/10.1037/dev0000141

Douglass, S., & Umaña-Taylor, A. J. (2017). Examining discrimination, ethnic-racial identity status, and youth public regard among Black, Latino, and White adolescents. *Journal of Research on Adolescence*, *27*(1), 155–172. https://doi.org/10.1111/jora.12262

Drasin, H., Beals, K. P., Elliott, M. N., Lever, J., Klein, D. J., & Schuster, M. A. (2008). Age cohort differences in the developmental milestones of Gay men. *Journal of Homosexuality*, *54*(4), 381–399. https://doi.org/10.1080/00918360801991372

Duan, L., Chou, C.-P., Andreeva, V., & Pentz, M. (2009). Trajectories of peer social influences as long-term predictors of drug use from early through late adolescence. *Journal of Youth & Adolescence*, *38*(3), 454–465. https://doi.org/10.1007/s10964-008-9310-y

Dudovitz, R. N., Chung, P. J., & Wong, M. D. (2017). Teachers and coaches in adolescent social networks are associated with healthier self-concept and decreased substance use. *Journal of School Health*, *87*(1), 12–20. https://doi.org/10.1111/josh.12462

Durwood, L., McLaughlin, K. A., & Olson, K. R. (2017). Mental health and self-worth in socially transitioned transgender youth. *Journal of the American Academy of Child and Adolescent Psychiatry*, *56*(2), 116–123.e2. https://doi.org/10.1016/j.jaac.2016.10.016

Dykstra, V. W., Willoughby, T., & Evans, A. D. (2020). A Longitudinal examination of the relation between lie-telling, secrecy, parent-child relationship quality, and depressive symptoms in late-childhood and adolescence. *Journal of Youth and Adolescence*, *49*(2), 438–448. https://doi.org/10.1007/s10964-019-01183-z

East, P. L., Khoo, S. T., Reyes, B. T., & Coughlin, L. (2006). AAP report on pregnancy in adolescents. *Perspectives on Sexual & Reproductive Health*, *10*, 12.

Easterbrooks, M. A., Chaudhuri, J. H., Bartlett, J. D., & Copeman, A. (2011). Resilience in parenting among young mothers: Family and ecological risks and opportunities. *Children and Youth Services Review*, *33*(1), 42–50. https://doi.org/10.1016/j.childyouth.2010.08.010

Ellis, W. E., & Zarbatany, L. (2017). Understanding processes of peer clique influence in late childhood and early adolescence. *Child Development Perspectives*, *11*(4), 227–232. https://doi.org/10.1111/cdep.12248

Else-Quest, N. M., & Morse, E. (2015). Ethnic variations in parental ethnic socialization and adolescent ethnic identity: A Longitudinal study. *Cultural Diversity and Ethnic Minority Psychology*, *21*(1), 54–64. https://doi.org/10.1037/a0037820

Englund, M. M., Siebenbruner, J., Oliva, E. M., Egeland, B., Chung, C.-T., & Long, J. D. (2013). The developmental significance of late adolescent substance use for early adult functioning. *Developmental Psychology*, *49*(8), 1554–1564. https://doi.org/10.1037/a0030229

Erdley, C. A., & Day, H. J. (2017a). Friendship in childhood and adolescence. In M. Hojjat & A. Moyer (Eds.), *The psychology of friendship* (pp. 3–19). Oxford University Press.

Erdley, C. A., & Day, H. J. (2017b). Friendship in childhood and adolescence. In M. Hojjat & A. Moyer (Eds.), *The Psychology of friendship* (pp. 3–20). Oxford University Press. https://doi.org/10.1093/acprof:oso/9780190222024.003.0001

Erikson, E. H. (1950). *Childhood and society* (2nd ed.). Norton.

Erol, R. Y., & Orth, U. (2011). Self-esteem development from age 14 to 30 years: A longitudinal study. *Journal of Personality and Social Psychology*, *101*(3), 607–619. https://doi.org/10.1037/a0024299

Esnaola, I., Sesé, A., Antonio-Agirre, I., & Azpiazu, L. (2020). The development of multiple self-concept dimensions during adolescence. *Journal of Research on Adolescence*, *30*(S1), 100–114. https://doi.org/10.1111/jora.12451

Ethier, K. A., Kann, L., & McManus, T. (2018). Sexual intercourse among high school students — 29 states and United States overall, 2005–2015. *MMWR. Morbidity and Mortality Weekly Report*, *66*(5152), 1393–1397. https://doi.org/10.15585/mmwr.mm665152a1

Exner-Cortens, D., Eckenrode, J., & Rothman, E. (2013). Longitudinal associations between teen dating violence victimization and adverse health outcomes. *Pediatrics*, *131*(1), 71–78. https://doi.org/10.1542/peds.2012-1029

Farrell, A. D., Thompson, E. L., & Mehari, K. R. (2017). Dimensions of peer influences and their relationship to adolescentsâ€TM aggression, other problem behaviors and prosocial behavior. *Journal of Youth and Adolescence*, *46*, 1351–1369. https://doi.org/10.1007/s10964-016-0601-4

Farrington, D. P., & Loeber, R. (2000). Epidemiology of juvenile violence. *Juvenile Violence*, *9*, 733–748.

Federal Bureau of Invesigation. (2019). *Table 38 arrests by age, 2018*. 2018 Crime in the United States. https://ucr.fbi.gov/crime-in-the-u.s/2018/crime-in-the-u.s.-2018/topic-pages/tables/table-38

Ferguson, G. M., Hafen, C. A., & Laursen, B. (2010). Adolescent psychological and academic adjustment as a function of discrepancies between actual and ideal self-perceptions. *Journal of Youth and Adolescence*, *39*(12), 1485–1497. https://doi.org/10.1007/s10964-009-9461-5

Finer, L. B., & Philbin, J. M. (2013). Sexual initiation, contraceptive use, and pregnancy among young adolescents. *Pediatrics*, *131*(5), 886–891. https://doi.org/10.1542/peds.2012-3495

Fiorilli, C., Grimaldi Capitello, T., Barni, D., Buonomo, I., & Gentile, S. (2019). Predicting adolescent depression: The Interrelated roles of self-esteem and interpersonal stressors. *Frontiers in Psychology*, *10*(MAR), 565. https://doi.org/10.3389/fpsyg.2019.00565

Flannery, D. J., Hussey, D., & Jefferis, E. (2005). Adolescent delinquency and violent behavior. In T. P. Gullotta & G. R. Adams (Eds.), *Handbook of adolescent behavioral problems: Evidence-based approaches to prevention and treatment* (pp. 415–438). Springer Science + Business Media.

Forrest, L. N., Zuromski, K. L., Dodd, D. R., & Smith, A. R. (2017). Suicidality in adolescents and adults with binge-eating disorder: Results from the national comorbidity survey replication and adolescent supplement. *International Journal of Eating Disorders*, *50*(1), 40–49. https://doi.org/10.1002/eat.22582

Fortenberry, J. D. (2013). Puberty and adolescent sexuality. *Hormones and Behavior*, *64*(2), 280–287. https://doi.org/10.1016/j.yhbeh.2013.03.007

Foshee, V. A., McNaughton Reyes, H. L., Tharp, A. T., Chang, L.-Y., Ennett, S. T., Simon, T. R., Latzman, N. E., & Suchindran, C. (2015). Shared longitudinal predictors of physical peer and dating violence. *The Journal of Adolescent Health : Official Publication of the Society for Adolescent Medicine*, *56*(1), 106–112. https://doi.org/10.1016/j.jadohealth.2014.08.003

Foshee, V. A., McNaughton Reyes, H. L., Vivolo-Kantor, A. M., Basile, K. C., Chang, L.-Y., Faris, R., & Ennett, S. T. (2014). Bullying as a longitudinal predictor of adolescent dating violence. *The Journal of Adolescent Health : Official Publication of the Society for Adolescent Medicine*, *55*(3), 439–444. https://doi.org/10.1016/j.jadohealth.2014.03.004

French, D. C., & Cheung, H. S. (2018). Peer relationships. In J. E. Lansford & P. Banati (Eds.), *Handbook of adolescent development research and its impact on global*. Oxford University Press. https://global.oup.com/academic/product/handbook-of-adolescent-development-research-and-its-impact-on-global-policy-9780190847128? q=adolescent global&lang=en&cc=us#

Fuligni, A. J., & Tsai, K. M. (2015). Developmental flexibility in the age of globalization: Autonomy and identity development among immigrant adolescents. *Annual Review of Psychology*, *66*(1), 411–431. https://doi.org/10.1146/annurev-psych-010814-015111

Furman, W., Collibee, C., Lantagne, A., & Golden, R. L. (2019). Making movies instead of taking snapshots: Studying change in youth's romantic relationships. *Child Development Perspectives*, *13*(3), 135–140. https://doi.org/10.1111/cdep.12325

Furman, W., & Rose, A. J. (2015). Friendships, romantic relationships, and peer relationships. In W. M. Bukowski, B. Laursen, & K. H. Rubin (Eds.), *Handbook of child psychology and developmental science* (pp. 1–43). John Wiley & Sons, Inc. https://doi.org/10.1002/9781118963418.childpsy322 Bukowski

Future of Sex Education Initiative. (2012). National sexuality education standards: Core content and skills, K-12. *Journal of School Health*, *82*, 1–42. https://siecus.org/wp-content/uploads/2018/07/National-Sexuality-Education-Standards.pdf

Galambos, N. L., Berenbaum, S. A., & McHale, S. M. (2009). Gender development in adolescence. In R. M. Lerner & L. Steinberg (Eds.), *Handbook of adolescent psychology* (Vol. 1, pp. 305–357). John Wiley & Sons, Inc. https://doi.org/10.1002/9780470479193.adlpsy001011

Galliher, R. V., McLean, K. C., & Syed, M. (2017). An integrated developmental model for studying identity content in context. *Developmental Psychology*, *53*(11), 2011–2022. https://doi.org/10.1037/dev0000299

Gates, G. J. (2011). *How many people are lesbian, gay, bisexual and transgender?* https://escholarship.org/uc/item/09h684x2

Ge, X., Natsuaki, M. N., Neiderhiser, J. M., & Reiss, D. (2009). The longitudinal effects of stressful life events on adolescent depression are buffered by parent-child closeness. *Development & Psychopathology*, *21*(2), 621–635. https://doi.org/10.1017/s0954579409000339

Gibbs, J. C., Basinger, K. S., Grime, R. L., & Snarey, J. R. (2007). Moral judgment development across cultures: Revisiting Kohlberg's universality claims. *Developmental Review*, *27*(4), 443–500. https://doi.org/10.1016/j.dr.2007.04.001

Gilligan, C. (1982). *In a different voice: Psychological theory and women's development*. Harvard University Press.

Giordano, P. C., Soto, D. A., Manning, W. D., & Longmore, M. A. (2010). The characteristics of romantic relationships associated with teen dating violence. *Social Science Research*, *39*(6), 863–874. https://doi.org/10.1016/j.ssresearch.2010.03.009

Glenn, C. R., Kleiman, E. M., Kellerman, J., Pollak, O., Cha, C. B., Esposito, E. C., Porter, A. C., Wyman, P. A., & Boatman, A. E. (2020). Annual research review: A Meta-analytic review of worldwide suicide rates in adolescents. *Journal of Child Psychology and Psychiatry*, *61*(3), 294–308. https://doi.org/10.1111/jcpp.13106

Goforth, A. N., Pham, A. V., & Oka, E. R. (2015). Parent-child conflict, acculturation gap, acculturative stress, and behavior problems in Arab American adolescents. *Journal of Cross-Cultural Psychology*, *46*(6), 821–836. https://doi.org/10.1177/0022022115585140

Golden, N. H., Katzman, D. K., Sawyer, S. M., Ornstein, R. M., Rome, E. S., Garber, A. K., Kohn, M., & Kreipe, R. E. (2015). Update on the medical management of eating disorders in adolescents. *The Journal of Adolescent Health : Official Publication of the Society for Adolescent Medicine*, *56*, 370–375. https://doi.org/10.1016/j.jadohealth.2014.11.020

Goldschmidt, A. B., Wall, M. M., Zhang, J., Loth, K. A., & Neumark-Sztainer, D. (2016). Overeating and binge eating in emerging adulthood: 10-year stability and risk factors. *Developmental Psychology, 52*(3), 475–483. https://doi.org/10.1037/dev0000086

Gonzales-Backen, M. A., Meca, A., Lorenzo-Blanco, E. I., Des Rosiers, S. E., Córdova, D., Soto, D. W., Cano, M. Á., Oshri, A., Zamboanga, B. L., Baezconde-Garbanati, L., Schwartz, S. J., Szapocznik, J., & Unger, J. B. (2018). Examining the temporal order of ethnic identity and perceived discrimination among Hispanic immigrant adolescents. *Developmental Psychology, 54*(5), 929–937. https://doi.org/10.1037/dev0000465

Gonzalez Avilés, T., Finn, C., & Neyer, F. J. (2021). Patterns of romantic relationship experiences and psychosocial adjustment from adolescence to young adulthood. *Journal of Youth and Adolescence, 50*, 550–562. https://doi.org/10.1007/s10964-020-01350-7

Goodson, P., Buhi, E. R., & Dunsmore, S. C. (2006). Self-esteem and adolescent sexual behaviors, attitudes, and intentions: A Systematic review. *Journal of Adolescent Health, 38*(3), 310–319. https://doi.org/10.1016/J.JADOHEALTH.2005.05.026

Graham, S., Munniksma, A., & Juvonen, J. (2014). Psychosocial benefits of cross-ethnic friendships in urban middle schools. *Child Development, 85*(2), 469–483. https://doi.org/10.1111/cdev.12159

Gray, K. M., & Squeglia, L. M. (2018). Research Review: What have we learned about adolescent substance use? *Journal of Child Psychology and Psychiatry and Allied Disciplines, 59*, 618–627. https://doi.org/10.1111/jcpp.12783

Greenberg, J. S. (2017). *exploring the dimensions of human sexuality.* Jones & Bartlett.

Gremmen, M. C., Dijkstra, J. K., Steglich, C., & Veenstra, R. (2017). First selection, then influence: Developmental differences in friendship dynamics regarding academic achievement. *Developmental Psychology, 53*(7), 1356–1370. https://doi.org/10.1037/dev0000314

Griffith, S. F., & Grolnick, W. S. (2013). Parenting in Caribbean families: A look at parental control, structure, and autonomy support. *Journal of Black Psychology, 40*(2), 166–190. https://doi.org/10.1177/0095798412475085

Grossman, A. H., Park, J. Y., & Russell, S. T. (2016). Transgender youth and suicidal behaviors: Applying the interpersonal psychological theory of suicide. *Journal of Gay & Lesbian Mental Health, 20*(4), 329–349. https://doi.org/10.1080/19359705.2016.1207581

Grotevant, H. D., Thorbecke, W., & Meyer, M. L. (1982). An extension of Marcia's identity status interview into the interpersonal domain. *Journal of Youth and Adolescence, 11*(1), 33–47. https://doi.org/10.1007/BF01537815

Gruenenfelder-Steiger, A. E., Harris, M. A., & Fend, H. A. (2016). Subjective and objective peer approval evaluations and self-esteem development: A test of reciprocal, prospective, and long-term effects. *Developmental Psychology, 52*(10), 1563–1577. https://doi.org/10.1037/dev0000147

Guttmacher Institute. (2014). *American teens' sexual and reproductive health* (Issue 9/5/07. Author. http://www.guttmacher.org/pubs/fb_ATSRH.html

Guttmacher Institute. (2017). *Adolescent sexual and reproductive health in the United States.* Fact Sheet. https://www.guttmacher.org/fact-sheet/american-teens-sexual-and-reproductive-health

Haas, A. P., Eliason, M., Mays, V. M., Mathy, R. M., Cochran, S. D., D'Augelli, A. R., Silverman, M. M., Fisher, P. W., Hughes, T., Rosario, M., Russell, S. T., Malley, E., Reed, J., Litts, D. A., Haller, E., Sell, R. L., Remafedi, G., Bradford, J., Beautrais, A. L., & Clayton, P. J. (2011). Suicide and suicide risk in lesbian, gay, bisexual, and transgender populations: Review and recommendations. *Journal of Homosexuality, 58*(1), 10–51. https://doi.org/10.1080/00918369.2011.534038

Hadiwijaya, H., Klimstra, T. A., Vermunt, J. K., Branje, S. J. T., & Meeus, W. H. J. (2017). On the development of harmony, turbulence, and independence in parent–adolescent relationships: A five-wave longitudinal study. *Journal of Youth and Adolescence, 46*, 1772–1788. https://doi.org/10.1007/s10964-016-0627-7

Hagman, J., Gardner, R. M., Brown, D. L., Gralla, J., Fier, J. M., & Frank, G. K. W. (2015). Body size overestimation and its association with body mass index, body dissatisfaction, and drive for thinness in anorexia nervosa. *Eating and Weight Disorders - Studies on Anorexia, Bulimia and Obesity, 20*(4), 449–455. https://doi.org/10.1007/s40519-015-0193-0

Hall, S. P., & Brassard, M. R. (2008). Relational support as a predictor of identity status in an ethnically diverse early adolescent sample. *Journal of Early Adolescence, 28*(1), 92–114. https://doi.org/10.1177/0272431607308668

Hamidullah, S., Thorpe, H. H. A., Frie, J. A., Mccurdy, R. D., & Khokhar, J. Y. (2020). Adolescent substance use and the brain: Behavioral, cognitive and neuroimaging correlates. *Frontiers in Human Neuroscience, 14*, 298. https://doi.org/10.3389/fnhum.2020.00298

Harding, J. F., Hughes, D. L., & Way, N. (2017). Racial/ethnic differences in mothers' socialization goals for their adolescents. *Cultural Diversity and Ethnic Minority Psychology, 23*(2), 281–290. https://doi.org/10.1037/cdp0000116

Harries, M. D., Paglia, H. A., Redden, S. A., & Grant, J. E.-M. (2018). Age at first sexual activity: Clinical and cognitive associations. *Annals of Clinical Psychiatry : Official Journal of the American Academy of Clinical Psychiatrists, 30*(2), 102–112. http://www.ncbi.nlm.nih.gov/pubmed/29697711

Harris, M. A., Gruenenfelder-Steiger, A. E., Ferrer, E., Donnellan, M. B., Allemand, M., Fend, H., Conger, R. D., & Trzesniewski, K. H. (2015). Do parents foster self-esteem? Testing the prospective impact of parent closeness on adolescent self-esteem. *Child Development, 86*(4), 995–1013. https://doi.org/10.1111/cdev.12356

Harris-McKoy, D., & Cui, M. (2012). Parental control, adolescent delinquency, and young adult criminal behavior. *Journal of Child and Family Studies, 22*(6), 836–843. https://doi.org/10.1007/s10826-012-9641-x

Hart, J. R., Coates, E. E., & Smith-Bynum, M. A. (2019). Parenting style and parent-adolescent relationship quality in African American mother-adolescent dyads. *Parenting, 19*(4), 318–340. https://doi.org/10.1080/15295192.2019.1642085

Harter, S. (2012a). Emerging self-processes during childhood and adolescence. In M. R. Leary & J. P. Tangney (Eds.), *Handbook of self and identity* (pp. 680–715). Guilford.

Harter, S. (2012b). *The construction of the self: Developmental and sociocultural foundations* (2nd ed.). Guilford Pubn.

Hartup, W. W., & Stevens, N. (1997). Friendships and adaptation in the life course. *Psychological Bulletin, 121*, 355–370.

Hatchel, T., Valido, A., De Pedro, K. T., Huang, Y., & Espelage, D. L. (2019). Minority stress among transgender adolescents: The role of peer victimization, school belonging, and ethnicity. *Journal of Child and Family Studies*, *28*, 2467–2476. https://doi.org/10.1007/s10826-018-1168-3

Hazel, C. E., Walls, N. E., & Pomerantz, L. (2019). Gender and sexual minority students' engagement with school: The impacts of grades, feeling Unsafe, and gay/straight alliances. *Contemporary School Psychology*, *23*, 432–443. https://doi.org/10.1007/s40688-018-0199-5

Heine, S. J., & Hamamura, T. (2007). In search of East Asian self-enhancement. *Personality and Social Psychology Review*, *11*(1), 4–27. https://doi.org/10.1177/1088868306294587

Herpertz-Dahlmann, B., Dempfle, A., Konrad, K., Klasen, F., Ravens-Sieberer, U., & group, T. B. study. (2015). Eating disorder symptoms do not just disappear: The Implications of adolescent eating-disordered behaviour for body weight and mental health in young adulthood. *European Child & Adolescent Psychiatry*, *24*(6), 675–684. https://doi.org/10.1007/s00787-014-0610-3

Hiatt, C., Laursen, B., Mooney, K. S., & Rubin, K. H. (2015). Forms of friendship: A person-centered assessment of the quality, stability, and outcomes of different types of adolescent friends. *Personality and Individual Differences*, *77*, 149–155. https://doi.org/10.1016/j.paid.2014.12.051

Hiatt, C., Laursen, B., Stattin, H., & Kerr, M. (2017). Best friend influence over adolescent problem behaviors: Socialized by the satisfied. *Journal of Clinical Child & Adolescent Psychology*, *46*(5), 695–708. https://doi.org/10.1080/15374416.2015.1050723

Hoeben, E. M., Meldrum, R. C., Walker, D., & Young, J. T. N. (2016). The role of peer delinquency and unstructured socializing in explaining delinquency and substance use: A State-of-the-art review. *Journal of Criminal Justice*, *47*, 108–122. https://doi.org/10.1016/j.jcrimjus.2016.08.001

Hoeve, M., Dubas, J. S., Gerris, J. R. M., van der Laan, P. H., & Smeenk, W. (2011). Maternal and paternal parenting styles: Unique and combined links to adolescent and early adult delinquency. *Journal of Adolescence*, *34*(5), 813–827. https://doi.org/10.1016/j.adolescence.2011.02.004

Hofer, C., Eisenberg, N., Spinrad, T. L., Morris, A. S., Gershoff, E., Valiente, C., Kupfer, A., & Eggum, N. D. (2013). Mother-adolescent conflict: Stability, change, and relations with externalizing and internalizing behavior problems. *Social Development (Oxford England)*, *22*(2), 259–279. https://doi.org/10.1111/sode.12012

Hofmann, V., & Müller, C. M. (2018). Avoiding antisocial behavior among adolescents: The positive influence of classmates' prosocial behavior. *Journal of Adolescence*, *68*, 136–145. https://doi.org/10.1016/j.adolescence.2018.07.013

Holman, D. M., Benard, V., Roland, K. B., Watson, M., Liddon, N., & Stokley, S. (2014). Barriers to human papillomavirus vaccination among US adolescents. *JAMA Pediatrics*, *168*(1), 76. https://doi.org/10.1001/jamapediatrics.2013.2752

Huang, D. Y. C., Murphy, D. A., & Hser, Y.-I. (2011). Parental monitoring during early adolescence deters adolescent sexual initiation: Discrete-time survival mixture analysis. *Journal of Child and Family Studies*, *20*(4), 511–520. https://doi.org/10.1007/s10826-010-9418-z

Huey, M., Hiatt, C., Laursen, B., Burk, W. J., & Rubin, K. (2017). Mother–adolescent conflict types and adolescent adjustment: A Person-oriented analysis. *Journal of Family Psychology*, *31*(4), 504–512. https://doi.org/10.1037/fam0000294

Hughes, D. L., Del Toro, J., Harding, J. F., Way, N., & Rarick, J. R. D. (2016). Trajectories of discrimination across adolescence: Associations with academic, psychological, and behavioral outcomes. *Child Development*, *87*(5), 1337–1351. https://doi.org/10.1111/cdev.12591

Hughes, D. L., Del Toro, J., & Way, N. (2017). Interrelations among dimensions of ethnic-racial identity during adolescence. *Developmental Psychology*, *53*(11), 2139–2153. https://doi.org/10.1037/dev0000401

Hughes, D. L., Witherspoon, D., Rivas-Drake, D., & West-Bey, N. (2009). Received ethnic–racial socialization messages and youths' academic and behavioral outcomes: Examining the mediating role of ethnic identity and self-esteem. *Cultural Diversity and Ethnic Minority Psychology*, *15*(2), 112–124. https://doi.org/10.1037/a0015509

Huguley, J. P., Wang, M. Te., Vasquez, A. C., & Guo, J. (2019). Parental ethnic-racial socialization practices and the construction of children of color's ethnic-racial identity: A research synthesis and meta-analysis. *Psychological Bulletin*, *145*(5), 437–458. https://doi.org/10.1037/bul0000187

Ioverno, S., Belser, A. B., Baiocco, R., Grossman, A. H., & Russell, S. T. (2016). The protective role of gay-straight alliances for Lesbian, Gay, bisexual, and questioning students: A prospective analysis. *Psychology of Sexual Orientation and Gender Diversity*, *3*(4), 397–406. https://doi.org/10.1037/sgd0000193

Isomaa, R., Isomaa, A.-L., Marttunen, M., Kaltiala-Heino, R., & Björkqvist, K. (2009). The prevalence, incidence and development of eating disorders in finnish adolescents—a two-step 3-year follow-up study. *European Eating Disorders Review*, *17*(3), 199–207. https://doi.org/10.1002/erv.919

Jackman, D. M., & MacPhee, D. (2017). Self-Esteem and future orientation predict adolescents' risk engagement. *The Journal of Early Adolescence*, *37*(3), 339–366. https://doi.org/10.1177/0272431615602756

Jaffee, S., & Hyde, J. S. (2000). Gender differences in moral orientation: A meta-analysis. *Psychological Bulletin*, *126*(5), 703.

Jaramillo, N., Buhi, E. R., Elder, J. P., & Corliss, H. L. (2017). Associations between sex education and contraceptive use among heterosexually active, adolescent males in the United States. *The Journal of Adolescent Health : Official Publication of the Society for Adolescent Medicine*, *60*(5), 534–540. https://doi.org/10.1016/j.jadohealth.2016.11.025

Jeha, D., Usta, I., Ghulmiyyah, L., & Nassar, A. (2015). A review of the risks and consequences of adolescent pregnancy. *Journal of Neonatal-Perinatal Medicine*, *8*(1), 1–8. https://doi.org/10.3233/NPM-15814038

Jespersen, K., Kroger, J., & Martinussen, M. (2013). Identity status and moral reasoning: A Meta-analysis. *Identity*, *13*(3), 266–280. https://doi.org/10.1080/15283488.2013.799472

Johns, M. M., Beltran, O., Armstrong, H. L., Jayne, P. E., & Barrios, L. C. (2018). Protective factors among transgender and gender variant youth: A systematic review by socioecological level. *The Journal of Primary Prevention*, *39*(3), 263–301. https://doi.org/10.1007/s10935-018-0508-9

Johnson, A. Z., Sieving, R. E., Pettingell, S. L., & McRee, A.-L. (2015). The roles of partner communication and relationship status in adolescent contraceptive use. *Journal of Pediatric Health Care : Official Publication of National Association of Pediatric Nurse Associates & Practitioners*, *29*(1), 61–69. https://doi.org/10.1016/j.pedhc.2014.06.008

Johnston, LD., O'Malley, PM., & Bachman, JG, et al.. (2019). *Monitoring the future national results on adolescent drug use: Overview of key findings, 2001*. National Institute on Drug Abuse.

Jordan, J. W., Stalgaitis, C. A., Charles, J., Madden, P. A., Radhakrishnan, A. G., & Saggese, D. (2019). Peer crowd identification and adolescent health behaviors: Results from a statewide representative study. *Health Education and Behavior*, *46*(1), 40–52. https://doi.org/10.1177/1090198118759148

Jugert, P., Leszczensky, L., & Pink, S. (2020). Differential influence of same- and cross-ethnic friends on ethnic-racial identity development in early adolescence. *Child Development*, *91*(3), 949–963. https://doi.org/10.1111/cdev.13240

Juster, R.-P., Smith, N. G., Ouellet, É., Sindi, S., & Lupien, S. J. (2013). Sexual orientation and disclosure in relation to psychiatric symptoms, diurnal cortisol, and allostatic load. *Psychosomatic Medicine*, *75*(2), 103–116. https://doi.org/10.1097/PSY.0b013e3182826881

Kaestle, C. E. (2019). Sexual orientation trajectories based on sexual attractions, partners, and identity: A Longitudinal investigation from adolescence through young adulthood using a U.S. representative sample. *The Journal of Sex Research*, *56*(7), 811–826. https://doi.org/10.1080/00224499.2019.1577351

Kågesten, A., Gibbs, S., Blum, R. W., Moreau, C., Chandra-Mouli, V., Herbert, A., & Amin, A. (2016). Understanding factors that shape gender attitudes in early adolescence globally: A mixed-methods systematic review. *PLOS ONE*, *11*(6), e0157805. https://doi.org/10.1371/journal.pone.0157805

Kaiser Family Foundation. (2014). *Sexual health of adolescents and young adults in the United States*. Henry J. Kaiser Family Foundation. http://kff.org/womens-health-policy/fact-sheet/sexual-health-of-adolescents-and-young-adults-in-the-united-states/

Kann, L., Kinchen, S., Shanklin, S. L., Flint, K. H., Kawkins, J., Harris, W. A., Lowry, R., Olsen, E. O., McManus, T., Chyen, D., Whittle, L., Taylor, E., Demissie, Z., Brener, N., Thornton, J., Moore, J., Zaza, S., & Centers for Disease Control and Prevention. (2014). Youth risk behavior surveillance--United States, 2013. *Morbidity and Mortality Weekly Report. Surveillance Summaries (Washington, D.C. : 2002)*, *63*(Suppl 4), 1–168. http://www.ncbi.nlm.nih.gov/pubmed/24918634

Kann, L., McManus, T., Harris, W. A., Shanklin, S. L., Flint, K. H., Queen, B., Lowry, R., Chyen, D., Whittle, L., Thornton, J., Lim, C., Bradford, D., Yamakawa, Y., Leon, M., Brener, N., & Ethier, K. A. (2018). Youth risk behavior surveillance — United States, 2017. *MMWR Surveillance Summaries*, *67*(8), 1. https://doi.org/10.15585/MMWR.SS6708A1

Kantor, L., & Levitz, N. (2017). Parents' views on sex education in schools: How much do Democrats and Republicans agree? *PLoS One*, *12*(7), e0180250. https://doi.org/10.1371/journal.pone.0180250

Kapetanovic, S., Rothenberg, W. A., Lansford, J. E., Bornstein, M. H., Chang, L., Deater-Deckard, K., Di Giunta, L., Dodge, K. A., Gurdal, S., Malone, P. S., Oburu, P., Pastorelli, C., Skinner, A. T., Sorbring, E., Steinberg, L., Tapanya, S., Uribe Tirado, L. M., Yotanyamaneewong, S., Peña Alampay, L., & Bacchini, D. (2020). Cross-cultural examination of links between parent–adolescent communication and adolescent psychological problems in 12 cultural groups. *Journal of Youth and Adolescence*, *49*(6), 1225–1244. https://doi.org/10.1007/s10964-020-01212-2

Kapetanovic, S., & Skoog, T. (2021). The Role of the family's emotional climate in the links between parent-adolescent communication and adolescent psychosocial functioning. *Journal of Abnormal Child Psychology*, *49*(2), 141–154. https://doi.org/10.1007/s10802-020-00705-9

Kapetanovic, S., Skoog, T., Bohlin, M., & Gerdner, A. (2019). Aspects of the parent-adolescent relationship and associations with adolescent risk behaviors over time. *Journal of Family Psychology*, *33*(1), 1–11. https://doi.org/10.1037/fam0000436

Karoly, H. C., Ross, J. M., Ellingson, J. M., & Feldstein Ewing, S. W. (2020). Exploring Cannabis and Alcohol co-use in adolescents: A narrative review of the evidence. *Journal of Dual Diagnosis*, *16*(1), 58–74. https://doi.org/10.1080/15504263.2019.1660020

Katzman, D. K. (2005). Medical complications in adolescents with Anorexia Nervosa: A review of the literature. *International Journal of Eating Disorders*, *37*, 52–59.

Kawabata, Y., & Crick, N. R. (2011). The significance of cross-racial/ethnic friendships: Associations with peer victimization, peer support, sociometric status, and classroom diversity. *Developmental Psychology*, *47*(6), 1763–1775. https://doi.org/10.1037/a0025399

Keel, P. K. (2014). Bulimia Nervosa. In R. L. Cautin & S. O. Lilienfeld (Eds.), *The encyclopedia of clinical psychology*. John Wiley & Sons, Inc. http://onlinelibrary.wiley.com/doi/10.1002/9781118625392.wbecp251/abstract? deniedAccessCustomisedMessage=&userIsAuthenticated=false

Keizer, R., Helmerhorst, K. O. W., & van Rijn-van Gelderen, L. (2019). Perceived quality of the mother–adolescent and father–adolescent attachment relationship and adolescents' self-esteem. *Journal of Youth and Adolescence*, *48*(6), 1203–1217. https://doi.org/10.1007/s10964-019-01007-0

Kerr, M., Stattin, H., & Burk, W. J. (2010). A reinterpretation of parental monitoring in longitudinal perspective. *Journal of Research on Adolescence*, *20*(1), 39–64. https://doi.org/10.1111/j.1532-7795.2009.00623.x

Keski-Rahkonen, A., & Mustelin, L. (2016). Epidemiology of eating disorders in Europe. *Current Opinion in Psychiatry*, *29*(6), 340–345. https://doi.org/10.1097/YCO.0000000000000278

Kessler, R. C., Berglund, P. A., Chiu, W. T., Deitz, A. C., Hudson, J. I., Shahly, V., Aguilar-Gaxiola, S., Alonso, J., Angermeyer, M. C., Benjet, C., Bruffaerts, R., de Girolamo, G., de Graaf, R., Maria Haro, J., Kovess-Masfety, V., O'Neill, S., Posada-Villa, J., Sasu, C., Scott, K., & Xavier, M. (2013). The prevalence and correlates of binge eating disorder in the World Health Organization World Mental Health Surveys. *Biological Psychiatry*, *73*(9), 904–914. https://doi.org/10.1016/j.biopsych.2012.11.020

Kindelberger, C., Mallet, P., & Galharret, J. (2020). Diversity of romantic experiences in late adolescence and their contribution to identity formation. *Social Development*, *29*(2), 615–634. https://doi.org/10.1111/sode.12415

Kiselica, M. S., & Kiselica, A. M. (2014). The complicated worlds of adolescent fathers: Implications for clinical practice, public policy, and research. *Psychology of Men & Masculinity, 15*(3), 260.

Klaczynski, P. A., Felmban, W. S., & Kole, J. (2020). Gender intensification and gender generalization biases in pre-adolescents, adolescents, and emerging adults. *British Journal of Developmental Psychology, 38*(3), 415–433. https://doi.org/10.1111/bjdp.12326

Klimstra, T. A., Kuppens, P., Luyckx, K., Branje, S., Hale, W. W., Oosterwegel, A., Koot, H. M., & Meeus, W. H. J. (2016). Daily dynamics of adolescent mood and identity. *Journal of Research on Adolescence, 26*(3), 459–473. https://doi.org/10.1111/jora.12205

Knox, P. L., Fagley, N. S., & Miller, P. M. (2004). Care and Justice moral orientation among African American college students. *Journal of Adult Development, 11*(1), 41–45.

Kobak, R., Abbott, C., Zisk, A., & Bounoua, N. (2017). Adapting to the changing needs of adolescents: Parenting practices and challenges to sensitive attunement. *Current Opinion in Psychology, 15*, 137–142. https://doi.org/10.1016/j.copsyc.2017.02.018

Kohlberg, L. (1969). Stage and sequence: The cognitive-developmental approach to socialization. In D. A. Goslin (Ed.), *Handbook of socialization* (pp. 347–480). Rand McNally.

Kohlberg, L., Levine, C., & Hewer, A. (1983). Moral stages: A Current formulation and a response to critics. *Contributions to Human Development, 10*, 174.

Kohlberg, L., & Ryncarz, R. A. (1990). Beyond justice reasoning: Moral development and consideration of a seventh stage. In C. N. Alexander & E. J. Langer (Eds.), *Higher stages of human development: Perspectives on adult growth* (pp. 191–207). Oxford University Press.

Korlat, S., Foerst, N. M., Schultes, M.-T., Schober, B., Spiel, C., & Kollmayer, M. (2021). Gender role identity and gender intensification: Agency and communion in adolescents' spontaneous self-descriptions. *European Journal of Developmental Psychology.* https://doi.org/10.1080/17405629.2020.1865143

Kosciw, J. G., Palmer, N. A., & Kull, R. M. (2015). Reflecting resiliency: Openness about sexual orientation and/or gender identity and its relationship to well-being and educational outcomes for LGBT students. *American Journal of Community Psychology, 55*(1–2), 167–178. https://doi.org/10.1007/s10464-014-9642-6

Kroger, J. (2015). Identity development through adulthood: The move toward 'wholeness'. In K. C. McLean & M. Syed (Eds.), *The Oxford handbook of identity development* (pp. 65–80). Oxford University Press.

Kroger, J., Martinussen, M., & Marcia, J. E. (2010). Identity status change during adolescence and young adulthood: A Meta-analysis. *Journal of Adolescence, 33*(5), 683–698. https://doi.org/10.1016/j.adolescence.2009.11.002

Kyere, E., & Huguley, J. P. (2020). Exploring the process by which positive racial identity develops and influences academic performance in Black youth: Implications for social work. *Journal of Ethnic and Cultural Diversity in Social Work, 29*(4), 286–304. https://doi.org/10.1080/15313204.2018.1555502

Lansford, J. E., Costanzo, P. R., Grimes, C., Putallaz, M., Miller, S., & Malone, P. S. (2009). Social Network Centrality and Leadership Status: Links with Problem Behaviors and Tests of Gender Differences. *Merrill-Palmer Quarterly, 55*(1), 1–25.

Lansford, J. E., Laird, R. D., Pettit, G. S., Bates, J. E., & Dodge, K. A. (2014). Mothers' and fathers' autonomy-relevant parenting: Longitudinal links with adolescents' externalizing and internalizing behavior. *Journal of Youth and Adolescence, 43*(11), 1877–1889. https://doi.org/10.1007/s10964-013-0079-2

Lansford, J. E., Staples, A. D., Bates, J. E., Pettit, G. S., & Dodge, K. A. (2013). Trajectories of mothers' discipline strategies and interparental conflict: Interrelated change during middle childhood. *Journal of Family Communication, 13*(3), 178–195. https://doi.org/10.1080/15267431.2013.796947

Lara, L. A. S., & Abdo, C. H. N. (2016). Age at time of initial sexual intercourse and health of adolescent girls. *Journal of Pediatric and Adolescent Gynecology, 29*(5), 417–423. https://doi.org/10.1016/J.JPAG.2015.11.012

Laursen, B. (2017). Making and keeping friends: The Importance of being similar. *Child Development Perspectives, 11*(4), 282–289. https://doi.org/10.1111/cdep.12246

Lavender, J. M., Utzinger, L. M., Cao, L., Wonderlich, S. A., Engel, S. G., Mitchell, J. E., & Crosby, R. D. (2016). Reciprocal associations between negative affect, binge eating, and purging in the natural environment in women with bulimia nervosa. *Journal of Abnormal Psychology, 125*(3), 381–386. https://doi.org/10.1037/abn0000135

Lee, C. G., Seo, D.-C., Torabi, M. R., Lohrmann, D. K., & Song, T. M. (2018). Longitudinal trajectory of the relationship between self-esteem and substance use from adolescence to young adulthood. *Journal of School Health, 88*(1), 9–14. https://doi.org/10.1111/josh.12574

Leenders, I., & Brugman, D. D. (2005). Moral/non-moral domain shift in young adolescents in relation to delinquent behaviour. *British Journal of Developmental Psychology, 23*(1), 65–79.

Legate, N., Ryan, R. M., & Weinstein, N. (2012). Is coming out always a "Good Thing"? Exploring the relations of autonomy support, outness, and wellness for Lesbian, Gay, and Bisexual individuals. *Social Psychological and Personality Science, 3*(2), 145–152. https://doi.org/10.1177/1948550611411929

Lerner, R. M., & Israeloff, R. (2007). *The good teen: Rescuing adolescence from the myths of the storm and stress years.* Crown.

Leung, R. K., Toumbourou, J. W., & Hemphill, S. A. (2014). The effect of peer influence and selection processes on adolescent alcohol use: A Systematic review of longitudinal studies. *Health Psychology Review, 8*(4), 426–457. https://doi.org/10.1080/17437199.2011.587961

Levine, J. A., Emery, C. R., & Pollack, H. (2007). The Well-Being of children born to teen mothers. *Journal of Marriage and Family, 69*(1), 105–122. https://doi.org/10.1111/j.1741-3737.2006.00348.x

Li, M., Fu, X., Xie, W., Guo, W., Li, B., Cui, R., & Yang, W. (2020). Effect of early life stress on the epigenetic profiles in depression. *Frontiers in Cell and Developmental Biology, 8*, 867. https://doi.org/10.3389/fcell.2020.00867

Lillevoll, K. R., Kroger, J., & Martinussen, M. (2013). Identity status and anxiety: A Meta-analysis. *Identity, 13*(3), 214–227. https://doi.org/10.1080/15283488.2013.799432

Lindberg, L., Santelli, J., & Desai, S. (2016). Understanding the decline in adolescent fertility in the United States, 2007–2012. *Journal of Adolescent Health, 59*(5), 577–583. https://doi.org/10.1016/j.jadohealth.2016.06.024

Lionetti, F., Palladino, B. E., Moses Passini, C., Casonato, M., Hamzallari, O., Ranta, M., Dellagiulia, A., & Keijsers, L. (2019). The development of parental monitoring during adolescence: A Meta-analysis. *European Journal of Developmental Psychology, 16*(5), 552–580. https://doi.org/10.1080/17405629.2018.1476233

Lippold, M. A., Greenberg, M. T., & Feinberg, M. E. (2011). A Dyadic approach to understanding the relationship of maternal knowledge of youths' activities to youths' problem behavior among rural adolescents. *Journal of Youth and Adolescence, 40*(9), 1178–1191. https://doi.org/10.1007/s10964-010-9595-5

Lisdahl, K. M., Gilbart, E. R., Wright, N. E., & Shollenbarger, S. (2013). Dare to delay? The impacts of adolescent alcohol and marijuana use onset on cognition, brain structure, and function. *Frontiers in Psychiatry, 4*, 53. https://doi.org/10.3389/fpsyt.2013.00053

Liu, R. T., & Mustanski, B. (2012). Suicidal ideation and self-harm in lesbian, gay, bisexual, and transgender youth. *American Journal of Preventive Medicine, 42*(3), 221–228. https://doi.org/10.1016/j.amepre.2011.10.023

LoBraico, E. J., Brinberg, M., Ram, N., & Fosco, G. M. (2020). Exploring processes in day-to-day parent–adolescent conflict and angry mood: Evidence for circular causality. *Family Process, 59*(4), 1706–1721. https://doi.org/10.1111/famp.12506

Lock, J. (2011). Evaluation of family treatment models for eating disorders. *Current Opinion in Psychiatry, 24*(4), 274–279. https://doi.org/10.1097/YCO.0b013e328346f71e

Lopez-Larson, M. P., Rogowska, J., Bogorodzki, P., Bueler, C. E., McGlade, E. C., & Yurgelun-Todd, D. A. (2012). Cortico-cerebellar abnormalities in adolescents with heavy marijuana use. *Psychiatry Research: Neuroimaging, 202*(3), 224–232. https://doi.org/10.1016/j.pscychresns.2011.11.005

Lopez-Tamayo, R., LaVome Robinson, W., Lambert, S. F., Jason, L. A., & Ialongo, N. S. (2016). Parental monitoring, association with externalized behavior, and academic outcomes in Urban African-American Youth: A Moderated mediation analysis. *American Journal of Community Psychology, 57*(3–4), 366–379. https://doi.org/10.1002/ajcp.12056

Lorenzetti, V., Hoch, E., & Hall, W. (2020). Adolescent cannabis use, cognition, brain health and educational outcomes: A Review of the evidence. *European Neuropsychopharmacology, 36*, 169–180. https://doi.org/10.1016/j.euroneuro.2020.03.012

Lubman, D. I., Cheetham, A., & Yücel, M. (2015). Cannabis and adolescent brain development. *Pharmacology & Therapeutics, 148*, 1–16. https://doi.org/10.1016/j.pharmthera.2014.11.009

Lucas-Thompson, R., Seiter, N. S., & Lunkenheimer, E. S. (2020). Interparental conflict, attention to angry interpersonal interactions, and adolescent anxiety. *Family Relations, 69*(5), 1041–1054. https://doi.org/10.1111/fare.12505

Lussier, A. A., Hawrilenko, M., Wang, M., Choi, K. W., Cerutti, J., Zhu, Y., & Dunn, E. C. (2021). Genetic susceptibility for major depressive disorder associates with trajectories of depressive symptoms across childhood and adolescence. *Journal of Child Psychology and Psychiatry, 62*, 895–904. https://doi.org/10.1111/jcpp.13342

Madsen, S. D., & Collins, W. A. (2011). The Salience of adolescent romantic experiences for romantic relationship qualities in young adulthood. *Journal of Research on Adolescence, 21*(4), 789–801. https://doi.org/10.1111/j.1532-7795.2011.00737.x

Maheux, A. J., Evans, R., Widman, L., Nesi, J., Prinstein, M. J., & Choukas-Bradley, S. (2020). Popular peer norms and adolescent sexting behavior. *Journal of Adolescence, 78*, 62–66. https://doi.org/10.1016/j.adolescence.2019.12.002

Mahfouda, S., Moore, J. K., Siafarikas, A., Zepf, F. D., & Lin, A. (2017). Puberty suppression in transgender children and adolescents. *The Lancet Diabetes & Endocrinology, 5*(10), 816–826. https://doi.org/10.1016/S2213-8587(17)30099-2

Malhi, N., Oliffe, J. L., Bungay, V., & Kelly, M. T. (2020). Male perpetration of adolescent dating violence: A Scoping review. *American Journal of Men's Health, 14*(5), 155798832096360. https://doi.org/10.1177/1557988320963600

Malti, T., & Latzko, B. (2010). Children's moral emotions and moral cognition: Towards an integrative perspective. *New Directions for Child & Adolescent Development, 2010*(129), 1–10. https://doi.org/10.1002/cd.272

Mann, F. D., Patterson, M. W., Grotzinger, A. D., Kretsch, N., Tackett, J. L., Tucker-Drob, E. M., & Harden, K. P. (2016). Sensation seeking, peer deviance, and genetic influences on adolescent delinquency: Evidence for person-environment correlation and interaction. *Journal of Abnormal Psychology, 125*(5), 679–691. https://doi.org/10.1037/abn0000160

Marceau, K., Nair, N., Rogers, M. L., & Jackson, K. M. (2020). Lability in parent- and child-based sources of parental monitoring is differentially associated with adolescent substance use. *Prevention Science, 21*(4), 568–579. https://doi.org/10.1007/s11121-020-01094-7

Marcia, J. E. (1966). Development and validation of ego-identity status. *Journal of Personality and Social Psychology, 3*(5), 551–558.

Marcia, J. E. (2002). Identity and psychosocial development in adulthood. *Identity, 2*(1), 7–28. https://doi.org/10.1207/S1532706XID0201_02

Markiewicz, D., & Doyle, A. B. (2016). Best friends. In R. J. R. Levesque (Ed.), *Encyclopedia of adolescence* (pp. 1–8). Springer Publishing Company. https://doi.org/10.1007/978-3-319-32132-5_314-2

Markus, H. R., & Kitayama, S. (2010). Cultures and selves: A cycle of mutual constitution. *Perspectives on Psychological Science, 5*(4), 420–430. https://doi.org/10.1177/1745691610375557

Marshall, E. J. (2014). Adolescent alcohol use: Risks and consequences. *Alcohol and Alcoholism (Oxford, Oxfordshire), 49*(2), 160–164. https://doi.org/10.1093/alcalc/agt180

Martin, J., Hamilton, B., & Osterman, M. (2018). *Births in the United States, 2017; data brief, no. 318*. NCHS Data Brief. https://www.cdc.gov/nchs/data/databriefs/db318.pdf

Marx, R. A., & Kettrey, H. H. (2016). Gay-straight alliances are associated with lower levels of school-based victimization of LGBTQ+ youth: A systematic review and meta-analysis. *Journal of Youth and Adolescence, 45*(7), 1269–1282. https://doi.org/10.1007/s10964-016-0501-7

Marzilli, E., Cerniglia, L., & Cimino, S. (2018). A narrative review of binge eating disorder in adolescence: Prevalence, impact, and psychological treatment strategies. *Adolescent Health, Medicine and Therapeutics, 9*, 17–30. https://doi.org/10.2147/AHMT.S148050

Masche, J. G. (2010). Explanation of normative declines in parents' knowledge about their adolescent children. *Journal of Adolescence, 33*(2), 271–284. https://doi.org/10.1016/j.adolescence.2009.08.002

Mason, W. A., & Spoth, R. L. (2011). Longitudinal associations of alcohol involvement with subjective well-being in adolescence and prediction to alcohol problems in early adulthood. *Journal of Youth and Adolescence*, *40*(9), 1215–1224. https://doi.org/10.1007/s10964-011-9632-z

Maughan, B., Collishaw, S., & Stringaris, A. (2013). Depression in childhood and adolescence. *Journal of the Canadian Academy of Child and Adolescent Psychiatry = Journal de l'Académie Canadienne de Psychiatrie de l'enfant et de l'adolescent*, *22*(1), 35–40. http://www.pubmedcentral.nih.gov/articlerender.fcgi? artid=3565713&tool=pmcentrez&rendertype=abstract

McAdams, D. P., & Zapata-Gietl, C. (2015). Three strands of identity development across the human life course. In K. C. McLean & M. Syed (Eds.), *The oxford handbook of identity development* (pp. 81–96). Oxford University Press. https://doi.org/10.1093/oxfordhb/9780199936564.013.006

McClelland, S. I., & Tolman, D. L. (2014). Adolescent sexuality. In T. Tio (Ed.), *Encyclopedia of critical psychology* (pp. 40–47). Springer Publishing Company.

McConnell, E. A., Birkett, M., & Mustanski, B. (2016). Families matter: Social support and mental health trajectories among Lesbian, Gay, Bisexual, and Transgender youth. *Journal of Adolescent Health*, *59*(6), 674–680. https://doi.org/10.1016/J.JADOHEALTH.2016.07.026

McCoy, S. S., Dimler, L. M., Samuels, D. V., & Natsuaki, M. N. (2019). Adolescent susceptibility to deviant peer pressure: Does gender matter? *Adolescent research review*, *4*(1), 59–71. https://doi.org/10.1007/s40894-017-0071-2

McCrea, K. T., Richards, M., Quimby, D., Scott, D., Davis, L., Hart, S., Thomas, A., & Hopson, S. (2019). Understanding violence and developing resilience with African American youth in high-poverty, high-crime communities. *Children and Youth Services Review*, *99*, 296–307. https://doi.org/10.1016/j.childyouth.2018.12.018

McKinney, C., & Renk, K. (2011). A multivariate model of parent-adolescent relationship variables in early adolescence. *Child Psychiatry and Human Development*, *42*(4), 442–462. https://doi.org/10.1007/s10578-011-0228-3

McLean, K. C., Syed, M., Way, N., & Rogers, O. (2015). [T]hey Say black men won't make it, but i know i'm gonna make it. In K. C. McLean & M. Syed (Eds.), *The oxford handbook of identity development* (pp. 269–287). Oxford University Press. https://doi.org/10.1093/oxfordhb/9780199936564.013.032

McQuillan, G., Kruszon-Moran, D., Markowitz, L. E., Unger, E. R., & Paulose-Ram, R. (2017). Prevalence of HPV in adults aged 18–69: United States, 2011–2014. *NCHS Data Briefs, 280*. https://www.cdc.gov/nchs/data/databriefs/db280.pdf

Meeus, W. H. J. (2011). The Study of adolescent identity formation 2000-2010: A Review of longitudinal research. *Journal of Research on Adolescence (Blackwell Publishing Limited)*, *21*(1), 75–94. https://doi.org/10.1111/j.1532-7795.2010.00716.x

Meeus, W. H. J. (2016). Adolescent psychosocial development: A review of longitudinal models and research. *Developmental Psychology*, *52*(12), 1969–1993. https://doi.org/10.1037/dev0000243

Mercer, N., Crocetti, E., Branje, S., van Lier, P., & Meeus, W. (2017). Linking delinquency and personal identity formation across adolescence: Examining between- and within-person associations. *Developmental Psychology*, *53*(11), 2182–2194. https://doi.org/10.1037/dev0000351

Merrin, G. J., Davis, J. P., Berry, D., & Espelage, D. L. (2019). Developmental changes in deviant and violent behaviors from early to late adolescence: Associations with parental monitoring and peer deviance. *Psychology of Violence*, *9*(2), 196–208. https://doi.org/10.1037/vio0000207

Meruelo, A. D., Castro, N., Cota, C. I., & Tapert, S. F. (2017). Cannabis and alcohol use, and the developing brain. *Behavioural Brain Research*, *325*, 44–50. https://doi.org/10.1016/j.bbr.2017.02.025

Micali, N., Solmi, F., Horton, N. J., Crosby, R. D., Eddy, K. T., Calzo, J. P., Sonneville, K. R., Swanson, S. A., & Field, A. E. (2015). Adolescent eating disorders predict psychiatric, high-risk behaviors and weight outcomes in young adulthood. *Journal of the American Academy of Child & Adolescent Psychiatry*, *54*(8), 652–659.e1, . https://doi.org/10.1016/J.JAAC.2015.05.009

Miconi, D., Moscardino, U., Ronconi, L., & Altoè, G. (2017). Perceived parenting, self-esteem, and depressive symptoms in immigrant and non-immigrant adolescents in Italy: A multigroup path analysis. *Journal of Child and Family Studies*, *26*(2), 345–356. https://doi.org/10.1007/s10826-016-0562-y

Miech, R. A., Johnston, L. D., O'Malley, P. M., Bachman, J. G., Schulenberg, J. E., & Patrick, M. E. (2017). *Monitoring the future national survey results on drug use, 1975–2016: Volume I, Secondary school students*. http://www.monitoringthefuture.org/pubs/monographs/mtf-vol1_2016.pdf

Miething, A., Almquist, Y. B., Edling, C., Rydgren, J., & Rostila, M. (2017). Friendship trust and psychological well-being from late adolescence to early adulthood: A Structural equation modelling approach. *Scandinavian Journal of Public Health*, *45*(3), 244–252. https://doi.org/10.1177/1403494816680784

Miller, J. G. (2018). Physiological mechanisms of prosociality. *Current Opinion in Psychology*, *20*, 50–54. https://doi.org/10.1016/J.COPSYC.2017.08.018

Miller-Cotto, D., & Byrnes, J. P. (2016). Ethnic/racial identity and academic achievement: A Meta-analytic review. *Developmental Review*, *41*, 51–70. https://doi.org/10.1016/j.dr.2016.06.003

Mims, L. C., & Williams, J. L. (2020). "They told me what I was before I could tell them what I was": Black girls' ethnic-racial identity development within multiple worlds. *Journal of Adolescent Research*, *35*(6), 754–779. https://doi.org/10.1177/0743558420913483

Miranda-Mendizábal, A., Castellví, P., Parés-Badell, O., Almenara, J., Alonso, I., Blasco, M. J., Cebrià, A., Gabilondo, A., Gili, M., Lagares, C., Piqueras, J. A., Roca, M., Rodríguez-Marín, J., Rodríguez, T., Soto-Sanz, V., Vilagut, G., & Alonso, J. (2017). Sexual orientation and suicidal behaviour in adolescents and young adults: Systematic review and meta-analysis. *The British Journal of Psychiatry*, *211*, 77–87. http://bjp.rcpsych.org/content/early/2017/02/20/bjp.bp.116.196345

Monahan, K. C., Steinberg, L., Cauffman, E., & Mulvey, E. P. (2013). Psychosocial (im)maturity from adolescence to early adulthood: Distinguishing between adolescence-limited and persisting antisocial behavior. *Development and Psychopathology*, *25*, 1093–1105. https://doi.org/10.1017/S0954579413000394

Moore, S. R., Harden, K. P., & Mendle, J. (2014). Pubertal timing and adolescent sexual behavior in girls. *Developmental Psychology*, *50*(6), 1734–1745. https://doi.org/10.1037/a0036027

Moreno, O., Janssen, T., Cox, M. J., Colby, S., & Jackson, K. M. (2017). Parent-adolescent relationships in Hispanic versus Caucasian families: Associations with alcohol and marijuana use onset. *Addictive Behaviors, 74*, 74–81. https://doi.org/10.1016/J.ADDBEH.2017.05.029

Müller-Oehring, E. M., Kwon, D., Nagel, B. J., Sullivan, E. V., Chu, W., Rohlfing, T., Prouty, D., Nichols, B. N., Poline, J.-B., Tapert, S. F., Brown, S. A., Cummins, K., Brumback, T., Colrain, I. M., Baker, F. C., De Bellis, M. D., Voyvodic, J. T., Clark, D. B., Pfefferbaum, A., & Pohl, K. M. (2018). Influences of age, sex, and moderate alcohol drinking on the intrinsic functional architecture of adolescent brains. *Cerebral Cortex, 28*(3), 1049–1063. https://doi.org/10.1093/cercor/bhx014

Mustanski, B., Andrews, R., & Puckett, J. A. (2016). The Effects of Cumulative Victimization on Mental Health Among Lesbian, Gay, Bisexual, and Transgender Adolescents and Young Adults. *American Journal of Public Health, 106*(3), 527–533. https://doi.org/10.2105/AJPH.2015.302976

Mustanski, B., & Liu, R. T. (2013). A longitudinal study of predictors of suicide attempts among lesbian, gay, bisexual, and transgender youth. *Archives of Sexual Behavior, 42*(3), 437–448. https://doi.org/10.1007/s10508-012-0013-9

National Institute of Mental Health. (2019). *Major depression.* https://www.nimh.nih.gov/health/statistics/major-depression.shtml

Natsuaki, M. N., Shaw, D. S., Neiderhiser, J. M., Ganiban, J. M., Harold, G. T., Reiss, D., & Leve, L. D. (2014). Raised by depressed parents: Is it an environmental risk? *Clinical Child and Family Psychology Review, 17*(4), 357–367. https://doi.org/10.1007/s10567-014-0169-z

Negriff, S., Susman, E. J., & Trickett, P. K. (2011). The developmental pathway from pubertal timing to delinquency and sexual activity from early to late adolescence. *Journal of Youth and Adolescence, 40*(10), 1343–1356. https://doi.org/10.1007/s10964-010-9621-7

Nelson, S. C., Syed, M., Tran, A. G. T. T., Hu, A. W., & Lee, R. M. (2018). Pathways to ethnic-racial identity development and psychological adjustment: The differential associations of cultural socialization by parents and peers. *Developmental Psychology, 54*(11), 2166–2180. https://doi.org/10.1037/dev0000597

Nesi, J., Widman, L., Choukas-Bradley, S., & Prinstein, M. J. (2017). Technology-based communication and the development of interpersonal competencies within adolescent romantic relationships: A Preliminary investigation. *Journal of Research on Adolescence, 27*(2), 471–477. https://doi.org/10.1111/jora.12274

Niolon, P. H., Vivolo-Kantor, A. M., Latzman, N. E., Valle, L. A., Kuoh, H., Burton, T., Taylor, B. G., & Tharp, A. T. (2015). Prevalence of teen dating violence and co-occurring risk factors among middle school youth in high-risk urban communities. *Journal of Adolescent Health, 56*(2), S5–S13. https://doi.org/10.1016/j.jadohealth.2014.07.019

Nogueira Avelar e Silva, R., van de Bongardt, D., van de Looij-Jansen, P., Wijtzes, A., & Raat, H. (2016). *Mother- and father-adolescent relationships and early sexual intercourse. Pediatrics, 138*(6), e2016782. http://pediatrics.aappublications.org/content/138/6/e20160782

Office for National Statistics. (2015). *What are the top causes of death by age and gender?* http://visual.ons.gov.uk/what-are-the-top-causes-of-death-by-age-and-gender/

Office of Juvenile Justice and Delinquency Prevention. (2014). *Statistical briefing book.* http://www.ojjdp.gov/ojstatbb/

Office of Juvenile Justice and Delinquency Prevention. (2019). *Juvenile arrest rate trends.* https://www.ojjdp.gov/ojstatbb/crime/JAR_Display.asp? ID=qa05261

Onetti, W., Fernández-García, J. C., & Castillo-Rodríguez, A. (2019). Transition to middle school: Self-concept changes. *PLoS One, 14*(2), e0212640. https://doi.org/10.1371/journal.pone.0212640

Orth, U. (2017). The lifespan development of self-esteem. In J. Specht (Ed.), *Personality development across the lifespan* (pp. 181–195). Elsevier. https://doi.org/10.1016/B978-0-12-804674-6.00012-0

Oshri, A., Carlson, M. W., Kwon, J. A., Zeichner, A., & Wickrama, K. K. A. S. (2017). Developmental growth trajectories of self-esteem in adolescence: Associations with child neglect and drug use and abuse in young adulthood. *Journal of Youth and Adolescence, 46*(1), 151–164. https://doi.org/10.1007/s10964-016-0483-5

Oxford, M. L., Gilchrist, L. D., Lohr, M. J., Gillmore, M. R., Morrison, D. M., & Spieker, S. J. (2005). Life course heterogeneity in the transition from adolescence to adulthood among adolescent mothers. *Journal of Research on Adolescence, 15*(4), 479–504.

Panagiotakopoulos, L. (2018). Transgender medicine - puberty suppression. *Reviews in Endocrine and Metabolic Disorders, 19*(3), 221–225. https://doi.org/10.1007/s11154-018-9457-0

Panchaud, C., & Anderson, R. (2014). *A definition of comprehensive sexuality education. Demystifying data: A guide to using evidence to improve young people's sexual health and rights.* https://www.guttmacher.org/sites/default/files/report_downloads/demystifying-data-handouts_0.pdf

Pariseau, E. M., Chevalier, L., Long, K. A., Clapham, R., Edwards-Leeper, L., & Tishelman, A. C. (2019). The relationship between family acceptance-rejection and transgender youth psychosocial functioning. *Clinical Practice in Pediatric Psychology, 7*(3), 267–277. https://doi.org/10.1037/cpp0000291

Pazol, K., Whiteman, M. K., Folger, S. G., Kourtis, A. P., Marchbanks, P. A., & Jamieson, D. J. (2015). Sporadic contraceptive use and nonuse: Age-specific prevalence and associated factors. *American Journal of Obstetrics and Gynecology, 212*(3), 324.e1–324.e8. https://doi.org/10.1016/j.ajog.2014.10.004

Pedersen, E. R., Osilla, K. C., Miles, J. N. V., Tucker, J. S., Ewing, B. A., Shih, R. A., & D'Amico, E. J. (2017). The role of perceived injunctive alcohol norms in adolescent drinking behavior. *Addictive Behaviors, 67*, 1–7. https://doi.org/10.1016/j.addbeh.2016.11.022

Pei, R., Lauharatanahirun, N., Cascio, C. N., O'Donnell, M. B., Shope, J. T., Simons-Morton, B. G., Vettel, J. M., & Falk, E. B. (2020). Neural processes during adolescent risky decision making are associated with conformity to peer influence. *Developmental Cognitive Neuroscience, 44*, 100794. https://doi.org/10.1016/j.dcn.2020.100794

Petersen, I. T., Lindhiem, O., LeBeau, B., Bates, J. E., Pettit, G. S., Lansford, J. E., & Dodge, K. A. (2018). Development of internalizing problems from adolescence to emerging adulthood: Accounting for heterotypic continuity with vertical scaling. *Developmental Psychology, 54*(3), 586–599. https://doi.org/10.1037/dev0000449

Phinney, J. S., & Ong, A. D. (2007). Conceptualization and measurement of ethnic identity: Current status and future directions. *Journal of Counseling Psychology, 54*(3), 271–281. https://doi.org/10.1037/0022-067.54.3.271

Pike, K. M., Hoek, H. W., & Dunne, P. E. (2014). Cultural trends and eating disorders. *Current Opinion in Psychiatry, 27*(6), 436–442. https://doi.org/10.1097/YCO.0000000000000100

Pinquart, M., & Gerke, D. C. (2019). Associations of parenting styles with self-esteem in children and adolescents: A Meta-analysis. *Journal of Child and Family Studies, 28*, 2017–2035. https://doi.org/10.1007/s10826-019-01417-5

Piquero, A. R., & Moffitt, T. E. (2013). Moffitt's developmental taxonomy of antisocial behavior. In G. Bruinsma & D. Weisburd (Eds.), *Encyclopedia of criminology and criminal justice* (pp. 3121–3127). Springer.

Plöderl, M., Wagenmakers, E.-J., Tremblay, P., Ramsay, R., Kralovec, K., Fartacek, C., & Fartacek, R. (2013). Suicide risk and sexual orientation: A Critical review. *Archives of Sexual Behavior, 42*(5), 715–727. https://doi.org/10.1007/s10508-012-0056-y

Poppen, P. (1974). Sex differences in moral judgment. *Personality and Social Psychology Bulletin, 1*(1), 313–315. https://doi.org/10.1177/0146167274001001106

Poulin, F., & Chan, A. (2010). Friendship stability and change in childhood and adolescence. *Developmental Review, 30*(3), 257–272. https://doi.org/10.1016/j.dr.2009.01.001

Power, F. C., Higgins, A., & Kohlberg, L. (1989). *Lawrence Kohlberg's approach to moral education.* Columbia University Press.

Preckel, F., Niepel, C., Schneider, M., & Brunner, M. (2013). Self-concept in adolescence: A Longitudinal study on reciprocal effects of self-perceptions in academic and social domains. *Journal of Adolescence, 36*(6), 1165–1175. https://doi.org/10.1016/j.adolescence.2013.09.001

Price-Feeney, M., Green, A. E., & Dorison, S. (2020). Understanding the mental health of transgender and nonbinary youth. *Journal of Adolescent Health, 66*(6), 684–690. https://doi.org/10.1016/j.jadohealth.2019.11.314

Priess, H. A., & Lindberg, S. M. (2018). Gender intensification. In R. J. R. Levesque (Ed.), *Encyclopedia of adolescence* (pp. 1135–1142). Springer New York. https://doi.org/10.1007/978-1-4419-1695-2_391

Puckett, J. A., Cleary, P., Rossman, K., Mustanski, B., & Newcomb, M. E. (2018). Barriers to gender-affirming care for transgender and gender nonconforming individuals. *Sexuality Research and Social Policy, 15*(1), 48–59. https://doi.org/10.1007/s13178-017-0295-8

Rafferty, Y., Griffin, K. W., & Lodise, M. (2011). Adolescent motherhood and developmental outcomes of children in early head start: The Influence of maternal parenting behaviors, well-being, and risk factors within the family setting. *American Journal of Orthopsychiatry, 81*(2), 228–245. https://doi.org/10.1111/j.1939-0025.2011.01092.x

Ragelienė, T. (2016). Links of adolescents identity development and relationship with peers: A Systematic literature review. *Journal of the Canadian Academy of Child and Adolescent Psychiatry = Journal de l'Academie Canadienne de Psychiatrie de l'enfant et de l'adolescent, 25*(2), 97–105. http://www.ncbi.nlm.nih.gov/pubmed/27274745

Raifman, J., Charlton, B. M., Arrington-Sanders, R., Chan, P. A., Rusley, J., Mayer, K. H., Stein, M. D., Austin, S. B., & McConnell, M. (2020). Sexual orientation and suicide attempt disparities among US adolescents: 2009-2017. *Pediatrics, 145*(3), e20191658. https://doi.org/10.1542/peds.2019-1658

Reel, J. J. (2012). *Eating disorders: An Encyclopedia of causes, treatment, and prevention.* ABC-CLIO.

Renk, K., Liljequist, L., Simpson, J. E., & Phares, V. (2005). Gender and age differences in the topics of parent-adolescent conflict. *Family Journal, 13*(2), 139–149. https://doi.org/10.1177/1066480704271190

Richmond, A. D., Laursen, B., & Stattin, H. (2019). Homophily in delinquent behavior: The Rise and fall of friend similarity across adolescence. *International Journal of Behavioral Development, 43*(1), 67–73. https://doi.org/10.1177/0165025418767058

Rivas-Drake, D., Hughes, D., & Way, N. (2009). A Preliminary analysis of associations among ethnic-racial socialization, ethnic discrimination, and ethnic identity among urban sixth graders. *Journal of Research on Adolescence, 19*(3), 558–584. https://doi.org/10.1111/j.1532-7795.2009.00607.x

Rivas-Drake, D., Seaton, E. K., Markstrom, C., Quintana, S., Syed, M., Lee, R. M., Schwartz, S. J., Umaña-Taylor, A. J., French, S., & Yip, T. (2014). Ethnic and racial identity in adolescence: Implications for psychosocial, academic, and health outcomes. *Child Development, 85*(1), 40–57. https://doi.org/10.1111/cdev.12200

Rivas-Drake, D., Umaña-Taylor, A. J., Schaefer, D. R., & Medina, M. (2017). Ethnic-racial identity and friendships in early adolescence. *Child Development, 88*(3), 710–724. https://doi.org/10.1111/cdev.12790

Rizzo, C. J., Joppa, M., Barker, D., Collibee, C., Zlotnick, C., & Brown, L. K. (2018). Project date SMART: A Dating Violence (DV) and sexual risk prevention program for adolescent girls with prior DV exposure. *Prevention Science, 19*, 416–442. https://doi.org/10.1007/s11121-018-0871-z

Robinson, J. P., & Espelage, D. L. (2013). Peer victimization and sexual risk differences between lesbian, gay, bisexual, transgender, or questioning and nontransgender heterosexual youths in grades 7-12. *American Journal of Public Health, 103*(10), 1810–1819. https://doi.org/10.2105/AJPH.2013.301387

Rodgers, R. F., Watts, A. W., Austin, S. B., Haines, J., & Neumark-Sztainer, D. (2017). Disordered eating in ethnic minority adolescents with overweight. *International Journal of Eating Disorders, 50*(6), 665–671. https://doi.org/10.1002/eat.22652

Rodríguez-Meirinhos, A., Vansteenkiste, M., Soenens, B., Oliva, A., Brenning, K., & Antolín-Suárez, L. (2020). When is parental monitoring effective? A Person-centered analysis of the role of autonomy-supportive and psychologically controlling parenting in referred and non-referred adolescents. *Journal of Youth and Adolescence, 49*(1), 352–368. https://doi.org/10.1007/s10964-019-01151-7

Romero, A. J., Edwards, L. M., Fryberg, S. A., & Orduña, M. (2014). Resilience to discrimination stress across ethnic identity stages of development. *Journal of Applied Social Psychology, 44*(1), 1–11. https://doi.org/10.1111/jasp.12192

Rose, A. J., & Asher, S. R. (2017). The Social tasks of friendship: Do boys and girls excel in different tasks? *Child Development Perspectives, 11*(1), 3–8. https://doi.org/10.1111/cdep.12214

Rote, W. M., & Smetana, J. G. (2016). Beliefs about parents' right to know: Domain differences and associations with change in concealment. *Journal of Research on Adolescence*, *26*, 334–344. https://doi.org/10.1111/jora.12194

Rote, W. M., Smetana, J. G., & Feliscar, L. (2020). Longitudinal associations between adolescent information management and mother-teen relationship quality: Between-versus within-family differences. *Developmental Psychology*, *56*(10), 1935–1947. https://doi.org/10.1037/dev0000947

Rueger, S. Y., Chen, P., Jenkins, L. N., & Choe, H. J. (2014). Effects of perceived support from mothers, fathers, and teachers on depressive symptoms during the transition to middle school. *Journal of Youth and Adolescence*, *43*(4), 655–670. https://doi.org/10.1007/s10964-013-0039-x

Rulison, K., Patrick, M. E., & Maggs, J. (2015). Linking peer relationships to substance use across adolescence. In R. A. Zucker & S. A. Brown (Eds.), *The Oxford handbook of adolescent substance abuse* (Vol. 1). Oxford University Press. https://doi.org/10.1093/oxfordhb/9780199735662.013.019

Russell, S. T., & Fish, J. N. (2016). Mental health in Lesbian, Gay, Bisexual, and Transgender (LGBT) youth. *Annual Review of Clinical Psychology*, *12*(1), 465–487. https://doi.org/10.1146/annurev-clinpsy-021815-093153

Russell, S. T., Pollitt, A. M., Li, G., & Grossman, A. H. (2018). Chosen name use is linked to reduced depressive symptoms, suicidal ideation, and suicidal behavior among transgender youth. *The Journal of Adolescent Health : Official Publication of the Society for Adolescent Medicine*, *63*(4), 503–505. https://doi.org/10.1016/j.jadohealth.2018.02.003

Saewyc, E. M. (2011). Research on adolescent sexual orientation: Development, health disparities, stigma, and resilience. *Journal of Research on Adolescence*, *21*(1), 256–272. https://doi.org/10.1111/j.1532-7795.2010.00727.x

Safer, J. D., & Chan, K. J. (2019). Review of medical, socioeconomic, and systemic barriers to transgender care. In L. Poretsky & W. C. Hembree (Eds.), *Transgender Medicine* (pp. 25–38). Humana Press. https://doi.org/10.1007/978-3-030-05683-4_2

Samarova, V., Shilo, G., & Diamond, G. M. (2014). Changes in youths' perceived parental acceptance of their sexual minority status over time. *Journal of Research on Adolescence*, *24*(4), 681–688. https://doi.org/10.1111/jora.12071

Sanchez, D., Whittaker, T. A., Hamilton, E., & Arango, S. (2017). Familial ethnic socialization, gender role attitudes, and ethnic identity development in Mexican-origin early adolescents. *Cultural Diversity and Ethnic Minority Psychology*, *23*(3), 335–347. https://doi.org/10.1037/cdp0000142

Sánchez-Queja, I., Oliva, A., & Parra, Á. (2017). Stability, change, and determinants of self-esteem during adolescence and emerging adulthood. *Journal of Social and Personal Relationships*, *34*(8), 1277–1294. https://doi.org/10.1177/0265407516674831

Santelli, J., Kantor, L. M., Grilo, S. A., Speizer, I. S., Lindberg, L. D., Heitel, J., Schalet, A. T., Lyon, M. E., Mason-Jones, A. J., McGovern, T., Heck, C. J., Rogers, J., & Ott, M. A. (2017). Abstinence-only-until-marriage: An Updated review of U.S. policies and programs and their impact. *Journal of Adolescent Health*, *61*(3), 273–280. https://doi.org/10.1016/J.JADOHEALTH.2017.05.031

Savin-Williams, R. C. (2016). Sexual orientation: Categories or continuum? Commentary on Bailey et al. *Psychological Science in the Public Interest*, *17*(2), 37–44. https://doi.org/10.1177/1529100616637618

Savin-Williams, R. C. (2019). Developmental trajectories and milestones of sexual-minority youth. In S. Lamb & J. Gilbert (Eds.), *The Cambridge handbook of sexual development* (pp. 156–179). Cambridge University Press. https://doi.org/10.1017/9781108116121.009

Savin-Williams, R. C., & Cohen, K. M. (2015). Developmental trajectories and milestones of Lesbian, Gay, and Bisexual young people. *International Review of Psychiatry*, *27*(5), 357–366. https://doi.org/10.3109/09540261.2015.1093465

Savin-Williams, R. C., Dubé, E. M., & Dube, E. M. (1998). Parental reactions to their child's disclosure of a Gay/Lesbian identity. *Family Relations*, *47*(1), 7. https://doi.org/10.2307/584845

Savin-Williams, R. C., & Ream, G. L. (2003). Sex variations in the disclosure to parents of same-sex attractions. *Journal of Family Psychology*, *17*(3), 429–438. https://doi.org/10.1037/0893-3200.17.3.429

Savin-Williams, R. C., & Ream, G. L. (2007). Prevalence and stability of sexual orientation components during adolescence and young adulthood. *Archives of Sexual Behavior*, *36*(3), 385–394. https://doi.org/10.1007/s10508-006-9088-5

Schaffhuser, K., Allemand, M., & Schwarz, B. (2017). The development of self-representations during the transition to early adolescence: The role of gender, puberty, and school transition. *The Journal of Early Adolescence*, *37*(6), 774–804. https://doi.org/10.1177/0272431615624841

Schagen, S. E. E., Cohen-Kettenis, P. T., Delemarre-van de Waal, H. A., & Hannema, S. E. (2016). Efficacy and safety of gonadotropin-releasing hormone agonist treatment to suppress puberty in gender dysphoric adolescents. *The Journal of Sexual Medicine*, *13*(7), 1125–1132. https://doi.org/10.1016/j.jsxm.2016.05.004

Schwartz, S. J., Luyckx, K., & Crocetti, E. (2015). What have we learned since schwartz (2001)? In K. C. McLean & M. Syed (Eds.), *The oxford handbook of identity development* (pp. 539–561). Oxford University Press. https://doi.org/10.1093/oxfordhb/9780199936564.013.028

Sears, H. A., Sandra Byers, E., & Lisa Price, E. (2007). The co-occurrence of adolescent boys' and girls' use of psychologically, physically, and sexually abusive behaviours in their dating relationships. *Journal of Adolescence*, *30*(3), 487–504. https://doi.org/10.1016/j.adolescence.2006.05.002

Seaton, E. K., Yip, T., & Sellers, R. M. (2009). A Longitudinal examination of racial identity and racial discrimination among African American adolescents. *Child Development*, *80*(2), 406–417. https://doi.org/10.1111/j.1467-8624.2009.01268.x

Sedgh, G., Finer, L. B., Bankole, A., Eilers, M. A., & Singh, S. (2015). Adolescent pregnancy, birth, and abortion rates across countries: Levels and recent trends. *The Journal of Adolescent Health : Official Publication of the Society for Adolescent Medicine*, *56*(2), 223–230. https://doi.org/10.1016/j.jadohealth.2014.09.007

Shin, H., & Ryan, A. M. (2014). Early adolescent friendships and academic adjustment: Examining selection and influence processes with longitudinal social network analysis. *Developmental Psychology*, *50*(11), 2462–2472. https://doi.org/10.1037/a0037922

Silva, K., Ford, C. A., & Miller, V. A. (2020). Daily parent-teen conflict and parent and adolescent well-being: The Moderating role of daily and person-level warmth. *Journal of Youth and Adolescence, 49*(8), 1601–1616. https://doi.org/10.1007/s10964-020-01251-9

Silveri, M. M., Dager, A. D., Cohen-Gilbert, J. E., & Sneider, J. T. (2016a). Neurobiological signatures associated with alcohol and drug use in the human adolescent brain. *Neuroscience & Biobehavioral Reviews, 70*, 244–259. https://doi.org/10.1016/j.neubiorev.2016.06.042

Silveri, M. M., Dager, A. D., Cohen-Gilbert, J. E., & Sneider, J. T. (2016b). Neurobiological signatures associated with alcohol and drug use in the human adolescent brain. *Neuroscience & Biobehavioral Reviews, 70*, 244–259. https://doi.org/10.1016/J.NEUBIOREV.2016.06.042

Simons, J. S., Wills, T. A., & Neal, D. J. (2014). The many faces of affect: A multilevel model of drinking frequency/quantity and alcohol dependence symptoms among young adults. *Journal of Abnormal Psychology, 123*(3), 676–694. https://doi.org/10.1037/a0036926

Simons, L., Schrager, S. M., Clark, L. F., Belzer, M., & Olson, J. (2013). Parental support and mental health among transgender adolescents. *Journal of Adolescent Health, 53*(6), 791–793. https://doi.org/10.1016/j.jadohealth.2013.07.019

Skinner, O. D., & McHale, S. M. (2016). Parent–adolescent conflict in African American families. *Journal of Youth and Adolescence, 45*(10), 2080–2093. https://doi.org/10.1007/s10964-016-0514-2

Smetana, J. G. (2011). Adolescents' social reasoning and relationships with parents: Conflicts and coordinations within and across domains. In E. Amsel & J. C. Smetana (Eds.), *Adolescent vulnerabilities and opportunities: Developmental and constructivist perspectives* (pp. 139–158,). Cambridge University Press.

Smetana, J. G., Jambon, M., & Ball, C. (2014). The Social domain approach to children's moral and social judgments. In M. Killen & J. G. Smetana (Eds.), *Handbook of moral development* (pp. 23–44). Psychology Press. https://doi.org/10.4324/9780203581957

Smetana, J. G., & Rote, W. M. (2019). Adolescent–parent relationships: Progress, processes, and prospects. *Annual Review of Developmental Psychology, 1*(1), 41–68. https://doi.org/10.1146/annurev-devpsych-121318-084903

Smink, F. R. E., van Hoeken, D., & Hoek, H. W. (2013). Epidemiology, course, and outcome of eating disorders. *Current Opinion in Psychiatry, 26*(6), 543–548. https://doi.org/10.1097/YCO.0b013e328365a24f

Smink, F. R. E., van Hoeken, D., Oldehinkel, A. J., & Hoek, H. W. (2014). Prevalence and severity of DSM-5 eating disorders in a community cohort of adolescents. *The International Journal of Eating Disorders, 47*(6), 610–619. https://doi.org/10.1002/eat.22316

Smith, T. E., & Leaper, C. (2006). Self-perceived gender Typicality and the peer context during adolescence. *Journal of Research on Adolescence, 16*(1), 91–104. https://doi.org/10.1111/j.1532-7795.2006.00123.x

Smith-Darden, J. P., Kernsmith, P. D., Reidy, D. E., & Cortina, K. S. (2017). In search of modifiable risk and protective factors for teen dating violence. *Journal of Research on Adolescence, 27*(2), 423–435. https://doi.org/10.1111/jora.12280

Spear, L. P. (2018). Effects of adolescent alcohol consumption on the brain and behaviour. *Nature Reviews Neuroscience, 19*(4), 197–214. https://doi.org/10.1038/nrn.2018.10

Spencer, M. B., Swanson, D. P., & Harpalani, V. (2015). Development of the self. In M. E. Lamb (Ed.), *Handbook of child psychology and developmental science* (pp. 1–44). John Wiley & Sons, Inc. https://doi.org/10.1002/9781118963418.childpsy318

Stalgaitis, C. A., Navarro, M. A., Wagner, D. E., & Walker, M. W. (2020). Who uses tobacco products? Using peer crowd segmentation to identify youth at risk for cigarettes, cigar products, Hookah, and E-Cigarettes. *Substance Use and Misuse, 55*(7), 1045–1053. https://doi.org/10.1080/10826084.2020.1722698

Statistics Canada. (2015). *The 10 leading causes of death, 2011*. http://www.statcan.gc.ca/pub/82-625-x/2014001/article/11896-eng.htm

Steinberg, L., & Monahan, K. C. (2007). Age differences in resistance to peer influence. *Developmental Psychology, 43*(6), 1531–1543. https://doi.org/10.1037/0012-1649.43.6.1531

Stevens, E. N., Lovejoy, M. C., & Pittman, L. D. (2014). Understanding the relationship between actual: Ideal discrepancies and depressive symptoms: A Developmental examination. *Journal of Adolescence, 37*(5), 612–621. https://doi.org/10.1016/j.adolescence.2014.04.013

Stice, E., Gau, J. M., Rohde, P., & Shaw, H. (2017). Risk factors that predict future onset of each DSM-5 eating disorder: Predictive specificity in high-risk adolescent females. *Journal of Abnormal Psychology, 126*(1), 38–51. https://doi.org/10.1037/abn0000219

Sumter, S. R., Bokhorst, C. L., & Westenberg, P. M. (2018). Resistance and conformity. In R. J. R. Levesque (Ed.), *Encyclopedia of adolescence* (pp. 3149–3160). Springer International Publishing. https://doi.org/10.1007/978-3-319-33228-4_327

Syed, M., Walker, L. H. M., Lee, R. M., Umana-Taylor, A. J., Zamboanga, B. L., Schwartz, S. J., Armenta, B. E., & Huynh, Q.-L. (2013). A two-factor model of ethnic identity exploration: Implications for identity coherence and well-being. *Cultural Diversity and Ethnic Minority Psychology, 19*(2), 143–154. https://doi.org/10.1037/a0030564

Takagi, M., Youssef, G., & Lorenzetti, V. (2016). Neuroimaging of the human brain in adolescent substance users. In D. De Micheli, A. L. M. Andrade, E. A. da Silva, & M. L. O. de Souza Formigoni (Eds.), *Drug abuse in adolescence* (pp. 69–99). Springer International Publishing. https://doi.org/10.1007/978-3-319-17795-3_6

Tang, S., Davis-Kean, P. E., Chen, M., & Sexton, H. R. (2016). Adolescent pregnancy's intergenerational effects: Does an adolescent mother's education have consequences for her children's achievement? *Journal of Research on Adolescence, 26*, 180–193. https://doi.org/10.1111/jora.12182

Tarry, H., & Emler, N. (2007). Attitude, values and moral reasoning as predictors of delinquency. *British Journal of Developmental Psychology, 25*(2), 169–183. https://doi.org/10.1348/026151006x113671

Taylor, J. L. (2009). Midlife Impacts of Adolescent Parenthood. *Journal of Family Issues, 30*(4), 484–510.

Thapar, A., Collishaw, S., Pine, D. S., & Thapar, A. K. (2012). Depression in adolescence. *Lancet, 379*(9820), 1056–1067. https://doi.org/10.1016/S0140-6736(11)60871-4

Thoma, B. C., Salk, R. H., Choukas-Bradley, S., Goldstein, T. R., Levine, M. D., & Marshal, M. P. (2019). Suicidality disparities between transgender and cisgender adolescents. *Pediatrics, 144*(5), e20191183. https://doi.org/10.1542/peds.2019-1183

Thomas, J. J., Eddy, K. T., Ruscio, J., Ng, K. L., Casale, K. E., Becker, A. E., & Lee, S. (2015). Do Recognizable lifetime eating disorder phenotypes naturally occur in a culturally Asian population? A Combined latent profile and taxometric approach. *European Eating Disorders Review*, *23*(3), 199–209. https://doi.org/10.1002/erv.2357

Titzmann, P. F., Brenick, A., & Silbereisen, R. K. (2015). Friendships fighting prejudice: A Longitudinal perspective on adolescents' cross-group friendships with immigrants. *Journal of Youth and Adolescence*, *44*(6), 1318–1431. https://doi.org/10.1007/s10964-015-0256-6

Toomey, R. B., Syvertsen, A. K., & Shramko, M. (2018). Transgender adolescent suicide behavior. *Pediatrics*, *142*(4), e20174218. https://doi.org/10.1542/peds.2017-4218

Trinh, S. L., Lee, J., Halpern, C. T., & Moody, J. (2019). Our buddies, ourselves: The role of sexual homophily in adolescent friendship networks. *Child Development*, *90*(1), e132–e147. https://doi.org/10.1111/cdev.13052

Trost, K., Eichas, K., Ferrer-Wreder, L., & Galanti, M. R. (2020). The study of family context: Examining its role for identity coherence and adolescent adjustment for Swedish adolescents. *The Journal of Early Adolescence*, *40*(2), 165–196. https://doi.org/10.1177/0272431619833479

Trucco, E. M. (2020). A review of psychosocial factors linked to adolescent substance use. *Pharmacology Biochemistry and Behavior*, *196*, 172969. https://doi.org/10.1016/j.pbb.2020.172969

Trucco, E. M., Colder, C. R., Wieczorek, W. F., Lengua, L. J., & Hawk, L. W. (2014). Early adolescent alcohol use in context: How neighborhoods, parents, and peers impact youth. *Development and Psychopathology*, *26*(2), 425–436. https://doi.org/10.1017/S0954579414000042

Twenge, J. M., & Park, H. (2019). The Decline in adult activities among U.S. adolescents, 1976–2016. *Child Development*, *90*(2), 638–654. https://doi.org/10.1111/cdev.12930

Uddin, M., Jansen, S., & Telzer, E. H. (2017). Adolescent depression linked to socioeconomic status? Molecular approaches for revealing premorbid risk factors. *BioEssays*, *39*(3), 1600194. https://doi.org/10.1002/bies.201600194

Ueno, K. (2005). Sexual orientation and psychological distress in adolescence: Examining interpersonal stressors and social support processes. *Social Psychology Quarterly*, *68*(3), 258–277.

Uji, M., Sakamoto, A., Adachi, K., & Kitamura, T. (2013). The impact of authoritative, authoritarian, and permissive parenting styles on children's later mental health in Japan: Focusing on parent and child gender. *Journal of Child and Family Studies*, *23*(2), 293–302. https://doi.org/10.1007/s10826-013-9740-3

Umaña-Taylor, A. J. (2016). Ethnic-Racial identity conceptualization, development, and youth adjustment. In L. Balter & C. S. Tamis-LeMonda (Eds.), *Child psychology: A handbook of contemporary issues* (p. 505). Routledge.

Umaña-Taylor, A. J. (2016). A post-racial society in which ethnic-racial discrimination still exists and has significant consequences for youths' adjustment. *Current Directions in Psychological Science*, *25*(2), 111–118. https://doi.org/10.1177/0963721415627858

Umaña-Taylor, A. J., Guimond, A. B., Updegraff, K. A., & Jahromi, L. (2013). A longitudinal examination of support, self-esteem, and mexican-origin adolescent mothers' parenting efficacy. *Journal of Marriage and the Family*, *75*(3), 746–759. https://doi.org/10.1111/jomf.12019

U.S. Bureau of Labor Statistics. (2021). *Occupational outlook handbook: 2021*. https://www.bls.gov/ooh/

Vagi, K. J., Rothman, E. F., Latzman, N. E., Tharp, A. T., Hall, D. M., & Breiding, M. J. (2013). Beyond correlates: A review of risk and protective factors for adolescent dating violence perpetration. *Journal of Youth and Adolescence*, *42*(4), 633–649. https://doi.org/10.1007/s10964-013-9907-7

van de Bongardt, D., Reitz, E., Sandfort, T., & Deković, M. (2014). A Meta-Analysis of the relations between three types of peer norms and adolescent sexual behavior. *Personality and Social Psychology Review: An Official Journal of the Society for Personality and Social Psychology, Inc*, *19*, 203–234. https://doi.org/10.1177/1088868314544223

Van Dijk, M. P. A., Branje, S., Keijsers, L., Hawk, S. T., Hale, W. W., & Meeus, W. (2014). Self-Concept clarity across adolescence: Longitudinal associations with open communication with parents and internalizing symptoms. *Journal of Youth and Adolescence*, *43*(11), 1861–1876. https://doi.org/10.1007/s10964-013-0055-x

Van Doorn, M. D., Branje, S. J. T., & Meeus, W. H. J. (2011). Developmental changes in conflict resolution styles in parent-adolescent relationships: A four-wave longitudinal study. *Journal of Youth and Adolescence*, *40*(1), 97–107. https://doi.org/10.1007/s10964-010-9516-7

Van Hoorn, J., Crone, E. A., & Van Leijenhorst, L. (2017a). Hanging out with the right crowd: Peer influence on risk-taking behavior in adolescence. *Journal of Research on Adolescence*, *27*(1), 189–200. https://doi.org/10.1111/jora.12265

Van Hoorn, J., Crone, E. A., & Van Leijenhorst, L. (2017b). Hanging out with the right crowd: Peer influence on risk-taking behavior in adolescence. *Journal of Research on Adolescence*, *27*(1), 189–200. https://doi.org/10.1111/jora.12265

van Hoorn, J., Meuwese, R., Rieffe, C., & Crone, E. A. (2016). Peer influence on prosocial behavior in adolescence. *Journal of Research on Adolescence*, *26*(1), 90–100. https://doi.org/10.1111/jora.12173

Vance, S. R., Ehrensaft, D., & Rosenthal, S. M. (2014). Psychological and medical care of gender nonconforming youth. *Pediatrics*, *134*(6), 1184–1192. https://doi.org/10.1542/peds.2014-0772

Vanhalst, J., Luyckx, K., Scholte, R. H. J., Engels, R. C. M. E., & Goossens, L. (2013). Low self-esteem as a risk factor for loneliness in adolescence: Perceived - but not actual - social acceptance as an underlying mechanism. *Journal of Abnormal Child Psychology*, *41*(7), 1067–1081. https://doi.org/10.1007/s10802-013-9751-y

Vincke, J., & van Heeringen, K. (2002). Confidant support and the mental wellbeing of Lesbian and Gay young adults: A longitudinal analysis. *Journal of Community & Applied Social Psychology*, *12*(3), 181–193. https://doi.org/10.1002/casp.671

von Soest, T., Wichstrøm, L., & Kvalem, I. L. (2016). The development of global and domain-specific self-esteem from age 13 to 31. *Journal of Personality and Social Psychology*, *110*(4), 592–608. https://doi.org/10.1037/pspp0000060

Vosylis, R., Erentaitė, R., & Klimstra, T. (2020). The material context of adolescent identity formation: A family economic stress approach. *Identity, 21*, 200–218. https://doi.org/10.1080/15283488.2020.1836491

Vrangalova, Z., & Savin-Williams, R. C. (2011). Adolescent sexuality and positive well-being: A Group-norms approach. *Journal of Youth and Adolescence, 40*(8), 931–944. https://doi.org/10.1007/s10964-011-9629-7

Wagnsson, S., Lindwall, M., & Gustafsson, H. (2014). Participation in organized sport and self-esteem across adolescence: The mediating role of perceived sport competence. *Journal of Sport & Exercise Psychology, 36*(6), 584–594. https://doi.org/10.1123/jsep.2013-0137

Walker, T. Y., Elam-Evans, L. D., Yankey, D., Markowitz, L. E., Williams, C. L., Fredua, B., Singleton, J. A., & Stokley, S. (2019). National, regional, state, and selected local area vaccination coverage among adolescents aged 13–17 years — United States, 2018. *MMWR. Morbidity and Mortality Weekly Report, 68*(33), 718–723. https://doi.org/10.15585/mmwr.mm6833a2

Wall-Wieler, E., Roos, L. L., & Nickel, N. C. (2016). Teenage pregnancy: The impact of maternal adolescent childbearing and older sister's teenage pregnancy on a younger sister. *BMC Pregnancy and Childbirth, 16*(1), 120. https://doi.org/10.1186/s12884-016-0911-2

Wang, C., Xia, Y., Li, W., Wilson, S. M., Bush, K., & Peterson, G. (2016). Parenting behaviors, adolescent depressive symptoms, and problem behavior: The role of self-esteem and school adjustment difficulties among Chinese adolescents. *Journal of Family Issues, 37*, 520–542. https://doi.org/10.1177/0192513X14542433

Wang, M.-T., Dishion, T. J., Stormshak, E. A., & Willett, J. B. (2011). Trajectories of family management practices and early adolescent behavioral outcomes. *Developmental Psychology, 47*(5), 1324–1341. https://doi.org/10.1037/a0024026

Wang, M.-T., & Sheikh-Khalil, S. (2014). Does parental involvement matter for student achievement and mental health in high school? *Child Development, 85*(2), 610–625. https://doi.org/10.1111/cdev.12153

Warner, T. D. (2018). Adolescent sexual risk taking: The distribution of youth behaviors and perceived peer attitudes across neighborhood contexts. *Journal of Adolescent Health, 62*(2), 226–233. https://doi.org/10.1016/J.JADOHEALTH.2017.09.007

Watson, R. J., Adjei, J., Saewyc, E., Homma, Y., & Goodenow, C. (2017). Trends and disparities in disordered eating among heterosexual and sexual minority adolescents. *International Journal of Eating Disorders, 50*(1), 22–31. https://doi.org/10.1002/eat.22576

Watson, R. J., Grossman, A. H., & Russell, S. T. (2019). Sources of social support and mental health among LGB youth. *Youth & Society, 51*(1), 30–48. https://doi.org/10.1177/0044118X16660110

Weisz, A. N., & Black, B. M. (2002). Gender and moral reasoning: African American youth respond to dating dilemmas. *Journal of Human Behavior in the Social Environment, 5*(1), 35–52.

Wentzel, K. R. (2014). Prosocial behavior and peer relations in adolescence. In G. C. L. M. Padilla-Walker (Ed.), *Prosocial development: A multidimensional approach* (pp. 178–200). Oxford University Press.

Weymouth, B. B., Buehler, C., Zhou, N., & Henson, R. A. (2016). A meta-analysis of parent-adolescent conflict: Disagreement, hostility, and youth maladjustment. *Journal of Family Theory & Review, 8*(1), 95–112. https://doi.org/10.1111/jftr.12126

White, C. N., & Warner, L. A. (2015). Influence of family and school-level factors on age of sexual initiation. *The Journal of Adolescent Health : Official Publication of the Society for Adolescent Medicine, 56*(2), 231–237. https://doi.org/10.1016/j.jadohealth.2014.09.017

White, R. M. B., Knight, G. P., Jensen, M., & Gonzales, N. A. (2018). Ethnic socialization in neighborhood contexts: Implications for ethnic attitude and identity development among mexican-origin adolescents. *Child Development, 89*(3), 1004–1021. https://doi.org/10.1111/cdev.12772

Williams, T. S., Connolly, J., Pepler, D., Laporte, L., & Craig, W. (2008). Risk models of dating aggression across different adolescent relationships: A developmental psychopathology approach. *Journal of Consulting and Clinical Psychology, 76*(4), 622–632. https://doi.org/10.1037/0022-006x.76.4.622

Willoughby, T., & Hamza, C. A. (2011). A longitudinal examination of the bidirectional associations among perceived parenting behaviors, adolescent disclosure and problem behavior across the high school years. *Journal of Youth and Adolescence, 40*(4), 463–478. https://doi.org/10.1007/s10964-010-9567-9

Wilson, G. T., Grilo, C. M., & Vitousek, K. M. (2007). Psychological treatment of eating disorders. *American Psychologist, 62*(3), 199–216.

Wincentak, K., Connolly, J., & Card, N. (2017). Teen dating violence: A meta-analytic review of prevalence rates. *Psychology of Violence, 7*(2), 224–241. https://doi.org/10.1037/a0040194

Winters, A. M. (2020). Theoretical foundations: Delinquency risk factors and services aimed at reducing ongoing offending. *Child and Adolescent Social Work Journal, 37*(3), 263–269. https://doi.org/10.1007/s10560-020-00655-7

Witwer, E., Jones, R., & Lindberg, L. (2018). *Sexual behavior and contraceptive and condom use among U.S. high school students, 2013–2017.* https://doi.org/10.1363/2018.29941

Wouters, S., Doumen, S., Germeijs, V., Colpin, H., & Verschueren, K. (2013). Contingencies of self-worth in early adolescence: The Antecedent role of perceived parenting. *Social Development, 22*(2), 242–258. https://doi.org/10.1111/sode.12010

Xu, J., Kochanek, K. D., Murphy, S. L., & Arias, E. (2014). Mortality in the United States, 2012. *NCHS Data Brief, 168*, 1–8. http://europepmc.org/abstract/med/25296181

Ybarra, M. L., Price-Feeney, M., & Mitchell, K. J. (2019). A cross-sectional study examining the (In)congruency of sexual identity, sexual behavior, and romantic attraction among adolescents in the US. *Journal of Pediatrics, 214*, 201–208. https://doi.org/10.1016/j.jpeds.2019.06.046

Yip, T. (2014). Ethnic identity in everyday life: The influence of identity development status. *Child Development, 85*(1), 205–219. https://doi.org/10.1111/cdev.12107

Yip, T. (2018). Ethnic/Racial identity—a double-edged sword? Associations with discrimination and psychological outcomes. *Current Directions in Psychological Science, 27*(3), 170–175. https://doi.org/10.1177/0963721417739348

Yip, T., Wang, Y., Mootoo, C., & Mirpuri, S. (2019). Moderating the association between discrimination and adjustment: A meta-analysis of ethnic/racial identity. *Developmental Psychology, 55*(6), 1274–1298. https://doi.org/10.1037/dev0000708

Yuen, W. S., Chan, G., Bruno, R., Clare, P., Mattick, R., Aiken, A., Boland, V., McBride, N., McCambridge, J., Slade, T., Kypri, K., Horwood, J., Hutchinson, D., Najman, J., De Torres, C., & Peacock, A. (2020). Adolescent alcohol use trajectories: Risk factors and adult outcomes. *Pediatrics, 146*(4), e20200440. https://doi.org/10.1542/peds.2020-0440

Zapolski, T. C. B., Fisher, S., Banks, D. E., Hensel, D. J., & Barnes-Najor, J. (2017). Examining the protective effect of ethnic identity on drug attitudes and use among a diverse youth population. *Journal of Youth and Adolescence, 46*(8), 1702–1715. https://doi.org/10.1007/s10964-016-0605-0

Zucker, K. J. (2017). Epidemiology of gender dysphoria and transgender identity. *Sexual Health, 14*(5), 404. https://doi.org/10.1071/SH17067

CHAPTER 11

Adwan-Shekhidem, H., & Atzmon, G. (2018). The epigenetic regulation of telomere maintenance in aging. In A. Moskalev & A. M. Vaiserman (Eds.), *Epigenetics of aging and longevity* (pp. 119–136). Elsevier. https://doi.org/10.1016/B978-0-12-811060-7.00005-X

Allen, T. D., Johnson, R. C., Kiburz, K. M., & Shockley, K. M. (2013). Work-family conflict and flexible work arrangements: deconstructing flexibility. *Personnel Psychology, 66*(2), 345–376. https://doi.org/10.1111/peps.12012

Alschuler, M., & Yarab, J. (2018). Preventing student veteran attrition: What more can we do? *Journal of College Student Retention: Research. Theory & Practice, 20*(1), 47–66. https://doi.org/10.1177/1521025116646382

American Psychiatric Association. (2013). *Diagnostic and statistical manual of mental disorders DSM-V* (5th ed.).

Andrews, J. A., Hampson, S. E., Severson, H. H., Westling, E., & Peterson, M. (2016). Perceptions and use of E-cigarettes across time among emerging adults. *Tobacco Regulatory Science, 2*(1), 70–81. https://doi.org/10.18001/TRS.2.1.8

Andrews, J. A., & Westling, E. (2016). Substance use in emerging adulthood. In J. J. Arnett (Ed.), *The Oxford handbook of emerging adulthood* (Vol. 1). Oxford University Press. https://doi.org/10.1093/oxfordhb/9780199795574.013.20

Arnett, J J. (2014). Presidential address: The emergence of emerging adulthood. *Emerging Adulthood, 2*(3), 155–162. https://doi.org/10.1177/2167696814541096

Arria, A. M., Caldeira, K. M., Allen, H. K., Vincent, K. B., Bugbee, B. A., & O'Grady, K. E. (2016). Drinking like an adult? Trajectories of alcohol use patterns before and after college graduation. *Alcoholism: Clinical and Experimental Research, 40*(3), 583–590. https://doi.org/10.1111/acer.12973

Arsenis, N. C., You, T., Ogawa, E. F., Tinsley, G. M., & Zuo, L. (2017). Physical activity and telomere length: Impact of aging and potential mechanisms of action. *Oncotarget, 4*, 45008–45019. https://doi.org/10.18632/oncotarget.16726

Athanasou, J. A. (2002). Vocational pathways in the early part of a career: An Australian study. *Career Development Quarterly, 51*(1), 78–86.

Atran, S., & Medin, D. (2008). *The native mind and the cultural construction of nature*. MIT Press. http://psycnet.apa.org/index.cfm? fa=search.displayRecord&UID=2007-18941-000

Azofeifa, A., Mattson, M. E., Schauer, G., McAfee, T., Grant, A., & Lyerla, R. (2016). National estimates of marijuana use and related indicators ? National survey on drug use and health, United States, 2002-2014. *MMWR. Surveillance Summaries, 65*(11), 1–28. https://doi.org/10.15585/mmwr.ss6511a1

Babb, S., Malarcher, A., Schauer, G., Asman, K., & Jamal, A. (2017). Quitting smoking among adults — United States, 2000–2015. *MMWR. Morbidity and Mortality Weekly Report, 65*(52), 1457–1464. https://doi.org/10.15585/mmwr.mm6552a1

Bae, H., & Kerr, D. C. R. (2020). Marijuana use trends among college students in states with and without legalization of recreational use: Initial and longer-term changes from 2008 to 2018. *Addiction, 115*(6), 1115–1124. https://doi.org/10.1111/add.14939

Baines, H. L., Turnbull, D. M., & Greaves, L. C. (2014). Human stem cell aging: Do mitochondrial DNA mutations have a causal role? *Aging Cell, 13*(2), 201–205. https://doi.org/10.1111/acel.12199

Barthel, F. P., Wei, W., Tang, M., Martinez-Ledesma, E., Hu, X., Amin, S. B., Akdemir, K. C., Seth, S., Song, X., Wang, Q., Lichtenberg, T., Hu, J., Zhang, J., Zheng, S., & Verhaak, R. G. W. (2017). Systematic analysis of telomere length and somatic alterations in 31 cancer types. *Nature Genetics, 49*(3), 349–357. https://doi.org/10.1038/ng.3781

Batista, A. N. R., Garcia, T., Franco, E. A. T., Azevedo, P. S., Barbosa, M. F., Zornoff, L. A. M., Minicucci, M. F., De Paiva, S. A. R., Zucchi, J. W., De Godoy, I., & Tanni, S. E. (2020). Comparison of morphometry and ventricular function of healthy and smoking young people. *BMC Cardiovascular Disorders, 20*(1), 1–7. https://doi.org/10.1186/s12872-020-01372-w

Belsky, D. W., Caspi, A., Arseneault, L., Baccarelli, A., Corcoran, D., Gao, X., Hannon, E., Harrington, H. L., Rasmussen, L. J. H., Houts, R., Huffman, K., Kraus, W. E., Kwon, D., Mill, J., Pieper, C. F., Prinz, J., Poulton, R., Schwartz, J., Sugden, K., . . . Moffitt, T. E, . . (2020). Quantification of the pace of biological aging in humans through a blood test, the DunedinPoAm DNA methylation algorithm. *ELife, 9*, 1–56. https://doi.org/10.7554/eLife.54870

Belsky, D. W., Caspi, A., Houts, R., Cohen, H. J., Corcoran, D. L., Danese, A., Harrington, H., Israel, S., Levine, M. E., Schaefer, J. D., Sugden, K., Williams, B., Yashin, A. I., Poulton, R., & Moffitt, T. E. (2015). Quantification of biological aging in young adults. *Proceedings of the National Academy of Sciences of the United States of America, 112*(30), E4104–E4110. https://doi.org/10.1073/pnas.1506264112

Bengtson, V., Settersten, R., Kennedy, B. K., & Smith, J. (2016). *Handbook of theories of aging*. Springer. https://books.google.com/books?hl=en&lr=&id=xyUODAAAQBAJ&oi=fnd&pg=PP1&dq=Handbook+of+Theories+of+Aging&ots=HcqHpnqUSb&sig=N0fLW1BpGC2CxTGHHO3hbj5l4Gc

Bentov, Y., Yavorska, T., Esfandiari, N., Jurisicova, A., & Casper, R. (2011). The contribution of mitochondrial function to reproductive aging. *Journal of Assisted Reproduction & Genetics, 28*(9), 773–783. https://doi.org/10.1007/s10815-011-9588-7

Blackburn, E. H., Epel, E. S., Lin, J., Sfeir, A., Lange, T. de., Blackburn, E. H., Greider, C. W., Szostak, J. W., Xie, Z., Jay, K. A., Smith, D. L., Zhang, Y., Liu, Z., Zheng, J., Tian, R., Li, H., Blackburn, E. H., Armanios, M., Blackburn, E. H., . . . Blau, H. M, . . (2015). Human telomere biology: A contributory and interactive factor in aging, disease risks, and protection. *Science, 350*(6265), 1193–1198. https://doi.org/10.1126/science.aab3389

Bonnie, R. J., Stroud, C., & Breiner, H. (2015). *Investing in the health and well-being of young adults*. National Academies Press.

Bozick, R., & DeLuca, S. (2011). Not making the transition to college: School, work, and opportunities in the lives of American youth. *Social Science Research, 40*(4), 1249–1262. https://doi.org/10.1016/j.ssresearch.2011.02.003

Brahem, S., Mehdi, M., Elghezal, H., & Saad, A. (2011). The effects of male aging on semen quality, sperm DNA fragmentation and chromosomal abnormalities in an infertile population. *Journal of Assisted Reproduction & Genetics, 28*(5), 425–432. https://doi.org/10.1007/s10815-011-9537-5

Brandon, P. D., & Temple, J. B. (2007). Family provisions at the workplace and their relationship to absenteeism, retention, and productivity of workers: Timely evidence from prior data. *Australian Journal of Social Issues, 42*(4), 447–460.

Brochado, S., Soares, S., & Fraga, S. (2017). A scoping review on studies of cyberbullying prevalence among adolescents. *Trauma, Violence, & Abuse, 18*(5), 523–531. https://doi.org/10.1177/1524838016641668

Bronkema, R., & Bowman, N. A. (2017). A residential paradox?: Residence hall attributes and college student outcomes. *Journal of College Student Development, 58*(4), 624–630. https://doi.org/10.1353/csd.2017.0047

Bronkema, R. H., & Bowman, N. A. (2019). Close campus friendships and college student success. *Journal of College Student Retention: Research, Theory & Practice, 21*(3), 270–285. https://doi.org/10.1177/1521025117704200

Brooks, R., & Everett, G. (2008). The predominance of work-based training in young graduates' learning. *Journal of Education & Work, 21*(1), 61–73. https://doi.org/10.1080/13639080801956966

Brown, A. E., Carpenter, M. J., & Sutfin, E. L. (2011). Occasional smoking in college: Who, what, when and why? *Addictive Behaviors, 36*(12), 1199–1204. https://doi.org/10.1016/j.addbeh.2011.07.024

Calk, R., & Patrick, A. (2017). Millennials through the looking glass: Workplace motivating factors. *Journal of Business Inquiry, 16*(2), 131–139. https://journals.uvu.edu/index.php/jbi/article/view/81

Campisi, J. (2013). Aging, cellular senescence, and cancer. *Annual Review of Physiology, 75*, 685–705. https://doi.org/10.1146/annurev-physiol-030212-183653

Campos-Vazquez, R. M., & Gonzalez, E. (2020). Obesity and hiring discrimination. *Economics and Human Biology, 37*, 100850. https://doi.org/10.1016/j.ehb.2020.100850

Cannon, S. M., Einstein, G. P., & Tulp, O. L. (2017). Analysis of telomere length in aging and age-related illness. *The FASEB Journal, 31*(1 Suppl.), 935.2. http://www.fasebj.org/content/31/1_Supplement/935.2.short

Carlson, D. S., Grzywacz, J. G., Ferguson, M., Hunter, E. M., Clinch, C. R., & Arcury, T. A. (2011). Health and turnover of working mothers after childbirth via the work-family interface: An analysis across time. *The Journal of Applied Psychology, 96*(5), 1045–1054. https://doi.org/10.1037/a0023964

Carnes, A. M. (2017). Bringing work stress home: The impact of role conflict and role overload on spousal marital satisfaction. *Journal of Occupational and Organizational Psychology, 90*(2), 153–176. https://doi.org/10.1111/joop.12163

Carroll, J. M., Humphries, M., & Muller, C. (2018). Mental and physical health impairments at the transition to college: Early patterns in the education-health gradient. *Social Science Research, 74*, 120–131. https://doi.org/10.1016/j.ssresearch.2018.05.002

Centers for Disease Control. (2020). Current cigarette smoking among adults in the United States. *CDC*. https://www.cdc.gov/tobacco/data_statistics/fact_sheets/adult_data/cig_smoking/

Centers for Disease Control. (2021). *WISQARS leading causes of death reports, 1981 - 2019*. https://webappa.cdc.gov/sasweb/ncipc/leadcause.html

Cheng, H. L., Medlow, S., & Steinbeck, K. (2016). The health consequences of obesity in young adulthood. *Current Obesity Reports, 5*(1), 30–37. https://doi.org/10.1007/s13679-016-0190-2

Chooi, Y. C., Ding, C., & Magkos, F. (2019). The epidemiology of obesity. *Metabolism: Clinical and Experimental, 92*, 6–10. https://doi.org/10.1016/j.metabol.2018.09.005

Christensen, R. K., Moon, K. K., & Whitford, A. B. (2021). Genetics and sector of employment. *International Public Management Journal*. https://doi.org/10.1080/10967494.2020.1802631

Cohen, R., & Shikora, S. (2020). Fighting weight bias and obesity stigma: A call for action. *Obesity Surgery, 30*(5), 1623–1624. https://doi.org/10.1007/s11695-020-04525-0

Colizzi, M., Tosato, S., & Ruggeri, M. (2020). Cannabis and cognition: Connecting the dots towards the understanding of the relationship. *Brain Sciences, 10*(3), 133. https://doi.org/10.3390/brainsci10030133

Combs, G. M., & Milosevic, I. (2016). Workplace discrimination and the wellbeing of minority women: Overview, prospects, and implications. In M. L. Connerley & J. Wu (Eds.), *Handbook on well-being of working women* (pp. 17–31). Springer. https://doi.org/10.1007/978-94-017-9897-6_2

Compton, W. M., Han, B., Hughes, A., Jones, C. M., & Blanco, C. (2017). Use of marijuana for medical purposes among adults in the United States. *JAMA, 317*(2), 209. https://doi.org/10.1001/jama.2016.18900

Corder, K., Winpenny, E., Love, R., Brown, H. E., White, M., & van Sluijs, E. (2019). Change in physical activity from adolescence to early adulthood: A systematic review and meta-analysis of longitudinal cohort studies. *British Journal of Sports Medicine, 53*, 496–503. https://doi.org/10.1136/bjsports-2016-097330

Cornman, J. C., Glei, D. A., Goldman, N., Ryff, C. D., & Weinstein, M. (2015). Socioeconomic status and biological markers of health: An examination of adults in the United States and Taiwan. *Journal of Aging and Health, 27*(1), 75–102. https://doi.org/10.1177/0898264314538661

Côté, J. E. (2014). The dangerous myth of emerging adulthood: An evidence-based critique of a flawed developmental theory. *Applied Developmental Science, 18*(4), 177–188. http://www.tandfonline.com/doi/abs/10.1080/10888691.2014.954451#.VTOQ7JMug8Q

Côté, M., & Bégin, C. (2020). Review of the experience of weight-based stigmatization in romantic relationships. *Current Obesity Reports*, *9*(3), 280–287. https://doi.org/10.1007/s13679-020-00383-0

Covarrubias, R., & Fryberg, S. A. (2015). Movin' on up (to college): First-generation college students' experiences with family achievement guilt. *Cultural Diversity and Ethnic Minority Psychology*, *21*(3), 420–429. https://doi.org/10.1037/a0037844

Cowan, B. (2020). *Short-run effects of COVID-19 on U.S. worker transitions*. https://doi.org/10.3386/w27315

Cservenka, A., & Brumback, T. (2017). The burden of binge and heavy drinking on the brain: Effects on adolescent and young adult neural structure and function. *Frontiers in Psychology*, *8*, 1111. https://doi.org/10.3389/fpsyg.2017.01111

Deak, J. D., Miller, A. P., & Gizer, I. R. (2019). Genetics of alcohol use disorder: A review. *Current Opinion in Psychology*, *27*, 56–61. https://doi.org/10.1016/j.copsyc.2018.07.012

de Siqueira, J. V. V., Almeida, L. G., Zica, B. O., Brum, I. B., Barceló, A., & de Siqueira Galil, A. G. (2020). Impact of obesity on hospitalizations and mortality, due to COVID-19: A systematic review. *Obesity Research & Clinical Practice*, *14*(5), 398–403. https://doi.org/10.1016/j.orcp.2020.07.005

Dijkhuis, R., de Sonneville, L., Ziermans, T., Staal, W., & Swaab, H. (2020). Autism symptoms, executive functioning and academic progress in higher education students. *Journal of Autism and Developmental Disorders*, *50*(4), 1353–1363. https://doi.org/10.1007/s10803-019-04267-8

DiPietro, L., Buchner, D. M., Marquez, D. X., Pate, R. R., Pescatello, L. S., & Whitt-Glover, M. C. (2019). New scientific basis for the 2018 U.S. physical activity guidelines. *Journal of Sport and Health Science*, *8*(3), 197–200. https://doi.org/10.1016/j.jshs.2019.03.007

Dodig, S., Čepelak, I., & Pavić, I. (2019). Hallmarks of senescence and aging. *Biochemia Medica*, *29*(3). https://doi.org/10.11613/BM.2019.030501

Duxbury, L., Stevenson, M., & Higgins, C. (2018). Too much to do, too little time: Role overload and stress in a multi-role environment. *International Journal of Stress Management*, *25*, 250–266. https://doi.org/10.1037/str0000062

Edwards, R., Carter, K., Peace, J., & Blakely, T. (2013). An examination of smoking initiation rates by age: Results from a large longitudinal study in New Zealand. *Australian and New Zealand Journal of Public Health*, *37*(6), 516–519. http://www.ncbi.nlm.nih.gov/pubmed/24892149

Elias, R., & White, S. W. (2018). Autism goes to college: Understanding the needs of a student population on the rise. *Journal of Autism and Developmental Disorders*, *48*(3), 732–746. https://doi.org/10.1007/s10803-017-3075-7

Enoch, M.-A. (2013). Genetic influences on the development of alcoholism. *Current Psychiatry Reports*, *15*(11), 412. https://doi.org/10.1007/s11920-013-0412-1

Farsalinos, K. E., & Polosa, R. (2014). Safety evaluation and risk assessment of electronic cigarettes as tobacco cigarette substitutes: A systematic review. *Therapeutic Advances in Drug Safety*, *5*(2), 67–86. https://doi.org/10.1177/2042098614524430

Fedarko, N. S. (2018). Theories and mechanisms of aging. In J. G. Reves, S. R. Barnett, J. R. McSwain, & G. A. Rooke (Eds.), *Geriatric anesthesiology* (pp. 19–25). Springer International Publishing. https://doi.org/10.1007/978-3-319-66878-9_2

Feldman, R. S. (2017). *The first year of college: Research, theory, and practice on improving the student experience and increasing retention. Cambridge*. https://books.google.com/books?id=G9BCDwAAQBAJ&dq=The+first-generation+student+experience+:+implications+for+campus+practice,+and+strategies+for+improving+persistence+and+success&lr=&source=gbs_navlinks_s

Ferguson, R. F., & Lamback, S. (2014). *Creating pathways to prosperity: A blueprint for action. Report issued by the pathways to prosperity project at the Harvard Graduate School of Education and the Achievement Gap Initiative at Harvard University*. http://www.agi.harvard.edu/pathways/CreatingPathwaystoProsperityReport2014.pdf

Ferrucci, L., Gonzalez-Freire, M., Fabbri, E., Simonsick, E., Tanaka, T., Moore, Z., Salimi, S., Sierra, F., & de Cabo, R. (2020). Measuring biological aging in humans: A quest. *Aging Cell*, *19*(2), e13080. https://doi.org/10.1111/acel.13080

Flament, F., Bazin, R., & Piot, B. (2013). Effect of the sun on visible clinical signs of aging in Caucasian skin. *Clinical, Cosmetic and Investigational Dermatology*, *6*, 221. https://doi.org/10.2147/CCID.S44686

Ford, N. D., Patel, S. A., & Narayan, K. M. V. (2017). Obesity in low- and middle-income countries: Burden, drivers, and emerging challenges. *Annual Review of Public Health*, *38*(1), 145–164. https://doi.org/10.1146/annurev-publhealth-031816-044604

Fryar, C. D., Carroll, M. D., & Afful, J. (2021). Prevalence of overweight, obesity, and severe obesity among adults aged 20 and over: United States, 1960–1962 through 2017–2018. *National Center for Health Statistics Health E-Stats; NHANES*. https://doi.org/10.1001/jama.2020.14590

Fulgoni, V., & Drewnowski, A. (2019). An economic gap between the recommended healthy food patterns and existing diets of Minority Groups in the US National Health and Nutrition Examination Survey 2013–14. *Frontiers in Nutrition*, *6*, 37. https://doi.org/10.3389/fnut.2019.00037

Garcia, P. R. J. M., Restubog, S. L. D., Bordia, P., Bordia, S., & Roxas, R. E. O. (2015). Career optimism: The roles of contextual support and career decision-making self-efficacy. *Journal of Vocational Behavior*, *88*, 10–18. https://doi.org/10.1016/j.jvb.2015.02.004

Gawlik, K. S., Melnyk, B. M., & Tan, A. (2018). An epidemiological study of population health reveals social smoking as a major cardiovascular risk factor. *American Journal of Health Promotion*, *32*(5), 1221–1227. https://doi.org/10.1177/0890117117706420

Gerstorf, D., Hülür, G., Drewelies, J., Willis, S. L., Schaie, K. W., & Ram, N. (2020). Adult development and aging in historical context. *American Psychologist*, *75*(4), 525–539. https://doi.org/10.1037/amp0000596

Ghosh, A., Coakley, R. C., Mascenik, T., Rowell, T. R., Davis, E. S., Rogers, K., Webster, M. J., Dang, H., Herring, L. E., Sassano, M. F., Livraghi-Butrico, A., Van Buren, S. K., Graves, L. M., Herman, M. A., Randell, S. H., Alexis, N. E., & Tarran, R. (2018). Chronic E-cigarette exposure alters the human bronchial epithelial proteome. *American Journal of Respiratory and Critical Care Medicine*, *198*(1), 67–76. https://doi.org/10.1164/rccm.201710-2033OC

Golbidi, S., Daiber, A., Korac, B., Li, H., Essop, M. F., & Laher, I. (2017). Health benefits of fasting and caloric restriction. *Current Diabetes Reports*, *17*(12), 1–11. https://doi.org/10.1007/s11892-017-0951-7

Goniewicz, M. L., Lingas, E. O., & Hajek, P. (2013). Patterns of electronic cigarette use and user beliefs about their safety and benefits: An internet survey. *Drug and Alcohol Review, 32*(2), 133–140. https://doi.org/10.1111/j.1465-3362.2012.00512.x

Gonzáles-Figueroa, E., & Young, A. M. (2005). Ethnic identity and mentoring among Latinas in professional roles. *Cultural Diversity and Ethnic Minority Psychology, 11*(3), 213–226.

Gordon, M. (2017). *Individual-level and socio-contextual influences on body mass index and achievement in adolescence to young adulthood. Journal of Adolescent and Family Health, 8*(1), 1. https://scholar.utc.edu/jafh/vol8/iss1/1

Govindaraju, D., Atzmon, G., & Barzilai, N. (2015). Genetics, lifestyle and longevity: Lessons from centenarians. *Applied & Translational Genomics, 4*, 23–32. https://doi.org/10.1016/j.atg.2015.01.001

Hales, C. M., Carroll, M. D., Fryar, C. D., & Ogden, C. L. (2020). *Prevalence of obesity and severe obesity among adults: United States, 2017-2018 key findings data from the National Health and Nutrition Examination Survey (NCHS Data Brief No. 360)*. https://stacks.cdc.gov/view/cdc/85451

Hall, W. (2014). What has research over the past two decades revealed about the adverse health effects of recreational cannabis use? *Addiction, 110*(1), 19–35. https://doi.org/10.1111/add.12703

Halpern, D. F. (2005). How time-flexible work policies can reduce stress, improve health, and save money. *Stress & Health: Journal of the International Society for the Investigation of Stress, 21*(3), 157–168. https://doi.org/10.1002/smi.1049

Hamer, R., & van Rossum, E. J. (2017). Six languages in education—Looking for postformal thinking. *Behavioral Development Bulletin, 22*(2), 377–393. https://doi.org/10.1037/bdb0000030

Hansen, J. C. (2020). Holland, John. In B. J. Carducci, C. S. Nave, J. S. Mio, & R. E. Riggio (Eds.), *The Wiley encyclopedia of personality and individual differences* (pp. 621–625). Wiley. https://doi.org/10.1002/9781119547181.ch368

Hayflick, L. (1996). *How and why we age*. Ballantine Books.

Heinonen, I., Helajärvi, H., Pahkala, K., Heinonen, O. J., Hirvensalo, M., Pälve, K., Tammelin, T., Yang, X., Juonala, M., Mikkilä, V., Kähönen, M., Lehtimäki, T., Viikari, J., & Raitakari, O. T. (2013). Sedentary behaviours and obesity in adults: The cardiovascular risk in young finns study. *BMJ Open, 3*(6), e002901. https://doi.org/10.1136/bmjopen-2013-002901

Herbert, C., Meixner, F., Wiebking, C., & Gilg, V. (2020). Regular physical activity, short-term exercise, mental health, and well-being among University Students: The results of an online and a laboratory study. *Frontiers in Psychology, 11*, 509. https://doi.org/10.3389/fpsyg.2020.00509

Herrenkohl, T. I., Hong, S., Klika, J. B., Herrenkohl, R. C., & Russo, M. J. (2013). Developmental impacts of child abuse and neglect related to adult mental health, substance use, and physical health. *Journal of Family Violence, 28*(2), 191–199. https://doi.org/10.1007/s10896-012-9474-9

Herrera, B. M., Keildson, S., & Lindgren, C. M. (2011). Genetics and epigenetics of obesity. *Maturitas, 69*(1), 41–49. https://doi.org/10.1016/j.maturitas.2011.02.018

Hewitt, B., Baxter, J., & Western, M. (2006). Family, work and health: The impact of marriage, parenthood and employment on self-reported health of Australian men and women. *Journal of Sociology, 42*(1), 61–78.

Higgins, C. A., Duxbury, L. E., & Lyons, S. T. (2010). Coping with overload and stress: Men and women in dual-earner families. *Journal of Marriage and Family, 72*(4), 847–859. https://doi.org/10.1111/j.1741-3737.2010.00734.x

Holland, J. L. (1997). *Making vocational choices: A theory of vocational personalities and work environments* (3rd ed.). Psychological Assessment Resources.

Hope, J. (2017). Review policy recommendations to support adult learners. *Recruiting & Retaining Adult Learners, 19*(7), 8. https://doi.org/10.1002/nsr.30238

Huang, Y., Heflin, C. M., & Validova, A. (2021). Material hardship, perceived stress, and health in early adulthood. *Annals of Epidemiology, 53*, 69–75.e3. https://doi.org/10.1016/j.annepidem.2020.08.017

Huerta, T. R., Walker, D. M., Mullen, D., Johnson, T. J., & Ford, E. W. (2017). Trends in E-cigarette awareness and perceived harmfulness in the U.S. *American Journal of Preventive Medicine, 52*(3), 339–346. https://doi.org/10.1016/j.amepre.2016.10.017

Hwang, C. L., Piano, M. R., Thur, L. A., Peters, T. A., Da Silva, A. L. G., & Phillips, S. A. (2020). The effects of repeated binge drinking on arterial stiffness and urinary norepinephrine levels in young adults. *Journal of Hypertension, 38*(1), 111–117. https://doi.org/10.1097/HJH.0000000000002223

Igielnik, R. (2021). *More working parents now say child care amid COVID-19 has been difficult | Pew Research Center. Fact Tank: News in the Numbers*. https://www.pewresearch.org/fact-tank/2021/01/26/a-rising-share-of-working-parents-in-the-u-s-say-its-been-difficult-to-handle-child-care-during-the-pandemic/

Ilacqua, A., Izzo, G., Emerenziani, G. Pietro., Baldari, C., & Aversa, A. (2018). Lifestyle and fertility: The influence of stress and quality of life on male fertility. *Reproductive Biology and Endocrinology, 16*(1), 115. https://doi.org/10.1186/s12958-018-0436-9

Institute for Veterans and Military Families. (2019). *Student veterans a valuable asset to higher education*. https://ivmf.syracuse.edu/wp-content/uploads/2019/12/Student-Vets_Valuable-AssetFINAL-11.6.19.pdf

Jasienska, G., Bribiescas, R. G., Furberg, A.-S., Helle, S., & Núñez-de la Mora, A. (2017). Human reproduction and health: An evolutionary perspective. *The Lancet, 390*(10093), 510–520. https://doi.org/10.1016/S0140-6736(17)30573-1

Jiang, Z., Newman, A., Le, H., Presbitero, A., & Zheng, C. (2019). Career exploration: A review and future research agenda. *Journal of Vocational Behavior, 110*, 338–356. https://doi.org/10.1016/j.jvb.2018.08.008

Jimenez, A., Piña-Watson, B., & Manzo, G. (2021). Resilience through family: Family support as an academic and psychological protective resource for Mexican descent first-generation college students. *Journal of Hispanic Higher Education*, 153819272098710. https://doi.org/10.1177/1538192720987103

Johnson, M. K., Mortimer, J. T., & Heckhausen, J. (2020). Work value transmission from parents to children: Early socialization and delayed activation. *Work and Occupations, 47*(1), 83–119. https://doi.org/10.1177/0730888419877445

Johnson, S. L., Dunleavy, J., Gemmell, N. J., & Nakagawa, S. (2015). Consistent age-dependent declines in human semen quality: A systematic review and meta-analysis. *Ageing Research Reviews, 19C*, 22–33. https://doi.org/10.1016/j.arr.2014.10.007

Jones, K. P., Peddie, C. I., Gilrane, V. L., King, E. B., & Gray, A. L. (2016). Not so subtle: A meta-analytic investigation of the correlates of subtle and overt discrimination. *Journal of Management, 42*(6), 1588–1613. https://doi.org/10.1177/0149206313506466

Jury, M., Smeding, A., Stephens, N. M., Nelson, J. E., Aelenei, C., & Darnon, C. (2017). The experience of low-SES students in higher education: Psychological barriers to success and interventions to reduce social-class inequality. *Journal of Social Issues, 73*(1), 23–41. https://doi.org/10.1111/josi.12202

Kanny, D., Liu, Y., Brewer, R. D., & Lu, H. (2013). *Binge drinking - United States, 2011. Morbidity and Mortality Weekly Report. Surveillance Summaries, 62*(Suppl. 3), 77–80. http://www.ncbi.nlm.nih.gov/pubmed/24264494

Kantamneni, N., McCain, M. R. C., Shada, N., Hellwege, M. A., & Tate, J. (2018). Contextual factors in the career development of prospective first-generation college students. *Journal of Career Assessment, 26*(1), 183–196. https://doi.org/10.1177/1069072716680048

Kenney, W. L., Wilmore, J., & Costill, D. L. (2020). *Physiology of sport and exercise* (6th ed.). Human Kinetics.

Kerr, D. C. R., Bae, H., & Koval, A. L. (2018). Oregon recreational marijuana legalization: Changes in undergraduates' marijuana use rates from 2008 to 2016. *Psychology of Addictive Behaviors, 32*(6), 670–678. https://doi.org/10.1037/adb0000385

Kerr, W. C., Lui, C., & Ye, Y. (2018). Trends and age, period and cohort effects for marijuana use prevalence in the 1984-2015 US National Alcohol Surveys. *Addiction, 113*(3), 473–481. https://doi.org/10.1111/add.14031

Khazan, O., & Harris, A. (2020). The limited child-care options for essential workers. *The Atlantic*. https://www.theatlantic.com/politics/archive/2020/09/limited-child-care-options-essential-workers/615931/

King, E. B., Madera, J. M., Hebl, M. R., Knight, J. L., & Mendoza, S. A. (2006). What's in a name? A multiracial investigation of the role of occupational stereotypes in selection decisions. *Journal of Applied Social Psychology, 36*(5), 1145–1159.

King, P. M., & Kitchener, K. S. (2016). Cognitive development in the emerging adult. In J. J. Arnett (Ed.), *The Oxford handbook of emerging adulthood* (pp. 105–125). Oxford University Press. https://doi.org/10.1093/oxfordhb/9780199795574.013.14

Knight, W., Wessel, R. D., & Markle, L. (2018). Persistence to graduation for students with disabilities: Implications for performance-based outcomes. *Journal of College Student Retention: Research, Theory & Practice, 19*(4), 362–380. https://doi.org/10.1177/1521025116632534

Kossek, E. E., & Lautsch, B. A. (2018). Work–life flexibility for whom? Occupational status and work–life inequality in upper, middle, and lower level jobs. *Academy of Management Annals, 12*(1), 5–36. https://doi.org/10.5465/annals.2016.0059

Krei, M. S., & Rosenbaum, J. E. (2000). Career and college advice to the forgotten half: What do counselors and vocational teachers advise? *Teachers College Record, 103*(5), 823–842. http://eric.ed.gov/?id=EJ638357

Kroon, E., Kuhns, L., & Cousijn, J. (2021). The short-term and long-term effects of cannabis on cognition: Recent advances in the field. *Current Opinion in Psychology, 38*, 49–55. https://doi.org/10.1016/j.copsyc.2020.07.005

Kuhn, D. (2013). Reasoning. In P. D. Zelazo (Ed.), *The Oxford handbook of developmental psychology: Body and mind* (Vol. 1, pp. 744–764). Oxford University Press. https://doi.org/10.1093/oxfordhb/9780199958450.013.0026

Kultalahti, S., & Viitala, R. (2015). Generation Y – Challenging clients for HRM? *Journal of Managerial Psychology, 30*(1), 101–114. https://doi.org/10.1108/JMP-08-2014-0230

Kuntsche, E., Kuntsche, S., Thrul, J., & Gmel, G. (2017). Binge drinking: Health impact, prevalence, correlates and interventions. *Psychology & Health, 32*(8), 976–1017. https://doi.org/10.1080/08870446.2017.1325889

Kwarteng, J. L., Schulz, A. J., Mentz, G. B., Israel, B. A., & Perkins, D. W. (2017). Independent effects of neighborhood poverty and psychosocial stress on obesity over time. *Journal of Urban Health, 94*(6), 791–802. https://doi.org/10.1007/s11524-017-0193-7

Labouvie-Vief, G. (2006). Emerging structures of adult thought. In J. J. Arnett & J. L. Tanner (Eds.), *Emerging adults in America: Coming of age in the 21st century* (pp. 59–84). American Psychological Association.

Labouvie-Vief, G. (2015). *Integrating emotions and cognition throughout the lifespan*. Springer. https://doi.org/10.1007/978-3-319-09822-7

Lagouge, M., & Larsson, N.-G. N.-G. (2013). The role of mitochondrial DNA mutations and free radicals in disease and ageing. *Journal of Internal Medicine, 273*(6), 529–543. https://doi.org/10.1111/joim.12055

Lakerveld, J., & Mackenbach, J. (2017). The upstream determinants of adult obesity. *Obesity Facts, 10*(3), 216–222. https://doi.org/10.1159/000471489

Lam, P. H., Chiang, J. J., Chen, E., & Miller, G. E. (2021). Race, socioeconomic status, and low-grade inflammatory biomarkers across the lifecourse: A pooled analysis of seven studies. *Psychoneuroendocrinology, 123*, 104917. https://doi.org/10.1016/j.psyneuen.2020.104917

Lapsley, D., & Hardy, S. A. (2017). Identity formation and moral development in emerging adulthood. In L. M. Padilla-Walker & L. J. Nelson (Eds.), *Flourishing in emerging adulthood: Positive development during the third decade of life* (pp. 14–39). Oxford University Press. https://doi.org/10.1093/acprof:oso/9780190260637.003.0002

Larson, N. I., Story, M. T., & Nelson, M. C. (2009). Neighborhood environments. *American Journal of Preventive Medicine, 36*(1), 74-81.e10. https://doi.org/10.1016/j.amepre.2008.09.025

Lau-Barraco, C., Linden-Carmichael, A. N., Hequembourg, A., & Pribesh, S. (2017). Motivations and consequences of alcohol use among heavy drinking nonstudent emerging adults. *Journal of Adolescent Research, 32*(6), 667–695. https://doi.org/10.1177/0743558416630812

Lavie, C. J., Ozemek, C., Carbone, S., Katzmarzyk, P. T., & Blair, S. N. (2019). Sedentary behavior, exercise, and cardiovascular health. *Circulation Research, 124*(5), 799–815. https://doi.org/10.1161/CIRCRESAHA.118.312669

Lawson, K. M. (2018). Mechanisms underlying parent–Child occupational consistency: A critical review. *Community, Work and Family, 21*(3), 272–291. https://doi.org/10.1080/13668803.2017.1284761

Lee, C. E., Day, T. L., Carter, E. W., & Taylor, J. L. (2021). Examining growth among college students with intellectual and developmental disability: A longitudinal study. *Behavior Modification*, *45*(2), 324–348. https://doi.org/10.1177/0145445520982968

Lee, C. M., Maggs, J. L., Neighbors, C., & Patrick, M. E. (2011). Positive and negative alcohol-related consequences: Associations with past drinking. *Journal of Adolescence*, *34*(1), 87–94. https://doi.org/10.1016/j.adolescence.2010.01.009

Leech, T. G., Jacobs, S., & Watson, D. (2020). Factors associated with binge drinking during the transition into adulthood: Exploring associations within two distinct young adult age ranges. *Substance Abuse: Research and Treatment*, *14*, 1178221820951781. https://doi.org/10.1177/1178221820951781

Leung, J., Chiu, C. Y. V., Stjepanović, D., & Hall, W. (2018). Has the legalisation of medical and recreational cannabis use in the USA affected the prevalence of cannabis use and cannabis use disorders? *Current Addiction Reports*, *5*(4), 403–417. https://doi.org/10.1007/s40429-018-0224-9

Li, S., Nguyen, T. L., Wong, E. M., Dugué, P. A., Dite, G. S., Armstrong, N. J., Craig, J. M., Mather, K. A., Sachdev, P. S., Saffery, R., Sung, J., Tan, Q., Thalamuthu, A., Milne, R. L., Giles, G. G., Southey, M. C., & Hopper, J. L. (2020). Causes of variation in epigenetic aging across the lifespan. *medRxiv*. https://doi.org/10.1101/2020.05.10.20097030

Lin, Y. H., Chen, Y. C., Tseng, Y. C., Tsai, S. T., & Tseng, Y. H. (2020). Physical activity and successful aging among middle-aged and older adults: A systematic review and meta-analysis of cohort studies. *Aging*, *12*(9), 7704–7716. https://doi.org/10.18632/aging.103057

Lipari, R. N., Hughes, A., & Bose, J. (2016). Driving under the influence of alcohol and illicit drugs. In *The CBHSQ Report*. Substance Abuse and Mental Health Services Administration (US). http://www.ncbi.nlm.nih.gov/pubmed/28252900

Lodato, M. A., & Walsh, C. A. (2019). Genome aging: Somatic mutation in the brain links age-related decline with disease and nominates pathogenic mechanisms. *Human Molecular Genetics*, *28*(R2), R197–R206. https://doi.org/10.1093/hmg/ddz191

Loprinzi, P. D., Pazirei, S., Robinson, G., Dickerson, B., Edwards, M., & Rhodes, R. E. (2020). Evaluation of a cognitive affective model of physical activity behavior. *Health Promotion Perspectives*, *10*(1), 88. https://doi.org/10.15171/hpp.2020.14

Lovell, M. E., Akhurst, J., Padgett, C., Garry, M. I., & Matthews, A. (2020). Cognitive outcomes associated with long-term, regular, recreational cannabis use in adults: A meta-analysis. *Experimental and Clinical Psychopharmacology*, *28*(4), 471–494. https://doi.org/10.1037/pha0000326

Lunau, T., Bambra, C., Eikemo, T. A., van der Wel, K. A., & Dragano, N. (2014). A balancing act? Work-life balance, health and well-being in European welfare states. *European Journal of Public Health*, *24*(3), 422–427. https://doi.org/10.1093/eurpub/cku010

MacDonald, K. (2018). A review of the literature: The needs of nontraditional students in postsecondary education. *Strategic Enrollment Management Quarterly*, *5*(4), 159–164. https://doi.org/10.1002/sem3.20115

MacLean, P. S., Wing, R. R., Davidson, T., Epstein, L., Goodpaster, B., Hall, K. D., Levin, B. E., Perri, M. G., Rolls, B. J., Rosenbaum, M., Rothman, A. J., & Ryan, D. (2015). NIH working group report: Innovative research to improve maintenance of weight loss. *Obesity (Silver Spring Md.)*, *23*(1), 7–15. https://doi.org/10.1002/oby.20967

Maddux, W. W., & Yuki, M. (2006). The "ripple effect": Cultural differences in perceptions of the consequences of events. *Personality and Social Psychology Bulletin*, *32*(5), 669–683. https://doi.org/10.1177/0146167205283840

Mahmoud, A. B., Reisel, W. D., Grigoriou, N., Fuxman, L., & Mohr, I. (2020). The reincarnation of work motivation: Millennials vs older generations. *International Sociology*, *35*(4), 393–414. https://doi.org/10.1177/0268580920912970

Maier, K. S. (2005). Transmitting educational values: Parent occupation and adolescent development. In B. Schneider & L. J. Waite (Eds.), *Being together, working apart: Dual-career families and the work-life balance* (pp. 396–418). Cambridge University Press.

Marcho, C., Oluwayiose, O. A., & Pilsner, J. R. (2020). The preconception environment and sperm epigenetics. *Andrology*, *8*(4), 924–942. https://doi.org/10.1111/andr.12753

Martin, J. A., Hamilton, B. E., Osterman, M. J. K., & Driscoll, A. K. (2019). Births: Final data for 2018. *National Vital Statistics Reports*, 68(13). https://www.cdc.gov/nchs/data/nvsr/nvsr68/nvsr68_13-508.pdf

Martins, W. P., & Jokubkiene, L. (2017). Assessment of the functional ovarian reserve. In S. Guerriero, W. P. Martins, & J. L. Alcazar (Eds.), *Managing ultrasonography in human reproduction* (pp. 3–12). Springer International Publishing. https://doi.org/10.1007/978-3-319-41037-1_1

Mather, K. A., Jorm, A. F., Parslow, R. A., & Christensen, H. (2011). Is telomere length a biomarker of aging? A review. *The Journals of Gerontology. Series A, Biological Sciences and Medical Sciences*, *66*(2), 202–213. https://doi.org/10.1093/gerona/glq180

Mather, M. (2012). The emotion paradox in the aging brain. *Annals of the New York Academy of Sciences*, *1251*, 33–49. https://doi.org/10.1111/j.1749-6632.2012.06471.x

Matthews, T. J., & Hamilton, B. E. (2016). *Mean age of mothers is on the rise: United States, 2000–2014 (NCHS Data Brief No. 232)*. https://www.cdc.gov/nchs/products/databriefs/db232.htm

Maugeri, G., Castrogiovanni, P., Battaglia, G., Pippi, R., D'Agata, V., Palma, A., Di Rosa, M., & Musumeci, G. (2020). The impact of physical activity on psychological health during Covid-19 pandemic in Italy. *Heliyon*, *6*(6), e04315. https://doi.org/10.1016/j.heliyon.2020.e04315

Mayhew, M. J., Rockenbach, A. N., Bowman, N. A., Seifert, T. A., Wolniak, G. C., Pascarella, E. T., & Terenzini, P. Y. (2016). *How college affects students: 21st century evidence that higher education works* (Vol. 3). Wiley.

McCrady, B. S. (2017). Alcohol Use Disorders. In D. McKay, J. S. Abramowitz, & E. A. Storch (Eds.), *Treatments for psychological problems and syndromes* (pp. 235–247). John Wiley & Sons, Ltd. https://doi.org/10.1002/9781118877142.ch16

McDonald, R. B. (2014). *Biology of aging*. Garland Science.

McGarry, K. (2018). The skills gap: Employers expect more than what college grads offer. *The James G. Martin Center for Academic Renewal*. https://www.jamesgmartin.center/2018/04/skills-gap-employers-expect-college-grads-offer/

McLeod, J. D., Meanwell, E., & Hawbaker, A. (2019). The experiences of college students on the autism spectrum: A comparison to their neurotypical peers. *Journal of Autism and Developmental Disorders*, *49*(6), 2320–2336. https://doi.org/10.1007/s10803-019-03910-8

Merrill, J. E., & Carey, K. B. (2016). Drinking over the lifespan: Focus on college ages. *Alcohol Research: Current Reviews*, *38*(1), 103–114. http://www.ncbi.nlm.nih.gov/pubmed/27159817

Miech, R. a., Johnston, L. D., O'Malley, P. M., Bachman, J. G., Schulenberg, J. E., & Patrick, M. E. (2017). *Monitoring the future national survey results on drug use, 1975–2016: Vol. I, secondary school students*. http://www.monitoringthefuture.org/pubs/monographs/mtf-vol1_2016.pdf

Mikels, J. A., Löckenhoff, C. E., Maglio, S. J., Goldstein, M. K., Garber, A., & Carstensen, L. L. (2010). Following your heart or your head: Focusing on emotions versus information differentially influences the decisions of younger and older adults. *Journal of Experimental Psychology. Applied*, *16*(1), 87–95. https://doi.org/10.1037/a0018500

Milholland, B., Suh, Y., & Vijg, J. (2017). Mutation and catastrophe in the aging genome. *Experimental Gerontology*, *94*, 34–40. https://doi.org/10.1016/j.exger.2017.02.073

Mitteldorf, J. (2016). An epigenetic clock controls aging. *Biogerontology*, *17*(1), 257–265. https://doi.org/10.1007/s10522-015-9617-5

Miura, Y.., & Endo, T.. (2010). Survival responses to oxidative stress and aging. *Geriatrics & Gerontology International*, *10*, S1–S9. https://doi.org/10.1111/j.1447-0594.2010.00597.x

Monaghan, D. B., & Attewell, P. (2015). The community college route to the bachelor's degree. *Educational Evaluation and Policy Analysis*, *37*(1), 70–91. https://doi.org/10.3102/0162373714521865

Montesanto, A., Latorre, V., Giordano, M., Martino, C., Domma, F., & Passarino, G. (2011). The genetic component of human longevity: Analysis of the survival advantage of parents and siblings of Italian nonagenarians. *European Journal of Human Genetics*, *19*(8), 882–886. https://doi.org/10.1038/ejhg.2011.40

Morgan, W. B., Elder, K. B., & King, E. B. (2013). The emergence and reduction of bias in letters of recommendation. *Journal of Applied Social Psychology*, *43*(11), 2297–2306. https://doi.org/10.1111/jasp.12179

Moshman, D., & Moshman, D. (2011). *Adolescent rationality and development: Cognition, morality, and identity.* Psychology Press. https://books.google.com/books?id=Fl2vkqcMqMsC&dq=moshman+adolscence&lr=&source=gbs_navlinks_s

Moskalev, A. A., Aliper, A. M., Smit-McBride, Z., Buzdin, A., & Zhavoronkov, A. (2014). Genetics and epigenetics of aging and longevity. *Cell Cycle*, *13*(7), 1063–1077. https://doi.org/10.4161/cc.28433

Mouzon, D. M., Taylor, R. J., Woodward, A. T., & Chatters, L. M. (2017). Everyday racial discrimination, everyday non-racial discrimination, and physical health among African-Americans. *Journal of Ethnic & Cultural Diversity in Social Work*, *26*(1–2), 68–80. https://doi.org/10.1080/15313204.2016.1187103

Müller, L., Di Benedetto, S., & Pawelec, G. (2019). The immune system and its dysregulation with aging. In J. R. Harris & V. I. Korolchuk (Eds.), *Biochemistry and cell biology of ageing: Part II clinical science* (Vol. 91, pp. 21–43). Springer New York. https://doi.org/10.1007/978-981-13-3681-2_2

Murthy, V. H. (2017). E-cigarette use among youth and young adults. *JAMA Pediatrics*, *171*(3), 209. https://doi.org/10.1001/jamapediatrics.2016.4662

Mylona, E. K., Shehadeh, F., Fleury, E., Kalligeros, M., & Mylonakis, E. (2020). Neighborhood-level analysis on the impact of accessibility to fast food and open green spaces on the prevalence of obesity. *The American Journal of Medicine*, *133*(3), 340–346-e1. https://doi.org/10.1016/j.amjmed.2019.08.024

National Association of College and Employers. (2017). *The class of 2017 student survey report*. https://www.naceweb.org/store/2017/the-class-of-2017-student-survey-report/

National Association of Colleges and Employers. (2018). *Job outlook 2018*.

National Center for Education Statistices. (2021). *Total fall enrollment in degree-granting postsecondary institutions, by control and level of institution, attendance status, and age of student: 2017*. https://nces.ed.gov/programs/digest/d19/tables/dt19_303.55.asp?current=yes

National Center for Education Statistics. (2017). Immediate college enrollment rate. *Condition of Education*. https://nces.ed.gov/programs/coe/indicator_cpa.asp

National Center for Education Statistics. (2019). Fast facts: Students with disabilities (60). *Fast Facts*. https://nces.ed.gov/fastfacts/display.asp?id=60

National Center for Education Statistics. (2020). Undergraduate retention and graduation rates - indicator April (2020). *The Condition of Education*. https://nces.ed.gov/programs/coe/indicator_ctr.asp

National Center for Education Statistics. (2021a). Immediate college enrollment rate - indicator April (2020). *The Condition of Education*. https://nces.ed.gov/programs/coe/indicator_cpa.asp

National Center for Education Statistics. (2021b). *Percentage of persons 25 to 29 years old with selected levels of educational attainment, by race/ethnicity and sex: Selected years, 1920 through 2019*. https://nces.ed.gov/programs/digest/d19/tables/dt19_104.20.asp

National Center for Education Statistics. (2021c). Total fall enrollment in degree-granting postsecondary institutions, by level of enrollment, sex, attendance status, and race/ethnicity or nonresident alien status of student: Selected years, 1976 through 2018. *Digest of Education Statistics*. https://nces.ed.gov/programs/digest/d19/tables/dt19_306.10.asp?current=yes

National Council on Alcoholism and Drug Dependence. (2015). *Alcohol and crime*. https://ncadd.org/learn-about-alcohol/alcohol-and-crime

National Highway Traffic Safety Administration. (2016). *Alcohol impaired driving. Traffic Safety Facts - 2015*. https://crashstats.nhtsa.dot.gov/Api/Public/ViewPublication/812357

Ndobo, A., Faure, A., Boisselier, J., & Giannaki, S. (2018). The ethno-racial segmentation jobs: The impacts of the occupational stereotypes on hiring decisions. *Journal of Social Psychology*, *158*(6), 663–679. https://doi.org/10.1080/00224545.2017.1389685

Neha, K., Haider, M. R., Pathak, A., & Yar, M. S. (2019). Medicinal prospects of antioxidants: A review. *European Journal of Medicinal Chemistry*, *178*, 687–704. https://doi.org/10.1016/j.ejmech.2019.06.010

Nicklas, J. M., Huskey, K. W., Davis, R. B., & Wee, C. C. (2012). Successful weight loss among obese U.S. adults. *American Journal of Preventive Medicine*, *42*(5), 481–485. https://doi.org/10.1016/j.amepre.2012.01.005

Nurkkala, M., Kaikkonen, K., Vanhala, M. L., Karhunen, L., Keränen, A.-M., & Korpelainen, R. (2015). Lifestyle intervention has a beneficial effect on eating behavior and long-term weight loss in obese adults. *Eating Behaviors*, *18*, 179–185. https://doi.org/10.1016/j.eatbeh.2015.05.009

Nutter, S., Russell-Mayhew, S., Arthur, N., & Ellard, J. H. (2018). Weight bias as a social justice issue: A call for dialogue. *Canadian Psychology/Psychologie Canadienne*, *59*(1), 89–99. https://doi.org/10.1037/cap0000125

Office of the Surgeon General. (2016). *A report of the surgeon general—Executive summary.*

Ojalehto, B., & Medin, D. (2015a). Emerging trends in culture and concepts. In R. A. Scott & M. C. Buchmann (Eds.), *Emerging trends in the social and behavioral sciences* (pp. 1–15). John Wiley & Sons, Inc. https://doi.org/10.1002/9781118900772.etrds0064

Ojalehto, B., & Medin, D. (2015b). Perspectives on culture and concepts. *Annual Review of Psychology*, *66*(1), 249–275. https://doi.org/10.1146/annurev-psych-010814-015120

Olmedillas del Moral, M., Fröhlich, N., Figarella, K., Mojtahedi, N., & Garaschuk, O. (2020). Effect of caloric restriction on the in vivo functional properties of aging microglia. *Frontiers in Immunology*, *11*, 750. https://doi.org/10.3389/fimmu.2020.00750

Opresko, P. L., & Shay, J. W. (2017). Telomere-associated aging disorders. *Ageing Research Reviews*, *33*, 52–66. https://doi.org/10.1016/j.arr.2016.05.009

Orzano, A. J., & Scott, J. G. (2004). Diagnosis and treatment of obesity in adults: An applied evidence-based review. *The Journal Of The American Board Of Family Practice / American Board Of Family Practice*, *17*(5), 359–369.

Osam, E. K., Bergman, M., & Cumberland, D. M. (2017). An integrative literature review on the barriers impacting adult learners' return to college. *Adult Learning*, *28*(2), 54–60. https://doi.org/10.1177/1045159516658013

Parker, D., & Heflin, M. (2020). Biology of aging. In R. A. Rosenthal, M. E. Zenilman, & M. R. Katlic (Eds.), In *Principles and practice of geriatric surgery* (pp. 37–50). Springer International Publishing. https://doi.org/10.1007/978-3-319-47771-8_3

Parker, K., Horowitz, J. M., & Minkin, R. (2020). How coronavirus has changed the way Americans work. *Pew Research Center.* https://www.pewresearch.org/social-trends/2020/12/09/how-the-coronavirus-outbreak-has-and-hasnt-changed-the-way-americans-work/

Patrick, M. E., Bray, B. C., & Berglund, P. A. (2016). Reasons for marijuana use among young adults and long-term associations with marijuana use and problems. *Journal of Studies on Alcohol and Drugs*, *77*(6), 881–888. https://doi.org/10.15288/jsad.2016.77.881

Patton, L. D., Renn, K. A., Guido-DiBrito, F., & Quaye, S. J. (2016). *Student development in college: Theory, research, and practice.* Wiley.

Payne, V. G., & Isaacs, L. D. (Larry D. (2020). *Human motor development: A lifespan approach* (10th ed.). Routledge.

PayScale. (2020a). *2020 racial wage gap - Compensation research from PayScale*. https://www.payscale.com/data/racial-wage-gap

PayScale. (2020b). Gender pay gap statistics for 2020. *PayScale.* https://www.payscale.com/data/gender-pay-gap

Pedić, L., Pondeljak, N., & Šitum, M. (2020). Recent information on photoaging mechanisms and the preventive role of topical sunscreen products. *Acta Dermatovenerologica Alpina, Pannonica et Adriatica*, *25*(4), 201–207. https://doi.org/10.15570/actaapa.2020.40

Perry, W. G. (1970). *Forms of intellectual and ethical development in the college years: A scheme.* Jossey-Bass.

Phillips, L. T., Stephens, N. M., & Townsend, S. S. M. (2016). *Access is not enough: Cultural mismatch persists to limit first-generation students' opportunities for achievement throughout college.* https://www.scholars.northwestern.edu/en/publications/access-is-not-enough-cultural-mismatch-persists-to-limit-first-ge

Pieh, C., Budimir, S., & Probst, T. (2020). The effect of age, gender, income, work, and physical activity on mental health during coronavirus disease (COVID-19) lockdown in Austria. *Journal of Psychosomatic Research*, *136*, 110186. https://doi.org/10.1016/j.jpsychores.2020.110186

Piercy, K. L., Troiano, R. P., Ballard, R. M., Carlson, S. A., Fulton, J. E., Galuska, D. A., George, S. M., & Olson, R. D. (2018). The physical activity guidelines for Americans. *JAMA*, *320*(19), 2020. https://doi.org/10.1001/jama.2018.14854

Pifferi, F., & Aujard, F. (2019). Caloric restriction, longevity and aging: Recent contributions from human and non-human primate studies. *Progress in Neuro-Psychopharmacology and Biological Psychiatry*, *95*, 109702. https://doi.org/10.1016/j.pnpbp.2019.109702

Pratt, I. S., Harwood, H. B., Cavazos, J. T., & Ditzfeld, C. P. (2019). Should I stay or should I go? Retention in first-generation college students. *Journal of College Student Retention: Research, Theory & Practice*, *21*(1), 105–118. https://doi.org/10.1177/1521025117690868

Puhl, R. M., Heuer, C. A., & Brownell, K. D. (2011). Stigma and social consequences of obesity. In P. G. Kopelman, I. D. Caterson, & W. H. Dietz (Eds.), *Clinical obesity in adults and children* (pp. 25–40). Wiley-Blackwell. https://doi.org/10.1002/9781444307627.CH3

Puhl, R. M., Himmelstein, M. S., & Pearl, R. L. (2020). Weight stigma as a psychosocial contributor to obesity. *The American Psychologist*, *75*(2), 274–289. https://doi.org/10.1037/amp0000538

Rabourn, K. E., BrckaLorenz, A., & Shoup, R. (2018). Reimagining student engagement: How nontraditional adult learners engage in traditional postsecondary environments. *Journal of Continuing Higher Education*, *66*(1), 22–33. https://doi.org/10.1080/07377363.2018.1415635

Radford, A. W., Cominole, M., & Skomsvold, P. (2015). Demographic and enrollment characteristics of nontraditional undergraduates: 2011-12. *Department of Education*. http://www.voced.edu.au/content/ngv:70505

Rao, M., Afshin, A., Singh, G., & Mozaffarian, D. (2013). Do healthier foods and diet patterns cost more than less healthy options? A systematic review and meta-analysis. *BMJ Open*, *3*(12), e004277. https://doi.org/10.1136/bmjopen-2013-004277

Reckdenwald, A., Ford, J. A., & Murray, B. N. (2016). Alcohol use in emerging adulthood: Can Moffitt's developmental theory help us understand binge drinking among college students? *Journal of Child & Adolescent Substance Abuse*, *25*(6), 497–503. https://doi.org/10.1080/1067828X.2015.1103347

Redman, L. M., Smith, S. R., Burton, J. H., Martin, C. K., Il'yasova, D., & Ravussin, E. (2018). Metabolic slowing and reduced oxidative damage with sustained caloric restriction support the rate of living and oxidative damage theories of aging. *Cell Metabolism, 27*(4). https://doi.org/10.1016/j.cmet.2018.02.019

Rehm, J. (2011). The risks associated with alcohol use and alcoholism. *Alcohol Research & Health: The Journal of the National Institute on Alcohol Abuse and Alcoholism, 34*(2), 135–143. https://doi.org/Fea-AR&H-65

Rhodes, R. E., Janssen, I., Bredin, S. S. D., Warburton, D. E. R., & Bauman, A. (2017). Physical activity: Health impact, prevalence, correlates and interventions. *Psychology & Health, 32*(8), 942–975. https://doi.org/10.1080/08870446.2017.1325486

Rimfeld, K., Ayorech, Z., Dale, P. S., Kovas, Y., & Plomin, R. (2016). Genetics affects choice of academic subjects as well as achievement. *Scientific Reports, 6*(1), 1–9. https://doi.org/10.1038/srep26373

Roberts, S. B., & Rosenberg, I. (2006). Nutrition and aging: Changes in the regulation of energy metabolism with aging. *Physiological Reviews, 86*(2), 651–667. https://doi.org/10.1152/physrev.00019.2005

Robinson, E., Boyland, E., Chisholm, A., Harrold, J., Maloney, N. G., Marty, L., Mead, B. R., Noonan, R., & Hardman, C. A. (2021). Obesity, eating behavior and physical activity during COVID-19 lockdown: A study of UK adults. *Appetite, 156*, 104853. https://doi.org/10.1016/j.appet.2020.104853

Robinson, E., Sutin, A., & Daly, M. (2017). Perceived weight discrimination mediates the prospective relation between obesity and depressive symptoms in U.S. and U.K. adults. *Health Psychology, 36*(2), 112–121. https://doi.org/10.1037/hea0000426

Roh, E., & Choi, K. M. (2020). Health consequences of sarcopenic obesity: A narrative review. *Frontiers in Endocrinology, 11*, 332. https://doi.org/10.3389/fendo.2020.00332

Rosenbaum, J. E., & Person, A. E. (2003). Beyond college for all: Policies and practices to improve transitions into college and jobs. *Professional School Counseling, 6*(4), 252.

Ross-Gordon, J. M. (2011). Research on adult learners: Supporting the needs of a student population that is no longer nontraditional. *Peer Review, 3*(1), 26–29. http://www.aacu.org/publications-research/periodicals/research-adult-learners-supporting-needs-student-population-no

RTI International. (2019a). *First-generation college students: Demographic characteristics and postsecondary enrollment.* https://firstgen.naspa.org/files/dmfile/FactSheet-01.pdf

RTI International. (2019b). *First-generation college students' employment.* https://firstgen.naspa.org/files/dmfile/FactSheet-04.pdf

Russo, M., Shteigman, A., & Carmeli, A. (2016). Workplace and family support and work–life balance: Implications for individual psychological availability and energy at work. *The Journal of Positive Psychology, 11*(2), 173–188. https://doi.org/10.1080/17439760.2015.1025424

Sanchez-Sanchez, J. L., Izquierdo, M., Carnicero-Carreño, J. A., García-García, F. J., & Rodríguez-Mañas, L. (2020). Physical activity trajectories, mortality, hospitalization, and disability in the Toledo study of healthy aging. *Journal of Cachexia, Sarcopenia and Muscle, 11*(4), 1007–1017. https://doi.org/10.1002/jcsm.12566

Sandoval, W. A., Greene, J. A., & Bråten, I. (2016). Understanding and promoting thinking about knowledge. *Review of Research in Education, 40*(1), 457–496. https://doi.org/10.3102/0091732X16669319

Sansone, V. A., & Tucker Segura, J. S. (2020). Exploring factors contributing to college success among student veteran transfers at a four-year university. *Review of Higher Education, 43*(3), 888–916. https://doi.org/10.1353/rhe.2020.0011

Schoon, I., & Polek, E. (2011). Teenage career aspirations and adult career attainment: The role of gender, social background and general cognitive ability. *International Journal of Behavioral Development, 35*(3), 210–217. https://doi.org/10.1177/0165025411398183

Schöttker, B., Brenner, H., Jansen, E. E. H., Gardiner, J., Peasey, A., Kubínová, R., Pająk, A., Topor-Madry, R., Tamosiunas, A., Saum, K.-U. K., Holleczek, B., Pikhart, H., Bobak, M., Barzilai, N., Huffman, D., Muzumdar, R., Bartke, A., Chung, H., Cesari, M., . . . Tosukhowong, P. (2015). Evidence for the free radical/oxidative stress theory of ageing from the CHANCES consortium: A meta-analysis of individual participant data. *BMC Medicine, 13*(1), 300. https://doi.org/10.1186/s12916-015-0537-7

Schuch, F. B., Bulzing, R. A., Meyer, J., Vancampfort, D., Firth, J., Stubbs, B., Grabovac, I., Willeit, P., Tavares, V. D. O., Calegaro, V. C., Deenik, J., López-Sánchez, G. F., Veronese, N., Caperchione, C. M., Sadarangani, K. P., Abufaraj, M., Tully, M. A., & Smith, L. (2020). Associations of moderate to vigorous physical activity and sedentary behavior with depressive and anxiety symptoms in self-isolating people during the COVID-19 pandemic: A cross-sectional survey in Brazil. *Psychiatry Research, 292*, 113339. https://doi.org/10.1016/j.psychres.2020.113339

Schuh-Huerta, S. M., Johnson, N. A., Rosen, M. P., Sternfeld, B., Cedars, M. I., & Reijo Pera, R. A. (2012). Genetic variants and environmental factors associated with hormonal markers of ovarian reserve in Caucasian and African American women. *Human Reproduction, 27*(2), 594–608. https://doi.org/10.1093/humrep/der391

Schulenberg, J. E., Johnston, L. D., O'malley, P. M., Bachman, J. G., Miech, R. A., & Patrick, M. E. (2020). *Monitoring the Future national survey results on drug use, 1975–2019: Vol. II, College students and adults ages 19–60.* http://www.monitoringthefuture.org//pubs/monographs/mtf-vol2_2019.pdf

Schwartz, R. (2017). Legalize marijuana without the smoke. *CMAJ, 189*(4), E137–E138. https://doi.org/10.1503/cmaj.161203

Shockley, K. M., Shen, W., DeNunzio, M. M., Arvan, M. L., & Knudsen, E. A. (2017). Disentangling the relationship between gender and work-family conflict: An integration of theoretical perspectives using meta-analytic methods. *Journal of Applied Psychology, 102*(12), 1601–1635. https://doi.org/10.1037/apl0000246

Silins, E., Horwood, L. J., Patton, G. C., Fergusson, D. M., Olsson, C. A., Hutchinson, D. M., Spry, E., Toumbourou, J. W., Degenhardt, L., Swift, W., Coffey, C., Tait, R. J., Letcher, P., Copeland, J., & Mattick, R. P. (2014). Young adult sequelae of adolescent cannabis use: An integrative analysis. *The Lancet Psychiatry, 1*(4), 286–293. https://doi.org/10.1016/S2215-0366(14)70307-4

Silventoinen, K., & Konttinen, H. (2020). Obesity and eating behavior from the perspective of twin and genetic research. *Neuroscience & Biobehavioral Reviews, 109*, 150–165. https://doi.org/10.1016/j.neubiorev.2019.12.012

Simons, J. S., Wills, T. A., & Neal, D. J. (2014). The many faces of affect: A multilevel model of drinking frequency/quantity and alcohol dependence symptoms among young adults. *Journal of Abnormal Psychology, 123*(3), 676–694. https://doi.org/10.1037/a0036926

Simons-Morton, B., Haynie, D., Liu, D., Chaurasia, A., Li, K., & Hingson, R. (2016). The effect of residence, school status, work status, and social influence on the prevalence of alcohol use among emerging adults. *Journal of Studies on Alcohol and Drugs, 77*(1), 121–132. https://doi.org/10.15288/JSAD.2016.77.121

Sinnott, J. D. (1998). *The development of logic in adulthood: Postformal thought and its applications*. Plenum.

Sinnott, J. D. (2003). Postformal thought adn adult development: Living in balance. In J. Demick & C. Andreoletti (Eds.), *Handbookof adult development* (pp. 221–238). Kluwer.

Sinnott, J. D., Hilton, S., Wood, M., & Douglas, D. (2020). Relating flow, mindfulness, cognitive flexibility, and postformal thought: Two studies. *Journal of Adult Development, 27*(1), 1–11. https://doi.org/10.1007/s10804-018-9320-2

Sirgy, M. J., & Lee, D. J. (2018). Work-life balance: An integrative review. *Applied Research in Quality of Life, 13*(1), 229–254. https://doi.org/10.1007/s11482-017-9509-8

Soneji, S., Barrington-Trimis, J. L., Wills, T. A., Leventhal, A. M., Unger, J. B., Gibson, L. A., Yang, J., Primack, B. A., Andrews, J. A., Miech, R. A., Spindle, T. R., Dick, D. M., Eissenberg, T., Hornik, R. C., Dang, R., & Sargent, J. D. (2017). Association between initial use of e-cigarettes and subsequent cigarette smoking among adolescents and young adults: A systematic review and meta-analysis. *JAMA Pediatrics, 171*(8), 788–797. https://doi.org/10.1001/jamapediatrics.2017.1488

Soria, K. M., & Johnson, M. (2017). High-impact educational practices and the development of college students' pluralistic outcomes. *College Student Affairs Journal, 35*(2), 100–116. https://doi.org/10.1353/csj.2017.0016

Speakman, J. R., & Mitchell, S. E. (2011). Caloric restriction. *Molecular Aspects of Medicine, 32*(3), 159–221. https://doi.org/10.1016/j.mam.2011.07.001

Spini, D., Jopp, D. S., Pin, S., & Stringhini, S. (2016). The multiplicity of aging: Lessons for theory and conceptual development from longitudinal studies. In V. L. Bengtson & R. Settersten (Eds.), *Handbook of theories of aging* (3rd ed., pp. 669–692). Springer. https://books.google.com/books?hl=en&lr=&id=xyUODAAAQBAJ&oi=fnd&pg=PP1&dq=Handbook+of+Theories+of+Aging&ots=HbrErnpUXd&sig=FEah_aZzSiPRBgKIwXVlbSnZ_os#v=onepage&q=Handbook of Theories of Aging&f=false

Spokane, A. R., & Cruza-Guet, M. C. (2005). Holland's theory of vocational personalities in work environments. In S. D. Brown & R. W. Lent (Eds.), *Career development and counseling: Putting theory and research to work* (pp. 24–41). John Wiley & Sons Inc.

Stahl, E., Ferguson, L., & Kienhues, D. (2016). Diverging information and epistemic change. In I. B. Jeffrey, A. Greene, & W. A. Sandoval (Eds.), *Handbook of epistemic cognition* (pp. 330–342). Routledge. https://doi.org/10.4324/9781315795225-30

Stavro, K., Pelletier, J., & Potvin, S. (2013). Widespread and sustained cognitive deficits in alcoholism: A meta-analysis. *Addiction Biology, 18*(2), 203–213. https://doi.org/10.1111/j.1369-1600.2011.00418.x

Stephens, N. M., Fryberg, S. A., Markus, H. R., Johnson, C. S., & Covarrubias, R. (2012). Unseen disadvantage: How American universities' focus on independence undermines the academic performance of first-generation college students. *Journal of Personality and Social Psychology, 102*(6), 1178–1197. https://doi.org/10.1037/a0027143

Stillman, C. M., Esteban-Cornejo, I., Brown, B., Bender, C. M., & Erickson, K. I. (2020). Effects of exercise on brain and cognition across age groups and health states. *Trends in Neurosciences, 43*(7). https://doi.org/10.1016/j.tins.2020.04.010

Substance Abuse and Mental Health Services Administration. (2014). *Results from the 2013 National Survey on Drug Use and Health: Summary of national findings*. http://www.samhsa.gov/data/sites/default/files/NSDUHresultsPDFWHTML2013/Web/NSDUHresults2013.pdf

Sue, D. W., Capodilupo, C. M., Torino, G. C., Bucceri, J. M., Holder, A. M. B., Nadal, K. L., & Esquilin, M. (2007). Racial microaggressions in everyday life: Implications for clinical practice. *American Psychologist, 62*(4), 271–286. https://doi.org/10.1037/0003-066X.62.4.271

Sumartiningsih, S., Lin, H.-F., & Lin, J.-C. (2019). Cigarette smoking blunts exercise-induced heart rate response among young adult male smokers. *International Journal of Environmental Research and Public Health, 16*(6), 1032. https://doi.org/10.3390/ijerph16061032

Super, D. E. (1990). A life-span, life-space approach to career development. In D. Brown & L. Brooks (Eds.), *Career choice and development: Applying contemporary theories to practice* (2nd ed., pp. 197–261). Jossey-Bass.

Syed, M. (2016). Emerging adulthood: Developmental stage, theory, or nonsense? In J. J. Arnett (Ed.), *The Oxford handbook of emerging adulthood* (pp. 11–25). Oxford University Press. https://doi.org/10.1093/oxfordhb/9780199795574.013.9

Symonds, W. C., Schwartz, R., & Ferguson, R. F. (2011). *Pathways to prosperity: Meeting the challenge of preparing young Americans*. http://www.sawdc.com/media/5959/pathways_to_prosperity_feb2011.pdf

Tan, W. C., & Sin, D. D. (2018). What are the long-term effects of smoked marijuana on lung health? *CMAJ, 190*(42), E1243–E1244. https://doi.org/10.1503/cmaj.181307

Tavolacci, M. P., Berthon, Q., Cerasuolo, D., Dechelotte, P., Ladner, J., & Baguet, A. (2019). Does binge drinking between the age of 18 and 25 years predict alcohol dependence in adulthood? A retrospective case-control study in France. *BMJ Open, 9*(5), e026375. https://doi.org/10.1136/bmjopen-2018-026375

Tchernof, A., & Després, J.-P. (2013). Pathophysiology of human visceral obesity: An update. *Physiological Reviews, 93*(1), 359–404. https://doi.org/10.1152/physrev.00033.2011

Terry-McElrath, Y. M., O'Malley, P. M., Johnston, L. D., & Schulenberg, J. E. (2019). Young adult longitudinal patterns of marijuana use among US National samples of 12th grade frequent marijuana users: A repeated-measures latent class analysis. *Addiction, 114*(6), 1035–1048. https://doi.org/10.1111/add.14548

Terry-McElrath, Y. M., Patrick, M. E., O'Malley, P. M., & Johnston, L. D. (2018). The end of convergence in developmental patterns of frequent marijuana use from ages 18 to 30: An analysis of cohort change from 1976–2016. *Drug and Alcohol Dependence, 191*, 203–209. https://doi.org/10.1016/j.drugalcdep.2018.07.002

Teychenne, M., White, R. L., Richards, J., Schuch, F. B., Rosenbaum, S., & Bennie, J. A. (2020). Do we need physical activity guidelines for mental health: What does the evidence tell us? *Mental Health and Physical Activity, 18*, 100315. https://doi.org/10.1016/j.mhpa.2019.100315

Tison, G. H., Avram, R., Kuhar, P., Abreau, S., Marcus, G. M., Pletcher, M. J., & Olgin, J. E. (2020). Worldwide effect of COVID-19 on physical activity: A descriptive study. *Annals of Internal Medicine, 173*(9), 767–770. https://doi.org/10.7326/M20-2665

Tobin, D. J. (2017). Introduction to skin aging. *Journal of Tissue Viability, 26*(1), 37–46. https://doi.org/10.1016/j.jtv.2016.03.002

Traboulsi, H., Cherian, M., Abou Rjeili, M., Preteroti, M., Bourbeau, J., Smith, B. M., Eidelman, D. H., & Baglole, C. J. (2020). Inhalation toxicology of vaping products and implications for pulmonary health. *International Journal of Molecular Sciences, 21*(10), 3495. https://doi.org/10.3390/ijms21103495

Triana, M. C., Jayasinghe, M., & Pieper, J. R. (2015). Perceived workplace racial discrimination and its correlates: A meta-analysis. *Journal of Organizational Behavior, 36*(4), 491–513. https://doi.org/10.1002/job.1988

Tuononen, T., Parpala, A., & Lindblom-Ylänne, S. (2019). Graduates' evaluations of usefulness of university education, and early career success–A longitudinal study of the transition to working life. *Assessment and Evaluation in Higher Education, 44*(4), 581–595. https://doi.org/10.1080/02602938.2018.1524000

Ulrich, S., & Freer, B. D. (2020). From the military to college and beyond: Growing a culturally sensitive program to support veteran success. *Journal of Clinical Psychology, 76*(5), 905–915. https://doi.org/10.1002/jclp.22925

United States Department of Health and Human Services. (2014). *National survey on drug use and health, 2013*. https://doi.org/10.3886/ICPSR35509.v1

Unsworth, S. J., Levin, W., Bang, M., Washinawatok, K., Waxman, S. R., & Medin, D. (2012). Cultural differences in children's ecological reasoning and psychological closeness to nature: Evidence from menominee and European American children. *Journal of Cognition and Culture, 12*(1–2), 17–29. https://doi.org/10.1163/156853712X633901

U.S. Bureau of Labor Statistics. (2015). *Labor force statistics from the current population survey: Employment status of the civilian noninstitutional population by age, sex, and race*. http://www.bls.gov/cps/cpsaat03.htm

US Bureau of Labor Statistics. (2016). *Median years of tenure with current employer for employed wage and salary workers by age and sex, selected years, 2006-16*.

U.S. Bureau of Labor Statistics. (2017). *Employment characteristics of families summary*. https://www.bls.gov/news.release/famee.nr0.htm

U.S. Bureau of Labor Statistics. (2019). *Number of jobs, labor market experience, and earnings growth: Results from a national longitudinal survey summary*. https://www.bls.gov/news.release/nlsoy.nr0.htm

U.S. Bureau of Labor Statistics. (2020a). *Employee tenure summary*. https://www.bls.gov/news.release/tenure.nr0.htm

U.S. Bureau of Labor Statistics. (2020b). Labor force characteristics by race and ethnicity, 2019: BLS reports: U.S. Bureau of Labor Statistics. *BLS Reports*. https://www.bls.gov/opub/reports/race-and-ethnicity/2019/home.htm

U.S. Bureau of Labor Statistics. (2020c). *Labor market activity, education, and partner status among Americans at age 33: Results from a longitudinal survey*. https://www.bls.gov/news.release/pdf/nlsyth.pdf

US Bureau of Labor Statistics. (2021). Employed persons by detailed occupation, sex, race, and Hispanic or Latino ethnicity. *Labor Force Statistics from the Current Population Survey*. https://www.bls.gov/cps/cpsaat11.htm

U.S. Department of Agriculture, & U.S. Department of Health and Human Services. (2020). *Dietary guidelines for Americans, 2020–2025*. Retrieved from https://www.dietaryguidelines.gov/sites/default/files/2020-12/Dietary_Guidelines_for_Americans_2020-2025.pdf

U.S. Department of Health and Human Services. (2014). *The health consequences of smoking—50 years of progress. A report of the surgeon general*. http://www.surgeongeneral.gov/library/reports/50-years-of-progress/

U.S. Department of Health and Human Services. (2018). *Physical activity guidelines for Americans* (2nd ed.). US Dept of Health and Human Services.

U.S. Department of Labor. (2020). Mothers and families. *U.S. Department of Labor*. https://www.dol.gov/agencies/wb/data/mothers-and-families

U.S. News & World Report. (2016). *Time & money*. https://mediakit.usnews.com/downloads/insights/USN_PartnerInsights_Strayer.pdf

Valko, M., Jomova, K., Rhodes, C. J., Kuča, K., & Musílek, K. (2016). Redox- and non-redox-metal-induced formation of free radicals and their role in human disease. *Archives of Toxicology, 90*(1), 1–37. https://doi.org/10.1007/s00204-015-1579-5

Van Houten, B., Santa-Gonzalez, G. A., & Camargo, M. (2018). DNA repair after oxidative stress: Current challenges. *Current Opinion in Toxicology, 7*, 9–16. https://doi.org/10.1016/J.COTOX.2017.10.009

Vasquez-Salgado, Y., Greenfield, P. M., & Burgos-Cienfuegos, R. (2015). Exploring home-school value conflicts. *Journal of Adolescent Research, 30*(3), 271–305. https://doi.org/10.1177/0743558414561297

Vella, C. A., Taylor, K., & Nelson, M. C. (2020). Associations of leisure screen time with cardiometabolic biomarkers in college-aged adults. *Journal of Behavioral Medicine, 43*(6), 1014–1025. https://doi.org/10.1007/s10865-020-00161-2

Villanti, A. C., Johnson, A. L., Rath, J. M., Williams, V., Vallone, D. M., Abrams, D. B., Hedeker, D., & Mermelstein, R. J. (2017). Identifying "social smoking" U.S. young adults using an empirically-driven approach. *Addictive Behaviors, 70*, 83–89. https://doi.org/10.1016/j.addbeh.2017.02.004

Vilorio, D. (2016). Earnings and unemployment rates by educational attacinment, 2015. *Career Outlook - US Bureau of Labor Statistics*. https://www.bls.gov/careeroutlook/2016/data-on-display/education-matters.htm

Walker, B. B., Shashank, A., Gasevic, D., Schuurman, N., Poirier, P., Teo, K., Rangarajan, S., Yusuf, S., & Lear, S. A. (2020). The local food environment and obesity: Evidence from three cities. *Obesity, 28*(1), 40–45. https://doi.org/10.1002/oby.22614

Ward, L., Siegel, M. J., & Davenport, Z. (2012). First generation college students: Understanding and improving the experience from recruitment to commencement. *Jossey-Bass*. http://psycnet.apa.org/record/2012-23668-000

Watson, T. L., & Blanchard-Fields, F. (1998). Thinking with your head and your heart: Age differences in everyday problem-solving strategy preferences. *Aging, Neuropsychology, and Cognition*, *5*(3), 225–240.

Wessel, R. D., Jones, J. A., Markle, L., & Westfall, C. (2009). Retention and graduation of students with disabilities: Facilitating student success. *Journal of Postsecondary Education and Disability*, *21*(3), 116–125. http://www.ahead.org/publications/jped

White, S. W., Elias, R., Salinas, C. E., Capriola, N., Conner, C. M., Asselin, S. B., Miyazaki, Y., Mazefsky, C. A., Howlin, P., & Getzel, E. E. (2016). Students with autism spectrum disorder in college: Results from a preliminary mixed methods needs analysis. *Research in Developmental Disabilities*, *56*, 29–40. https://doi.org/10.1016/j.ridd.2016.05.010

Wilbur, T. G. (2021). Stressed but not depressed: A longitudinal analysis of first-generation college students, stress, and depressive symptoms. *Social Forces*, *100*, 56–85. https://doi.org/10.1093/sf/soaa091

Williams, M. G., & Lewis, J. A. (2019). Gendered racial microaggressions and depressive symptoms among black women: A moderated mediation model. *Psychology of Women Quarterly*, *43*(3), 368–380. https://doi.org/10.1177/0361684319832511

Williams, M. T. (2020). Microaggressions: Clarification, evidence, and impact. *Perspectives on Psychological Science*, *15*(1), 3–26. https://doi.org/10.1177/1745691619827499

Windle, M. (2020). Maturing out of alcohol use in young adulthood: Latent class growth trajectories and concurrent young adult correlates. *Alcoholism: Clinical and Experimental Research*, *44*(2), 532–540. https://doi.org/10.1111/acer.14268

Winslow, S. (2005). Work-family conflict, gender, and parenthood, 1977-1997. *Journal of Family Issues*, *26*(6), 727–755. https://doi.org/10.1177/0192513X05277522

Witteveen, D., & Attewell, P. (2021). Delayed time-to-degree and post-college earnings. *Research in Higher Education*, *62*(2), 230–257. https://doi.org/10.1007/s11162-019-09582-8

Xi, H., Li, C., Ren, F., Zhang, H., & Zhang, L. (2013). Telomere, aging and age-related diseases. *Aging Clinical and Experimental Research*, *25*(2), 139–146. https://doi.org/10.1007/s40520-013-0021-1

Xu, Z., Duc, K. D., Holcman, D., & Teixeira, M. T. (2013). The length of the shortest telomere as the major determinant of the onset of replicative senescence. *Genetics*, *194*(4), 847–857. https://doi.org/10.1534/genetics.113.152322

Yamin, C. K., Bitton, A., & Bates, D. W. (2010). E-cigarettes: A rapidly growing Internet phenomenon. *Annals of Internal Medicine*, *153*(9), 607–609. https://doi.org/10.7326/0003-4819-153-9-201011020-00011

Yang, J., Hu, J., & Zhu, C. (2021). Obesity aggravates COVID-19: A systematic review and meta-analysis. *Journal of Medical Virology*, *93*(1), 257–261. https://doi.org/10.1002/jmv.26237

Zeidler, D. L., Sadler, T. D., Applebaum, S., & Callahan, B. E. (2009). Advancing reflective judgment through socioscientific issues. *Journal of Research in Science Teaching*, *46*(1), 74–101. https://doi.org/10.1002/tea.20281

Zhang, C., Brook, J. S., Leukefeld, C. G., & Brook, D. W. (2016). Trajectories of marijuana use from adolescence to adulthood as predictors of unemployment status in the early forties. *The American Journal on Addictions*, *25*(3), 203–209. https://doi.org/10.1111/ajad.12361

Zhang, L. (1999). A comparison of U.S. and Chinese University students' cognitive development: The cross-cultural applicability of Perry's theory. *Journal of Psychology*, *133*(4), 425–440.

Zhang, L. (2004). The Perry scheme: Across cultures, across approaches to the study of human psychology. *Journal of Adult Development*, *11*(2), 123–138.

Zheng, Y., Manson, J. E., Yuan, C., Liang, M. H., Grodstein, F., Stampfer, M. J., Willett, W. C., & Hu, F. B. (2017). Associations of weight gain from early to middle adulthood with major health outcomes later in life. *JAMA*, *318*(3), 255. https://doi.org/10.1001/jama.2017.7092

Ziegler, D. V., Wiley, C. D., & Velarde, M. C. (2015). Mitochondrial effectors of cellular senescence: Beyond the free radical theory of aging. *Aging Cell*, *14*(1), 1–7. https://doi.org/10.1111/acel.12287

CHAPTER 12

Acevedo, B. P., & Aron, A. (2009). Does a long-term relationship kill romantic love? *Review of General Psychology*, *13*(1), 59–65. https://doi.org/10.1037/a0014226

Adamczyk, K. (2017). Voluntary and involuntary singlehood and young adults' mental health: An investigation of mediating role of romantic loneliness. *Current Psychology*, *36*(4), 888–904. https://doi.org/10.1007/s12144-016-9478-3

Afifi, T. O., Cox, B. J., & Enns, M. W. (2006). Mental health profiles among married, never-married, and separated/divorced mothers in a nationally representative sample. *Social Psychiatry & Psychiatric Epidemiology*, *41*(2), 122–129. https://doi.org/10.1007/s00127-005-0005-3

Agüero, J. M. (2021). COVID-19 and the rise of intimate partner violence. *World Development*, *137*, 105217. https://doi.org/10.1016/j.worlddev.2020.105217

Ahmadabadi, Z., Najman, J. M., Williams, G. M., Clavarino, A. M., & D'Abbs, P. (2021). Gender differences in intimate partner violence in current and prior relationships. *Journal of Interpersonal Violence*, *36*(1–2), 915–937. https://doi.org/10.1177/0886260517730563

Amato, P. R. (2010). Research on divorce: Continuing trends and new developments. *Journal of Marriage & Family*, *72*(3), 650–666. https://doi.org/10.1111/j.1741-3737.2010.00723.x

Amato, P. R., & Irving, S. (2006). Historical trends in divorce in the United States. In M. A. Fine & J. H. Harvey (Eds.), *Handbook of divorce and relationship dissolution* (pp. 41–57). Lawrence Erlbaum Associates Publishers.

Amato, P. R., & Sobolewski, J. M. (2004). The effects of divorce on fathers and children: Nonresidential fathers and stepfathers. In M. E. Lamb (Ed.), *The role of the father in child development* (4th ed., pp. 341–367). John Wiley & Sons Inc.

Anderson, J. W. (2016). Sternberg's triangular theory of love. In C. L. Shehan (Ed.), *Encyclopedia of family studies* (pp. 1–3). John Wiley & Sons, Inc. https://doi.org/10.1002/9781119085621.wbefs058

Andrews, J. A., & Westling, E. (2016). Substance use in emerging adulthood. In J. J. Arnett (Ed.), *The Oxford handbook of emerging adulthood* (Vol. 1). Oxford University Press. https://doi.org/10.1093/oxfordhb/9780199795574.013.20

Arnett, J. J. (2003). Conceptions of the transition to adulthood among emerging adults in American ethnic groups. *New Directions for Child & Adolescent Development, 2003*(100), 63–76.

Arnett, J. J. (2016a). Identity development from adolescence to emerging adulthood. In K. C. McLean & M. Syed (Eds.), *The Oxford handbook of identity development* (pp. 53–64). Oxford University Press. https://doi.org/10.1093/oxfordhb/9780199936564.013.009

Arnett, J. J. (2016c). *The Oxford handbook of emerging adulthood* (Vol. 1). Oxford University Press. https://doi.org/10.1093/oxfordhb/9780199795574.001.0001

Arnett, J. J. (2019). Conceptual foundations of emerging adulthood. In J. J. Arnett & J. L. Murray (Eds.), *Emerging adulthood and higher education: A new student development paradigm* (pp. 11–24). Routledge.

Arnett, J. J., & Mitra, D. (2018). Are the features of emerging adulthood developmentally distinctive? A comparison of ages 18–60 in the United States. *Emerging Adulthood, 8*, 412–419. https://doi.org/10.1177/2167696818810073

Arnett, J. J., & Mitra, D. (2020). Are the features of emerging adulthood developmentally distinctive? A comparison of ages 18–60 in the United States. *Emerging Adulthood, 8*(5), 412–419. https://doi.org/10.1177/2167696818810073

Arnett, J. J., & Padilla-Walker, L. M. (2015). Brief report: Danish emerging adults' conceptions of adulthood. *Journal of Adolescence, 38*, 39–44. https://doi.org/10.1016/J.ADOLESCENCE.2014.10.011

Arnett, J. J., & Schwab, J. (2012). *The Clark University poll of emerging adults: Thriving, struggling, and hopeful.* http://www2.clarku.edu/clark-poll-emerging-adults/pdfs/clark-university-poll-emerging-adults-findings.pdf

Arnett, J. J., Žukauskienė, R., & Sugimura, K. (2014). The new life stage of emerging adulthood at ages 18–29 years: Implications for mental health. *The Lancet Psychiatry, 1*(7), 569–576. https://doi.org/10.1016/S2215-0366(14)00080-7

Ascigil, E., Wardecker, B. M., Chopik, W. J., & Edelstein, R. S. (2021). Division of baby care in heterosexual and lesbian parents: Expectations versus reality. *Journal of Marriage and Family, 83*(2), 584–594. https://doi.org/10.1111/jomf.12729

Avison, M., & Furnham, A. (2015). Personality and voluntary childlessness. *Journal of Population Research, 32*(1), 45–67. https://doi.org/10.1007/s12546-014-9140-6

Aykutoğlu, B., & Uysal, A. (2017). The relationship between intimacy change and passion: A dyadic diary study. *Frontiers in Psychology, 8*, 2257. https://doi.org/10.3389/fpsyg.2017.02257

Bahns, A. J. (2019). Preference, opportunity, and choice: A multilevel analysis of diverse friendship formation. *Group Processes & Intergroup Relations, 22*, 233–252. https://doi.org/10.1177/1368430217725390

Baranowska-Rataj, A., Matysiak, A., & Mynarska, M. (2013). Does lone motherhood decrease women's happiness? Evidence from qualitative and quantitative research. *Journal of Happiness Studies, 15*(6), 1457–1477. https://doi.org/10.1007/s10902-013-9486-z

Barrett, B. J. (2015). *Domestic violence in the LGBT community.* NASW Press and Oxford University Press. https://doi.org/10.1093/acrefore/9780199975839.013.1133

Barry, C. M., Madsen, S. D., Nelson, L. J., Carroll, J. S., & Badger, S. (2009). Friendship and romantic relationship qualities in emerging adulthood: Differential associations with identity development and achieved adulthood criteria. *Journal of Adult Development, 16*(4), 209–222. https://doi.org/10.1007/s10804-009-9067-x

Bartel, S. J., Sherry, S. B., Molnar, D. S., Mushquash, A. R., Leonard, K. E., Flett, G. L., & Stewart, S. H. (2017). Do romantic partners influence each other's heavy episodic drinking? Support for the partner influence hypothesis in a three-year longitudinal study. *Addictive Behaviors, 69*, 55–58. https://doi.org/10.1016/J.ADDBEH.2017.01.020

Batalova, J. A., & Cohen, P. N. (2002). Premarital cohabitation and housework: Couples in cross-national perspective. *Journal of Marriage & Family, 64*(3), 743–755.

Baumbusch, J. L. (2004). Unclaimed treasures: Older women's reflections on lifelong singlehood. *Journal of Women & Aging, 16*(1/2), 105–121.

Bendall, C. (2010). The domestic violence epidemic in South Africa: Legal and practical remedies. *Women's Studies, 39*(2), 100–118. https://doi.org/10.1080/00497870903459275

Berkman, L. F., Zheng, Y., Glymour, M. M., Avendano, M., Börsch-Supan, A., & Sabbath, E. L. (2015). Mothering alone: Cross-national comparisons of later-life disability and health among women who were single mothers. *Journal of Epidemiology and Community Health, 69*(9), 865–872. https://doi.org/10.1136/jech-2014-205149

Bernardi, L., & Mortelmans, D. (2018). *Lone parenthood in the life course* (Vol. 8). Springer International Publishing. https://doi.org/10.1007/978-3-319-63295-7

Bersamin, M. M., Zamboanga, B. L., Schwartz, S. J., Donnellan, M. B., Hudson, M., Weisskirch, R. S., Kim, S. Y., Agocha, V. B., Whitbourne, S. K., & Caraway, S. J. (2014). Risky business: Is there an association between casual sex and mental health among emerging adults? *The Journal of Sex Research, 51*(1), 43–51. https://doi.org/10.1080/00224499.2013.772088

Beyer, K., Wallis, A. B., & Hamberger, L. K. (2015). Neighborhood environment and intimate partner violence. *Trauma, Violence, & Abuse, 16*(1), 16–47. https://doi.org/10.1177/1524838013515758

Beyers, W., & Seiffge-Krenke, I. (2010). Does identity precede intimacy? Testing Erikson's theory on romantic development in emerging adults of the 21st century. *Journal of Adolescent Research, 25*(3), 387–415. https://doi.org/10.1177/0743558410361370

Björkenstam, E., Hallqvist, J., Dalman, C., & Ljung, R. (2013). Risk of new psychiatric episodes in the year following divorce in midlife: Cause or selection? A nationwide register-based study of 703,960 individuals. *The International Journal of Social Psychiatry, 59*(8), 801–804. https://doi.org/10.1177/0020764012461213

Bleidorn, W., Buyukcan-Tetik, A., Schwaba, T., van Scheppingen, M. A., Denissen, J. J. A., & Finkenauer, C. (2016). Stability and change in self-esteem during the transition to parenthood. *Social Psychological and Personality Science, 7*(6), 560–569. https://doi.org/10.1177/1948550616646428

Bookwala, J., & Jacobs, J. (2004). Age, marital processes, and depressed affect. *Gerontologist, 44*(3), 328–338.

Bos, H. M. W., Kuyper, L., & Gartrell, N. K. (2018). A population-based comparison of female and male same-sex parent and different-sex parent households. *Family Process, 57*(1), 148–164. https://doi.org/10.1111/famp.12278

Bourassa, K. J., Sbarra, D. A., & Whisman, M. A. (2015). Women in very low quality marriages gain life satisfaction following divorce. *Journal of Family Psychology, 29*(3), 490–499. https://doi.org/10.1037/fam0000075

Bowen, E., Ball, A., Jones, A. S., & Miller, B. (2021). Toward many emerging adulthoods: A theory-based examination of the features of emerging adulthood for cross-systems youth. *Emerging Adulthood, 9*, 189–201. https://doi.org/10.1177/2167696821989123

Boyle, M. H., Georgiades, K., Cullen, J., & Racine, Y. (2009). Community influences on intimate partner violence in India: Women's education, attitudes towards mistreatment and standards of living. *Social Science & Medicine, 69*(5), 691–697. https://doi.org/10.1016/j.socscimed.2009.06.039

Brandel, M., Melchiorri, E., & Ruini, C. (2018). The dynamics of eudaimonic well-being in the transition to parenthood: Differences between fathers and mothers. *Journal of Family Issues, 39*, 2572–2589. https://doi.org/10.1177/0192513X18758344

Breiding, M. J., Chen, J., & Black, M. C. (2014). *Intimate partner violence in the United States - 2010*. https://www.ncjrs.gov/App/Publications/abstract.aspx?ID=267363

Breiding, M. J., Smith, S. G., Basile, K. C., Walters, M. L., Chen, J., & Merrick, M. T. (2014). Prevalence and Characteristics of sexual violence, stalking, and intimate partner violence victimization — National intimate partner and sexual violence survey, United States, 2011. *Morbidity and Mortality Weekly Report, 63*(SS08), 1–18. https://www.cdc.gov/mmwr/preview/mmwrhtml/ss6308a1.htm

Brewster, M. E. (2017). Lesbian women and household labor division: A systematic review of scholarly research from 2000 to 2015. *Journal of Lesbian Studies, 21*(1), 47–69. https://doi.org/10.1080/10894160.2016.1142350

Buggs, S. G. (2017). Does (mixed-)race matter? The role of race in interracial sex, dating, and marriage. *Sociology Compass, 11*(11), e12531. https://doi.org/10.1111/soc4.12531

Busch, H., & Hofer, J. (2012). Self-regulation and milestones of adult development: Intimacy and generativity. *Developmental Psychology, 48*(1), 282–293. https://doi.org/10.1037/a0025521

Butters, R. P., Droubay, B. A., Seawright, J. L., Tollefson, D. R., Lundahl, B., & Whitaker, L. (2021). Intimate partner violence perpetrator treatment: Tailoring interventions to individual needs. *Clinical Social Work Journal, 49*, 391–404. https://doi.org/10.1007/s10615-020-00763-y

Cao, H., Zhou, N., Fine, M., Liang, Y., Li, J., & Mills-Koonce, W. R. (2017). Sexual minority stress and same-sex relationship well-being: A meta-analysis of research prior to the U.S. Nationwide Legalization of Same-Sex Marriage. *Journal of Marriage and Family, 79*(5), 1258–1277. https://doi.org/10.1111/jomf.12415

Carey, K. B., Norris, A. L., Durney, S. E., Shepardson, R. L., & Carey, M. P. (2018). Mental health consequences of sexual assault among first-year college women. *Journal of American College Health, 66*, 480–486. https://doi.org/10.1080/07448481.2018.1431915

Carpenter, C., Eppink, S., Gonzales, G. J., & McKay, T. (2021). *Effects of access to legal same-sex marriage on marriage and health. Journal of Policy Analysis and Management, 40*(2), 376–411. https://doi.org/10.1002/pam.22286

Caspi, A., Herbener, E. S., & Ozer, D. J. (1992). Shared experiences and the similarity of personalities: A longitudinal study of married couples. *Journal of Personality and Social Psychology, 62*(2), 281–291. https://doi.org/10.1037/0022-3514.62.2.281

Centers for Disease Control and Prevention. (2018). *The National intimate partner and sexual violence survey: 2015 data brief — Updated release*. https://stacks.cdc.gov/view/cdc/60893

Central Intelligence Agency. (2021). Total fertility rate. *The World Factbook*. https://www.cia.gov/the-world-factbook/field/total-fertility-rate/country-comparison

Chang, A., & Simmons-Duffin, S. (2017). Same-sex spouses turn to adoption to protect parental rights: NPR. *NPR: All Things Considered*. https://www.npr.org/2017/09/22/551814731/same-sex-spouses-turn-to-adoption-to-protect-parental-rights

Chen, S., & van Ours, J. C. (2018). Subjective well-being and partnership dynamics: Are same-sex relationships different? *Demography, 55*(6), 2299–2320. https://doi.org/10.1007/s13524-018-0725-0

Cherlin, A. J. (2013). Health, marriage, and same-sex partnerships. *Journal of Health and Social Behavior, 54*(1), 64–66. https://doi.org/10.1177/0022146512474430

Church, E. (2004). *Understanding stepmothers: Women share their struggles, successes, and insights*. Harper Collins.

Chzhen, Y., & Bradshaw, J. (2012). Lone parents, poverty and policy in the European Union. *Journal of European Social Policy, 22*(5), 487–506. https://doi.org/10.1177/0958928712456578

Claxton, S., & Van Dulmen, M. (2016). Casual sexual relationships and experiences in emerging adulthood. In J. J. Arnett (Ed.), *The oxford handbook of emerging adulthood* (pp. 245–261). Oxford University Press. https://doi.org/10.1093/oxfordhb/9780199795574.013.002

Cohen, P., Kasen, S., Chen, H., Hartmark, C., & Gordon, K. (2003). Variations in patterns of developmental transitions in the emerging adulthood period. *Developmental Psychology, 39*(4), 657. http://www.ncbi.nlm.nih.gov/pubmed/12859120

Collins, A., & van Dulmen, M. (2006). Friendships and romance in emerging adulthood: Assessing distinctiveness in close relationships. In J. J. Arnett & J. L. Tanner (Eds.), *Emerging adults in America: Coming of age in the 21st century* (pp. 219–234). American Psychological Association.

Copen, C. E., Daniels, K., & Mosher, W. D. (2013). First premarital cohabitation in the United States: 2006–2010 National survey of family growth. *National Health Statistics Reports, 64*, 1–15. http://bibliobase.sermais.pt:8008/BiblioNET/Upload/PDF3/002491.pdf

Copen, C. E., Daniels, K., Vespa, J., Mosher, W. D., Daniels, K., Vespa, J., & Mosher, W. D. (2012). First marriages in the United States: Data from the 2006–2010 national survey of family growth. *National Health Statistics Reports, 49*(49), 1–21. http://www.ncbi.nlm.nih.gov/pubmed/22803221

Copp, J. E., Giordano, P. C., Manning, W. D., & Longmore, M. A. (2016). Couple-level economic and career concerns and intimate partner violence in young adulthood. *Journal of Marriage and the Family, 78*(3), 744–758. https://doi.org/10.1111/jomf.12282

Côté, J. E. (2014). The dangerous myth of emerging adulthood: An evidence-based critique of a flawed developmental theory. *Applied Developmental Science, 18*(4), 177–188. http://www.tandfonline.com/doi/abs/10.1080/10888691.2014.954451#.VTOQ7JMug8Q

Damaske, S., Bratter, J. L., & Frech, A. (2017). Single mother families and employment, race, and poverty in changing economic times. *Social Science Research, 62*, 120–133. https://doi.org/10.1016/j.ssresearch.2016.08.008

David-Barrett, T., Rotkirch, A., Carney, J., Behncke Izquierdo, I., Krems, J. A., Townley, D., McDaniell, E., Byrne-Smith, A., & Dunbar, R. I. M. (2015). Women favour dyadic relationships, but men prefer clubs: Cross-cultural evidence from social networking. *PLoS One, 10*(3), e0118329. https://doi.org/10.1371/journal.pone.0118329

Debrot, A., Meuwly, N., Muise, A., Impett, E. A., & Schoebi, D. (2017). More than just sex. *Personality and Social Psychology Bulletin, 43*(3), 287–299. https://doi.org/10.1177/0146167216684124

de Guzman, N. S., & Nishina, A. (2017). 50 years of loving: Interracial romantic relationships and recommendations for future research. *Journal of Family Theory & Review, 9*(4), 557–571. https://doi.org/10.1111/jftr.12215

DeLongis, A., & Zwicker, A. (2017). Marital satisfaction and divorce in couples in stepfamilies. *Current Opinion in Psychology, 13*, 158–161. https://www.sciencedirect.com/science/article/pii/S2352250X16301932

DePaulo, B. (2014). A singles studies perspective on mount marriage. *Psychological Inquiry, 25*(1), 64–68. https://doi.org/10.1080/1047840X.2014.878173

Devries, K. M., Mak, J. Y. T., García-Moreno, C., Petzold, M., Child, J. C., Falder, G., Lim, S., Bacchus, L. J., Engell, R. E., Rosenfeld, L., Pallitto, C., Vos, T., Abrahams, N., & Watts, C. H. (2013). Global health. The global prevalence of intimate partner violence against women. *Science (New York, N.Y.), 340*(6140), 1527–1528. https://doi.org/10.1126/science.1240937

Dew, J., Britt, S., & Huston, S. (2012). Examining the relationship between financial issues and divorce. *Family Relations, 61*(4), 615–628. https://doi.org/10.1111/j.1741-3729.2012.00715.x

Dion, K. L., & Dion, K. K. (1993). Gender and ethnocultural comparisons in styles of love. *Psychology of Women Quarterly, 17*(4), 463–473.

Don, B. P., & Mickelson, K. D. (2014). Relationship satisfaction trajectories across the transition to parenthood among low-risk parents. *Journal of Marriage and Family, 76*(3), 677–692. https://doi.org/10.1111/jomf.12111

Doodson, L. J. (2014). Understanding the factors related to stepmother anxiety: A qualitative approach. *Journal of Divorce & Remarriage, 55*(8), 645–667. https://doi.org/10.1080/10502556.2014.959111

Doss, B. D., & Rhoades, G. K. (2017). The transition to parenthood: Impact on couples' romantic relationships. *Current Opinion in Psychology, 13*, 25–28. https://doi.org/10.1016/J.COPSYC.2016.04.003

Dribe, M., & Stanfors, M. (2009). Does parenthood strengthen a traditional household division of labor? Evidence from Sweden. *Journal of Marriage & Family, 71*(1), 33–45. https://doi.org/10.1111/j.1741-3737.2008.00578.x

du Bois-Reymond, M. (2016). Emerging adulthood theory and social class. In J. J. Arnett (Ed.), *The Oxford handbook of emerging adulthood* (Vol. 1). Oxford University Press. https://doi.org/10.1093/oxfordhb/9780199795574.013.37

Dworkin, E. R., Ullman, S. E., Stappenbeck, C., Brill, C. D., & Kaysen, D. (2018). Proximal relationships between social support and PTSD symptom severity: A daily diary study of sexual assault survivors. *Depression and Anxiety, 35*(1), 43–49. https://doi.org/10.1002/da.22679

Edwards, K. M., Sylaska, K. M., & Neal, A. M. (2015). Intimate partner violence among sexual minority populations: A critical review of the literature and agenda for future research. *Psychology of Violence, 5*(2), 112–121.

Eickmeyer, K. J. (2019). Cohort trends in union dissolution during young adulthood. *Journal of Marriage and Family, 81*(3), 760–770. https://doi.org/10.1111/jomf.12552

Eickmeyer, K. J., & Manning, W. D. (2018). Serial cohabitation in young adulthood: Baby boomers to millennials. *Journal of Marriage and Family, 80*(4), 826–840. https://doi.org/10.1111/jomf.12495

Eisenberg, M. E., Spry, E., & Patton, G. C. (2015). From emerging to established: Longitudinal patterns in the timing of transition events among Australian emerging adults. *Emerging Adulthood, 3*(4), 277–281. https://doi.org/10.1177/2167696815574639

Ellerbe, C. Z., Jones, J. B., & Carlson, M. J. (2018). Race/ethnic differences in nonresident fathers' involvement after a nonmarital birth*. *Social Science Quarterly, 99*(3), 1158–1182. https://doi.org/10.1111/ssqu.12482

Emezue, C. (2020). Digital or digitally delivered responses to domestic and intimate partner violence during COVID-19. *JMIR Public Health and Surveillance, 6*(3), e19831. https://doi.org/10.2196/19831

Eng, S., Li, Y., Mulsow, M., & Fischer, J. (2010). Domestic violence against women in Cambodia: Husband's control, frequency of spousal discussion, and domestic violence reported by Cambodian Women. *Journal of Family Violence, 25*(3), 237–246. https://doi.org/10.1007/s10896-009-9287-7

Erikson, E. H. (1950). *Childhood and society* (2nd ed.). Norton.

Eriksson, P. L., Wängqvist, M., Carlsson, J., & Frisén, A. (2020). Identity development in early adulthood. *Developmental Psychology, 56*(10), 1968–1983. https://doi.org/10.1037/dev0001093

Facio, A., & Micocci, F. (2003). Emerging adulthood in Argentina. In J. J Arnett & N. L. Galambos (Eds.), *New directions in child development: Exploring cultural conceptions ofthe transition to adulthood* (Vol. 100, pp. 21–31). Jossey-Bass.

Farr, R. H., Bruun, S. T., & Patterson, C. J. (2019). Longitudinal associations between coparenting and child adjustment among lesbian, gay, and heterosexual adoptive parent families. *Developmental Psychology, 55*, 2547–2560. https://doi.org/10.1037/dev0000828

Fedewa, A. L., Black, W. W., & Ahn, S. (2014). Children and adolescents with same-gender parents: A meta-analytic approach in assessing outcomes. *Journal of GLBT Family Studies, 11*(1), 1–34. https://doi.org/10.1080/1550428X.2013.869486

Feliciano, C., & Rumbaut, R. G. (2018). Varieties of ethnic self-identities: Children of immigrants in middle adulthood. *RSF, 4*(5), 26–46. https://doi.org/10.7758/rsf.2018.4.5.02

Feliciano, C., & Rumbaut, R. G. (2019). The evolution of ethnic identity from adolescence to middle adulthood: The case of the immigrant second generation. *Emerging Adulthood*, *7*(2), 85–96. https://doi.org/10.1177/2167696818805342

Finer, L. B., & Zolna, M. R. (2016). Declines in unintended pregnancy in the United States, 2008–2011. *New England Journal of Medicine*, *374*(9), 843–852. https://doi.org/10.1056/nejmsa1506575

Fletcher, G. J. O., Kerr, P. S. G., Li, N. P., & Valentine, K. A. (2014). Predicting romantic interest and decisions in the very early stages of mate selection. *Personality and Social Psychology Bulletin*, *40*(4), 540–550. https://doi.org/10.1177/0146167213519481

Frejka, T. (2017). Childlessness in the United States. In M. Kreyenfeld & D. Konietzka (Eds.), *Childlessness in Europe: Contexts, causes, and consequences* (pp. 159–179). Springer. https://doi.org/10.1007/978-3-319-44667-7_8

Frost, D. M., Meyer, I. H., & Hammack, P. L. (2015). Health and well-being in emerging adults' same-sex relationships: Critical questions and directions for research in developmental science. *Emerging Adulthood (Print)*, *3*(1), 3–13. https://doi.org/10.1177/2167696814535915

Gadassi, R., Bar-Nahum, L. E., Newhouse, S., Anderson, R., Heiman, J. R., Rafaeli, E., & Janssen, E. (2016). Perceived partner responsiveness mediates the association between sexual and marital satisfaction: A daily diary study in newlywed couples. *Archives of Sexual Behavior*, *45*, 109–120. https://doi.org/10.1007/s10508-014-0448-2

Galatzer-Levy, I. R., Mazursky, H., Mancini, A. D., & Bonanno, G. A. (2011). What we don't expect when expecting: Evidence for heterogeneity in subjective well-being in response to parenthood. *Journal of Family Psychology*, *25*(3), 384–392. https://doi.org/10.1037/a0023759

Ganong, L., Jensen, T., Sanner, C., Russell, L., Coleman, M., & Chapman, A. (2019). Linking Stepfamily functioning, marital quality, and steprelationship quality. *Family Relations*, *68*(4), 469–483. https://doi.org/10.1111/fare.12380

Gao, G. (2001). Intimacy, passion and commitment in Chinese and US American romantic relationships. *International Journal of Intercultural Relations*, *25*(3), 329–342.

Garcia, J. R., Reiber, C., Massey, S. G., & Merriwether, A. M. (2012). Sexual hookup culture: A review. *Review of General Psychology*, *16*(2), 161–176. https://doi.org/10.1037/a0027911

Gartrell, N., & Bos, H. (2010). US National longitudinal lesbian family study: Psychological adjustment of 17-year-old adolescents. *Pediatrics*, *126*(1), 28–36. https://doi.org/10.1542/peds2009-3153

Gato, J., Santos, S., & Fontaine, A. M. (2017). To have or not to have children? That is the question. Factors influencing parental decisions among lesbians and gay men. *Sexuality Research and Social Policy*, *14*(3), 310–323. https://doi.org/10.1007/s13178-016-0268-3

Gillespie, B. J., Lever, J., Frederick, D., & Royce, T. (2015). Close adult friendships, gender, and the life cycle. *Journal of Social and Personal Relationships*, *32*(6), 709–736. https://doi.org/10.1177/0265407514546977

Giordano, P. C., Manning, W. D., Longmore, M. A., & Flanigan, C. M. (2012). Developmental shifts in the character of romantic and sexual relationships from adolescence to young adulthood. In A. Booth, S. L. Brown, N. S. Landale, W. D. Manning, & S. M. McHale (Eds.), *Early adulthood in a family context* (pp. 133–164). Springer. https://doi.org/10.1007/978-1-4614-1436-0_9

Goldberg, A. E., Downing, J. B., & Moyer, A. M. (2012). Why parenthood, and why now?: Gay men's motivations for pursuing parenthood. *Family Relations*, *61*(1), 157–174. http://www.ncbi.nlm.nih.gov/pubmed/22563135

Goldberg, S. K., & Conron, K. L. (2018). How many same-sex couples in the US are raising children?. *Williams Institute*. https://williamsinstitute.law.ucla.edu/publications/same-sex-parents-us/

Goldsen, J., Bryan, A. E. B., Kim, H.-J., Muraco, A., Jen, S., & Fredriksen-Goldsen, K. I. (2017). Who says i do: The changing context of marriage and health and quality of life for LGBT older adults. *The Gerontologist*, *57*(Suppl. 1), S50–S62. https://doi.org/10.1093/geront/gnw174

Gonzaga, G. C., Campos, B., & Bradbury, T. (2007). Similarity, convergence, and relationship satisfaction in dating and married couples. *Journal of Personality and Social Psychology*, *93*(1), 34–48.

Gosangi, B., Park, H., Thomas, R., Gujrathi, R., Bay, C. P., Raja, A. S., Seltzer, S. E., Balcom, M. C., McDonald, M. L., Orgill, D. P., Harris, M. B., Boland, G. W., Rexrode, K., & Khurana, B. (2021). Exacerbation of physical intimate partner violence during COVID-19 pandemic. *Radiology*, *298*(1), E38–E45. https://doi.org/10.1148/radiol.2020202866

Gottman, J., & Gottman, J. (2017). The natural principles of love. *Journal of Family Theory & Review*, *9*(1), 7–26. https://doi.org/10.1111/jftr.12182

Graham, J. M. (2011). Measuring love in romantic relationships: A meta-analysis. *Journal of Social and Personal Relationships*, *28*(6), 748–771. https://doi.org/10.1177/0265407510389126

Grandgenett, H. M., Steel, A. L., Brock, R. L., & DiLillo, D. (2021). Responding to disclosure of sexual assault: The potential impact of victimization history and rape myth acceptance. *Journal of Interpersonal Violence*. https://doi.org/10.1177/0886260519898429

Greenstein, T. N. (2009). National context, family satisfaction, and fairness in the division of household labor. *Journal of Marriage & Family*, *71*(4), 1039–1051. https://doi.org/10.1111/j.1741-3737.2009.00651.x

Grover, S., & Helliwell, J. F. (2014). *How's life at home? New evidence on marriage and the set point for happiness*. http://www.nber.org/papers/w20794

Guzzo, K. B. (2014). Trends in cohabitation outcomes: Compositional changes and engagement among never-married young adults. *Journal of Marriage and the Family*, *76*(4), 826–842. https://doi.org/10.1111/jomf.12123

Hadley, R., & Hanley, T. (2011). Involuntarily childless men and the desire for fatherhood. *Journal of Reproductive and Infant Psychology*, *29*(1), 56–68. https://doi.org/10.1080/02646838.2010.544294

Hall, J. A. (2016). Same-sex friendships. In C. R Berger, M. E Roloff, S. R Wilson, J. P. Dillard, J. Caughlin, & D. Solomon (Eds.), *The International encyclopedia of interpersonal communication* (pp. 1–8). John Wiley & Sons, Inc. https://doi.org/10.1002/9781118540190.wbeic138

Hanzal, A., & Segrin, C. (2009). The role of conflict resolution styles in mediating the relationship between enduring vulnerabilities and marital quality. *Journal of Family Communication*, *9*(3), 150–169. https://doi.org/10.1080/15267430902945612

Härkönen, J. (2015). Divorce. In J. Treas, J. Scott, & M. Richards (Eds.), *The Wiley Blackwell companion to the sociology of families* (pp. 303–322). Wiley-Blackwell.

Harris, E. A. (2017). Same-sex parents still face legal complications. *New York Times*. https://www.nytimes.com/2017/06/20/us/gay-pride-lgbtq-same-sex-parents.html

Hartup, W. W., & Stevens, N. (1999). Friendships and adaptation across the life span. *Current Directions in Psychological Science*, *8*, 76–79.

Hatzenbuehler, M. L. (2014). Structural stigma and the health of lesbian, gay, and bisexual populations. *Current Directions in Psychological Science*, *23*(2), 127–132. https://doi.org/10.1177/0963721414523775

Helms, H. M., Walls, J. K., Crouter, A. C., & McHale, S. M. (2010). Provider role attitudes, marital satisfaction, role overload, and housework: A dyadic approach. *Journal of Family Psychology: JFP:. Journal of the Division of Family Psychology of the American Psychological Association (Division 43)*, *24*(5), 568–577. https://doi.org/10.1037/a0020637

Hendrick, C., & Hendrick, S. S. (2004). Sex and romantic love: Connects and disconnects. In J. H. Harvey, A. Wenzel, & S. Sprecher (Eds.), *The handbook of sexuality in close relationships* (pp. 159–182). Lawrence Erlbaum Associates Publishers.

Hendry, L. B., & Kloep, M. (2010). How universal is emerging adulthood? An empirical example. *Journal of Youth Studies*, *13*(2), 169–179. https://doi.org/10.1080/13676260903295067

Hennon, C. B., Hildenbrand, B., & Schedle, A. (2008). Stepfamilies and children. In T. P. Gullotta & G. M. Blau (Eds.), *Family influences on childhood behavior and development: Evidence-based prevention and treatment approaches* (pp. 161–185). Routledge/Taylor & Francis Group.

Henrich, J., Heine, S. J., & Norenzayan, A. (2010). The weirdest people in the world? *Behavioral and Brain Sciences*, *33*(2–3), 61–83. https://doi.org/10.1017/S0140525X0999152X

Herbenick, D., Reece, M., Schick, V., Sanders, S. A., Dodge, B., & Fortenberry, J. D. (2010). Sexual behavior in the United States: Results from a national probability sample of men and women ages 14–94. *The Journal of Sexual Medicine*, *7*(Suppl. 5), 255–265. https://doi.org/10.1111/J.1743-6109.2010.02012.X

Hiekel, N., Liefbroer, A. C., & Poortman, A.-R. (2014). Understanding diversity in the meaning of cohabitation across Europe. *European Journal of Population*, *30*(4), 391–410. https://doi.org/10.1007/s10680-014-9321-1

Hock, R. (2015). *Human sexuality*. Pearson.

Holt, L. J., Mattanah, J. F., & Long, M. W. (2018). Change in parental and peer relationship quality during emerging adulthood. *Journal of Social and Personal Relationships*, *35*(5), 743–769. https://doi.org/10.1177/0265407517697856

Hsueh, A. C., Morrison, K. R., & Doss, B. D. (2009). Qualitative reports of problems in cohabiting relationships: Comparisons to married and dating relationships. *Journal of Family Psychology*, *23*(2), 236–246. https://doi.org/10.1037/a0015364

Huijts, T., Kraaykamp, G., & Subramanian, S. V. (2011). Childlessness and psychological well-being in context: A multilevel study on 24 European countries. *European Sociological Review*, *29*(1), 32–47. https://doi.org/10.1093/esr/jcr037

Huxhold, O., Miche, M., & Schüz, B. (2014). Benefits of having friends in older ages: Differential effects of informal social activities on well-being in middle-aged and older adults. *The Journals of Gerontology. Series B, Psychological Sciences and Social Sciences*, *69*(3), 366–375. https://doi.org/10.1093/geronb/gbt029

Hyde, J. S., & DeLamater, J. D. (2017). *Understanding human sexuality*. McGraw Hill.

Jackson, J. B. (2018). The ambiguous loss of singlehood: Conceptualizing and treating singlehood ambiguous loss among never-married adults. *Contemporary Family Therapy*, *40*(2), 210–222. https://doi.org/10.1007/s10591-018-9455-0

Jackson, J. B., Miller, R. B., Oka, M., & Henry, R. G. (2014). Gender differences in marital satisfaction: A meta-analysis. *Journal of Marriage and Family*, *76*(1), 105–129. https://doi.org/10.1111/jomf.12077

Jasinski, J., Blumenstein, L., & Morgan, R. (2014). Testing Johnson's typology: Is there gender symmetry in intimate terrorism? *Violence and Victims*, *29*(1), 73–88. https://doi.org/10.1891/0886-6708.VV-D-12-00146

Jensen, T. M., & Ganong, L. H. (2020). Stepparent–child relationship quality and couple relationship quality: Stepfamily household type as a moderating influence. *Journal of Family Issues*, *41*(5), 589–610. https://doi.org/10.1177/0192513X19881669

Jensen, T. M., & Howard, M. O. (2015). Perceived stepparent–Child relationship quality: A systematic review of stepchildren's perspectives. *Marriage & Family Review*, *51*(2), 99–153. https://doi.org/10.1080/01494929.2015.1006717

Jose, A., O'Leary Daniel, K., & Moyer, A. (2010). Does premarital cohabitation predict subsequent marital stability and marital quality? A meta-analysis. *Journal of Marriage & Family*, *72*(1), 105–116. https://doi.org/10.1111/j.1741-3737.2009.00686.x

Kail, B. L., Acosta, K. L., & Wright, E. R. (2015). State-level marriage equality and the health of same-sex couples. *American Journal of Public Health*, *105*(6), 1101–1105. https://doi.org/10.2105/AJPH.2015.302589

Karakurt, G., Koç, E., Çetinsaya, E. E., Ayluçtarhan, Z., & Bolen, S. (2019). Meta-analysis and systematic review for the treatment of perpetrators of intimate partner violence. *Neuroscience and Biobehavioral Reviews*, *105*, 220–230. https://doi.org/10.1016/j.neubiorev.2019.08.006

Katz-Wise, S. L., Priess, H. A., & Hyde, J. S. (2010). Gender-role attitudes and behavior across the transition to parenthood. *Developmental Psychology*, *46*(1), 18–28. https://doi.org/10.1037/a0017820

Kaufman-Parks, A. M., DeMaris, A., Giordano, P. C., Manning, W. D., & Longmore, M. A. (2018). Familial effects on intimate partner violence perpetration across adolescence and young adulthood. *Journal of Family Issues*, *39*, 1933–1961. https://doi.org/10.1177/0192513X17734586

Kimmes, J. G., Mallory, A. B., Spencer, C., Beck, A. R., Cafferky, B., & Stith, S. M. (2019). A meta-analysis of risk markers for intimate partner violence in same-sex relationships. *Trauma, Violence, and Abuse*, *20*(3), 374–384. https://doi.org/10.1177/1524838017708784

King, B. M. (2019). *Human sexuality today*. Pearson.

Kirkner, A., Relyea, M., & Ullman, S. E. (2018). PTSD and problem drinking in relation to seeking mental health and substance use treatment among sexual assault survivors. *Traumatology, 24*(1), 1–7. https://doi.org/10.1037/trm0000126

Kline, N. K., Berke, D. S., Rhodes, C. A., Steenkamp, M. M., & Litz, B. T. (2021). Self-blame and PTSD following sexual assault: A longitudinal analysis. *Journal of Interpersonal Violence, 36*(5–6), NP3153–NP3168. https://doi.org/10.1177/0886260518770652

Ko, K. J., Berg, C. A., Butner, J., Uchino, B. N., & Smith, T. W. (2007). Profiles of successful aging in middle-aged and older adult married couples. *Psychology and Aging, 22*(4), 705–718.

Koball, H. L., Moiduddin, E., Henderson, J., Goesling, B., & Besculides, M. (2010). What do we know about the link between marriage and health? *Journal of Family Issues, 31*(8), 1019–1040. https://doi.org/10.1177/0192513X10365834

Koert, E., & Daniluk, J. C. (2017). When time runs out: Reconciling permanent childlessness after delayed childbearing. *Journal of Reproductive and Infant Psychology, 35*(4), 342–352. https://doi.org/10.1080/02646838.2017.1320363

Koivunen, J. M., Rothaupt, J. W., & Wolfgram, S. M. (2009). Gender dynamics and role adjustment during the transition to parenthood: Current perspectives. *Family Journal, 17*(4), 323–328. https://doi.org/10.1177/1066480709347360

Koropeckyj-Cox, T., & Pendell, G. (2007). Attitudes about childlessness in the United States. *Journal of Family Issues, 28*(8), 1054–1082.

Koropeckyj-Cox, T., Romano, V. R., & Moras, A. (2007). Through the lenses of gender, race, and class: Students' perceptions of childless/childfree individuals and couples. *Sex Roles, 56*(7/8), 415–428.

Krebs, C., Breiding, M. J., Browne, A., & Warner, T. (2011). The association between different types of intimate partner violence experienced by women. *Journal of Family Violence, 26*(6), 487–500. https://doi.org/10.1007/s10896-011-9383-3

Kreider, R. M., Ellis, R., & U. S. Bureau of the Census. (2011). *Number, timing, and duration of marriages and divorces: 2009. Current population reports*. https://www.census.gov/prod/2011pubs/p70-125.pdf

Kreyenfeld, M., & Konietzka, D. (2017). Analyzing childlessness. In M. Kreyenfeld & D. Konietzka (Eds.), *Demographic research monographs* (pp. 3–15). Springer. https://doi.org/10.1007/978-3-319-44667-7_1

Kulik, L., & Havusha-Morgenstern, H. (2011). Does cohabitation matter? Differences in initial marital adjustment among women who cohabited and those who did not. *Families in Society: The Journal of Contemporary Social Services, 92*(1), 120–127.

Kuo, J. C. L., & Raley, R. K. (2016). Diverging Patterns of union transition among cohabitors by race/ethnicity and education: Trends and marital intentions in the United States. *Demography, 53*(4), 921–935. https://doi.org/10.1007/s13524-016-0483-9

Kuperberg, A. (2014). Age at coresidence, premarital cohabitation, and marriage dissolution: 1985-2009. *Journal of Marriage and Family, 76*(2), 352–369. https://doi.org/10.1111/jomf.12092

Kuperberg, A., & Padgett, J. E. (2016). The role of culture in explaining college students' selection into hookups, dates, and long-term romantic relationships. *Journal of Social and Personal Relationships, 33*(8), 1070–1096. https://doi.org/10.1177/0265407515616876

Kurdek, L. A. (2006). Differences between partners from heterosexual, gay, and lesbian cohabiting couples. *Journal of Marriage & Family, 68*(2), 509–528.

Lamidi, E. (2016). *FP-16-05 a quarter century change in nonmarital births: Differences by educational attainment*. National Center for Family and Marriage Research Family Profiles. https://scholarworks.bgsu.edu/ncfmr_family_profiles/48

Lamidi, E. O., Manning, W. D., & Brown, S. L. (2019). Change in the stability of first premarital cohabitation among women in the United States, 1983–2013. *Demography, 56*(2), 427–450. https://doi.org/10.1007/s13524-019-00765-7

Landberg, M., Lee, B., & Noack, P. (2019). What alters the experience of emerging adulthood? How the experience of emerging adulthood differs according to socioeconomic status and critical life events. *Emerging Adulthood, 7*(3), 208–222. https://doi.org/10.1177/2167696819831793

Langenderfer-Magruder, L., Whitfield, D. L., Walls, N. E., Kattari, S. K., & Ramos, D. (2016). Experiences of intimate partner violence and subsequent police reporting among lesbian, gay, bisexual, transgender, and queer adults in Colorado. *Journal of Interpersonal Violence, 31*(5), 855–871. https://doi.org/10.1177/0886260514556767

Lapsley, D., & Hardy, S. A. (2017). Identity formation and moral development in emerging adulthood. In L. M. Padilla-Walker & L. J. Nelson (Eds.), *Flourishing in emerging adulthood: Positive development during the third decade of life* (pp. 14–39). Oxford University Press. https://doi.org/10.1093/acprof:oso/9780190260637.003.0002

Laughland-Booÿ, J., Skrbiš, Z., & Newcombe, P. (2018). Identity and intimacy: A longitudinal qualitative study of young Australians. *Journal of Adolescent Research, 33*(6), 725–751. https://doi.org/10.1177/0743558416684959

Lavelle, B., & Smock, P. J. (2012). Divorce and women's risk of health insurance loss. *Journal of Health and Social Behavior, 53*(4), 413–431. https://doi.org/10.1177/0022146512465758

Lavner, J. A., & Bradbury, T. N. (2012). Why do even satisfied newlyweds eventually go on to divorce? *Journal of Family Psychology, 26*(1), 1–10. https://doi.org/10.1037/a0025966

Lavner, J. A., & Bradbury, T. N. (2014). Marital satisfaction change over newlywed years. In A. C. Michalos (Ed.), *Encyclopedia of quality of life and well-being research* (pp. 3811–3815). Springer Netherlands. https://doi.org/10.1007/978-94-007-0753-5_3856

Lavner, J. A., Waterman, J., & Peplau, L. A. (2014). Parent adjustment over time in gay, lesbian, and heterosexual parent families adopting from foster care. *The American Journal of Orthopsychiatry, 84*(1), 46–53. https://doi.org/10.1037/h0098853

Le, Y., McDaniel, B. T., Leavitt, C. E., & Feinberg, M. E. (2016). Longitudinal associations between relationship quality and coparenting across the transition to parenthood: A dyadic perspective. *Journal of Family Psychology, 30*(8), 918–926. https://doi.org/10.1037/fam0000217

LeBlanc, N. J., Brown, M., & Henin, A. (2020). Anxiety disorders in emerging adulthood. In E. Bui, M. E. Charney, & A. W. Baker (Eds.), *Clinical handbook of anxiety disorders* (pp. 157–173). Springer. https://doi.org/10.1007/978-3-030-30687-8_8

Lehmann, V., Tuinman, M. A., Braeken, J., Vingerhoets, A. J. J. M., Sanderman, R., & Hagedoorn, M. (2015). Satisfaction with relationship status: Development of a new scale and the role in predicting well-being. *Journal of Happiness Studies*, *16*(1), 169–184. https://doi.org/10.1007/s10902-014-9503-x

Leikas, S., Ilmarinen, V.-J., Verkasalo, M., Vartiainen, H.-L., & Lönnqvist, J.-E. (2018). Relationship satisfaction and similarity of personality traits, personal values, and attitudes. *Personality and Individual Differences*, *123*, 191–198. https://doi.org/10.1016/J.PAID.2017.11.024

Lesthaeghe, R. J., López-Colás, J., & Neidert, L. (2016). The social geography of unmarried cohabitation in the USA, 2007–2011. In A. Esteve & R. J. Lesthaeghe (Eds.), *Cohabitation and marriage in the Americas: Geo-historical legacies and new trends* (pp. 101–131). Springer International Publishing. https://doi.org/10.1007/978-3-319-31442-6_4

Lewis, N. A., & Yoneda, T. (2021). Within-couple personality concordance over time: The importance of personality synchrony for perceived spousal support. *The Journals of Gerontology: Series B*, *76*(1), 31–43. https://doi.org/10.1093/geronb/gbaa163

Lewis, R. J., Mason, T. B., Winstead, B. A., & Kelley, M. L. (2017). Empirical investigation of a model of sexual minority specific and general risk factors for intimate partner violence among lesbian women. *Psychology of Violence*, *7*(1), 110–119. https://doi.org/10.1037/vio0000036

Li, N. P., Yong, J. C., Tov, W., Sng, O., Fletcher, G. J. O., Valentine, K. A., Jiang, Y. F., & Balliet, D. (2013). Mate preferences do predict attraction and choices in the early stages of mate selection. *Journal of Personality and Social Psychology*, *105*(5), 757–776. https://doi.org/10.1037/a0033777

Lichter, D. T., Sassler, S., & Turner, R. N. (2014). Cohabitation, post-conception unions, and the rise in nonmarital fertility. *Social Science Research*, *47*, 134–147. https://doi.org/10.1016/j.ssresearch.2014.04.002

Livingston, G. (2018). *U.S. women more likely to have children than a decade ago | Pew Research Center. Pew Research Center.* https://www.pewresearch.org/social-trends/2018/01/18/theyre-waiting-longer-but-u-s-women-today-more-likely-to-have-children-than-a-decade-ago/

Lodi-Smith, J., Spain, S. M., Cologgi, K., & Roberts, B. W. (2017). Development of identity clarity and content in adulthood. *Journal of Personality and Social Psychology*, *112*(5), 755–768. https://doi.org/10.1037/pspp0000091

Lutz-Zois, C. J., Bradley, A. C., Mihalik, J. L., & Moorman-Eavers, E. R. (2006). Perceived similarity and relationship success among dating couples: An idiographic approach. *Journal of Social & Personal Relationships*, *23*(6), 865–880.

Maggs, J. L., Jager, J., Patrick, M. E., & Schulenberg, J. (2012). Social role patterning in early adulthood in the USA: Adolescent predictors and concurrent wellbeing across four distinct configurations. *Longitudinal and Life Course Studies*, *3*(2), 190–210.

Mallette, J. K., Futris, T. G., Oshri, A., & Brown, G. L. (2020). Paternal support and involvement in unmarried fragile families: Impacts on long-term maternal mental health. *Family Process*, *59*(2), 789–806. https://doi.org/10.1111/famp.12456

Mancini, A. D., Bonanno, G. A., & Clark, A. E. (2011). Stepping off the hedonic treadmill. *Journal of Individual Differences*, *32*(3), 144–152. https://doi.org/10.1027/1614-0001/a000047

Manning, W. D. (2013). *Trends in cohabitation: Over twenty years of change, 1987-2010 (FP-13-12)*. National Center for Family & Marriage Research.

Manning, W. D. (2015). Cohabitation and child wellbeing. *The Future of Children*, *25*(2), 51–66.

Manning, W. D. (2020). Young adulthood relationships in an era of uncertainty: A case for cohabitation. *Demography*, *57*(3), 799–819. https://doi.org/10.1007/s13524-020-00881-9

Manning, W. D., Smock, P. J., & Kuperberg, A. (2021). Cohabitation and marital dissolution: A comment on Rosenfeld and Roesler (2019). *Journal of Marriage and Family*, *83*(1), 260–267. https://doi.org/10.1111/jomf.12724

Markey, P. M., & Markey, C. N. (2007). Romantic ideals, romantic obtainment, and relationship experiences: The complementarity of interpersonal traits among romantic partners. *Journal of Social & Personal Relationships*, *24*(4), 517–533.

Markstrom, C. A., & Kalmanir, H. M. (2001). Linkages between the psychosocial stages of identity and intimacy and the ego strengths of fidelity and love. *Identity*, *1*(2), 179–196.

Martin, J. A., Hamilton, B. E., Osterman, M. J. K., & Driscoll, A. K. (2019). Births: Final data for 2018. *National Vital Statistics Reports*, *68*(13). https://www.cdc.gov/nchs/products/index.htm

Matthews, T. J., & Hamilton, B. E. (2002). Mean age of mother, 1970–2000. *National Vital and Statistics Reports*, *51*(1). https://www.cdc.gov/nchs/data/nvsr/nvsr51/nvsr51_01.pdf

Mayseless, O., & Scharf, M. (2003). What does it mean to be an adult? The Israeli experience. *New Directions for Child & Adolescent Development*, *2003*(100), 5–20.

McNulty, J. K., Wenner, C. A., & Fisher, T. D. (2016). Longitudinal associations among relationship satisfaction, sexual satisfaction, and frequency of sex in early marriage. *Archives of Sexual Behavior*, *45*(1), 85–97. https://doi.org/10.1007/s10508-014-0444-6

Mgoqi-Mbalo, N., Zhang, M., & Ntuli, S. (2017). Risk factors for PTSD and depression in female survivors of rape. *Psychological Trauma: Theory, Research, Practice, and Policy*, *9*(3), 301–308. https://doi.org/10.1037/tra0000228

Mikucka, M., & Rizzi, E. (2020). The parenthood and happiness link: Testing predictions from five theories. *European Journal of Population*, *36*(2), 337–361. https://doi.org/10.1007/s10680-019-09532-1

Mills, M., Rindfuss, R. R., McDonald, P., & te Velde, E. (2011). Why do people postpone parenthood? Reasons and social policy incentives. *Human Reproduction Update*, *17*(6), 848–860.

Mitchell, L. L., & Syed, M. (2015). Does college matter for emerging adulthood? Comparing developmental trajectories of educational groups. *Journal of Youth and Adolescence*, *44*(11), 2012–2027. https://doi.org/10.1007/s10964-015-0330-0

Moorman, J. D. (2020). Socializing singlehood: Personal, interpersonal, and sociocultural factors shaping black women's single lives. *Psychology of Women Quarterly*, *44*(4), 431–449. https://doi.org/10.1177/0361684320939070

Moreira, D. N., & Pinto da Costa, M. (2020). The impact of the Covid-19 pandemic in the precipitation of intimate partner violence. *International Journal of Law and Psychiatry*, *71*, 101606. https://doi.org/10.1016/j.ijlp.2020.101606

Movement Advancement Project. (2018). *Foster and adoption laws*. http://www.lgbtmap.org/equality-maps/foster_and_adoption_laws

Musick, K., & Michelmore, K. (2018). Cross-national comparisons of union stability in cohabiting and married families with children. *Demography*, *55*(4), 1389–1421. https://doi.org/10.1007/s13524-018-0683-6

Napper, L. E., Montes, K. S., Kenney, S. R., & LaBrie, J. W. (2016). Assessing the personal negative impacts of hooking up experienced by college students: Gender differences and mental health. *The Journal of Sex Research*, *53*(7), 766–775. https://doi.org/10.1080/00224499.2015.1065951

National Center for Health Statistics. (2019). NSFG - listing I - Key statistics from the national survey of family growth. *Key Statistics from the National Survey of Family Growth*. https://www.cdc.gov/nchs/nsfg/key_statistics/i_2015-2017.htm#impaired

Neff, L. A., & Karney, B. R. (2017). Acknowledging the elephant in the room: How stressful environmental contexts shape relationship dynamics. *Current Opinion in Psychology*, *13*, 107–110. https://doi.org/10.1016/J.COPSYC.2016.05.013

Nelson, L. J. (2009). An examination of emerging adulthood in Romanian college students. *International Journal of Behavioral Development*, *33*(5), 402–411. https://doi.org/10.1177/0165025409340093

Nelson, L. J. (2021). The theory of emerging adulthood 20 years later: A look at where it has taken us, what we know now, and where we need to go. *Emerging Adulthood*, *9*, 179–188. https://doi.org/10.1177/2167696820950884

Nelson, L. J., Badger, S., & Wu, B. (2004). The influence of culture in emerging adulthood: Perspectives of Chinese college students. *International Journal of Behavioral Development*, *28*, 26–36.

Nelson, L. J., & Luster, S. S. (2016). "Adulthood" by whose definition? In J. J. Arnett (Ed.), *The Oxford handbook of emerging adulthood* (pp. 421–437). Oxford University Press. https://doi.org/10.1093/oxfordhb/9780199795574.013.24

Nelson, S. K., Kushlev, K., & Lyubomirsky, S. (2014). The pains and pleasures of parenting: When, why, and how is parenthood associated with more or less well-being? *Psychological Bulletin*, *140*(3), 846–895. https://doi.org/10.1037/a0035444

Nelson-Coffey, S. K., Killingsworth, M., Layous, K., Cole, S. W., & Lyubomirsky, S. (2019). Parenthood is associated with greater well-being for fathers than mothers. *Personality and Social Psychology Bulletin*, *45*(9), 1378–1390. https://doi.org/10.1177/0146167219829174

Newkirk, K., Perry-Jenkins, M., & Sayer, A. G. (2017). Division of household and childcare labor and relationship conflict among low-income new parents. *Sex Roles*, *76*(5–6), 319–333. https://doi.org/10.1007/s11199-016-0604-3

Ng, T. K., & Cheng, H. K. C. (2010). The effects of intimacy, passion, and commitment on satisfaction in romantic relationships among Hong Kong Chinese people. *Journal of Psychology in Chinese Societies*, *11*(2), 123–146. https://scholars.cityu.edu.hk/en/publications/the-effects-of-intimacy-passion-and-commitment-on-satisfaction-in-romantic-relationships-among-hong-kong-chinese-people(0c2c7a34-d084-40a3-a3ef-ca4a84cb2a80).html

Nicolaisen, M., & Thorsen, K. (2017). What are friends for? Friendships and loneliness over the lifespan—From 18 to 79 years. *The International Journal of Aging and Human Development*, *84*(2), 126–158. https://doi.org/10.1177/0091415016655166

Obidoa, C. A., Dodor, B. A., Tackie-Ofosu, V., Obidoa, M. A., Kalisch, H. R., & Nelson, L. J. (2019). Perspectives on markers of adulthood among emerging adults in Ghana and Nigeria. *Emerging Adulthood*, *7*(4), 270–278. https://doi.org/10.1177/2167696818778906

O'Connor, J., Cusano, J., McMahon, S., & Draper, J. (2018). Students' articulation of subtle rape myths surrounding campus sexual assault. *Journal of College Student Development*, *59*(4), 439–455. https://doi.org/10.1353/csd.2018.0041

Ogolsky, B. G., Dennison, R. P., & Monk, J. K. (2014). The role of couple discrepancies in cognitive and behavioral egalitarianism in marital quality. *Sex Roles*, *70*(7–8), 329–342. https://doi.org/10.1007/s11199-014-0365-9

O'Laughlin, E. M., & Anderson, V. N. (2001). Perceptions of parenthood among young adults: Implications for career and family planning. *American Journal of Family Therapy*, *29*(2), 95–108.

Olmstead, S. B. (2020). A decade review of sex and partnering in adolescence and young adulthood. *Journal of Marriage and Family*, *82*(2), 769–795. https://doi.org/10.1111/jomf.12670

Olmstead, S. B., Conrad, K. A., & Anders, K. M. (2018). First semester college students' definitions of and expectations for engaging in hookups. *Journal of Adolescent Research*, *33*(3), 275–305. https://doi.org/10.1177/0743558417698571

Orchowski, L. M., Untied, A. S., & Gidycz, C. A. (2013). Social reactions to disclosure of sexual victimization and adjustment among survivors of sexual assault. *Journal of Interpersonal Violence*, *28*(10), 2005–2023. https://doi.org/10.1177/0886260512471085

Ortiz-Ospina, E., & Roser, M. (2020). Marriages and divorces. *Our World in Data*. https://ourworldindata.org/marriages-and-divorces

Park, Y., Impett, E. A., & MacDonald, G. (2021). Singles' Sexual satisfaction is associated with more satisfaction with singlehood and less interest in marriage. *Personality and Social Psychology Bulletin*, *47*, 741–752. https://doi.org/10.1177/0146167220942361

Peitzmeier, S. M., Malik, M., Kattari, S. K., Marrow, E., Stephenson, R., Agénor, M., & Reisner, S. L. (2020). Intimate partner violence in transgender populations: Systematic review and meta-analysis of prevalence and correlates. *American Journal of Public Health*, *110*(9), E1–E14. https://doi.org/10.2105/AJPH.2020.305774

Pepping, C. A., MacDonald, G., & Davis, P. J. (2018). Toward a psychology of singlehood: An attachment-theory perspective on long-term singlehood. *Current Directions in Psychological Science*, *27*(5), 324–331. https://doi.org/10.1177/0963721417752106

Perelli-Harris, B., & Gassen, N. S. (2012). How similar are cohabitation and marriage? Legal approaches to cohabitation across Western Europe. *Population and Development Review*, *38*(3), 435–467. https://doi.org/10.1111/j.1728-4457.2012.00511.x

Perrig-Chiello, P., Hutchison, S., & Morselli, D. (2014). Patterns of psychological adaptation to divorce after a long-term marriage. *Journal of Social and Personal Relationships*, *32*(3), 386–405. https://doi.org/10.1177/0265407514533769

Perrin, E. C., & Siegel, B. S. (2013). Promoting the well-being of children whose parents are gay or lesbian. *Pediatrics*, *131*(4), e1374–e1383. https://doi.org/10.1542/peds.2013-0377

Peterson, B. D., Gold, L., & Feingold, T. (2007). The experience and influence of infertility: Considerations for couple counselors. *Family Journal, 15*(3), 251–257.

Pettee, K. K., Brach, J. S., Kriska, A. M., Boudreau, R., Richardson, C. R., Colbert, L. H., Satterfield, S., Visser, M., Harris, T. B., Ayonayon, H. N., & Newman, A. B. (2006). Influence of marital status on physical activity levels among older adults. *Medicine & Science in Sports & Exercise, 38*(3), 541–546.

Pollitt, A. M., Robinson, B. A., & Umberson, D. (2018). Gender conformity, perceptions of shared power, and marital quality in same- and different-sex marriages. *Gender & Society : Official Publication of Sociologists for Women in Society, 32*(1), 109–131. https://doi.org/10.1177/0891243217742110

Pollmann-Schult, M. (2018). Parenthood and life satisfaction in Europe: The role of family policies and working time flexibility. *European Journal of Population, 34*(3), 387–411. https://doi.org/10.1007/s10680-017-9433-5

Popenoe, D. (2009). Cohabitation, marriage, and child wellbeing: A cross-national perspective. *Society, 46*(5), 429–436. https://doi.org/10.1007/s12115-009-9242-5

Preisner, K., Neuberger, F., Bertogg, A., & Schaub, J. M. (2020). Closing the happiness gap: The decline of gendered parenthood norms and the increase in parental life satisfaction. *Gender & Society, 34*(1), 31–55. https://doi.org/10.1177/0891243219869365

Prendergast, S., & MacPhee, D. (2018). Family resilience amid stigma and discrimination: A conceptual model for families headed by same-sex parents. *Family Relations, 67*(1), 26–40. https://doi.org/10.1111/fare.12296

Pylyser, C., De Mol, J., Loeys, T., & Buysse, A. (2019). Father Reflections on doing family in stepfamilies. *Family Relations, 68*(4), 500–511. https://doi.org/10.1111/fare.12377

Raley, J. A., Fisher, W. M., Halder, R., & Shanmugan, K. (2013). Child custody and homosexual/bisexual parents: A survey of judges. *Journal of Child Custody, 10*(1), 54–67. https://doi.org/10.1080/15379418.2013.781843

Raley, R. K., & Sweeney, M. M. (2020). Divorce, repartnering, and stepfamilies: A decade in review. *Journal of Marriage and Family, 82*(1), 81–99. https://doi.org/10.1111/jomf.12651

Ramos Salazar, L. (2015). The negative reciprocity process in marital relationships: A literature review. *Aggression and Violent Behavior, 24*, 113–119. https://doi.org/10.1016/j.avb.2015.05.008

Ratelle, C. F., Carbonneau, N., Vallerand, R. J., & Mageau, G. (2013). Passion in the romantic sphere: A look at relational outcomes. *Motivation and Emotion, 37*(1), 106–120. https://doi.org/10.1007/s11031-012-9286-5

Ravert, R. D., Stoddard, N. A., & Donnellan, M. B. (2018). A content analysis of the methods used to study emerging adults in six developmental journals from 2013 to 2015. *Emerging Adulthood, 6*(3), 151–158. https://doi.org/10.1177/2167696817720011

Reczek, C. (2020). Sexual- and gender-minority families: A 2010 to 2020 decade in review. *Journal of Marriage and Family, 82*(1), 300–325. https://doi.org/10.1111/jomf.12607

Reed, R. A., Pamlanye, J. T., Truex, H. R., Murphy-Neilson, M. C., Kunaniec, K. P., Newins, A. R., & Wilson, L. C. (2020). Higher rates of unacknowledged rape among men: The role of rape myth acceptance. *Psychology of Men and Masculinity, 21*(1), 162–167. https://doi.org/10.1037/men0000230

Reeder, H. (2017). "He's like a brother": The social construction of satisfying cross-sex friendship roles. *Sexuality & Culture, 21*(1), 142–162. https://doi.org/10.1007/s12119-016-9387-5

Richards, T. N., Tillyer, M. S., & Wright, E. M. (2017). Intimate partner violence and the overlap of perpetration and victimization: Considering the influence of physical, sexual, and emotional abuse in childhood. *Child Abuse & Neglect, 67*, 240–248. https://doi.org/10.1016/J.CHIABU.2017.02.037

Riggle, E. D. B., Rostosky, S. S., & Horne, S. G. (2010). Psychological distress, well-being, and legal recognition in same-sex couple relationships. *Journal of Family Psychology, 24*(1), 82–86. https://doi.org/10.1037/a0017942

Riggle, E. D. B., Wickham, R. E., Rostosky, S. S., Rothblum, E. D., & Balsam, K. F. (2017). Impact of civil marriage recognition for long-term same-sex couples. *Sexuality Research and Social Policy, 14*(2), 223–232. https://doi.org/10.1007/s13178-016-0243-z

Robles, T. F. (2014). Marital quality and health: Implications for marriage in the 21st century. *Current Directions in Psychological Science, 23*(6), 427–432. https://doi.org/10.1177/0963721414549043

Rollè, L., Giardina, G., Caldarera, A. M., Gerino, E., & Brustia, P. (2018, August). When intimate partner violence meets same sex couples: A review of same sex intimate partner violence. *Frontiers in Psychologym, 9*. https://doi.org/10.3389/fpsyg.2018.01506

Roper, S. W., Fife, S. T., & Seedall, R. B. (2020). The intergenerational effects of parental divorce on young adult relationships. *Journal of Divorce and Remarriage, 61*(4), 249–266. https://doi.org/10.1080/10502556.2019.1699372

Rosenfeld, M. J. (2014). Couple longevity in the era of same-sex marriage in the United States. *Journal of Marriage and Family, 76*(5), 905–918. https://doi.org/10.1111/jomf.12141

Rostosky, S. S., & Riggle, E. D. B. (2017). Same-sex couple relationship strengths: A review and synthesis of the empirical literature (2000–2016). *Psychology of Sexual Orientation and Gender Diversity, 4*(1), 1–13. https://doi.org/10.1037/sgd0000216

Roy, R. N., Schumm, W. R., & Britt, S. L. (2014). Voluntary versus involuntary childlessness. In R. N. Roy, W. R. Schumm, & S. L. Britt (Eds.), *Transition to parenthood* (pp. 49–68). Springer.

Rubin, H., & Campbell, L. (2012). Day-to-day changes in intimacy predict heightened relationship passion, sexual occurrence, and sexual satisfaction: A dyadic diary analysis. *Social Psychological and Personality Science, 3*(2), 224–231. https://doi.org/10.1177/1948550611416520

Ryan, K. M. (2019). Rape mythology and victim blaming as a social construct. In W. T. O'Donohue & P. A. Schewe (Eds.), *Handbook of Sexual assault and sexual assault prevention* (pp. 151–174). Springer International Publishing. https://doi.org/10.1007/978-3-030-23645-8_9

Salary.com. (2021a). *Director of student services | Salary.com.* https://www.salary.com/tools/salary-calculator/director-of-student-services

Salary.com. (2021b). *Resident director salary | Salary.com.* https://www.salary.com/research/salary/posting/resident-director-salary

Sánchez Gassen, N., & Perelli-Harris, B. (2015). The increase in cohabitation and the role of union status in family policies: A comparison of 12 European countries. *Journal of European Social Policy, 25*(4), 431–449. https://doi.org/10.1177/0958928715594561

Sarkisian, N., & Gerstel, N. (2016). Does singlehood isolate or integrate? Examining the link between marital status and ties to kin, friends, and neighbors. *Journal of Social and Personal Relationships*, *33*(3), 361–384. https://doi.org/10.1177/0265407515597564

Sassler, S., & Lichter, D. T. (2020). Cohabitation and marriage: Complexity and diversity in union-formation patterns. *Journal of Marriage and Family*, *82*(1), 35–61. https://doi.org/10.1111/jomf.12617

Sassler, S., & Miller, A. J. (2011). Class differences in cohabitation processes. *Family Relations*, *60*(2), 163–177. https://doi.org/10.1111/j.1741-3729.2010.00640.x

Sbarra, D. A., & Coan, J. A. (2017). Divorce and health: Good data in need of better theory. *Current Opinion in Psychology*, *13*, 91–95. https://doi.org/10.1016/j.copsyc.2016.05.014

Sbarra, D. A., Hasselmo, K., & Bourassa, K. J. (2015). Divorce and health: Beyond individual differences. *Current Directions in Psychological Science*, *24*(2), 109–113. https://doi.org/10.1177/0963721414559125

Sbarra, D. A., Law, R. W., & Portley, R. M. (2011). Divorce and death: A meta-analysis and research agenda for clinical, social, and health psychology. *Perspectives on Psychological Science*, *6*(5), 454–474. https://doi.org/10.1177/1745691611414724

Schmidt, L., Sobotka, T., Bentzen, J. G., & Nyboe Andersen, A. (2012). Demographic and medical consequences of the postponement of parenthood. *Human Reproduction Update*, *18*(1), 29–43. https://doi.org/10.1093/humupd/dmr040

Schwartz, S. J. (2016). Turning point for a turning point. *Emerging Adulthood*, *4*(5), 307–317. https://doi.org/10.1177/2167696815624640

Schwartz, S. J., Zamboanga, B. L., Luyckx, K., Meca, A., & Ritchie, R. A. (2013). Identity in emerging adulthood: Reviewing the field and looking forward. *Emerging Adulthood*, *1*(2), 96–113. https://doi.org/10.1177/2167696813479781

Schwartz, S. J., Zamboanga, B. L., Luyckx, K., Meca, A., & Ritchie, R. A. (2016). Identity in emerging adulthood. In J. J. Arnett (Ed.), *The Oxford handbook of emerging adulthood* (pp. 401–420). Oxford University Press. https://doi.org/10.1093/oxfordhb/9780199795574.013.001

Seabrook, R. C., Ward, L. M., & Giaccardi, S. (2018). Why is fraternity membership associated with sexual assault? Exploring the roles of conformity to masculine norms, pressure to uphold masculinity, and objectification of women. *Psychology of Men and Masculinity*, *19*(1), 3–13. https://doi.org/10.1037/men0000076

Seiffge-Krenke, I. (2003). Testing theories of romantic development from adolescence to young adulthood: Evidence of a developmental sequence. *International Journal of Behavioral Development*, *27*(6), 519–531. https://doi.org/10.1080/01650250344000145

Shapiro, D. N., & Stewart, A. J. (2011). Parenting stress, perceived child regard, and depressive symptoms among stepmothers and biological mothers. *Family Relations*, *60*(5), 533–544. https://doi.org/10.1111/j.1741-3729.2011.00665.x

Sharon, T. (2016). Constructing adulthood: Markers of adulthood and well-being among emerging adults. *Emerging Adulthood*, *4*(3), 161–167. https://doi.org/10.1177/2167696815579826

Sharp, E. A., & Ganong, L. (2007). Living in the gray: Women's experiences of missing the marital transition. *Journal of Marriage and Family*, *69*(3), 831–844. https://doi.org/10.1111/j.1741-3737.2007.00408.x

Shortt, J. W., Low, S., Capaldi, D. M., Eddy, J. M., & Tiberio, S. S. (2016). Predicting intimate partner violence for at-risk young adults and their romantic partner - NCJ 250668. *National Criminal Justice Reference Service*. https://www.ncjrs.gov/App/Publications/abstract.aspx?ID=272836

Shulman, S., & Connolly, J. (2013). The challenge of romantic relationships in emerging adulthood: Reconceptualization of the field. *Emerging Adulthood*, *1*(1), 27–39. https://doi.org/10.1177/2167696812467330

Shulman, S., Seiffge-Krenke, I., Scharf, M., Boiangiu, S. B., & Tregubenko, V. (2018). The diversity of romantic pathways during emerging adulthood and their developmental antecedents. *International Journal of Behavioral Development*, *42*(2), 167–174. https://doi.org/10.1177/0165025416673474

Simon, K. A., Tornello, S. L., Farr, R. H., & Bos, H. M. W. (2018). Envisioning future parenthood among bisexual, lesbian, and heterosexual women. *Psychology of Sexual Orientation and Gender Diversity*, *5*(2), 253–259. https://doi.org/10.1037/sgd0000267

Simpson, J. A., & Rholes, W. S. (2019). Adult attachment orientations and well-being during the transition to parenthood. *Current Opinion in Psychology*, *25*, 47–52. https://doi.org/10.1016/J.COPSYC.2018.02.019

Sinozich, S., & Langton, L. (2014). *Rape and sexual assault victimization among college-age females, 1995–2013*. https://assets.documentcloud.org/documents/1378364/rsavcaf9513.pdf

Sirsch, U., Dreher, E., Mayr, E., & Willinger, U. (2009). What does it take to be an adult in Austria?: Views of adulthood in Austrian adolescents, emerging adults, and adults. *Journal of Adolescent Research*, *24*(3), 275–292.

Smith, S. G., Basile, K. C., Gilbert, L. K., Merrick, M. T., Patel, N., Walling, M., & Jain, A. (2017). *National Intimate Partner and Sexual Violence Survey (NISVS): 2010-2012 state report*. https://stacks.cdc.gov/view/cdc/46305

Smithson, M., & Baker, C. (2008). Risk orientation, loving, and liking in long-term romantic relationships. *Journal of Social & Personal Relationships*, *25*(1), 87–103. https://doi.org/10.1177/0265407507086807

Smock, P. J., & Schwartz, C. R. (2020). The demography of families: A review of patterns and change. *Journal of Marriage and Family*, *82*(1), 9–34. https://doi.org/10.1111/jomf.12612

Sorokowski, P., Sorokowska, A., Butovskaya, M., Karwowski, M., Groyecka, A., Wojciszke, B., & Pawłowski, B. (2017). Love influences reproductive success in humans. *Frontiers in Psychology*, *8*, 1922. https://doi.org/10.3389/fpsyg.2017.01922

Sorokowski, P., Sorokowska, A., Karwowski, M., Groyecka, A., Aavik, T., Akello, G., Alm, C., Amjad, N., Anjum, A., Asao, K., Atama, C. S., Atamtürk Duyar, D., Ayebare, R., Batres, C., Bendixen, M., Bensafia, A., Bizumic, B., Boussena, M., Buss, D. M., . . . Sternberg, R. J. (2021). Universality of the triangular theory of love: Adaptation and psychometric properties of the triangular love scale in 25 countries. *Journal of Sex Research*, *58*(1), 106–115. https://doi.org/10.1080/00224499.2020.1787318

Sprecher, S., Econie, A., & Treger, S. (2019). Mate preferences in emerging adulthood and beyond: Age variations in mate preferences and beliefs about change in mate preferences. *Journal of Social and Personal Relationships*, *36*(10), 3139–3158. https://doi.org/10.1177/0265407518816880

Stanca, L. (2012). Suffer the little children: Measuring the effects of parenthood on well-being worldwide. *Journal of Economic Behavior & Organization*, *81*(3), 742–750. https://doi.org/10.1016/j.jebo.2010.12.019

Stegen, H., Switsers, L., & De Donder, L. (2021). Life stories of voluntarily childless older people: A retrospective view on their reasons and experiences. *Journal of Family Issues*, *47*, 1536–1558. https://doi.org/10.1177/0192513X20949906

Steinhoff, A., & Keller, M. (2020). Pathways from childhood sociomoral sensitivity in friendship, insecurity, and peer rejection to adult friendship quality. *Child Development*, *91*(5), e1012–e1029. https://doi.org/10.1111/cdev.13381

Stepler, R. (2017). Number of cohabiting Americans rises, especially among those 50+ | Pew Research Center. *Pew Research Center*. http://www.pewresearch.org/fact-tank/2017/04/06/number-of-u-s-adults-cohabiting-with-a-partner-continues-to-rise-especially-among-those-50-and-older/

Sternberg, R. J. (2004). A triangular theory of love. In H. T. Reis & C. E. Rusbult (Eds.), *Close relationships: Key readings* (pp. 213–227). Taylor & Francis.

Stewart, A. L. (2014). The Men's Project: A sexual assault prevention program targeting college men. *Psychology of Men & Masculinity*, *15*(4), 481–485. https://doi.org/10.1037/a0033947

Sumter, S. R., Valkenburg, P. M., & Peter, J. (2013). Perceptions of love across the lifespan: Differences in passion, intimacy, and commitment. *International Journal of Behavioral Development*, *37*(5), 417–427. https://doi.org/10.1177/0165025413492486

Swanson, J. A. (2016). Trends in literature about emerging adulthood. *Emerging Adulthood*, *4*(6), 391–402. https://doi.org/10.1177/2167696816630468

Syed, M. (2016). Emerging adulthood: Developmental stage, theory, or nonsense? In J. J. Arnett (Ed.), *The Oxford handbook of emerging adulthood* (pp. 11–25). Oxford University Press. https://doi.org/10.1093/oxfordhb/9780199795574.013.9

Syed, M., & Mitchell, L. L. (2016). How race and ethnicity shape emerging adulthood. In J. J. Arnett (Ed.), *The Oxford handbook of emerging adulthood* (pp. 87–101). Oxford University Press. https://doi.org/10.1093/oxfordhb/9780199795574.013.005

Tanner, J. L. (2016). Mental health in emerging adulthood. In J. J. Arnett (Ed.), *The Oxford handbook of emerging adulthood* (pp. 499–520). Oxford University Press. https://doi.org/10.1093/oxfordhb/9780199795574.013.30

Tanner, J. L. (2018). Emerging adulthood. In R. F. Levant (Ed.), *Encyclopedia of adolescence* (pp. 1149–1157). Springer.

Tarzia, L., Forsdike, K., Feder, G., & Hegarty, K. (2020). Interventions in health settings for male perpetrators or victims of intimate partner violence. *Trauma, Violence, and Abuse*, *21*(1), 123–137. https://doi.org/10.1177/1524838017744772

Taylor, L. S., Fiore, A. T., Mendelsohn, G. A., & Cheshire, C. (2011). "Out of my league": A real-world test of the matching hypothesis. *Personality & Social Psychology Bulletin*, *37*(7), 942–954. https://doi.org/10.1177/0146167211409947

Taylor, Z. E., & Conger, R. D. (2014). Risk and resilience processes in single-mother families: An interactionist perspective. In Z. Sloboda & H. Petras (Eds.), *Defining prevention science* (pp. 195–217). Springer US. https://doi.org/10.1007/978-1-4899-7424-2

Taylor, Z. E., & Conger, R. D. (2017). Promoting strengths and resilience in single-mother families. *Child Development*, *88*(2), 350–358. https://doi.org/10.1111/cdev.12741

Thielemans, G., Fallesen, P., & Mortelmans, D. (2021). Division of household labor and relationship dissolution in Denmark 2001–2009. *Journal of Family Issues*, *42*, 1582–1606. https://doi.org/10.1177/0192513X20949890

Thomas, R. J. (2019). Sources of friendship and structurally induced homophily across the life course. *Sociological Perspectives*, *62*(6), 822–843. https://doi.org/10.1177/0731121419828399

Tidwell, N. D., Eastwick, P. W., & Finkel, E. J. (2013). Perceived, not actual, similarity predicts initial attraction in a live romantic context: Evidence from the speed-dating paradigm. *Personal Relationships*, *20*(2), 199–215. https://doi.org/10.1111/j.1475-6811.2012.01405.x

Tillyer, M. S., & Wright, E. M. (2013). Intimate Partner violence and the victim-offender overlap. *Journal of Research in Crime and Delinquency*, *51*(1), 29–55. https://doi.org/10.1177/0022427813484315

Timonen, V., & Doyle, M. (2014). Life-long singlehood: Intersections of the past and the present. *Ageing and Society*, *34*(10), 1749–1770. https://doi.org/10.1017/S0144686X13000500

Tornello, S. L., Kruczkowski, S. M., & Patterson, C. J. (2015). Division of labor and relationship quality among male same-sex couples who became fathers via surrogacy. *Journal of GLBT Family Studies*, *11*(4), 375–394. https://doi.org/10.1080/1550428X.2015.1018471

Trillingsgaard, T., Baucom, K. J. W., & Heyman, R. E. (2014). Predictors of change in relationship satisfaction during the transition to parenthood. *Family Relations*, *63*(5), 667–679. https://doi.org/10.1111/fare.12089

Trottier, D., Benbouriche, M., & Bonneville, V. (2021). A meta-analysis on the association between rape myth acceptance and sexual coercion perpetration. *Journal of Sex Research*, *58*, 375–382. https://doi.org/10.1080/00224499.2019.1704677

Turell, S. C., Brown, M., & Herrmann, M. (2018). Disproportionately high: An exploration of intimate partner violence prevalence rates for bisexual people. *Sexual and Relationship Therapy*, *33*(1–2), 113–131. https://doi.org/10.1080/14681994.2017.1347614

Twenge, J. M., Sherman, R. A., & Wells, B. E. (2015). Changes in American adults' sexual behavior and attitudes, 1972–2012. *Archives of Sexual Behavior*, *44*(8), 2273–2285. https://doi.org/10.1007/s10508-015-0540-2

Ueda, P., Mercer, C. H., Ghaznavi, C., & Herbenick, D. (2020). Trends in frequency of sexual activity and number of sexual partners among adults aged 18 to 44 years in the US, 2000-2018. *JAMA Network Open*, *3*(6), e203833. https://doi.org/10.1001/jamanetworkopen.2020.3833

Umaña-Taylor, A. J. (2016). Ethnic-racial identity conceptualization, development, and youth adjustment. In L. Balter & C. S. Tamis-LeMonda (Eds.), *Child psychology: A handbook of contemporary issues* (p. 505). Routledge.

Umaña-Taylor, A. J., Quintana, S. M., Lee, R. M., Cross, W. E., Rivas-Drake, D., Schwartz, S. J., Syed, M., Yip, T., & Seaton, E. (2014). Ethnic and racial identity during adolescence and into young adulthood: An integrated conceptualization. *Child Development, 85*(1), 21–39. https://doi.org/10.1111/cdev.12196

Umberson, D., Donnelly, R., & Pollitt, A. M. (2018). Marriage, Social control, and health behavior: A dyadic analysis of same-sex and different-sex couples. *Journal of Health and Social Behavior, 59*(3), 429–446. https://doi.org/10.1177/0022146518790560

United Nations. (2019). *World marriage data*. https://population.un.org/MarriageData/index.html#/home

United Nations Statistics Division. (2014). *Demographic yearbook: 2013*. http://unstats.un.org/unsd/demographic/products/dyb/dyb2.htm

United Nations Statistics Division. (2017). *Divorces and crude divorce rates by urban/rural residence: 2011 - 2015. United Nations demographic yearbook: 2015*. https://unstats.un.org/Unsd/demographic/products/dyb/dyb2015/Table25.pdf

U.S. Bureau of Labor Statistics. (2021). *Occupational outlook handbook: 2021*. https://www.bls.gov/ooh/

U.S. Bureau of the Census. (2015). *Table A1. Marital status of people 15 years and over, by age, sex, and personal earnings: 2019. America's families and living arrangements: 2019*. http://www.census.gov/hhes/families/data/cps2014A.html

U.S. Census Bureau. (2019). *Table A1. Marital status of people 15 years and over, by age, sex, and personal earnings: 2019. America's families and living arrangements: 2019*. https://www.census.gov/data/tables/2019/demo/families/cps-2019.html

U.S. Census Bureau. (2020). *Historical marital status tables; esimated median age of first marriage by sex: 1890-present*. https://www.census.gov/data/tables/time-series/demo/families/marital.html

U.S. Department of Agriculture. (2017). *Families projected to spend an average of $233,610 raising a child born in 2015 | USDA*. https://www.usda.gov/media/press-releases/2017/01/09/families-projected-spend-average-233610-raising-child-born-2015

U.S. Department of Health and Human Services. (2019). *National vital statistics report*.

Van Rijn - Van Gelderen, L., Ellis-Davies, K., Huijzer-Engbrenghof, M., Jorgensen, T. D., Gross, M., Winstanley, A., Rubio, B., Vecho, O., Lamb, M. E., & Bos, H. M. (2020). Determinants of non-paid task division in gay-, lesbian-, and heterosexual-parent families with infants conceived using artificial reproductive techniques. *Frontiers in Psychology, 11*, 914. https://doi.org/10.3389/fpsyg.2020.00914

van Scheppingen, M. A., Chopik, W. J., Bleidorn, W., & Denissen, J. J. A. (2019). Longitudinal actor, partner, and similarity effects of personality on well-being. *Journal of Personality and Social Psychology, 117*(4), e51–e70. https://doi.org/10.1037/pspp0000211

van Scheppingen, M. A., Denissen, J. J. A., & Bleidorn, W. (2018). Stability and change in self-control during the transition to parenthood. *European Journal of Personality, 32*(6), 690–704. https://doi.org/10.1002/per.2172

van Scheppingen, M. A., & Leopold, T. (2020). Trajectories of life satisfaction before, upon, and after divorce: Evidence from a new matching approach. *Journal of Personality and Social Psychology, 119*, 1444–1458. https://doi.org/10.1037/pspp0000270

Vanassche, S., Swicegood, G., & Matthijs, K. (2012). Marriage and children as a key to happiness? Cross-national differences in the effects of marital status and children on well-being. *Journal of Happiness Studies, 14*(2), 501–524. https://doi.org/10.1007/s10902-012-9340-8

Vasilenko, S. A., & Lefkowitz, E. S. (2018). Sexual behavior and daily affect in emerging adulthood. *Emerging Adulthood, 6*(3), 191–199. https://doi.org/10.1177/2167696818767503

Vechiu, C. (2019). The role of hypermasculinity as a risk factor in sexual assault perpetration. In W. T. O'Donohue & P. A. Schewe (Eds.), *Handbook of sexual assault and sexual assault prevention* (pp. 257–273). Springer International Publishing. https://doi.org/10.1007/978-3-030-23645-8_15

Vespa, J. (2014). Historical trends in the marital intentions of one-time and serial cohabitors. *Journal of Marriage and Family, 76*(1), 207–217. https://doi.org/10.1111/jomf.12083

Vosylis, R., & Klimstra, T. (2021). How does financial life shape emerging adulthood? Short-term longitudinal associations between perceived features of emerging adulthood, financial behaviors, and financial well-being. *Emerging Adulthood*, 216769682090897. https://doi.org/10.1177/2167696820908970

Wang, W., & Parker, K. (2014). *Record share of Americans have never married*. http://www.pewsocialtrends.org/2014/09/24/record-share-of-americans-have-never-married/

Waren, W., & Pals, H. (2013). Comparing characteristics of voluntarily childless men and women. *Journal of Population Research, 30*(2), 151–170. https://doi.org/10.1007/s12546-012-9103-8

Watson, R. J., Snapp, S., & Wang, S. (2017). What we know and where we go from here: A review of lesbian, gay, and bisexual youth hookup literature. *Sex Roles, 77*(11–12), 801–811. https://doi.org/10.1007/s11199-017-0831-2

Weger, H. (2016). Cross-sex friendships. In C. R. Berger, M. E. Roloff, S. R. Wilson, J. P. Dillard, J. Coughlin, & D. Solomon (Eds.), *The international encyclopedia of interpersonal communication* (pp. 1–6). John Wiley & Sons, Inc. https://doi.org/10.1002/9781118540190.wbeic131

Weisskirch, R. S. (2018). Psychosocial intimacy, relationships with parents, and well-being among emerging adults. *Journal of Child and Family Studies, 27*(11), 3497–3505. https://doi.org/10.1007/s10826-018-1171-8

Widarsson, M., Engström, G., Rosenblad, A., Kerstis, B., Edlund, B., & Lundberg, P. (2013). Parental stress in early parenthood among mothers and fathers in Sweden. *Scandinavian Journal of Caring Sciences, 27*(4), 839–847. https://doi.org/10.1111/j.1471-6712.2012.01088.x

Wider, W., Suki, N. M., Lott, M. L., Nelson, L. J., Low, S. K., & Cosmas, G. (2021). Examining criteria for adulthood among young people in Sabah (East Malaysia). *Journal of Adult Development, 28*, 194–206. https://doi.org/10.1007/s10804-020-09367-9

Wiersma, J. D., Fischer, J. L., Harrington Cleveland, H., Reifman, A., & Harris, K. S. (2010). Selection and socialization of drinking among young adult dating, cohabiting, and married partners. *Journal of Social and Personal Relationships, 28*(2), 182–200. https://doi.org/10.1177/0265407510380083

Wight, R. G., Leblanc, A. J., & Lee Badgett, M. V. (2013). Same-sex legal marriage and psychological well-being: Findings from the California Health Interview Survey. *American Journal of Public Health, 103*(2), 339–346. https://doi.org/10.2105/AJPH.2012.301113

Wildsmith, E., Manlove, J., & Cook, E. (2018, August 8). Dramatic increase in the proportion of births outside of marriage in the United States from 1990 to 2016 - Child Trends. *Child Trends*. https://www.childtrends.org/publications/dramatic-increase-in-percentage-of-births-outside-marriage-among-whites-hispanics-and-women-with-higher-education-levels

Wilhite, E. R., & Fromme, K. (2021). The differential influence of drinking, sensation seeking, and impulsivity on the perpetration of unwanted sexual advances and sexual coercion. *Journal of Interpersonal Violence, 36*(3–4), 1437–1454. https://doi.org/10.1177/0886260517742151

Williams, C. D., Byrd, C. M., Quintana, S. M., Anicama, C., Kiang, L., Umaña-Taylor, A. J., Calzada, E. J., Pabón Gautier, M., Ejesi, K., Tuitt, N. R., Martinez-Fuentes, S., White, L., Marks, A., Rogers, L. O., & Whitesell, N. (2020). A lifespan model of ethnic-racial identity. *Research in Human Development, 17*(2–3), 99–129. https://doi.org/10.1080/15427609.2020.1831882

Williams, L., Kabamalan, M., & Ogena, N. (2007). Cohabitation in the Philippines: Attitudes and behaviors among young women and men. *Journal of Marriage & Family, 69*(5), 1244–1256.

Wilson, L. C., & Miller, K. E. (2016). Meta-analysis of the prevalence of unacknowledged rape. *Trauma, Violence, & Abuse, 17*(2), 149–159. https://doi.org/10.1177/1524838015576391

Wolf, R. (2017). Supreme Court rules for same-sex parents' birth certificate rights in Arkansas case. *USA Today*. https://www.usatoday.com/story/news/politics/2017/06/26/supreme-court-hear-challenge-same-sex-parents-birth-certificate/102427194/

Wood, D., Crapnell, T., Lau, L., Bennett, A., Lotstein, D., Ferris, M., & Kuo, A. (2018). Emerging adulthood as a critical stage in the life course. In N. Halfon, C. B. Forrest, R. M. Lerner, & E. M. Faustman (Eds.), *Handbook of life course health development* (pp. 123–143). Springer International Publishing. https://doi.org/10.1007/978-3-319-47143-3_7

World Health Organization. (2005). *World Health Organization multi-country study on women's health and domestic violence against women*. http://www.who.int/gender/violence/who_multicountry_study/en/index.html

Wrzus, C., Zimmermann, J., Mund, M., & Neyer, F. J. (2017). Friendships in young and middle adulthood. In M. Hojjat & A. Moyer (Eds.), *The psychology of friendship* (pp. 21–38). Oxford University Press. https://doi.org/10.1093/acprof:oso/9780190222024.003.0002

CHAPTER 13

AAUW. (2017). *The simple truth about the gender pay gap (Spring 2017)*. http://www.aauw.org/research/the-simple-truth-about-the-gender-pay-gap/

Ackerman, P. L., & Beier, M. E. (2006). Determinants of domain knowledge and independent study learning in an adult sample. *Journal of Educational Psychology, 98*(2), 366–381. 10.1037/0022-0663.98.2.366

Adams, G. A., & Rau, B. L. (2011). Putting off tomorrow to do what you want today: Planning for retirement. *The American Psychologist, 66*(3), 180–192. https://doi.org/10.1037/a0022131

Agorastos, A., Pervanidou, P., Chrousos, G. P., & Baker, D. G. (2019). Developmental trajectories of early life stress and trauma: A narrative review on neurobiological aspects beyond stress system dysregulation. *Frontiers in psychiatry, 10*, 118. https://doi.org/10.3389/fpsyt.2019.00118

Aldwin, C. M., & Levenson, M. R. (2001). Stress, coping, and health at midlife: A developmental perspective. In M. E. Lachman (Ed.), *Handbook of midlife development* (pp. 188–214). John Wiley & Sons Inc.

Almeida, S., Rato, L., Sousa, M., Alves, M. G., & Oliveira, P. F. (2017). Fertility and sperm quality in the aging male. *Current Pharmaceutical Design, 23*, 4429–4437. https://doi.org/10.2174/1381612823666170503150313

American Diabetes Association. (2014). Standards of medical care in diabetes--2014. *Diabetes care, 37*(Suppl 1), S11–66. https://doi.org/10.2337/dc13-S011

American Society of Plastic Surgeons. (2017). *2016 Plastic surgery statistics report*. www.plasticsurgery.org

American Society of Plastic Surgeons. (2020). *2020 National plastic surgery statistics*. https://www.plasticsurgery.org/documents/News/Statistics/2020/plastic-surgery-statistics-report-2020.pdf

Anderson, N. D., & Craik, F. I. M. (2017). 50 years of cognitive aging theory. *The Journals of Gerontology Series B: Psychological Sciences and Social Sciences, 72*(1), 1–6. https://doi.org/10.1093/geronb/gbw108

Anderson, W. F., Rosenberg, P. S., Prat, A., Perou, C. M., & Sherman, M. E. (2014). How many etiological subtypes of breast cancer: Two, three, four, or more? *Journal of the National Cancer Institute, 106*(8), dju165–dju165. https://doi.org/10.1093/jnci/dju165

Araujo, A. B., O'Donnell, A. B., Brambilla, D. J., Simpson, W. B., Longcope, C., Matsumoto, A. M., & McKinlay, J. B. (2004). Prevalence and incidence of androgen deficiency in middle-aged and older men: Estimates from the Massachusetts male aging study. *The Journal of Clinical Endocrinology and Metabolism, 89*(12), 5920–5926. https://doi.org/10.1210/jc.2003-031719

Arnson, Y., Rozanski, A., Gransar, H., Otaki, Y., Doris, M., Wang, F., Friedman, J., Hayes, S., Thomson, L., Tamarappoo, B., Slomka, P., Dey, D., & Berman, D. (2017). Hormone replacement therapy is associated with less coronary atherosclerosis and lower mortality. *Journal of the American College of Cardiology, 69*(11), 1408. https://doi.org/10.1016/S0735-1097(17)34797-6

Avis, N. E., Brockwell, S., & Colvin, A. (2005). A universal menopausal syndrome? *American Journal of Medicine, 118*(12), 1406. 10.1016/j.amjmed.2005.10.010

Avis, N. E., Crawford, S. L., Greendale, G., Bromberger, J. T., Everson-Rose, S. A., Gold, E. B., Hess, R., Joffe, H., Kravitz, H. M., Tepper, P. G., Thurston, R. C., & Study of Women's Health Across the Nation. (2015). Duration of menopausal vasomotor symptoms over the menopause transition. *JAMA Internal Medicine, 175*(4), 531–539. https://doi.org/10.1001/jamainternmed.2014.8063

Avis, N. E., Stellato, R., Crawford, S., Bromberger, J., Ganz, P., Cain, V., & Kagawa-Singer, M. (2001). Is there a menopausal syndrome? Menopausal status and symptoms across racial/ethnic groups. *Social Science & Medicine, 52*(3), 345.

Avolio, B. J., & Sosik, J. J. (1999). A life-span framework for assessing the impact of work on white-collar workers. In S. L. Willis & J. D. Reid (Eds.), *Life in the middle: Psychological and social development in middle age* (pp. 249–274). Academic Press.

Ayala Calvo, J.-C., & García, G. M. (2018). Hardiness as moderator of the relationship between structural and psychological empowerment on burnout in middle managers. *Journal of Occupational and Organizational Psychology, 91*, 362–384. https://doi.org/10.1111/joop.12194

Backé, E.-M., Seidler, A., Latza, U., Rossnagel, K., & Schumann, B. (2012). The role of psychosocial stress at work for the development of cardiovascular diseases: A systematic review. *International Archives of Occupational and Environmental Health, 85*(1), 67–79. https://doi.org/10.1007/s00420-011-0643-6

Badimon, L., Chagas, P., & Chiva-Blanch, G. (2017). Diet and cardiovascular disease: Effects of foods and nutrients in classical and emerging cardiovascular risk factors. *Current Medicinal Chemistry, 26*(19), 3639–3651. https://doi.org/10.2174/0929867324666170428103206

Baker, D. P., Eslinger, P. J., Benavides, M., Peters, E., Dieckmann, N. F., & Leon, J. (2015). The Cognitive impact of the education revolution: A possible cause of the Flynn Effect on population IQ. *Intelligence, 49*, 144–158. https://doi.org/10.1016/j.intell.2015.01.003

Ballesteros, S., Mayas, J., Prieto, A., Ruiz-Marquez, E., Toril, P., & Reales, J. M. (2017). Effects of video game training on measures of selective attention and working memory in older adults: Results from a randomized controlled trial. *Frontiers in Aging Neuroscience, 9*, 354. https://doi.org/10.3389/fnagi.2017.00354

Baltes, M. M., & Carstensen, L. L. (2003). The process of successful aging: Selection, optimization and compensation. In U. M. Staudinger & U. Lindenberger (Eds.), *Understanding human development: Dialogues with lifespan psychology* (pp. 81–104). Kluwer Academic Publishers.

Barbur, J. L., & Rodriguez-Carmona, M. (2015). Color vision changes in normal aging. In A. J. Elliot, M. D. Fairchild, & A. Franklin (Eds.), *Handbook of color psychology* (p. 740). Cambridge University Press. http://openaccess.city.ac.uk/12513/

Barnes-Farrell, J. L., & Matthews, R. A. (2007). Age and work attitudes. In K. S. Shultz & G. A. Adams (Eds.), *Aging and work in the 21st century* (pp. 139–162). Lawrence Erlbaum Associates Publishers.

Bartone, P. T., Jarle, Eid., & Sigurd, W. Hystad. (2016). Training hardiness for stress resilience. In N. Maheshwari & V. V. Kumar (Eds.), *Military psychology: Concepts, trends and interventions* (pp. 231–248). Sage Publications.

Bartsch, L. M., Loaiza, V. M., & Oberauer, K. (2019). Does limited working memory capacity underlie age differences in associative long-term memory? *Psychology and Aging, 34*(2), 268–281. https://doi.org/10.1037/pag0000317

Basaria, S. (2013). Reproductive aging in men. *Endocrinology and metabolism clinics of North America, 42*(2), 255–270. https://doi.org/10.1016/j.ecl.2013.02.012

Benjamin, E. J., Virani, S. S., Callaway, C. W., Chamberlain, A. M., Chang, A. R., Cheng, S., Chiuve, S. E., Cushman, M., Delling, F. N., Deo, R., de Ferranti, S. D., Ferguson, J. F., Fornage, M., Gillespie, C., Isasi, C. R., Jiménez, M. C., Jordan, L. C., Judd, S. E., Lackland, D., & American Heart Association Council on Epidemiology and Prevention Statistics Committee and Stroke Statistics Subcommittee. (2018). Heart disease and stroke statistics-2018 update: A report from the American heart association. *Circulation, 137*(12), e67–e492. https://doi.org/10.1161/CIR.0000000000000558

Benkhadra, K., Mohammed, K., Al Nofal, A., Carranza Leon, B. G., Alahdab, F., Faubion, S., Montori, V. M., Abu Dabrh, A. M., Zúñiga Hernández, J. A., Prokop, L. J., & Murad, M. H. (2015). Menopausal hormone therapy and mortality: A systematic review and meta-analysis. *The Journal of Clinical Endocrinology & Metabolism, 100*(11), 4021–4028. https://doi.org/10.1210/jc.2015-2238

Benz, C. C. (2008). Impact of aging on the biology of breast cancer. *Critical Reviews in Oncology/Hematology, 66*(1), 65–74. 10.1016/j.critrevonc.2007.09.001

Beyene, Y. (1986). Cultural significance and physiological manifestations of menopause a biocultural analysis. *Culture, Medicine and Psychiatry, 10*(1), 47–71. https://doi.org/10.1007/BF00053262

Beyene, Y., & Martin, M. C. (2001). Menopausal experiences and bone density of Mayan women in Yucatan, Mexico. *American Journal Of Human Biology: The Official Journal Of The Human Biology Council, 13*(4), 505–511.

Biessels, G. J., & Whitmer, R. A. (2020). Cognitive dysfunction in diabetes: how to implement emerging guidelines. *Diabetologia, 63*, 3–9. https://doi.org/10.1007/s00125-019-04977-9

Blom, V., Richter, A., Hallsten, L., & Svedberg, P. (2018). The associations between job insecurity, depressive symptoms and burnout: The role of performance-based self-esteem. *Economic and Industrial Democracy, 39*(1), 48–63. https://doi.org/10.1177/0143831X15609118

Bratt, C., Abrams, D., Swift, H. J., Vauclair, C.-M., & Marques, S. (2018). Perceived age discrimination across age in Europe: From an ageing society to a society for all ages. *Developmental Psychology, 54*(1), 167–180. https://doi.org/10.1037/dev0000398

Braver, T. S., & West, R. (2008). Working memory, executive control, and aging. In F. I. M. Craik & T. A. Salthouse (Eds.), *The handbook of aging and cognition* (3rd ed., pp. 311–372). Psychology Press.

Brown, R. E. (2016). Hebb and cattell: The genesis of the theory of fluid and crystallized intelligence. *Frontiers in Human Neuroscience, 10*, 606. https://doi.org/10.3389/fnhum.2016.00606

Brydon, L., Strike, P. C., Bhattacharyya, M. R., Whitehead, D. L., McEwan, J., Zachary, I., & Steptoe, A. (2010). Hostility and physiological responses to laboratory stress in acute coronary syndrome patients. *Journal of Psychosomatic Research, 68*(2), 109–116. https://doi.org/10.1016/j.jpsychores.2009.06.007

Bugg, J. M., Zook, N. A., DeLosh, E. L., Davalos, D. B., & Davis, H. P. (2006). Age differences in fluid intelligence: Contributions of general slowing and frontal decline. *Brain & Cognition, 62*(1), 9–16. 10.1016/j.bandc.2006.02.006

Burgoyne, A. P., Hambrick, D. Z., & Altmann, E. M. (2019). Is working memory capacity a causal factor in fluid intelligence? *Psychonomic Bulletin and Review, 26*(4), 1333–1339. https://doi.org/10.3758/s13423-019-01606-9

Campbell, K. L., Lustig, C., & Hasher, L. (2020). Aging and inhibition: Introduction to the special issue. *Psychology and Aging, 35*(5), 605–613. https://doi.org/10.1037/pag0000564

Cano, M. (2021). Racial/ethnic differences in US drug overdose mortality, 2017–2018. *Addictive Behaviors, 112*, 106625. https://doi.org/10.1016/j.addbeh.2020.106625

Case, A., & Deaton, A. (2017). Mortality and morbidity in the 21st century. *Brookings Papers on Economic Activity, 2017*(Spring), 397–476. https://doi.org/10.1353/eca.2017.0005

Castelo-Branco, C., & Davila, J. (2015). Menopause and aging skin in the elderly. In M. A. Farage, K. W. Miller, N. F. Woods, & H. I. Maibach (Eds.), *Skin, mucosa and menopause* (pp. 345–357). Springer Berlin Heidelberg. https://doi.org/10.1007/978-3-662-44080-3_25

Centers for Disease Control. (2020). *National diabetes statistics report 2020. Estimates of diabetes and its burden in the United States*. https://www.cdc.gov/diabetes/pdfs/data/statistics/national-diabetes-statistics-report.pdf

Centers for Disease Control. (2021). *WISQARS leading causes of death reports, 1981 - 2019*. https://webappa.cdc.gov/sasweb/ncipc/leadcause.html

Centers for Disease Control and Prevention. (2016). QuickStats: Percentage distribution of respondent-assessed health status among adults aged ≥25 years, by Completed education — national health interview survey, United States, 2015. *MMWR: Morbidity & Mortality Weekly Report, 65*, 1383. https://www.cdc.gov/mmwr/volumes/65/wr/mm6548a8.htm

Chamani, I. J., & Keefe, D. L. (2019). Epigenetics and female reproductive aging. *Frontiers in Endocrinology, 10*, 473. https://doi.org/10.3389/fendo.2019.00473

Charkhabi, M. (2019). Quantitative job insecurity and well-being: Testing the mediating role of hindrance and challenge appraisals. *Frontiers in Psychology, 9*, 2776. https://doi.org/10.3389/fpsyg.2018.02776

Chelmow, D., Pearlman, M. D., Young, A., Bozzuto, L., Dayaratna, S., Jeudy, M., Kremer, M. E., Scott, D. M., & O'Hara, J. S. (2020). Executive summary of the early-onset breast cancer evidence review conference. *Obstetrics and Gynecology, 135*, 1457–1478. https://doi.org/10.1097/AOG.0000000000003889

Chen, E., & Miller, G. E. (2013). Socioeconomic status and health: Mediating and moderating factors. *Annual Review of Clinical Psychology, 9*(1), 723–749. https://doi.org/10.1146/annurev-clinpsy-050212-185634

Chen, T., & Li, D. (2007). The roles of working memory updating and processing speed in mediating age-related differences in fluid intelligence. *Aging, Neuropsychology & Cognition, 14*(6), 631–646.

Cheng, Y. J., Kanaya, A. M., Araneta, M. R. G., Saydah, S. H., Kahn, H. S., Gregg, E. W., Fujimoto, W. Y., & Imperatore, G. (2019). Prevalence of diabetes by race and ethnicity in the United States, 2011-2016. *JAMA - Journal of the American Medical Association, 322*(24), 2389–2398. https://doi.org/10.1001/jama.2019.19365

Chevalère, J., Lemaire, P., & Camos, V. (2020). Age-related changes in Verbal working memory strategies. *Experimental Aging Research, 46*(2), 93–127. https://doi.org/10.1080/0361073X.2020.1716152

Chlebowski, R. T., Barrington, W., Aragaki, A. K., Manson, J. E., Sarto, G., O'Sullivan, M. J., Wu, D., Cauley, J. A., Qi, L., Wallace, R. L., & Prentice, R. L. (2017). Estrogen alone and health outcomes in black women by African ancestry. *Menopause, 24*(2), 133–141. https://doi.org/10.1097/GME.0000000000000733

Chopra, S., Shaw, M., Shaw, T., Sachdev, P. S., Anstey, K. J., & Cherbuin, N. (2018). More highly myelinated white matter tracts are associated with faster processing speed in healthy adults. *NeuroImage, 171*, 332–340. https://doi.org/10.1016/j.neuroimage.2017.12.069

Chrisler, J. C. (2008). The menstrual cycle in a biopsychosocial context. In F. L. Denmark & M. A. Paludi (Eds.), *Psychology of women: A handbook of issues and theories* (2nd ed., pp. 400–439). Praeger Publishers/Greenwood Publishing Grou.

Colom, R., Flores-Mendoza, C. E., & Abad, F. J. (2007). Generational changes on the draw-a-man test: A comparison of brazilian Urban and rural children tested in 1930, 2002 AND 2004. *Journal of Biosocial Science, 39*(01), 79. https://doi.org/10.1017/S0021932005001173

Cornelis, M. C., Wang, Y., Holland, T., Agarwal, P., Weintraub, S., & Morris, M. C. (2019). Age and cognitive decline in the UK Biobank. *PLOS One, 14*(3), e0213948. https://doi.org/10.1371/journal.pone.0213948

Craik, F. I. M., & Rose, N. S. (2012). Memory encoding and aging: A neurocognitive perspective. *Neuroscience and Biobehavioral Reviews, 36*(7), 1729–1739. https://doi.org/10.1016/j.neubiorev.2011.11.007

Curtin, S. C., & Arias, E. (2018). Mortality trends by race and ethnicity among adults aged 25 and over: United States, 2000-2017 key findings data from the national vital statistics system. *NCHS Data Brief, 342*. https://www.cdc.gov/nchs/products/index.htm.

Daniëls, N. E. M., Bartels, S. L., Verhagen, S. J. W., Van Knippenberg, R. J. M., De Vugt, M. E., & Delespaul, P. A. E. G. (2020). Digital assessment of working memory and processing speed in everyday life: Feasibility, validation, and lessons-learned. *Internet Interventions, 19*, 100300. https://doi.org/10.1016/j.invent.2019.100300

Dasgupta, D., & Ray, S. (2017). Is menopausal status related to women's attitudes toward menopause and aging? *Women & Health, 57*, 311–328. https://doi.org/10.1080/03630242.2016.1160965

Davis, D., Bendayan, R., Muniz Terrera, G., Hardy, R., Richards, M., & Kuh, D. (2017). Decline in search speed and verbal memory over 26 years of midlife in a British birth cohort. *Neuroepidemiology, 49*(3–4), 121–128. https://doi.org/10.1159/000481136

Davis, D. S., Sbrocco, T., Odoms-Young, A., & Smith, D. M. (2010). Attractiveness in African American and Caucasian women: Is beauty in the eyes of the observer? *Eating Behaviors, 11*(1), 25–32. https://doi.org/10.1016/j.eatbeh.2009.08.004

DeBono, N. L., Robinson, W. R., Lund, J. L., Tse, C. K., Moorman, P. G., Olshan, A. F., & Troester, M. A. (2018). Race, menopausal hormone therapy, and invasive breast cancer in the carolina breast cancer study. *Journal of Women's Health, 27*(3), 377–386. https://doi.org/10.1089/jwh.2016.6063

DeFronzo, R. A., & Abdul-Ghani, M. (2011). Assessment and treatment of cardiovascular risk in prediabetes: Impaired glucose tolerance and impaired fasting glucose. *The American Journal of Cardiology, 108*(3), 3B–24B. https://doi.org/10.1016/j.amjcard.2011.03.013

Delanoë, D., Hajri, S., Bachelot, A., Mahfoudh Draoui, D., Hassoun, D., Marsicano, E., & Ringa, V. (2012). Class, gender and culture in the experience of menopause. A comparative survey in Tunisia and France. *Social Science & Medicine*, *75*(2), 401–409. https://doi.org/10.1016/j.socscimed.2012.02.051

Deligkaris, P., Panagopoulou, E., Montgomery, A. J., & Masoura, E. (2014). *Job burnout and cognitive functioning: A systematic review.* http://www.tandfonline.com/doi/abs/10.1080/02678373.2014.909545

Dennis, H., & Thomas, K. (2007). Ageism in the workplace. *Generations*, *31*(1), 84–89.

de Salis, I., Owen-Smith, A., Donovan, J. L., & Lawlor, D. A. (2018). Experiencing menopause in the UK: The interrelated narratives of normality, distress, and transformation. *Journal of Women & Aging*, *30*, 520–540. https://doi.org/10.1080/08952841.2018.1396783

Dillaway, H. E. (2008). "Why can't you control this?" How women's interactions with intimate partners define menopause and family. *Journal of Women & Aging*, *20*(1/2), 47–64.

Ditzen, B., Schmidt, S., Strauss, B., Nater, U. M., Ehlert, U., & Heinrichs, M. (2008). Adult attachment and social support interact to reduce psychological but not cortisol responses to stress. *Journal of Psychosomatic Research*, *64*(5), 479–486. https://doi.org/10.1016/j.jpsychores.2007.11.011

Donatelle, R. (2004). *Health: The basics*. Benjamin Cummings.

Donohue, S. M., & Heywood, J. S. (2014). Job satisfaction and gender: An expanded specification from the NLSY. *International Journal of Manpower*, *25*, 211–238. http://www.emeraldinsight.com/doi/abs/10.1108/01437720410536007

Drydakis, N., MacDonald, P., Chiotis, V., & Somers, L. (2018). Age discrimination in the UK labour market. Does race moderate ageism? An experimental investigation. *Applied Economics Letters*, *25*(1), 1–4. https://doi.org/10.1080/13504851.2017.1290763

Ehlert, U., & Fischbacher, S. (2013). Reproductive health. In M. D. Gellman & J. R. Turner (Eds.), *Encyclopedia of Behavioral Medicine* (pp. 1658–1665). Springer New York. https://doi.org/10.1007/978-1-4419-1005-9

Elgamal, S. A., Roy, E. A., & Sharratt, M. T. (2011). Age and verbal fluency: the mediating effect of speed of processing. *Canadian Geriatrics Journal: CGJ*, *14*(3), 66–72. https://doi.org/10.5770/cgj.v14i3.17

Elias, M. F., & Dore, G. A. (2016). Cardiovascular Disease. In S. K. Whitbourne (Ed.), *The encyclopedia of adulthood and aging* (pp. 1–4). John Wiley & Sons, Inc. https://doi.org/10.1002/9781118521373.wbeaa216

Ellingsen, V. J., & Ackerman, P. L. (2016). Fluid-Crystallized theory of intelligence. In *The Encyclopedia of adulthood and aging* (pp. 1–5). John Wiley & Sons, Inc. https://doi.org/10.1002/9781118521373.wbeaa022

Endo, Y., Nourmahnad, A., & Sinha, I. (2020). Optimizing Skeletal Muscle anabolic response to resistance training in aging. *Frontiers in Physiology*, *11*, 874. https://doi.org/10.3389/fphys.2020.00874

Ericsson, A., & Pool, R. (2016). *Peak: Secrets from the new science of expertise*. Houghton Mifflin.

Ericsson, K. A. (2014). Expertise. *Current biology : CB*, *24*(11), R508–510. https://doi.org/10.1016/j.cub.2014.04.013

Ericsson, K. A. (2017). Expertise and individual differences: The search for the structure and acquisition of experts' superior performance. *Wiley Interdisciplinary Reviews: Cognitive Science*, *8*(1–2), e1382. https://doi.org/10.1002/wcs.1382

Ericsson, K. A., & Moxley, J. H. (2013). Experts' superior memory: From accumulation of chunks to building memory skills that mediate improved performance and learning. In D. S. L. Timothy & J. Perfect (Eds.), *The SAGE handbook of applied memory* (pp. 404–420). Sage.

Esler, M. (2017). Mental stress and human cardiovascular disease. *Neuroscience & Biobehavioral Reviews*, *74*, 269–276. https://doi.org/10.1016/J.NEUBIOREV.2016.10.011

Espeland, M. A., Bryan, R. N., Goveas, J. S., Robinson, J. G., Siddiqui, M. S., Liu, S., Hogan, P. E., Casanova, R., Coker, L. H., Yaffe, K., Masaki, K., Rossom, R., & Resnick, S. M. (2013). Influence of type 2 diabetes on brain volumes and changes in brain volumes: Results from the Women's Health Initiative Magnetic Resonance Imaging studies. *Diabetes Care*, *36*(1), 90–97. https://doi.org/10.2337/dc12-0555

Fadde, P. J., & Sullivan, P. (2020). Developing expertise and expert performance. In M. J. Bishop, E. Boling, J. Elen, & V. Svihla (Eds.), *Handbook of research in educational communications and technology* (pp. 53–72). Springer International Publishing. https://doi.org/10.1007/978-3-030-36119-8_4

Federal Interagency Forum on Aging-Related Statistics. (2016). *Older Americans 2016 key indicators of well-being*. https://agingstats.gov/docs/LatestReport/Older-Americans-2016-Key-Indicators-of-WellBeing.pdf

Federal Reserve. (2020). *Report on the economic well-being of U.S. households in 2018*. https://www.federalreserve.gov/publications/2019-economic-well-being-of-us-households-in-2018-retirement.htm

Federico, F., Marotta, A., Orsolini, M., & Casagrande, M. (2021). Aging in cognitive control of social processing: Evidence from the attention network test. *Aging, Neuropsychology, and Cognition*, *28*(1), 128–142. https://doi.org/10.1080/13825585.2020.1715336

Ferry, A. V., Anand, A., Strachan, F. E., Mooney, L., Stewart, S. D., Marshall, L., Chapman, A. R., Lee, K. K., Jones, S., Orme, K., Shah, A. S. V., & Mills, N. L. (2019). Presenting symptoms in men and women diagnosed with myocardial infarction using sex-specific criteria. *Journal of the American Heart Association*, *8*(17), e012307. https://doi.org/10.1161/JAHA.119.012307

Finkelstein, L. M., Ryan, K. M., & King, E. B. (2013). What do the young (old) people think of me? Content and accuracy of age-based metastereotypes. *European Journal of Work and Organizational Psychology*, *22*(6), 633–657. https://doi.org/10.1080/1359432X.2012.673279

Firooz, A., Rajabi-Estarabadi, A., Zartab, H., Pazhohi, N., Fanian, F., & Janani, L. (2017). The influence of gender and age on the thickness and echo-density of skin. *Skin Research and Technology*, *23*(1), 13–20. https://doi.org/10.1111/srt.12294

Flynn, J. R. (1984). The mean IQ of Americans: Massive gains 1932 to 1978. *Psychological Bulletin*, *95*(1), 29–51. https://doi.org/10.1037/0033-2909.95.1.29

Flynn, J. R. (2012). *Are we getting smarter?* Cambridge University Press. https://doi.org/10.1017/CBO9781139235679

Flynn, J. R., & Rossi-Casé, L. (2012). IQ gains in Argentina between 1964 and 1998. *Intelligence*, *40*(2), 145–150. https://doi.org/10.1016/j.intell.2012.01.006

Forcier, K., Stroud, L. R., & Papandonatos, G. D. (2006). Links between physical fitness and cardiovascular reactivity and recovery to psychological stressors: A meta-analysis. *Health Psychology*, *25*(6), 723–739.

Franks, P. W., & Pare, G. (2016). Putting the genome in context: Gene-environment interactions in type 2 diabetes. *Current Diabetes Reports*, *16*(7), 57. https://doi.org/10.1007/s11892-016-0758-y

Freund, A. M., & Baltes, P. B. (2007). Toward a theory of successful aging: Selection, optimization, and compensation. In R. Fernández-Ballesteros (Ed.), *Geropsychology: European perspectives for an aging world* (pp. 239–254). Hogrefe & Huber Publishers.

Friedman, H. S., & Kern, M. L. (2014). Personality, well-being, and health*. *Annual Review of Psychology*, *65*(1), 719–742. https://doi.org/10.1146/annurev-psych-010213-115123

Fuentecilla, J. L., Liu, Y., Huo, M., Kim, K., Birditt, K. S., Zarit, S. H., & Fingerman, K. L. (2020). Midlife adults' daily support to children and parents: Implications for diurnal cortisol. *Journal of Aging and Health*, *32*(9), 926–936. https://doi.org/10.1177/0898264319863994

Gaines, B., Dugan, A., & Cherniack, M. (2018). The relationship between retirement expectations and job insecurity among the aging us workforce. *Innovation in Aging*, *2*(Suppl. 1), 1005–1005. https://doi.org/10.1093/geroni/igy031.3714

Gambacciani, M., & Levancini, M. (2014). Hormone replacement therapy and the prevention of postmenopausal osteoporosis. *Przeglad Menopauzalny = Menopause Review*, *13*(4), 213–220. https://doi.org/10.5114/pm.2014.44996

Garcia, G. A., Khoshnevis, M., Yee, K. M. P., Nguyen, J. H., Nguyen-Cuu, J., Sadun, A. A., & Sebag, J. (2018). The effects of aging vitreous on contrast sensitivity function. *Graefe's Archive for Clinical and Experimental Ophthalmology*, *256*, 919–925. https://doi.org/10.1007/s00417-018-3957-1

Gaydosh, L., Hummer, R. A., Hargrove, T. W., Halpern, C. T., Hussey, J. M., Whitsel, E. A., Dole, N., & Harris, K. M. (2019). The depths of despair among US adults entering midlife. *American Journal of Public Health*, *109*(5), 774–780. https://doi.org/10.2105/AJPH.2019.305002

Geerligs, L., Maurits, N. M., Renken, R. J., & Lorist, M. M. (2014). Reduced specificity of functional connectivity in the aging brain during task performance. *Human Brain Mapping*, *35*(1), 319–330. https://doi.org/10.1002/hbm.22175

Gerber, M., & Pühse, U. (2009). Do exercise and fitness protect against stress-induced health complaints? A review of the literature. *Scandinavian Journal of Public Health*, *37*(8), 801–819. https://doi.org/10.1177/1403494809350522

Gershon, A., Johnson, S. L., & Miller, I. (2013). Chronic stressors and trauma: Prospective influences on the course of bipolar disorder. *Psychological Medicine*, *43*(12), 2583–2592. https://doi.org/10.1017/S0033291713000147

Giasson, H. L., Queen, T. L., Larkina, M., & Smith, J. (2017). Age group differences in perceived age discrimination: Associations with self-perceptions of aging. *The Gerontologist*, *57*(Suppl. 2), S160–S168. https://doi.org/10.1093/geront/gnx070

Gil-Cazorla, R., Shah, S., & Naroo, S. A. (2016). A review of the surgical options for the correction of presbyopia. *The British Journal of Ophthalmology*, *100*, 62–70. https://doi.org/10.1136/bjophthalmol-2015-306663

Gilbert, R., & Constantine, K. (2005). When strength can't last a lifetime: Vocational challenges of male workers in early and middle adulthood. *Men and Masculinities*, *7*(4), 424–433. 10.1177/1097184X03257582

Glei, D. A., & Preston, S. H. (2020). Estimating the impact of drug use on US mortality, 1999-2016. *PLOS One*, *15*(1), e0226732. https://doi.org/10.1371/journal.pone.0226732

Gold, D. T. (2016). Bone. In *The encyclopedia of adulthood and aging* (pp. 1–5). John Wiley & Sons, Inc. https://doi.org/10.1002/9781118521373.wbeaa300

Gold, E. B., Crawford, S. L., Avis, N. E., Crandall, C. J., Matthews, K. A., Waetjen, L. E., Lee, J. S., Thurston, R., Vuga, M., & Harlow, S. D. (2013). Factors related to age at natural menopause: Longitudinal analyses from SWAN. *American Journal of Epidemiology*, *178*(1), 70–83. https://doi.org/10.1093/aje/kws421

Goodman, A. (2020). Menopause and society: The association of educational level, social status, and financial status with positive versus negative perceptions about menopause. *Menopause*, *27*(6), 630–631. https://doi.org/10.1097/GME.0000000000001563

Grabe, S., & Hyde, J. S. (2006). Ethnicity and body dissatisfaction among women in the United States: A meta-analysis. *Psychological Bulletin*, *132*(4), 622–640. https://doi.org/10.1037/0033-2909.132.4.622

Graf, A. S., Long, D. M., & Patrick, J. H. (2017). Successful aging across adulthood: Hassles, uplifts, and self-assessed health in daily context. *Journal of Adult Development*, *24*(3), 216–225. https://doi.org/10.1007/s10804-017-9260-2

Grindler, N. M., Allsworth, J. E., Macones, G. A., Kannan, K., Roehl, K. A., & Cooper, A. R. (2015). Persistent organic pollutants and early menopause in U.S. Women. *PloS One*, *10*(1), e0116057. https://doi.org/10.1371/journal.pone.0116057

Gruber, N., Mosimann, U. P., Müri, R. M., & Nef, T. (2013). Vision and night driving abilities of elderly drivers. *Traffic Injury Prevention*, *14*(5), 477–485. https://doi.org/10.1080/15389588.2012.727510

Gujral, U.P.., Mohan, V.., Pradeepa, R.., Deepa, M.., Anjana, R.M.., Mehta, N.K.., & Narayan, K.M.. (2016). Ethnic variations in diabetes and prediabetes prevalence and the roles of insulin resistance and β-cell function: The CARRS and NHANES studies. *Journal of Clinical & Translational Endocrinology*, *4*, 19–27. https://doi.org/10.1016/J.JCTE.2016.02.004

Gupta, P., Sturdee, D. W., & Hunter, M. S. (2006). Mid-age health in women from the Indian subcontinent (MAHWIS): General health and the experience of menopause in women. *Climacteric*, *9*(1), 13–22.

Gupta, S., Tao, L., Murphy, J. D., Camargo, M. C., Oren, E., Valasek, M. A., Gomez, S. L., & Martinez, M. E. (2019). Race/ethnicity-, socioeconomic status-, and anatomic subsite-specific risks for gastric cancer. *Gastroenterology*, *156*(1), 59–62.e4. https://doi.org/10.1053/j.gastro.2018.09.045

Gutin, I., & Hummer, R. A. (2020). Occupation, employment status, and "despair"-associated mortality risk among working-aged U.S. adults, 1997–2015. *Preventive Medicine*, *137*, 106129. https://doi.org/10.1016/j.ypmed.2020.106129

Hambrick, D. Z., Burgoyne, A. P., Macnamara, B. N., & Ullén, F. (2018). Toward a multifactorial model of expertise: Beyond born versus made. *Annals of the New York Academy of Sciences, 1426*, 284–295. https://doi.org/10.1111/nyas.13586

Hannan, M. T., Broe, K. E., Cupples, L. A., Dufour, A. B., Rockwell, M., & Kiel, D. P. (2012). Height loss predicts subsequent hip fracture in men and women of the Framingham study. *Journal of Bone and Mineral Research: The Official Journal of the American Society for Bone and Mineral Research, 27*(1), 146–152. https://doi.org/10.1002/jbmr.557

Hannon, K. (2010). Dealing with the hormone dilemma. *U.S. News & World Report, 147*(2), 51–52.

Hanson, M. (2019). The Inheritance of cardiovascular disease risk. *Acta Paediatrica, 108*(10), 1747–1756. https://doi.org/10.1111/apa.14813

Hanspal, T., Weber, A., & Wohlfart, J. (2020). Income and wealth shocks and expectations during the COVID-19 pandemic. *CEBI Working Paper Series, 13*(20). https://doi.org/10.2139/ssrn.3578472

Haring, R., Ittermann, T., Völzke, H., Krebs, A., Zygmunt, M., Felix, S. B., Grabe, H. J., Nauck, M., & Wallaschofski, H. (2010). Prevalence, incidence and risk factors of testosterone deficiency in a population-based cohort of men: Results from the study of health in Pomerania. *The Aging Male: The Official Journal of the International Society for the Study of the Aging Male, 13*(4), 247–257. https://doi.org/10.3109/13685538.2010.487553

Hartley, A. A., & Maquestiaux, F. (2016). Attention. In *The encyclopedia of adulthood and aging* (pp. 1–5). John Wiley & Sons, Inc. https://doi.org/10.1002/9781118521373.wbeaa133

Hartshorne, J. K., & Germine, L. T. (2015). When does cognitive functioning peak? The asynchronous rise and fall of different cognitive abilities across the life span. *Psychological Science, 26*(4), 433–443. https://doi.org/10.1177/0956797614567339

Hayslip, B. J., Panek, P. E., & Patrick, J. H. (2007). *Adult development and aging* (4th ed.). Krieger Publishing Company.

Heidemeier, H., & Staudinger, U. M. (2015). Age differences in achievement goals and motivational characteristics of work in an ageing workforce. *Ageing and society, 35*, 809–836. https://doi.org/10.1017/S0144686X13001098

Helfer, K. S., Merchant, G. R., & Wasiuk, P. A. (2017). Age-related changes in objective and subjective speech perception in complex listening environments. *Journal of Speech Language and Hearing Research, 60*(10), 3009. https://doi.org/10.1044/2017_JSLHR-H-17-0030

Heraty, N., & McCarthy, J. (2015). Unearthing psychological predictors of financial planning for retirement among late career older workers: Do self-perceptions of aging matter? *Work, Aging and Retirement, 1*, wav008. https://doi.org/10.1093/workar/wav008

Herzmann, G., & Curran, T. (2011). Experts' memory: An ERP study of perceptual expertise effects on encoding and recognition. *Memory & Cognition, 39*(3), 412–432. https://doi.org/10.3758/s13421-010-0036-1

Hessel, P., Kinge, J. M., Skirbekk, V., & Staudinger, U. M. (2018). Trends and determinants of the Flynn effect in cognitive functioning among older individuals in 10 European countries. *Journal of Epidemiology and Community Health, 72*(5), 383–389. https://doi.org/10.1136/jech-2017-209979

Hickey, M., Elliott, J., & Davison, S. L. (2012). Hormone replacement therapy. *BMJ (Clinical Research Ed.), 344*, e763. https://doi.org/10.1136/bmj.e763

Hill-Briggs, F., Adler, N. E., Berkowitz, S. A., Chin, M. H., Gary-Webb, T. L., Navas-Acien, A., Thornton, P. L., & Haire-Joshu, D. (2021). Social determinants of health and diabetes: A scientific review. *Diabetes Care, 44*, 258–279. https://doi.org/10.2337/dci20-0053

Holt, R. I. G., Phillips, D. I. W., Jameson, K. A., Cooper, C., Dennison, E. M., & Peveler, R. C. (2013). The Relationship between depression, anxiety and cardiovascular disease: Findings from the Hertfordshire cohort study. *Journal of Affective Disorders, 150*(1), 84–90. https://doi.org/10.1016/j.jad.2013.02.026

Horn, J. L., & Cattell, R. B. (1966). Refinement and test of the theory of fluid and crystallized general intelligences. *Journal of Educational Psychology, 57*(5), 253–270.

Horn, J. L., & Noll, J. (1997). Human cognitive capabilities: Gf-Gc theory. In D. P. Flanagan, J. L. Genshaft, & P. L. Harrison (Eds.), *Contemporary intellectual assessment: Theories, tests, and issues* (pp. 53–91). Guilford Press.

Houston, K. A., King, J., Li, J., & Jemal, A. (2018). Trends in prostate cancer incidence rates and prevalence of prostate specific antigen screening by socioeconomic status and regions in the United States, 2004 to 2013. *Journal of Urology, 199*(3), 676–682. https://doi.org/10.1016/j.juro.2017.09.103

Howard, B. V., Van Horn, L., Hsia, J., Manson, J. E., Stefanick, M. L., Wassertheil-Smoller, S., LaCroix, A. Z., Langer, R. D., Lasser, N. L., Lewis, C. E., Limacher, M. C., Margolis, K. L., Mysiw, J., Ockene, J. K., Parker, L. M., Perri, M. G., Phillips, L., Prentice, R. L., & Robbins, J. (2006). Low-fat diet and weight change in postmenopausal women. *JAMA: Journal of the American Medical Association, 296*, 394–395.

Howell, L. C., & Beth, A. (2002). Midlife Myths and realities: Women reflect on their experiences. *Journal of Women & Aging, 14*(3/4), 189.

Hu, X., Kaplan, S., & Dalal, R. S. (2010). An examination of blue-versus white-collar workers' conceptualizations of job satisfaction facets. *Journal of Vocational Behavior, 76*(2), 317–325. https://doi.org/10.1016/j.jvb.2009.10.014

Hu, Y., van Lenthe, F. J., Borsboom, G. J., Looman, C. W. N., Bopp, M., Burström, B., Dzúrová, D., Ekholm, O., Klumbiene, J., Lahelma, E., Leinsalu, M., Regidor, E., Santana, P., de Gelder, R., & Mackenbach, J. P. (2016). Trends in socioeconomic inequalities in self-assessed health in 17 European countries between 1990 and 2010. *Journal of Epidemiology and Community Health, 70*(7), 644–652. https://doi.org/10.1136/jech-2015-206780

Huang, K.-E., Xu, L., Nasri, N. I., & Jaisamrarn, U. (2010). The Asian menopause survey: Knowledge, perceptions, hormone treatment and sexual function. *Maturitas, 65*(3), 276–283. https://doi.org/10.1016/j.maturitas.2009.11.015

Hvas, L., & Dorte Effersøe, G. (2008). Discourses on menopause - Part II: How do women talk about menopause?. *Health: An Interdisciplinary Journal for the Social Study of Health, Illness & Medicine, 12*(2), 177–192. https://doi.org/10.1177/1363459307086842

Infurna, F. J., Gerstorf, D., & Lachman, M. E. (2020). Midlife in the 2020s: Opportunities and challenges. *American Psychologist, 75*(4), 470–485. https://doi.org/10.1037/amp0000591

James, E. R., Salas-Huetos, A., Gostick, A. R., Carrell, D. T., Aston, K. I., & Jenkins, T. G. (2021). Aging of male and female gametes. In T. Tollefsbol (Ed.), *Epigenetics and reproductive health* (pp. 253–267). Elsevier. https://doi.org/10.1016/b978-0-12-819753-0.00013-1

Jannasch, F., Kroger, J., & Schulze, M. B. (2017). Dietary patterns and type 2 diabetes: A systematic literature review and meta-analysis of prospective studies. *The Journal of Nutrition, 147*(6), 1174–1182. https://doi.org/10.3945/jn.116.242552

Jemal, A., Thun, M. J., Ward, E. E., Henley, S. J., Cokkinides, V. E., & Murray, T. E. (2008). Mortality from leading causes by education and race in the United States, 2001. *American Journal of Preventive Medicine, 34*(1), 1–8.

Jeong, Y. J., Aldwin, C. M., Igarashi, H., & Spiro, A. (2016). Do hassles and uplifts trajectories predict mortality? Longitudinal findings from the VA normative aging study. *Journal of Behavioral Medicine, 39*(3), 408–419. https://doi.org/10.1007/s10865-015-9703-9

Juster, R.-P., Bizik, G., Picard, M., Arsenault-Lapierre, G., Sindi, S., Trepanier, L., Marin, M.-F., Wan, N., Sekerovic, Z., Lord, C., Fiocco, A. J., Plusquellec, P., McEwen, B. S., & Lupien, S. J. (2011). A transdisciplinary perspective of chronic stress in relation to psychopathology throughout life span development. *Development and Psychopathology, 23*(3), 725–776. https://doi.org/10.1017/S0954579411000289

Kalayinia, S., Goodarzynejad, H., Maleki, M., & Mahdieh, N. (2018). Next generation sequencing applications for cardiovascular disease. *Annals of Medicine, 50*(2), 91–109. https://doi.org/10.1080/07853890.2017.1392595

Karlamangla, A. S., Miller-Martinez, D., Lachman, M. E., Tun, P. A., Koretz, B. K., & Seeman, T. E. (2014). Biological correlates of adult cognition: midlife in the United States (MIDUS). *Neurobiology of Aging, 35*(2), 387–394. https://doi.org/10.1016/j.neurobiolaging.2013.07.028

Kehr, H. M., Strasser, M., & Paulus, A. (2018). Motivation and volition in the workplace. In J. Heckhausen & H. Heckhausen (Eds.), *Motivation and action* (pp. 819–852). Springer International Publishing. https://doi.org/10.1007/978-3-319-65094-4_19

Kelch-Oliver, K. (2011). The Experiences of African American grandmothers in grandparent-headed families. *The Family Journal, 19*(1), 73–82. https://doi.org/10.1177/1066480710388730

Keller, K., & Engelhardt, M. (2013). Strength and muscle mass loss with aging process. Age and strength loss. *Muscles, Ligaments and Tendons Journal, 3*(4), 346–350. http://europepmc.org/articles/PMC3940510/? report=abstract

Kennedy, Q., Taylor, J. L., Reade, G., & Yesavage, J. A. (2010). Age and expertise effects in aviation decision making and flight control in a flight simulator. *Aviation, Space, and Environmental Medicine, 81*(5), 489–497. http://www.pubmedcentral.nih.gov/articlerender.fcgi? artid=2905035&tool=pmcentrez&rendertype=abstract

Ketch, C., Weedin, E., & Gibson, B. A. (2017). Management of the symptoms of perimenopause. In D. Shoupe (Ed.), *Handbook of gynecology* (pp. 487–497). Springer International Publishing. https://doi.org/10.1007/978-3-319-17798-4_44

Keteepe-Arachi, T., & Sharma, S. (2017). Cardiovascular disease in women: Understanding symptoms and risk factors. *European Cardiology Review, 12*(1), 10–13. https://doi.org/10.15420/ecr.2016:32:1

Khan, N., Afaq, F., & Mukhtar, H. (2010). Lifestyle as risk factor for cancer: Evidence from human studies. *Cancer Letters, 293*(2), 133–143. https://doi.org/10.1016/j.canlet.2009.12.013

Khan, S. D. (2017). Aging and male reproduction. In K. Gunasekaran & N. Pandiyan (Eds.), *Male infertility* (pp. 197–206). Springer India. https://doi.org/10.1007/978-81-322-3604-7_13

Kievit, R. A., Fuhrmann, D., Borgeest, G. S., Simpson-Kent, I. L., & Henson, R. N. A. (2018). The Neural determinants of age-related changes in fluid intelligence: A pre-registered, longitudinal analysis in UK Biobank. *Wellcome Open Research, 3*, 38. https://doi.org/10.12688/wellcomeopenres.14241.2

Kish, J. K., Yu, M., Percy-Laurry, A., & Altekruse, S. F. (2014). Racial and ethnic disparities in cancer survival by neighborhood socioeconomic status in surveillance, epidemiology, and end results (SEER) registries. *Journal of the National Cancer Institute. Monographs, 2014*(49), 236–243. https://doi.org/10.1093/jncimonographs/lgu020

Koh, K. K., Han, S. H., Oh, P. C., Shin, E. K., & Quon, M. J. (2010). Combination therapy for treatment or prevention of atherosclerosis: Focus on the lipid-RAAS interaction. *Atherosclerosis (00219150), 209*(2), 307–313. https://doi.org/10.1016/j.atherosclerosis.2009.09.007

Kollbaum, P. S., & Bradley, A. (2020). Correction of presbyopia: old problems with old (and new) solutions. *Clinical and Experimental Optometry, 103*(1), 21–30. https://doi.org/10.1111/cxo.12987

Kotsopoulos, J., Huzarski, T., Gronwald, J., Moller, P., Lynch, H. T., Neuhausen, S. L., Senter, L., Demsky, R., Foulkes, W. D., Eng, C., Karlan, B., Tung, N., Singer, C. F., Sun, P., Lubinski, J., & Narod, S. A. (2016). Hormone replacement therapy after menopause and risk of breast cancer in BRCA1 mutation carriers: A case-control study. *Breast Cancer Research and Treatment, 155*(2), 365–373. https://doi.org/10.1007/s10549-016-3685-3

Kramer, A. F., & Madden, D. J. (2008). Attention. In F. I. M. Craik & T. A. Salthouse (Eds.), *The handbook of aging and cognition* (3rd ed., pp. 189–249). Psychology Press.

Kuehn, B. M. (2020). In Alzheimer research, glucose metabolism moves to center stage. *Journal of the American Medical Association, 323*, 297–299. https://doi.org/10.1001/jama.2019.20939

Künstler, E. C. S., Penning, M. D., Napiórkowski, N., Klingner, C. M., Witte, O. W., Müller, H. J., Bublak, P., & Finke, K. (2018). Dual task effects on visual attention capacity in normal aging. *Frontiers in Psychology, 9*, 1564, . https://doi.org/10.3389/fpsyg.2018.01564

Lachman, M. E., Teshale, S., & Agrigoroaei, S. (2015). Midlife as a pivotal period in the life course: Balancing growth and decline at the crossroads of youth and old age. *International Journal of Behavioral Development, 39*(1), 20–31. https://doi.org/10.1177/0165025414533223

Langton, C. R., Whitcomb, B. W., Purdue-Smithe, A. C., Sievert, L. L., Hankinson, S. E., Manson, J. A. E., Rosner, B. A., & Bertone-Johnson, E. R. (2020). Association of parity and breastfeeding with risk of early natural menopause. *JAMA Network Open, 3*(1), e1919615. https://doi.org/10.1001/jamanetworkopen.2019.19615

Larney, S., & Hall, W. (2019). A major expansion of opioid agonist treatment is needed to reduce overdose deaths in the USA. *The Lancet Public Health*, e77–e78. https://doi.org/10.1016/S2468-2667(19)30001-5

Lê-Scherban, F., Brenner, A. B., Hicken, M. T., Needham, B. L., Seeman, T., Sloan, R. P., Wang, X., & Diez Roux, A. V. (2018). Child and adult socioeconomic status and the cortisol response to acute stress: Evidence from the multi-ethnic study of atherosclerosis. *Psychosomatic Medicine*, *80*(2), 184–192. https://doi.org/10.1097/PSY.0000000000000543

Lee, Y.-A., & Goto, Y. (2015). Chronic stress effects on working memory: Association with prefrontal cortical tyrosine hydroxylase. *Behavioural Brain Research*, *286*, 122–127. https://doi.org/10.1016/j.bbr.2015.03.007

Leigh-Paffenroth, E. D., & Elangovan, S. (2011). Temporal processing in low-frequency channels: Effects of age and hearing loss in middle-aged listeners. *Journal of the American Academy of Audiology*, *22*(7), 393–404. https://doi.org/10.3766/jaaa.22.7.2

Leong, A., Porneala, B., Dupuis, J., Florez, J. C., & Meigs, J. B. (2016). Type 2 diabetes genetic predisposition, obesity, and all-cause mortality risk in the U.S.: A multiethnic analysis. *Diabetes Care*, *39*(4), 539–546. http://care.diabetesjournals.org/content/39/4/539.short

Linz, S., & Semykina, A. (2013). Job satisfaction, expectations, and gender: Beyond the European union. *International Journal of Manpower*, *34*(6), 584–615. https://doi.org/10.1108/IJM-06-2013-0149

Liu, J., & Eden, J. (2007). Experience and attitudes toward menopause in Chinese women living in Sydneyâ€"A cross sectional survey. *Maturitas*, *58*(4), 359–365.

Lobo, R. A. (2017). Hormone-replacement therapy: Current thinking. *Nature Reviews Endocrinology*, *13*(4), 220–231. https://doi.org/10.1038/nrendo.2016.164

Logan, A. J., & Baker, J. (2007). Cross-sectional and longitudinal profiles of age related decline in golf performance. *Journal of Sport & Exercise Psychology*, *29*, S15–S15.

Lorenc, E. S., Mallett, R., & Lewis-Peacock, J. A. (2021). Distraction in visual working Memory: Resistance is not futile. *Trends in Cognitive Sciences*, *25*, 228–239. https://doi.org/10.1016/j.tics.2020.12.004

Low, E., Crewther, S. G., Ong, B., Perre, D., & Wijeratne, T. (2017). Compromised motor dexterity confounds processing speed task outcomes in stroke patients. *Frontiers in Neurology*, *8*, 484. https://doi.org/10.3389/fneur.2017.00484

Lubbadeh, T. (2020). International review of management and marketing job burnout: A general literature review. *International Review of Management and Marketing*, *10*(3), 2020. https://doi.org/10.32479/irmm.9398

Lustig, C., Hasher, L., & Tonev, S. T. (2006). Distraction as a determinant of processing speed. *Psychonomic Bulletin & Review*, *13*(4), 619–625.

Lynn, R. (2009). What has caused the Flynn effect? Secular increases in the Development Quotients of infants. *Intelligence*, *37*(1), 16–24. https://doi.org/10.1016/j.intell.2008.07.008

Maddi, S. R. (2013). Personal hardiness as the basis for resilience. In *Hardiness: Turning stressful circumstances into resilient growth* (pp. 7–17). Springer Netherlands. https://doi.org/10.1007/978-94-007-5222-1

Maddi, S. R. (2016). Hardiness as a pathway to resilience under stress. In U. Kumar (Ed.), *The routledge international handbook of psychosocial resilience* (p. 104). Routledge.

Maddi, S. R. (2020a). Personality hardiness. In K. Sweeny, M. L. Robbins, & L. M. Cohen (Eds.), *The Wiley encyclopedia of health psychology* (pp. 439–445). Wiley. https://doi.org/10.1002/9781119057840.ch94

Maddi, S. R. (2020b). Resiliency and Hardiness. In B. J. Carducci, C. S. Nave, J. S. Mio, & R. E. Riggio (Eds.), *The Wiley encyclopedia of personality and individual differences* (pp. 393–398). Wiley. https://doi.org/10.1002/9781118970843.ch330

Madi, A., & Cui, G. (2020). Regulation of immune cell metabolism by cancer cell oncogenic mutations. *International Journal of Cancer*, *147*(2), 307–316. https://doi.org/10.1002/ijc.32888

Madsen, R., & Birkelund, R. (2016). Women's experiences during myocardial infarction: Systematic review and meta-ethnography. *Journal of Clinical Nursing*, *25*(5–6), 599–609. https://doi.org/10.1111/jocn.13096

Magee, W. (2015). Effects of gender and age on pride in work, and job satisfaction. *Journal of Happiness Studies*, *16*(5), 1091–1115. https://doi.org/10.1007/s10902-014-9548-x

Malinen, O.-P., & Savolainen, H. (2016). The Effect of perceived school climate and teacher efficacy in behavior management on job satisfaction and burnout: A longitudinal study. *Teaching and Teacher Education*, *60*, 144–152. https://doi.org/10.1016/j.tate.2016.08.012

Marchiondo, L. A., Gonzales, E., & Williams, L. J. (2019). Trajectories of perceived workplace age discrimination and long-term associations with mental, self-rated, and occupational health. *The Journals of Gerontology: Series B*, *74*(4), 655–663. https://doi.org/10.1093/geronb/gbx095

Marshall, B. L. (2007). Climacteric redux?. *Men & Masculinities*, *9*(4), 509–529.

Marsland, A. L., Walsh, C., Lockwood, K., & John-Henderson, N. A. (2017). The effects of acute psychological stress on circulating and stimulated inflammatory markers: A systematic review and meta-analysis. *Brain, Behavior, and Immunity*, *64*, 208–219. https://doi.org/10.1016/J.BBI.2017.01.011

Mayes, J. L. (2021). Urban noise levels are high enough to damage auditory sensorineural health. *Cities & Health*, *5*(1–2), 96–102. https://doi.org/10.1080/23748834.2019.1577204

McDaniel, D., Farris, P., & Valacchi, G. (2018). Atmospheric skin aging-Contributors and inhibitors. *Journal of Cosmetic Dermatology*, *17*(2), 124–137. https://doi.org/10.1111/jocd.12518

McEwen, B. S. (2018). Neurobiological and systemic effects of chronic stress. *Chronic Stress*, *1*, 247054701769232. https://doi.org/10.1177/2470547017692328

McLeod, P., Sommerville, P., & Reed, N. (2005). Are automated actions beyond conscious access? In J. Duncan, P. McLeod, & L. Phillips (Eds.), *Measuring the Mind* (pp. 359–371). Oxford University Press.

McNamara, M., Batur, P., & DeSapri, K. T. (2015). In the clinic. Perimenopause. *Annals of Internal Medicine*, *162*(3), ITC1–15. https://doi.org/10.7326/AITC201502030

Mehta, K. M., & Yeo, G. W. (2017). Systematic review of dementia prevalence and incidence in United States race/ethnic populations. *Alzheimer's & Dementia*, *13*(1), 72–83. https://doi.org/10.1016/j.jalz.2016.06.2360

Meister, H., Wenzel, F., Gehlen, A. K., Kessler, J., & Walger, M. (2020). Static and dynamic cocktail party listening in younger and older adults. *Hearing Research*, *395*, 108020. https://doi.org/10.1016/j.heares.2020.108020

Mielck, A., Vogelmann, M., Leidl, R., Mielck, A., Reitmeir, P., Vogelmann, M., Leidl, R., Franks, P., Lubetkin, E., Melnikow, J., Jia, H., Zack, M., Moriarty, D., Fryback, D., Luo, N., Johnson, J., Shaw, J., Feeny, D., Coons, S., & Williams, A, . . (2014). Health-related quality of life and socioeconomic status: Inequalities among adults with a chronic disease. *Health and Quality of Life Outcomes*, *12*(1), 58. https://doi.org/10.1186/1477-7525-12-58

Miller, T. A., Allen, R. H., Kaunitz, A. M., & Cwiak, C. A. (2018). Contraception for midlife women: A review. *Menopause*, *25*, 817–827. https://doi.org/10.1097/GME.0000000000001073

Mitchell, W. K., Williams, J., Atherton, P., Larvin, M., Lund, J., & Narici, M. (2012). Sarcopenia, dynapenia, and the impact of advancing age on human skeletal muscle size and strength; A quantitative review. *Frontiers in Physiology*, *3*, 260. https://doi.org/10.3389/fphys.2012.00260

Morrissey, M. (2019). *The State of American retirement savings*. Economic Policy Institute. https://www.epi.org/publication/the-state-of-american-retirement-savings/

Morrow, D. G., Menard, W. E., Ridolfo, H. E., Stine-Morrow, E. A. L., Teller, T., & Bryant, D. (2003). Expertise, cognitive Ability, and age effects on pilot communication. *International Journal of Aviation Psychology*, *13*(4), 345.

Morrow, D. G., & Schriver, A. (2007). External support for pilot communication: Implications for age-related design. *International Journal of Cognitive Technology*, *12*(1), 21–30.

Moxley, J. H., & Charness, N. (2013). Meta-analysis of age and skill effects on recalling chess positions and selecting the best move. *Psychonomic Bulletin & Review*, *20*(5), 1017–1022. https://doi.org/10.3758/s13423-013-0420-5

Mroczek, D. K., Stawski, R. S., Turiano, N. A., Chan, W., Almeida, D. M., Neupert, S. D., & Spiro, A. (2015). Emotional reactivity and mortality: Longitudinal findings from the VA normative aging study. *Journals of Gerontology - Series B Psychological Sciences and Social Sciences*, *70*(3), 398–406. https://doi.org/10.1093/geronb/gbt107

Munukka, M., Koivunen, K., von Bonsdorff, M. B., Sipilä, S., Portegijs, E., Ruoppila, I., & Rantanen, T. (2020). Birth cohort differences in cognitive performance in 75- and 80-year-olds: A comparison of two cohorts over 28 years. *Aging Clinical and Experimental Research*, *33*(1), 57–65. https://doi.org/10.1007/s40520-020-01702-0

Murphy, N., Alderman, P., Voege Harvey, K., & Harris, N. (2017). Women and heart disease: An evidence-based update. *The Journal for Nurse Practitioners*, *13*(9), 610–616. https://doi.org/10.1016/j.nurpra.2017.07.011

Naicker, K., Johnson, J. A., Skogen, J. C., Manuel, D., Øverland, S., Sivertsen, B., & Colman, I. (2017). Type 2 diabetes and comorbid symptoms of depression and anxiety: Longitudinal associations with mortality risk. *Diabetes Care*, *40*(3), 352–358. https://doi.org/10.2337/dc16-2018

National Cancer Institute. (2020). *Cancer statistics - National cancer institute*. https://www.cancer.gov/about-cancer/understanding/statistics

National Center for Health Statistics. (2015). *Deaths: Final data for 2013. National vital statistics reports*. http://www.cdc.gov/nchs/data/nvsr/nvsr64/nvsr64_02.pdf

Nenclares, P., & Harrington, K. J. (2020). The biology of cancer. *Medicine*, *48*, 67–72. https://doi.org/10.1016/j.mpmed.2019.11.001

Neugarten, B. L. (1968). The Awareness of middle aging. In B. L. Neugarten (Ed.), *Middle age and aging* (pp. 137–147). University of Chicago Press.

Neumark, D., Burn, I., Button, P., Neumark, D., Burn, I., & Button, P. (2017). *Age discrimination and hiring of older workers*. FRBSF Economic Letter. https://econpapers.repec.org/article/fipfedfel/00121.htm

Ng, T. W. H., & Feldman, D. C. (2010). The relationships of age with job attitudes: A meta-analysis. *Personnel Psychology*, *63*(3), 677–718. https://doi.org/10.1111/j.1744-6570.2010.01184.x

Nguyen, B. T., Han, X., Jemal, A., & Drope, J. (2016). Diet quality, risk factors and access to care among low-income uninsured American adults in states expanding Medicaid vs. states not expanding under the affordable care act. *Preventive Medicine*, *91*, 169–171. https://doi.org/10.1016/J.YPMED.2016.08.015

Nickels, S., Truong, T., Hein, R., Stevens, K., Buck, K., Behrens, S., Eilber, U., Schmidt, M., Häberle, L., Vrieling, A., Gaudet, M., Figueroa, J., Schoof, N., Spurdle, A. B., Rudolph, A., Fasching, P. A., Hopper, J. L., Makalic, E., Schmidt, D. F., & Chang-Claude, J, . . (2013). Evidence of gene-environment interactions between common breast cancer susceptibility loci and established environmental risk factors. *PLoS Genetics*, *9*(3), e1003284. https://doi.org/10.1371/journal.pgen.1003284

Niessen, L. W., Mohan, D., Akuoku, J. K., Mirelman, A. J., Ahmed, S., Koehlmoos, T. P., Trujillo, A., Khan, J., & Peters, D. H. (2018). Tackling socioeconomic inequalities and non-communicable diseases in low-income and middle-income countries under the sustainable development agenda. *The Lancet*, *391*, 2036–2046. https://doi.org/10.1016/S0140-6736(18)30482-3

Nilsson, J., Thomas, A. J., O'Brien, J. T., & Gallagher, P. (2014). White matter and cognitive decline in aging: A focus on processing speed and variability. *Journal of the International Neuropsychological Society: JINS*, *20*(3), 262–267. https://doi.org/10.1017/S1355617713001458

Nisbett, R. E., Aronson, J., Blair, C., Dickens, W., Flynn, J., Halpern, D. F., & Turkheimer, E. (2013). Intelligence: New findings and theoretical developments. *American Psychologist*, *67*(2), 130–159. https://doi.org/10.1037/a0026699

Nosek, M., Kennedy, H. P., & Gudmundsdottir, M. (2012). Distress during the menopause transition: A rich contextual analysis of midlife women's narratives. *SAGE Open*, *2*(3), 2158244012455178. https://doi.org/10.1177/2158244012455178

O'Connor, D. B., Thayer, J. F., & Vedhara, K. (2021). Stress and health: A review of psychobiological processes. *Annual Review of Psychology*, *72*(1), 663–688. https://doi.org/10.1146/annurev-psych-062520-122331

Ohira, T., Hozawa, A., Iribarren, C., Daviglus, M. L., Matthews, K. A., Gross, M. D., & Jacobs, D. R. (2008). Longitudinal association of serum carotenoids and tocopherols with hostility: The CARDIA study. *American Journal of Epidemiology*, *167*(1), 42.

Old, S. R., & Naveh-Benjamin, M. (2008). Differential effects of age on item and associative measures of memory: A meta-analysis. *Psychology and Aging, 23*(1), 104–118. https://doi.org/10.1037/0882-7974.23.1.104

Oltmanns, J., Godde, B., Winneke, A. H., Richter, G., Niemann, C., Voelcker-Rehage, C., Schömann, K., & Staudinger, U. M. (2017). Don't lose your brain at work – The role of recurrent novelty at work in cognitive and brain aging. *Frontiers in Psychology, 8*, 117. https://doi.org/10.3389/fpsyg.2017.00117

Ormerod, T. C. (2005). Planning and ill-defined problems. In R. Morris & G. Ward (Eds.), *The cognitive psychology of planning*. Psychology Press.

Ostchega, Y., Fryar, C. D., Nwankwo, T., & Nguyen, D. T. (2017). *Hypertension prevalence among adults aged 18 and over: United States, 2017-2018 key findings data from the national health and nutrition examination survey*. https://www.cdc.gov/nchs/products/index.htm.

Owsley, C., McGwin, G., Jackson, G. R., Kallies, K., & Clark, M. (2007). Cone- and rod-mediated dark adaptation impairment in age-related maculopathy. *Ophthalmology, 114*(9), 1728–1735.

Palta, P., Schneider, A. L. C., Biessels, G. J., Touradji, P., & Hill-Briggs, F. (2014). Magnitude of cognitive dysfunction in adults with type 2 diabetes: A meta-analysis of six cognitive domains and the most frequently reported neuropsychological tests within domains. *Journal of the International Neuropsychological Society: JINS, 20*(3), 278–291. https://doi.org/10.1017/S1355617713001483

Panay, N., Hamoda, H., Arya, R., & Savvas, M. (2013). The 2013 British menopause society & women's health concern recommendations on hormone replacement therapy. *Menopause International, 19*(2), 59–68. https://doi.org/10.1177/1754045313489645

Paramei, G. V., & Oakley, B. (2014). Variation of color discrimination across the life span. *Journal of the Optical Society of America. A, Optics, Image Science, and Vision, 31*(4), A375–84. https://doi.org/10.1364/JOSAA.31.00A375

Park, D. C., & Festini, S. B. (2017). Theories of mem##ory and ##: A L##ook at the pas##t and a glimp##se of the future. *The Journals of Gerontology Series B: Psychological Sciences and Social Sciences, 72*(1), 82–90. https://doi.org/10.1093/geronb/gbw066

Parrado, C., Mercado-Saenz, S., Perez-Davo, A., Gilaberte, Y., Gonzalez, S., & Juarranz, A. (2019). Environmental stressors on skin aging. mechanistic insights. *Frontiers in Pharmacology, 10*, 759. https://doi.org/10.3389/fphar.2019.00759

Passow, S., Westerhausen, R., Wartenburger, I., Hugdahl, K., Heekeren, H. R., Lindenberger, U., & Li, S.-C. (2012). Human aging compromises attentional control of auditory perception. *Psychology and Aging, 27*(1), 99–105. https://doi.org/10.1037/a0025667

Perlmutter, M., Kaplan, M., & Nyquest, L. (1990). Development of adaptive competence in adulthood. *Human Development, 33*, 185–197.

Perron, R. (2018). *The value of experience: Age discrimination against older workers persists*. https://doi.org/10.26419/res.00177.002

Peters, P., Van der Heijden, B. I. J. M., Spurk, D., De Vos, A., & Klaassen, R. (2019). Please don't look at me that way. An empirical study into the effects of age-based (Meta-)stereotyping on employability enhancement among older supermarket workers. *Frontiers in Psychology, 10*, 249. https://doi.org/10.3389/fpsyg.2019.00249

Peters, S. A. E., Huxley, R. R., & Woodward, M. (2014). Diabetes as a risk factor for stroke in women compared with men: A systematic review and meta-analysis of 64 cohorts, including 775 385 individuals and 12 539 strokes. *The Lancet, 383*(9933), 1973–1980. https://doi.org/10.1016/S0140-6736(14)60040-4

Piazza, J. R., Stawski, R. S., & Sheffler, J. L. (2019). Age, daily stress processes, and allostatic load: A longitudinal study. *Journal of Aging and Health, 31*(9), 1671–1691. https://doi.org/10.1177/0898264318788493

Pietschnig, J., & Voracek, M. (2015). One century of global IQ gains: A formal meta-analysis of the flynn effect (1909-2013). *Perspectives on Psychological Science, 10*(3), 282–306. https://doi.org/10.1177/1745691615577701

Quaranta, N., Coppola, F., Casulli, M., Barulli, M. R., Panza, F., Tortelli, R., Solfrizzi, V., Sabbà, C., & Logroscino, G. (2015). Epidemiology of age related hearing loss: A review. *Hearing, Balance and Communication, 13*, 77–81. https://doi.org/10.3109/21695717.2014.994869

Ramchandran, K., Zeien, E., & Andreasen, N. C. (2019). Distributed neural efficiency: Intelligence and age modulate adaptive allocation of resources in the brain. *Trends in Neuroscience and Education, 15*, 48–61. https://doi.org/10.1016/j.tine.2019.02.006

Rey-Mermet, A., & Gade, M. (2018). Inhibition in aging: What is preserved? What declines? A meta-analysis. *Psychonomic Bulletin and Review, 25*(5), 1695–1716. https://doi.org/10.3758/s13423-017-1384-7

Rey-Mermet, A., Gade, M., & Oberauer, K. (2018). Should we stop thinking about inhibition? Searching for individual and age differences in inhibition ability. *Journal of Experimental Psychology: Learning Memory and Cognition, 44*(4), 501–526. https://doi.org/10.1037/xlm0000450

Robert, L., & Labat-Robert, J. (2016). Skin. *The encyclopedia of adulthood and aging*, 1–4. https://doi.org/10.1002/9781118521373.wbeaa165

Roberts, R. O., Knopman, D. S., Przybelski, S. A., Mielke, M. M., Kantarci, K., Preboske, G. M., Senjem, M. L., Pankratz, V. S., Geda, Y. E., Boeve, B. F., Ivnik, R. J., Rocca, W. A., Petersen, R. C., & Jack, C. R. (2014). Association of type 2 diabetes with brain atrophy and cognitive impairment. *Neurology, 82*(13), 1132–1141. https://doi.org/10.1212/WNL.0000000000000269

Roring, R. W., & Charness, N. (2007). A multilevel model analysis of expertise in chess across the life span. *Psychology and Aging, 22*(2), 291–299.

Rossi, A. S. (2004). The menopausal transition and aging processes. In O. G. Brim, C. D. Ryff, & R. C. Kessler (Eds.), *How healthy are we?: A national study of well-being at midlife* (pp. 153–201). University of Chicago Press.

Rowe, G., Hasher, L., & Turcotte, J. (2010). Interference, aging, and visuospatial working memory: The role of similarity. *Neuropsychology, 24*(6), 804–807. https://doi.org/10.1037/a0020244

Rowell, S. F., Green, J. S., Teachman, B. A., & Salthouse, T. A. (2016). Age does not matter: Memory complaints are related to negative affect throughout adulthood. *Aging & Mental Health, 20*(12), 1255–1263. https://doi.org/10.1080/13607863.2015.1078284

Roy, T., & Lloyd, C. E. (2012). Epidemiology of depression and diabetes: A systematic review. *Journal of Affective Disorders, 142*(Suppl), S8–21. https://doi.org/10.1016/S0165-0327(12)70004-6

Rubin, L. R., Fitts, M. L., & Rubin, L. R. (2003). "Whatever feels good in my soul": Body ethics and aesthetics among African American and Latina women. *Culture, Medicine and Psychiatry, 27*(1), 49–75. https://doi.org/10.1023/A:1023679821086

Salthouse, T. A. (1984). Effects of age and skill in typing. *Journal of Experimental Psychology: General, 113*, 345–371.

Salthouse, T. A. (2012). Consequences of age-related cognitive declines. *Annual Review of Psychology, 63*, 201–226. https://doi.org/10.1146/annurev-psych-120710-100328

Salthouse, T. A. (2016). Continuity of cognitive change across adulthood. *Psychonomic Bulletin & Review, 23*(3), 932–939. https://doi.org/10.3758/s13423-015-0910-8

Salthouse, T. A. (2017). Neural correlates of age-related slowing. In C. Roberto, N. Lars, & C. P. Denise (Eds.), *Cognitive neuroscience of aging: Linking cognitive and cerebral aging* (pp. 259–272). ozford.

Salthouse, T. A., & Madden, D. J. (2013). Information processing speed and aging. In J. DeLuca & J. H. Kalmar (Eds.), *Information processing speed in clinical populations* (pp. 221–239). Psychology Press.

Salthouse, T. A., & Pink, J. E. (2008). Why is working memory related to fluid intelligence? *Psychonomic Bulletin & Review, 15*(2), 364–371. http://www.pubmedcentral.nih.gov/articlerender.fcgi?artid=2485208&tool=pmcentrez&rendertype=abstract

Sampselle, C. M., Harris, V., Harlow, S. D., & Sowers, M. (2002). Midlife development and menopause in African American and Caucasian women. *Health Care for Women International, 23*(4), 351–363.

Sandvik, A. M., Bartone, P. T., Hystad, S. W., Phillips, T. M., Thayer, J. F., & Johnsen, B. H. (2013). Psychological hardiness predicts neuroimmunological responses to stress. *Psychology, Health & Medicine, 18*(6), 705–713. https://doi.org/10.1080/13548506.2013.772304

Santoro, N. (2016). Perimenopause: From research to practice. *Journal of Women's Health, 25*(4), 332–339. https://doi.org/10.1089/jwh.2015.5556

Santoro, N., Rceca, C., Peters, B. A., & Neal-Perry, G. (2021). The menopause transition: Signs, symptoms, and management options. *The Journal of Clinical Endocrinology & Metabolism, 106*(1), 1–15. https://doi.org/10.1210/clinem/dgaa764

Schaie, K. W. (2013). *Developmental influences on adult intelligence: The seattle longitudinal study.* Oxford University Press,.

Schaie, K. W. (2016). The longitudinal study of adult cognitive development. In R. J. Sternberg, S. T. Fiske, & D. J. Foss (Eds.), *Scientists making a difference: One Hundred eminent behavioral and brain* (pp. 218–222). Cambridge.

Schieman, S., & Koltai, J. (2017). Discovering pockets of complexity: Socioeconomic status, stress exposure, and the nuances of the health gradient. *Social Science Research, 63*, 1–18. https://doi.org/10.1016/J.SSRESEARCH.2016.09.023

Schmiedek, F. (2017). Development of cognition and intelligence. In J. Specht (Ed.), *Personality development across the lifespan* (pp. 309–323). Elsevier. https://doi.org/10.1016/B978-0-12-804674-6.00019-3

Schwartz, B. L., & Frazier, L. D. (2005). Tip-of-the-tongue states and aging: Contrasting psycholinguistic and metacognitive perspectives. *Journal of General Psychology, 132*(4), 377–391.

Sebastiani, P., Andersen, S. L., Sweigart, B., Du, M., Cosentino, S., Thyagarajan, B., Christensen, K., Schupf, N., & Perls, T. T. (2020). Patterns of multi-domain cognitive aging in participants of the long life family study. *GeroScience, 42*(5), 1335–1350. https://doi.org/10.1007/s11357-020-00202-3

Segerstrom, S. C., & O'Connor, D. B. (2012). Stress, health and illness: Four challenges for the future. *Psychology & Health, 27*(2), 128–140. https://doi.org/10.1080/08870446.2012.659516

Seidman, S. N., & Weiser, M. (2013). Testosterone and mood in aging men. *The Psychiatric Clinics of North America, 36*(1), 177–182. https://doi.org/10.1016/j.psc.2013.01.007

Shanafelt, T. D., Hasan, O., Dyrbye, L. N., Sinsky, C., Satele, D., Sloan, J., & West, C. P. (2015). Changes in burnout and satisfaction with work-life balance in physicians and the general US working population between 2011 and 2014. *Mayo Clinic Proceedings, 90*(12), 1600–1613. https://doi.org/10.1016/j.mayocp.2015.08.023

Sharma, M., & Rush, S. E. (2014). Mindfulness-based stress reduction as a stress management intervention for healthy individuals. *Journal of Evidence-Based Complementary & Alternative Medicine, 19*(4), 271–286. https://doi.org/10.1177/2156587214543143

Shiels, M. S., Berrington de González, A., Best, A. F., Chen, Y., Chernyavskiy, P., Hartge, P., Khan, S. Q., Pérez-Stable, E. J., Rodriquez, E. J., Spillane, S., Thomas, D. A., Withrow, D., & Freedman, N. D. (2019). Premature mortality from all causes and drug poisonings in the USA according to socioeconomic status and rurality: An analysis of death certificate data by county from 2000–15. *The Lancet Public Health, 4*(2), e97–e106. https://doi.org/10.1016/S2468-2667(18)30208-1

Shippee, T. P., Wilkinson, L. R., Schafer, M. H., & Shippee, N. D. (2019). Long-term effects of age discrimination on mental health: The role of perceived financial strain. *The Journals of Gerontology: Series B, 74*, 664–674. https://doi.org/10.1093/geronb/gbx017

Shores, M. M. (2014). The Implications of low testosterone on mortality in men. *Current Sexual Health Reports, 6*(4), 235–243. https://doi.org/10.1007/s11930-014-0030-x

Shoss, M. K. (2017). Job insecurity: An integrative review and agenda for future research. *Journal of Management, 43*(6), 1911–1939. https://doi.org/10.1177/0149206317691574

Siegel, R. L., Miller, K. D., & Jemal, A. (2018). Cancer statistics, 2018. *CA: A Cancer Journal for Clinicians, 68*(1), 7–30. https://doi.org/10.3322/caac.21442

Sin, N. L., Graham-Engeland, J. E., Ong, A. D., & Almeida, D. M. (2015). Affective reactivity to daily stressors is associated with elevated inflammation. *Health Psychology, 34*(12), 1154–1165. https://doi.org/10.1037/hea0000240

Sinaki, M. (2021). Osteoporosis. In D. X. Cifu (Ed.), *Braddom's physical medicine and rehabilitation* (pp. 690–714.e3). Elsevier. https://doi.org/10.1016/B978-0-323-62539-5.00034-5

Smith, R., Frazer, K., Hyde, A., O'Connor, L., & Davidson, P. (2018). "Heart disease never entered my head": Women's understanding of coronary heart disease risk factors. *Journal of Clinical Nursing, 27*(21–22), 3953–3967. https://doi.org/10.1111/jocn.14589

Song, J., Mailick, M. R., Greenberg, J. S., Ryff, C. D., & Lachman, M. E. (2016). Cognitive aging in parents of children with disabilities. *The Journals of Gerontology Series B: Psychological Sciences and Social Sciences, 71*(5), 821–830. https://doi.org/10.1093/geronb/gbv015

Sörensen, S., White, K., & Ramchandran, R. S. (2016). Vision in mid and late life. In *The Encyclopedia of adulthood and aging* (pp. 1–5). John Wiley & Sons, Inc. https://doi.org/10.1002/9781118521373.wbeaa189

Stephens, P. J., Tarpey, P. S., Davies, H., Van Loo, P., Greenman, C., Wedge, D. C., Nik-Zainal, S., Martin, S., Varela, I., Bignell, G. R., Yates, L. R., Papaemmanuil, E., Beare, D., Butler, A., Cheverton, A., Gamble, J., Hinton, J., Jia, M., Jayakumar, A., & Stratton, M. R. (2012). The Landscape of cancer genes and mutational processes in breast cancer. *Nature, 486*(7403), 400–404. https://doi.org/10.1038/nature11017

Stevenson, J. (2017). Is HRT a cardiovascular risk for older women? *Maturitas, 100,* 116. https://doi.org/10.1016/j.maturitas.2017.03.331

Stokes, J. E., & Moorman, S. M. (2020). Sticks and stones: Perceived age discrimination, well-being, and health over a 20-year period. *Research on Aging, 42*(3–4), 115–125. https://doi.org/10.1177/0164027519894875

Stone, A. A., Schneider, S., & Broderick, J. E. (2017). Psychological stress declines rapidly from age 50 in the United States: Yet another well-being paradox. *Journal of Psychosomatic Research, 103,* 22–28. https://doi.org/10.1016/j.jpsychores.2017.09.016

Stubbs, B., Veronese, N., Vancampfort, D., Prina, A. M., Lin, P. Y., Tseng, P. T., Evangelou, E., Solmi, M., Kohler, C., Carvalho, A. F., & Koyanagi, A. (2017). Perceived stress and smoking across 41 countries: A global perspective across Europe, Africa, Asia and the Americas. *Scientific Reports, 7*(1), 1–8. https://doi.org/10.1038/s41598-017-07579-w

Stypinska, J., & Turek, K. (2017). Hard and soft age discrimination: The dual nature of workplace discrimination. *European Journal of Ageing, 14*(1), 49–61. https://doi.org/10.1007/s10433-016-0407-y

Sussman, M., Trocio, J., Best, C., Mirkin, S., Bushmakin, A. G., Yood, R., Friedman, M., Menzin, J., Louie, M., Lewis, V., Woods, N., Mitchell, E., Utian, W., Goodman, N., Cobin, R., Ginzburg, S., Katz, I., Woode, D., Blumel, J., & Gallia, C. (2015). Prevalence of menopausal symptoms among mid-life women: Findings from electronic medical records. *BMC Women's Health, 15*(1), 58, . https://doi.org/10.1186/s12905-015-0217-y

Swift, A., Liew, S., Weinkle, S., Garcia, J. K., & Silberberg, M. B. (2021). The facial aging process from the "Inside out.". *Aesthetic Surgery Journal, 41,* 1107–1119. https://doi.org/10.1093/asj/sjaa339

Swirsky, L. T., & Spaniol, J. (2019). Cognitive and motivational selectivity in healthy aging. *Wiley Interdisciplinary Reviews: Cognitive Science, 10*(6), e1512. https://doi.org/10.1002/wcs.1512

Sylvain-Roy, S., Lungu, O., & Belleville, S. (2014). Normal aging of the attentional control functions that underlie working memory. *The Journals of Gerontology. Series B, Psychological Sciences and Social Sciences, 70*(5), gbt166-. https://doi.org/10.1093/geronb/gbt166

Taylor, P., Mcloughlin, C., Meyer, D., & Brooke, E. (2017). *Everyday discrimination in the workplace, job satisfaction and psychological wellbeing: age differences and moderating variables.* https://doi.org/10.1017/S0144686X12000438

te Nijenhuis, J. (2013). The Flynn effect, group differences, and g loadings. *Personality and Individual Differences, 55*(3), 224–228. https://doi.org/10.1016/j.paid.2011.12.023

Terrell, K. (2017). *Studies show age discrimination still persists.* AARP - Work & JObs. https://www.aarp.org/work/working-at-50-plus/info-2017/age-discrimination-online-fd.html? intcmp=AE-WOR-W50-AD-R2-C1

Trahan, L. H., Stuebing, K. K., Fletcher, J. M., & Hiscock, M. (2014). The Flynn effect: A meta-analysis. *Psychological Bulletin, 140*(5), 1332–1360. https://doi.org/10.1037/a0037173

Turner, A. I., Smyth, N., Hall, S. J., Torres, S. J., Hussein, M., Jayasinghe, S. U., Ball, K., & Clow, A. J. (2020). Psychological stress reactivity and future health and disease outcomes: A systematic review of prospective evidence. *Psychoneuroendocrinology, 114,* 104599. https://doi.org/10.1016/j.psyneuen.2020.104599

Unsworth, N., Fukuda, K., Awh, E., & Vogel, E. K. (2014). Working memory and fluid intelligence: Capacity, attention control, and secondary memory retrieval. *Cognitive Psychology, 71,* 1–26. https://doi.org/10.1016/j.cogpsych.2014.01.003

Vainionpää, K., & Topo, P. (2006). The Construction of male menopause in Finnish popular magazines. *Critical Public Health, 16*(1), 19–34.

van Dooren, F. E. P., Nefs, G., Schram, M. T., Verhey, F. R. J., Denollet, J., & Pouwer, F. (2013). Depression and risk of mortality in people with diabetes mellitus: A systematic review and meta-analysis. *PloS One, 8*(3), e57058. https://doi.org/10.1371/journal.pone.0057058

Vestergren, P., & Nilsson, L.-G. (2011). Perceived causes of everyday memory problems in a population-based sample aged 39-99. *Applied Cognitive Psychology, 25*(4), 641–646. https://doi.org/10.1002/acp.1734

Vogt, D. S., Rizvi, S. L., & Shipherd, J. C. (2008). Longitudinal investigation of reciprocal relationship between stress reactions and hardiness. *Personality and Social Psychology Bulletin, 34*(1), 61–73. 10.1177/0146167207309197

von Känel, R., Princip, M., Holzgang, S. A., Fuchs, W. J., van Nuffel, M., Pazhenkottil, A. P., & Spiller, T. R. (2020). Relationship between job burnout and somatic diseases: A network analysis. *Scientific Reports, 10*(1), 18438. https://doi.org/10.1038/s41598-020-75611-7

Wang, J., & Puel, J.-L. (2020). Presbycusis: An update on cochlear mechanisms and therapies. *Journal of Clinical Medicine, 9*(1), 218. https://doi.org/10.3390/jcm9010218

Warren, C. S., Gleaves, D. H., & Rakhkovskaya, L. M. (2013). Score reliability and factor similarity of the sociocultural attitudes towards appearance questionnaire-3 (SATAQ-3) among four ethnic groups. *Journal of Eating Disorders, 1*(1), 14. https://doi.org/10.1186/2050-2974-1-14

Wells, F. (2014). *2014 Wells fargo middle class retirement study.* https://www08.wellsfargomedia.com/downloads/pdf/com/retirement-employee-benefits/insights/2014-retirement-study.pdf

Wettstein, M., & Wahl, H.-W. (2016). Hearing. In *The encyclopedia of adulthood and aging* (pp. 1–5). John Wiley & Sons, Inc. https://doi.org/10.1002/9781118521373.wbeaa202

Wiegand, C., Raschke, C., & Elsner, P. (2017). Skin aging: A brief summary of characteristic changes. In M. A. Farage, K. W. Miller, & H. I. Maibac (Eds.), *Textbook of aging skin* (pp. 55–65). Springer Berlin Heidelberg. https://doi.org/10.1007/978-3-662-47398-6_5

Williams, J., Allen, L., Wickramasinghe, K., Mikkelsen, B., Roberts, N., & Townsend, N. (2018). A systematic review of associations between non-communicable diseases and socioeconomic status within low- and lower-middle-income countries. *Journal of Global Health*, *8*(2), 020409. https://doi.org/10.7189/jogh.08.020409

Williams, R. L. (2013). Overview of the Flynn effect. *Intelligence*, *41*(6), 753–764. https://doi.org/10.1016/j.intell.2013.04.010

Wolffsohn, J. S., & Davies, L. N. (2019). Presbyopia: Effectiveness of correction strategies. *Progress in Retinal and Eye Research*, *68*, 124–143. https://doi.org/10.1016/j.preteyeres.2018.09.004

Wong, J. C. H., O'Neill, S., Beck, B. R., Forwood, M. R., & Khoo, S. K. (2020). A 5-year longitudinal study of changes in body composition in women in the perimenopause and beyond. *Maturitas*, *132*, 49–56. https://doi.org/10.1016/j.maturitas.2019.12.001

Woolf, S. H., Chapman, D. A., Buchanich, J. M., Bobby, K. J., Zimmerman, E. B., & Blackburn, S. M. (2018). Changes in midlife death rates across racial and ethnic groups in the United States: Systematic analysis of vital statistics. *BMJ (Online)*, *362*, k3096. https://doi.org/10.1136/bmj.k3096

Yeves, J., Bargsted, M., Cortes, L., Merino, C., & Cavada, G. (2019). Age and perceived employability as moderators of job insecurity and job satisfaction: A moderated moderation model. *Frontiers in Psychology*, *10*, 799. https://doi.org/10.3389/fpsyg.2019.00799

Zanto, T. P., & Gazzaley, A. (2017). Cognitive control and the ageing brain. In T. Egner (Ed.), *The Wiley handbook of cognitive control* (pp. 476–490). Wiley.

Zaval, L., Li, Y., Johnson, E. J., & Weber, E. U. (2015). Complementary contributions of fluid and crystallized intelligence to decision making across the life span. In T. M. Hess, J. Strough, & C. E. Löckenhoff (Eds.), *Aging and decision making* (pp. 149–168). Elsevier. https://doi.org/10.1016/B978-0-12-417148-0.00008-X

Zhang, S., & Duan, E. (2018). Fighting against skin aging: The way from bench to bedside. *Cell Transplantation*, *27*, 729–738. https://doi.org/10.1177/0963689717725755

Zhang, W., Yu, Z., & Ruan, Q. (2020). Presbycusis-related tinnitus and cognitive impairment: Gender differences and common mechanisms. In S. Akarsu (Ed.), *An overview and management of multiple chronic conditions*. IntechOpen. https://doi.org/10.5772/intechopen.90956

Zou, M. (2015). Gender, work orientations and job satisfaction. *Work, Employment & Society*, *29*(1), 3–22. https://doi.org/10.1177/0950017014559267

CHAPTER 14

Adams-Price, C. E., Nadorff, D. K., Morse, L. W., Davis, K. T., & Stearns, M. A. (2018). The creative benefits scale. *The International Journal of Aging and Human Development*, *86*(3), 242–265. https://doi.org/10.1177/0091415017699939

Alter, A. L., & Hershfield, H. E. (2014). People search for meaning when they approach a new decade in chronological age. *Proceedings of the National Academy of Sciences of the United States of America*, *111*(48), 17066–17070. https://doi.org/10.1073/pnas.1415086111

American Association of Retired Persons. (2002). *The grandparent study:2002 Report*. Author.

An, J. S., & Cooney, T. M. (2006). Psychological well-being in mid to late life: The role of generativity development and parent-child relationships across the lifespan. *International Journal of Behavioral Development*, *30*(5), 410–421.

Arnett, J. J. (2018). Happily stressed: The complexity of well-being in midlife. *Journal of Adult Development*, *25*, 270–278. https://doi.org/10.1007/s10804-018-9291-3

Attar-Schwartz, S., Tan, J.-P., Buchanan, A., Flouri, E., & Griggs, J. (2009). Grandparenting and adolescent adjustment in two-parent biological, lone-parent, and step-families. *Journal of Family Psychology*, *23*(1), 67–75. https://doi.org/10.1037/a0014383

Aumann, K., Galinsky, E., Sakai, K., Brown, M., & Bond, J. T. (2010). *The elder care study: Everyday realities and wishes for change*. Families and Work Institute.

Avis, N. E., Colvin, A., Karlamangla, A. S., Crawford, S., Hess, R., Waetjen, L. E., Brooks, M., Tepper, P. G., & Greendale, G. A. (2017). Change in sexual functioning over the menopausal transition. *Menopause*, *24*(4), 379–390. https://doi.org/10.1097/GME.0000000000000770

Balsam, K. F., Rothblum, E. D., & Wickham, R. E. (2017). Longitudinal predictors of relationship dissolution among same-sex and heterosexual couples. *Couple and Family Psychology: Research and Practice*, *6*(4), 247–257. https://doi.org/10.1037/cfp0000091

Barańczuk, U. (2019). The five factor model of personality and emotion regulation: A meta-analysis. *Personality and Individual Differences*, *139*, 217–227. https://doi.org/10.1016/j.paid.2018.11.025

Barnes, J., Gardiner, J., Sutcliffe, A., & Melhuish, E. (2013). The parenting of preschool children by older mothers in the United Kingdom. *European Journal of Developmental Psychology*, *11*(4), 397–419. https://doi.org/10.1080/17405629.2013.863728

Barrett, A. E., & Montepare, J. M. (2015). "It's about time": Applying life span and life course perspectives to the study of subjective age. *Annual Review of Gerontology and Geriatrics*, *35*(1), 55–77. https://doi.org/10.1891/0198-8794.35.55

Battersby, A., & Phillips, L. (2016). In the end it all makes sense. *The International Journal of Aging and Human Development*, *83*(2), 184–204. https://doi.org/10.1177/0091415016647731

Baum, N., Rahav, G., & Sharon, D. (2005). Changes in the self-concepts of divorced women. *Journal of Divorce & Remarriage*, *43*(1), 47–67. https://doi.org/10.1300/J087v43n01_03

Baumeister, R. F., & Landau, M. J. (2018). Finding the meaning of meaning: Emerging insights on four grand questions. *Review of General Psychology*, *22*(1), 1–10. https://doi.org/10.1037/gpr0000145

Beaumont, S. L., & Pratt, M. M. (2011). Identity processing styles and psychosocial balance during early and middle adulthood: The role of identity in intimacy and generativity. *Journal of Adult Development*, *18*(4), 172–183. https://doi.org/10.1007/s10804-011-9125-z

Behler, R., Donnelly, R., & Umberson, D. (2019). Psychological distress transmission in same-sex and different-sex marriages. *Journal of Health and Social Behavior, 60*(1), 18–35. https://doi.org/10.1177/0022146518813097

Bekhet, A. K. (2015). Resourcefulness in African American and caucasian American caregivers of persons with dementia: Associations with perceived burden, depression, anxiety, positive cognitions, and psychological well-being. *Perspectives in Psychiatric Care, 51*(4), 285–294. https://doi.org/10.1111/ppc.12095

Belsky, J., Jaffee, S., Hsieh, K.-H., & Silva, P. A. (2001). Child-rearing antecedents of intergenerational relations in young adulthood: A prospective study. *Developmental Psychology, 37*(6), 801–813. https://doi.org/10.1037/0012-1649.37.6.801

Bem, S. L. (1985). Androgyny and gender schema theory: A conceptual and empirical integration. In T. B. Sondregger (Ed.), *Nebraska symposium on motivation, 1984: Psychology and gender* (pp. 76–103). University of Nebraska Press.

Bergland, A., Nicolaisen, M., & Thorsen, K. (2014). Predictors of subjective age in people aged 40-79 years: A five-year follow-up study. The impact of mastery, mental and physical health. *Aging & Mental Health, 18*(5), 653–661. https://doi.org/10.1080/13607863.2013.869545

Beutel, M. E., Glaesmer, H., Wiltink, J., Marian, H., & Brähler, E. (2010). Life satisfaction, anxiety, depression and resilience across the life span of men. *The Aging Male : The Official Journal of the International Society for the Study of the Aging Male, 13*(1), 32–39. http://informahealthcare.com/doi/abs/10.3109/13685530903296698

Birditt, K. S., Antonucci, T. C., & Tighe, L. (2012). Enacted support during stressful life events in middle and older adulthood: An examination of the interpersonal context. *Psychology and Aging, 27*(3), 728–741. https://doi.org/10.1037/a0026967

Birditt, K. S., Manalel, J. A., Kim, K., Zarit, S. H., & Fingerman, K. L. (2017). Daily interactions with aging parents and adult children: Associations with negative affect and diurnal cortisol. *Journal of Family Psychology, 31*, 699–709. https://doi.org/10.1037/fam0000317

Blanchflower, D. G. (2021). Is happiness U-shaped everywhere? Age and subjective well-being in 145 countries. *Journal of Population Economics, 34*(2), 575–624. https://doi.org/10.1007/s00148-020-00797-z

Bleidorn, W., & Hoppwood, C. J. (2019). Stability and change in personality traits over the lifespan. In D. P. McAdams, R. L. Shiner, & J. L. Tackett (Eds.), *Handbook of personality development* (pp. 237–252). The Guilford Press. https://psycnet.apa.org/record/2018-63285-014

Bleidorn, W., Hopwood, C. J., & Lucas, R. E. (2018). Life events and personality trait change. *Journal of Personality, 86*(1), 83–96. https://doi.org/10.1111/jopy.12286

Bleidorn, W., Klimstra, T. A., Denissen, J. J. A., Rentfrow, P. J., Potter, J., & Gosling, S. D. (2013). Personality maturation around the world: A cross-cultural examination of social-investment theory. *Psychological Science, 24*(12), 2530–2540. https://doi.org/10.1177/0956797613498396

Blieszner, R. (2014). The worth of friendship: Can friends keep us happy and healthy? *Generations, 38*(1), 24–30. http://www.ingentaconnect.com/content/asag/gen/2014/00000038/00000001/art00005

Bloch, L., Haase, C. M., & Levenson, R. W. (2014). Emotion regulation predicts marital satisfaction: More than a wives' tale. *Emotion (Washington, DC.), 14*(1), 130–144. https://doi.org/10.1037/a0034272

Bolin, K., Lindgren, B., & Lundborg, P. (2008). Your next of kin or your own career?: Caring and working among the 50+ of Europe. *Journal of Health Economics, 27*(3), 718–738. https://doi.org/10.1016/j.jhealeco.2007.10.004

Bosley-Smith, E. R., & Reczek, C. (2018). Before and after "i do": Marriage processes for mid-life gay and lesbian married couples. *Journal of Homosexuality, 65*(14), 1985–2004. https://doi.org/10.1080/00918369.2017.1423213

Bouchard, G. (2018). A dyadic examination of marital quality at the empty-nest phase. *The International Journal of Aging and Human Development, 86*(1), 34–50. https://doi.org/10.1177/0091415017691285

Brim, O. G., Ryff, C. D., & Kessler, R. C. (Eds.). (2004). *How healthy are we?: A national study of well-being at midlife*. In *The John D. and Catherine T. MacArthur foundation series on mental health and development. Studies on successful midlife development*. University of Chicago Press.

Brondolo, E., Blair, I. V., & Kaur, A. (2018). Biopsychosocial mechanisms linking discrimination to health: A focus on social cognition. In B. Major, J. F. Dovidio, & B. G. Link (Eds.), *The Oxford handbook of stigma, discrimination, and health* (Vol. 1). Oxford University Press. https://doi.org/10.1093/oxfordhb/9780190243470.013.8

Brown, S. L., Lin, I. F., Hammersmith, A. M., & Wright, M. R. (2019). Repartnering following gray divorce: The roles of resources and constraints for women and men. *Demography, 56*(2), 503–523. https://doi.org/10.1007/s13524-018-0752-x

Buczak-Stec, E., König, H. H., & Hajek, A. (2019). The link between sexual satisfaction and subjective well-being: A longitudinal perspective based on the German Ageing Survey. *Quality of Life Research, 28*(11), 3025–3035. https://doi.org/10.1007/s11136-019-02235-4

Bundick, M. J., Remington, K., Morton, E., & Colby, A. (2021). The contours of purpose beyond the self in midlife and later life. *Applied Developmental Science, 25*(1), 62–82. https://doi.org/10.1080/10888691.2018.1531718

Burr, J. A., & Mutchler, J. E. (1999). Race and ethnic variation in norms of filial responsibility among older persons. *Journal of Marriage & the Family, 61*(3), 674–687. 10.2307/353569

Bybee, J. A., & Wells, Y. V. (2003). The development of possible selves during adulthood. In J. Demick & C. Andreoletti (Eds.), *Handbook of adult development* (pp. 257–270). Kluwer Academic/Plenum Publishers.

Camberis, A.-L., McMahon, C. A., Gibson, F. L., & Boivin, J. (2016). Maternal age, psychological maturity, parenting cognitions, and mother-infant interaction. *Infancy, 21*(4), 396–422. https://doi.org/10.1111/infa.12116

Caputo, J. (2019). Crowded nests: Parent–adult child coresidence transitions and parental mental health following the great recession. *Journal of Health and Social Behavior, 60*(2), 204–221. https://doi.org/10.1177/0022146519849113

Carlo, G., Koller, S., Raffaelli, M., & De Guzman, M. R. T. (2007). Culture-related strengths among Latin American families: A case study of Brazil. *Marriage & Family Review, 42*(3), 335–360.

Carpenter, C. S., Eppink, S. T., Gonzales, G., & McKay, T. (2021). Effects of access to legal same-sex marriage on marriage and health. *Journal of Policy Analysis and Management*, *40*(2), 376–411. https://doi.org/10.1002/pam.22286

Chen, F., Mair, C. A., Bao, L., & Yang, Y. C. (2015). Race/ethnic differentials in the health consequences of caring for grandchildren for grandparents. *The Journals of Gerontology. Series B, Psychological Sciences and Social Sciences*, *70*, 793–803. https://doi.org/10.1093/geronb/gbu160

Chen, J., Krahn, H. J., Galambos, N. L., & Johnson, M. D. (2019). Wanting to be remembered: Intrinsically rewarding work and generativity in early midlife. *Canadian Review of Sociology/Revue Canadienne de Sociologie*, *56*(1), 30–48. https://doi.org/10.1111/cars.12228

Cheng, T. C., Powdthavee, N., & Oswald, A. J. (2017). Longitudinal evidence for a midlife nadir in human well-being: Results from four data sets. *The Economic Journal*, *127*(599), 126–142. https://doi.org/10.1111/ecoj.12256

Chrouser Ahrens, C. J., & Ryff, C. D. (2006). Multiple roles and well-being: Sociodemographic and psychological moderators. *Sex Roles*, *55*(11–12), 801–815.

Cichy, K. E., Lefkowitz, E. S., Davis, E. M., & Fingerman, K. L. (2013). "You are such a disappointment!": Negative emotions and parents' perceptions of adult children's lack of success. *The Journals of Gerontology. Series B, Psychological Sciences and Social Sciences*, *68*(6), 893–901. https://doi.org/10.1093/geronb/gbt053

Clarke-Stewart, A., & Brentano, C. (2006). *Divorce: Causes and consequences*. Yale University Press.

Coall, D. A., & Hertwig, R. (2011). Grandparental investment: A relic of the past or a resource for the future? *Current Directions in Psychological Science*, *20*(2), 93–98. https://doi.org/10.1177/0963721411403269

Cohen, S. A., Sabik, N. J., Cook, S. K., Azzoli, A. B., & Mendez-Luck, C. A. (2019). Differences within differences: Gender inequalities in caregiving intensity vary by race and ethnicity in informal caregivers. *Journal of Cross-Cultural Gerontology*, *34*(3), 245–263. https://doi.org/10.1007/s10823-019-09381-9

Condon, J., Luszcz, M., & McKee, I. (2018). The transition to grandparenthood: A prospective study of mental health implications. *Aging & Mental Health*, *22*(3), 336–343. https://doi.org/10.1080/13607863.2016.1248897

Cook, S. K., Snellings, L., & Cohen, S. A. (2018). Socioeconomic and demographic factors modify observed relationship between caregiving intensity and three dimensions of quality of life in informal adult children caregivers. *Health and Quality of Life Outcomes*, *16*(1), 1–12. https://doi.org/10.1186/s12955-018-0996-6

Costa, P. T., McCrae, R. R., & Löckenhoff, C. E. (2019). Personality across the life span. *Annual Review of Psychology*, *70*(1), 423–448. https://doi.org/10.1146/annurev-psych-010418-103244

Costa, R. M., & Brody, S. (2012). Sexual satisfaction, relationship satisfaction, and health are associated with greater frequency of penile–Vaginal intercourse. *Archives of Sexual Behavior*, *41*(1), 9–10. https://doi.org/10.1007/s10508-011-9847-9

Cowan, H. R. (2019). Can a good life be unsatisfying? Within-person dynamics of life satisfaction and psychological well-being in late midlife. *Psychological Science*, *30*(5), 697–710. https://doi.org/10.1177/0956797619831981

Cox, K. S., Wilt, J., Olson, B., & McAdams, D. P. (2010). Generativity, the big five, and psychosocial adaptation in midlife adults. *Journal of Personality*, *78*(4), 1185–1208. https://doi.org/10.1111/j.1467-6494.2010.00647.x

Crowley, J. E. (2019). Gray divorce: Explaining midlife marital splits. *Journal of Women and Aging*, *31*(1), 49–72. https://doi.org/10.1080/08952841.2017.1409918

Czekierda, K., Banik, A., Park, C. L., & Luszczynska, A. (2017). Meaning in life and physical health: Systematic review and meta-analysis. *Health Psychology Review*, *11*, 387–418. https://doi.org/10.1080/17437199.2017.1327325

Dare, J., & Green, L. (2011). Rethinking social support in women's midlife years: Women's experiences of social support in online environments. *European Journal of Cultural Studies*, *14*(5), 473–490. https://doi.org/10.1177/1367549411412203

Dare, J. S. (2011). Transitions in midlife women's lives: Contemporary experiences. *Health Care for Women International*, *32*(2), 111–133. https://doi.org/10.1080/07399332.2010.500753

Davis, E. M., Kim, K., & Fingerman, K. L. (2018). Is an empty nest best?: Coresidence with adult children and parental marital quality before and after the great recession. *The Journals of Gerontology Series B: Psychological Sciences and Social Sciences*, *73*(3), 372–381. https://doi.org/10.1093/geronb/gbw022

Deary, I. J., Pattie, A., & Starr, J. M. (2013). The stability of intelligence from age 11 to age 90 years : The lothian birth cohort of 1921. *Psychologiical Science*, *24*, 2361–2368. https://doi.org/10.1177/0956797613486487

Degges-White, S., & Kepic, M. (2020). Friendships, subjective age, and life satisfaction of women in midlife. *Adultspan Journal*, *19*(1), 39–53. https://doi.org/10.1002/adsp.12086

DeLamater, J. (2012). Sexual expression in later life: A review and synthesis. *Journal of Sex Research*, *49*(2/3), 125–141. https://doi.org/10.1080/00224499.2011.603168

Denissen, J. J. A., Luhmann, M., Chung, J. M., & Bleidorn, W. (2019). Transactions between life events and personality traits across the adult lifespan. *Journal of Personality and Social Psychology*, *116*(4), 612–633. https://doi.org/10.1037/pspp0000196

de Quadros-Wander, S., McGillivray, J., & Broadbent, J. (2013). The influence of perceived control on subjective wellbeing in later life. *Social Indicators Research*, *115*(3), 999–1010. https://doi.org/10.1007/s11205-013-0243-9

Doerwald, F., Zacher, H., Van Yperen, N. W., & Scheibe, S. (2021). Generativity at work: A meta-analysis. *Journal of Vocational Behavior*, *125*, 103521. https://doi.org/10.1016/j.jvb.2020.103521

Dolbin-MacNab, M. L. (2006). Just like raising your own? Grandmothers'TM perceptions of parenting a second time around. *Family Relations*, *55*(5), 564–575.

Doley, R., Bell, R., Watt, B., & Simpson, H. (2015). Grandparents raising grandchildren: Investigating factors associated with distress among custodial grandparent. *Journal of Family Studies*, *21*(2), 1–19. https://doi.org/10.1080/13229400.2015.1015215

Drewelies, J., Wagner, J., Tesch-Römer, C., & Heckhausen, J. (2017). Perceived control across the second half of life: The role of physical health and social integration. *Psychology and Aging*, *32*(1), 76–92. https://doi.org/10.1037/pag0000143

Edwards, O. W., & Benson, N. F. (2010). A four-factor social support model to mediate stressors experienced by children raised by grandparents. *Journal of Applied School Psychology, 26*(1), 54–69. https://doi.org/10.1080/15377900903368862

Ellis, R. R., & Simmons, T. (2014). *Coresident grandparents and their grandchildren: 2012*. https://www.census.gov/content/dam/Census/library/publications/2014/demo/p20-576.pdf

Erikson, E. H. (1959). *Identity and the life cycle, Volume 1* (Vol. 64). Norton.

Fang, S. C., Rosen, R. C., Vita, J. A., Ganz, P., & Kupelian, V. (2015). Changes in erectile dysfunction over time in relation to framingham cardiovascular risk in the Boston Area Community Health (BACH) Survey. *The Journal of Sexual Medicine, 12*(1), 100–108. https://doi.org/10.1111/jsm.12715

Fincham, F. D., Beach, S. R. H., & Davila, J. (2007). Longitudinal relations between forgiveness and conflict resolution in marriage. *Journal of Family Psychology, 21*(3), 542–545.

Fingerman, K. L. (2000). `We had a nice little chat': Age and generational differences in mothers' and daughters'. *Journals of Gerontology Series B: Psychological Sciences & Social Sciences, 55B*(2), 95.

Fingerman, K. L. (2001). A Distant closeness: Intimacy between parents and their children in later life. *Generations, 25*(2), 26.

Fingerman, K. L., Cheng, Y.-P., Birditt, K., & Zarit, S. (2012). Only as happy as the least happy child: Multiple grown children's problems and successes and middle-aged parents' well-being. *The Journals of Gerontology. Series B, Psychological Sciences and Social Sciences, 67*(2), 184–193. https://doi.org/10.1093/geronb/gbr086

Fingerman, K. L., Cheng, Y.-P., Wesselmann, E. D., Zarit, S., Furstenberg, F., & Birditt, K. S. (2012). Helicopter parents and landing pad kids: Intense parental support of grown children. *Journal of Marriage and Family, 74*(4), 880–896. https://doi.org/10.1111/j.1741-3737.2012.00987.x

Fingerman, K. L., Hay, E. L., & Birditt, K. S. (2004). The Best of ties, the worst of ties: Close, problematic, and ambivalent social relationships. *Journal of Marriage & Family, 66*(3), 792–808.

Fingerman, K. L., Kim, K., Birditt, K. S., & Zarit, S. H. (2016). The Ties that bind: Midlife Parents' Daily experiences with grown children. *Journal of Marriage and Family, 78*(2), 431–450. https://doi.org/10.1111/jomf.12273

Fingerman, K. L., & Suitor, J. J. (2017). Millennials and their parents: Implications of the new young adulthood for midlife adults. *Innovation in Aging, 1*(3), igx026. https://doi.org/10.1093/geroni/igx026

Fiori, K. L., & Denckla, C. A. (2015). Friendship and happiness among middle-aged adults. In M. Demir (Ed.), *Friendship and happiness* (pp. 137–154). Springer Netherlands. https://doi.org/10.1007/978-94-017-9603-3_8

Freund, A. M. (2017). Motivational changes across adulthood: The Role of goal representations for adult development and aging. In R. A. Scott & S. Kosslyn (Eds.), *Emerging trends in the social and behavioral sciences* (pp. 1–15). John Wiley & Sons, Inc. https://doi.org/10.1002/9781118900772.etrds0424

Freund, A. M., & Ritter, J. O. (2009). Midlife crisis: A debate. *Gerontology, 55*(5), 582–591. https://doi.org/10.1159/000227322

Friedman, E. M., Park, S. S., & Wiemers, E. E. (2017). New estimates of the sandwich generation in the 2013 panel study of income dynamics. *The Gerontologist, 41*(2), 191–196. https://doi.org/10.1093/geront/gnv080

Friedman, H. S., & Kern, M. L. (2014). Personality, well-being, and health*. *Annual Review of Psychology, 65*(1), 719–742. https://doi.org/10.1146/annurev-psych-010213-115123

Fry, C. L. (1985). Culture, behavior, and aging in the comparative perspective. In J. E. Birren & K. W. Schaie (Eds.), *Handbook of the psychology of aging* (2nd ed., pp. 216–244). Van Nostrand Reinhold Company.

Fry, R. (2016). *For first time in modern era, living with parents edges out other living arrangements for 18- to 34-Year-Olds*. Pew Research Center. http://www.pewsocialtrends.org/2016/05/24/for-first-time-in-modern-era-living-with-parents-edges-out-other-living-arrangements-for-18-to-34-year-olds/

Fry, R., Passel, J. S., & Cohn, D. (2020, September 4). A majority of young adults in the U.S. live with their parents for the first time since the Great Depression. *Pew Research Center*. https://www.pewresearch.org/fact-tank/2020/09/04/a-majority-of-young-adults-in-the-u-s-live-with-their-parents-for-the-first-time-since-the-great-depression/

Fry, R., Passel, J. S., & Cohn, D. (2020, September 4). *A majority of young adults in the U.S. live with their parents for the first time since the Great Depression*. Pew Research Center. https://www.pewresearch.org/fact-tank/2020/09/04/a-majority-of-young-adults-in-the-u-s-live-with-their-parents-for-the-first-time-since-the-great-depression/

Fuller-Thomson, E., & Minkler, M. (2001). American grandparents providing extensive child care to their grandchildren: Prevalence and profile. *The Gerontologist, 41*(2), 201–209. https://doi.org/10.1093/geront/41.2.201

Garcia, M. A., & Umberson, D. (2019). Marital strain and psychological distress in same-sex and different-sex couples. *Journal of Marriage and Family, 81*(5), 1253–1268. https://doi.org/10.1111/jomf.12582

Gelman, C. R., Tompkins, C. J., & Ihara, E. S. (2013). The complexities of caregiving for minority older adults: Rewards and challenges. In K. E. Whitfield (Ed.), *Handbook of minority aging* (pp. 313–328). Springer.

Geurts, T., Van Tilburg, T. G., & Poortman, A.-R. (2012). The grandparent-grandchild relationship in childhood and adulthood: A matter of continuation? *Personal Relationships, 19*(2), 267–278. https://doi.org/10.1111/j.1475-6811.2011.01354.x

Goldsen, J., Bryan, A. E. B., Kim, H.-J., Muraco, A., Jen, S., & Fredriksen-Goldsen, K. I. (2017). Who says i do: The changing context of marriage and health and quality of life for LGBT older adults. *The Gerontologist, 57*(Suppl. 1), S50–S62. https://doi.org/10.1093/geront/gnw174

Graham, E. K., & Lachman, M. E. (2012). Personality stability is associated with better cognitive performance in adulthood: Are the stable more able? *The Journals of Gerontology. Series B, Psychological Sciences and Social Sciences, 67*(5), 545–554. https://doi.org/10.1093/geronb/gbr149

Graham, E. K., Rutsohn, J. P., Turiano, N. A., Bendayan, R., Batterham, P. J., Gerstorf, D., Katz, M. J., Reynolds, C. A., Sharp, E. S., Yoneda, T. B., Bastarache, E. D., Elleman, L. G., Zelinski, E. M., Johansson, B., Kuh, D., Barnes, L. L., Bennett, D. A., Deeg, D. J. H., Lipton, R. B., . . . Mroczek, D. K. (2017). Personality predicts mortality risk: An integrative data analysis of 15 international longitudinal studies. *Journal of Research in Personality*, *70*, 174–186. https://doi.org/10.1016/J.JRP.2017.07.005

Griggs, J., Tan, J.-P., Buchanan, A., Attar-Schwartz, S., & Flouri, E. (2010). 'They've always been there for me': Grandparental involvement and child well-being. *Children & Society*, *24*(3), 200–214. https://doi.org/10.1111/j.1099-0860.2009.00215.x

Grossman, M. R., & Gruenewald, T. L. (2017). Caregiving and perceived generativity: A positive and protective aspect of providing care? *Clinical Gerontologist*, *40*(5), 435–447. https://doi.org/10.1080/07317115.2017.1317686

Grover, S., & Helliwell, J. F. (2014). *How's life at home? New evidence on marriage and the set point for happiness*. http://www.nber.org/papers/w20794

Grundström, J., Konttinen, H., Berg, N., & Kiviruusu, O. (2021). Associations between relationship status and mental well-being in different life phases from young to middle adulthood. *SSM-Population Health*, *14*, 100774. https://doi.org/10.1016/j.ssmph.2021.100774

Grundy, E., & Henretta, J. C. (2006). Between elderly parents and adult children: A new look at the intergenerational care provided by the "sandwich generation.". *Ageing & Society*, *26*(5), 707–722. http://eprints.lse.ac.uk/53680/

Guo, M., Kim, S., & Dong, X. (2019). Sense of Filial obligation and caregiving burdens among chinese immigrants in the United States. *Journal of the American Geriatrics Society*, *67*(S3), S564–S570. https://doi.org/10.1111/jgs.15735

Gutmann, D. L. (1985). The parental imperative revisited: Towards a developmental psychology of adulthood and later life. In J. Meacham (Ed.), *Contributions to human development* (pp. 31–60). S Karger AG. https://doi.org/10.1159/000411472

Hampson, S. E., Edmonds, G. W., Barckley, M., Goldberg, L. R., Dubanoski, J. P., & Hillier, T. A. (2016). A big five approach to self-regulation: Personality traits and health trajectories in the Hawaii longitudinal study of personality and health. *Psychology, Health & Medicine*, *21*(2), 152–162. https://doi.org/10.1080/13548506.2015.1061676

Hank, K., Cavrini, G., Di Gessa, G., & Tomassini, C. (2018). What do we know about grandparents? Insights from current quantitative data and identification of future data needs. *European Journal of Ageing*, 1–11. https://doi.org/10.1007/s10433-018-0468-1

Härkönen, J. (2015). Divorce. In J. Treas, J. Scott, & M. Richards (Eds.), *The wiley blackwell companion to the sociology of families* (pp. 303–322). Wiley-Blackwell.

Harris, M. A., & Orth, U. (2020). The link between self-esteem and social relationships: A meta-analysis of longitudinal studies. *Journal of Personality and Social Psychology*, *119*(6), 1459–1477. https://doi.org/10.1037/pspp0000265

Hayslip, B., Blumenthal, H., & Garner, A. (2015). Social support and grandparent caregiver health: One-year longitudinal findings for grandparents raising their Grandchildren. *The Journals of Gerontology Series B: Psychological Sciences and Social Sciences*, *70*(5), 804–812. https://doi.org/10.1093/geronb/gbu165

Hayslip, B., Fruhauf, C. A., & Dolbin-MacNab, M. L. (2017). Grandparents raising Grandchildren: What have we learned over the past decade? *The Gerontologist*, *57*(10), 1196. https://doi.org/10.1093/geront/gnx106

Hayslip, Jr, B., & Blumenthal, H. (2016). Grandparenthood: A developmental perspective. In M. H. Meyer & E. Daniele (Eds.), *ChallengGerontology: Changes, challenges, and solutionses* (pp. 271–298). Praeger.

Heckhausen, J., & Brim, O. G. (1997). Perceived problems for self and others: Self-protection by social downgrading throughout adulthood. *Psychology and Aging*, *12*(4), 610–619. http://www.ncbi.nlm.nih.gov/pubmed/9416630

Heckhausen, J., Wrosch, C., & Schulz, R. (2010). A Motivational theory of life-span development. *Psychological Review*, *117*(1), 32–60. https://doi.org/10.1037/a0017668

Heintzelman, S. J., & King, L. A. (2014). Life is pretty meaningful. *The American Psychologist*, *69*(6), 561–574. https://doi.org/10.1037/a0035049

Henderson, C. E., Hayslip, J. B., Sanders, L. M., & Louden, L. (2009). Grandmother—Grandchild relationship quality predicts psychological adjustment among youth from divorced families. *Journal of Family Issues*, *30*(9), 1245–1264.

Herbenick, D., Reece, M., Hensel, D., Sanders, S., Jozkowski, K., & Fortenberry, J. D. (2011). Association of lubricant use with women's Sexual pleasure, sexual satisfaction, and genital symptoms: A prospective daily diary study. *The Journal of Sexual Medicine*, *8*(1), 202–212. https://doi.org/10.1111/j.1743-6109.2010.02067.x

Herbenick, D., Reece, M., Schick, V., Sanders, S. A., Dodge, B., & Fortenberry, J. D. (2010). Sexual behavior in the United States: Results from a national probability sample of men and women ages 14–94. *The Journal of Sexual Medicine*, *7*(s5), 255–265. https://doi.org/10.1111/J.1743-6109.2010.02012.X

Hill, P. L., Turiano, N. A., Mroczek, D. K., & Roberts, B. W. (2012). Examining concurrent and longitudinal relations between personality traits and social well-being in adulthood. *Social Psychological and Personality Science*, *3*(6), 698–705. https://doi.org/10.1177/1948550611433888

Holt-Lunstad, J. (2017). Friendship and health. In M. Hojjat & A. Moyer (Eds.), *The psychology of friendship* (pp. 233–248). Oxford University Press. https://psycnet.apa.org/record/2016-59521-014

Hooker, S. A., Masters, K. S., & Park, C. L. (2018). A meaningful life is a healthy life: A conceptual model linking meaning and meaning salience to health. *Review of General Psychology*, *22*(1), 11–24. https://doi.org/10.1037/gpr0000115

Hughes, M. L., & Lachman, M. E. (2018). Social comparisons of health and cognitive functioning contribute to changes in subjective age. *The Journals of Gerontology Series B: Psychological Sciences and Social Sciences*, *73*, 816–824. https://doi.org/10.1093/geronb/gbw044

Huo, M., Kim, K., Zarit, S. H., & Fingerman, K. L. (2018). Support grandparents give to their adult Grandchildren. *The Journals of Gerontology: Series B*, *73*, 1006–1015. https://doi.org/10.1093/geronb/gbw208

Hutteman, R., Hennecke, M., Orth, U., Reitz, A. K., & Specht, J. (2014). Developmental tasks as a framework to study personality development in adulthood and old age. *European Journal of Personality*, *28*(3), 267–278.

Huxhold, O., Miche, M., & Schüz, B. (2014). Benefits of having friends in older ages: Differential effects of informal social activities on well-being in middle-aged and older adults. *The Journals of Gerontology. Series B, Psychological Sciences and Social Sciences, 69*(3), 366–375. https://doi.org/10.1093/geronb/gbt029

Infurna, F. J., Gerstorf, D., & Lachman, M. E. (2020). Midlife in the 2020s: Opportunities and challenges. *American Psychologist, 75*(4), 470–485. https://doi.org/10.1037/amp0000591

Infurna, F. J., Gerstorf, D., Ram, N., Schupp, J., & Wagner, G. G. (2011). Long-term antecedents and outcomes of perceived control. *Psychology and Aging, 26*(3), 559–575. https://doi.org/10.1037/a0022890

Infurna, F. J., & Okun, M. A. (2015). Antecedents and outcomes of level and rates of change in perceived control: The moderating role of age. *Developmental Psychology, 51*(10), 1420–1437. https://doi.org/10.1037/a0039530

Işık, Ş., & Ü Zbe, N. (2015). Personality traits and positive/negative affects: An analysis of meaning in life among adults. *Kuram ve Uygulamada Egitim Bilimleri, 15*(3), 587–595. https://doi.org/10.12738/estp.2015.3.2436

Ivery, J. M., & Muniz, G. R. (2017). Caregiving transitions: Developmental and gendered perspectives. *Journal of Human Behavior in the Social Environment, 27*(4), 311–320. https://doi.org/10.1080/10911359.2017.1284028

Jackson, J. B., Miller, R. B., Oka, M., & Henry, R. G. (2014). Gender differences in marital satisfaction: A meta-analysis. *Journal of Marriage and Family, 76*(1), 105–129. https://doi.org/10.1111/jomf.12077

James, J. B., & Lewkowicz, C. (1995). Rethinking the gender identity crossover hypothesis: A test of a new model. *Sex Roles, 32*(3), 185–207.

Jones, C. J., Peskin, H., & Livson, N. (2011). Men's and women's change and individual differences in change in femininity from age 33 to 85: Results from the intergenerational studies. *Journal of Adult Development, 18*(4), 155–163. https://doi.org/10.1007/s10804-010-9108-5

Jones, C., Peskin, H., & Wandeler, C. (2017). Femininity and dominance across the Lifespan: Longitudinal findings from two cohorts of women. *Journal of Adult Development, 24*(1), 22–30. https://doi.org/10.1007/s10804-016-9243-8

Jones, P. S., Winslow, B. W., Lee, J. W., Burns, M., & Zhang, X. E. (2011). Development of a caregiver empowerment model to promote positive outcomes. *Journal of Family Nursing, 17*(1), 11–28. https://doi.org/10.1177/1074840710394854

Kamo, Y. (1998). Asian grandparents. In M. E. Szinovacz (Ed.), *Handbook on grandparenthood* (pp. 97–112). Greenwood Press/Greenwood Publishing Group.

Kandler, C., Bleidorn, W., Riemann, R., Spinath, F. M., Thiel, W., & Angleitner, A. (2010). Sources of cumulative continuity in personality: A longitudinal multiple-rater twin study. *Journal of Personality and Social Psychology, 98*(6), 995–1008. https://doi.org/10.1037/a0019558

Karraker, A., & Latham, K. (2015). In sickness and in health? Physical illness as a risk factor for marital dissolution in later life. *Journal of Health and Social Behavior, 56*(1), 59–73. https://doi.org/10.1177/0022146514568351

Keyes, C. L. M., & Westerhof, G. J. (2012). Chronological and subjective age differences in flourishing mental health and major depressive episode. *Aging & Mental Health, 16*(1), 67–74. https://doi.org/10.1080/13607863.2011.596811

Kiecolt-Glaser, J. K. (2018). Marriage, divorce, and the immune system. *American Psychologist, 73*(9), 1098–1108. https://doi.org/10.1037/amp0000388

Kim, K., Bangerter, L. R., Liu, Y., Polenick, C. A., Zarit, S. H., & Fingerman, K. L. (2016). Middle-Aged offspring's support to aging parents with emerging disability. *The Gerontologist, 20*, gnv686. https://doi.org/10.1093/geront/gnv686

King, A. R., Russell, T. D., & Veith, A. C. (2017). Friendship and mental health functioning. In M. Hojjat & A. Moyer (Eds.), *The psychology of friendship* (pp. 249–266). : Oxford University Press. https://psycnet.apa.org/record/2016-59521-015

King, B. M. (2019). *Human sexuality today.* Pearson.

King, L. A., & Hicks, J. A. (2021). The science of meaning in life. *Annual Review of Psychology, 72*(1), 561–584. https://doi.org/10.1146/annurev-psych-072420-122921

Knodel, J., & Chayovan, N. (2009). Intergenerational relationships and family care and support for thai elderly. *Ageing International, 33*(1–4), 15–27. https://doi.org/10.1007/s12126-009-9026-7

Ko, H.-J., Hooker, K., Geldhof, G. J., & McAdams, D. P. (2016). Longitudinal purpose in life trajectories: Examining predictors in late midlife. *Psychology and Aging, 31*(7), 693–698. https://doi.org/10.1037/pag0000093

Kohl, N. M., Mossakowski, K. N., Sanidad, I. I., Bird, O. T., & Nitz, L. H. (2019). Does the health of adult child caregivers vary by employment status in the United States? *Journal of Aging and Health, 31*(9), 1631–1651. https://doi.org/10.1177/0898264318782561

Kolodziejczak, K., Drewelies, J., Deeg, D. J. H., Huisman, M., & Gerstorf, D. (2020). Perceived importance and enjoyment of sexuality in late Midlife: Cohort differences in the Longitudinal Aging Study Amsterdam (LASA). *Sexuality Research and Social Policy*, 1–15. https://doi.org/10.1007/s13178-020-00486-2

Kornadt, A. E., Hess, T. M., Voss, P., & Rothermund, K. (2018). Subjective age across the life span: A differentiated, longitudinal approach. *The Journals of Gerontology Series B: Psychological Sciences and Social Sciences, 73*, 767–777. https://doi.org/10.1093/geronb/gbw072

Krahn, H. J., Johnson, M. D., & Galambos, N. L. (2021). Intrinsically rewarding work and generativity in Midlife: The long arm of the job. *Work and Occupations, 48*, 184–206. https://doi.org/10.1177/0730888420964942

Kroencke, L., Kuper, N., Bleidorn, W., & Denissen, J. (2021). How does substance use affect personality development? Disentangling between- and within-person effects. *Social Psychological and Personality Science, 12*(4), 517–527. https://doi.org/10.1177/1948550620921702

Kross, E., Gard, D., Deldin, P., Clifton, J., & Ayduk, O. (2012). "Asking why" from a distance: Its cognitive and emotional consequences for people with major depressive disorder. *Journal of Abnormal Psychology, 121*(3), 559–569. https://doi.org/10.1037/a0028808

Krzastek, S. C., Bopp, J., Smith, R. P., & Kovac, J. R. (2019). Recent advances in the understanding and management of erectile dysfunction. *F1000Research, 8*. https://doi.org/10.12688/f1000research.16576.1

Lachman, M. E., Agrigoroaei, S., & Rickenbach, E. H. (2015). Making sense of control: Change and consequences. In *Emerging trends in the social and behavioral sciences* (pp. 1–16). Wiley. https://doi.org/10.1002/9781118900772.etrds0209

Lachman, M. E., Teshale, S., & Agrigoroaei, S. (2015). Midlife as a pivotal period in the life course: Balancing growth and decline at the crossroads of youth and old age. *International Journal of Behavioral Development*, *39*(1), 20–31. https://doi.org/10.1177/0165025414533223

Lapp, L. K., & Spaniol, J. (2016). Aging and self-discrepancy: Evidence for adaptive change across the life span. *Experimental Aging Research*, *42*(2), 212–219. https://doi.org/10.1080/0361073X.2016.1132900

Lavelle, B., & Smock, P. J. (2012). Divorce and women's risk of health insurance loss. *Journal of Health and Social Behavior*, *53*(4), 413–431. https://doi.org/10.1177/0022146512465758

Lee, Y., Tang, F., Kim, K. H., & Albert, S. M. (2015). The vicious cycle of parental caregiving and financial well-being: A longitudinal study of women. *The Journals of Gerontology Series B: Psychological Sciences and Social Sciences*, *70*(3), 425–431. https://doi.org/10.1093/geronb/gbu001

Lefkowitz, E. S., & Fingerman, K. L. (2003). Positive and negative emotional feelings and behaviors in mother-daughter ties in late life. *Journal of Family Psychology*, *17*(4), 607–617.

Lefkowitz, E. S., & Zeldow, P. B. (2006). Masculinity and femininity predict optimal mental health: A belated test of the androgyny hypothesis. *Journal of Personality Assessment*, *87*(1), 95–101.

Lemaster, P., Delaney, R., & Strough, J. (2017). Crossover, degendering, or...? A multidimensional approach to life-span gender development. *Sex Roles*, *76*(11–12), 669–681. https://doi.org/10.1007/s11199-015-0563-0

Leopold, T. (2018). Gender differences in the consequences of divorce: A study of multiple outcomes. *Demography*, *55*(3), 769–797. https://doi.org/10.1007/s13524-018-0667-6

Leopold, T., & Skopek, J. (2015). The demography of grandparenthood: An international profile. *Social Forces*, *94*, 801–832. https://doi.org/10.1093/sf/sov066

Leszko, M., Elleman, L. G., Bastarache, E. D., Graham, E. K., & Mroczek, D. K. (2016). Future directions in the study of personality in adulthood and older age. *Gerontology*, *62*(2), 210–215. https://doi.org/10.1159/000434720

Levinson, D. J. (1978). *The seasons of a man's life*. Knopf.

Levinson, D. J. (1996). *The seasons of a woman's life*. Knopf.

Lilgendahl, J. P., & McAdams, D. P. (2011). Constructing stories of self-growth: How individual differences in patterns of autobiographical reasoning relate to well-being in midlife. *Journal of Personality*, *79*(2), 391–428. https://doi.org/10.1111/j.1467-6494.2010.00688.x

Lin, I.-F., & Brown, S. L. (2021). The economic consequences of gray divorce for women and Men. *The Journals of Gerontology: Series B*. https://doi.org/10.1093/geronb/gbaa157

Löckenhoff, C. E., De Fruyt, F., Terracciano, A., McCrae, R. R., De Bolle, M., Costa, P. T., Aguilar-Vafaie, M. E., Ahn, C., Ahn, H., Alcalay, L., Allik, J., Avdeyeva, T. V., Barbaranelli, C., Benet-Martinez, V., Blatný, M., Bratko, D., Cain, T. R., Crawford, J. T., Lima, M. P., . . . Yik, M. (2009). Perceptions of aging across 26 cultures and their culture-level associates. *Psychology and Aging*, *24*(4), 941–954. https://doi.org/10.1037/a0016901

Lodi-Smith, J., & Roberts, B. W. (2007). Social investment and personality: A meta-analysis of the relationship of personality traits to investment in work, family, religion, and volunteerism. *Personality and Social Psychology Review*, *11*(1), 68–86. https://doi.org/10.1177/1088868306294590

Lodi-Smith, J., & Roberts, B. W. (2010). Getting to know me: Social role experiences and age differences in self-concept clarity during adulthood. *Journal of Personality*, *78*(5), 1383–1410. https://doi.org/10.1111/j.1467-6494.2010.00655.x

López Ulloa, B. F., Møller, V., & Sousa-Poza, A. (2013). How does subjective well-being evolve with age? A literature review. *Journal of Population Ageing*, *6*(3), 227–246. https://doi.org/10.1007/s12062-013-9085-0

Lorenz, F. O., Wickrama, K. A. S., Conger, R. D., & Elder, G. H. J. (2006). The short-term and decade-long effects of divorce on women's midlife health. *Journal of Health and Social Behavior*, *47*(2), 111–125.

Lucas, R. E., & Donnellan, M. B. (2011). Personality development across the life span: Longitudinal analyses with a national sample from Germany. *Journal of Personality & Social Psychology*, *101*(4), 847–861. https://doi.org/10.1037/a0024298

Luhmann, M., Hofmann, W., Eid, M., & Lucas, R. E. (2012). Subjective well-being and adaptation to life events: A meta-analysis. *Journal of Personality and Social Psychology*, *102*(3), 592–615. https://doi.org/10.1037/a0025948

Luthar, S. S., & Ciciolla, L. (2016). What it feels like to be a mother: Variations by children's developmental stages. *Developmental Psychology*, *52*(1), 143–154. https://doi.org/10.1037/dev0000062

Mac Dougall, K., Beyene, Y., & Nachtigall, R. D. (2012). "Inconvenient biology:" Advantages and disadvantages of first-time parenting after age 40 using in vitro fertilization. *Human Reproduction (Oxford, England)*, *27*(4), 1058–1065. https://doi.org/10.1093/humrep/des007

Mancini, A. D., Bonanno, G. A., & Clark, A. E. (2011). Stepping off the hedonic treadmill. *Journal of Individual Differences*, *32*(3), 144–152. https://doi.org/10.1027/1614-0001/a000047

Margolis, R. (2016). The changing demography of grandparenthood. *Journal of Marriage and Family*, *78*(3), 610–622. https://doi.org/10.1111/jomf.12286

Marks, N. F., Bumpass, L. L., & Jun, H. (2004). Family roles and well-being during the middle life course. In O. G. Brim, C. D. Ryff, & R. C. Kessler (Eds.), *How healthy are we?: A national study of well-being at midlife* (pp. 514–549). University of Chicago Press.

Mausbach, B. T., Roepke, S. K., Chattillion, E. A., Harmell, A. L., Moore, R., Romero-Moreno, R., Bowie, C. R., & Grant, I. (2012). Multiple mediators of the relations between caregiving stress and depressive symptoms. *Aging & Mental Health*, *16*(1), 27–38. https://doi.org/10.1080/13607863.2011.615738

Mazzuca, S., Kafetsios, K., Livi, S., & Presaghi, F. (2019). Emotion regulation and satisfaction in long-term marital relationships: The role of emotional contagion. *Journal of Social and Personal Relationships, 36*(9), 2880–2895. https://doi.org/10.1177/0265407518804452

McAdams, D. P. (2014). The life narrative at midlife. *New Directions for Child and Adolescent Development, 2014*(145), 57–69. https://doi.org/10.1002/cad.20067

McAdams, D. P., & Olson, B. D. (2010). Personality development: Continuity and change over the life course. *Annual Review of Psychology, 61*(1), 517–542. https://doi.org/10.1146/annurev.psych.093008.100507

McCrae, R. R. (2002). The maturation of personality psychology: Adult personality development and psychological well-being. *Journal of Research in Personality, 36*(4), 307–317.

McCrae, R. R., & Costa, Jr, P. T. (2008). The five-factor theory of personality. In O. P. John, R. W. Robins, & L. A. Pervin (Eds.), *Handbook of personality psychology: Theory and research* (3rd ed., pp. 159–181). Guilford Press.

McCrae, R. R., & Costa, P. T. J. (2006). Cross-cultural perspectives on adult personality trait development. In D. K. Mroczek & T. D. Little (Eds.), *Handbook of personality development* (pp. 129–145). Lawrence Erlbaum Associates Publishers.

McCrae, R. R., Terracciano, A., & The Personality Profiles of Cultures Project. (2005). Universal features of personality traits from the observer's perspective: Data from 50 cultures. *Journal of Personality and Social Psychology, 88*, 547–561.

McKeering, H., & Pakenham, K. I. (2000). Gender and generativity issues in parenting: Do fathers benefit more than mothers from involvement in child care activities? *Sex Roles, 43*(7), 459–480.

McNulty, J. K., Wenner, C. A., & Fisher, T. D. (2016). Longitudinal associations among relationship satisfaction, sexual satisfaction, and frequency of sex in early marriage. *Archives of Sexual Behavior, 45*(1), 85–97. https://doi.org/10.1007/s10508-014-0444-6

Mehta, C., Wilson, J., & Smirles, K. E.-S. (2021). Gender segregation and its correlates at midlife and beyond. *The International Journal of Aging and Human Development, 93*, 675–699. https://doi.org/10.1177/0091415020974624

Meier, A., Musick, K., Fischer, J., & Flood, S. (2018). Mothers' and fathers' well-being in parenting across the arch of child development. *Journal of Marriage and Family, 80*(4), 992–1004. https://doi.org/10.1111/jomf.12491

Mendoza, A. N., Fruhauf, C. A., & MacPhee, D. (2020). Grandparent caregivers' resilience: Stress, support, and coping predict life satisfaction. *International Journal of Aging and Human Development, 91*(1), 3–20. https://doi.org/10.1177/0091415019843459

Meng, J., Martinez, L., Holmstrom, A., Chung, M., & Cox, J. (2017). Research on social networking sites and social support from 2004 to 2015: A narrative review and directions for future research. *Cyberpsychology, Behavior, and Social Networking, 20*(1), 44–51. https://doi.org/10.1089/cyber.2016.0325

MetLife Mature Market Institute, National Alliance for Caregiving, & Center for Long Term Care Research and Policy. (2011). *The MetLife study of caregiving costs to working caregivers: Double jeopardy for baby boomers caring for their parents.* https://www.caregiving.org/wp-content/uploads/2011/06/mmi-caregiving-costs-working-caregivers.pdf

Milojev, P., & Sibley, C. G. (2017). Normative personality trait development in adulthood: A 6-year cohort-sequential growth model. *Journal of Personality and Social Psychology, 112*(3), 510–526. https://doi.org/10.1037/pspp0000121

Mitchell, B. A. (2010). Happiness in midlife parental roles: A contextual mixed methods analysis. *Family Relations, 59*(3), 326–339. http://cat.inist.fr/?aModele=afficheN&cpsidt=23030811

Mitchell, B. A. (2016). Empty nest. In C. L. Shehan (Ed.), *Encyclopedia of family studies* (pp. 1–4). John Wiley & Sons, Inc. https://doi.org/10.1002/9781119085621.wbefs008

Mitchell, B. A., & Lovegreen, L. D. (2009). The empty nest syndrome in midlife families: A multimethod exploration of parental gender differences and cultural dynamics. *Journal of Family Issues, 30*(12), 1651–1670.

Montgomery, R. J. V., Rowe, J. M., & Kosloski, K. (2007). Family caregiving. In J. A. Blackburn & C. N. Dulmus (Eds.), *Handbook of gerontology: Evidence-based approaches to theory, practice, and policy* (pp. 426–454). John Wiley & Sons Inc.

Moore, C. S., Grant, M. D., Zink, T. A., Panizzon, M. S., Franz, C. E., Logue, M. W., Hauger, R. L., Kremen, W. S., & Lyons, M. J. (2014). Erectile dysfunction, vascular risk, and cognitive performance in late middle age. *Psychology and Aging, 29*, 163–172. https://doi.org/10.1037/a0035463

Moore, R. M., Allbright-Campos, M., & Strick, K. (2017). Childlessness in midlife. *The Family Journal, 25*(1), 40–47. https://doi.org/10.1177/1066480716679647

Moore, S. M., & Rosenthal, D. A. (2015). Personal growth, grandmother engagement and satisfaction among non-custodial grandmothers. *Aging & Mental Health, 19*(2), 136–143. https://doi.org/10.1080/13607863.2014.920302

Morgan, J., & Robinson, O. (2013). Intrinsic aspirations and personal meaning across adulthood: Conceptual interrelations and age/sex differences. *Developmental Psychology, 49*(5), 999–1010. https://doi.org/10.1037/a0029237

Mroczek, D. K., Spiro, A. I. I. I., & Griffin, P. W. (2006). Personality and aging. In J. E. Birren & K. W. Schaire (Eds.), *Handbook of the psychology of aging* (6th ed., pp. 363–377). Elsevier.

Muise, A., Schimmack, U., & Impett, E. A. (2016). Sexual frequency predicts greater well-being, but more is not always better. *Social Psychological and Personality Science, 7*(4), 295–302. https://doi.org/10.1177/1948550615616462

Mustillo, S., Li, M., & Wang, W. (2021). Parent work-to-family conflict and child psychological well-being: Moderating role of grandparent coresidence. *Journal of Marriage and Family, 83*(1), 27–39. https://doi.org/10.1111/jomf.12703

Nantais, C., & Stack, M. (2020). Generativity versus stagnation. In V. Zeigler-Hill & T. K. Shackelford (Eds.), *Encyclopedia of personality and individual differences* (pp. 1–3). Springer International Publishing. https://doi.org/10.1007/978-3-319-28099-8_589-1

Nelson, N. A., & Bergeman, C. S. (2021). Development of generative concern across mid- to later life. *The Gerontologist, 61*(3), 430–438. https://doi.org/10.1093/geront/gnaa115

Neuberger, F. S., & Haberkern, K. (2013). Structured ambivalence in grandchild care and the quality of life among European grandparents. *European Journal of Ageing, 11*(2), 171–181. https://doi.org/10.1007/s10433-013-0294-4

Newton, N., & Stewart, A. J. (2010). The middle ages: Change in women's personalities and social roles. *Psychology of Women Quarterly*, *34*(1), 75–84. https://doi.org/10.1111/j.1471-6402.2009.01543.x

Nomaguchi, K. M., & Milkie, M. A. (2003). Costs and rewards of children: The effects of becoming a parent on adults' lives. *Journal of Marriage & Family*, *65*(2), 356–374.

Nomaguchi, K., & Milkie, M. A. (2020). Parenthood and well-being: A decade in review. *Journal of Marriage and Family*, *82*(1), 198–223. https://doi.org/10.1111/jomf.12646

Ogolsky, B. G., Dennison, R. P., & Monk, J. K. (2014). The role of couple discrepancies in cognitive and behavioral egalitarianism in marital quality. *Sex Roles*, *70*(7–8), 329–342. https://doi.org/10.1007/s11199-014-0365-9

Orth, U. (2017). The lifespan development of self-esteem. In J. Specht (Ed.), *Personality development across the lifespan* (pp. 181–195). Elsevier. https://doi.org/10.1016/B978-0-12-804674-6.00012-0

Orth, U., Erol, R. Y., & Luciano, E. C. (2018). Development of self-esteem from age 4 to 94 Years: A meta-analysis of longitudinal studies. *Psychological Bulletin*, *144*(10), 1045–1080. https://doi.org/10.1037/bul0000161

Orth, U., Trzesniewski, K. H., & Robins, R. W. (2010). Self-esteem development from young adulthood to old age: A cohort-sequential longitudinal study. *Journal of Personality and Social Psychology*, *98*(4), 645–658. https://doi.org/10.1037/a0018769

Oshio, A., Taku, K., Hirano, M., & Saeed, G. (2018). Resilience and big five personality traits: A meta-analysis. *Personality and Individual Differences*, *127*, 54–60. https://doi.org/10.1016/j.paid.2018.01.048

Park, C. L. (2010). Making sense of the meaning literature: An integrative review of meaning making and its effects on adjustment to stressful life events. *Psychological Bulletin*, *136*(2), 257–301. https://doi.org/10.1037/a0018301

Parker, K., & Patten, E. (2013). *The sandwich generation rising financial burdens for middle-aged Americans*. http://www.pewsocialtrends.org/2013/01/30/the-sandwich-generation/

Parker, K., & Wang, W. (2013). *Modern parenthood roles of moms and dads converge as they balance work and family*. http://www.pewsocialtrends.org/2013/03/14/modern-parenthood-roles-of-moms-and-dads-converge-as-they-balance-work-and-family/

Pasupathi, M., & Mansour, E. (2006). Adult age differences in autobiographical reasoning in narratives. *Developmental Psychology*, *42*(5), 798–808.

Pearson, A. L., Bentham, G., Day, P., Kingham, S., Flegal, K., Carroll, M., Ogden, C., Curtin, L., Hill, J., Wyatt, H., Reed, G., Peters, J., Bohdjalian, A., Langer, F., Shakeri-Leidenmühler, S., Gfrerer, L., Ludvik, B., Zacherl, J., Prager, G., . . . Brug, J. (2014). Associations between neighbourhood environmental characteristics and obesity and related behaviours among adult New Zealanders. *BMC Public Health*, *14*(1), 553. https://doi.org/10.1186/1471-2458-14-553

Perrig-Chiello, P., Hutchison, S., & Morselli, D. (2014). Patterns of psychological adaptation to divorce after a long-term marriage. *Journal of Social and Personal Relationships*, *32*(3), 386–405. https://doi.org/10.1177/0265407514533769

Peterson, L. M., Stock, M. L., Monroe, J., Molloy-Paolillo, B. K., & Lambert, S. F. (2020). Racial exclusion causes acute cortisol release among emerging-adult African Americans: The role of reduced perceived control. *Journal of Social Psychology*, *160*(5), 658–674. https://doi.org/10.1080/00224545.2020.1729685

Pilar Matud, M., Bethencourt, J. M., & Ibáñez, I. (2014). Relevance of gender roles in life satisfaction in adult people. *Personality and Individual Differences*, *70*, 206–211. https://doi.org/10.1016/j.paid.2014.06.046

Pillemer, K., & Suitor, J. J. (2014). Who provides care? A prospective study of caregiving among adult siblings. *The Gerontologist*, *54*(4), 589–598. https://doi.org/10.1093/geront/gnt066

Pillemer, K., Suitor, J. J., Riffin, C., & Gilligan, M. (2017). Adult children's problems and mothers' well-being. *Research on Aging*, *39*(3), 375–395. https://doi.org/10.1177/0164027515611464

Pinquart, M., & Wahl, H.-W. (2021). Subjective age from childhood to advanced old age: A meta-analysis. *Psychology and Aging*, *35*(3), 394–406. https://doi.org/10.1037/pag0000600

Polenick, C. A., Birditt, K. S., & Zarit, S. H. (2018). Parental support of adult children and middle-aged couples' marital satisfaction. *The Gerontologist*, *58*(4), 663–673. https://doi.org/10.1093/geront/gnx021

Polenick, C. A., Seidel, A. J., Birditt, K. S., Zarit, S. H., & Fingerman, K. L. (2017). Filial obligation and marital satisfaction in middle-aged couples. *The Gerontologist*, *57*(3), 417–428. https://doi.org/10.1093/geront/gnv138

Pollitt, A. M., Robinson, B. A., & Umberson, D. (2018). Gender conformity, perceptions of shared power, and marital quality in same- and different-sex marriages. *Gender & Society : Official Publication of Sociologists for Women in Society*, *32*(1), 109–131. https://doi.org/10.1177/0891243217742110

Pollmann-Schult, M. (2014). Parenthood and life satisfaction: Why don't children make people happy? *Journal of Marriage and Family*, *76*(2), 319–336. https://doi.org/10.1111/jomf.12095

Power, R., & Pluess, M. (2015). Heritability estimates of the Big Five personality traits based on common genetic variants. *Translational Psychiatry*, *5*, e604. https://doi.org/10.1038/tp.2015.96

Pudrovska, T. (2009). Parenthood, stress, and mental health in late midlife and early old age. *The International Journal of Aging & Human Development*, *68*(2), 127–147. https://doi.org/10.2190/AG.68.2.b

Pulkkinen, L., Feldt, T., & Kokko, K. (2005). Personality in young adulthood and functoning in middle age. In S. L. Willis & M. Martin (Eds.), *Middle adulthood: A lifespan perspective* (pp. 99–141). Sage.

Quinn-Nilas, C., Milhausen, R. R., McKay, A., & Holzapfel, S. (2018). Prevalence and predictors of sexual problems among midlife Canadian adults: Results from a national survey. *Journal of Sexual Medicine*, *15*(6), 873–879. https://doi.org/10.1016/j.jsxm.2018.03.086

Rammstedt, B., Spinath, F. M., Richter, D., & Schupp, J. (2013). Partnership longevity and personality congruence in couples. *Personality and Individual Differences*, *54*(7), 832–835. https://doi.org/10.1016/j.paid.2012.12.007

Rapoport, E., Muthiah, N., Keim, S. A., & Adesman, A. (2020). Family well-being in grandparent-versus parent-headed households. *Pediatrics*, *146*(3). https://doi.org/10.1542/PEDS.2020-0115

Rastrelli, G., Corona, G., & Maggi, M. (2018). Testosterone and sexual function in men. *Maturitas, 112*, 46–52. https://doi.org/10.1016/j.maturitas.2018.04.004

Rathunde, K., & Isabella, R. (2017). Play, flow, and tailoring identity in middle adulthood. In J. D. Sinnott (Ed.), *Identity flexibility during adulthood* (pp. 211–232). Springer International Publishing. https://doi.org/10.1007/978-3-319-55658-1_14

Riley, L. D., & Bowen, C. (2005). The sandwich generation: Challenges and coping strategies of multigenerational families. *Family Journal, 13*(1), 52–58. https://doi.org/10.1177/1066480704270099

Roberts, B. W., & Caspi, A. (2003). The cumulative continuity model of personality development: Striking a balance between continuity and change in personality traits across the life course. In M. Ursula & U. Lindenberger (Eds.), *Understanding human development: Dialogues with lifespan psychology* (pp. 183–214). Kluwer Academic.

Roberts, B. W., & Mroczek, D. (2008). Personality trait change in adulthood. *Current Directions in Psychological Science, 17*(1), 31–35. https://doi.org/10.1111/j.1467-8721.2008.00543.x

Robinson, S. A., & Lachman, M. E. (2017). Perceived control and aging: A mini-review and directions for future research. *Gerontology, 63*(5), 435–442. https://doi.org/10.1159/000468540

Röcke, C., & Lachman, M. E. (2008). Perceived trajectories of life satisfaction across past, present, and future: Profiles and correlates of subjective change in young, middle-aged, and older adults. *Psychology and Aging, 23*(4), 833–847. https://doi.org/10.1037/a0013680

Rokach, R., Cohen, O., & Dreman, S. J. (2004). Who pulls the trigger? Who initiates divorce among over 45-year-olds. *Journal of Divorce & Remarriage, 42*(1/2), 61–83. https://doi.org/10.1300/J087v42n01_03

Rosenberg, S. D., Rosenberg, H. J., & Farrell, M. P. (1999). The midlife crisis revisited. In S. L. Willis & J. D. Reid (Eds.), *Life in the middle: Psychological and social development in middle age* (pp. 47–73). Academic Press.

Rote, S. M., & Moon, H. (2016). Racial/ethnic differences in caregiving frequency: Does immigrant status matter? *The Journals of Gerontology Series B: Psychological Sciences and Social Sciences, 73*(6), gbw106. https://doi.org/10.1093/geronb/gbw106

Ryff, C. D. (1991). Possible selves in adulthood and old age: A tale of shifting horizons. *Psychology and Aging, 6*(2), 286–295.

Ryff, C. D. (1995). Psychological well-being in adult life. *Current Directions in Psychological Science, 4*(4), 99–104. 10.1111/1467-8721.ep10772395

Ryff, C. D. (2014). Psychological well-being revisited: Advances in the science and practice of eudaimonia. *Psychotherapy and Psychosomatics, 83*(1), 10–28. https://doi.org/10.1159/000353263

Sakraida, T. J. (2005). Common themes in the divorce transition experience of midlife women. *Journal of Divorce & Remarriage, 43*(1/2), 69–88. https://doi.org/10.1300/J087v43n01_04

Salary.com. (2021). Retrieved from https://www.salary.com/

Sanders, M. R., & Turner, K. M. T. (2018). The importance of parenting in influencing the lives of children. In M. R. Sanders & A. Morawska (Eds.), *Handbook of parenting and child development across the lifespan* (pp. 3–26). Springer International Publishing. https://doi.org/10.1007/978-3-319-94598-9_1

Saxbe, D., Rossin-Slater, M., & Goldenberg, D. (2018). The transition to parenthood as a critical window for adult health. *American Psychologist, 73*(9), 1190–1200. https://doi.org/10.1037/amp0000376

Sbarra, D. A., & Coan, J. A. (2017). Divorce and health: Good data in need of better theory. *Current Opinion in Psychology, 13*, 91–95. https://doi.org/10.1016/j.copsyc.2016.05.014

Sbarra, D. A., Hasselmo, K., & Bourassa, K. J. (2015). Divorce and health: Beyond individual differences. *Current Directions in Psychological Science, 24*(2), 109–113. https://doi.org/10.1177/0963721414559125

Sbarra, D. A., Law, R. W., & Portley, R. M. (2011). Divorce and death: A meta-analysis and research agenda for clinical, social, and health psychology. *Perspectives on Psychological Science, 6*(5), 454–474. https://doi.org/10.1177/1745691611414724

Sbarra, D. A., Smith, H. L., & Mehl, M. R. (2012). When leaving your ex, love yourself: Observational ratings of self-compassion predict the course of emotional recovery following marital separation. *Psychological Science, 23*(3), 261–269. https://doi.org/10.1177/0956797611429466

Schneller, D. P., & Arditti, J. A. (2004). After the breakup: Interpreting divorce and rethinking intimacy. *Journal of Divorce & Remarriage, 42*(1), 1–37.

Schober, P. S. (2013). The parenthood effect on gender inequality: Explaining the change in paid and domestic work when british couples become parents. *European Sociological Review, 29*(1), 74–85. https://doi.org/10.1093/esr/jcr041

Schwaba, T., & Bleidorn, W. (2018). Individual differences in personality change across the adult life span. *Journal of Personality, 86*(3), 450–484. https://doi.org/10.1111/jopy.12327

Seiffge-Krenke, I. (2010). Predicting the timing of leaving home and related developmental tasks: Parents' and children's perspectives. *Journal of Social & Personal Relationships, 27*(4), 495–518. https://doi.org/10.1177/0265407510363426

Shamloul, R., & Ghanem, H. (2013). Erectile dysfunction. *The Lancet, 381*(9861), 153–165. https://doi.org/10.1016/S0140-6736(12)60520-0

Shane, J., Hamm, J., & Heckhausen, J. (2019). Subjective age at work: Feeling younger or older than one's actual age predicts perceived control and motivation at work. *Work, Aging and Retirement, 5*(4), 323–332. https://doi.org/10.1093/workar/waz013

Shane, J., & Heckhausen, J. (2019). Motivational theory of lifespan development. In B. Baltes, C. Rudolph, & H. Zacher (Eds.), *Work across the lifespan* (pp. 111–134). Elsevier. https://doi.org/10.1016/B978-0-12-812756-8.00005-0

Sheppard, P., & Monden, C. (2019). Becoming a first-time grandparent and subjective well-being: A fixed effects approach. *Journal of Marriage and Family, 81*(4), 1016–1026. https://doi.org/10.1111/jomf.12584

Shinan-Altman, S., & Werner, P. (2019). Subjective age and its correlates among middle-aged and older adults. *The International Journal of Aging and Human Development, 88*(1), 3–21. https://doi.org/10.1177/0091415017752941

Shiota, M. N., & Levenson, R. W. (2007). Birds of a feather don't always fly farthest: Similarity in Big Five personality predicts more negative marital satisfaction trajectories in long-term marriages. *Psychology and Aging, 22*(4), 666–675.

Silverstein, M., & Marenco, A. (2001). How Americans enact the grandparent role across the family life course. *Journal of Family Issues*, *22*(4), 493–522.

Simon, J. A. (2011). Identifying and treating sexual dysfunction in postmenopausal women: The role of estrogen. *Journal of Women's Health (2002)*, *20*(10), 1453–1465. https://doi.org/10.1089/jwh.2010.2151

Simon, R. W., & Caputo, J. (2019). The costs and benefits of parenthood for mental and physical health in the United States: The importance of parenting stage. *Society and Mental Health*, *9*(3), 296–315. https://doi.org/10.1177/2156869318786760

Smith, G. C., & Hancock, G. R. (2010). Custodial grandmother-grandfather dyads: Pathways among marital distress, grandparent dysphoria, parenting practice, and grandchild adjustment. *Family Relations*, *59*(1), 45–59. https://doi.org/10.1111/j.1741-3729.2009.00585.x

Smith, J., & Freund, A. M. (2002). The dynamics of possible selves in old age. *Journals of Gerontology Series B: Psychological Sciences & Social Sciences*, *57B*(6), 492.

Smith, R. L., Gallicchio, L., & Flaws, J. A. (2017). Factors affecting sexual activity in midlife women: Results from the midlife health study. *Journal of Women's Health*, *26*(2), 103–108. https://doi.org/10.1089/jwh.2016.5881

Sneed, J. R., Whitbourne, S. K., Schwartz, S. J., & Huang, S. (2012). The relationship between identity, intimacy, and midlife well-being: Findings from the Rochester Adult Longitudinal Study. *Psychology and Aging*, *27*(2), 318–323. https://doi.org/10.1037/a0026378

Soenens, B., Vansteenkiste, M., & Beyers, W. (2019). Parenting adolescents. In M. H. Bornstein (Ed.), *Handbook of parenting*. Routledge. https://doi.org/10.4324/9780429440847-4

Soliz, J. (2015). Communication and the grandparent-grandchild relationship. In C. R. Berger, M. E. Roloff, S. R. Wilson, J. P. Dillard, J. Coughlin, & D. Solomon (Eds.), *The international encyclopedia of interpersonal communication* (pp. 1–5). John Wiley & Sons, Inc. https://doi.org/10.1002/9781118540190.wbeic221

Soto, C. J. (2015). Is happiness good for your personality? Concurrent and prospective relations of the big five with subjective well-being. *Journal of Personality*, *83*(1), 45–55. https://doi.org/10.1111/jopy.12081

Soto, C. J., John, O. P., Gosling, S. D., & Potter, J. (2011). Age differences in personality traits from 10 to 65: Big Five domains and facets in a large cross-sectional sample. *Journal of Personality and Social Psychology*, *100*(2), 330–348. https://doi.org/10.1037/a0021717

Srivastava, S., John, O. P., Gosling, S. D., & Potter, J. (2003). Development of personality in early and middle adulthood: Set like plaster or persistent change? *Journal of Personality and Social Psychology*, *84*, 1041–1053.

Steger, M. F., Oishi, S., & Kashdan, T. B. (2009). Meaning in life across the life span: Levels and correlates of meaning in life from emerging adulthood to older adulthood. *The Journal of Positive Psychology*, *4*(1), 43–52. https://doi.org/10.1080/17439760802303127

Steger, M. F., Oishi, S., & Kesebir, S. (2011). Is a life without meaning satisfying? The moderating role of the search for meaning in satisfaction with life judgments. *The Journal of Positive Psychology*, *6*(3), 173–180. https://doi.org/10.1080/17439760.2011.569171

Steinberg, L. (2001). We know some things: Parent-adolescent relationships in retrospect and prospect. *Journal of Research on Adolescence*, *11*(1), 1–19.

Steinberg, L., Icenogle, G., Shulman, E. P., Breiner, K., Chein, J., Bacchini, D., Chang, L., Chaudhary, N., Di Giunta, L., Dodge, K. A., Fanti, K. A., Lansford, J. E., Malone, P. S., Oburu, P., Pastorelli, C., Skinner, A. T., Sorbring, E., Tapanya, S., Tirado, L. M. U., . . . Takash, H. M. S. (2018). Around the world, adolescence is a time of heightened sensation seeking and immature self-regulation. *Developmental Science*, *21*(2), e12532. https://doi.org/10.1111/desc.12532

Steiner, L. M., Suarez, E. C., Sells, J. N., & Wykes, S. D. (2011). Effect of age, initiator status, and infidelity on women's divorce adjustment. *Journal of Divorce & Remarriage*, *52*(1), 33–47. https://doi.org/10.1080/10502556.2011.534394

Stephan, Y., Caudroit, J., Jaconelli, A., & Terracciano, A. (2014). Subjective age and cognitive functioning: A 10-year prospective study. *The American Journal of Geriatric Psychiatry : Official Journal of the American Association for Geriatric Psychiatry*, *22*(11), 1180–1187. https://doi.org/10.1016/j.jagp.2013.03.007

Stephan, Y., Sutin, A. R., & Terracciano, A. (2018). Subjective age and mortality in three longitudinal samples. *Psychosomatic Medicine*, *80*(7), 659–664. https://doi.org/10.1097/PSY.0000000000000613

Strickhouser, J. E., Zell, E., & Krizan, Z. (2017). Does personality predict health and well-being? A metasynthesis. *Health Psychology*, *36*(8), 797–810. https://doi.org/10.1037/hea0000475

Stuifbergen, M. C., Van Delden, J. J. M., & Dykstra, P. A. (2008). The implications of today's family structures for support giving to older parents. *Ageing & Society*, *28*(3), 413–434. 10.1017/S0144686X07006666

Sutcliffe, A. G., Barnes, J., Belsky, J., Gardiner, J., & Melhuish, E. (2012). The health and development of children born to older mothers in the United Kingdom: Observational study using longitudinal cohort data. *BMJ (Clinical Research Ed.)*, *345*(aug21_1), e5116. https://doi.org/10.1136/bmj.e5116

Syed, M., & McLean, K. C. (2018). Erikson's theory of psychosocial development. In E. Braaten & B. Willoughby (Eds.), *The SAGE encyclopedia of intellectual and developmental disorders* (pp. 577–581). PsyArXiv. https://doi.org/10.17605/OSF.IO/ZF35D

Symoens, S., Van de Velde, S., Colman, E., & Bracke, P. (2014). Divorce and the multidimensionality of men and women's mental health: The role of social-relational and socio-economic conditions. *Applied Research in Quality of Life*, *9*(2), 197–214. https://doi.org/10.1007/s11482-013-9239-5

Tanis, M., van der Louw, M., & Buijzen, M. (2017). From empty nest to Social Networking Site: What happens in cyberspace when children are launched from the parental home? *Computers in Human Behavior*, *68*, 56–63. https://doi.org/10.1016/J.CHB.2016.11.005

Tearne, J. E. (2015). Older maternal age and child behavioral and cognitive outcomes: A review of the literature. *Fertility and Sterility*, *103*(6), 1381–1391. https://doi.org/10.1016/j.fertnstert.2015.04.027

Terracciano, A., Stephan, Y., Aschwanden, D., Lee, J. H., Sesker, A. A., Strickhouser, J. E., Luchetti, M., & Sutin, A. R. (2021). Changes in subjective age during COVID-19. *The Gerontologist*, *61*(1), 13–22. https://doi.org/10.1093/geront/gnaa104

Thiele, D. M., & Whelan, T. A. (2008). The relationship between grandparent satisfaction, meaning, and generativity. *International Journal of Aging & Human Development*, *66*(1), 21–48.

Thomas, H. N., Hamm, M., Hess, R., & Thurston, R. C. (2018a). Changes in sexual function among midlife women: "I'm older... and I'm wiser.". *Menopause*, *25*(3), 286–292. https://doi.org/10.1097/GME.0000000000000988

Thomas, H. N., Hamm, M., Hess, R., & Thurston, R. C. (2018b). Changes in sexual function among midlife women. *Menopause*, *25*, 286–292. https://doi.org/10.1097/GME.0000000000000988

Thomas, H. N., Hess, R., & Thurston, R. C. (2015). Correlates of sexual activity and satisfaction in midlife and older women. *Annals of Family Medicine*, *13*(4), 336–342. https://doi.org/10.1370/afm.1820

Thomas, H. N., Neal-Perry, G. S., & Hess, R. (2018). Female sexual function at midlife and beyond. *Obstetrics and Gynecology Clinics of North America*, *45*, 709–722. https://doi.org/10.1016/j.ogc.2018.07.013

Thomas, H. N., & Thurston, R. C. (2016). A biopsychosocial approach to women's sexual function and dysfunction at midlife: A narrative review. *Maturitas*, *87*, 49–60. https://doi.org/10.1016/j.maturitas.2016.02.009

Toothman, E. L., & Barrett, A. E. (2011). Mapping midlife: An examination of social factors shaping conceptions of the timing of middle age. *Advances in Life Course Research*, *16*(3), 99–111. https://doi.org/10.1016/j.alcr.2011.08.003

Tosi, M. (2020). Boomerang kids and parents' well-being: Adaptation, stressors, and social norms. *European Sociological Review*, *36*(3), 460–473. https://doi.org/10.1093/esr/jcz068

Tracy, E. L., & Utz, R. L. (2020). For better or for worse: Health and marital quality during midlife. *Journal of Aging and Health*, *32*(10), 1625–1635. https://doi.org/10.1177/0898264320948305

Trillingsgaard, T., & Sommer, D. (2018). Associations between older maternal age, use of sanctions, and children's socio-emotional development through 7, 11, and 15 years. *European Journal of Developmental Psychology*, *15*(2), 141–155. https://doi.org/10.1080/17405629.2016.1266248

Turiano, N. A., Chapman, B. P., Agrigoroaei, S., Infurna, F. J., & Lachman, M. (2014). Perceived control reduces mortality risk at low, not high, education levels. *Health Psychology*, *33*(8), 883–890. https://doi.org/10.1037/hea0000022

Turiano, N. A., Chapman, B. P., Gruenewald, T. L., & Mroczek, D. K. (2015). Personality and the leading behavioral contributors of mortality. *Health Psychology: Official Journal of the Division of Health Psychology, American Psychological Association*, *34*(1), 51–60. https://doi.org/10.1037/hea0000038

U.S. Bureau of Labor Statistics. (2021). *Occupational Outlook Handbook: 2021*. Retrieved from https://www.bls.gov/ooh/

U.S. Bureau of the Census. (2015). *Table A1. Marital status of people 15 years and over, by age, sex, personal earnings, race, and hispanic origin: 2014*. America's Families and Living Arrangements: 2014. http://www.census.gov/hhes/families/data/cps2014A.html

US Census Bureau. (2017). *National grandparents day 2017: Sept. 10*. Facts for Features. https://www.census.gov/newsroom/facts-for-features/2017/grandparents-day.html

Vandewater, E., & Stewart, A. (2006). Paths to late midlife well-being for women and men: The importance of identity development and social role quality. *Journal of Adult Development*, *13*(2), 76–83.

Vargas Lascano, D. I., Galambos, N. L., Krahn, H. J., & Lachman, M. E. (2015). Growth in perceived control across 25 years from the late teens to midlife: The role of personal and parents' education. *Developmental Psychology*, *51*(1), 124–135. https://doi.org/10.1037/a0038433

Villar, F. (2012). Successful ageing and development: The contribution of generativity in older age. *Ageing and Society*, *32*(07), 1087–1105. https://doi.org/10.1017/S0144686X11000973

Villar, F., Celdrán, M., & Triadó, C. (2012). Grandmothers offering regular auxiliary care for their grandchildren: An expression of generativity in later life? *Journal of Women & Aging*, *24*(4), 292–312. https://doi.org/10.1080/08952841.2012.708576

von Hippel, C., Adhia, A., Rosenberg, S., Austin, S. B., Partridge, A., & Tamimi, R. (2019). Sexual function among women in midlife: Findings from the nurses' health study II. *Women's Health Issues*, *29*(4), 291–298. https://doi.org/10.1016/j.whi.2019.04.006

Voss, P., Kornadt, A. E., & Rothermund, K. (2017). Getting what you expect? Future self-views predict the valence of life events. *Developmental Psychology*, *53*(3), 567–580. https://doi.org/10.1037/dev0000285

Vukasović, T., & Bratko, D. (2015). Heritability of personality: A meta-analysis of behavior genetic studies. *Psychological Bulletin*, *141*(4), 769–785. https://doi.org/10.1037/bul0000017

Walther, A., Mahler, F., Debelak, R., & Ehlert, U. (2017). Psychobiological protective factors modifying the association between age and sexual health in men: Findings from the men's health 40+ study. *American Journal of Men's Health*, *11*(3), 737–747. https://doi.org/10.1177/1557988316689238

Wang, H., & Amato, P. R. (2000). Predictors of divorce adjustment: Stressors, resources, and definitions. *Journal of Marriage & the Family*, *62*(3), 655–668.

Wang, W., & Parker, K. (2014). *Record share of Americans have never married*. http://www.pewsocialtrends.org/2014/09/24/record-share-of-americans-have-never-married/

Wang, Y.-N., Shyu, Y.-I. L., Chen, M.-C., & Yang, P.-S. (2011). Reconciling work and family caregiving among adult-child family caregivers of older people with dementia: Effects on role strain and depressive symptoms. *Journal of Advanced Nursing*, *67*(4), 829–840. https://doi.org/10.1111/j.1365-2648.2010.05505.x

Wängqvist, M., Lamb, M. E., Frisén, A., & Hwang, C. P. (2015). Child and adolescent predictors of personality in early adulthood. *Child Development*, *86*(0), 1253–1261. https://doi.org/10.1111/cdev.12362

Werner, E. E. (1991). Grandparent-grandchild relationships amongst US ethnic groups. In P. K. Smith (Ed.), *The psychology of grandparenthood: An international perspective* (pp. 68–82). Taylor & Frances/Routledge.

Wethington, E. (2000). Expecting stress: Americans and the "midlife crisis.". *Motivation and Emotion*, *24*(2), 85–103.

Wethington, E., Kessler, R. C., & Pixley, J. E. (2004). Turning points in adulthood. In O. G. Brim, C. D. Ryff, & R. C. Kessler (Eds.), *How healthy are we?: A national study of well-being at midlife* (pp. 586–613). University of Chicago Press.

Whitbeck, L., & Hoyt, D. R. (1994). Early family relationships, intergenerational solidarity, and support provided to parents by. *Journal of Gerontology, 49*(2), S85.

White, S. M., Wojcicki, T. R., & McAuley, E. (2012). Social cognitive influences on physical activity behavior in middle-aged and older adults. *The Journals of Gerontology Series B: Psychological Sciences and Social Sciences, 67B*(1), 18–26. https://doi.org/10.1093/geronb/gbr064

Whitley, D. M., & Fuller-Thomson, E. (2017). African-American solo grandparents raising grandchildren: A representative profile of their health status. *Journal of Community Health, 42*(2), 312–323. https://doi.org/10.1007/s10900-016-0257-8

Williams, M. N. (2011). The changing roles of grandparents raising grandchildren. *Journal of Human Behavior in the Social Environment, 21*(8), 948–962. https://doi.org/10.1080/10911359.2011.588535

Williams, N., & Torrez, D. J. (1998). Grandparenthood among Hispanics. In M. E. Szinovacz (Ed.), *Handbook on grandparenthood* (pp. 87–96). Greenwood Press/Greenwood Publishing Group.

Wilt, J., Cox, K., & McAdams, D. P. (2010). The eriksonian life story: Developmental scripts and psychosocial adaptation. *Journal of Adult Development, 17*(3), 156–161. https://doi.org/10.1007/s10804-010-9093-8

Wray, S. (2007). Women making sense of midlife: Ethnic and cultural diversity. *Journal of Aging Studies, 21*(1), 31–42. https://doi.org/10.1016/j.jaging.2006.03.001

Wrzus, C., Wagner, G. G., & Riediger, M. (2016). Personality-situation transactions from adolescence to old age. *Journal of Personality and Social Psychology, 110*(5), 782–799. https://doi.org/10.1037/pspp0000054

Wrzus, C., Zimmermann, J., Mund, M., & Neyer, F. J. (2017). Friendships in young and middle adulthood. In M. Hojjat & A. Moyer (Eds.), *The psychology of friendship* (pp. 21–38). Oxford University Press. https://doi.org/10.1093/acprof:oso/9780190222024.003.0002

Yancura, L. A., Barnett, M. A., Sano, Y., & Mammen, S. (2020). Context matters: Nonresident grandparent contributions to low-income rural families. *Child & Family Social Work, 25*(2), 267–276. https://doi.org/10.1111/cfs.12682

Yavorsky, J. E., Dush, C. M. K., & Schoppe-Sullivan, S. J. (2015). The production of inequality: The gender division of labor across the transition to parenthood. *Journal of Marriage and the Family, 77*(3), 662–679. https://doi.org/10.1111/jomf.12189

Zarit, S. H., & Eggebeen, D. J. (2002). Parent-child relationships in adulthood and later years. In M. H. Bornstein (Ed.), *Handbook of parenting: Vol. 1: Children and parenting* (2nd ed., pp. 135–161). Lawrence Erlbaum Associates Publishers.

Zhan, H. J. (2004). Willingness and expectations: Intergenerational differences in attitudes toward filial responsibility in China. *Marriage & Family Review, 36*(1/2), 175–200. 10.1300/J002v36n01_08

Zondervan-Zwijnenburg, , M. A. J., Veldkamp, S. A. M., Neumann, A., Barzeva, S. A., Nelemans, S. A., Beijsterveldt, C. E. M., Branje, S. J. T., Hillegers, M. H. J., Meeus, W. H. J., Tiemeier, H., Hoijtink, H. J. A., Oldehinkel, A. J., & Boomsma, D. I. (2020). Parental age and offspring childhood mental health: A multi-cohort, population-based investigation. *Child Development, 91*(3), 964–982. https://doi.org/10.1111/cdev.13267

CHAPTER 15

Aarsland, D., Creese, B., Politis, M., Chaudhuri, K. R., Ffytche, D. H., Weintraub, D., & Ballard, C. (2017). Cognitive decline in Parkinson disease. *Nature Reviews Neurology, 13*(4), 217–231. https://doi.org/10.1038/nrneurol.2017.27

Abeysinghe, A. A. D. T., Deshapriya, R. D. U. S., & Udawatte, C. (2020). Alzheimer's disease; a review of the pathophysiological basis and therapeutic interventions. *Life Sciences, 256*, 117996. https://doi.org/10.1016/j.lfs.2020.117996

Abrams, A. P. (2014). Physiology of aging of older adults: Systemic and oral health considerations. *Dental Clinics of North America, 58*(4), 729–738. https://doi.org/10.1016/j.cden.2014.06.002

Ackerman, P. L., & Beier, M. E. (2006). Determinants of domain knowledge and independent study learning in an adult sample. *Journal of Educational Psychology, 98*(2), 366–381. https://doi.org/10.1037/0022-0663.98.2.366

Adams, D. R., Kern, D. W., Wroblewski, K. E., McClintock, M. K., Dale, W., & Pinto, J. M. (2018). Olfactory dysfunction predicts subsequent dementia in older U.S. adults. *Journal of the American Geriatrics Society, 66*(1), 140–144. https://doi.org/10.1111/jgs.15048

Administration on Aging. (2014). *A profile of older Americans: 2014*. http://www.aoa.acl.gov/Aging_Statistics/Profile/index.aspx

Aigner, T., Haag, J., Martin, J., & Buckwalter, J. (2007). Osteoarthritis: Aging of matrix and cells - going for a remedy. *Current Drug Targets, 8*(2), 325–331. https://doi.org/10.2174/138945007779940070

Ailshire, J. A., Beltrán-Sánchez, H., & Crimmins, E. M. (2015). Becoming centenarians: Disease and functioning trajectories of older US Adults as they survive to 100. *The Journals of Gerontology. Series A, Biological Sciences and Medical Sciences, 70*(2), 193–201. https://doi.org/10.1093/gerona/glu124

Alejandro, S.-L., Fabian, S.-G., Helios, P.-G., Carmen, F.-L., Enzo, E., Alejandro, L., & Nuria, G. (2015). Where are supercentenarians located? A worldwide demographic study. *Rejuvenation Research, 18*, 14–19. http://online.liebertpub.com/doi/abs/10.1089/rej.2014.1609

Alzheimer's Association. (2018). *2018 Alzheimer's disease facts and figures*. Alzheimer's Association.

Alzheimer's Association. (2021). *Alzheimer's disease facts and figures - 2021*. https://www.alz.org/media/documents/alzheimers-facts-and-figures.pdf

Alzheimer's Disease International. (2015). *World Alzheimer report 2014: Dementia and risk reduction*. http://www.alz.co.uk/research/world-report-2014

American Academy of Ophthalmology. (2011). *Eye health statistics at a glance*. http://www.aao.org/newsroom/upload/Eye-Health-Statistics-April-2011.pdf

American Cancer Society. (2019). *Cancer facts & figures. 2019* https://www.cancer.org/content/dam/cancer-org/research/cancer-facts-and-statistics/annual-cancer-facts-and-figures/2019/cancer-facts-and-figures-2019.pdf

American Psychiatric Association. (2013). *Diagnostic and statistical manual of mental disorders DSM-V* (5th ed.). Author.

Andersen, K., Lolk, A., Martinussen, T., & Kragh-Sørensen, P. (2010). Very mild to severe dementia and mortality: A 14-year follow-up – The odense study. *Dementia & Geriatric Cognitive Disorders, 29*(1), 61–67. https://doi.org/10.1159/000265553

Angara, P., Tsang, D. C., Hoffer, M. E., & Snapp, H. A. (2021). Self-perceived hearing status creates an unrealized barrier to hearing healthcare utilization. *Laryngoscope, 131*(1), E289–E295. https://doi.org/10.1002/lary.28604

Ang, M. J., & Afshari, N. A. (2021). Cataract and systemic disease: A review. In *Clinical and experimental ophthalmology* (Vol. 49, pp. 118–127). Blackwell Publishing. https://doi.org/10.1111/ceo.13892

Anstey, K. J., Hofer, S. M., & Luszcz, M. A. (2003). A latent growth curve analysis of late-life sensory and cognitive function over 8 years: Evidence for specific and common factors underlying change. *Psychology and Aging, 18*(4), 714–726. 10.1037/0882-7974.18.4.714

Arai, Y., Sasaki, T., & Hirose, N. (2017). Demographic, phenotypic, and genetic characteristics of centenarians in Okinawa and Honshu, Japan: Part 2 Honshu, Japan. *Mechanisms of Ageing and Development, 165,* 80–85. https://doi.org/10.1016/J.MAD.2017.02.005

Archambeau, K., Forstmann, B., Van Maanen, L., & Gevers, W. (2020). Proactive interference in aging: A model-based study. *Psychonomic Bulletin and Review, 27*(1), 130–138. https://doi.org/10.3758/s13423-019-01671-0

Ardelt, M. (1998). Social crisis and individual growth: The long-term effects of the great depression. *Journal of Aging Studies, 12*(3), 291.

Ardelt, M. (2010). Are older adults wiser than college students? A comparison of two age cohorts. *Journal of Adult Development, 17*(4), 193–207. https://doi.org/10.1007/s10804-009-9088-5

Ardelt, M., Pridgen, S., & Nutter-Pridgen, K. L. (2018). The relation between age and three-dimensional wisdom: Variations by wisdom dimensions and education. *The Journals of Gerontology: Series B, 73,* 1339–1349. https://doi.org/10.1093/geronb/gbx182

Armstrong, N. J., Mather, K. A., Thalamuthu, A., Wright, M. J., Trollor, J. N., Ames, D., Brodaty, H., Schofield, P. R., Sachdev, P. S., & Kwok, J. B. (2017). Aging, exceptional longevity and comparisons of the Hannum and Horvath epigenetic clocks. *Epigenomics, 9*(5), 689–700. https://doi.org/10.2217/epi-2016-0179

Artistico, D., Orom, H., Cervone, D., Krauss, S., & Houston, E. (2010). Everyday challenges in context: The influence of contextual factors on everyday problem solving among young, middle-aged, and older adults. *Experimental Aging Research, 36*(2), 230–247. https://doi.org/10.1080/03610731003613938

Ash, A. S., Kroll-Desrosiers, A. R., Hoaglin, D. C., Christensen, K., Fang, H., & Perls, T. T. (2015). Are members of long-lived families healthier than their equally long-lived peers? Evidence from the long life family study. *The Journals of Gerontology. Series A, Biological Sciences and Medical Sciences, 70,* 971–976. https://doi.org/10.1093/gerona/glv015

Aslan, U. B., Cavlak, U., Yagci, N., Akdag, B., Stewart, A. L., Miller, C. J., & Bloch, D. A. (2008). Balance performance, aging and falling: A comparative study based on a Turkish sample. *Archives of Gerontology and Geriatrics, 46*(3), 283–292. https://doi.org/10.1016/j.archger.2007.05.003

Atkinson-Clement, C., Pinto, S., Eusebio, A., & Coulon, O. (2017). Diffusion tensor imaging in Parkinson's disease: Review and meta-analysis. *NeuroImage: Clinical, 16,* 98–110. https://doi.org/10.1016/J.NICL.2017.07.011

Attems, J., Walker, L., & Jellinger, K. A. (2015). Olfaction and aging: A mini-review. *Gerontology, 61*(6), 485–490. https://doi.org/10.1159/000381619

Avila, J. F., Rentería, M. A., Jones, R. N., Vonk, J. M. J., Turney, I., Sol, K., Seblova, D., Arias, F., Hill-Jarrett, T., Levy, S. A., Meyer, O., Racine, A. M., Tom, S. E., Melrose, R. J., Deters, K., Medina, L. D., Carrión, C. I., Díaz-Santos, M., Byrd, D. A. R., . . . Manly, J. J. (2021). Education differentially contributes to cognitive reserve across racial/ethnic groups. *Alzheimer's and Dementia, 17*(1), 70–80. https://doi.org/10.1002/alz.12176

Avis, N. E., Brockwell, S., & Colvin, A. (2005). A universal menopausal syndrome? *American Journal of Medicine, 118*(12), 1406. 10.1016/j.amjmed.2005.10.010

Avis, N. E., & Crawford, S. (2006). Menopause: Recent research findings. In S. K. Whitbourne & S. L. Willis (Eds.), *The baby boomers grow up: Contemporary perspectives on midlife* (pp. 75–109). Lawrence Erlbaum Associates Publishers.

Babcock, K. R., Page, J. S., Fallon, J. R., & Webb, A. E. (2021). Adult hippocampal neurogenesis in aging and Alzheimer's disease. *Stem Cell Reports, 16,* 681–693. https://doi.org/10.1016/j.stemcr.2021.01.019

Baddeley, A. (2020). Memory. In *Memory.* Routledge. https://doi.org/10.4324/9780429449642-15

Ball, N., Teo, W. P., Chandra, S., & Chapman, J. (2019). Parkinson's disease and the environment. *Frontiers in Neurology, 10,* 218. https://doi.org/10.3389/fneur.2019.00218

Baltes, M. M., & Carstensen, L. L. (2003). The process of successful aging: Selection, optimization and compensation. In U. M. Staudinger & U. Lindenberger (Eds.), *Understanding human development: Dialogues with lifespan psychology* (pp. 81–104). Kluwer Academic Publishers.

Baltes, P. B., & Staudinger, U. M. (2000). Wisdom: A metaheuristic (pragmatic) to orchestrate mind and virtue toward excellence. *American Psychologist, 55*(1), 122–136. 10.1037/0003-066X.55.1.122

Banerjee, G., Kim, H. J., Fox, Z., Jäger, H. R., Wilson, D., Charidimou, A., Na, H. K., Na, D. L., Seo, S. W., & Werring, D. J. (2017). MRI-visible perivascular space location is associated with Alzheimer's disease independently of amyloid burden. *Brain, 140*(4), 1107–1116. https://doi.org/10.1093/brain/awx003

Barengo, N. C., Antikainen, R., Borodulin, K., Harald, K., & Jousilahti, P. (2017). Leisure-time physical activity reduces total and cardiovascular mortality and cardiovascular disease incidence in older adults. *Journal of the American Geriatrics Society, 65*(3), 504–510. https://doi.org/10.1111/jgs.14694

Barulli, D., & Stern, Y. (2013). Efficiency, capacity, compensation, maintenance, plasticity: Emerging concepts in cognitive reserve. *Trends in Cognitive Sciences, 17*(10), 502–509. https://doi.org/10.1016/j.tics.2013.08.012

Bechshøft, R. L., Malmgaard-Clausen, N. M., Gliese, B., Beyer, N., Mackey, A. L., Andersen, J. L., Kjær, M., & Holm, L. (2017). Improved skeletal muscle mass and strength after heavy strength training in very old individuals. *Experimental Gerontology, 92,* 96–105. https://doi.org/10.1016/J.EXGER.2017.03.014

Beier, M. E., & Ackerman, P. L. (2005). Age, ability, and the role of prior knowledge on the acquisition of new domain knowledge: Promising results in a real-world learning environment. *Psychology and Aging, 20*(2), 341–355. 10.1037/0882-7974.20.2.341

Bellou, V., Belbasis, L., Tzoulaki, I., Evangelou, E., & Ioannidis, J. P. A. (2016). Environmental risk factors and Parkinson's disease: An umbrella review of meta-analyses. *Parkinsonism & Related Disorders, 23*, 1–9. https://doi.org/10.1016/j.parkreldis.2015.12.008

Benjamin, E. J., Virani, S. S., Callaway, C. W., Chamberlain, A. M., Chang, A. R., Cheng, S., Chiuve, S. E., Cushman, M., Delling, F. N., Deo, R., de Ferranti, S. D., Ferguson, J. F., Fornage, M., Gillespie, C., Isasi, C. R., Jiménez, M. C., Jordan, L. C., Judd, S. E., Lackland, D., . . . American Heart Association Council on Epidemiology and Prevention Statistics Committee and Stroke Statistics Subcommittee. (2018). Heart disease and stroke statistics-2018 update: A report From the American Heart Association. *Circulation, 137*(12), e67–e492. https://doi.org/10.1161/CIR.0000000000000558

Berkes, M., Calvo, N., Anderson, J. A. E., & Bialystok, E. (2021). Poorer clinical outcomes for older adult monolinguals when matched to bilinguals on brain health. *Brain Structure and Function, 226*(2), 415–424. https://doi.org/10.1007/s00429-020-02185-5

Bernasconi, A. A., Wiest, M. M., Lavie, C. J., Milani, R. V., & Laukkanen, J. A. (2021). Effect of omega-3 dosage on cardiovascular outcomes: An updated meta-analysis and meta-regression of interventional trials. *Mayo Clinic Proceedings, 96*(2), 304–313. https://doi.org/10.1016/j.mayocp.2020.08.034

Bernstein, M. (2017). Nutritional needs of the older adult. *Physical Medicine and Rehabilitation Clinics of North America, 28*(4), 747–766. https://doi.org/10.1016/j.pmr.2017.06.008

Berntsen, D., & Rubin, D. C. (2002). Emotionally charged autobiographical memories across the life span: The recall of happy, sad, traumatic and involuntary memories. *Psychology and Aging, 17*(4), 636–652. 10.1037/0882-7974.17.4.636

Bettens, K., Sleegers, K., & Van Broeckhoven, C. (2013). Genetic insights in Alzheimer's disease. *The Lancet Neurology, 12*(1), 92–104. https://doi.org/10.1016/S1474-4422(12)70259-4

Bialystok, E. (2021). Bilingualism: Pathway to cognitive reserve. *Trends in Cognitive Sciences, 25*, 355–364. https://doi.org/10.1016/j.tics.2021.02.003

Bielak, A. A. M. (2010). How can we not 'Lose It' if we still don't understand how to 'Use It'? Unanswered Questions about the influence of activity participation on cognitive performance in older age – A mini-review. *Gerontology, 56*(5), 507–519. https://doi.org/10.1159/000264918

Bigelow, R. T., Reed, N. S., Brewster, K. K., Huang, A., Rebok, G., Rutherford, B. R., & Lin, F. R. (2020). Association of hearing loss with psychological distress and utilization of mental health services among adults in the United States. *JAMA Network Open, 3*(7), 2010986, . https://doi.org/10.1001/jamanetworkopen.2020.10986

Birney, D. P., & Sternberg, R. J. (2011). The development of cognitive abilities. In M. H. Bornstein & M. E. Lamb (Eds.), *Developmental science: An advanced textbook* (6th ed., pp. 353–388). Psychology Press.

Bishop, A. J., Martin, P., MacDonald, M., & Poon, L. (2010). Predicting happiness among centenarians. *Gerontology, 56*(1), 88–92. https://doi.org/10.1159/000272017

Bisiacchi, P. S., Borella, E., Bergamaschi, S., Carretti, B., & Mondini, S. (2008). Interplay between memory and executive functions in normal and pathological aging. *Journal of Clinical & Experimental Neuropsychology, 30*(6), 723–733. https://doi.org/10.1080/13803390701689587

Bittner, N., Jockwitz, C., Franke, K., Gaser, C., Moebus, S., Bayen, U. J., Amunts, K., & Caspers, S. (2021). When your brain looks older than expected: combined lifestyle risk and BrainAGE. *Brain Structure and Function, 226*(3), 621–645. https://doi.org/10.1007/s00429-020-02184-6

Blasiak, J. (2020). Senescence in the pathogenesis of age-related macular degeneration. *Cellular and Molecular Life Sciences, 77*, 789–805. https://doi.org/10.1007/s00018-019-03420-x

Blauwendraat, C., Nalls, M. A., & Singleton, A. B. (2020). The genetic architecture of Parkinson's disease. *The Lancet Neurology, 19*(2), 170–178. https://doi.org/10.1016/S1474-4422(19)30287-X

Bleicher, K., Cumming, R. G., Naganathan, V., Seibel, M. J., Sambrook, P. N., Blyth, F. M., Le Couteur, D. G., Handelsman, D. J., Creasey, H. M., & Waite, L. M. (2011). Lifestyle factors, medications, and disease influence bone mineral density in older men: Findings from the CHAMP study. *Osteoporosis International: A Journal Established as Result of Cooperation between the European Foundation for Osteoporosis and the National Osteoporosis Foundation of the USA, 22*(9), 2421–2437. https://doi.org/10.1007/s00198-010-1478-9

Blennow, K., Mattsson, N., Schöll, M., Hansson, O., & Zetterberg, H. (2015). Amyloid biomarkers in Alzheimer's disease. *Trends in Pharmacological Sciences, 36*(5), 297–309. https://doi.org/10.1016/j.tips.2015.03.002

Bloemendaal, M., Zandbelt, B., Wegman, J., van de Rest, O., Cools, R., & Aarts, E. (2016). Contrasting neural effects of aging on proactive and reactive response inhibition. *Neurobiology of Aging, 46*, 96–106. https://doi.org/10.1016/j.neurobiolaging.2016.06.007

Blondell, S. J., Hammersley-Mather, R., & Veerman, J. L. (2014). Does physical activity prevent cognitive decline and dementia?: A systematic review and meta-analysis of longitudinal studies. *BMC Public Health, 14*(1), 510. https://doi.org/10.1186/1471-2458-14-510

Blumberg, J., Bailey, R., Sesso, H., & Ulrich, C. (2018). The evolving role of multivitamin/multimineral supplement use among adults in the age of personalized nutrition. *Nutrients, 10*(2), 248. https://doi.org/10.3390/nu10020248

Bonanni, L., Franciotti, R., Delli Pizzi, S., Thomas, A., & Onofrj, M. (2018). Lewy body dementia. In D. Galimberti & E. Scarpini (Eds.), *Neurodegenerative diseases* (pp. 297–312). Springer International Publishing. https://doi.org/10.1007/978-3-319-72938-1_14

Borella, E., Carretti, B., Riboldi, F., & De Beni, R. (2010). Working memory training in older adults: Evidence of transfer and maintenance effects. *Psychology and Aging, 25*, 767–778. https://doi.org/10.1037/a0020683

Boulos, C., Salameh, P., & Barberger-Gateau, P. (2017). Social isolation and risk for malnutrition among older people. *Geriatrics & Gerontology International, 17*(2), 286–294. https://doi.org/10.1111/ggi.12711

Bove, F., Fraix, V., Cavallieri, F., Schmitt, E., Lhommée, E., Bichon, A., Meoni, S., Pélissier, P., Kistner, A., Chevrier, E., Ardouin, C., Limousin, P., Krack, P., Benabid, A. L., Chabardès, S., Seigneuret, E., Castrioto, A., & Moro, E. (2020). Dementia and subthalamic deep brain stimulation in Parkinson disease: A long-term overview. *Neurology, 95*(4), E384–E392. https://doi.org/10.1212/WNL.0000000000009822

Bowles, R. P., & Salthouse, T. A. (2003). Assessing the age-related effects of proactive interference on working memory tasks using the Rasch model. *Psychology and Aging, 18*(3), 608–615. 10.1037/0882-7974.18.3.608

Boyer, K. A., Andriacchi, T. P., & Beaupre, G. S. (2012). The role of physical activity in changes in walking mechanics with age. *Gait & Posture, 36*(1), 149–153. https://doi.org/10.1016/j.gaitpost.2012.02.007

Brai, E., Hummel, T., & Alberi, L. (2020). Smell, an underrated early biomarker for brain aging. *Frontiers in Neuroscience, 14*, 792. https://doi.org/10.3389/fnins.2020.00792

Brandão, D., Ribeiro, O., Afonso, R. M., & Paúl, C. (2017). Escaping most common lethal diseases in old age: Morbidity profiles of Portuguese centenarians. *European Geriatric Medicine, 8*(4), 310–314. https://doi.org/10.1016/J.EURGER.2017.04.011

Braun, S. M. G., & Jessberger, S. (2014). Adult neurogenesis: mechanisms and functional significance. *Development, 141*(10), 1983–1986. https://doi.org/10.1242/dev.104596

Braun, U., Muldoon, S. F., & Bassett, D. S. (2015). On human brain networks in health and disease. *eLS*, 1–9. https://doi.org/10.1002/9780470015902.a0025783

Braver, T. S., & West, R. (2008). Working memory, executive control, and aging. In F. I. M. Craik & T. A. Salthouse (Eds.), *The handbook of aging and cognition* (3rd ed., pp. 311–372). Psychology Press.

Brehmer, Y., Westerberg, H., & Bäckman, L. (2012). Working-memory training in younger and older adults: Training gains, transfer, and maintenance. *Frontiers in Human Neuroscience, 6*, 63. https://doi.org/10.3389/fnhum.2012.00063

Brewster, K. K., Hu, M.-C., Zilcha-Mano, S., Stein, A., Brown, P. J., Wall, M. M., Roose, S. P., Golub, J. S., & Rutherford, B. R. (2020). Age-related hearing loss, late-life depression, and risk for incident dementia in older adults. *The Journals of Gerontology: Series A, 76*(5), 827–834. https://doi.org/10.1093/gerona/glaa242

Brustio, P. R., Rabaglietti, E., Formica, S., & Liubicich, M. E. (2018). Dual-task training in older adults: The effect of additional motor tasks on mobility performance. *Archives of Gerontology and Geriatrics, 75*, 119–124. https://doi.org/10.1016/j.archger.2017.12.003

Buford, T. W., Anton, S. D., Judge, A. R., Marzetti, E., Wohlgemuth, S. E., Carter, C. S., Leeuwenburgh, C., Pahor, M., & Manini, T. M. (2010). Models of accelerated sarcopenia: Critical pieces for solving the puzzle of age-related muscle atrophy. *Ageing Research Reviews, 9*(4), 369–383. https://doi.org/10.1016/j.arr.2010.04.004

Busche, M. A., & Hyman, B. T. (2020). Synergy between amyloid-β and tau in Alzheimer's disease. In *Nature neuroscience* (Vol. 23, pp. 1183–1193). Nature Research. https://doi.org/10.1038/s41593-020-0687-6

Calapai, G., Bonina, F., Bonina, A., Rizza, L., Mannucci, C., Arcoraci, V., Laganà, G., Alibrandi, A., Pollicino, C., Inferrera, S., & Alecci, U. (2017). A randomized, double-blinded, clinical trial on effects of a vitis vinifera extract on cognitive function in healthy older adults. *Frontiers in Pharmacology, 8*, 776. https://doi.org/10.3389/fphar.2017.00776

Carson, V. B., Vanderhorst, K., & Koenig, H. G. (2015). *Care giving for Alzheimer's disease: A compassionate guide for clinicians and loved ones*. Springer.

Carstensen, L. L., & DeLiema, M. (2018). The positivity effect: A negativity bias in youth fades with age. *Current Opinion in Behavioral Sciences, 19*, 7–12. https://doi.org/10.1016/j.cobeha.2017.07.009

Cawthon, P. M., Shahnazari, M., Orwoll, E. S., & Lane, N. E. (2016). Osteoporosis in men: Findings from the osteoporotic fractures in men study (MrOS). *Therapeutic Advances in Musculoskeletal Disease, 8*(1), 15–27. https://doi.org/10.1177/1759720X15621227

Čekanauskaitė, A., Skurvydas, A., Žlibinaitė, L., Mickevičienė, D., Kilikevičienė, S., & Solianik, R. (2020). A 10-week yoga practice has no effect on cognition, but improves balance and motor learning by attenuating brain-derived neurotrophic factor levels in older adults. *Experimental Gerontology, 138*, 110998. https://doi.org/10.1016/j.exger.2020.110998

Centers for Disease Control. (2015). *Web-based Injury Statistics Query and Reporting System (WISQARS)* . National Center for Injury Prevention and Control.

Centers for Disease Control. (2018). *Fatal injury reports, national, regional and state, 1981 – 2016*. Web-Based Injury Statistics Query and Reporting System. https://webappa.cdc.gov/sasweb/ncipc/mortrate.html

Chapko, D., McCormack, R., Black, C., Staff, R., & Murray, A. (2018). Life-course determinants of cognitive reserve (CR) in cognitive aging and dementia – A systematic literature review. *Aging & Mental Health, 22*, 915–926. https://doi.org/10.1080/13607863.2017.1348471

Charlton, K. E., Batterham, M. J., Bowden, S., Ghosh, A., Caldwell, K., Barone, L., Mason, M., Potter, J., Meyer, B., & Milosavljevic, M. (2013). A high prevalence of malnutrition in acute geriatric patients predicts adverse clinical outcomes and mortality within 12 months. *E-SPEN Journal, 8*(3), e120–e125. https://doi.org/10.1016/j.clnme.2013.03.004

Chen, X., Hertzog, C., & Park, D. C. (2017). Cognitive predictors of everyday problem solving across the lifespan. *Gerontology, 63*(4), 372–384. https://doi.org/10.1159/000459622

Cheng, Y. J., Kanaya, A. M., Araneta, M. R. G., Saydah, S. H., Kahn, H. S., Gregg, E. W., Fujimoto, W. Y., & Imperatore, G. (2019). Prevalence of diabetes by race and ethnicity in the United States, 2011-2016. *JAMA -. Journal of the American Medical Association, 322*(24), 2389–2398. https://doi.org/10.1001/jama.2019.19365

Cheslock, M., & De Jesus, O. (2021, February 18). Presbycusis. In *StatPearls*. StatPearls Publishing. http://www.ncbi.nlm.nih.gov/pubmed/32644646

Cheung, C., Wyman, J. F., Bronas, U., McCarthy, T., Rudser, K., & Mathiason, M. A. (2017). Managing knee osteoarthritis with yoga or aerobic/strengthening exercise programs in older adults: A pilot randomized controlled trial. *Rheumatology International, 37*(3), 389–398. https://doi.org/10.1007/s00296-016-3620-2

Chin, A. L., Negash, S., & Hamilton, R. (2011). Diversity and disparity in dementia: The impact of ethnoracial differences in Alzheimer disease. *Alzheimer Disease and Associated Disorders, 25*(3), 187–195. https://doi.org/10.1097/WAD.0b013e318211c6c9

Choi, J. S., Jang, S. S., Kim, J., Hur, K., Ference, E., & Wrobel, B. (2021). Association between olfactory dysfunction and mortality in US adults. *JAMA Otolaryngology - Head and Neck Surgery, 147*(1), 49–55. https://doi.org/10.1001/jamaoto.2020.3502

Cho, S. J., & Stout-Delgado, H. W. (2020). Aging and lung disease. *Annual Review of Physiology, 82*, 433–459. https://doi.org/10.1146/annurev-physiol-021119-034610

Cicchino, J. B., & McCartt, A. T. (2015). Critical older driver errors in a sample of serious U.S. crashes. *Accident Analysis & Prevention, 80*, 211–219.

Clapp, W. C., Rubens, M. T., Sabharwal, J., & Gazzaley, A. (2011). Deficit in switching between functional brain networks underlies the impact of multitasking on working memory in older adults. *Proceedings of the National Academy of Sciences of the United States of America, 108*(17), 7212–7217. https://doi.org/10.1073/pnas.1015297108

Coats, R. O., Waterman, A. H., Ryder, F., Atkinson, A. L., & Allen, R. J. (2021). Following instructions in working memory: Do older adults show the enactment advantage? *The Journals of Gerontology. Series B, Psychological Sciences and Social Sciences, 76*(4), 703–710. https://doi.org/10.1093/geronb/gbaa214

Connell, C. M., Scott Roberts, J., McLaughlin, S. J., & Akinleye, D. (2009). Racial differences in knowledge and beliefs about Alzheimer disease. *Alzheimer Disease & Associated Disorders, 23*(2), 110–116. https://doi.org/10.1097/WAD.0b013e318192e94d

Cooper, C., Javaid, M. K., & Arden, N. (2014). Epidemiology of osteoarthritis. In N. Arden, F. Blanco, C. Cooper, A. Guermazi, D. Hayashi, D. Hunter, M. K. Javaid, F. Rannou, J.-Y. Roemer, & F. W. Reginster (Eds.), *Atlas of osteoarthritis* (pp. 21–36). Springer Healthcare Ltd. https://doi.org/10.1007/978-1-910315-16-3_2

Corlier, F., Hafzalla, G., Faskowitz, J., Kuller, L. H., Becker, J. T., Lopez, O. L., Thompson, P. M., & Braskie, M. N. (2018). Systemic inflammation as a predictor of brain aging: Contributions of physical activity, metabolic risk, and genetic risk. *NeuroImage, 172*, 118–129. https://doi.org/10.1016/j.neuroimage.2017.12.027

Corrada, M. M., Brookmeyer, R., Paganini-Hill, A., Berlau, D., & Kawas, C. H. (2010). Dementia incidence continues to increase with age in the oldest old: The 90+ Study. *Annals of Neurology, 67*(1), 114–121. https://doi.org/10.1002/ana.21915

Corriveau, R. A., Bosetti, F., Emr, M., Gladman, J. T., Koenig, J. I., Moy, C. S., Pahigiannis, K., Waddy, S. P., & Koroshetz, W. (2016). The science of vascular contributions to cognitive impairment and dementia (VCID): A framework for advancing research priorities in the cerebrovascular biology of cognitive decline. *Cellular and Molecular Neurobiology, 36*(2), 281–288. https://doi.org/10.1007/s10571-016-0334-7

Crews, J. E., Chou, C.-F., Stevens, J. A., & Saaddine, J. B. (2016). Falls among persons aged ?65 years with and without severe vision impairment ? United States, 2014. *Morbidity and Mortality Weekly Report, 65*(17), 433–437. https://doi.org/10.15585/mmwr.mm6517a2

Daselaar, S., & Cabeza, R. (2005). Age-related changes in hemispheric organization. In R. Cabeza, L. Nyberg, & D. C. Park (Eds.), *Cognitive neuroscience of aging: Linking cognitive and cerebral aging* (pp. 325–353). Oxford University Press.

da Silva Costa, A. A., Moraes, R., Hortobágyi, T., & Sawers, A. (2020). Older adults reduce the complexity and efficiency of neuromuscular control to preserve walking balance. *Experimental Gerontology, 140*, 111050. https://doi.org/10.1016/j.exger.2020.111050

Davey, A., Elias, M. F., Siegler, I. C., Lele, U., Martin, P., Johnson, M. A., Hausman, D. B., & Poon, L. W. (2010). Cognitive function, physical performance, health, and disease: Norms from the Georgia centenarian study. *Experimental Aging Research, 36*(4), 394–425. https://doi.org/10.1080/0361073x.2010.509010

de Graaf, C., Polet, P., & van Staveren, W. A. (1994). Sensory perception and pleasantness of food flavors in elderly subjects. *Journal of Gerontology, 49*(3), 93–P99. https://doi.org/10.1093/geronj/49.3.P93

De la Rosa, A., Olaso-Gonzalez, G., Arc-Chagnaud, C., Millan, F., Salvador-Pascual, A., García-Lucerga, C., Blasco-Lafarga, C., Garcia-Dominguez, E., Carretero, A., Correas, A. G., Viña, J., & Gomez-Cabrera, M. C. (2020). Physical exercise in the prevention and treatment of Alzheimer's disease. *Journal of Sport and Health Science, 9*(5), 394–404. https://doi.org/10.1016/j.jshs.2020.01.004

Denney, N. W., Pearce, K. A., & Palmer, A. M. (1982). A developmental study of adults' performance on traditional and practical problem-solving tasks. *Experimental Aging Research, 8*(2), 115–118. https://doi.org/10.1080/03610738208258407

Dong, H., Zhou, W., Wang, P., Zuo, E., Ying, X., Chai, S., Fei, T., Jin, L., Chen, C., Ma, G., & Liu, H. (2020). Comprehensive analysis of the genetic and epigenetic mechanisms of osteoporosis and bone mineral density. *Frontiers in Cell and Developmental Biology, 8*, 194. https://doi.org/10.3389/fcell.2020.00194

Dong, X., Milholland, B., & Vijg, J. (2016). Evidence for a limit to human lifespan. *Nature, 538*(7624), 257–259. https://doi.org/10.1038/nature19793

Doroudgar, S., Chuang, H. M., Perry, P. J., Thomas, K., Bohnert, K., & Canedo, J. (2017). Driving performance comparing older versus younger drivers. *Traffic Injury Prevention, 18*(1), 41–46. https://doi.org/10.1080/15389588.2016.1194980

Douaud, G., Refsum, H., de Jager, C. A., Jacoby, R., Nichols, T. E., Smith, S. M., & Smith, A. D. (2013). Preventing Alzheimer's disease-related gray matter atrophy by B-vitamin treatment. *Proceedings of the National Academy of Sciences of the United States of America, 110*(23), 9523–9528. https://doi.org/10.1073/pnas.1301816110

Dumas, J. A. (2017). Physical activity and the hippocampus in older adults. *The American Journal of Geriatric Psychiatry : Official Journal of the American Association for Geriatric Psychiatry, 25*(3), 218–219. https://doi.org/10.1016/j.jagp.2016.12.005

Dunn, A. R., O'Connell, K. M. S., & Kaczorowski, C. C. (2019). Gene-by-environment interactions in Alzheimer's disease and Parkinson's disease. *Neuroscience and Biobehavioral Reviews, 103*, 73–80. https://doi.org/10.1016/j.neubiorev.2019.06.018

Emre, M., Ford, P. J., Bilgiç, B., & Uç, E. Y. (2014). Cognitive impairment and dementia in Parkinson's disease: Practical issues and management. *Movement Disorders, 29*(5), 663–672. https://doi.org/10.1002/mds.25870

Erickson, K. I., Raji, C. A., Lopez, O. L., Becker, J. T., Rosano, C., Newman, A. B., Gach, H. M., Thompson, P. M., Ho, A. J., & Kuller, L. H. (2010). Physical activity predicts gray matter volume in late adulthood: The Cardiovascular Health Study. *Neurology, 75*(16), 1415–1422. https://doi.org/10.1212/WNL.0b013e3181f88359

Erickson, K. I., Voss, M. W., Prakash, R. S., Basak, C., Szabo, A., Chaddock, L., Kim, J. S., Susie, H., Alves, H., White, S. M., Wojcicki, T. R., Mailey, E., Vieira, V. J., Martin, S. A., Pence, B. D., Woods, J. A., McAuley, E., & Kramer, A. F. (2011). Exercise training increases size of hippocampus and improves memory. *Proceedings of the National Academy of Sciences of the United States of America*, *108*(7), 3017–3022. https://doi.org/10.1073/pnas.1015950108

Falck, R. S., Davis, J. C., Best, J. R., Crockett, R. A., & Liu-Ambrose, T. (2019). Impact of exercise training on physical and cognitive function among older adults: A systematic review and meta-analysis. *Neurobiology of aging*, *79*, 119–130. https://doi.org/10.1016/j.neurobiolaging.2019.03.007

Farage, M. A., Miller, K. W., & Maibach, H. I. (2015). Degenerative changes in aging skin. In M. A. Farage, K. W. Miller, & H. I. Maibach (Eds.), *Textbook of aging skin* (pp. 1–18). Springer. https://doi.org/10.1007/978-3-642-27814-3_4-2

Farrell, M. C., Giza, R. J., & Shibao, C. A. (2020). Race and sex differences in cardiovascular autonomic regulation. In In *Clinical autonomic research* (Vol. 30, pp. 371–379). Springer Science and Business Media Deutschland GmbH. https://doi.org/10.1007/s10286-020-00723-z

Farzaei, M. H., Bahramsoltani, R., Abbasabadi, Z., Braidy, N., & Nabavi, S. M. (2019). Role of green tea catechins in prevention of age-related cognitive decline: Pharmacological targets and clinical perspective. *Journal of Cellular Physiology*, *234*(3), 2447–2459. https://doi.org/10.1002/jcp.27289

Farzaneh-Far, R., Lin, J., Epel, E. S., Harris, W. S., Blackburn, E. H., & Whooley, M. A. (2010). Association of Marine omega-3 fatty acid levels with telomeric aging in patients with coronary heart disease. *Journal of the American Medical Association*, *303*(3), 250–257.

Feng, J., Choi, H. S., Craik, F. I. M., Levine, B., Moreno, S., Naglie, G., & Zhu, M. (2018). Adaptive response criteria in road hazard detection among older drivers. *Traffic Injury Prevention*, *19*(2), 141–146. https://doi.org/10.1080/15389588.2017.1373190

Fenn, A. M., Corona, A. W., & Godbout, J. P. (2013). Aging and the immune system. In A. W. Kusnecov & H. Anisman (Eds.), *The Wiley-Blackwell handbook of psychoneuroimmunology* (pp. 313–329). John Wiley & Sons Ltd. https://doi.org/10.1002/9781118314814

Festa, E. K., Ott, B. R., Manning, K. J., Davis, J. D., & Heindel, W. C. (2013). Effect of cognitive status on self-regulatory driving behavior in older adults: An assessment of naturalistic driving using in-car video recordings. *Journal of Geriatric Psychiatry and Neurology*, *26*(1), 10–18. https://doi.org/10.1177/0891988712473801

Fielding, R. A., Guralnik, J. M., King, A. C., Pahor, M., McDermott, M. M., Tudor-Locke, C., Manini, T. M., Glynn, N. W., Marsh, A. P., Axtell, R. S., Hsu, F.-C., & Rejeski, W. J. (2017). Dose of physical activity, physical functioning and disability risk in mobility-limited older adults: Results from the LIFE study randomized trial. *PLoS One*, *12*(8), e0182155. https://doi.org/10.1371/journal.pone.0182155

Fierini, F. (2020). Mixed dementia: Neglected clinical entity or nosographic artifice? *Journal of the Neurological Sciences*, *410*, 116662. https://doi.org/10.1016/j.jns.2019.116662

Firth, J., Stubbs, B., Vancampfort, D., Schuch, F., Lagopoulos, J., Rosenbaum, S., & Ward, P. B. (2018). Effect of aerobic exercise on hippocampal volume in humans: A systematic review and meta-analysis. *NeuroImage*, *166*, 230–238. https://doi.org/10.1016/J.NEUROIMAGE.2017.11.007

Frank, C. R., Xiang, X., Stagg, B. C., & Ehrlich, J. R. (2019). Longitudinal associations of self-reported vision impairment with symptoms of anxiety and depression among older adults in the United States. *JAMA Ophthalmology*, *137*(7), 793–800. https://doi.org/10.1001/jamaophthalmol.2019.1085

Frankenberg, C., Knebel, M., Degen, C., Siebert, J. S., Wahl, H. W., & Schröder, J. (2021). Autobiographical memory in healthy aging: A decade-long longitudinal study. *Aging, Neuropsychology, and Cognition*. https://doi.org/10.1080/13825585.2020.1859082

Frank-Wilson, A. W., Farthing, J. P., Chilibeck, P. D., Arnold, C. M., Davison, K. S., Olszynski, W. P., & Kontulainen, S. A. (2016). Lower leg muscle density is independently associated with fall status in community-dwelling older adults. *Osteoporosis International*, *27*(7), 2231–2240. https://doi.org/10.1007/s00198-016-3514-x

Fransen, M., McConnell, S., Harmer, A. R., Van Der Esch, M., Simic, M., & Bennell, K. L. (2015). Exercise for osteoarthritis of the knee: A Cochrane systematic review. *British Journal of Sports Medicine*, *49*(24), 1554–1557. https://doi.org/10.1136/bjsports-2015-095424

Freeman, S., Garcia, J., & Marston, H. R. (2013). Centenarian self-perceptions of factors responsible for attainment of extended health and longevity. *Educational Gerontology*, *39*(10), 717–728. https://doi.org/10.1080/03601277.2012.750981

Frisoni, G. B., Boccardi, M., Barkhof, F., Blennow, K., Cappa, S., Chiotis, K., Démonet, J.-F., Garibotto, V., Giannakopoulos, P., Gietl, A., Hansson, O., Herholz, K., Jack, C. R., Nobili, F., Nordberg, A., Snyder, H. M., Ten Kate, M., Varrone, A., Albanese, E., . . . Winblad, B. (2017). Strategic roadmap for an early diagnosis of Alzheimer's disease based on biomarkers. *The Lancet Neurology*, *16*(8), 661–676. https://doi.org/10.1016/S1474-4422(17)30159-X

Gaesser, B., Sacchetti, D. C., Addis, D. R., & Schacter, D. L. (2011). Characterizing age-related changes in remembering the past and imagining the future. *Psychology and Aging*, *26*, 80–84. https://doi.org/10.1037/a0021054

Gahche, J. J., Bailey, R. L., Potischman, N., & Dwyer, J. T. (2017). Dietary supplement use was very high among older adults in the United States in 2011–2014. *The Journal of Nutrition*, *147*(10), 1968–1976. https://doi.org/10.3945/jn.117.255984

Gallaway, P., Miyake, H., Buchowski, M., Shimada, M., Yoshitake, Y., Kim, A., & Hongu, N. (2017). Physical activity: A viable way to reduce the risks of mild cognitive impairment, Alzheimer's disease, and vascular dementia in older adults. *Brain Sciences*, *7*(2), 22. https://doi.org/10.3390/brainsci7020022

Gannon, O. J., Robison, L. S., Custozzo, A. J., & Zuloaga, K. L. (2019). Sex differences in risk factors for vascular contributions to cognitive impairment & dementia. *Neurochemistry International*, *127*, 38–55. https://doi.org/10.1016/j.neuint.2018.11.014

Gerstorf, D., Ram, N., Hoppmann, C., Willis, S. L., & Schaie, K. W. (2011). Cohort differences in cognitive aging and terminal decline in the Seattle longitudinal study. *Developmental Psychology*, *47*(4), 1026–1041. https://doi.org/10.1037/a0023426

Gonçalves, J. T., Schafer, S. T., & Gage, F. H. (2016). Adult neurogenesis in the hippocampus: From stem cells to behavior. *Cell*, *167*(4), 897–914. https://doi.org/10.1016/j.cell.2016.10.021

Govindaraju, D., Atzmon, G., & Barzilai, N. (2015). Genetics, lifestyle and longevity: Lessons from centenarians. *Applied & Translational Genomics*, *4*, 23–32. https://doi.org/10.1016/j.atg.2015.01.001

Gow, A. J., Corley, J., Starr, J. M., & Deary, I. J. (2012). Reverse causation in activity-cognitive ability associations: The Lothian Birth Cohort 1936. *Psychology and Aging*, *27*(1), 250–255. https://doi.org/10.1037/a0024144

Granacher, U., Muehlbauer, T., & Gruber, M. (2012). A qualitative review of balance and strength performance in healthy older adults: Impact for testing and training. *Journal of Aging Research*, *2012*, 708905. https://doi.org/10.1155/2012/708905

Greene, N. R., Naveh-Benjamin, M., & Cowan, N. (2020). Adult age differences in working memory capacity: Spared central storage but deficits in ability to maximize peripheral storage. *Psychology and Aging*, *35*(6), 866–880. https://doi.org/10.1037/pag0000476

Groot, C., Hooghiemstra, A. M., Raijmakers, P. G. H. M., van Berckel, B. N. M., Scheltens, P., Scherder, E. J. A., van der Flier, W. M., & Ossenkoppele, R. (2016). The effect of physical activity on cognitive function in patients with dementia: A meta-analysis of randomized control trials. *Ageing Research Reviews*, *25*, 13–23. https://doi.org/10.1016/j.arr.2015.11.005

Grootswagers, P., de Regt, M., Domić, J., Dronkers, J., Visser, M., Witteman, B., Hopman, M., & Mensink, M. (2020). A 4-week exercise and protein program improves muscle mass and physical functioning in older adults – A pilot study. *Experimental Gerontology*, *141*, 111094. https://doi.org/10.1016/j.exger.2020.111094

Grossman, H., Bergmann, C., & Parker, S. (2006). Dementia: A brief review. *Mount Sinai Journal of Medicine*, *73*(7), 985–992.

Gurland, B. J., Wilder, D. E., Lantigua, R., Stern, Y., Chen, J., Killeffer, E. H., & Mayeux, R. (1999). Rates of dementia in three ethnoracial groups. *International Journal of Geriatric Psychiatry*, *14*(6), 481–493. http://www.ncbi.nlm.nih.gov/pubmed/10398359

Gutchess, A. H., & Boduroglu, A. (2015). Cognition in adulthood across cultures. In L. A. Jensen (Ed.), *The Oxford handbook of human development and culture* (pp. 621–636). Oxford University Press. https://doi.org/10.1093/oxfordhb/9780199948550.013.38

Guzmán-Vélez, E., Warren, D. E., Feinstein, J. S., Bruss, J., & Tranel, D. (2016). Dissociable contributions of amygdala and hippocampus to emotion and memory in patients with Alzheimer's disease. *Hippocampus*, *26*(6), 727–738. https://doi.org/10.1002/hipo.22554

Hamilton, J. M., Landy, K. M., Salmon, D. P., Hansen, L. A., Masliah, E., & Galasko, D. (2012). Early visuospatial deficits predict the occurrence of visual hallucinations in autopsy-confirmed dementia with Lewy bodies. *The American Journal of Geriatric Psychiatry: Official Journal of the American Association for Geriatric Psychiatry*, *20*(9), 773–781. https://doi.org/10.1097/JGP.0b013e31823033bc

Hanagasi, H. A., Tufekcioglu, Z., & Emre, M. (2017). Dementia in Parkinson's disease. *Journal of the Neurological Sciences*, *374*, 26–31. https://doi.org/10.1016/j.jns.2017.01.012

Haring, A. E., Zhuravleva, T. Y., Alperin, B. R., Rentz, D. M., Holcomb, P. J., & Daffner, K. R. (2013). Age-related differences in enhancement and suppression of neural activity underlying selective attention in matched young and old adults. *Brain Research*, *1499*, 69–79. https://doi.org/10.1016/j.brainres.2013.01.003

Hartmann, C. J., Fliegen, S., Groiss, S. J., Wojtecki, L., & Schnitzler, A. (2019). An update on best practice of deep brain stimulation in Parkinson's disease. *Therapeutic Advances in Neurological Disorders*, *12*, 1756286419838096. https://doi.org/10.1177/1756286419838096

Hase, Y., Horsburgh, K., Ihara, M., & Kalaria, R. N. (2018). White matter degeneration in vascular and other ageing-related dementias. *Journal of Neurochemistry*, *144*(5), 617–633. https://doi.org/10.1111/jnc.14271

Hedden, T., & Gabrieli, J. D. E. (2004). Insights into the ageing mind: A view from cognitive neuroscience. *Nature Reviews. Neuroscience*, *5*(2), 87–96. https://www.nature.com/articles/nrn1323

Heesterbeek, T. J., Lorés-Motta, L., Hoyng, C. B., Lechanteur, Y. T. E., & den Hollander, A. I. (2020). Risk factors for progression of age-related macular degeneration. *Ophthalmic and Physiological Optics*, *40*, 140–170. https://doi.org/10.1111/opo.12675

Hill-Briggs, F., Adler, N. E., Berkowitz, S. A., Chin, M. H., Gary-Webb, T. L., Navas-Acien, A., Thornton, P. L., & Haire-Joshu, D. (2021). Social determinants of health and diabetes: A scientific review. *Diabetes Care*, *44*, 258–279. https://doi.org/10.2337/dci20-0053

Hindin, S. B., & Zelinski, E. M. (2012). Extended practice and aerobic exercise interventions benefit untrained cognitive outcomes in older adults: A meta-analysis. *Journal of the American Geriatrics Society*, *60*(1), 136–141. https://doi.org/10.1111/j.1532-5415.2011.03761.x

Hirsch, L., Jette, N., Frolkis, A., Steeves, T., & Pringsheim, T. (2016). The incidence of Parkinson's disease: A systematic review and meta-analysis. *Neuroepidemiology*, *46*(4), 292–300. https://doi.org/10.1159/000445751

Hoenig, M. C., Bischof, G. N., Hammes, J., Faber, J., Fliessbach, K., van, Eimeren T., & Drzezga, A. (2017). Tau pathology and cognitive reserve in Alzheimer's disease. *Neurobiology of Aging*, *57*, 1–7. https://doi.org/10.1016/j.neurobiolaging.2017.05.004

Holtzer, R., Epstein, N., Mahoney, J. R., Izzetoglu, M., & Blumen, H. M. (2014). Neuroimaging of mobility in aging: A targeted review. *The Journals of Gerontology. Series A, Biological Sciences and Medical Sciences*, *69*(11), 1375–1388. https://doi.org/10.1093/gerona/glu052

Hoppmann, C. A., & Blanchard-Fields, F. (2010). Goals and everyday problem solving: Manipulating goal preferences in young and older adults. *Developmental Psychology*, *46*(6), 1433–1443. https://doi.org/10.1037/a0020676

Hort, J., O'Brien, J. T., Gainotti, G., Pirttila, T., Popescu, B. O., Rektorova, I., Sorbi, S., & Scheltens, P. (2010). EFNS guidelines for the diagnosis and management of Alzheimer's disease. *European Journal of Neurology*, *17*(10), 1236–1248. https://doi.org/10.1111/j.1468-1331.2010.03040.x

Horton, W. S., Spieler, D. H., & Shriberg, E. (2010). A corpus analysis of patterns of age-related change in conversational speech. *Psychology and Aging*, *25*, 708–713. https://doi.org/10.1037/a0019424

Hsu, C. L., Best, J. R., Davis, J. C., Nagamatsu, L. S., Wang, S., Boyd, L. A., Hsiung, G. R., Voss, M. W., Eng, J. J., & Liu-Ambrose, T. (2018). Aerobic exercise promotes executive functions and impacts functional neural activity among older adults with vascular cognitive impairment. *British Journal of Sports Medicine*, *52*(3), 184–191. https://doi.org/10.1136/bjsports-2016-096846

Hsu, Y. H., Xu, X., & Jeong, S. (2020). Genetic determinants and pharmacogenetics of osteoporosis and osteoporotic fracture. *Contemporary endocrinology*, 485–506. https://doi.org/10.1007/978-3-319-69287-6_25

Huntley, J. D., Hampshire, A., Bor, D., Owen, A. M., & Howard, R. J. (2017). The importance of sustained attention in early Alzheimer's disease. *International Journal of Geriatric Psychiatry*, *32*(8), 860–867. https://doi.org/10.1002/gps.4537

Iadecola, C. (2013). The pathobiology of vascular dementia. *Neuron*, *80*(4), 844–866. https://doi.org/10.1016/j.neuron.2013.10.008

Igarashi, H., Levenson, M. R., & Aldwin, C. M. (2018). The development of wisdom: A social ecological approach. *Journals of Gerontology - Series B Psychological Sciences and Social Sciences*, *73*(8), 1350–1358. https://doi.org/10.1093/geronb/gby002

Imoscopi, A., Inelmen, E. M., Sergi, G., Miotto, F., & Manzato, E. (2012). Taste loss in the elderly: epidemiology, causes and consequences. *Aging Clinical and Experimental Research*, *24*(6), 570–579. https://doi.org/10.3275/8520

Insurance Institute for Highway Safety. (2021). *Older drivers*. https://www.iihs.org/topics/older-drivers

Ishioka, Y. L., Gondo, Y., Fuku, N., Inagaki, H., Masui, Y., Takayama, M., Abe, Y., Arai, Y., & Hirose, N. (2016). Effects of the APOE ε4 allele and education on cognitive function in Japanese centenarians. *AGE*, *38*(5–6), 495–503. https://doi.org/10.1007/s11357-016-9944-8

Jackson, J. D., Rentz, D. M., Aghjayan, S. L., Buckley, R. F., Meneide, T.-F., Sperling, R. A., & Amariglio, R. E. (2017). Subjective cognitive concerns are associated with objective memory performance in Caucasian but not African-American persons. *Age and Ageing*, *46*(6), 988–993. https://doi.org/10.1093/ageing/afx077

Jacoby, L. L., Wahlheim, C. N., Rhodes, M. G., Daniels, K. A., & Rogers, C. S. (2010). Learning to diminish the effects of proactive interference: Reducing false memory for young and older adults. *Memory & Cognition*, *38*(6), 820–829. https://doi.org/10.3758/mc.38.6.820

Jäncke, L., Sele, S., Liem, F., Oschwald, J., & Merillat, S. (2020). Brain aging and psychometric intelligence: A longitudinal study. *Brain Structure and Function*, *225*(2), 519–536. https://doi.org/10.1007/s00429-019-02005-5

Jerome, G. J., Ko, S., Kauffman, D., Studenski, S. A., Ferrucci, L., & Simonsick, E. M. (2015). Gait characteristics associated with walking speed decline in older adults: Results from the Baltimore Longitudinal Study of Aging. *Archives of Gerontology and Geriatrics*, *60*(2), 239–243. https://doi.org/10.1016/j.archger.2015.01.007

Jeste, D. V., & Lee, E. E. (2019). The emerging empirical science of wisdom: Definition, measurement, neurobiology, longevity, and interventions. In *Harvard review of psychiatry* (Vol. 27, pp. 127–140). Lippincott Williams and Wilkins. https://doi.org/10.1097/HRP.0000000000000205

Jilla, A. M., Johnson, C. E., & Huntington-Klein, N. (2021). Hearing aid affordability in the United States. *Disability and Rehabilitation: Assistive Technology*. https://doi.org/10.1080/17483107.2020.1822449

Jin, J. (2018). Prevention of falls in older adults. *Journal of the American Medical Association*, *319*(16), 1734. https://doi.org/10.1001/jama.2018.4396

Jin, S., Trope, G. E., Buys, Y. M., Badley, E. M., Thavorn, K., Yan, P., Nithianandan, H., & Jin, Y. P. (2019). Reduced social participation among seniors with self-reported visual impairment and glaucoma. *PLoS One*, *14*(7), e0218540. https://doi.org/10.1371/journal.pone.0218540

Johansson, J., Nordstrom, A., Gustafson, Y., Westling, G., & Nordstrom, P. (2017). Increased postural sway during quiet stance as a risk factor for prospective falls in community-dwelling elderly individuals. *Age and Ageing*, *10*(Suppl. 4), 1–6. https://doi.org/10.1093/ageing/afx083

Jopp, D. S., Boerner, K., & Rott, C. (2016). Health and disease at age 100. *Deutsches Arzteblatt International*, *113*(12), 203–210. https://doi.org/10.3238/arztebl.2016.0203

Josephs, K. A., Dickson, D. W., Tosakulwong, N., Weigand, S. D., Murray, M. E., Petrucelli, L., Liesinger, A. M., Senjem, M. L., Spychalla, A. J., Knopman, D. S., Parisi, J. E., Petersen, R. C., Jack, C. R., & Whitwell, J. L. (2017). Rates of hippocampal atrophy and presence of post-mortem TDP-43 in patients with Alzheimer's disease: A longitudinal retrospective study. *The Lancet Neurology*, *16*(11), 917–924. https://doi.org/10.1016/S1474-4422(17)30284-3

Joubert, C., Davidson, P. S. R., & Chainay, H. (2018). When do older adults show a positivity effect in emotional memory? *Experimental Aging Research*, *44*(5), 455–468. https://doi.org/10.1080/0361073X.2018.1521498

Kaiser, M. J., Bauer, J. M., Rämsch, C., Uter, W., Guigoz, Y., Cederholm, T., Thomas, D. R., Anthony, P. S., Charlton, K. E., Maggio, M., Tsai, A. C., Vellas, B., & Sieber, C. C. (2010). Frequency of malnutrition in older adults: A multinational perspective using the mini nutritional assessment. *Journal of the American Geriatrics Society*, *58*(9), 1734–1738. https://doi.org/10.1111/j.1532-5415.2010.03016.x

Kalaria, R. N. (2018). The pathology and pathophysiology of vascular dementia. *Neuropharmacology*, *134*, 226–239. https://doi.org/10.1016/j.neuropharm.2017.12.030

Kang, S. W., Jeon, S., Yoo, H. S., Chung, S. J., Lee, P. H., Sohn, Y. H., Yun, M., Evans, A. C., & Ye, B. S. (2019). Effects of Lewy body disease and Alzheimer disease on brain atrophy and cognitive dysfunction. *Neurology*, *92*(17), E2015–E2026. https://doi.org/10.1212/WNL.0000000000007373

Kaniewski, M., Stevens, J. A., Parker, E. M., & Lee, R. (2015). An introduction to the centers for disease control and prevention's efforts to prevent older adult falls. *Frontiers in Public Health*, *2*, e119. https://doi.org/10.3389/fpubh.2014.00119

Karbach, J., & Verhaeghen, P. (2014). Making working memory work: A meta-analysis of executive-control and working memory training in older adults. *Psychological Science*, *25*(11), 2027–2037. https://doi.org/10.1177/0956797614548725

Karelitz, T. M., Jarvin, L., Sternberg, R. J., Karelitz, T. M., Jarvin, L., & Sternberg, R. J. (2010). The meaning of wisdom and its development throughout life. In W. F. Overton (Ed.), *The Handbook of life-span development* (pp. 837–881). John Wiley & Sons, Inc. https://doi.org/10.1002/9780470880166.hlsd001023

Kavé, G., Eyal, N., Shorek, A., & Cohen-Mansfield, J. (2008). Multilingualism and cognitive state in the oldest old. *Psychology and Aging*, *23*(1), 70–78. https://doi.org/10.1037/0882-7974.23.1.70

Kessels, R. P. C., Meulenbroek, O., Fernandez, G., & Olde Rikkert, M. G. M. (2010). Spatial working memory in aging and mild cognitive impairment: Effects of task load and contextual cueing. *Aging, Neuropsychology & Cognition*, *17*(5), 556–574. https://doi.org/10.1080/13825585.2010.481354

Khanuja, K., Joki, J., Bachmann, G., & Cuccurullo, S. (2018). Gait and balance in the aging population: Fall prevention using innovation and technology. *Maturitas*, *110*, 51–56. https://doi.org/10.1016/j.maturitas.2018.01.021

Khoury, R., Nair, A., & Grossberg, G. T. (2019). Can lifestyle modifications delay or prevent Alzheimer's disease? *Current Psychiatry, 18*(1), 29–38. www.facebook.com/

Kok, A. A. L., Aartsen, M. J., Deeg, D. J. H., & Huisman, M. (2015). Capturing the diversity of successful aging: An operational definition based on 16-year trajectories of functioning. *The Gerontologist, 57*(2), gnv127. https://doi.org/10.1093/geront/gnv127

Kondo, K., Kikuta, S., Ueha, R., Suzukawa, K., & Yamasoba, T. (2020). Age-related olfactory dysfunction: Epidemiology, pathophysiology, and clinical management. *Frontiers in Aging Neuroscience, 12*. https://doi.org/10.3389/fnagi.2020.00208

Korczyn, A. D., Vakhapova, V., & Grinberg, L. T. (2012). Vascular dementia. *Journal of the Neurological Sciences, 322*(1–2), 2–10. https://doi.org/10.1016/j.jns.2012.03.027

Kramer, A. F., & Colcombe, S. (2018). Fitness effects on the cognitive function of older adults: A meta-analytic study—Revisited. *Perspectives on Psychological Science, 13*(2), 213–217. https://doi.org/10.1177/1745691617707316

Kuys, S. S., Peel, N. M., Klein, K., Slater, A., & Hubbard, R. E. (2014). Gait speed in ambulant older people in long term care: A systematic review and meta-analysis. *Journal of the American Medical Directors Association, 15*(3), 194–200. https://doi.org/10.1016/j.jamda.2013.10.015

Lafreniere, D., & Parham, K. (2019). Sensory health and healthy aging: Hearing and smell. In P. P. Coll (Ed.), *Healthy aging* (pp. 145–158). Springer International Publishing. https://doi.org/10.1007/978-3-030-06200-2_13

Lamotte, G., Skender, E., Rafferty, M. R., David, F. J., Sadowsky, S., & Corcos, D. M. (2015). Effects of progressive resistance exercise training on the motor and nonmotor features of Parkinson's disease: A review. *Kinesiology Review, 4*, 11–27. https://doi.org/10.1123/kr.2014-0074

Larsson, M., Oberg-Blåvarg, C., & Jönsson, F. U. (2009). Bad odors stick better than good ones: Olfactory qualities and odor recognition. *Experimental Psychology, 56*(6), 375–380. https://doi.org/10.1027/1618-3169.56.6.375

Lavallée, M. M., Gandini, D., Rouleau, I., Vallet, G. T., Joannette, M., Kergoat, M.-J., Busigny, T., Rossion, B., & Joubert, S. (2016). A qualitative impairment in face perception in Alzheimer's disease: Evidence from a reduced face inversion effect. *Journal of Alzheimer's Disease, 51*(4), 1225–1236. https://doi.org/10.3233/JAD-151027

Lee, Y.-A., & Goto, Y. (2015). Chronic stress effects on working memory: Association with prefrontal cortical tyrosine hydroxylase. *Behavioural Brain Research, 286*, 122–127. https://doi.org/10.1016/j.bbr.2015.03.007

Lemere, C. (2013). Alzheimer's disease and down syndrome. *Alzheimer's & Dementia, 9*(4), 513. https://doi.org/10.1016/j.jalz.2013.04.223

Leversen, J. S. R., Haga, M., Sigmundsson, H., Rebollo, I., & Colom, R. (2012). From children to adults: Motor performance across the life-span. *PLoS One, 7*(6), e38830. https://doi.org/10.1371/journal.pone.0038830

Li, J.-Q., Tan, L., Wang, H.-F., Tan, M.-S., Tan, L., Xu, W., Zhao, Q.-F., Wang, J., Jiang, T., & Yu, J.-T. (2016). Risk factors for predicting progression from mild cognitive impairment to Alzheimer's disease: A systematic review and meta-analysis of cohort studies. *Journal of Neurology, Neurosurgery & Psychiatry, 87*(5), 476–484. https://doi.org/10.1136/jnnp-2014-310095

Lin, J. B., Tsubota, K., & Apte, R. S. (2016). A glimpse at the aging eye. *Aging and Mechanisms of Disease, 2*, 16003. https://doi.org/10.1038/npjamd.2016.3

Liu, H., Paige, N. M., Goldzweig, C. L., Wong, E., Zhou, A., Suttorp, M. J., Munjas, B., Orwoll, E., & Shekelle, P. (2008). Screening for osteoporosis in men: A systematic review for an American College of Physicians Guideline. *Annals of Internal Medicine, 148*(9), 685–701.

Li, W.-F., Hou, S.-X., Yu, B., Li, M.-M., Férec, C., Chen, J.-M., Wen-Feng, L., Shu-Xun, H., Bin, Y., Meng-Meng, L., Férec, C., & Jian-Min, C. (2010). Genetics of osteoporosis: Accelerating pace in gene identification and validation. *Human Genetics, 127*(3), 249–285. https://doi.org/10.1007/s00439-009-0773-z

Löckenhoff, C. E., & Carstensen, L. L. (2007). Aging, emotion, and health-related decision strategies: Motivational manipulations can reduce age differences. *Psychology and Aging, 22*(1), 134–146. 10.1037/0882-7974.22.1.134

Long, J. M., & Holtzman, D. M. (2019). Alzheimer disease: An update on pathobiology and treatment strategies. *Cell, 179*, 312–339. https://doi.org/10.1016/j.cell.2019.09.001

Lönnqvist, J. (2010). Cognition and mental ill-health. *European Psychiatry, 25*(5), 297–299. https://doi.org/10.1016/j.eurpsy.2010.01.006

Loprinzi, P. D., Edwards, M. K., Crush, E., Ikuta, T., & Del Arco, A. (2018). Dose–response association between physical activity and cognitive function in a national sample of older adults. *American Journal of Health Promotion, 32*(3), 554–560. https://doi.org/10.1177/0890117116689732

Lorente-Cebrián, S., Costa, A. G. V., Navas-Carretero, S., Zabala, M., Laiglesia, L. M., Martínez, J. A., & Moreno-Aliaga, M. J. (2015). An update on the role of omega-3 fatty acids on inflammatory and degenerative diseases. *Journal of Physiology and Biochemistry, 71*(2), 341–349. https://doi.org/10.1007/s13105-015-0395-y

Lorente-Cebrián, S., Costa, A. G. V., Navas-Carretero, S., Zabala, M., Martínez, J. A., & Moreno-Aliaga, M. J. (2013). Role of omega-3 fatty acids in obesity, metabolic syndrome, and cardiovascular diseases: A review of the evidence. *Journal of Physiology and Biochemistry, 69*(3), 633–651. https://doi.org/10.1007/s13105-013-0265-4

Lyu, F., Wu, D., Wei, C., & Wu, A. (2020). Vascular cognitive impairment and dementia in type 2 diabetes mellitus: An overview. *Life Sciences, 254*, 117771. https://doi.org/10.1016/j.lfs.2020.117771

Maass, A., Düzel, S., Goerke, M., Becke, A., Sobieray, U., Neumann, K., Lövden, M., Lindenberger, U., Bäckman, L., Braun-Dullaeus, R., Ahrens, D., Heinze, H.-J., Müller, N. G., & Düzel, E. (2015). Vascular hippocampal plasticity after aerobic exercise in older adults. *Molecular Psychiatry, 20*(5), 585–593. https://doi.org/10.1038/mp.2014.114

Mares, J. A., Millen, A. E., Lawler, T. P., & Blomme, C. K. (2017). Diet and supplements in the prevention and treatment of eye diseases. In A. M. Coulston, C. J. Boushey, & M. Ferruzzi (Eds.), *Nutrition in the prevention and treatment of disease* (pp. 393–434). Elsevier. https://doi.org/10.1016/B978-0-12-802928-2.00019-9

Margrett, J., Martin, P., Woodard, J. L., Miller, L. S., MacDonald, M., Baenziger, J., Siegler, I. C., Davey, A., & Poon, L. (2010). Depression among centenarians and the oldest old: Contributions of cognition and personality. *Gerontology, 56*(1), 93–99. https://doi.org/10.1159/000272018

Markus, H. S., & Schmidt, R. (2019). Genetics of vascular cognitive impairment. *Stroke, 50*, 765–772. https://doi.org/10.1161/STROKEAHA.118.020379

Marras, C., Canning, C. G., & Goldman, S. M. (2019). Environment, lifestyle, and Parkinson's disease: Implications for prevention in the next decade. *Movement Disorders, 34*, 801–811. https://doi.org/10.1002/mds.27720

Matar, E., Shine, J. M., Halliday, G. M., & Lewis, S. J. G. (2020). Cognitive fluctuations in Lewy body dementia: Towards a pathophysiological framework. *Brain, 143*, 31–46. https://doi.org/10.1093/brain/awz311

Mather, M., & Carstensen, L. L. (2005). Aging and motivated cognition: The positivity effect in attention and memory. *Trends in Cognitive Sciences, 9*(10), 496–502. https://doi.org/10.1016/j.tics.2005.08.005

Matthews, K. A., Xu, W., Gaglioti, A. H., Holt, J. B., Croft, J. B., Mack, D., & McGuire, L. C. (2019). Racial and ethnic estimates of Alzheimer's disease and related dementias in the United States (2015–2060) in adults aged ≥65 years. *Alzheimer's and Dementia, 15*(1), 17–24. https://doi.org/10.1016/j.jalz.2018.06.3063

Mattle, M., Chocano-Bedoya, P. O., Fischbacher, M., Meyer, U., Abderhalden, L. A., Lang, W., Mansky, R., Kressig, R. W., Steurer, J., Orav, E. J., & Bischoff-Ferrari, H. A. (2020). Association of dance-based mind-motor activities with falls and physical function among healthy older adults: A systematic review and meta-analysis. *JAMA Network Open, 3*(9), 2017688. https://doi.org/10.1001/jamanetworkopen.2020.17688

Mayeda, E. R., Glymour, M. M., Quesenberry, C. P., & Whitmer, R. A. (2016). Inequalities in dementia incidence between six racial and ethnic groups over 14 years. *Alzheimer's & Dementia, 12*(3), 216–224. https://doi.org/10.1016/j.jalz.2015.12.007

Mckee, M. M., Choi, H. J., Wilson, S., Dejonckheere, M. J., Zazove, P., Levy, H., & Bowers, B. J. (2019). Determinants of hearing aid use among older Americans with hearing loss. *Gerontologist, 59*(6), 1171–1181. https://doi.org/10.1093/geront/gny051

Meeus, B., Verstraeten, A., Crosiers, D., Engelborghs, S., Van den Broeck, M., Mattheijssens, M., Peeters, K., Corsmit, E., Elinck, E., Pickut, B., Vandenberghe, R., Cras, P., De Deyn, P. P., Van Broeckhoven, C., & Theuns, J. (2012). DLB and PDD: A role for mutations in dementia and Parkinson disease genes? *Neurobiology of Aging, 33*(3), 629.e5–629.e18, . https://doi.org/10.1016/j.neurobiolaging.2011.10.014

Mehta, K. M., & Yeo, G. W. (2017). Systematic review of dementia prevalence and incidence in United States race/ethnic populations. *Alzheimer's & Dementia, 13*(1), 72–83. https://doi.org/10.1016/j.jalz.2016.06.2360

Melby-Lervåg, M., Redick, T. S., & Hulme, C. (2016). Working memory training does not improve performance on measures of intelligence or other measures of "Far Transfer": Evidence from a meta-analytic review. *Perspectives on Psychological Science : A Journal of the Association for Psychological Science, 11*(4), 512–534. https://doi.org/10.1177/1745691616635612

Mikels, J. A., Larkin, G. R., Reuter-Lorenz, P. A., & Cartensen, L. L. (2005). Divergent trajectories in the aging mind: Changes in working memory for affective versus visual information with age. *Psychology and Aging, 20*(4), 542–553. https://doi.org/10.1037/0882-7974.20.4.542

Miller, D. B., & O'Callaghan, J. P. (2015). Biomarkers of Parkinson's disease: Present and future. *Metabolism, 64*(3), S40–S46. https://doi.org/10.1016/j.metabol.2014.10.030

Miller, L. S., Mitchell, M. B., Woodard, J. L., Davey, A., Martin, P., & Poon, L. W. (2010). Cognitive performance in centenarians and the oldest old: Norms from the Georgia centenarian study. *Aging, Neuropsychology & Cognition, 17*(5), 575–590. https://doi.org/10.1080/13825585.2010.481355

Mirelman, A., Bonato, P., Camicioli, R., Ellis, T. D., Giladi, N., Hamilton, J. L., Hass, C. J., Hausdorff, J. M., Pelosin, E., & Almeida, Q. J. (2019). Gait impairments in Parkinson's disease. *The Lancet Neurology, 18*(7), 697–708. https://doi.org/10.1016/S1474-4422(19)30044-4

Mirelman, A., Herman, T., Brozgol, M., Dorfman, M., Sprecher, E., Schweiger, A., Giladi, N., Hausdorff, J. M., AGS, G., Tinetti, M., Lamb, S., Jorstad-Stein, E., Hauer, K., Becker, C., Tinetti, M., Speechley, M., Ginter, S., Buchner, D., Larson, E., . . . Giladi, N. (2012). Executive function and falls in older adults: New findings from a five-year prospective study link fall risk to cognition. *PLoS One, 7*(6), e40297. https://doi.org/10.1371/journal.pone.0040297

Mitchell, P., Liew, G., Gopinath, B., & Wong, T. Y. (2018). Age-related macular degeneration. *The Lancet, 392*(10153), 1147–1159. https://doi.org/10.1016/S0140-6736(18)31550-2

Mojon-Azzi, S. M., Sousa-Poza, A., & Mojon, D. S. (2008). Impact of low vision on well-being in 10 European countries. *Ophthalmologica, 222*(3), 205–212. https://doi.org/10.1159/000126085

Mok, R. M., Myers, N. E., Wallis, G., & Nobre, A. C. (2016). Behavioral and neural markers of flexible attention over working memory in aging. *Cerebral Cortex, 26*(4), 1831–1842. https://doi.org/10.1093/cercor/bhw011

Mortensen, L., Meyer, A. S., & Humphreys, G. W. (2006). Age-related effects on speech production: A review. *Language & Cognitive Processes, 21*(1–3), 238–290. https://doi.org/10.1080/01690960444000278

Müller, L., Di Benedetto, S., & Pawelec, G. (2019). The immune system and its dysregulation with aging. In J. R. Harris & V. I. Korolchuk (Eds.), *Biochemistry and cell biology of ageing: Part II clinical science* (Vol. 91, pp. 21–43). Springer. https://doi.org/10.1007/978-981-13-3681-2_2

Munawar, K., Kuhn, S. K., & Haque, S. (2018). Understanding the reminiscence bump: A systematic review. *PLoS One, 13*(12), e0208595. https://doi.org/10.1371/journal.pone.0208595

Muscari, A., Giannoni, C., Pierpaoli, L., Berzigotti, A., Maietta, P., Foschi, E., Ravaioli, C., Poggiopollini, G., Bianchi, G., Magalotti, D., Tentoni, C., & Zoli, M. (2010). Chronic endurance exercise training prevents aging-related cognitive decline in healthy older adults: A randomized controlled trial. *International Journal of Geriatric Psychiatry, 25*(10), 1055–1064.

Nachtigall, M. J., Nazem, T. G., Nachtigall, R. H., & Goldstein, S. R. (2013). Osteoporosis risk factors and early life-style modifications to decrease disease burden in women. *Clinical Obstetrics and Gynecology, 56*(4), 650–653. https://doi.org/10.1097/GRF.0b013e3182aa1daf

Nair, A. K., Sabbagh, M. N., Tucker, A. M., & Stern, Y. (2014). Cognitive reserve and the aging brain. In A. K. Nair & M. N. Sabbagh (Eds.), *Geriatric neurology* (pp. 118–125). John Wiley & Sons, Ltd. https://doi.org/10.1002/9781118730676

Naj, A. C., & Schellenberg, G. D. (2017). Genomic variants, genes, and pathways of Alzheimer's disease: An overview. *American Journal of Medical Genetics Part B: Neuropsychiatric Genetics, 174*(1), 5–26. https://doi.org/10.1002/ajmg.b.32499

National Center for Health Statistics. (2018). *Selected diseases and conditions among adults aged 18 and over, by selected characteristics: United States, 2016. Tables of Summary Health Statistics.* https://www.cdc.gov/nchs/nhis/shs/tables.htm

National Council on Aging. (2021). *Get the facts on healthy aging.* https://www.ncoa.org/article/get-the-facts-on-healthy-aging

National Parkinson Foundation. (2008). *About Parkinson's disease.* National Parkinson Foundation. http://www.parkinson.org/NETCOMMUNITY/Page.aspx?pid=225&srcid=201

Nebel, R. A., Aggarwal, N. T., Barnes, L. L., Gallagher, A., Goldstein, J. M., Kantarci, K., Mallampalli, M. P., Mormino, E. C., Scott, L., Yu, W. H., Maki, P. M., & Mielke, M. M. (2018). Understanding the impact of sex and gender in Alzheimer's disease: A call to action. *Alzheimer's and Dementia, 14*(9), 1171–1183. https://doi.org/10.1016/j.jalz.2018.04.008

Neely, A. S., & Nyberg, L. (2021). Working memory training in late adulthood. In J. Rummel (Ed.), *Current issues in memory* (pp. 319–336). Routledge. https://doi.org/10.4324/9781003106715-20

NIH Osteoporosis and Related Bone Diseases National Resource Center. (2007). *Osteoporosis.* National Institutes of Health. http://www.niams.nih.gov/Health_Info/Bone/Osteoporosis/default.asp

Oberauer, K. (2019). Working memory and attention – A conceptual analysis and review. *Journal of Cognition, 2*(1), 1–23. https://doi.org/10.5334/joc.58

O'Brien, J. T., & Thomas, A. (2015). Vascular dementia. *The Lancet, 386*(10004), 1698–1706. https://doi.org/10.1016/S0140-6736(15)00463-8

Ogawa, T., Annear, M. J., Ikebe, K., & Maeda, Y. (2017). Taste-related sensations in old age. *Journal of Oral Rehabilitation, 44*(8), 626–635. https://doi.org/10.1111/joor.12502

Okonkwo, O. C., Cohen, R. A., Gunstad, J., Tremont, G., Alosco, M. L., & Poppas, A. (2010). Longitudinal trajectories of cognitive decline among older adults with cardiovascular disease. *Cerebrovascular Diseases, 30*(4), 362–373. https://doi.org/10.1159/000319564

Olsen, R. K., Pangelinan, M. M., Bogulski, C., Chakravarty, M. M., Luk, G., Grady, C. L., & Bialystok, E. (2015). The effect of lifelong bilingualism on regional grey and white matter volume. *Brain Research, 1612*, 128–139. https://doi.org/10.1016/j.brainres.2015.02.034

Ortiz-Peregrina, S., Ortiz, C., Salas, C., Casares-López, M., Soler, M., & Anera, R. G. (2020). Intraocular scattering as a predictor of driving performance in older adults with cataracts. *PLoS One, 15*(1), e0227892. https://doi.org/10.1371/journal.pone.0227892

Osorio, A., Fay, S., Pouthas, V., & Ballesteros, S. (2010). Ageing affects brain activity in highly educated older adults: An ERP study using a word-stem priming task. *Cortex: A Journal Devoted to the Study of the Nervous System and Behavior, 46*(4), 522–534. https://doi.org/10.1016/j.cortex.2009.09.003

Ossher, L., Flegal, K. E., & Lustig, C. (2013). Everyday memory errors in older adults. *Neuropsychology, Development, and Cognition. Section B, Aging, Neuropsychology and Cognition, 20*(2), 220–242. https://doi.org/10.1080/13825585.2012.690365

Owens, R. E. (2015). *Language development: An introduction.* Pearson.

Owsley, C., Ghate, D., & Kedar, S. (2018). Vision and aging. In M. Rizzo, S. Anderson, & B. Fritzsch (Eds.), *The Wiley handbook on the aging mind and brain* (pp. 296–314). Wiley Blackwell. https://doi.org/10.1002/9781118772034.ch15

Paillard, T., Rolland, Y., de Souto Barreto, P., Kalil-Gaspar, P., Marcuzzo, S., & Achaval, M. (2015). Protective effects of physical exercise in Alzheimer's Disease and Parkinson's disease: A narrative review. *Journal of Clinical Neurology, 11*(3), 212. https://doi.org/10.3988/jcn.2015.11.3.212

Paneni, F., DiazCañestro, C., Libby, P., Lüscher, T. F., & Camici, G. G. (2017). The aging cardiovascular system: Understanding it at the cellular and clinical levels. *Journal of the American College of Cardiology, 69*(15), 1952–1967. https://doi.org/10.1016/J.JACC.2017.01.064

Panula, J., Pihlajamäki, H., Mattila, V. M., Jaatinen, P., Vahlberg, T., Aarnio, P., & Kivelä, S. L. (2011). Mortality and cause of death in hip fracture patients aged 65 or older-a population-based study. *BMC Musculoskeletal Disorders, 12*(1), 105.

Park, J., Lee, O., & McKee, M. (2021). Association between hearing loss and suicidal ideation among middle-aged and older adults. *Aging & Mental Health*, 1–8. https://doi.org/10.1080/13607863.2021.1919991

Parnetti, L., Gaetani, L., Eusebi, P., Paciotti, S., Hansson, O., El-Agnaf, O., Mollenhauer, B., Blennow, K., & Calabresi, P. (2019). CSF and blood biomarkers for Parkinson's disease. *The Lancet Neurology, 18*(6), 573–586. https://doi.org/10.1016/S1474-4422(19)30024-9

Parrado, C., Mercado-Saenz, S., Perez-Davo, A., Gilaberte, Y., Gonzalez, S., & Juarranz, A. (2019). Environmental stressors on skin aging. Mechanistic insights. *Frontiers in Pharmacology, 10*, 759. https://doi.org/10.3389/fphar.2019.00759

Paúl, C., Ribeiro, O., & Santos, P. (2010). Cognitive impairment in old people living in the community. *Archives of Gerontology & Geriatrics, 51*(2), 121–124. https://doi.org/10.1016/j.archger.2009.09.037

Paul, L. (2011). Diet, nutrition and telomere length. *The Journal of Nutritional Biochemistry, 22*(10), 895–901. https://doi.org/10.1016/j.jnutbio.2010.12.001

Payne, V. G., & Isaacs, L. D. (2020). *Human motor development : A lifespan approach* (10th ed.). Routledge.

PBS Newshour. (2020, January 2). 3 ways that the U.S. population will change over the next decade. *PBS NewsHour.* https://www.pbs.org/newshour/nation/3-ways-that-the-u-s-population-will-change-over-the-next-decade

Peters, A., & Kemper, T. (2012). A review of the structural alterations in the cerebral hemispheres of the aging rhesus monkey. *Neurobiology of Aging, 33*(10), 2357–2372. https://doi.org/10.1016/j.neurobiolaging.2011.11.015

Peters, C. H., Sharpe, E. J., & Proenza, C. (2020). Cardiac pacemaker activity and aging. *Annual Review of Physiology, 82*, 21–43. https://doi.org/10.1146/annurev-physiol-021119-034453

Peterson, M. D., Rhea, M. R., Sen, A., & Gordon, P. M. (2010). Resistance exercise for muscular strength in older adults: A meta-analysis. *Ageing Research Reviews*, *9*(3), 226–237. https://doi.org/10.1016/j.arr.2010.03.004

Peterson, M. D., & Serra, J. A. (2021). Exercise interventions to prevent and improve sarcopenia. In A. J. Cruz-Jentoft & J. E. Morley (Eds.), *Sarcopenia* (p. 305). Wiley.

Pichora-Fuller, M. K. (2020). Hearing and cognitive aging. In O. Braddick (Ed.), *Oxford research encyclopedia of psychology*. Oxford University Press. https://doi.org/10.1093/acrefore/9780190236557.013.367

Pike, C. J. (2017). Sex and the development of Alzheimer's disease. *Journal of Neuroscience Research*, *95*(1–2), 671–680. https://doi.org/10.1002/jnr.23827

Piolino, P., Coste, C., Martinelli, P., Macé, A.-L., Quinette, P., Guillery-Girard, B., & Belleville, S. (2010). Reduced specificity of autobiographical memory and aging: Do the executive and feature binding functions of working memory have a role? *Neuropsychologia*, *48*(2), 429–440. https://doi.org/10.1016/j.neuropsychologia.2009.09.035

Piolino, P., Desgranges, B., Clarys, D., Guillery-Girard, B., Taconnat, L., Isingrini, M., & Eustache, F. (2006). Autobiographical memory, autonoetic consciousness, and self-perspective in aging. *Psychology and Aging*, *21*(3), 510–525. 10.1037/0882-7974.21.3.510

Pliatsikas, C., Moschopoulou, E., & Saddy, J. D. (2015). The effects of bilingualism on the white matter structure of the brain. *Proceedings of the National Academy of Sciences*, *112*(5), 1334–1337. https://doi.org/10.1073/pnas.1414183112

Postuma, R. B., Berg, D., Stern, M., Poewe, W., Olanow, C. W., Oertel, W., Obeso, J., Marek, K., Litvan, I., Lang, A. E., Halliday, G., Goetz, C. G., Gasser, T., Dubois, B., Chan, P., Bloem, B. R., Adler, C. H., & Deuschl, G. (2015). MDS clinical diagnostic criteria for Parkinson's disease. *Movement Disorders*, *30*(12), 1591–1601. https://doi.org/10.1002/mds.26424

Poulose, S. M., Miller, M. G., Scott, T., & Shukitt-Hale, B. (2017). Nutritional factors affecting adult neurogenesis and cognitive function. In *Advances in nutrition* (Vol. 8, pp. 804–811). American Society for Nutrition. https://doi.org/10.3945/an.117.016261

Prakash, R. S., Voss, M. W., Erickson, K. I., & Kramer, A. F. (2015). Physical activity and cognitive vitality. *Annual Review of Psychology*, *66*(1), 769–797. https://doi.org/10.1146/annurev-psych-010814-015249

Pringsheim, T., Jette, N., Frolkis, A., & Steeves, T. D. L. (2014). The prevalence of Parkinson's disease: A systematic review and meta-analysis. *Movement Disorders*, *29*(13), 1583–1590. https://doi.org/10.1002/mds.25945

Punt, D. (2020, October 1). *The world's oldest people and their secrets to a long life | Guinness World Records*. Guinness Book of World Records. . https://www.guinnessworldrecords.com/news/2020/10/the-worlds-oldest-people-and-their-secrets-to-a-long-life-632895

Quaranta, N., Coppola, F., Casulli, M., Barulli, M. R., Panza, F., Tortelli, R., Solfrizzi, V., Sabbà, C., & Logroscino, G. (2015). Epidemiology of age related hearing loss: A review. *Hearing, Balance and Communication*, *13*, 77–81. https://doi.org/10.3109/21695717.2014.994869

Quiñones, A. R., Kaye, J., Allore, H. G., Botoseneanu, A., & Thielke, S. M. (2020). An agenda for addressing multimorbidity and racial and ethnic disparities in Alzheimer's disease and related dementia. *American Journal of Alzheimer's Disease and Other Dementias*, *35*, 1533317520960874. https://doi.org/10.1177/1533317520960874

Raj, T., Chibnik, L. B., McCabe, C., Wong, A., Replogle, J. M., Yu, L., Gao, S., Unverzagt, F. W., Stranger, B., Murrell, J., Barnes, L., Hendrie, H. C., Foroud, T., Krichevsky, A., Bennett, D. A., Hall, K. S., Evans, D. A., & De Jager, P. L. (2017). Genetic architecture of age-related cognitive decline in African Americans. *Neurology Genetics*, *3*(1), e125. https://doi.org/10.1212/NXG.0000000000000125

Raman, M. R., Schwarz, C. G., Murray, M. E., Lowe, V. J., Dickson, D. W., Jack, C. R., & Kantarci, K. (2016). An MRI-based atlas for correlation of imaging and pathologic findings in Alzheimer's disease. *Journal of Neuroimaging*, *26*(3), 264–268. https://doi.org/10.1111/jon.12341

Rautiainen, S., Gaziano, J. M., Christen, W. G., Bubes, V., Kotler, G., Glynn, R. J., Manson, J. E., Buring, J. E., & Sesso, H. D. (2017). Effect of baseline nutritional status on long-term multivitamin use and cardiovascular disease risk. *JAMA Cardiology*, *2*(6), 617. https://doi.org/10.1001/jamacardio.2017.0176

Raz, N., & Daugherty, A. M. (2018). Pathways to brain aging and their modifiers: Free-radical-induced energetic and neural decline in senescence (FRIENDS) model - A mini-review. *Gerontology*, *64*(1), 49–57. https://doi.org/10.1159/000479508

Rea, I. M., & Mills, K. I. (2018). Living long and aging well. In A. Moskalev & A. M. Vaiserman (Eds.), *Epigenetics of aging and longevity* (pp. 137–152). Elsevier. https://doi.org/10.1016/B978-0-12-811060-7.00006-1

Reed, A. E., & Carstensen, L. L. (2012). The theory behind the age-related positivity effect. *Frontiers in Psychology*, *3*, 339. https://doi.org/10.3389/fpsyg.2012.00339

Reed, A. E., Chan, L., & Mikels, J. A. (2014). Meta-analysis of the age-related positivity effect: Age differences in preferences for positive over negative information. *Psychology and Aging*, *29*(1), 1–15. https://doi.org/10.1037/a0035194

Reed, N. S., Garcia-Morales, E., & Willink, A. (2021). Trends in hearing aid ownership among older adults in the United States from 2011 to 2018. *JAMA Internal Medicine*, *181*(3), 383–385. https://doi.org/10.1001/jamainternmed.2020.5682

Reilly, W., & Ilich, J. (2017). Prescription drugs and nutrient depletion: How much is known? *Advances in Nutrition*, *8*(1), 23–23. https://doi.org/10.1093/advances/8.1.23

Rektorova, I., Rusina, R., Hort, J., & Matej, R. (2009). The degenerative dementias. In R. P. Lisak, D. D. Truong, W. M. Carroll, & R. Bhidayasiri (Eds.), *International neurology: A clinical approach* (pp. 126–137). Wiley-Blackwell.

Reuter-Lorenz, P. A., & Cappell, K. A. (2008). Neurocognitive aging and the compensation hypothesis. *Current Directions in Psychological Science*, *17*(3), 177–182. https://doi.org/10.1111/j.1467-8721.2008.00570.x

Richmond, R. L., Law, J., & KayLambkin, F. (2012). Morbidity profiles and lifetime health of Australian centenarians. *Australasian Journal on Ageing*, *31*(4), 227–232. https://doi.org/10.1111/j.1741-6612.2011.00570.x

Rizzo, G., Arcuti, S., Martino, D., Copetti, M., Fontana, A., & Logroscino, G. (2015). Accuracy of clinical diagnosis of Parkinson's disease: A systematic review and bayesian meta-analysis (S36.001). *Neurology, 84*(14_Suppl.), S36.001. http://www.neurology.org/content/84/14_Supplement/S36.001.short

Roberts, J. S., Connell, C. M., Cisewski, D., Hipps, Y. G., Demissie, S., & Green, R. C. (2003). Differences between African Americans and whites in their perceptions of Alzheimer disease. *Alzheimer Disease and Associated Disorders*, *17*(1), 19–26. http://www.ncbi.nlm.nih.gov/pubmed/12621316

Rodriguez, F. S., Zheng, L., & Chui, H. C. (2019). Psychometric characteristics of cognitive reserve: How high education might improve certain cognitive abilities in aging. *Dementia and Geriatric Cognitive Disorders*, *47*(4–6), 335–344. https://doi.org/10.1159/000501150

Roh, D., Lee, D. H., Kim, S. W., Kim, S. W., Kim, B. G., Kim, D. H., & Shin, J. H. (2021). The association between olfactory dysfunction and cardiovascular disease and its risk factors in middle-aged and older adults. *Scientific Reports*, *11*(1), 1248. https://doi.org/10.1038/s41598-020-80943-5

Rosano, C., Guralnik, J., Pahor, M., Glynn, N. W., Newman, A. B., Ibrahim, T. S., Erickson, K., Cohen, R., Shaaban, C. E., MacCloud, R. L., & Aizenstein, H. J. (2017). Hippocampal response to a 24-month physical activity intervention in sedentary older adults. *The American Journal of Geriatric Psychiatry*, *25*(3), 209–217. https://doi.org/10.1016/j.jagp.2016.11.007

Rubin, D. C. (2000). Autobiographical memory and aging. In D. C. Park & N. Schwarz (Eds.), *Cognitive aging: A primer* (pp. 131–149). Psychology Press.

Russell-Goldman, E., & Murphy, G. F. (2020). The pathobiology of skin aging: New insights into an old dilemma. *American Journal of Pathology*, *190*(7), 1356–1369. https://doi.org/10.1016/j.ajpath.2020.03.007

Ryan, S. M., & Nolan, Y. M. (2016). Neuroinflammation negatively affects adult hippocampal neurogenesis and cognition: Can exercise compensate? *Neuroscience & Biobehavioral Reviews*, *61*, 121–131. https://doi.org/10.1016/j.neubiorev.2015.12.004

Ryu, S., Atzmon, G., Barzilai, N., Raghavachari, N., & Suh, Y. (2016). Genetic landscape of APOE in human longevity revealed by high-throughput sequencing. *Mechanisms of Ageing and Development*, *155*, 7–9. https://doi.org/10.1016/J.MAD.2016.02.010

Saad, M., Fausto, N., & Maisch, N. (2018). Vitamins and dietary supplements for the older adult. *American Journal of Therapeutics*, *25*(1), e173–e182. https://doi.org/10.1097/MJT.0000000000000669

Sailor, K. A., Schinder, A. F., & Lledo, P.-M. (2017). Adult neurogenesis beyond the niche: Its potential for driving brain plasticity. *Current Opinion in Neurobiology*, *42*, 111–117. https://doi.org/10.1016/j.conb.2016.12.001

Salthouse, T. A. (2011). Neuroanatomical substrates of age-related cognitive decline. *Psychological Bulletin*, *137*(5), 753–784. https://doi.org/10.1037/a0023262

Salthouse, T. A. (2012). Consequences of age-related cognitive declines. *Annual Review of Psychology*, *63*, 201–226. https://doi.org/10.1146/annurev-psych-120710-100328

Salthouse, T. A., & Madden, D. J. (2013). Information processing speed and aging. In J. DeLuca & J. H. Kalmar (Eds.), *Information processing speed in clinical populations* (pp. 221–239). Psychology Press.

Samanez-Larkin, G. R., Robertson, E. R., Mikels, J. A., Carstensen, L. L., & Gotlib, I. H. (2009). Selective attention to emotion in the aging brain. *Psychology and Aging*, *24*(3), 519–529. https://doi.org/10.1037/a0016952

Sampaio-Baptista, C., & Johansen-Berg, H. (2017). White Matter plasticity in the adult brain. *Neuron*, *96*(6), 1239–1251. https://doi.org/10.1016/J.NEURON.2017.11.026

Sandlin, D., McGwin, G., & Owsley, C. (2014). Association between vision impairment and driving exposure in older adults aged 70 years and over: A population-based examination. *Acta Ophthalmologica*, *92*(3), e207–e212. https://doi.org/10.1111/aos.12050

Savica, R., Grossardt, B. R., Rocca, W. A., & Bower, J. H. (2018). Parkinson disease with and without Dementia: A prevalence study and future projections. *Movement Disorders*, *33*(4), 537–543. https://doi.org/10.1002/mds.27277

Schaie, K. W. (2013). *Developmental influences on adult intelligence: The Seattle longitudinal study.* Oxford University Press,.

Schelke, M. W., Hackett, K., Chen, J. L., Shih, C., Shum, J., Montgomery, M. E., Chiang, G. C., Berkowitz, C., Seifan, A., Krikorian, R., & Isaacson, R. S. (2016). Nutritional interventions for Alzheimer's prevention: A clinical precision medicine approach. *Annals of the New York Academy of Sciences*, *1367*(1), 50–56. https://doi.org/10.1111/nyas.13070

Schiffman, S. S. (2009). Effects of aging on the human taste system. *Annals of the New York Academy of Sciences*, *1170*(1), 725–729. https://doi.org/10.1111/j.1749-6632.2009.03924.x

Schroots, J. J. F., van, Dijkum C., & Assink, M. H. J. (2004). Autobiographical memory from a life span perspective. *International Journal of Aging & Human Development*, *58*(1), 69–85, . https://doi.org/10.2190/7A1A-8HCE-0FD9-7CTX

Schubert, C. R., Cruickshanks, K. J., Fischer, M. E., Huang, G.-H., Klein, B. E. K., Klein, R., Pankow, J. S., & Nondahl, D. M. (2012). Olfactory impairment in an adult population: The Beaver Dam offspring study. *Chemical Senses*, *37*(4), 325–334. https://doi.org/10.1093/chemse/bjr102

Schwartz, B. L., & Frazier, L. D. (2005). Tip-of-the-tongue states and aging: Contrasting psycholinguistic and metacognitive perspectives. *Journal of General Psychology*, *132*(4), 377–391.

Sebastiani, P., & Perls, T. T. (2012). The genetics of extreme longevity: Lessons from the new England centenarian study. *Frontiers in Genetics*, *3*, 277. https://doi.org/10.3389/fgene.2012.00277

Senderovich, H., Tang, H., & Belmont, S. (2017). The Role of exercises in osteoporotic fracture prevention and current care gaps. Where are we now? Recent Updates. *Rambam Maimonides Medical Journal*, *8*(3), e0032. https://doi.org/10.5041/rmmj.10308

Sergi, G., Bano, G., Pizzato, S., Veronese, N., & Manzato, E. (2017). Taste loss in the elderly: Possible implications for dietary habits. *Critical Reviews in Food Science and Nutrition*, *57*(17), 3684–3689. https://doi.org/10.1080/10408398.2016.1160208

Shadyab, A. H., & LaCroix, A. Z. (2015). Genetic factors associated with longevity: A review of recent findings. *Ageing Research Reviews*, *19*, 1–7. https://doi.org/10.1016/j.arr.2014.10.005

Shafto, M. A., Stamatakis, E. A., Tam, P. P., & Tyler, L. K. (2010). Word retrieval failures in old age: The relationship between structure and function. *Journal of Cognitive Neuroscience*, *22*(7), 1530–1540. https://doi.org/10.1162/jocn.2009.21321

Shafto, M. A., & Tyler, L. K. (2014). Language in the aging brain: The network dynamics of cognitive decline and preservation. *Science*, *346*(6209), 583–587. https://doi.org/10.1126/science.1254404

Shors, T. J. (2014). The Adult Brain Makes New Neurons, and Effortful Learning Keeps Them Alive. *Current Directions in Psychological Science*, *23*(5), 311–318. https://doi.org/10.1177/0963721414540167

Siderowf, A., Aarsland, D., Mollenhauer, B., Goldman, J. G., & Ravina, B. (2018). Biomarkers for cognitive impairment in Lewy body disorders: Status and relevance for clinical trials. *Movement Disorders : Official Journal of the Movement Disorder Society*, *33*(4), 528–536. https://doi.org/10.1002/mds.27355

Sinaki, M. (2021). Osteoporosis. In D. X. Cifu (Ed.), *Braddom's physical medicine and rehabilitation* (pp. 690–714.e3). Elsevier. https://doi.org/10.1016/B978-0-323-62539-5.00034-5

Sinnott, J. D. (2003). Postformal thought adn adult development: Living in balance. In J. Demick & C. Andreoletti (Eds.), *Handbookof adult development* (pp. 221–238). Kluwer.

Siris, E. S., Adler, R., Bilezikian, J., Bolognese, M., Dawson-Hughes, B., Favus, M. J., Harris, S. T., Jan de Beur, S. M., Khosla, S., Lane, N. E., Lindsay, R., Nana, A. D., Orwoll, E. S., Saag, K., Silverman, S., & Watts, N. B. (2014). The clinical diagnosis of osteoporosis: A position statement from the National Bone Health Alliance Working Group. *Osteoporosis International*, *25*(5), 1439–1443. https://doi.org/10.1007/s00198-014-2655-z

Sorond, F. A., Cruz-Almeida, Y., Clark, D. J., Viswanathan, A., Scherzer, C. R., De Jager, P., Csiszar, A., Laurienti, P. J., Hausdorff, J. M., Chen, W. G., Ferrucci, L., Rosano, C., Studenski, S. A., Black, S. E., & Lipsitz, L. A. (2015). Aging, the central nervous system, and mobility in older adults: Neural mechanisms of mobility impairment. *The Journals of Gerontology Series A: Biological Sciences and Medical Sciences*, *70*(12), 1526–1532. https://doi.org/10.1093/gerona/glv130

Spalding, K. L., Bergmann, O., Alkass, K., Bernard, S., Salehpour, M., Huttner, H. B., Boström, E., Westerlund, I., Vial, C., Buchholz, B. A., Possnert, G., Mash, D. C., Druid, H., & Frisén, J. (2013). Dynamics of hippocampal neurogenesis in adult humans. *Cell*, *153*(6), 1219–1227. https://doi.org/10.1016/j.cell.2013.05.002

Spartano, N. L., Davis-Plourde, K. L., Himali, J. J., Andersson, C., Pase, M. P., Maillard, P., Decarli, C., Murabito, J. M., Beiser, A. S., Vasan, R. S., & Seshadri, S. (2019). Association of accelerometer-measured light-intensity physical activity with brain volume: The Framingham Heart Study. *JAMA Network Open*, *2*(4), e192745–e192745. https://doi.org/10.1001/jamanetworkopen.2019.2745

Srinivasan, V., Braidy, N., Chan, E. K. W., Xu, Y.-H., & Chan, D. K. Y. (2016). Genetic and environmental factors in vascular dementia: An update of blood brain barrier dysfunction. *Clinical and Experimental Pharmacology and Physiology*, *43*(5), 515–521. https://doi.org/10.1111/1440-1681.12558

Staudinger, U. M., & Baltes, P. B. (1996). Interactive minds: A facilitative setting of wisdom-related performance? *Journal of Personality & Social Psychology*, *71*(4), 746–762.

Staudinger, U. M., Dörner, J., & Mickler, C. (2005). Wisdom and personality. In R. J. Sternberg & J. Jordan (Eds.), *A handbook of wisdom: Psychological perspectives* (pp. 191–219). Cambridge University Press.

Staudinger, U. M., Kessler, E.-M., & Dörner, J. (2006). Wisdom in social context. In K. W. Schaie & L. L. Carstensen (Eds.), *Social structures, aging, and self-regulation in the elderly* (pp. 33–67). Springer Publishing Co.

Stepankova, H., Lukavsky, J., Buschkuehl, M., Kopecek, M., Ripova, D., & Jaeggi, S. M. (2014). The malleability of working memory and visuospatial skills: A randomized controlled study in older adults. *Developmental Psychology*, *50*(4), 1049–1059. https://doi.org/10.1037/a0034913

Stern, Y., Barnes, C. A., Grady, C., Jones, R. N., & Raz, N. (2019). Brain reserve, cognitive reserve, compensation, and maintenance: Operationalization, validity, and mechanisms of cognitive resilience. *Neurobiology of Aging*, *83*, 124–129. https://doi.org/10.1016/j.neurobiolaging.2019.03.022

Stillman, C. M., Esteban-Cornejo, I., Brown, B., Bender, C. M., & Erickson, K. I. (2020). Effects of exercise on brain and cognition across age groups and health states. *Trends in Neurosciences*, *43*(7), 533–543. https://doi.org/10.1016/j.tins.2020.04.010

St-Laurent, M., Abdi, H., Burianová, H., & Grady, C. L. (2011). Influence of aging on the neural correlates of autobiographical, episodic, and semantic memory retrieval. *Journal of Cognitive Neuroscience*, *23*(12), 4150–4163. https://doi.org/10.1162/jocn_a_00079

Storbeck, J., & Maswood, R. (2016). Happiness increases verbal and spatial working memory capacity where sadness does not: Emotion, working memory and executive control. *Cognition and Emotion*, *30*(5), 925–938. https://doi.org/10.1080/02699931.2015.1034091

Strough, J., Patrick, J. H., & Swenson, L. M. (2003). Strategies for solving everyday problems faced by grandparents: The role of experience. In B. Hayslip Jr & J. H. Patrick (Eds.), *Working with custodial grandparents* (pp. 257–275). Springer Publishing Co.

Studenski, S. (2011). Gait speed and survival in older adults. *JAMA*, *305*(1), 50. https://doi.org/10.1001/jama.2010.1923

Swenor, B. K., Wang, J., Varadaraj, V., Rosano, C., Yaffe, K., Albert, M., Simonsick, E. M., & Magaziner, J. (2019). Vision impairment and cognitive outcomes in older adults: The health ABC study. *Journals of Gerontology - Series A Biological Sciences and Medical Sciences*, *74*(9), 1454–1460. https://doi.org/10.1093/gerona/gly244

Sylvain-Roy, S., Lungu, O., & Belleville, S. (2014). Normal aging of the attentional control functions that underlie working memory. *The Journals of Gerontology. Series B, Psychological Sciences and Social Sciences*, *70*(5), gbt166-. https://doi.org/10.1093/geronb/gbt166

Takahashi, R. H., Nagao, T., & Gouras, G. K. (2017). Plaque formation and the intraneuronal accumulation of ?-amyloid in Alzheimer's disease. *Pathology International*, *67*(4), 185–193. https://doi.org/10.1111/pin.12520

Taubert, M., Roggenhofer, E., Melie-Garcia, L., Muller, S., Lehmann, N., Preisig, M., Vollenweider, P., Marques-Vidal, P., Lutti, A., Kherif, F., & Draganski, B. (2020). Converging patterns of aging-associated brain volume loss and tissue microstructure differences. *Neurobiology of Aging*, *88*, 108–118. https://doi.org/10.1016/j.neurobiolaging.2020.01.006

Tautvydaitė, D., Antonietti, J. P., Henry, H., von Gunten, A., & Popp, J. (2017). Relations between personality changes and cerebrospinal fluid biomarkers of Alzheimer's disease pathology. *Journal of Psychiatric Research*, *90*, 12–20. https://doi.org/10.1016/j.jpsychires.2016.12.024

ten Brinke, L. F., Bolandzadeh, N., Nagamatsu, L. S., Hsu, C. L., Davis, J. C., Miran-Khan, K., & Liu-Ambrose, T. (2015). Aerobic exercise increases hippocampal volume in older women with probable mild cognitive impairment: A 6-month randomised controlled trial. *British Journal of Sports Medicine*, *49*(4), 248–254. https://doi.org/10.1136/bjsports-2013-093184

Tobin, D. J. (2017). Introduction to skin aging. *Journal of Tissue Viability*, *26*(1), 37–46. https://doi.org/10.1016/j.jtv.2016.03.002

Toda, T., Parylak, S. L., Linker, S. B., & Gage, F. H. (2019). The role of adult hippocampal neurogenesis in brain health and disease. *Molecular Psychiatry*, *24*(1), 67–87. https://doi.org/10.1038/s41380-018-0036-2

Tosto, G., Bird, T. D., Bennett, D. A., Boeve, B. F., Brickman, A. M., Cruchaga, C., Faber, K., Foroud, T. M., Farlow, M., Goate, A. M., Graff-Radford, N. R., Lantigua, R., Manly, J., Ottman, R., Rosenberg, R., Schaid, D. J., Schupf, N., Stern, Y., Sweet, R. A., & Mayeux, R. (2016). The role of cardiovascular risk factors and stroke in familial Alzheimer Disease. *JAMA Neurology*, *73*(10), 1231. https://doi.org/10.1001/jamaneurol.2016.2539

Tricco, A. C., Thomas, S. M., Veroniki, A. A., Hamid, J. S., Cogo, E., Strifler, L., Khan, P. A., Robson, R., Sibley, K. M., MacDonald, H., Riva, J. J., Thavorn, K., Wilson, C., Holroyd-Leduc, J., Kerr, G. D., Feldman, F., Majumdar, S. R., Jaglal, S. B., Hui, W., & Straus, S. E. (2017). Comparisons of interventions for preventing falls in older adults. *JAMA*, *318*(17), 1687. https://doi.org/10.1001/jama.2017.15006

Trinchero, M. F., Buttner, K. A., Sulkes Cuevas, J. N., Temprana, S. G., Fontanet, P. A., Monzón-Salinas, M. C., Ledda, F., Paratcha, G., & Schinder, A. F. (2017). High plasticity of new granule cells in the aging hippocampus. *Cell Reports*, *21*(5), 1129–1139. https://doi.org/10.1016/J.CELREP.2017.09.064

Truong, D. D., & Wolters, E. C. (2009). Recognition and management of Parkinson's disease during the premotor (prodromal) phase. *Expert Review of Neurotherapeutics*, *9*(6), 847–857. https://doi.org/10.1586/ern.09.50

Tu, K. N., Lie, J. D., Wan, C. K. V., Cameron, M., Austel, A. G., Nguyen, J. K., Van, K., & Hyun, D. (2018). Osteoporosis: A review of treatment options. *Pharmacy and Therapeutics*, *43*, 92–104.

Turana, Y., Tengkawan, J., Chia, Y. C., Hoshide, S., Shin, J., Chen, C. H., Buranakitjaroen, P., Nailes, J., Park, S., Siddique, S., Sison, J., Ann Soenarta, A., Chin Tay, J., Sogunuru, G. P., Zhang, Y., Wang, J. G., & Kario, K. (2019). Hypertension and dementia: A comprehensive review from the HOPE Asia Network. *Journal of Clinical Hypertension*, *21*(8), 1091–1098. https://doi.org/10.1111/jch.13558

Turner, G. R., & Spreng, R. N. (2012). Executive functions and neurocognitive aging: Dissociable patterns of brain activity. *Neurobiology of Aging*, *33*(4), 826.e1–e13, . https://doi.org/10.1016/j.neurobiolaging.2011.06.005

Unsworth, N., Miller, A. L., & Robison, M. K. (2021). Are individual differences in attention control related to working memory capacity? A latent variable mega-analysis. *Journal of Experimental Psychology: General*, *150*, 1332–1357. https://doi.org/10.1037/xge0001000

U.S. Department of Health and Human Services. (2018). *The physical activity guidelines for Americans* (2nd ed.). U.S. Department of Health and Human Services. https://doi.org/10.1001/jama.2018.14854

van Bokhorst-de van der Schueren, M. A. E., Lonterman-Monasch, S., de Vries, O. J., Danner, S. A., Kramer, M. H. H., & Muller, M. (2013). Prevalence and determinants for malnutrition in geriatric outpatients. *Clinical Nutrition*, *32*(6), 1007–1011. https://doi.org/10.1016/j.clnu.2013.05.007

van den Broeke, C., de Burghgraeve, T., Ummels, M., Gescher, N., Deckx, L., Tjan-Heijnen, V., Buntinx, F., & van den Akker, M. (2018). Occurrence of malnutrition and associated factors in community-dwelling older adults: Those with a recent diagnosis of cancer are at higher risk. *The Journal of Nutrition, Health & Aging*, *22*(2), 191–198. https://doi.org/10.1007/s12603-017-0882-7

Van Dijk, K. R. A., Van Gerven, P. W. M., Van Boxtel, M. P. J., Van Der Elst, W., & Jolles, J. (2008). No protective effects of education during normal cognitive aging: Results from the 6-year follow-up of the maastricht aging study. *Psychology & Aging*, *23*(1), 119–130. 10.1037/0882-7974.23.1.119

van Heesbeen, H. J., & Smidt, M. P. (2019). Entanglement of genetics and epigenetics in Parkinson's disease. *Frontiers in Neuroscience*, *13*, 277. https://doi.org/10.3389/fnins.2019.00277

van Nispen, R. M. A., Vreeken, H. L., Comijs, H. C., Deeg, D. J. H., & van Rens, G. H. M. B. (2016). Role of vision loss, functional limitations and the supporting network in depression in a general population. *Acta Ophthalmologica*, *94*(1), 76–82. https://doi.org/10.1111/aos.12896

Verhaeghen, P., Steitz, D. W., Sliwinski, M. J., & Cerella, J. (2003). Aging and dual-task performance: A meta-analysis. *Psychology and Aging*, *18*(3), 443–460. https://doi.org/10.1037/0882-7974.18.3.443

Vermunt, L., Sikkes, S. A. M., van den Hout, A., Handels, R., Bos, I., van der Flier, W. M., Kern, S., Ousset, P. J., Maruff, P., Skoog, I., Verhey, F. R. J., Freund-Levi, Y., Tsolaki, M., Wallin, Å. K., Olde Rikkert, M., Soininen, H., Spiru, L., Zetterberg, H., Blennow, K., & . . . Coley, N. (2019). Duration of preclinical, prodromal, and dementia stages of Alzheimer's disease in relation to age, sex, and APOE genotype. *Alzheimer's and Dementia*, *15*(7), 888–898. https://doi.org/10.1016/j.jalz.2019.04.001

Vestergren, P., & Nilsson, L.-G. (2011). Perceived causes of everyday memory problems in a population-based sample aged 39-99. *Applied Cognitive Psychology*, *25*(4), 641–646. https://doi.org/10.1002/acp.1734

Vinters, H. V., Zarow, C., Borys, E., Whitman, J. D., Tung, S., Ellis, W. G., Zheng, L., & Chui, H. C. (2018). Review: Vascular dementia: Clinicopathologic and genetic considerations. *Neuropathology and Applied Neurobiology*, *44*(3), 247–266. https://doi.org/10.1111/nan.12472

Visschedijk, J., Achterberg, W., van Balen, R., & Hertogh, C. (2010). Fear of falling after hip fracture: A systematic review of measurement instruments, prevalence, interventions, and related factors. *Journal of the American Geriatrics Society*, *58*(9), 1739–1748. https://doi.org/10.1111/j.1532-5415.2010.03036.x

Vitlic, A., Lord, J. M., & Phillips, A. C. (2014). Stress, ageing and their influence on functional, cellular and molecular aspects of the immune system. *Age*, *36*(3), 9631. https://doi.org/10.1007/s11357-014-9631-6

Voelcker-Rehage, C., & Alberts, J. L. (2007). Effect of motor practice on dual-task performance in older adult. *Journals of Gerontology: Series B: Psychological Sciences and Social Sciences*, *62*(3), 141–148.

Vondracek, S. F. (2010). Managing osteoporosis in postmenopausal women. *American Journal of Health-System Pharmacy, 67*, S9–S19. https://doi.org/10.2146/ajhp100076

Walker, J. (2008). Osteoporosis: Pathogenesis, diagnosis and management. *Nursing Standard, 22*(17), 48–56.

Walker, Z., Possin, K. L., Boeve, B. F., & Aarsland, D. (2015). Lewy body dementias. *Lancet, 386*(10004), 1683–1697. https://doi.org/10.1016/S0140-6736(15)00462-6

Walker, Z., Possin, K. L., Boeve, B. F., & Aarsland, D. (2017). Lewy body dementias. *Focus, 15*(1), 85–100. https://doi.org/10.1176/appi.focus.15105

Wang, J., Sun, X., & Yang, Q. X. (2016). Early aging effect on the function of the human central olfactory system. *The Journals of Gerontology Series A: Biological Sciences and Medical Sciences, 21*(2), glw104. https://doi.org/10.1093/gerona/glw104

Wang, S., Luo, X., Barnes, D., Sano, M., & Yaffe, K. (2014). Physical activity and risk of cognitive impairment among oldest-old women. *The American Journal of Geriatric Psychiatry: Official Journal of the American Association for Geriatric Psychiatry, 22*(11), 1149–1157. https://doi.org/10.1016/j.jagp.2013.03.002

Wang, S., & Young, K. M. M. (2014). White matter plasticity in adulthood. *Neuroscience, 276*, 148–160. https://doi.org/10.1016/j.neuroscience.2013.10.018

Weeks, J. C., & Hasher, L. (2017). Divided attention reduces resistance to distraction at encoding but not retrieval. *Psychonomic Bulletin and Review, 24*(4), 1268–1273. https://doi.org/10.3758/s13423-016-1210-7

Welmer, A.-K., Rizzuto, D., Laukka, E. J., Johnell, K., & Fratiglioni, L. (2016). Cognitive and physical function in relation to the risk of injurious falls in older adults: A population-based study. *The Journals of Gerontology Series A: Biological Sciences and Medical Sciences, 68*(5), glw141. https://doi.org/10.1093/gerona/glw141

Weststrate, N. M., & Glück, J. (2017). Hard-earned wisdom: Exploratory processing of difficult life experience is positively associated with wisdom. *Developmental Psychology, 53*(4), 800–814. https://doi.org/10.1037/dev0000286

Wettstein, M., & Wahl, H.-W. (2016). Hearing. In S. K. Whitbourne (Ed.), *The encyclopedia of adulthood and aging* (pp. 1–5). John Wiley & Sons, Inc. https://doi.org/10.1002/9781118521373.wbeaa202

White, J., Greene, G., Kivimaki, M., & Batty, G. D. (2018). Association between changes in lifestyle and all-cause mortality: The Health and Lifestyle Survey. *Journal of Epidemiology and Community Health, 72*, 711–714. https://doi.org/10.1136/jech-2017-210363

Windle, G., Hughes, D., Linck, P., Russell, I., & Woods, B. (2010). Is exercise effective in promoting mental well-being in older age? A systematic review. *Aging & Mental Health, 14*(6), 652–669. https://doi.org/10.1080/13607861003713232

Wiseman, F. K., Al-Janabi, T., Hardy, J., Karmiloff-Smith, A., Nizetic, D., Tybulewicz, V. L. J., Fisher, E. M. C., & Strydom, A. (2015). A genetic cause of Alzheimer disease: Mechanistic insights from Down syndrome. *Nature Reviews Neuroscience, 16*(9), 564–574. https://doi.org/10.1038/nrn3983

Witte, A. V., Kerti, L., Hermannstädter, H. M., Fiebach, J. B., Schreiber, S. J., Schuchardt, J. P., Hahn, A., & Flöel, A. (2014). Long-chain omega-3 fatty acids improve brain function and structure in older adults. *Cerebral Cortex, 24*(11), 3059–3068. https://doi.org/10.1093/cercor/bht163

Wong, B. I., Lecompte, M., & Yang, L. (2021). The age-related associative deficit simulated by relational divided attention: Encoding strategy and recollection. *Memory, 29*(3), 406–415. https://doi.org/10.1080/09658211.2021.1898645

Woodside, J. V., McGrath, A. J., Lyner, N., & McKinley, M. C. (2015). Carotenoids and health in older people. *Maturitas, 80*(1), 63–68. https://doi.org/10.1016/j.maturitas.2014.10.012

World health Organization. (2012). *Dementia: A public health priority.* http://www.alzheimer.ca/en/sk/Get-involved/Raise-your-voice/~/media/WHO_ADI_dementia_report_final.ashx

World Health Organization. (n.d). *Dementia.* https://www.who.int/news-room/fact-sheets/detail/dementia

Wright, N. C., Saag, K. G., Dawson-Hughes, B., Khosla, S., & Siris, E. S. (2017). The impact of the new National Bone Health Alliance (NBHA) diagnostic criteria on the prevalence of osteoporosis in the USA. *Osteoporosis International, 28*(4), 1225–1232. https://doi.org/10.1007/s00198-016-3865-3

Xu, J. (2016). Mortality among centenarians in the United States, 2000-2014. *NCHS Data Brief, 233*(233), 1–8. http://www.ncbi.nlm.nih.gov/pubmed/26828422

Xu, W., Yu, J.-T., Tan, M.-S., & Tan, L. (2015). Cognitive reserve and Alzheimer's disease. *Molecular Neurobiology, 51*(1), 187–208. https://doi.org/10.1007/s12035-014-8720-y

Yorgason, J. B., Draper, T. W., Bronson, H., Nielson, M., Babcock, K., Jones, K., Hill, M. S., & Howard, M. (2018). Biological, psychological, and social predictors of longevity among utah centenarians. *The International Journal of Aging and Human Development, 87*, 225–243. https://doi.org/10.1177/0091415018757211

Zacher, H., & Staudinger, U. M. (2018). Wisdom and well-being. In E. Diener, S. Oishi, & L. Tay (Eds.), *Handbook of well-being.* DEF publishers.

Zanto, T. P., & Gazzaley, A. (2019). Aging of the frontal lobe. In M. D'Esposito & J. H. Grafman (Eds.), *Handbook of clinical neurology* (Vol. 163, pp. 369–389). Elsevier B.V. https://doi.org/10.1016/B978-0-12-804281-6.00020-3

Zhang, W., Song, M., Qu, J., & Liu, G. H. (2018). Epigenetic modifications in cardiovascular aging and diseases. *Circulation Research, 123*(7), 773–786. https://doi.org/10.1161/CIRCRESAHA.118.312497

CHAPTER 16

Abu-Raiya, H., Pargament, K. I., Krause, N., & Ironson, G. (2015). Robust links between religious/spiritual struggles, psychological distress, and well-being in a national sample of American adults. *American Journal of Orthopsychiatry, 85*(6), 565–575. https://doi.org/10.1037/ort0000084

Adams, G. A., Prescher, J., Beehr, T. A., & Lepisto, L. (2002). Applying work-role attachment theory to retirement decision-making. *International Journal of Aging & Human Development, 54*(2), 125–137. https://doi.org/10.2190/JRUQ-XQ2N-UP0A-M432

Adams, K. B., Leibbrandt, S., & Moon, H. (2011). A critical review of the literature on social and leisure activity and wellbeing in later life. *Ageing & Society, 31*(4), 683–712. https://doi.org/10.1017/s0144686x10001091

Adams, R. G. (2017). Friendship during the later Years. In C. L. Shehan (Ed.), *The blackwell encyclopedia of sociology* (pp. 1–2). John Wiley & Sons, Ltd. https://doi.org/10.1002/9781405165518.wbeosf069.pub2

Adams, R. G., Blieszner, R., & De Vries, B. (2000). Definitions of friendship in the third age: Age, gender, and study location effects. *Journal of Aging Studies*, *14*(1), 117.

Adams, R. G., & Taylor, E. M. (2015). Friendship and happiness in the third age. In M. Demir (Ed.), *Friendship and happiness* (pp. 155–169). Springer Netherlands. https://doi.org/10.1007/978-94-017-9603-3_9

Agrigoroaei, S., Lee-Attardo, A., & Lachman, M. E. (2017). Stress and subjective age: Those with greater financial stress look older. *Research on Aging*, *39*(10), 1075–1099. https://doi.org/10.1177/0164027516658502

American Association of Retired Persons. (2002). *The grandparent study:2002 report*. Author.

American Association of Retired Persons. (2008). *Update on the aged 55+ worker: 2007*. Author.

Anderberg, P., & Berglund, A.-L. (2010). Elderly persons' experiences of striving to receive care on their own terms in nursing homes. *International Journal of Nursing Practice*, *16*(1), 64–68. https://doi.org/10.1111/j.1440-172X.2009.01808.x

Andonian, L., & MacRae, A. (2011). Well older adults within an urban context: Strategies to create and maintain social participation. *The British Journal of Occupational Therapy*, *74*(1), 2–11. https://doi.org/10.4276/030802211X12947686093486

Atchley, R. C. (1989). A Continuity theory of normal aging. *The Gerontologist*, *29*(2), 183–190. https://doi.org/10.1093/geront/29.2.183

Atchley, R. C. (2016). Aging, religion, and spirituality. In C. L. Shehan (Ed.), *The blackwell encyclopedia of sociology* (pp. 1–3). John Wiley & Sons, Ltd. https://doi.org/10.1002/9781405165518.wbeoss220.pub2

Ball, M. M., Whittington, F. J., Perkins, M. M., Patterson, V. L., Hollingworth, C., King, S. V., & Combs, B. L. (2000). Quality of life in assisted living facilities: Viewpoints of residents. *Journal of Applied Gerontology*, *19*(3), 304–325.

Barbosa, L. M., Monteiro, B., & Murta, S. G. (2016). Retirement adjustment predictors—A systematic review. *Work, Aging and Retirement*, *2*(2), 262–280.

Barer, B. M. (2001). The "grands and greats" of very old black grandmothers. *Journal of Aging Studies*, *15*(1), 1.

Barrett, A. E., & Gumber, C. (2020). Feeling old, body and soul: The effect of aging body reminders on age identity. *Journals of Gerontology - Series B Psychological Sciences and Social Sciences*, *75*(3), 625–629. https://doi.org/10.1093/geronb/gby085

Bauer, M., Haesler, E., & Fetherstonhaugh, D. (2016). Let's talk about sex: Older people's views on the recognition of sexuality and sexual health in the health-care setting. *Health Expectations*, *19*(6), 1237–1250. https://doi.org/10.1111/hex.12418

Bell, S., Reissing, E. D., Henry, L. A., & VanZuylen, H. (2017). Sexual activity after 60: A systematic review of associated factors. *Sexual Medicine Reviews*, *5*(1), 52–80. https://doi.org/10.1016/j.sxmr.2016.03.001

Bell, T., Hill, N., & Stavrinos, D. (2020). Personality determinants of subjective executive function in older adults. *Aging and Mental Health*, *24*(11), 1935–1944. https://doi.org/10.1080/13607863.2019.1667300

Bender, A., Jox, R. J., Grill, E., Straube, A., & Lulé, D. (2015). Persistent vegetative state and minimally conscious state: A systematic review and meta-analysis of diagnostic procedures. *Deutsches Ärzteblatt International*, *112*(14), 235–242. https://doi.org/10.3238/arztebl.2015.0235

Bengtson, V. L., & DeLiema, M. (2016). Theories of aging and social gerontology: Explaining how social factors influence well-being in later life. In M. H. Meyer & E. A. Daniele (Eds.), *Gerontology: Changes, challenges, and solutions [2 volumes]: Changes, challenges, and solutions* (pp. 25–56). ABC-CLIO.

Bengtson, V. L., Silverstein, M., Putney, N. M., & Harris, S. C. (2015). Does religiousness increase with age? Age changes and generational differences over 35 years. *Journal for the Scientific Study of Religion*, *54*(2), 363–379. https://doi.org/10.1111/jssr.12183

Bergland, A., Nicolaisen, M., & Thorsen, K. (2014). Predictors of subjective age in people aged 40-79 years: A five-year follow-up study. The impact of mastery, mental and physical health. *Aging & Mental Health*, *18*(5), 653–661. https://doi.org/10.1080/13607863.2013.869545

Blanner, C., Mejldal, A., Prina, A. M., Munk-Jørgensen, P., Ersbøll, A. K., & Andersen, K. (2020). Widowhood and mortality: A Danish nationwide register-based cohort study. *Epidemiology and Psychiatric Sciences*, *29*, e149. https://doi.org/10.1017/S2045796020000591

Blanner Kristiansen, C., Kjær, J. N., Hjorth, P., Andersen, K., & Prina, A. M. (2019). Prevalence of common mental disorders in widowhood: A systematic review and meta-analysis. In *Journal of affective disorders* (Vol. 245, pp. 1016–1023). Elsevier B.V. https://doi.org/10.1016/j.jad.2018.11.088

Blieszner, R., & Ogletree, A. M. (2017). We get by with a little help from our friends: Aging together in tandem, and meeting the challenges of older age. *Generations*, *41*(2), 55–62.

Blieszner, R., Ogletree, A. M., & Adams, R. G. (2019). Friendship in later life: A research agenda. *Innovation in Aging*, *3*(1), 1–18. https://doi.org/10.1093/geroni/igz005

Böckerman, P., Ilmakunnas, P., Böckerman, P., & Ilmakunnas, P. (2017). Do good working conditions make you work longer? Evidence on retirement decisions using linked survey and register data. *IZA Discussion Papers, No. 10964*, *10964*. https://econpapers.repec.org/paper/izaizadps/dp10964.htm

Bogg, T., & Roberts, B. W. (2013). The case for conscientiousness: Evidence and implications for a personality trait marker of health and longevity. *Annals of Behavioral Medicine : A Publication of the Society of Behavioral Medicine*, *45*(3), 278–288. https://doi.org/10.1007/s12160-012-9454-6

Bordia, P., Read, S., & Bordia, S. (2020). Retiring: Role identity processes in retirement transition. *Journal of Organizational Behavior*, *41*(5), 445–460. https://doi.org/10.1002/job.2438

Breheny, M., & Griffiths, Z. (2017). "I had a good time when I was young": Interpreting descriptions of continuity among older people. *Journal of Aging Studies*, *41*, 36–43. https://doi.org/10.1016/J.JAGING.2017.03.003

Brennan-Ing, M., Kaufman, J. E., Larson, B., Gamarel, K. E., Seidel, L., & Karpiak, S. E. (2021). Sexual health among Lesbian, Gay, Bisexual, and Heterosexual older adults: An exploratory analysis. *Clinical Gerontologist*, *44*(3), 222–234. https://doi.org/10.1080/07317115.2020.1846103

Brison, K. J. (1995). You will never forget: Narrative, bereavement, and worldview among Kwanga women. *Ethos*, *23*(4), 474–488. https://doi.org/10.1525/eth.1995.23.4.02a00060

Brisson, C. D., Hsieh, Y.-T., Kim, D., Jin, A. Y., & Andrew, R. D. (2014). Brainstem neurons survive the identical ischemic stress that kills higher neurons: Insight to the persistent vegetative state. *PloS One*, *9*(5), e96585. https://doi.org/10.1371/journal.pone.0096585

Brown, S. L., Bulanda, J. R., & Lee, G. R. (2012). Transitions into and out of cohabitation in later life. *Journal of Marriage and the Family*, *74*(4), 774–793. https://doi.org/10.1111/j.1741-3737.2012.00994.x

Brown, S. L., & Kawamura, S. (2010). Relationship quality among cohabitors and marrieds in older adulthood. *Social Science Research*, *39*(5), 777–786. https://doi.org/10.1016/j.ssresearch.2010.04.010

Brown, S. L., & Wright, M. R. (2016). Older adults' attitudes toward cohabitation: Two decades of change. *The Journals of Gerontology Series B: Psychological Sciences and Social Sciences*, *71*(4), 755–764. https://doi.org/10.1093/geronb/gbv053

Brown, S. L., & Wright, M. R. (2017). Marriage, cohabitation, and divorce in later life. *Innovation in Aging*, *1*(2), igx015. https://doi.org/10.1093/geroni/igx015

Buglass, E. (2010). Grief and bereavement theories. *Nursing Standard*, *24*(41), 44–47. http://cat.inist.fr/?aModele=afficheN&cpsidt=22958713

Bureau of the Census. (2017). *Age and sex of all people, family members and unrelated individuals iterated by income-to-poverty ratio and race*. Current Population Survey - Poverty Status: POV-34. https://www.census.gov/data/tables/time-series/demo/income-poverty/cps-pov/pov-34.html

Butler, R. N. (1963). The Life review: An interpretation of reminiscence in the aged. *Psychiatry: Interpersonal and Biological Processes*, *26*(1), 65–76. http://www.tandfonline.com/doi/abs/10.1521/00332747.1963.11023339? journalCode=upsy20

Butler, S. S., & Eckart, D. (2007). Civic engagement among older adults in a rural community: A case study of the senior companion program. *Journal of Community Practice*, *15*(3), 77.

Caldwell, J. T., Lee, H., & Cagney, K. A. (2019). Disablement in context: Neighborhood characteristics and their association with frailty onset among older adults. *The Journals of Gerontology: Series B*, *74*(7), e40–e49. https://doi.org/10.1093/geronb/gbx123

Calvo, E., Haverstick, K., & Sass, S. A. (2009). Gradual retirement, sense of control, and retirees' happiness. *Research on Aging*, *31*(1), 112–135.

Candy, B., Holman, A., Leurent, B., Davis, S., & Jones, L. (2011). Hospice care delivered at home, in nursing homes and in dedicated hospice facilities: A systematic review of quantitative and qualitative evidence. *International Journal of Nursing Studies*, *48*(1), 121–133. https://doi.org/10.1016/j.ijnurstu.2010.08.003

Carstensen, L. L., & Mikels, J. A. (2005). At the intersection of emotion and cognition. Aging and the positivity effect. *Current Directions in Psychological Science*, *14*(3), 117–121. https://doi.org/10.1111/j.0963-7214.2005.00348.x

Carstensen, L. L., Turan, B., Scheibe, S., Ram, N., Ersner-Hershfield, H., Samanez-Larkin, G. R., Brooks, K. P., & Nesselroade, J. R. (2011). Emotional experience improves with age: Evidence based on over 10 years of experience sampling. *Psychology and Aging*, *26*(1), 21–33. https://doi.org/10.1037/a0021285

Chappell, N., Gee, E., McDonald, L., & Stones, M. (2003). *Aging in contemporary Canada. Pearson education canada*. Pearson.

Chasteen, A. L., & Madey, S. F. (2003). Belief in a just world and the perceived injustice of dying young or old. *OMEGA -Journal of Death and Dying*, *47*(4), 313–326. https://doi.org/10.2190/W7H7-TE9E-1FWN-B8XD

Cherry, K. E., Walker, E. J., Brown, J. S., Volaufova, J., LaMotte, L. R., Welsh, D. A., Su, L. J., Jazwinski, S. M., Ellis, R., Wood, R. H., & Frisard, M. I. (2013). Social engagement and health in younger, older, and oldest-old adults in the Louisiana healthy aging study. *Journal of Applied Gerontology: The Official Journal of the Southern Gerontological Society*, *32*(1), 51–75. https://doi.org/10.1177/0733464811409034

Choi, Y. J., & Matz-Costa, C. (2017). Perceived neighborhood safety, social cohesion, and psychological health of older adults. *The Gerontologist*, *58*(1), gnw187. https://doi.org/10.1093/geront/gnw187

Clarke, P., Morenoff, J., Debbink, M., Golberstein, E., Elliott, M. R., & Lantz, P. M. (2014). Cumulative exposure to neighborhood context: Consequences for health transitions over the adult life course. *Research on Aging*, *36*(1), 115–142. https://doi.org/10.1177/0164027512470702

Coelho, A., de Brito, M., & Barbosa, A. (2018). Caregiver anticipatory grief. *Current Opinion in Supportive and Palliative Care*, *12*, 52–57. https://doi.org/10.1097/SPC.0000000000000321

Cohen, R. (1967). *The Kanuri of Bornu*. Holt, Rinehart and Winston.

Cohen-Mansfield, J., Skornick-Bouchbinder, M., & Brill, S. (2017). Trajectories of end of life: A systematic review. *The Journals of Gerontology: Series B*, *27*, 998. https://doi.org/10.1093/geronb/gbx093

Cohn, D., & Passel, J. S. (2018). *Record 64 million Americans live in multigenerational households . Pew Research Center*. Retrieved from http://www.pewresearch.org/fact-tank/2018/04/05/a-record-64-million-americans-live-in-multigenerational-households

Cohn, D., & Passel, J. S. (2018). *Record 64 million Americans live in multigenerational households | Pew research center*. Fact Tank - Pew Research Center. http://www.pewresearch.org/fact-tank/2018/04/05/a-record-64-million-americans-live-in-multigenerational-households/

Coleman, M., & Ganong, L. (2008). Normative beliefs about sharing housing with an older family member. *International Journal of Aging & Human Development*, *66*(1), 49–72. http://www.ncbi.nlm.nih.gov/pubmed/18429483

Connor, S. R. (2018). *Hospice and palliative care*. Taylor and Francis.

Corr, C. A. (2019). The 'five stages' in coping with dying and bereavement: Strengths, weaknesses and some alternatives. *Mortality*, *24*, 405–417. https://doi.org/10.1080/13576275.2018.1527826

Corr, C. A. (2021). Should We Incorporate the Work of Elisabeth Kübler-Ross in Our Current Teaching and Practice and, If So, How? *Omega*, *83*, 706–728. https://doi.org/10.1177/0030222819865397

Corr, C. A., & Corr, D. M. (2013). Culture, socialization, and dying. In D. K.. Meagher, D. E. Balk, & D. Klass (Eds.), *Handbook of thanatology* (2 ed., Issue 11282, pp. 31–36). Routledge. https://doi.org/10.4324/9780203767306-10

Corr, C. A., Corr, D. M., & Doka, K. J. (2019). *Death and dying, life and living* (8th ed.). Cengage.

Cosby, R. (2020). Older African American adults: Understanding the role of the Black church's support in the community. *Journal of Religion and Spirituality in Social Work*, *39*(4), 353–371. https://doi.org/10.1080/15426432.2020.1780183

Counts, D. A., & Counts, D. R. (1985). I'm not dead yet? Aging and death: Processes and experiences in Kalia. In D. A. Counts & D. R. Counts (Eds.), *Aging and its transformations* (pp. 131–156). University of America Press.

Cox, K. S., Wilt, J., Olson, B., & McAdams, D. P. (2010). Generativity, the big five, and psychosocial adaptation in midlife adults. *Journal of Personality*, *78*(4), 1185–1208. https://doi.org/10.1111/j.1467-6494.2010.00647.x

Cranford, R. (2004). Diagnosing the permanent vegetative state. *AMA Journal of Ethics*, *6*(8), 350–352.

Curlin, F. A., Nwodim, C., Vance, J. L., Chin, M. H., & Lantos, J. D. (2008). To die, to sleep: US physicians' religious and other objections to physician-assisted suicide, terminal sedation, and withdrawal of life support. *The American Journal of Hospice & Palliative Care*, *25*(2), 112–120. https://doi.org/10.1177/1049909107310141

Damman, M., Henkens, K., & Kalmijn, M. (2015). Missing work after retirement: The role of life histories in the retirement adjustment process. *The Gerontologist*, *55*(5), 802–813. https://doi.org/10.1093/geront/gnt169

Dandy, K., & Bollman, R. D. (2008). *Seniors in rural Canada. Rural and Small Town Canada Analysis Bulletin*, *7*(8). http://globalag.igc.org/ruralaging/world/2008/ruralcanada.pdf

Darbonne, A., Uchino, B. N., & Ong, A. D. (2012). What mediates links between age and well-being? A Test of social support and interpersonal conflict as potential interpersonal pathways. *Journal of Happiness Studies*, *14*(3), 951–963. https://doi.org/10.1007/s10902-012-9363-1

Davies, E. M. M., Van der Heijden, B. I. J. M., & Flynn, M. (2017). Job satisfaction, retirement attitude and intended retirement age: A conditional process analysis across workers' level of household income. *Frontiers in Psychology*, *8*, 891. https://doi.org/10.3389/fpsyg.2017.00891

De Stefano, R., Muscatello, M. R. A., Bruno, A., Cedro, C., Mento, C., Zoccali, R. A., & Pandolfo, G. (2020). Complicated grief: A systematic review of the last 20 years. *International Journal of Social Psychiatry*, *67*(5), 492–499. https://doi.org/10.1177/0020764020960202

De Vaus, D., Wells, Y., Kendig, H., & Quine, S. (2007). Does gradual retirement have better outcomes than abrupt retirement? Results from an Australian panel study. *Ageing & Society*, *27*(5), 667–682.

Debrot, A., Meuwly, N., Muise, A., Impett, E. A., & Schoebi, D. (2017). More than just sex. *Personality and Social Psychology Bulletin*, *43*(3), 287–299. https://doi.org/10.1177/0146167216684124

DeLamater, J. (2012). Sexual expression in later life: A review and synthesis. *Journal of Sex Research*, *49*(2/3), 125–141. https://doi.org/10.1080/00224499.2011.603168

DeLamater, J., & Koepsel, E. (2015). Relationships and sexual expression in later life: A biopsychosocial perspective. *Sexual and Relationship Therapy*, *30*(1), 37–59. https://doi.org/10.1080/14681994.2014.939506

DeLiema, M., & Bengtson, V. L. (2017). Activity theory, disengagement theory, and successful aging. In N. A. Pachana (Ed.), *Encyclopedia of geropsychology* (pp. 15–20). Springer Singapore. https://doi.org/10.1007/978-981-287-082-7_102

DeNavas-Walt, C., & Proctor, B. D. (2014). *Income and poverty in the United States: 2013*. http://www.census.gov/hhes/www/poverty/data/incpovhlth/2013/

Dennis, D. (2008). *Living, dying, grieving*. Jones & Bartlett.

DeZutter, J., Toussaint, L., & Leijssen, M. (2014). Forgiveness, ego-integrity, and depressive symptoms in community-dwelling and residential elderly adults. *Journals of gerontology Series B: Psychological Sciences and Social Sciences*, *71*, 786–797. https://doi.org/10.1093/geronb/gbu146

Doskoch, P. (2011). Many men 75 and older consider sex important and remain sexually active. *Perspectives on Sexual and Reproductive Health*, *43*(1), 67–68. https://doi.org/10.1363/4306711

Dunbar, R. I. M. (2018). The anatomy of friendship. *Trends in Cognitive Sciences*, *22*, 32–51. https://doi.org/10.1016/j.tics.2017.10.004

Dykstra, P. A., & Fokkema, T. (2010). Relationships between parents and their adult children: A West European typology of late-life families. *Ageing and Society*, *31*(04), 37–59. https://doi.org/10.1017/S0144686X10001108

Egeland, M., Zunszain, P. A., & Pariante, C. M. (2015). Molecular mechanisms in the regulation of adult neurogenesis during stress. *Nature Reviews Neuroscience*, *16*(4), 189–200. https://doi.org/10.1038/nrn3855

Eisma, M. C., Tamminga, A., Smid, G. E., & Boelen, P. A. (2021). Acute grief after deaths due to COVID-19, natural causes and unnatural causes: An empirical comparison. *Journal of affective disorders*, *278*, 54–56. https://doi.org/10.1016/j.jad.2020.09.049

Elliott O'dare, C., Timonen, V., & Conlon, C. (2019). Forum Article Intergenerational friendships of older adults: Why do we know so little about them? *Ageing & Society*, *39*(1), 1–16.

Elwert, F., & Christakis, N. A. (2008). The effect of widowhood on mortality by the causes of death of both spouses. *American Journal of Public Health*, *98*(11), 2092–2098.

English, T., & Carstensen, L. L. (2014). Selective narrowing of social networks across adulthood is associated with improved emotional experience in daily life. *International Journal of Behavioral Development*, *38*(2), 195–202. https://doi.org/10.1177/0165025413515404

English, T., & Carstensen, L. L. (2016). Socioemotional selectivity theory. In N. A. Pachana (Ed.), *Encyclopedia of geropsychology* (pp. 1–6). Springer Publishing Company. https://doi.org/10.1007/978-981-287-080-3_110-1

Ennis, J., & Majid, U. (2020). The Widowhood effect: Explaining the adverse outcomes after spousal loss using physiological stress theories, marital quality, and attachment. *Family Journal*, *28*(3), 241–246. https://doi.org/10.1177/1066480720929360

Ennis, J., & Majid, U. (2021). "Death from a broken heart": A systematic review of the relationship between spousal bereavement and physical and physiological health outcomes.. *Death Studies*, *45*, 538–551. https://doi.org/10.1080/07481187.2019.1661884

Erikson, E. H.. (1950). (2nd ed.). New York: Norton.

Erikson, E. H. (1959). *Identity and the Life Cycle* (Vol. 1). New York: Norton.

Esposito, M., Sylvers, D., Clarke, P., Finlay, J., Jang, J. B., & Tang, S. (2020). Black-White inequities in perception of access to neighborhood resources among older adults. *Innovation in Aging*, *4*(Suppl. 1), 704–704. https://doi.org/10.1093/geroni/igaa057.2472

Fagundes, C. P., Murdock, K. W., LeRoy, A., Baameur, F., Thayer, J. F., & Heijnen, C. (2018). Spousal bereavement is associated with more pronounced ex vivo cytokine production and lower heart rate variability: Mechanisms underlying cardiovascular risk? *Psychoneuroendocrinology*, *93*, 65–71. https://doi.org/10.1016/j.psyneuen.2018.04.010

Fagundes, C. P., & Wu, E. L. (2020). Matters of the heart: Grief, morbidity, and mortality. *Current Directions in Psychological Science*, *29*(3), 235–241. https://doi.org/10.1177/0963721420917698

Fehr, R. (2012). Is retirement always stressful? The potential impact of creativity. *American Psychologist*, *67*(1), 76–77. https://doi.org/10.1037/a0026574

Feldman, D. C., & Beehr, T. A. (2011). A three-phase model of retirement decision making. *The American Psychologist*, *66*(3), 193–203. https://doi.org/10.1037/a0022153

Fernández Lorca, M. B., & Valenzuela, E. (2021 in press). Religiosity and subjective wellbeing of the elderly in Chile: A mediation analysis. *Journal of Religion, Spirituality and Aging*. https://doi.org/10.1080/15528030.2020.1839624

Field, N. P., Gal-Oz, E., & Bonanno, G. A. (2003). Continuing bonds and adjustment at 5 years after the death of a spouse. *Journal of Consulting and Clinical Psychology*, *71*(1), 110–117. https://doi.org/10.1037/0022-006x.71.1.110

Fields, N. L., & Dabelko-Schoeny, H. (2016). Aging in place. In S. K. Whitbourne (Ed.), *The encyclopedia of adulthood and aging* (pp. 1–5). John Wiley & Sons, Inc. https://doi.org/10.1002/9781118521373.wbeaa106

Fingerman, K. L., & Charles, S. T. (2010). It takes two to Tango: Why older people have the best relationships. *Current Directions in Psychological Science (Sage Publications Inc.)*, *19*(3), 172–176. https://doi.org/10.1177/0963721410370297

Fleischmann, M., Xue, B., & Head, J. (2020). Mental health before and after retirement - assessing the relevance of psychosocial working conditions: The whitehall II prospective study of British Civil servants. *Journals of Gerontology - Series B Psychological Sciences and Social Sciences*, *75*(2), 403–413. https://doi.org/10.1093/geronb/gbz042

Fonda, S. J., Clipp, E. C., & Maddox, G. L. (2002). Patterns in functioning among residents of an affordable assisted living housing facility. *Gerontologist*, *42*(2), 178.

Freak-Poli, R., Kirkman, M., De Castro Lima, G., Direk, N., Franco, O. H., & Tiemeier, H. (2017). Sexual activity and physical tenderness in older adults: Cross-sectional prevalence and associated characteristics. *The Journal of Sexual Medicine*, *14*(7), 918–927. https://doi.org/10.1016/j.jsxm.2017.05.010

Freedman, V. A., & Spillman, B. C. (2014). The residential continuum from home to nursing home: Size, characteristics and unmet needs of older adults. *The Journals of Gerontology. Series B, Psychological Sciences and Social Sciences*, *69*(7), S42–S50. https://doi.org/10.1093/geronb/gbu120

Freund, A. M., & Smith, J. (1999). Methodological comment: Temporal stability of older person's spontaneous self-definition. *Experimental Aging Research*, *25*(1), 95.

Fry, R. (2019). *Baby Boomers are in the workforce later in life than past generations*. https://www.pewresearch.org/fact-tank/2019/07/24/baby-boomers-us-labor-force/

Galek, K., Flannelly, K. J., Ellison, C. G., Silton, N. R., & Jankowski, K. R. B. (2015). Religion, meaning and purpose, and mental health. *Psychology of Religion and Spirituality*, *7*(1), 1–12. https://doi.org/10.1037/a0037887

Gall, T. L., Evans, D. R., & Howard, J. (1997). The retirement adjustment process: Changes in the well-being of male retirees across time. *The Journals of Gerontology: Series B: Psychological Sciences and Social Sciences*, *52*(3), 110–P117. https://doi.org/10.1093/geronb/52B.3.P110

Gamertsfelder, E. M., Seaman, J. B., Tate, J., Buddadhumaruk, P., & Happ, M. B. (2016). Prevalence of advance directives among older adults admitted to intensive care units and requiring mechanical ventilation. *Journal of Gerontological Nursing*, *42*(4), 34–41. https://doi.org/10.3928/00989134-20151124-02

Geurts, T., Van Tilburg, T. G., & Poortman, A.-R. (2012). The grandparent-grandchild relationship in childhood and adulthood: A matter of continuation? *Personal Relationships*, *19*(2), 267–278. https://doi.org/10.1111/j.1475-6811.2011.01354.x

Gillespie, B. J., Lever, J., Frederick, D., & Royce, T. (2015). Close adult friendships, gender, and the life cycle. *Journal of Social and Personal Relationships*, *32*(6), 709–736. https://doi.org/10.1177/0265407514546977

Gilligan, M., Karraker, A., & Jasper, A. (2018). Linked lives and cumulative inequality: A multigenerational family life course framework. *Journal of Family Theory & Review*, *10*(1), 111–125. https://doi.org/10.1111/jftr.12244

Glass, T. A., Mendes De Leon, C. F., Bassuk, S. S., & Berkman, L. F. (2006). Social engagement and depressive symptoms in late life. *Journal of Aging & Health*, *16*(4), 604–628.

Goldsen, J., Bryan, A. E. B., Kim, H.-J., Muraco, A., Jen, S., & Fredriksen-Goldsen, K. I. (2017). Who says I do: The changing context of marriage and health and quality of life for LGBT older adults. *The Gerontologist*, *57*(Suppl. 1), S50–S62. https://doi.org/10.1093/geront/gnw174

Gonzales, E., Lee, Y., Padula, W. V., & Jung, L. S. (2018). Exploring the consequences of discrimination and health for retirement by race and ethnicity: Results from the health and retirement study. *CRR WP 2018-6*. https://doi.org/10.2139/ssrn.3240735

Gopinath, B., Liew, G., Burlutsky, G., McMahon, C. M., & Mitchell, P. (2017). Visual and hearing impairment and retirement in older adults: A population-based cohort study. *Maturitas*, *100*, 77–81. https://doi.org/10.1016/j.maturitas.2017.03.318

Graham, E. K., James, B. D., Jackson, K. L., Willroth, E. C., Boyle, P., Wilson, R., Bennett, D. A., & Mroczek, D. K. (2021). Associations between personality traits and cognitive resilience in older adults. *Journals of Gerontology - Series B Psychological Sciences and Social Sciences*, *76*(1), 6–19. https://doi.org/10.1093/GERONB/GBAA135

Graham, E. K., & Lachman, M. E. (2012). Personality stability is associated with better cognitive performance in adulthood: Are the stable more able? *The Journals of Gerontology. Series B, Psychological Sciences and Social Sciences*, *67*(5), 545–554. https://doi.org/10.1093/geronb/gbr149

Grosse, C., & Grosse, A. (2015). Assisted suicide: Models of legal regulation in selected European countries and the case law of the European court of human rights. *Medicine, Science, and the Law*, *55*(4), 246–258. https://doi.org/10.1177/0025802414540636

Grotz, C., Matharan, F., Amieva, H., Pérès, K., Laberon, S., Vonthron, A.-M., Dartigues, J.-F., Adam, S., & Letenneur, L. (2017). Psychological transition and adjustment processes related to retirement: Influence on cognitive functioning. *Aging & Mental Health*, *21*, 1310–1316. https://doi.org/10.1080/13607863.2016.1220920

Grundy, E., & Henretta, J. C. (2006). Between elderly parents and adult children: A new look at the intergenerational care provided by the "Sandwich Generation.". *Ageing & Society*, *26*(5), 707–722. http://eprints.lse.ac.uk/53680/

Guo, Q., & Jacelon, C. S. (2014). An integrative review of dignity in end-of-life care. *Palliative Medicine*, *28*(7), 931–940. https://doi.org/10.1177/0269216314528399

Gurrentz, B., & Mayol-Garcia, Y. (2021, April 22). *Love and loss among older adults*. https://www.census.gov/library/stories/2021/04/love-and-loss-among-older-adults.html

Hagestad, G. O. (2018). Interdependent lives and relationships in changing times: A life-course view of families and aging. In R. Settersten (Ed.), *Lives in time and place and invitation to the life course* (pp. 135–159). Routledge. https://doi.org/10.4324/9781315224206-6

Hao, Y. (2008). Productive activities and psychological well-being among older adults. *Journals of Gerontology: Series B: Psychological Sciences and Social Sciences*, *63*(2), S64–s72.

Harvard Medical School ad Hoc Committee. (1968). A definition of irreversible Coma. *JAMA*, *205*(6), 337. https://doi.org/10.1001/jama.1968.03140320031009

Hatch, L. R., & Bulcroft, K. (2004). Does long-term marriage bring less frequent disagreements? Five explanatory frameworks. *Journal of Family Issues*, *25*(4), 465–495. 10.1177/0192513X03257766

Hayward, R. D., & Krause, N. (2013). Changes in church-based social support relationships during older adulthood. *The Journals of Gerontology. Series B, Psychological Sciences and Social Sciences*, *68*(1), 85–96. https://doi.org/10.1093/geronb/gbs100

Hearn, S., Saulnier, G., Strayer, J., Glenham, M., Koopman, R., & Marcia, J. E. (2011). Between integrity and despair: Toward construct validation of Erikson's eighth stage. *Journal of Adult Development*, *19*, 1–20. https://doi.org/10.1007/s10804-011-9126-y

Heckhausen, J., & Brim, O. G. (1997). Perceived problems for self and others: Self-protection by social downgrading throughout adulthood. *Psychology and Aging*, *12*(4), 610–619. http://www.ncbi.nlm.nih.gov/pubmed/9416630

Henning, G., Hansson, I., Berg, A. I., Lindwall, M., & Johansson, B. (2017). The role of personality for subjective well-being in the retirement transition – Comparing variable- and person-oriented models. *Personality and Individual Differences*, *116*, 385–392. https://doi.org/10.1016/j.paid.2017.05.017

Henning, G., Stenling, A., Bielak, A. A. M., Bjälkebring, P., Gow, A. J., Kivi, M., Muniz-Terrera, G., Johansson, B., & Lindwall, M. (2021). Towards an active and happy retirement? Changes in leisure activity and depressive symptoms during the retirement transition. *Aging and Mental Health*, *25*(4), 621–631. https://doi.org/10.1080/13607863.2019.1709156

Henry, N. J. M., Berg, C. A., Smith, T. W., & Florsheim, P. (2007). Positive and negative characteristics of marital interaction and their association with marital satisfaction in middle-aged and older couples. *Psychology and Aging*, *22*(3), 428–441.

Heybroek, L., Haynes, M., & Baxter, J. (2015). Life satisfaction and retirement in Australia: A longitudinal approach. *Work, Aging and Retirement*, *1*(2), 166–180. https://doi.org/10.1093/workar/wav006

Holden, C. A., Collins, V. R., Handelsman, D. J., Jolley, D., & Pitts, M. (2014). Healthy aging in a cross-sectional study of Australian men: What has sex got to do with it? *The Aging Male : The Official Journal of the International Society for the Study of the Aging Male*, *17*(1), 25–29. https://doi.org/10.3109/13685538.2013.843167

Homan, K. J., & Boyatzis, C. J. (2010). Religiosity, sense of meaning, and health behavior in older adults. *International Journal for the Psychology of Religion*, *20*(3), 173–186. https://doi.org/10.1080/10508619.2010.481225

Horowitz, M. M. (1967). *Morne- paysan: Peasant village in martinique*. Holt, Rinehart and Winston.

Houghton, K. (2021). *Getting a prescription to die remains tricky across the U.S. | time*. Time. https://time.com/5950396/aid-in-dying-2021/

Howe, C., Matthews, L. R., & Heard, R. (2010). Work to retirement: A snapshot of psychological health in a multicultural Australia population. *Work: Journal of Prevention, Assessment & Rehabilitation*, *36*(2), 119–127.

Hughes, M. L., Geraci, L., & De Forrest, R. L. (2013). Aging 5 years in 5 minutes: The effect of taking a memory test on older adults' subjective age. *Psychological Science*, *24*(12), 2481–2488. https://doi.org/10.1177/0956797613494853

Hughes, M. L., & Touron, D. R. (2021). Aging in context: Incorporating everyday experiences into the study of subjective age. *Frontiers in Psychiatry*, *12*, 633234. https://doi.org/10.3389/fpsyt.2021.633234

Huo, M., Kim, K., Zarit, S. H., & Fingerman, K. L. (2018). Support grandparents give to their adult grandchildren. *The Journals of Gerontology: Series B*, *73*, 1006–1015. https://doi.org/10.1093/geronb/gbw208

Huyck, M. H., & Gutmann, D. L. (2006). Men and their wives: Why are some married men vulnerable at midlife? In V. H. Bedford & B. Formaniak Turner (Eds.), *Men in relationships: A new look from a life course perspective* (pp. 27–50). Springer Publishing Co.

Hyde, Z. Z., Flicker, L., Hankey, G. J., Almeida, O. P., McCaul, K. A., Chubb, S. A. P. A. P., & Yeap, B. B. (2010). Prevalence of sexual activity and associated factors in men aged 75 to 95 years. *Annals of Internal Medicine*, *153*(11), 693–702. https://doi.org/10.7326/0003-4819-153-11-201012070-00002

James, J.B., & Zarrett, N. (2006). Ego integrity in the lives of older women. *Journal of Adult Development*, *13*, 61–75. 10.1007/s10804-006-9003-2

Jecker, N. S. (2006). Euthanasia. In R. Schulz (Ed.), *The encyclopedia of aging* (4th ed., pp. 392–394). Springer Publishing Company.

Jecker, N. S. (2011). Medical futility and the death of a child. *Journal of Bioethical Inquiry*, *8*(2), 133–139. https://doi.org/10.1007/s11673-011-9288-0

Jenkins, K. R., Pienta, A. M., & Horgas, A. L. (2002). Activity and health-related quality of life in continuing care retirement communities. *Research on Aging*, *24*(1), 124.

Jeste, D. V., & Oswald, A. J. (2014). Individual and societal Wisdom: Explaining the Paradox of human aging and high well-being. *Psychiatry: Interpersonal and Biological Processes*, *4*, 317–330. http://www.tandfonline.com/doi/abs/10.1521/psyc.2014.77.4.317

Johnson, K. J., & Mutchler, J. E. (2014). The emergence of a positive gerontology: From disengagement to social involvement. *The Gerontologist*, *54*(1), 93–100. https://doi.org/10.1093/geront/gnt099

Joshi, S., Mooney, S. J., Rundle, A. G., Quinn, J. W., Beard, J. R., & Cerdá, M. (2017). Pathways from neighborhood poverty to depression among older adults. *Health & Place*, *43*, 138–143. https://doi.org/10.1016/J.HEALTHPLACE.2016.12.003

Kandler, C., Kornadt, A. E., Hagemeyer, B., & Neyer, F. J. (2015). Patterns and sources of personality development in old age. *Journal of Personality and Social Psychology*, *109*(1), 175–191. https://doi.org/10.1037/pspp0000028

Kaplan, D. B., & Berkman, B. J. (2021). *Religion and spirituality in older people*. Merck Manual. https://www.merckmanuals.com/home/older-people's-health-issues/social-issues-affecting-older-people/religion-and-spirituality-in-older-people

Kastenbaum, R. J., & Moreman, C. M. (2018). *Death, society, and human experience* (12th ed.). Routledge.

Kemp, E. A., & Kemp, J. E. (2002). Older couples: New romances: Finding & keeping love in later life. In E. A. Kemp & J. E. Kemp (Eds.), *Older couples: New romances: Finding & keeping love in later life*. Celestial Arts.

Kent de Grey, R. G., & Uchino, B. N. (2020). The health correlates and consequences of friendship. In K. Sweeny, K., M. L. Robbins, & L. M. Cohen. (Eds.), *The Wiley encyclopedia of health psychology* (pp. 239–245). Wiley. https://doi.org/10.1002/9781119057840.ch72

Kenyon, B. L. (2001). Current research in children's conceptions of death: A critical review. *OMEGA - Journal of Death and Dying*, *43*(1), 63–91. https://doi.org/10.2190/0X2B-B1N9-A579-DVK1

Keyes, C. L. M., & Reitzes, D. C. (2007). The role of religious identity in the mental health of older working and retired adults. *Aging & Mental Health*, *11*(4), 434–443. 10.1080/13607860601086371

Keyes, K. M., Pratt, C., Galea, S., McLaughlin, K. A., Koenen, K. C., & Shear, M. K. (2014). The Burden of loss: Unexpected death of a loved one and psychiatric disorders across the life course in a national study. *American Journal of Psychiatry*, *171*(8), 864–871. https://doi.org/10.1176/appi.ajp.2014.13081132

Khan, A. (2014). *For young and old, it's wise to have a living will to state health-care wishes. U.S. News & World Report*. http://health.usnews.com/health-news/health-wellness/articles/2014/12/19/why-you-need-a-living-will-even-at-age-18

Kim, J., Smith, T. W., & Kang, J. (2015). Religious affiliation, religious service attendance, and mortality. *Journal of Religion and Health*, *54*(6), 2052–2072. https://doi.org/10.1007/s10943-014-9902-7

King, A. C., Salvo, D., Banda, J. A., Ahn, D. K., Chapman, J. E., Gill, T. M., Fielding, R. A., Demons, J., Tudor-Locke, C., Rosso, A., Pahor, M., & Frank, L. D. (2017). Preserving older adults' routine outdoor activities in contrasting neighborhood environments through a physical activity intervention. *Preventive Medicine*, *96*, 87–93. https://doi.org/10.1016/J.YPMED.2016.12.049

King, B. M., Carr, D. C., Taylor, M. G., & Pruchno, R. (2019). Depressive symptoms and the buffering effect of resilience on widowhood by gender. *Gerontologist*, *59*(6), 1122–1130. https://doi.org/10.1093/geront/gny115

King, V., & Scott, M. E. (2005). A comparison of cohabiting relationships among older and younger adults. *Journal of Marriage & Family*, *67*(2), 271–285.

Ko, K. J., Berg, C. A., Butner, J., Uchino, B. N., & Smith, T. W. (2007). Profiles of successful aging in middle-aged and older adult married couples. *Psychology and Aging*, *22*(4), 705–718.

Kornadt, A. E., Hess, T. M., Voss, P., & Rothermund, K. (2018). Subjective age across the life span: A differentiated, longitudinal approach. *The Journals of Gerontology Series B: Psychological Sciences and Social Sciences*, *73*, 767–777. https://doi.org/10.1093/geronb/gbw072

Kornadt, A. E., & Rothermund, K. (2012). Internalization of age stereotypes into the self-concept via future self-views: A general model and domain-specific differences. *Psychology and Aging*, *27*(1), 164–172. https://doi.org/10.1037/a0025110

Kotter-Grühn, D., Kornadt, A. E., & Stephan, Y. (2016). Looking beyond chronological age: Current knowledge and future directions in the study of subjective age. *Gerontology*, *62*(1), 86–93. https://doi.org/10.1159/000438671

Krause, N. (2005). God-Mediated control and psychological well-being in late life. *Research on Aging*, *27*(2), 136–164. https://doi.org/10.1177/0164027504270475

Kristensen, P., Weisæth, L., Hussain, A., & Heir, T. (2015). Prevalence of psychiatric disorders and functional impairment after loss of A family member: A longitudinal study after the 2004 tsunami. *Depression and Anxiety*, *32*(1), 49–56. https://doi.org/10.1002/da.22269

Kübler-Ross, E. (1969). On death and dying. In E. Kübler-Ross (Ed.), *On death and dying*. Collier Books/Macmillan Publishing Co.

Kübler-Ross, E. (1974). Questions and answers on death and dying. In E. Kübler-Ross (Ed.), *Questions and answers on death and dying*. Collier Books/Macmillan Publishing Co.

Kwak, S., Kim, H., Chey, J., & Youm, Y. (2018). Feeling how old i am: Subjective age is associated with estimated brain age. *Frontiers in Aging Neuroscience*, *10*, 168. https://doi.org/10.3389/fnagi.2018.00168

Lancel, M., Stroebe, M., & Eisma, M. C. (2020). Sleep disturbances in bereavement: A systematic review. *Sleep medicine reviews*, *53*, 101331. https://doi.org/10.1016/j.smrv.2020.101331

Lang, F. R., Featherman, D. L., & Nesselroade, J. R. (1997). Social self-efficacy and short-term variability in social relationships: The macarthur successful aging studies. *Psychology and Aging*, *12*(4), 657–666.

Laureys, S., Celesia, G. G., Cohadon, F., Lavrijsen, J., León-Carrión, J., Sannita, W. G., Sazbon, L., Schmutzhard, E., von Wild, K. R., Zeman, A., & Dolce, G. (2010). Unresponsive wakefulness syndrome: A new name for the vegetative state or apallic syndrome. *BMC Medicine*, *8*(1), 68. https://doi.org/10.1186/1741-7015-8-68

Lawrence, A. R., & Schigelone, A. R. S. (2002). Reciprocity beyond dyadic relationships: Aging-related communal coping. *Research on Aging*, *24*(6), 684–704. 10.1177/016402702237187

Lee, D. M., Nazroo, J., O'Connor, D. B., Blake, M., & Pendleton, N. (2016). Sexual health and well-being among older men and women in england: Findings from the english longitudinal study of ageing. *Archives of Sexual Behavior*, *45*(1), 133–144. https://doi.org/10.1007/s10508-014-0465-1

Lee, E.-K. O., & Sharpe, T. (2007). Understanding religious/spiritual coping and support resources among African American older adults: A mixed-method approach. *Journal of Religion, Spirituality & Aging*, *19*(3), 55–75. https://doi.org/10.1300/J496v19n03_05

Leming, M., & Dickinson, G. (2020). *Understanding dying, death, and bereavement* (9th ed.). Cengage Learning,.

Lin, I. F., Brown, S. L., Wright, M. R., & Hammersmith, A. M. (2018). Antecedents of gray divorce: A life course perspective. *Journals of Gerontology - Series B Psychological Sciences and Social Sciences*, *73*(6), 1022–1031. https://doi.org/10.1093/geronb/gbw164

Lucas, R. E., & Donnellan, M. B. (2011). Personality development across the life span: Longitudinal analyses with a national sample from Germany. *Journal of Personality & Social Psychology*, *101*(4), 847–861. https://doi.org/10.1037/a0024298

Luchetti, M., Terracciano, A., Stephan, Y., & Sutin, A. R. (2015). Personality and cognitive decline in older adults: Data from a longitudinal sample and meta-analysis. *The Journals of Gerontology. Series B, Psychological Sciences and Social Sciences*, *71*(4), 591–601. https://doi.org/10.1093/geronb/gbu184

Lunney, J. R., Lynn, J., Foley, D. J., Lipson, S., & Guralnik, J. M. (2003). Patterns of functional decline at the end of life. *JAMA*, *289*(18), 2387. https://doi.org/10.1001/jama.289.18.2387

Maciejewski, P. K., Zhang, B., Block, S. D., & Prigerson, H. G. (2007). An empirical examination of the stage theory of grief. *JAMA*, *297*(7), 716–723. https://doi.org/10.1001/jama.297.7.716

Manning, L. K., & Miles, A. (2018). Examining the effects of religious attendance on resilience for older adults. *Journal of Religion and Health*, *57*(1), 191–208. https://doi.org/10.1007/s10943-017-0438-5

Manvelian, A., & Sbarra, D. A. (2020). Marital status, close relationships, and all-cause mortality: Results from a 10-year study of nationally representative older adults. *Psychosomatic Medicine*, *82*(4), 384–392. https://doi.org/10.1097/PSY.0000000000000798

Marsh, H. W., Nagengast, B., & Morin, A. J. S. (2012). Measurement invariance of big-five factors over the life span: ESEM tests of gender, age, plasticity, maturity, and La Dolce Vita effects. *Developmental Psychology*, *49*(6), 1194–1218. https://doi.org/10.1037/a0026913

Mathis, A. L., Rooks, R. N., Tawk, R. H., & Kruger, D. J. (2017). Neighborhood influences and BMI in Urban older adults. *Journal of Applied Gerontology*, *36*(6), 692–708. https://doi.org/10.1177/0733464815584670

McAuliffe, L., Bauer, M., & Nay, R. (2007). Barriers to the expression of sexuality in the older person: The role of the health professional. *International Journal of Older People Nursing*, *2*(1), 69–75.

McCoy, A., Rauer, A., & Sabey, A. (2017). The meta marriage: Links between older couples' relationship narratives and marital satisfaction. *Family Process*, *56*(4), 900–914. https://doi.org/10.1111/famp.12217

McCrae, R. R., Terracciano, A., & The Personality Profiles of Cultures Project. (2005). Universal features of personality traits from the observer's perspective: Data from 50 cultures. *Journal of Personality and Social Psychology*, *88*, 547–561.

McDonald, L., & Robb, A. L. (2004). The economic legacy of divorce and separation for women in old age. *Canadian Journal on Aging*, *23*, S83–s97.

McMahan, J. (2001). Brain death, cortical death and persistent vegetative state. In H. Kuhse & R. Singer (Eds.), *A companion to bioethics* (pp. 250–260). Blackwell.

McMahan True, M., Pisani, L., & Oumar, F. (2001). Infant – mother attachment among the Dogon of mali. *Child Development*, *72*(5), 1451.

Menec, V. H., Shooshtari, S., Nowicki, S., & Fournier, S. (2010). Does the relationship between neighborhood socioeconomic status and health outcomes persist into very old age? A population-based study. *Journal of Aging & Health*, *22*(1), 27–47. https://doi.org/10.1177/0898264309349029

Mills, S. (2012). Sounds to soothe the soul: music and bereavement in a traditional South Korean death ritual. *Mortality*, *17*(2), 145–157. https://doi.org/10.1080/13576275.2012.675231

Moos, N. L. (1994). An integrative model of grief. *Death Studies*, *19*(4), 337–364. http://eric.ed.gov/?id=EJ511322

Morrill, M. S., & Westall, J. (2019). Social security and retirement timing: Evidence from a national sample of teachers. *Journal of Pension Economics and Finance*, *18*(4), 549–564. https://doi.org/10.1017/S1474747218000422

Morrissey, M. (2019). *The state of American retirement savings*. Economic Policy Institute. https://www.epi.org/publication/the-state-of-american-retirement-savings/

Mortazavi, S. S., Assari, S., Alimohamadi, A., Rafiee, M., & Shati, M. (2020). Fear, loss, social isolation, and incomplete grief due to COVID-19: A recipe for a psychiatric pandemic. *Basic and Clinical Neuroscience*, *11*(2), 225–232. https://doi.org/10.32598/bcn.11.covid19.2549.1

Mortimore, E., Haselow, D., Dolan, M., Hawkes, W. G., Langenberg, P., Zimmerman, S., & Magaziner, J. (2008). Amount of social contact and hip fracture mortality. *Journal of the American Geriatrics Society*, *56*(6), 1069–1074.

Mõttus, R., Luciano, M., Starr, J. M., Pollard, M. C., & Deary, I. J. (2013). Personality traits and inflammation in men and women in their early 70s: The Lothian birth cohort 1936 study of healthy aging. *Psychosomatic Medicine*, *75*(1), 11–19. https://doi.org/10.1097/PSY.0b013e31827576cc

Mroczek, D. K. (2020). Personality and healthy aging in 1945 and 2020: Reflecting on 75 Years of research and theory. *Journals of Gerontology - Series B Psychological Sciences and Social Sciences*, *75*, 471–473. https://doi.org/10.1093/geronb/gbz125

Mroczek, D. K., Weston, S. J., & Willroth, E. C. (2020). *A lifespan perspective on the interconnections between personality, health, and optimal aging* (pp. 191–202). Springer Publishing Company. https://doi.org/10.1007/978-3-030-32053-9_12

Muratore, A. M., & Earl, J. K. (2015). Improving retirement outcomes: The role of resources, pre-retirement planning and transition characteristics. *Ageing and Society*, *35*(10), 2100–2140. https://doi.org/10.1017/S0144686X14000841

Nakajima, S. (2018). Complicated grief: Recent developments in diagnostic criteria and treatment. *Philosophical Transactions of the Royal Society B: Biological Sciences*, *373*. https://doi.org/10.1098/rstb.2017.0273

Newman, D. A., Jeon, G., & Hulin, C. L. (2012). In M. Wang (Ed.), *Retirement attitudes: Considering etiology, measurement, attitude-behavior relationships, and attitudinal ambivalence*. Oxford University Press. https://doi.org/10.1093/oxfordhb/9780199746521.013.0090

Newport, F. (2006). *Religion most important to blacks, women, and older Americans: Gallup poll.* . Retrieved from http://www.gallup.com/poll/25585/Religion-Most-Important-Blacks-Women-Older-Americans.aspx

Nguyen, A. W. (2020). Religion and mental health in racial and ethnic minority populations: A review of the literature. *Innovation in Aging*, *4*(5), 1–13. https://doi.org/10.1093/geroni/igaa035

O'Brien, E. L., Hess, T. M., Kornadt, A. E., Rothermund, K., Fung, H., & Voss, P. (2017). Context influences on the subjective experience of aging: The impact of culture and domains of functioning. *The Gerontologist*, *57*(Suppl. 2), S127–S137. https://doi.org/10.1093/geront/gnx015

O'Connor, M. F. (2019). Grief: A brief history of research on how body, mind, and brain adapt. *Psychosomatic Medicine*, *81*, 731–738. https://doi.org/10.1097/PSY.0000000000000717

Oi, K. (2021). Does retirement get under the skin and into the head? Testing the pathway from retirement to cardio-metabolic risk, then to episodic memory. *Research on Aging*, *43*(1), 25–36. https://doi.org/10.1177/0164027520941161

Oregon Public Health Division, C. for H. S. (2021). *Oregon death with dignity act: 2020 data summary*. www.healthoregon.org/dwd

Orth, U., & Robins, R. W. (2019). Development of self-esteem across the lifespan. In D. P. McAdams, R. L. Shiner, & J. L. Tackett (Eds.), *Handbook of personality development* (pp. 328–344). Guilford. https://psycnet.apa.org/record/2018-63285-019

Otani, H., Yoshida, S., Morita, T., Aoyama, M., Kizawa, Y., Shima, Y., Tsuneto, S., & Miyashita, M. (2017). Meaningful communication before death, but not present at the time of death itself, is associated with better outcomes on measures of depression and complicated grief among bereaved family members of cancer patients. *Journal of Pain and Symptom Management*, *54*(3), 273–279. https://doi.org/10.1016/j.jpainsymman.2017.07.010

Palacios-Ceña, D., Carrasco-Garrido, P., Hernández-Barrera, V., Alonso-Blanco, C., Jiménez-García, R., & Fernández-de-las-Peñas, C. (2012). Sexual behaviors among older adults in Spain: Results from a population-based national sexual health survey. *The Journal of Sexual Medicine*, *9*(1), 121–129. https://doi.org/10.1111/j.1743-6109.2011.02511.x

Payscale.com. (2021). *User design salary*. https://www.payscale.com/research/US/Job=UX_Designer/Salary

Pew Research Center. (2009). *Growing Old in America: Expectations vs. Reality*. Retrieved from http://www.pewsocialtrends.org/2009/06/29/growing-old-in-america-expectations-vs-reality/ Pew Research Center

Pew Research Center. (2013). *Views on end - of - Life medical treatments*. http://www.pewforum.org/2013/11/21/views-on-end-of-life-medical-treatments/

Pinquart, M., & Schindler, I. (2007a). Changes of life satisfaction in the transition to retirement: A latent-class approach. *Psychology & Aging*, *22*(3), 442–455. 10.1037/0882-7974.22.3.442

Pinquart, M., & Schindler, I. (2007b). Changes of life satisfaction in the transition to retirement: A latent-class approach. *Psychology and Aging*, *22*(3), 442–455. https://doi.org/10.1037/0882-7974.22.3.442

Pinquart, M., & Wahl, H.-W. (2021). Subjective age from childhood to advanced old age: A meta-analysis. *Psychology and Aging*, *36*(3), 394–406. https://doi.org/10.1037/pag0000600

Postigo, J. M. L., & Honrubia, R. L. (2010). The Co-residence of elderly people with their children and grandchildren. *Educational Gerontology*, *36*(4), 330–349. https://doi.org/10.1080/03601270903212351

Powell-Wiley, T. M., Gebreab, S. Y., Claudel, S. E., Ayers, C., Andrews, M. R., Adu-Brimpong, J., Berrigan, D., & Davis, S. K. (2020). The relationship between neighborhood socioeconomic deprivation and telomere length: The 1999–2002 national health and nutrition examination survey. *SSM - Population Health*, *10*, 100517. https://doi.org/10.1016/j.ssmph.2019.100517

Pushkar, D., Chaikelson, J., Conway, M., Etezadi, J., Giannopoulus, C., Li, K., & Wrosch, C. (2010). Testing continuity and activity variables as predictors of positive and negative affect in retirement. *The Journals of Gerontology: Series B: Psychological Sciences and Social Sciences*, *65*(1), 42–49. https://doi.org/10.1093/geronb/gbp079

Quine, S., Wells, Y., de Vaus, D., & Kendig, H. (2007). When choice in retirement decisions is missing: Qualitative and quantitative findings of impact on well-being. *Australasian Journal on Ageing*, *26*(4), 173–179.

Radwany, S., Albanese, T., Clough, L., Sims, L., Mason, H., & Jahangiri, S. (2009). End-of-life decision making and emotional burden: Placing family meetings in context. *The American Journal of Hospice & Palliative Care*, *26*(5), 376–383. https://doi.org/10.1177/1049909109338515

Rao, J. K., Anderson, L. A., Lin, F.-C., & Laux, J. P. (2014). Completion of advance directives among U.S. consumers. *American Journal of Preventive Medicine*, *46*(1), 65–70. https://doi.org/10.1016/j.amepre.2013.09.008

Rasheed, M. N., & Rasheed, J. M. (2003). Rural African American older adults and the Black helping tradition. *Journal of Gerontological Social Work*, *41*(1/2), 137–150.

Ready, R. E., Carvalho, J. O., & Åkerstedt, A. M. (2012). Evaluative organization of the self-concept in younger, midlife, and older adults. *Research on Aging*, *34*(1), 56–79. https://doi.org/10.1177/0164027511415244

Reed, T. D., & Neville, H. A. (2014). The Influence of religiosity and spirituality on psychological well-being among black women. *Journal of Black Psychology*, *40*(4), 384–401. https://doi.org/10.1177/0095798413490956

Reitz, A. K., & Staudinger, U. M. (2017). Getting older, getting better? Toward understanding positive personality development across adulthood. In J. Specht (Ed.), *Personality development across the lifespan* (pp. 219–241). Elsevier. https://doi.org/10.1016/B978-0-12-804674-6.00014-4

Reitzes, D.C., & Mutran, E.J. (2004). The transition to retirement: Stages and factors that influence retirement adjustment. *International Journal of Aging & Human Development, 59*, 63–84.

Renz, M.., Reichmuth, O.., Bueche, D.., Traichel, B.., Mao, M. S.., Cerny, T.., & Strasser, F.. (2018). Fear, Pain, Denial, and Spiritual Experiences in Dying Processes. *American Journal of Hospice and Palliative Medicine, 35*(3), 478–491. http://dx.doi.org/10.1177/1049909117725271

Richardson, V., & Kilty, K.M. (1991). Adjustment to retirement: Continuity vs. discontinuity. *International Journal of Aging & Human Development, 33*, 151–169.

Robles, T. F., Menkin, J. A., Robles, T. F., & Menkin, J. A. (2015). Social relationships and health in older adulthood. In R. A. Scott & M. C. Buchmann (Eds.), *Emerging trends in the social and behavioral sciences* (pp. 1–15). John Wiley & Sons, Inc. https://doi.org/10.1002/9781118900772.etrds0310

Ronneberg, C. R., Miller, E. A., Dugan, E., & Porell, F. (2016). The protective effects of religiosity on depression: A 2-year prospective study. *The Gerontologist, 56*, 421–431. https://doi.org/10.1093/geront/gnu073

Rosenblatt, P. C. (2008). Grief across cultures: A review and research agenda. In M. S. Stroebe, R. O. Hansson, H. Schut, W. Stroebe, & E. Van den Blink (Eds.), *Handbook of bereavement research and practice: Advances in theory and intervention* (pp. 207–222). American Psychological Association.

Rosnick, C. B., Small, B. J., & Burton, A. M. (2010). The effect of spousal bereavement on cognitive functioning in a sample of older adults. *Aging, Neuropsychology & Cognition, 17*(3), 257–269. https://doi.org/10.1080/13825580903042692

Rubin, D. C., & Berntsen, D. (2006). People over forty feel 20% younger than their age: Subjective age across the lifespan. *Psychonomic Bulletin & Review, 13*(5), 776–780.

Sander, J., Schupp, J., & Richter, D. (2017). Getting together: Social contact frequency across the life span. *Developmental Psychology, 53*(8), 1571–1588. https://doi.org/10.1037/dev0000349

Sanford, A. M., Orrell, M., Tolson, D., Abbatecola, A. M., Arai, H., Bauer, J. M., Cruz-Jentoft, A. J., Dong, B., Ga, H., Goel, A., Hajjar, R., Holmerova, I., Katz, P. R., Koopmans, R. T. C. M., Rolland, Y., Visvanathan, R., Woo, J., Morley, J. E., & Vellas, B. (2015). An international definition for "nursing home&quot. *Journal of the American Medical Directors Association, 16*(3), 181–184. https://doi.org/10.1016/j.jamda.2014.12.013

Santini, Z. I., Koyanagi, A., Tyrovolas, S., Mason, C., & Haro, J. M. (2015). The association between social relationships and depression: A systematic review. *Journal of Affective Disorders, 175*, 53–65. https://doi.org/10.1016/j.jad.2014.12.049

Schmitz, A. (2021). Gendered experiences of widowhood and depression across Europe: The role of loneliness and financial resources from a longitudinal perspective. *Journal of Affective Disorders, 280*, 114–120. https://doi.org/10.1016/j.jad.2020.11.091

Schoenfeld, T. J., & Gould, E. (2013). Differential effects of stress and glucocorticoids on adult neurogenesis. In C. Belzung & P. Wigmore (Eds.), *Neurogenesis and neural plasticity* (pp. 139–164). Springer Publishing Company. https://doi.org/10.1007/7854_2012_233

Segel-Karpas, D., Ayalon, L., & Lachman, M. E. (2018). Loneliness and depressive symptoms: The moderating role of the transition into retirement. *Aging & Mental Health, 22*(1), 135–140. https://doi.org/10.1080/13607863.2016.1226770

Seiger Cronfalk, B., Ternestedt, B.-M., & Norberg, A. (2017). Being a close family member of a person with dementia living in a nursing home. *Journal of Clinical Nursing, 26*(21–22), 3519–3528. https://doi.org/10.1111/jocn.13718

Sewdas, R., de Wind, A., van der Zwaan, L. G. L., van der Borg, W. E., Steenbeek, R., van der Beek, A. J., & Boot, C. R. L. (2017). Why older workers work beyond the retirement age: a qualitative study. *BMC Public Health, 17*(1), 672. https://doi.org/10.1186/s12889-017-4675-z

Shaw, B. A. (2005). Anticipated support from neighbors and physical functioning during later life. *Research on Aging, 27*(5), 503–525. 10.1177/0164027505277884

Sheehan, N. W., & Petrovic, K. (2008). Grandparents and their adult grandchildren: Recurring themes from the literature. *Marriage & Family Review, 44*(1), 99–124.

Sheldon, K.M., & Kasser, T. (2001). Getting older, getting better? Personal strivings and psychological maturity across the life span. *Developmental Psychology, 37*, 491–501.

Shelton, A. (2013). Social security: Still lifting many older americans out of poverty. *AARP*. http://blog.aarp.org/2013/07/01/social-security-still-lifting-many-older-americans-out-of-poverty/

Shin, S. H., Kim, G., & Park, S. (2018). Widowhood status as a risk factor for cognitive decline among older adults. *American Journal of Geriatric Psychiatry, 26*(7), 778–787. https://doi.org/10.1016/j.jagp.2018.03.013

Shinan-Altman, S., & Werner, P. (2019). Subjective age and its correlates among middle-aged and older adults. *The International Journal of Aging and Human Development, 88*(1), 3–21. https://doi.org/10.1177/0091415017752941

Siegel, K., & Weinstein, L. (2008). Anticipatory grief reconsidered. *Journal of Psychosocial Oncology, 1*(2), 61–73. https://doi.org/10.1300/J077v01n02_04

Siguaw, J. A., Sheng, X., & Simpson, P. M. (2018). Biopsychosocial and retirement factors influencing satisfaction with life. *International Journal of Aging and Human Development, 85*, 332–353. https://doi.org/10.1177/0091415016685833

Sims, T., Hogan, C. L., & Carstensen, L. L. (2015). Selectivity as an emotion regulation strategy: Lessons from older adults. *Current Opinion in Psychology, 3*, 80–84. https://doi.org/10.1016/j.copsyc.2015.02.012

Sirrine, E. H., Salloum, A., & Boothroyd, R. (2018). Predictors of continuing bonds among bereaved adolescents. *Omega (United States), 76*(3), 237–255. https://doi.org/10.1177/0030222817727632

Skatacka, K., & Gerymski, R. (2019). Sexual activity and life satisfaction in older adults. *Psychogeriatrics, 19*(3), 195–201. https://doi.org/10.1111/psyg.12381

Smith, J., & Freund, A. M. (2002). The Dynamics of Possible Selves in Old Age. *Journals of Gerontology Series B: Psychological Sciences & Social Sciences, 57B*(6), 492.

Smith, K. V., Wild, J., & Ehlers, A. (2020). The masking of mourning: Social disconnection after bereavement and its role in psychological distress. *Clinical Psychological Science : A Journal of the Association for Psychological Science, 8*(3), 464–476. https://doi.org/10.1177/2167702620902748

Social Security Administration. (2016). *Fact sheet - Social security: Social security is important to women*. Fact Sheet. https://www.ssa.gov/news/press/factsheets/ss-customer/women-ret.pdf

Social Security Administration. (2018). *Fact sheet: Social security*. Fact Sheet. https://www.ssa.gov/news/press/factsheets/basicfact-alt.pdf

Soto, C. J. (2015). Is happiness good for your personality? Concurrent and prospective relations of the big five with subjective well-being. *Journal of Personality, 83*(1), 45–55. https://doi.org/10.1111/jopy.12081

Srinivasan, S., Glover, J., Tampi, R. R., Tampi, D. J., & Sewell, D. D. (2019). Sexuality and the older adult. *Current Psychiatry Reports, 21*, 1–9. https://doi.org/10.1007/s11920-019-1090-4

Stephan, Y., Caudroit, J., Jaconelli, A., & Terracciano, A. (2014). Subjective age and cognitive functioning: A 10-year prospective study. *The American Journal of Geriatric Psychiatry : Official Journal of the American Association for Geriatric Psychiatry, 22*(11), 1180–1187. https://doi.org/10.1016/j.jagp.2013.03.007

Stephan, Y., Chalabaev, A., Kotter-Grühn, D., & Jaconelli, A. (2013). "Feeling younger, being stronger": An experimental study of subjective age and physical functioning among older adults. *The Journals of Gerontology. Series B, Psychological Sciences and Social Sciences, 68*(1), 1–7. https://doi.org/10.1093/geronb/gbs037

Stephan, Y., Sutin, A. R., Canada, B., & Terracciano, A. (2017). Personality and frailty: Evidence from four samples. *Journal of Research in Personality, 66*, 46–53. https://doi.org/10.1016/J.JRP.2016.12.006

Stephan, Y., Sutin, A. R., Luchetti, M., & Terracciano, A. (2021). An older subjective age is related to accelerated epigenetic aging. *Psychology and Aging*. https://doi.org/10.1037/pag0000607

Stephan, Y., Sutin, A. R., & Terracciano, A. (2018). Subjective age and mortality in three longitudinal samples. *Psychosomatic Medicine, 80*(7), 659–664. https://doi.org/10.1097/PSY.0000000000000613

Stephan, Y., Sutin, A. R., Wurm, S., & Terracciano, A. (2021). Subjective aging and incident cardiovascular disease. *The Journals of Gerontology. Series B, Psychological Sciences and Social Sciences, 76*(5), 910–919. https://doi.org/10.1093/geronb/gbaa106

Stepler, R. (2016). Smaller share of women ages 65 and older are living Alone | Pew research center. *Pew Research Center*. http://www.pewsocialtrends.org/2016/02/18/smaller-share-of-women-ages-65-and-older-are-living-alone/

Stepler, R. (2016). *Smaller share of women ages 65 and older are living alone. Pew Research Center*. Retrieved from http://www.pewsocialtrends.org/2016/02/18/smaller-share-of-women-ages-65-and-older-are-living-alone/

Stepler, R. (2017). Number of cohabiting Americans rises, especially among those 50+ | Pew research center. *Pew Research Center*. http://www.pewresearch.org/fact-tank/2017/04/06/number-of-u-s-adults-cohabiting-with-a-partner-continues-to-rise-especially-among-those-50-and-older/

Story, T. N., Berg, C. A., Smith, T. W., Beveridge, R., Henry, N. J. M., & Pearce, G. (2007). Age, marital satisfaction, and optimism as predictors of positive sentiment override in middle-aged and older married couples. *Psychology and Aging, 22*(4), 719–727.

Stroebe, M., Boerner, K., & Schut, H. (2017). Grief. In V. Zeigler-Hill & T. K. Shackelford (Eds.), *Encyclopedia of personality and individual differences* (pp. 1–5). Springer International Publishing. https://doi.org/10.1007/978-3-319-28099-8_520-1

Stroebe, M., & Schut, H. (2010). The dual process model of coping with bereavement: A decade on. *Omega: Journal of Death and Dying, 61*(4), 273–289. https://doi.org/10.2190/OM.61.4.b

Stroebe, M., & Schut, H. (2016). Overload: A missing link in the dual process model?. *OMEGA - Journal of Death and Dying, 74*(1), 96–109. https://doi.org/10.1177/0030222816666540

Stroebe, M., Schut, H., & Boerner, K. (2010). Continuing bonds in adaptation to bereavement: Toward theoretical integration. *Clinical Psychology Review, 30*(2), 259–268. https://doi.org/10.1016/j.cpr.2009.11.007

Stroebe, M., Schut, H., & Boerner, K. (2017). cautioning health-care professionals: Bereaved persons are misguided through the stages of grief. . *OMEGA -Journal of Death and Dying, 74*(4), 455–473. https://doi.org/10.1177/0030222817691870

Stroope, S., Cohen, I. F. A., Tom, J. C., Franzen, A. B., Valasik, M. A., & Markides, K. S. (2017). Neighborhood perception and self-rated health among Mexican American older adults. *Geriatrics & Gerontology International, 17*(12), 2559–2564. https://doi.org/10.1111/ggi.13089

Subramanian, S. V., Elwert, F., & Christakis, N. (2008). Widowhood and mortality among the elderly: The modifying role of neighborhood concentration of widowed individuals. *Social Science & Medicine, 66*(4), 873–884. 10.1016/j.socscimed.2007.11.029

Syme, M. L., Klonoff, E. A., Macera, C. A., & Brodine, S. K. (2013). Predicting sexual decline and dissatisfaction among older adults: The role of partnered and individual physical and mental health factors. *The Journals of Gerontology. Series B, Psychological Sciences and Social Sciences, 68*(3), 323–332. https://doi.org/10.1093/geronb/gbs087

Tang, F. (2008). Socioeconomic disparities in voluntary organization involvement among older adults. *Nonprofit & Voluntary Sector Quarterly, 37*(1), 57–75.

Tang, S., & Chow, A. Y. M. (2017). How do risk factors affect bereavement outcomes in later life? An exploration of the mediating role of dual process coping. *Psychiatry Research, 255*, 297–303. https://doi.org/10.1016/j.psychres.2017.06.001

Taylor, A., & Gosney, M. A. (2011). Sexuality in older age: Essential considerations for healthcare professionals. *Age and Ageing, 40*(5), 538–543. https://doi.org/10.1093/ageing/afr049

Teitelbaum, J., & Shemie, S. (2016). Brain death. In M. M. Smith, G. G. Citerio, & W. A. I. Kofke (Eds.), *Oxford textbook of neurocritical care* (pp. 390–398). Oxford University Press. https://doi.org/10.1093/med/9780198739555.003.0029

Teno, J. M., Weitzen, S., Fennell, M. L., & Mor, V. (2001). Dying trajectory in the last year of life: Does cancer trajectory fit other diseases? *Journal of Palliative Medicine*, *4*(4), 457–464. https://doi.org/10.1089/109662101753381593

Thiele, D. M., & Whelan, T. A. (2008). The relationship between grandparent satisfaction, meaning, and generativity. *International Journal of Aging & Human Development*, *66*(1), 21–48.

Thompson, W. K., Charo, L., Vahia, I. V., Depp, C., Allison, M., & Jeste, D. V. (2011). Association between higher levels of sexual function, activity, and satisfaction and self-rated successful aging in older postmenopausal women. *Journal of the American Geriatrics Society*, *59*(8), 1503–1508. https://doi.org/10.1111/j.1532-5415.2011.03495.x

Toth, M., Palmer, L., Bercaw, L., Voltmer, H., & Karon, S. L. (2021). Trends in the use of residential settings among older adults. *The Journals of Gerontology: Series B*. https://doi.org/10.1093/geronb/gbab092

Trevino, K. M., Litz, B., Papa, A., Maciejewski, P. K., Lichtenthal, W., Healy, C., & Prigerson, H. G. (2018). Bereavement challenges and their relationship to physical and psychological adjustment to loss. *Journal of Palliative Medicine*, *21*(4), 479–488. https://doi.org/10.1089/jpm.2017.0386

Uno, C., Okada, K., Matsushita, E., Satake, S., & Kuzuya, M. (2021). Friendship-related social isolation is a potential risk factor for the transition from robust to prefrailty among healthy older adults: A 1-year follow-up study. *European Geriatric Medicine*, *12*(2), 285–293. https://doi.org/10.1007/s41999-020-00422-y

U.S. Bureau of Labor Statistics. (2020). *Civilian labor force participation rate by age, sex, race, and ethnicity : U.S. Bureau of labor statistics*. Employment Projections. https://www.bls.gov/emp/tables/civilian-labor-force-participation-rate.htm

U.S. Bureau of Labor Statistics. (2021). *Occupational Outlook Handbook: 2021*. Retrieved from https://www.bls.gov/ooh/

U.S. Federal Reserve. (2018). *Report on the economic well-being of U.S. Households in 2016 - May 2017*. . https://www.federalreserve.gov/publications/2017-economic-well-being-of-us-households-in-2016-retirement.htm

Vaillant, G. E. (1994). "Successful aging" and psyochsocial well-being: Evidence from a 45-year study. In E. H . Thompson (Ed.), *Older men's lives* (pp. 22–41). SAGE.

Vaillant, G. E. (2004). Positive aging. In P.A. Linley & S. Joseph (Eds.), *Positive psychology in practice* (pp. 561–578). John Wiley.

van Bilsen, P. M. A., Hamers, J. P. H., Groot, W., & Spreeuwenberg, C. (2008). Sheltered housing compared to independent housing in the community. *Scandinavian Journal of Caring Sciences*, *22*(2), 265–274. 10.1111/j.1471-6712.2007.00529.x

Van Cauwenberg, J., Cerin, E., Timperio, A., Salmon, J., Deforche, B., & Veitch, J. (2017). Is the association between park proximity and recreational physical activity among mid-older aged adults moderated by park quality and neighborhood conditions? *International Journal of Environmental Research and Public Health*, *14*(2), 192. https://doi.org/10.3390/ijerph14020192

van der Maas, P. (1991). Euthanasia and other medical decisions concerning the end of life. *The Lancet*, *338*(8768), 669–674. https://doi.org/10.1016/0140-6736(91)91241-L

van Solinge, H., & Henkens, K. (2008). Adjustment to and satisfaction with retirement: Two of a kind? *Psychology and Aging*, *23*(2), 422–434.

Waldinger, R. J., & Schulz, M. S. (2010). What's love got to do with it? Social functioning, perceived health, and daily happiness in married octogenarians. *Psychology and Aging*, *25*(2), 422–431. https://doi.org/10.1037/a0019087

Wallace, C. L., Wladkowski, S. P., Gibson, A., & White, P. (2020). Grief during the COVID-19 pandemic: Considerations for palliative care providers. *Journal of Pain and Symptom Management*, *60*(1), e70–e76. https://doi.org/10.1016/j.jpainsymman.2020.04.012

Wang, L., Koenig, H. G., Al Shohaib, S., & Wang, Z. (2020). Religiosity, depression and telomere length in Chinese older adults. *Journal of Affective Disorders*, *260*, 624–628. https://doi.org/10.1016/j.jad.2019.09.066

Wang, M. (2007). Profiling retirees in the retirement transition and adjustment process: Examining the longitudinal change patterns of retirees' psychological well-being. *Journal of Applied Psychology*, *92*(2), 455–474.

Wang, M., Henkens, K., & van Solinge, H. (2011). A review of theoretical and empirical advancements. *The American Psychologist*, *66*(3), 204–213. https://doi.org/10.1037/a0022414

Weiss, A., Costa, P. T., Karuza, J., Duberstein, P. R., Friedman, B., & McCrae, R. R. (2005). Cross-Sectional age differences in personality among medicare patients aged 65 to 100. *Psychology and Aging*, *20*(1), 182–185. https://doi.org/10.1037/0882-7974.20.1.182

Weiss, D., & Lang, F. R. (2012). "They" are old but "I" feel younger: Age-group dissociation as a self-protective strategy in old age. *Psychology and Aging*, *27*(1), 153–163. https://doi.org/10.1037/a0024887

Weitzen, S., Teno, J. M., Fennell, M., & Mor, V. (2003). Factors associated with site of death: A national study of where people die. *Medical Care*, *41*(2), 323–335. https://doi.org/10.1097/01.MLR.0000044913.37084.27

Whitbourne, S. K. (2007). *Adult development and aging: Biopsychosocial perspectives*. Wiley.

Whiting, P., & Bradley, L. J. (2007). Artful witnessing of the story: Loss in aging adults. *Adultspan: Theory Research & Practice*, *6*(2), 119–128.

Windsor, T. D., Anstey, K. J., & Rodgers, B. (2008). Volunteering and psychological well-being among young-old adults: How much is too much? *Gerontologist*, *48*(1), 59–70.

Wöhrmann, A. M., Fasbender, U., & Deller, J. (2017). Does more respect from leaders postpone the desire to retire? Understanding the mechanisms of retirement decision-making. *Frontiers in Psychology*, *8*, 1400. https://doi.org/10.3389/fpsyg.2017.01400

Wortman, J., Lucas, R. E., & Donnellan, M. B. (2012). Stability and change in the big five personality domains: Evidence from a longitudinal study of Australians. *Psychology and Aging*, *27*(4), 867–874. https://doi.org/10.1037/a002932210.1037/a0029322.supp(Supplemental)

Wright, M. R., & Brown, S. L. (2017). Psychological well-being among older adults: The role of partnership status. *Journal of Marriage and Family*, *79*(3), 833–849. https://doi.org/10.1111/jomf.12375

Wright, P. M., & Hogan, N. S. (2008). Grief theories and models: Applications to Hospice nursing practice. *Journal of Hospice & Palliative Nursing*, *10*(6), 350–356.

Wrzus, C., Hänel, M., Wagner, J., & Neyer, F. J. (2013). Social network changes and life events across the life span: A meta-analysis. *Psychological Bulletin*, *139*(1), 53–80. https://doi.org/10.1037/a0028601

Wu, Y.-T., Prina, A. M., Jones, A. P., Barnes, L. E., Matthews, F. E., Brayne, C., & Medical Research Council Cognitive Function and Ageing Study. (2015). Community environment, cognitive impairment and dementia in later life: Results from the cognitive function and ageing study. *Age and Ageing*, *44*(6), 1005–1011. https://doi.org/10.1093/ageing/afv137

Wu, Z., & Schimmele, C. M. (2007). Uncoupling in late life. *Generations*, *31*(3), 41–46.

Yadav, K. N., Gabler, N. B., Cooney, E., Kent, S., Kim, J., Herbst, N., Mante, A., Halpern, S. D., & Courtright, K. R. (2017). Approximately one in three us adults completes any type of advance directive for end-of-life care. *Health Affairs*, *36*(7), 1244–1251. https://doi.org/10.1377/hlthaff.2017.0175

Yeung, D. Y., & Zhou, X. (2017). Planning for retirement: Longitudinal effect on retirement resources and post-retirement well-being. *Frontiers in Psychology*, *8*, 1300. https://doi.org/10.3389/fpsyg.2017.01300

Ysseldyk, R., Haslam, S. A., & Haslam, C. (2013). Abide with me: Religious group identification among older adults promotes health and well-being by maintaining multiple group memberships. *Aging & Mental Health*, *17*(7), 869–879. https://doi.org/10.1080/13607863.2013.799120

Zacher, H., & Kirby, G. (2015). Remaining time. In S. K. Whitbourne (Ed.), *The encyclopedia of adulthood and aging* (pp. 1–5). John Wiley & Sons, Inc. https://doi.org/10.1002/9781118521373.wbeaa059

Zimmer, Z., Jagger, C., Chiu, C.-T., Ofstedal, M. B., Rojo, F., & Saito, Y. (2016). Spirituality, religiosity, aging and health in global perspective: A review. *SSM - Population Health*, *2*, 373–381. https://doi.org/10.1016/J.SSMPH.2016.04.009

NAME INDEX

SUBJECT INDEX